S0-BAC-280

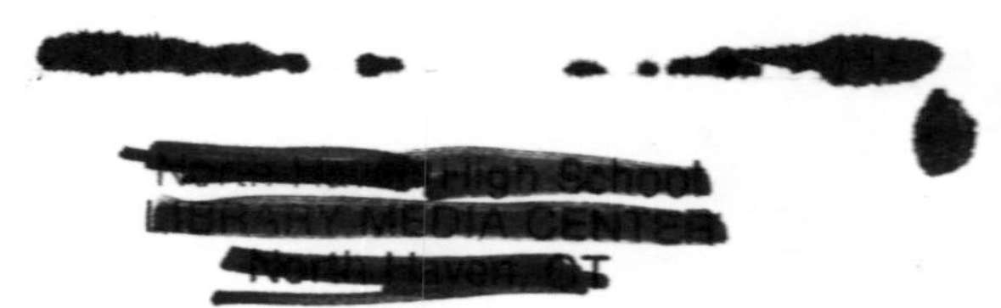

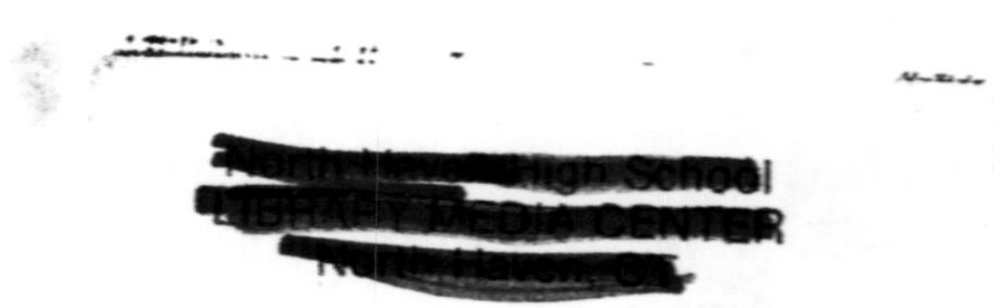

DRAMA

CRITICISM

Guide to Gale Literary Criticism Series

For criticism on	Consult these Gale series
Authors now living or who died after December 31, 1999	*CONTEMPORARY LITERARY CRITICISM (CLC)*
Authors who died between 1900 and 1999	*TWENTIETH-CENTURY LITERARY CRITICISM (TCLC)*
Authors who died between 1800 and 1899	*NINETEENTH-CENTURY LITERATURE CRITICISM (NCLC)*
Authors who died between 1400 and 1799	*LITERATURE CRITICISM FROM 1400 TO 1800 (LC)* *SHAKESPEAREAN CRITICISM (SC)*
Authors who died before 1400	*CLASSICAL AND MEDIEVAL LITERATURE CRITICISM (CMLC)*
Authors of books for children and young adults	*CHILDREN'S LITERATURE REVIEW (CLR)*
Dramatists	*DRAMA CRITICISM (DC)*
Poets	*POETRY CRITICISM (PC)*
Short story writers	*SHORT STORY CRITICISM (SSC)*
Black writers of the past two hundred years	*BLACK LITERATURE CRITICISM (BLC)* *BLACK LITERATURE CRITICISM SUPPLEMENT (BLCS)*
Hispanic writers of the late nineteenth and twentieth centuries	*HISPANIC LITERATURE CRITICISM (HLC)* *HISPANIC LITERATURE CRITICISM SUPPLEMENT (HLCS)*
Native North American writers and orators of the eighteenth, nineteenth, and twentieth centuries	*NATIVE NORTH AMERICAN LITERATURE (NNAL)*
Major authors from the Renaissance to the present	*WORLD LITERATURE CRITICISM, 1500 TO THE PRESENT (WLC)* *WORLD LITERATURE CRITICISM SUPPLEMENT (WLCS)*

ISSN 1056-4349

Criticism of the Most Significant and Widely Studied Dramatic Works from all the World's Literatures

VOLUME 13

Linda Pavlovski, Editor

Detroit
New York
San Francisco
London
Boston
Woodbridge, CT

STAFF

Library of Congress Catalog Card Number 92-648805
ISBN 0-7876-3141-8
ISSN 1056-4349
Printed in the United States of America

10 9 8 7 6 5 4 3 2 1

Contents

Preface

Drama Criticism (*DC*) is principally intended for beginning students of literature and theater as well as the average playgoer. The series is therefore designed to introduce readers to the most frequently studied playwrights of all time periods and nationalities and to present discerning commentary on dramatic works of enduring interest. Furthermore, *DC* seeks to acquaint the reader with the uses and functions of criticism itself. Selected from a diverse body of commentary, the essays in *DC* offer insights into the authors and their works but do not require that the reader possess a wide background in literary studies. Where appropriate, reviews of important productions of the plays discussed are also included to give students a heightened awareness of drama as a dynamic art form, one that many claim is fully realized only in performance.

DC was created in response to suggestions by the staffs of high school, college, and public libraries. These librarians observed a need for a series that assembles critical commentary on the world's most renowned dramatists in the same manner as Gale's *Short Story Criticism* (*SSC*) and *Poetry Criticism* (*PC*), which present material on writers of short fiction and poetry. Although playwrights are covered in such Gale literary criticism series as *Contemporary Literary Criticism* (*CLC*), *Twentieth-Century Literary Criticism* (*TCLC*), *Nineteenth-Century Literature Criticism* (*NCLC*), *Literature Criticism from 1400 to 1800* (*LC*), and *Classical and Medieval Literature Criticism* (*CMLC*), *DC* directs more concentrated attention on individual dramatists than is possible in the broader, survey-oriented entries in these Gale series. Commentary on the works of William Shakespeare may be found in *Shakespearean Criticism* (*SC*).

Scope of the Series

By collecting and organizing commentary on dramatists, *DC* assists students in their efforts to gain insight into literature, achieve better understanding of the texts, and formulate ideas for papers and assignments. A variety of interpretations and assessments is offered, allowing students to pursue their own interests and promoting awareness that literature is dynamic and responsive to many different opinions.

Approximately five to ten authors are included in each volume, and each entry presents a historical survey of the critical response to that playwright's work. The length of an entry is intended to reflect the amount of critical attention the author has received from critics writing in English and from foreign critics in translation. Every attempt has been made to identify and include the most significant essays on each author's work. In order to provide these important critical pieces, the editors sometimes reprint essays that have appeared elsewhere in Gale's literary criticism series. Such duplication, however, never exceeds twenty percent of a *DC* volume.

Organization of the Book

A *DC* entry consists of the following elements:

- The **Author Heading** consists of the playwright's most commonly used name, followed by birth and death dates. If an author consistently wrote under a pseudonym, the pseudonym is listed in the author heading and the real name given in parentheses on the first line of the introduction. Also located at the beginning of the introduction are any name variations under which the dramatist wrote, including transliterated forms of the names of authors whose languages use nonroman alphabets.

- The **Introduction** contains background information that introduces the reader to the author and the critical debates surrounding his or her work.

- A **Portrait of the Author** is included when available.

- The list of **Principal Works** is divided into two sections. The first section contains the author's dramatic pieces and is organized chronologically by date of first performance. If this has not been conclusively determined, the composition or publication date is used. The second section provides information on the author's major works in other genres.

- Essays offering **overviews and general studies of the dramatist's entire literary career** give the student broad perspectives on the writer's artistic development, themes, and concerns that recur in several of his or her works, the author's place in literary history, and other wide-ranging topics.

- **Criticism** of individual plays offers the reader in-depth discussions of a select number of the author's most important works. In some cases, the criticism is divided into two sections, each arranged chronologically. When a significant performance of a play can be identified (typically, the premier of a twentieth-century work), the first section of criticism will feature **production reviews** of this staging. Most entries include sections devoted to **critical commentary** that assesses the literary merit of the selected plays. When necessary, essays are carefully excerpted to focus on the work under consideration; often, however, essays and reviews are reprinted in their entirety. Footnotes are reprinted at the end of each essay or excerpt. In the case of excerpted criticism, only those footnotes that pertain to the excerpted texts are included.

- Critical essays are prefaced by brief **Annotations** explicating each piece.

- A complete **Bibliographic Citation,** designed to help the interested reader locate the original essay or book, precedes each piece of criticism.

- An annotated bibliography of **Further Reading** appears at the end of each entry and suggests resources for additional study. In some cases, significant essays for which the editors could not obtain reprint rights are included here. Boxed material following the further reading list provides references to other biographical and critical sources on the author in series published by Gale.

Cumulative Indexes

A **Cumulative Author Index** lists all of the authors that appear in a wide variety of reference sources published by the Gale Group, including *DC.* A complete list of these sources is found facing the first page of the Author Index. The index also includes birth and death dates and cross references between pseudonyms and actual names.

A **Cumulative Nationality Index** lists all authors featured in *DC* by nationality, followed by the number of the *DC* volume in which their entry appears.

A **Cumulative Title Index** lists in alphabetical order the individual plays discussed in the criticism contained in *DC.* Each title is followed by the author's last name and corresponding volume and page numbers where commentary on the work is located. English-language translations of original foreign-language titles are cross-referenced to the foreign titles so that all references to discussion of a work are combined in one listing.

Citing *Drama Criticism*

When writing papers, students who quote directly from any volume in *Drama Criticism* may use the following general formats to footnote reprinted criticism. The first example pertains to material drawn from periodicals, the second to materials reprinted from books.

Susan Sontag, "Going to the Theater, Etc.," *Partisan Review* XXXI, no. 3 (Summer 1964), 389-94; excerpted and reprinted in *Drama Criticism,* vol. 1, ed. Lawrence J. Trudeau (Detroit: Gale Research, 1991), 17-20.

Eugene M. Waith, *The Herculean Hero in Marlowe, Chapman, Shakespeare and Dryden* (Chatto & Windus, 1962); excerpted and reprinted in *Drama Criticism,* vol. 1, ed. Lawrence J. Trudeau (Detroit: Gale Research, 1991), 237-47.

Suggestions are Welcome

Readers who wish to suggest new features, topics, or authors to appear in future volumes, or who have other suggestions or comments are cordially invited to call, write, or fax the Managing Editor:

Managing Editor, Literary Criticism Series

The Gale Group

27500 Drake Road

Farmington Hills, MI 48331-3535

1-800-347-4253 (GALE)

Fax: 248-699-8054

Acknowledgments

The editors wish to thank the copyright holders of the excerpted criticism included in this volume and the permissions managers of many book and magazine publishing companies for assisting us in securing reproduction rights. We are also grateful to the staffs of the Detroit Public Library, the Library of Congress, the University of Detroit Mercy Library, Wayne State University Purdy/Kresge Library Complex, and the University of Michigan Libraries for making their resources available to us. Following is a list of the copyright holders who have granted us permission to reproduce material in this volume of *DC*. Every effort has been made to trace copyright, but if omissions have been made, please let us know.

COPYRIGHTED EXCERPTS IN *DC*, VOLUME 13, WERE REPRODUCED FROM THE FOLLOWING PERIODICALS:

Bulletin of the Comediantes, v. 33, Spring, 1981 for "Tirso's Don Juan and the Opposing Self" by Everett W. Hesse./v. 37, Summer, 1985 for "Love, Matrimony and Desire in the Theatre of Tirso de Molina" by Henry W. Sullivan./v. 40, Summer, 1988 for "Tirso de Molina's Idea of 'Tragedia'" by David H. Darst./v. 40, Winter, 1988 for "Language and Seduction in 'El Burlador de Seville'" by James Mandrell./v. 42, Summer, 1990 for "The 'Burlador' and the 'Burlados': A Sinister Connection" by Raymond Conlon. All reproduced by permission of the authors.—***The Centennial Review,*** v. XXXII, Summer, 1988 for "Megan Terry and Family Talk" by Judith Babnich. Copyright © *The Centennial Review,* 1988. All rights reserved. Reproduced by permission of the publisher and author.—***Commonweal,*** v. CXVIII, May 3, 1991. Copyright © 1991 Commonweal Publishing Co., Inc. Reproduced by permission of Commonweal Foundation.—***Comparative Drama,*** v. 25, Winter, 1991/92. © copyright 1991-92, by the Editors of Comparative Drama. Reproduced by permission.—***Critica Hispanica,*** v. 9, 1987. Reproduced by permission.—***Drama,*** 1988 for a lecture delivered on October 21, 1987 by Alan Ayckbourn. © Haydonning 1988./Autumn, 1973 for "Plays in Performance" by J. W. Lambert and others. Both reproduced by permission.—***The Drama Review,*** v. 21, December, 1977 for "Two Pages a Day" by Megan Terry. Copyright © 1977, *The Drama Review.* Reproduced by permission of the publisher and the author.—***Forum for Modern Language Studies,*** v. XXII, July, 1986. Reproduced by permission.—***The French Review,*** v. LVIII, March, 1985; v. 62, April, 1989; v. 66, October, 1992. Copyright 1985, 1989, 1992 by the American Association of Teachers of French. All reproduced by permission.—***French Studies,*** v. XLV, April, 1991. Reproduced by permission.—***Hispanic Review,*** v. 58, Summer, 1990. Reproduced by permission.—***History of European Ideas,*** v. 20, 1995. Copyright © 1995 Elsevier Science Ltd. All rights reserved. Reproduced by permission.—***The Hudson Review,*** v. XLIV, Summer, 1991. Copyright © 1991 by The Hudson Review, Inc. Reproduced by permission.—***Kentucky Romance Quarterly,*** v. 29, 1982. Copyright © 1982 Helen Dwight Reid Educational Foundation. Reproduced with permission of the Helen Dwight Reid Educational Foundation, published by Heldref Publications, 1319 18th Street, NW, Washington, DC 20036-1802.—***L' Esprit Créateur,*** v. XXXVI, Spring, 1996. Copyright © 1996 by L'Esprit Créateur. Reproduced by permission.—***MLN,*** v. 90, April, 1975. © copyright 1975 by The Johns Hopkins University Press. All rights reserved. Reproduced by permission.—***Modern Drama,*** v. XXVI, March, 1983; v. XXVII, December, 1984. Copyright © 1983, 1984 University of Toronto, Graduate Centre for Study of Drama. Both reproduced by permission.—***Modern Languages Journal,*** v. 70, June, 1989. Reproduced by permission.—***Modern Languages,*** v. LIX, September, 1978. Reproduced by permission.—***The Nation,*** New York, v. 252, April 8, 1991. © 1991 *The Nation magazine*/The Nation Company, Inc. Reproduced by permission.—***The New Leader,*** v. LXXV, June 1-15, 1992. © 1992 by The American Labor Conference on International Affairs, Inc. Reproduced by permission.—***Nottingham French Studies,*** v. 29, Spring, 1990; v. 33, Spring, 1994. © The University of Nottingham 1990, 1994. Both reproduced by permission.—***Papers on French Seventeenth Century Literature,*** v. XV, 1988; v. XVI, 1989; v. XXII, 1995. © 1988, 1989, 1995 PFSCL. All reproduced by permission.—***PMLA,*** v. 89, January, 1974. Copyright © 1974 by the Modern Language Association of America. Reproduced by permission of the Modern Language Association of America.—***Renascence,*** v. XXXVII, Summer, 1985. © copyright, 1985, Marquette University Press. Reproduced by permission.—***Romance Languages Annual,*** v. 1, 1989; v. 6, 1994. © 1990, 1995 by Purdue Research Foundation. All rights reserved. Both reproduced by permission.—***Romance Notes,*** v. XXIII, Winter, 1982; v. XXXII, Fall, 1991. Both reproduced by permission.—***The Romanic Review,*** v. 45, 1974. © The Trustees of Columbia University. Reproduced by permission.—***Studies in American Drama, 1945-Present,*** v. 2, 1987; v. 4, 1989. Copyright © by Philip C. Kolin and Colby H. Kullman. Both reproduced by permission.—***Theatre Journal,*** v. 34, October, 1982. © 1982 University and College Theatre Association of the American Theatre Association. Reproduced by permission of The Johns Hopkins University Press.—***The Times Educational Supplement,*** March 15, 1991 for "Plotting Success" by Reva Klein. © The Times Supplements Limited 19 Reproduced from *The Times Educational Supplement* by permission of the author.—***Times Literary Supplement,*** November 1, 1991; August 19, 1992; August 13, 1993. © The Times Supplements Limited 1991, 1992, 1993. All reproduced from

The Times Literary Supplement by permission.—***The University of Mississippi Studies in English,*** v. X, 1992. Copyright © 1992 The University of Mississippi. Reproduced by permission.—***Variety,*** May 4, 1992. Reproduced by permission.

COPYRIGHTED EXCERPTS IN *DC*, VOLUME 13, WERE REPRODUCED FROM THE FOLLOWING BOOKS:

Bermel, Albert. From "Fears into Laughs," in ***One Act Comedies of Moliere.*** Second edition. Translated by Albert Bermel. Frederick Ungar Publishing Co., 1975. Copyright © 1975 by Albert Bermel. Reproduced by permission.—Betsko, Kathleen, and Rachel Koenig. From an interview in ***Interviews with Contemporary Women Playwrights.*** Beech Tree Books, 1987. Copyright © 1987 by Kathleen Betsko and Rachel Koenig. All rights reserved. Reprinted by permission of HarperCollins Publishers, Inc.—Breslauer, Jan and Helene Keyssar. From "Making Magic Public: Megan Terry's Traveling Family Circus," in ***Making A Spectacle: Feminist Essays on Contemporary Women's Theatre.*** Edited by Lynda Hart. The University of Michigan Press, 1989. Copyright © by The University of Michigan 1989. All rights reserved. Reproduced by permission.—Cave, Richard Allen. From ***New British Drama in Performance on the London Stage: 1970 to 1985.*** Colin Smythe, 1987. Copyright © 1987 by Richard Allen Cave. All rights reserved. Reproduced by permission.—Kauffmann, Stanley. From ***Persons of the Drama: Theater Criticism and Comment.*** Harper & Row, Publishers, 1976. Copyright © 1966 by Stanley Kauffmann. All rights reserved. Reprinted by permission of Brandt & Brandt Literary Agents, Inc.—Keyssar, Helene. From ***Feminist Theatre.*** Macmillan, 1984. © Helene Keyssar 1984. All rights reserved. Reproduced by permission.—Londre, Felica Hardison. From an interview in ***Speaking on Stage: Interviews with Contemporary American Playwrights.*** Edited by Philip C. Konlin and Colby H. Kullman. The University of Alabama Press, 1996. Copyright © 1996. All rights reserved. Reproduced by permission of the publisher and the author.—Marranca, Bonnie. From ***American Playwrights: A Critical Survey, Vol. 1.*** by Bonnie Marranca and Gautam Dasgupta. Drama Book Specialists, 1981. Copyright © 1981 by Bonnie Marranca and Gautam Dasgupta. All rights reserved. Reproduced by permission of the author.—McKendrick, Melveena. From "Tirso de Molina and the other Lopistas," in ***Theatre in Spain, 1490-1700.*** Cambridge University Press, 1989. © Cambridge University Press 1989. Reproduced by permission.—Soufas, Teresa Scott. From ***Melancholy and the Secular Mind in Spanish Golden Age Literature.*** University of Missouri Press, 1990. Copyright © 1990 by The Curators of the University of Missouri. All rights reserved. Reproduced by permission.—Taylor, John Russell. From "Art and Commerce: The New Drama in the West End Marketplace," in ***Contemporary English Drama.*** Edited by C. W. E. Bigsby. Edward Arnold, 1981. Copyright © Edward Arnold (Publishers) Ltd. 1981. Reproduced by permission.—Taylor, John Russell. From ***The Second Wave: British Drama for the Seventies.*** Hill and Wang, 1971. Copyright © 1971 by John Russell Taylor. All rights reserved. Reproduced by permission of The Peters Fraser and Dunlop Group Limited on behalf of John Russell Taylor.

PHOTOGRAPHS APPEARING IN *DC*, VOLUME 13, WERE RECEIVED FROM THE FOLLOWING SOURCES:

Ayckbourn, Alan, photograph. AP/Wide World Photos. Reproduced by permission.—Molière, engraving. The Library of Congress.—Tirso de Molina, engraving. The Library of Congress.

Alan Ayckbourn
1939-

English playwright and lyricist.

INTRODUCTION

One of Great Britain's most popular and prolific playwrights, Ayckbourn is best known for his intricately plotted and inventively staged plays that explore daily middle-class life and marriage. In works that successfully balance tragic subject matter with comic events, Ayckbourn frequently centers on what he perceives as the monotony and emotional torment underlying his characters' lives and examines such themes as loneliness, unintentional cruelty and self-interest.

BIOGRAPHICAL INFORMATION

Ayckbourn was born April 12, 1939, in London. Influenced by his mother, a romance-fiction writer, Ayckbourn began writing at an early age. He attended Haileybury School in 1952, devoting most of his time to writing plays and acting. Ayckbourn toured with several repertory companies and worked as assistant stage manager before he began his relationship with the Studio Theatre Company in the small resort town of Scarborough. There Ayckbourn gained experience in all aspects of theater under the direction of Stephen Joseph, an innovative stage manager who had introduced the concept of theater-in-the-round to England. During this period, Ayckbourn wrote several light comedies that he had admittedly created as vehicles to advance his own acting career. Ayckbourn's first significant work, *Standing Room Only* (1961), which concerns a London bus driver and his family who are caught in a twenty-year traffic jam, is his only absurdist drama. After receiving harsh reviews for *Xmas v. Mastermind* (1962) and *Mr. Whatnot* (1963), Ayckbourn took a financially secure position at the BBC in 1965, producing radio dramas while concurrently writing plays for the theater. His first success came when the farce *Relatively Speaking* (1967) opened in London to wide critical acclaim.

MAJOR WORKS

Ayckbourn's prolific output prompted numerous critics to remark that his total number of plays now surpasses that of Shakespeare. Many of Ayckbourn's plays present the foibles of middle-class married life within the structure of the "well-made" play. For example, in such early plays as *Relatively Speaking* (1967) and *How the Other Half Loves* (1969), Ayckbourn utilizes the conventions of mistaken identities and misunderstandings, complicated plots and precisely timed exits and entrances to humorously explore marital infidelities. *How the Other Half Loves* also presents a good example of how Ayckbourn uses staging techniques to transcend space and time. The play has two separate settings that are superimposed onstage so that actions occurring in different places at different times are seen simultaneously. *Time and Time Again* (1971) and *Absurd Person Singular* (1972) mark the beginning of plays in which Ayckbourn created more fully developed characters in the context of what he termed "the truly hilarious dark play." *Absurd Person Singular*, for instance, concerns three unhappily married couples who take turns entertaining one another on three successive Christmas Eves. One of the wives repeatedly attempts suicide by various ludicrous means in front of the other guests while they remain cruelly unaware of her pain. *A Small Family Business* (1987), which depicts the moral decline of an entire family through a series of humorous and complicated plot twists, is, nevertheless, noted for its unhappy conclusion: a drug-addicted daughter sits alone in her room injecting heroin while downstairs her family celebrates their entry into the drug trade. Continuing to emphasize the dark side of everyday existence, *Woman in Mind* (1985) charts the mental breakdown of Susan, the wife of a self-centered pastor. At first she fantasizes about an ideal family; however, her fantasy world eventually degenerates into uncontrollable hallucinations, and she is left utterly alone as her real family remains oblivious to her emotional needs.

CRITICAL RECEPTION

Though Ayckbourn's reputation is based primarily on his ability to write entertaining comedies, most critics agree that his plays convey serious themes concerning the failures and tragedies of ordinary life as well as the moral and cultural decline of society. In particular, such plays as *A Small Family Business* and *Woman in Mind* not only depict the foibles of individuals, but are noted for addressing such social issues as drug abuse, the shortcomings Ayckbourn perceives in organized religion, and the manipulative qualities of the media, most evident in *Man of the Moment* (1988), in which a villainous character is made a hero by television journalists. Characterizing Ayckbourn's critical status, Michael Billington called him "the best comic dramatist since Molière," while Peter Hall has asserted that, "in 100 years' time, when he's forgiven for being successful, people will read his plays as an accurate reflection of English life in the 1960s, '70s and '80s. They represent a very important social document."

PRINCIPAL WORKS

Plays

The Square Cat [as Roland Allen] 1959
Love After All [as Roland Allen] 1959
Dad's Tale [as Roland Allen] 1960
Standing Room Only [as Roland Allen] 1961
Xmas v. Mastermind 1962
Mr. Whatnot 1963
Meet My Father 1965 [also performed as *Relatively Speaking*] 1967
The Sparrow 1967
**Mixed Doubles: An Entertainment on Marriage* 1969
How the Other Half Loves 1969
The Story So Far 1970 [also performed as *Me Times Me Times Me* (revised edition), 1972, and *Family Circles* (revised edition), 1978]
Ernie's Incredible Illucinations 1971
Time and Time Again 1971
Absurd Person Singular 1972
***The Norman Conquests* 1973
Absent Friends 1974
†*Confusions* 1974
Bedroom Farce 1975
Just Between Ourselves 1976
Ten Times Table 1977
Joking Apart 1978
Men on Women on Men [with Paul Todd] 1978
Sisterly Feelings 1979
Taking Steps 1979
Season's Greetings 1980
Suburban Strains [with Paul Todd] 1980
Way Upstream 1981
Intimate Exchanges 1982
It Could Be Any One of Us 1983
A Chorus of Disapproval 1984
The Westwoods 1984
Woman in Mind: December Bee 1985
Henceforeward . . . 1987
A Small Family Business 1987
Man of the Moment 1988
Mr. A's Amazing Maze Plays 1988
The Inside Outside Slide Show 1989
Invisible Friends 1989
The Revengers' Comedies 1989
Body Language 1990
This Is Where We Came In 1990
Wildest Dreams 1991
Time of My Life 1992
Dreams from a Summer House 1992
Communicating Doors 1994
Haunting Julia 1994
The Musical Jigsaw Play 1994
A Word from Our Sponsor 1995
By Jeeves 1996
The Champion of Paribanou 1996
Things We Do for Love 1997

*This work includes the plays *Countdown* and *We Who Are About To.*

**This work includes the plays *Table Manners*, *Living Together*, and *Round and Round the Garden.*

†This work includes the one-act plays *Mother Figure*, *Drinking Companion*, *Between Mouthfuls*, *Gosforth's Fete* and *A Talk in the Park.*

AUTHOR COMMENTARY

Alan Ayckbourn (essay date 1987)

A lecture delivered on October 21, 1987, in *Drama*, No. 167, 1988, pp. 5–7.

[*The following excerpt highlights a talk given by Ayckbourn, in which he voices his concerns about the future of the commercial play.*]

Most of my talks start off with different titles and end up roughly the same—a sort of history of me. Anyway, this time I wanted at least to start differently, even if I end up in the same place. I want to draw your attention to what I consider to be an endangered species; it's called the good commercial play. There are still a few of us practising it out there, but it is becoming increasingly difficult to develop. There are several reasons why.

The first is down to the fact that a lot of work is being done by community or group theatres—splendid work too, except that what's happening is that these plays are what I call Event Theatre—plays that are often developed and done *in situ* to cover a particular event, something pressingly social like, say, the miners' strike. But very often they don't move any further than that. They die with the group doing them, and so there is no play left over to move forward. You might note, for instance, how few productions have been seen of even a show like *Nicholas Nickelby*. The play that you can take off the shelf and do, is actually not as much in evidence as it used to be.

The second reason, possibly, is due to the fact that a lot of theatres are consigning the new writers to the studio end of the business—the low risk end. I would say that studio writing is fine and good, for *very new writers*. But for writers to survive they have got to come out of the greenhouse at some stage. One of the great benefits I had was to experience commercial pressures: to do more, that is, than just deliver a play. If you are always being sheltered by productions of, say, *King Lear*, assorted Agatha Christies and Alan Ayckbourn—we always tend to get bracketed together—then in truth, as a writer, you remain playing to small houses in small theatres, or to no houses in small theatres. As one regional director said to me, there's a lot of very good work being done developing new writers in studio theatres but whoever saw a second production of most of these plays? A writer learns a lot from repetition of his work—at least he does if he is canny.

The third, the most obvious but probably the biggest reason, is the shrinking budgets, the move away from government finance, the smaller amounts available for smaller theatres outside London where new dramatists, one hopes, are coming—a play is an expensive thing. It's easy enough—comparatively easy anyway—to get a small scale production in a small theatre, but it's that next stage, to play among the big league, that is getting tougher. At Scarborough we spend a lot of time encouraging new writers, but it is not really a matter of receiving a script and saying 'this looks good' and just doing it. Often it's a matter of recruiting and creating a working relationship with an individual who you have a hunch might write a play in five years.

In my own case I was lucky enough. I was an actor looking to be a star, who happened to arrive in a theatre where there was one of the most remarkable men I've met—Stephen Joseph. The theatre in Scarborough bears his name. He had a rather eccentric habit of encouraging *anyone* who worked in his theatre to write—the box office assistant etc. We had a lot of playwrights wandering round that theatre at any one time. But, in my case, the eight or nine plays I had done in the privacy of my own home, although reasonable, had never shown any development. Because a playwright doesn't just develop in isolation. One of the saddest sights is seeing the work of an unproduced author who's written for forty years and who's *stayed absolutely still*. The only thing that has got better is his typing.

Until a play goes through the mill, you can't begin to get a feedback as to what is working and what isn't. I was more interested, in point of fact, in acting during the early times I am now talking about and so, under Stephen's prompting, I wrote a wonderful vehicle for myself; it was designed to show just how good an actor I was. As an ASM I had observed from the wings for two years, a lot of how a play was put together. I knew that if you wanted to be a star you came on at the end of the first act, so I wrote my character in at the last line of Act 1. I stayed on for the next two acts and I gave myself all the laugh lines. In a fit of enthusiasm I wrote myself in as a guitar-playing, singing, dancing pop singer; none of which I could actually *do*. The first act was traumatic and I was sick several times before I came on. When I did come on it was to find myself in a play that I completely failed to recognise as mine. But, what remained with me, was the experience of the very first laugh of the play—it may have been just a titter—a few minutes in. That was very exciting, like gunsmoke to a warhorse. After that I seriously began to think about writing more . . . vehicles for myself. The next play, therefore, was destined to show me in *four* roles. I stole the plot from the *Marriage Of Figaro*, disguising it slightly. *The Guardian*—or *Manchester Guardian* as it was then called—described it as a 'witless' piece. Nor did I get very good reviews as an actor. Still failing to heed the call, I went on to write a third play, and this time I wrote a mere *eight* parts for myself. I came on and off in a monstrously bad series of false moustaches. The play died without trace. It was then—around then—that I hit on the idea of putting *other* actors in, in the hope that they would do something for my plays that I so conspicuously could not. About the same time Stephen guided me gently away from acting towards directing.

So, I developed two careers at once. On the one hand I was directing and on the other hand I was a writer delivering plays at regular intervals to Stephen and his company: I think the first thing to be said about the whole business of starting to write (I may be repeating myself) was that I had been fortunate enough to be put in at the sharp end. I was writing plays in a company running on a shoestring in a town, Scarborough, in the North East of England; a town not known for its theatrical innovation. It was a variety town in summer and in winter it had no theatre at all. Here we were doing a totally unknown form of theatre—theatre in the round—by totally unknown writers, actors and directors; it was the first outside London fringe I suppose. We are talking here, don't forget, about the early 'sixties. We were all earning nothing. We were the first company not to play the National Anthem, which immediately branded us as communists, and it meant that nobody came because of that, as well as for the other, reasons. My plays were supposed to earn us the money to live until next week. So the onus was well and truly upon me. My colleagues in the dressing room were putting pressure upon me to write something they could do. If we were all going to starve in force nine gales in Scarborough then the least I could do was to provide them with something worth acting in.

On the other hand, I had to satisfy the needs of a very disparate audience coming not at all from the traditional theatre-going public. The thing about Scarborough is that it is a holiday town, and people tend to behave abnormally when they're on holiday. They do daring things, like going to the theatre. For many people in our audiences, the nearest they had got to a live actor was the television set (thus the classic overheard remark when the lights went up one evening of . . . 'oooh, it's in colour'). What we got from these audiences was instant involvement, to the point often—irritatingly sometimes it's true—of very loud comment. They became involved. Coming, as I do, from the rather more laid-back Southern regions, I found it very stimulating. And every night I was experiencing—as an actor to begin with being right in the middle of the whole thing—how a play was progressing. Perhaps, as importantly, I was also noticing how the plays were failing. In that respect theatre in the round is very useful. From any angle one is watching the audience. I'm a great audience watcher even today.

But even then, and later when we moved to Stoke-on-Trent, no West End managements looked anywhere near us. Incidentally, it is interesting to note that although I was greeted as an overnight success, I'd had some ten plays unproduced, and it wasn't until my seventh produced work—so *seventeen* plays in all—that I got one nibble from a West End management. It was a long business and a long investment by that theatre which, by the end, was doing reasonably nicely, but not more, from my work. It's an interesting thing that a new playwright can sometimes deliver, quite out of the blue, a most magnificent first script. But if you are lucky enough to produce it, the difficulty will start on the second or third piece. Because, you see, the trouble with playwriting is that it is beset with rules. I always compare it with furniture making rather than with any other kind of writing.

To create a play you need a great knowledge of construction. The whole thing is to hold an audience's attention for two hours. Narrative, character, development and dialogue are all a crucial part of the process. They are basic rules, but only after you have learned them can you consider breaking them. At one point Stephen suggested that I write, for once, a well-made play. *The well-made play*—to a young dramatist this is an insulting term. It suggests that you are selling out. But it intrigued me as an exercise when I was writing the first of my plays that was really commercially successful—***Relatively Speaking***. I remember sitting down and trying to write a piece that was, if you like, actor-proof, a play that would have a mechanism in it that would need only the slightest of pushes to make it work. In doing so I had to apply all my mind and technique to such an extent that I became very depressed. In fact I kept putting it off. I remember Stephen phoned me and asked if I yet had a title; titles of my plays always come first. I said 'not yet'. He said that the leaflets were going to press so I clutched, from the air, a title . . . *Meet My Mother*, I'll call it that. So he said he'd put it in. A couple of days later he called and told me that he had changed it to ***Meet My Father***—it looked better on the programme. I said 'fair enough, that'll fit'. In fact I hadn't started it yet. This was the play (it was eventually finished) that caught the eye of a West End impressario. The casting, although difficult, was eventually first rate Michael Hordern, Celia Johnson, Richard Briers and Jennifer Hilary, and we went out on tour.

With this play I had a stroke of good fortune. It happened to arrive at a point when the French Window was almost forgotten—it *was* a play, I blush to confess, with French Windows. The hairy men had moved in—the heavy, post Osborne, Pinter mob, and realism was the course of the day. In came this rather charming vehicle with a rather embarrassed author in tow, who wanted to be associated with that heavy mob, not with this cosy little piece. As it happened the piece was received rapturously but it probably set me back a couple of years. I was known as Mr SitCom. Mr Light Ent. I tend to wince even now when people say—thirty four plays later—that this is still the best thing I've written.

It was a couple of years later that I was to meet the first of my mega-stars, Robert Morley, when I wrote ***How The Other Half Loves***. I didn't write it for him, I actually wrote it for my company. The thing I was learning was how to write for groups of actors. I've never been against the star system. What I've hated is the idea of a vehicle for a star, and I've always tried to write equal parts, equal shares for actors. I hope I've never written a part that I wouldn't have played myself. To that extent I was writing team plays. But I came to a head on collision for the first time with Robert Morley. He was due to play one sixth of a play of mine which increasingly became one third, one half and then three quarters. Now, if you employ Robert Morley there is no point trying to pretend he isn't there. He is very very big, and big too with his audiences. People who pay to see plays by unknown writers in fact pay to see people like Robert Morley. So, in the end one let him out of his cage and he rampaged about the play, and it was the longest run I've ever had. He said, very sweetly, to me at the end—he knew I was wincing a lot as yet another scene vanished— . . . I've left a trail of sadder but richer writers behind me'. I was forced to agree with him.

As for my writing now many years on, Scarborough has given me, if nothing else, the right to take daring risks, and the right to fail. I now realise that I have a double obligation: to an audience—one has to entertain them as a practical writer; but one has also to give them something else besides. And balancing these two aspects is a fine, indeed a keen edged manoeuvre. In the end, it is the tight rope that a commercial play has to be willing to tread. You can offend more people than you please, or you can just make the work so trite and glib that you avoid the central issues. But audiences don't forgive you for that either. So, the 'commercial play' - defined simply as a play that people pay to come and see in large numbers, and which is done several times. My main fear is that the conditions for writers like myself, who have had the theatre and funds to do it, will just not be around in a few years. They may even be fading out now.

I'm going to fade out now. I wonder if you would like to ask me some questions, because I'm red-hot on questions.

Question: You have been very unpretentious and self-deprecatory about your method, in the sense that you talk as if you were merely a technician, yet it must be clear to most people who've seen your plays that there is a very deep human content in them. Some might even put it so high as Chekhovian content. Do you not agree that there's some personal pressure which works in you as well as the apparent technical approach that you adopt?

Answer: Yes. I am interested in how people treat each other. There's obviously a huge male/female rift in many of my plays. There is also I think, recently, a concern about the moral state of the nation. The last play, ***A Small Family Business***, was described, rightly I think, as a morality play. It is about the nature of honesty. Without sounding too 'revivalist preacher', it struck me that we were in danger of having no agreed moral code any longer. Now it was exactly what any of us chose to make it. We all had an idea of what we considered to be honest, that to steal the office pencil was OK, to steal the desk was probably not. I tried, in that play, to take us very gently from things we would all condone to matters that none of us should condone, murder and drug peddling. Yes, I do talk technically, mainly because when you talk about other things you get rather near your creative centre. And I find it very difficult to say things which, outside the context of my plays, don't sound, well, rather trite.

Reva Klein (essay date 1991)

SOURCE: "Plotting Success," in *The Times Educational Supplement*, No. 3898, March 15, 1991, p. 34.

[*In the following essay, Ayckbourn discusses* Invisible Friends, *a work he considers to be a morality play.*]

"I may not have a lot of things, but I do have technique." I suppose it comes from doing the same job for 33 years. Despite his standing as one of the most successful playwrights in the English-speaking world today, Alan Ayckbourn is nothing if not humble. The award-winning writer and director who describes himself as someone who is "known for making plots like watches" is in London rehearsing his new family play ***Invisible Friends*** at the National Theatre. When it opened last year at Ayckbourn's own theatre, the Stephen Joseph in Scarborough, *The Times* hailed it as "one of the best examples of children's drama . . . since Peter Pan".

Ayckbourn himself wouldn't be caught dead calling his own work "children's drama", preferring instead the concept of mixed-age, family audiences where children and parents sit and laugh and get scared and feel sad together. "Those are the best sort of audiences," he says, "not just dragooned kids being told to sit and shut up by fearsome teachers."

Invisible Friends he calls a shorter, more resolved version of his adult play ***Woman In Mind***, a moving piece about a depressed woman, lonely in her middle-aged marriage, who retreats into a fantasy world. What audiences at the National will be seeing is more lighthearted, but equally concerned with loneliness, alienation and the power of the imagination.

It's about young Lucy, who's fed up with her family, and no wonder. Her mother is depressed, her father appears to be narcoleptic and her heavy metal-obsessed brother is simply on another planet. Lucy invents an imaginary friend who fulfils all her needs. All's fun and games until, in the second act, the appearance of the imaginary friend's brother and father signifies a shift towards the sinister and dangerous. Resolution arrives just in time, and Lucy and her family all live, if not happily ever after, at least more at ease with each other.

Ayckbourn considers the play to be, like his other work, "a half concealed morality play". A firm opponent of the type of children's theatre that he scathingly calls "junior agit-prop", he just as firmly believes in the capacity of children to grasp complicated messages. "In the last few years, from seeing children sitting with parents in adult theatre wide awake throughout, it began to occur to me that many of us are excluding children from theatre for the wrong reasons and that when we did things specifically for them, they were condescending. It was then that I decided to try to write for family audiences the same sort of things I do for adults. This type of theatre is my adult theatre except that it's pared down."

His first two forays into what he admits to having conceived as children's theatre were long ago and dreadful enough, he chuckles, to have nearly put him off writing. Last year's ***Mr A's Amazing Maze Plays*** was, if not overwhelmingly successful, interesting enough to whet his appetite for more.

OVERVIEWS AND GENERAL STUDIES

John Russell Taylor (essay date 1971)

SOURCE: "Three Farceurs: Alan Ayckbourn, David Gregan, Simon Gray," in *The Second Wave: British Drama for the Seventies*, Hill and Wang, 1971, pp. 155-71.

[In the following excerpt, Taylor examines the works of Ayckbourn, David Cregan, and Simon Gray—playwrights who, in Taylor's opinion, are re-examining traditional theatrical genres.]

We tend to expect plays by new writers to be in some sense *avant-garde*, and the newer the writer the more *avant-garde* the play. We even sometimes seem to suggest that it is the young writer's duty to be *avant-garde*, and chastise him if he is falling short of this ideal by writing straightforward, old-fashioned sorts of plays. But of course, there is no necessary connection between youth and deliberate modernity. Indeed, one of the salient characteristics of the newer British drama has been exploration of a different sort: the re-examination and revivification of forms of the past, reclaiming for serious attention techniques and genres which have fallen into disuse or at least into intellectual disrepute.

One obvious example of this process is the new interest shown by several of our younger dramatists in the most 'theatrical' of theatrical genres, melodrama and farce. Sometimes, perhaps, they have been prompted to look again by the influence of Brecht, with his theoretical advocacy of the endistancing techniques natural to farce in order to induce a more critical attitude in audiences towards what is going on on stage. Sometimes, rather, it may be the influence of Theatre of the Absurd, Ionesco in particular, with its emphasis on the mechanical nature of farce, farce's shameless manipulation of its human puppets for the purposes of plotting, as a useful way of demonstrating the absurdity of the human condition. And sometimes, no doubt, it is just because the dramatists concerned enjoy traditional farce on its own familiar terms, and see no reason why they should not constructively exercise their enjoyment and pass it on to audiences supped full of horrors.

Alan Ayckbourn must surely belong wholeheartedly to this last group. Of all our younger dramatists he is the one who has most consistently and uncompromisingly avoided any suggestion of deeper meaning in his plays. Try as we may we cannot find any trace of social or political indoctrination masquerading as harmless diversion, let alone of cosmic anguish. His prime determination is unmistakably to make us laugh and keep us laughing, and all his considerable technical gifts are marshalled to that end alone. It is a tight-rope, and a particularly dangerous, vertiginous tight-rope at that, since if the writer stumbles he has no safety net of deeper significance to fall into: if his plays are not funny they are nothing. And while we are inclined to accept serious intent, however muffed, as a mitigating circumstance for a dramatist, unreasonably enough we see no merit at all in the dramatist who tries to make us laugh and fails.

Fortunately, this has not yet happened to Alan Ayckbourn. Even his less successful plays have always had at least that going for them. No doubt a lot of his basic theatrical instinct comes from the years he spent in the rough-and-tumble of provincial theatre, as actor, ASM, writer and general odd-job man. He was born in London in 1939, was educated at Haileybury till the age of seventeen, and has worked in the theatre, one way or another, ever since. Acting jobs came and went in rep at Worthing, Leatherhead and Oxford, and finally with Stephen Joseph's Studio Theatre in Scarborough, Stoke-on-Trent and elsewhere. During his time with the Studio Theatre he acted a wide variety of roles (I remember seeing him once, devastatingly, in drag as the dictatorial Cook in David Campton's *Little Brother, Little Sister*) and began to write under the pen name of Roland Allen. His earliest plays were actuated primarily by the desire to give himself show parts as an actor, but as time went on he became more interested in writing *per se*, and less interested in acting.

The first real success of his writing in this phase was ***Standing Room Only*** (1961), in which the elements of his later style are clearly visible. The situation undeniably has overtones of Theatre of the Absurd. The play postulates a future (but probably not too far distant future) in which London has finally become immobilized by that great, ultimate traffic jam which there is no untangling. As a result of this, thousands of Londoners have resigned themselves to staying where the jam left them, camping out in cars and buses all over the West End. The action of the play takes place on a double-decker bus stuck in Shaftesbury Avenue, and it retails a few hours in the lives of five characters who have taken up permanent residence in it with considerable comic adroitness, if at times some slight sense of strain at spinning out one joke quite so far. On the other hand, it already suggests Ayckbourn's particular speciality, the comedy of embarrassment, with its characters trying desperately to continue living normal, respectable, suburban lives in these very eccentric, public conditions.

Though there was talk of a West End production for ***Standing Room Only***, it never actually materialized. Ayckbourn's first West End airing came instead with ***Mister Whatnot***, staged by the Studio Theatre at Stoke-on-Trent in 1963 and at the Arts the following year. The oddity of this play was that it is about three-quarters mimed: the hero, a piano-tuner let loose in a stately home, never says a word throughout, and much of the rest of the action is conducted wordlessly. The piano-tuner falls in love with a Lord's daughter, and after various vicissitudes succeeds in marrying her in the teeth of the family's objections and in spite of her fiancé, an effete but eminently suitable candidate for her hand. One might suppose that the main inspiration for the play was silent film comedy, but in fact its closest connections seem to be with the films of the Marx Brothers, and there are sections of the action which look like conscious tributes to Harpo in particular. For instance, there is a big meal-table scene in which our hero hides beneath the tablecloth and progressively eats and drinks his way round the table, to the puzzlement and consternation of the diners, who remain unaware of his presence and cannot understand why glasses and plates which, they could have sworn, were full a moment ago are now empty.

The audiences were amused, but the play got a mixed press and did not run. Not so with Ayckbourn's next West End play, ***Relatively Speaking*** (1967). This at once established itself as a major popular success, and went on to be translated into a dozen or more languages and produced all over the world. It is an essay in sheer mechanical ingenuity—the spinning-out of one joke beyond any reasonable possibility—and works as much on the audience's nerves (will he or won't he be able to come up with yet one more twist?) as directly on their funny bone. It thereby achieves the curious effect of being at once forced and funny. It turns entirely on one endless misunderstanding. Greg, a rather innocent young man involved in a serious affair with a not-so-innocent girl, decides he wants to marry her, and therefore wants to meet her family. She is evasive about this, but tells him that an address he finds scribbled on a cigarette-packet is that of her parents, whom she is going to visit that Sunday. So, come Sunday our hero turns up at a house in the country to introduce himself as Virginia's fiancé. But as we know, or very rapidly guess, the occupants are not her parents at all, but her former lover (an older man) and the lover's unsuspecting wife. If this were Feydeau that would be the beginning, and endless complications would follow. In any case, it would be only one thread in an intricate mesh of inter-related intrigues. But for Ayckbourn that is all there is to it.

The four people concerned are the entire cast, and the whole comedy is extracted from the possible patterns of misunderstanding which can be found in this one basic situation. It has to begin with a couple of pretty obvious falsities: when Greg arrives at 'The Willows' he is made to behave as surely no young man in the world would behave, and certainly as no one as shy and socially self-conscious as he would, by marching in, not introducing himself at all (not even 'I'm Greg - Ginny's fiancé') and remaining sublimely unconscious of the total mystification his arrival causes. Why? Obviously, because the play would stop there and then if he were permitted to say any more. The comedy then derives entirely from variations on embarrassment, with the well-bred hosts trying vainly to find out who their unexpected guest is and what the hell he wants without appearing to do so. If the degree of evasiveness Greg manages unconsciously to achieve is beyond the capacity (or incapacity) of any sane person, the responses of the older couple are beautifully observed and hysterically funny.

The first act curtain, predictably enough, is the arrival of Ginny, come to satisfy her curiosity about her ex-lover's wife. (Another improbability which is a little hard to swallow, incidentally, for how on earth would she explain her appearance there without giving the game away if the unexpected presence of Greg did not remove the necessity?) Now the lady of the house feels fairly happy: here is the missing link, in that she knows Virginia works for her husband, and can therefore imagine some reason why she and her fiancé should have turned up this bright Sunday morning. But for the husband complications are only just starting. After freeing his mind of the understandable confusion that it is his wife rather than his 'daughter' ex-mistress that the young man wants to marry, he then has to cope with the problem of keeping up the pretence that the girl is his daughter for Greg while not arousing his wife's suspicions in the process. Once committed to this ticklish situation, he warms to his task and starts embroidering things for Greg with a string of splendidly embarrassing reminiscences of his 'daughter's' childhood, when she was so fat she was almost circular and was known as 'Jumbo Ginny'. Eventually, when this situation too has been milked for as many laughs as possible, all the complications get sorted out, even if no one ends up much the wiser. At each stage in the play there is present, shadowy but haunting, the feeling that the next moment it may just come to a stop, that even Ayckbourn's considerable ingenuity may run out and he will not be able to find another trick to keep things going in despite of all reason. It doesn't, and he does; the tight-rope is successfully walked even though we are sometimes too uncomfortably conscious of the abyss which yawns beneath.

Much the same could be said of Ayckbourn's next full-length play to reach the West End, ***How the Other Half Loves*** (1970). Here again mechanical ingenuity is the making, and at times almost the breaking of the play. The initial situation is again quite simple: we meet two families, the Fosters (upper-middle class) and the Phillipses (on their way up), linked by the fact that the husbands both work in the same firm, and that Mrs Foster is having a secret affair with Mr Phillips. The play would be quite slight and conventional, were it not for one brilliant technical device (a little like Peter Shaffer's switching of light values in *Black Comedy*) which makes it. This consists of superimposing the two households in one set, which is alternately or as a rule simultaneously the Fosters' drawing-room and the Phillips's living-room. The walls are variegated with patches of their different decorative schemes (pseudo-damask wallpaper and distemper-contemporary), their sofa and chairs mix Harrods-grand with suburban-inventive, and when the table is laid for dinner it is half linen and crystal, half paper napkins and tumblers from the shop round the corner.

This enables simultaneous actions in the two houses to be not only crosscut but intertwined. It turns out that a hapless and socially out-of-their-depth couple, the Featherstones (he works in the clerical department) have been hit upon by both guilty parties in the little game of marital infidelity as an alibi and consequently have to take embarrassing part in two simultaneous and variously excruciating dinner-parties at the same table. This sequence is the climax and really the *raison d'être* of the play. The Featherstones, almost equally ill at ease socially with both the Fosters and the Phillipses, find matters even worse when they are unwittingly forced to provide a smokescreen for Fiona Foster and Bob Phillips during an awkward dinner-table conversation which they never quite begin to grasp the drift of. Especially since they are seen by us as undergoing these two ordeals at the same time, staggering conversationally from one end of the table to the other, with the minor upsets of one occasion being picked up immediately in the talk of the other (Featherstone knocks something over in one, his hostess in the other speeds to mop it up).

But the superimposition device is used with great ingenuity throughout, as characters walk round each other, deliver insults in each other's face, sublimely, mutually unaware, and talk in apparently unrelated snatches of dialogue which nevertheless for us pick up one another, re-echoing or briskly deflating. It is only after the dinner-parties when the double set becomes single and all the complications are disentangled, that the play drifts into anti-climax. But where it is funny it is very funny indeed, with a dash and conviction which makes all question of whether Ayckbourn can qualify (on the grounds of technical innovation) as a 'new dramatist' or must be written down (on the grounds of his subject-matter and flighty approach to it) as a crass conservative sublimely irrelevant.

Not, I think, that one would ever be tempted to classify Ayckbourn as an important dramatist. He knows his limitations and seems to work very happily within them. Though not many of his plays have turned up in London, he is quite prolific, still writing plays for the Scarborough company where he started at the rate of about one a year (latest ***The Story So Far***, 1970), and writing them off if they flop. He has also written a number of shorter pieces, such as ***Countdown***, a sketch in the marital diversion ***Mixed Doubles*** (1969) about a long-married couple continuing their own interior-monologue reveries while the husband tells a joke, and ***Ernie's Incredible Illucinations*** (1969), a playlet for children about a boy with an embarrassing gift for materializing his fantasies. If Ayckbourn looks certain to remain, at best, one of our most reliable light entertainers, there are, after all, many worse things to be. . . .

J. W. Lambert, E. Shorter, R. Craig, J. Peter (essay date 1973)

SOURCE: "Plays in Performance," in *Drama, London* No. 110, Autumn, 1973, pp. 17-29.

[*In the following excerpt, the authors discuss trends and review plays in London theater.*]

Time to sober up, to return to the straight, though luckily not the strait, and still less narrow, theatre. In particular to the commercial (or as it would prefer independent) theatre, which has produced a by no means contemptible clutch of comedies. Unquestionably first among them is Alan Ayckbourn's tongue-twistingly titled ***Absurd Person Singular*** (Criterion). Those of us who have managed ever since ***Relatively Speaking*** to enjoy Mr. Ayckbourn's plays without condescension must observe with rueful amusement his gradual promotion by the *beau monde* into what in fact he always was, something more than a deft contriver of after-dinner amusement; after all, ***How the Other Half Loves*** even managed (unlike Ustinov's *Half-way up a Tree*) to survive the inevitable transmogrification imposed by the mischievous enormity of Robert Morley. ***Time and Time Again*** is an astonishing demonstration of how to use farce techniques for sharp social comment and insight into human nature. And ***Absurd Person Singular*** repeats the process. If I have a reservation it is that there is here less humanity; clarity of vision begins to seem at times a little flushed with *Schadenfreude*. Nevertheless the piece is enormously enjoyable as well as lethal in its portraits of six assorted middle-class English on three successive Christmas Eves. First we are in the speckless kitchen of Sidney and Jane; he a small tradesman, she an obsessive if muddle-headed housewife, entertaining their bank manager and his socially superior lady and a young architect and his difficult wife. Farcical disasters proliferate. So far, so good. Next we are in the progressive young architect's cluttered mess of a kitchen; his neurotic wife keeps attempting suicide, the bank manager's wife is floating out on a tide of alcohol, the visiting small tradesman's wife busies herself with cleaning up—and the curtain falls on a mood of still uproariously funny but increasingly chill hysteria as the sextet, in varying stages of collapse, join one by one in singing 'The Twelve Days of Christmas'.

Last comes the big-house kitchen-sitting room of the bank manager, with some sort of an air of comfortable traditional values about it. But there is no heating, the bank manager's wife is upstairs, by now a hopeless alcoholic, he himself has withdrawn into a fog of affable indifference, the young architect's career has collapsed (though his suicidal wife has, all unexplained, turned into a briskly competent young woman). Enter the former small tradesman, now well on the way to big money as a property developer. With appalling geniality he sets the others, all too literally, dancing to his tune, and the play ends with a gruesomely funny demonstration of the power of money.

Eric Thompson's direction most skilfully paces the personal and professional development of the six: Alan Tagg's sets neatly sum up the character of each *ménage*. Perhaps Richard Briers, as the manic tradesman on the make, and Sheila Hancock as the bank manager's lost wife, offer dazzling caricatures, but I shouldn't care to quibble. Certainly Bridget Turner's quintessential housewife, Anna Calder-Marshall's obsessively wrecked young architect's wife, David Burke as the shaggy, aggressive, womanizing pride of the polytechnic and Michael Aldridge as the gently fading bank manager weave a superbly comic, sharply cruel portrait of a very real society. . . .

John Russell Taylor (essay date 1981)

SOURCE: "Art and Commerce: The New Drama in the West End Marketplace," in *Contemporary English Drama*, edited by C. W. E. Bigsby, Edward Arnold, 1981, pp. 177-88.

[*In the following excerpt, Taylor discusses whether the New Drama loses its ideals in an effort to be commercially successful, pointing out that Ayckbourn has maintained the ideal while achieving success.*]

. . . The main distinguishing feature of the New Drama was that in various ways its writers challenged our view of reality, or even denied that it existed at all ('What have I seen', inquired one of Pinter's characters, 'the scum or the essence?'). Traditional dramatists, on the other hand, however much they might challenge our received ideas about intellectual, social, political or moral issues, usually left reality as such alone: maybe they recognized that it was 'a joint pretence' on which we all depended to continue (Pinter again), but if so they were certainly not going to hint as much to their audiences. In the 1970s two important dramatists at least diverged from the New Drama norm by seeming to assume, and allowing us comfortingly to assume, that while the whole truth might not be known, it was not of its nature unknowable.

They were, of course, Alan Ayckbourn and Simon Gray. Apart from their success with a vast, non-specialized public they have virtually nothing else in common. It is altogether possible that Simon Gray nurtures fantasies of deeper significance for his works: his play for the National Theatre, *Close of Play* (1979), certainly roused a lot of discussion of what was real and what was imaginary (were this benighted family on an awful weekend get-together all imagined by the mute father who remains centre-stage throughout, or was he imagined by them, or were they maybe all dead?). But unfortunately the piece gave much too much the impression of having been deliberately devised as a tribute to Experiment to impress the critics (which on the whole it didn't) and dutifully bore National Theatre audiences (which on the whole it did). One could hardly take it seriously as a statement about the identity-crisis of our own times or something of the sort. And at least, once he had got that out of his system, Gray returned cheerfully to his natural stamping-ground in *Stage Struck*, Agatha Christie with intellect.

Ayckbourn, happily, has never been troubled with delusions of deeper significance. Of his whole very theatrically orientated generation (he was born in 1939) he has probably been the most complete, all-round man of the theatre. He began at the age of seventeen as an actor in provincial rep, ending up with Stephen Joseph's Studio Theatre company in Scarborough and Stoke on Trent. Here he did just about everything, as actor, director, ASM, general odd-job man and also, eventually, writer under the name of Roland Allen. His first play to reach London (briefly) was ***Mr Whatnot*** in 1964; his first resounding success was ***Relatively Speaking***, produced in Scarborough in 1965 as ***Meet My Father*** and in London in 1967. Since then he has established himself as far and away our most prolific dramatist as well as our most staggering commercial success, with, at one point, no fewer than five plays running simultaneously in London. (It might be added, parenthetically, that he seems to be very specifically a British taste; his plays have never done so well elsewhere, and certainly not in New York.) In recent years he has also been in general control of his own theatre at Scarborough, where he tries out many more plays than London theatregoers could ever suspect, more even than see the light of day in the South, difficult though that is to imagine.

At least Ayckbourn's plays are all of a piece, middle-class plays for middle-class audiences, set wherever in the scampi-belt the garden gnomes grow thickest. Certainly he began with out-and-out farce, and has moved little by little into character comedy, but not, apparently, with any of the comedian's traditional desire to play Hamlet. Rather, he has created his own comic world, and if from time to time he feels inclined to probe it a little deeper, he never shows any signs of ceasing to see it as comic at all. One or two of his plays manage a hint or two of melancholy just beneath the surface: ***Time and Time Again*** (1971-72), perhaps, and ***Joking Apart*** (1979) begin, particularly the latter, to mirror a certain menopausal dissatisfaction with life on the part of Ayckbourn's characters if not, we may presume, of Ayckbourn himself. But in general he is content to recolonize for the English theatre those territories of society which have been lying fallow since *French Without Tears* began to seem intolerably elitist and out of touch with life (which is to say, some time before it came to look like a charming period piece and long before it began to seem again to be a play which had something of lasting validity to say about youth and growing up and life).

Ayckbourn is in fact an interesting and exceptional dramatist because what turns him on in his plays is so evenly divided between the creation of character and milieu, and the element of purely technical challenge. In ***Relatively Speaking*** the technical challenge seems to be uppermost: one would guess that Ayckbourn has set out quite deliberately to make the most out of the least, to see just how far one farcical joke (a misunderstanding involving a girl's fiancé in the belief that her older lover is actually her father) can be taken without cracking under the strain. Admittedly this is your basic stuff of farce, and that is the way it is developed. But to make so much capital out of the one simple situation—especially for an author who, as we have subsequently had ample evidence, is hardly short of ideas—does appear to invite comment on the prestidigitatory side of the proceedings: we must, surely, be meant to be aware of (to vary the metaphor) just how dangerous a tightrope our dramatist is treading. Hope/fear that he will fall is all part of the fun.

But since ***Relatively Speaking*** Ayckbourn has managed to keep his elements in better balance. If the human element is more prominent and important in ***How the Other Half Loves*** (1970), so is the purely technical. The trick of the play, in fact, resides, as with *Black Comedy*, in one technical device which, once the audience grasps it, becomes an enjoyable talking-point in itself, being not only used, but displayed for all it is worth. In this case it is the notion of combining two households in one set, super-imposed and intertwined. The set is half pseudo-grand, with damask wallpaper and Harrods' traditional furniture, half struggling *Guardian*-reader, with distemper and nappies drying; the two households are equally contrasted, linked only by the fact that the two husbands work in the same firm and that, secretly, Mrs Foster (grand) is having an affair with Mr Phillips (ambitious). The actions that go on in the two rooms alternate and often get inextricably involved with each other as a character in one will narrowly miss collision with a character in the other or apparently (from the audience's point of view) deliver a resounding insult fairly and squarely in the face of his victim, without either party on stage being aware of it. The climax of farcical ingenuity comes with the dinner scene, when an innocent third family, which has been used as an alibi by both philanderers, finds itself embarrassingly involved in two simultaneous dinner parties, full of ambiguity and devastating cross-reference, at a table which is half linen and crystal, half paper napkins and tumblers from the local supermarket.

It is possible to suspect that without the mechanical complication Ayckbourn's plays might turn out to be pretty thin. But one might as well wonder what Feydeau would be like without his clockwork precision of intrigue: that, after all, is the prime source of his creativity. Ayckbourn is a little bit more interested in his people as people than Feydeau, but finally he is interested in them only within the context of the complex structures he devises to set them in motion, and it would be unrealistic to complain that these structures are only an elaborate cover he adopts to disguise from us the limitations of his human vision. Certainly when he does not have the structural complexity, as in, say, ***Ten Times Table*** (1978), his plays can seem pretty frail and long drawn out. Also one can well see in that play how heavily he may depend on having the right actor to bulk out the role with his or her own personality: a Tom Courtenay or Penelope Keith role may well thin to vanishing point when played by anyone else.

But on the other hand, in one of his really complicated works, like ***The Norman Conquests*** (1974), the characters do take on intricacy too. The three plays which make up ***The Norman Conquests***, played in repertory on consecutive nights, are in some ways an extension of the idea of ***How the Other Half Loves***, turning it, in a sense, inside out. This time all the romantic and other intrigues are going on in the same house at the same time, during another ghastly weekend. So while we are watching people popping in and out of the garden at just the right wrong moments, we are probably wondering what on earth can be going on in the dining room or the drawing room. The classical answer is that nothing is: the characters are existent only when and where we see them, and there is no point asking how many children Lady Macbeth had or other such questions which presuppose that there is a larger reality of which what we see in the theatre is but a small segment. But, says Ayckbourn, what if I, the dramatist, know perfectly well what is going on elsewhere, and choose to tell you? Hence, we have these three plays, the action of which is for the most part simultaneous: put them together in your mind, and you know exactly where everyone is and what he or she is doing for just about every moment of the time covered.

Moreover, just in terms of time spent you have that much more acquaintance with the characters than any one play would give you. You come to know them in much the same way that you know your neighbours, and however improbable your neighbours may seem, it would never occur to you to doubt their existence: extent of acquaintance can conveniently stand in for depth and intensity. And thirdly, it is necessary for the complete working of the scheme that each one of the plays shall be self-sufficient and make perfect dramatic sense if seen without the other two. Of course, it may be hoped also that the first one you see (it could be any of the three) will be sufficiently entertaining and intriguing to send you back for more. And if this succeeds, it is a triumph of sheer theatrical expertise: one cannot imagine the effect being equal in any other medium, simply because here the stage's natural limitations are being turned into a decided advantage, whereas in a film, for instance, nothing could be simpler than to shift the locale from one room to another at will, and therefore nothing less interesting.

By the time of Ayckbourn's real emergence as a dramatist the New Drama itself was already old and settled enough to make questions of whether he really belonged to it, or was, rather, an entrenched conservative dressed up in a certain amount of technical gimmickry but none the less catering essentially for the complacencies of Aunt Edna, seem completely beside the point. New drama, old drama, what's the difference? The world is divided into plays that work and plays that don't. Most of Ayckbourn's do, and if he is finally Ben Travers for the 1970s, at least it is for the 1970s, not the 1930s. The New Drama has changed the expectations even of audiences who would never dream of enjoying one of those modern plays—very much as Shaw remarked in the 1890s 'A modern manager need not produce *The Wild Duck*, but he must be very careful not to produce a play which will seem insipid and old-fashioned to playgoers who have seen *The Wild Duck*, even though they may have hissed it.' Even a conservative audience is quite a bit different in its expectations today from how it was ten years ago, and it is ridiculous to berate a commercially successful dramatist for taking advantage of this difference without, as it were, having put in his stint of experimental unpopularity in order to deserve it. . . .

Simon Gray might well complain that he suffers from his own success: audiences and critics have been too quick to feel they have him taped, and react with quite unreasonable hostility if he tries anything different, as he has most spectacularly with *Close of Play*. But the fact is that he is best at what he is best known for, and applauding his enterprise in trying to do something different is not the same as admitting its success. It would seem that he is self-conscious about being, with Alan Ayckbourn, our most solidly popular, commercially bankable playwright during the 1970s. Like Robert Bolt before him, he would like to be taken differently, more seriously, and from time to time makes deliberate attempts in that direction. It is true that comedians seldom feel they are getting their just desserts: another successful commercial dramatist with higher aspirations, Alan Bennett, remarked when receiving his *Evening Standard* award for *Getting On* as the Best Comedy of 1971, that 'To be given the award for Best Comedy is rather like taking great care and love nurturing your finest marrow but when you take it to the show you find you have won the prize for best cucumber.'

Fortunately no such qualms seem to afflict Alan Ayckbourn. Or if they do, he wisely keeps them to himself. In his work the old and the new, art and commerce, are immaculately fused, so that it does not really matter in what light you choose to see his plays, they are just unarguably there. He offers a model for what the unpretentious but not contemptible commercial theatre of the 1970s (and after) should or may be like. Significantly, it seems that commercial and comic have to be synonymous: we are still waiting to see whether such a thing as a tragedy or even a strong drama can belong just as unmistakably to our own time and still achieve just as indisputable a broad-based popular success. Maybe *Equus* has done it: at any rate, it stands out as the only play of the 1970s which can put in a serious claim. But otherwise, funny can find the middle-brow public, while serious has to be either safely classic or dangerously contemporary. Perhaps the 1980s, and the changes they will inevitably bring in theatregoing tastes and habits, will also produce a playwright who can comfortably bridge the gap and produce that popular, modern, British tragedy that the world has supposedly been waiting for ever since *The Deep Blue Sea*.

Elmer M. Blistein (essay date 1983)

SOURCE: "Alan Ayckbourn: Few Jokes, Much Comedy," in *Modern Drama*, Vol. XXVI, No. 1, March, 1983, pp. 26-36.

[*In the following excerpt, Blistein praises Ayckbourn's comedies, focusing on his use of setting and time.*]

As *The Comedy of Errors* unties all its knots, as it finally reaches a moment of repose after a hectic and bewildering sequence of events, only two members of the dramatis personae are left on stage. They are identical twins, and they have just been reunited after thirty-three or twenty-five or twenty-three years. (Shakespeare is very precise about hours in this play, but he is cavalier in his treatment of years.) These identical twins, servants, have been crucial to the action, and they are the last to leave the stage. Twelve lines before *Exeunt*, Dromio of Syracuse says to his twin brother from Ephesus,

> There is a fat friend at your master's house,
> That kitchen'd me for you today at dinner.
>
> (V.i. 414-415)

Fine word, "kitchen'd," even though the *OED* suggests that used as a transitive verb it is obsolete, and so rare that it may even be a *hapax legomenon*.

Dromio is "kitchen'd" only once. The audience and readers of Alan Ayckbourn's ***Absurd Person Singular*** (1972) are kitchened for three acts of the three-act play on three successive Christmas Eves: first in "Sidney *and* Jane Hopcroft*'s kitchen of their small suburban house. Last Christmas*"; then in "Geoffrey *and* Eva Jackson*'s kitchen in their fourth-floor flat. This Christmas*"; finally in "*The* Brewster-Wrights' *kitchen. Next Christmas.*"[1]

The "*Last*," the "*This*," and the "*Next*" may give us pause for a moment, but the joke—if, indeed, it exists—is a mild one and may safely be disregarded. The setting may not be disregarded. We have all experienced comedies set in drawing rooms, in forests, in fields, in marketplaces, on seacoasts, on beaches, on piers, in bedrooms, in dining rooms, on porches, in gardens, but it took an Alan Ayckbourn to exploit to its fullest the comic potential of the unromantic, practical, even banal kitchen.

We should not be surprised. Settings have always been important in Ayckbourn's plays. In ***Standing Room Only*** (1961), one of his earliest efforts, the setting is a bus caught in a traffic jam on Shaftesbury Avenue. The time is the early twenty-first century, and the bus has been in the traffic jam so long that the driver's "two grown-up daughters have never known any other home, and indeed he has come to think that the bus's destination board announces his name, Hammersmith, with the letters Brdwy after it being his recommendation from London Transport: 'Best Ruddy Driver We've 'ad Yet'."[2]

In ***How the Other Half Loves*** (1969), the setting and the manipulation of time are far more complex than either the characters or the dialogue. Ayckbourn's opening stage direction tells us "*The* Curtain *rises to reveal two living rooms, partially lit. Not a composite setting but with two rooms contained and overlapping in the same area.*"[3] The overlap is so arranged that Fiona and Frank Foster and Teresa and Bob Phillips can entertain Mary and William Detweiler at separate dinner parties on the same stage at the same time. The audience, that is, watches the separate dinner parties taking place simultaneously. Actually, the Foster dinner is on Thursday evening and the Phillips dinner is on Friday evening. No, it is not all done with mirrors and fine wire, although we do expect some legerdemain when the program tells us that Act One, Scene 2 takes place on "Thursday And Friday Night" (p. 3). The uppercase conjunction simply requires the Detweilers to have swivel chairs that enable them to turn from the Phillips table to the Foster table at will, the playwright's will, for their complicated performance in this scene.

In ***Bedroom Farce*** (1975), all of the action takes place in three bedrooms which belong to Ernest and Delia, Malcolm and Kate, and Nick and Jan (p. 161). By means of cross-fades the audience's attention is drawn to one bedroom or another, but all are in view at all times. Just as another couple is needed to complicate the action in ***How the Other Half Loves***, so another couple, Trevor and Susannah, Ernest and Delia's son and daughter-in-law, is required to complicate the action in ***Bedroom Farce***. It may be of some interest that the French adaptation called the play *3 Lits pour 8*, and the advertising poster showed the upper portion of the *8* attached to the lower portion of the *3*.[4] Susannah and Trevor complicate matters by bringing their marital problems to all three bedrooms. At the conclusion they find themselves in Kate's and Malcolm's bed. Kate had urged Malcolm to take a bath to calm his nerves, after Trevor had arrived to say how sorry he and Susannah were that they had ruined Kate's and Malcolm's party. When Susannah joined Trevor in the bedroom and eventually in the bed, Kate prudently decided to find out how Malcolm was managing. When Trevor and Susannah are alone together, Susannah gives a strange but inevitable curtain speech that ends with her repeating for the third time in the play her incantation, her prayer, her mantra:

> Yes.
>
> [Trevor *cuddles up to her*]
>
> [*She holds his head in her arms*]
>
> . . . I've been thinking. We must do something about our house. I think that's important. I want to start trying to make it more of a home. I—haven't been very good at that. I mean, somewhere nice . . . then you'll want to come home all the more, won't you? And I'll try and cook. I mean, really cook . . . and make sure you have some clean clothes in the morning and . . . well. You know what I mean, don't you? Trevor? Trevor . . . ?
>
> [Trevor *is asleep*]
>
> [*alone*] Oh . . . I am confident in myself. I have confidence in myself. I am not unattractive. I am attractive. People still find me attractive . . .
>
> [*Lights fade slowly during this*]
>
> Curtain (p. 229)

It may be significant that the *Three Plays* version of what Susannah has called her "exercises" (p. 178) omits from her curtain speech the three sentences which had twice previously closed her mantra: "I am not afraid of people. People are not frightening. There is nothing to be frightened of" (pp. 178, 207). The Samuel French acting edition includes them, properly I think.[5]

Ayckbourn's most popular and, perhaps, most interesting manipulations of setting and time occur in ***The Norman Conquests*** (1973).[6] Ian Watson describes ***The Norman Conquests*** succinctly and accurately: "Three self-contained plays, featuring the same people at the same house over the same weekend. Each play stands as a complete entity and can be performed independently of the other two; although in practice, all three are usually played on consecutive nights, to be seen in any order."[7] I am not so sure about "any order." I prefer ***Round and Round the Garden*** for the first play in the sequence (only a lavishly sententious critic would call ***The Norman Conquests*** a trilogy). ***Table Manners*** ought to be second, and ***Living Together*** ought to be third. My not-so-arbitrary preference is based on the time given for the first scene in each play's opening stage direction: in *Garden*, the first scene takes place in "*The garden, Saturday, 5:30 p.m.*" (p. 1); in *Table*, the first scene takes place in "*The dining-room, Saturday, 6 p.m.*" (p. 1); and in ***Living***, the first scene is in "*The sitting-room, Saturday, 6:30 p.m.*" (p. 1). To make ***Garden*** an envelope of sorts for all three plays, its last scene is the latest of the three; it takes place on Monday at 9 a.m. (p. 37). The last scenes of ***Table*** (p. 48) and ***Living*** (p. 40) take place on Monday at 8 a.m.

The three plays present six characters in search not of an author but of something less tangible. Annie, the spinster, seeks love and escape, but not necessarily in that order. Ruth, her myopic sister who refuses to wear glasses because of vanity, according to some, but because glasses irritate her sinuses, according to her, is looking for continuing success in her never-described career. Reg, their brother, really wants little out of life. He merely wants some people to play the board games he invents and an occasional person to laugh at his jokes as he is so willing to laugh at others'. Sarah, his shrewish, dominating wife, is the kind of person John Donne had in mind when he said, ". . . O, to some / Not to be martyrs is a martyrdom" ("The Litany," ll. 89-90). She seeks perfection in an imperfect world whose imperfections she has not only richly augmented, but also magnified. Tom, a bachelor and a veterinarian, is a kindly but dim soul who prefers animals to people, but who likes Annie and needs somebody to direct him into her arms. And finally, there is Norman, Ruth's errant husband, whose "Conquests" are ironically chronicled, and not merely in the title. In the social spectrum, Norman belongs at the infrared end; he is a social anarchist persuaded that social contracts are for other people, not him. Married to Ruth, he has already bedded—perhaps "rugged" would be a better term—Annie, the previous Christmas when Ruth was upstairs sick in bed. This weekend he manages to bed his wife, Ruth, on the same rug, and then replies in response to her "It's nice on the rug," "I told you it was. It can be our rug" (***Living***, p. 40). Norman and Annie's rug, Norman and Ruth's rug, but not yet—and probably never—Norman and Sarah's rug, even though at one point in the hectic activities of the weekend, Sarah has just about agreed to go off with Norman for a couple of days to, perhaps, Bournemouth (***Living***, p. 48).

And going away with Norman is what this involved action is all about. After the Christmas interlude on the furry rug, Norman and Annie had taken about six months to make arrangements by telephone and letter to spend a weekend together in Hastings. Discovering that Hastings was all booked, Norman made, or said he made,[8] reservations in East Grinstead, and had purchased himself a new pair of pyjamas because, as Annie suggests, "just because you're unfaithful there's no need for your pyjamas to be as well"

(*Garden*, p. 8). Sarah had grudgingly agreed to come with Reg to take care of the offstage presence, Annie's, Ruth's, and Reg's mother, while Annie had a brief holiday. By her officious probing, Sarah discovered with whom Annie was going away, saw to it that the plan was canceled, called Ruth to inform her of her husband's and sister's attempted peccadillo and to insist that Ruth come at once to confront Norman. Norman, frustrated, gets blind drunk on homemade dandelion and parsnip wine—the thought of either makes a gourmand, let alone a gourmet, gag—and adds more confusion to the sixes and sevens that already exist.

But then there is that offstage presence. Annie, the spinster, needed somebody to spell her so she could go off for a weekend, for she is responsible for her bedridden mother. This mother never makes an appearance fortunately, if all we hear about her is true. She is described by Sarah, her daughter-in-law, as a tart. It seems clear from what her children, Reg, Ruth, and Annie, say about her that she may be charitably described as a woman who just seems to have liked men other than her husband. She is bedridden because, as Annie says to Ruth, and with some compassion: "She just has no desire to get up. No reason to. So she doesn't. Sad, really. Her whole life was centred round men, wasn't it? When they lost interest in her, she lost interest in herself" (*Living*, p. 31).

Here, then, are three plays with twelve scenes, in three different settings, at eleven different times. Surely confusion should be worse confounded, but that does not happen. The story line is clear, for the integration of the three plays is skillfully done and highlighted by pertinent action, not merely movement. In the first scene of *Table*, Sarah, the whining shrew (that description is not an oxymoron in Sarah's case), throws a biscuit tin at Reg, her husband (p. 15), and Annie appears with a dustpan (p. 16). In the first scene of *Living*, Annie, Tom, and Norman hear the clatter; Annie leaves to discover the cause, reappears for a moment with a dustpan and brush as she goes to help clean up the mess (pp. 12-13); and Reg mentions the matter twice more in the second scene (pp. 17-18).

In the first scene of *Table*, Sarah sends Reg to check on Norman and Annie in the sitting room (p. 12), because she does not trust them alone together. Reg enters just as Annie has "*impulsively*" kissed Norman on the cheek because he looks "so limp. Like an old tea towel." Reg picks up a wastepaper basket to justify his statement that he has "just come in for something," and exits (*Living*, p. 6). Sarah then impels, and I choose the word advisedly, Tom to the sitting room (*Table*, p. 13), and he joins Annie and Norman (*Living*, p. 7).

Dialogue, too, integrates the plays. Norman, overcome by dandelion and parsnip wine (he may also have drunk some carrot wine, but that is not clear), becomes melancholy and weepy as he mournfully intones a half-dozen times: "Nobody loves me. . . . Nobody loves me at all," "(*to Sarah*) Nobody loves me. (*To Annie*) Nobody loves me . . ." (*Garden*, pp. 15-16, 24); "Nobody loves me. Nobody loves me any more" (*Living*, p. 27). When he delivers these lines, both Annie and Sarah have a sympathetic yen for him, even though we should not call that yen love. Ruth is not yet on the scene, but she is married to him, and by the following scene she is snuggled in the sitting-room rug with him as she says, "It's nice on the rug" (*Living*, p. 40). Both Tom and Reg have commented that he is a pleasant fellow, and will say so again, so Norman's "Nobody loves me" may safely be translated that Norman does not love himself.

Ruth's attitude toward Norman may be described as liberated, amused, occasionally bemused, but certainly not as sadly resigned. Consider a dialogue she has with Sarah:

> Ruth Sarah dear, I've been married to Norman for five years. I have learnt through bitter experience that the last thing to do with Norman is to take him seriously. That's exactly what he wants. . . .
>
> Sarah I'm amazed you've stayed with him. I really am.
>
> Ruth Well, I don't really look at it that way. I rather think of him as staying with me. After all, I make all the payments on the house, most of the furniture is mine. It has crossed my mind, in moments of extreme provocation, to throw him out—but I don't know, I think I must be rather fond of him. It's a bit like owning an oversized unmanageable dog, being married to Norman. He's not very well house-trained, he needs continual exercising—mental and physical—and it's sensible to lock him up if you have visitors. Otherwise he mauls them. But I'd hate to get rid of him.
>
> Sarah That's all very well if you keep him under proper control. When he goes upsetting other people's lives. Annie's, for example . . .
>
> Ruth You really can't blame Norman entirely, you know. He only jumps up at people who encourage him. It's a general rule, if you don't want him licking your face, don't offer him little titbits. I don't mean just Annie either. (*Garden*, p. 25)

A dog is, at least, animate. When Ruth has a conversation with Annie about Norman, she now compares him to something inanimate, a book. Norman is an assistant librarian, and I suspect the emphasis should be on the word assistant:

> Annie I'm sorry. I never for a minute intended to take Norman away from you or anything.
>
> Ruth Forget it. You couldn't possibly take Norman away from me. That assumes I own him in the first place. I've never done that. I always feel with Norman that I have him on loan from somewhere. Like one of his library books. I'll get a card one day informing me he's overdue and there's a fine to pay on him. (*Table*, p. 36)

Norman would not, it seems, object to the comparison. He does not initiate, but freely uses the same comparison when speaking about Annie and himself in a conversation with Sarah. She has accused him of stealing Annie away from Tom. He denies the possibility of theft:

NORMAN I wasn't stealing her, I was borrowing her. For the week-end.

SARAH Make her sound like one of your library books.

NORMAN She was borrowing me, too. It was mutual. It was a friendly loan. We never intended to upset anybody. We both agreed. That was the joy of it, don't you see? Nobody need ever to have known. (***Living***, pp. 4-5)

In this case Norman is talking to the wrong person. Sarah believes that all such information should be imparted to others, particularly if the information could possibly cause pain.

There is one line which Norman repeats so often, about a dozen times in the three plays, that it acts like a reprise. The line deals with Norman's desire to make people, particularly women, happy. Ruth has just kissed Norman at his request, and this dialogue ensues:

NORMAN Are you happy?

RUTH What?

NORMAN Do I make you happy at all?

RUTH Well . . .

NORMAN Say you're happy.

RUTH Why? Is it important?

NORMAN Yes. I want you to be happy. I want everyone to be happy. I want to make everyone happy. It's my mission in life . . .

RUTH Yes, all right, Norman. Well, let's not worry about other people too much, just concentrate on making me happy, will you? The other people will have to try to be happy without you, won't they?

NORMAN But you are happy?

RUTH Yes, I'm fairly happy. (***Living***, p. 45)

The first we had heard about Norman's desire to make someone happy was at breakfast on the morning after Norman's drunkenness. Sarah, Annie, and Reg were doing their best to ignore Norman, so he indulged in a lengthy dialogue about his and other people's behavior. After Sarah and Annie left the room as a result of one of Norman's outrageous statements, only Reg was left to listen to Norman wallowing in his self-pity:

I suppose you think I'm cruel, too, don't you? Well, I've damn good cause to be, haven't I? I mean, nobody's thought about my feelings, have they? It's all Annie - Annie - Annie—what about me? I was going to give her everything. Well, as much as I could. My whole being. I wanted to make her happy for a week-end, that's all. (***Table***, p. 22)

The reprise is heard again toward the end of *Table*, when Norman, having suggested an assignation to Sarah, says: "I'd like to make you happy, Sarah. . . . Is that wrong of me? To want to see you happy? . . . I'd very much like to make you happy" (p. 50). Two sides later, after a few entrances and exists, Sarah and Norman are alone for a moment and this considered dialogue occurs:

SARAH Reg gets home about half past six in the evening on weekdays.

NORMAN Busy man.

SARAH If you feel like giving me a ring, any time. I'm usually tied to the house. I don't get out much.

NORMAN I'd make you happy, Sarah.

SARAH Yes.

NORMAN 'Bye-bye.

Norman goes out to the house, eating the last of his toast. Sarah looks thoughtful. She gives a pleased grunt. (p. 52)

The adjective "pleased" and the noun "grunt" tell us how Sarah reacts to Norman's proposition. How Norman reacts to her suggestion to call her is not difficult to ascertain, and his reaction is enhanced rather than vitiated by the speeches and action just before the final curtain some three sides later:

Annie flies at Norman and clings on to him

ANNIE Oh, Norman. . . . (*muffled*) I want . . .

NORMAN Eh?

ANNIE I want . . .

NORMAN I can't hear you. What?

ANNIE (*in a wail*) I want to go to East Grinstead.

NORMAN (*soothing her*) All right. Fine. I'll take you. I'll take you.

ANNIE (*tearfully*) Will you?

NORMAN Just say the word. Come on now, don't cry. I'll make you happy. Don't worry. I'll make you happy.

Norman hugs her to him. Annie clings on. Norman looks towards the window, then out front, smiling happily

CURTAIN. (p. 55)

This passage certainly should be the coda, not another reprise. So far as the audience can figure out, Norman has been reconciled with his wife (***Living***, p. 45), has an assignation pending with Sarah (***Table***, pp. 50, 52), and a promised assignation with Annie (***Table***, p. 55). The plays, after all, are called ***The Norman Conquests***. Whatever the case for William the Norman, our Norman is a bastard in the colloquial if not in the literal sense. He cannot end up as a conqueror. He must get his comeuppance so that our bourgeois prejudices may be appeased. So, at the end of ***Garden*** Ayckbourn destroys our social anarchist. As departure time arrives, Norman's car will not start. Reg gets a rope in order to pull Norman's car to the top of an incline so that he can get started. Reg warns Norman to give him sufficient time to get out of the way before Norman releases his hand brake.

What happens is obvious. Norman's car crashes into the back of Reg's. All must stay for another day. The myopic but insightful Ruth turns to Norman and this colloquy concludes the plays:

> RUTH If I didn't know you better, I'd say you did all that deliberately.
>
> NORMAN Me? Why should I want to do that?
>
> SARAH Huh.
>
> NORMAN Give me one good reason why I'd do a thing like that?
>
> RUTH Offhand, I can think of three.
>
> *Pause*
>
> NORMAN Ah. (*Brightening*) Well, since we're all here, we ought to make the most of it, eh? What do you say?
>
> *Norman smiles round at the women in turn*
>
> *Ruth gets up and without another word goes into the house* (*After her*) Ruth . . .
>
> *He turns to Annie but she too, rises and goes into the house* Annie . . .
>
> *He turns to Sarah. She, likewise, rises and follows the others* Sarah!
>
> *Norman is left alone, bewildered, then genuinely hurt and indignant* (*Shouting after them*) I only wanted to make you happy.
>
> CURTAIN. (p. 49)

Here is the coda, not another reprise. By outrageous behavior, by clever words, by dexterous hands, by eliciting sympathy when he is tipsy or drunk, Norman has managed to seduce—I do not think that is the wrong word; Norman manages to lead all three aside, at least temporarily, into the primrose path of dalliance—his wife, her sister, and her sister-in-law. If they all reject him at the end, if the moral indignation of all Pecksniffian audiences is assuaged, a cynic may well consider that united the women stand, divided they fall. When Norman is one-on-one with a woman, he is successful. Consider the last scenes of ***Living*** and ***Table***.

Norman does want to make people, especially women, happy. If he knows only one, two, three, four ways to do that—behavior (outrageous), words (clever), hands and other body parts (dexterous), sympathy (elicited by tipsiness)—neither Reg nor Tom knows even one. But Norman's method is not rape, despite Annie's comment: "Norman doesn't bother with secret signals at all. It was just wham, thump and there we both were on the rug" (***Table***, p. 5). Norman, and perhaps he does achieve conquests after all, makes three women happy occasionally; there is no evidence that either Tom or Reg ever makes any woman happy at any time. So, although Norman is merely the title character of ***The Norman Conquests***, he is more important as an eponym than Cymbeline or King John. Sarah may be "fifth Business," but Norman runs the show, and we are luckier and, yes, happier for it.

For what sets Ayckbourn apart from most contemporary writers of comedy is the fact, as Walter Kerr and others have noted,[9] that he can make us laugh without writing one-liners. His comedy depends upon the adroit juxtaposition of episodes, the clever manipulation of time, the dexterous use of props. In Ayckbourn's plays, a lawn chair, a biscuit tin, a rug, an easy-to-assemble-yourself dressing table, a wastepaper basket are more important than a clever line. He can write one-liners, but he seems to want to subordinate them to visual effects.

Ayckbourn's progress in the theater from actor to assistant stage manager to technical stage manager to director may have influenced the path his writing would take. But certainly over the last two decades he has given us comedies that test the traditional limits of time, place, and action. Events that normally happen offstage are brought onstage in ***Absurd Person Singular***. In ***The Norman Conquests***, although Ayckbourn requires three plays to accomplish the feat, every offstage action is brought onstage, and every onstage action has repercussions offstage. The solving of Rubik's Cube becomes child's play in comparison. But Ayckbourn has more than cleverness to offer. He writes comedies about people who genuinely concern us in situations that appear to be inevitable. What more can we ask?

Notes

1. Alan Ayckbourn, *Absurd Person Singular*, in *Three Plays: Absurd Person Singular, Absent Friends, and Bedroom Farce* (New York, 1979), pp. 15, 45, 71. All quotations from this play and *Bedroom Farce* are from this edition.
2. *Standing Room Only* has not been published. This description is taken from Ian Watson, *Conversations with Ayckbourn* (London, 1981), p. 176.
3. Alan Ayckbourn, *How the Other Half Loves* (New York, 1971), p. 5.
4. Watson, *Conversations*, p. 162.
5. Alan Ayckbourn, *Bedroom Farce* (New York, 1977), p. 58.
6. *The Norman Conquests* comprises three plays: *Round and Round the Garden* (New York, 1975), *Table Manners* (New York, 1975), and *Living Together* (New York, 1975). All quotations from these plays are taken from these editions.
7. Watson, *Conversations*, p. 180.
8. Norman plays fast and loose with the truth so often in his courtship (a fine Victorian word) routines so frequently, that it is difficult to determine when he is telling the truth in factual matters. Is he telling the truth or is he lashing out in frustration when he

yells after Annie, who has run out on his monologue: "I didn't even book the hotel. I knew you wouldn't come. You didn't have the guts." (*Table*, p. 22)?

9. Walter Kerr, in "Hail the Conquering Ayckbourn," *The New York Times*, 14 December 1975, describes *The Norman Conquests* as "this happy saga of mishaps among the mismatched" (Sec. 2, p. 1), and goes on later to say, "As for Mr. Ayckbourn, he's a sly one. He doesn't write one-liners . . ." (Sec. 2, p. 5). And in "Ayckbourn, Ex-Actor, Now Plays Singular Writer of Comedies," *The New York Times*, 11 October 1974, Mel Gussow says, "he writes 'comedy of people' rather than 'line comedy'." Gussow then goes on to quote Ayckbourn:"'No one comes out of the theater singing my lines,' he said. 'Actually they're not very good jokes because they're made by the characters themselves. To them, it's totally unfunny, but it's funny to the audience'" (p. 30, cols. 2-3).

Malcom Page (essay date 1983)

SOURCE: "The Serious Side of Alan Ayckbourn," in *Modern Drama*, Vol. XXVI, No. 1, March, 1983, pp. 36-46.

[*In the following excerpt, Page discusses how Ayckbourn's work deals with the many serious aspects of being human.*]

The comedies of Alan Ayckbourn have featured prominently in the British theatre in the last fifteen years. His earliest plays were the lightest and purest of comedies, giving him the reputation of being the most undemanding of entertainers. This initial reputation has obscured the depth and the seriousness of some of his plays, particularly those of 1974-78: ***Absent Friends, Just Between Ourselves***, and ***Joking Apart***.

Ayckbourn's first big success, ***Relatively Speaking***, staged in London in 1967,[1] led John Russell Taylor to judge that Ayckbourn "avoided any suggestion of deeper meaning," that one would not classify him as "important," and that he "looks certain to remain, at best, one of our most reliable light entertainers. . . ."[2] In 1973, Michael Billington pronounced that Ayckbourn's "sole aim is to make us laugh. His plays contain no messages, offer no profound vision of the universe, tell us nothing about how to live our lives."[3] John Elsom in 1977 stressed technique: ". . . Ayckbourn is the nearest British equivalent to Feydeau—in his skill, wit, neat characteristics and style."[4] Even in 1981, Hilary Spurling could assert: "Not the least engaging of Alan Ayckbourn's many virtues is the fact that—unlike pretty well every other comic genius in the theatre between Pinero and Pinter—he has never let himself be fooled into thinking he was a serious playwright."[5] Though Ayckbourn's work changed, judgments such as these have been slow to alter.

A few critics have recognized the growing seriousness of the plays and tried to grasp the new emphases in various fashions. Billington in 1974: "Ayckbourn is a left-wing writer using a right-wing form; and even if there is nothing strident, obvious or noisy about his socialism, it is none the less apparent that he has a real detestation for the money-grubber, the status-seeker and the get-rich-quicker."[6] Julian Jebb in 1977: "It does not seem in the least inappropriate to evoke Chekhov when writing about . . . [Ayckbourn]. Like the master, he sees life as it is—and life as it ought to be."[7] Martin Bronstein in 1980: "I'm puzzled why Alan Ayckbourn hasn't been clutched to the bosom of the Women's Liberation Movement as being their writer. He's the only contemporary playwright who shows the real plight of the average woman in today's world."[8]

Ayckbourn has in fact outlined in numerous interviews precisely what his designs are, aware that he is developing towards the kind of comedy he hopes eventually to achieve—and he has himself claimed to be following Chekhov. As early as 1970, he said: "I'd like to finish up writing tremendously human comedies—Chekhovian comedy in a modern way."[9] Seven years later, he had the same model: ". . . I want to move further into the Chekhovian field, exploring attitudes to death, loneliness, etc.—themes not generally dealt with in comedy."[10] In 1975, he remarked that in his later plays, "The characters aren't necessarily getting nastier, but I do feel that they're getting sadder."[11] He explains: "it seems to me that the deeper you go into a character, the sadder the play must inevitably become."[12] He has another term for the changing tone in an interview in 1977: ". . . I started with broad farce and I've been getting more and more gloomy ever since." Here also he expressed an aim: "You can at most make people see their fellows in a new light. . . ."[13] In a Preface dated 1976, he accepted seriousness and the pursuit of truth:

> As a nation, we show a marked preference for comedy when it comes to playgoing, as any theatre manager will tell you. At the same time, over a large area of the stalls one can detect a faint sense of guilt that there is something called enjoyment going on. . . . It's to do with the mistaken belief that because it's funny, it can't be serious—which of course isn't true at all. Heavy, no; serious, yes. . . . [I]t can be funny, but let's make it truthful.[14]

And in 1979 he offered an aim which sounds as though it might easily be "heavy": "It seems to me a good thing if you can outline some of the small areas of grey angst in people's minds."[15]

That Ayckbourn displays extraordinary technical ingenuity in his plays is by now well-known and needs little discussion. ***Absurd Person Singular*** (1972) has its three scenes on three consecutive Christmas Eves, in three different kitchens, featuring the same three married couples: a quite fastidious tidiness. ***The Norman Conquests*** (1973) is a trilogy about one week-end; it shows what is happening in a dining-room, sitting-room and garden, the plays designed to make sense in any order, or indeed if only one is seen. (I am left wanting a fourth play set in the bedroom occupied by the unseen mother.) Characteristically, the final play contains both the beginning and end of the cycle. The structure makes a serious point, too: "that if we see only part of a situation, we can jump to the wrong conclusions about the whole."[16] Ayckbourn's plotting remains as skilled—and as schematic—in the next plays. ***Bedroom Farce*** (1975) somehow steers eight people into three on-stage bedrooms. ***Just Between Ourselves*** (1976) turns on fours: scenes on four Saturdays, three months between each, for two couples—and a car on-stage. ***Joking Apart*** (1978) also has four scenes, each four years apart (including Boxing Day and Guy Fawkes's Night), bringing together the same seven people each time.

The risk when Ayckbourn sets himself insoluble problems and then proceeds to solve them is that these may become the whole justification of the play. Two other dramas may give more attention to the display of technique than they do to character and human truth. ***Sisterly Feelings*** (1979) has alternative second and third acts (the choice of which is to be played determined by tossing a coin at the end of Acts 1 and 2) leading to the same fourth act. ***Taking Steps*** (1979) is set on different floors of a three-storey house, yet performed in the round, so that there is "really" only one floor; as a result, the play is more successful in the Scarborough in-the-round theatre than in a West End theatre.

While these skills are frequently dazzling, Ayckbourn claims our attention for his insights about people: he prompts us to laugh, then to care about the character and to make a connection with ourselves, our own behaviour, and possibly beyond to the world in which we live. Through ***Absurd Person Singular***, Ayckbourn first explores a dual response: that these are his creations to amuse us, and that they are also suffering human beings. Here he turns from displaying the fatuity and absurdity of his people to examining their unhappiness and what might be done about it. In the second of the three acts, Eva, almost silent, attempts suicide by various means in her kitchen, while other people drift in—ignoring the pathetic, unhappy woman in their midst—and try to solve a number of domestic problems. This scene, intended to be simultaneously comic and serious, fails: Ayckbourn appears callous, heartless. Max Wyman wrote of the 1976 production at the Arts Club Theatre, Vancouver: ". . . ***Absurd Person Singular*** seems to me to be a cruel, dreadfully brittle play. . . . [F]or all its social comment it is reduced, ultimately to the theatrical equivalent of laughing at the limbless. . . . I felt uncomfortable with its flippant approach to human misery—and with the brainless guffaws of those who think multiple attempts at suicide are funny. . . ."[17] Not till ***Just Between Ourselves*** does Ayckbourn manage to write the scene that is both amusing and disturbing. ***Just Between Ourselves***, the earlier ***Absent Friends***, and the later ***Joking Apart*** are the three Plays Serious—which are nevertheless also comedies.

Absent Friends (1974), the first piece that is a "play" rather than a "comedy," remains Ayckbourn's most restrained, sombre, and subdued work. Five friends gather for a Saturday afternoon tea-party to cheer Colin, whom they have not seen for three years and whose fiancée, Carol, drowned two months before. They expect that Colin will not want to talk about Carol, but in fact he speaks of her both readily and cheerfully. The end of the first act reveals the basic notion of ***Absent Friends***:

> Colin . . . Because I've been denied my own happiness, I don't envy or begrudge you yours. I just want you to know that, despite everything that happened, in a funny sort of way, I too am very happy.
>
> (*He smiles round at them serenely. A silence. A strange whooping noise. It is* Diana *starting to weep hysterically. Unable to contain herself, she rushes out. After a moment,* Marge *fumbles for her handkerchief and blows her nose loudly.* John, *looking sickly, gives* Colin *a ghastly smile. . . .*[18]

There is, of course, a paradox here: the people with ample reason to be happy are not. Further, the contented Colin lacks the tact and sensitivity to understand his impact.

The three women emerge as very unhappy people. Marge, for example, is married to a sick, bedridden man who wanted to be a cricketer but became a fire-prevention officer instead; she puts her energy into choosing shoes and cleaning stains off chairs. Evelyn's husband, John, seems to have placed Evelyn accurately: "she has absolutely no sense of humour. Which is very useful since it means you never have to waste your time trying to cheer her up. Because she's permanently unhappy. Misery is her natural state" (p. 165). Unlike most Ayckbourn males, John sees something of the situation, but not his own responsibility or what might be done. Diana is Ayckbourn's fullest study of a woman in decline after marrying and entering her thirties; she explains: ". . . I was the bright one in our family but I can't keep up with Paul sometimes. When he has one of his moods, I think to myself, now if I was really clever, I could probably talk him round or something, but I mean the thing is, really and truly, and I know I'm running myself down when I say this, I don't think I'm really enough for him" (pp. 106-107). In the second act—in one of those Ayckbourn passages which start out as funny and become deadly serious about a human being in misery—she bursts out: ". . . I had this burning ambition, you see, to join the Canadian Royal Mounted Police. . . . People used to say 'You can't join the Mounted Police. You're a little girl. Little girls don't join the Mounted Police. Little girls do nice things like typing and knitting and nursing and having babies.' So I married Paul instead. Because they refused to let me join the Mounted Police" (p. 160).

Absent Friends is sad because youth is behind all of the characters and only Colin, lucky in his temperament, can take a rose-tinted-spectacles view:

> Colin Remember that fabulous picnic?
>
> Diana All I remember is running from one car to the other in the rain with the thermos flask.

COLIN And we found a great place for tea.

PAUL Where they overcharged us.

COLIN It was great. I'll always remember that. (p. 152)

Colin's return has a disastrous impact on Diana and Paul. Perhaps, however, if we seek affirmation, his impact on Marge and John may be judged beneficial. Although Ayckbourn's plays are not located with geographical precision (for instance, ***Norman Conquests*** informs us only that the place is within reach of East Grinstead), it is nevertheless clear that ***Absent Friends*** sketches in the limitations, the boredom, the humdrum of a small town rather than suburbia.

Just Between Ourselves (1976) shows how a well-meaning husband drives his wife to insanity through relentless cheerfulness and optimism. The following passage from the first scene illustrates how Dennis habitually treats his wife, Vera:

DENNIS . . . I'll give you a little tip shall I? A little tip when you're next using an electric kettle. They work far better when you don't keep slinging them on the floor.

VERA I couldn't help it. I just caught it with my elbow.

DENNIS . . . Caught it with her elbow. . . . If I told you, Mr. Andrews, the things my wife had caught with her elbow . . .

VERA . . . All right.

DENNIS You would not believe it, Mr. Andrews, cups, saucers, dinner plates, radio sets . . .

NEIL Really.

DENNIS Whole trays of glasses.

VERA Dennis . . .

DENNIS And that's just for this month. You ever want a demolition job doing, Mr. Andrews, she's your woman. (*he laughs*)

(NEIL *joins in halfheartedly.*
VERA *less so still.*)

Elbows going away like pistons . . .

NEIL Well, I suppose we all tend to . . . occasionally.

DENNIS Yes, quite (*hugging* VERA) I was only joking, love, only joking. I'm always pulling her leg, aren't I, love?[19]

This is typical of Ayckbourn in his vein of lightly concealed seriousness: we laugh twice at Dennis's amusing lines, then wince and recognize the implications of being always on the receiving end of put-down humour. Vera's last plea for Dennis to communicate with her is moving:

VERA . . . I need help, Dennis.

DENNIS Yes, but don't you see, you're not being clear, Vee. You say help but what sort of help do you mean?

VERA Just help. From you.

DENNIS Yes. Well, look, tell you what. When you've got a moment, why don't you sit down, get a bit of paper and just make a little list of all the things you'd like me to help you with. Things you'd like me to do, things that need mending or fixing and then we can talk about them and see what I can do to help. All right?

(VERA *does not reply.*) (pp. 56-57)

The contrast between Dennis's practicality and Vera's inarticulate emotionalism could hardly be clearer.

Taking place on Dennis's birthday, the second scene ends in a melancholy way with a disastrous tea-party at which everyone tries not to focus on the forgotten birthday cake and the likelihood of accidents by the tense Vera. The third scene concludes with the greatest moment in Ayckbourn's work, an episode wildly funny and deeply tragic, when Vera goes insane. While Dennis has become entangled inside the car with the steering-wheel, seat-belts, and a neighbouring woman Pam, to whom he is demonstrating the car, Vera quarrels with her mother-in-law and pursues her with a roaring electric drill. Then Pam slumps onto the car horn, which "*blasts loudly and continuously*"; and Neil comes in with a birthday cake, switching on lights, thus "*bathing the scene in a glorious technicolour,*" and singing "Happy birthday to you" (p. 63). Ayckbourn dreams of writing "a truly hilarious dark play"[20]: this he has achieved, at least for these five minutes.

Four months later we see Vera again, sitting silently in her garden in January. The people responsible hover round her, assuring each other that she is getting better. Throughout this chilling scene, Vera stares out blankly, speechless, motionless, as grim an image as any in Beckett, grimmer than almost any scene anywhere in comedy. Here the laughter of the first three scenes dies on the lips, as the audience see what poor Vera has come to and how the man responsible is as far as ever from realizing his responsibility.

The other couple parallel the marriage quite closely. Pam has settled for passivity, being merely the loyal stay-at-home wife like Diana of ***Absent Friends***. Having considered night-classes, she decides: "I think that was just a lovely dream, Neil. I'm getting too old for that" (p. 36). They have sexual problems, too. She is depressed in the third scene, for she recognizes of her husband: "That man is destroying me. He is systematically destroying me. I was the youngest supervisor they'd ever had. I had prospects" (p. 60). So she leaves Neil—for a week. In the final scene, she is still talking of her need to acquire qualifications:

DENNIS What are you planning to do, then?

PAM Well, I was considering public relations.

DENNIS Ah.

NEIL I thought you said you were going into the prison service.

PAM That was a joke. (p. 69)

This exchange suggests that communication between Pam and Neil has not improved.

Robin Thornber writes: "where the manic black comedy of ***Absent Friends*** dealt with death and our refusal to recognize it, this play is about growing old—an even more sombre theme because you can't ignore it."[21] Although this description strives to find a truth for all five characters, ***Just Between Ourselves*** is really Vera and Dennis's play. Billington is more accurate in describing the theme as "what Terence Rattigan once called the real *vice Anglais*: fear of expressing emotion . . . The total gesture is one of fierce attack on what E.M. Forster called 'the under-developed heart'."[22] Yet Dennis is no villain: he can be faulted only for insensitivity, ignorance, thoughtlessness. Bernard Levin has identified the new power of ***Just Between Ourselves***: "the verdict must be that with this play Mr. Ayckbourn has grown up. . . . Alan Ayckbourn has gained an immense reputation with a series of plays in which puppets dance most divertingly on their strings. Here he has cut the strings and then stuck the knife into the puppets. They bleed."[23]

The third "serious" play, ***Joking Apart*** (1978), sets its four scenes on special occasions: Guy Fawkes's Night, Boxing Day, a girl's eighteenth birthday. The stage includes the corner of a tennis-court, offering glimpses of the action in two games, and a croquet-lawn just off, with balls rolling on from time to time. The structural innovation is that the scenes are four years apart, so that we see seven characters over a period of twelve years, from their twenties to their thirties.

Joking Apart is a study of winners and losers. Richard and Anthea, for example, are likeable, generous, hospitable people. They are also enormously successful: happy, energetic, their two children a credit to them, Richard's furniture-import business flourishing. No one can put a finger on the secret of their success—some mixture of luck, instinct, talent. In contrast, their neighbours Hugh and Louise are losers. Hugh is a failure as vicar, his sermons being muddled and inaudible, his temperament too youthful for the elderly parishioners. He does not care for his timid, ineffectual wife, Louise, who descends to unbalance, her behaviour in the last scene caused by the latest dose of the latest drug. Their son is a handful when small and ignores them in his teens, treating them in fact as "a couple of deaf-mute family retainers" (p. 207). Richard can be directly reproached for offending this couple only once, when he impetuously tears down and burns the dividing fence. Intended as a way of opening up his garden to the neighbours, this gesture is seen by Louise as the loss of her own tiny garden. Anthea upsets Hugh by her very presence, the contrast between her exuberance and Louise's passivity inspiring Hugh to love—as he confesses while both are distracted by a tennis-game.

There are three other characters in the picture. Another couple are Richard's business partners: Sven, a Finn, and his wife, Olive. Richard's business acumen gradually makes Sven think himself a failure, so that he becomes resigned to being second-rate—and Olive takes her mood from him. After eight years, Sven accepts the challenge to play tennis with Richard—and wins, only to be crushed when it turns out that Richard had played left-handed. Four years later, Sven is victim to a heart attack, confined to a chair, a mere spectator. In the sad decline of this couple, Richard and Anthea's immediate role is slight. Finally, there is Brian. Like Hugh, he is silently devoted to Anthea; and Anthea seems insensitive in not grasping this devotion, ready though she is to be a week-end hostess to Brian and his girl-friends.

In general, the degree of blame attached to Richard and Anthea is small. Perhaps a critic should more accurately emphasize Sven's envy and resentment, and to a degree the same flaws in the other four hangers-on. Ayckbourn illuminates the sadness intrinsic to the condition that the world has its born winners, and the less obvious fact that other people shrink through contrasting themselves with these winners. The final mood is wistful, downbeat, even elegiac - though the occasion is a girl's eighteenth birthday party, and she may be able to shrug off the middle-aged losers, and winners.[24]

These three "serious" plays at first look to be very different from the rest of the *oeuvre*. Ayckbourn himself encouraged the distinction by describing ***Just Between Ourselves*** and ***Joking Apart*** (but not ***Absent Friends***) as his "winter" plays, written for the winter months when his theatre performs for the local Scarborough audience rather than for the summer visitors who seek only laughter from the theatre.[25] Consequently, when ***Bedroom Farce*** was advertised throughout its long London run with the quotation from the *Daily Express*, "If you don't laugh, sue me," it clearly identified the kind of play it was. Yet some of the lighter plays of the seventies also challenge an accepted rule of contemporary comedy: that the audience does not take home the sorrows of the characters after the show. This convention—a matter of both the dramatist's style and the audience's expectations—verges on breakdown when Ayckbourn shifts from farce to real people in real trouble.

These realistic plays leave much to the director and actors: whether or not suffering humanity is to be drawn out, perhaps at the expense of our laughing so readily at the actions. ***The Norman Conquests*** extensively studies two troubled marriages, and shows pity for unfortunate Annie as well, trapped into looking after her bedridden mother and unable in the end to take off for even one stolen week-end in East Grinstead. In watching *Bedroom Farce*, the audience can laugh only as long as they remember that the man contorted with the pain of a bad back is an actor exercising his craft (as with suicidal Eva in ***Absurd Person Singular***, this is one of the moments when Ayckbourn is either heartless or audacious). The neurotic Susannah in ***Bedroom Farce*** is not so far from victims like Vera of ***Just Between Ourselves*** and Louise of ***Joking Apart***:

whereas Susannah is distanced by the familiar framework of comedy, the other two women are not.

While Ayckbourn was writing shrewdly and on the whole sadly of human behaviour, ***Absurd Person Singular*** suggested that he aspired to be a social critic, too. In this play, the property-speculating shopkeeper rises during the dramatic action to pass the architect and bank manager, reversing the normal pecking order. This comedy prompted Ronald Bryden's eloquent interpretation:

> [Ayckbourn] simply demonstrates, in terms audiences have to recognise as fact, the tragic absurdity of some of the things our society forces on human beings. . . . The final scene, in which [the property-speculator] . . . forces them in their own stronghold to play the humiliating party-games they evaded at his party two years before, is as cuttingly vivid an image of the England of the Poulson affair as any British playwright is likely to offer us. It may not send anyone into Piccadilly to man the barricades, but I think it may make many of its audiences think twice before voting again for the free market economy, individual enterprise and the competitive principle.[26]

Such precise attention to occupations and social change is not found again in Ayckbourn's work. The playwright is not faulting society for the madness of Vera and the decline of Louise; he indicts the insensitive people around them.

Ayckbourn's subject generally embraces people between the ages of twenty-five and forty (his age at the time of writing); of the middle class (upper middle for the old couple Ernest and Delia in ***Bedroom Farce***; lower middle in ***Absent Friends***); living in English suburbia in the present. His recurring theme is marriage, usually its miseries: his happiest couple, Richard and Anthea of ***Joking Apart***, have never bothered to get married. In ***Bedroom Farce***, for example, Jan is flighty and at least potentially unfaithful to Nick; the newly-weds Malcolm and Kate share a love of playfulness but probably do not know when to stop; and Trevor and Susannah put all their energies into talk, self-analysis, and anxiety, giving themselves no chance for a stable relationship. In ***Just Between Ourselves***, both men neglect their wives' real needs, and each assumes that his own marriage is the only possible kind: Neil has no idea of what is happening, while Dennis conceals from himself the failings in his marriage. The causes are less clear in ***Joking Apart***, but failure looks to be inevitable: Olive submerges herself as helpmate to Sven; and Hugh is unable to care for Louise when the charming Anthea lives at the bottom of the garden.

Looking at individuals, Ayckbourn shows and condemns thoughtlessness and insensitivity. He studies people who are cheerful, well-meaning, and amiable, yet stir up every kind of trouble and unhappiness in their circles. Dennis of ***Just Between Ourselves*** is most savagely treated, confident that he understands his wife while he drives her insane. Trevor of ***Bedroom Farce*** is rude and inconsiderate, sublimely wrapped up in himself and his troubles; sure that if he says "Sorry" often enough he merits forgiveness, understanding, and a bed for the night. In ***Absent Friends***, Colin radiates good humour in such a way that he deepens his friends' discontent. Most subtly, the sunny dispositions and good fortune of Richard and Anthea in ***Joking Apart*** add to the sense of failure within their circle. Ayckbourn looks steadily at people in pain and shows that being human, having any involvement with others, is difficult and fraught with problems. Which aspect of human nature will he next examine? Ayckbourn is forty-three in 1983, his writing career probably less than half over. I look forward especially to more winter plays—more efforts to write "the truly hilarious dark play."

Notes

1. *Relatively Speaking* was performed in Scarborough in 1965 (as *Meet My Father*). Three dates may be cited for Ayckbourn's plays: the *première* in Scarborough, Yorkshire; the first London performance, usually about a year later; and the date of publication. Hereafter I cite the Scarborough date: Ayckbourn says the plays are always written immediately before rehearsals start; see, e.g., John Heilpern, "Theatrical Five-Day Wonder," *The Observer*, 13 February 1977, p. 14. I should note here that the London production of *Joking Apart* (1979) and the White Rock, B.C., Summer Theatre production of *Just Between Ourselves* (1980) prompted me to take Ayckbourn seriously, and that my commentary also draws on performances of the plays in Scarborough, Pitlochry, Harrogate, Vancouver, and on television.
2. John Russell Taylor, *The Second Wave* (London, 1971), pp. 156, 162.
3. Michael Billington, "Ayckbourn, Alan," in *Contemporary Dramatists*, ed. James Vinson (New York, 1973), p. 60.
4. John Elsom, rev. of *Three Plays*, by Alan Ayckbourn, *Gambit*, 8, No. 30 (1977), 108.
5. Hilary Spurling, "Side by Side in Scarborough," *Times Literary Supplement*, 13 February 1981, p. 166.
6. "Michael Billington Assesses the Significance of Alan Ayckbourn," *The Guardian*, 14 August 1974, p. 11.
7. Julian Jebb, "*Just Between Ourselves*," *Plays and Players*, 24 (June 1977), 28.
8. Martin Bronstein, rev. of *Three Plays: Joking Apart, Just Between Ourselves, Ten Times Table*, by Alan Ayckbourn, *Scene Changes*, 8 (January-February 1980), 40.
9. "Farceur, Relatively Speaking: Robin Thornber Interviews Alan Ayckbourn," *The Guardian*, 7 August 1970, p. 8.
10. Ayckbourn, as quoted in Oleg Kerensky, *The New British Drama* (London, 1977), p. 129.

11. Alan Ayckbourn and Michael Coveney, "Scarborough Fare" (interview), *Plays and Players*, 22 (September 1975), 18.

12. Ayckbourn, as quoted in Ray Connolly, "Atticus: Ayckbourn, with Music," *Sunday Times*, 8 February 1981, p. 32.

13. Ayckbourn, as quoted in Kerensky, p. 129.

14. Alan Ayckbourn, Preface, *Three Plays: Bedroom Farce, Absent Friends, and Absurd Person Singular* (Harmondsworth, 1979), p. 8.

15. Ayckbourn, as quoted in Janet Watts, "Absurd Persons, Plural and Suburban," *The Observer*, 4 March 1979, p. 39.

16. John Elsom, "A Clutch of Ayckbourn," *The Listener*, 31 July 1975, p. 152.

17. Max Wyman, "A Stove, the Stuff of Comic Melodrama," *Vancouver Sun*, 25 June 1976, p. 39.

18. Alan Ayckbourn, *Absent Friends*, in *Three Plays: Bedroom Farce* . . . , pp. 144-145; subsequent references in the text.

19. Alan Ayckbourn, *Just Between Ourselves*, in *Three Plays: Joking Apart, Ten Times Table, Just Between Ourselves* (London, 1979), pp. 16-17; subsequent references in the text.

20. Ayckbourn, as quoted in Ian Watson, "Ayckbourn of Scarborough," *Municipal Entertainment*, 5 (May 1978), p. 11.

21. Robin Thornber, "*Just Between Ourselves*," *The Guardian*, 30 January 1976, p. 10.

22. Michael Billington, "*Between Ourselves*," *The Guardian*, 21 April 1977, p. 10.

23. Bernard Levin, "Theatre: Mr. Ayckbourn Changes Trains," *Sunday Times*, 24 April 1977, p. 37.

24. A fourth "serious" play is the unpublished *Family Circles* (Scarborough, 1970, as *The Story So Far*; Orange Tree, Richmond, November 1978). Benedict Nightingale commented: "Emotionally, it is bleaker than any of his plays except *Just Between Ourselves*, and no less cynical about the domestic dovecote . . ." ("Stay Single," *New Statesman*, 1 December 1978, p. 763).

25. Alan Ayckbourn, Preface, *Three Plays: Joking Apart* . . . , p. 7.

26. Ronald Bryden, "*Absurd Person Singular*," *Plays and Players*, 20 (August 1973), 41.

Richard Allen Cave (essay date 1987)

SOURCE: "New Forms of Comedy: Ayckbourn and Stoppard," in *New British Drama in Performance on the London Stage: 1970 to 1985*, Colin Smythe, 1987, pp. 56-100.

[*In the following excerpt, Cave examines how Ayckbourn's focus on character development has blurred the dividing lines between the different styles of comedy.*]

If Nichol's and Frayn's experiments with the form of domestic comedy and farce seem intent on defining the nature and function of these two styles, Alan Ayckbourn's prolific output seems designed to question whether what till now were believed to be *necessary* limitations in these styles of comedy, the "carefully engineered partial" views of events referred to above, are really necessary at all. By imposing a series of quite arbitrary limitations on himself (usually the consequences of writing primarily for the small-scale Library Theatre in Scarborough), Ayckbourn has steadily transformed the subject matter of comedy and farce making them a vehicle for stringent psychological analysis, especially of the waste lands of the middle class sensibility. Ayckbourn has said that he felt his progress as a dramatist demanded that he should "try and get more comedy from character and less from artificially induced situations". Interestingly the more that character has become his focus the more he has begun to blur the dividing lines between different styles of comic writing: satirical comedy can suddenly erupt into farce (***Ten Times Table***); domestic comedy can pass through farce into a dark, mordant mood (***Just Between Ourselves***); while black comedy he has redefined as a dispassionate view of a middle-class household that is "positively knee-deep in home truths" (***Living Together***).

One of Ayckbourn's first West End successes of the Seventies, ***How the Other Half Loves*** (Lyric, 1970), offered an image which has proved emblematic of the directions in which his more recent plays would move: two rooms intersected on stage so that characters ostensibly in different locations could work beside or around each other while being quite oblivious of the other's presence. This illustrates not only Ayckbourn's immensely inventive way with settings (he has never found it essential to have quantities of doors before he can create farce) but also his preoccupation with the invisible walls that people create around themselves. Obsessional minds have long been the butt of comedy and Ayckbourn is not averse to exploiting this device; what is unusual is his increasing tendency to shift our perspective suddenly so that we perceive the unconscious motive that generates the obsession, which quite changes the quality of our laughter. The obsessions are not sexual but rather the products of minds coping with a totally shallow, benighted existence as in the case of the wives in ***Absurd Person Singular*** (Criterion, 1973): "When you've lain in bed for any length of time, on your own . . . with just your thoughts, don't you find your whole world just begins to crowd in on you? . . . You just lie there thinking, oh God, it could've been so much better if only I'd had the sense to do so and so—you finish up lying there utterly filled with self-loathing" [p. 87]. Or the obsessions may be compensating for an emotional void in the characters' experience as with Sarah and Annie in ***The Norman Conquests*** (Greenwich and Globe, 1974), who despise the ramshackle Norman but are helpless to stave off his advances once he promises them a little happiness. When Ayckbourn does turn to an apparently conventional setting and idiom in ***Bedroom Farce*** (Lyttleton, 1977), it is to show that the express desire of the occupiers of all three bedrooms is for a good night's sleep. That they are prevented from this by the squabbles of Susannah and Trevor has got nothing to do with infidelities enjoyed or planned; it is simply that Susannah and Trevor can only find peace when they have totally discomfitted everyone else (when they do finally get together, they quite unconcernedly dispossess Kate and Malcolm of their bed for the night). *Bedroom Farce* is not about adultery or permissiveness but is a wry look at the quixotic ways in which couples contrive to live together amicably; it is less concerned with the capriciousness of wicked instincts than the waywardness of affection in regulating marital harmony.

Much of Ayckbourn's comic invention is directed at marriages in which that pattern of adjustment is not fair to both partners. Desperation provides the momentum for many a conventional farce where "desperate" takes the meaning "reckless"; Ayckbourn pursues this line but will suddenly shift his perspective to explore the darker significances of "desperate" as "extremely serious" and "without hope". Act Two Scene One of ***Just Between Ourselves*** (Queen's, 1977) shows the genial Dennis esconced in his private den at the back of the garage preparing a birthday treat for his mother, Marjorie: it involves decking the place out with coloured lights and giving a final sanding to a new workbox he has made for her. Throughout his efforts are disrupted by first a neighbouring husband, Neil, and then his wife, Pam, giving their respective accounts of why their marriage has failed. Pam gets very drunk on the birthday wine. Dennis's attempt to extricate her from his car into which she has tumbled is viewed by Marjorie, who now inopportunely arrives, as scandalous; her scathing innuendoes attract the attention of Dennis's wife, Vera, whose inadequacy as a spouse for her son has been relentlessly the subject of Marjorie's conversation. Marjorie sees the scene with Pam as vindication of her opinion and this drives Vera to breaking-point. Fortunately the flex on Dennis's sanding drill is too short for Vera to reach Marjorie's face when she grabs it with lethal intent. Seeking to protect his mother, Dennis abandons Pam who falls prone over the steering wheel, sounding the horn which is Neil's signal to switch on the fairy lights and arrive with a candlelit cake singing "Happy birthday to you!". Here are many of the hallmarks of good farce: the monster mother-in-law about to get her come-uppance; the mouse cornered once too often who becomes a raging fury; the helplessly inert body getting in everyone's way; the misunderstood accident that gives rise in the spectator's mind to a string of lubricious interpretations; the inappropriately timed arrival of an unsuspecting innocent into a seeming madhouse; and the credible domestic detail (the too-short flex) that just stops the situation short of tragedy. It is all too fast-moving for us to stop and think of the degrees of desperation that have brought the situation about. There are times—and this is one of them—when Ayckbourn appears to distrust farce for engineering that partial view which obviates our need for care. Those two characters sharing a stagespace in ***How the Other Half Loves*** but ignoring each other can be funny or callous depending on one's perspective and how attuned one's sensitivity is. In ***Just Between Ourselves*** Ayckbourn's interest is in character not situation. The short second scene of the Act shows Vera, now in a catatonic daze, seated in the garden in mid-January rather than share the house with Marjorie while Dennis, ever-genial, vows his wife is getting better by the day. The situation is bizarre but it leaves the audience profoundly uneasy. The opening act had intimated the tensions between Vera and Marjorie—but to his wife's pleas that he help more around the house (Vera is too polite and too timid to speak openly of how Marjorie tyrannises over her) Dennis turns a deaf ear. His den is his sanctum, his means of creating harmony between himself and his world. As the play goes on Dennis's genial joking, the camaraderie of his "Just between ourselves now" is seen to be a strategy for keeping painful experience at bay. His recurrent snorts of laughter in time cut our laughter dead because by the final scene we realise the extent to which in seeing Dennis's world as the stuff of farce we are sharing his deliberately limited perspective. Doubtless we no more see ourselves as cruel than Dennis does; but, by changing perspective, the play shames us into caring. Ayckbourn cleverly manipulates the form and nature of farce to make us aware how holding unquestioningly to certain attitudes and assumptions we unwittingly do violence to others.

Not all Ayckbourn's experiments with the form of farce are as successful as this or the bravura technical achievement of the three interlocking plays that make up ***The Norman Conquests. Sisterly Feelings*** (Olivier, 1980) attempted to explore the play of chance and choice in shaping the individual life by creating a structure in which the two leading actresses could twice during performance opt at the toss of a coin to play one of two alternative scenes. The fact that all the possible combinations led invariably to the same final scene meant that the structure became imprisoning rather than liberating. Two sisters are seen contemplating whether or not to pursue an affair with a handsome stranger; the final scene shows them back with their respective partners. One admired the ingenuity of the transitions between scenes, but the emphatic assertion of the *status quo* at the end made the sisters seem little more than dilettante flirts while the overall theme seemed to be that the comfort of the known will always have a stronger attraction than the risky and the unpredictable, which rather runs counter to Ayckbourn's claim that he believes characters should "retain the dignity of resolving their own destinies". The structure seemed too elaborate for it all to be an anecdote about people lacking the courage to be unconventional and singular; there is scant sense of human dignity involved in that observation on character.

Ayckbourn has also several times tried to make his social criticism covertly political. That there is a power-hungry Hitler inside little Sydney Hopcroft in ***Absurd Person***

Singular is evident from the way in the first act he scares his wife Jane into being a slave to his passion for order and cleanliness; the final image of him making all their friends dance to his orders and play humiliating party games, however, seems too stark a transition at the close of an act that, though already dark in mood, has looked with compassion at the spiritual desolation of Eva and Marion, the social demise of Geoffrey and the marital *angst* of Ronald. It is not that the insight is misguided—such lost souls could credibly be swept up into the schemes of a rising entrepreneurial demon like Sydney—the problem is that the dramatic method has shifted into the surreal and expressionistic without due preparation. In a play that has moved like ***Just Between Ourselves*** from comedy of manners through farce to a sombre realism, the transition is one too many and so the whole structure suddenly risks seeming contrived. The Fascist overtones are discomfitting in the wrong way; as they are in the frankly allegorical ***Way Upstream*** (Lyttleton, 1982): the pirating of a private launch touring the rivers of England (this ship of state) by a petty dictator goes unchallenged till the submissive Alistair rebels when his wife Emma is threatened with walking the plank; the worm turns, gains control of the boat and steers through Armageddon Bridge to sunlight and a naked frolic, as if Eden has been regained. The ultra-realism (a navigable boat on a stage full of water) did not merge well with political allegory, and the farce-convention (little man makes good) by which the play achieved its conclusion reduced the portentous to the bathetic. The boundaries of comic expression resisted stretching in that fashion. ***Ten Times Table*** (Globe, 1978) succeeds while it remains a satirical comedy about the way factions on committees polarise each other to wider and wider extremes till the real purpose of their coming together (here to organise a civic pageant) is lost sight of as the will to power seizes everyone's imagination uncontrollably. As the day of the pageant approaches the two sides are clearly intent on turning the simulation of a chapter of local history (the army's suppression of a labourers' revolt) into a genuine battle. The Socialists are particularly keen to re-write history and convert what was formerly a martyrdom into a decisive military *coup*. The shift to farce for the final scene during the pageant misfires because Ayckbourn seems uncertain about what is the appropriate tone to sustain here: there are hints of black comedy (an offstage wounding and an offstage rape), but the dominant mood is that of a jolly skit on amateur dramatics with a bizarre hobby-horse and ill-fitting costumes, drunken actors and a deaf pianist who blithely plays on through the riot. Surprisingly for Ayckbourn, the end was misjudged in being *comfortable* (a descent into whimsy) when shock was called for. One is left wondering with these three instances whether Ayckbourn's much-boasted facility for conceiving plays in the few days that precede the date allotted for their rehearsal might not, given the newness for him here of the subject matter and the consequent problems with tone, have merited some pause for study and revision. ***Ten Times Table*** fails for want of the conviction to follow through the logic that its progress through four excellent scenes has set in motion. Overall Ayckbourn is at his best reinvigorating the forms of domestic comedy, when his technical virtuosity makes us *feel* how life's richest comic ironies are from the standpoint of the victims utterly catastrophic.

Stoppard is another prolific dramatist whose work tends to fall short of the best when it becomes overtly political. His richest and most rewarding comedies are those that experiment with the possibilities of comic form to illuminate the nature of imagination. Like Ayckbourn, Stoppard is preoccupied with the way individuals' desperation and recklessness spring from a deep-rooted despair at the over-tidy efficiency, pragmatism and self-interest of the modern world, where commercial values risk governing every aspect of the human condition. His finest plays—*Rosencrantz and Guildenstern are Dead, Jumpers, Travesties*—are essentially about blindness, usually moral blindness, which is equated with a dangerous failure of imagination in the characters, who cannot engage adequately in consequence with the world in which they are situated. The cleverness of his art is to make us engage with those worlds far more subtly than the characters can do themselves and, since *Rosencrantz and Guildenstern are Dead*, Stoppard has generally achieved this by deploying an art of travesty, where much of the humour depends for its effect on the audience's familiarity with the plot, conventions or style of a well-known play or popular theatrical format. Travesty perhaps needs definition here. It is not with Stoppard simply a matter of destructive burlesque, a debunking (as in several of Peter Nichols' works) of a form of theatre he finds morally questionable; nor is it a self-conscious exploration as with Bennett and Frayn of a particular genre in order to reach some psychological understanding of its nature and its relation to an audience's needs. Stoppard's usage is quite different too from the structure Ayckbourn has devised for his most recent work, ***A Chorus of Disapproval*** (Olivier, 1985), which looks at an amateur operatic society's rehearsals of *The Beggar's Opera* and draws some ironic parallels between the cupidity and lusts of Gay's characters in Hanoverian England and the actors and actresses who now impersonate them. The difference between Ayckbourn's and Stoppard's use of travesty is that one produces a closed, the other an open form of comedy. Ayckbourn's prevailing irony infers that, though times and fashions change, humankind will still find subtle ways of transgressing the biblical commandment against coveting a neighbour's ox, ass, and wife. While there is great ingenuity in the way the parallels are drawn, the play's development does become increasingly predictable, which is not helped by the device of playing what is chronologically the last scene of the play first in the actual performance so that the outcome is clear from the start. As a consequence the characters have only a limited freedom within which to develop, being confined by the structure Ayckbourn has imposed on the action and the pessimism it infers. Travesty in Stoppard enriches rather than questions one's appreciation of the play that acts as his prototype; travesty becomes itself a creative act of the imagination.

Thomas M. Disch (essay date 1991)

SOURCE: A review of *Henry IV and others*, in *The Nation*, New York, Vol. 252, No. 13, April 8, 1991, pp. 458-60.

[*In the following excerpt, Disch attributes Broadway's future to plays written by Ayckbourn, Neil Simon and others.*]

The good news from Broadway comes in the familiar form of comedies by Neil Simon and Alan Ayckbourn, the most consistently popular and prolific purveyors to commercial theater in New York and London. Ayckbourn's plays have not had nearly the success on Broadway that they've had on the West End, and so for two of them to be playing at once is almost like having an Ayckbourn festival, albeit of a retrospective nature, since both plays have had to wait a fair while to cross the Atlantic. ***Absent Friends*** (1974), at the Manhattan Theatre Club (technically not Broadway, but just around the corner), is the older of the two and conceptually the more modest. Its story hinges on the visit, after a long absence, of Colin, the recently bereaved member of a small coven of suburbanites whom the years have turned rancid. Colin is a monster of positive thinking and smarminess and bullies his old chums into exhuming the delusions of their youth, until one of them finally cracks. It's *The Iceman Cometh* in reverse, with, instead of Bowery bums, five twitty Brits getting their noses rubbed in the terrible truth. Peter Frechette as Colin can't help but steal the show, and Brenda Blethyn, a mainstay of the National Theatre, has been imported to play Diana, a British variant of the traditional Mad Housewife. Her culminating mad scene may strike some as inauthentic, not to say preposterous, as it asks us to believe that the secret sorrow of her life is that she could not join the Royal Canadian Mounted Police and wear their wonderful red uniform. Those who would cavil at that would probably also object to *Peter Pan* as unrealistic and *The Wind in the Willows* as farfetched. Like most prolific comic writers, Ayckbourn writes for his own private crew of commedia dell'arte figures—comic stereotypes who are costumed with new quirks and foibles in successive plays. There is the Adulterous Wife, who in this play is notable for being sullen and laconic (played by Gillian Anderson); the Philandering Husband (David Purdham); the Bumbling Innocent (John Curless); and a more vain and determinedly shallow version of the Mad Housewife (Ellen Parker). Ayckbourn's forte as a comedian of manners, and the secret of his success in England, is an ambivalent fondness/contempt for "middling" existence, for people who aren't overly bright or capable or attractive and their ordinary confusions, stupidities and hypocrisies. Rather than excoriate he laughs, or sometimes only smiles wryly, and he expects his audiences to be of a similar disposition. In America audiences tend to prefer either a more sentimental treatment of such matters (such as Neil Simon offers) or a more savage one, but I've never seen an Ayckbourn play I didn't like. ***Absent Friends*** may not be one of his best, but it's quite good enough, and it's cheering to know that Lynne Meadow, who directed it and is the artistic director of the Manhattan Theatre Club, has made a long-term commitment to mounting more of his plays.

Taking Steps, at the Circle in the Square Theatre, probably is among Ayckbourn's best, with one of the author's patented high-concept premises. To wit, the central arena stage represents three levels of the same house—attic, bedroom and lounge—and the connecting corridors and stairways. Events take place concurrently on all three levels without the characters being aware of those not on their floor. Six familiar figures from Ayckbourn's central casting department inhabit his conceptual funhouse: the Bumbler (who this time is the star, and is drolly overdone by Spike McClure); the Adulterous Wife (Jane Summerhays); the Old Sot (Christopher Benjamin); the Young Bore (Jonathan Hogan); a variant of the Mad Housewife, a fiancée in peril of marrying the Young Bore (Pippa Pearthree); and also, a dishonest contractor of the lower orders (Bill Buell). The plot is much more fanciful than that of ***Absent Friends***, involving elaborate mistaken identities and belief in ghosts. Again, the point of such folderol is not to hold up the mirror to nature but to create an artificial pattern of events that has the power to surprise and delight. As so often in farce, one must give the author time to wind up all the clockwork mechanisms that will eventually come into play, which means that for the first half-hour or so one must attend closely without a lot of immediate mirth. Whether Alan Strachan's direction was to some degree responsible for the opening *longueurs* I wouldn't know without seeing an alternative production. ***Absent Friends*** seemed more of a piece, but comedy of manners is a more tractable genre than farce. If I could say which of the two to plump for, it would be ***Taking Steps***. . . .

George Weales (essay date 1991)

SOURCE: "Downstairs, Upstairs: Lost in Yonkers, Steps and Friends," in *Commonweal*, Vol. CXVIII, No. 9, May 3, 1991, pp. 293-94.

[*In the following excerpt, Weales compares and contrasts Ayckbourn and Neil Simon in reviewing* Lost in Yonkers, Taking Steps *and* Absent Friends.]

One of the commonplaces of casual criticism is to suggest or to deny that there are strong similarities between Neil Simon and Alan Ayckbourn. Benedict Nightingale was in the denial column recently (*New York Times*, February 10) in an article preceding the opening of two early Ayckbourn plays, ***Taking Steps*** (1979), which is still playing at the Circle in the Square, and ***Absent Friends*** (1974), which played the usual limited run at Manhattan Theatre Club. Both playwrights are phenomenally successful in their own countries and not much admired abroad, and their styles are certainly very different. What they have in common is a very black view of human possibilities and a desire to illustrate it in comfortable, comic surroundings. Not even the sentimental endings of Simon's recent autobiographical work can mask the sense of impending disaster that is more obvious in broadly comic works like *Last of the Red Hot Lovers* and *The Prisoner of Second Avenue*. It is customary to talk about how Ayckbourn's comedies have darkened in the last decade or so, but I cannot recall that the fun and games of the earlier ones grew out of any sanguine sense of human relationships.

Taking Steps is a farce about sex and real estate in which one woman decides not to leave her boring husband, another decides to run away from her even more boring fiancé (he puts himself to sleep when he talks), and the boring husband decides to buy a white elephant of a house none of them wants. The play is full of not very funny devices about the wrong persons being in the wrong beds and someone's being trapped in a closet and an offstage motorcycle that elicits verbal caresses of the word Yamaha. The main device, however, involves the kind of scenic trickery that Ayckbourn has used on other occasions. This time, the single set depicts three rooms, one atop another, the room identified in each case by particular articles of furniture; the characters share performance space but go unseen, however ludicrous their behavior, by the other characters, momentarily at rest, who are presumably on other floors.

In the preface to the published version of the play, Ayckbourn says, "unfortunately, it's possible to gain only an inkling of a play's merit from reading it. The real test occurs on a stage." This is clearly true of ***Taking Steps***. Tristram, the young solicitor who is so shy that he is practically tongue-tied, is tedious on the page, but on stage, as played by Spike McClure, he is very funny. So too with the bores, who are simply boring on the page, but funnily boring in the flesh, and the stairway business is more amusing than one might expect from a visual tiptoe gag that is endlessly repeated. There is not much substance to ***Taking Steps***, but none is intended. It is for fun or for nothing and, happily, it is often for fun.

There is more to ***Absent Friends***. It is about a group of insufferable people who have been brought together by Diana, who is determined that they should console the even more insufferable Colin on the death of his fiancée. It turns out that they never much liked him when they were presumed to be his friends, they have not seen him for years, and he is so smugly comfortable in his memories of his beloved that her presumed perfections give him the excuse to diagnose them incorrectly and prescribe unlikely happy endings to their insurmountable problems—of which there are plenty. Much of the play is funny, in a flesh-crawling way, although Diana's husband is too much of a bully and the sluttish Evelyn, with whom he had it off (sort of) in the back seat of his car, is too involved in her own boredom to be comic—at least as they were played at MTC. Brenda Blethyn, on the other hand, gave a hilarious performance as Diana, even during the character's final breakdown at the end of the play, an intensely painful moment that was one laugh after another. The crowd of crocks above Kravitz's Kandy Store could have learned a trick or two about laughing angst from Diana and from Brenda Blethyn.

Richard Hornby (essay date 1992)

SOURCE: "Ayckbourn in New York," in *The Hudson Review*, Vol. XLIV, No. 2, Summer, 1991, pp. 285-91.

[*In the following essay, Hornby praises Ayckbourn's plays.*]

The plays of Alan Ayckbourn have the reputation in New York of being box office poison. Fabulously successful in the rest of the world, whether in English or in translation (the Germans are especially fond of him), they have usually flopped here, when they have been done at all. One production was so bad that the audience ended up prompting the lead actor. We have thus managed to miss out on some of the most stimulating, unusual, and hilarious British plays of the past decade.

The first sign of possible change was a successful production a few seasons back of Ayckbourn's ***Woman in Mind*** at the Manhattan Theatre Club. A comedy about a woman slipping into schizophrenia (believe it or not!), it starred the droll and delightful Stockard Channing, who was largely responsible for its success. Besides, the Manhattan Theatre Club, and its artistic director Lynne Meadow, have long experience with contemporary British drama, knowing how to play the stylish, subtle, non-realistic material that most American actors and directors find incomprehensible.

Inspired by the fortunate outcome of ***Woman in Mind***, two productions of Ayckbourn plays opened this past season in New York, ***Taking Steps*** and ***Absent Friends***. These are early plays, dating from the seventies, which is unfortunate; most of his best work has been done in the past ten years, including ***Chorus of Disapproval*** and ***A Small Family Business***, comic masterpieces yet to be seen here. Nevertheless, ***Taking Steps*** and ***Absent Friends*** are so much better than most of what passes for playwriting in America these days that their productions could not have been more welcome.

Taking Steps is a farce dedicated to Ben Travers, whose plays at the Aldwych Theatre in London in the twenties were exemplars of farcical construction. A stock device in farce going back to ancient Roman theatre is the use of doors; the audience, knowing what is behind the doors, breathtakingly anticipates entrances and exits through them, which sometimes lead to comic confrontations and sometimes to hilarious near misses. Ayckbourn, writing for his own theatre in Scarborough in northern England, could not use doors because the stage is in the round. He therefore hit upon the device of having the action take place on three levels—the living room, bedroom, and attic—of a Victorian house, all of which are depicted simultaneously on the stage floor. Two sets of stairs are also depicted on the floor, with the actors going up and down in pantomime. Thus the entrances and exits and discoveries and near misses all take place with the actors in full view. There are also a lot of visual jokes, as when one of the characters, a dancer, prances across the stage in the "bedroom," while the other actors, who are of course actually right beside her, look upward to see the "living room" chandelier swaying. So masterful is Ayckbourn with his device that it is always perfectly clear where everyone is, even when there are characters on all three floors at once.

This obsession with the technicalities of playwriting is typical of Ayckbourn, whose plays include devices like a play within the play, or retelling the same story in three related plays in three parts of the same house, or the tossing of a coin to determine where the plot in a particular performance will go. Ayckbourn is as technically intricate as his contemporary, Tom Stoppard, if you stop to think about it—but you rarely do, because the devices are so clear and unforced. Furthermore, Stoppard writes about artists, intellectuals, and political leaders, while Ayckbourn typically focuses on very ordinary middle-class folk, who exhibit a "suburban blandness," as a character says of one of his unlikely heroes. Somehow, Ayckbourn manages to write funny plays about dull people.

In ***Taking Steps***, the action revolves around Roland Crabbe, an arrogant, wealthy, alcoholic manufacturer of buckets, who is living in the Victorian house but cannot decide whether to buy it from the desperate owner, Leslie Bainbridge. Roland's marriage to Elizabeth, a dancer, is also in a state of limbo; as the play opens, she is about to leave him, only three and a half months after their wedding. Elizabeth's brother Mark is trying to console her, despite the fact that his own fiancée, Kitty, recently abandoned him at the altar, and has since been picked up by the police on a charge of soliciting. Thus, all the characters are in the process of "taking steps" in their lives, but are not really going anywhere, just as the stairs on the set do not really lead to other floors. Even Elizabeth winds up returning to her boorish husband, but, in a "bed trick" (as literary critics call it) worthy of Shakespeare's *Measure for Measure* or Wycherley's *The Country Wife*, ends up unwittingly making love to her husband's befuddled young lawyer, Tristram Watson.

Such trickery was typical of Ben Travers, as are the confusions arising from a ghost story (Tristram thinks Elizabeth is the ghost of a murdered prostitute), and from a suicide note that gets attributed to the wrong person. Beneath all the fun, however, there are darker themes that Ayckbourn will explore more fully in later plays: Roland's alcoholism is more than just a comic device, while his callousness and ruthlessness would be disturbing if we had time to stop and think about them. The two love relationships in the play—between Roland and Elizabeth, and Mark and his former fiancée, Kitty—are both disasters, while Kitty's suicide note is funny only because it is wrongly attributed to Roland. Furthermore, there is an underlying theme of non-communication: Tristram stammers, Elizabeth's goodbye note is illegible, Kitty's suicide note goes awry, Mark is such a boring speaker that he puts people asleep (including himself at one point!), and Roland repeatedly mixes up his clichés, correcting himself and then pompously correcting the correction. ("This is the real McKay. McCoy. Some people say McCoy, I say McKay.") Misunderstanding is a central technique of farce, but it can also be a comment on the deterioration of relationships in modern society. The characters in *Taking Steps* might as well be on different floors even when, like the actors, they are side by side. Lack of communication is one of the major themes of serious modern dramatists like Brecht, Ionesco, Beckett, and Pinter, and as Pinter himself has remarked, Ayckbourn is an ultimately very serious playwright.

The New York production of ***Taking Steps*** was at the uptown Circle in the Square, which usually operates in a thrust configuration, but which was opened up nicely into a full arena, as at Scarborough. Such a configuration is none too popular with directors and designers; sightlines are a constant problem, and there is no façcade with which to establish locale. Nevertheless, a stage fully in the round creates a marvelous feeling of intimacy between performers and audience when it is handled well, as it certainly was here. The clarity of the play was partly the result of director Alan Strachan's deft staging, and partly of James Morgan's ingenious set. The cast was a mixture of British and American actors, but they all seemed as English as cold toast and wet weather, and their acting was both precise and very funny. Particularly good were Christopher Benjamin (English) as Roland, and Spike McClure (American) as Tristram. Other recent mixed casts on Broadway have not been so felicitous; it was nice to see our own actors holding their ground with the more experienced and better trained Brits.

Absent Friends, written earlier than ***Taking Steps***, is less intricately constructed, but darker in tone. The action revolves around an amiable young fellow named Colin, whose fiancée has recently drowned. Diane, wife of one of his old friends, Paul, has arranged a tea party so that they, along with two other old friends, John and Gordon, can console Colin. The irony is that Colin seems perfectly resigned to his loss, and that he sentimentalizes endlessly about his friends despite the fact that their marriages are all fiascoes. Paul, an inveterate philanderer, has had a back seat sexual encounter with Evelyn, John's bored, churlish wife. John knows about the affair, but is forced to keep quiet because he is dependent on Paul for business. Gordon, a hypochondriac, never even makes it to the tea party; he constantly demands his wife's attention by phone, however, recalling Tolstoy's remark that a family is a tyranny ruled by its sickest member. Colin consistently misinterprets his friends' problems, offering mawkish "solutions" that are comical by their very irrelevance. Because they see him as being in mourning, however, they can neither enlighten him, nor tell him to shut up.

Absent Friends, then, is once again about mutual misunderstandings that reflect non-communication at a deeper level. The comedy is somewhat predictable, but the satire on contemporary suburban life is deft, and the individual characters are each vividly drawn. The trouble with the play is that it does not go anywhere; there is a climax, of sorts, when Diane suffers an emotional breakdown in the second act, but it does not resolve any of the characters' conflicts or change any of their relationships. Colin, of course, sees the breakdown through rose-colored glasses, so that he ends as he began, happier by far with the idealized memories of his dead fiancée than his friends are with their living, breathing, repulsive spouses. It is an obvious irony, though not an ineffectual one.

The Manhattan Theatre Club production of ***Absent Friends***, directed as usual by Lynne Meadow, was brisk, intelligent, and poignant. I particularly liked John Lee Beatty's set, a light, open, suburban living room whose spotlessness came to seem ominous. Placed at a graceful angle to the audience, it facilitated movement and meaningful groupings, and gave a good sense of being part of a larger whole. The offstage kitchen and upstairs bedroom are significant to the action; Beatty's setting led your imagination, via intriguing halls and stairways, to those important unseen locations.

As with ***Taking Steps***, the cast of ***Absent Friends*** was a mixture of British and American actors. (There must be a lot of Americans performing in England these days, because Equity will only allow as many of their actors to work here as British Equity allows American actors to work there.) Brenda Blethyn, an actress I have seen many times on the London stage, was noteworthy as Diana, all chipper, neat, and efficient, desperately trying to maintain a façade with her nagging, supercilious husband, until her breakdown came like a sudden summer thunderstorm. Blethyn's face actually turned bright red as she raged about the unfairness of her life, starting with the frustration of her childhood dream of joining the Royal Canadian Mounted Police, a failure that seemed like original sin. When she finally dumped a pitcher of cream on her husband's stupid head, we all cheered.

The remainder of the cast, though all adequate, varied in quality. David Purdham as Paul was a perfect foil for Blethyn, handsome and charming (making his success with women comprehensible) yet, in a remarkably understated way, a despotic brute. Gillian Anderson, an American actress trained in England, was hilarious as the surly Evelyn, while John Curless as her cuckolded husband was delightfully athletic, swooping about the stage in imagined soccer games, his physical agitation covering up his emotional repression. Ellen Parker as Marge was less effective; her unseen husband never came to life for me in their many phone conversations, and she seemed too American. Her accent was accurate as regard to broadening the vowels and dropping the Rs, but did not get the pitch variation; English people toot up and down the scale, while Americans speak their mother tongue in a dead monotone that is usually a giveaway when they try to sound foreign. Peter Frechette as Colin had the same problem, and similarly was a bit too open, too aggressive, too emotional for a self-deluded Englishman. . . .

Hugh Rorrison (essay date 1994)

SOURCE: "Reception of and Critical Response to Botho Strauss and Alan Ayckbourn in Britain and Germany," in *History of European Ideas*, Vol. 20, No. 1-3, 1995, pp. 43-7.

[*In the following essay, Rorrison compares and contrasts Botho Strauss of Germany and Ayckbourn of Britain, concluding that while both are successful in their own theatrical cultures, it may be difficult to become mainstream in both.*]

Botho Strauss and Alan Ayckbourn both write comedies, both are prolific, Ayckbourn rather more so than Strauss, though Strauss as a writer of fiction and essays has the wider range. Both are commentators on contemporary manners, both are satirists of the consumer society, and both are widely performed in their respective countries and abroad. Of each it has been claimed that it is to their plays social historians of future centuries will turn to discover how we live now. They use the same material much of the time. Michael Billington lists the recurring themes in Ayckbourn as 'disillusionment with marriage, horror at masculine insensitivity towards women, dislike of do-gooders and bullish opportunists, sympathy with the feckless and incompetent'.[1] Strauss shares all these, though his emphasis is more on '*Beziehungskiste*', emancipated relationships and post-sixties sexual partnerships. The two writers often use the same comic strategies: the husband's unequal struggle with the kitchen equipment in *Kalldewey Farce*[2] has its parallel in Jerome's problems with his robot servant, Nan 300F, in ***Henceforward . . .***[3] However the way they structure their material, and the effects they aim at are different, and differ in ways that are determined by the cultural conventions and audience expectations in their respective countries.

Their two names were linked polemically in 1978 by Peter Zadek, the director who had just completed a string of informal, improvisational Shakespeare productions in Bochum and Hamburg. His radically crude approach aroused critical controversy, attracted media attention and sold seats, but it had a cultural purpose. Zadek believed that Shakespeare had been systematically gentrified by the German theatre. Claiming that in his time Shakespeare was popular art, not high art, Zadek's project was to bring popular audiences back to Shakespeare and simultaneously to widen the social base of the stodgily middle-class German subsidised theatre. He saw in Ayckbourn a useful ally.

In 1978 Zadek published a polemical report on the London stage[4] in which he praised the street credibility of the productions he had seen in the West End. This was real theatre: theatre which not only attracted a general public but also produced writers of quality. Ayckbourn was a prime example. He had achieved critical recognition with ***Relatively Speaking*** (1965) and ***How the Other Half Loves*** (1969), but the technical ingenuity which had revitalised English drawing-room comedy was beginning to look merely mechanical by 1978, when Zadek pronounced him a writer of comic dialogue of the precision of Marivaux (whom the Germans had just discovered), who was humane, refreshing and progressive, funnier than Nestroy, and much more accessible than Botho Strauss, who for his part (according to Zadek) could, but for reasons of status dare not, write like Ayckbourn for a broader public.

> 'Strauß is *the* German boulevard dramatist, but he can only write in that vein with a bad conscience, so he has to conceal it'.[5]

Since Zadek's article German reviews of Ayckbourn productions invariably address the issue of whether the play is real comedy or just boulevard, whereas hostile critics snipe at Strauss as boulevard pretending to be comedy.

What is boulevard? The *Cambridge Guide to World Theatre* defines it only as a historical form of commercial theatre in Paris in the late-nineteenth century, not as a general category. When English critics use the term to describe light comedy, it is mildly derogatory rather than witheringly dismissive. From a German point of view it is something lowbrow foreigners go in for. Challenged by Zadek, critic Michael Merschmeier defined it as theatre which was unprovocative and unchallenging, which peopled the stage with figures similar to the audience but restricted their discourse to the innocuous. To call theatre boulevard in Germany is to say it cannot be taken seriously.[6]

To see how the term applies to Strauss and Ayckbourn, two plays will now be compared in which the action is set on rehearsal stages, the former's *Visitors* which he designates as a comedy, and the latter's ***A Chorus of Disapproval***, for which, as usual, Ayckbourn gives no designation.[7]

None of Strauss's plays has a linear plot. *Visitors* opens with a rehearsal. Karl Joseph, an old ham of the Gründgens generation, plays a discredited professor of gene-technology, and Max, a recent emigrant from the G.D.R. (it is 1988) acts his assistant. These two are joined by Edna Gruber, a retired actress much concerned about ecology and animal welfare, making a come-back as the professor's daughter. Max, while trying to maintain a presence beside these domineering old pros, is also campaigning against 'sick realism', so debates about style and scientific ethics runs through the posturing.

Separately Strauss demonstrates Max's private life. He is living with Lena the wealthy daughter of parents who own vineyards and laundrettes. This is '*Beziehungskiste*', focussing on Max's insecurity and drinking, and Lena's support and loyalty as well as her need for the 'three little words', he cannot bring himself to say.

Beside and through these two realistic strands of action runs a surreal one in which Max and Lena appear as their own doubles and Edna Gruber as an apparition. Here the Max-Lena relationship is explored in another dimension where Lena ends by strangling Max. This plot travels through a landscape of alienation—all-night bar, fairground stall in no-man's-land, and finally the theatre cloakroom, where Max, as the Man from the Audience, complains to the cloakroom lady that the play he has just come out of is so close to his life, that he resents paying to see it. Whether this is Max acting the Man from the Audience, or the same actor doubling as the Man from the Audience, we never know. It soon becomes clear that on the stage another Man from the Audience is complaining to another cloakroom lady about the play he has just come out of . . . Strauss has set up an elaborate *mise-en-abime* as an enigmatic joke.

The end of the play neatly ties off all three strands. Max the actor has his part back. In her surreal incarnation Lena strangles Max, but he reappears as the Man from the Audience, and then in a final coda as Max the lover, finally able to tell Lena *he loves her.*

There is a high degree of sophistication in this interplay of different plot levels and roles, and it often looks as if it were designed for comic effect, although the incidence of laughs on the videotape of the Hamburg Thalia Theater production is not high. The accelerating interplay of the various strands of action in the final phase intensifies the confusion and leaves the ending whimsically (or is it philosophically?) open. One is tempted to call it post-Modern surrealism.

Ayckbourn's ***A Chorus of Disapproval*** is a mechanism of a different order. It has a linear plot and starts with an ending: the curtain is coming down to tumultuous applause on the Pendon Amateur Light Opera Society's production of *The Beggar's Opera*. So the play starts with a flourish which it maintains with astutely placed duets and trios from *The Beggar's Opera* in a sustained exercise in theatrical intertextuality. Gay's lines become comic aspersions on the amateurs who are delivering them.

After taking his bow and receiving his congratulations Macheath reverts to simple Guy Jones who is being ostracised by the rest of the cast. To explain why they are doing this, the play then shifts back to the day he arrived for his audition. Guy, recently widowed, is first given a minor part, but progresses to the lead via the beds of two senior members' wives, because these other members of the cast mistakenly believe he can help them make a killing on some development land. This is the misunderstanding that triggers the comedy. By the end his new friends realise their error and turn against him. Their code of behaviour typifies the enterprise culture.

Once the naïve central newcomer is placed in a competitive group where nobody believes anybody and self-interest rules, the outcome is inevitable, though not predictable. Ayckbourn has a facility for constructing human situations whose centre of gravity is so placed that they generate their own comic momentum, and provided the characters are plausible, a British audience will happily go along with the resultant fun as part of life's rich tapestry. German audiences, and even more German critics, are inclined to be bored by the apparent lack of significance. Partly this is due to loss of specificity in translation. Conversely a German audience will accept, even if it doesn't understand, the complicated structure of a Strauss play as part of life's impenetrable mystery, while a British audience finds it merely pretentious. Philistinism may be operating here. British critics though are eager to be kind to foreign plays.

Ayckbourn's characters are insecure and neurotic small-town types and they have problems, but not identity problems.

Of the eccentric minor character Jarvis Huntley-Pyke we are told that he is 'in his late fifties—the epitome of the 'knowing Northerner'. He is little more than a running gag until Guy naïvely tells him people are trying to swindle him, whereupon Jarvis tells the story of his development, land, a tale of generations of exploitation and pseudo-philanthropy. Here a trivial character reveals a callous, mercenary streak that brings the ethics of Thatcherite individualism sharply into focus. An anecdote develops naturally out of the plot, unmasking not only the teller, but also his class.

When Dafydd, director of *The Beggar's Opera*, confides in Guy that his wife is frigid, Guy is already, inadvertantly, the wife's lover:

> Dafydd: . . . I call her my Swiss Army Wife, you know. No man should be without one. It's just that she's—she's got a blade missing . . .

The boy scout metaphor turns the confession into a joke to hide Dafydd's British embarrassment in sexual matters, but the tannoy is on and his confidences are broadcast over the theatre. The comic surface reveals levels of domestic anguish without wallowing in them. When Dafydd finds out about his wife and Guy just before curtain up on the first night, he curses his guts but also wishes him luck as Macheath for the show, a British compromise you might say, but a touch that is typical of Ayckbourn's affectionate amusement at people's human foibles. His characters' awfulness and the constant misfortunes the plot brings upon them produce constant laughs.

Dafydd's compulsion to complete the production as his marriage crumbles, despite his awareness of the philistinism of small-town England, points to an essential function of art in at least his life.

Strauss's characters inhabit an emancipated world. They behave in public in a way that Ayckbourn's people keep private. They experience identity problems with a much greater intellectual awareness. Consider how Max tries to dispel Edna Gruber's doubts about her self and her acting:

> Max: No, you are the one, only you still have the power to raise your voice above the petty, the moderate, the trivial. For you acting is still something sacred . . . And everybody, right down to the most mediocre dwarf senses it, experiences the shudder which never fails, when you, the actress, liberate him from his pitiable condition.[8]

Edna's response undercuts Max's rhetoric with jokey pathos, but the fact remains that these figures are capable of a pathos which would be inadmissible in Ayckbourn. Max invokes the sublime function of art, and he can do so with the conviction that he is touching a belief his audience's share. Art as a mode of access to the transcendental is an integral part of Strauss's authorial project. His minor characters tend to be symbolic.

What Ayckbourn and Strauss share is an eye for behaviour and an ear for language that will transfer to the stage. Consequently there is much that could be seen as banal incident, were it not embedded in the authors' disparate dramatic structures. It must also be said that they fit into different sectors of the market. Strauss's plays are quickly premiered at major houses like the Berlin Schaubühne. They then trickle down through the state theatre system. Ayckbourn is usually performed by small regional theatres (*Landesbühnen*), by touring companies, or the occasional commercial theatres. In England Strauss is adjudged too commercially risky by even the top national companies, and has only been professionally performed four times. Ayckbourn brings out his plays in his own theatre in Scarborough (or occasionally at the Royal National Theatre), and they then go to the West End, in both cases catering for audiences who demand to be entertained, that is made to laugh. They will not be bored for the sake of Art. Ayckbourn is a product of British audiences' insistence on entertainment and his reflections on society have to be integrated into effective comic structures. Strauss can rely on audiences who see theatre as animated literature. Each is mainstream in his own country, but the likelihood of the two theatrical cultures assimilating to the point where both could be mainstream in both is remote.

Notes

1. Michael Billington, *Alan Ayckbourn* (Macmillan, London, 1983), p. 1.
2. Botho Strauss, *Kalldewey Farce* (DTV Munich, 1984), p. 23ff.
3. Alan Ayckbourn, *Henceforward . . .* (Faber and Faber, London, 1988), p. 9ff.
4. In *Die Zeit* (8 December 1978).
5. Theater Heute, 1989/13, p. 29.
6. Theater Heute, 1984/13, p. 92.
7. Botho Strauss, *Besucher* (Munich, Hanser, 1988); Alan Ayckbourn, *A Chorus of Disapproval* (Faber and Faber, London, 1986).

8. Botho Strauss, *Besucher* (Munich, Hanser, 1988), p. 48.

ABSURD PERSON SINGULAR

PRODUCTION REVIEWS

Stanley Kauffmann (review date 1976)

SOURCE: "New Plays: *Absurd Person Singular*," in *Persons of the Drama: Theater Criticism and Comment*, Harper & Row, Publishers, 1976, pp. 245-48.

[*In the following excerpt, Kauffman favorably reviews Ayckbourn's* Absurd Person Singular, *pointing out that the play should be categorized as film slapstick rather than comedy or farce.*]

Alan Ayckbourn has been trumpeted as the Neil Simon of England. Untrue. Neil Simon is a master of middlebrow, smart-cracking social comedy, a manufacturer of character comment that probes just enough to make us laugh indulgently and like ourselves a wee bit more. To judge by ***Absurd Person Singular***, the first Ayckbourn play produced here, he has no such interest. (He has had several other big London successes besides this one.) ***Singular*** shows him to be much more the Mack Sennett of England—fifty percent of Sennett, anyway.

Ayckbourn calls his play a comedy, but it is farce; and essentially it is not theater farce, it is film slapstick. The great farces of Feydeau and Courteline and Pinero are complicated machines of egocentric desire in monochromatic characters, people who desperately want something or other and bump violently into or frantically evade or breathlessly deceive others. Ayckbourn makes no such machine. His characters are monochrome, all right, but few of them *want* anything very much: they just behave in certain ways that are sharply and quickly defined. One wife is a compulsive housecleaner who has an addiction to cleaning, no matter whose house she's in. Another wife is a compulsive, socially pretentious drinker. And so on. The result is a series of situations that lead to physical complications that lead to more physical complications. The play is so much like a series of Sennett set-ups that it could very easily be played completely silent with fifteen or twenty subtitles.

Ayckbourn understands the secret of this kind of laugh-building. Each of his nests of structures begins with an action that is perfectly credible for its doer and then proceeds perfectly logically: the comedy comes from the fact that this logic has nothing to do with the logic of the other people. For instance, a husband angrily sends his wife out to buy the soda she forgot to get for the party going on inside the living room. They are both anxious that the guests—business bigshots whom they are eager to impress—should not know of the lapse. The wife goes out the kitchen door, into pouring rain, with raincoat and big hat and boots, her evening dress underneath. When she returns, the kitchen door is locked, and she hovers outside the window like a wet ghost, ducking when one of the guests comes in from the living room. Finally she has to go in the front door pretending to be someone else until she can get to the kitchen and change. She has behaved perfectly logically according to her pattern: that pattern simply has nothing to do with what the others, or we, would call sensible.

The three acts are three Christmas Eve parties with the same three couples (and one couple who never appear), each party in the home of a different couple. It's suburbia, but there's no more attempt at suburban satire than is inescapable, in our culture, in merely choosing the setting. The charms of these bourgeoisie remain discreet. The first act is in a climbing couple's kitchen, with the guests leaking in from offstage (an eccentric device previously used by Wolfgang Bauer in *Party for Six*). The second act is in the home of a philandering incompetent architect and the wife he is driving batty. The third act is in the home of a moldering middle-aged banking couple. During the play the first couple get prosperous, the second have domestic turbulence, the third molder more as the wife boozes more, but none of this is closely related to or caused by the action of the play we see.

Except for the batty wife's non-suicide. Her attempts to self-destruct are the basis of the funniest act, the second, in her home. The laughs come from the fact that no one—except her husband, the cause of her trouble, who has gone to chase down a doctor—understands how neurotic she is or what she is trying to do. She just moves mute and doggedly doomed through their busy, chattering incomprehension. She leaves a suicide note on a table: someone else, who needs a scrap of paper to write something on, grabs it and turns it over to use the other side. She sticks her head in the oven preparatory to turning on the gas: the compulsive housecleaner friend thinks she's worried about the dirtiness of the stove and immediately helps out by cleaning it. The neurotic stands on a table to hang herself from a lightfixture and pulls off the socket: the banker thinks she's trying to repair the fixture and climbs up on the table to help. By the time the distraught husband returns, everything has proceeded to a point, with strict logic, entirely disconnected from the point at which he left.

As hinted above, most of the dialogue itself is quite unfunny. Ayckbourn almost seems to flirt with the idea of an Ionesco-like barrage of banalities, which may be the source of the "absurd" in his title, but the dialogue never quite gets to that level of self knowledge. If this play were not well *done*, it would be worse than unfunny, it would be embarrassing.

But it is well done indeed, which brings us to the other fifty percent of Mack Sennett—the director. (Sennett wrote *and* directed his films.) Eric Thompson has got the shortest end of any stick that I've seen in a long time. His name occurs in most reviews of ***Singular*** in a subordinate clause about the direction near the end. I speak strictly proportionately but quite seriously when I say that Thompson's contribution to ***Singular*** is no less than Peter Brook's was to *Marat/Sade*. I never expected to see such good farce playing again on our stage. I have seen these six actors before, some of them many times, so I know how much Thompson has done with them.

Ayckbourn himself may have helped: he has been an actor and he directs the first tryout productions of his plays in Scarborough, far from London. But Thompson, also an ex-actor, directs the plays in London and has built this one with the frivolous ingenuity of one of those huge matchstick castles. Timing is precise; concentration is utter. And Thompson has solved the age-old problem of theater farce that Sennett never had to face. When there are two or three or ten actors in a film scene and only one of them is doing something, the director just cuts away from the others, closes in on the main man so that the others won't be standing around with the proverbial egg on their faces. But the stage director can't send the other actors offstage: he has to find some way to keep the others both neutral and supportive of whatever Number-One-at-the-moment is doing. Thompson handles this well in every case, and there are lots of cases. Mostly it's a matter of eyes. Thompson has given his actors careful instruction about what they ought to be thinking about and looking at when they are not figuratively center, so that they are really in the scene, not just actors waiting for cues, without being distracting. The whole thing is put together with superlative craft.

So there are good farce performances from Carole Shelley, the only English member of a cast that does well with English accents; Richard Kiley, that fine romantic actor who almost made *Man of La Mancha* bearable; Larry Blyden; and Geraldine Page, enjoyably overarticulating her platitudes as the lush. Even the oleaginous Tony Roberts is tolerable (he's the architect). And, heaven be praised, I have lived long enough to write a favorable word about Sandy Dennis. As the glazed neurotic, wandering around her kitchen, trying patiently to kill herself, she is very, very funny.

Half the laurels at least, then, to Eric Thompson. If you never expected again to see a play in which a man carrying a bowl of potato chips is startled and whooshes them up into the air; in which another man is repairing electric wires when someone accidentally turns on the switch and the current makes him do a skeleton dance; and certainly never expected to see such things done well, then ***Absurd Person Singular*** will refresh you. Historically, it's interesting too: silent-film comedy fed on the theater of its day, and now it's feeding back into its source.

ABSENT FRIENDS

PRODUCTION REVIEWS

J.K.L. Walker (review 1992)

SOURCE: A review of *Absent Friends*, in *Times Literary Supplement*, No. 4663, August 19, 1992, p. 16.

[*In the following review, Walker suggests Ayckbourn's* Absent Friends *leaves an audience less than satisfied.*]

Absent Friends is not one of Alan Ayckbourn's funniest plays, but then, nor was it intended to be. When it came to London from Scarborough in 1975, with Richard Briers in the role of Colin, the happy innocent who creates havoc in the lives of his old friends, the play met with a mixed critical reception, one reviewer dismissing it as "woefully limp", with a weak plot and unconvincing characters. Despite this, the play achieved a respectable nine-month run and has since often been seen as one of Ayckbourn's best, a tragi-comedy that perceptively reveals the futility and bitterness underlying conventional suburban marriage.

The plot is simple. A group of friends assembles one Saturday afternoon for a tea-party to welcome Colin, a former member of the group (played in this revival by Gary Bond), and to console him for the death by drowning of his fiancée. This well-meant act of charity goes disastrously wrong, as marital and extra-marital tensions shatter the atmosphere before Colin's arrival. Paul, a successful and charmless bully (Michael Melia), in whose house the party is to be held (in Bernard Culshac's set, all shiny-buttoned green-leatherette furniture and with the gin and Scotch optics behind the corner bar), is revealed to have made a joyless, back-seat conquest of the scornful, gum-chewing, black-faced Evelyn (Jane Slavin) ("about as exciting as being made love to by a sack of clammy cement"), with the connivance of her husband John (John Salthouse), sycophantically dependent on Paul to put business his way. Paul's wife Diana (Susie Blake), the originator of the party, and her friend Marge (Cherith Mellor), seem, with the relentless banality of their chat, to offer suburban normality in counterpoint to this rather sleazy trio, but it soon becomes evident from Marge's telephone conversations with her bedridden husband Gordon—another one-time member of the group—that she has reduced the aspiring county cricketer to a condition of infantile hypochondria; while Diana's party manners, already strained by Paul's boorish behaviour, disintegrate as her suspicion of Paul's infidelity with Evelyn finally crystallizes.

Here, then, is Ayckbourn on the true face of middle-class marriage and long-time acquaintanceship: boredom, indifference, mutual dislike, restless male egotism barely held in check by a domestic convention that has shaped women into dispensers of tea and triviality. And it is into this wasteland of lost hopes and brutalized feelings that Ayckbourn at last looses Colin, a beaming sentimentalist, his gaze locked firmly on the golden past, a glad-handing bank-clerk in rimless glasses and a pearl-grey suit, delighted to meet his old friends again and bearing under his arm photograph albums of his drowned girlfriend. The fact of the girl's death is quickly disposed of in a halting speech from Diana, interrupted by ill-tempered comments from Paul, and a boosterish reply from Colin, and soon they are all cooing and clucking over the photographs as if they were holiday snaps—as many of them turn out to be.

By this stage of the evening—despite the efforts of a highly professional cast—some doubts are beginning to appear, and one is tempted to echo the grumbles about the weakness of the plot. Surely Colin's character would be well known to such old friends, who might then be less than surprised at such remorseless optimism in the face of bereavement. And is a fiancée, rather than a wife of long standing, quite strong enough a peg on which to hang this ironic inversion? As Colin goes on unerringly, with his blindly idealized reminiscences of the past, to put a hatchet to the weakest joints of the present, causing Diana to empty the cream jug over Paul's head and, finally, to be supported from the room in hysterics, one wonders whether such a character is sustainable outside the realms of farce. Ayckbourn himself has declared his intention in ***Absent Friends*** to experiment with a simpler style, eschewing his mastery of comic ingenuity, "deliberately stopping at points where, perhaps, one could have broadened into more obvious farce". It may be that the dissatisfaction one feels with the play reflects an inadequate balance of the genres.

Ayckbourn has perfect pitch for the cadences of trite, everyday conversation, a gift that has not deserted him here, where it is put to good use to signal painful no-go areas in relationships rather than comic mutual incomprehension. Such naturalism may not, however, be enough to throw the moral weight where it is needed, leaving members of the audience at liberty to identify according to their predispositions: "God, weren't the men awful!" (surely Ayckbourn's point) may be balanced by "But the women were so boring!" (which might surprise him).

A SMALL FAMILY BUSINESS

PRODUCTION REVIEWS

Jeremy Gerard (essay date 1992)

SOURCE: A review of *A Small Family Business,* in *Variety*, May 4, 1992, p. 191.

[*In the following essay,* A Small Family Business *and its supporters are given a harsh review.*]

Those who feel that subsidized theater ought to do more than subsidize Broadway have a great new case study with ***A Small Family Business***. Why, critics might reasonably ask, is the Manhattan Theater Club devoting its considerable resources to the lavish staging of a middling comedy by England's most prolific playwright?

To be fair, the company created a commercial subsidiary, MTC Prods. Inc., to co-produce ***Business*** directly on Broadway. But the principals are artistic director Lynne Meadow and managing director Barry Grove—director and executive producer, respectively, of the production at the Music Box.

Meadow and Grove need answer to no one regarding their long record for presenting some of the most adventurous theater in New York (particularly, in recent seasons, on the second stage at their City Center home base). They're nothing if not eclectic, which explains why they've also chosen to become Ayckbourn acolytes. But Ayckbourn has fared poorly on Broadway under more conventional circumstances, and this $1.5 million production isn't likely to win many converts to the cause.

A Small Family Business is a classical, if not classic, farce in which nearly all of the family's members are corrupt, corruptible and exceedingly acquisitive. The business is the manufacture of home furnishings. Some of the products have mysteriously shown up bearing Italian designer names and selling, in a case of reverse knockoff, at a markup—frequently before the stuff is barely off the drawing board.

In the opening scene, Jack McCracken (Brian Murray) arrives home in an overstimulated mood and begins a hilarious seduction of his wife, Poppy (Jane Carr)—to the snickering amusement of the family members secreted in the den for a surprise celebration. The reason for the party is that Poppy's senile father, Ken (Thomas Hill), has decided to turn the firm over to Jack.

The old man confides in Jack about the ripoffs and compels him to hire private investigator Benedict Hough (Anthony Heald) to get to the bottom of things. Unsurprisingly, Jack soon learns that his various siblings and in-laws are all in on the side action—and that everyone has something on everyone else. By play's end, this upright prig has become downright dirty.

Business sports plenty of typical British sex comedy gags, including one ravenous sister-in-law (Caroline Lagerfelt) who has entertained each of the five Rivetti brothers (all played by Jake Weber) and another, (Patricia Conolly) who is convinced that eating in public is obscene. Though the finale has a dreary, end-of-the-'80s aspect, it doesn't fully justify what's gone on before.

Murray is earnest but surprisingly effortful as Jack, though that could be said of the overall production. Meadow has launched it at a fever pitch, and after a couple of hours one comes away feeling hectored. Most of the performances are above average, though Heald seems to be giving a master class in tics, brow-furrowing and lip-curling.

The show has a certain giddy grace, underscored by flashing, pinball-style lights between scenes and those still, and disturbing, final moments. There's an exceptionally handsome set by John Lee Beatty; six rooms double-decked in a suburban household that, true to the family business, is sleekly anonymous—all blond veneer and polished metals that gleam under Peter Kaczorowski's lights. And Ann Roth's costumes are, as always, the kind of clothes you know these characters live in.

The result is a big So what? That $1.5 million may have been spent well, but on the evidence at the Music Box, it wasn't spent wisely.

Stefan Kanfer (essay date 1992)

SOURCE: A review of *A Small Family Business,* in *The New Leader,* Vol. LXXV, No. 7, June 1-15, 1992, p. 31.

[*In the following excerpt, Kanfer reviews Ayckbourn's* A Small Family Business.]

Alan Ayckbourn's ***A Small Family Business***, a British import, can be enjoyed on two levels: The action takes place upstairs and downstairs in a suburban house. Jack McCracken (Brian Murray) is a British executive with a short fuse and a vast ego. His father-in-law, Ken Ayers (Thomas Hill), has grown too potty to carry on at Ayers and Graces, a failing furniture manufacturing concern. So Jack leaves the frozen food business and takes over, gathering the family around for a pep talk. From now, he vows, matters will be different. Squabbles, inefficiency, white-collar theft will be replaced with the only things that matter: honesty, decency and above all "simple basic trust." For without these the family—indeed, the world—is doomed. Chorus of assent, nods and raised glasses.

The aura of good feeling is punctured by an ominous knock. Enter Benedict Hough (Anthony Heald), a squinting private eye whose specialty is blackmail. He has bad news. Jack's adolescent daughter, Samantha (Amelia Campbell), has been caught shoplifting. This turns out to be the most trivial disclosure of the evening. Further investigation reveals that termites have been at the roots, branches and leaves of the family tree. Jack's brother Cliff (Mark Arnott) is involved in grand larceny. So is Cliff's wife Anita (Caroline Lagerfelt). To gain her sizable wardrobe and pricey automobiles, she has been bedding down with the five thieving Rivetti brothers, all from the Cosa Nostra, all ripping off A & G's designs, and all played by the amazing Jake Weber. Even Jack's sweet, wide-eyed wife Poppy (Jane Carr) has been making off with paper clips.

Nobody is pure but Jack, and each ungainly cleanup gets him deeper into the morass. Theft leads to coverups, coverups to payoffs, payoffs to debt. Each sin is accompanied by a hilarious hide-and-seek game, with lovers disappearing into closets, brother selling out brother, and extortionists raising their prices. Only one solution presents itself. Hough, who knows everything and wants £50,000 to keep the lid on, must be terminated with extreme prejudice. So he is, in a most bizarre manner. And as the sleuth goes, so goes honesty, decency and simple basic trust.

Ayckbourn directed his own production of ***Family Business*** at London's Royal National Theater. It is difficult to imagine how he could have excelled Lynn Meadow's metronomic staging at the Music Box. The single element that might be improved is diction. The cast is mixed English and American, and several colonials are not up to the intonations. Still, this is a minor quibble in a seriocomic triumph. Ann Roth's costumes vary ingeniously between the dowdiness of the Queen Mum and the kinky glamour of Madonna, and John Lee Beatty's inventive set allows four subplots to go on simultaneously.

Despite his bulk, Murray displays the light touch of a gadfly gradually succumbing to DDT. Campbell, who was outstanding in last year's *Our Country's Good*, is especially memorable as the daughter acting out the corruption she sees around her. Lagerfelt manages to be sexy, desperate and risible, a rare talent for pretty actresses on either side of the ocean. The playwright has often been called the English Neil Simon. That comparison will not stand. Alan Ayckbourn is the English Alan Ayckbourn, *sui generis*, master of that rarest and most difficult genre, the moral farce.

THE REVENGERS' COMEDIES

PRODUCTION REVIEWS

Tom Morris (review date 1991)

SOURCE: A review of *The Revengers' Comedies*, in *Times Literary Supplement,* No. 4622, November 1, 1991, p. 18.

[*In the following review, Morris unfavorably reviews* The Revengers' Comedies, *focusing on the play's weak plot and unbelievable characters.*]

Every character in this play is wound up, placed on the stage and allowed to potter to its doom without turning to right or left. Although Alan Ayckbourn invokes the rich heritage of revenge tragedy, and his promoters have spattered the programme with portentous quotations from Nietzsche, Heraclitus and Gaboriau, this kind of fatedness is the natural province of farce. The humiliations of his hero, well played as a sort of tragic Winnie-the-Pooh by Griff Rhys Jones, are compelling because he can't see his way out of them.

The Revengers' Comedies is meticulously structured in twos. Not only is it performed in two episodes over two evenings, there are also two central characters, two locations, two comic situations and two love stories. Jones plays guileless Henry Bell, too nice to get on in the city; Lia Williams plays Karen Knightley, a mad, fantastical woman-child. Henry's world is the London office block of the international consortium Lembridge Tennit. Karen's is Furtherfield House, complete with creaky staircase, suits of armour and a servants' wing. The two characters meet in despair as they prepare to jump off Albert Bridge. Thrown together by circumstance, they plot to avoid suicide by taking revenge, and to avoid detection by swapping their revenges. Karen will engineer the downfall of Bruce Tick, whose promotion has made Henry redundant, and Henry will do the same for Imogen Staxton-Billing who has reclaimed her husband from Karen's embraces. Thus naive and likeable Henry is hopelessly at sea in a village where women are chattels and duelling is not uncommon while ruthless Karen rises like a death-watch beetle through the humourless ranks of Lembridge Tennit. Her affair with Henry is characterized by shrieking and wild sex: Henry's affair with his intended victim Imogen by suffocated sobs and kisses stolen in the chicken run.

The central performances are strong and as precise as the plot. But Ayckbourn also finds room to decorate his script—as Roger Glossop decorates his lavish country house sets—with baroque details of character and staging. Adam Godley as Karen's goofy brother Oliver, invests his tiny role with an integrity and pathos that far outgrows his service to the plot. All this is sure to delight audiences, as are the set-pieces of typecast comedy that form the bulk of the play, and which are reinforced by his characters' names. Tracey Willingforth is an up-front secretary, Jeremy Pride is pleased with himself and Mrs Bulley is a bully. There is a danger, however, that such humour becomes thoughtless. One of Karen's tricks at Lembridge Tennit is to persuade Mr Pride's brusque middle-aged secretary that her bachelor boss is in love with her, causing both of their downfalls. Like Malvolio, she dolls herself up and moons about like a ninny, but the trick hangs too easily on the premiss that all unattractive secretaries are secretly in love with their bosses. Ayckbourn's delivery of jokes has always been like giving the audience sweets until suddenly they get one with pepper in it, but I'm not convinced that this one was supposed to be hot.

In invoking ***The Revenger' Tragedies*** in his title, Ayckbourn was surely aiming at a more ambitious blend of tone than he in fact delivers. He may have noticed that the comic blindness of Karen's victims is similar, for example, to Othello's, but he fails to couple that idea with any significant investigation of what revenge might mean to Henry or to her. Reviewing the original Scarborough production of this play in the *TLS* in 1977, John Wilders wrote that Ayckbourn's plots are "wholly improbable and can therefore be developed in any direction with no need for credibility." For this flexibility a price must be paid which a revenge play can ill afford: it leaves plot and character essentially without motive.

TIME OF MY LIFE

PRODUCTION REVIEWS

Patrick O'Connor (review date 1993)

SOURCE: A review of *Time of My Life*, in *Times Literary Supplement*, No. 4715, August 13, 1993, p. 17.

[*In the following review, O'Connor describes Ayckbourn's* Time of My Life *as a horror story filled with symbolism.*]

Alan Ayckbourn's forty-fourth play, ***Time of My Life***, is a horror story, set in "Calvinu's restaurant—Time: past, present and future". The Stratton family—parents, two sons, daughter-in-law and the younger's son's new girlfriend—are gathered to celebrate mother's birthday. During the course of the evening a table on either side of the stage, the centre of which is occupied by the family banquet, shows the progress of the elder son and his estranged wife in the future, and on the opposite side, in the past, the doomed courtship of the younger son and his date, Maureen (Sophie Heyman), a punk hair-dresser from the wrong end of town. During the second scene, early in the evening, we learn that a car crash will result in the death of the father (Anton Rodgers) on the way home.

Laura (Gwen Taylor), the mother, is a sharply-spoken, critical organizer. Marriage for her is a form of business: she folds the wrapping-paper from her birthday presents, winds the ribbon neatly, and waits for the departure of the children to badmouth their gifts and their partners. The punk drinks too much and exits to throw up in the gents, having mistaken the door. Throughout the play, the symbolism of the females vomiting over their men's lives in one way or another, no matter how little they seem to deserve it, prepares us for a triple rejection. After three Remy Martins, the mother lets slip, or chooses the moment to reveal, that her own extra-marital fling took place in 1974, in the back of a car, with her husband's late brother. The shock of this revelation triggers his consumption of most of a bottle of blue liqueur, the reckless ride and instant death.

Ayckborn denies the mother, played with ferocious drive by Gwen Taylor, even a moment's softness. "We were never great lovers, were we?" she asks her husband before recalling, "That's the end of the swinging sixties, I thought to myself"—when they purchased single beds "in August 1970". She has seen off any rivals, with a bottle of nail-polish remover and a quiet word in the ladies, and later dispatches the punk girl with the news that it was her behaviour at dinner that so upest her husband that it lead to his death.

If the main theme of the play is that of the Furies, destroying the men physically or psychologically—even the beloved younger son Adam (Stephen Mapes) is reduced to waiting at table, dressed in an embroidered tarboosh, while his brother (Richard Garnett) is left homeless, unemployed and divorced—the extent of the misery on stage makes the laughter, which all comes from the verbal quips, a harsh comment. Laura chooses a family of stray dogs in preference to her own grandchildren.

Ayckbourn's use of food and the rituals of family gatherings around the table, on picnics, or cooking provides a constant thread in his work. The heroine of ***Time of My Life,*** or at least the one character whose actions seem to suggest the author's approval, is the daughter-in-law, Stephanie (Karen Drury). She hardly eats at all, and throughout the evening, during the half-dozen or so different appointments at which we see her story unfold, she asks vainly for still water, not sparkling, and it is her triumph over the waiters and her husband that, in the final scene, she sends back the fizzy stuff and gets *eau-plat*.

The restaurant's cuisine is unidentifiable, the only dish described being melon and pineapple soaked in passion-flower juice. Nevertheless, its Balkan music and desperate waiters, only one of whom speaks English, suggest the extent to which the absence of compassion implicit in the family's collapse contributes towards our own reprehensible failure when confronted by emotions and hatreds tragically beyond our control or understanding.

FURTHER READING

Criticism

Ayckbourn, Alan. *Three Plays*. New York: Grove Press, Inc., 1977.

A collection of plays by Ayckbourn with a preface by the writer discussing his views on the works.

Evans, Barbara Lloyd, and Garth Lloyd Evans. *Plays in Review*. London: Batsford Academic and Educational, 1985.

A collection of critical reviews of authors and their work including Ayckbourn and his plays.

Hanks, Robert et al. Reviews of *Communicating Doors*, by Alan Ayckbourn. *Theatre Record*, no. 16 (September 3, 1995).

Provides a number of reviews on Ayckbourn's play. *Communicating Doors*.

Page, Malcolm. *File on Ayckbourn*. London: Methuen Drama, Michelin House, 1989.

Contains an overview of Ayckbourn's life and career, reviews of his work, comments made by the author himself and a list of sources for further reading.

Additional coverage of Ayckbourn's life and career is contained in the following sources published by the Gale Group: *Contemporary Authors*, Vols. 21-24R; *Contemporary Authors New Revision Series*, Vols. 31, 59; *Contemporary Literary Criticism*, Vols. 5, 8, 18, 33, 74; *DISCovering Authors: British*; *DISCovering Authors: Dramatists Module*; *Dictionary of Literary Biography*, Vol. 13; *Major 20th-Century Writers*, Editions 1, 2.

Molière
1632-1673

(Pseudonym of Jean Baptiste Poquelin) French dramatist.

INTRODUCTION

Molière is widely recognized as one of the greatest comic writers of seventeenth-century France and one of the foremost dramatists in world literature. In such masterpieces as *Le Tartuffe* (1664; *Tartuffe*), *Dom Juan* (1665; *Don Juan*), and *Le misantrope* (1666; *The Misanthrope*), he succeeded in elevating the traditional status of French comedy from farcical buffoonery to that of an influential forum for social criticism. Molière thus profoundly influenced the development of modern comedy and established comic drama as a legitimate literary medium, equal to tragedy in its ability to portray aspects of human nature

BIOGRAPHICAL INFORMATION

Born in Paris, Molière was the eldest of six children of a well-to-do upholsterer to King Louis VIII. Molière developed an early passion for theater, attended Paris's finer schools, briefly studied law, and inherited his father's position at court. In 1642 he met and became romantically involved with actress Madeleine Béjart. Béjart's family strongly influenced Molière, who formally renounced his royal appointment to pursue a theatrical career. He adopted the pseudonym Molière to respect his father's desire to avoid associations with the theater and established the L'Illustre Théatre (The Illustrious Theater) with Béjart's family. For thirteen years, Molière struggled as an actor, director, and stage director, even spending time in a debtor's prison, and began adapting Italian *commedia dell'arte* farces. Returning to Paris in 1658, Molière's troupe staged his farce *Le dépit amoureux* (1656; *The Amorous Quarrel*); the play was greeted with overwhelming enthusiasm, and the production earned them both the favor of Louis XIV and the privilege of sharing a theater with the famous Italian performers of Scaramouche. The following year, he satirized French society and manners with *Les précieuses ridicules* (1659; *The Affected Ladies*). Molière's portrayal of pretentiousness in high society was so accurate that it outraged numerous aristocrats who believed themselves the target of the dramatist's parody. Molière thus earned the first of many influential enemies; thereafter, his life and plays were almost always at the center of controversy. He married the twenty-one-year-old Armande Béjart, thought to be the daughter or younger sister of Madeleine Béjart, in 1662. The marriage was rife with difficulties and is often considered the inspiration for many of Molière's subsequent works, including his most commercially successful play, *L'école des femmes* (1662; *A School for Women*). Plagued with recurrent illnesses due primarily to exhaustion from overworking, the dramatist was diagnosed a hypochondriac by doctors angered by Molière's parodies of their profession. He died of a lung disorder in 1673 following the fourth performance of his final comedy, *Le malade imaginaire* (1673; *The Hypochondriac*). Denied both the ministrations of a priest and interment in consecrated ground because of his profession, he was granted a secular funeral after Louis XIV intervened on his behalf.

MAJOR WORKS

While Molière's early plays are generally divided between full-length *comédies litteraires in verse, such as Dom Garcie de Navarre (1661; Don Garcie of Navarre), and one-act farces, such as Les précieuses ridicules ;* from *L'école des femmes* onwards these two forms became fused.

Despite its success, *L'éecole des femmes* was attacked by Molière's enemies as immoral and sacrilegious, and Molière was accused of incest and labeled a cuckold. The controversy surrounding him increased, however, with the production of his most renowned work, *Tartuffe*, which skewered and/or offended several aspects of upper-class French society, the Roman Catholic Church, and the the influential underground society, Compagnie du Saint Sacrement, which boasted many powerful and influential members. Although *Tartuffe* was extremely popular with audiences and was acclaimed by Louis XIV, the Archbishop of Paris issued a decree threatening to excommunicate anyone performing, attending, or even reading the play. It was not until 1669—after the bulk of political and religious power had shifted away from his most adamant opponents—that Molière was permitted to perform publicly the final version of the play. In the midst of the controversy, Molière produced *Don Juan*, a cynical recasting of the legend of the irreligious libertine who embraces hypocrisy and commits unpardonable sins. *Don Juan*'s sensitive subject matter invited further censorship from outraged church officials, who had the play suppressed after only fifteen performances. In 1667, Molière submitted a five-act revision of *Tartuffe* called *L'imposteur* in which he renamed Tartuffe Paulphe, secularized the hypocrite's priestly mien, and subdued the overtly religious attacks of the original play. This attempt to pacify church officials was unsuccessful, however, and he petitioned Louis XIV for an official reprieve. The King's personal support of Molière was unfailing, and it is possible that without his royal favor and protection, the dramatist might well have been executed for heresy. Following the controversy surrounding *Tartuffe*, Molière resorted on several occasions to writing less consequential farces.

CRITICAL RECEPTION

Despite attempts by traditionalists, religious leaders, and medical professionals to discredit Molière's work during his lifetime, his detractors had little effect on his theatrical success. His plays were extremely popular and, despite claims that he was merely a mediocre farceur, rival playwrights and companies soon began almost uniformly imitating his dramatic style. In England, Molière's work was widely imitated and evaluated, with many English critics ranking him beside Ben Jonson. That most Restoration dramatists were familiar with his works is evidenced in the nearly forty plays that appeared prior to 1700 in which such authors as John Dryden, William Wycherley, Aphra Behn, and Thomas Shadwell adapted, translated, or borrowed freely from his comedies. Molière's positive reputation in England continued to flourish during the eighteenth century. In France, however, public and critical opinion of his works declined drastically. In the early nineteenth century, during the French Restoration, Molière's comedies regained preeminence among dramatic critics and enjoyed a tremendous resurgence of public popularity. His work was also embraced by Romanticists as detailing a revolutionary, almost tragic, individualism that transcended rigid classicism. Twentieth-century scholars have addressed a number of issues concerning Molière and his works, and the majority of critical assessments has been positive. In general, scholars have continued the objective scholarly work instigated by such nineteenth-century scholars as Sainte-Beuve, Ferdinand Brunetiere, and Gustave Larroumet, probing virtually every literary, scientific, and historical aspect of the dramatist and his work. While scholars still seek philosophical, ethical, and religious messages in Molière's comedies, critical interest has, in many instances, shifted away from assessments of Molière's didactic intent toward purely aesthetic examinations of his comic technique.

PRINCIPAL WORKS

Plays

La jalousie de Barbouillé [*The Jealousy of Le Barbouillé*] 1645?

Le médecin volant [*The Flying Doctor*] 1645?

L'estourdy; ou, Le contre-temps [*The Blunderer; or, The Counterplots*] 1653; also published as *L'étourdi*, 1888

Le dépit amoureux [*The Amorous Quarrel*] 1656

Le précieuses ridicules [*The Affected Ladies*] 1659

Sganarelle ou Le cocu imaginaire [*The Imaginary Cuckold*] 1660

Dom Garcie de Navarre; ou, Le prince jaloux [*Don Garcie of Navaarre; or, The Jealous Prince*] 1661

L'école des maris [*A School for Husbands*] 1661

Les fâcheux [*The Impertinents;* also translated as *The Bores*] 1661

L'école des femmes [*A School for Women;* also translated as *The School for Wives*] 1662

La critique de "L'école des femmes" [*"The School for Women" Criticised*] 1663

L'impromptu de Versailles [*The Impromptu of Versailles*] 1663

Le mariage forcé [*The Forced Marriage*] 1664

La Princesse d'Élide [*The Princess of Elis, being the Second Day of the Pleasures of the Inchanted Island*] 1664

Le Tartuffe [*Tartuffe: or, The Hypocrite;* also translated as *Tartuffe: or, The Imposter*] 1664; revised versions also performed as *L'imposteur*, 1667, and *Le Tartuffe; ou, L'imposteur*, 1669

Dom Juan; ou, Le festin de pierre [*Don John; or, The Libertine;* also translated as *Don Juan; or, The Feast with the Statue*] 1665

Le médecin malagré lui [*The Forced Physician;* also translated as *The Doctor in Spite of Himself*] 1666

Le misantrope [*The Misanthrope; or, Man-Hater;* also translated as *The Misanthrope*] 1666

Amphitryon [*Amphitryon; or, The Two Sosias*] 1668

L'avare [*The Miser*] 1668

George Dandin; ou, Le mary confondu [*George Dandin; or, The Wanton Wife*] 1668

Monsieur de Pourceaugnac [*Monsieur de Pourceaugnac; or, Squire Treloobу*] 1669

Le bourgeois gentilhomme [*The Gentlemen Cit;* also translated as *The Bourgeois Gentlemen*] 1670

Les fourberies de Scapin [*The Cheats of Scapin;* also translated as *The Rogueries of Scapin*] 1671

Psiché [with Pierre Corneille] [*Psiché;* also translated as *Psyche*] 1671

La femmes savantes [*The Learned Ladies*] 1672

Le malade imaginaire [*The Hypochondriac;* also translated as *The Imaginary Invalid*] 1673

The Works of Mr. de Molière 6 vols., 1714

The Dramatic Works of Mr. de Molière 6 vols., 1875-76

The Plays of Molière in French with an English Translation 8 vols., 1902-07

OVERVIEWS AND GENERAL STUDIES

Albert Bermel (excerpt date 1975)

SOURCE: "Fears into Laughs," in *One Act Comedies of Moliere,* second edition, translated by Albert Bermel, Frederick Ungar Publishing Co., 1975, pp. 1-10.

[*In the following essay, Bermel discusses the balance between comedy and tragedy in Molière's theater.*]

Molière's longer plays have often unsettled critics who like to keep their genres clean and uncomplicated. ***The Misanthrope, Tartuffe, The School for Wives, George Dandin, Don Juan, The Miser,*** and ***The Learned Ladies*** are richly comic yet they contain scenes that are disturbing, if not distressing, to sit through, and they end by stirring up in us a discord of emotions. The genre merchants will not be defeated, though. They have found an answer, a general repository for Molière's drama, the tragicomedy. If redefining the plays in this way helps to keep alive the human quality of Molière's characters, and to kill off the stilted, grimacing, artificial performance, that would-be reconstruction of British "style", then the tragicomic assumption does serve a theatrical purpose. But the dangers of categorizing persist.

There is not an overall balance in Molière between comedy and tragedy, for the tragic sense and effects are partially concealed. My own impression, after watching many Molière productions, is that the glints of bitterness and darkness register better on an audience when the actors do not seem to push for them. If the productions are not funny, very funny, they are not worth doing. Roger Planchon's peerless ***Tartuffe,*** for example, was greeted by continuous open bursts of laughter; the audience felt uneasy *while* it was enjoying itself. George Saintsbury called Molière "the Master of the Laugh,"[1] but there is more than one kind of laugh. Lionel Abel has written that Molière "lifted comedy to a level of artistry and refinement it had never had before nor has had since"[2]; and John Palmer emphasizes the variety of Molière's comedy when he says that "no man has more finely smiled or more broadly laughed." For the comic actor, then, Molière's full-length plays provide not only rewarding roles, but tests of intelligence, sincerity, and versatility. Can the same be said of the one-acts? It can insofar as many of their situations and characters prefigure the ones in the longer plays, or in some instances, duplicate them. Even into the most rollicking of his short plays Molière manages to slip hints and glimpses of somber thoughts and feelings. . . .

But what stands out in these less ambitious works is their twofold comedy, a balance, sometimes a clash, between formal and informal entertainment. On the one side we find a colloquial, rough quality—humor—which proceeds from characters who do not mean to look and sound funny; on the other side we find studied, polished wit that enables other characters to be funny by intention. (Some characters, of course, are both humorous and witty.) The humor, especially the naturalness of its language, was inspired by Molière's years as a traveling performer and enhanced by his knack for clothing dialogue in sentences that appear suspiciously ordinary and uncalculated. The formal wit has mixed origins; it comes partly from the strained, literary mannerisms of seventeenth-century France, partly from his responses to the Court spectators in the mature period of his career, and partly from his striving for new, elevated comic forms.

Molière's training as actor and author began during fifteen years on the road while he circulated among provincial audiences, appearing on a converted tennis court in Agen or Fontenaye,[3] in the consular palace at Narbonne, or in the city halls of Lyon, Nantes, and other large towns. His early sketches and plays, worked up from commedia dell'arte skits of the Italian troupes who visited France frequently in the early seventeenth century, were shot through with popular sight gags, jokes (*burli*), and stage buffoonery (*lazzi*). Like the commedia scenarios they were populated by traditional and familiar figures: the pedant, the cuckold, the tightfisted father, the scheming servants, the aching lovers, the Pistol-like soldier-braggart who refuses to fight. The matter of these entertainments was not altogether primitive and the staging fairly elaborate. Molière's company wore splendid costumes and, in spite of the hasty preparations and a certain helping of improvisation, the actors performed with finesse. The troupe's provincial patrons, such as the Prince de Conti and the Duc d'Epernon, may have enjoyed the boisterous bits of business—stage beatings, pratfalls, and raw jokes—but must also have expected some subtlety in the writing and presentation. Only two of these early efforts survive, ***The Jealous Husband*** and ***The Flying Doctor***; into them Molière had already begun to infuse literary distinction. He adapted the situations from who knows how many sources, not only from the commedia routines, but also from Plautus and Terence (he is said to have known Terence's work by heart in Latin), and from unnumbered sixteenth- and seventeenth-century dramatists in Spain, France, and Italy. The knockabout humor of these playlets exploited such satisfying, vintage themes as the triumphs of love over greed, youth over age, and honesty over pretence. Later Molière was to investigate these themes more rigorously and, in his longer plays, to present avaricious, aging, and pretentious characters with a combined severity and understanding that have never been surpassed.

In the transitions from early to late plays another theatrical element persisted. It has affinities with folk art because it predates the commedia dell'arte and goes back to wandering performers of the middle ages. It also has affinities with improvisation because it consists of set pieces or bravura turns done by specialized players and by nobody else, so that the author adapts his scripts to the solos done by certain "masks," that is, actors in character. Each of these turns might be compared with an aria used over and over, with negligible variations, in different operas. A succession of such arias—a doctor's followed by an outraged father's and a betrayed lover's—added up to a revue format linked by a flimsy thread of story. The format, obtrusive in the one-act plays, becomes disguised after Molière tremendously strengthens the story line for his large, complex dramas, but it is very much there. The big speeches of Alceste, Acaste, Don Juan, Philaminte, Dandin, Orgon, Tartuffe, and Sosie, superb as monologues, retain the flavor of those solo comic acts. So do the recurring scenes, such as the one in which a maidservant mocks her master (in, say, ***The Middle-Class Nobleman***); there must have been a maid's-laughing-and-giggling act which one of the women in the Molière company excelled in, and he made room for it. Some critics have been disappointed that in his very late play ***Scapin*** Molière returned to commedia scenes, characters, and *lazzi*; the truth is that he had never abandoned them.

Yet we should not underestimate Molière's contributions to the solo turns. The Scholar's long speeches in ***The Jealous Husband*** and the Lawyer's puffy address to Sganarelle in ***The Flying Doctor*** have obviously been painstakingly planned and composed, even if they were drawn from existing material. The formal side of Molière's writing thus shows up in these first two of his plays and may have done in such lost plays as ***The Woodcutter*** and ***Gorgibus in the Sack.*** In the next two plays the literary notes resound strikingly. ***Two Precious Maidens Ridiculed*** takes literature as one of its dominant themes and enters the fringes of Parisian high society; while ***The Imaginary Cuckold*** is written in rhyming verse. In the former play he was not tilling new ground, for there had been at least two previous plays about the *précieuses* of Paris; but in this play Molière acquired what we recognize today as his own satirical tone, probably because the dialogue is based on his personal experiences. In a play written by one of his enemies, a character calls Molière "a dangerous man . . . he goes nowhere without his eyes and ears." He had visited the fashionable Blue Room in the *hôtel* (mansion) of Mme de Rambouillet, dedicated nearly forty years before to cultural discussions, and its imitation, the salon of Mlle de Scudéry on the rue de Beauce, where *précieuses* and their admirers sat in alcoves and buried one another in verbal bouquets. In reproducing their grotesquely sententious exchanges, Molière did not forget to add a generous ration of lowbrow comedy, as when Mascarille makes his entry into the play in a sedan and tries to bully the porters out of their payments, or when he and his fellow valet are thrashed at the end by their masters and forced to strip down in public. The contrast between formality and informality in this play is dramatized when the author juxtaposes the affectations of the girls and the valets with the spontaneous speech patterns of the father, the suitors, and the maid.

By the time he came to write ***The Imaginary Cuckold*** in 1660 he had tried his hand at verse drama in two five-act comedies, ***The Bungler,*** 1655, and ***The Loving Quarrel,*** 1656, and had developed a rhythmic style that was not merely supple enough to accommodate the comedy but actually helped to point it up by skillful use of rhyme, meter, and ictus.

Molière practiced his art at a time when *esprit* (meaning both wit and intelligence) and "correct" form were prized as artistic ends and enforced, if not legislated, by the French Academy. Tragedy was looked up to as literature's summit. Molière performed a number of tragic roles and kept a stock of other authors' tragedies in his repertory. Yet he apparently was unconvincing in serious roles. He could turn his gifts to superb account in mimicry and comedy, but contemporary reports say he lacked the measured, ringing voice that tragic acting then required. If you can't beat the game and don't want to join it, invent your own. One theory has it that Molière's desire to cast comedy in poetic forms may have had something to do with his incapacity as a tragedian; by lifting the standards of comedy he might be able to bring it on a par with tragedy. But no artist sets out to create art that is *equal* to other art. Molière, I surmise, tried to demonstrate that finely wrought comedy can throw surprising light on a potentially tragic situation. It is easy to say with twentieth-century hindsight—or by foreseeing the past, as Paulhan has it—that Molière was bound to succeed in this lofty enterprise. Boileau had told him that his most rollicking speech was "often worth a learned sermon," but it must have been difficult at that time for anybody, Molière included, to be sure that "serious" comedy was a feasible objective; then, suddenly, here was ***The Imaginary Cuckold,*** its formal and informal constituents in near equilibrium: a farce in poetry.[4] Coming from somebody else the hybrid might have worn the features of a monster; from Molière it proved to be a dramatic innovation. In addition, it proved a success, but Molière's rivals did not acknowledge its qualities any more than they subsequently admired the full-length plays in verse.

The remaining three plays in this book are also weddings of opposites. ***The Rehearsal at Versailles*** contains a heartfelt exposition of some of Molière's beliefs as a playwright and methods as an actor, but the disruptive sequences—the niggling questions of La Thorillière and the clamor of the courtiers—are quickfire comedy. ***The Forced Marriage*** pits a dimwitted bourgeois against long-winded scholars and sham nobility until he gives up all hope, a stranger lost in exotic vocabularies. And ***The Seductive Countess*** is ***Two Precious Maidens Ridiculed*** translated into a provincial setting where the heroine's sentiments sound even more out of place.

Together these plays represent seven of Molière's ten one-act plays. The other three are omitted for different reasons. ***The Criticism of the School for Wives*** was born of the controversy that followed the early productions of ***The School for Wives*** and becomes an orphan when separated from the parent play. ***Pastorale Comique,*** a slight divertissement, was addressed to Louis XIV's vanity. ***The Sicilian,*** a longer, more substantial divertissement, depends for many of its effects on colossal machinery; some recently built college theatres have vastly more sophisticated plant and equipment than was needed for the original production at Saint-Germain-en-Laye and could handle this comedy-ballet with dispatch, but, as the old stage saw goes, it doesn't read as well as it probably plays. The remaining seven comedies can fairly be called the cream of Molière's one-acts, and in their diversity are not unrepresentative of his work as a whole, even if they never touch the emotional and dialectical sublimity of ***Don Juan, Tartuffe, The Misanthrope,*** and ***The School for Wives.***

In addition to the ten one-acts, Molière wrote two two-acts, nine three-acts, and twelve five-acts; from this diversity we assume that he was aware of the importance of unfolding an action at the right length and with the right strength. In this respect his one-act comedies are models; they run their courses without forcing the speed; they put on a nice dash just before the end, and stop before they are winded or simply moving forward mechanically. A one-act play makes an especially memorable impression when it arises from a single situation; Molière hews scrupulously to this discipline; he enriches the situation with humorous twists and embellishments brought about by the presence of rogues and their marks, fools, but he does not stray too far off the main track. By codifying and at the same time renewing a number of theatrical conventions, Molière realized a new kind of brief comedy, compact, organized, and peopled with figures who stand for quickly recognizable clusters of attributes.

Since the playwright's death in 1673 the growing Molière industry has ground out dozens of editions and interpretations of his drama; the card files are overflowing, and periodicals such as the *Moliériste,* published for a decade during the last century, have devoted themselves to keeping up with new information and criticism. Because not much is known of Molière's first thirty-six years, stray documents about the birth of his wife or the death of his mistress's mother, Marie Hervé, have been pored over for clues, and Molière's life and writings reexamined in the light of the new data, however trifling. Molière as man, author, and performer has undergone many evaluations, and it is not possible (or desirable) to be dogmatic about him or the meanings of his work.

A casual reading of his plays and prefaces suggests that he abhorred extreme behavior, pleading for a sane, middle course in human activity. Accordingly, certain earlier critics and biographers, like Brunetière, formulated a Moliéresque "philosophy" that images him forth as an insufferably wise old advice-donor. "He possessed a quality," says Voltaire, "that sets him apart from Corneille, Racine, Boileau, and La Fontaine: he was a philosopher in theory *and* practice." This remark from one of the shrewdest commentators on human affairs and literature can easily be misinterpreted, and often has been. It is true that a sense of conventional morality, a belief in the powers of common sense and common decency and moderation, does appear to inform the plays. Let us suppose, for the sake of the argument, that Molière was trying to promote moderation among his contemporaries. What is moderation? Surely it involves the suppression of personal whims, mannerisms, and irrational impulses; it calls for an adherence to social norms. We thus have a portrait of Molière as *un homme moyen raisonnable*; his reasonable characters become his mouthpieces, his villains and fools his targets; we then take him (if we are reasonable ourselves and follow the argument through) to be *the* playwright of conformity, as the Goncourt brothers did.[5]

Such a conclusion is at odds with the spirit of the plays themselves. It may be going too far to say that Molière sides with his villains and fools, but it is fair to notice that the extreme characters like Harpagon the miser, Orgon the outrageously jealous host of Tartuffe, Arnolphe the selfish, tormented guardian, and Alceste, the self-appointed conscience of mankind are the backbones of the plays they appear in, and Molière may well have felt a certain affection for them, otherwise he would not have looked into them so piercingly or been able to make them so amuse and worry us. Nor would he have been able to play them, as he did, with such conviction. On the other hand, the sensible figures who plead for natural behavior do not hold leading roles. They are neither as colorful nor as appealing as the villains and fools. They could almost be transplanted, like the scenes in the early comedies, from one play to another. It is hard to imagine that they were not conceived for the sake of dramatic opposition and to give each comedy's fantastic branchings-out roots in the real world.

From the plays to the author. Palmer remarks that "nothing is more dangerous or misleading than to look for an author in his works," and the same might be said of searching for the meaning of an author's works in his life. Not that the life and works tell us nothing about each other; rather, one offers only wispy clues to the other. The transmutation of experience into art encompasses distortions we have no way of assessing. What, for instance, are we to make of Molière's middle-class background from studying the comedies? By piecing together isolated sentences and sentiments we can decide that he detested what Bernard

Shaw calls middle-class morality *and* that he thought it the basis for a life of contentment;[6] that he rebelled against his father *and* respected him. We can discover that he "really" loved his wife and that he "really" hated her. We can psychologize at a distance and say with Ramón Fernández that Molière releases his private vexations through his extreme characters and then balances his drama with the commonsensical characters who represent the thoughtful, deliberative side of his personality. Such observations remove us from the plays; they whisk us speculatively on a tour of the author's corpse. Which keeps its silence.

It seems to me a tortuous procedure to apply Molière's plays to his life only in order to refer deductions about his life back again to the plays. We are liable to miss the sharpness and specificity of Molière's actual portraits. If we study the bigger portraits one at a time we notice that most of them have lineaments in common, despite the generous differences in their outward features. Behind the comic words and gestures, palpitated by obsessive behavior patterns—Jourdain's extravagance, Harpagon's avarice, the (dissimilar) snobbery of Alceste, Dandin, and Philaminte, the possessiveness of Orgon and Arnolphe—there lurk fears. Fears of going unheeded, unrecognized, unloved. Each of these characters wants to be master (or mistress) of a household, a metaphor for being in control of oneself, able to hold up to the world an acceptable image of oneself. The fears and their consequences are hilarious to watch, but terrifying for the characters to undergo because they spring from desperation; the plays, instead of allaying those fears, make them come true. In Molière's funniest moments we are never far from nightmare, the inexorable acting out of the worst that could happen. It is not that events exactly get out of control; rather, the more the characters try to exert control the more they bring to pass what they most dread. Arnolphe finally *is* a cuckold; Dandin makes *and publicly shows* himself inferior to his wife; Alceste, in his rejection of Célimène, turns out to be no better than other people in the Parisian *haut monde* whom he despises. These characters are born losers. We laugh; they do not. Dandin says *"Marchand qui perd ne peut rire"*—the loser cannot laugh. With a few exceptions, these characters fear being unloved because they are unable to give love or, indeed, much else.[7] They have little or nothing to give, and that is what they receive. They have made their empty beds and must lie in them.

Now, we do not need to conclude that Molière is handing out practical advice to the lovelorn—give of your affection and ye shall receive. He would surely be among the first to understand that such advice is fruitless, like instructing a dog how to behave like a cat. He saw in his time people, perhaps including himself, who strove to cope with their fears in ways that could only aggravate those fears and ultimately realize them. Neither in the long plays nor the short ones do I see any implicit remedies. But why should one expect remedies? A playwright has no obligation to turn healer; in Molière healers are all quacks. Like the Greeks and Shakespeare before him, like his acquaintances Corneille and Racine, like Ibsen and Pirandello and Chekhov after him,[8] Molière analyzed life and clothed his analysis in theatrical forms that have allowed his vision to live more vividly than his contemporaries' prosaic reports.

A contributor to *The Oxford Companion to the Theatre* believes that Molière's plays are "universal in their application, yet untranslatable. In transit, the wit evaporates and only a skeleton plot is left. This, however, will not deter people from trying to translate them—a fascinating preoccupation." It is true that Molière, who made many enemies during his lifetime, has all too often since his death needed protection from his translating friends. But Richard Wilbur's versions of ***The Misanthrope, Tartuffe,*** and ***The School for Wives,*** and Tony Harrison's modernized ***The Misanthrope,*** set in the time of De Gaulle, all follow the French devotedly without sacrificing style and simplicity in their English verse. This book has a more modest objective: to bring the vernacular side of the short comedies into play. Up-to-the-minute slang is not the answer; in addition to dating too rapidly, it wrenches the plays out of their period and environment. But nor does it help to take the sentences practically word for word from the French, as some translators have done, finishing up with a computerized English that makes the plays sound like Restoration comedies composed by an illiterate.

Ten years ago when the first edition of these translations was published I started to enunciate some principles of translating Molière into a language that is actable. Today I think that literary principles, when offered by a translator as by an author, are useless excuses, apologies, self-justification. All that matters is results. A translator works by instinct. He has to trust his ear, his senses. He is lucky or unlucky. But his luck is more likely to hold as long as he feels unabated respect and love for the plays in their original form.

Notes

1. The authors and books referred to here are listed in the bibliography, except where otherwise stated.
2. *Metatheatre* (New York: Hill & Wang, Inc., 1963), p. 64.
3. The tennis courts did not have makeshift stages, as has sometimes been suggested; they were transformed into serviceable playhouses.
4. The topic of Molière as *farceur* is discussed in Gustave Lanson's essay, and by the director Jacques Copeau (see bibliography).
5. *Pages from the Goncourt Journal,* ed. and trans. by Robert Baldick (New York: Oxford University Press, 1962), p. 49.
6. Molière was Shaw's favorite playwright. See Archibald Henderson, *George Bernard Shaw: Man of the Century* (New York: Appleton-Century-Crofts, 1956), p. 502.
7. The exceptions include Monsieur Jourdain and Argan, whose escapades end fairly happily, and also

Don Juan and Amphitryon, who are special cases that I hope to discuss at more length elsewhere.

8. In *Men and Masks* (see bibliography) Lionel Gossman devotes a detailed chapter called "After Molière" (pp. 252-306) to the effects of Molière's "unflinching honesty" on later European writers.

Henry Phillips (essay date 1989)

SOURCE: "Molière and *Tartuffe:* Recrimination and Reconciliation," in *The French Review,* Vol. 62, No. 5, April, 1989, pp. 749-63.

[*In the following essay, Phillips examines the changing attitudes towards Molière's drama, focusing on the criticisms of the church.*]

The year 1922 marked the three-hundredth anniversary of Molière's birth. An occasion, one might think, to celebrate unequivocally the life and work of one of the three great dramatists of the seventeenth century in France and indeed one of the great figures of French literature. After all, the controversies over ***Tartuffe*** and ***Dom Juan,*** and especially over ***L'Ecole des femmes*** had surely abated by then, leaving the way open for the consecration of a supreme representative of the culture of France. Everybody could at least agree on that. Not quite.

The tercentenary revived, in a particularly acute fashion, arguments over Molière's ***Tartuffe,*** which had raged fitfully throughout the nineteenth century. The more general context was in any event the relations between the Church and the theater, especially in the former's attitudes to actors. It should be recalled that the so-called *querelle du théâtre* in the seventeenth and eighteenth centuries in France had pitted those who believed drama to have a morally improving function against those who, like Nicole, Bossuet, and Rousseau, saw in it a corrupting and socially disruptive influence.[1] Generally speaking, basic attitudes condemning the public theater, actors, and above all actresses could still be found in the early decades of the twentieth century.[2] But the tercentenary celebrations, while certainly critical of Molière, at the same time offered an opportunity for reflexion, with the result that 1922 became something of a watershed in the relations between Church and theater. Old problems were raised, but, happily, moves towards their resolution were undertaken by both sides. In this article, I shall give some prominence to those who wrote in various Catholic journals during the year of the celebrations. The debate, however, was carried on well into the 1930s and beyond. I have therefore chosen a thematic rather than a purely chronological perspective.

Molière had in fact always constituted a problem for literary critics who, in the nineteenth and early twentieth centuries, had sometimes shown great hostility towards Molière's alleged anticlericalism. Even the great Lanson himself expressed reservations over ***Tartuffe,*** and saw in Molière a Voltairian *avant la lettre.*[3] The comic playwright was, wrote Lanson, profoundly ignorant of Christianity: "il ne le comprend pas." (526) But this view did not seriously threaten Molière's unquestionable claim to greatness. Lanson concluded that: "Molière est, en effet, peut-être le plus exactement, largement et complètement français." His genius, in comparison to La Fontaine's, possessed "les qualités françaises portées à un degré supérieur de puissance et de netteté." (530) Even more ardent supporters of Molière were disturbed by the possibilities of flaws in the playwright's reputation. Doumic offers a glimpse of the potential embarrassment surrounding the whole question of Molière's sincerity at the time of the *querelle de **Tartuffe*** when he remarks: "Avouez qu'il serait au moins fâcheux que Molière n'eût pris la parole que pour nous tromper." (Quoted in Reyval, *L'Eglise et le théâtre* 15). Reyval reacts to those who make the charge that Molière was not only anticlerical but a liar and an imposter by an assertion that seems to start from the wrong end: "Je suis trop molièriste pour m'associer à eux." (*L'Eglise et le théâtre* 16)

The Catholic Church, however, was the institution for whom Molière's place in French culture remained a highly sensitive issue. As I have indicated, their concern did not begin with the tercentenary year. Louis Veuillot, the influential, extremist Catholic journalist of the second half of the nineteenth century, had, in 1877, set out in often strident terms the grievance of the Church against Molière and ***Tartuffe.*** The tercentenary simply provided the opportunity to focus these grievances in terms of the degree to which Molière could be regarded as representative of "l'esprit français." Undoubtedly, the subtext to the arguments advanced also focuses on a certain conception of society, and how far religious attitudes should form a part of that conception. In a sense, Catholic writers were challenging judgments issuing from the predominantly lay dissemination of culture in the Third Republic.

Indeed the position of Lanson regarding Molière's place in French culture I have cited earlier was, it seems, typical of the period 1880-1914 when Molière achieved a sort of secular canonisation as a model of the national genius of France. Ralph Albanese, Jr. records how the playwright was seen as representative of "la vieille race gauloise". What is even more significant is that the author of ***Tartuffe*** is illustrative of a transformation in the role of Ancien Régime literature in secondary school programs as a result of the new republican cultural ideology. The notion of "l'esprit français" was taken in hand by the school system to the extent that there was created "toute une personnalité, une âme, bref, un fonds d'identité nationale inspirant une tradition académique parfaitement fixe" (Albanese 36). More fundamentally: "un des aspects essentiels de la vision républicaine de la modernité réside dans l'invention d'une transcendance bourgeoise: la sacralisation des arts, la valorisation de la culture comme succédané de la religion représentent des conséquences immédiates d'une idéologie laïque face au cléricalisme toujours menaçant" (Albanese 41). The situation I shall describe relating to the tercentenary and after, as I have suggested, was in some ways a ripost to the creation of this "Panthéon scolaire et laïque" (Albanese 42).

The contributors to the debate in 1922 (and subsequently) had however no desire to evict Molière from the Pantheon altogether. It was rather a question of qualifying his claim to fame. The most authoritative voice in the arguments surrounding the celebration of Molière's birth was Jean Calvet, a prominent Catholic scholar who was to become Doyen of the Faculté libre des Lettres de Paris. Writing in the *Cahiers Catholiques* of 10 January 1922, his stated intention is to "réviser ses (=Molière) titres à la divinisation." Calvet knows that his intervention will be regarded as "outrecuidance ridicule" in the eyes of freethinkers "qui se laissent imposer par la critique consacrée des fétichismes littéraires ou sociaux." He thus situates himself in polemical opposition to certain social and literary currents. But, he adds, "nous voulons voir clair et, en admirant Molière, marquer ses limites, parce qu'il en a" ("Le Centenaire" 977). Moreover, if one takes the view that Molière is really the most perfect and worthy expression of "l'esprit français," then "il y aurait là un abus de confiance contre quoi nous protesterions" (978).

This *cri de cœur* is, unsurprisingly, echoed in H. Gaillard de Champris's volume on *Les Ecrivains classiques,* volume IV of the *Histoire de la littérature française* under the direction of Calvet himself. Molière, however great as an observer of humanity and as a writer, has his limits. Indeed Molière is condemned by the nature of his admirers who are seen as "d'excellents bourgeois à qui ont manqué le sens de la grande poésie, l'inquiétude philosophique et à plus forte raison, le sentiment religieux." That they should regard him as representative of "l'esprit français" is "une prétention exorbitante et, dans une certaine mesure, injurieuse" (117-18).

Typically for this period of Molière criticism, the issue turns in part on the playwright's "philosophy" which is, Calvet asserts, Molière's principal claim to represent "l'esprit français." What is this philosophy in practice? It is perceived as lying in the ridicule of family life and paternal authority in ***George Dandin*** ("Le Centenaire" 981-82), and in the contempt for a religious education exemplified in ***L'Ecole des femmes*** (979). It is true that the servants in his plays proclaim "les principes de sa sagesse" which often contain a certain aphoristic common sense. But the laughter provoked in the comedies "a presque toujours une odeur," so that it is not to Molière that we have recourse in order to learn "le secret des vertus de notre race" (982). Calvet's wording recalls Lanson's description of Molière's greatness when he denies that the playwright represents "parfaitement et totalement l'esprit français" (981).

The real obstacle to an unequivocal acceptance of an immaculate Molière is obviously ***Tartuffe,*** which all Catholic commentators regard as embodying the very worst in his theater (along with certain aspects of ***Dom Juan***). That ***Tartuffe*** should find acceptance with freethinkers is, according to Calvet, understandable. What is more difficult to accommodate is, on the one hand, university critics who "d'un ton pénétré et solennel" declare that the true meaning of the Gospel is to be found at Port-Royal, and on the other, claim a few pages later that Molière was careful not to attack true piety, only hypocrisy, and that he even rendered a service to Christianity in providing a portrait of the ideal Christian ("Le Centenaire" 980).

Tartuffe is the main target too of two articles in the *Revue des objections* (15 January 1922) attributed to Père Coubet who also wished to restrict the nature of the celebrations. Molière is not, however, regarded as a mediocre playwright (in many respects that is precisely the problem). Coubet indeed identifies as praiseworthy "son génie, son esprit caustique, sa verve désopilante" and, generally speaking, his profound knowledge of the resources and expression of the French language, all of which have placed him in the first rank of classical writers ("Le Tricentenaire" 3). In this sense, even ***Tartuffe*** has its good points ("Le Tartuffe" 10). But a distinction must be made between "le talent et la moralité." At this level, there is no point in seeking in his drama "une idée généreuse, un noble caractère, de la beauté morale." Quite simply, "l'homme de bien ou n'existe pas pour lui ou lui est indifférent" ("Le Tricentenaire" 5). The distinction between morality and talent is clearly adhered to by Gaillard de Champris. There are those who congratulate Molière for being a comic playwright simply intent on making people laugh: let us hope that they do not then raise him "à la dignité de grand moraliste, sinon de grand philosophe, et ne proposent pas ses enseignments à l'admiration, à la docilité des peuples reconnaissants" (116).

The content of Molière's philosophy inevitably leads to a discussion of the exact nature of his Christianity. The central focus here is on Cléante's description of the real "dévot." Much has been written and speculated upon in this context.[4] My aim is not, however, to arbitrate in that particular debate, but merely to give some account of the concerns of those who felt most directly implicated in what was interpreted as an attack on a certain conception of spirituality and worship offered by Tartuffe, but more insidiously by Orgon.

In his interesting *Essai sur la séparation de la religion et de la vie: Molière est-il chrétien?,* Calvet attempts to relate the question of Molière's Christianity to certain historical trends still in evidence in the seventeenth century. He argues that Molière's plays retain the vestiges of that sort of Humanism which sought to reconcile "les deux sagesses," that is to say, the Christian and the pagan (10). Furthermore, Molière completes a stage in French thought initiated by Montaigne, namely the separation of religion from life in general, "en formulant les lois de la vie de société." What is meant by this is that religious questions have their own place and do not impinge on a form of life in society: "l'homme qui veut vivre en société ne doit apporter dans la société que ce qu'il a de commun avec les autres hommes; il a le devoir de s'appliquer à leur donner du plaisir par sa tolérance et par ses sourires" (71). Montaigne and Molière thus managed to introduce into "notre idéal national" a sort of secular secession which, precisely, is rejected by modern religious thought (11). For Calvet, moreover, Molière holds that real Christianity is a natural religion, "un déïsme de bon ton se conformant à la coutume des lieux" (72). Perhaps at the root of Calvet's position is a rejection of the domination of a lay culture where even religion becomes just another feature of social existence, in a predominantly lay educational and cultural system. Gaillard de Champris in some way echoes Calvet's opinion in that Molière is believed to express through Cléante the view that religion is, like all other practical problems, a relative one: "Or le christianisme est la religion de l'absolu" (115). For Molière not only is religion devoid of real content, but it has no privileged position in the world.

For Calvet and others, one of their principal objections to Molière and ***Tartuffe*** is that the latter is considered to offer a model of real Christianity, when a tradition existed in the seventeenth century which gave a much sounder model of spirituality in society and which remains relevant to twentieth-century France. Calvet in fact undertakes no less than a defense of the Catholic Reform which sought through such figures as Bossuet, Bourdaloue, and, above all, St François de Sales, to evangelize seventeenth-century society in all its aspects.[5] Indeed, Molière's plays, especially ***Tartuffe,*** run directly—and consciously—counter to this tradition in that they constitute a reply on behalf of the young Louis XIV and his court to attempts to curb their revelling and sexual licence. Molière was thus engaged in a polemic where "il réclame avec le Roi, avec la jeune Cour, non seulement le droit à la douceur de vivre, mais celui d'accommoder l'esprit de l'Evangile aux convenances mondaines et aux exigences de la nature" (Gaillard de Champris 59). This is a constant theme from Veuillot onwards, the latter believing the ***Princesse d'Elide*** (not without reason) to be an apology for the king's amorous adventures (50-51). He also believes that Louis XIV approved of ***Tartuffe*** for making his censors look ridiculous (151).

Calvet, however, does not adhere to a simplistic view of ***Tartuffe*** and ***Dom Juan.*** Although he agrees with the idea of Molière as the Court's advocate in the face of the new spirituality, which had its representatives even among those close to the king, he believes that Molière spoke for the "mondains" rather than for the "libertins" ("Le Centenaire" 978-79). Indeed, under the protection of the King, the playwright certainly attacked the "dévots [. . .] qui limitent les libertés de la vie," as in ***Tartuffe,*** but also the "libertins" "qui heurtent le bon sens", as in ***Dom Juan*** (*Essai* 124). ***Dom Juan*** is regarded as a critique of atheism (88).

According to some, Orante and Daphné, the prudes mentioned by Cléante, were used in an attack on the *dévots* at court, for whom the direct models were reckoned to be the Duchesse de Navailles and Madame de Soissons, both of whom had criticized Louis's sexual conduct. But Calvet rejects this personalised interpretation of the play (Tartuffe too has his model), preferring to see in Tartuffe a symbol of what Molière wished to attack (*Essai* 73). More seriously Orgon's character provides the real opportunity for the frontal assault on the new spirituality: "le procès qui est fait ici du chrétien réformé et par conséquent de la réforme elle-même, est sans quartier et sans nuance" (68). As for presenting real "dévots" through Cléante, "ce sont des ombres, qui portent les noms d'ombres" (70). We must therefore renounce the old idea espoused by "la critique universitaire" of ***Tartuffe*** as a satire of religious hypocrisy. The play marks rather the culmination of the conflict between "l'esprit chrétien de réforme morale" and "l'esprit du monde jouisseur" ("Le Centenaire" 979-80). Calvet admits that the Counter-Reformation in France was not without its excesses (*Essai* 34). But this is clearly no reason to suppress in favor of Molière as representing the true "esprit français" the reputation and standing of the Catholic Reformers: "les ouvriers de la Réforme Catholique sont l'honneur de leur temps et leur œuvre d'assainissement moral s'impose au respect de l'histoire" (62). The limits to Molière's own reputation lie precisely in his attempt to cast doubt on the existence of Counter-Reformation heroism. In this context, Corneille is a much worthier figure. Molière "est l'homme pour qui la sainteté n'a pas de sens" (72-73).

For many commentators a more fundamental question than the religious content of the plays was whether Molière himself was a Christian, or more accurately what sort of Christian he was, because, interestingly, the view of Molière as an atheist, among the authors and writers I have read, is exceptional. The closest a writer comes to an accusation of atheism is when Henri d'Alméras describes Molière as possessing "une religion de façade," which was necessary because his dependent position and the times prevented him from declaring himself openly as a freethinker (85). But, as we all know, Molière performed his Easter communion the year before he died. Is that not something in his favor? Henri d'Alméras believes that this proves nothing in itself: "pratiquer n'est pas croire" (83). Other writers are a little more generous, but by no means entirely complimentary. Coubet believes at least Molière's act of Easter devotion to have probably been sincere. But it was not enough: an act of contrition ought to have inspired in him "une attitude plus franche et plus courageuse. Mais il faut bien avouer que la franchise et le courage n'étaient pas son fort." Instead, offering himself as spokesman for a debauched court and then pillorying its adversaries as hypocrites was in itself an act of hypocrisy and cowardice. Molière was "'un pauvre homme' de piètre moralité" ("Le Tartuffe" 16).

As I have remarked, Calvet rejects the view of Molière as a "libertin." Nor is Cléante's role "une précaution hypocrite." Molière may have been mistaken about real Christianity, but he was a Christian, or wanted to be, "comme l'est un déïste de bonne foi qui va parfois à la messe" (*Essai* 82-83). Mauriac believes that, too indifferent to metaphysics to probe deeply into religious questions, Molière was simply against "la démesure chrétienne," and against "la malédiction chrétienne contre ce que Pascal appelle l'usage délicieux et criminel du monde" (270).

The implicit assumption behind these very qualified opinions of Molière's status as a Christian is that he was incompetent to deal fully, and with the necessary understanding, with a matter of religion, in fact a conclusion already reached by writers in the seventeenth century. Inevitably, Molière's personal life is adduced as evidence against him. His own morality was, according to Coubet, "fort médiocre" given the deplorable nature of his home life. The consequences for his plays are therefore obvious ("Le Tricentenaire" 4). For Gaillard de Champris, religion is "un sujet réservé" which requires special knowledge, "une délicatesse de sentiments, une dignité, une pureté de vie qui ne sont pas, en général, l'apanage des auteurs comiques, encore moins des comédiens." Even allowing for Molière's sincerity, the way he poses the problem in ***Tartuffe*** proves his total incompetence to handle such things (114-15). Both ***Tartuffe*** and ***Dom Juan,*** despite the fact that Molière may have believed himself to be a Christian, demonstrate "l'insuffisance de sa formation chrétienne" (114). Gaillard de Champris further regrets that Molière introduced matters of this sort into the theater, which is hardly the appropriate forum (116). Calvet had enlarged on this idea in his *Essai* where Molière's intention is identified as distinguishing "la vérité de la grimace" and "la vertu de ses exagérations ou de ses conrefaçons." Such discrimination is not proper to the theater where the audience is "simpliste, distrait et paresseux" (40). Even Albert Reyval regards the subject of ***Tartuffe*** as somewhat delicate: its treatment by a moralist or a theologian, rather than a playwright, would have borne the stamp of greater authority (*L'Eglise, la comédie* 28).

What is evident from my discussion already is that ***Tartuffe*** is not just a play. Molière's choice of subject meant that it transcended the boundaries of comedy and art, however much one may attempt to justify it by providing a theory of the ridiculous, as in the ***Lettre sur la comédie de l'Imposteur.*** Contemporaries such as Bourdaloue and Massillon perceived how serious the effects of the play could be on practising Christians, afraid, because of their visible acts of worship, of being put in the same category as Tartuffe. More than this, however, the consequences of Molière's choice of subject and his manner of dealing with it transcend his own epoch. The play was and is dangerous. To what extent, then, can Molière be held personally responsible for the damage it continues to cause in the eyes of the commentators who are the object of this study? Did he know what he was doing?

Mauriac bears a definite grudge against Molière for not having admitted or agreed that, by means of Orgon and Tartuffe, he struck at the heart of Christianity (270), when the instincts of all those around him told them that the whole of Christianity was indicted by a caricature so subtle and so devious that it just had to be deliberate (266). Mauriac is therefore certain that the playwright was well enough aware that he was providing a poisoned weapon for the enemies of the Christian faith for centuries to come (270). Another writer, while not believing that Molière directly incited feeling against the Church, nonetheless finds it difficult to believe that he could not have perceived the use the Church's enemies would make of ***Tartuffe*** ("L'Eglise et le théâtre" 32). Veuillot too affirms that Molière knew exactly how people in the future would take advantage of his play for their own purposes and that the weapon he had forged would not be allowed to rust with age (164). Veuillot is indeed the source of a much repeated view that, when anticlerical feeling needed to be aroused, ***Tartuffe*** was performed (1). For Coubet freemasons have constant recourse to the play in their drive against religion ("Le Tartuffe" 13). Clearly ***Tartuffe*** in its turn became a pawn in the incessant conflict which raged between religious and anti-religious factions in French society before 1939.[6] Let us leave the last word on this particular aspect of the debate with the reviewer of Reyval's book of 1924: "Le ***Tartuffe,*** considéré en lui-même et abstraction faite des intentions de son auteur, est incontestablement une des pièces qui ont fait le plus de tort à l'Eglise" ("L'Eglise et le théâtre" 28).

Hostility to Molière does not entirely eliminate charity, for, however great Molière's responsibility, deliberate or otherwise, in undermining the Church, his death and the circumstances surrounding it are a cause of considerable embarrassment and unease to Catholicism's modern representatives. No commentator is prepared ultimately to justify the treatment Molière received, although all plead the necessity to understand the reason for the Church's attitude at the time. Typical is Coubet, at least in the way he asks the initial question: "Cette sévérité du clergé n'a-t-elle pas été excessive? L'Eglise n'a-t-elle pas fait preuve d'intolérance et d'obscurantisme, de méchanceté et d'injustice envers ce grand génie? Cette attitude appelle une explication, et le tricentenaire de Molière rentre par ce côté dans le domaine de l'apologétique" ("Le Tricentenaire" 4). Later Coubet argues that it is not surprising that Molière appeared in the clergy's eyes as a dangerous and corrupting mind: "Et nous comprenons dès lors, même si nous ne l'approuvons pas sur tous les points, l'attitude qu'eurent à son endroit plusieurs des prêtres de Saint-Eustache, sa paroisse" (9). Reyval's reviewer is less grudging. Surely, the Church had a just grievance, but this was no reason for a priest to reject Molière at his final agony ("L'Eglise et le théâtre" 33). After all, another writer tells us, Molière's dying moments included "de vifs sentiments de foi et de repentir." He therefore died a good Christian ("La Mort" 17). The conduct of the two priests who refused to attend cannot therefore be approved. But the judgment is not all black for the Church. Its rigour was regrettable but explicable: "Molière avait tout fait pour la mériter." Today, however, things would have been different. Even then he can add: "l'intolérance reprochée à la religion se réduit à peu de chose. Elle n'exprime pas un jugement solennel de l'Eglise, ni son attitude habituelle, mais seulement la rigueur de quelques ecclésiastiques qui en portaient la responsabilité" (20-21). The spirit of the Church is embodied rather in the *curé* of Passy who assisted Molière's widow in her intercession with the King (19). In a sense, this writer's viewpoint has an element of truth. The Catholic Church of the seventeenth century was by no means unanimous in its condemnation of theater and the treatment of actors with regard to the sacraments. Few clerics, however, had any time for actors (even less for actresses), and it is unquestionable that hostility to the theater was more widespread than he wishes to believe. But clearly the aim of the exercise is now less categorical than the attack on ***Tartuffe*** might imply and can be classified as one of damage limitation. Molière's defenders, of course, have no reservations. Reyval, no anticlerical, regards Molière's death as "l'un des plus douloureux et, disons-le, des plus regrettables épisodes de la lutte de l'Eglise contre le théâtre" (*L'Eglise, la comédie* 80).

The concern among Catholic commentators I have described, even qualified, nonetheless marks a turning point in relations between Church and theater in France. From 1922 on, one is able to identify what may be termed a revisionist attitude towards the rigorist position evinced by many religious moralists who participated in the *querelle du théâtre* of the seventeenth century. Their positions are now seen either to have been wrong or at the very least to be outdated. Incredibly, the principal victim of these developments is Bossuet whose *Maximes et réflexions sur le théâtre* of 1694 mark the culmination of the seventeenth-century stage controversy. More significant in the context of this article is that the *Maximes* contain a withering attack on the person and plays of Molière.

The general position is put by Coubet. Even in 1922 he could assert that Bossuet's opinion was excessive in its severity: he was, we know, a rigorist in almost all things: "ici, il l'est, croyons-nous, un peu trop" ("Le Tricentenaire" 6). Other views on Bossuet's *Maximes* are more specific and heavily critical. Père Deman, reflecting on Urbain and Levesque's edition of the *Maximes,* disagrees with the editors that "la finesse de l'analyse psychologique garde toute sa valeur." Nor is the work "une impressionnante leçon de morale". He replies instead that "l'idéal des *Maximes* n'est pas trop élevé, il est déplacé." Moreover, the French are too inclined to believe (i.e. mistaken in that belief) that Bossuet's morality is "l'infaillible expression de la morale chrétienne" (194-95). He points further to a number of deficiencies in Bossuet's arguments against Caffaro (a Theatine monk who was unwise enough to write a defense of theater which was published at the head of an edition of Boursault's works), including the lack of rigour in his interpretation of Plato and the prejudiced use of quotations from St Augustine (183). In addition, "Bossuet nous déconcerte quand il se met en peine de démontrer que le divertissement est indigne des chrétiens." (189)

During the seventeenth century, those who espoused the cause of drama often sought justification for their views in St. Thomas Aquinas's *Summa,* where in Question 168 of the *Secunda Secundae* he offers what was perceived as a favorable view of the actor's contribution to the relaxation of the individual. Basically he denies that, as long as certain conditions are fulfilled, acting and play-going are sinful.[7] We know that Richelieu held to the views of St Thomas, and certainly D'Aubignac quotes them in his *Dissertation sur la condamnation des théâtres* of 1666. Caffaro made Question 168 the basis of his defense of drama. Bossuet and many others, on the other hand, vigorously protested against what they regarded as a total misinterpretation of the Angelic Doctor. Several of the modern commentators I have quoted here, however, resurrect the standard Thomist line. One writer argues that only scandalous performances are to be condemned ("L'Eglise" 35), and Père Antoine de Parvillez denies that any proof exists to suggest that the theater is always, and "par une nécessité de nature," immoral, thus implicitly arguing that drama is "indifferent" and dependent rather on the use to which it is put (219). The classic Thomist position is summarized by Père Gillet in an edition of the *Figaro:*

> En ce qui concerne les comédiens, nous n'avons plus le droit de les rejeter en marge de l'humanité sous prétexte qu'en divertissant les hommes, ils contribuent à les démoraliser, puisqu'au contraire il est naturel aux hommes de se divertir et qu'il peut y avoir, même du point de vue moral, de beaux et de bons divertissements. (Quoted by Reyval, *L'Eglise, la comédie* 110)

But Bossuet's legacy, it must be said, is not considered to be completely negative. It is especially his conclusions which are now seen as obsolete. Père Carré, a major figure in the reconciliation of Church and theater, can speak of the *Maximes* as "admirables de ton et de langue, mais pleines d'outrance." Bossuet's work did, however, enormous damage to relations between the two institutions (*L'Eglise* 26-27). Carré can therefore at the same time regret Bossuet's rigorism but admire "avec quelle ampleur il a posé les termes du débat" (29). For Parvillez, Bossuet properly called our attention to our moral accountability in terms of the way we amuse ourselves (224), and the prelate's views would have been relevant to parts of the contemporary theater, especially "la pudeur éteinte" of actresses (225-26). Even Deman argues that Bossuet has a point about carnal love and covetousness (187-88). Carré finds the important contribution in Bossuet's work to be his emphasis on "la commotion de l'esprit" experienced by actors who must give the whole of themselves to a role, which then leads to the alienation of the self ("De Molière" 173-74). Carré, however, denies the mechanistic conclusions of the Eagle of Meaux, whereby the actor of necessity becomes an immoral being (*L'Eglise* 37).

The grave reservations modern Catholic commentators have both over the circumstances surrounding the death of Molière and over the extremist position of Bossuet imply a break in continuity with the stage controversy of the seventeenth century. It is time to call a halt. Deman states unequivocally: "il n'est point bon que l'on prolonge ces querelles." Such arguments present a quite erroneous impression of the real task of Christian morality (196). Quite simply, these "querelles" give modern Catholicism a bad name. Indeed the very nature of the French Church is deemed to have radically changed. Many writers, even Veuillot, utterly reject the *gallican* side to the seventeenth-century "querelle". During this period, Roman bishops, unlike many (but not all) of their counterparts in France, never formally condemned actors by excluding them from the sacraments unless they renounced their profession.[8] Reyval, in 1924, obviously reacting to the 1922 debate, quotes a particularly telling remark of Claudel who saw in Bossuet's *Maximes* "une manifestation particulière de cet esprit défensif de retranchement et de retrait qui fut celui de notre gallicanisme" (95). It is interesting, Reyval adds, to contrast the rigorist attitude of the Gallican clergy of 1673 with "l'attitude bienveillante du clergé plus *catholique* de 1922" (82-83, my emphasis).

The reference to an "attitude bienveillante" obviously suggests that, in Reyval's opinion at least, relations between the Church and the theater were transformed in some practical way. Indeed, from the time of the tercentenary celebrations, one witnesses an increasingly formal rapprochement between the two institutions. In the first instance, the initiative came from representatives of the theater. Georges Le Roy, a sociétaire of the Comédie Française, and his wife, the actress Jeanne Delvair, sought permission for a requiem mass for Molière. Le Roy wrote to Cardinal Dubois, archbishop of Paris, with his suggestion on 18 January 1922. The mass would close the tercentenary celebrations. It was first requested that the mass be celebrated in Notre-Dame de Paris or at the Eglise Saint-Roch. On 21 January, Cardinal Dubois replied, giving his blessing to the proposed event, but stating that it was not his place to take the initiative. He also argued that a service at Notre-Dame would be difficult to organise and his preferred location was Saint-Eustache. The mass was eventually celebrated at Saint-Roch on 17 February, although not in the presence of the cardinal "qu'un engagement formel avait seul empêché de présider lui-même la cérémonie" (Reyval, *L'Eglise, la comédie* 135).[9] Was the Cardinal being cautious?

True to the abandonment of the Gallican position in favour of a more "Catholic" one, the formal reconciliation went beyond the national boundaries of France. In 1957 Pope Pius XII received a delegation of actors from the Comédie Française in March after a performance of Montherlant's *Port-Royal,* and the seventy-fourth general Congregation of Vatican II (23 November 1963) included the theater in its deliberations on appropriate means of social communication. These deliberations were solemnised by a decree of Paul VI promulgated on 4 December, 1963 (Gaquère 64). The most significant occasion in the whole process of reconciliation was the tercentenary of Bossuet's ordination when artists held a mass for the repose of Bossuet's soul (Carré, *L'Eglise* 46).

The Church in France was, however, to play a greater role in the reconciliation of Church and theater. From the 1920s George Le Roy had ambitions to implant the Church within the theatrical domain itself in a sort of Salesian endeavor to make provision for a form of worship (in the broad sense of the term) appropriate to the theatrical profession. Seeking formal approval for his intention to form an association of Christian actors, he was received in 1925 by Pius XI who apparently told him: "Ne tenez pas compte des outrances de votre grand Bossuet, vous avez votre place dans l'Eglise" (Carré, "De Molière" 172). The association was to be called the *Fédération pour la défense artistique et morale du théâtre de France.* A committee of eminent people would provide the necessary guidance, and with the active collaboration of daily newspapers and periodicals, there would be a "comité de lecture qui devait procéder à la composition du répertoire" and "une corporation d'artistes exécutants, aussi recommandables par leur valeur morale que par leur qualité professionnelle" (Reyval, *L'Eglise, la comédie* 156-58). But the federation failed to attract the necessary attention of significant personalities.

But through perseverance the Union catholique du théâtre was formed in 1927 with 800 members and included among its founder members Gaston Baty. It was reconstituted after the Second World War (in 1947) with Père Carré as its spiritual adviser.[10] Its aim, according to Article III of its statutes, was to gather together "en vue d'affirmer leur vie spirituelle, les professionnels du Spectacle (Théâtre, Concert, Cinéma, etc.): auteurs, compositeurs, artistes, artisans etc." A mass was to be celebrated every Sunday in the Church of the Dominicans of the Faubourg Saint-Honoré (St. Thomas Aquinas was a Dominican . . .), and twice a month artists would come for some instruction in their faith.

Père Carré obviously saw the Union as a part of the regeneration of lay Catholicism. As he writes:

> Depuis vingt-cinq ans, ce qui s'est passé, c'est—dans le monde du théâtre comme dans les autres milieux—l'éveil à un idéal religieux conciliant la profession et la vie . . . Or, chez beaucoup, nous assistons à une prise de conscience grandissante des possibilités concrètes, quotidiennes, d'incarnation de la vocation chrétienne. Dès lors, pourquoi refuser l'accord entre les exigences de l'art et celles de la foi? Faut-il, là, faire exception? (*L'Eglise* 51)

The need of "une sorte de paroisse spirituelle" is strengthened by actors constituting "un milieu déterminé, sans cloisons étanches par rapport aux autres, mais cohérent" (52-53). Through a "centre spirituel," the world of the theater can thus be evangelised. It would provide moreover a means whereby actors and actresses could discover a religious solution to the particular problems of their profession. Carré's book provides interesting views on the specific spiritual needs of performing artists and contains psychological insights of a certain subtlety, far removed at least in their conclusions, from those of Bossuet. (See in particular *L'Eglise* 61-65).

The events and attitudes I have outlined in this article are of interest from a variety of points of view. In some ways they demonstrate the tenacity of certain judgments over a very wide expanse of time. Sometimes one could be forgiven for thinking that what one is reading has come straight out of the seventeenth century. But this tenacity (some might say obduracy) also has its historical significance. It is often redolent of the defensive and conservative nature of French Catholicism before 1945. The attitudes I have described are also part of the religious divide and the trench warfare which raged between the Church and anticlericals in the Third Republic. Even after 1922, it is still possible to perceive the shifts of position I have analyzed as an attempt on behalf of the Church to recuperate certain aspects of French culture rather than an attempt at peaceful co-existence. But there is no question that the tercentenary celebrations of Molière's birth triggered a greater openness towards performing artists and the theater in general (despite gravely expressed reservations concerning the modern repertory). This eventually resulted in a genuine concern for the spiritual welfare of the profession. Calvet wrote in defense of the Catholic Reform. The change in attitudes post-1922 seems to represent what was best in the spirit of that movement.

Notes

1. A full account of the seventeenth-century stage controversy in France is offered by Bourquin, Moffat, and Phillips. J. Barish has recently published a work on the subject which covers the same subject outside as well as in France.
2. The Protestant Synod of Privas in 1912 stipulated that: "Il ne sera loisible aux fidèles d'assister aux comédies, tragédies, farces, et autres jeux, joués en public ou en particulier, vu que, de tout temps, cela a été défendu entre les chrétiens comme apportant la corruption des mœurs, mais surtout quand l'Ecriture sainte est profanée" (Gaquère 21-22). For the Carême of 1922 Père Janvier preached a sermon condemning the sort of theater which offers "l'apologie de l'amour coupable, des passions sensuelles, sinon de la débauche, et de l'impiété" (Quoted in Reyval, *L'Eglise et le théâtre* 107-08).
3. La Pommeraye had already declared in 1877 that it would be an anachronism to interpret Molière in this way (12).
4. Among the most recent contributions to the question of the religious implications of *Tartuffe,* see especially Raymond Picard's article where he in fact echoes many of the points raised by Calvet, although of course not in any polemical way.
5. Calvet attempts to establish a link between Molière's attack on preciosity and the Catholic Reform. St François de Sales had introduced "la préciosité dans la piété, la distinction dans la manière de se tenir devant Dieu." Many "précieuses" belonged to the "monde dévot" (*Essai* 39).
6. For an interesting account of nineteenth- and early twentieth-century French catholicism, see Zeldin, who provides other valuable bibliographical references.
7. On the question of St Thomas's position in this context, see Phillips 158sq and 179-82.
8. An excellent account of the French use of the model diocesan ritual published by Pope Paul V in 1614 is given by Jean Dubu. He points out that Bossuet never altered his ritual to include actors among those most susceptible to be refused the sacraments.
9. Details of the arrangements for the mass are to be found in both works of Reyval and Carré's book. Paul Souday in fact claimed that the mass was an *attack* on Molière's memory since he was an atheist. The archivist of the Comédie Française provided documentary proof of the opposite and Souday's position was repudiated (Reyval, *L'Eglise et le théâtre* 86-88).
10. There were precedents for such societies in England, France and the USA. Reyval mentions the Actors' Church Union organised by the Rev Anstruther Cardew (who was particularly concerned about the plight of dancing girls), the Catholic Theater Guild, whose chairman was the Rev Sidney Smith S.J., and a society entitled Catholiques des beaux-arts founded by M. Regnault, a distinguished Parisian architect, with 1000 members, for the most part musicians (*L'Eglise et le théâtre* 144-47).

David Shaw (essay date 1991)

SOURCE: "Molière's Temporary Happy Endings," in *French Studies,* Vol. XLV, No. 2, April, 1991, pp. 129-42.

[*In the following essay, Shaw examines Molière's use of comic denouements, contending that they suggest that real-life endings are not always happy.*]

Many would say that Molière's plays end happily. Tartuffe is arrested, Harpagon finds his money, Philaminte sees the error of her ways: the obstacle is removed, the lovers can marry, order is restored, the celebrations can commence. But this is not the whole picture. His plays do not all end on a note of unrestrained happiness. If the ending of ***Tartuffe*** anticipates the 'doux hymen' to come, ***George Dandin*** ends with talk of suicide. If ***Les Femmes savantes*** ends with the marriage of Clitandre and Henriette, ***Le Misanthrope*** ends with the separation of Alceste and Célimène. The pattern is not obvious.

It has been claimed that Molière's endings are poor, victims of the pressure under which he worked. 'Que n'ai-je toujours été le maître de mon temps!', he says in Voltaire's *Temple du Goût,* 'j'aurais trouvé des dénouements plus heureux'.[1] Mornet argues that his endings are implausible, careless, mere concessions to fashion: 'Ses dénouements sont rarement vraisemblables [. . .]. Molière assurément imagine n'importe quoi. Son indifférence s'explique par celle de ses contemporains'.[2]

But this does not really stand up. If the endings are careless and conventional, why are they so varied? The denouement of ***Le Misanthrope*** is highly *un*conventional, for a comedy, *because* it stems logically from what we know of the characters. There is no indication that Molière considered this denouement any less important than the rest of the play, which is perhaps his most carefully crafted work. His endings are clearly *not* uniformly conventional nor even, in some cases, conventionally happy: as such they deserve more attention than they customarily receive.[3]

Up to a point, his endings seem perfectly orthodox. For example, he generally respects the 'restoration of order' principle common to tragedy and comedy. In tragedy, once the monster is eliminated, normality can resume. In comedy, the antipathetic obstacle figure must renounce his claims so that the young people can be happy and the audience content. Molière generally accepts this format: Arnolphe and Orgon, Harpagon and Jourdain, Philaminte and Argan all withdraw their objections just in time and the plays end in symbolic rejoicing.

Similarly, most of his plays end with a marriage. The theorists stipulated that endings should be as complete as possible with the fate of all characters known and settled. This usually meant the marriage of the main characters, a convention frequently respected in tragedy and virtually omnipresent in tragicomedy and comedy. In tragicomedy the convention was so strong that historical accuracy was no match for it: in Magnon's *Tite* (1660), for example, Titus ends up by *marrying* Berenice!

The tyranny of the 'happy marriage' convention, coupled with the remorseless tidiness of classical theatre, often gave rise to double, and even triple, marriages. There are two marriages at the end of both ***Dom Garcie de Navarre*** and ***L'Avare.*** For some theorists, such multiple marriages were more or less a requirement:

> Les poètes doivent disposer toutes choses de sorte que ceux qui sont les amis du héros et qui se sont intéressés dans tous ses malheurs participent autant qu'il est possible à sa bonne fortune [. . .]. De là vient qu'il se fait toujours plusieurs mariages à la fin des comédies, et les choses se débrouillent de telle manière que tout le monde est content, et que les spectateurs se retirent pleinement satisfaits.[4]

Thus, Rotrou's tragicomedy *Laure persécutée* (1639) and, remarkably, Corneille's tragedy *Agésilas* (1666) both culminate in three marriages. So do ***L'Étourdi*** and ***Le Bourgeois Gentilhomme.*** Even in ***Le Misanthrope,*** if Alceste and Célimène go their separate ways, there is still the marriage of Philinte and Éliante to signify a happy ending. And Philinte's quixotic intention, expressed in the final line, to go on seeking to bring them together is clearly another acknowledgement of the importance of this convention.

A third characteristic of the seventeenth-century comedy denouement is the 'recognition', the belated revelation of some unsuspected identity or relationship which opens the way to the happy marriage. It might be a lover discovering a partner thought lost, as in Brosse's *Songes des hommes éveillés* (1646), or, more frequently, the reuniting of members of a family long separated, as in D'Ouville's *Aimer sans savoir qui* (1646). These separations are often ascribed to romantic adventures involving shipwreck, pirates, gypsies, etc. Such endings occur frequently enough in Molière's plays for students to refer to them as 'typical Molière endings'! In the last two scenes of ***L'École des femmes,*** for example, we learn that Agnès has a father and that the bride whom Horace's father has chosen for him turns out conveniently to be Agnès herself. Similarly, at the end of ***L'Avare,*** the man Harpagon had in mind for his daughter turns out to be the father of both his steward and his intended bride! This family separation involved both shipwreck *and* pirates.

Molière's endings are also broadly conventional in terms of the number of characters on stage as the final words are spoken. The practice of assembling as many actors as possible at the denouement was universally respected.[5] The idea seems to have been to create an impression of completeness, with everyone involved in the celebrations. One also suspects that the actors liked to share in the applause at the end of a performance, however small their role. The phenomenon was common to all forms of theatre. Corneille actually modified the ending of *Nicomède* to take account of it:

> D'abord j'avais fini la pièce sans les [Prusias and Flaminius] faire revenir [. . .] mais le goût des spectateurs, que nous avons accoutumés à voir rassembler tous nos personnages à la conclusion de cette sorte de poème, fut cause de ce changement où je me résolus pour leur donner plus de satisfaction, bien qu'avec moins de régularité. (*Nicomède, Examen*)

This remark underlines the tyranny of the fashion, which sometimes probed the limits of verisimilitude. At the end of Corneille's own *Clitandre,* with the exception of the wicked Pymante who is in prison, all the main characters are reunited, together with the corpses of two minor characters, Lycaste and Géronte, killed in the opening act!

In comedy the characters do not die; one therefore often finds the stage very crowded during the final scene. Molière's plays generally respect the tradition. There are nine characters on stage at the end of ***L'École des maris,*** ten at the end of ***Tartuffe,*** eleven at the end of ***L'Avare*** and no fewer than twelve at the end of ***L'Impromptu de Versailles.*** In the latter play, as in ***Scapin, La Critique*** and ***L'École des maris,*** the entire cast is on stage for the final scene. Moreover, when Molière wrote ***Le Dépit amoureux,*** based on *L'Interesse,* by the Italian author Secchi, he added several scenes, absent from the original, whose only function seems to be to allow the entire troupe to gather on stage at the end. He was thus quite comfortable with this aspect of the traditional denouement.

A final feature of his endings which might be thought of as traditional is the willingness of his characters to address the final lines directly to the audience. Originating in farce, this device is reasonably common in the comedies of the first half of the century. The idea was to bring the audience back to reality with an amusing surprise. One finds the device in plays such as Scarron's *Jodelet, ou le Maître Valet* and Corneille's *La Suite du Menteur,* both performed in 1645. Scherer notes that such denouements were condemned by the theorists and claims that they died out: 'Aussi l'âge classique renonce-t-il presque entièrement à cette forme de dénouement'.[6] The device may not have been to the taste of critics such as Chapelain, but it certainly did not die out. On the contrary, it was a regular feature of Molière's denouements: from ***L'Étourdi*** to *Scapin,* a dozen or so of his plays end with lines addressed directly to the audience or with some remark drawing attention to the dramatic illusion.[7] At the end of ***L'École des maris,*** for example, the stage direction '*Au parterre*' clearly indicates where the final lines are to be directed; while at the end of ***La Critique*** the characters wonder, Pirandello-like, how to make their conversations into a play.

Thus, in five significant respects Molière's endings contain traditional elements: the obstacle character who relents, recognition scenes, the happy marriage, the gathering together of most of the cast, and jokes concerning the dramatic illusion. It is easy to see why his endings are sometimes thought of as being merely conventional.

However, such judgements raise more questions than they resolve. Much that is interesting about Molière's denouements is excluded by these categories. If they contain elements which are traditional, they also contain much that is difficult to fit into any conventional pattern. Let us look at them again.

It has been argued that Molière's indifference towards his denouements is revealed most clearly in the final lines of ***La Critique de l'École des femmes.*** The characters are uncertain how to bring their play to an end because 'il ne saurait y avoir ni mariage ni reconnaissance' (scene 6), and they settle for the announcement that supper is served. Quentin Hope interprets this as a demonstration of the careless way Molière arrives at his denouements: 'Molière appears to be saying that when it comes to ending your play, use a marriage and recognition scene if you can, otherwise seize on the first pretext to hand'.[8] This judgement does the ending less than justice. ***La Critique de l'École des femmes*** is a polemical play in which Molière pokes fun at a range of theatrical conventions and claims the right to entertain his public as he chooses. By expressly regretting the impossibility of a recognition scene or marriage, he is smilingly drawing our attention to another convention, that of the traditional denouement. By highlighting the formula, he is underlining its artificiality.

There is a similar joke at the end of ***L'Étourdi.*** As everyone else is happily betrothed, Mascarille announces, six lines from the end of the play, that he too would like to get married:

> Vous voilà tous pourvus. N'est-il point quelque fille
> Qui pût accommoder le pauvre Mascarille?
>
> (ll. 2063-64)

Upon which Anselme announces, three lines from the end, that he has someone in mind for Mascarille: the latter promptly accepts, without even knowing the identity of the lady. In this implausible bid to marry off everyone in sight, it is again difficult to see anything but a parody of the usual convention.

This self-awareness is incorporated, in a more sophisticated way, into the endings of other plays. The devices he uses to bring about his denouements are generally no more implausible than those of his rivals. But one does have the impression that he enjoys underlining the artificiality of the convention. Thus, in ***Tartuffe,*** the reversal comes as late and as unexpectedly as possible. At line 1902, with just sixty lines to go, there is no hint of a way out. Orgon's family has lost everything: even the legal system seems to be on Tartuffe's side. The play is saved from tragedy by the royal intervention, a veritable *rex ex machina* which nothing allows us to anticipate.

In the same vein, the artificiality of the recognition scenes at the end of ***L'École des femmes*** is underlined with a particularly blatant piece of stylization. Agnès's real father appears and his story is told by Chrysalde and Oronte. The adventure they describe, all sudden flights and exotic exile, is completely conventional. More interesting is the way they are made to tell it. The description takes the form of ten pairs of rhyming couplets, eight of them beginning with the word *et,* with the two narrators taking it in turn to recite them.[9] The symmetry is perfect. The artificiality of the convention is thus highlighted to the point of parody: stylistically separated from the rest of the text, the sequence is shown to be a ritual whose only role is to bring the play speedily to a happy ending. To some extent, the exaggerated complications provide a useful palliative: 'The artificiality of the recognition scene determines the note of the denouement, reminding the spectator that this is "only a comedy" and preventing him from becoming excessively concerned about the discomfiture of Arnolphe'.[10]

But it can be argued that such exaggeration simultaneously serves a quite different purpose. Molière's subjects—charlatanism, women's rights, religious hypocrisy, aristocratic perversity, etc—are more substantial and controversial than was the norm for comedy; and he is interested in character rather than plot. For both these reasons, he tends to create serious situations which are difficult to bring to a plausible happy ending. A play based on mistaken identity, such as Boisrobert's *Belle Invisible* (1656), leads fairly logically to a recognition scene; a play about a believable religious hypocrite does not. In real life the events described in ***L'École des femmes, Tartuffe*** and

L'Avare would end unhappily. But Molière's deliberately contrived endings underline the gulf between art and reality. By exaggerating the artificiality of his denouements he is paying lip service to the convention of the happy ending while ironically suggesting that real-life Arnolphes, Tartuffes and Harpagons would not be so miraculously checked.

Equally interesting is his handling of the number of people onstage at the end of his plays. If, as we have seen, he is often orthodox in this matter, the endings of plays like ***Dom Juan*** and ***Le Misanthrope*** seem dramatically to flout the crowded stage convention. At the beginning of the final scene of ***Dom Juan,*** there are three characters on stage, as there have been for most of the play. But, after the statue drags Don Juan down to Hell, Sganarelle remains emphatically alone. Far from being a signal for general rejoicing, his final 'Mes gages!' speech is an expression of anguish. He has lost his job and faces a bleak future. Even his claim that everyone (but him) is happy leaves us unconvinced: Monsieur Dimanche has still not been paid.

Rather than closing the play on a conventional note of reconciliation, these lines provide a final twist to our appreciation of Sganarelle's character. Uniquely among seventeenth-century curtain lines, they were judged so shocking that they had to be cut. In conventional terms, it would have been more acceptable to end the play with the destruction of Don Juan. Sganarelle's final lines provide a ludicrous contrast with the divine intervention which he has just witnessed. We are unexpectedly returned to the physical world and so we laugh. But at the back of our minds, we wonder what will happen next: if the fate of the impious Don Juan has been settled, that of the materialistic Sganarelle has not. A note of ironic uncertainty remains.

Several other Molière plays end with a hint of dispersal, rather than joyous assembly. The plot of ***Amphitryon*** consists of Jupiter's morally dubious bid to obtain the sexual favours of Alcmène by taking on the appearance of her husband, Amphitryon. The tone of the final lines, unlike that of the usual communal celebration, is one of discreet reserve, as Sosie concludes, with a wink to the audience:

> Et que chacun chez soi doucement se retire. Sur telles affaires toujours Le meilleur est de ne rien dire.
>
> (ll. 1941-43)

Amphitryon's humiliation is implicit in his silence, Alcmène's presence is precluded by the *bienséances* and, as Sosie says in his final speech, 'les phrases sont embarrassantes'. The ending corresponds to the prologue discussion between Mercure and La Nuit on the immoral activities of the gods. A celebration in the conventional theatrical mode would have been in poor taste. Rather than celebrating a legal union, the denouement seeks to play down an act of adultery: discreet silence and dispersal, rather than the usual rejoicing. The moral ambiguity of the situation is underlined, albeit with a knowing smile, by the unusual nature of the ending.

An even more striking instance of Molière's willingness to move beyond the conventional format occurs at the end of ***Le Misanthrope.*** Through the final act, the stage has gradually filled: as the final scene commences, there are eight characters on stage, the entire cast in fact, with the exception of three insignificant servant roles. The ending thus promises to be of the traditional kind. But Molière is teasing us: he gives us a glimpse of a conventional ending before moving on to something quite different. Throughout the last scene the stage gradually empties, as six of the characters hear unpalatable truths and successively withdraw. After Célimène and Alceste have gone their separate ways, Philinte and Éliante resolve to pursue them in a bid to reunite them. At the final curtain, the stage is empty.

Scherer claims that dispersal at the denouement is a sign of a sad ending: 'C'est la fuite devant le dénouement, qui en manifeste la tristesse, alors que l'afflux des personnages en scène impliquait une certaine allégresse, réclamée par le public'.[11]

He supports this statement with reference to plays by Rotrou and Corneille in which this is clearly the case, as they all end with a lone character expressing various shades of unhappiness.[12] He is on more shaky ground, however, in claiming that the ending of ***Le Misanthrope*** is similarly gloomy: 'On trouve une forme semblable de dénouement, et elle est bien mélancolique aussi, dans le ***Misanthrope*** de Molière'.[13]

Such a statement requires qualification. If the only permissible token of happiness at the end of a comedy is multiple marriages involving all the main characters, then the ending of ***Le Misanthrope*** is clearly a sad one. If, however, one is prepared to consider an ending more in line with the principle of *vraisemblance,* the case for a sad interpretation may seem less overwhelming.

The point of the play is that Alceste and Célimène are incompatible. They may love each other, but they could not live together. Each time they meet, they quarrel. The final scene suggests that, for all their efforts, a real understanding is impossible: unlike Kate and Petruchio, they are temperamentally unsuited.

However, despite the latent pathos, Molière retains a marvellous lightness of touch. The ending is, to say the least, ambiguous. The temptations of conventional artificiality are for once resisted. Alceste and Célimène are given the opportunity to compromise, to see the error of their ways in the traditional way that usually leads to marriage. But this time it does not happen. Célimène's reluctant offer to marry Alceste is pure form: it is a typically indirect way of saying that she prefers life in society to marriage with him. Alceste declines because she cannot accept him on his terms. Their parting is the only logical solution and neither gives the impression of being particularly unhappy about it. To have condemned them to marriage would have implied a much more painful ending. Many of Molière's other eponymous characters have wedding plans which fall through, but that does not make them tragic. As Harpagon's happiness depends not on marriage but on being reunited with his money, so Alceste's only hope of happiness lies in the world outside Célimène's salon. We do not see him achieve it, but the possibility is there. The ending of ***Le Misanthrope*** may be challenging; it may leave us wondering what will become of Alceste; but it is not necessarily melancholy.

I have argued elsewhere that ***Le Misanthrope*** represents the high water mark of formal classical comedy.[14] Alceste and Célimène, by retaining their theatrical integrity to the end, are the embodiment of *vraisemblance*. They do not undergo some implausible change of heart in the interests of a cosy ending. Here we touch on a revolutionary feature of Molière's endings. However contrived the happy ending, the main character remains unrepentant. Philaminte is still a pedant, Orgon a fanatic and Harpagon a miser. Molière's plays are concerned with fundamental traits of character so that his heroes are not to be converted in the traditional way.

Comedy is therefore maintained to the end. In the conventional seventeenth-century format, the fifth act of a comedy lacks sparkle. When the plot is just a series of misunderstandings, there is little purchase for humour at the denouement: the author is simply explaining the complications, tying up loose ends. But Molière's unreconstructed *imaginaires* remain incorrigibly themselves. The denouement has to be fitted round them and the comic tension lasts through the final scene. Harpagon churlishly agrees to the double wedding on condition that Anselme will pay for it; after Tartuffe's arrest, Orgon, moving from one extreme to the other, memorably condemns all men of virtue; and Sganarelle, having witnessed a miracle, can think only of his wages.

If ***Dom Juan*** ends with Sganarelle's lament, it is not the only Molière play to end on a note of comic exasperation. As in Sganarelle's case, this is usually voiced by a disgruntled figure who has been by-passed by the denouement. One recalls the other Sganarelle's blanket condemnation of women at the end of ***L'École des maris*** and the curse on literature by Gorgibus at the end of ***Les Précieuses ridicules,*** his final explosion conveying the hopeless, incomprehending rage of a little man railing against an irresistible force:

> Et vous, qui êtes cause de leur folie, sottes billevesées, pernicieux amusements des esprits oisifs, romans, vers, chansons, sonnets et sonnettes, puissiez-vous être à tous les diables! (scene 17)

This is another way of maintaining comic momentum as long as possible, the function of such outbursts being that of an antidote to the ritual of the happy ending.

Fixity of character is also a springboard for the spectacular nonsense at the end of the best comedy-ballets. In ***Le Malade imaginaire,*** it is impossible to reason with Argan. He cannot understand that he is wrong to require his daughter to marry a doctor: rational argument cannot reach him. The other characters therefore resort to the medical ceremony, a subterfuge designed to flatter his neurosis and overcome his objection to Cléante. He is fooled into thinking that he is being made a doctor, and therefore in no need of a medical son-in-law. Behind the fantasy, there runs at least a thread of logic. It would have been ludicrous for Argan to lose his awe of doctors: the colourful finale ensures a happy ending even though the dotty old hypochondriac remains true to his character.

The curmudgeon forced to take part in the dance is actually a joke which occurs at the end of most of the comedy-ballets. The most dramatic example occurs in ***L'Amour médecin.*** The prudent Clitandre has brought with him, in addition to a lawyer for the wedding contract, a troupe of dancers and musicians which he uses as a kind of spiritual tranquillizer:

> Ce sont des gens dont je me sers tous les jours pour pacifier avec leur harmonie les troubles de l'esprit. (III, 7)

As Sganarelle watches the dancing, Clitandre tries to steal away with his daughter and the dancers themselves prevent Sganarelle from intervening. The play's final speech therefore goes like this:

> SGANARELLE: Comment diable! [*Il veut aller après Clitandre et Lucinde, les danseurs le retiennent*] Laissez-moi aller, laissez-moi aller, vous dis-je. [*Les danseurs le retiennent toujours.*] Encore? [*Ils veulent faire danser Sganarelle de force.*] Peste des gens! (III, 8)

This is really an explicit version of what happens in more sophisticated form in other comedy-ballets: the dancers' intervention keeps Sganarelle frustrated—and therefore amusing—until the music soothes his anger.

This device is one key to the problematic ending of ***George Dandin.*** Taken at face value, the play's final lines contain a threat of suicide. Deceived by his wife and despised by her snobbish parents, Dandin apparently threatens to drown himself:

> Ah! je n'y vois plus de remède. Lorsqu'on a, comme moi, épousé une mauvaise femme, le meilleur parti qu'on puisse prendre, c'est de s'aller jeter dans l'eau, la tête la première. (III, 15)

Here, Molière seems to be standing the conventional denouement on its head. Dandin is alone on stage and wishing himself unmarried; far from celebrating anything, he is unhappy, it would seem, to the point of contemplating suicide. All the usual trappings of the comedy denouement are missing. When comic characters talk of dying, it is normally an empty threat. When Scapin or Argan claim to be near death, we have no reason to take them seriously. But Dandin is different: it would not be difficult to imagine a man in his position truly desperate. So is this ending as grim as it seems?

The answer lies partly in the fact that ***George Dandin*** was written as a comedy-ballet. Félibien's *Relation de la Fête de Versailles* makes it clear that, in the original production, conceived as part of the *Grand Divertissement royal,* the verb *noyer* had nothing to do with death:

> Enfin un de ses amis lui conseille de noyer dans le vin toutes ses inquiétudes, et l'emmène pour joindre sa troupe, voyant venir la foule des bergers amoureux.[15]

In the original performance, therefore, the tone of the ending was alcoholic rather than tragic: after Dandin's final expression of frustration, he was surrounded by dancers, who carried him off to the inn, where he drowned only his sorrows. Like Sganarelle, the character thus retained all his comic, out-of-step-with-the-world integrity right up to the end of the comedy proper, at which point he allowed himself to be distracted by an invitation to join the dance. Reassured of the absurdity of the aspiring lower orders, the court could not possibly have seen tragedy in this ending.

However, when the play transferred to the Palais-Royal, it lost its dancers. Molière could not afford to offer to the public the lavish musical and balletic interludes that the royal purse had subsidized. But he seems to have thought it unnecessary to change the final lines. This was presumably because the logic of the comedy-ballet ending is implicit throughout the play. Dandin lacks the stature to be tragic. He is a grotesque peasant, a rustic Monsieur Jourdain who has married above his station and is paying for it. He is too dull to interest his wife and too inarticulate to impress her appalling parents. He actually dismisses the idea of suicide as a romantic whim (III, 8). He is a splendidly prosaic creation whose impotence inspires laughter rather than sympathy.

Even the troublesome final line should be seen as another illustration of his mediocrity. The image of the unhappily married husband expressing his frustration via the idea of throwing himself headfirst into water was a comic commonplace in French literature from the Middle Ages onward. In an interesting article on ***George Dandin,***[16] Joan Crow shows that the image, originally inspired by lines in Juvenal's Sixth Satire, recurs in works as diverse as the *Quinze Joyes de mariage,* the *Roman de la Rose* and Chappuzeau's comedy *L'Avare dupé,* performed in 1663. Unoriginal to the end, Dandin is thus expressing his impotence in more or less proverbial wisdom rather than stating a personal intention. And from what we know of Molière's acting style, one imagines that he would have given the last line unmistakable comic resonance, perhaps through some stage business hinting at the alcoholic solution offered by the comedy-ballet finale. There is no evidence that contemporaries found any reason to disagree with Robinet's judgement that the play was 'archicomique'.[17]

In some of Molière's comedy-ballets, as we have seen, a happy ending is achieved when the obstacle characters are convinced by others that they are what they are not. Jourdain is persuaded that he has acquired nobility, Argan that he has been made a doctor. These illusions persist to the final curtain. At the end of ***Les Précieuses ridicules,*** there is a curious variant on this. Mascarille is a valet whom his master disguises as a nobleman, in order to take revenge on the disdainful *précieuses.* He plays his part brilliantly; Madelon and Cathos are duly captivated and then mortified when his true identity is announced.[18] According to normal farce practice, the play should have ended there, with Mascarille reverting to his servant identity. But Mascarille goes on playing the part. When his master strips him almost naked, he unexpectedly complains with the same high-flown language he has used throughout:

> O fortune! quelle est ton inconstance! Traiter comme cela un marquis!
>
> (scenes 15 and 16)

And the half-naked servant continues to bewail his fate with the language of an aristocrat: the comic mask seems to be fixed. He never accepts his old identity and we are left wondering what the future holds for him.

The same thing happens at the end of ***Le Médecin malgré lui.*** All seems resolved: Léandre has conveniently come into a fortune, the lovers can marry and Sganarelle is no longer to be hanged. But he does not acknowledge that he has only been masquerading as a doctor and, in his last speech, announces to his wife that he means to continue the pretence:

> . . . prépare-toi désormais à vivre dans un grand respect avec un homme de ma conséquence, et songe que la colère d'un médecin est plus à craindre qu'on ne peut croire. (III, 11)

We have no way of knowing whether he is serious. But it would be quite in character and, again, the remark introduces a pleasantly ambiguous note at a point where comedy often degenerates into banality.

Such ambiguity is perhaps the most characteristic feature of Molière's denouements. Even when there is a recognizable happy ending, one often has the impression that little has actually changed. If Valère and Cléante can marry their sweethearts, the cause of the problem, Harpagon's avarice, has not been eradicated. If Don Juan is suppressed, Sganarelle remains behind. It is no coincidence that Sganarelle speaks both the first and the last lines of the play. Both are concerned with the physical world, his anxiety over his wages at the end recalling his praise of tobacco at the beginning. The world of materialism and credulity which spawned Don Juan remains intact: one feels he will be back.

There is similar symmetry in ***Le Médecin malgré lui***: Sganarelle's truculent threat to his wife at the end recalls the domestic quarrel they were having at the beginning. The circle is complete. Although the lovers can marry, the play leaves no impression of lasting harmony. The curtain falls before Martine can reply. But the struggle will continue. The play could begin all over again.

The ending of ***Le Misanthrope*** is also ambiguous enough to suggest a continuous cycle. Alceste's rejection of Célimène need not mean the end of the affair. He was even ruder to her at the end of Act IV, and has long been aware of the illogical nature of their relationship ('Il est vrai; ma raison me le dit chaque jour' (l. 247)). So the revelations of the final scene tell him nothing new. There is often a gap between what he says and what he does. He talks of fleeing to his 'desert' in the opening scene but repeatedly shows reluctance even to leave the room; he claims to be brutally frank, but tries not to hurt Oronte's feelings. So it is possible that he will again fail to carry out his threat. The play closes, as it opened, with an expression of concern from Philinte. As he pursued Alceste on stage in Act I, so he now follows him off. Their endless dialogue might be about to resume.

Some of the other solutions also have a temporary ring. Jourdain's daughter can marry her Cléonte because her father thinks the latter is the son of the Grand Turk: one might wonder how long such a fundamentally honest young man will be able to keep up the pretence. The happy outcome of ***Le Malade imaginaire,*** which depends on Argan believing that he has become a doctor, seems equally precarious. The final line of ***Le Mariage forcé*** ('Allons nous réjouir, et célébrer cet heureux mariage') may seem utterly conventional: but the archetypal end-of-comedy formula takes on a hollow ring when we remember that this marriage concerns a bride who, three scenes earlier, has promised her lover that she will be a widow within six months.

It is clear that Molière's denouements are as rich and varied a feature of his plays as any other. From ***Le Misanthrope*** to the humblest farce, they are admirably crafted. In Jouvet's words, 'ils sont de la plus parfaite et de la plus fine convention théâtrale'.[19] If they show orthodox traits, they are also ironic and self-aware. They demonstrate respect for stage convention but also willingness to go beyond it. Like the rest of his theatre, they can be witty, stimulating, even shocking.

Unusually for the time, they ensure that the comedy continues into the final scene. The last line of ***Dom Juan*** is one of the most dangerously comic in Molière's theatre. One could infer from his endings alone that his desire to amuse was greater than his crusading zeal: one might, for example, question his claim to 'corriger les gens en les divertissant',[20] when his own characters are so endearingly incapable of mending their ways.

But the function of these comic denouements is also a serious one. They suggest that in real life things might turn out less happily. They suggest that the solution arrived at may anyway be a temporary one, lasting only long enough to bring the curtain down on a happy ending. Some of his characters clearly have a future as well as a past. The enemies of spontaneity, nature and common sense can be briefly neutralized. But there is no proof that they can be lastingly checked. The forces of reason can win the odd battle, but the war will continue. Men and women are shown to be incorrigibly pretentious and irrational, inflexible and gullible. With a few exceptions, they are not blamed, they just are. There are no conversions. The ultimate wisdom of a Molière play often lies, not in the words of the *raisonneur,* but in the final scene.

Notes

1. Voltaire, *Œuvres complètes,* Kehl edition (1784), ll. 834-36.
2. Daniel Mornet, *Molière,* Connaissance des Lettres (Paris, Hatier-Boivin, 1962), p. 127.
3. The best recent studies in this area are Quentin M. Hope, 'Molière's Curtain Lines', *French Studies,* XXVI (1972), 143-55, R. D. Fraser and S. F. Rendall, 'The Recognition Scene in Molière's Theater', *Romanic Review,* 64 (1973), 16-31 and C. J. Gossip, 'Arnolphe, Alceste and Comic Closure', *French Studies Bulletin,* 36 (1990), 5-7.
4. P. Bernard Lamy, *Nouvelles réflexions sur l'art poétique* (Paris, A. Pralard, 1668), pp. 150-51.
5. However, according to Jacques Scherer, this tradition did not pre-date classicism. See his *La Dramaturgie classique en France* (Paris, Nizet, 1964), p. 141.
6. Ibid., p. 144.
7. See *L'Étourdi, Sganarelle, Les Précieuses ridicules, L'École des maris, La Critique de l'École des femmes, L'Impromptu de Versailles, Dom Juan, Le Médecin malgré lui, Amphitryon, George Dandin, Le Bourgeois Gentilhomme, Les Fourberies de Scapin.*
8. Hope, 'Molière's Curtain Lines', p. 143.
9. *L'École des femmes,* ll. 1741-59.
10. Fraser and Rendall, 'The Recognition Scene', p. 26.
11. Scherer, *La Dramaturgie classique,* p. 144.
12. Ibid., p. 143. The plays are two tragi-comedies by Rotrou, *Cléagenor et Doristée* (1634) and *L'Heureuse Constance* (1635), and two consecutive comedies by Corneille, *La Suivante* (1633) and *La Place Royale* (1633).
13. Scherer, *La Dramaturgie classique,* p. 144.
14. David Shaw, 'Le Misanthrope and Classical Comedy', *Modern Languages,* 55, no. 1 (1974), 16-26.
15. André Félibien, *Relations de la Fête de Versailles du 18 juillet 1668,* quoted by Despois and Mesnard, *Œuvres de Molière* (Paris, Hachette, 1881), VI, 614-40 (p. 622).

16. Joan Crow, 'Reflections on *George Dandin*', in *Molière: Stage and Study. Essays in Honour of W. G. Moore,* edited by W. D. Howarth and M. Thomas (Oxford, Clarendon Press, 1973), pp. 3-12.
17. *Lettre en vers,* 12 July 1668.
18. *Les Précieuses ridicules,* scene 15.
19. Quoted by W. G. Moore in *Molière: A New Criticism* (Oxford, Clarendon Press, 1949), p. 83.
20. *Placet présenté au Roi sur la comédie du Tartuffe,* 31 August 1664.

Robert Kenny (essay date 1994)

SOURCE: "Molière's Tower of Babel: *Monsieur de Pourceaugnac* and the Confusion of Tongues," in *Nottingham French Studies,* Vol. 33, No. 1, Spring, 1994, pp. 59-70.

[*In the following essay, Kenny explores Molière's struggles in creating the new genre of musical-comedy.*]

Much modern criticism has positively re-evaluated Molière's *comédies-ballets* in the context of the argument for a 'third manner' Molière who turns away from high comedy of language towards an irrational world of fantasy and illusion. Gérard Defaux and Claude Abraham make this case eloquently in spite of the somewhat embarrassing presence of ***Les Femmes savantes,*** while more recently Patrick Dandrey has disagreed radically with this thesis, particularly with reference to the musical coherence of the *comédie-ballet.*[1] The tripartite division of Molière's thought and work, though it contains many useful insights, is largely the result of neat academic hindsight and the deification of Molière the classical genius. It is perhaps worth noting that this critical view in a more benign form is already present in Sainte-Beuve's *notice* for his edition of the *Oeuvres*; 'De la farce franche et un peu grosse du début, on se sera élevé, en passant par le naïf, le sérieux, le profondément observé, jusqu'à la fantaisie du rire dans toute sa pompe et au gai sabbat le plus délirant.' Sainte-Beuve clearly recognised and celebrated the late *comédies-ballets* as 'ces fusées[. . .] d'éblouissante gaieté' and places them on a level with *A Midsummer Night's Dream* and *The Tempest.*[2] Late nineteenth-century criticism took a more solemn turn and for far too long a more just evaluation of the *comédies-ballets* has been hindered by the fact that the music, singing and dancing have been truncated or simply excised from performances which reduce the plays to abridged and aesthetically unsatisfying approximations of spoken comedy. More recently, critics have remembered, as Alain pointed out many years ago, 'Shakespeare acteur, Molière acteur, ce ne sont point des hasards' and have reexamined the works as blueprints for performance rather than judging them merely as printed literary texts.

In doing this they are belatedly complying with Molière's express wishes. In the preface to ***L'Amour médecin*** he admits that his new genre was the hybrid but happy result of an urgent royal command. As such it had no corpus of pre-existing conventions to govern its structure and Molière, Lully and Beauchamp, as seasoned men of the theatre, were engaged in a new art of improvisation. Nevertheless, as Sainte-Beuve remarked, 'Le génie se fait de chaque nécessité une inspiration' and Molière saw at once the potential for this new form of music theatre. The prologue is sung by 'La Comédie, La Musique, Le Ballet' personified, and they agree on a new form of theatrical harmony; 'Quittons, quittons notre vaine querelle, / Ne nous disputons point nos talents tour à tour; / Et d'une gloire plus belle / Piquons-nous en ce jour. / Unissons-nous tous trois d'une ardeur sans seconde, / Pour donner du plaisir au plus grand roi du monde' Donneau de Visé was among the first to note the originality of Molière's *trouvaille;* 'Il a, le premier, inventé la manière de mêler des scènes de musique et des ballets dans ses comédies et trouvé par là un nouveau secret de plaire qui avait été jusqu'alors inconnu.' In his preface Molière presciently warns future *readers* of the *comédies-ballets* that they must become *metteurs en scène* if they are to appreciate the genre; 'Il n'est pas nécessaire de vous avertir qu'il y a beaucoup de choses qui dépendent de l'action. On sait bien que les comédies ne sont faites que pour être jouées, et je ne conseille de lire celle-ci [***L'Amour médecin***] qu'aux personnes qui ont des yeux pour découvrir, dans la lecture, tout le jeu du théâtre.' In such conditions 'Vous les verriez dans un état beaucoup plus supportable; et les airs et les symphonies de l'incomparable M. Lully, mêlés à la beauté des voix et à l'adresse des danseurs, leur donnent, sans doute, des grâces dont ils ont toutes les peines du monde à se passer.'

As early as 1661 in his *Avertissement* to ***Les Fâcheux,*** Molière had bemoaned the lack of rehearsal time which obliged him to invent a new genre in which the ballets were hastily stitched into the course of the action, with the result that 'certains endroits du ballet n'entrent pas dans la comédie aussi naturellement que d'autres.' Nevertheless he goes on to reveal that he is genuinely intrigued by the theatrical potential of this mingling of genres; 'Quoi qu'il en soit, c'est un mélange qui est nouveau pour nos théâtres [. . .] et, comme tout le monde l'a trouvé agréable, il peut servir d'idée à d'autres choses qui pourraient être méditées avec plus de loisir' Molière was to meditate on this 'mélange' throughout the remainder of his career, often putting what are surely his own thoughts into the mouths of his characters on the stage. In ***La Princesse d'Élide*** in 1664, he makes a decisive addition to his 'mélange' by a massive introduction of vocal music. Molière himself, in the role of Moron, celebrates the extension of his talents to include singing, not without an ironic dig at the fanciful conventions of pastoral lyricism; 'Jusqu'au revoir. Pour moi, je reste ici, et j'ai une petite conversation à faire avec ces arbres et ces rochers.' In the third *intermède,* as Philis resists his advances, Moron clearly voices Molière's own feelings on the current vogue for vocal music; '. . . si je savais chanter, j'en ferais bien mieux mes affaires. La plupart des femmes aujourd'hui se laissent prendre par les oreilles; elles sont cause que tout le monde se mêle de musique, et l'on ne réussit auprès d'elles que par les petites chansons [. . .] Il faut que j'apprenne à chanter pour faire comme les autres . . .' A satyr arrives and Moron begs 'mon ami, tu sais bien ce que tu m'as promis il y a longtemps: apprends-moi à chanter, je te prie.' The lesson gets nowhere and in a later scene Molière-Moron laments his relative lack of musicianship, surely in an implied contrast with his great collaborator-rival, Lully; 'Morbleu! que n'ai-je de la voix! Ah! nature marâtre, pourquoi ne m'as-tu pas donné de quoi chanter comme à un autre? [. . .] Mais pourquoi est-ce je ne puis pas chanter? N'ai-je pas un estomac, un gosier et une langue comme un autre? Oui, oui, allons: je veux chanter aussi . . .' One further speech in ***La Princesse d'Élide*** contains a tribute to the power of song. At the end of Act IV, in the remarkably poignant monologue which prefigures exactly the tone of Marivaux's 'surprise de l'amour', the Princess calls on the singers in these words; 'O vous, admirables personnes, qui par la douceur de vos chants avez l'art d'adoucir les plus fâcheuses inquiétudes, approchez-vous d'ici, de grâce, et tâchez de charmer avec votre musique le chagrin où je suis.'

In these years of experiment and collaboration (on stage as well as off) between ***Les deux Baptiste,*** as Mme de Sévigné called them, Lully learned much from Molière; as Philippe Beaussant points out in his introduction to Mark Minkowski's recording of scenes from the *comédies-ballets,* 'nous comprenons que, bien avant *Cadmus et Hermione,* son premier opéra, Lully ait pu concevoir le récitatif à la française. Il existe des exemples achevés de récitatif "lulliste" dans les scènes pastorales de ***George Dandin*** ou dans ***Les Amants magnifiques,*** mais l'ébauche s'y trouve déjà dans ***La Princesse d'Élide.***' But it is also in that work that one of the keys may be found to the quarrel between the two men, namely the presence in Molière, alongside grace and elegance, of 'le comique le plus endiablé [. . .] que la Tragédie lyrique au ton soutenu bannira peu à peu.'[3] In the last great *comédies-ballets* Molière-Moron continues to mock the excessively wilting and affected aspects of pastoral convention. Much as he admired the delicate minor-key laments of Lully's lovelorn nymphs and shepherds, his own artistic temperament inclined him to exploit singing and dancing for more comic effects. In ***Le Sicilien,*** Adraste orders a serenade which must be 'tendre et passionnée, quelque chose qui m'entretienne dans une douce rêverie'. The slave Hali counsels him against 'le bémol'. 'Monsieur je tiens pour le bécarre. Vous savez que je m'y connais. Le bécarre me charme; hors du bécarre, plus de salut en harmonie.'[4] In the end Hali offers a trio in which two lovesick shepherds lament 'tout remplis de langueur [. . .] sur bémol. [. . .] Là-dessus vient un berger joyeux avec un bécarre admirable, qui se moque de leur faiblesse.' One cannot help reading into this amusing exchange and Moron's earlier complaint an aspect of the temperamental tension between Molière and Lully, a tension which released remarkable creative energy before reaching breaking-point in 1670-71.

Critics have dealt extensively with the last two *comédies-ballets,* insisting on the dramatic and psychological relevance of the musical scenes to the comedy as a whole. The most fervent admirers of the genre have insisted on the richly satisfying homogeneity of the constituent elements. Philippe Beaussant, for instance, admires 'l'imbrication du chant de la danse et de la comédie. Elle est exemplaire dès leur première oeuvre commune, elle éclate dans ***La Princesse d'Élide.*** L'action parlée et l'action chantée s'enchaînent sans rupture et se marient, de même que l'action jouée et l'action dansée.'[5] Well, up to a point. Many of the *entrées de ballet* have no justification other than as pure choreographic spectacle but, as in present-day musicals, they are none the worse for that. Jacques Copeau maintained that '***George Dandin*** me paraissait fermé aux attractions du divertissement.'[6] ***Le Bourgeois gentilhomme*** contains ninety minutes of music and is rarely seen with *Le Ballet des Nations.* The intervention of Polichinelle in ***Le Malade imaginaire*** is barely comprehensible for a non-specialist audience, unaware that it continues in parodic form Molière's long reflection on the relative merits of words and music. Most recently, Patrick Dandrey has been utterly, and surely most unfairly, dismissive of the value of the musical scenes; 'le divertissement [. . .] ne fait que se surajouter assez artificiellement à l'intrigue et à son dénouement. [. . .] Et puis [. . .] quel rôle jouent les ritournelles et trémoussements de Lully dans l'action dramatique des autres comédies-ballets?'[7] 'Trémoussements' indeed. A word most memorably uttered by Monsieur Jourdain.

One returns again to Molière's own reminder that 'les comédies ne sont faites que pour être jouées'. Diderot perceived this more clearly than Dandrey when he remarked 'Si l'on croit qu'il y ait beaucoup d'hommes plus capables de faire ***Pourceaugnac*** que ***Le Misanthrope,*** on se trompe.' Of all the *comédies-ballets,* and I include the last two, ***Monsieur de Pourceaugnac*** is perhaps the most formally coherent, a perfect fusion of singing, dancing and acting in the service of pure entertainment. It may be appreciated in the theatre at one and the same time as a gloriously gratuitous comic spectacle and as a further contribution to Molière's conscious inner dialogue on the nature and function of comic theatre. Music is essential to both the performance and understanding of ***Pourceaugnac.*** Without it, the piece is amputated, unbalanced, unsatisfying. Not that Molière's comic writing lacks wit, grace and verve, far from it. But the spoken scenes are paced and structured to lead into and out of the musical scenes in a way which makes both integral parts of the intrigue. Lully's music frames the entire piece; Molière obviously does not resent this but gives the last word to music for reasons which will shortly become clear.

Pourceaugnac is an excellent example of the overall internal coherence of Molière's output, of what one might call the dialectical, rather than monolinear, growth of his work. The purified essence of ***La Jalousie du Barbouillé*** and ***Le Médecin volant*** is present alongside clear pre-echoes of the world of M. Jourdain and Argan. As one attempts to unravel the apparently simple texture of the work the threads of a surprisingly rich thematic tapestry are revealed and each deserves separate consideration.

Molière never forgot his early years as a wandering *farceur,* nor his debt to the traditions and techniques of the *commedia dell'arte.* In ***Pourceaugnac*** he both openly acknowledges his debt and transforms and revivifies common material. The opening musical invocation 'Répands charmante nuit' has its obvious parallel in the dark openings and night scenes of the *commedia* (cf. ***Le Sicilien,*** scene 1; 'Il fait noir comme dans un four: le ciel s'est habillé ce soir en Scaramouche.') Gustave Attinger, in the course of his classic account of Molière's links with the *commedia,* points out that the action of the whole of Act I and the first two scenes of Act II are based in precise detail on an Italian *canevas, Policinello pazzo per forza,* and that later scenes including the debts alleged by the 'marchand flamand' and the arrival of an abandoned wife and her children are to be found in the *canevas, Policinello burlato.*[8] In other words, the bare bones of most of the action are borrowed but brilliantly improved by Molière. In the *canevas,* every trick played on Policinello is revealed by a speaker in advance, thus destroying the element of surprise for the audience. Molière, on the other hand, never allows Sbrigani to reveal the next twist of his wicked imagination. It is surely with this in mind that he makes Eraste say to Julie (and the audience) 'Ne vous demandez pas tous les ressorts que nous ferons jouer; vous en aurez le divertissement; et comme aux comédies; il est bon de vous laisser le plaisir de la surprise, et de ne vous avertir point de tout ce qu'on vous fera voir.' Molière drives the point home in the last act where Sbrigani's final tricks are announced to Eraste in inaudible whispered exchanges. Molière gives us two abandoned wives instead of one and a whole 'volée d'enfants'. We may also see an acknowledgement of *commedia* sources in the fact that *médecins grotesques* and the *matassins* with their *clystères* sing their entire scene in Italian, transforming an earthy old commonplace into a brightly paced comic interlude of music and dancing. Another Italian device which Molière exploited repeatedly is the use of pattern dialogue and rapid-fire, symmetrical exchanges. Such exchanges are found throughout ***Pourceaugnac,*** often in situations which suggest that they may have been accompanied by refined versions of Italian *lazzi.* Let us conclude this far from exhaustive list with a reminder that Molière also borrowed from the Italians (as well as from French farce) that procession of pedantic professionals (and professional pedants) whose utterances, far from throwing light on any situation, serve only to obfuscate meaning and confuse the actors and the action. Such obfuscation and confusion are a central aspect of ***Pourceaugnac***'s comic action and also of its more serious sub-text.

Jacques Copeau saw the essential action of the play as a 'poursuite' and this is surely one of the keys to its success in the theatre. Much of the vitality of the spoken action comes from the relentless forward drive of the chase. No sooner is the theme established with great economy in the opening scenes, culminating in Sbrigani's 'Ma foi! voici notre homme: songeons à nous' than the hunt is on for this 'gibier' who is 'homme enfin à donner dans tous les panneaux qu'on lui présentera.' The rhythm of the entire play could be marked *accelerando,* with only occasional brief pauses to allow the audience to draw breath, to emphasise the rhythm by comic contrast or to allow Sbrigani to prepare his next trick. Sbrigani's 'gibier' is not merely M. de Pourceaugnac but also Oronte who falls just as readily into the trap for 'le beau-père est aussi dupe que le gendre.' Molière has divided between the two older men a number of character types; the pretentious provincial in Paris, the lascivious older suitor, the irascible authoritarian father-figure. Neither is a match for the protean transformations or the rapid footwork of Sbrigani and his friends in an intrigue which moves to the rhythm of dance, a *pas de deux, de trois, de quatre,* punctuated and crowned by the entries of the entire corps de ballet. Attinger, quoting Copeau, noted that 'tout se déroule dans une cadence qui postule la choréographie' and that 'la musique et la danse communiquent à toute la pièce un rythme de ballet'.[9] To this observation should be added Robert McBride's very pertinent assertion that 'Le théâtre de Molière fourmille de scènes qui sont autant de petits ballets parfaitement orchestrés et cohérents à l'intérieur de ce grand ballet des incompatibles qu'est une de ses comédies.'[10] Thanks to Sbrigani, Julie's incompatibility with Pourceaugnac is ironically inverted into feigned desire and at the end of the play Eraste joins Julie in a *pas de deux* of feigned incompatibility. By the time Sbrigani allows Pourceaugnac and Oronte to meet, he has ensured that they are in the first stages of an incompatibility which grows more pronounced as the play proceeds. A possibly shameful medical complaint, two wives and a host of children are incompatible with 'ce fâcheux mariage que mon père s'est mis en tête.' Finally Pourceaugnac is utterly incompatible with all those around him. According to Copeau 'C'est un mannequin en butte à toutes les avanies qui ont été délibérément concertées contre lui [. . .] On pourrait dire qu'il ne se mêle pas à la comédie, mais se borne à lui faire tête. C'est le jeu adverse qui se développe en dehors de lui, autour de lui et contre lui . . .'.[11]

The verbal and visual choreography of the entire play is based largely around two types of movement, both of which contribute to the 'poursuite'. The first is a double movement which is alternately centrifugal and centripetal. A whole series of characters, real and disguised, come from the furthest-flung and most 'ex-centric' corners of France and beyond, all drawn to Paris, the metropolitan centre of cultural and social refinement and, within Paris, to that classic setting for comic intrigue, the 'place publique'. The two young couples run in to set the plot in motion then scatter in all directions, only meeting again in the finale. Pourceaugnac comes up from Limoges to play the gentleman and is chased onto the stage by the mocking crowd which met him at the coach-stop, just as he will at the very end be chased off by the entire company. Along the way we meet a bewildering cavalcade of characters and caricatures who claim to have come from afar. Sbrigani, first from Naples, then as the merchant from Flanders, no mean linguistic jump for an actor; Lucette from Pézénas in the deep South and Nérine from St-Quentin up in Picardy; grotesque doctors who sing in Italian and 'lawyers' who while singing in French quote legal precedents from almost every nation in Western Europe; drunken Swiss guards with their guttural Germanic drivel. In the finale we meet gypsies from . . . heaven alone knows where. The bemused Oronte is left spinning in the midst of these linguistically and geographically bewildering entrances and exits, hardly even recognising the 'language' spoken by his own daughter. The other important movement is circular. The balletic chase sends Pourceaugnac, and at times Oronte, round in ever-decreasing and ever more frenzied circles until the atmosphere is one of demented vertigo. As Pourceaugnac is finally expelled from the whirligig Eraste brings Julie back from her supposed 'fuite' and Oronte is brought back from his flight of paternal excentricity. The three high points of the circular chase are the dance of the *matassins* with their *clystères,* the swarm of 'wives' and children around Pourceaugnac who cries 'Au secours! Où fuirai-je? Je n'en puis plus', and the ballet of 'Avocats, Procureurs et Sergents' who whirl around the would-be 'gentilhomme limousin' at his last appearance in male attire. . . . The comic chase is present from Molière's very earliest works and in its crudest form it is simply another of the things he borrowed from the *commedia*; but in ***Pourceaugnac*** it is so refined by music and choreography that it acquires a grace and symmetry which might almost be described as elegant.

Monsieur de Pourceaugnac is perhaps the most self-consciously theatrical of all Molière's *comédies-ballets,* perhaps even of all his plays. With the exception of Oronte and the two speaking doctors, every actor on stage is playing a character who is playing another character. Within the play another play is being performed with Pourceaugnac and Oronte as its spectators and victims. Eraste announces this structure 'comme aux comédies' in the first scene and Nérine puns 'nous lui jouerons tant de pièces'. Sbrigani, the genial stage-manager, says to his co-plotters 'vous nous tiendrez prêts au besoin les autres acteurs de la comédie' and Eraste reinforces the theme when he urges Julie 'Au moins, Madame, souvenez-vous bien de votre rôle [. . .] pour mieux couvrir notre jeu . . .'. Pourceaugnac is playing a role which he finds increasingly difficult to sustain and his pathetically repeated bleating 'Je suis gentilhomme limousin' rings ever more hollow until in the third act he too is obliged to take on an even more spurious and comic identity, a travesty of a travesty!

Much of the delight of the intrigue comes from dramatic irony, the sustained disparity between what various characters wrongly believe to be taking place among themselves onstage, what others know to be true, and the further irony of the presence of the audience. It is surely as another deliberate irony that Molière gives Pourceaugnac the line 'Est-ce une comédie que nous jouons ici?' at the only moment in the play when the true answer, delivered in good faith by the doctors, is 'Non.' For the doctors, who are real doctors, are themselves victims of the plot and their diagnoses, perfectly sound and sensible in the medicine of the day, only become ridiculous in that they are addressed to a man who is not a melancholy hypochondriac but a hearty bumpkin in search of a good dinner. In scene after scene, language, far from contributing to rational communication, serves only to cloud the issue, to misinform and to disinform. The wariness of academic pedantry which Molière originally borrows from the *commedia* becomes in his work a sustained reflection on the dangers and limitations of language. The theme is already present in ***La Jalousie du Barbouillé*** where all the supposed wisdom of 'le docteur' is irrelevant jargon and incomprehensible Latin. When this garrulous pedant attempts to bring harmony to the quarrelling family the result is that everyone ends up speaking at once and understanding nothing. This is the very first appearance of what might be called the theme of Babel and it is underlined by the fact that it results in the doctor's fall to the ground. Learned language impedes all communication in ***Dépit amoureux*** II,6, leaving the pedant Métaphraste to muse ironically on a 'world turned upside down' from which language and therefore meaning are absent. A similar theme is further elaborated in ***Le Mariage forcé,*** where the two pedants are far less capable of telling Sganarelle what he needs to know than a couple of flighty gypsies, whose singing and dancing perhaps reveal a glimmer of truth.

Every speech in ***Monsieur de Pourceaugnac*** contributes to the *décalage* between appearance and reality. Language at its most plausible is also at its most mendacious and leads ultimately to the total absurdity of a man stripped of his identity and of his clothes, mimicking the voice of a 'femme du bel air'. In the third act Pourceaugnac literally loses his own voice and becomes one more caricature among the cackling voices of Babel. This confusion of tongues is one of the most powerful effects created by Molière in the play. Sbrigani has kept his Neapolitan accent; Pourceaugnac's French is richly spiced with 'l'accent du Midi'; the doctors' Parisian French is incomprehensible thanks to their subject matter and their Latin interpolations; the *matassins* sing in Italian; the 'marchand flamand' speaks double-Dutch; Nérine chews her words 'à la Picarde'. But the climax of this proliferation of competing voices comes with the arrival from Pézenas of Lucette who, abandoning completely any semblance of Cartesian or Gallic clarity, takes flight into a torrent of Gascon from which virtually all meaning has fled. It is surely no coincidence that at such a comic high point of the action Molière decided to replace French with the most extended pieces of babble in his entire work. Nor is it an accident that the structure of Lucette's speech is a parody of a form which demanded an intense purity and clarity of diction, namely, Racinian tragedy. In the last long speech of her first scene, Lucette becomes a burlesque Ariadne, 'abandounado à las mourtéles doulous que yeu ressenti de sas perfidos acciûs'. The following scene is another *Ballet des Incompatibles* in which a pair of fishwives, one (the actor

Hubert) in drag, outdo each other in incomprehensibility, and the entire scene is crowned by the meaningless prattle of children, *enfant=infans*=speechless. It is from this high point of absurdity onwards that Pourceaugnac is persuaded to divest himself of his own intended role, his legal jargon, his precious clothes and his voice, so that in the scene with the two *suisses* (in reality friends of Sbrigani) all three voices on stage are counterfeit. And all this was engineered by Sbrigani who Pourceaugnac believed to the last to be 'le seul honnête homme que j'aie trouvé dans cette ville.' When, moments later, an exhausted Oronte concludes the betrothal of the young lovers with the conventional 'Ah! que de bruit! [. . .] Ah, ah, ah!' there is, in performance, a far more than conventional sigh of relief that the babble of tongues is about to be stilled.

If the performance were to end at this point with a perfunctory 'allons quérir un notaire!' ***Pourceaugnac*** could be seen as a wilfully perverse tale of heartless mockery and deception, a cruel Parisian confidence trick played on an elderly gentleman (Oronte was the last role played by the one-eyed and lame Béjart) and a harmless and gullible booby up from the sticks (Molière losing his Armande-Julie). But this is not a black comedy or theatre of cruelty; it is, as Eraste told Julie, a 'divertissement' from the moments of *noirceur* in the real world of Molière's moral comedy. Respecting as it does the unity of time, the action is a perfect example of the 'folle journée', a day of pure and harmless madness on which all proprieties and conventions may, without negative moral implications, be thrown to the winds. In other words, as in the other late *comédies-ballets,* it is Shrove Tuesday, 'Carnaval', when a temporary inversion of order into disorder is a salutary, cathartic and curative process. As we are warned in *La Comtesse d' Escarbagnas,* 'C'est sans vous offenser Madame, et les comédies veulent ces sortes de choses'; in Mme Jourdain's words we are in a world of 'carême(s)-prenant(s)' and it is 'temps d'aller en masque'. In ***Le Malade imaginaire*** Béralde further reassures us that 'le Carnaval autorise cela' and at the end of ***Pourceaugnac,*** Eraste says 'nous pouvons jouir du divertissement de la saison.' Molière played Pourceaugnac, Jourdain and Argan, and, as Covielle points out 'Tout cela sent un peu sa comédie [. . .] et il est homme à y jouer son rôle à merveille.' The reiterated references to 'theatre in the theatre' remind us that we are in a privileged space of fantasy, as Plautus said 'in festivo loco',[12] a place in which the insoluble moral ambiguities of the real world and the linguistic ambiguities of apparently logical discourse are momentarily vanquished in favour of a new language of harmonious reconciliation. For Molière the dramatist, the confusion of tongues when all speak at once leads to Babel; for the Molière of the *comédies-ballets,* music transforms and elevates the babble into vocal harmony.

Music enfolds and informs the entire structure of ***Monsieur de Pourceaugnac.*** The time of spoken dialogue and the tempo of music are carefully balanced throughout, creating, in the theatre, a measured and aesthetically satisfying experience which is difficult to glean from the printed page. A grandiose overture boldly asserts the importance of music in the ensuing action, and its rapid second section with breathless overlapping entries seems to prefigure the relentless 'poursuite'. The *Sérénade* which follows has an integral role in the dramatic structure. Eraste says to the musicians and singers, 'Suivez les ordres que je vous ai donnés pour la sérénade. Pour moi, je me retire, et ne veux point paraître ici.' The solos and the trio serve as an exposition, telling in brief of the predicament of Julie and Eraste whose love is crossed by tyrannical parents. This is a clever and economical way of establishing the love theme, for there is little time for wooing once the chase has begun. Although promising a happy outcome, the music remains wistful and elegiac and even the trio 'Aimons-nous donc', with its plaintive falling phrases, seems more a hopeful prayer than a bold assertion. An energetic ballet then enacts a brief quarrel and reconciliation, preparing the audience for the role of dance in the action. The endless verbiage of the doctors is a perfect example of what Béralde calls 'le roman de la médecine' and bears little relation to reality. The doctors only succeed in making a perfectly healthy man feel confused and irritable and before administering their own dubious remedies they call on the 'douceur exhilarante de la musique' to calm his spirits. Thus the doctors are part of the malady not the cure. The cure, for the audience, if not yet for Pourceaugnac, lies in the conjunction of comedy, ballet and music. All three personified in ***L'Amour médecin*** declared that 'Sans nous tous les hommes / Deviendraient mal sains, / Et c'est nous qui sommes / Leurs grands médecins.' As soon as the doctors' pompous and dotty music begins we leave the real world for the first flight into comic fantasy in what Copeau called the 'espaces béants de la musique'. The music begins in a mock-doleful minor mode (which Molière had called 'le bémol') then moves on to an elegant dance rhythm in which the singers urge us to banish melancholy with singing, dancing, laughter, wine and snuff! The 'clystère' scene is purified by music and dance ('un beau bécarre') and becomes a stylised ballet of whirling dervishes which concludes the first act. The second act similarly moves towards a fantastic musical climax of grotesque lawyers, in which the lugubrious music of the slow lawyer and the rapid patter of the stuttering lawyer eventually overlap and become incomprehensible, except as an exhilaratingly rhythmic musical and balletic pattern.

The presence of these structurally coherent and dramatically relevant musical scenes at the outset, and at the end of the first two acts, sets up a powerful aesthetic expectation of music, song and dance at the close of the last act. This is of course realised but the function of the finale is different from the earlier *intermèdes.* One simply cannot agree with Patrick Dandrey that the musical finale of ***Pourceaugnac*** is merely 'un prolongement redondant'. True, it is not exactly a part of the action but it is a crucial part of the structures we have tried to examine. For Molière, 'la fin d'une vraie et pure comédie' now demands the absolution of all conflict into musical harmony. Language and plot dissolve as all the 'acteurs de la comédie' return to be reconciled with each other and the audience in a celebration of harmless folly and laughter, what Sainte-Beuve called Molière's 'Purs ébats, son rire étincelant, redoublé, presque sans cause en se prolongeant, désintéressé du réel, comme une flamme folâtre qui voltige de plus belle après que la combustion grossière a cessé, un rire des dieux, suprême, inextinguible.'[13] The stage directions remind us that the whole company '[cherche] à se donner des plaisirs innocents' at the end of what might, as in ***L'École des maris,*** be called 'le stratagème adroit d'un innocent amour.' The text of the final chorus makes it clear that Pourceaugnac, who has played *Policinello* for our delight, is included in the rejoicing; 'Lorsque pour rire on s'assemble / Les plus sages ce me semble / sont ceux qui sont les plus fous.' What had been impossible in speech has been realised in the conjunction of words and music. The triumphant chords of C and G major remind us that 'Hors du bécarre plus de salut en harmonie.' The solos of the finale are delivered by a couple of 'Égyptiens'. Paradoxically this is one last echo of the theme of excentricity of which we spoke earlier. These picturesque nomads now take the centre of the stage to wish good fortune to the entire company, and their exquisitely delicate duet ('les biens, la gloire', a brief moment of relative bémol) is a surprisingly poignant reminder of the vanity of human wishes. In the final curtain call, the voices of reason and erudition, 'le divin Hippocrate', Aristotle and his 'trois opérations de l'esprit', the babble of Neapolitan, Gascon, Picard, Limousin, Dutch, Italian, German and Latin, all are silenced to receive a Gypsy's blessing in music, and to respond in an impressively grandiose four-voiced harmony which triumphs over Babel. In ***Monsieur de Pourceaugnac,*** Molière-Moron who longed to learn to sing, finally realised his dream and created a prototypically coherent musical-comedy.

Notes

1. Gérard Defaux, *Molière ou les métamorphoses du comique* (Lexington: French Forum, 1980); Claude Abraham, *On the structure of Molière's comédies-ballets,* Papers on French Seventeenth Century Literature, 1984; Patrick Dandrey, *Molière ou l'esthétique du ridicule* (Paris: Klincksieck, 1992), p.270.
2. Sainte-Beuve ed., Molière, *Oeuvres Complètes* (Paris: Lecou, 1853), p.24.
3. Philippe Beaussant, sleeve-notes to Lully-Molière, *Comédies-Ballets,* Erato CD 2292-45286-2.
4. Molière is here using the words *bémol* and *bécarre* to signify minor and major keys, not sharps and naturals.
5. Philippe Beaussant, loc. cit..
6. Jacques Copeau, *Registres II, Molière* (Paris: Gallimard, 1976), p.265.
7. Patrick Dandrey, loc. cit..
8. Gustave Attinger, *L'Esprit de la commedia dell'arte dans le théâtre français* (Neuchâtel: La Baconnière, 1950), pp. 137-8.
9. Ibid., p.159.
10. Robert McBride, 'Molière, le Languedoc et le Ballet des Incompatibles', in *La Vie théâtrale dans les provinces du Midi* (Paris: Jean-Michel Place, 1980), p.135. In this ballet Molière made one of his earliest appearances *travesti en femme.* Pourceaugnac was his last such appearance, although it could be said that at the end of both *Le Bourgeois gentilhomme* and *Le Malade imaginaire* Molière is equally 'cross-dressed' in garments which mark him out as a creature from a fantasy world.
11. Jacques Copeau, op.cit., p.269.
12. Plautus, *Miles gloriosus,* vv.83-85.
13. Sainte-Beuve, loc. cit.

Noël A. Peacock (essay date 1994)

SOURCE: "Translating Molière for the English Stage," in *Nottingham French Studies,* Vol. 33, No. 1, Spring, 1994, pp. 83-91.

[*In the following essay, Peacock discusses the issues surrounding the translation of Molière's plays, focusing on three types of translators: conservationists, modernists, and postmodernists.*]

> If we are not careful, Molière could become one of the obstacles to a united Europe. How can you trade freely, let alone merge with a nation whose best comedy does not travel?[1]

This ironic taunt by John Peter in 1987, which could so easily have been taken for a backbench salvo in the Maastricht debate in 1993, gives expression to the disquiet, shared by numerous actors, directors, and especially theatre box-office managers, at the lack of performable translations of Molière in English. The dramatic ineffectiveness, not to mention unspeakability, of certain versions, has given a misleading impression of the great comic dramatist, even to the point of causing *The Daily Telegraph*'s drama critic, Charles Spencer—paradoxically—to suspect 'that there was nothing wrong with Molière that a sense of humour wouldn't have put right [. . .]'.[2] One of the problems is the discrepancy between page and stage: many translations are aimed at publication rather than at performance. The result is that they are often confined to library bookshelves and dusted down by those engaged in academic study and not by theatre practitioners. As John Fowles has indicated, Molière has been consigned to a theatrical limbo in Britain, to the status of a study dramatist: 'on the whole we don't know what to do with him so we leave him alone'.[3] Molière himself, in his much-cited prefatory advice in ***L'Amour médecin,*** limited readership to those willing to exercise their theatrical imagination:

> et je ne conseille de lire celle-ci qu'aux personnes qui ont des yeux pour découvrir dans la lecture tout le jeu du théâtre.

A translator's unawareness of the practicalities of the theatre may be illustrated from the embarrassment inflicted on an actor by Henri Van Laun, whose recently republished translation of ***Le Misanthrope***[4] assigns to the plain speaking Alceste a line whose pedantry gives another dimension to Molière's humour:

> . . . your ebullitions of tenderness know no bounds.
> Zounds!

Another problem is the low status accorded to the art of translating. Promotion Boards and Research Assessment Panels seem to pay scant attention to translations, whatever their intrinsic merits. Theatre managers tend to be equally dismissive in awarding minimal royalties (one translator recently received 3% of royalties, with the author receiving 10%).

This paper, then, will explore theatrically successful solutions to the problem of translating Molière for the English stage. The 'translators' have been placed into three categories: *conservationists, modernisers* and *post-modernisers.* The nomenclature is used rather idiosyncratically, and has been preferred to the more conventional critical suffixes (conservatives, modernists and post-modernists), which tend, these days, to lead to confusion, and to be viewed pejoratively. By *conservationists,* I understand those who wish to preserve all the outward features of the seventeenth-century structure, albeit in a renewed form; by *modernisers,* those who have upgraded certain aspects for the modern age; by *post-modernisers,* those who have knocked down and rebuilt the main structure but have used some of the original materials. The boundaries between the different kinds of terminological architecture are, however, somewhat fluid.

Firstly, the *conservationists,* whose main emphasis is on fidelity to the original. The leading modern exponent, Richard Wilbur, produced a line-by-line translation in iambic pentameters of ***The Misanthrope*** (1955), ***Tartuffe*** (1963), ***The School for Wives*** (1971) and ***The Learned Ladies*** (1978). The only major liberties taken were in suggesting no one period and in the use of a modern idiom. Wilbur was highly critical of contemporary modernisations in which the loss of a credible social frame for him entailed a loss of meaning. He cited the example of a translation in which Alceste entered a twentieth-century American living room in hippy attire, a ten-speed bicycle under his arm, insisting 'tell it like it is'. In Wilbur's preface to ***The Learned Ladies*** (1978), he expressed the hope that all readers would envision his translation in a 'just historical perspective'. Wilbur's translations were praised for their elegance, wit and accuracy. The elevated tone given by the versification helped him to retain Molière's parody of tragic diction.

In America, his work was regarded as 'the nearest thing to Molière that we have';[5] his ***Tartuffe*** was awarded a share of the Bollingen translation prize in 1963. In Britain, however, very quotable strictures applied by some of his first reviewers have perhaps had a dissuasive effect on directors. W. A. Darlington (*The Daily Telegraph,* 22 November 1967) dimissed the mode of expression as an 'uninspired jog-trot translation' evocative of the doggerel that used to be reeled out in Victorian pantomimes; 'trumpery translation' exclaimed Harold Hobson (*The Sunday Times,* 25 August 1974); Sean Day-Lewis (*The Daily Telegraph,* 28 November 1971) pleaded for 'lines not chimes'; and Tony Harrison damned Wilbur with faint praise: '[His ***Tartuffe*** and ***Misanthrope***] are hard polished closet drama'.[6] Wilbur's rehabilitation in England has come from performances of his ***Misanthrope*** in Manchester and London in 1981, and, most recently, in the highly successful ***School for Wives*** (running at the Almeida Theatre, London, from December 1993 to January 1994), which has earned him the accolade of 'prince among contemporary translators'.[7]

Ian Maclean's revision (in 1989) of George Gravely's ***Precious Provincials, Don Juan, The Reluctant Doctor, The Miser, The Would-Be-Gentleman*** and *Scapin the Schemer,* and his own version of ***George Dandin,*** have not sacrificed academic rigour to theatrical expediency. Maclean has preserved Gravely's awareness of the exigencies of the stage without falsifying the meaning of the original. Gravely's expression, which was probably somewhat archaic even at the time of composition,[8] has been rendered into modern prose. However, Maclean emphasises the timelessness of Molière's art in retaining, albeit with a glossary for the reader, Molière's allusions to contemporary society and culture.[9]

Halfway between *conservationist* and *moderniser,* Miles Malleson was one of the first of the postwar 'translators' to subject Molière's texts to the theatrical emendations appropriate to the English stage. A modern languages graduate, with access to the original French versions, Malleson debunked the notion that Molière's scripts were sacred texts, to which not one jot or tittle could be added and from which nothing could be taken away. Malleson kept to a large extent the French setting and plot but adopted a modern idiom. The dramatic movement was altered by repetitions, disruption of long speeches with laconic interjections from audiences on stage (indignant fathers, so-called *raisonneurs,* and impetuous children). Central traits of character were sharpened to give comic emphasis. (Like Molière, Malleson, as an actor-playwright, was not unmindful of the need to create good parts for himself!) Malleson's quite free adaptations of ***Sganarelle*** (1955), ***L'École des femmes*** (1954), ***Tartuffe*** (1950), ***Le Misanthrope*** (1956), ***L'Avare*** (1948), ***Le Bourgeois gentilhomme*** (1951) and ***Le Malade imaginaire*** (1959), would on occasion omit minor roles (for example, the lawyer in ***The School for Wives,*** 'Un Parent de sa Femme' and Villebrequin in ***Sganarelle***), or on occasion, add speeches and scenes (for example, the extra scene in ***The School for Wives,*** in which he dramatizes Horace's fall from the ladder). Malleson's ***Tartuffe,*** which takes the form of a play within a play, is an imaginative attempt to situate, in a theatrical and historical context, Molière's problematic five-act play. Malleson provides by way of preface an anachronistic reworking of scenes from ***L'Impromptu de Versailles,*** in which the King is seen interrupting a rehearsal in order to command a performance of ***Tartuffe.*** The visible presence of the Supreme Spectator throughout the latter spectacle prepares the audience for the panegyric to Louis which so many critics and directors have found embarrassing.[10]

Despite the modern idiom, Malleson's focus is rather traditional: his *imaginaire* is an entirely comic figure, misguided but not totally unlikeable. Malleson's work retained its popularity for about three decades, and even now, is a source for adaptors unfamiliar with the original French versions.

Recent *modernisers* have, however, been more bold. Two adaptations of ***L'Avare*** highlight the generic ambiguities which critics have discerned in Molière's text. Jeremy Sams's version, written for Stephen Pimlott's production at The National Theatre in 1991, has been described as a 'black comedy', or a 'white tragedy'. In both the translation and the production, Harpagon emerges as a 'financier for our times', rather than as the 'traditional pantaloon'. Sams's main innovation lies in his manipulation of registers. The ostentatiously low diction has justifiably been criticised for going beyond the verbal restraints recognised by even the most intemperate of Molière's rogues and obsessionals.[11] The vituperative lexis is, however, not gratuitously shocking, but is perhaps intended to intensify a linguistic contrast inherent in the original, namely between the worlds of romance and of money. The *confessio amantis* of both Élise and Valère, conveyed by Molière in exaggeratedly precious prose, is expressed by Sams in rhythmic verse, which at times creeps into rhyme (in Act I, scene i). Sams has further recourse to verse upon the entry of Anselme at the end of the play to denote the rise in emotional temperature. Critical opinion was extremely divided: 'Charnel-house Molière' cried Benedict Nightingale in *The Times* (11 May 1991); 'one of the best Molière productions I have seen anywhere, ever' was John Peter's retort in *The Sunday Times* (12 May 1991).

In Mike Alfreds's farcical modernisation of ***L'Avare*** (1990, for The Oxford Stage Company) the currency is updated to that of the single European Monetary System. The world of romance is conveyed by rhyming couplets. These preserve, albeit in a less subtle form, Molière's parody of the lovers' earnest protestations:

> I know I must do what I'm told
>
> Fathers know better because they're old
>
> Ignore this scandal
>
> Your father is the one we have to handle.

Alfreds's rendering is, as he styled it himself, 'a beggar's burlesque', with its origins in pantomime, or even, as one reviewer facetiously remarked, the 'Carry On Tradition'.[12]

The most influential *moderniser,* however, remains Tony Harrison, whose updating of ***The Misanthrope*** (1973) to De Gaulle's Paris of 1966, encouraged a radical reexamination of the presuppositions underpinning translation of Molière. Harrison condemned the almost 'fetishistic' belief in the fixity of the text:

> It seems to me that one could do worse than treat a translation as one does a décor or production as endlessly renewable.[13]

For Harrison, a translation is inextricably linked to a production. It is subject to endless emendations and updating, and has a limited lifespan. For ***The Misanthrope,*** Harrison's method was a collaborative one, incorporating insights from the producer John Dexter and from the principal actors; votes were taken to decide on the best readings where alternatives were given. The originality of Harrison's enterprise lay not solely in the topical transposition but also in the fusion of epigrams and colloquialisms, and in an eclectic versification:

> I have made use of a couplet similar to the one I used in *The Loiners,* running the lines over, breaking up sentences, sometimes using the odd half-rhyme to subdue the chime, playing off the generally colloquial tone and syntax against the formal structure, letting the occasional couplet leap out as an epigram in moments of devastation or wit. My floating *'s* is a way of linking the couplet at the joint and speeding up the pace by making the speaker deliver it as almost one line not two [. . .]. I have made use of the occasional Drydenian triplet, and, once in Act III, of something I call a 'switchback' rhyme, a device I derive from the works of George Formby [. . .].[14]

Some of his inventions are rather questionable, such as turning the 'tribunal des Maréchaux' into a midnight meeting of the Members of the French Academy at *Maxim's,* presided over by André Malraux; or assigning to Éliante, whose language in Molière is replete with abstract expressions, the occasional vulgarity: 'his monstrous mistress with enormous bubs'. However, as *The Times*'s reviewer acknowledged (16 March 1989), Harrison's translation set an unsurpassed standard in the reworking of French classics, 'combining the maximum idiomatic freedom with the severest metrical precision, and yielding strings of marvellous new jokes unknown to Molière but perfectly in keeping with his comedy'. But, as Harrison predicted, his work dated quickly. In the revival at the National Theatre in 1989, the play had slipped back into a 'comic never-never land'. De Gaulle's Paris was very different from that of Mitterand, and even from that of Giscard d'Estaing.

Nevertheless, Harrison raised the status of the translator to that of co-dramatist. The new direction was followed by John Fowles, the author of *The Collector, The Magus* and *The French Lieutenant's Woman,* and a former student of French literature at Oxford. His translation of ***Dom Juan,*** which, he claimed, was 'done with the help of one of my old Oxford professors', left an old London professor with some reservations:

> I can give John Fowles a mark of only alpha-double-minus stroke beta-plus [. . .]. There are some inadvertent mistranslations.[15]

Fowles's conception of the play was, however, highly innovative, as he indicated in an interview with John Higgins of *The Times* (6 April 1981):

> . . . ***Dom Juan*** is [. . .] about the use and abuse of language. I see Juan as a semiologist, a kind of early Roland Barthes.

Fowles's eponymous hero constructs and deconstructs the language of his interlocutors. His servant, Sganarelle also communicates on a higher verbal plane (for example, 'vous ne m'en aviez rien dit' is rendered by 'you hadn't vouchsafed me a clarification'; 'je vous dirai franchement' by 'I must tell you without circumloquacity').

Ranjit Bolt's 1987 version of ***Les Femmes savantes*** (entitled *The Sisterhood*) and his ***Tartuffe*** (1991) were also written under the sign of Harrison, whose ***Misanthrope*** had been an inspiration to Bolt since he first saw it at the Old Vic at the age of 15.[16] Topicality in *The Sisterhood* included: a discussion of deconstructionists leading to the *femmes savantes*'s rejection of Derrida, Lacan and Foucault; their adopting a Marxist response to Trissotin's poem; Ariste's reported luncheon with Raymond Barre; Martine's confusion of *decompose* and *deconstruct*; and the upgrading of Trissotin's violet-coloured carriage (the subject of his poem) to a purple Porsche.[17]

Bolt's ***Tartuffe*** evokes a new swaggartly-topical soteriology. The quasi-messianic pretensions of his Tartuffe are parodied by Cléante's ironic question as he watches Tartuffe pour out a glass of wine:

> Have you been sent to save us from sin?
>
> And what was the water before I came in?

Bolt's self-conscious rhyming, however clever and witty, tends to attenuate any satiric barbs implicit in the translation. In Sir Peter Hall's production in 1991 at The Playhouse Theatre, London, the actors were encouraged to end-stop each line, thus calling attention to the unconventional juxtapositions:

> I must say my [pause]
>
> Erotic tinder isn't half so dry.
>
> What earthly happiness is equated to [pause]
>
> The happiness of being loved by you.
>
> Look at him, he's totally besotted [pause]
>
> If there's Tartuffo-mania he's got it!

As for the third group of 'translators', the *post-modernisers* have transformed, or even severed links with, their French source. Their parentage may, paradoxically, be traced to the Restoration dramatists, who, like unwanted orphans were abandoned by eighteenth-century 'formalists' and nineteenth-century 'moralists'. These dramatists eschewed literal translation and adaptation. The most faithful among them tended to paraphrase Molière. The majority, however, perceived the need to transform their source to cater for the different tastes of English and French audiences. Molière's respect for the *bienséances* was found to be less appealing to seventeenth-century English audiences whose penchant for realism led dramatists to attenuate French stylisation and to lower the status of some of the characters.[18] In their search for theatrical elements likely to appeal to their public, Restoration dramatists often had little regard for the aesthetic coherence of the plays from which they pillaged. Very few Restoration comedies could, even loosely, be termed translations of Molière.[19] In fact, some compositions combined incidents from different plays.[20]

Into the category of *post-modernisers* may also be placed Neil Bartlett and Jatinda Verma. In Bartlett's version of ***Le Misanthrope*** (1988), the link with the French past is cut: the setting is Célimène's ritzy *pied à terre* in the newly-fashionable London Docklands. The Court of Louis XIV together with its power-crazed retinue has become the world of contemporary media chic, with its obsequious fashion followers. The cast is reduced to six (most probably for practical rather than for ideological reasons, there being only six actors in the Red Shift company for whom the play was written). Bartlett's Alceste is a waspish literary critic and journalist from North of the Border who finds himself isolated amongst the media moguls and the fashionable yuppie set. The *wearer o' the green* is referred to as *Tartan Teddie*. Oronte's role is expanded to include the speeches of the marquesses.

Bartlett has retained the twelve-syllable alexandrine, which gives metrical formality to his anachronistic licence. The adaptation, commended for an epigrammatic brilliance reminiscent of Oscar Wilde, is full of media jargon. Philinte's opening line 'Qu'est-ce donc?' is rendered by 'What's up doc?'; his justification of complacency, by: 'They're part of the package, part of being a man'. Oronte's sonnet, which is read off the back of a pack of Sobranies, becomes transfixed on the London underground:

> My love is like a Northern Line Station
>
> I get stuck on it [. . .].

The image is sustained:

> Being a man what should I do
>
> But tend upon the timetable of my desire.

Oronte's composition provokes a rare direct statement from Célimène: 'His mind is as bland as his verse'. Alceste's language too is invaded by the vulgarity of media-speak as well as by the lexis sometimes associated with his northern temperament. The linguistic lobotomy performed on Molière's *atrabilaire* is perhaps best illustrated in the 'translation' of Alceste's mock-heroic exit:

> Crippled by injustice, spat upon by shits,

> I'll book a one-way ticket out of this abyss.
>
> Trahi de toutes parts, accablés d'injustices,
>
> Je vais sortir d'un gouffre où triomphent les vices [. . .].

Molière's high moral discourse has to give way to the language of expediency and of commerce. This is the price for a 'Misanthrope for our times'!

Bartlett's ***School for Wives*** (written for the Derby Playhouse in 1990) transposes the French setting to modern-day Derby. Arnolphe is a smug Tory City Councillor, who mouths Thatcherite slogans on morality while at the same time keeping in a little house a black girl from a one-parent family (Molière's Agnès). Ethical questions in Molière are thus given by Bartlett an ethnic dimension.

Ethnicity is a key issue in Jatinda Verma's recreation of ***Tartuffe*** for the National Theatre in 1990. An out-of-favour Hindu Poet, Pandit Ravi Varma, is commissioned by a bigoted Muslim leader, the Moghul Emperor Aurangzeb (1618-1707) to provide a version of ***Tartuffe*** to mark the visit to the Indian Court of one of Molière's friends, the traveller François Bernier. *Tartuffe* is portrayed as a 'faking fakir' who flagellates himself in mock-repentance with scrunched-up dhoti, and who guzzles Indian delicacies while Organ's wife is grievously stricken with an attack of dum-dum fever.

In this play-within-a-play, the role of the translator is given self-conscious prominence. In his programme note, Jatinda Verma indicates that the translator's art entails transforming the original. In support of his argument he cites Salman Rushdie's notion of cultural identity:

> . . . [is] not the entire national culture based on the principle of borrowing whatever clothes [seem] to fit, Aryan, Mughal, British, take-the-best-and-leave-the-rest? (*The Satanic Verses*)

The written text of Verma's created translator is subjected to a significant emendation. His ending leaves Orgon and his family as penniless exiles. The Moghul Emperor requires, however, a flattering postscriptum which approximates to Molière's introduction of the Exempt. The *imperator ex machina* closure seems gratuitous. In fact, as Jim Hiley quipped in *The Listener* (8 March 1990), it is 'almost as if Salman Rushdie had renounced *The Satanic Verses*'. At one level, the 'phoney aesthetic' is politically subversive in its ironic presentation of the fundamentalist despot's censure of the poet's dénouement. At another level, Verma's invention reopens the debate over the *Ur-tartuffe* and invites fresh speculation with regard to Molière's original three-act composition in 1664.

In conclusion, let us assess briefly the significance of these adaptations for Molière studies. In the first place, the trend towards radical revisionism reflects the growing tendency in France to replace the authority of the text by that of the director. Even in recent translations in which there is a professed adherence to the text, there is a modification of setting (for example, Derek Mahon's ***School for Wives*** (1986) is set just before the July Revolution of 1830, with Arnolphe based in Avignon but aspiring to the nobility of Paris as represented by Horace and Oronte). It is not insignificant that a number of the 'translations' have been undertaken by theatrical directors, and for a particular company and production. Sometimes their work has been based on a translation and not on the original French version.[21]

Secondly, the mode of expression is becoming increasingly concrete and colloquial. Even John Fowles's literary rendering of ***Dom Juan*** contained 'frank twentieth-century terms in place of seventeenth-century decorum',[22] which caused purists no little disquiet. A new low verbal threshold was set by Jeremy Sams. However, to judge from reviews, this has already been lowered by the earthy, boisterous tone of Nick Dear's ***Le Bourgeois gentilhomme*** (National Theatre 1992). It will be interesting to follow the theatrical fortunes of Ian Maclean's revision of George Gravely's more high-flown translations, and of his own version of ***George Dandin.***

Thirdly, the divorce between stage and study is perhaps not as marked as it might appear. Though these adaptations obviously cannot be recommended as parallel texts, they give theatrical expression to debates in criticism: for example, the problematic ending of ***Tartuffe***; the comic possibilities offered by Molière's versification (a largely unexplored area in Molière studies); those seemingly embarrassing passages—for example, the first two scenes and the ending of ***L'Avare***; Cléante's long speeches in ***Tartuffe***; generic problems—for example, is ***L'Avare*** a comedy, a farce or a dark play, or all three things combined in a single aesthetic?

Finally, these adaptations raise fundamental questions with regard to the art of translating Molière for the English stage. Do the aesthetics of performance justify the sacrifice of accuracy? Should the preposition in the title of the translation be changed from *by* to *after* Molière? Should the authors discussed above be termed *traducers* or *translators?* Such questions cannot, however, be answered within the scope of this paper. It is sufficient to say that, however faithful the translation, if it is incapable of stimulating the theatrical imagination of director, actors and audience, it fails the litmus test of all drama. The works discussed pass the above test—sometimes with distinction. Yet, if I may have recourse to an old cliché, even some of the more traditionally orientated versions may be seen as a betrayal of the original. However, such betrayal is paradoxically a faithful one, if judged by the 'spirit' and not the 'letter' of Molière's dramaturgy. For the 'translators' are contributing to a revival of interest in Molière,[23] not least among a new generation of theatregoers, beyond whose philological grasp the original versions would otherwise perhaps forever lie.

Notes

1. *The Sunday Times,* 18 October 1987.
2. *The Daily Telegraph,* 31 March 1990.

3. *The Times,* 6 April 1981.
4. First published in 1876 (by William Paterson, Edinburgh) and revived in 1992 (by Dover Publications, New York).
5. See John Simon, 'Translation or Adaptation', in *From Parnassus: Essays in honor of Jacques Barzun,* edited by D. B. Weiner and W. R. Keylor (New York: Harper and Row, 1976), 147-57; Noël Peacock, *Molière in Scotland* (Glasgow: University of Glasgow French and German Publications, 1993), pp. 43, 75-76, 121-22, 139, 180.
6. Tony Harrison, 'Molière Nationalized', *Revue d'histoire du théâtre* (1973), 169-86 (p. 169).
7. John Gross's commendation in *The Sunday Telegraph* (12 December 1993) is consistent with that of other reviewers: Michael Billington, *The Guardian* (10 December 1993): 'Richard Wilbur's sprightly translation'; the drama critic of *The Independent* (15 December 1993): 'Richard Wilbur's enjoyably inventive translation'; George Craig, *TLS,* 4733 (17 December 1993): 'Richard Wilbur's translation is assured and sensitive. There are some memorable rhymes [. . .].'
8. Maclean considers the style somewhat similar to that of Restoration dramatists. Gravely's versions of *Les Précieuses ridicules, Le Médecin malgré lui* and *Les Fourberies de Scapin* were originally undertaken in 1916; his *L'Avare* in 1919. Gravely revised these translations in 1945, and added in 1948 translations of *Dom Juan* and *Le Bourgeois gentilhomme* (see Ian Maclean, *Molière: Don Juan and Other Plays* (Oxford: OUP, 1989), p. xxi).
9. For example, 'Trivelino', 'Aronce [. . .] Clélie', '*Cirrus the Great*', '*petit coucher*', 'Great Comedians', 'Perdrigeon', 'Gombaud and Macée'.
10. For further discussion of Malleson's adaptations see: J. Copley, 'On Translating Molière into English', *Durham University Journal,* 52 (1959-60), 116-24; Peacock, op. cit., pp. 9-10, 23-25, 60-61, 69-73, 117-18, 159-61, 192-93, 212-13.
11. See, for example: Stephen Bamforth, 'Reflections on the National Theatre's New *Miser* (9 May 1991)', *FSB,* 40 (Autumn 1991), 18-20: '. . . racy to be sure, but not quite the sort of thing you expect from French classical theatre, not even Molière's'; Malcolm Bowie, 'Greed's Epic Poet', *TLS,* 4598 (17 May 1991): 'A small blemish, perhaps, in a production where such all-in gusto often works well but Molière's writing deserves better than this'.
12. Charles Spencer, *The Daily Telegraph,* 31 March 1990.
13. Harrison, art. cit., p. 172.
14. Harrison's introduction to *The Misanthrope* (London: Rex Collings, 1973), p. vi.
15. John Weightman, *TLS,* 4072 (17 April 1981).
16. See Robert Gore Langton's interview with Ranjit Bolt in *The Times,* 4 June 1990.
17. See the review in the *TLS,* 4420 (18 December 1987) by Maya Slater.
18. For example, in Wycherley's *The Plain Dealer,* Molière's sophisticated *coquette,* Célimène, is vulgarised into the unambiguously promiscuous Olivia; *l'homme aux rubans verts* is transformed into a coarse, blustering sailor.
19. There are only five generally accepted translations: Sir William D'Avenant's *Sganarelle* in *The Playhouse to be Let,* John Dryden's *Amphitryon,* Thomas Otway's *The Cheats of Scapin,* Thomas Medbourne's *Tartuffe or the French Puriton,* and Sir John Vanbrugh's *The Mistake.*
20. The eclecticism of the Restoration dramatists can be seen in Edward Ravenscroft's *Scaramouch,* which brings together elements of *Le Mariage forcé, Les Fourberies de Scapin* and *Le Bourgeois gentilhomme,* or in his *Mamamouchi,* which was based on *Le Bourgeois gentilhomme* and *Monsieur de Pourceaugnac.*
21. For example, Jatinda Verma openly acknowledged in his programme note that his *Tartuffe* was based on a translation from the French by Philippe Cherbonnier.
22. See Weightman, art. cit.
23. See, for example, the number of performances since 1989 in London, a theatrical centre previously regarded as unpropitious to productions of Molière: 1989—*Le Misanthrope* (Neil Bartlett, Young Vic), *The Misanthrope* (Tony Harrison, National); 1990—*The Miser* (Mike Alfreds, Young Vic), *Tartuffe* (Jatinda Verma, National), *Tartuffe* (David Bryer, Palace [Watford]); 1991—*The Miser* (Jeremy Sams, National), *Tartuffe* (Ranjit Bolt, Playhouse); 1992—*Le Bourgeois gentilhomme* (Nick Dear, National); 1993—*The School for Wives* (Richard Wilbur, Almeida).

Larry W. Riggs (essay date 1994)

SOURCE: "Desire, Disclosure, and Power: Molière's Unmasking of Hegemonic Ideology," in *Romance Languages Annual,* Vol. 6, No. 1, 1994, pp. 144-50.

[*In the following essay, Riggs discusses the relationships between desire, discourse, and the institutionalized world as presented in Molière's comedies.*]

> . . . the ocularcentrism of modernity, the hegemony of vision, the the installation of the reign of the despotic eye, is also a verbocentrism, the consciousness of the book, and an egocentrism, the consciousness of a separated, detached atom of individuality.—Robert D. Romanyshyn

In his *Jameson, Althusser, Marx,* William Dowling demonstrates that an ideological discourse contains a system of abstract rules and implies a system of concrete institutions. I would argue that such a discourse is, in fact, constituted by the ambition or desire to produce such a system of institutions, such a social and cultural *world.* The discourse and the institutions constitute, legitimate, and perpetuate one another. I will attempt to persuade you that it is just this relationship among desire, discourse, and an institutionalized world that is at issue in Molière's major comedies. A concretized, materialized discourse is an institutionalized desire, an ambitious hallucination transformed into a social world. This definition enables us to see that, for Molière, it is important to denounce ideological ambitions that aim to institutionalize a kind of ventriloquism: a hegemony, in the etymological sense, in which all voices are instruments of the single, central voice of power.

According to Jean Duvignaud, "La dérision trouble la cohérence des systèmes, des structures, et la gravité des observateurs" (11). If Molière's major comedies lampoon his *ridicules'* absolutist ambitions, it is, at the same time, because that is the vocation of comedy and because Molière and his contemporaries lived the establishment of a modern culture driven by desire for abstraction, universalization, and institutionalization. In effect, as I have argued elsewhere ("Intimations"), Molière's comedy tries to do what post-modernist thought mandates: demolishing closures, creating in meaning systems openings that prevent epistemological sclerosis, studying the motives that drive representation, making of language itself the main focus of critical consciousness. Signification, as a function of desire and power, is always at the heart of Moliéresque drama. In the period when modern culture's hegemony was establishing itself, Molière contested the major codes of that modernity (see Vernet).

The "idées souverainistes," in Robert Mandrou's phrase (39), which the *ridicules* have in common with the real absolutists of the time, like their reflexive repression of dissent, reflect absolutist rationalism's ruthless hostility to cultural resistance. Reason, in the modern, universalist sense, is fundamentally paranoid: as a function of the will to universalization, it is obliged to fear all particularities. The quest for complete mastery of nature, the attempt to construct a world reflecting and supporting a whole and transcendental self, is illusory and perpetuates fear (Albanese). The dystopia that the *ridicules'* mad "cognitive utopia" (Tyler 132) would be, if it were realized, is inherent in modern civilization's epistemological imperialism. The *ridicule* is the repressed double of the transcendental Cartesian subject.

The desire to control, manipulate, and even re-create nature which modern, techno-scientistic culture and Molière's *ridicules* have in common, regards every manifestation of nature that escapes the totalizing generalizations of instrumental knowledge and normative discourse as an intolerable threat. The comic character who aspires to be the only subject of desire in his or her "realm" shares with absolutist monarchy and instrumentalist modernism this fear of all that is heterodox or plurivocal.

In the plays I study here, as in modern, pedagogico-therapeutic culture, a pedagogical imperative operates on the profoundest level. Molière forces us to recognize two dangerous aspects of the *ridicules'* desire to live in a world made by and of words: first, normative discourse hides the tyrannical preacher/pedagogues' motives and ambitions; second, the therapeutic, imperialistic attitude justified and imposed by such discourse creates a cultural environment wherein people will, in fact, have to live. Words are an important focus of comic scrutiny precisely because they can construct the world "hallucinated" by the would-be tyrant. As Benjamin Bennett puts it, one of comic theater's essential functions is to prevent excessive privileging of literary, textual signs (10).

From Arnolphe to Dom Juan and Alceste, from Harpagon to Monsieur Jourdain and Argan, Molière's *ridicules* want to be proprietors of a power legitimated and perpetuated by definitive knowledge. They are driven by fear and by desire for mastery. Each wants to be the sole transcendental subject of an unchallenged hegemony. Their megalomania is a refusal of drama, of the presence of the Other, of the absence that always gnaws away at dreams of absolutist plenitude. This absence and drama are present as the origin of fear and desire and as the ultimate message of the plays. Laughter recognizes and enacts these lacunae in our being and our knowledge: laughter reaffirms the primacy of the body; it is a physical act. By ending with laughter and, quite often, with a marriage and a feast, comedies celebrate appetite, openings, fertility (see Tobin). They show that control means closure, sclerosis, starvation, sterility. Pleasure and nourishment come to us in the form of exchanges through openings. To open one's mouth to laugh is to prepare for pleasure and nourishment, to acknowledge the inseparability of body and mind.

The *ridicules* always try to disguise their lust for power as devotion to principle, whether the principle be Arnolphe's *méthode,* Alceste's sincerity, the supposed ascetic idealism of the *femmes savantes,* or Orgon's religious zeal. Each wants to live in a world entirely structured by his or her normative discourse, while Molière undermines their project and celebrates their failure.

General discussion of appetite or desire in Molière leads to productive consideration of power and its legitimate or illegitimate uses as Molière sees them. The relation between power and pleasure is an important Moliéresque preoccupation. Consumption—of food, of words and texts, of flattery—is a pervasive theme. Molière's most energetic condemnation is reserved for those whose pleasure *is power.* As Ronald Tobin has recently emphasized, comedy is closely connected with the celebratory ritual of feasting. The conviviality of a feast, like that of a pluralistic society, is destroyed when the powerful seek pleasure by denying others access to pleasure.

Molière recognizes that the order of the social world is always linguistic and that language always expresses desires. He dramatizes tension between speech, or drama, and text. He understands the temptation to use words as privileged signifiers to establish power for the Self over the Other and to disguise the desire for power as devotion to principles. It is illuminating to see how often this drama turns on attempts to impose *text* as a means of escaping pluralistic, dramatic communication.

The relation between print and power has been studied in literary works from Rabelais and Cervantes to George Orwell and beyond. Here, obviously, I want to deal with Molière. The French comedian lived on the border between drama and literature and during the period of rapid centralization of French politics, language, and culture. Max Vernet has quite recently elucidated Molière's critique of the modernity emerging in his time. The plays dramatize a cultural battle that had begun in earnest one hundred fifty years earlier.

Theorists of absolutism, ambitious literary figures, and aggressively evangelical moralists throughout Western Europe recognized the power of print. In each case, the nation-building, absolutist project involved institutionalizing a national language, always a synthetic distillate of dialects; attacking regionalisms; and creating a professional class of writers, critics, and jurists whose expertise was in reading, writing, and inculcating the new language. Textualization of consciousness, or colonization of subjective "space" by authoritative discourses concretized in printed texts, is an important feature of early modern culture. Resistance to this process quickly came to be defined as perverse, as a threatening *otherness* obstructing the progress of Reason. Print, despite its impersonal appearance, has always been saturated with desire for power. Molière dramatizes and analyzes the kinds of personal fears and motives that drive attempts to engineer reality and consciousness and to stamp out unorthodox forms of discourse.

Molière's use of his own artistic voice involved him in a number of grave disputes. The adherents of *préciosité,* most notably Madeleine de Scudéry, were "scandalized" by ***Les Précieuses ridicules*** and managed to have that play banned for two weeks. Coming at the beginning of their career in Paris, that interdiction could have made it impossible for Molière's troupe to survive. A bit later, of course, the *parti dévot* succeeded in having ***Tartuffe*** banned. This crisis lasted five years. Most of the major plays analyze the effects of univocalist ideologies of conversion. They ridicule domestic hegemonies while underlining the analogies between those burlesque tyrannies and the reality of increasing cultural and moral authoritarianism in seventeenth-century France.

Molière's comic types are oblivious to the voice of their desire, which is audible to us in their discourse. They are oblivious, also, to the desire in the voices of those who flatter their ambition. The *femmes savantes,* like Orgon, in ***Le Tartuffe,*** are the dupes of their chosen authority figures precisely because they desire unquestioned authority for themselves. These would-be domestic tyrants want to transform complex, dramatic, familial networks, which resemble the feudal order, into absolutist entities, with all authority residing in a single figure and all "communication" going in one direction. Molière shows that absolutism would convert a family—or a society—into the collective equivalent of a single diseased personality: into a collective solipsism.

Terry Eagleton has said that "bourgeois dreams of transcendence tend to be foolish fantasies" (100). The learned ladies' abstractionist Utopia certainly qualifies as a foolish fantasy. In ridiculing it, however, Molière denounces the masked desire in all transcendentalist discourse. He also lampoons official aesthetics, or the organized production of taste, as a formula for repressive mediocrity. Taste is always desire cycled through and disciplined by a normative discourse. In the ladies' Utopia, *they* would control the discourse; that discourse would institutionalize their desires and interests.

Molière knows the implications of this. The play exposes the ladies' textual world as a palimpsest: their lust for power, prestige, and artificially intensified sexual enjoyment constantly *shows through* their immaterialist rhetoric. When hallucinations are successfully realized, they become dictatorships. This is exactly what the ladies have in mind. They define resistance as defectiveness. Their normative discourse is oppression disguised as therapy for the culturally defective.

Les Femmes savantes examines closely the way personal motives and physical desires can be disguised by transforming them into such normative language. The ladies' system is a method for acquiring power and prestige. They present it as an ascetic aspiration toward "higher" consciousness and an evangelical zeal to bring this consciousness to others. The ladies thus join in the classicist/*précieux* effort to control *eros* by encoding it in *logos*—to domesticate desire by controlling linguistic expression. Molière mocks this ambition as both unrealistic and hypocritical: language can only *disguise* desire. Normative language can hide, and serve, the pleasure of controlling others' access to pleasure. It cannot serve as a means to or expression of authentic transcendence. The body is always present as means and motive.

This purported mastery of emotion is part of classicism's effort to mask the consolidation of political power as cultural and psychological progress. This supposed "progress" toward mental control of physical impulses is both an instrument and a justification of some people's growing hegemony over others. Molière, like other writers from Rabelais to Orwell, is aware of the way language habits are used to validate political hierarchies. He was involved in hard, serious battles for cultural, and therefore for political, influence.

Préciosité, which subjects communication to a vocabulary of abstract words and rites, is a perfect example of what Bennett calls excessive privileging of literary language

(10). Desires are submitted to synthetic linguistic formulas; people try to speak like books. This discipline claims to civilize material interests and desires by denying them explicit expression. Its arbiters are writers and grammarians. Explicit references to desire are banished from *précieux* discourse. The supposed conquest of nature is thus inscribed in language itself. However, the conquest of nature is always in reality the conquest of certain elements of society by others. Molière shows how this ersatz transcendence of desire becomes an *instrument* of desire.

In their relations with the hack *précieux* poet, Trissotin, the ladies show an infantile reverence for the literary language they associate with the desired transformation of their status. They treat words as magical possessions, as talismanic objects capable of producing metamorphoses. In Act 3, scene 2, Trissotin answers the ladies' "prayers" by reciting some of his verses. The subtext of appetite in the ladies' attitude to Trissotin has already been betrayed by Bélise who, in the previous scene, says that the poems are "Repas friands qu'on donne à mon oreille" (line 716), and begs the poet: "Faites tôt, et hâtez nos plaisirs" (line 718). The ladies clearly intend to enjoy extreme pleasure while claiming the moral superiority of "ascetics" and blocking others' access to pleasure.

The words are status symbols, and their display is intended to weld this little group together and validate their superiority. The meal-metaphor—"Servez-nous promptement votre aimable repas" (line 746)—and the repeated sexual overtones—"On s'en meurt de plaisir" (line 810)—emphasize the physical basis of all motivation. Trissotin obviously succeeds by pretending to substitute literary signs for bodily needs and by marketing this technique as a status symbol. Molière portrays the ladies' *consumption* of the poem as a process of ventriloquism: their subjectivity is literally constituted from literary products even as they think of themselves as original. They ingest and regurgitate Trissotin's bookish words.

The fact that the poem is actually one by a real *précieux* scribbler of the time emphasizes the issue of textuality. The textual coincidence also emphasizes the issue of *reproduction* as a means of colonizing the consciousness of naïve language-consumers. The ladies' desire for power and prestige makes them the creatures of professional textualizers. Language is, in effect, using them to talk to itself and to achieve its own spread. Molière recognizes that the motives for a text's production and propagation always "show through." At the play's end, of course, Trissotin's own very material motives will be revealed.

After their ecstatic session with Trissotin, the ladies begin to speak of their plans for an Academy where *everything* will be taught. The foundation of this universalist institution will be their absolute control over language. Moreover, as they speak of their school, the language of power, already familiar in their speech, returns: "Vous verrez nos *status* quand ils seront tous faits" (line 920): "Nous serons par *nos lois* les *juges* des ouvrages. / Par *nos lois,* prose et vers, tout nous sera *soumis*" (lines 922-23; my emphasis). The self-idealizations of any dominant group are disguised and universalized through institutions, most notably through *schools.* The ladies' "aspirations" are really toward the exercise of a power whose legitimacy will be beyond question. This kind of power cannot be questioned because it is masked as impersonal idealism. In addition, it is impossible to question a power which is completely identified with the language in which complaints would have to be expressed and with the institutions where that language is taught. The ladies clearly aim at perfect power over the *subjective* experience of their "subjects." They hope to practice a "terroristic signification" much like that referred to by Jean Baudrillard (Poster 4).

It is evident that the ladies' desire for personal power motivates their "spiritualism." In her conflict with the cook, Martine, Philaminte asserts the independence of mind from *nourishment.* Molière argues that only those who inhabit a hallucinatory world *made of words* can assert the superiority of "spirit" over body. References to Vaugelas and Cotin emphasize that the ladies' world is constructed by and from texts. At the same time, Molière shows us that textual worlds are constructed in order to realize desires, and that the desires masked by attacks on desire are the most dangerous ones.

Tartuffe is another fascinating study of power and pleasure. The play attacks desire's disguises in their most impenetrable citadel: religion, morality, and preaching. Tartuffe himself is a crude figure whose physical appetites are rather obvious. He is *gros* and *gras.* He eats and drinks greedily. He uses the language of devoutness to pursue sexual ends. The play dissects the power-pleasure nexus on a more profound and more subversive level, however: speech, both in itself and as a means of reducing others to silence, is a source of *pleasure* for the tyrannical characters. Beginning with Madame Pernelle in the first scene, they constantly interrupt and pontificate. First Orgon, and then Tartuffe himself, are brought low by their excessive desire to express their power in language. Speech—and texts—are means of penetrating and consuming others. Competition for the privilege of manipulating signs is an extension of more physical conflicts.

The point here is that, if speech itself is both an expression and an extension of pleasure, then the ultimate hypocrisy is to *preach* asceticism to the silenced Other. Molière's long battle against the univocalist forces in seventeenth-century France is at its most intense in ***Le Tartuffe.*** The lust being unmasked is not merely that of a seedy, hypocritical buffoon; it is that of all authoritarian moralism.

In ***Tartuffe,*** Orgon and Madame Pernelle's relationship with Tartuffe parallels the learned ladies' fascination with Trissotin. From the beginning of the play, it is clear that language, power, and pleasure are at issue. Tartuffe is literally identified by Orgon with weighty, moralizing *texts*: Orgon recommends that his family, too fond of pleasure, read *La Fleur des saints,* a large book of moralizing clichés. Orgon's character parodies the dream of an all founding Word. Tartuffe's devoutness is a quasi-textual creation: it is made out of pious words and gestures. Molière makes us aware that *dévotion* is a performance. Like the learned ladies, then, Orgon has learned the "technique" of ignoring the biological, the bodily basis of all performances. The return, or revenge, of the body and of desire is fundamental in this play, too.

The desire for control is explicitly linked by Molière with Orgon's almost mystical respect for *documents.* Orgon is in a hurry to institutionalize his desires in the form of legally binding texts. He wants his *desire* to be the environment his family lives in. He has a marriage contract binding his daughter to Tartuffe, and a formal transfer of his wealth to Tartuffe, drawn-up. Orgon wants to institutionalize a new order chartered by authoritative texts and permitting him to escape from personal relations and obligations. He wants to disguise this desire for a world emanating from him as a quest for moral improvement. In fact, he is afraid of his family. He wants to imprison their subjectivity within legal, documentary walls and to take pleasure in blocking their pleasures.

Tartuffe corresponds rather nicely to the Church as legitimator of absolutist hegemony and to Louis XIV's militantly orthodox Jesuit counsellors. The battle for discursive dominance in Orgon's household reflects the one going on in France. Tartuffe provides both a source of religious discourse slanted to Orgon's advantage and a flattering mirror or double reinforcing Orgon's conception of himself as analogous to God. However, Tartuffe proves to be a palimpsest. Transcendentalist discourse thinly veils strong, earthy desires.

Orgon's eyes are opened to the truth about Tartuffe only when his ears are opened to the latter's *voice.* When Orgon hides under a table while Tartuffe is speaking with Orgon's wife, Elmire, Tartuffe's personal voice breaks through his pseudo-scriptural rhetoric. When he cannot see the mesmerizing representative of his *vision,* he is returned to the acoustic space of dramatic being. The eye is aggressive; it selects its objects and isolates or abstracts it from all context. Its focus is always *motivated.* However, in modernist culture, vision is identified with clarity and objectivity. The ear, on the other hand, can neither select its "object" nor close itself. That is why the illusory absolutist world of Orgon collapses only when, hidden under the table from where he can no longer see and be mesmerized by his idol, the dupe is forced to hear Tartuffe's voice.

Orgon's solipsistic universe evaporates when Orgon hears this voice, which expresses the desire of a rival. Orgon's mask falls off in the instant when Tartuffe's lust becomes *audible* to him. The motives behind Tartuffe's devout rhetoric show through when Tartuffe believes he is within reach of his object, which is *pleasure.* He is revealed as a competing *appetite.* The play-within-the-play thus has the same aim as the play proper: transcendentalist rhetoric is exposed as merely a mask for competitive desire. Orgon and Madame Pernelle, like the learned ladies, are first the dupes of their *own* desires disguised as a disinterested quest for "higher" reality. There can be no unmotivated quest, and no "transcendent" motives. The "gros et gras" Tartuffe could have been an honest Rabelaisian, but his effort to pass for a saintly ascetic leads to his downfall. The body takes its revenge, then, on both Orgon and Tartuffe. The hierarchical division of body and spirit, the model and basis for all other hierarchies, collapses.

Throughout ***Le Tartuffe,*** it is emphasized that language emanates from *bodies.* As it emerges from his body and tries to penetrate Elmire, Tartuffe's discourse makes it clear that his body is the motive as well as the means of his utterances. Language is a weapon and a symptom, not a transparent medium of truth.

Gorgibus, in ***Le Cocu imaginaire,*** also wants absolute power over his household. His method is to force his daughter to read moralizing texts. He specifically recommends Pibrac's *Les Quatrains, Les Tablettes de la Vie et de la Mort* by Matthieu, and the Spanish Dominican Luis de Granada's *Guide des pécheurs.* Gorgibus says to Célie that "si vous n'aviez lu que ces moralités, / Vous sauriez un peu mieux suivre mes volontés" (lines 39-40). Gorgibus's concern for Célie's soul is merely a mask for his will-to-power.

Gorgibus thus insists that Célie perfect her *submission to his will* by reading certain texts. He strongly resembles Arnolphe, the foolish tyrant of ***L'Ecole des femmes.*** Arnolphe's method, as he calls it, has the same goal as Gorgibus's: he wants to create a woman whose submission to his desire is perfect, whose very being is submission. Arnolphe wants to make himself entirely safe from infidelity, and he has educated Agnès with this goal alone in view. His technique is one of physical and mental incarceration. Agnès lives within the confines of Arnolphe's house, and he controls her access to people and experiences. As is the case for Gorgibus, a key to Arnolphe's technique for engineering a submissive woman is moralistic literature. Arnolphe and Gorgibus regard texts as the means to domesticate their female charges just as modern genetic engineers domesticate "wild," unpredictable genes by subjecting them to rewriting. The two types imitate religious proselytizers and rationalist universalizers in reducing problems to a matter of manipulating information

In Act 3, scene 2, Arnolphe has Agnès read from what he calls "un écrit important / Qui vous enseignera l'office de la femme" (lines 741-42). The book is *Les Maximes du Mariage.* The resemblance between this book—Agnès reads *ten* maxims—and the Ten Commandments was one of the reasons for the ***Querelle de L'Ecole des femmes.*** This scene begins with Arnolphe telling Agnès what he expects of her, and saying "imprimez-le-vous bien" (line 678). Arnolphe clearly expects that Agnès will be perfectly obedient because her subjectivity will be composed entirely of texts expressing the absoluteness of her obligation to him. His desire will be the force that creates her. He wants to use moralistic texts to engineer a subjectivity of subjection for Agnès, to control the way she allocates her attention, and to determine the nature of her experience.

The action of the play turns on Arnolphe's failure to control Agnès's access to communication from outside and to determine her production of words. As she voices her pleasure and desire, Arnolphe's textual "architecture" crumbles. Agnès gains control over the allocation of her attention, over her production and reception of language. Her liberation begins when she uses language to express *her* desires. Appropriately, she first does this through a *window*—the inevitable breach in Arnolphe's textual preserve.

Arnolphe's system of architectural and textual walls is intended to create and preserve his power over a woman. Like the learned ladies, he sees education as normalization and "feminization," as a process for creating—imprinting—the Other's subjectivity. He sees people with whom Agnès might come into contact as rival teachers. In berating her for her "infidelity," he says "Il faut qu'on vous ait mise à quelque bonne *école*" (line 1497; my emphasis). This is an inadvertent admission that Arnolphe really understands the relation between desire and moralism. He speaks like a moralizing book because he knows univocal control is threatened by rival discourses.

Another of Molière's characters who tries to speak like a book is Dom Juan: "vous parlez tout comme un livre," Sganarelle says to his master, in the opening scene of ***Dom Juan.*** Much of this play's comedy, and much of its meditation on power, turn on the linguistic differences between Sganarelle and Dom Juan. Sganarelle, like Martine, the cook in ***Les Femmes savantes,*** is superstitious and uses language like a peasant, while his master speaks the language of rationalism. To speak like a book is to reproduce orally the conventions of a written code. This gives to speech the air of having a source "above" the level of personal, dialogic communication and desire. Speech that seems to be like a text thus has authority no one would be willing to accord to a mere personal voice. Power's service to appetite is disguised as normative discourse. In Dom Juan's case, the reality of power is always discernible under the pretense of reason.

Dom Juan is not really rational: others' acceptance of his "arguments" depends on his power in the social system, not on his persuasiveness. His intelligence and reasonableness are no more at issue than is his personal attractiveness. In terms of both *eros* and *logos,* he trades on his social advantages. Molière thus suggests that rational communication is in a problematical relation with the exercise of power. He would agree with Jürgen Habermas that real community will be realized only when there is unlimited speech, free from constraint by the dominance of ideology or neurosis (xvii).

Dom Juan's major characteristic, and the essence of "speaking like a book," is, then, his refusal of *dialogue.* Sganarelle's speech is deformed in at least two ways by his master's discourse of power: first, Sganarelle consciously avoids the kind of coherence that would make him Dom Juan's discursive *rival;* secondly, his oral, folkloric discourse is unable to match Dom Juan's bookishness in a society that has already decided to sanctify the superstition of Reason above all others. Thus, Sganarelle is obligated to *pretend* to be more ignorant than he is. Dom Juan's dominance has nothing to do with possessing "truth"; it suffices that he possesses *power.* No satisfactory dialogue can develop in this situation. Being and drama can reassert themselves only through Dom Juan's complete destruction.

The marginalizing, or silencing, of plurivocality (see Gaines) is clearly an extremely important issue in ***Dom Juan.*** Molière's own voice had been silenced by powerful figures in seventeenth-century France. The servant's obligatory inarticulateness and caution in expressing quite appropriate thoughts mirror Molière's own situation. Dom Juan refuses to listen to Sganarelle's indirect warnings, and his refusal has disastrous results. The nobleman resembles the powerful in France who tried to silence Molière rather than heed his warnings about their abuses. Molière, who played the part of Sganarelle, speaks "through" the character when the latter says that "la crainte en moi fait l'office du zèle, bride mes sentiments, et me réduit d'applaudir bien souvent à ce que mon âme déteste" (Act 1, scene 1). From inside his partial disguise as Sganarelle, then, Molière meditates on the effects of discursive tyranny. The connection between this play and ***Tartuffe*** becomes explicit when, in Act 5, Dom Juan becomes a religious hypocrite.

Molière denounces discursive monopoly. He carefully, "inarticulately," mocks *his* masters as he plays the part of a servile but worried valet whose discourse is interrupted, distorted, or silenced by a master who ignores very sensible warnings. Dom Juan does, in effect, precisely what Molière's enemies had done by banning ***Tartuffe.*** Like Sganarelle's disjointed speeches, this play says what the interdiction of ***Le Tartuffe*** prevented Molière from saying more directly.

By converting his "nobility," insofar as nobility is supposed to have a moral dimension, into an imposture, Dom Juan has undermined the whole social system's credibility. Hegemonic power undermines its own basis. It also destroys the mutuality that, finally, even the most powerful need if their power is to have any real meaning. Molière attacks, through the story of Dom Juan, the univocalism of French absolutism. His own difficulties were a direct consequence of the period's increasing moral and cultural authoritarianism.

In the universe of ***Dom Juan,*** we can already see what Rousseau will denounce as the detachment of desire from real physical needs. Such detachment, and Molière sees this as clearly as Rousseau will, produces a generalized, insatiable desire. This desire characterizes modern civilization which was, in Molière's time, already on the way to becoming the civilization of consumption. It is only on the level of abstraction that desire can be unlimited, and Dom Juan is as much an abstractionist as any *femme savante.* Their semiotic voracity makes these characters into signs devouring other signs. We have seen this clearly in the scenes where the learned ladies metaphorically "devour" Trissotin's poem. When Dom Juan decomposes the peasant girl Charlotte's body into a set of partial objects in order to admire it more eloquently (Act 2, scene 2), he makes her into a sort of pretext for a rhetorical exercise; by changing her body into a collection of words, Dom Juan disguises his desire as literature. By doing this, he transforms himself into a machine for manufacturing verbiage. By talking like a book, Dom Juan masks his own corporal substance. All of his substance will be consumed by the flames of a generalized desire which Molière disguises as divine retribution.

I hope it is evident that we would benefit from applying these ideas to other Molièresque plays. In ***Le Misanthrope,*** Alceste is an excellent example of the old alliance between light and power (Riggs "Optics"). That alliance, which is fundamental to the origins, in Greek thought, of modern epistemological imperialism (Blumenberg 46), is at the heart of Alceste's identification of control with an independent, definitive perspective. After all, it is Alceste who echoes Descartes by saying that "Les doutes sont fâcheux plus que tout autre chose" (line 1122) and who wants to be told only "ce qu'avec clarté l'on peut me faire voir" (line 1124). Arsinoé plays the Mephistophelean role we have seen Tartuffe and Trissotin playing when she assures Alceste that she will give him "une pleine lumière" (line 1126) on Célimène. Célimène thus becomes, in my opinion, the archetype of the object of a knowledge which wills itself to be absolute and objective. Alceste's rhetorical devotion to sincerity is a mask for his desire to possess the object of his invasive knowledge. Like the other *ridicules,* Alceste attempts to construct for himself a transcendental subjectivity justifying a therapeutic attitude toward others. It is also important to note that, like the other major *ridicules,* Alceste identifies power with text: he believes he possesses Célimène definitively when Arsinoé has given him what she claims Célimène has *written* (see Riggs "Purloined").

In his analysis of ***Le Misanthrope,*** Vernet says that "Célimène . . . avec les autres pervertisseurs de signes . . . complètent la galerie de ceux qui espèrent une récompense du travail d'indifférenciation qu'ils font subir aux mots ou aux choses" (263). Célimène's art is that of writing caricatural portraits. Nothing could be more abstract than such caricatures: they fix living beings in the immobility of texts and make definitive the angle of vision of their composer. Célimène wants to be the privileged reader, and thus the writer, of her world. Her desire, as much as that of Alceste, is unmasked by the play.

In ***L'Avare,*** Harpagon's disordered appetite for gold, that paradoxical substance which seems to materialize the abstract value of money, is so closely related to death that he is obliged to *bury* the object of his desire. He will be unable to enjoy the feast that closes the play and defeats his effort to starve all who have lived under his power.

Whether literally or figuratively, all of Molière's *ridicules* are forced to perform the comic pirouette, that ineluctable performance which, along with laughter, returns the body to its rightful prominence. Molière never stops reminding us that the most "rational" universalism derives its imperialistic energy from personal, material desires. He reminds us, in other words, that culture is the materialization of motives, of desires, and that every human activity is a performance. No performance is disinterested.

Molière forces us to face the anxiety engendered by awareness that the ridiculous aspiring transcendental ego is the reflection of our own personal and cultural ambitions. This is what Orgon experiences when he hears Tartuffe's lust in his speech and what we experience in laughing at our lust for control. Molière's comedy, just as much as the Freudian unconscious, subverts the would-be definitive language of the Subject. The comic pirouette sketches the emptiness at the center of Being; it and the laughter it provokes acknowledge the encounter between desire and its limits.

There is a body in every costume, just as it is always a body that speaks and writes. Although we have increasingly identified knowledge and power with vision and reading, desire always has a *voice.* The petty domestic tyrannies ridiculed and undermined by Molière are would-be copies of real absolutism, whose ubuesque core it is, in my view, Molière's purpose to show. The domain each *ridicule* would like to dominate would be constituted and sustained by a normative univocality, an unquestionably legitimate hegemony. The *ridicule* wants to be the master and proprietor of a world that would be, in fact, nothing more than the materialization of that desire.

Finally, comedy shows us that chance, gaps, and openings are our "salvation." Nourishment—intellectual or physical—comes to us only through openings. Closure is famine. Our visualist, transcendentalist, textualist epistemology, which defines knowledge as a kind of technique bestowing the power to manipulate the world, ties us to the *ridicules.* It is only by accepting—indeed, by *celebrating*—the unmasking of the desires that constitute and perpetuate that epistemology that we can see pleasure and mutuality, nourishment and surprise, are inseparable.

Works Cited

Albanese, Ralph, Jr. *Le Dynamisme de la peur chez Molière: une analyse socio-culturelle de Dom Juan, Tartuffe, et L'Ecole des femmes.* Jackson: University of Mississippi Romance Monographs, 1976.

Bennett, Benjamin. *Theater as Problem: Modern Drama and Its Place in Literature.* Ithaca: Cornell UP, 1990.

Blumenberg, Hans. "Light as Metaphor for Truth." Levin 30-62.

Clifford, James, and George Marcus, eds. *Writing Culture: The Poetics and Politics of Ethnography.* Berkeley: U of California P, 1986.

Dowling, William. *Jameson, Althusser, Marx: An Introduction to the Political Unconscious.* Ithaca: Cornell UP, 1984.

Duvignaud, Jean. *Le Propre de l'homme: histoires du rire et de la dérision.* Paris: Hachette, 1985.

Eagleton, Terry. *The Function of Criticism: From the Spectator to Post-Structuralism.* London: New Left Books, 1984.

Gaines, James F. *Social Structures in Molière's Theater.* Columbus: Ohio State UP, 1984.

Habermas, Jürgen. *Legitimation Crisis.* Trans. Thomas McCarthy. Boston: Beacon, 1975.

Levin, David Michael, ed. *Modernity and the Hegemony of Vision.* Berkeley: U of California P, 1993.

———. "Introduction." Levin 1-29.

Mandrou, Robert, *L'Europe absolutiste: raison et raison d'état 1649-1775.* Paris: Fayard, 1977.

Molière, Jean-Baptiste Poquelin. *Oeuvres complètes.* Paris: Garnier Frères, 1966-69.

Poster, Mark. ed. *Jean Baudrillard: Selected Writings.* Stanford: Stanford UP, 1988.

Riggs, Larry W. "Another Purloined Letter: Text, Transparency, and Transcendence in *Le Misanthrope.*" *The French Review* 66.1 (October 1992): 26-37.

———. "Intimations of Post-Structuralism: Subversion of the Classicist Subject in *Les Femmes savantes and Le Tartuffe.*" *Literature, Interpretation, Theory* 2 (1990): 59-75.

———. "The Optics of Power and the Hazards of Judgment in Molière's *Le Misanthrope.*" *Nottingham French Studies* 18.2 (October 1979): 1-13.

Romanyshyn, Robert D. "The Despotic Eye and Its Shadow: Media Image in the Age of Literacy." Levis 339-60.

Tobin, Ronald W. *Tarte à la crème—Comedy and Gastronomy in Molière's Theater.* Columbus: Ohio State UP, 1990.

Tyler, Stephen. "Post-Modern Ethnography: From Document of the Occult to Occult Document." Clifford and Marcus 122-40.

Vernet, Max. *Molière: côté jardin, côté cour.* Paris: Nizet, 1991.

James F. Gaines (essay date 1996)

SOURCE: "Molière and Marx: Prospects for a New Century," in *L'Esprit Createur,* Vol. XXXVI, No. 1, Spring, 1996, pp. 21-30.

[*In the following essay, Gaines delineates the connection between Marx and Molière.*]

Of all the avatars of structuralism that fueled the critical imagination during the third quarter of this century, none now seems more doomed than Marxism. The social-philosophical colossus that once commanded respect from worldwide scholars (in many cases, all too literally) finds itself banned in Russia, micro-miniaturized in Western Europe, and forgotten like a dimestore turtle in Asia, as Deng Chaiao-Ping uses his last breath to revive the merchant class and Castro holds photo-ops with the *Chevaliers du taste-vin.* The former reverend fathers of leftist thought, like Louis Althusser, and their fellow travelers, including Sartre and Foucault, are bespattered with the shame of little murders, club-footed deceptions, and careless propagation not of revolution, but of the AIDS virus. Yet at the very time when Marxism seems to have attained its absolute nadir, there may be some sense in examining a kind of intellectual counter-investment strategy, returning to see if there are any salvageable elements amid the rubble of its once-proud towers.

To recapitulate historically—for that, after all, was one of its great watchwords—the impetus for Marxist criticism of seventeenth-century literature did not come primarily from Marx himself, whose literary pronouncements are mainly limited to cryptic passages in the *German Ideology,* where notions about the secondary role of literature as a product of ideology are associated with an odd collective concept of the process of early modern artistic creation.[1] Nor were seventeenth-century studies much indebted to Engels, nor Lenin, nor even Revolutionary-era writers like Gorky or Mayakovsky, whose views were largely framed by the dichotomy between decadence and utilitarian futurism, but to Stalinist-era thinkers like Boris Porchnev.[2]

Although mainly a social historian, Porchnev influenced subsequent Marxist images of the century of Louis XIV by laying down the broad outlines of class struggle, in which authoritarian monarchs played off a haughty, but extravagant and ineffectual nobility against a greedy bourgeoisie, with the help of a nefarious and frequently homicidal clergy, while all of the above exploited a downtrodden mass of peasants. One problem with the official party line was that it left little room for literature, since writing was lumped together with the rest of art as a frivolous superstructural indulgence or worse, and the "popular" element in seventeenth-century literature was so restricted that even highly motivated communists seldom bestirred themselves to seek it out.[3] In light of recent historical research, we also know today that much of Porchnev's paradigm was faulty: even the peasant revolts which he highlighted, far from anticipating proletarian action, were more often than not fomented by nobles or burghers and grafted onto concepts of a (horrors!) religious or spiritual nature. More creative readings than Porchnev's were, it is true, being formulated by marginalized leftists such as Bakhtin and Bulgakov, but their works would have to await the end of the Stalin, and in some cases Khrushchev, eras before becoming widely known, even in the communist world.

It is significant that the greatest opus of Marxist literary structuralism, Lucien Goldmann's *Le Dieu caché* (Paris: Gallimard, 1959), adopted a much more subtle "genetic" approach that sought to link class origins indirectly with intellectual expression through the mediating factor of ideology, which he called "la vision du monde." Unfortunately, Goldmann's fascination with Pascal's and Racine's participation in the Jansenist experience led him to a tenuous association between the relatively restricted ranks of the *trésoriers de France* and a much broader pietistic movement. One wonders what would have become of genetic structuralism if Goldmann had focussed his efforts on Molière instead. As it was, the prevalent Marxist voice on Molière became that of the crypto-Stalinist John Cairncross, who strove to identify the playwright as an eminent bourgeois libertine. Without really intending to, Cairncross's argument reverted to the positions of nineteenth-century positivists and Catholic revivalists such as Brunetière and Faguet. His method consisted of classification by association, insisting that, since Molière consorted with known libertines such as Bernier and Chapelle, he was consequently a libertine himself.[4] As for the case for Molière the skeptic, it was developed far more convincingly by Robert McBride, without the straitjacket of early proletarian ideology.[5] Nevertheless, Cairncross's image of a socially active dramatist firing off volleys against the reactionary clergy and sneaking in a few potshots at neo-feudalism was exciting and played to the popular-culture revisionist view of a century full of lusty musketeers and Capitaine Fracasses. The perdurable power of this myth can still be seen not only in the media adaptations of Ariane Mnouchkine (including her film *Molière*) and Roger Planchon, but also most recently in the film, *la Reine Margot.*

Cairncross's principal obstacle was the same bourgeois misdefinition that tripped up Goldmann, but instead of an overly narrow view of the bourgeoisie, his became far too vague and anachronistic. For Cairncross, Molière belongs by birth to a "bourgeoisie commerçante et industrielle" (39), despite the fact that his family and its milieu were neither *commerçante* in the seventeenth-century sense of the word, nor in any way industrial, but had roots instead in both the shopkeeper stratum and in the realm of the *officers,* by virtue of his father's (and later his own) venal post of *tapissier du roi.* More importantly, however, he was bourgeois because he was fundamentally anti-noble. In his haste to counter Bénichou's ideas about Molière as spokesman for a worldly court *morale,* Cairncross exaggerates the playwright's castigation of bogus *anoblis* like Arnolphe, George "Monsieur de la Dandinière" Dandin, and "Monseigneur" le Mamamouchi Jourdain into a full-scale campaign against social mobility through office-holding (57-58). Such a broad condemnation is necessary to the thesis that Molière despised all *gentilshommes,* whoever they may be or strive to be. This fault is all the less excusable because of the concurrent research revelations of the Annales school of historians.

Far more complex and detailed than the model of seventeenth-century dynamics developed by party-line Marxism, the concepts of the Annales school were ironically developed by a method that went straight back to Marx's original economic analysis, with a careful attention to the interaction between social standing, power, and financial/market function. Their findings, especially represented in the works of Roland Mousnier, Pierre Goubert, and Fernand Braudel, reveal a society arranged not on the theoretical models of (mainly) endogamous medieval orders or money-based Marxist proletarian/bourgeois divisions, but on a minutely graduated system of *états, conditions* or *dignités* that featured both limited exogamy and limited mobility. On the one hand, local loyalties of family, extended *parentèle,* and rural or municipal bodies were far more important in determining identity and behavior than any of the more sweeping categories that began to emerge in the eighteenth century. However, collective concerns maintained a delicate balance with a more (but rarely exclusively) personal drive for land and office-holding. Thus, there was no easy Cartesian graphing along bourgeois/proletarian axes for the seventeenth-century Frenchman, who always had to be careful to weigh appetite against obligation and to beware of a vast plurality of Others ready to judge his slightest actions. The mentality of this largely pre-capitalist *société des états* permeates Molière's works and resists, to some degree, all attempts at recuperation by more recent ideological systems.

Beginning in 1963, the same year that Cairncross's and Porchnev's books were published in Paris, the publishing house of Éditions Sociales began a series of individual Molière plays with introductions featuring leftist viewpoints. These rather divergent studies often present more subtle analyses than the Cairncross paradigm.[6] For instance, the treatment of ***Le Misanthrope*** by Édouard Lop and André Sauvage (1963) links bourgeois and aristocratic influences, as well as the author's personal peculiarities, in the formulation of *honnêteté* appearing in that play. However, the tendency to present each play as a battleground of distinct, exterior social forces, more or less in the manner of a collectivist *roman à clef,* yields very mixed results. Suzanne Rossat-Mignod's notion of a progressive feminism in ***L'École des femmes*** (1964) would probably not pass muster by standards of today's feminist criticism, and the politically timely allusions in the introduction to ***Les Femmes savantes*** by Jean Cazalbou and Denise Sevely (1971), though published seven years later, are even more far-fetched. Rossat-Mignod's reading of ***Tartuffe*** (1970) succeeds mainly in beating the dead horse of a-historical interpretation, while failing to articulate the play with the unique dilemma of the *officier* groups in the mid-1660's. Guy Leclerc's disappointing presentation of ***Dom Juan*** (1968) is so closely tied to a celebration of the eponym's allegedly exemplary libertinism that it reduces the rest of the cast to truncated representative types.

It is significant, if not ironic, that the Éditions Sociales series, always more influential in the realms of French popular culture than in scholarly circles, ceased in 1971, at the very moment when a pointedly leftist version of Molière was dominating the theatre. Patrice Chéreau's ***Dom Juan*** and Roger Planchon's ***Tartuffe*** were the most acclaimed of a sequence of loosely Marxist interpretations that had begun about ten years earlier. Strongly imprinted by the "spirit of '68," these stagings framed the plays as confrontations between subversion (the title characters) and repression (Church and State). Supported by ingenious set designs and compellingly emotional acting that often made one forget one was watching what had ideologically become a *pièce à thèse,* these productions also had the good fortune to emerge at a point in theatrical history where the intensity of ritual (eventually culminating in Ariane Mnouchkine's productions) was displacing long-prevalent notions of character and plot, a conjuncture that actually gave their inconsistencies a certain positive value. Subsequent, sometimes more thoughtful productions of these masterpieces, such as the 1978-79 Comédie-Française and 1981 National Theatre versions of *Dom Juan,* have suffered somewhat by comparison with the lingering *éclat* of the Chéreau and Planchon plays, with the result that much directorial effort has been veering toward texts that had formerly languished in relative neglect, such as ***George Dandin, Les Fourberies de Scapin,*** and ***L'Avare.***

Working on the basis of research by earlier critics such as Lionel Gossman, Jacques Guicharnaud, Judd Hubert, and Jean Alter, a group of North American critics came forward during the 1970's and 1980's to apply Annales thinking to the social analysis of Molière. Works of this group include Ralph Albanese's *Le Dynamisme de la peur chez Molière,* my own *Social Structures in Molière's Theater,* Harold Knutson's *The Triumph of Wit,* Larry Riggs's *Molière and Plurality,* and Max Vernet's *Molière, côté cour, côté jardin.* Though there is a tremendous range of difference in these books with respect to critical values and the interpretation of the plays, they all strive in large measure to present social interpretations that break free of the predetermined party-line Marxist grid and that appreciate the diversity and internal contradictions of the seventeenth-century bourgeoisie as dynamic forces in the texts.

While often employing what would popularly be considered "Marxist" vocabulary and methods of determining social affiliation, the North American sociocritical school treats many central axioms of Marxism as problems rather than as established facts. These problematical topics include the determining influence of material status over consciousness, the existence of a coherent hegemonistic superstructure, the function of money within a production system based on surplus value, the notion of "class" itself as a valid operant classification, and the various historical and anthropological explanations given for these phenomena by Marx and his followers. All are concerned with the ambiguities of representation in a canon as socially rich and diverse as Molière's, and the general trend among them is to reject one-dimensional assessments of authorial intentionality on either side of the traditional Marxist class barrier, thus subscribing fully neither to Bénichou's Molière *aristocrate mondain,* nor *to Cairncross's Molière bourgeois militant.* The North Americans share a view of an effervescent social structure in the process of rapid evolution, where identity had to be constantly reaffirmed and redefined by contextual reaction and where the most fundamental terms, such as bourgeois, *roturier,* or *noble* were subject to historically and socially variable interpretations. Moreover, the very existence of the individual becomes an ongoing drama that finds natural expression on the theatrical stage.

North American sociocritics have also succeeded where many old-fashioned Marxist critics failed, in establishing a basis for understanding the polyphony in Molière's (and indeed almost any) comic theater. Cairncross's analyses, for instance, revived the outmoded figure of the *raisonneur* in a slightly different guise, with Dom Juan and Alceste as social critics instead of Sganarelle and Philinte as social defenders. This was necessary because Marxism postulates a single (even if collective), authoritative (even if against the perceived social authority), militant voice in any worthwhile (non-decadent) work of art. The North Americans attempt in very divergent ways to distinguish the separate voices in a work and to interrelate them, harmoniously or not, as the overall shape of the work demands. In Albanese's work, this exploration is organized around the provocation, reception, or rejection of fear, for fear is never a singular phenomenon, and its plural aspects are highlighted by the political tenor of Albanese's analysis. In my *Social Structures,* the polyphonic emphasis was on a qualitatively differentiated hierarchy, and particularly on the discordances created when changes unsanctioned by the hierarchical whole disrupted the relationships between existing groups within the system. Knutson's work incorporates social polyphony with his earlier archetypal research to study the historical development of Molièresque forms as they mutate into British Restoration comedy, focusing on the multifaceted issue of deception and *duperie* (I would further maintain that his conclusions are applicable to French comedy of the last quarter of the century as well). Riggs articulates a junction with several important features of deconstructive theory as he shows how Molière systematically resists the formation of any univocal discourse. Vernet, for his part, adopts the viewpoint that a Molière "play" is in reality a very complex philosophical game, where the fate of the hand depends on the interaction of multiple players.

Although this school has opened numerous perspectives for a post-Marxist age, no treatment of our subject would be even nearly complete without a discussion of Jacques Derrida's *Specters of Marxism.*[7] It is a strikingly un-Marxist assessment of the topic, one which deals with what is basically materialistic in an eminently symbolic way, a deconstructive autopsy that takes place in the absence of a *corpus delicti,* that is, mainly without consideration of past or present socio-politico-economic contexts.[8]

Derrida's book is based on a rather tricky philosophical triple play: Shakespeare to Hegel to Marx to Valéry. From time to time one catches a glimpse of Walter Benjamin roaming in this strange infield like an extra shortstop; Derrida draws heavily upon his wonderful formula of the *Schein des Scheinloses* (even making its translation, "the appearance of the inapparent," the title of his final chapter!), without, as far as I can determine, ever fully crediting his Judeo-German teammate. (Benjamin himself would no doubt merely have heaved a sigh at this little ellipsis—*il en a vu d'autres.*) Marx, not quite completely dead yet (*pace* Benoist, Fukuyama et al.), rises like the spectral figure of Hamlet's father to cast a withering call for justice upon a new, and mostly reluctant, generation. Much discussion is given, in an exhaustively Derridean way, to the explication of how "the time is out of joint." Though Derrida generally avoids the abominable double adverb "already, always" so dear to Marxists, one gets the idea after a few dozen pages that he means the same thing.

There are a few interesting bits of sleight of hand in Derrida's argument. Firstly, one has to mention the clever way he slips an atheistic axiom into the discourse, devaluing "spiritual" values even while glossing the notion of the spectral (17), and making Marx's (im)material existence the central point of any history (hence teleology and eschatology) (13).

Derrida's efforts remind one of a recent film. Burrowing into the rich fossil remains of the early modern period, he tries to find some of the fundamental living matter of Communism. Ingeniously splicing it together with frog DNA (no pun intended) collected from amphibians of the PCF and other ponds, he dreams of recreating the mighty Marxosaurus that once stalked Cold War Era swamps, striking terror into the hearts of mammalo-capitalists everywhere. But as Jeff Goldblum so aptly put it in the film, these creatures had their day and they struck out; the fuzzy little fur-bearing finance rodents endured. No amount of tinkering by (social) scientists can obviate the evolutionary fact—one that Marx, as an ardent evolutionist, would undoubtedly have ratified: Derrida's intellectual Jurassic Park of Marxism is a bust from the beginning. Ironically, the philosopher falls victim to an ill that he himself analyzes in the book, the so-called "Marcellus effect," in which some people, like Marcellus the guard in *Hamlet,* assume that scholars are capable of everything, even spectral intervention.

Perhaps part of the problem with Derrida's analysis is that it is based on a tacit misunderstanding common to "Anglo-Saxon," French and Soviet students of early communism. For if Marx refers repeatedly to Hamlet as an example, it is not because he considers that Hamlet represents any type of inheritance passed on to the British, the French, or the Russians, nor even to the as-yet nonexistent International. Marx was a child of his age, and when he referred to Shakespeare's figure, he meant, as all good Germans of the Romantic age did, that "Deutschland ist Hamlet!"[9] This is not to say that Derrida's appropriation of the symbol and the "conjuring" is entirely without pertinence, but it is thrown seriously out of focus if one forgets the (like it or not) German nationalistic context from which Marx was operating. If one remembers that Lenin himself was astonished that fate decreed Russia should be the home state of communism, one can imagine what the reaction of Marx's ghost would have really been, on learning that the International was to be quartered in the Kremlin, rather than Frankfurt, Berlin, or at least London! Perhaps, as John Reed eventually came to believe, that is where the times really started to get "out of joint."

But to return to Derrida, is there any possibility that Marxism, or even one of the Marxisms he conjures, can be raised? What can still be useful? One thing that is clear is that it makes little sense to turn to Marx for a causal or genetic explanation of early modern culture. One needs only an elementary grounding in late twentieth-century anthropology to appreciate how seriously flawed are Marx's notions about free labor, pastoral tribalism, and the evolution of community property in precapitalist society. This should hardly be surprising, since besides his confessed debt to Proudhon, Marx has little to build on except Rousseau and other more or less utopian theorists of noble savagery. One does well to remember, after all, that it was not Marx who invented atheistic determinism, but the Enlightenment philosophers.

If there are parts of the apparatus still fit for service, they are certainly the ones that Marx fashioned after his own observations of nineteenth-century reality: the alienation of human agency in the industrial production process, the rising dominance of commodities and a commodity mentality, and the problematic status of exchange. Perhaps one possible direction for those who do not wish to approach Habermas's rationalism is the autonomist approach advocated by Michael Ryan in relation to studies of modern culture.[10]

Closer to Molière, Pierre Force's recent study, *Molière ou le prix des choses* (Paris: Nathan, 1994), shows a very fruitful development in the direction of French exchange theory, based most directly on the work of Pierre Bourdieu, but encompassing fascinating articulations with previous notions of exchange all the way back to Rousseau (surprisingly, not the *Lettre à D'Alembert,* but the *Rêveries du promeneur solitaire!*) and to Aristotle's *Nicomachean Ethics.* According to Force, the goal of Moliéresque comedy is to highlight the very "injustice" (221) at which Derrida takes aim, but which takes the particular comic form of imbalance and disorder (likewise points of focus in my *Social Structures,* 169-230). Ridicule results from any defect on either the giving or the receiving end, especially in the failure to evaluate properly (or sometimes, as in ***Dom Juan,*** to even identify) the terms of an exchange (223). Although Force does not cite it in this instance, the first scene of ***Le Malade imaginaire,*** where Argan ridiculously "capitalizes" his enemas and purgatives, thus serves as an apt capstone for the Molière canon. It also illustrates a second ironic insight, that those who seek to hegemonize the rules of exchange inevitably emerge as more risible characters than those they seek to manipulate. The ineffectiveness of Molière's bumbling, would-be authoritarians certainly turns Marxism, with its inescapable reflex to take itself seriously, quite upside-down.

Indeed, laughter in its most general and collective form constitutes a fitting conclusion to this overview and a worthy subject for the future. The reception of comedy is always an experience that impacts on the individual, but a given reader or spectator is never really alone, for a play by its very nature requires a multiplication of artistic consciousness, not only through the characters "on stage," but through the forever-implied presence of an audience. Furthermore, as Jean-Marie Apostolidès has pointed out, in seventeenth-century France, that audience always included the virtual presence of the king himself, the symbolic embodiment of the entire hierarchy. Even when, as in ***Amphitryon,*** the king (or the king's king) is the object of irony, the reader/spectator is invited to laugh with the king. The historical moments when new comedies are able to emerge to manifest a fleeting sense of social balance, perhaps even a type of social communion, are rather rare, but even in their re-creation, these plays convey a powerful sense of ritual recommitment to society. If, in the cherished formula *castigat ridendo mores,* the first verb is a singular of artistic vector, the second always must be plural, for, as Molière learned with ***Dom Garcie de Navarre,*** sublime interpersonal insights are no good on stage unless the audience shares the laughter. It is time to go beyond Bakhtin's work on the carnavalesque (surely one of the richest and earliest fruits of neo-Marxist thought) more fully to comprehend a context which was not just another text, but an experience that transcends scripture, and perhaps politics, too.

Notes

1. See for example *Literature and Art by Karl Marx and Frederick Engels* (New York: International Publishers, 1947), 3-14 and 74-76. Although Marx reportedly had rather wide literary interests, his theoretical pronouncements seem to have been especially shaped by tensions with contemporaries such as Max Stirner and Eugène Sue; see for example Marx and Engels, *On Literature and Art,* ed. Lee Baxandall and Stefan Morawski (New York: International General, 1973), 77-79.

2. The most available version is the 1963 reedition, *Les Soulèvements popularies en France de 1623 à 1648* (Paris: SEVPEN), but the work itself, like its political underpinning, dates from a much earlier period.

3. It is hard to cite a writer of truly "common" origin from this period. Even those who are accused of the most unremitting "realism," Sorel, Furetière, minor dramatists such as Brécourt and Chevalier, could scarcely qualify as proletarians or peasants, and their analyses of popular milieux were strictly views *à vol d'oiseau.* The definitive study of early modern lower classes in French literature is Pierre Ronzeaud's *Peuple et représentations* (Aix: Université de Provence, 1988); see esp. 40-52. In fact, the first efforts to appropriate Molière as a pre-Revolutionary partisan date from before the Soviet period, as Ralph Albanese shows in "Molière devant la socio-critique," *Œuvres et Critiques,* 6, 1 (1981): 57-66, see esp. n. 14.

4. *Molière bourgeois et libertin* (Paris: Nizet, 1963). This method has not changed much over the following years. See "Molière subversif," the first seven pages of Cairncross's *L'Humanité de Molière* (Paris: Nizet, 1988). Although Cairncross attributes the title of his anthology of essays to the well-known article on *Dom Juan* by James Doolittle, which he includes, one cannot quite efface the appearance of another publication under the title *L'Humanité,* and the efforts to recycle old class-based analyses remind me of a news agent I once frequented on the boulevard Saint-Germain who was always trying to interest his clients in the well-worn issues being dredged up again by the *Huma* of the 70's.

5. Contrast, for instance, McBride's *The Sceptical Vision of Molière: A Study in Paradox* (New York: Barnes and Noble, 1977), where one finds a careful discussion of *Dom Juan* in its philosophical context (79-106), with the almost socialist-realist approach that Cairncross still maintains in a recent article ("A Structural Approach to Molière's *Dom Juan.*" *Continuum* 4 [1992]: 1-7). It is equally interesting to set McBride's "precocious" reading of *Amphitryon* (160-86) next to another not-quite-new-historicist article, "The Uses of History: Molière and Louis XIV Revisited," *ELF* 58 (1993): 25-31.

6. Ralph Albanese's "Molière devant la socio-critique" presents a particularly nuanced and valuable analysis of the Éditions Sociales series.

7. I refer to Peggy Kamuf's translation, *Specters of Marx* (New York: Routledge, 1994), because it is much more easily procured than the 1993 original by Éditions Galilée, and because Kamuf often introduces interesting observations of her own in attempting to handle Derrida's deliberate punning and language play.

8. There are a couple of exceptions: Derrida insists on an anti-Stalinist disclaimer to distance himself from the Hungarian repression and events thereafter, and he adds a catty swipe at the Danes for rejecting the Maestricht Accords.

9. The quote came from the poet Ferdinand Freiligrath. See Russell A. Berman, "Faust, Germany, and Unification," *South Central Review,* 12 (1995): 1-15.

10. *Politics and Culture: Working Hypotheses for a Post-Revolutionary Society* (Baltimore: Johns Hopkins, 1989), 46-61. Ryan's ideas are closely based on those of the Italian leftist, Antonio Negri.

L'IMPROMPTU DE VERSAILLES

CRITICAL COMMENTARY

Cecile Lindsay (essay date 1982)

SOURCE: "Molière in the Post-Structuralist Age: *L'Impromptu de Versailles*," in *Theatre Journal,* Vol. 34, No. 3, October, 1982, pp. 373-83.

[*In the following essay, Lindsay provides an in-depth look at Molière's* L'Impromptu de Versailles, *commenting on possible reasons why the play has been overlooked.*]

Molière's ***L'Impromptu de Versailles*** (***The Rehearsal at Versailles***) has not, over the critical ages, received much attention. Traditionally considered a marginal element in Molière's repertoire, the ***Impromptu*** has in the main been a singularly, even signally neglected work. For in the vicissitudes of literary history since the classical era, the fortunes of Molière's plays have provided an accurate gage of critical changes through successive generations. In ***The Misanthrope,*** for example, the *honnête homme* Philinte flattered the classical era's notions of restraint, moderation, and social adjustment, while the Romantics saw in Alceste a noble and kindred spirit whose keen sense of personal integrity made him near-tragically unsuited for life in the degraded society of more pliant folk. Existentialist criticism of ***The Misanthrope,*** on the other hand, has more recently indicted Alceste for his exemplary bad faith and self-deception. That the ascendancy or decline of Alceste's star can be correlated with the tides of literary criticism has been a scholarly staple since the eighteenth century formulated the textbook question of Molière-Alceste versus Molière-Philinte. While ***The Misanthrope*** has been one of the most popular of Molière's works, the ***Impromptu*** ranks only slightly higher in frequency of performance and study than such unimposing pieces as ***Le Médecin volant (The Flying Physician)*** and Molière's embarassing attempt at heroic drama, ***Dom Garcie de Navarre.*** Yet the ***Impromptu***'s more modest fortunes are equally a gage of the critical ages or, more precisely, of a critical "coming of age," for the ***Impromptu*** is in many senses a post-structuralist *pièce de résistance,* a hard gem of a play that has until now resisted interpretive efforts, but which stages some of the major tenets of post-structuralist criticism. The ***Impromptu*** is a marginal text for a critical era obsessed with the marginal, a hopelessly fragmented play about the frustrations and rewards of fragmentation; it raises the question of power, performance, and the role of the intellectual in social critique. It offers as well a dazzling argument for intertextuality, reflexivity, and autonomy in the domain of artistic production; it finally leaves us balanced on a precarious undecidability between paradoxical interpretations.

The ***Impromptu*** was written in eight days in the Fall of 1663, and was performed at Versailles, apparently at the request of Louis XIV. It constituted Molière's last theatrical word in the heated "war of comedies" which broke out soon after the arrival in Paris (in 1658) of Molière's provincial theatrical troupe. Molière's first comedies, among them ***Les Précieuses ridicules, Sganarelle,*** and ***L'Ecole des femmes,*** had enjoyed an extraordinary public success that provoked consternation in the capital's theatrical community and threatened to upstage the prestigious Hôtel de Bourgogne, the official dramatic troupe of Paris, which esteemed tragedy only. Not only did Molière annex both public and royal favor (with rewards at once moral and financial), but he dared parody the acting style of the reigning tragedians as well as the mores and manners of the court nobility. Rivalry simmered until the brilliant triumph of ***L'Ecole des femmes,*** in December, 1662, which was hotly attacked by the critics as indecent and shocking. Molière's witty and satiric response, ***La Critique de L'Ecole des femmes,*** earned him several new enemies, among them Pierre and Thomas Corneille, who felt themselves the target of certain well-placed barbs. An angry pamphlet was published by one author who saw himself satirized in the ***Critique*** and who sought to champion the cause of writers, actors, women, and nobles as well as that of religion and propriety. The actors of the Hôtel de Bourgogne then presented their own counteroffensive with a strident attack on Molière in *Le Portrait du Peintre,* a reputedly collaborative effort by Corneille and other illustrious figures that was signed by an aspiring young dramatist named Boursault. The aspersions cast shifted from the professional to the personal realm, exploiting Molière's reputed marital problems (he had recently wed a young actress in his troupe), and suggesting that his new wife was in reality the daughter of his former mistress and thus his own daughter. Possibly affronted by the violence of the attack directed at a royal favorite, the King appears to have ordered a prompt theatrical response. It is to this exigency that the ***Impromptu de Versailles*** owes its genesis and its name.[1]

The scene is the *salle de comédie,* the King's private theatre at Versailles, where the play was, in effect, first performed. The members of the cast are Molière and his troupe, who play themselves rehearsing a new and still untitled play that is to be performed in two hours before the King, who had commissioned it. Alone on stage in the first scene, Molière conjures up his troupe, like the Creator, by calling their names. The mutinous actors complain upon entering that they have not had sufficient time to memorize their roles, while Molière frantically tries to call them to order, lamenting the difficulty of the director's task: "Actors—impossible creatures to handle."[2] Of the purportedly commissioned play, we hear only fragments from which we gather that its subject is a reply to Boursault's *Le Portrait du Peintre.* This rehearsed play features the mandatory ridiculous marquis (played by Molière) and the *honnête homme* (Brécourt), a young gentleman who champions Molière and explains his theatrical satires as social, not personal, commentary. The major portion of the ***Impromptu,*** however, is given over to Molière's stage directions and frantic conversations with his actors, a series of lively exchanges which provide a "backstage" glimpse of the actor/director/author's craft in action, as well as a scene of conjugal dispute between Molière and his young wife. Thus, the ***Impromptu*** at first seems to present a case of theatrical *mise en abyme,* a play-within-a-play that provides an occasion for discussing the nature of drama while it allows the bracketing of Molière's satiric barbs within the internal play. The ***Impromptu***'s general effect is disarmingly frank, spontaneous, and engaging. But the rehearsal is not, strictly speaking, a real play; it is really a *pre*-play playfully presenting the "real" actors to an audience which is not really supposed to be present yet. The spectator is, as one commentator has noted, both *devant* (in front of) and *avant* (temporally before) the completed, integral play.[3] For despite the fragmented structure and confusion between "play" and "real," the ***Impromptu*** as performed is a patent and paradoxical whole. The focus shifts within this whole from "rehearsal" to "play" as the actors lapse in and out of character, momentarily assume another's role, or repeat words a "real" person supposedly said.

This dizzying shift in focus is further augmented by the insertion of yet another element, a third play: a play *manqué,* an aborted sketch of a response to his critics which Molière has, for a variety of reasons, abandoned. In an attempt to avoid giving a performance for which the troupe is manifestly unprepared, one of the actresses suggests that Molière perform alone:

> When the king asked you for a reply to the criticism of your other work, why didn't you write the play about the Bourgogne actors [*cette comédie des comédiens*], which you've often described to us? It would have been perfect for this occasion. When the critics did their satirical portrait of you they left themselves wide open, and your portrait of them would be a much more accurate picture than theirs was of you. They tried to spoof your comic acting, but they weren't imitating you at all, only the roles you were playing, your makeup, and the mannerisms you adopted in trying to draw a comic character from life. But if you mock an actor in a *serious* part, you'll come very close to mocking him as a man, because serious acting doesn't allow him to cover up his personal faults with ridiculous tricks and comic gestures. (pp. 100-01)

Thus begins Molière's counterattack on the critics who saw him in the cuckolded husband of the ***École des femmes,*** as well as his satire of the bombastic style of his rivals at the Hôtel de Bourgogne. After claiming to have abandoned the project of parodying the tragedians because he had not had sufficient time to study their performances, Molière is nevertheless persuaded to sketch out the rejected scenario in which a poet proposes a play to a troupe of actors newly arrived from the provinces. When a slender, presentable young man is designated as the actor who plays kings, the pompous poet rejects both his natural delivery of lines and his unkingly physique, proposing instead a parodic imitation of the well-known actor Montfleury. This third *mise en abyme* of the play allows Molière to satirize his enemies, to flatter young King Louis, and to propose a more "realistic" brand of acting.

The interpolation of the third play-within-the-play has, however, cost the troupe valuable rehearsal time, and they desperately resume the discussion, and subsequently the performance, of the "real" or commissioned play. In the movement back and forth between the three plays, the *commedia dell arte* tone of improvisation and burlesque gives rise to an *ars comica* in which Molière enunciates his theories on comedy's proper subject, form, and function. When the rehearsal of the "real" play begins, Molière adopts the role of a ridiculous marquis who quarrels with an equally absurd peer over the question of which of the two had been parodied by Molière in the ***Critique de l'École des femmes.*** Molière's ironic differentiation into an actor playing himself playing a role in which he refers to himself as author is vertiginously multiplied when another character (Brécourt) becomes the spokesman for Molière's theatrical theory: "The business of comedy is to present the flaws common to all men, and especially the men of our time. It would be impossible for Molière to dream up people who resembled nobody you've ever met. If he is going to be challenged with pillorying every living person who has the same faults as his characters, he will indeed have to stop writing plays" (p. 110). The pronouncement of this thesis on the social role of comedy is accompanied by a subtle threat aimed at Molière's detractors which links the noble ideal of artistic freedom to the more pragmatic end of not robbing the King of his royal diversions.

If the lofty formulation of poetic autonomy covers over a more political aim, it also enters into frank conflict with the ***Impromptu***'s own practices. For despite its profession of disinterested and generalized social critique, the play unquestionably contains (as did the ***Critique***) an unflattering portrait of a contemporary author (Donneau de Visé) and satiric use of speeches from various Corneillian tragedies. Moreover, Boursault and his play are explicitly named and attacked in the rehearsed play when the ridiculous marquis boasts about *Le Portrait du peintre*:

> His name is Boursault, and he is indeed listed as author on the placards, but I'll let you all in on a secret. A number of people had a hand in the writing. . . . All the playwrights and actors in Paris look on Molière as their main enemy, so we united against him. Every one of us has added a brush stroke to the portrait, but we refrained from publishing our names. People would have thought it too easy if he were crushed by the whole of Parnassus at once. We want to make his defeat more shameful by giving the credit to an unknown writer. (p. 113)[4]

If Molière's accusation here is clearly exaggerated, his final judgment, voiced by Brécourt, is doubtless more accurate: "I've looked at the script, and since the most amusing lines in it are lifted from Molière's own work, he won't object if the audience likes them" (p. 115). When Molière's spokesman modestly concludes that Molière should make no public response to the latest attacks—a successful new play comprising the most delicious revenge—one of the actresses breaks character to interrupt the rehearsal and express her surprise at Molière's restraint: "If I were you, I'd arrange things differently. Everybody expects you to make a vigorous reply, and from what I heard of the way you were dealt with in that comedy, you have every right to come back at them; I hope you won't spare a single one" (p. 115).

At this point, Molière too steps out of his role and appears to speak in his own name, as Molière the author-director. Having placed within the rejected play and the rehearsed scenario some genuinely nasty barbs destined for his rivals and critics, and having paradoxically claimed via Brécourt that he would not return the calumnies directed at him, Molière now speaks in his own voice, ostensibly in the "real," virtuously and vehemently refusing suggestions that he venge himself. Even still, even as he makes an impassioned public declaration, he gives Boursault one last shot:

> You'd be doing him too much honor to impersonate him in front of such a distinguished gathering. He couldn't ask for more. He's a man who has nothing to lose. He chooses to attack me because that is one way of getting his name known. Well, I intend to make a public announcement to this effect: I will not answer their criticisms or their countercriticisms. They can say the very worst things of my plays; I don't mind. I willingly offer up my plays, my face, my gestures, my words, my tone of voice. I sacrifice my tricks of the trade for them to use as they will. I have no objections to whatever they take, if only the audience likes it. But in yielding all this to them, I reserve the rest as my own property. [They must not touch on the type of subjects which I am told they have attacked in their plays.] That is all I will politely ask of this honest gentleman whom they've engaged to write their play, and that is the only retaliation they shall have from me. (p. 117)[5]

The ***Impromptu*** concludes shortly after this somewhat self-righteous and slightly dishonest declaration with the King's benevolent permission to put off the performance until a later date. For all its brevity the ***Impromptu*** presents a dense and complicated, often paradoxical structure; it is a play (or two) at once within a play and *without* the play: the play is in a sense never performed—the fiction is that the King never sees the rehearsed play, or at least must go without the play for the time being. And yet the ***Impromptu*** as multiple play-within-play *was* played, probably on the 18th or 19th of October, 1663; and it was played without, that is, exterior to, the play, for it took place in the *real* domain of a genuine professional struggle. The proof is in the plum bestowed on Molière after the ***Impromptu***'s lively success: the troupe was awarded a pension, and the King stood godfather to Molière's first child by his new wife.

The ***Impromptu***'s complex structure and strategies make it a play particularly attractive to the concerns of post-structuralism. The triple play-within-a-play multiplies roles, confuses identities, and provides the context for a vertiginously specular criticism of theatre by theatre. Neither the rejected *comédie des comédiens* nor the rehearsed play takes place in its entirety—even the rehearsal is necessarily incomplete and fragmented, interrupted at every turn by visitors and by the actors themselves. Nor is the play's language wholly Molière's: in the parodic *comédie des comédiens*, Molière counterfeits the emphatic style of tragic diction by imitating his rival actors in speeches taken from the most popular dramas of Corneille, the period's reigning tragic author. More is at stake in this intertextual war than the lambasting of theatrical rivals, however. Tragedy itself is the target of Molière's attack, and, beyond tragedy, the metaphysical and political values embodied in the heroic genre. Corneille's heroes still transmitted the old, independent spirit of the feudal nobility whom Louis XIV had politically emasculated after the Fronde, in his successful effort to place himself at the head of a unified, centralized state. While Corneille's *Cinna* gave a lesson in kingly conduct, Molière's ***Impromptu*** contented itself with providing a mirror of the king's omnipotence, benevolence, and wisdom. Proposing to substitute a more natural, practical, and self-ironizing style for the grandiose and philosophizing style of the tragic author, Molière signals his allegiance to the modern state and its new structure of power. The intertextual perversion and parody of Corneille's theatre opens up the play's apparent closure to a dialogue between external value systems. Just as the distinction between what is purportedly real and what is really a play is constantly transgressed in the ***Impromptu***'s performance, the integrality of Molière's textual production is willfully violated.

The same strategic aims govern both types of transgression. Molière's principal tactic in the ***Impromptu*** is to interrupt and disrupt the normal properties of classical theatrical performance and composition: unity, illusion, closure. By means of a unified, integral spectacle, the classical dramatist created, if not the illusion of reality, then the illusion of meaningfulness, of coherence, of logical and significant closure. The disruption of these conventional theatrical properties allows Molière to redefine theatre, to present his version of what is properly theatrical, to propose his own *ars comica.* In his distribution of roles and in his directions to his actors, Molière demonstrates his theory of theatrical realism: the role must conform to the actor's own personality, and diction should reproduce natural speech. Thus he counsels his spokesman: "Brécourt, your part is exactly the same as that of Dorante in the last play,[6] an honest man at Court. Look thoughtful, speak in a natural voice, and gesticulate as little as possible" (p. 105). When, at the end of the play, Molière seems to speak in his own voice in a spontaneous public declaration, he forcefully separates proper from improper theatrical subjects. While professional matters of composition, diction, and gesture are fair game for the satire of rivals, Molière points out, the personal lives of actors or authors are inappropriate and unseemly subjects for public comment. Molière is thereby able to return with righteous indignation the charges of indecency and impropriety directed at him by the court's old guard of moralists, out-doing the *dévots* by changing the rules of piety and establishing new guidelines for moral behavior. Based on the premise that distinctions must be made and maintained between public and private domains, between general satire and personal vendetta, between legitimate criticism and prudish quibbling, these new guidelines are calculated to please a monarch bent on establishing a modern, secular, and rational state.

Having determined what theatre must not do, Molière can complete his version of what it can and should accomplish. Here, too, the strategy throughout the ***Impromptu*** is one of interruption and disruption; the proper nature of theatre is elaborated through the constant fracturing of theatrical convention. When the actors initially rebel at performing an unknown script, Molière abandons the rehearsal in order to evoke his own dilemma: "To stage a comedy for this kind of audience is no joke. These are not easy people to amuse or impress. They laugh only when they feel like it" (p. 99). With unerring diplomacy, Molière seeks first of all to produce a work which will merit the approval of a discerning and intelligent king. Nor is the good judgment of the public slighted; some of the cleverest gibes directed at his rivals concern the public reception of their plays: "Why should he write these wicked comedies for all Paris to see, with people in them we all recognize? Why doesn't he write like Monsieur Lysidas[7] who never attacks a soul? You never hear another playwright say a word against him. His works may not be popular, but they don't offend or provoke anybody and we all agree that they're elegantly written" (p. 114). The financial success and public acclaim of Molière's comedies were a modern measure of theatrical efficacy when opposed to the critical approval granted his rivals' more correct but less entertaining compositions.

The standard enunciation of Molière's theory of comedy comes during the rehearsed play, when Brécourt defends Molière against the two marquis by quoting what he overheard Molière himself say: "His aim, he said, is to portray types, not individuals, and all of the people who appear in his plays are imaginary, phantoms if you like; he invents them as he goes along, in such a way as to entertain the audience . . ." (p. 109). *Instruire et plaire*: Molière's recipe for comedy calls for the correction of contemporary vices through laughter. The comic author takes on the function of social critic. Mixing the rehearsal, the rehearsed, and the purportedly spontaneous, the ***Impromptu*** presents theatre in the act of defining its own nature and goals. It proposes itself as a play that will respond to criticism while at the same time itself constituting a criticism of other theatrical productions. In this way, the ***Impromptu*** erases the distinction between art and its criticism, just as it blurs the boundaries between the real and the play by its vertiginous, virtuoso shifts.

The "real" is thus both inserted in and ousted from the ***Impromptu.*** The play performed in October, 1663 responded to a (probably) real command and to a very real attack from several quarters. The play's triumph allowed Molière to emerge from the fray in a much better condition, professionally and financially. Playing themselves, the actors are given the opportunity to indulge the audience's curiosity about their personalities and personal lives. Molière's spat with his wife tantalizes a public that already believes him a cuckold, yet it ultimately obscures more than clarifies the couple's relations. Molière and his troupe flirtatiously offer a glimpse of their (or their victims') real lives only to claim exemption, in the name of satire, when their plays are mistakenly taken for reality. Molière makes an impassioned case for the autonomy of art when he insists that personality be divorced from production, and that social critique not bow to partisan pressure. In this way, the ***Impromptu*** playfully appears to put the "real" on stage only to better throw it off.

This gesture—feigning one thing in order to effect another—comprises, finally, Molière's characteristic operation in the ***Impromptu.*** And it is in its ability to deal with what is generally perceived to be paradox and contradiction that post-structuralism makes one of its most important contributions, at least in respect to Molière's play. Paradox informs the ***Impromptu***: proposing itself as a sort of anti-play, a rehearsal that is constantly disrupted by spontaneous interjections, the ***Impromptu*** is neither spontaneous nor disrupted, nor even really a rehearsal. It is, rather, an intricate and imbricated structure, an integral play in its own right whose strategical success takes place on several levels. Molière's multiple roles comprise the principal carrier of the play's paradoxes. By the time Molière indignantly cries out against personal calumny in the public theatre, he has already roundly attacked Boursault for his ambition and ridiculed the young playwright's lack of reputation. When he seems to break character to argue for the strict separation of private and professional personae, Molière is able to carry off an audacious gamble: he wagers that his audience will be so dazzled by his virtuoso contradictions that it will either forget the earlier evidence, opting to believe his final, virtuous stance, or else applaud his daring insincerity. In either case, Molière's political aim is achieved; his rivals are at once made to seem ridiculous and menaced with the monarch's displeasure. In every instance and at every turn in the play, Molière has it both ways, and always his own way.

Yet just as he undercuts his own appeal for the separation of private man and public actor by irremediably confusing the two in his own case, Molière undoes his own argument for the autonomy of the aesthetic by destroying the distinction between the two types of discourse, artistic and critical. Paradoxically, of course, the ***Impromptu***'s strength derives from this simultaneous postulation and erosion of distinctions; all the levels and forms of discourse in the ***Impromptu***—be they personal or professional, self-reflexive or didactic, "spontaneous" or openly calculated—serve to empower the performer. Molière's strategic parry in the "war of comedies" of 1663 transforms comedy into power. Transgressing all the limits his critical era placed on theatrical production, Molière's performance of the ***Impromptu*** was in a sense a *performative* accomplishing, by the very fact of its being pronounced, a variety of aims in the realm of the real: probably revenge and possibly education, but most certainly profit both political and material. The ***Impromptu***'s singular importance lies in its ability to break down the distinctions that are conventionally made between actors and roles, between forms of discourse, and between art and reality, while at the same time claiming to assert and define those very distinctions. It is in this characteristic gesture that the ***Impromptu*** has posed its greatest problems for critics in the three hundred-odd years since its performance, and it is in this gesture that this marginal play comprises a post-structuralist treasure.

All the complications and confusions in the ***Impromptu*** are, finally, about identity; who are the satirized individuals? when are the actors playing themselves and when are they playing themselves adopting a role? are they ever just themselves? do we ever see Molière the man? The frustration and possible mistakes as to identity mirror the critical dilemma this play has always posed: the difficulty or even the impossibility of deciding between alternative interpretations which are not simply dissimilar, but squarely antithetical. While Molière's contemporary critics were wholly obsessed with identifying the various individuals under attack in the ***Impromptu,*** commentators in the next century felt the play had lost its interest since the people named or aimed at were no longer alive. Voltaire vehemently rejected the play precisely because it identified too clearly its targets: "It is a cruel and excessive satire in which Boursault is openly named. Even the license of ancient Greek comedy could go no further. Both Boursault's and Molière's satire should have been suppressed in the name of propriety and public honesty."[8] The ***Impromptu*** was not performed even once during the eighteenth century.

While the nineteenth century twice revived the play (in 1838 and in 1880), it had definitively become a marginal element in Molière's work. Théophile Gautier classified the ***Impromptu*** among "those charming plays that we never get to see,"[9] but critics of the 1880 production characterized the play as "without any importance at all in the work of our great author."[10] Scholars and critics of the nineteenth century who did take an interest in the ***Impromptu*** were no longer preoccupied with the questions of identity posed by the play, but saw the piece instead as an enunciation of Molière's theories on directing, acting, and the nature of theatre.

The twentieth century has evinced a growing renewal of interest in the ***Impromptu,*** both in terms of performance and study. While one commentator saw Molière himself erupt unmasked on the stage, "Appearing on the stage among his troupe at work, Molière no longer uses the weapons of a writer; he thinks aloud, forgets himself. He speaks as an injured man. He rejects trickery; he is there alive, vibrant, at work . . . ,"[11] later "New Critics" have rejected the notion of Molière's genuine unmasking at the end of the play, seeing instead in the ***Impromptu*** a forceful demonstration of the autonomy of the aesthetic in which Molière recedes behind a brilliant series of multiple masks. The New Critical analyses of the ***Impromptu*** have opted to view the play as a self-enclosed, autonomous *art poétique.*[12]

Whereas earlier criticism responded to the ***Impromptu***'s simultaneous presentation of what was viewed as two antithetical interpretations by choosing either to view the play in terms of its identification with a given reality, or to see it as a self-contained reflection on theatre by theatre, two more recent analyses have attempted to place the metatheatrical elements in the play within the context of its political efficacy. In "La Critique du théâtre au théâtre," Jacques Nichet sees the ***Impromptu*** as a collective critical activity involving audience as well as actor and serving to question the traditional values of the dominant ideology.[13] In his 1972 essay Marc Fumaroli argues that the ***Impromptu*** forms a microcosmic version of Louis XIV's solar universe: Molière mirrors in miniature the difficulties and triumphs, the cleverness and intelligence, of the young king's reign; the *art poétique* doubles as a flattering vision of Louis's own *art de régner.*[14] Both essays move toward the recognition that Molière's play is at once a declaration of allegiance to a newly constituted power, and an empowering discourse. In the last ten years, analysis has begun, albeit on a small scale, to rehearse the ***Impromptu***'s singular contribution to critical thought. Moreover, we are now in a critical age propitious for dealing with a work which has up to now resisted interpretation. We are no longer forced to choose between two approaches we consider to be antithetical, but can, like Molière, opt for the rewards of the undecidable.

Notes

1. For the historical conditions surrounding this genesis, see Percy Addison Chapman, *The Spirit of Molière, An Interpretation* (Princeton, N.J.: Princeton Univ. Press, 1940), pp. 164-171 and Sylvie Chavalley, "l'Impromptu de Versailles," *Molière: Stage and Study* (Oxford: Clarendon Press, 1973), pp. 228-41.
2. Molière, *The Rehearsal at Versailles,* tr. Albert Bermel, *One-Act Comedies of Molière* (New York: Frederick Ungar Publishing Co., 1962), p. 98. Subsequent citations from this edition will be noted in parentheses in the text.
3. Marc Fumaroli, "Microcosme comique et macrocosme solaire: Molière, Louis XIV, et *l'Impromptu de Versailles,*" *Revue des Sciences Humaines* 37, No. 145 (January-March 1972), 106.
4. More literally, "to an author without any reputation" (un auteur sans réputation).
5. The sentence within brackets is my own translation.
6. *La Critique de l'Ecole des femmes.*
7. In *La Critique de l'Ecole des femmes* as well as in the *Impromptu,* Molière satirizes Donneau de Visé in the character of Lysidas, a pedantic and pompous poet.

8. Cited in the documentation accompanying *l'Impromptu de Versailles* (Paris: Nouveaux Classiques Larousse, 1968), p. 168. The translation is mine.
9. Cited by Chevalley in "*l'Impromptu de Versailles,*" p. 244. The translation is mine.
10. Chevalley, p. 244.
11. Pierre Brisson, *Molière, sa vie et ses oeuvres* (1942), cited in *l'Impromptu de Versailles* (Nouveaux Classiques Larousse), p. 190; the translation is mine.
12. See Robert Nelson, "*l'Impromptu de Versailles* Reconsidered," French Studies 11 (1957), 305-14, and *The Play within a Play; the Dramatist's Conception of his Art: Shakespeare to Anouilh* (New Haven: Yale Univ. Press, 1958).
13. Jacques Nichet, "La Critique du théâtre au théâtre: Aristophane, Molière, Brecht," *Littérature,* 9 (February 1973), 31-46.
14. "Microcosme comique et macrocosme solaire," 102-3.

TARTUFFE

CRITICAL COMMENTARY

Quentin M. Hope (essay date 1974)

SOURCE: "Place and Setting in *Tartuffe,*" in *Publications of the Modern Language Association of America,* Vol. 89, No. 1, January, 1974, pp. 42-9.

[*In the following essay, Hope maintains that the setting of Molière's* Tartuffe *had a distinctive, expressive function.*]

The theme of place and setting in the classical theater has attracted far more attention in Racine than in Molière.[1] The action of most Racine tragedies is inseparable from certain deeply expressive settings: altar, temple, sea and seaport, labyrinth, seraglio, and a palace which seems to imprison its occupants. There is also in Racine the evocative use of place names recalling a dark past or foretelling a brilliant future. Burning Troy is the backdrop of *Andromaque* and imperial Rome the illusory goal of *Mithridate.* Some of Racine's most memorable lines evoke places ("Dans l'Orient désert quel devint mon ennui") or suggest them ("Vous mourûtes aux bords où vous fûtes laissée").

These prestigious allusions to place belong to the world of heroic exploit and imperial grandeur rather than to a comic setting. Place can be significant in comedy, however. One has only to remember the many Shakespeare comedies in which the scene shifts from court to country and often back again as in *The Winter's Tale.* The contrast between the polish and corruption of civilized life and the gross and primitive simplicity of rustic life is a fundamental theme of Shakespearean comedy, the denouement offering, most often, a reconciliation of the two extremes. Even in a comedy like *The Merchant of Venice,* the title of which suggests an exclusively urban setting, the scene changes from the hustle and bustle of the Rialto and the lawcourts to Portia's country dwelling where the atmosphere encourages intimate feelings, introspection, and lyricism.

Place and setting are not as expressive and symbolic in Molière as in Shakespeare. Furthermore, place, climate, season, and all the material circumstances that surround the play are obviously less important in the classical theater than in either the romantic theater with its emphasis on local color or the naturalist theater with its emphasis on man as a product of his environment. It is fair to ask whether the subject of place in Molière really exists. A play has to take place somewhere, after all, and the necessities of the plot usually require a few references to place and setting. One could argue that Molière simply sketches in background with a rapid, careless hand so that he can focus attention on what counts for him: the rhythm of the dialogue, the balance of one scene against another, the confrontation of the characters, and so on. But a rereading of Molière with particular attention to setting and place references suggests that they do contribute something measurable and significant to Molière's dramaturgy.

The *pastorales* belong in a category apart. Setting counts for a great deal in these plays, as the name of the genre shows. Everything takes place in Greece, most often in the Vale of Tempe: "l'agréable vallée de Tempé." Eternal springtime reigns amidst flowers, woods, fountains, grottoes, shepherds, shepherdesses, satyrs, nymphs, dryads, and fauns. These plays where the setting is most emphasized are also the most conventional that Molière wrote, and, in spite of a certain faded charm, the least interesting.

The other plays take place either in the house or out in the street, or as in ***L'Ecole des femmes*** hesitate ambivalently between the two. The street is, more precisely, a *carrefour* or *place publique.* This is the traditional setting for Plautus and Terence and for the *commedia dell'arte.* As one might expect, Molière uses it in his early plays; but later plays too are set out of doors: ***George Dandin, Les Fourberies de Scapin,*** and ***Monsieur de Pourceaugnac.*** Funny things happen on the way to the forum that cannot so easily be made to happen in a drawing room: abductions, serenades, chance encounters, nighttime escapades involving mistaken identity. Traditionally, the town is a seaport and the denouement is shipped in by sea. Molière shows a preference for Messina. Even when the scene is not specifically Italian the readiness with which characters reveal private feelings and secrets in public suggests a Mediterranean setting. It is understandable that Italian street corners and public squares with their well-known resemblance to stage sets and their obvious theatrically are often the sets chosen by stage designers for these outdoor plays.

The weather, too, in the outdoor comedies, has a Mediterranean clemency, or at least the young lovers find it suitable for their amorous enterprises. The jealous husband or guardian uses it as an excuse to keep his ward in the house—Dom Pèdre in ***Le Sicilien***: "Allons, rentrons ici . . . le temps se couvre un peu" (Sc. viii). The valets in particular complain about being outdoors night and day in all kinds of weather. Hali in ***Le Sicilien***: "Le ciel s'est habillé ce soir en Scaramouche, et je ne vois pas une étoile qui montre le bout de son nez. Sotte condition que celle d'un esclave" (Sc. i). Sosie in ***Amphitryon***: "Jour et nuit, grêle, vent, péril, chaleur, froidure / dès qu'ils parlent il faut voler" (ll. 172-73). These are feelings shared by Sganarelle in ***Dom Juan.*** The most perfect expression of the *topos* comes not in Molière, however, but in the aria that Mozart gives to Leporello at the beginning of *Don Giovanni.*

Needless to say, slapstick is not banned from the stage when Molière moves his play indoors. Rough-and-tumble action, mistaken identity, miraculous denouements based on chance encounter can happen in the town house of Harpagon or Monsieur Jourdain as well as in a public square of Messina or Naples. But the comedy is somewhat higher toned, the gestures less sweeping, the deceptions less crude. Thus, the distinction between outdoor and indoor plays, while not to be drawn too sharply, remains valid. Setting contributes to tonality and resonance.

Tartuffe belongs to the category of plays that take place inside, and in particular to those that take place in a bourgeois house in Paris. Place plays a particularly distinctive role in it. The world in which Molière's characters live can be seen as a series of concentric circles: props, set, house, city, province, universe. The places they live in and the things that surround them are in varying degrees atmospheric and expressive. In ***Tartuffe*** material objects, the props and the house itself, and the places alluded to—Paris and province, heaven and earth, palace and prison—have a particular importance.

Tartuffe takes place in Orgon's house. The most notable thing about the place is that it shelters an unwelcome intruder: Tartuffe himself. Whether he is on stage or not Tartuffe's presence is felt throughout the play. His false spirituality is clothed in real flesh. "Un homme est de chair," as he says to Elmire. From Dorine we learn that he has red ears and a florid complexion, and that he is an unappetizing fellow:

> Et je vous verrais nu, du haut jusques en bas
> Que toute votre peau ne me tenterait pas.
>
> (ll. 867-68)

We see him eating, belching, sleeping, letching. Like Arsinoé in ***Le Misanthrope,*** "il a de l'amour pour les réalités." In the seduction scene of Act IV he distrusts Elmire's "propos si doux." A master of sweet talk himself, he knows what value to set on it. He demands "des réalités," namely the favors of Elmire which he expects to enjoy without delay. This body, whose physical appetites are so precisely evoked, lives in a world of real and palpable things. The hypocrite who pretends to have renounced "les choses de ce monde" has more props, on or off stage, than any other character in Molière. He eats partridge and leg of lamb, sleeps soundly in a warm bed, drinks four great draughts of wine. He has not been on stage more than a moment or two before we find out about the rod and the hairshirt which he keeps up in his room, and discover the handkerchief which he takes out of his pocket and gives to Dorine so that she may cover her overexposed bosom. A moment later he is taking a lively interest in the material of Elmire's dress ("l'étoffe en est mœlleuse") and inspecting the lacework of her bodice up close. When Cléante corners him in an argument, his pocket watch, a symbol of a regulated and pious life, reminds him that it is time for prayers and offers him a pretext for leaving the room.

> Il est, monsieur, trois heures et demie:
> Certain devoir pieux me demande là-haut,
> Et vous m'excuserez de vous quitter si tôt.
>
> (ll. 1266-68)

He appears to be equipped for all emergencies. When Elmire has a simulated coughing fit he draws a box of licorice from his pocket and offers it to her: "Vous plaît-il un morceau de ce jus de réglisse?" (l. 1498). There is unctuosity even in that simple line, and something that dimly suggests the association between candy and fawning hypocrisy encountered so often in Shakespeare.

Madame Pernelle is the first to define the world in which the characters in ***Tartuffe*** live. While berating the individual members of the family, she denounces the whole atmosphere of the house. She sees liberty, disorder, and anarchy everywhere. The house is ruled by a lord of misrule: "On n'y respecte rien, chacun y parle haut, / Et c'est tout justement la cour du roi Pétaut" (ll. 11-12). This is rhythmically echoed in her final outburst: "C'est véritablement la tour de Babylone, / Car chacun y babille et tout du long de l'aune" (ll. 161-62). The two place references (*la cour du roi Pétaut* and *la tour de Babylone*[2]) balance off. She complains at length that she never has a chance to talk. "Propos oisifs, chansons, fariboles . . . mille caquets divers" (ll. 154, 159)—that is all she ever hears. Cléante is forever preaching, Dorine is a "forte en gueule"—"Voyez la langue," "Taisez-vous," "Madame à jaser tient le dé tout le jour" (l. 143). They counterattack in the same terms. Dorine: "Pourquoi . . . en faire un vacarme à nous rompre la tête?" (l. 82). Cléante: "A tous les sots caquets n'ayons donc nul égard" (l. 100). In spite of her prejudice and vehemence, what Madame Pernelle says has the truth of any good caricature. As the author of the *Lettre sur l'imposteur* says, "Elle réussit si bien que le spectateur ôtant . . . ce qu'elle y met du sien . . . reçoit une volupté très sensible d'être informé dès l'abord . . . par une voie si fidèle et si agréable" (in Molière, *Œuvres,* ed. Despois et Mesnard, IV, 532). There is a lot of talking in Orgon's house, tempers flare up quickly, and conversations soon turn into clattering arguments ending with threats of violence. "Je ne mâche point ce que j'ai sur le cur," (l. 40) says Madame Pernelle, and the others follow her example. With the exception of the timid Mariane, they are a talkative and outspoken lot. Tartuffe himself affirms it when at the denouement he turns to the *exempt* and says, "Délivrez-moi, Monsieur, de la criaillerie" (l. 1897). Their frankness sets off his hypocrisy.

Madame Pernelle also offers a distorted but vivid glimpse of the neighborhood Orgon's family lives in and of their active social life: carriages rolling up before the door, lackeys laughing and joking, visits, dances, gatherings, and other inventions of the devil. To listen to Madame Pernelle you would imagine that the life of the family is made up of song, games, gossip, and a succession of noisy parties. It is true that Damis, Mariane, Valère, Cléante, Elmire, and Dorine are people who enjoy the pleasures of life. ***Tartuffe*** was supposed to form part of *Les Plaisirs de l'île enchantée,* the entertainment offered by the young Louis XIV to his mistress Louise de la Vallière. Tartuffe is a spoilsport who interrupts the pleasures of an urbane and sophisticated family. Molière's other contribution to *Les Plaisirs de l'île enchantée,* ***La Princesse d'Elide,*** celebrates the joys and pangs of love in a rustic setting. The pleasures evoked in ***Tartuffe*** are urban and specifically Parisian, yet Paris itself is an enchanted island, as Dorante says in Corneille's *Le Menteur*:

> Paris semble à mes yeux un pays de romans.
> J'y croyais ce matin voir une île enchantée.
>
> (ll. 552-53)

Orgon's family is less bedazzled by the splendors of Paris than the provincial Dorante is, but no less determined to enjoy them. *Les bals, les conversations, les assemblées, les visites* are delights which they cherish. The theater, too, no doubt. Although there are no allusions in ***Tartuffe*** to the entertainment offered by a Molière comedy as there are in ***Le Misanthrope*** and in ***Le Malade imaginaire,*** such youthful and broad-minded people surely must form part of the audience at the Palais Royal.

"Hors de Paris il n'y a pas de salut pour les honnêtes gens," says Mascarille in ***Les Précieuses ridicules*** (Sc. ix). To which Cathos replies: "C'est une vérité incontestable." Dorine agrees wholeheartedly with these sentiments, as is obvious from the picture she draws of what life will be like for Mariane when she is married to Tartuffe.

> Vous irez par le coche en sa petite ville,
> Qu'en oncles et cousins vous trouverez fertile,
> Et vous vous plairez fort à les entretenir.
> D'abord chez le beau monde on vous fera venir.
> Vous irez visiter, pour votre bienvenue,
> Madame la baillive et Madame l'élue,
> Qui d'un siège pliant vous feront honorer.
> Là, dans le carnaval, vous pourrez espérer
> Le bal et la grand' bande, à savoir, deux musettes,
> Et parfois Fagotin et les marionnettes;
>
> (ll. 657-66)

This passage is one of those which serves to orient the play firmly in time and place, giving its characters a well-defined habitation, a past, and a future. In addition to this satiric glimpse into the future, there are in ***Tartuffe*** a number of glimpses into the past: Orgon as supporter of the throne during the Fronde, his first wife and her exemplary conduct, Monsieur Loyal, former servant of Orgon's father, Orgon's encounter in church with Tartuffe, Tartuffe himself as protagonist of "un long détail d'actions toutes noires" (l. 1925). One might well ask what Tartuffe would be doing in this little town. The path to heaven does not usually lead through the provinces. On the contrary, Cléante's reference in Act I to "ces dévots de place . . . qui . . . prêchent la retraite au milieu de la cour" (l. 372) suggests that Tartuffe plans to remain in Paris and to continue making his way up the ladder. Presumably, Dorine supposes he would go to the country to recover the title and property he had lost because of his neglect of worldly things. That is merely the pretext for the passage, however. Its purpose is to cast ridicule on provincial life, as Molière does in ***Monsieur de Pourceaugnac, George Dandin***, and ***La Comtesse d'Escarbagnas,*** and to support the theme of the delights of Paris, the bright Babylon. Everything Dorine says implies a sorry contrast for Mariane between the life she leads in Paris and the life she would lead in a small provincial city. Instead of her urbane and sympathetic uncle Cléante, the numberless uncles and cousins of Tartuffe, instead of Parisian parties and dances, formal calls on the wives of the local dignitaries, instead of the Palais Royal, a trained monkey and a marionette show, instead of the real *beau monde* of Paris, its feeble and ridiculous imitation. It is a contrast that Molière uses in many plays. Paris is the capital of social life and fashion ("nos rubans, notre rouge et nos mouches," l. 206), of entertainment, of comedy, liberty, and youth. *La province,* be it country, or small town, or *désert,* is the domain of solitude, severity, sobriety in manners and clothing, and of everything that Sganarelle in ***L'Ecole des maris*** means by "l'ancienne honnêteté": constraint, puritanism, masculine tyranny, and female subservience. Its inhabitants are unfashionable, boring, and ridiculous.

Only in ***Le Misanthrope*** are the corruption, superficiality, and hypocrisy of Parisian life denounced by a character who engages at least part of the sympathy of his audience. Alceste would, no doubt, find the snobbishness of Mariane and Dorine, the horror they feel at the prospect of living anywhere except in Paris, as shocking as Tartuffe's hypocrisy itself. But the sympathetic characters in ***Tartuffe*** all consider the pleasures of Paris to be very much worth pursuing, and it is only the play's *cabale des dévots*—Tartuffe, Orgon, Madame Pernelle, and the servant Laurent—who denounce them.

Madame Pernelle buttresses her attack on the family by telling them that their way of life scandalizes the whole neighborhood. She reports an "éclat fâcheux dans tout le voisinage" (l. 90). Everyone is talking. This elicits a counterattack from Dorine, no mean gossip herself, in which the censors are censured, and an enlightened little sermon from Cléante on the futility of trying to keep people from gossiping. That does not prevent him later on from expressing the same concern about what people are saying when he tells Tartuffe how scandalized everyone is by his presence in the Orgon household:

> Oui, tout le monde en parle, et vous m'en pouvez croire,
> L'éclat que fait ce bruit n'est point à votre gloire.
>
> (ll. 1185-86)

The characters in ***Tartuffe*** live in a world populated by people who talk about them and sit in judgment on them. Orgon reports the gossip he has heard about Valère: "à jouer on dit qu'il est enclin" (l. 523). Dorine warns him that if he takes Tartuffe as a son-in-law he will be ridiculed: "je ne puis souffrir / qu'aux brocards d'un chacun vous alliez vous offrir" (ll. 547-48). Mariane is afraid of what the public will say if she displays her love for Valère without conventional girlish reticence: "Et veux-tu que mes feux par le monde étalés . . ." (l. 635). Elmire suggests that an appeal to the public will invalidate the contract whereby Tartuffe has become the owner of Orgon's house:

> Allex faire éclater l'audace de l'ingrat
> Ce procédé détruit la vertu du contrat.
>
> (ll. 1823-24)

No one is more aware of this large and impressionable audience than Tartuffe himself, the character who plays to an audience every moment of his life. He is an expert on public opinion and knows or pretends to know what people think of him: "Tout le monde me prend pour un homme de bien" (l. 1099). He knows the power of the spoken word and the efficacy of silence:

> Le scandale du monde est ce qui fait l'offense,
> Et ce n'est pas pécher que pécher en silence.
>
> (ll. 1505-06)

Tartuffe never forgets *le monde* and *les choses de ce monde* which he has pretended to renounce. The people in the background watching, admiring, despising, and gossiping give their own perspective to the play and throw the dominant figure into dramatic relief.

Fear of scandal and the provocation of scandal have an important part to play in ***Tartuffe.*** This is natural enough. Scandal is endemic to the theater. The dramatist may not always set out, as he does in ***Tartuffe,*** to portray scandalous doings, but he almost always seeks to shake, to shock, to have some more than passing impact on his audience. He aims at what we call a gut response: as Molière puts it, good plays are "des choses qui nous prennent par les entrailles" (***La Critique de l'école des femmes,*** Sc. vi). It is to direct or reinforce this response of theater audiences to the scandalous, outrageous, or ridiculous behavior of his protagonists that Molière furnishes them with an offstage audience and shows their impact on these outsiders. Molière's characters are frequently reminded that they are being watched by a public with a sharp sense of the ridiculous or a keen nose for scandal—a public both urbane and urban which dramatizes their actions. Chrysalde to Arnolphe in ***L'Ecole des femmes***: "Gare qu'aux carrefours on ne vous tympanise" (l. 72). Philinte to Alceste in ***Le Misanthrope***: "Je vous dirai tout franc que cette maladie, / Partout où vous allez donne la comédie" (ll. 105-06). Anselme to Pandolfe in ***L'Etourdi***: "De grâce, n'allez pas divulguer un tel conte; / On en ferait jouer quelque farce à ma honte" (ll. 619-20).

Madame Pernelle adds another dimension to the world the characters live in when she tells them what destination Tartuffe has in mind for them: "C'est au chemin du Ciel qu'il prétend vous conduire" (l. 53). *Le ciel,* a key word in ***Tartuffe,*** spoken for the first time in this line, is a euphemism for God, but there are instances where it keeps more than a trace of its primary meaning. Tartuffe contrives to mention *le ciel* as often as possible and no doubt reminds us of its presence by gesture as well. "Ses roulements d'yeux et son ton radouci"—a line from Alceste's description of *le franc scélérat* in ***Le Misanthrope*** (l. 127)—fits Tartuffe very well. Nothing, in fact, expresses piety more theatrically than eyes rolling heavenward, a favorite facial expression of baroque art and one that seems inseparable from the part of Tartuffe. Tartuffe is on intimate terms with heaven—*au mieux du monde,* as Orgon puts it—and gives the impression of being in almost constant communication with the heavenly father. Whether he is looking up to grace from on high or turning his back on the things of this world, everything he talks about takes on an intensely physical aspect. Paris may be just outside the door, but when Tartuffe speaks heaven is right over the roof. His imperturbable and tireless repetition of the word—"l'interêt du ciel, la gloire du ciel, la volonté du ciel"—helps persuade his victims that he has the key to heaven in his back pocket.

The opening scene of ***Tartuffe*** has much to say about the setting and atmosphere in which the action will take place: a noisy, disputatious, outspoken household; a neighborhood buzzing with talk and gossip; a family accustomed to the pleasures offered by a sociable, lively capital city that finds itself invited against its will to abandon earthly pursuits and to follow an intruder up the straight and narrow path to heaven. The whole scene is framed by an opening line which promises an exit: "Allons, Flipote, allons" (l. 1), and a final line which echoes it: "marchons, gaupe, marchons" (l. 171). It is, in fact, an exit scene, the longest and, with the possible exception of Monsieur Purgon's whirlwind exit in Act III of ***Le Malade imaginaire,*** the most expressive in Molière's theater.

Entrances and exits are crucial moments in the structure of any play. Many of them in ***Tartuffe*** are dramatically underscored and echo one another. Characters leave the house with a malediction like Madame Pernelle or are thrown out like Damis, Tartuffe, and Monsieur Loyal. They enter to take possession of the house or to be reconciled with the family. Entrances and exits underline the double significance of the house in ***Tartuffe.*** It is at once a possession symbolizing and guaranteeing Orgon's social standing and a shelter protecting and preserving the intimacy of family life. It is both *pignon sur rue* and *foyer.* Entrances and exits to this privileged place also provide, through the open door, glimpses of the world outside.

Orgon's first entrance follows Madame Pernelle's exit. She leaves a house where she sees nothing but disorder and disrespect. He returns to a house where he sees nothing but prosperity and piety. "Tout semble y prospérer," (l. 300) he says beatifically to his brother-in-law. Tartuffe has brought about this happy state of affairs, and Orgon can talk about nothing else.

The scene takes as its point of departure a situation often used in drama: the return of the lord and master. In tragedy, the absences of the father like Thésee or Mithridate are motivated by warlike or heroic enterprises which impart a certain prestige to the absent figure. In most Molière comedies the reasons are less specific and far humbler. Orgon, like Arnolphe in ***L'Ecole des femmes,*** has gone to spend a few days in the country, presumably to oversee his property. He has certainly not been on vacation. We learn from Cléante's greeting that it is not the season to enjoy the pleasures of rustic life: "La campagne à présent n'est pas beaucoup fleurie" (l. 225). We have seen Dorine's depressing view of small-city life. This one glimpse of the countryside is not much more cheerful. It is the only reference to nature in the whole play. This is typical. In most Molière comedies, except for the *pastorales,* the setting is urban, and most of the infrequent allusions to nature suggest there is danger in leaving town. Dom Juan plans an abduction by water and is nearly drowned, then journeys through a forest and is attacked by robbers. Elise in ***L'Avare*** owes her life to her fiancé, Valère, who saved her from drowning, and he in turn is the survivor of a shipwreck. It is small wonder that Molière's characters rarely venture beyond the city walls. Who knows what dangers may await them? The fathers in Molière whose business takes them out of town could all exclaim with Sganarelle in ***L'Amour médecin***: "Ah! l'étrange chose que la vie! Et que je puis bien dire avec ce grand philosophe de l'antiquité, que qui terre a, guerre a" (Act I, Sc. i). They would do well to remember Scapin's warning that it is best to expect the worst any time one returns from a trip.

> Pour peu qu'un père de famille ait été absent de chez lui, il doit promener son esprit sur tous les fâcheux accidents que son retour peut rencontrer, se figurer sa maison brûlée, son argent dérobé, sa femme morte, son fils estropié, sa fille subornée; et ce qu'il trouve qu'il ne lui est point arrivé, l'imputer à bonne fortune.
>
> (Act II, Sc. v)

Orgon's inquiries on his return are a commonplace of the comic theater: "Tout s'est-il, ces deux jours, passé de bonne sorte? / Qu'est-ce qu'on fait céans? . . . Comme est-ce qu'on s'y porte?" (ll. 229-30). This might be Arnolphe in ***L'Ecole des femmes***: "Hé bien! Alain, comment se porte-t-on ici?" (l. 221). The surprise comes when we learn that it is not his wife, son, or daughter that concerns him, but only Tartuffe. He has learned from Tartuffe a new imperturbability in the face of the disasters that the returning father must learn to expect:

> Et je verrais mourir frère, enfants, mère et femme
> Que je m'en soucierais autant que de cela.
>
> (ll. 278-79)

By a fundamental dramatic irony this entrance where Orgon can think of no one but Tartuffe is balanced by an exit where Tartuffe himself ejects Orgon from his own house and dispossesses him. The peripeteia, the moment which in Boileau's words "change tout, donne à tout une face imprévue," turns on the question of the ownership of the house. Everything has changed because the property has changed hands. Orgon says to Tartuffe, "Il faut, tout sur le champ, sortir de la maison" (l. 1556) to which Tartuffe replies, "C'est à vous d'en sortir, vous qui parlez en maître" (l. 1557). Until the last scene it appears that Tartuffe is right: Orgon is no longer master of his own house and will be obliged to leave it. Monsieur Loyal serves a notice of eviction, Valère enters to hasten his departure with the news of his imminent arrest, and just as he is making a precipitous exit, Tartuffe and the *exempt* appear to lead him off to prison.

As for Tartuffe, we do not see his entrance. Before the play begins he has already established himself as the dominant force in the household and the problem is how to get rid of him. The scene in Act III when he finally appears is a false exit. He says to his servant Laurent: "Si l'on vient pour me voir, je vais aux prisonniers / Des aumônes que j'ai partager les deniers" (ll. 855-56). There is dramatic irony here, too. Tartuffe will indeed go to prison but not yet and not of his own free will. Orgon's house is not a house that you step out of casually. Characters leave in a rage or are thrown out with a curse. "Comme un criminel chassez-moi de chez vous" (l. 1084) says Tartuffe to Orgon when he is denounced by Damis. He has the tyrant's trick of threatening to leave in order to establish his presence more securely: "Je crois qu'il est besoin, mon frère, que j'en sorte . . . Laissez-moi vite, en m'éloignant d'ici / Leur ôter tout sujet de m'accuser ainsi" (ll. 1154, 1163-64). In Act IV, when Cléante urges him to withdraw, Tartuffe interrupts and, far from leaving the house, goes upstairs where an unspecified pious duty calls him. When he finally does leave, his threats make it clear that he will reappear to take possession of his property.

When a bourgeois like Orgon loses his house, he loses his identity. The bourgeois in Molière considers his house, his wife, and his children as property. Typically, he wants to keep everything for himself. His house is particularly dear to him, however, since his status depends on it, a bourgeois being by definition a person who owns property in the city. A bourgeois stripped of his possessions descends to the level of a Tartuffe before his meeting with Orgon, "un gueux . . . qui n'avait pas de souliers / Et dont l'habit entier valait bien six deniers" (ll. 64-65). That is what happens in the play.

Tartuffe rises as Orgon falls. Orgon was a man of wisdom and courage. "Pour servir son prince, il montra du courage" (l. 182). At the beginning of the last scene he expects to be led off to prison by order of the King. Tartuffe in the meanwhile has become what Orgon was, a trusted servant of the King. He plays the part with his usual zeal and aplomb: "L'intérêt du prince est mon premier devoir" (l. 1880). They have exchanged roles. Tartuffe was the creature of Orgon, Orgon becomes the creature of Tartuffe, "un homme à mener par le nez" (l. 1524). Orgon is psychologically dependent on Tartuffe from the start, but he has done nothing irreparable until the donation. He has learned from Tartuffe to express contempt for the ties that bind him to his family and to his worldly possessions, to his house and to his home. The donation following upon his son's disinheritance closes the gap between words and deeds. Living in a dream world, however, Orgon will not realize the hard meaning of what he has done until Monsieur Loyal has moved in with ten strong men who will help Orgon and his family move out in the morning. All this "sans scandale et sans bruit" (l. 1784). There is an ironical echo here of Madame Pernelle's attack on the household's noisy and scandalous life. The eviction of Orgon's family will no doubt bring more excitement to the neighborhood and more delight to its gossips than anything Madame Pernelle could have imagined. Orgon will be in prison, his family on the street, and Tartuffe installed in the house as its new owner.

Valère's appearance at the end also echoes a theme from the beginning of the play. Cléante argues that the parties and social gatherings of Paris life are not at all incompatible with virtue and goodness of heart. This is one of the commonplaces of libertine thought. Orgon reports that Valère does not go to church as often as he should, and is probably something of a gambler as well. But it is Valère, the spurned suitor, who comes to Orgon's rescue with a carriage and a thousand louis. Valère has a well-connected friend who values friendship over justice (another libertine commonplace) and who has the delicacy and thoughtfulness to violate a state secret and inform him of Orgon's imminent arrest. ***Tartuffe*** is not only a condemnation of bigotry and hypocrisy, but, through Valère, an affirmation of the innocence and goodness not only of those "dévots de cœur" whom Cléante enumerates, but also in a more general way, of all the attractive young people who enjoy "les bals, les conversations, les assemblées," gambling, theater, fashionable dress, all the pleasures that you can find in Paris and nowhere else.

Valère is powerless against the evil represented by Tartuffe, however. It is only the King who can correct such abuses. The miraculous denouement recalls the crowning advantage of living in Paris: the opportunity to bask in the radiant presence of the Sun-King. The imagery of *l'exempt*'s speech suggests the solar attributes of Louis XIV. He is an enemy of darkness, horror, crookedness, traps, deceptions, and frauds. A flood of light emanates from him and suffuses the scene. He sees straight and he sees all: "Un prince dont les yeux se font jour dans les cœurs . . . une droite vue . . . Il a percé par ses vives clartés, / Des replis de son cur toutes les lâchetés" (l. 1907, l. 1910, ll. 1919-20). The black misdeeds and dark plotting of Tartuffe have cast a heavy shadow on the scene. By removing him the King restores to the scene its brightness and purity, and, to borrow a line from *Phèdre,* "rend au jour qu'il souillait toute sa pureté." Louis' palace is so close that as soon as the curtain falls the whole family will go kneel before him in gratitude.

Tartuffe is unique in the particular importance it gives to the house itself, but many of its place references have their counterpart in other Molière comedies: apart from costume (so important in Molière that it deserves to be treated separately), props form the characters' most immediate environment. Parallels to the props which characterize Tartuffe are the catalog of worn-out, ugly, antiquated, and useless objects which Harpagon foists off on a borrower in ***L'Avare,*** or conversely, the objects symbolic of aristocratic rank and refinement among which Monsieur Jourdain moves with such delight and bewilderment. In most Molière comedies, as in ***Tartuffe,*** the audience is reminded that the characters inhabit a neighborhood where malicious gossip abounds. Harpagon finds this out when he asks Maître Jacques what people are saying about him, and Madame Jourdain knows precisely what the neighbors will say if her daughter marries a nobleman. Dorine's satiric attack on provincial life is echoed and expanded in a half-dozen plays. With the more distant place references in Molière we move from the real to the fantastic. They come from the charlatans who, like Tartuffe referring to *le ciel,* seek to bedazzle their victims, or from the long-lost relatives who bring a happy ending in from overseas. Thus Covielle tells Monsieur Jourdain, "j'ai voyagé par tout le monde," to which Monsieur Jourdain answers with his usual childish wonder: "Je pense qu'il y a bien loin en ce pays-là" (Act IV, Sc. iii). Toinette in ***Le Malade imaginaire*** also comes from afar: "Je suis médecin passager qui vais de ville en ville, de province en province, de royaume en royaume" (Act III, Sc. x). Dramatically, these hoaxes are not sharply distinguishable from the miraculous denouements which also are brought in unexpectedly by world travelers: Thomas d'Alburcy from Naples in ***L'Avare,*** Enrique, the long-lost relative from America, in ***L'Ecole des femmes.***

The affirmation of the pleasures of Paris implicit in ***Tartuffe*** is repeated in several other plays. It is revealing, however, to turn from the denouement of ***Tartuffe*** with its family gathering at the feet of the King, to the denouement of ***Le Misanthrope*** where the group scatters and the protagonist bids farewell to Paris with a final denunciation: "Je vais sortir d'un gouffre où triomphent les vices" (l. 1804). Alceste departs in search of some remote and as yet undiscovered place where a man of honor can dwell in freedom:

> Et chercher sur la terre un endroit écarté
> Où d'être homme d'honneur on ait la liberté.
>
> (ll. 1805-06)

The contrast is enlightening. Molière's characters seem to live in a world whose constituent elements are sufficiently stable so that one can imagine a character from one play moving into the other. In fact, *le franc scélérat* who wins his case against Alceste in ***Le Misanthrope*** seems to be none other than Tartuffe himself. But *le franc scélérat* remains a shadowy figure in ***Le Misanthrope*** and never puts in an appearance in Célimène's salon. Paris may be the same city in ***Le Misanthrope*** as in ***Tartuffe*** but it is seen in such a harsh light that its features are hard to recognize.

The quaint notion that Molière was somehow a clumsy or careless dramatist who slapped his plays together with little care for anything except characters and ideas has been so thoroughly discredited that today we may tend to the other extreme and see in elements of his dramaturgy that are merely trivial or conventional the working out of some design. It may well be that in some of his plays the setting and place references simply furnish a painted backdrop as usable in one play as in another. Certainly in ***Tartuffe,*** however—and no doubt in ***Le Misanthrope*** as well—they have a distinctive expressive function and are integrated into an esthetic whole.

Notes

1. All references to Molière's works are taken from Molière, *Œuvres,* edition Despois et Mesnard (Paris: Hachette, 1878).
2. The motif of Paris as Babylon would be worth tracing from the kind of sermon Molière is parodying here through Henry James's "the bright Babylon" to the "cité orientale" which Proust evokes in *Sodome et Gomorrhe.*

Myrna Kogan Zwillenberg (essay date 1975)

SOURCE: "Dramatic Justice in *Tartuffe*," in *Modern Language Notes,* Vol. 90, No. 4, April, 1975, pp. 583-90.

[*In the following essay, Zwillenberg explores Molière's use of justice in* Tartuffe.]

Few will quarrel with the judgment that Molière's ***Tartuffe*** is a masterpiece, yet those who agree on the excellence of the play frequently express hostility and confusion about the intervention of the King at the end. The King's justice, it is argued, may be thorough and effective, but it is so unexpected as to cast doubt upon the dramatic coherence of the entire comedy. Probably, Molière himself is responsible for this reaction, having resorted to a *deus ex machina* that appears to defy internal resolution. By relying on a device which introduces a new character possessed of sweeping powers, he seems to be saying that there is a break between dramatically motivated expectations of justice and the King's own dazzling display of power and omniscience.

The earliest extant criticism of the play (thought to be written by Molière) is the *Lettre sur la comédie de l'Imposteur,* a pamphlet which circulated after the 1664 version of ***Tartuffe.*** In it the author assumes the conventional posture of an Aristotelian critic who defends the portrayal of the Hypocrite as a moral corrective to vice. The King's justice does not surprise this critic; on the contrary, he saves his greatest praise for the dénouement:

> Il me semble que si, dans tout le reste de la pièce, l'auteur a égalé tous les anciens et surpassé tous les modernes, on peut dire que dans ce dénouement il s'est surpassé lui-même, n'ayant rien de plus grand, de plus magnifique et de plus merveilleux, et cependant rien de plus naturel, de plus heureux et de plus juste. . . ."[1]

Today such hyperbole and its critical perspective seem quaint at best.[2] Nevertheless, the *Lettre* remains more than a charming, but useless antique. The author of that document, like so many generations of spectators after him, sensed the relationship between the tensions generated by the figure of Tartuffe and the audience's desire that he not go unpunished at the end of the play. The comic and unsympathetic nature of the character suggests that he is a ridiculous figure destined to lose the protection of his mask, opaque only to Orgon and his mother. Indeed, it seems safe to say that a final triumph by Tartuffe would betray the comic essence of the play: the folly of both Tartuffe and Orgon would not be amusing if comedy were to dissolve into melodrama, leaving the hypocrite victorious over a helpless family.

Interestingly enough, the author of the *Lettre* skirts completely the issue of Orgon's complicity in Tartuffe's rise to power. This embarrassing omission, no doubt motivated by a desire to defend, rather than analyse the play, has long since been corrected. Lionel Gossman, notably, has summarized modern critical opinion: "Tartuffe cannot be given credit for having bamboozled Orgon. Orgon is as much Tartuffe's creator as Tartuffe himself."[3]

Here it seems, we are arriving at the heart of the dilemma. The comic tensions provoking audience laughter are directly related to situations and characters perceived as unjust. Even where no legal breaches occur—as in the case of Orgon's decision to marry off his daughter to Tartuffe or to banish and disinherit his son—the injustice of such actions is manifest to the audience. To be sure, Molière has taken the precaution of signaling such incidents by having the servant Dorine express her exaggerated moral outrage, a significant device which pinpoints the areas meant to be ridiculous. But even if Dorine were not present, the excessive authority exercised over the sympathetic characters by both Orgon and Tartuffe would be cause enough to desire that they receive their just desserts.

When considered in the light of a need for closure, however, this type of scenario poses thorny problems.

Audience expectations of dramatic justice, nurtured through the repeated exposure of comic folly, demand confirmation, usually in the form of order replacing comic disorder. But if there are two strong comic figures, it would surely not do to foil only one of the protagonists. Dramatic justice, in the case of ***Tartuffe,*** would seem to necessitate the punishment of Orgon and the hypocrite, two figures whose outrageous behavior constitutes an aberration we are willing to enjoy as a comic spectacle, but only with the knowledge that it will not go unchecked.

This conclusion may help to explain the traditional hostility to the dénouement. Even if the ending did not include a *deus ex machina,* it would still be difficult to justify, as a solution, an ending that treats one comic figure so harshly and the other so lightly.

However, a fundamental error in this reasoning derives, I believe, from a narrow view of justice as a final rather than evolving concept. Seventeenth-century theoreticians traditionally considered only the final reversal in a series to be the dénouement,[4] but if one takes into consideration the comic tensions engendered by a multiplicity of evolving characters and situations, it might be more proper to expand the dénouement to include the relaxation of all the major tensions. Moreover, appreciation of the gradual nature of such an extended process might make it possible to perceive not only the means employed, but also its effect upon the dynamics of the play.

Perhaps the most important factor is that the roles of the protagonists do evolve in the course of the play. If one compares, for example, Orgon's early posture of power and insensitivity with his plight in Act IV, scene 7, when Tartuffe announces control over the family's wordly possessions, it becomes clear that the lines of comic force have shifted. Nor is the role of Orgon the only one to change, for this scene also heralds a major change in the role of the hypocrite. Functioning formerly as Orgon's alter-ego and as a ridiculous figure inspiring laughter,[5] he now appears as a menace whose power threatens the internal equilibrium of the comic process.

This striking scene, with its overwhelming reversals, may hold a key to the final proceedings. First of all, it separates the lines of force which permitted Orgon and Tartuffe to function as comic accomplices. This is important because it strengthens the individuality of each figure at the same time it separates the fate of one from the other. Secondly, it serves as a dénouement of sorts because it humbles Orgon, punishing him for his folly and humilating him for his blindness. All of his unjust acts make him ripe for humiliation, and Tartuffe's assumption of power provides at least partial justice in the spectacle of Orgon's helpless rage.

But it would be erroneous to see in this scene any complete comic closure for the play.[6] Orgon deserves to be humiliated, but not in so abject—and one could add, unfunny—a manner, and certainly not by a figure who is at least as guilty of misconduct as he. In brief, this pivotal scene shifts the focus to Tartuffe's power, but resolves only a fraction of the tensions present.

If Orgon cannot dispel Tartuffe's power, who is left to do it? A rapid glance at the remaining cast of characters offers little hope of a solution. The docile daughter Marianne cannot even openly challenge her father. Damis, with his adolescent rage and simplistic idealism, has, of course, been banished. Elmire, the discreet and self-effacing wife, would appear to have some chance for success, but she already seems exhausted, having expended all her energy in the plot to trick Tartuffe, a plot so contrary to her nature that she feels obliged to apologize for it. Dorine and Cléante perceive the situation most clearly, but for all their talking, they have been lacking the force and prestige to bring about any significant change. That leaves only old Madame Pernelle, who shares with her son Orgon the blindness and gullibility which make of her another accomplice, rather than a possible savior for the family.

Boileau's suggested dénouement, which would have the family judge and then perhaps chase Tartuffe from the house in a farcical manner, is deftly dismissed by Professor Scherer, who points out that the family, devoid of its legal documents, is hardly in a position to judge Tartuffe.[7] This simple fact, coupled with the dramatic havoc to be created by changing the formerly weak character of the family, would therefore make such a solution impossible. Also, once again, a concerted effort by Orgon and his family would bypass the important issue of Orgon's guilt and posture as a comic figure.

The burden of comic closure falls to Act V which, it will appear, deals with the problem in steps. The proceedings of Act IV have given ample proof of Tartuffe's true nature even to a mind as closed as that of Orgon. Therefore, Orgon's awakening comes as the proper and logical first step. Scene 2 brings the return of Damis, welcomed home by a chastened father. The rhythm then changes, bringing comic relief in the obstinate ramblings of Madame Pernelle during Scene 3. In Scene 5, after she has seen for herself the crimes perpetrated by Tartuffe's henchman, Monsieur Loyal, she, too, awakens to the truth, exclaiming: "Je suis tout ébaubie, et je tombe des nues!" Valère's offer of aid in the following scene puts the final touch on the reunion and shows him to be a worthy husband for Marianne. All would thus seem to be very sweet just before the play's final scene—except for the significant fact that the problems have again only partially been solved. This is the moment of the arrival of the Exempt, representative of the police and the King. The play's final scene is also the moment for the play's greatest reversal, the *deus ex machina* that resolves all of the difficulties still remaining.

It should be noted that this ending does have its supporters, and in recent years most of the arguments have centered about the thematic justification for the King's intervention.[8] Given the theme of abused authority, set in motion in the play's initial scene and sustained throughout the comedy, the validity of introducing a supreme authority figure at its close seems largely justified. However, thematic coherence alone would not explain Molière's recourse to so spectacular an ending. Indeed, as mentioned earlier, the surprise of the Exempt's arrival, his silence, and then his startling revelation of the reasons for his appearance suggest a structural breach as powerful as any thematic link.

Clearly then, any full explanation for the *deus ex machina* must look to structural as well as thematic criteria. One clue can be found in the spectacle of Act V. These scenes are usually cited to show that Molière had reached a dead-end: that "real life" drama has brought Orgon and his family to contrition and reconciliation, without a happy ending. However, this interpretation ignores two structural details that have dominated the comedy: the impulse to justice and the pattern of comic equilibrium.

When considered as a dramatic device, the first part of the fifth act reveals itself to be a period of apprehension that makes the coming storm more impressive. The weakness of the sympathetic figures cries out for a strong and just reversal precisely because the comic structure of the play (which descends at times to a farcical level) makes highly unlikely a final victory for the villain of the piece.

Molière's careful attention to detail in Act V would also support this view. The reunion of the family, the conversion of Madame Pernelle, the hope of a wedding for the young lovers *if* Tartuffe's dastardly plot can be thwarted—all combine to create an emotionally charged cliff-hanger. Nor is the solution a particularly difficult one, for having disposed of the other major problems, Molière need solve only one more: foiling Tartuffe.

However, the climate of suspense means that any solution to the dilemma will have to match the emotional heights reached in the first part of Act V. A wink and a pardon, as in ***L'Avare,*** will not suffice, nor will a happy carnival setting, as in le ***Bourgeois Gentilhomme***; on the contrary, a tonic chord will have to be very forceful.

In the final scene timing is all-important. Molière exploits the suspense to an extreme, allowing Tartuffe his final vindictive tirade in the presence of the Exempt whose initial silence seems to bear witness to the hypocrite's victory. This is the moment for the play's most startling reversal, and it comes only after Tartuffe himself has set the trap:

> Tartuffe, à l'Exempt.
> Délivrez-moi, Monsieur, de la criaillerie,
> Et daignez accomplir votre ordre, je vous prie.
> L'Exempt
>
> Oui, *c'est trop demeurer* sans doute à l'accomplir:
> Votre bouche *à propos* m'invite à le remplir;
> Et pour l'exécuter, suivez-moi tout à l'heure
> Dans la prison qu'on doit vous donner pour demeure.
>
> (1897-1902)

No dramatic or linguistic flourish is spared in this or in the Exempt's following speech. One listens in stunned silence to a litany of the King's superhuman qualities and to the sentence he has decreed. Not only for the family, but for the spectator as well, the words bring sweet relief that comes from a reprieve from fear. The intolerable cloud of injustice which has loomed menacingly overhead is slowly lifted, leaving the pure light of *le roi Soleil.* The impulses to justice and to comic equilibrium have been fulfilled after all, and the structural integrity of the play is intact. To be sure, the suspense was painful, but the pleasure is all the more intense for it.

Another major aspect of the dénouement, distinct from the orchestration of the scene, is the means by which Tartuffe is punished and order restored to the household: Tartuffe is discovered as a result of *past* crimes, and Orgon is excused because of *past* favors rendered to the King during the Fronde. The text is very explicit on both points, noting with respect to Tartuffe that he is:

> un fourbe renommé
> Dont sous un autre nom il étoit informé,
> Et c'est un long détail d'actions toutes noires
> Dont on pourroit former des volumes d'histories.
>
> (1923-26)

As for Orgon's pardon, it is the result of a favor dating back about twenty years:

> Et c'est le prix qu'il donne au zèle qu'autrefois
> On vous vit témoigner en appuyant ses droits
>
> (1939-40)

When these two aspects, the surprise of the *deus ex machina* and the device of relating both the punishment and the pardon to the past, are examined in the light of tensions generated earlier, the ending appears anything but arbitrary.

First of all, the intervention of the King resolves all of the major tensions remaining: it punishes Tartuffe, recognizes and then excuses Orgon's culpability, restores family harmony, and guarantees that such excesses will not soon take place again. In brief, it unties all the knots (and does not merely chop them off, as a wag suggested) at the same time it releases the tensions resulting from the Tartuffe-Orgon fraternity. The audience is rewarded for its correct perception of comic forces by the spectacle of seeing the guilty defeated, and it also experiences the pleasure of suspense preceding the welcome reversal which terminates the play.

Secondly, the device of reverting back in time reveals itself to be a beautifully simple measure for solving a complex problem gracefully. Punishing Tartuffe by other means, such as a judgment by the family or an invalidation of the contract in the courts, would have still left unsolved the matter of Orgon's complicity. Moreover, this sort of ending would have been devoid of the éclat which comes from Tartuffe's final blunder, exposed for all to see in the refracted light of the reversal. Nor is the problem of Orgon's crimes ignored; they are simply separated from those of Tartuffe, permitting the King to treat each individually.

This is not to say, however, that the substance of the ending is inferior to its form. On the contrary, the device of making the King the agent of justice more than adequately meets the specific needs of the ending. The impulse to dramatic justice, which has been growing more intense throughout Act V, finds an appropriate carrier in the person of the King. Only a figure of superhuman stature could see into the hearts of men, and only he could remember good and evil dating back to the Fronde. In fact, by putting on stage the one mortal figure capable of transcending time, Molière has solved the greatest problem still remaining. Certainly, no solution is possible in the present, but an earlier time, free of complications, easily meets the need for an outside form of justice.

The point is that Molière has paced himself in such a way as to exploit all of the dramatic potential in Tartuffe's rise to power and in his subsequent, inevitable fall. Like an elastic band stretched to its breaking point, the action of Act V creates increased audience apprehension proportional to the growing threat of disaster. Unlike the subtle play of forces which marked the period of complicity between the two comic figures, the technique here is linear and cumulative, building up force for a reversal whose shock is equal to the suspense preceding it.

On the other hand, this does not mean that just any final reversal will have the desired effect. It is the mark of an expert craftsman that the means employed correspond so perfectly to the tensions generated earlier. Moreover, this would appear to be Molière's primary consideration, rather than any attempt to explain the King's interest in Orgon's dilemma. Although such interest comes as a great surprise, it is one which strengthens the force of the Exempt's pronouncements. Surely, a monarch who knows all things past and present should cause little wonder that his perception of injustice is accurate. Just how accurate becomes apparent in his balanced dispensation of justice, which corresponds not only to past crimes or favors, but also to the dramatic exigency of relaxing the tensions caused by the ascendance of a villain.

Looking back to Act IV, scene 6, the dénouement further reveals itself to be the second stage of a process begun much earlier. From a pattern of balanced complicity Molière moved to the imbalance of allowing Tartuffe apparent victory, at the expense of the family's humiliation and helplessness. This permitted him to relax one major tension deriving from the injustice of Orgon's abuse of authority. However, it left another major tension, that of Tartuffe's unjust rise to power, which then demanded an even greater reversal to redress the balance. And since a satisfying solution could ignore neither Orgon's earlier complicity, nor his present helplessness, dramatic equilibrium could be restored only by an outside agent able to transcend the present. Also, by choosing the one figure capable of perceiving all the divisions, justice could be dispensed with an even hand.

When examined in the light of both structural and dramatic exigencies, therefore, Molière's recourse to a *deus ex machina* emerges as a fitting vehicle for the resolution of comic tensions. It effectively restores the equilibrium of the comic universe, releases all remaining tensions, and confirms the validity of the spectator's perception. ***Tartuffe*** may disappoint those looking for "real life" drama, but the play itself has no such pretensions. Its internal comedy, nourished by examples of injustice, constitutes a closely controlled dramatic mechanism whose evolving plan leads us to expect a just ending. ***Tartuffe*** clearly fulfills this expectation, and provides masterful comedy in the process.

Notes

1. The *Lettre* consulted for this study appears in the Despois-Mesnard edition of Molière's works (Paris, 1878), IV, 529-66. This edition is also the source for direct references to the play.
2. As Jacques Scherer and others have pointed out, the force of the argument, for all its attractiveness, suffers from an excess of uncritical praise.
3. Lionel Gossman, *Men and Masks: A Study of Molière* (Baltimore, 1963), p. 110.
4. See Jacques Scherer, *La Dramaturgie classique en France* (Paris, 1950), pp. 125-26.
5. Three such moments, grouped by Marcel Gutwirth, are the handkerchief scene where Tartuffe tangles with Dorine ("Couvrez ce sein que je ne saurois voir . . ." III,2), his grotesque attempts at seduction in his first meeting with Elmire (III,3), and his recourse to the truth, in the fervent hope he will not be believed, after being denounced by Damis (III,6). See *Molière ou l'invention comique* (Paris, 1966), pp. 179-83.
6. John Cairncross's theory, in *New Light on Molière: Tartuffe; Elomire Hypocondre* (Genève, 1956), of the three-act "Urtartuffe" of 1664, ending with Orgon chasing Tartuffe from the house, would be only slightly more satisfying. Since Orgon is largely responsible for Tartuffe's rise to power, it would be difficult to appreciate an ending which failed to take that fact into consideration.
7. Jacques Scherer, *Structures de Tartuffe* (Paris, 1966), p. 192.
8. Scherer cites the King's role as "roi-père" and the probability that he has followed the fortunes of Orgon (*Structures de Tartuffe*, pp.200-207). See also Judd Hubert, *Molière and the Comedy of Intellect* (Berkeley, 1962); and Jacques Guicharnaud, *Molière, une aventure théâtrale* (Paris, 1963).

Andrew McKenna (essay date 1989)

SOURCE: "*Tartuffe*, Representation and Difference," in

Papers on French Seventeenth Century Literature, Vol. XVI, No. 30, 1989, pp. 76-93.

[*The following essay, McKenna discusses Molière's* Tartuffe, *focusing on misinterpretations embodied within the work that serve to entrap its audience.*]

Molière's ***Le Tartuffe, ou l'Imposteur*** is a play about sex, religion and politics, the canonical topics of adult conversation. It affords the requisite opportunities for a radical critique of desire, the sacred, and power, the canonical topics of our demystifying fervor—with which we often remystify readers by the use of such terms as theophallogocentrism. Moreover, it is a text whose misunderstanding-misinterpretation is inscribed within it, thereby deploying tactics of entrapment (of reader or spectator) which are deemed by many as indispensable to strategies identified as deconstructive. Finally, it is a text in which psychological and rhetorical structures are imbricated, mutually implicated and complicated, so that the allegory of true and false devotion unfolds as an allegory of reading. As a consequence, its analysis serves in this essay as the occasion for interrelating a critique of representation and difference, as exhibited most notably in the writings of Jacques Derrida and Jacques Lacan, with a critique of violence and desire, particularly as we find it in the writings of René Girard.

Orgon-"orgueil": if that word-play has any validity, it suggets that pride is the inscribed subject of the play, the literal and figurative subject in the twofold sense of the noun "subject": as the principle of identity, of action, the locus of agency; and as the matter, the theme, the topic. Orgon imposes Tartuffe on his household in order to dominate its members in a way that exceeds the authority and mastery he already enjoys as *pater familias,* as undisputed head of the household. His daughter Mariane, whom he would marry to Tartuffe, provides the formula for Orgon's ascendancy:

> Contre un père absolu que veux-tu que je fasse?
>
> Un père, je l'avoue, a sur nous tant d'empire Que je n'ai jamais eu la force de rien dire. (II, iii)

But the spectator has already witnessed in an earlier scene that Orgon is not satisfied with such mastery. He seeks control from within the minds and hearts of those subordinate to him:

> Mariane: Qui voulez vous, mon pére, que je dise Qui me touche le coeur, et qu'il me serait doux De voir par votre choix devenir mon époux?
>
> Orgon: Tartuffe.
>
> Mariane: Il n'en est rien, mon père, je vous jure, Pourquoi me faire dire une telle imposture?
>
> Orgon: Mais je veux que cela solt une vérité: Et c'est assez pour vous que je l'aie arrêté. (II,i)

The principle impostor of Molière's play, as critics like Gossman and Guicharnaud have not failed to point out, is Orgon himself, for whom "devotion", the subordination of all conduct and attitudes to absolute, transcendent values, is but a mask, a means to an end: domination. It is one of the fundamental ironies of the play that absolute values are no such thing here: they are relative to the tyrannical ambition of the father. It is a symmetrical irony that Tartuffe, who is enlisted in the service of this goal, should enjoy indisputable mastery over Orgon, who calls him his "brother", but who dotes on him like a lover on his mistress:

> Dorinne
>
> Il l'appelle son frère et l'aime dans son âme Cent fois plus qu'il ne fait mère, fils, fille, et femme.
>
> . . . . .
>
> Il le choie, il l'embrasse, et pour une maîtresse On ne saurait je pense, avoir plus de tendresse:
>
> . . . . .
>
> Enfin il en est fou; c'est son tout, son héros; Il l'admire à tous coups, le cite à tout propos; Ses moindres actions lui semblent des miracles, Et tous les mots qu'il dit sont pour lui des oracles.
>
> (I, ii)

Dorine's hyperbolic metaphors translate the relation of Orgon to Tartuffe as one of idolatry. Orgon is a member of a religion whose god is, undecidably perhaps, himself and Tartuffe. The desire to be god or to play at being god is structurally destined to idolatry, which we define as devotion to a false god, to a mere representation, a signifier. Religious devotion, as institutionalized in the seventeenth century, is the appropriate focus for Molière's critique of representation, which is inseparable from his critique of desire. For what idolatry signifies is the desire of the other's desire. This takes the form of worship of the other's desire. Orgon's subjugation to Tartuffe emulates, is the model for the desired subjugation of his family: his adoration of Tartuffe replicates the adoration he seeks from his family. Tartuffe is to Orgon as Orgon would be to his family—and as Elmire will be for Tartuffe. There is no center to this structure other than the other's desire, which explains why, at the geometrical center of the play (III,iii), Tartuffe in turn is lead to express his desire for Elmire in the language of slavish devotion: "J'aurai toujours pour vous, ô suave merveille, / Une dévotion à nulle autre pareille." "Hubris" and humiliation alternate with each other; like signifier and signified for the Saussurean sign, they are two sides of the same indivisible page, of the same "interdividual" desire (Girard, *Des Choses cachées* III).

To speak of Dorine's discourse, or anyone else's, as metaphorical hyperbole here is perhaps redundant, both metaphor and hyperbole being but discursive equivalents of speaking "as if" (Johnson 62-76). The ontological question then arises: what is not "as if", what is not translation, and correlatively, what is that is not "always already" being translated? The interest of such questions (of representation as rhetoric) is evidenced by Orgon's inability to predicate Tartuffe's superior essence: "C'est un homme

. . . qui, . . . ha! un homme . . . un homme enfin" (I,v). Tartuffe's divine difference consists in nothing else than in Orgon's election of him as a lever by which he seeks absolute power over his family. Orgon's inept tautology here, in the context of his (self-)defense of Tartuffe before the remonstrations of Cléante, translates the vacuity of his own bid for absolute sovereignty: "Qui suit bien ses leçons goûte une paix profonde, / Et comme du fumier regarde tout le monde" (I,v). His peace is constructed on the virtual annihilation of all around him. He does not wish this, but the transcendence which this represents. Similarly, when he intones "Allons, ferme, mon coeur, point de faiblesse humaine" in response to his daughter's entreaties (IV, iii), we rightly suspect that it is the "humaine" rather than the "faiblesse" that he seeks to transcend.

We might recall a symmetrical dilemma posed by La Bruyère, whose portrait of the true dévot (*Les Caractères,* "De la mode," § 23) reads like the negative exposure of the false (§ 2l). This textual structure issues from a social structure which Michael Koppisch has analyzed as *The Dissolution of Character* in La Bruyère's world: what has indeed dissolved, as the author notes, is "the substantiality of man's very essence" (112) in a world given over to the comparison of appearances. Molière too is a comic witness to this dissolution, above all to its potential for violent rivalry.

Orgon's all out devotion to Tartuffe is consonant with the totalitarian character of his desire. Such a desire is properly metaphysical: it has no object in its quest for a transcendence which, as such, forever eludes it: it knows no term, unless it be that of pride, which we invoke in the original sense of "hubris", a rivalry with divinity connoting a hybrid relation, a relation of doubles. It is in this sense that pride is everywhere the subject, the sovereign principle and the principle of deluded sovereignty in Molière's comedy. The Prince, who intervenes from above and without, Dorine, the servant who mediates symmetrically from beneath and consequently outside the circuit of desire and power, and finally Elmire, the faithful wife, are all prominent exceptions to the rule of pride, of mimetic desire, which dominates the action of the play. The Prince is exempt from the struggle because he is deemed or ordained as one confident in his possession of power: Dorine, because she is symmetrically confident in her lack of it: Elmire, because she is confident in her indifference to it. All the other character's are pawns in Molière's power play.

Madame Pernelle, a caricature of her son, sets the tone in her peremptory denunciation of a household whose offense is that "de me complaire on ne prend nul souci": "Oui, je sors de chez Vous fort mal édifiée: / Dans toutes mes leçons j'y suis contrariée" (I, i). As each member of the household is cut off, progressively, at their first (Dorine: "Si . . ."; Damis: "Mais . . ."), second (Mariane: "Je crois . . ."), third (Elmire: "Mais, ma mère . . ."), and fourth word (Cléante: "Mais, Madame, après tout . . ."), we know that dictatorship, not worship, is at issue. Sganarelle, whose first words in ***Le Médecin malgré lui*** are "Non, je te dis que je n'en veux rien faire, et que c'est à moi de parler et d'être le maître," is in the wings. The wife-beater in Molière's farce is the violent heresiarch of sexual difference, just as the slap Madame Pernelle will give to her servant marks her as the heresiarch of social (and moral-intellectual) difference:

> *(Donnant un soufflet à Filpote)*
>
> Allons,vous, vous rêvez, et bayez aux cornellles. Jour de Dieu! je saurai vous frotter les oreilles. Marchons, gaupe, marchons. (I,i)

"Listen! Hear me, first and last," she is saying with a violence toward her servant which represents the violence of her bid for moral ascendancy. "Violence," as Girard has noted, "will come to an end only after it has had the last word and that word has been accepted as divine" (*Violence* 135). In Madame Pernelle's words we have the fated union of violence and the sacred, which is what transpires when hierarchical institutions governing social differences break down. As Girard notes, "The withering away of the transcendental influence means that there is no longer the slightest difference between a desire to save the city and unbridled ambition, between genuine piety and the desire to claim divine status for oneself" (ibid.). Religious devotion testifies to a sacrificial crisis, a crisis of eroding differences, which pervades Molière's world. The radical privatization of worship, a new religious form born of the Counter-Reformation (Argan 22-3), embodies a crisis of consciousness, of subjectivity released willy-nilly from adherence to absolute values, or, much the same thing, from their credible public representation. That Molière's Dom Juan should contemplate the career of a hypocrite, of a "faux dévot," as the displacement and perfection of his career as seducer-rapist, as heresiarch of desire, is pertinent in this regard. Dom Juan's panic individualism and Orgon's panic abdication are complementary expressions of this same crisis, as is the totalitarian "sincerity" of Alceste. It is expressed as a crisis of "character" in La Bruyère, where this term designates a unified totality, a principle of identity and agency whose dissolution in mimetic bondage to the desires of others has been traced by Michael Koppisch through succeeding editions of *Les Caractères* within the courtier's own lifetime.

Madame Pernelle's violence is a transparent refutation of her piety, which Dorine does not fall to detect, indeed to thematize, in Orgon:

> Orgon: Te talras-tu, serpent, dont les traits effrontés . . . ?
>
> Dorine: Ah! vous êtes dévot, et vous vous emportez? (II, ii)

Physical violence accompanies verbal abuse: it is the apposite *dramatization* of the sacred which is being bid for in the play. Violence will out in a competition for power in which the individual will, the principle of autonomous agency, has no role to play. For the latter is but an object of desire rather than a source or origin of agency.

Molière's sense of the sovereignty of violence, as it issues from mimetic desire, is born out in the conduct of Damis. As true and loyal son in his righteous indignation at the attempted seduction of Elmilre by Tartuffe, Damis differs not a wit, nor by a word, from the "emportement" of his outrageous father against all around him.

> Et la bonté du Ciel m'y semble avoir conduit Pour confondre l'orgueil d'un traltre qui me nuit, Pour m'ouvrir une voie à prendre la vengeance De son hypocrisie et de son insolence, A détromper mon père, et lui mettre en plein jour L'âme d'un scélérat qui vous parle de l'amour. (III,iv)

The first two verses of Damis's outburst might have been uttered by Orgon. His election of Tartuffe in spite of the opposition of his family, i.e., because of the opposition of his family, betrays the reactive, relative force of his desire:

> Mais plus on fait d'effort afin de l'en bannir, Plus j'en veux employer à l'y mieux retenir; Et je vais me hâter de lui donner ma fille, Pour confondre l'orgueil de toute ma famllle. (III,vi)

Orgon's desire to retain Tartuffe is a function—a reaction and an invitation—of others' desire to be rid of him, of which Damis's desire is the most strident, the most like the desire of his father in its imperious violence:

> Que la foudre sur l'heure achève mes destins, Qu'on me traite partout du plus grand des faquins, S'il est aucun respect ni pouvolr qul m'arrête, Et si je ne fais pas quelque coup de ma tête! (III,i)

The insubordination of the son emulates the imperious will of the father and is accordingly bound to oppose it; bound indeed by the double bind that destines the son (or the disciple) to oppose the father (the model) wherever and whenever he seeks to resemble him (Girard, *Violence* 145-8). Once again Damis's words on Tartuffe might just as well have been those of Orgon on Damis. The father's "coup de tête" responds like clockwork (tic/toc) to the son's resistance to his will—the will being merely that which opposes what resists it, or the mystified imitation of a rival desire:

> DAMIS: A recevoir sa main on pense l'obliger?
>
> ORGON: Oui, traître, et dès ce soir, pour vous faire enrager. Ah! je vous brave tous, et vous ferai connaître Qu'il faut qu'on m'obéisse et que je suis le maître. Allons, qu'on se rétracte, et qu'à l'instant, fripon, On se jette à ses pieds pour demander pardon.
>
> DAMIS: Qui, moi, de ce coquin, qui, par ses impostures . . .
>
> ORGON: Ah! tu résistes, gueux, et lui dis des injures? Un baton! un baton! ne me retenez pas. (III,vi)

In the midst of the conflict between father and son, Tartuffe, for his part, has only to confess the literal truth for Orgon to confuse his language with the rhetoric of devotion:

> Chaque instant de ma vie est chargé de souillures: Elle n'est qu'un amas de crimes et d'ordures:
>
> Pourquoi sur un tel fait m'être si favorable? Savez-vous, après tout, de quoi je suis capable? Vous fiez-vous, mon frère, à mon extérieur? Et, pour tout ce qu'on voit, me croyez-vous meilleur?
>
> (III,Vi)

Tartuffe's essentially rhetorical question to Orgon questions the essence of rhetoric for Molière's audience. The intemporal rhetoric of original sin disguises Tartuffe's temporal, concrete, literal transgression by its very hyperbole. Tartuffe performs a *quid pro quo,* metonymical in its structure, by which a whole displaces one of its parts, the doctrine of original sin being just such a generalization of particulars, just such a hypostasis of experience. Orgon's folly consists in just such a total investment in figure, a massive *quid pro quo* whereby the sign is ever taken for the thing itself, whereby the name is invested with an essence. The *quid pro quo* follows from the *qui pro quo* whereby he takes himself for a master. He takes himself for being what he is, whereupon, by a predictable contortion of the ontological project, he usurps the power—let us call it theoroyalogical—which is infinitely beyond and above him and which makes him what he is. Orgon, in the manner of Hugo as portrayed by Cocteau, "est un fou qui se croit Orgon." His identity can only be restored to him by the Prince, in whom divine power is invested. The latter's intervention at the close of the play is indeed a *deus ex machina* but it is not fortuitous. Rather it is one whose logic is motivated by the crisis of identity and of difference which informs the play from the outset.

Princely clairvoyance is by definition exempt, as declared by the character bearing that name, from fraudulent illusions (V,vii)—but only, of course, in principle, that is as the imaginary and appropriately off-stage locus of authority, as a sovereign, autonomous will immune to mimetic rivalry. One has only to read Saint-Simon to know that no such will exists, to know that Louis XIV was no less madly and destructively jealous of his royal prerogatives, no less prey to mimetic rivalry and no less deleterious to his household and kingdom than Orgon. Saint-Simon's Tartuffe is Madame de Maintenon, throughout; Louis's model-rival for Saint-Simon is the Prince of Orange. (For Louis's rivalry with his own court at large, consult the episode in the *Mémoires* concerning Courtenvaux [II: 516-18]; for his rivalry with his own minister, Louvois, consult IV: 958ff.) Molière's investment in such a principle is doubtless obligatory in view of his need of royal patronage. But in view of his analyses of desire and hubris, it is probable that his monarchism is informed by the same political intelligence as Pascal's: to foreclose violent rivalry (consult §§ 89, 294, 299, 310, 313 in the Brunschweig edition of the *Pensées*). Orgon's radical "méconnaissance", which is infallibly that of "His Majesty the Ego" (Freud), accounts for the way his own words have an unconsciously double meaning which, at another level, the literal, redounds to his mockery:

> Je vois qu'il [Tartuffe] reprend tout, et qu'à ma femme même, Il prend, pour mon honneur, un intérêt extrême; Il m'avertit des gens qui lui font les yeux doux, Et plus que moi six fois il s'en montre jaloux. (I, v)

What is a "point d'honneur" for Orgon is punctuated by a "point d'ironie" for the public. Double meanings in this play are but the linguistic modality of the rivalry of doubles which informs the psychological conflict of the play.

Only those who, out of their own tyrannical ambition, wish to be fooled by him are fooled by Tartuffe: Orgon, Madame Pernelle. Other characters, his brother Cléante signally, are fooled by Orgon when they believe that Orgon is actually fooled by Tartuffe. Cléante believes that his brother is blind, not that he is tyrannical. Cléante believes in his brother's good faith: he consequently remains blind to his brother's tyrannical ambition. Cléante sees the comedy of devotion being played by Tartuffe, but does not see the comedy being played by his brother Orgon. Cléante knows that true piety does not parade itself before us in the manner of Tartuffe, that the word is not the thing, that one must not always trust appearances, etc. (I,v). But Cléante is helpless to enlighten his brother, who must be blindfolded by his wife in order to hear the truth. Like Molière's other "raisonneurs", (Philinte in ***Le Misanthrope,*** Chrysale in ***L'Ecole des femmes***), Cléante is a nominalist. He believes as much in the exteriority of truth to falsehood as in that of the word to the thing itself. Today we would call him logocentric, and rightly so: analysis of his remonstrations to Orgon (I,v) would but demonstrate Derrida's maxim: "Chacun de nous est le mystagogue *et l'Aufklarer* d'un autre" ("D'un ton . . ." 462).

Because the thing is not itself, not even that thing we call hypocrisy. I do not mean that there is no such thing as hypocrisy, but that there is no such thing in itself. Hypocrisy as the difference between saying and doing, between the word and the thing, between appearance and being, mask and the real, etc., is opposed to sincerity, authenticity, true devotion, etc. This opposition, like others of its stamp, breaks down in Molière's comedy. What is comic is just this breakdown of antinomies, just this loss of difference. It is the presumption, the error, the sin of hypocrisy to impute to others an evil which is not in oneself, or to judge others by standards one does not apply to onself. That is the injustice of hypocrisy, its inequity. It is in the name of that injustice, and for the sake of equity, that Orgon's household urges the expulsion of Tartuffe from its midst. He condemns indulgence in the flesh while avid in carnal self-indulgence. Hypocrisy is the name for this duplicity, this internal difference, or difference within, evidence for which invalidates the difference the hypocrite makes between himself and others. Molière's comedy is not for all that reducible to a condemnation of hypocrisy. That is what hypocrites do: denounce the difference between virtues we profess and vices we practice, between sign and referent, theory and practice. There is a profound hypocrisy in denouncing hypocrisy, which is always the hypocrisy of the other. Differ*a*nce, as difference within, invades hypocrisy as it does every other substantial determination or judgment. Molière's comedy does not merely condemn hypocrisy—for all, including hypocrites, do that—but deconstructs it, by revealing its subjection to desire, by revealing it as but one of the many detours of desire.

Conflict in Molière is not a matter of individual character, nor of psychological stereotypes. It is the consequence of the mimetic structure of desire, of which such notions as character or personality are the illusory effects, the imaginary reflection. Or, to speak more precisely and psychoanalytically, they are the reflection, as we read of it in Lacan's "Mirror Stage," of the Imaginary, which is ever the image of the other as a complete being, the image of completeness which is every only apprehended in the other. Orgon's existence, which Dorine has correctly diagnosed as madness, is imaginary in just such a Lacanian sense: he mistakes the Symbolic for the Real (cf. *Séminaire II* 66-72). Whence the structural homology between Lacan's "Mirror Stage" and Girard's dialectics of mimetic desire, where "Le désir selon l'autre" (Girard) takes another for its model of autonomous selfhood: it takes the other, whole in its apparent otherness (as is the reflection of the self in the mirror for Lacan's *infans*) as Wholly Other, or, much the same thing, Holy Other, this delusion being the ground of Orgon's worship of Tartuffe. Both Lacan and Girard are engaged in deconstructing that ideological construct of Western secular humanism called the Subject, which is variously identified as the sovereign ego, as the autonomous will. It is what Molière "always already" reveals as an imposture, as it emerges from the vacation of the center formerly occupied by the divinity.

For the will is not the center of subjective agency in Molière's play, it is the object of competitive desire. Molière thoroughly anticipates Freud's insistence that "*the Ego is not master in its own house*" (S.E. XVII: 144). Such indeed might have been the subtitle of this play, or its translation. We need not, for all that, subscribe to very arcane machinations of the unconscious. It is sufficient for the ego to desire mastery, as Orgon does, or to imagine it, as Arnolphe does in ***L'Ecole des femmes,*** to find itself opposed by rival doubles. This is altogether Alceste's situation in ***Le Misanthrope***; his targeting of the coquettish Célimène as the object of his desire is preposterous to the reasoning of Philinte, who is as duped by Alceste's imposture as Cléante by Orgon's. Alceste's attraction to Célimène finds its rationale, its origin, unsuspected by either Alceste or Philinte, in the rivals surrounding her, as in Célimène herself, both rival and model of his "own" desire.

Lacan's observations are richly apposite here: "C'est qu'Alceste est fou et que Molière le montre comme tel,—très justement en ceci que dans sa belle âme il ne reconnait pas qu'il concourt lui-même au désordre contre lequel il s'insurge" (*Ecrits* 173). Translation: "Célimène, c'est le même, c'est lui-même." (In response to this essay, Robert

Nelson further ventured "ça le mène": yes, that too, as long as we transliterate "ça" as "Sa". For it is not, despite his protestations to the contrary about blind passion, any Freudian *id* that leads Alceste on, but the signifier, the "signifiant" or "Sa", in its abbreviated form: for the object of desire is but the signifier of another's desire.)

"C'est cette passion de démontrer à tous son unicité" that Lacan labels *"l'agression suicidaire du narcissisme"* (*Ecrits* 174). But to speak thus of narcissism is to deprive it of any center which in not located in others. Thus Orgon's bid for uniqueness, for transcendence, transforms all around him into mortal rivals:

> Oui, je deviens tout autre avec son entretien:
>
> Il m'enseigne à n'avoir affection pour rien,
>
> De toutes amitiés il détache mon âme;
>
> Et je verrais mourir frère, enfants, mère et femme,
>
> Que je m'en soucierais autant que de cela. (I, v)

Orgon utters a properly sacrificial vow, the immolation of all to his divinity. Orgon's discovery of a rival "frère ennemi" in Tartuffe himself, who becomes a rival for the possession of his wife, is a necessary consequence of this radical decentering, to which no one is immune, not even Tartuffe, least of all Tartuffe. Tartuffe will be as easily duped by Elmire as Orgon by Tartuffe, for as Elmir states. "Non: on est aisément dupé par ce q'on aime. / Et l'amour propre engage à se tromper soi-même" (IV, iii). These verses apply as well to Orgon as to Tartuffe, of whom they are said. They find their apt summary, their structuring principle, in the title of Lacan's *Séminaire XXI: Les Non-dupes errent.*

The unconscious in Molière, as in Lacan, is "structured like a language" because language is structured by the desire of the other. The symmetrical "mal-entendu" which takes place between Mariane and Valère, lovers and rivals at once, displays the dynamics of this law, to which all are subject whose "amour propre", whose desire, whose pride, is "engagé". Mariane balks at making too frank a declaration of love when she complains to Dorine: "Ferai-je dans mon choix voir un coeur trop épris?" (II, iii). When the lovers confront each other over Mariane's marriage to Tartuffe, there ensues a verbal duel which is formally reminiscent of stychomythia in Corneille:

> VALÈRE: Moi, je vous l'ai donné pour vous plaire, Madame.
>
> MARIANE: Et moi, je le suivrai pour vous faire plaisir. (II, iv)

They say the same thing because, like Don Diègue and Don Gomès in *Le Cid,* they desire the same thing, which in Corneille's play is royal recognition and which in Molière's play is, more to the point, each other's desire. For lack of a better word, we call this sentiment: love, and Lacan: "agression suidicaire du narcissisme." Valère for his part is finally bound to name its admixture with pride: "Un coeur qui nous oublie engage notre gloire." The hostilty of the lovers is as mimetic as their affection, which is only too susceptible to Racinian affectation, as Valère utters lines we might have heard from Oreste, Hermione or Pyrrhus in *Andromaque*: "Et cette lâcheté jamais ne se pardonne, / De montrer de l'amour pour qui nous abandonne." For all such characters, "il y va de ma gloire," as we read in Racine. "Le désir," writes Girard, "s'attache à la gloire mais la gloire n'est que l'objet auquel s'attache le désir" ("Racine . . ." 587).

For Dorine, who is external to this structure, and therefore cannot fail to mark its symmetry, this is "sottise des deux parts:" "Vous êtes fous tous les deux." In Dorine Molière has staged and thematized the role of the observer, whom we might conceive as the psychoanalyst at his or her ideal, imaginary or impossible best: immune to transference and countertransference, this figure can enunciate the truth of the structure, the truth of desire: "A vous dire le vrai les amants sont bien fous!" The madness of the lovers is a veritable "aliénation mentale," whereby the desire of each is captive of the symmetrical, reciprocal and consequently conflictual desire of the other. The lovers only react to each other's desire and are in no way in command of their own. Each is prey to the other's desire in a hybrid relation in which no one is in charge but desire itself. As Girard states, "Si le désir est le même pour tous les hommes, s'il n'y a jamais qu'un même désir, il n'y a pas de raison de ne pas faire de lui le veritable 'sujet' de la structure, sujet qui se ramène d'ailleurs à la mimésis" (*Des Choses cachées* 327).

This alterity of self to self, this difference within the self such that each self is not so different from another as it is from itself, this constitutive alienation or "folie" is the psychological modality of Derridean "differance", where the "a" testifies to the difference within a sign or entity rather than to the difference between signs or entitities, such as we have in a binary opposition ("La Différance" in *Marges*). In other words, the psychological modality of differance is desire itself, to whose internal division Lacan's paradoxical formula, "agresion/suicidaire," testifies as well. Post-structruralism is just that problematic of difference as exercising signs, entities, institutions alike: from within. Intersubjective conflict (difference) is ruled by intrasubjective differance, whereby the ever-mimetic reclamations of autonomous subjectivity are prey to their symmetrical "origin" in the other, their arbitrary point of origination in the desire of the other. It is the subject's "possession" by the desire of other subjects to which Molière gives everywhere the name "folie". Orgon says as much when he unwittingly remarks of Tartuffe: "Oui, je deviens tout autre avec son entretien." In fact he is literally beside himself, "hors de lui," a condition which is no less true when he fawns over Tartuffe than when he rages against his household. "Vous avez là, ma fille, une peste avec vous," he says of Dorine,

> Avec qui sans péché je ne saurais plus vivre.
>
> Je me sens hors d'état maintenant de poursuivre:

> Ses discours insolents m'ont mis l'esprit en feu,
>
> Et je vais prendre l'air pour me rasseoir un peu. (II, ii)

Orgon's lines, particularly for their reference to a plague, serve to remind us that the conflict of this play in theme and substance is tragic: the violent opposition of father and son, the ruin of a household owing to the hubris of its master. It has, alas, been too often played as tragic, usually by the representation of an all too nasty Tartuffe, who is nonetheless as much the comic dupe of his own pride as other characters in the play. Our hatred, our diabolization of Tartuffe, our consecration of his difference, as of some sovereign ill will, only guarantees his stay among us, for it requires the postulate of a supreme good will which we are only too readily prone to confuse with our own person: His Majesty the Ego, the subject as irreducible substance, indeed such a will as Molière invests in his fabulously off-stage Prince (V, vii). Molière deconstructs the subject, as he is bound to do when he dramatizes its interaction with other subjects, where he uncovers its fundamentally dialectical character, its reactive substance, its unsubstantial, volatile structure.

This is nowhere as evident as in the character of Tartuffe himself: he likewise falls prey to the illusion of mastery in his own house, which is the necessary and sufficient condition for his own downfall. He can don and doff his mask at will, it appears—to him as to all about him. It is that will, or power, or mastery, which is the object of desire. In his gluttonous satisfaction of his appetites, as described by Dorine (I, iv), Tartuffe does not know himself as prey to this desire, but mistakes himself as master of his destiny—though his gluttony is but the physical caricature of Orgon's metaphysical desire. Tartuffe is as much a buffoon as a rascal, and should be played as such. There is no fool like one's own fool, and that is what Tartuffe is. It is ever the case with the "dupe double" in Molière that he (or she) is fooled by others because he is first and foremost duped by himself (cf. Livingston).

Only our blind faith in the psychological unity of character, our belief in the autonomy of the desiring subject, could wish to decide whether Tartuffe speaks from the heart or the head when he attempts the seduction of Elmire. It is just such unity—theoroyalogical, psychologocentric, etc.—that is undone by the play. That belief is just the trap that the play in its entirety springs upon us: that we can know the outside from the inside, judge essences by appearances, sentiments by words, character as intention, etc. That is Orgon's error and all too frequently our own, as "hypocrite lecteur" of Tartuffe. Precisely because we know that Tartuffe is not a true "dévot", whose thoughts are only heaven bound, whose desire is only for salvation, we cannot be sure that his devotion to Elmire is not genuine, as least at the stage of his first declaration. The ambiguity of Tartuffe's language testifies to his psychological and emotional difference, his difference from within, from himself, whereby we cannot know for sure what he is saying because he does not know. His posture is, strictly speaking, structurally speaking, undecidable. His ignorance in this respect is just what constitutes our knowledge, and the comic pleasure we take in it.

Readers of ***Le Misanthrope*** know at any rate that no truth is to be decided on the basis of what is sincere in the expression of sentiments, or on the basis of the unity of character that a notion like sincerity advertises. Tartuffe is too often played as if Molière had never written ***Le Misanthrope,*** i.e. as if Molière were Jean-Jacques Rousseau, whose resolutely tragic identification with Alceste, in his *Lettre à d'Alembert sur les spectacles,* is so notorious. The connection with the author of *La Nouvelle Héloïse* is instructive. For Tartuffe's verses compose one of the most passionate declarations of love we find in all of Molière: it rivals with the best of them in all of classical French literature:

> Que si vous contemplez d'une âme un peu bénigne
>
> Les tribulations de votre esclave indigne,
>
> S'il faut que vos bontés veuillent me consoler
>
> Et jusqu'à mon néant daignent se ravaler,
>
> J'aurai toujours pour vous, ô suave merveille,
>
> Une dévotion à nulle autre pareille. (III, iii)

To worship a woman in the place of, or as, celestial divinity is simply to manifest the detours, the displacements to which desire is susceptible. In his representation of desire as idolatry, Molière invites us to consider every passionate lover as a "faux dévot", or to conceive the "faux dévot" as the exemplar of the passionate lover. In the ardent lover's discourse, adoration is misplaced or displaced towards a mortal creature: the language properly addressed to a divinity is improperly, that is rhetorically, figuratively, addressed to a human: the essentially hyperbolic nature of rhetoric, its detour or perversion of terms from their "proper" reference is exhibited. Rhetoric is just that detour, distortion, turning or troping endemic to poetry as to desire itself. I am, of course, employing a logocentric, "metaphysical" notion of rhetoric, whose functioning depends upon a belief in the proper sense of words as original to their meaning. Such a notion of direct vs. indirect reference, of literal vs. figurative representation is superseded by contemporary speculation on language (cf. Gans, *The Origin of Language,* chs I and II on the relation between desire as deferral and representation as structurally metaphorical). It is just that notion that is undecidable in Molière, especially in Tartuffe's discourse to Elmire. Such consideration would take us a long way towards understanding the profound (or "unconscious") tartuffery of Rousseau's Saint-Preux, not to mention that of Rousseau himself, who more than once filled the role of a Tartuffe to the households which took him in. Such consideration should doubtless extend to Baudelaire, whose tartuffery, especially in his love poetry, is strategic and self-conscious, with the result that desire as sadomasochistic excess, the "agression suicidaire" of "L'Héautontimoroumdnos" and of "Le Voyage", is fused with the poet's vocation. This vocation announces itself accordingly as the revelation of hypocrisy in the justly famous address "Au lecteur" which concludes "Hypocrite lecteur, mon semblable, mon frère!" For this too, Molière sets the stage and we are fools upon it when, with the violent Orgon (V, i), we proudly rejoice in the expulsion of tartuffery.

Works Cited

Argan, Giulio Carlo. *The Europe of the Capitals: 1600-1700.* Geneva: Skira, 1964.

Derrida, Jacques. *Marges de la Philosophie.* Paris: Minuit, 1972.

———. "D'un ton apocalyptique adopté naguère en philosophie" in *Les Fins de l'homme: A Partir du travail de Jacques Derrida.* eds. Ph. Lacoue-Labarthe and Jean-Luc Nancy. Paris: Galilée, 1981.

Freud, Sigmund. *Standard Edition of the Complete Psychological Works of Sigmund Freud.* eds. James Strachey et al. London: Hogarth, 1953-74.

Gans. Eric. *The Origin of Language: A Formal Theory of Representation.* Berkeley: University of California, 1981.

Girard, René. *Violence and the Sacred.* trans. Patrick Gregory. Baltimore: Johns Hopkins, 1978.

———. "Racine, Poète de la Gloire." *Critique* (June 1964).

———. *Des Choses cachées depuis la fondation du monde.* Paris: Grasset, 1978.

Gossman, Lionel. *Men and Masks: A Study of Molière.* Baltimore: Johns Hopkins, 1963.

Guicharnaud, Jacques. *Molière: Une Aventure théâtrale.* Paris: Gallimard, 1963.

Johnson, Barbara. *Défigurations du lanquaqe poétique: La Seconde Révolution baudelairienne.* Paris: Flammarion, 1979.

Koppisch, Michael. *The Dissolution of Character: Changing Perspectives in La Bruyère "Caractères".* Lexington, Kentucky: French Forum, 1981.

Lacan. Jacques. *Ecrits.* Paris: Seuil, 1966.

———. *Séminaire II: Le Moi dans la théorie de Freud et dans la technique de la psychanalyse.* Paris: Seuil, 1978.

Livingston, Paisley. "Comic Treatment: Molière and the Farce of Medicine." *MLN.* Vol. 94. No. 4 (1979).

Saint-Simon. *Mémoires.* Paris: Gallimard, Pléiade ed., 1961.

Peter H. Nurse (essay date 1989)

SOURCE: "*Tartuffe*: Comedy or Drama?" in *Modern Languages Journal,* Vol. 70, No. 2, June, 1989, pp. 118-22.

[*In the following essay, Nurse surveys aspects of Molière's* Tartuffe, *examining the long disputed question as to which genre it belongs: pure comedy, satirical comedy,* drame bourgeois, *or tragedy.*]

If ambiguity is one of the necessary characteristics of a masterpiece, then ***Tartuffe*** clearly qualifies for such a distinction, for, together with ***Dom Juan*** and ***Le Misanthrope,*** it is one of the plays which has consistently stirred controversy since its first performance. The critical arguments centre on two interrelated problems, one of them specific and one more general, namely: how should the character of Tartuffe himself be interpreted, and to what kind of dramatic *genre* should the play be assigned, with the choice ranging between pure comedy (with a large dose of farce), satirical comedy, *drame bourgeois* (anticipating the 18th-century category of that name) and, finally, tragedy. However, if the latter rates a mention, it is mainly because of a famous pronouncement by Goethe referring to the 'eminently tragic situations' in such plays as ***Tartuffe*** or ***L'Avare*** where family conflicts led to fathers cursing their sons. This encouraged somewhat inflated statements such as Jules Janin's remark in 1839 that '***Le Tartuffe*** est la plus terrible tragédie qui soit sortie de la tête des hommes'. I think no one would today pursue this line, which is only of interest in so far as it highlights the problem of how far the play goes beyond the normal boundaries of the comic. This article will limit itself to the question of the dramatic tone of the play and the possible moral implications of its vision.

The kind of controversy caused by ***Tartuffe*** first made its appearance with the fierce polemics which surrounded ***L'Ecole des Femmes*** in 1663. It flared up again with the banning of ***Tartuffe*** in 1664 (denounced as a work 'absolutely harmful to religion'), a ban that lasted for five years with only a brief interruption in 1667. Meanwhile the situation was aggravated by the almost certain banning of ***Dom Juan*** in 1665, since the play disappeared permanently from Molière's repertory after only a handful of performances.

It is this historical perspective that no doubt accounts for the fact that a major critical tradition persists which sees Molière's theatre as voicing a kind of naturalistic philosophy, with its roots in Renaissance humanism, from which it derived its celebration of natural instinct and its unremitting mockery of those who sought to repress it. Largely concomitant with this view is the notion that Molière is essentially a satirist with a more or less coherent ideology expressing indignation at certain vices such as puritan intolerance, religious hypocrisy and avarice. Opinions differ as to how subversive this ideology was, some stressing the free-thinking, virtually pagan, *libertinage,* others emphasising the so-called 'bourgeois' ethic of *bon sens* and moderation supposedly echoed by the *raisonneur* figures like Cléante in ***Tartuffe*** or Philinte in ***Le Misanthrope.*** Both of these sub-groups accept that Molière is a committed author with a positive moral programme, and perhaps the leading exponent of this critical tendency is Professor Antoine Adam, author of the outstanding *Histoire de la Littérature française au XVIIe siècle* (1952). For Adam, from 1661 onwards with ***L'Ecole des Maris*** and ***L'Ecole des Femmes,*** Molière's comedy is no longer gratuitous, no longer a simple satire of ridiculous fashions. These plays now reveal his thinking on the moral problems of his age, showing him to be firmly behind the new optimism characteristic of the 'société galante' of the *salon* world:

> Une grand idée l'inspirait: sa foi dans la vocation morale du théâtre. C'était depuis plus d'un siècle l'enseignement de l'humanisme. Molière, comme ses maîtres, croyait que la scène est "l'ecole des moeurs" et qu'il appartient au théâtre de rappeler sans cesse les principes de la vraie morale, qui n'est pas soumission aux préjugés mais noblesse et générosité. Il ne pouvait prévoir qu'un jour certains lui reprocheraient d'enseigner une morale de la médiocrité et de la platitude. Il pouvait encore moins imaginer que, pour mieux le louer, d'étonants historiens refuseraient de voir en lui autre chose qu'un amuseur.

It is this last sentence which recalls that there is indeed another flourishing critical tradition, still vocal, which rejects the whole idea of a committed author with a coherent moral vision. Spearheaded by Professor René Bray, in his book: *Molière, homme de théâtre* (1954), these critics emphasise the pure theatricality of Molière's work, with its roots in medieval French farce and Italian *commedia dell'arte*. For Bray, the plays constitute an imaginary world, and when we enter it as spectators, we abandon our everyday social persons. It is a domain of pure illusion, alien to all considerations of pragmatic morality, so that we cannot be said to be dealing with satire in the strict sense of the word, but with pure comedy. And so René Bray writes: 'Quand il peint Tartuffe ou Dom Juan, le poète cherche non pas à ridiculiser un hypocrite ou un libertin, mais à en dégager la force comique.' It is typical of Bray's book that it begins with a chapter entitled: 'Molière, pense-t-il?' and concludes with a negative. Critics who share this persuasion clearly attach little value to Molière Preface to ***Tartuffe*** where he underlines the didactic and polemical character of the play: this is seen as special pleading forced upon the playwright by his enemies' denunciation of the subversiveness of the work.

Inevitably, when one turns to examine ***Tartuffe*** in order to measure it against these different critical perspectives, it is at first sight difficult to believe the play could ever have been quite so innocent of moral and ideological significance, given the furore it aroused when first put on in 1664. On that occasion, only three acts were performed and we do not know whether this was an early version complete in three acts or whether it was just the first three acts of the play more or less as we now have it. One theory argues that it was probably roughly Acts I, III and IV of the final draft. However, all this is pure speculation; all we know, apart from the published 1669 text, is that Molière put on a compromise five-act version in 1667, known to us in some close detail from an anonymous pamphlet published in its defence that same year, called the *Lettre sur la comédie de l'Imposteur,*—an invaluable document not least for the evidence it offers of the nature of Molière's production. The 1667 version seems to have been quite close to the final text; at all events, it was again speedily banned and Molière was not free to give regular public performances until 1669.

As was remarked at the beginning of this [essay], the problem of the dramatic tone of the play is essentially bound up with the question of how we view Tartuffe, whose character is problematic in a much more fundamental sense than that of the protagonist, Orgon, played by Molière himself. Orgon is recognisably cast in the same comic mould as the other great creations brought to life by the playwright's acting skills. Like Arnolphe, Alceste or Argan, he meets perfectly the conditions of the comic first defined by Plato in one of his dialogues when he wrote:

> Mirth is generally evoked by the sight of self-ignorance or self-conceit, as when a man fancies himself richer, more handsome, more virtuous or wiser than he really is; and this mirth must be occasioned by one who is powerless to inflict hurt on others, otherwise he would not be a source of mirth but of danger.

This spells out the sense in which Orgon is what Molière called an *imaginaire,* or fantasist, playing out the rôle of a *dévot,* affecting to repress natural instinct, but in fact deeply self-indulgent. This point is admirably highlighted in the 1667 *Lettre* where it comments on Act IV, scene 3 (lines 1279-1293) in which Orgon insists that his daughter Mariane must accept Tartuffe as her husband:

> D'abord Mariane se jette à ses genoux et le harangue si bien qu'elle le touche. On voit cela dans la mine du pauvre homme; et c'est cela qui est un trait admirable de l'entêtement ordinaire aux bigots, pour montrer comme ils se défont de toutes les inclinations naturelles et raisonnables. Car celui-ci, se sentant attendrir, se ravise tout d'un coup et se dit à soimême, croyant faire une chose fort héroïque,—"Ferme, ferme, mon coeur, point de faiblesse humaine!"

Cloaking his authoritarian bullying in puritanical language, Orgon urges his daughter to mortify her senses. It is a replay of Arnolphe's hypocritical tactics with Agnès, and with both characters Molière exploits a vein of mock-heroic comedy to satirise bigotry.

The reference in the *Lettre* to the 'inclinations naturelles et raisonnables' which the bigot suppresses recalls an earlier scene (Act I, scene 5) where Orgon has boasted of the spiritual lesson he learned from Tartuffe:

> Qui suit ses leçons goûte une paix profonde
>
> Et comme du fumier regarde tout le monde.
>
> Oui, je deviens tout autre avec son entretien,
>
> Il m'enseigne à n'avoir affection pour rien,
>
> De toutes amitiés il détache mon âme;

> Et je verrais mourir frère, enfants, mère et femme,
>
> Que je m'en soucierais autant que cela.
>
> (273-279)

Cléante's ironic rejoinder:

> Les sentiments humains, mon frère, que voilà!

has far-reaching implications when one remembers that Orgon is here echoing one of the most problematic of Christ's saying in the Gospels—namely, Luke 14, verse 26: 'If any man come to me and hate not his father and mother and wife and children and brethren and sisters, yea his own life also, he cannot be my disciple.' Passages such as this certainly suggest why the *parti dévot* was so hostile to the play, but that becomes even more apparent when we turn to the rôle of Tartuffe himself. In this respect there is one piece of evidence which almost certainly tells us something quite specific about the character as presented in the early version of 1664. It is the *Placet* of 1667, in which Molière explains how he has modified the appearance of his hypocrite, dressing him as a fashionable man of the world:

> En vain j'ai déguisé le personnage sous l'ajustement d'un homme du monde; j'ai eu beau lui donner un petit chapeau, de grands cheveux, un grande collet, une épée et des dentelles sur tout l'habit . . . tout cela n'a rien servi.

If we take the opposite of each of these details—*grand chapeau, petits cheveux, petit collet,* no sword and plain coat—we have Tartuffe's probable dress and appearance in 1664: in other words a man of clerical garb. Indeed, Furetière, in his *Dictionnaire Universel* (1690) specifically glosses *petit-collet* as 'un homme qui s'est mis dans la dévotion.' Professor Adam is right to say that there was ambiguity about the hypocrite's exact status, but clearly he was near enough to suggesting a priest for the *dévots* to be enraged:

> L'un des traits les plus curieux de la société française à cette époque, c'est l'existence d'une classe sociale mal définie, intermédiaire entre le clergé et les laïcs . . . Faut-il même parler des prêtres régulièrement ordonnés qui vivaient à Paris sans charge déterminée en marge de la hiérarchie dans une indépendance à peu près complète? Il était donc possible à Molière de laisser dans le vague la véritable condition de Tartuffe. Celui-ci appartenait à cette classe incertaine. Etaitil prêtre? Molière ne le dit pas, mais il ne dit pas le contraire nulle part.

So much for Tartuffe's appearance and status; but what of the way he was played? Once again, the problem is clearly stated by Professor Adam:

> On hésite à définir Tartuffe. Faut-il voir en lui un calculateur profond qui mène son jeu avec une froide lucidité? Est-il au contraire un rustre dont toute la force est d'instinct, une sorte de bête de proie, un gros animal qui finira par tomber lourdement dans le piège? Machiavel ou Raspoutine? Ou bien même Machiavel *et* Raspoutine, figure mal cohérente où Molière a mêlé des traits incompatibles?

The text itself provides evidence for both views. We are told he is 'gros et gras, le teint frais et la bouche vermeille' with a greedy appetite suggesting crude manners. Dorine says that when he first arrived he was a shoeless beggar, and Damis calls him a *pied plat,* which is defined as 'un paysan, un homme grossier, un gueux.' On the other hand, Dorine concedes that he is wily and will be difficult to trip up. He is well versed in the language of religious mysticism: in the first seduction scene with Elmire (III, 3), he exploits the neo-Platonic idea that in loving her, he is loving the reflection of the Divine Being. And again, in the second seduction scene (IV, 5), Tartuffe shows he is well versed in Jesuit casuistry, notably 'l'art de diriger l'intention' attacked by Pascal in the *Lettres provinciales.*

Historians of the theatre suggest that actors playing the rôle of Tartuffe have seldom managed to reconcile these two aspects of the character and have usually settled for one or the other. This is how the point is made by the critic Jules Lemaître:

> Du temps de Molière, conformément à sa pensée, Tartuffe fut joué en 'comique' et même en 'valet comique' . . . 'Aussi l'habitude de jouer chaque soir Hector ou Crispin avait rétréci le talent des comédiens, circonscrit leur horizon: leur unique tâche étant de faire rire, Tartuffe fut joué comme *valet,* et peu à peu, ce grand rôle ne fut plus qu'un sournois plaisant et cynique dont les charges et les paillardises égayaient le public. Cette grossière interprétation du rôle devint la tradition . . .'
>
> Mais un beau jour on s'avisa que Tartuffe ne devait pas faire rire à ce point . . . Mieux qu'aucun de ses devanciers, M. Worms a sauvé Tartuffe du ridicule. Ce qu'il a exprimé peut-être le plus fortement, c'est l'ardente passion sensuelle dont Tartuffe est dévoré. Il lui a prêté aussi une sorte d'âpreté triste, une allure sombre et fatale, et qui fait songer tant^t à don Salluste, tantôt à Iago. Enfin il semble qu'il ait voulu surtout nous rendre sensible cette idée, que Tartuffe se perd parce qu'il aime. Et, en même temps, il nous a montré un scélérat si élégant, d'une pâleur si distinguée dans son costume noir, si spécial par l'ironie sacrilège qu'il mêle à ses discours, que, si Elmire lui résiste, ce ne peut plus être chez elle dégoût et répugnance . . . Oh! qu'à ce moment le premier Tartuffe, le bedeau, le truand d'église, est loin de nos yeux et de notre souvenir!
>
> (*Les Deux Tartuffe,* 1896)

Such evidence of theatrical tradition explains why different producers and actors can arrive at completely contrasting dramatic tonalities. If a clownish element enters into the rôle, the play obviously moves towards more naked farce, as was the case when Leonard Rossiter acted Tartuffe. If, on the other hand, you play the hypocrite as a cool calculating seducer, a sinister note is quickly established. That was how the celebrated producer, Roger Planchon, chose to present the play when he brought his French company to the National Theatre in London in the 70s. Here is an extract of *The Times*'s report on the production:

> And in the second half, the pretence to comedy all but vanishes. When Orgon refuses to relent over the Tartuffe marriage, Mariane is carried off in a state of hysterical frenzy. The trick that removes the scales from Orgon's eyes is likewise played for terror. It seems that a rape is about to take place over the table; and when Tartuffe quits the room, Elmire whips the cloth away and orders her husband out in a paroxysm of wrath.

The *Lettre* of 1667 offers significant evidence that Molière himself similarly stresed the darker side of the action, for here is how it comments on the fifth Act:

> Permettez-moi de vous faire remarquer que l'esprit de tout cet acte et son seul effet et but jusqu'ici n'a été que de représenter les affaires de cette pauvre famille dans la dernière désolation par la violence et l'impudence de l'imposteur, jusque-là qu'il paraît que c'est une affaire sans ressource dans les formes, de sorte qu'à moins de quelque dieu qui y mette la main, c'est à dire de la machine . . . tout est déploré.

On the other hand it is similarly the *Lettre* which reminds us of the comic pattern in the way the hypocrite was played in the two crucial seduction scenes. Here quite unambiguously the emphasis is upon the conception of a man who, though normally wily and controlled, loses his head through passion, so that he imperils his own scheme to take possession of Orgon's household. In other words, it is the classic ironic formula of the *trompeur trompé,* or, to use the fashionable metaphor, the case of an over-reaching trickster whose mask slips to give himself away. This is particularly apparent when the *Lettre* describes Act III, scene 2 where Dorine tells him that Elmire has asked to see him:

> Enfin elle fait son message, et il le reçoit avec une joie qui le décontenance et le jette un peu hors de son rôle: et c'est ici que l'on voit représentée mieux que nulle part ailleurs la force de l'amour et les grands et beaux jeux que cette passion peut faire, par les effets involontaires qu'il produit dans l'âme de toutes la plus concertée.

There then follows the step-by-step description of each of the private interviews with Elmire; first, that in Act III, scene 3:

> A peine la dame paraît que notre cagot la reçoit avec empressement qui, bien qu'il ne soit pas fort grand, paraît extraordinaire dans une homme de sa figure . . . Les choses étant dans cet état, et, pendant ce dévotieux entretien, notre cagot s'approchant toujours de la dame même sans y penser, à ce qu'il semble, à mesure qu'elle s'éloigne; enfin il lui prend la main, comme par manière de geste . . . et, tenant cette main il la presse si fort entre les siennes qu'elle est contrainte de lui dire—'Que vous me serrez fort', à quoi il répond soudain, se recueillant et s'apercevant de son transport: 'C'est par excès de zèle.' Un moment après, il s'oublie de nouveau, et promenant sa main sur le genou de la dame, elle lui dit, confuse de sa liberté, 'ce que fait là sa main?' Il répond, aussi surpris que la première fois, qu' 'il trouve son étoffe moelleuse', et pour rendre plus vraisemblable cette défaite, par un artifice fort naturel, il continue de considérer son ajustement . . . Enfin, enflammé par tous ces petits commencements, par la présence d'une femme bien faite qu'il adore et qui le traite avec beaucoup de civilité, et par les doucerurs arrachées à la première découverte d'une passion amoureuse, il lui fait sa déclaration . . . Il s'étend admirablement là-dessus et lui fait si bien sentir son humanité et sa faiblesse pour elle qu'il ferait presque pitié s'il n'était interrompu par Damis.

Everything here stresses the idea of a man out of control, undone by instinct, resulting in a *défaite,* as is again the case with the second interview, where the commentator uses similar metaphors such as 'il commence à s'aveugler'. The second interview is in fact based on an even more classic comic formula, namely: *à trompeur, trompeur et demi.* To trick Tartuffe, Elmire exploits the ambiguities of the contemporary language of gallantry, as used by *coquettes* to save appearances. She can thus explain her reserve in the earlier scene as a typical coquette's ploy for egging on the suitor.

With both Orgon and Tartuffe, the comic mechanism of deflation repeatedly points to the same moral implications, suggesting a view of the human condition which gives primacy to what the 1667 *Lettre* called 'les inclinations naturelles et raisonnables'. Hence the label of 'naturalism' often applied to the underlying philosophy; and, as Paul Bénichou writes in his brilliant *Morales du Grand Siècle* (1948), the term is appropriate in so far as it expresses the surrender of human pretensions to the all-powerful facts of experience. The whole of Molière's moral system, he says, consists of knowing how to yield to a certain number of facts, and, throughout his work, the force of custom defies justice just as much as the force of our desires defies social codes of behaviour.

It is when Bénichou concludes that it is in this sense that Molière's work is 'amoral' that one sees better why critics like René Bray contest the legitimacy of speaking of 'la morale de Molière' and prefer to talk of 'pure theatre' with its roots in farce. However, what is distinctive about plays like ***Tartuffe*** is that they anchor the action in a recognisable social reality, justifying the playwright's contention that he was not dealing with abstractions but with 'les hommes de notre siècle'. That, of course, explains why ***Tartuffe*** can no longer be contained within the boundaries of 'pure comedy' and why we are here faced with a hybrid genre in which the *drame* threatens to take over. And this, as was remarked at the beginning of this article, is exactly related to the process by which Tartuffe himself ceases to be a purely comic character, because, in Plato's terminology, he changes from a source of mirth into a source of danger. Only the King can save Orgon's household from this threat, just as in reality it was Louis XIV who finally checked the *parti dévot* in 1669.

DOM JUAN

CRITICAL COMMENTARY

David Shaw (essay date 1978)

SOURCE: "Egoism and Society: A Secular Interpretation of Molière's *Dom Juan*," in *Modern Languages*, Vol. LIX, No. 3, September, 1978, pp. 121-30.

[*In the following essay, Shaw considers Molière's ambiguity towards the issues brought forth in* Dom Juan.]

That ***Dom Juan*** is the most 'difficult' play in the whole Molière canon is something of a critical commonplace: fault has repeatedly been found with its alleged incoherence:

> ***Dom Juan*** révèle une incohérente ténèbre . . . Molière, comme jamais, donne l'impression de ne tendre, pour l'immédiat, qu'à ficeler de bric et de brac, un succes au hasard des prises, des échos, des coins de table. [J. Audiberti, *Molière Dramaturge.* L'Arche, 1954, p. 73.] . . . l'intrigue reste décousue, incomplète. [G. Michaut, *Les Luttes de Molière.* Hachette, 1925, p. 148.]

> Cette tragédie-comédie fantasque et bouffonne est une macédoine incroyable de tous les genres: elle est étrange, elle est bizarre, elle est hybride, elle est obscure en diable. [J. Lemaître, *Impressions de théâtre.* Paris, 1888, 1920, I, 57.]

Its seemingly endless succession of ambiguities and false trails might indeed suggest, at first sight, a hastily composed baroque tangle of conflicting ideas, a confused answer to the ban on ***Tartuffe.*** On the other hand, is it not possible, without hurting one's back, to see in the play a paradoxical kind of order, even simplicity, which, in fact, probes many of the usual assumptions made about Molière?

Perhaps the most fundamental assumption questioned by the play is the famous theory of the 'raisonneur'. The popular idea of 'Molière's point of view' being presented in each play by one character owes its respectability almost entirely to the wholly exceptional role of Cléante in ***Tartuffe.*** This character's function is almost entirely polemical: it was largely developed after the 1664 ban in order to underline the careful distinction between true and false piety. In the other major plays, however, the function of characters like Chrysalde, Ariste, Philinte, Béralde, etc., is primarily comic, intended to form the maximum comic contrast with the central character rather than to state an attitude identifiable beyond doubt as that of Molière.

If one thing is certain about ***Dom Juan,*** it is that it contains no single character likely to be taken for Molière's mouthpiece. The sympathy we undoubtedly feel, in varying degrees, for Elvire, Don Carlos and Don Louis is always contaminated by admiration of the way in which Don Juan outwits them. Given the size of his role and his constant willingness to give moral advice to his master, Sganarelle comes closest to the traditional concept of the 'raisonneur'. But we are, surely not expected to identify Molière with such a pathetic buffoon. Indeed, in view of the evident link between the two plays, one might even have been tempted to suggest an angry parody of the clearly drawn factions in ***Tartuffe*** if it were possible to know more about the enigmatic 1664 version of this play.

In the absence of an obvious 'spokesman', the most contradictory interpretations of ***Dom Juan*** have been seriously put forward. Perhaps the standard reading is that the play is a furious reply to the critics of ***Tartuffe*** and that the key is the diatribe on hypocrisy at the beginning of the final act. Having seen his prudent condemnation of hypocrisy vilified and banned by clerics with vested interests, Molière is now, according to this theory, retaliating with an attack on the fundamental tenets of Christianity itself. As Don Juan is evidently Molière's mouthpiece on medicine and hypocrisy, might he not have the same function everywhere else in the play? He is therefore a witty, elegant, superior creature offered up for our admiration. His superiority is constantly underlined by the stupid credulity of Sganarelle, equally fearful of Devil, werewolf, 'moine bourru' and God, and in whose mouth even the most traditional proofs of the existence of God sound comically naive. We cannot admire Sganarelle: he is cowardly, gluttonous and more than a little cynical. 'Il n'y a pas de mal' he says [III,2] when inviting the hermit to blaspheme, and he resorts to crude violence in order to avoid paying his debts [IV,3] without even the excuse of his master's menacing presence.

The impression of parody is heightened by the nature of the two speeches from Sganarelle within which all the play's action is framed. From a strictly Christian point of view, the denouement would clearly have been more satisfactory if the play had ended at the very moment of Don Juan's death. But, with Sganarelle's final cry 'Mes gages! mes gages!', the comic perspective is fully restored. The play's final statement, far from underlining the demonstrated power of divine wrath suggests that heaven is rather irrelevant. At the moment Sganarelle discovers he has been right all along, he is shown unmoved by the fact and totally preoccupied with material values.

The curious tribute to tobacco, at the beginning of the play, is interesting for the same reason. At first sight it seems almost a parody of the conventional exposition of the time: it tells us little about Don Juan himself and seems to have no relevance to the ensuing action. However, for a seventeenth century spectator, the significance of the allusion would have been quite specific. Tobacco, which had been introduced into France in the sixteenth century as a treatment for migraine, was, in 1665, still sold only on prescription. The purely social use of tobacco had been expressly forbidden by the ecclesiastical authorities who feared, rightly or wrongly, that it increased the power of the Devil over the user. Both snuff takers and smokers thus officially faced excommunication. Nevertheless, the enormous popularity of tobacco was such that a flourishing black market was established and in 1674 its sale was finally legalised by a Colbert always quick to spot new sources of state revenue through taxation. To speak of tobacco in 1665 was therefore to speak of a popular but illegal physical indulgence totally opposed by the Church. To praise it in Sganarelle's glowing terms was therefore to cock an unmistakable snook at the *parti des devots*. The mention of Aristotle in the opening line and the link forged between tobacco and virtue constitute virtually a direct parody of the orthodox position concerning tobacco. Sganarelle's statements on Christianity are thus largely devalued in advance and all the play's action is framed between two expressions of downright materialism pronounced by heaven's principal spokesman.

However, in spite of all this, it is difficult to accept the play as nothing but an apology for atheism. In 1665, such an enterprise would still have been highly dangerous; for a theatre director with Molière's responsibilities it was more or less unthinkable. Indeed, it has been argued, by critics of the standing of Michaut and Jouvet, that ***Dom Juan*** should in fact be seen as a clumsy defence of Christianity with Sganarelle as a simple, but basically sympathetic, defender of heavenly interests. The original play on the Don Juan theme was, of course, a highly edifying work by an austere religious. The Don Juan in Tirso de Molina's *El Burlador de Sevilla* is a debauched, violent young man who never actually denies the existence of God: his sin is overconfidence: he tries to lead a totally immoral life with the intention of reforming at a later date. But he puts off his repentance too long and is finally carried off by the statue while calling for a priest. Our play is therefore basically similar to the original: Don Juan is visibly wrong and the Christians are finally vindicated by the action of the statue. Warnings of his impending fate rain down on Don Juan from beginning to end. He sometimes appears frankly odious, as when he needlessly curses his dignified old father. His marked lack of curiosity when confronted with supernatural phenomena could moreover be construed as fear and when he draws his sword to attack a ghost he comes close to ridicule.

In one sense, Molière's play is even *more* edifying than any of the Spanish, French or Italian versions. He adds symbolic characters: the veiled spectral lady and 'le Temps avec sa faux à la main' figure in no other version. Further, Don Juan's achievements are really very few in number: he seduces Elvire only by marrying her, fails to obtain even a kiss from Charlotte and does not succeed in persuading the hermit to blaspheme. His actual crimes are far less numerous than those of his predecessors: if he killed the commander, it was apparently in a duel ('Ne l'ai-je pas bien tué?' he asks in 1,2); if he persuaded Elvire to leave her convent, it seems as if she was a very willing party to the abduction. No question of the murder and rape of which earlier Don Juans were guilty; and no suggestion in the play that Elvire had actually taken vows or intended to become a nun. It is therefore arguable that, like Phèdre, Don Juan is condemned less for actual crimes than for sacrilegious attitudes.

But again, this is not a satisfactory explanation of the play's teasing complexity: too many important elements remain outside it. Any interpretation which attempts to reduce the play to the level of a simple religious treatise runs the risk of raising more problems than it solves. Unless the play is totally and obscurely ambiguous, there must be a third, less simplistic, interpretation.

One of the major preoccupations of the classical age was how to define the relationship between reason and passion. All the major writers are concerned with the problem. Corneille seems to feel that some men are capable of dominating their passions through the exercise of reason; in Racine's theatre, on the other hand, man is usually the rather pathetic plaything of his emotions. Molière's attitude in this debate seems to have been quite subtle. ***L'Ecole des Femmes*** (1662) demonstrates that reason alone can never suffice and that it is dangerously absurd to attempt to ignore the natural feelings that everyone experiences. ***Tartuffe*** and ***Dom Juan*** examine the other side of the problem, showing the fatal power that the passions can develop if they are not moderated by reason. In ***Tartuffe,*** the force of criminal desire is, perhaps a little arbitrarily, neutralised by excessive self-confidence. But in ***Dom Juan,*** which represents the ultimate development of this line of argument, we have a terrible combination of limitless desire and total cynicism in a character who is also powerfully intelligent.

Sganarelle's portrait of Don Juan, in the opening scene, is highly significant:

> . . . un chien . . . qui passe cette vie en véritable bête brute . . . un grand seigneur méchant homme.

Don Juan's animality is indeed his most striking single characteristic. He acts as if nature is for him a kind of god, as if all desires may be realised if they derive from nature:

> . . . je rends à chacune les hommages et les tributs où la nature nous oblige. [I,2]

And he pursues his desires with a kind of relentless, single minded intelligence which makes him a terrible adversary:

> Il n'est rien qui puisse arrêter l'impétuosité de mes désirs . . . songeons seulement a ce qui nous peut donner du plaisir. [I,2]

It is therefore tempting to see in Don Juan the elemental force of egoism, a kind of incarnation of the most selfish facets of human nature liberated by his rank, his cynicism and his intelligence from all normal moral constraints. Instead of moderating his desires, his intelligence and judgement are placed squarely at their disposal.

At the same time, given his paradoxically total subservience to his physical desires and to his constant need to dominate, it is clear that Don Juan is not without his comic side. A tenuous kind of comedy, perhaps, but, as we have seen, there is certainly a duality about the character which sometimes makes him seem rather less independent than he claims to be. His need to dominate causes him to seek out a succession of difficult obstacles in order to prove again and again his own superiority. Hence the analogy with Alexander, the storming of a convent, the pursuit of the engaged girl, and so on. Worse than a sadist, he is totally indifferent to the feelings of other people who are to him mere objects to be exploited at his whim. His description of his attitude towards women is strikingly filled with military vocabulary:

> On goûte une douceur extrême à *réduire* par cent hommages un coeur . . . à voir de jour en jour *les petits progrès qu'on y fait, à combattre* . . . l'innocente pudeur d'une âme qui a peine à *rendre les armes, à forcer pied à pied toutes les petites résistances* qu'elle nous *oppose,* à *vaincre* les scrupules . . . [I,2] (my italics)

Women are mere objectives, adversaries to be conquered. He feels no affection: the only sentiment that he feels is the pleasure of triumph. The list of Don Juan's opponents is, in fact, bewilderingly varied: a man prepared to challenge, in quick succession, a noble woman, a hermit and a statue is evidently not following a carefully prepared plan. But it is clear that Don Juan derives a large part of his power precisely from the fact that he behaves in a totally unpredictable way. He is strong because, in a society based on codes and conventions of all kinds, he is the only one who respects none of them and because he is always prepared to *pretend* to accept any code of behaviour if it appears to offer him a new chance of conquest. Poor Gusman cannot believe that so visibly perfect a lover could fail to keep his word:

> . . . et je ne comprends point comme après tant d'amour et tant d'impatience *témoignée,* tant d'hommages pressants, de voeux, de soupirs et de larmes, tant de lettres passionnées, de protestations ardentes, et de serments réitérés, tant de transports enfin et tant d'emportements *qu'il a fait paraître* . . . je ne comprends pas, dis-je, comme, après tout cela, il aurait le coeur de pouvoir manquer à sa parole. [I,1] (my italics)

Gusman's conventional mind is thus easily taken in by Don Juan's hypocrisy.

We know that seventeenth-century polite society attached great importance to questions of precedence, to elegance, to codes of etiquette in general. There was thus a very real danger of appearance being taken for reality, elegance for merit, hypocrisy for virtue. Many of Molière's major comedies satirise a tendency to attach undue importance to facades and codes: the code of romanesque love in ***Les Précieuses Ridicules,*** that of refined society in ***Le Misanthrope,*** the facade of religiosity in ***Tartuffe,*** medical mystique in ***Le Malade Imaginatre,*** etc. But only in ***Don Juan*** are all these themes brought together in the context of one cynical, chameleon-like figure, in order to demonstrate the dangers facing a superficial society in its entirety.

Just for a moment, Elvire, in her first appearance, seems to have Don Juan's measure. She is aware that he has been playing a part for her benefit:

> Ah! que vous savez mal vous défendre pour un homme de cour . . . Que ne vous armez-vous le front d'une noble effronterie? Que ne me jurez-vous que vous êtes toujours dans les mêmes sentiments pour moi . . .? [I,3].

Her tone is that of the prompter reminding the actor of lines forgotten. But Don Juan is too clever to be neutralised in this way: one code having been declared inoperable by Elvire's irony, he simply switches to another, that of pious sincerity:

> Je vous avoue, Madame, que je n'ai point le talent de dissimuler, et que je porte un coeur sincère. [I,3]

And there is even heavier irony in the unexpected concentration of religious terms with which he continues: within the space of eight lines or so he mentions concepts like conscience, belief, sin, scruples, soul, vows, divine anger. He thus pays her the compliment of tacitly revealing his virtuosity but without giving her another chance to outflank him. This little confrontation is a kind of ironic prefiguration of the scene in act V where Don Juan again puts on his mask of piety to outwit his father. It has been suggested that the show of hypocrisy in the final act destroys the unity of the character: given Don Juan's courage and spirit, he would surely never stoop to such an unworthy ploy:

> Don Juan hypocrite, voila qui ne répond guere a l'idée que nous nous faisions de lui. [G. Michaut, op.cit. p. 150]

To argue thus is surely totally to misunderstand his nature; from one end of the play to the other he continually adopts whichever mask seems to him the most likely to have the effect he wants. That is the real source of his power.

The change of decor at the start of the second act represents a fairly violent visual shock. For the seventeenth century spectator, to pass from sumptuous palace to rustic sea coast was the greatest possible social contrast. But the dramatic parallel between the two settings is quickly obvious. The peasants of act II are far from being noble savages in the eighteenth-century sense: they are rather mean, petty people and are as preoccupied with formal codes of behaviour as are the courtiers. Like Harpagon, Pierrot believes that love can be bought: he cannot understand why his expressions of devotion, in the form of ribbons, blackbirds and hurdy-gurdy serenades, have not had a more tangible effect. His idea of how lovers should behave is simplistic and superficial: he is distressed because Charlotte does not imitate the dangerous horse-play of Thomasse, their lovelorn neighbour. He seems much more concerned that Charlotte should conform to this ideal than that she should actually have deep feelings. For her part, Charlotte feels her honour safe if she can make Don Juan marry her. The idea is traditional but clearly cannot be applied to Don Juan; he is 'l'épouseur du genre humain', for whom marriage is simply another convention which can sometimes be useful as a means to an end.

From act II onwards our attitude towards Don Juan becomes increasingly ambiguous. In spite of ourselves we admire his effortless superiority over the peasants; but, at the same time, he begins to demonstrate a kind of comic, and paradoxical, impotence. His plan to seduce the engaged girl was thwarted by the storm; he owes his life to a peasant. His reaction to the peasant girls is automatic: he desires them on seeing them. As we already know from Sganarelle, 'Dame, demoiselle, bourgeoise, paysanne, il ne trouve rien de trop chaud ni de trop froid pour lui' [I,1]. His sexual appetites ignore questions of rank or 'qualité', a lack of delicacy and taste which might have appeared faintly ridiculous to the seventeenth-century courtier. In scene 4, Don Juan's stylised confrontation with the two girls, Charlotte and Mathurine, conveys a clear image of how his own behaviour contains the seeds of his own defeat. He has made the same rash promises of marriage to both girls and now has to try, albeit brilliantly, to play them off against each other when they try to compare stories:

> *Mathurine.*—Quoi! Charlotte . . .
>
> *Don Juan,* bas à Mathurine.—Tout ce que vous lui direz sera inutile: elle s'est mis cela dans la tête.
>
> *Charlotte.*—Quement donc! Mathurine . . .
>
> *Don Juan,* bas à Charlotte.—C'est en vain que vous lui parlerez; vous ne lui ôterez point cette fantaisie. [II,4]

The scene is a masterly demonstration of virtuosity, but it only helps Don Juan evade exposure as a liar; ultimately, he seduces no-one, precisely because of the glib, automatic promises he has made to both. Don Juan, here on the defensive, is suddenly far removed from the lyrical disciple of Alexander of act I: we find him, not for the last time, having to use his considerable intelligence merely to extricate himself from embarrassing situations brought about by his own impetuous appetites. In a sense then, the fatal invitation made to the statue is already anticipated: like Tartuffe, Don Juan is incapable of profiting from his errors; like Tartuffe also, he finally tempts fortune once too often.

The discussion which opens the third act amply demonstrates the undogmatic nature of Don Juan's libertinage. The attack on medicine was, in itself, fairly predictable. Given the closeness of the links between the faculties of medicine and theology, it was normal for a libertine to mock the doctors. Indeed, part of the disapproval of Molière in pious circles stemmed from his tendency to see doctors as either fools or crooks. But Don Juan's very eloquence where medicine is concerned underlines his curious reticence on the subject of religion. His replies to Sganarelle's questions are suddenly evasive and monosyllabic:

> Laissons cela . . . Eh! . . . Oui, oui . . . Ah! ah! ah! . . . La peste soit du fat! etc. [III,1]

There is clearly no suggestion of an unexpected show of respect for Christianity, but it is equally clear that, whatever he is, Don Juan is not a doctrinaire atheist. He seems, quite simply, reluctant to get involved in a debate on a difficult question with an unworthy opponent: Don Juan has no real interest in arguing the case for atheism except in so far as it gives him another chance to prove his own superiority. With the hapless Sganarelle, his usual tactic, as here, is simply to lapse into silence and to permit his opponent to lose himself in his own hilariously muddled reasoning.

The poor hermit in scene 2 evidently seems to him a more worthy opponent. He promptly attempts to reduce him to the level of a self-interested beggar by turning against him the sense of his simple words: when the poor man innocently says that he prays 'pour la prospérité des gens de bien qui me donnent quelque chose', Don Juan seizes on this to make it seem as if the hermit is, in fact, praying for his own prosperity. But he finds in the hermit an unexpected bedrock of faith which constitutes a kind of elemental force more powerful than Don Juan himself; the hermit is thus cushioned against the temptations raised by the outrageous offer of the Louis d'or. This might be regarded as the first positive demonstration of divine power, more tangible even than the storm. But Don Juan, as always, is impervious to the hint and is more concerned with finding a way out of a discussion which he is not quite managing to dominate. He gives the Louis d'or to save face and because it is easier to give it than to put it back in his purse. His 'pour l'amour de l'humanité', far from signifying some complex system of rational humanism, is simply a glib and apathetic formula, a convenient means of escape like his sudden interest in saving Don Carlos from his assailants.

Again, therefore, Don Juan shows no appetite for a philosophical debate on the subject of Christianity: he quickly loses interest if the expected victory does not materialise quickly. Rather than a militant, free-thinking philosopher, Don Juan begins to look like the slave of a nature which prevents him even from asking questions. The enigmatic declarations—such as 'deux et deux sont quatre' and 'pour l'amour de l'humanité'—which have caused critics to find hidden depths in the character are, on the contrary, mere convenient clichés demonstrating a disturbingly total apathy in respect of everything but his own most immediate needs.

Elvire's brothers seem, at first, much less serious opponents. Don Carlos is hopelessly entangled in a complex code of honour of which he can see the shortcomings only too well. He is painfully conscious of being 'asservi par les lois de l'honneur au dérèglement de la conduite d'autrui, et de voir sa vie, son repos et ses biens dépendre de la fantaisie du premier téméraire . . .' [III,3]. He is a sensitive man and we sympathise with his attempt to reconcile his personal debt towards Don Juan with the demands of family honour. His is a subtle concept of honour worthy of the age of the 'honnête homme'. But his urbanity is such that Don Juan is easily able to exploit this attitude towards honour both by unexpectedly rescuing his own mortal enemy and then, as always, by simply adopting the same language as his chivalrous opponent, winning his respect by claiming to be jealous of his 'friend's' honour.

Alphonse is far less sympathetic: his conception of honour is much less subtle, much more brutally direct:

> Tous les services que nous rend une main ennemie ne sont d'aucun mérite pour engager notre âme . . . l'honneur est infiniment plus précieux que la vie . . . [III,4]

Anyone capable of saying that in 1665 would have appeared quaintly anachronistic: the heroic days of *Le Cid* were already a very distant memory. The snag is that Alphonse's unpleasant brutality promises to be rather more effective in dealing with Don Juan than Carlos' gentlemanly good manners: Carlos mistakenly assumes that Don Juan respects the same code as he and, as we have seen, Don Juan always gets the better of respecters of codes. Alphonse's more primitive thirst for vengeance would have posed him far more serious problems: it is a narrow escape.

A progression is now evident in the order of Don Juan's adventures. At the beginning of the play, he is a handsome, predatory animal who seeks out his prey and then moves in, seemingly infallibly, for the kill. Gradually, however, the kill becomes increasingly difficult to execute as he finds his plans thwarted by the storm, the peasant girls' jealousy, the hermit's faith, etc. Then, from act III onwards, it is Don Juan himself who becomes the prey, hunted by forces set in motion by his own nature. It is quite logical, therefore, that, having narrowly escaped death at the hands of Elvire's brothers, Don Juan should immediately taunt the commander's statue. For the invitation issued to the statue is no more frivolous than his other challenges, his constant tactic having been to reduce his opponents to the level of mere playthings. There is thus a certain dramatic irony in the way in which Don Juan himself will be eliminated by the most elemental *thing* of all, a lump of stone. It is as if only such an adversary could have the brutal, single-minded simplicity required to crush Don Juan's constant diversity which is, in itself, merely a sophisticated mask disguising the naked force of instinct.

The fourth act opens with a brief pause in the downward course of Don Juan's fortunes. The entries of Monsieur Dimanche and of Don Louis have been criticised for being ill-prepared and largely gratuitous additions. On the other hand, given the nature of Don Juan as he has been presented to us, Molière really had little alternative. Don Juan exists only in the present. He faces up to problems as they occur but is quite unable to make long term plans; that he is good at forgetting unpleasant experiences is amply demonstrated by his lame, almost absent-minded, explanation of the moving statue:

> . . . c'est une bagatelle, et nous pouvons avoir été trompés par un faux jour ou surpris de quelque vapeur qui nous ait troublé la vie. [IV,1]

Neither curiosity nor memory, it would seem, of the fact that two dangerous rendezvous now await him. M. Dimanche and Don Louis are characters trying not to suffer the same fate: they are more or less irksome figures from the past who insist on returning from the oblivion to which Don Juan has attempted to consign them. As we are seeing them largely through Don Juan's eyes, there was thus no other way to prepare for their appearance.

With M. Dimanche, Don Juan rediscovers his early panache in order to deny him the time to state his demand in any meaningful way. Again, he attempts to belittle his adversary by inviting him to supper and this time he is successful: in accordance with the rules of etiquette of the time, the tradesman has to refuse the aristocrat's invitation. Don Juan thus mockingly reminds Dimanche of the unbridgeable social gulf between them while, at the same time, effectively getting rid of him without paying him a sou. The contrast with the other supper invitation, so unexpectedly accepted by the statue, underlines the fact that Don Juan need only fear a supernatural which has as little respect as he has for man-made codes and conventions.

With his father, his reaction is quite different: panache gives way to unpleasant cynicism. It would, however, be wrong to see in this meeting a simple confrontation between good and evil: if the play is an allegory, it is a more complex allegory than that. Don Louis is certainly sympathetic but he is basically an anachronism: like Alphonse, he remains obsessed with simple, old-fashioned values, those of the past. His conception of virtue is very moving:

> Nous n'avons part à la gloire de nos ancêtres qu'autant que nous nous efforçons de leur ressembler. [IV,4]

But it is precisely this preoccupation with his ancestors in an idealised and black-and-white past which makes it so easy for Don Juan to fool him at the beginning of the final act. For Don Louis represents, perhaps better than any other character, the society which has spawned Don Juan, a society dominated by convention and rules of all kinds. Confronted by his father's eloquence, Don Juan refuses to meet him head on: 'Monsieur, si vous étiez assis, vous en seriez mieux pour parler.' [IV,4] It is another attempt to 'chosifier' the opponent: the sudden reminder of the physical plane in the middle of the well-drawn moral tirade effectively deflates his father. The tradition was of course for actors in tragedy to remain standing, whereas those in comedy tended to be seated. Don Juan is thus, in a sense, attempting to reduce Don Louis to the level of a mere obstacle, a 'père de comédie' like Gorgibus or Géronte. And at the end of the scene, Don Louis' impotent fury tends to conform to the role created for him by his son:

> Mais sache, fils indigne, que la tendresse paternelle est poussée à bout par tes actions, que je saurai, plus tôt

> que tu ne penses, mettre une borne à tes dérèglements, prévenir sur toi le courroux du ciel . . . [IV,4]

Pure bluster of course, as we see by his overjoyed reaction to Don Juan's feigned conversion in act V; he has indeed degenerated into a noisy but innocuous obstacle. Given the absence of true danger, Don Juan's curse of his father is unpleasantly gratuitous:

> Eh! mourez le plus tôt que vous pourrez, c'est le mieux que vous puissiez faire. [IV,5]

But he has been threatened and so his response is instinctive and brutal; the filial bond, more precious than life itself to Don Louis, is another value that means nothing at all to his son.

There then follows a series of return visits by characters that Don Juan would clearly rather not see again. They are all seeking Don Juan's salvation but the latter, obsessed as always by his pathetic desire to dominate, cannot appreciate this. No real communication is therefore possible. Elvire's sincere concern, in scene 6, serves only to stir up again Don Juan's old desire. When the statue is announced, we see again Don Juan's blinkered obstinacy: 'Allons voir, et montrons que rien ne me saurait ébranler.' [IV,7] And he greets the statue with another show of effusion, offering him wine and song and generally attempting, this time in vain, to reduce this new guest to the level of another M. Dimanche. Don Louis returns at the beginning of the final act and Don Juan, donning once more his mask of piety, makes the virtuous noises that are enough to send his father away happy.

The lyrical tirade which follows, extolling the benefits of hypocrisy, is clearly meant to balance the one in I,2 on the pleasures of amorous conquest. In both cases we have a description of the pleasure to be derived from a superior kind of trickery. The vocabulary is identical: the 'transports', 'larmes', and 'soupirs' of the first correspond exactly to the 'grimaces', 'roulement d'yeux' and 'soupir mortifie' of the second. And both culminate in a description of a kind of military campaign against conventional morality. The two main facets of Don Juan's libertinage, his sexual appetites and his religious scepticism, are thus highlighted in an almost self-consciously symmetrical way; far from being incoherent, the play in fact has a profound kind of order which transcends superficial questions of conventional neatness.

Moreover, the tirade on hypocrisy is framed between practical demonstrations of its possibilities and of its limits. If Don Louis, as we have seen, is just a passing irritation, Don Carlos, when he returns in V,3, is a much more difficult proposition. He is now obsessed, like his brother, by the idea of vengeance and Don Juan's hypocrisy immediately shows itself to be less effective against another obsession: Don Carlos refuses to recognise the particular mask that he is now wearing and so Don Juan has to agree to a dangerous duel.

The series of reappearances, which is becoming increasingly dangerous for Don Juan, is completed by that of the supernatural. Faced with the spectre, he again rejects the evidence of his eyes:

> Si le Ciel me donne un avis, il faut qu'il parle un peu plus clairement, s'il veut que je l'entende. [V,4]

In view of the profusion and the variety of the warnings that he has received, this remark epitomises Don Juan's ultimate refusal of reality. He naturally seeks to reduce the significance of the spectre by claiming to recognise its voice and by drawing his sword against it. As we have seen, this is a tactic which works very well with human opponents and their relative values. But to go on using it in the face of the implacable supernatural is patently absurd. This pathetic response to heaven's final offer of mercy demonstrates that, ultimately, all his power was based on an illusion: he cannot adapt to a reality different from his own vision of the world. In this, he paradoxically comes to resemble the Arnolphes, the Alcestes, the Argans, the Orgons, all the other 'inadaptés' who inhabit Molière's stage.

Society in ***Dom Juan*** is like an enormous stage production, with everyone accepting a particular role and a particular set of rules. Only Don Juan, good actor though he undoubtedly is, is incapable of accepting this discipline, but spends his time poking fun at, and exploiting for his own ends, the conventions which are visibly at the base of this society. As society is obviously imperfect, it might be argued that some of its conventional values could be usefully questioned. However, when these are merely replaced by cynical indifference towards the rights and feelings of others, the result is anarchy and chaos. Don Juan and the Christian ethic are clearly incompatible. A ray of hope may therefore be derived from the fact that the final victory is won by heaven and that Don Juan is destroyed. This was, after all, the main point of the original story. But the real conclusion of Molière's play is more complex than that: the effects of Don Juan's egoism are still appreciable even after his death. Sganarelle's very complacency about Don Juan's other victims demonstrates that the underlying danger has not been suppressed:

> Voilà par sa mort un chacun satisfait: Ciel offensé, lois violées, filles séduites, familles déshonorées, parents outragés, femmes mises à mal, maris poussés à bout, tout le monde est content. Il n'y a que moi seul de malheureux.

Sganarelle's continuing credulity forcibly reminds us that, on the level of society, heaven's intervention has really achieved very little. The debts have not been paid, Elvire is still dishonoured, the peasants have not regained their tranquil mediocrity and Sganarelle has actually lost his job. The final lines of the play therefore bring us back to earth, where the real problems remain largely unsolved, even after Don Juan's death. Sganarelle is convinced that this event, for most of the victims, signals the end of the problem: he thus demonstrates the concern with appearances which allowed Don Juan to dominate a whole society. Don Juan could reappear in a different guise and no-one would notice. If the play does at any moment go beyond comedy it is surely in the implications of its ending.

The key to any interpretation of the play is one's reaction to Don Juan himself. Sganarelle, although the source of most of the laughter, really presents fewer problems than his master. His function is to strike the maximum comic contrast with Don Juan: total gullibility and fear in the company of total scepticism and bravado. The presence of a 'raisonneur' would inevitably have weakened the argument as well as the comedy. Molière is showing us a whole society in danger through its obsession with rules and codes: a single wise and superior character would therefore have seemed a rather arbitrary exception. Sganarelle is shown torn between terror of his master, almost, but not quite, equal terror of heaven and his own basically sensuous nature. Moreover, far from floundering itself in the disorder of which it has often been accused, the play follows a precise line, Don Juan's character is developed in a logical manner and, in view of the warnings and signs, his end has almost the inevitability of tragedy. Molière does not seem to be arguing strongly either for or against Christianity, in ***Dom Juan*** at least. The attitude that permeates the play is already that of Philinte: society consists essentially of a series of conventions and codes, religion among them. While it is important to bear in mind the perhaps sobering reality underlying the codes, it is also vital to resist the youthful temptation to debunk them all at once, for fear of having nothing but naked egoism to put in their place.

Nathan Gross (essay date 1982)

SOURCE: "Obligation in *Dom Juan*," in *From Gestures to Idea: Esthetics and Ethics in Moliere's Comedy,* Columbia University Press, 1982, pp. 39-71.

[*In the following essay, Gross presents an in-depth discussion of Molière's* Dom Juan, *focusing on the gestural nature of the play.*]

Dom Juan, composed in the shadow of the banned ***Tartuffe,*** is a machine-play, a "spectacular" in the etymological sense, whose use of mechanical devices in the tomb and the Statue belongs to a pattern of gestures implicit in the text which shape the comedy's structure and meaning. Sganarelle's gestures during his opening speech supplement his praise of snuff. Like the allusions to kneeling in ***Tartuffe,*** they are recalled throughout the play and, in an entirely different sense, in his final speech as he cries for his wages. Molière, playing the role in 1665, must have brought the full tradition of comic turns and pranks, inflection and gesture of the Italian *commedia* to his delivery. But seventeen years had passed and Molière was dead when the play was first printed by La Grange, who, acting Dom Juan, may never have seen Sganarelle's gestures at the play's beginning or end. He was offstage, probably preparing to enter; and by 1682 memory of Molière's gestures during rehearsals would have dimmed. Even if the edition were based on Molière's own script, no detailed gestural directions would appear, since the author-director would need no written reminders. Besides, stage directions are rare enough in classical plays, and must be inferred from the speeches. La Grange included a few obvious indications: holding a snuffbox, falling down, and so on. The text must furnish other gestures as Molière might have directed: performance style, always a question of varying declamation and movement, reflects the text most closely when the playwright participates in the staging and realizes auctorial intentions.

When the curtains part, Sganarelle holds a snuffbox as an instrument for challenging the authority of Aristotle and philosophy on the subject of ethics. His mock-serious attitude jars with the patent absurdity of his statement, particularly in the mid-seventeenth century when snuff was considered a doubtful substance, a vice rather than a source of virtue.

> Quoi que puisse dire Aristote et toute la Philosophie, il n'est rien d'égal au tabac: c'est la passion des honnêtes gens, et qui vit sans tabac n'est pas digne de vivre. Non-seulement il réjouit et purge les cerveaux humains, mais encore il instruit les âmes à la vertu, et l'on apprend avec lui à devenir honnête homme.

The surprising juxtaposition of Aristotle and snuff provokes laughter: Aristotle said nothing about tobacco, which entered Europe as a result of Renaissance voyages of discovery in the New World. The declaration that life without snuff is not worthy of humans exemplifies Sganarelle's ridiculous reasoning, accompanied by pedantic gesture: the forefinger raised, the eyes staring at the snuffbox. This section may even be punctuated by a sneeze if Sganarelle takes snuff at this moment. (If he sampled it before the curtains opened, he may have sneezed before beginning the panegyric, in a startling opening gesture.) The sneeze marks the absurd assertion linking snuff and virtue: a gesture shows the foolishness of Sganarelle's claim that snuff is indispensable to virtue, the ethical and happy life which is sought by Aristotle in the *Nicomachean Ethics* and which is the principal aim of philosophy.

Sganarelle then develops the notion that snuff affects the *honnête homme* in society:

> Ne voyez-vous pas bien, dès qu'on en prend, de quelle manière obligeante on en use avec tout le monde, et comme on est ravi d'en donner à droit et à gauche, partout où l'on se trouve? On n'attend pas même qu'on en demande, et l'on court au-devant du souhait des gens: tant il est vrai que le tabac inspire des sentiments d'honneur et de vertu à tous ceux qui en prennent.

He offers snuff to people imagined all over the stage and to Gusman. This polite gesture has ramifications beyond social amenities, according to Sganarelle, for he would persuade Gusman that snuff leads to the good life. Sganarelle poses as a benefactor who does not wait to be asked for a gift of inestimable value if it miraculously confers honor and virtue. Were snuff such a wonder drug, Gusman would owe his bliss to Sganarelle. Could he ever adequately express his gratitude, or free himself of the debt with some commensurate action? Molière did not lightly choose his words as Sganarelle describes the "manière obligeante" of offering snuff by people "ravi" to pass it around. "Obliging," derived from *ob-ligare,* means "binding to," usually through service or favor; even the relatively rare "much obliged" still contains the notion of debt implied as an expression of gratitude. Sganarelle's civil gesture, performing the most valuable service, would place Gusman in his infinite debt; and while he should delight in conferring virtue upon Gusman, he is "ravi" because Gusman, unable to repay the obligation, must, as a virtuous man, acknowledge Sganarelle as the source of his happiness. Through Sganarelle, whose ridiculous speech and movements provoke laughter, Molière parodies civil gesture to raise the serious question of the dynamics of egoism underlying the practices of *bonnêteté.*

The encomium of snuff introduces Dom Juan's fundamental dilemma concerning the "dialectic of obligation": how to remain free of debts not easily reckoned in measurable, and consequently commensurable, terms; how to shun obligations that reduce him to infinite debtor status; and how to appear the boundless creditor of people to whom in fact he owes much. Dom Juan, Sganarelle, and most other characters expect a person performing a service or favor to enjoy an ethical advantage. The recipient is indebted to the benefactor until a commensurate service, rendered in payment, cancels the original debt. Most relationships among men occur within such a dialectic of obligation, and the favors are answerable: few services are infinite in worth. An offer of snuff, without the ultimate value Sganarelle attributes to it, typifies the polite gesture that creates a "social obligation," usually taken as a matter of course, and with a pinch of salt, in *honnête* circles. According to one point of view, however, Pascal's, La Rochefoucauld's, and Hobbes', civil gestures actually disguise the gentleman's self-interest, his *amour-propre,* his instinct to tyrannize by creating relationships of master-slave between himself as benefactor and his social peers. "Chaque moi est l'ennemi et voudrait être le tyran des autres" (Pensée 455 in Brunschvicg's standard numbering), even in polite society where conventional gesture establishes an appearance of civility without changing the fundamental nature of man, which breaks out in moments of stress and challenge.[1] Generous gestures are seen to spring from egoistic motives; mutually reciprocal "obliging" gestures sublimate the desire for irreversibly obligating acts. The dialectic of obligation is a version of Hegel's master-slave dialectic.

The basic ethical structure of ***Dom Juan*** concerns the debtor's response to his awareness of debt, particularly when life-and-death is at stake. That is rarely the case in comedy, or in real life; but in this play, after act I, it is a question of life-and-death at every moment. The play's larger content, which is the point of contact between the comedy and reality, concerns the basic relationship of life-and-death between God and man: the initial giving of life and, in a Christian framework, the remission of sins and the eternal salvation of the soul. Those gifts lie outside the dialectic of obligation, for reasons to be discussed in the context of the great scene of the Poor Man (III, ii). Dom Juan invents debts to himself to reverse relationships with creditors; he follows the strategy of a self-interested creditor to exaggerate his services and paralyze his debtor. But Dom Juan fails, trapped by situations of enormous debt and reduced to a paralyzed slave.

The final gesture in Sganarelle's praise of snuff epitomizes the strategy of reversing debtor relationships. "Mais c'est assez de cette matière. Reprenons un peu notre discours," he says, as transition to the subject of Elvire's pursuit of Dom Juan. *Matière* means both "subject" and "stuff": "enough of that subject (snuff)" and "enough of that material (snuff)." The double meaning indicates that Sganarelle relinquishes the snuffbox to Gusman; it does not reappear in the play because it belongs to Gusman, a character whose language marks him as closer than Sganarelle to elegant circles where snuffboxes are found. Sganarelle covers his embarrassment with the pun on *matière.* Gusman's gestural claim to the snuffbox startlingly provokes the intuition that Sganarelle played benefactor with Gusman's own snuff. Gusman must have offered a pinch before the curtains parted. Did Sganarelle intend the praise of snuff to distract from a simple social obligation while using Gusman's snuffbox to annul the obligation and create a debt of virtue and happiness toward himself by Gusman? That would summarize the pattern of Dom Juan's actions: attempts to cancel or distract from real obligations and embarrassments, while making creditors appear indebted to him. The snuff-speech provides a paradigm for later episodes, exaggerated to absurdity in words and gestures that partially veil its significance. The pun of the transition acts like a shock, making the audience quickly reconsider the praise of snuff and accompanying gestures, while it laughs at Sganarelle, forced to return the snuffbox to its owner: snuff has produced no virtue in this would-be pilferer.

Although Sganarelle fails to become Gusman's benefactor, he proceeds to establish superiority in judgment over Gusman and in ethics over Dom Juan through criticism of his master. Sganarelle again plays Gusman's benefactor with his character analysis, as he later acts the part with the peasants in act II, giving similar derogatory information about Dom Juan to elicit their gratitude. Some of his pleasure lingers when Dom Juan enters (I, ii): he answers Dom Juan casually, challenges Dom Juan's behavior, and wisecracks that he had not mentioned Elvire's presence because, "Monsieur, vous ne me l'avez pas demandé." He apparently feels no obligation to volunteer significant information! Dom Juan's own good mood shows in his eager account of constant infidelities, which develops Sganarelle's observation that Dom Juan "se plaît à se promener de liens en liens, et n'aime guère demeurer en place." Along with movement and change, those baroque categories, Molière stresses the breaking of bonds, *liens,* derived also from *ligare.* Dom Juan resembles a purveyor of snuff, who offers love to beauties all around him, creating obligations toward himself, and feeling no bonds toward the women chosen for seduction. After all, he is giving, they are taking.

He plays on the idea of engagement, a form of obligation: *gages*—wages—are pledges of good faith, and he introduces a more general obligation, dictated by nature, the only one he respects because it permits him to ignore the civil and legal obligations implied by marriage. "J'ai beau être engagé, l'amour que j'ai pour une belle n'engage point mon âme à faire injustice aux autres; je conserve des yeux pour voir le mérite de toutes, et rends à chacune les hommages et les tributs où la nature nous oblige." The speech leads to a comparison with Alexander the Great, wishing for new worlds, and with conquerors who cannot "se résoudre à borner leurs souhaits": "je me sens un coeur à aimer toute la terre," he exclaims. The image of a limitless conqueror is revealing in the light of the dialectic of obligation, for Alexander could leave conquests because it was in the nature of things that he move on without restriction from one place to another in order to satisfy his destiny. He operated on a level where ordinary obligations did not obtain. He owed nothing, while all was owed to him.

Sganarelle correctly perceives that Dom Juan talks like a book. Dom Juan follows the Petrarchist-précieux conceit of woman as a fortified place to be captured; and Alexander, in Molière's period, represented a type of romantic hero for whom women would abandon their virtue with no thought for tomorrows. (Alexander, of course, came to be a figure for Louis XIV as well.) But Sganarelle's remark suggests that happens only in fiction, while in reality women expect to be courted and wed within the dialectic of obligation. Dom Juan is not free, after all, to love "toute la terre," but is limited to a finite number of conventional women.

Molière does not delay in confronting Dom Juan with the most recent woman, whose presence creates an embarrassment Alexander never knew. Elvire comes to recall her husband to the bonds of marriage. Dom Juan's euphoria, culminating in the comparison with Alexander, is interrupted, and he shifts the burden of her vexation to Sganarelle who, also embarrassed, explains his and Dom Juan's departure with a reference to the comparison, now odious to Dom Juan because Elvire has proved it inaccurate. Molière allows Dom Juan a chance to seize the ethical advantage, however, after Elvire's enumeration of a courtier's conventional defenses; his response draws on what she should have argued: obligations to heaven, vows and pledges broken to marry him. He pretends to be her benefactor, instead of the faithless moral pauper he is. Like Sganarelle with the snuffbox, he borrows arguments Elvire had at her disposal and uses them hypocritically against her to establish her ethical inferiority.

Characteristically, he ignores her final imprecations and, after a pause for reflection, a strange stage direction for silent gesture, he goes off, his euphoria dampened but already on the upswing through his posture as Elvire's ethical superior and benefactor, and through his eagerness to break the bonds between a young couple whose happiness has aroused his desire.

In act I, obligations are engendered by: snuff, which creates a social obligation, an infinite one if snuff were really a means to a virtuous and happy life; and marriage, which creates legal and heaven-sanctioned obligations. Self-styled benefactors, Sganarelle and Dom Juan, behave exclusively for reasons of self-interest. In the remainder of the play, benefactors give life, and Dom Juan's relationships occur in a context of life-and-death. The stakes are increased infinitely; unlike those associated with snuff, they are real and everlasting. Dom Juan persists in mocking these terms with civil gestures meant to distract from the overwhelming debt of life he incurs, and to make him seem a creditor-benefactor instead of an infinite debtor. If his subterfuges are perceived as brilliant esthetic gestures, the point is missed, and Dom Juan cannot be appreciated as a comic creation. For the gestures do not hide the fact that no polite motion can countervail the gift of life. The crucial question, though, that Dom Juan's displays of virtuosity sidestep, is whether any recompense at all is required to offset this gift: is the gift of life contained within the dialectic of obligation?

Life-and-death may seem too serious a topic for a genre that usually excludes death. A protagonist may be laughed off the stage, but is not punished with death for errors and misdeeds. Dom Juan is exceptional, for death is ultimately the wages of his sin: his life is the pledge forfeited for breaking faith. Death, however, does not simply occur as a miraculous intervention to destroy Dom Juan, or as an opportunity to exploit machines on stage. The shadow of death is cast more and more deeply across the play from act II onwards; in act III the theme of life-and-death recurs in each episode; and the appearances of the Statue in subsequent acts are like visitations of Death personified.

When act II begins, Dom Juan has been saved from death by Pierrot. Against this background, the act's single episode exhibits Dom Juan's frustration and embarrassment when confronted by two peasant girls to whom he has promised marriage. A situation he has made turns against him. This reversal is typical of Molière's comic dramaturgy in other plays (for example, ***L'École des femmes*** and ***Les Femmes savantes***), and it is repeated in act III. But the ethical point supported by this basic comic action deals with a greater theme, the great lord's treatment of the benefactor who has saved his life. Pierrot's narrative of the rescue provides a context for the act, as Sganarelle's praise of snuff sets the context for Dom Juan in act I. Molière again uses gesture to bolster the text, even extending gesture to the language itself: the patois establishes character and makes the audience perceive that Dom Juan is beholden to a bumpkin. Pierrot intends his narrative to impress Charlotte, his fiancée, and consequently, while acting out the account, he stresses his own qualities of keen eyesight and shrewdness in persuading Lucas to bet against him on a sure thing. (A bet, incidentally, is another form of pledged obligation.) Molière emphasizes Pierrot's lack of specific moral worth: he is immodest, self-interested (he collected the bet from Lucas before setting out to the rescue), and more taken with the profit from his wager than with having saved a life. All that detracts not a whit from the fact that the great lord's life depends on him.

Pierrot is also bound to the dialectic of obligation, not with Dom Juan, however, from whom he asks no reward, but with Charlotte. His possessiveness shows in a demand that she respond to his attentions, as gifts and serenades obligate her to. Dom Juan's attempt to seduce Charlotte betrays his benefactor, who sets great store, in his engagement to Charlotte, on the dialectic of obligation reduced to the absurd level of serenades, tokens, and love-pinches. Dom Juan at no time mentions his debt to Pierrot. Worse, on learning of Charlotte's engagement, he courts her more ardently: "Quoi? une personne comme vous serait la femme d'un simple paysan! Non, non, c'est profaner tant de beautés . . ." He strikes Pierrot when the peasant claims his rights, but grows silent when Pierrot recalls the rescue: ". . . ça n'est pas bian de battre les gens, et ce n'est pas la récompense de v's avoir sauvé d'être nayé." Dom Juan threatens Pierrot again only after Pierrot regrets having saved him, as if the remark nullified Dom Juan's debt: "Si j'avais su ça tantôt, je me serais bien gardé de le tirer de gliau, et je gli aurais baillé un bon coup d'aviron sur la tête." Dom Juan reacts viciously when he feels himself quit of obligation by the expressed wish that he had been knocked underwater by Pierrot's oar. This manipulation of the dialectic of obligation is specious, for the fact of the rescue remains. Dom Juan seizes an opportunity to escape the debt easily, and to pose as Charlotte's benefactor.

Charlotte and Sganarelle also pose as benefactors, with regard to Pierrot. Charlotte tries to convert her broken engagement into a service: "Va, va, Pierrot, ne te mets point en peine: si je sis Madame, je te ferai gagner queuque chose, et tu apporteras du beurre et du fromage cheux nous." Playing the grande dame, the embarrassed obligee caught in the act imitates Dom Juan to appear the benefactor. She abjures the unmeasurable ethical values implicit in betrothal, and invents material values owed her. Sganarelle also pretends to serve Pierrot, and is struck for his pains. He intervenes to obligate Dom Juan's victims to himself; that is why he denounces his master, out of earshot, at the end of the act. But the debts do not take shape, as Dom Juan's slap and return make Sganarelle abandon his poses of philanthropy. His apparent pity for Pierrot turns into "peste soit du maroufle," while he must swallow Dom Juan's taunt, "Te voilà payé de ta charité." But charity the gesture cannot be, if a self-interested Sganarelle wants superiority and obligation. Such self-seeking is typical of all the characters in this act, none of whom respects ethical obligations and performs services disinterestedly. Pierrot comes closest to performing a service freely by saving Dom Juan; its selflessness is mitigated, however, by his insistence on the wager.

But Dom Juan's debt to Pierrot differs in nature from all the other obligations, actual and desired. Betrothal and the protection of victims seem pale next to the debt of life itself. The stakes of benefactor-obligee relationships are increased to that level in act III, where every episode involves life-and-death. While Dom Juan refuses in act II to acknowledge his debt of life to a peasant, from act III on he is disconcerted by the thought of owing his life to nearly every character introduced, from the hermit to the Statue. He is caught by the consequences of construing his debts, great and small, in terms of the dialectic of obligation. That attitude must now be examined, before we look at the events of act III, particularly the scene with the Poor Man.

Within the dialectic of obligation, a benefactor remains superior until the recipient of a service has rendered an equivalent one. Certain acts of great magnitude, however, produce unrepayable debts. The value implicit in giving or saving life, bestowing a great fortune, or raising to a rank of undeserved merit cannot easily be matched in equivalent action, because the benefactor will probably never be in need of such action. That creates a problem, for although people generally consider great gifts desirable, they are uncomfortable with the consciousness of debt such gifts induce. As Pascal noted, "trop de bienfaits irritent" (Pensée 72).

But immeasurable services do not properly belong to a dialectic of obligation, a movement back and forth between parties who hold a measurable, temporary ethical advantage: a pinch of snuff can be offered to the original purveyor, and it confers no boundless ethical values of virtue and happiness, Sganarelle to the contrary. Acts like saving life do not originate in a desire for moral slaves, but in grace and charity. (The whole question of *générosité* in Corneille is at issue here, incidentally.) A gap exists between common and commensurable action within the dialectic of obligation and acts of charity: in seventeenth-century terms it is an abyss. Pierrot did not save Dom Juan to alter or establish dynamics of power between himself as creditor and the nobleman as debtor. He seeks no reward, and does not speak as though Dom Juan were immeasurably beholden to him. He mentions a "récompense" strictly in reaction to Dom Juan's treachery. The peasant's behavior stands as an object lesson to the man saved, and to the audience, of an act of charity; and this point is strengthened by Molière's insistence on Pierrot's toeing the line on the dialectic of obligation where his fiancée is involved, and by Pierrot's relegation of importance to the keenness of his eyesight rather than to the actual rescue. Dom Juan acts ungratefully, feeling overwhelmingly burdened with a debt of life to Pierrot. He is comic not only because the situations he manipulates entrap and embarrass him, but especially because he is caught by the dialectic of obligation where it does not apply: he misinterprets a fundamental relationship of charity as equivalent to Sganarelle's pinch of snuff, a civil gesture that the valet claims to confer immeasurable, unpayable values and correspondingly large debts; he cannot imagine acts of grace committed without expectation or desire of reward or obligation. And this misconception demeans and reduces the sublime, the saving of life, to the ridiculous and the vicious, the pushing of snuff à la Sganarelle. The scenes with the Poor Man in act III and with Dom Louis and Done Elvire in act IV will permit Molière to expand the profound source of Dom Juan's comic nature to a similar misreading of the relationship of God to man, in another mistaken application of the dialectic of obligation.

Situations of life-and-death that should transcend the dialectic of obligation occur in every episode of the third act, which structurally telescopes and repeats three times the overall dramatic pattern of act II. The first two acts contain single situations, Dom Juan's flight from Elvire and his attempted seduction of the peasant girls. Act III, by contrast, contains no extended episode. Four incidents induce a comic rhythm, where Dom Juan's enjoyment and frustration, his euphoric inflation and deflation alternate. The structure is basic to Molière's plays and is most apparent in ***L'École des femmes.*** It contributes to the comic nature of the action, but as a factor of dramaturgy, not of the philosophic "comic vision" of the play. Dom Juan finds a scornful pleasure in discussing beliefs with Sganarelle; then the hermit's lesson in charity embarrasses him. He enjoys the ironies of his incognito after rescuing Dom Carlos, but loses the advantage when his own life is spared in turn. Finally, the Statue of the Commander accepts his mockingly extended invitation: the rest of the play works out the full deflation, and destruction, of Dom Juan as part of the comic rhythm pattern. In all these incidents death is an element. Dom Juan and Sganarelle joke about how doctors kill; they meet a man starving to death and learn of dangerous bandits in the wood. Carlos is nearly killed. Alonse demands Dom Juan's life on the spot. The act ends at the tomb of a man killed, not by doctors but by Dom Juan. The recurrent structural detail, and the consequent expectation that Dom Juan's euphoria and mockery at the tomb will eventually be followed by his deflation lend to the audience feelings of excitement—how will Molière arrange the deferred comeuppance?—and of assurance that the character it condemns will not triumph. If ancient tragedy uses dark oracles to prefigure the inevitable ending, Molière follows a classical esthetic and uses patterns of structure.

When act III begins, Dom Juan and Sganarelle are disguised, and Molière draws attention to Sganarelle's doctor costume by recalling Dom Juan's intention of exchanging clothing with his valet. The doctor suit permits an apparently casual reintroduction of the theme of life-and-death. Doctors, master and man agree, are not committed to saving life: their privileges alone count, and they may kill with impunity, demanding, and getting, boundless admiration and gratitude. Sganarelle believes in medicine because of the measureless consideration it confers on a doctor, even an impostor dressed as one. He believes in heaven, hell, the devil and the bogeyman for similar reasons: they are beyond him, and he stands in awe of them. Molière juxtaposes the beliefs on medicine and religion to suggest analogous qualities in the reasoning beneath the apparent foolishness of Sganarelle's argument. As the peasants bow to a man dressed in the mystery-bearing costume of a doctor, treating him with boundless respect no matter what in fact he is or does, so Sganarelle thinks of heaven as wondrously mysterious. Whether the doctor saves or kills the patient, he performs incomprehensible acts. Analogously, man and the world are full of mystery; they must have been created by a being whose nature and action, like the doctor's, are incomprehensible, before whose measureless power and essence Sganarelle bows in wonderment. Sganarelle trips himself up in farcical conclusion; the pratfall is an absurd counterpart of the moral attitude implied by his reasoning.

The argument from necessity and mystery is not original to Sganarelle. It may be taken as typical of a school of believers, including Pascal, who find in infinite *grandeur* and infinitesimal *petitesse* reasons, though irrational, for belief in God. But Sganarelle is no spokesman for any formal or popular theological position; his function is dramaturgic, to furnish a contrast for Dom Juan's rationalist credo: "Je crois, Sganarelle, que deux et deux sont quatre, et que quatre et quatre sont huit." Belief is simplified to the measurable and predictable. Dom Juan refuses to acknowledge what Sganarelle claims to be immeasurable, for which arithmetic—logical rationality—cannot account. (He would like to be limitless himself, hence the wish for new worlds to conquer, like Alexander; but Elvire's intrusion deflates the wish.) Sganarelle seems to state the position of the "esprit de finesse," lacking, however, the clarity of intuition and expression typical of this mode of perception, while Dom Juan states a case for the "esprit de géométrie," with the significant difference that he refuses to accept the promptings of intuition as a base on which to reason. Molière is not aping or parodying Pascal: the *Pensées* were not published until 1670. But could he have had prior knowledge of them? Molière seems to present a brief for what Henri Gouhier calls "un humanisme chrétien en train de tourner au christianisme humanisé."[2] At the least, Molière was familiar with the ideological context of *libertinage* whose terms Pascal knew and used. Molière's strategy parallels Pascal's, presenting two postures of the human mind, both of which separately are inadequate. Dom Juan's belief in "arithmetic" corresponds to his refusal to acknowledge and deal with obligations that are not strictly measurable and payable (even though he will not honor them either). He resists the notion of the infinite, since in that perspective nothing differentiates him from Sganarelle, or from Pierrot: "Dans la vue de ces infinis, tous les finis sont égaux" (*Pensée* 72). The dialectic of obligation itself withers in the face of the infinite. But while Dom Juan may shrug off Sganarelle's questions about heaven, the devil, and the bogeyman, just as he ignores relationships that conform to no manageable dialectic of obligation unless he holds the immeasurable advantage, his refusal to acknowledge belief does not mean that heaven, at least, does not exist, nor that the fact ever escapes him. To cite Pascal once more, "Tout ce qui est incompréhensible ne laisse pas d'être" (*Pensée* 430), and one could probably find a similar position in the Lucretian sources of seventeenth-century Epicurean *libertinage.*

The contrast between two and two are four, and the marvelous, inexplicable, and immeasurable, along with Dom Juan's pleasure over Sganarelle's clumsiness when he sees his servant trip, provide the context for the encounter with the Poor Man. As Dom Juan observes, Sganarelle's reasoning about the mystery-defying reason has made them lose their way. They must seek help from the poor hermit who happens to be there when they need him. If his directions are viewed in the perspective of the dialectic of obligation, the debt is measurable: eventually, Dom Juan could find a way out of the wood; and an equivalent gesture could easily be found in a piece of money or food. (If the forest is a symbolic place, signifying the perilous darkness of Dom Juan's soul, the debt is boundless. But seeing the scene as allegorical creates dramatic inconsistencies—until one realizes that the whole play is an allegory of divine charity. That will become clearer later in the discussion.) There is a greater peril to Dom Juan, and the warning about thieves in the wood, added by the hermit, engenders a much greater sense of debt in the dialectic of obligation, for it concerns life-and-death: "Mais je vous donne avis que vous devez vous tenir sur vos gardes, et que depuis quelque temps il y a des voleurs ici autour." Dom Juan's studiedly polite reply is meant to counter his debt in words: "Je te suis bien obligé, mon ami, et je rends grâce de tout mon coeur." The hermit says "je vous donne"; Dom Juan answers with "rendre," paying for precious advice with a polite formula, like Harpagon. While a coin would be more appropriate compensation to an obvious pauper, Dom Juan remains unmoved by the man's appearance. He combines polite words with the familiar "tu"—Sganarelle had used "vous"—to mark a *bonhomie* the Poor Man cannot use. The hermit then asks for charity. He needs alms to survive, like any hermit under vows of poverty: he is not without reason called "Francisque" in the cast of characters, even though the name is not spoken. (Did his costume suggest a mendicant's habit?) Dom Juan interprets the plea as a demand within the dialectic of obligation: "Ah! ah! je vois que ton avis est intéressé."

Dom Juan attacks the hermit's principles to distract from his own embarrassment, caused by the beggar's lesson in charity: "grâce" is not rendered through words, but in a saving deed or gesture that shows the effect of being touched by grace. All the fatuity and absurdity of Dom Juan's polite formula, "je te rends grâce de tout mon coeur," is revealed when he fails to respond to the hermit's obvious need. His heart is not touched. Neither he nor Sganarelle, each unmoved by tales of the doctors' victims, is capable of pity or conversion. Sganarelle even takes his master's part with the hermit, having learned his lesson after sympathizing with the peasants in act II. To cover his lack of charity, Don Juan resorts to schemes of finite obligations, like a bookkeeper tallying debts and credits in the mode of two and two are four, a concept unknown to the hermit faced with the peril of imminent starvation. Despite that concern, though, he is moved to caution two strangers about thieves in the wood; such warning, perhaps saving their life, cannot be compensated for within the bounded dialectic of obligation. Thinking in his usual manner, Dom Juan must feel himself once more in a situation of measureless debt, the kind he cannot acknowledge without recognizing his own smallness.

But Dom Juan is mistaken, for the hermit's request for alms cuts through the dialectic of obligation. He is in dire need: "Hélas, Monsieur, je suis dans la plus grande nécessité du monde"; "je vous assure, Monsieur, que le plus souvent je n'ai pas un morceau de pain á me mettre sous les dents." No one starving in a forest beats around the bush serving a potential benefactor with warnings in order to create a debt repayable with money or food. He straightforwardly asks for charity, just as the grasshopper loses all shyness when she realizes she may starve to death. (The *cigale* shows she understands the uncharitable nature of the ant when she offers to repay principal and interest, within the dialectic of obligation!)

The hermit does not argue with Dom Juan, but, insisting on his poverty and vocation, promises to respond gratefully to alms: "Je suis un pauvre homme, Monsieur, retiré tout seul dans ce bois depuis dix ans, et ne manquerai pas de prier le Ciel qu'il vous donne toute sorte de biens." Since Dom Juan is incapable of charitable giving, and because the hermit needs help, he answers Dom Juan's rebuff in terms similar to those of the dialectic of obligation, but on the infinite level that Dom Juan cannot bear. His life saved by Dom Juan's alms, he will pray for Dom Juan's salvation in a measureless sense. For a coin, the hermit will return something of infinite value well beyond two and two are four, adding to the debt already existing. Dom Juan is close to realizing an enormous return on his investment, winning the sweepstakes as it were; but the grand seigneur cannot be bettered by a hermit, even if he comes out the winner.

Both the hermit and Dom Juan are in mortal peril, though in different senses. The dark wood in traditional literature suggests the peril of the soul, from which only a figure of love as *caritas* can bring rescue, like Beatrice when she sends Vergil to Dante. This is another source of wonder, like the mysteries Sganarelle alluded to. That traditional meaning may color the hermit scene. Even without this coloring, however, the subject of the encounter remains charity in extreme situations of life-and-death. Dom Juan immediately, and deliberately, confuses the issue, making the hermit's warning seem intended to oblige him to pay a coin in return; he reads the warning as a civil gesture, without sensing the abyss between offering snuff and giving charity. Advice and coin are parts of a system of ethical values involved in the saving of life: and *the saving of life is the most exalted manner of imitating God.* This is no dialectic of obligation, but Charity with a capital C. The hermit, nearly a dead man whom Dom Juan can revive, invites Dom Juan to act according to an analogon with God that Dom Juan cannot understand because he misinterprets God's relationship to man as following the dialectic of obligation. God, however, does not push snuff. Dom Juan refuses to be moved to a charitable act by the Poor Man's extreme need. He is frustrated in his own terms, and, because he refuses to acknowledge charity, he is not converted to a system of values that would free him from the stultifying dialectic of obligation that deprives him of his fullest humanity. He prefers to spare himself embarrassment by compromising the hermit's ethical values.

The Poor Man's refusal to swear again frustrates Dom Juan. By raising the subject of self-interest, Dom Juan shows his sense of debt for the hermit's advice, and he finally agrees to pay off that imagined debt, cheaply enough, with a single gold piece. Dom Juan must hand over the coin because otherwise, in his own terms, he will remain immeasurably obligated to the hermit. He wants neither to owe nor to satisfy the debt, and getting the man to swear converts the coin into a reward for the blasphemy, in a kind of unholy bargain. Dom Juan will no longer owe, nor will he have paid the debt, and he will have destroyed the hermit's ethical values. When his browbeating fails, he tosses the Poor Man the gold piece "pour l'amour de l'humanité," upsetting the formula "pour l'amour de Dieu" to distract from his failure. The witty saying, however, cuts sharply along double edges, for the phrase contradicts the situation where it occurs. Repayment of the debt is a totally interested act; it is not charity. Giving for love of mankind, though, without expectation of reward and desire to rid himself of his sense of debt, would be charity. Giving disinterestedly "pour l'amour de l'humanité" constitutes an imitation of God, who gives and restores life, in creation and salvation, without expecting his creature ever can match such gifts in return. That is the recurrent theme of Augustine's *Confessions,* and it shapes Augustinian Catholicism as practiced by a Pascal who wonders whether God asks anything of man "sinon qu'il l'aime et le connaisse" (*Pensée* 430). God is the greatest benefactor possible, a philanthropist in the etymological sense, outside any dialectic of obligation.

Dom Juan's witty phrase turns ironically against him as a reminder of genuine free giving; it makes us draw distinctions between, on the one hand, Dom Juan's charity-devoid attempt to conceal embarrassment before the hermit's lesson in charity and, on the other hand, the God of charity, outside the dialectic of obligation, who gives "pour l'amour de l'humanité." The audience does not laugh at the intended stroke of wit, which instead pierces Dom Juan's desired concealment of defeat. He unwittingly parodies God's loving relationship to man, and does not understand how close he has come to escaping the dialectic of obligation with a free, disinterested act of charity. What should be a profound, religious, humanizing experience, the imitation of divine love, becomes a grandiose mocking gesture meant to save face.

This episode concerning charity in the extreme situation of life-and-death expands the vision of the play to include fundamental questions of God and man. Dom Juan's willful misinterpretation of the hermit's motive at the beginning of the scene makes him miss a rare chance to understand and imitate seriously God's relationship to man, to grasp the wonderful mystery Sganarelle had vainly reasoned about. That is genuinely sad, but Dom Juan remains comic. A tragic protagonist would face his shame and humiliation on understanding the significance of his action; he would convert to the ethical values implicit in the act whose form he had imitated, albeit unwittingly; and he then would face the consequences of conversion, whatever they might be, whatever the values might demand. That is the mechanism of Cornelian conversion and of Rotrou's *Saint Genest,* where the metaphor of performance as imitation is extended to the utmost limit: Genest learns to grasp the ethical content implicit in the play of conversion and martyrdom that he acts out. But Dom Juan remains dominated by the need to maintain the appearances of a dignity he lacks, not only when measured against God's infinite worth, but also when placed on the scale of the Poor Man, whose scruples are firm. He resists conversion, which could confer dignity, even though almsgiving closely imitates the divine act that should convert him, and us. Insistence on the dialectic of obligation, refusal to entertain the notion of free giving, determination to destroy the hermit's ethic, based on hope in God's loving charity: these deprive Dom Juan of an opportunity to correct a false perspective that condemns him to live without the full humanity he is capable of as one of God's creatures. But he is still not deprived of God's love or grace, since, although he misses the chance afforded by the crucial encounter with the Poor Man, it is not the last time Dom Juan is offered an opportunity to be moved and to act charitably in knowing or unwitting imitation of God.

An opportunity to save life, but not in imitation of God, arises right after Dom Juan tosses the Poor Man a coin. He may rush to rescue Dom Carlos because "la partie est inégale, et je ne dois pas souffrir cette lâcheté"; but he bore easily enough with unequal odds as he and Sganarelle ganged up on the hermit. Dom Juan creates an immeasurable debt of life that he does not expect Carlos to repay. Still disguised as a country gentleman, Dom Juan savors a private comedy of ironies, with the man seeking to kill him owing him life. Molière develops the scene (III, iii) to expand on Dom Juan's pleasure in toying with the idea of infinite obligation to himself. He cuts short Carlos' speech of thanks—"Souffrez, Monsieur, que je vous rende grâce d'une action si généreuse, et que . . ."—affecting modesty, and avoiding the possibility that an expression of gratitude, a polite verbal gesture, will reduce the debt as he tried to do in response to the hermit's warning. (Pierrot's impolite verbal gesture, it may be recalled, had nullified Dom Juan's debt to him in Dom Juan's eyes.) Carlos keeps mentioning the obligation after Dom Juan admits friendship with the man Carlos pursues:

> c'est bien la moindre chose que je vous doive, après m'avoir sauvé la vie . . .
>
> après ce que je vous dois, ce me serait une trop sensible douleur que vous fussiez de la partie . . .
>
> Faut-il que je vous doive la vie, et que Dom Juan soit de vos amis?

Dom Juan's pleasure evaporates during Carlos' debate with his brother on vengeance, when Carlos satisfies the debt Dom Juan had presumed to be immeasurable and unpayable. He is no longer "redevable de la vie" to Dom Juan, for, as two and two are four, so one life spared compensates for a life saved, one infinite value equals another. From the position of superiority and arrogance implicit in his private comedy, Dom Juan is diminished as Carlos satisfies, within the dialectic of obligation, a life-and-death debt. The debate between the brothers serves a dramatic purpose more important than the analysis of aristocratic behavior and vendetta, for it reduces Dom Juan to silence and shrinks his advantage to nothing.

Dom Juan voices vexation in his response to Carlos: "Je n'ai rien exigé de vous, et vous tiendrai ce que j'ai promis." In the light of the hermit scene, there may be another unwitting parody of God in these words, with Dom Juan pretending that he had not meant to obligate Carlos by saving his life. Of course he had not demanded that Carlos be sure to "rendre le bien que j'ai reçu de vous"; he should have preferred an attack by Elvire's brothers, less threatening than the band of thieves just driven off, to losing advantage over Carlos. He also vents rage on Sganarelle, whose scatological reply distracts from Dom Juan's frustration, allowing him, and the audience, to start building toward another brief life-and-death episode, in which pleasure is succeeded by disappointment, surprise, and fear. Molière uses jokes to make the audience lose track of Dom Juan's discomfort, duplicate his euphoria, and react more strongly when his pleasure vanishes. The comic rhythm generates a quasi-identification between protagonist and public. We recognize, however, that the euphoria is short-lived; and when the Statue agrees to come to dinner, we may be shocked by the supernatural element but are hardly surprised by the dramaturgy.

Dom Juan's invitation to the Statue parodies polite gesture. To the objection that visiting a man he killed is not "civile," Dom Juan argues, "Au contraire, c'est une visite dont je lui veux faire civilité, et qu'il doit recevoir de bonne grâce, s'il est galant homme." He goes "au-devant du souhait," as it were, like Sganarelle with the snuffbox, in a parody of civil behavior to obligate the Statue to himself, silly as that seems. Fresh from frustration with Dom Carlos, Dom Juan needs to be someone's creditor, even a statue's, as a concomitant of his sense of perpetual debt to God; and he desperately needs to amuse himself to forget the frustrations of his encounters with the Poor Man and Carlos. So he mocks the vanity of the Commander dressed as a Roman emperor in a grandiose tomb.

The measure of his frustration and despair is indicated by his reduction to parodying civil gestures with a statue, which, he is certain, cannot repay the simple, measurable obligation in an invitation to dinner. The scale of his gesture is radically reduced from the infinite scale of saving life on which the rest of act III occurs. But even the foolproof joke backfires and grows to that scale; the parody of ordinary civil gestures which conceal a latent will to dominate turns on Dom Juan and destroys him. The Statue will not only come to dinner, but will return the favor; and at the end of act V he will come for his guest as another civil gesture, just as Dom Juan parodically offers to see out his guests in act IV. Dom Juan calls the Statue to life, in another possible unwitting parody of divine action. In fact, though, the Statue is given movement as a divine miracle meant to restore Dom Juan to life—or to lead him to hell should he refuse conversion. True to the pattern of act III, Dom Juan's expectations about a debt that cannot be satisfied are frustrated; and the social debt, within the ordinary dialectic of obligation, that he had parodied to his surprise becomes one on the immeasurable scale of life-and-death. But Dom Juan misunderstands, as usual, fearing to incur an immeasurable debt, and refuses to convert. The parody of civil gesture that backfires sets in motion the mechanism of the Statue; and death, which spans the act from the doctor jokes to the substantial presence of the commander's funeral monument, will overarch the rest of the play.

From the parody of civil gesture in Sganarelle's snuff speech the action has led to Dom Juan's parodic gestures directed to the Statue. In act IV Dom Juan uses quasi-polite and parodic gestures to defuse the serious purpose of four unwelcome visitors, variants of the device of intruding *fâcheux,* who keep Dom Juan from enjoying distractions like those in acts II and III. He cannot dine in peace, even after dismissing the intruders with marks of courtesy, or impertinence, in the guise of civil gestures. In extending hospitable invitations to be seated—which recall his frustration in being kept from sitting at the table—or to stay for the night, or to be seen out by a punctilious host, his purpose concerns his advantage, not the comfort or pleasure of the guest. Superficial gestures are intended to manipulate obligations and avoid paying serious ethical debts.

In one recurrent gesture, Dom Juan offers to see out his guests. The "flambeau pour conduire Monsieur Dimanche," ordered by Dom Juan, occurs metaphorically in Dom Louis's speech: ancestral glory is "un flambeau qui éclaire aux yeux d'un chacun la honte de vos actions." Elvire leaves before Dom Juan can see her out: "ne faites aucune instance pour me conduire et songez seulement à profiter de mon avis," she says, rejecting polite gestures that defuse serious concerns. The Statue also rejects any accompaniment: "on n'a pas besoin de lumière, quand on est conduit par le ciel." (We shall see how the Statue returns the gesture at the end of act V, when the image of the torch is extended, in a familiar baroque poetic process, to match Dom Juan's torch in the flames of hell to which the Statue leads him.) After the first, farcical episode where Dom Juan dazzles Monsieur Dimanche, his civil, but cheap, gestures turn against Dom Juan, who cannot deflect the visitors' intention of counseling him.

The style for dealing with intruders is announced before Monsieur Dimanche enters. "Il est bon de les payer de quelque chose, et j'ai le secret de les renvoyer satisfaits sans leur donner un double." Faced, as it were, with a financial "lord" who wants an obligation honored—a meaning implicit in the derivation of "Dimanche" from *dominus*—Dom Juan substitutes imagined ethical values by insisting on the chair and by inquiring about his creditor's health and family. He raises in Dimanche a sense of boundless obligation to keep him from mentioning the finite material obligation. Dom Juan toys with the acknowledgment of his debt—puns run rampant on a vocabulary of interest, obligation, and profit—which, after all, belongs to the measurable mode of two and two are four, while he produces a sense of ethical worth in Dimanche, infinitely superior in nature to worth based on wealth. The merchant's reply, "Nous vous sommes infiniment obligés," is entirely accurate. "Tant de civilités et tant de compliments" render him ineffective as a moneylender collecting debts: paralyzed, he cannot follow his best interest, for fear that materialist concerns might diminish Dom Juan's esteem.

The instant replay between Monsieur Dimanche and Sganarelle shows in brutal terms what the master thinks of the creditor. Sganarelle throws him out; and his offer, "Je vais vous éclairer," refers less to torchlight than to enlightenment concerning Dom Juan's, and Sganarelle's, intention. The episode with Dimanche, interpolated by Molière into the plot of his sources, provides an easy victory for Dom Juan and furnishes a context for Dom Louis's visit, and for Dom Juan's impertinent put-down in the form of a "sit-down." In other circumstances, the remark, "Monsieur, si vous étiez assis, vous en seriez mieux pour parler," would denote respect for a father; here, it marks contempt, and is meant to distract from Dom Juan's vexation. His shifts from ethical concerns to a superficial polite gesture, however, cannot counter ethical debts to a father as progenitor, protector, counselor. Dom Juan's civil-contemptuous gestures with his father and with Elvire lend him no advantage: as in the hermit scene, *the audience does not laugh,* and even Sganarelle, shocked, disapproves. The dramaturgic strategy allows Dom Juan no immediate diversion. Embarrassing visits rapidly follow and are not defused by his interruptions. Dom Louis's long speech conditions us for Elvire's subsequent plea for conversion; both speeches, and the Statue's visit, stand out from their immediate contexts, which involve Sganarelle in brief episodes of farce that do not allow Dom Juan sufficient distraction.

The father's entrance stops the action. He analyzes Dom Juan's behavior and expounds a scheme of relationships governing men in the kingdom. He, and later Elvire, restate and develop themes of self-interest, obligation, and charity. But Dom Louis is not saintly; he is dominated by self-interest. Each stage of his quasi-Cornelian tirade dwells on his shame. His values exclude genuine conversion: Dom Juan is told to reform to restore the family's good name as a matter of conformity, not as a result of a change of heart. (This point of view is hardly Cornelian.) Self-interest frames his words: he had begged heaven for a son, he will implore heaven to destroy that son to purge his shame. His appeal to ancestral honor is not advice freely given for love of Dom Juan—the phrase "tendresse paternelle" seems out of place in the speech—but is intended to restore his own rank and honor at court. He is alarmed that he caused heaven to act not through grace in giving him a son but to rid itself of a pest, that he has invited punishment through his son's behavior, and that his self-interest has been justly rewarded: "ce fils, que j'obtiens en fatiguant le Ciel de voeux, est le chagrin et le supplice de cette vie même dont je croyais qu'il devait être la joie et la consolation." The king also has lost patience:

> De quel oeil, à votre avis, pensez-vous que je puisse voir cet amas d'actions indignes, dont on a peine, aux yeux du monde, d'adoucir le mauvais visage, cette suite continuelle de méchantes affaires, qui nous réduisent, à toutes heures, à lasser les bontés du Souverain, et qui ont épuisé auprès de lui le mérite de mes services et le crédit de mes amis?

Within a surviving feudalism and according to the dialectic of obligation, royal protection and aristocratic privileges represent payment for services. A second source of privilege, however, beyond the king's debt for service, lies in "bontés," royal favors. Once Dom Louis's measurable stock of credits is exhausted, he is reduced to begging for favors—as he had begged heaven for a son—and thus risking the king's displeasure. This second relationship of noble to king, outside the dialectic of obligation, cuts to the quick of the play. While the king satisfies debts for services rendered, he may grant favors because he loves the subject; but he may be wearied by importunate pleas, and the result may resemble heaven's "favor," extended not out of grace and love, but to teach a moral lesson in the monster that is Dom Juan. Molière used analogical reasoning in Sganarelle's argument in act III and does again here.

Once the king has honored his debts, the noble, subscribing to the dialectic of obligation, stands naked of value before him. Only the sovereign's grace can restore his dignity. His service had distinguished him from common people, but now he senses the enormous gap separating him from the king. The notion here is that there is no intrinsic worth, that only continued service can establish and maintain merit; this conception is worthy of Corneille, whose protagonists successfully enhance their nature through action. The dialectic of obligation had spared the noble the acknowledgment of the essential difference between himself and the sovereign. That explains Dom Juan's need to maintain and manipulate the dialectic of obligation; like us all, he cannot bear to contemplate himself as inferior in nature or reduced in stature.

These issues are related to those raised in the critical encounter with the Poor Man. The qualitative difference between sovereign and noble, as between God and creature, cannot be measured; the mode of being of one is not statable in terms of the other. Dom Juan refuses to contend with a measureless gap beyond which infinite power and being exist. He refuses to risk the moral paralysis of feeling reduced to nothing against the limitless value of king and God, and he concludes that only two and two are four makes sense in order to keep the vast difference in nature between himself and God-king from overwhelming him. He refuses, where he is concerned, to concede the gap in the great chain of being between the creator and the created which does not permit the continuity along the chain throughout creation to extend from creation upward to God. Dom Juan unwittingly imitated God's charity with the Poor Man; now it can be observed that, where others are concerned, he manipulates the dialectic of obligation as a deliberate parodic imitation of king and God to prove a gap in nature between himself and his victims. But that gap, unlike the one in the great chain of being between creator and creation, does not exist: Molière's Dom Juan never succeeds in establishing superiority. The specious ethical value he pretends to confer makes only a Charlotte or a Dimanche sense a gulf conjured up between them and the great lord; only they are rendered ineffectual before the parodically grace-ful lending of value that bridges such a gap, and emphasizes it. Dom Juan predicts Monsieur Dimanche's response on the model of his own—if he would allow himself to acknowledge his worthlessness in the perspective of king and God. But critical differences distinguish Dom Juan's conception of divine and royal relationships to creature and subject from seventeenth-century humanistic views, including Pascal's, according to which neither God nor king commands total abnegation of value from the creature or subject. And while Dom Juan acts through self-interest to paralyze his victims, God and king exercise grace to free their chosen. Dom Juan's signs of value remain gestural, empty, parodic; God's and the king's confer genuine worth derived from, but not diminishing, their own transcendent absolute value.

Father and son, Dom Louis and Dom Juan, mistakenly explain grace and favor with parameters of human behavior that promote moral paralysis in a super-dialectic of obligation. Grace and favor, however, are freely given: *per-donare, par-don, for-give,* through gift. They are extended for mysterious love of the creature—"pour l'amour de l'humanité"—to bridge the gap, to convert man so he may acknowledge and emulate in imitation, not parody, superior modes of being and begin to merit his redemption through actions imitative of the charity that touched the heart in conversion. These terms, reminiscent of Pascal and Corneille's strategy, are incompatible with the dialectic of obligation. They obviate the desire to indemnify others, by the gestural equivalents of offering snuff in daily life, and to forget the essential differences from God or king. In this light, the prayer "Forgive us our debts as we forgive our debtors" is pointless, for the context of grace and favor eliminates awareness of debt to God; we forgive our debts when, converted, we realize that pardon is the proper imitation of God, a form of charity. When we stop imagining God's relationship to us as a dialectic of obligation we can imitate God and grow closer to our prelapsarian nature; we begin to bridge the unclosable gap in the chain of being between God and man.

Molière's thought implicit in Dom Louis's speech draws upon Augustinian assumptions: God loves man in spite of sinfulness and fallen nature; to be restored to his nature before the Fall, man must recognize and respond to God's love; happiness consists of the imitation of God's charity subsequent to the recognition of God's love. This vision, of which Dom Louis remains unaware because of his self-interest, is extended and developed by Elvire. She comes to convert Dom Juan for love of him, in the sense of love as charity. The arrangement of her speech marks that concern. Its first section ends on the note of her lack of self-interest in visiting him: "[le Ciel] n'a laissé dans mon coeur pour vous qu'une flamme épurée de tout le commerce des sens, une tendresse toute sainte, un amour détaché de tout, qui n'agit que pour soi, et ne se met en peine que de votre intérêt." Dom Juan's mocking aside to Sganarelle, "Tu pleures, je pense," meant to distract from his embarrassment, only draws attention to the words "votre intérêt." After the interruption Elvire again stresses detachment, and begs for Dom Juan's conversion, as if her ultimate happiness were at stake.

> De grâce, Dom Juan, accordez-moi, pour dernière faveur, cette douce consolation; ne me refusez point votre salut, que je vous demande avec larmes; et si vous n'êtes point touché de votre intérêt, soyez-le au moins de mes prières, et m'épargnez le cruel déplaisir de vous voir condamné à des supplices éternels.

Sganarelle's aside, "pauvre femme," highlights a notion related to the king's favor and God's grace in the phrase "accordez-moi, pour dernière faveur." Dom Juan's salvation is posed as a favor extended to Elvire outside the dialectic of obligation. Her interest lies mysteriously in *his* salvation; by converting he would act analogously to king and God, who act without self-interest for the good of the subject and creature. Like the hermit, Elvire gives him an opportunity to imitate nonparodically God and king, and to escape the dialectic of obligation. She also places her beatitude in his hands, identifying her self-interest with his salvation. Elvire is in the literary tradition of female Christian mediators, deriving from Augustine's mother, Saint Monica, and self-interest cannot properly be attributed to her. She brings into sharp focus, through her example and her pleading, the meaning of concepts found in Dom Louis's speech; and she offers a nonmiraculous means of persuading Dom Juan to convert. The miracle of the Statue is an intervention of power, and a show of the lengths to which God will go to make the wayward creature convert. Elvire's attempt to convert Dom Juan is mysterious, but not miraculous. Her words suggest that the ethical life and happiness, promised by Sganarelle through snuff, are found by imitating God: "Pour l'amour de vous, ou pour l'amour de moi," Elvire pleads, echoing "pour l'amour de l'humanité" and the lesson of charity. She risks

Dom Juan's scorn, but, like the Poor Man, does not allow humiliation to dissuade her from charitable actions.

Dom Juan's contempt, particularly for departures from expected social behavior in other people, means nothing to her in the light of her conversion to ethical values. That is why she advises Dom Juan, on entering, not to comment on her unusual clothing—she is veiled—as he had in act I. She must have overheard his remark then as she entered: "est-elle folle, de n'avoir pas changé d'habit, et de venir en ce lieu-ci avec son équipage de campagne?" (The comment introduces the theme of clothing, dear to the Renaissance, which has not been followed in this discussion.) As she wards off attention to meaningless conventions of dress, so she declines and avoids Dom Juan's gestures of hospitality, refusing to stay for the night—an extension of offers to sit—or to be seen out. With social debts on a petty scale Dom Juan would counter or defuse the ethical obligation he mistakenly sees in Elvire's wish to convert him. It is true that she conjures up the dialectic of obligation by referring to a "récompense" in the last section of her speech; but a dialectic whose terms, Dom Juan's salvation and Elvire's happiness, are infinite, is no dialectic but a stasis of equal, eternal terms. Dom Juan cannot reduce, through parodic civil gestures, the enormity of what Elvire freely offers him, with no interest in being his creditor. In this, she resembles the God who purified her heart.

Nor can Dom Juan succeed in mocking the Statue, who visits in response to his invitation. The Statue enters in a context of farce: Dom Juan has asked Sganarelle to sit at dinner with him—a gesture showing the real significance, as mocking shows of courtesy, of other invitations to sit since he has the dishes removed before Sganarelle can touch them. Sganarelle serves again as a scapegoat for the embarrassment brought by Dom Louis and Elvire. Dom Juan extends courtesies to the Statue by asking Sganarelle to join the feast, to sing, and to toast the Commander's health, another contemptuous gesture, since the Commander is dead and Dom Juan killed him! The perfect host's every courteous gesture within the dialectic of obligation is designed to cover his amazement and to increase his guest's debt, while his commands to Sganarelle reveal the parodic nature of the gestures, meant to frighten the valet and to offend the Statue. But the Statue remains faithful to the dialectic of obligation initiated in the graveyard: he acquits himself of liability, no matter how contemptuous the original indebting gesture, by inviting Dom Juan in turn to dine. He delivers no moralizing speech, as the audience expects according to the pattern set by Dom Louis and Elvire (that speech is deferred until the end when the Statue, as host, may choose the subject of conversation, as it were); but the earlier visitors came for Dom Juan's reform, while the Statue visits because he is obliged to, in response to an invitation accepted.

The forces at play here are greater than in previous scenes, no less than divinity and death, infinite though concretized in the Statue. They nevertheless obey the comparatively petty laws of the dialectic of obligation; and it is according to those laws, the laws of two and two are four on a level of measurable and commensurable gestures, that Dom Juan is to be destroyed: in his own terms. Whereas he should recognize the presence of infinite forces in the miraculous Statue, he refuses, and the Statue obligingly responds in the only terms Dom Juan will acknowledge. Instruments Dom Juan uses to gain advantage, parodically, over the Statue of the Commander he had killed become instruments of his own destruction. The torch, passed by Dom Juan to Sganarelle as the fourth act ends to see the Statue out, gains its full significance at the play's end when the Statue returns the gesture, within the dialectic of obligation, but on an infinite scale, as only God can: the torch is repaid boundlessly and endlessly in the fires of hell. Dom Juan is finally made to acknowledge the presence of the infinite and everlasting, when the grace and favor of heaven are shown to be exhausted. The life-and-death situation ends in death, despite the extreme charity of the Statue.

The Statue visits, it is true, because he accepted Dom Juan's invitation. But within a pattern of decreasing self-interest on the part of the fourth-act visitors, the Statue has the least self-interest: in effect, as an instrument for Dom Juan's salvation, he acts despite his own interest within the aristocratic code and the dialectic of obligation. Charity succeeds vendetta; and only when Dom Juan refuses charity is he struck down, but not even then for the Commander's vengeance. The operation of grace through the Statue portrays the effects of conversion, the loss of the Commander's self-interest, and, only finally, the effects of a refusal to convert.

Dom Juan's hypocrisy and parody of conversion provide material for act V and trigger his destruction. As a hypocrite, he intends to put off those who press for his repentance while indulging his desires and placing enemies in his power. The strategy seems to work when the act begins, for Dom Louis believes his son and praises "la bonté du Ciel" for effecting conversion. He leaves to "rendre grâce au Ciel," still thinking of heaven's free gifts in the improper terms of the dialectic of obligation. Dom Juan's hypocritical posture as heaven's defender seems successful.

In the second scene his delight on fooling his father breaks out, and he eagerly describes for Sganarelle a gamut of gestures designed to satisfy his desires à la Tartuffe while he pretends to serve others as a spiritual and ethical guide. As in his explanation of inconstancy in love in I, iii, the Alexander speech, in this long discourse he is anxious to expound his thought to Sganarelle, to justify his behavior, and to enjoy the valet's shock. Both speeches recall Sganarelle's praise of snuff. Passing around a parody of religion, Dom Juan uses heaven as Sganarelle offered snuff in a parody of civil gesture. Sganarelle provoked laughter with his claims and Gusman was unimpressed; Dom Juan seemingly offers nothing less than salvation, and nobody laughs. Dom Juan's parodic gesture would place in his debt people ready for grace and real conversion, just as

Sganarelle meant to obligate the real owner of the snuffbox. But while a receiver of snuff can easily repay his benefactor in kind, no service matches the benefits of religion: eternal life and beatitude.

Dom Juan expects his gestures performed in the name of "le Ciel"—his response to Carlos' every objection in scene iii—to shield him and afford him ethical advantage. The structure of act V, a counterstructure to act IV, allows him increasing euphoria until the Spectre and the Statue appear. He refuses conversion, but for once honors his word, to join the Statue for dinner. The dialectic of obligation begun in the graveyard is thus satisfied, and the Statue, acting truly in heaven's name, leads Dom Juan to a death provoked by his refusal of grace and his abuse of heaven's name. As the sovereign must act to protect the state and his subjects from Tartuffe's ultimate crime, his false serving of the prince for his own self-interest, so heaven must renounce its grace and destroy Dom Juan for the sake of those creatures who are open to grace and salvation, lest Dom Juan's hypocrisy in the name of heaven threaten their spiritual welfare. Dom Juan receives the wages of sin because of God's love for man, "pour l'amour de l'humanité"; death, which has hovered over the play since act II, claims Dom Juan.

The matter of wages for years of service dominates Sganarelle's final, shocking speech. It contains no word of lament for his master, nor a moral. Molière concludes with a frustrated Sganarelle, bounding around the stage searching for signs of Dom Juan, demanding his wages of the air peopled with imaginary benefactors, like Harpagon pleading for his strongbox with the people he conjures up around him, then with the audience laughing at him. Sganarelle is also laughed at, as, obsessed, he shouts for his wages, again and again: at the beginning of the speech, "Mes gages! mes gages!"; at the end, "Mes gages! mes gages! mes gages!" La Grange, having disappeared through a trap door, could not have seen Molière's stage movements and may have wondered why he heard laughter following Dom Juan's damnation.

The gestural play no longer involves Sganarelle's polite offering of what was not his to obligate a circle of imagined snuff-takers. He gestures wildly to demand what is owed him in the dialectic of obligation that bound him to his master. Everyone is satisfied and content, made happy not by snuff, as it were, but by Dom Juan's death—and of course Sganarelle is wrong: no character is satisfied by Dom Juan's death. Sganarelle is left with nothing to show for his servitude, compromised by association with a wicked master. He had remained with Dom Juan in the expectation of payment: not for ethical values, but for material values contracted for and deliverable as part of a dialectic of obligation between master and servant. He is not like Sancho Panza, who remains faithful to Don Quixote long after it becomes apparent that any reward his master might bestow cannot compare with the ethical and spiritual ties between them.

Sganarelle is as comic as Dom Juan, perhaps more so, because the point escapes him. After witnessing miracles in a drama of divine charity, he can think only of the wages his master pledged to him. The last laugh is on Sganarelle, because the purveyor of snuff, cheated in the dialectic of obligation, should have learned from experience that his master never honored debts and because he is still concerned with material obligations when he, who had argued in act III for something wondrous responsible for man, has witnessed miracles of charity outside the dialectic of obligation. A comedy with reconciliation, or a tragedy, would end with a hymn to God's charity and power. But Sganarelle does not see beyond his wages. Like his master, he is totally bound to the dialectic of obligation—stultifying, reducing everything in the manner of two and two are four to the measure of only one element in man, and ultimately destructive of qualities deemed by the period of Molière and Pascal, of humanist freethinkers, noble and bourgeois gentlemen, believing philosophers and apologists for religion, to confer dignity and value on the incomprehensible monster, man.

Notes

1. Jan Miel has a pertinent discussion of this point in his *Pascal and Theology* (Baltimore: The Johns Hopkins University Press, 1969), pp. 170-71.
2. Henri Gouhier, "L'Inhumain Dom Juan," *La Table ronde* 119:67-73.

Larry W. Riggs (essay date 1987)

SOURCE: "Ethics, Debts, and Identity in Dom Juan," in *Romance Quarterly*, Vol. 34, No. 2, May, 1987, pp. 141-46.

[*In the following excerpt, Riggs explores the role of the individual in society as presented in Molière's* Dom Juan.]

In Molière's comedy, the desire to eliminate or avoid the risks in social and sexual relationships is a fundamental theme. The issue of debt, or obligation, is explicitly central in some of the plays, and it serves as a metaphor for the cohesiveness of society itself.[1] ***Dom Juan*** is a play in which this theme is particularly important, and whose progress explores the social implications of debt, risk, ethics, and identity. Like ***Le Tartuffe,*** whose interdiction forced Molière to write ***Dom Juan*** in order to have a new play to produce, ***Dom Juan*** studies the relationship between gestures and meaning as that relationship either supports and renews, or exploits and exhausts, social beliefs and ethical significances. A nobleman's effort to make himself independent of the very network of meanings and obligations that is the basis of his status as nobleman is an excellent vehicle for exploring the issue of identity and the ineluctably social ground of individuality.

Dom Juan dramatizes the refusal of ethical risk in such a way as to show that society can be either a stagnant, ceremonial game, circling toward total disillusionment, or a collective effort to conceive and realize values. It can be the latter only if the interdependence of identities and the primacy of ethically significant exchanges are recognized. As Dom Juan's deception reduces others' respect for him to the level of superstition, he becomes a phantom analogous to the *loup-garou* of Sganarelle's fantasies. Ethical meaning and social value can exist only in a context of substantial exchanges involving both risk and mutual benefit, and individual identity can be expressed and preserved only in ethically meaningful relationships.

The play begins with a burlesque praise of generous social gestures that states, in quasi-absurd fashion, the basic themes of the play. Molière does full justice to the complexities of his subject by having this overture performed by a character whose egotism is showing: Sganarelle illustrates the benefits of generous gestures by distributing imaginary pinches of *someone else's* snuff.[2] Indeed, the social consequences of gestures intended to create an impressive appearance of generosity without actually giving anything of substance are a principal preoccupation of this play. Gestures whose purpose ought to be to establish meaningful linkages among persons can be used to deceive and manipulate. This destroys both social cohesiveness and individual identity.

Sganarelle's burlesque "praise of tobacco" gives a brief glimpse of *honnête* society as, like any social group, a system of linkages established and preserved by gestures whose commonly accepted meanings express shared values. Immediately after his speech about the merits of tobacco, Sganarelle explains to Done Elvire's servant, Gusman, that Dom Juan has no respect for social gestures and institutions, nor for the meanings they reflect.

Marriage, as an institution and as a system of gestures reflecting obligation and benefit, is a major theme in ***Dom Juan.***[3] Dom Juan tries to remove all risk and obligation from this most fundamental of social relationships. However, he does not try to avoid marriage. On the contrary, he attempts to empty marriage—as gesture and as institution—of its significance and its power to obligate him by repeating and thereby trivializing it. Sganarelle describes the situation perfectly when he says: "Un mariage ne lui coûte rien à contracter" (Act I, sc. i). Dom Juan, despite the superficial differences, resembles the protagonists in Molière's other major comedies in that he destroys his *own* substance by destroying that of his relationships.[4]

The contradiction at the center of Dom Juan's effort to transcend the social network is that his successes in escaping from obligation depend largely on his *social status.* Even—or perhaps especially—the nobility is inextricably embedded in the context of social perceptions and meanings.[5] At least as much as Molière's other *ridicules,* Dom Juan is deluded: he believes that he can retain his identity while avoiding the risks of social interchange. The status of *gentilhomme* is meaningful only within a given context, and its possession, as Dom Louis forcefully reminds Dom Juan in Act IV, sc. iv, is a debt as well as a privilege: "Et qu'avez-vous fait dans le monde pour être gentilhomme? Croyez-vous qu'il suffise d'en porter le nom et les armes, et que ce nous soit une gloire d'être sortis d'un sang noble lorsque nous vivons en infâmes? Non, non, la naissance n'est rien où la vertu n'est pas."

By this definition, nobility is a dramatic quality: it exists in and depends on social interaction. It is a quality of relationships, not a static attribute permanently possessed by totally self-sufficient individuals. Thus, Dom Juan's principal advantage in dominating others is *itself* a debt and obligation. His identity is created and limited by the social meanings and expectations associated with his status. Like Molière's other comic leads, Dom Juan needs to have the authenticity and power of his identity confirmed by the same people whom he tries to reduce to a state of ethical nonexistence.[6] The very nature of his enterprise underlines the importance of others and of what they give to him, even as he tries to avoid all obligations to them. The inescapably social basis of Dom Juan's identity is emphasized by the fact that the peasant girl, Charlotte, is first attracted to Dom Juan by Pierrot's description of the nobleman's clothes. She is "softened up" for seduction, before she has seen Dom Juan's *person,* by an evocation of his *costume* (Act II, sc. i).

A particularly important aspect of Dom Juan's manipulation of obligations is that he tries to evade or "repay" real debts with empty gestures. The *Scène du Pauvre* (Act III, sc. ii) and Dom Juan's meeting with his bourgeois creditor, Monsieur Dimanche (Act IV, sc. iii), are excellent examples of his manipulation of gestures. In the *Scène du Pauvre,* Dom Juan and Sganarelle have just discovered that they are lost in the forest. Dom Juan has Sganarelle ask a passing man for directions. Significantly, it is Sganarelle who must *contract* the obligation, while Dom Juan reserves for himself the privilege of thanking the *Pauvre,* and thus discharging the debt. The poor man shows them their way and warns them of the presence of bandits in the forest. Having offered real assistance, he asks for thanks in a form more tangible than Dom Juan's "je te rends grâce de tout mon coeur." Dom Juan feigns surprise at the poor man's venality and offers him a gold coin if he will use God's name in vain.

Here, Dom Juan is trying to nullify the other's ethical substance and set himself up as the rival of God by showing that material self-interest governs even the hermit's behavior. At least as important, however, is Dom Juan's desire to escape from an obligation by obscuring the whole issue of mutuality. His efforts to reduce others to ethical nullity is, ultimately, self-destructive: he attempts to empty his relationships of meaning by merely "miming" gestures of generosity and commitment and in the process reduces *himself* to the level of Sganarelle's feigned distribution of snuff. By trying to extricate his identity and his freedom from the network of social dependencies, Dom Juan makes himself a phantom—a kind of dangerous clown. His only resource in this deluded deception is an advantage whose meaning and potency are social creations. Dom Juan "borrows" his status and gestures from the collective fund of meanings, but he does not replenish that fund by confirming the meanings. He exhausts trust as a social resource by overexploiting it. He wastes both personal and social resources and, thereby, undermines the ground of his own identity.

Dom Juan owes a financial debt to Monsieur Dimanche. However, he avoids paying it by overwhelming the creditor with purely formal gestures. Because he is a nobleman, the fund of impressive gestures is easily accessible to him. The very chairs in his house can be used to flatter Monsieur Dimanche and to make *him* feel indebted to Dom Juan. Monsieur Dimanche finds it impossible to mention Dom Juan's debt: "Il est vrai; il me fait tant de civilités et tant de compliments, que je ne saurais jamais lui demander de l'argent."

Again, as with his female conquests, Dom Juan exploits the advantages of his position in the system of social meanings as a way of gaining independence from those meanings. This independence is, ultimately, illusory. He intends to destroy the ethical significance of his relationships—their place in a context of debts or obligations—but his enterprise *depends on* gestures and reactions drawn from the collective fund of ethical significances. His entire identity is a form of debt, in that it is constructed of materials belonging to the collective realm.[7] As his father tells him, Dom Juan's nobility is a social resource which must be renewed often by authentically noble acts. Dom Louis speaks of his son's behavior as a waste of valuable resources: ". . . cette suite continuelle de méchantes affaires, qui nous réduisent, à toutes heures, à lasser les bontés du Souverain, et qui ont épuisé auprès de lui le mérite de mes services et le crédit de mes amis?" (Act IV, sc. iv).

Throughout this speech, Dom Louis makes it clear that noble status is, in a sense, borrowed from the ancestors who earned it and from the contemporaries who acknowledge and thus confirm it, and that it can be exhausted by overexploitation. Without noble acts, Dom Juan's status and therefore his identity are as phantasmagoric as Sganarelle's *loup-garou.* A *grand seigneur méchant homme* reduces nobility to a mere social superstition—the commoners' naive belief in the veracity of gestures and trappings without substance. Dom Juan is destroying his own and his family's credibility and converting himself into a phantom.

In the final analysis, Dom Juan refuses to acknowledge limits. His thirst for transcendent freedom rejects limits, and yet only limited entities can be valuable elements in meaningful exchanges. The statue of the slain Commander represents the ineluctability of limits. The statue is made of stone, and it commemorates a death, thus serving as a reminder of the materiality and finitude of life. At the same time, since it represents a man whom Dom Juan has killed, the statue symbolizes the inescapability of consequences in a human world which is a closed system, or network. Indeed, acts and persons have ethical significance precisely *because* the social world is a finite system. Dom Juan's hypocrisy, too, shows his attachment to the social world; he, like the other *ridicules,* wants to triumph over, and therefore *in,* the group.

Dom Juan, having sought to escape from ethical entanglements, can only disappear from the scene where ethical implications are explored. Sganarelle's anguished cry—"Mes gages, mes gages, mes gages"—serves as a final commentary on Dom Juan in two ways: first, it is a reminder that Dom Juan always avoided paying real debts; secondly, it confirms the suggestion in the play that those who refuse obligations can only be "phantoms" and reveals that Sganarelle's expectation of a reward for his loyal service has, in effect, been mere superstition. To the extent that Sganarelle has been an admirer and small-time imitator of Dom Juan, his desperation is poetic justice.

Dom Juan is, then, a play which dramatizes the perception that without the acknowledgement of mutual need and benefit, the human world would fly apart. The social world can have neither practical cohesiveness nor ethical significance without the acceptance of mutual indebtedness. Risk and limitation are inescapable, and Dom Juan's quest is futile. Marriage in *Dom Juan* represents the fundamental social reality which is composed of risk, limitation, benefit, and obligation.

Dom Juan's spurious transcendence depends on the perceptions, motivations, and reactions of his victims, and these depend on Dom Juan's ostensible place in the web of social meanings. His very successes in his chosen avenue of individuation confirm the contingency of his identity. He tries to individuate himself radically by escaping from risk and debt.[8] Virtually every scene in the play, however, brings proof that both risk and debt are inescapable. The *grand seigneur méchant homme* destroys the ethical substance of interactions by exploiting his status without renewing and legitimating its basis. Like Alceste in ***Le Misanthrope,*** Dom Juan hopes to receive all the benefits of social existence without paying its price. This is abundantly clear in Act V, wherein Dom Juan has explicitly chosen to become a hypocrite. All meaning would eventually evaporate from a system of purely manipulative gestures, and mutual respect would be reduced to a foolish superstition. Hypocrites choose and, little by little, *create* an ethically sterile world of dupes and phantoms. In such a world there can be only superstitious, irresponsible credulity, or nihilism. A world without lenders and debtors would lose its principle of coherence and meaningfulness. By virtue of his self-undermining egotism, Dom Juan clearly belongs in the gallery of Molièresque *ridicules.*

The critics who treat Dom Juan as a metaphysical rebel beating against the limits of human possibility, or as a lucid witness of the disintegration of his class fighting nobly for free individuality, miss two key points: first, Dom Juan is fundamentally similar to Molière's other egotists; and, secondly, Dom Juan's means of escaping from obligations and limiting *others'* freedom are social tricks permitted him by his status. The twentieth-century tendency to see in Dom Juan a hero of anti-conventional "authenticity" is anachronistic: in an elaborate, hierarchical social structure such as that of seventeenth-century France, the self is not separable from its roles and accoutrements. Honor, nobility, and ethical veracity depend on *deserving to be oneself*—on meriting one's "costume." We, on the other hand, tend to regard all structures and roles as mystifications and only the "naked" self as authentic. Thus, in our zeal to discover the truth of the unrelated self, we demand the abandonment of all that which actually sustains the identity. This is, of course, a version of the very predicament Molière warns against.[9]

Notes

1. Nathan Gross, *From Gesture to Idea: Esthetics and Ethics in Molière's Comedy* (Columbia University Press, 1982), p. 11.
2. Gross, p. 43.
3. G.J. Watson, *Drama: An Introduction* (New York: St. Martin's Press, 1983), p. 83. Professor Watson discusses the link between marriage as a traditional theme in comedy and as the fundamental social institution.
4. Kenneth Burke, *Language as Symbolic Action: Essays on Life, Literature, and Method* (University of California Press, 1966), p. 18.
5. Bruce Wilshire, *Role-Playing and Identity* (Indiana University Press, 1982), p. 44.
6. Wilshire, p. 185. On the decline of the nobility as an ethical entity, see Erica Harth, *Ideology and Culture in Seventeenth-Century France* (Cornell University Press, 1983), pp. 46ff; and Davis Bitton, *The French Nobility in Crisis* (Stanford University Press, 1969), pp. 78ff.
7. See my "Context and Convergence in the Comedy of *Le Misanthrope,*" *Romance Notes,* 25 (1984), 65-69.
8. Of course, Dom Juan shows no fear of *physical* risk. It is the *ethical* risk of real social interaction that he rejects.
9. For an example of what I regard as an anachronistic view of the issue of freedom in the play, see Laurent Romero, "Dom Juan ou les périls de la liberté: pour une critique dramatique intégrale," *Revue d'histoire du théâtre,* 31 (1979): 81-88.

Beryl Schlossman (essay date 1991)

SOURCE: "Disappearing Acts: Style, Seduction, and Performance in *Dom Juan,*" in *Modern Language Notes,* Vol. 106, No. 5, December, 1991, pp. 1030-47.

[*In the following essay, Schlossman evaluates Molière's approach to portraying* Dom Juan *indirectly through other character interpretations of him.*]

> Quel diable de style! Ceci est bien pis que le reste.
>
> (Molière, ***Dom Juan,*** V, iv)

Molière's ***Dom Juan ou le festin de pierre*** begins after Dom Juan's disappearing act. His absence in the first scene allows other characters to allude to his flight, and to present a 'disembodied' version of his rhetoric of seduction. Molière subtracts the initial seduction scenes from the Spanish and Italian theatres of Don Juan's desire. He suspends the lover's intrigues and presents Dom Juan indirectly, through Sganarelle's representation of him. Sganarelle offers an oblique representation of Dom Juan's fictions, his beautiful rhetoric, and his stylistic effects.

Sganarelle

Under the comic mask of the harlequin valet, the libertine Seducer first appears as the vanishing point of his beautiful rhetoric. The identity of the courtly intriguer is shifted from sword and mask to the verbal fictional performances of love; these performances are anticipated and seconded by the valet Sganarelle, who must speak for his master. Shortly before Molière invented the valet, Dominique Biancolelli performed his *commedia dell'arte* version of Don Juan in the theater that he shared with Molière's company. Like Dominique, Molière played the role of the valet rather than the Seducer.

Although there were several models for Dom Juan's harlequin valet, Molière chose to enter the scene in the new voice of one of his own characters. Sganarelle had appeared in his earliest farces; in ***Dom Juan,*** however, he resembles the type of Arlecchino-Arlequin, who constantly shifts his positions and allegiances without developing as a character.[1] Sganarelle's judgment of his master in the speeches that end the play is identical with the opinion he presents to Gusman in the first scene: "Ah! Monsieur, c'est le Ciel qui vous parle, et c'est un avis qu'il vous donne . . . Ah! Monsieur, rendezvous à tant de preuves, et jetez-vous vite dans le repentir [Ah! my lord, Heaven speaks to you, and gives you warning . . . Ah! my lord, surrender before so much evidence, and make haste to repent]" (V, iv; V, V).[2] In his role as Dom Juan's valet, Sganarelle emerges as a *commedia dell'arte* type, invented and signed by Molière.

More than any love object, Sganarelle is Dom Juan's destined partner; despite Sganarelle's ambivalence, he remains faithful to Dom Juan. Molière's transformation of the Italian Harlequin figures brings Sganarelle closer to the rhetorical edge of his master. Leporello will owe his status to him; it is an indirect tribute to Sganarelle's importance that Da Ponte's Don Giovanni pleads with Leporello not to leave him. Leporello warns his master: "non credeste di *sedurre i miei pari, Come le donne,* a forza di danari [don't think you can seduce men of my type like women, with money]." Leporello's surrender to Don Giovanni's pleading (and bribery) comically underlines the parallel between the dire mastery that Don Giovanni exercises over him and over women: the valet cannot resist the seductions of his master.

This exchange between the disgusted Leporello and his libertine master in *Don Giovanni* II, i, continues a dialogue that was broken off at Dona Elvira's appearance in I, iv. The dialogue parallels the scene between master and valet in Molière's I, ii: Dom Juan describes his plot for kidnapping the fiancée he saw earlier, and Don Giovanni evokes his new passion for a lady who has promised to meet him that evening (I, iv). Da Ponte echoes Molière's motif of flight. In both works, the valet guesses that the reason for their recent journey (away from Done Elvire, in both cases) is a new conquest.

In these scenes, Don Juan explains to his dismayed valet his notion of loving all women: "je me sens un coeur à aimer toute la terre; et comme Alexandre, je souhaiterais qu'il y eût d'autres mondes, pour y pouvoir étendre mes conquêtes amoureuses [I feel within me a heart for loving the whole earth; and like Alexander, I would desire the existence of other worlds, for the power to extend to them my amorous conquests" (I, ii). In *Don Giovanni* Act II, scene i, Da Ponte recalls Molière's "comme Alexandre" speech: "Io, che in me sento sí esteso sentimento, Vo'bene a tutte quante [I, who feel in myself so great a feeling, I love them all]." Da Ponte's unrecognized and unacknowledged source is Molière's ***Dom Juan.***

Spanish Flames

> Don Juan: Vite, adoréte, abraséme, tanto que tu amor me anima a que contigo me case. (Tirso de Molina, *El Burlador*)[3]

Before the Italian *commedia dell'arte*, the mediocre French renderings of Villiers and Dorimon, and the vanished text of Giliberto, a monk (and a popular playwright) who wrote under the pseudonym of Tirso de Molina created the first Don Juan in *El Burlador de Sevilla y Convidado de Piedra.* The popularity of *El Burlador* and certain textual coincidences with ***Dom Juan*** indicate the probability that Molière knew Tirso's text.

In *El Burlador,* Tirso invented Don Juan as a Baroque Christian "myth," as a dramatic representation, and as an example of the inconstant lover masquerading under the rhetorical banner of courtly love. During the late 1650's a series of successful and popular Don Juan portrayals derived from Tirso by the French and the Italians were staged in Paris. The extensive transcriptions and take-offs on the popular Spanish *comedia* set the scene for Molière's inventive use of the tradition: in addition to shifts in tone, genre, and ideology, the interpretive developments that he proposes in his approach to the subject reveal changes in the mode of representation that shapes his text.

The spectator of Tirso's *El Burlador* is both a voyeur and a witness: he is assailed by the unmediated and brutal visual evidence of Don Juan's seductions and acts of trickery. Tirso's play focuses on a repeated demand for Don Juan's repentance within the Catholic frame of the Spanish Baroque; this exhortation is combined with a morbid insistence on the vicissitudes of human flesh that is characteristic of Trauerspiel. Within a highly emblematic discourse, the topos of repentance and the theme of the flesh alternate with intrigue, seduction, and the Golden Age refinements of courtly love rhetoric.

Compared with Molière's writing, the Baroque "précieux" style of Tirso's play seems antiquarian. In *Le Dom Juan de Molière,* Jacques Arnavon refers to Tirso in the following terms: "the play gives off a very mixed odor . . . A dramatic fantasy on 'sin' . . . with . . . copious developments about the aforementioned sin, *very complacently explained and detailed . . . the style, when it is not weakened by preciousness,* . . . remains beautifully elevated. Tisbea, Catalinon, the valet, are not lacking in veracity despite *faults of taste*" (20-21).[4] Although Arnavon's negative reaction to it preceded the revalorization of the Baroque, it is indirectly substantiated by Benjamin's emphasis on the antiquarian element in his concept of Baroque dramatic representation as Trauerspiel.

Tirso's graphic and occasionally lurid vocabulary of sexuality provides a startling contrast to ***Dom Juan.*** *El Burlador* confirms its direct visual mode with a similar violence on the level of language: the simultaneous unfolding of elaborately coded emblematics and an anti-euphemistic literalness about the body challenges the refined idiom of the courtier. This could be described as one of the great paradoxes of Trauerspiel representation and Baroque art. In Tirso's play, an idiom of literal and unmediated eroticism infiltrates the refined conceits of love. Through the intrusions that he effects as skillfully as the best political intriguer, the Spanish forerunner of Molière's Dom Juan prefigures the knots of his rhetoric. In Sganarelle's words, Dom Juan proposed the most conventional knot—marriage: "Il ne se sert point d'autres pièges pour attraper les belles, et c'est un épouseur à toutes mains [He does not use any other traps to catch beautiful women, and he is a bridegroom ready for anything]" (I, i).

Act III of *El Burlador* condenses Don Juan's strategy in the following conventional terms: "I saw you, I adored you, I burned with so great a flame that my love for you urges me to marry you" (III, 246-48). This speech to the peasant Aminta captures the essence of the Seducer's rhetoric of beautiful lies. The Don Juans of Molière, Mozart, and the earlier *commedia dell'arte* versions could have made this speech. Its effect and its content mark the origin of Don Juan's poetics of desire presented in the conventional terms of love.

The result is a representation of love as "true" (desire) and "false" (the promise of marriage). It is precisely because Tirso's play uses a conventional idiom of love to tell the scandalous truth of eroticism that the fictional Don Juan became a central figure at the crossroads of Baroque literary tradition. Truth and falsehood are knotted together in the conceits of courtly love discourse, but Tirso's idiom of desire preserves its metaphoric power through the explicit contrast in Don Juan's discourse between the metaphoric and the literal. The oblique Molière uses the comic-dramatic ambivalence and the *commedia dell'arte* nuances of Sganarelle's portrayal to articulate this contrast and to filter Dom Juan's "beaux mystères" of transgression through the beautiful mysteries of his rhetoric. The rhetorical veil that is essential to Dom Juan's effects in the play is preserved by Sganarelle's discordances and the skillfully projected incoherences of his discourse.

Between Tirso and Molière, a major rhetorical shift has taken place. Its effects on ***Dom Juan*** are articulated in the relation between eroticism and poetic language, and in the new importance of aesthetics within the play. A new subversion is at work: "quel diable de style! [what a diabolical style!]." Molière's reshaping of the tradition into a vehicle for an oblique portrayal of desire and an emphasis on rhetoric makes of Dom Juan a stylist. Dom Juan's libertinage becomes an art form: aesthetics unfolds its charms before the horrified gaze of ethics.

Speaking as Sganarelle, Molière articulates Dom Juan's ultimate role, as a literary stylist. The complete passage reads: "Quel diable de style! Ceci est bien pis que le reste, et je vous aimerais bien mieux encore comme vous étiez auparavant [What a diabolical style! This is much worse than the rest, and I would like you so much better the way you were before]" (V, iv). The remark is directed at a Dom Juan who disguises his black intentions in the Tartuffian trappings of piety. The implacable logic of this choice is partly masked by Sganarelle's shocked reaction to the "new" Dom Juan, but the first act already revealed a Dom Juan who claimed God ("le Ciel") as his alibi for abandoning the dishonored Done Elvire, torn from her convent by his seductive discourse (I, iii).

When Dom Juan returns to this form of argument in Act V, Molière assimilates an eloquent explanation of religious hypocrisy and its negative powers within his portrait of the libertine. At this moment, Dom Juan comes dangerously close to an identification with the author (and the authority) of ***Tartuffe,*** who speaks out against the "dévots": the writer places himself for a few minutes under the banner of libertine rhetoric.

The valet's complaint about a diabolical style that is even worse than the rest can be taken literally; Sganarelle's allusion to Dom Juan's disguise can be read as an unconscious comment on the version of libertine "noirceur" that appears in ***Dom Juan ou le festin de pierre.*** More eloquent than the Don Juans of Tirso and the Italians, Molière's character emerges in the diabolical power of his style, in the tropes that bear the blackness of his fictions. The constant displacements of rhetoric drive the libertine Master into an endless "changement" of love objects. Style subsumes the real; Dom Juan's tropes carry out the fictions of the libertine and carry language over into the realm of consummated desire.

Dom Juan's ongoing "diable de style" claims mastery over the Real (Lacan's "Réel") until the end, when diabolical style leads to his infernal and unredeemable death. The supernatural elements of the play recast the rhetorical displacements of eroticism (the invitation, the offering of the hand, the inner flames of desire), in the allegorical encounter between the monument of the Commandeur and the condemned libertine.

Tirso's Don Juan expresses his desire on two rhetorical levels: the gallant "caballero" evokes the common poetic image of flames aroused by the object, and the great lord of noble blood and "pagñola arrogancia [Spanish arrogance]" (III, 745) demands that his object offer her hand to him in a gesture of solemn juridical and religious value. When Don Juan encounters the statue of the man he has murdered, he utters the first invitation. The Statue echoes Don Juan's motifs of erotic trickery and returns the invitation. He asks for Don Juan's hand, and transforms the lover's rhetorical flames into hellfire:

> Don Gonzale: Dame esa mano, no temas, la mano dame.
>
> Don Juan: Eso dices? Yo, temor? Que me abraso! No me abrases con tu fuego!
>
> Don Gonzale: Este es poco para el fuego que buscaste [Give me your hand, do not be afraid, give me your hand. What did you say? I, afraid? I am burning! Don't burn me with your fire! It is nothing compared to the fire you sought]
>
> (III, 944-49)

Molière's play maintains these parallel terms of seduction and punishment. The sacred overtones resonate retroactively when the Commandeur repeats Dom Juan's erotic motifs in the service of Heaven rather than the desires of the libertine. After Dom Juan repeats Sganarelle's invitation ("Le Seigneur Commandeur voudrait-il venir souper avec moi? [Would it please the Lord Commander to come dine with me?]" [III, v]) the Statue lowers his head in a sign of assent. Within the Stone Guest tradition, the impious young man who mocks the dead and the boundary between the living and the dead by uttering an invitation may still alter his fate, but in Molière's version, when the Statue comes at the appointed time to Dom Juan's table, he indicates that Dom Juan's time is up: "Dom Juan, c'est assez. Je vous invite à venir demain souper avec moi. En aurez-vous le courage? [Dom Juan, that is enough. I invite you to come tomorrow and dine with me. Will you have the courage?]" (IV, viii).

While Molière subtly uses his innovations—Done Elvire, Sganarelle, and the veil of rhetoric—to introduce art and the sublime into Tirso's framework of seduction, he preserves the three-fold structure of seduction in "El Burlador": the invitation or the gift of the word ("'la promesse que je vous ai donnée [the promise that I made to you]'" [III, iii]), the giving of the hand in return for the promise of marriage ("'abandonnez-moi seulement votre main [give me only your hand]'" [III, ii]), and the flames of love ("une ardeur sans égale [a passion without equal]," "le ravissement où je suis [the rapture that is mine]", [I, ii; II, ii]) that Pierrot comically describes when he finds Dom

Juan kissing Charlotte's hand: "Tout doucement, Monsieur, tenez-vous, s'il vous plaît. Vous vous échauffez trop [Take it easy, my lord, behave yourself, please. You are getting much too overheated]" (III, iii).

During the brief final scene (V, vi), the Statue speaks: "Arrêtez, Dom Juan: vous m'avez hier donné parole de venir manger avec moi [Stop, Dom Juan: yesterday you gave me your word to come and eat with me]," and Dom Juan agrees: "Oui." The heavenly "foudre [thunder]" that is aroused by a Luciferian refusal to repent in the preceding scene (V, v) when the feminine Spectre announced that only a minute remained for Dom Juan to save his soul ("S'il ne se repent ici, sa perte est résolue [if he does not repent here, his downfall is certain]") burns Dom Juan with an intimate fire that consumes him. "Le Ciel" repeats the "ardeur" of Dom Juan's burning passion ("l'impétuosité de mes désirs [the impetuousness of my desires]" [I, ii]); it displaces (seducere) or "translates" the power of metaphor. This sacred "translation" or "seduction" is encoded as the invisible: in the final interiority of the play, the inner fire that assails Dom Juan is no longer identified with his desire. The hand of the Other—"le Ciel"—is supernaturally dramatized in the last scenes through several allegorical forms.

Baroque Images

In Molière's text, these allegorical forms progressively lose their object-like character, their materiality and opacity; they become more elusive, ethereal, and evanescent. Spiritual and sublime, they enter the pure present tense. Modernist descendants include the Mallarmean point of a poetic enunciation and the mystical instant of ecstacy invoked by Benjamin's reading of Proust.[5] This present occurs in the fleeting moment of Dom Juan's fictions, in the artful instant staged by the Baroque image.

The allegorical progression that leads to the supreme vanishing point, the instant of representation bequeathed to modernity by the Baroque, begins in the beautiful "tombeau" (described by Dom Juan as a "magnifique demeure [magnificent dwelling]") that contains a "superbe mausolée" and the imposing marble likeness of the Commandeur's Statue. The appearance of this monumental representation is followed by a disembodied apparition of the feminine and suggestively Done Elvire-like Spectre. It appears first "en femme voilée [in the form of a veiled woman]," and then as a completely allegorical "figure" of "le Temps avec sa faux [Time with its scythe]," before it disappears completely ("s'envole") to return to the realm of sacred signs, "le Ciel." In the final instants of the play, the Spectre evaporates into the thin air of allegory, and the sacred receives its most minimal figure as the "invisible" of divine retribution, interiorized within the libertine body.

The feminine figure fades away; her ethical message arrives at the last moment, to guarantee the subtle allegorization of the invisible. The materiality of the libertine object implies the libertine doctrine of materialism that fled the spiritual element as Dom Juan eluded Done Elvire; at the end of Molière's play, the material opacity of the object approaches the zero point.

What remains after the sacrifice has been consummated? The process of allegorization that points toward the meaning and end of *jouissance* is figured in a synesthetic finale on stage, when the libertine body disappears. The terms are reversed: the "invisible fire" inside Dom Juan appears on stage, and suddenly it is Dom Juan who leaves the visible realm. All that remains before the spectator is the tableau of the last Baroque image of the "invisible": Heaven's "tonnerre [thunder]," the substanceless "éclairs [lightning bolts]" and "grands feux [great fires]" and the empty space of the abyss ("la terre s'ouvre et l'abîme [the earth opens and engulfs him]"). The uncensored edition of 1682, quoted by Couton, reveals Molière's intentions for the final overturning of Dom Juan's desire. This version completes Dom Juan's final sentence and stages the concluding fireworks with a Baroque flourish in the character of Molière's court "impromptus" and "divertissements":

> Dom Juan: O Ciel! que sens-je? Un feu invisible me brûle, je n'en puis plus et tout mon corps devient un brasier ardent. Ah!
>
> (Le tonnerre tombe avec un grand bruit et de grands éclairs sur Dom Juan; la terre s'ouvre et l'abîme; et il sort de grands feux à l'endroit où il est tombé)
>
> Dom Juan: [O Heaven! what do I feel? An invisible fire burns me, I can no longer bear it and my whole body becomes a burning blaze. Ah!
>
> (Thunder falls with a great noise and great strokes of lighting on Dom Juan; the earth opens and engulfs him; and great fires come from the spot where he fell)]
>
> (V, vi).[6]

Hellfire ends Molière's Night play of libertinage and "noirceur."

Night Shadows

Tirso de Molina's *El Burlador de Sevilla* begins with the following stage setting: "Room in the palace of the king of Naples. Night. There is no light." The curtain rises on the concluding moments of a consummated seduction: a typical victory for Don Juan is illustrated in the undisguised satisfaction that is articulated and displayed by Don Juan's love object, the duchess Isabela. In the first lines of the play, Tirso indicates the motives for her surrender. Don Juan says: "Duquesa, de nuevo os juro de cumplir el dulce sí"; Isabela answers with an anticipation of the legality of *jouissance*: "Mis glorias serán verdades," and Don Juan assures her: "Sí, mi bien" ["again I swear to give you the sweet consent; my raptures will be true / truly enjoyed; yes my treasure"] (I: 3-8). Isabela's turn of phrase ("mis glorias") conflates an image of sacred light with an image of theatrical and visible public presence in the resonance of a typical Baroque metaphor. She seems to be saying that the transient delights of *jouissance*, described as her "glories," will be made "true" (or permanent) when her lover marries her.

In this first instance of the infamous broken promise, the man to whom the duchess Isabela has given her sexual favors (upon receiving an assurance of the "sweet yes" of marriage) is disguised as the duke Octavio, her fiancé. The evanescence of Don Juan's proposal and the undisguised blackness of his motives are dramatically highlighted by the verbal exchange that follows and its interplay of literal sexual language and emblematically coded metaphoric imagery. Eroticism unfolds through a strategy of artifice and falsehood, compounded by an assumed identity, and the ubiquitous broken promise of marriage. Isabela's happiness leads her to the terrible discovery that sets the plot in motion: she wants to light up the dark room ("Quiero sacar una luz" [9]) and when the alarmed (although masked) Don Juan asks her why she wants light, she answers: "Para que el alma dé fe del bien que llego a gozar [In order that the soul/heart may show the enjoyment (*jouissance*) that I reach]" (11-12). The figures of speech that Isabela uses in this first scene refer to a sexual enjoyment that is inseparable from the honorable enjoyments of marriage. Don Juan replies: "Mataréte la luz yo" [I will put out the light]" (13). His refusal plunges her in the horrible darkness of sin and dishonor, when his "engaño" is discovered. Her good ("bien") turns to evil: her praises turn to lament. She begins by invoking heaven ("Ah, cielo!"), and asking the disguised ("embozado") Don Juan who he is.

Isabela's "glory" and the light she wants to illuminate it secretly resonate within a vocabulary of Baroque aesthetics, where the Glory is a Catholic representation of the halo of light that surrounds the Holy Spirit or its presence in manifestations of the Trinity, the Transfiguration, or the Resurrection. Isabela's "glory" seems to echo the hieratic and aristocratic overtones of Corneille's concept of "gloire," but the erotic and Christian contexts of her statement (and Tirso's play) locate the text of *El Burlador* and its descendants in the field of Baroque representation elaborated by Bernini rather than in the texts of French Classicism. Neither Molière nor Tirso can be understood according to Corneille's vocabulary, but the pervasive theme of "glorias" and the melancholic evanescence evoked by the scene between Isabela and the masked Don Juan who claims to be Octavio share a certain rhetorical power with Bernini's vision of the Gloria Petri. Bernini designed and sculpted the Glory in Saint Peter's Cathedral, a work that is considered by art historians to mark definitively the high point of the Baroque, during the time when Molière was writing and staging ***Dom Juan.***

The first lines of Tirso's play set up the opposition between light and dark, good and evil, heaven and hell. Don Juan's discursive technique of "engaño" is presented as a discourse of courtly love; it projects a fantasmatic unity of desire and marriage before the eyes of Don Juan's objects. In Tirso's portrayals of women, it is the feminine fantasy that shimmers on the distant horizon of distinguished ladies as well as peasants and fisher girls. Tirso illustrates it in the figures of Isabela's speech.

The discourse of love in the play is a balancing act or a counterpoint between Don Juan's undecidable mixture of punishment and pleasure and a projected feminine version of courtly love rhetoric. The feminine version surrenders to the evanescence and violence of eroticism Baroque style by dissolving it in the "happy ending" of the Law. Tirso typecasts his Baroque oppositions of love as masculine and feminine, but the black portrait of desire that is under the rhetorical masks of courtly love—Don Juan's sweet nothings and his victims' fantasies of wedding glory—seems to challenge any discourse of sexual unity with the hair-raising vision of the drives.

At the edge of the sculpted folds of Bernini's most hieratic and important tomb monuments, madcap skeletons are poised ready to reach out for the viewer, or hold up an hourglass emblem. The mystery that Freud found in the drives, those odd couples, was registered in the books of the Baroque as the mysterious proximity of death and love. The emblems of Trauerspiel marry them together . . . *Y'a de l'Un.* There is one. The Baroque found that union at the end of the line, in the figures of sex and death, or marriage and resurrection. Love is the ultimate conflation; it plays on both sides. Death and love, hearts and bones, are the end-points of Trauerspiel emblematics. Hamlet tells the truth: his father's life-line ultimately ends with the end of weddings. Tisbea also speaks the truth when she lovingly reminds Don Juan that he must think of his own death.

Isabela's thinly veiled rhetoric of erotic satisfaction confirms and counterpoints Don Juan's language: he is distinguished by his success, his sadism, and his sexual punishment of women, rendered inseparable from the ambiguities of *jouissance* in Tirso's representation. These elements of Tirso's first scene form the background of the tradition. The discourse of love is twofold, in Tirso's play and in the tradition of love stories that he enters, disrupts, and begins again in the name of Don Juan Tenorio. Tirso sets the masculine against the feminine; he portrays love as a battlefield of desire against marriage. On another level, he makes Don Juan into a disruptor of couples on the verge of blissful unity in marriage. In this sense, Don Juan figures the importunity of desire, its refusal to be domesticated in the house of marriage, and its inherent transgression. Tirso inscribes the figure of desire with the name of Lucifer.

Don Juan's negativity maintains a constant separation between his desire and the object: social and spiritual harmony are not on his agenda. The figure of Don Juan originates in the mythical stature of the fantasy of sexual harmony that Lacan designates in the statement "Il n'y a pas de rapport sexuel [there is no sexual relation]": the Don Juan tradition confirms this separation or disharmony by matching the terms of Don Juan's seductions and the motifs of his punishment. When the sweet talk of sexual harmony reaches its final destination, the "Other" as the ear of the heavenly Father, the Stone Guest—a monumental image of a powerful earthly father—is sent to arrange for the Seducer's disappearance into a fiery abyss.

Don Juan's negativity (his erotic powers of destruction) designates the black realities behind the discourse of courtly love. Catalinón tells his master: "Ya sé que eres castigo de las mujeres [I know that you are the punishment of women]" (I:894). When Don Juan pretends to be Mota in order to trick his friend's beloved cousin Ana, the musicians sing: "Todo este mundo es errar [This world is all illusion]" but the play clearly indicates that he, Don Juan, is the source of illusion. When Dona Ana realizes that the disguised Don Juan is not Mota, she condemns his misuse of a lover's language: "Falso!, [Liar!]" (II:507, 510). The Baroque motifs of illusion and inconstancy are tailor-made for Don Juan. They inform and motivate his erotics of trickery, his destruction of honor, and his violations of sanctity, chastity, and virginity.

Throughout the course of Tirso's play, however, it is the unfaithful and cavalier (!) attitude of women that is emphasized, rather than the dubious practices of the male nobility.[7] The social status of women condemns them to the punishments inflicted by Don Juan's irresistible seductions, but the consequences condemn them long after the sadistic Don Juan has been plunged into the fiery abyss, in spite of the happy ending that is provided when a patriarchal figure like a King or a "Commander" smooths things over with a lot of weddings. Molière does not include Tirso's happy ending; later versions, including the Mozart-Da Ponte opera, do not return to Tirso's final solution. After writing Mozart's libretto for *Don Giovanni,* Da Ponte knew what the implications of libertinage meant for the social continuity of the "non-rapport sexuel [sexual non-relation]"; his tragicomic unveiling of the "truth" of love in *Cosí Fan Tutte,* a late collaboration with Mozart, resonates with a tone of detached understanding that does not sound any less feminist for being the product of Da Ponte's identification with libertinage. The lighthearted yet melancholy conclusion of the opera shows the realism of the aging Don Alfonso, the "Philosopher" who has played all of the characters like marionettes after his two friends set the plot in motion by making a bet with him on the virtue of their fiancées. Their outrage at his initial insinuations is matched only by their fury when they realize that they have tricked their fiancées into being unfaithful to them. When they ask the "Philosopher" how they can punish the women they still love, he replies: "Marry them!"

Tirso's scene of eroticism is masked in the blackness of Night—the hours sacrificed to criminals, libertines, Specters, visions, and dreams—and the literary blackness of the unlit Spanish stage. Don Juan begins the play by extinguishing the light of Isabela's faith, honor, and "glories": her lamentation of libertine blackness resonates in the gap between Don Juan's two discourses of love, the courtly idiom of love that he uses to mask his identity and the "other" discourse of undisguised desire and conquest: "yo engañé y gocé a Isabela la duquesa [I tricked the duchess Isabela and enjoyed her flesh]" (I: 67-68). The double darkness of night and literary artifice leads to Molière's representation of libertine desire in ***Dom Juan***: the discrepancy between the figured and the literal idioms of eroticism (elaborate Trauerspiel emblematics and the "man-to-man" dialogue that Tirso moves from the royal palace of Naples to the sleaziest alley of Seville without changing a word) disappears in Molière's play. The new role of Sganarelle is associated with an oblique account of eroticism, the highlighting of seduction rather than trickery, and Molière's aesthetic investment in the rhetoric of desire. It is possible that Molière's subtlety and "délicatesse"—a notion that is a masterpiece of libertine strategy, because it implies that the Seducer has aesthetic principles that never allow him to use language unworthy of the courtier—brought out a possibility for "noirceur" (independently pursued in the eighteenth century) that made his play for more subversive than all the lurid potential of Tirso's several hundred works for the stage. The libertine is neither a pagan nor a hero; he is empowered to tell lies precisely because "la vérité du language est chrétienne [the truth of language is Christian]." Neither Molière nor Marguérite de Navarre made this declaration: several hundred years later, it was written by Georges Bataille,[8] another writer preoccupied with Dom Juan and the impossibility of truly domesticating eroticism. Through transgression and obscenity, revelation and the ineffable, the philosopher in the boudoir cannot get rid of language.

In *El Burlador,* when Don Juan enters the bedroom of a peasant bride, Aminta, she laments: "Ay de mí! yo soy perdida! En mi aposento a estas horas? [Woe is me! I am lost! In my room at such hours?]" (III: 205-06). He speaks for all his *donjuanesque* descendants when he replies: "Estas son las horas mías [Such are my hours]" (207). Don Juan tells her that he burned with a love that impels him to marry her; she gives herself to him, the self-styled "Burlador de Sevilla" who triumphantly names himself in an aside to the audience. Isabela's laments are heard in the lines that follow this episode; they are addressed to the Night, as if the horror and loss that were caused by Don Juan's gallantries and sealed in the metaphorics of light and darkness at the beginning of the play had expanded beyond the constellations of language to the impersonal and voiceless source of blackness: "Oh, máscara del día! Noche al fin tenebrosa, antípoda del sol, del sueño esposa! [Oh, mask of day! tenebrous shadowed Night, antipode of the sun, bride of sleep!]" (III: 303-305). Molière's emphasis on rhetoric moves in the opposite direction; the blackness of Night and flames of Hell shape Don Juan's libertine turns of phrase.

Masks and Hearts

At the beginning of Molière's play, Sganarelle puffs himself up with comically serious pronouncements about virtue designed to distract his interlocutor's attention from Don Juan. Gusman continues to question him about his master's "heart," however, and Sganarelle attempts to excuse Don Juan's behavior for reasons of "youth" and "nobility" ("sa qualité"). When Gusman responds to Sganarelle's cautious references to "l'autre" (his Master) and his euphemisms about his own "experience" by invoking "les saints noeuds du mariage [the holy knots of marriage]," Sganarelle trades mystery for mystery: "tu ne sais pas encore . . . quel homme est Dom Juan [you do not know yet . . . who Dom Juan is]." Gusman tries another tactic to gain information; he offers an explicit narration of Dom Juan's seduction of his mistress. The rhetorical parity continues; Sganarelle suddenly abandons his euphemisms and tells the "whole story" of his master's libertine practices. The rhetorical display that began with detachment and understatement concludes with hyperbole in an explosion of graphic epithets. Sganarelle provides a final affirmation of his word with his declared intent to deny the truth of what he has just announced.

Sganarelle's speech takes the form of a rhetorical abstract of the play: the valet's commentary conceals Dom Juan behind the blackness of his own masks and illuminates him with an infernal "portrait." Sganarelle paints his master as a libertine on the edge of eternal damnation: "Suffit qu'il faut que le courroux du Ciel l'accable quelque jour . . . [It suffices to say that heavenly wrath must descend on him some day]" (I, i).

Molière constructs Sganarelle's conversation in the first scene as the "stage" for an oblique and decisive performance: the absent Don Juan is masked and then revealed. But unlike the beginning of Tirso's play, the "light" shed on Dom Juan by Sganarelle turns into another mask—the rhetorical inflation of Dom Juan's evil powers through a series of titles: "un Diable, un Turc, un Hérétique, qui ne croit ni Ciel, ni loup-garou, qui passe cette vie en véritable bête brute, en pourceau d'Epicure, en vrai Sardanapale . . . [a Devil, a Turk, a Heretic, who does not believe in Heaven or werewolf, who spends this life as a truly untamed animal, as an Epicurean boar, as a true Sardanapalus]." This description combines the sacred and the comic in mock-heroic epithets of emblematic hyperbole: Sganarelle's version of the truth provides another smokescreen. The scene ends with Sganarelle's denial: "écoute, au moins je t'ai fait cette confidence avec franchise . . . mais s'il fallait qu'il en vînt quelque chose à ses oreilles, je dirais hautement que tu aurais menti [listen, at least I spoke to you in frank confidence . . . but if some part of it happened to reach his ear, I would say out loud that you had lied]." Sganarelle's series of negations and denegations conceals and reveals the truth about Dom Juan; after all, Sganarelle gives Gusman anything but a straight answer. Like other skilled illusionists of Baroque art, Sganarelle transfigures his subject and portrays him in a mythical and theatrical framework that stuns the viewer and stops him in his tracks.

Sganarelle gives Gusman an image of the "transported" lover ("tant d'transports enfin et tant d'emportements qu'il a fait paraître" [I, i]) that lingers as a fixed monument to libertine inconstancy. Gusman already knows that Dom Juan is a master of rhetoric: Sganarelle's answer instructs the squire in the pleasures and horrors of libertine desire that are the heart of Dom Juan's rhetoric, and the only heart of the libertine artificer. The "cruel and heartless" Burlador enters Molière's text in Sganarelle's words as the "coeur de tigre [tiger's heart]" (IV, vi) or the seduction-loving "coeur" of the "plus grand coureur du monde [the greatest chaser in the world]"; Dom Juan's heart is enchanted only by the allegorically impersonal otherness of Beauty. He states: "la beauté me ravit partout où je la trouve [beauty ravishes me everywhere I find it]," but allegory fades away for Dom Juan until later, when the sacred intervenes in the forms of statues, a veiled feminine specter, and so on.

Beauty is represented by one woman after another, and the "heart" of Dom Juan's calculating hommage to courtly love rhetoric covers up the unsentimental reality of desire: "une beauté me tient au coeur [a beauty occupies my heart]" (I, ii). Dom Juan's "impétuosité" anticipates the focus on the ceaselessness of the drives in Freud's metapsychology; the "heart" of courtly love talk masks the heartlessness of the burning flames of desire. In *Don Giovanni* (II, xiv), Da Ponte restages the "festin" scene between Done Elvire and Dom Juan, shortly before the arrival of the Statue. Parallel to Sganarelle's exclamation of "coeur de tigre!" (IV, vi), Leporello utters the revealing epithet of "cor di sasso [heart of stone]." In Molière, the reader has been prepared by Sganarelle's account of his master to understand that the nameless "beauty" will be in Dom Juan's "heart" only until her name can be inscribed in the list of his erotic acquisitions. Like the translated form of the murdered Commendatore, the monument of the Stone Guest, Don Juan's heart is made of stone.

Notes

1. A good example of this type is in Goldoni's *Il servitore di due padrone,* a play that documents *commedia dell'arte* in written form, according to Goldoni's explanation in his preface.
2. All translations are my own.
3. "I saw you, I adored you, I burned with so great a flame that my love for you urges me to marry you" (III: 246-48).
4. "la pièce dégage une odeur fort mêlée . . . Une fantaisie dramatique sur le 'péché' . . . avec . . . de copieux développements sur ledit péché, *fort complaisamment expliqué et détaillé . . . le style, lorsqu'il ne s'affadit pas en préciosité,* . . . y demeure d'une belle élévation. Tisbea, Catalinon, le valet, ne manquent pas de vérité *malgré des fautes de goût.*"
5. See the discussion of this question in Schlossman, *The Orient of Style* and "Proust and Benjamin: The Invisible Image."
6. See Molière, OC vol. 2, p. 1319. This variant is confirmed by Mahelot's *Mémoire* about the stage sets ordered by Molière for the play; the props for

the "foudroiement" of Act V included resin for the "éclairs" and a trap door (ibid., pp. 1299-1300).

7. In his introduction to Tirso's play, Pierre Guénoun makes a somewhat surprising attempt to justify—in the name of history—the misogynistic clichés and emblems piously uttered by most of the male characters: "Pour ne pas commettre d'erreur à ce sujet, il faut bien voir que *l'Espagne du XVIIe siècle était un corps* à tradition patriarcale *qui craquait de toutes parts* sous une poussée matriarcale particulièrement vive. Les pères avaient, théoriquement, à la romaine, droit de vie et de mort sur les mères et sur les filles qui se montraient légères. *En fait, les mères et les filles étaient si délurées que les pères n'avaient aucune autorité*" (my underlining). Guénoun presents Tirso's Spain as a threatened masculine body, a patriarch menaced by sexually provocative women. *El Burlador,* 11.
8. "Fragment sur le christianisme," 382.

Works Cited

Arnavon, Jacques. *Le Dom Juan de Molière.* Copenhagen: Glydendal, 1947.

Benjamin, Walter. *Ursprung des deutschen Trauerspiels.* Ed. Rolf Tiedemann. Frankfurt am Main: Suhrkamp, 1982.

Bévotte, Georges Gendarme de. *La Légende de Don Juan: son origine dans la littérature.* Paris: Hachette et Cie, 1911.

Freud, Sigmund. *Der Witz und seine Beziehung zum Unbewußten* (1905). Studienausgabe. Frankfurt am Main: S. Fischer Verlag, 1970.

———. *Psychologie des Unbewußten.* Studienausgabe. 1975.

Jurgens, Madeleine, and Maxfield-Miller, Elizabeth. *Cent ans de recherches sur Molière.* Paris: Imprimerie Nationale, 1963.

Lacan, Jacques. *Ecrits.* Paris: Seuil, 1968.

———. *Séminaire VII: L'Ethique de la psychanalyse.* Paris: Seuil, 1986.

———. *Séminaire XX: Encore.* Paris: Seuil, 1975.

Macchia, Giovanni. *Vita, avventure et morte di Don Giovanni.* Torino: Laterza Bari, 1976.

Molière. *Oeuvres complètes.* Ed. Georges Couton. 2 vols. Bibliothèque de la Pléïade. Paris: Gallimard, 1971.

Molina, Tirso de. *El Burlador de Sevilla y convidado de piedra.* Ed. Joaquin Casalduero. Letras Hispanicas 58. Madrid: Càtedra, 1978.

———. *El Burlador de Sevilla y convidado de piedra.* Ed. Pierre Guenoun. Paris: Aubier-Flammarion, 1968.

Pintard, René. *Le Libertinage érudit.* Paris: Boivin et Cie, 1943.

———. "Temps et lieux dans le *Dom Juan* de Molière." *Studi in onore di Italo Siciliano.* Florence: Olschki, 1966. II: 997-1006.

Rousset, Jean. *L'Intérieur et l'extérieur: Essai sur la poésie et sur le théâtre au XVIIe siècle.* Paris: José Corti, 1968.

———. *Le Mythe de Don Juan.* Paris: Armand Colin, 1978.

Schlossman, Beryl. *Joyce's Catholic Comedy of Language.* Madison: U of Wisconsin P, 1985.

———. *The Orient of Style: Modernist Allegories of Conversion.* Durham: Duke U P, 1991.

———. "(Pas) encore!—Baudelaire, Flaubert, and Don Giovanni." *Romanic Review,* forthcoming.

Spitzer, Leo. "The Spanish Baroque." *Representative Essays.* Ed. Alban K. Forcione, Herbert Lindenberger, and Madeline Sutherland. Stanford: Stanford UP, 1988. 125-39.

Joy Sylvester (essay date 1991)

SOURCE: "Molière's *Dom Juan*: Charity's Prodigal Son," in *Romance Notes,* Vol. XXXII, No.1, Fall, 1991, pp. 23-7.

[*In the following essay, Sylvester analyzes "la scène du Pauvre" from Molière's* Dom Juan—*a scene considered one of the most misunderstood in all of French drama.*]

What has been called "la scène du Pauvre" (III, 2) is one of the most important and controversial scenes in all of French drama. It occurs in the exact middle of the play and it is after this scene that the growing pattern of defeats that Dom Juan suffers increase both in pace and in importance (Guicharnaud 252-58). It also marks a change in Dom Juan's dramatic personality, for it is here that, for the first time, he actually takes the initiative and attacks religion in an active attempt to demonstrate that the truth resides within him and that he is in the right. It is, as J. Guicharnaud has pointed out, "la mise en action de l'incroyance de Dom Juan" (255). The danger that Dom Juan represents to society is multifaceted. He combines in himself many temptations, the power of a man accustomed to being a master, the prestige of a *grand seigneur* and the resources of his riches, but most of all he is dangerous because he represents the principle of disorder set against the order of the universe. His defeat at the hands of the *Pauvre* is thus highly significant because symbolically it constitutes his first combat with and defeat by *le Ciel.*

This scene is striking not only for its great audacity, but also because it is the only time in the play before the end when Dom Juan loses a combat. When the beggar asks him for alms, Dom Juan seizes the opportunity to prove at last that God and His goodness do not exist. In order to do this he uses a Socratic technique consisting of a series of cleverly asked questions designed to lead his interlocutor to uncovering the truths he carries within him. Let us examine the logic that Dom Juan uses and what precedes it in order to understand the cleverness of the manipulator and the importance of the defeat which he suffers. Dom Juan is pleased when *le Pauvre* asks him for alms, and he understands this plea as proceeding from selfish motives because he so scorns mankind that he refuses to believe in the existence of any totally generous gesture. He plays with *le Pauvre* and tortures him without pity in order to possess him (as he has succeeded in possessing so many others) by corrupting him. Sganarelle tries to stop this attempt at corruption, but he is unsuccessful against the firm will of his master.

Dom Juan wants to convince the *Pauvre* that God does not exist and his logic proceeds as follows:

a. If God exists, He is good and rewards prayer;

b. However: You pray fervently to God and you are unrewarded.

c. Since there is no reward, there is no Divine Goodness.

d. In the absence of Divine Goodness, there can be no God.

e. Therefore: God does not exist.

The Socratic irony attempted by Dom Juan fails here because the *Pauvre* does not understand it; it is too intellectual and sophisticated for him. Dom Juan thus must fall back on sheer corruption, a Satanic technique: logic fails, temptation remains, here in the form of gold. The *Pauvre,* a man of simple and sincere faith, obstinately refuses to blaspheme against God. For the first time Dom Juan loses his sangfroid, insisting with growing fury that the *Pauvre* must swear; he must triumph here, the stakes are high and he uses every means at his disposal to succeed. Even Sganarelle cajoles: "Va, va, jure un peu, il n'y a pas de mal" (III, 2). Dom Juan gives way to his fury revealing the anguish he himself is suffering. "Prends, le voilà, prends, te dis-je, mais jure donc." Here Dom Juan becomes a more somber figure, and he suffers a stunning defeat when the *Pauvre* stubbornly refuses to become a blasphemer and to renounce his belief. The *Pauvre*'s answer is very simple but utterly final: "Non, Monsieur, j'aime mieux mourir de faim." Dom Juan fails and the failure is important because it marks the triumph of religion over the corrupting atheism of this "grand seigneur méchant homme" (I, 1).

The next lines have stimulated conflicting interpretations and continue to puzzle most readers and spectators, for after this defeat Dom Juan hurls the louis d'or at the *Pauvre* with these words: "Va, va, je te le donne pour l'amour de l'humanité" (III, 2). Critics and actors alike read this line in many different ways; and each actor plays the scene in a different way, it may be played seriously, or offhandedly, thus making light of the incident. Is this a truly generous gesture on the part of Dom Juan, one acknowledging the superiority of the *Pauvre* and his own emotion in the face of unshakable goodness and faith? We might imagine that illumination will suddenly come to him and make of him an *homme généreux* or even his century's ideal, an *homme de bien*: we might instead take his words, "pour l'amour de l'humanité" literally; and see him as transformed into an enlightened lover of humanity and of mankind. Nothing in the rest of the play supports either of these possibilities. There is neither conversion to belief, nor respect for established order of any kind, nor evidence of a sudden illumination and awakening of generous love for mankind. Rather the placement of this encounter—at the midpoint of the action and at the beginning of Dom Juan's defeats—seems more likely to predict to its observers the protagonist's fate.

In spite of this defeat by the *Pauvre,* Dom Juan remains obstinately the same, logical in his character of the *révolté;* he does not accept the reality of such a defeat. The words "pour l'amour de l'humanité" and the haughty gesture of throwing the gold at the *Pauvre* affirm his scornful pride. He loses this battle, but he will not admit it; throwing the gold away reestablishes his position as the proud aristocrat who thus erases a defeat that he considers unworthy of him. Some critics have argued that he is indifferent to this defeat and that the gesture is one of "désinvolture et indifférence" (Guicharnaud 255). I prefer to see there a scornful gesture, reinforced by the words *amour* and *humanité.* From the heights to which he aspires, as a worthy adversary of heaven, Dom Juan can love nothing and no one but himself, and certainly not humanity, for by such a love he would admit that he also is a mere man and, as such, possessed of all the frailties inherent in the human condition. It is with this gesture that Dom Juan also rejects utterly the call to charity that the established society, his nobility, and religion urge upon him.

Caritas is the act of perfect love and the greatest of the theological virtues. Charity and love, however, are the two things of which Dom Juan is incapable. His statements and actions oppose all that charity in its fullest sense implies. The *Pauvre,* in his simplicity, and by the real charity of his love for God, confounds the false, blackmailing "charity" with which Dom Juan seeks to tempt him. The word "charité" occurs only once in the play and in a context that clearly devalues it. The occasion is in Act II, Scene 3. Dom Juan attempts to seduce the peasant girl, Charlotte, and her fiancé, the bumbling, rustic Pierrot, (who has just saved Dom Juan from drowning) tries to stop him. He is rewarded for his sincerity by Charlotte's indifference, by her obvious attraction to the handsome aristocrat and by immediate evidence of Dom Juan's physical superiority. Dom Juan begins to push and hit him when, in an uncharacteristically generous movement, Sganarelle, after attempting to restrain his master, counsels Pierrot to go away quietly. His advice fails. Pierrot "fièrement" insists: "Je vais lui dire, moi." Dom Juan gives a resounding slap intended for Pierrot, who ducks, and it is Sganarelle, caught in the middle, who receives the blow. Dom Juan delightedly cries out: "Te voilà payé de ta charité" (II, 3).[1] The farce and the comedy serve to underline the seriousness of what is being questioned here, what one may call the usefulness of charity. Of what use is charity and self-sacrifice if all it earns is a slap and a beating? Such is the lesson demonstrated by Dom Juan to Sganarelle and Pierrot.[2] Here, as elsewhere in the play, the farce is not gratuitous but rather serves to intensify the drama and one's consciousness of the multiplicity of duels that Dom Juan must fight in this play (Guicharnaud 229-44). There is the duel of the master against the muddled but bourgeois good sense of his valet, that of the ungrateful son against his own father, and so on in a direct progression to the duel of the rich and proud, unbelieving noble against the simple but sincere *Pauvre,* to the final, most important duel of all, that most basic of duels, the duel between the truly unbelieving *libertin* against the power of Heaven and thus of God. Here, as represented in that futile battle of the unbelieving *libertin* who is fundamentally incapable of charity and of love, one may draw the parallel between Dom Juan and the *libertins* of his century. For Dom Juan represents as did many *libertins* of his generation a negative force seeking through revolt to become a positive force. As Molière's text so compellingly suggests, Dom Juan is a negative force, incapable of either charity or love. He is chaos masquerading as order, and he must be destroyed to preserve the principle of order in the universe. Therefore, only transcendent power can destroy him. This destruction is prefigured in the scène du *Pauvre,* and one may be allowed to think with Molière's blessing that it is Dom Juan's contempt for charity as well as his lack of that virtue that lead to his damnation.

Notes

1. This recalls a sentence of the Préface to *Tartuffe* in which Molière speaks of his battle to save his play from the implacable enmity of the hypocrites who refuse to give up their harassment: "Ils n'en veulent point démordre; et, tous les jours encore, ils font crier en public des zélés indiscrets, qui me disent des injures pieusement et me damnent *par charité*" (629). [Emphasis mine]
2. This recalls Montherlant's famous phrase in *Le Cardinal d'Espagne*: "Les Œuvres charitables par lesquelles il cherche à se débarrasser de la Charité" (I,2).

Works Cited

Guicharnaud, Jacques. *Molière, une aventure théâtrale.* Paris: Gallimard, 1963. 229-44, 252-58.

Molière. *Œuvres complètes.* Ed. R. Jouanny. Paris: Classiques Garnier, 1962. Préface à *Tartuffe.* Vol. 2. 629.

Montherlant, Henry de. *Théâtre.* Paris: *Bibliothèque de la Pléiade,* 1972.

Michael Spingler (essay date 1992)

SOURCE: "The Actor and the Statue: Space, Time, and Court Performance in Molière's *Dom Juan,*" in *Comparative Drama,* Vol. 25, No. 4, Winter, 1991-92, pp. 351-68.

[*In the following essay, Spingler concentrates on the scenic structure of Molière's* Dom Juan *and how the space itself questions the codes that govern court society.*]

In ***Dom Juan,*** Molière inscribes the organized world of seventeenth-century French court life within a dramatic space which reflects the relationship between theatrical and social performance. In what follows, I will focus on how Molière's handling of the play's scenic structure questions the codes which govern life at court. Considered from the point of view of the actor's location and movement on stage, ***Dom Juan*** is an interrogation of the court's attempt to adjust the perception of time and space to its own needs, in particular the need to transform history into a repeatable script. The way Molière incorporates the spatial and temporal consciousness of the courtier into ***Dom Juan*** is at the heart of his critical representation of the court as a constructed performance which relies excessively on theatrical self-presentation.

By the mid-seventeenth century, court space in France had long been organized into a framed and coherent whole, a cultural and social field which was the ideal setting for the representation of prestige and power. Norbert Elias defines the French court as "an arena of activity" ("un champ d'activité") which is also "the reflection of a social unity in space."[1] The court was a privileged space, organized around the person of the King and his royal household, within which an aristocratic self-performance could be played out according to a commonly held code of behavior. The framed space of the court authenticated the performed self and gave aristocratic performance both focus and prestige by setting it off from the rest of the world. It was a closed system, a worldly version of such enclosed spaces as monasteries and convents, where time could be controlled, and privileged moments of history replayed, by the repetition of significant gestures which were considered to be endowed with shared and permanent meaning.

At court such theatrical matters as one's location in space and one's mastery of etiquette—that is, scripted social behavior—were of fundamental importance since they performed the political function of expressing and maintaining social prestige. Where one positioned oneself and how well one behaved according to the complex and draconian code of the court defined what one was. Elias observes that the court was a social structure which supported a network of relations which were essential to the maintenance of the common and peculiar identity of its members: "Un ordre hiérarchique plus ou moins rigide, une étiquette minutieuse leur servait de lien. La nécessité de s'imposer et de se maintenir au sein d'une telle formation sociale leur donnait un caractère particulier, celui de *l'homme de cour*" ("A more or less rigid hierarchical order and a scrupulous etiquette served to link them. The necessity of asserting and maintaining oneself within such a social formation gave them a particular stamp: that of the courtier").[2] The ideal was to be fixed in a *mise en scène* which emblematized the courtier's continuous participation in royal authority.

Molière challenges this notion of a rehearsed and scripted life through a complex dramaturgical strategy consisting of a set of self-referential theatrical operations which brings up the problem of the actor's position within the playing space of the stage. The playwright focuses on the courtier's reliance on two particular performance conventions, centricity and stillness, as fundamental marks of aristocratic privilege. Centricity reflects the courtier's need to occupy a space whose prestige as place comes from its proximity to power. Stillness is the sign of the desire of the courtier, once having achieved a position near the center, to remain rooted to the spot. In his espousal of stillness and centricity, the courtier emulated two kinds of performers: the statues who populated the gardens and palaces of the aristocracy and the statue-like actors who dominated the stage, especially in tragedy.

The seventeenth century saw statuary as the essence of perfect being frozen in stone or metal. Statues were in effect paradigmatic courtiers, and the nobility strove to possess as much of the unchanging perfection of the statue as possible. Jean-Marie Apostolidès observes that the codes which governed the courtier's appearance at court transformed him into something very much like a statue which would be impervious to the effects of time and history:

> The numerous undergarments, like stage drops, emphasize the theatricality of [the courtier's] stance which is further heightened by his brightly colored make-up. For the courtier, façade is everything. He builds himself up like a chateau and he is at his best when seen from a certain distance. Effectively lit by wax candles, halfway between the actor and the statue, the courtier seems to possess a distinct nature. As he ages, he does not become fat or go bald. His appearance does not change. The courtier is an essence which is impervious to the decay brought on by history.[3]

The immobility of the statue idealized both the absolutely unchanging social position which the courtier aspired to maintain as well as his or her imperviousness to time.

Not only did the statue emblematize the perfected bearing of the aristocrat at court, but it also provided the aesthetic model for the tragic actor. Both the actor and the courtier aspired to the static perfection of the statue as the idealized expression of the mirror relationship between the focused expression of theater and the arranged social space of the court. For both the actor and the courtier, a statue-like stillness accompanied by recitative comprised the ideal form of aristocratic performance.[4]

By presenting the aristocratic characters of ***Dom Juan*** as tragic actors who model their self-performance on the stillness of statues, Molière relocates the apparently supernatural phenomenon of the living statue and redefines it as an essential part of the constructed social reality of life at court. The supernatural premise of ***Dom Juan***'s ending—that is, the protagonist's supposed undoing by a statue which has miraculously come to life—then takes on a profoundly ironic significance since all the court characters in the play may be seen and played as animated statues endowed with the gift of speech. In other words, Don Juan both battles and flees from statues throughout the play.[5]

If we consider Don Juan's artistocratic adversaries both as statues and as tragic actors, we can then identify two fundamental strategies of "blocking" which form the basis of two major dramaturgical patterns in ***Dom Juan.*** The first involves the repeated efforts of Don Juan's noble adversaries to fix him and themselves within a framed space by the authority of their declamations which is supported both by theatrical convention and by social etiquette. Opposed to this are Don Juan's swift departures from the playing space, a flight which creates a pattern of dislocation that undermines the aristocratic construction of a stable, unchanging social identity. This second pattern consists of a fragmenting of framed court space into a profusion of discontinuous local settings. The opposing patterns form a complex structure in which certain scenes possess the static, centered unity of tragedy while the play as a whole unfolds according to the decentering energies of farce.[6] What makes Molière's treatment of the legend unique is not the changing scenes of the play but rather his manner of opposing to the framed locus of the court a decentered, polymorphous space which suggests both the openness of farce and the ungovernable nature of seventeenth-century French space beyond the confines of the court.[7]

Dona Elvira's first scene with Don Juan establishes the model for the scenes in which he is pitted against his aristocratic adversaries. Her objectives, as a representative of the court, are to place and keep Don Juan within the primary space of court representation—that is, to fix him in a courtly *mise en scène.* She uses the behavior codes of the court to compose a self-conscious, theatricalized version of their encounter, including for him an appropriate role and discourse meant to put him at a disadvantage. Thus she plays on his surprise at her unexpected appearance and says, "J'ai pitié de vous voir la confusion que vous avez" ("I feel sorry to see you so embarrassed") (I.iii.724).[8] Don Juan's presumed embarrassment then becomes her justification for demanding an explanation according to form: "Parlez, Dom Juan, je vous prie, et voyons de quel air vous saurez vous justifier" ("Speak, Don Juan, I pray you, and let's see what manner you'll find to justify yourself") (I.iii.723). Don Juan's crime against Dona Elvira seems less important here than the self-justifying performance that she expects of him. Dona Elvira's use of the expression "voyons de quel air" reveals her attempt to place herself in the position of spectator/judge who will assess the merit of Juan's defense according to the rules of court behavior. The word "air" in particular suggests that, for Dona Elvira, the form of Don Juan's defense, including the quality of his acting technique, will overshadow its content. Consequently, she accuses Don Juan not of betrayal but of not knowing the prescribed role of the perfect courtier: "Ah! que vous savez mal vous défendre pour un homme de cour, et qui doit être accoutumé à ces sortes de choses!" ("Ah! how badly you defend yourself for a courtier who should be used to this sort of thing!") (I.iii.724).

Considered closely, Dona Elvira's line contains an astonishingly revealing slip: she takes for granted that, as a courtier, Don Juan should be used to "ces sortes de choses." So, it is not his behavior as such that constitutes his crime but rather his refusal to explain his behavior according to the etiquette and language of the court. She even prompts him in this language and in its corresponding theatrical stance—that is, she instructs him in the art of court theatrical declamation:

> Que ne vous armez-vous le front d'une noble effronterie? Que ne me jurez-vous que vous êtes dans les mêmes sentiments pour moi, et que rien n'est capable de vous détacher de moi que la mort? Que ne me dîtes-vous que les affaires de la dernière conséquence vous ont obligé à partir sans m'en donner avis; qu'il faut que, malgré vous, vous demeuriez ici quelque temps, et que je n'ai qu'à m'en retourner d'où je viens, assurée que vous suivrez mes pas le plus tôt qu'il vous sera possible; qu'il est certain que vous brûlez de me rejoindre, et qu'éloigné de moi, vous souffrez ce que souffre un corps qui est séparé de son âme? Voilà comme il faut vous défendre, et non pas être interdit comme vous êtes. (I.iii.724-25)

> (Why don't you brazenly assume a noble stance? Why don't you swear that you still have the same feelings towards me and that only death could take you from me? Why don't you say that urgent business forced you to leave without letting me know, that you must stay here against your will, that all I have to do is go back with the assurance you will follow me as soon as possible, that you long to join me, and that, separated from me, you suffer the torment of a body which has been separated from its soul? That's how you should defend yourself instead of being tongue-tied like you are.)

Dona Elvira gives a lesson in court performance which betrays her deep desire to have Don Juan legitimize her aristocratic identity through the appropriateness of his own playing. We may indeed take her at her word when she says, "Voilà comme il faut vous défendre." As a representative of the court she seeks self-confirmation in her fellow actor's performance. As Apostolidès observes, "At court one acknowledges the other to the degree that the other is recognized as a likeness which reflects one's own image."[9] To be is to see oneself duplicated ceaselessly through a complex code of speech, gesture, manner (*air*), mask, and costume which Dona Elvira's society, in an unconscious stroke of irony, called *honnêteté.*

It is thus principally etiquette rather than morality which drives the characters of ***Dom Juan.*** The system of co-performers who enact mirroring identities within the centered and privileged space of court and stage provides a place for actors to play a repeatable fable of aristocratic identity. This fable consists of the narration of events in the past and, in the process, the evocation of the self who participated in them. What Dona Elvira asks of Don Juan, then, is not explanation or repentance but participation in a scene which can represent their love either in a present or past form. Indeed, what is important is not the continued existence of the love itself but its continued representation.

Consequently, Dona Elvira narrates a tableau from the past, the familiar tragic one of the blinding of reason by passion, which she presents as the originating source of the present scene she is playing with Don Juan:

> J'ai été assez bonne, je le confesse, ou plutôt assez sotte pour me vouloir tromper moi-même, et travailler à démentir mes yeux et mon jugement. J'ai cherché des raisons pour excuser à ma tendresse le relâchement d'amitié qu'elle voyait en vous; et je me suis forgé cent sujets légitimes d'un départ si précipité, pour vous justifier d'un crime dont ma raison vous accusoit. . . . et j'écoutois avec plaisir milles chimères ridicules qui vous peignoit innocent à mon coeur. (I.iii.723)

> (I was soft-hearted, or rather, I admit it, simple enough to lie to myself, and to deny what my eyes and judgment told me. I looked for reasons that would explain your cooling towards me. I made up a hundred convincing explanations for your sudden departure in order to defend you against the crime that my reason accused you of . . . and I took pleasure in entertaining a thousand ridiculous fantasies which convinced my heart of your innocence.)

It is clear that Dona Elvira wants the vividness of this evocative account to influence Don Juan's playing in the scene, for as we have seen it is precisely those *raisons,* those *sujets légitimes,* those *chimères ridicules* which she prompts him to recite when she accuses him later of not knowing his lines—i.e., of not knowing the language of the court. Thus the evocation of a powerful scene from the past is designed to be the justifying premise, the emotive origin, of a scripted present behavior which is fundamentally theatrical and based on image and representation rather than the real.

Dona Elvira's tale of her struggle with herself is more appropriate to tragic declamation than it is to comic speech. Moreover, the way she draws upon the past to move Don Juan seems to anticipate the triumph at court of the erotic rather than heroic tragedy which will be dominated by Racine.[10] Such tragedy was increasingly preoccupied with the question of seduction, in particular with the seductive power of the tragic protagonist to transfix and immobilize the other, and its structure was built around a series of encounters within framed settings. These encounters take the form of a scene which Roland Barthes claims functions as a *véritable fantasme,* a dream image subject to a "protocol of repetition" by which the protagonist can relive a significant instant.[11] Within such a tableau, the character's *tirade,* delivered in recitative, assumes an hypnotic function, and serves, as Barthes observes, "to restore the stillness of the power relationship."[12]

Nowhere is the erotic basis of Dona Elvira's "tragic" performance more evident than in her second appearance on stage in Act IV. Although she has returned ostensibly to urge Don Juan to repent, she soon makes indirectly, in yet another narration, a declaration of love whose erotic character she barely conceals: "Je vous ai aimé avec une tendresse extrème, rien au monde ne m'a été si cher que vous; J'ai oublié mon devoir pour vous, j'ai fait toutes choses pour vous . . ." ("I loved you deeply; nothing in the world was as dear to me as you; I forgot my duty for you, I gave everything to you") (IV.vi.765). A repetitive structure of verbs in the *passé composé* has a hypnotic effect both on the speaker and the listener. Indeed, it is to the erotic subtext which is present throughout the scene and which is expressed theatrically through Dona Elvira's costume (*habit négligé*) and performance manner (*air*) that Don Juan responds when he invites her to stay the night. As he explains to Sganarelle: "Sais-tu que . . . j'ai trouvé de l'agrément dans cette nouveauté bizarre, et que son habit négligé, son air languissant et ses larmes ont réveillé en moi quelques petits restes d'un feu éteint?" ("Do you realize that . . . I found something pleasing in that strange new style and that her disordered dress, pining manner, and tears reignited the last cinders of my passion?") (IV.vii.766) As Don Juan suggests, Elvira's attempt to convert him is thwarted by the seductive ambiguity of her theatrical performance. Dona Elvira reveals this in her final appeal to Don Juan when she says, "Je vous en conjure par tout ce qui est capable de vous toucher" ("I beg you in the name of everything which is capable of touching you") (IV.vi.766).

However, if we can attribute a subtext of seduction to Dona Elvira, we must see it in terms of the play's particular view that erotic power is inseparable from the social power to control a subject's placement in culture. Seduction is pandemic in ***Dom Juan*** because Molière sees that its fundamental model is embodied in court performance. Molière has in fact significantly altered the Don Juan legend in which Juan alone is seen as seducer. In Molière's play, all the characters are engaged in some form of seduction.

Don Louis' visit to his son in Act IV thus bears some curious resemblance to the encouters between Dona Elvira and Don Juan. This scene also is a duet in which a representative of the court tries to subject Don Juan to the authority of his discourse. Like Dona Elvira, Don Louis tries to recenter Don Juan within the courtly *mise en scène* by using tragic recitative to conjure a scene from the past. Although Don Louis relies on the power of a biblical tale told with patriarchal eloquence rather than an evocation of past love to make of Don Juan a passive and receptive listener, his address to his son is nevertheless filled with a passionate vocabulary which bears a striking resemblance to Dona Elvira's: "J'ai souhaité un fils avec des *ardeurs* non pareilles; je l'ai demandé sans relâche avec des *transports* incroyables . . ." ("I longed for a son with unequalled *ardor;* I repeatedly asked for one in a state of indescribable *ecstasy* . . .") (IV.iv.762; italics mine). In this case, however, as the conclusion of his apostrophe to his son makes clear, Don Louis explicitly addresses an anxiety to which Dona Elvira only indirectly alludes. There is a catastrophic break in the causal continuity of events; the son which Don Louis gets is revealed to be not the one he had prayed for: "et ce fils que j'obtiens en fatiguant le ciel de voeux, est le chagrin et le supplice de cette vie dont je croyois qu'il devoit être la joie et la consolation" ("and this son which I get by wearying heaven with my entreaties turns out to be the sorrow and the burden of that very life to which I hoped he would bring joy and consolation") (IV.iv.762). The unbearable possibility for the courtier that the past, present, and future may not be linked intensifies the father's insistence that his son follow the example of his ancestors, that he affirm his present worth by imitating an idealized, narratable past which may be as much mythical as historical.

The key is to repeat its image: Don Louis says, "Aussi nous n'avons part à la gloire de nos ancêtres qu'autant que nous nous efforçons de leur ressembler" ("Therefore, we only partake of the glory of our ancestors to the extent that we strive to resemble them") (IV.iv.763). Don Juan's refusal to imitate a model which has been inscribed into the social fabric is the source of Don Louis' reproaches to his son. Significantly, Don Louis refers to "cet amas d'actions indignes" ("this accumulation of unspeakable deeds") as possessing a "mauvais visage" ("an evil mien") as if it is the face that his son presents to the world which is at the core of his crimes. The outraged father's reproach to Don Juan resembles the reproach of the outraged wife in the following respect: Juan does not resemble the perfect courtier who is the model of court identity either as scripted role or as idealized ancestor. His refusal to enter into the court system of imitation and mirroring identities thus jeopardizes the aristocratic performance of idealized space and time.

Dona Elvira and Don Louis rely on the mesmerizing power of staged tableaux designed to transform the characters into entranced spectators of the frozen image of their own place within court culture. In her account of recent studies of "theater states" by Gertz and others, Aletta Biersack speaks of "actors [who] are instances of a type, members of societal segments, structurally positioned." Elsewhere in her essay she observes that members of such closed cultural structures act as "cultural types rather than as individuals. Their practices are thus structurally situated, relationally positioned."[13] The same could be said of Dona Elvira and Don Louis. That is, what they do and say is determined by their position and status as members of the court, defined as a theatricalized social field which controls the representation of space and time by substituting the effigy, the mask, and the costume for the person. It is for this reason that these characters, like actors on the tragic stage, behave as statues. Their stillness is the principal theatrical and social expression of an unchanging identity which is impervious to time. As depicted in ***Dom Juan,*** court society consists of an ensemble of statue-actors who have the ability to arrange themselves in hypnotic tableaux of power which they can repeat indefinitely as they play the double role of character and spectator, viewed object and viewing subject. As Lévi-Strauss observes, "A universe constructed as a closed system results in each of its members offering his own image as example while reflecting those of the others."[14]

Dona Elvira and Don Louis both call upon the court's authority to legitimize aristocratic identity in their attempt to control Don Juan. Don Louis in particular tries to threaten Don Juan with banishment from his class. Thus, threatening his son with his own ancestors, he claims that the light shed by their illustrious deeds will expose and dishonor the miscreant before the entire world: "tout ce qu'ils ont fait d'illustre ne vous donne aucun avantage; au contraire, l'éclat n'en rejaillit sur vous qu'à votre déshonneur, et leur gloire est un flambeau qui éclaire aux yeux d'un chacun la honte de vos actions" ("you will derive no advantage from their illustrious deeds; on the contrary, their lustre only redounds to your dishonor, and their glory is a torch which illuminates for everyone your shameful behavior") (IV.iv.763). We may find an explanation for Don Louis' threats in Elias' analysis of the court's policing of its members: "Lorsqu'une bonne société de ce genre refusait à un de ses membres le titre de 'membre,' il perdait son 'honneur' et avec lui un élément intégrant de son identité personnel" ("When an exclusive society such as this refused to give to one of its members the title of 'member,' he lost his 'honor' and, along with it, an integral part of his personal identity").[15] Don Louis and Dona Elvira draw their power from their ability to cast the other out of the group—that is, out of the mirror, off the stage. For them to exist is to be perceived, and to be perceived they must remain within the performance space. At court, one can never stop playing. William Levitan has observed that "Once within the formally self-contained world of Racinian drama, we cannot easily get out. Its motivation appears self-evident and closed to question, its sufficiency hardly in doubt."[16] The space outside of the place of performance is, as Barthes has argued, a negative space, a sort of anti-scene of danger, even death. Implicit in this ideal of performance is the idea that there is no existence worth considering outside of the framed space of baroque court representation.[17] The courtier-performer might well share in Hamm's warning to Clov: "Outside of here it's death."

Don Louis' threats, however, have no effect on his son, for it is precisely the outside that Don Juan seeks. It is Don Juan's refusal to remain within the *mise en scène* of his adversaries, his continual movement outside the frame which constitutes his most significant violation of the rules of the game. For Don Juan, remaining within a scene for too long is to be trapped. Throughout the play, he alludes repeatedly to his search for borders, margins, settings on the periphery. His ideal is constant movement and change. A key to his actions is his affirmation that no one will keep him bound for very long: "Quoi? tu veux qu'on se lie à demeurer au premier objet qui nous prend, qu'on renonce au monde pour lui, et qu'on n'ait plus d'yeux pour personne?" ("What! Do you want us to tie ourselves down to the first thing that captures our attention, that we retire from the world and never look at anyone else?") On the contrary, for him, "tout le plaisir de l'amour est dans le changement" ("all the joys of love are to be found in change") (I.ii.719). Change, for Don Juan, is primarily a matter of place as he makes clear when he compares his seductions to the conquests of Alexander: "J'ai sur ce sujet l'ambition des conquérants, qui volent perpetuellement de victoire en victoire, et ne peuvent se résoudre à borner leur souhaits. Il n'est rien qui puisse arrêter l'impétuosité de mes désirs: je me sens un coeur à aimer toute la terre; et comme Alexandre, je souhaitrois qu'il y eût d'autres mondes, pour y étendre mes conquêtes amoureuses" ("My ambitions in this matter rival those of the conquerors who dash from victory to victory and who cannot bear to limit their wants. Nothing can brake the impetuosity of my desires: I have a heart which is capable of loving the entire earth, and, like Alexander, I wish there were other worlds to which I could extend my amorous conquests") (I.ii.719-20). Before dismissing this as solely the rodomontade of a scoundrel, we would do well to be attentive to the spatial terms in which it is cast. Against an established ideal of being bound within a unified space (*demeurer, arrêter, borner*) Don Juan opposes a counter model which privileges swift movement from place to place (*volent, étendre, autres mondes*). His *libertinage* is a reflection of the mentality of the colonists, explorers, traders, and adventurers of the times. Sganarelle defines what might indeed be called wanderlust when he describes Don Juan's heart as "le plus grand coureur du monde; il se plaît à se promener de liens en liens, et n'aime guère demeurer en place" ("the greatest wanderer in the world; it loves to go from place to place and hates to stay in one spot") (I.i.718). Don Juan's desire emphasizes flight, change, and openness. In Act III he explains his waywardness to Sganarelle in specifically spatial terms: "je ne saurois me résoudre à renfermer mon coeur entre quatre murailles" ("I could never shut my heart up within four walls") (III.v.753). It is precisely this need for movement and flight that Dona Elvira recognizes in her curious use of "crime," "trahaison," and "départ si précipité" (I.iii.723) as synonyms.

It is this "départ si précipité" that defines the second major spatial pattern in the play which is organized around the Don's frequent and often unexpected exits. These exits are the occasion for a set of subversive theatrical operations organized around spatial and temporal displacement. The signifying link between Juan's departures and the play's multiple sets is inscribed in a pattern created by the endings of the first three acts and the beginnings of each subsequent act. In each of the acts' endings, there is an exchange between Don Juan and Sganarelle in which Don Juan begins his line with an "allons"—suggesting a rapid exit—and Sganarelle makes a reply that contains a reference to his master which would not be said if Don Juan were still on stage.

> Dom Juan: Allons songer à l'exécution de notre entreprise amoureuse.
>
> Sganarelle: Ah! quel abominable maître me vois-je obligé de servir. (I.iii.726)
>
> (Don Juan: Come on, let's start thinking about our amorous expedition.

Sganarelle: Ah! What a vile master I have got to serve.)

Dom Juan: Allons vite, c'est trop d'honneur que je vous fais, et bien heureux est le valet qui peut avoir la gloire de mourir pour son maître.

Sganarelle: Je vous remercie d'un tel honneur. O Ciel, puisqu'il s'agit de mort, fais-moi la grâce de n'être point pris pour un autre. (II.v.742.)

(Don Juan: Come along! Quickly now! You should appreciate the honor I am bestowing on you. Not every valet gets to die gloriously for his master.

Sganarelle: Thanks so much for the favor. Oh, God, if I must die let it not be because I was mistaken for someone else.)

Dom Juan: Allons, sortons d'ici.

Sganarelle: Voilà de mes esprits forts qui ne veulent rien croire. (III.v.756.)

(Don Juan: Come along! Let's get out of this place.

Sganarelle: So much for the smart ones who never believe in anything.)

In each of the acts the concluding image is that of a stage empty except for Sganarelle who, once he realizes he is alone, scurries comically to catch up with his master. The swift exit of Don Juan which leaves Sganarelle behind suggests that Don Juan is indeed faster than the play itself. It is as if the play and everyone in it must hurry between acts to catch up with the protagonist.

In contrast to the characters of classical tragedy who submit to the seductive fixity of the proscenium frame, Don Juan retains the freedom to disappear and to reappear in an entirely new and different space. The play's structure then as it moves from act to act is one of disjuncture and dislocation. Once Don Juan exits from a particular location, that setting is lost and there can be no return to it. His exits at the end of the act are the occasion of a radical change of world which is represented by the completely unrelated setting that begins the next act. The change of scenes between Acts I and II is the most striking and may serve as a model for the movement of the play from act to act. We shift from the courtyard of a palace to a sea coast, a space which is the antithesis of court space since it is the incarnation of a breaking point, the border between zones of radical difference, land and sea. Moreover the references to the sea suggest that immediately offstage begins a realm that is *other,* a realm that is a denial of the microcosm represented by the system of etiquette and positioning at court. For the sea is the setting of Pierrot's *récit* in which he tells Charlotte the story of Don Juan's shipwreck. This *récit* is a rustic parody of—and antithesis to—the elevated recitative of Dona Elvira, and Pierrot's patois indicates from the very start of Act II that the high ground that Elvira sought to occupy in the first act is gone. The codes and conventions of performance have changed, as the rustic comedy of Don Juan's attempted seduction of the two peasant girls, Charlotte and Mathurine, demonstrates. Moreover, even when it returns with Don Carlos, Don Alonso, and Don Louis, the refined language of the court is not the only discourse which will prevail in the play.

If we follow the pattern of displacement and dislocation in the play, we may view Don Juan's references to movement as something more than the use of a familiar metaphor to defend his desire and justify his seductions. Rather, his seductions now appear as an essential component of his subversive practice of breaking out of the borders of court self-representation while forcing others to follow him into uncharted space. Don Juan's practice of seduction is opposite to that embodied by court society in which the object of the seduction is immobilized within the frame of cultural performance. Juan's form of seduction, on the contrary, involves a displacement, suggested by the word *enlèvement,* a carrying of the person out of privileged space. Seduction for Don Juan means forcing the other, woman or man, to move, lifting her or him out of a setting. Dona Elvira is taken from the walls of a convent while Mathurine and Charlotte are tempted to move out of their rustic milieu, out of their culture, just as Monsieur Dimanche is taken out of his setting as "merchant collecting a bill" and recast in the setting of "friend invited to dinner." Thus the opposing terms of seduction in the play, immobilizing the other within the frame of cultural identity, or dislocating and resituating the other in unfamiliar space, are part of the opposing patterns of fixed tableaux versus movement, change, and spatial dislocation that organize the play.

The characters' dislocation is also reflected throughout by the play's remarkably complex and problematic geography. All through ***Dom Juan*** there is a preoccupation with paths, destinations, and their opposite, new and unfamiliar places in which characters can lose their way. In this sense, Act III is the unmappable center of the play, where all the characters, including Juan himself, are lost:

Dom Juan: Mais tout en raisonnant, je crois que nous sommes égarés. (III.i.746)

(Don Juan: Well, while we were arguing I think we got lost.)

Dom Carlos: Je m'étois par hasard égaré d'un frère et de tous ceux de notre suite. (III.iii.748)

(Don Carlos: I had, by accident, lost track of my brother and of our entire entourage.)

In Act III, the dislocated, lost characters of ***Dom Juan*** find themselves in an unchartable space where established social codes and the examples of the past no longer function as a map of self-definition. It is a space which Phillipe Perrot has identified as being the opposite of the unified, homogenous space of the court and which he calls "the tumultuous wandering world of the great feudal lords."[18] It is a dangerous and ungovernable world where rocky coasts upon which ships can wreck and men drown abut dark forests within which bewildered travelers are prey to bandits. As Le Pauvre warns, "Mais je vous donne avis que vous devez vous tenir sur vos gardes, et que depuis quelque temps il y a des voleurs ici autour" ("But let me warn you that you had better be on your guard because for some time there have been bandits around here") (III.ii.746). Here any lingering notions we may have about explaining the multiple settings of the play solely in terms of Molière's dutiful following of a pastoral or tragicomic tradition should be dispelled. For we are not dealing with the tamed, attenuated, garden-like countryside of the Pastoral but with true wilderness, a realm which is threatening because it is both unpredictable and uncontrollable.

Spatial dislocation leads to breaks in time in which neither traditional codes nor past events indicate the course of future behavior. This is the dilemma of Don Carlos and Don Alonso, Dona Elvira's two brothers, who were united in the common family quest of righting the wrong done to their sister, a quest which should mark out clearly the path of their future behavior. Now, because of his chance encounter with Don Juan while lost in the forest which results in his owing his life to his enemy, Don Carlos is cast in the improbable and unexpected role of Don Juan's defender and is forced to be his brother's adversary. Don Carlos thus embodies the temporal dilemma of the dislocated character in ***Dom Juan,*** for he now has two pasts upon which to draw—the one in which Don Juan has wronged his sister and the one in which he has saved his life. Instead of a continuous temporal duration in which past, present, and future are linked in a unity of dramatic action, ***Dom Juan*** presents us with a series of flukes, chance events, in which the future is unpredictable because the past has lost its unity. Don Alonso recognizes this dilemma when he says to his brother, "c'est hasarder notre vengeance de la reculer et l'occasion de la prendre peut ne plus revenir" ("we risk jeopardizing our revenge if we put it off and the chance may not come our way again") (III.iv.751). Straying from the path, losing one's bearings, is a spatial form of the dilemma of losing one's identity and thus falling into unconstructed history—history the individual subject is incapable of determining.

The third act of ***Dom Juan*** thus reinserts the courtier into a world of ungovernable space and time that court performance seeks to mask, and it is this anti-court space and time which the play's ambivalent and problematical ending affirms. The play's conclusion resumes the two dramaturgical patterns I have traced, and its artificiality and excessive theatricality provide an ultimately ironic and subversive resonance to the drama's final events. To begin with, it is particularly significant, given Dona Elvira's and Don Louis' efforts to control Don Juan throughout the play, that it is the Statue of the Commander who succeeds where they fail. For the Commander is the perfected model of what the other aristocratic characters aspire to be, the animated statue, the subject perfectly transformed into signifying effigy, a monument to his own, now narrativized past. Everything in the play thus ironically points to him as the perfect character to play with Don Juan the quintessentially theatricalized and morally conventional tableau of the damnation of the libertine.

The Statue thus appears on one level to be the avenger who puts an end to the series of escapes we have seen throughout the play. He appears for the final scene just as Don Juan orders Sganarelle to follow him:

> Dom Juan: Allons, suis-moi.
>
> La Statue: Arrêtez, Dom Juan. (V.v-vi.776.)
>
> (Don Juan: Come on, follow me.
>
> The Statue: Stop! Don Juan.)

The exchange is a reprise of the fundamental opposition between flight and stillness which organizes the play. Here, the Statue's "arrêtez" seems to break the pattern of exits established by Juan's frequently repeated "allons." Don Juan is stopped at the very moment of his exit; this time he will remain forever in the Statue's grasp, imprisoned within the frame of a moral and ideologically acceptable dramatic resolution.

Yet, it is the very pattern of exits established earlier in the play which suggests that Don Juan's exit is not prevented, only momentarily deferred. In theatrical terms it takes place an instant later in the form of Juan's disappearance through the stage trap. If we view Don Juan's damnation as an exit, then his established tendency to break out of the frame of court representation is once again affirmed. Theater is turned against itself as the artifice of stage machinery becomes the means of escaping from the enclosed space of performance. What on one level is perceived as a conventionally moral ending functions on the level of self-referential theater as a quintessentially spectacular exit, the last of a triumphantly ironic series, by which Don Juan leaves behind, once and for all, the confining world of the court's social theater. Moreover, it is significant that this final exit follows exactly the pattern established in the first three acts according to which Sganarelle is left behind on an empty stage.

The concluding picture of Sganarelle left alone on stage as he was at the end of the first three acts inscribes the concluding scene's subversive ambiguity. His cry for his wages ("mes gages") points clearly not only to Don Juan's absence but also to the irrevocable emptiness of the stage. It is little wonder that Molière's audience found that the servant's farcical lament, with its emphasis on wages unpaid and obligations unmet, was scandalously inappropriate to the moral "solemnity" of the moment. Instead of the reassuring stage picture of statue-like tragic actors declaiming in a fixed tableau, ***Dom Juan***'s ending leaves us with a final image of a clown running about an empty stage looking vainly for a master and a vanished world. With Sganarelle alone and crying for his wages there is nothing left for the courtier to imitate or repeat.

Dom Juan thus challenges court society as a corps of players who perform within a framed *mise en scène* where imitation and repetition transform aristocratic history into a chronicle of permanence. History perceived spatially as fixed tableau denies an alternative view which acknowledges the power of time to disrupt and dislocate constructions of culture and class. It is this second historical sense which ***Dom Juan,*** with its structure of flight and escape from enclosed stages, its sense of France as open, and finally empty wilderness, reflects. In ***Dom Juan,*** a clown is left to point to an empty stage which reveals the abyss of time hidden behind the masquerade of court performance. For Molière, the complex dramaturgical practice of at the same time creating and exposing the illusions of theater remains the most potent weapon against a world of illusion.

Notes

I am very grateful to Michèle L. Farrell for her comments on earlier versions of this essay.

1. Norbert Elias, *La Société de cour,* trans. Pierre Kamnintzer (Paris: Calmann-Lévy, 1974), pp. 18-19. All translations of quotations from French are mine.
2. Ibid., p. 9.
3. Jean-Marie Apostolidès, *Le Roi-Machine: Spectacle et politique au temps de Louis XIV* (Paris: Les Editions de Minuit, 1981), p. 53.
4. I use both 'recitative' and *tirade* to emphasize that in the seventeenth century the tragic declamation of long passages was closer to chant than it was to speech. Jacques Scherer comments on the remarkable number of *tirades* in *Dom Juan*: "There certainly are a great many long speeches for such an animated play" (*Sur le Dom Juan de Molière* [Paris: SEDES, 1967], p. 66). Scherer contrasts the long speeches with the rapid, staccato dialogue which also abounds in the play. This is the verbal equivalent of the tensional relation between stillness and movement which I trace.
5. Jacques Guicharnaud notes that the Bray-Scherer edition of *Dom Juan* alludes to the program of a company touring the provinces around 1670 which describes the set for the fifth act as "a theater with statues for as far as the eye can see" (*Molière: une aventure théâtrale* [Paris: Gallimard, 1963], p. 294n).
6. Shoshana Felman has a similar view when she points out that traditional criticism which sees the multiple settings as disconnected and, therefore, evidence of a lack of structure "fails to see that in this play, breaks constitute, paradoxically, the connecting principle itself" (*The Literary Speech Act: Don Juan, or Seduction in Two Languages* [Ithaca: Cornell Univ. Press, 1983], pp. 45-46).
7. Fernand Braudel describes "la France ancienne" (which he traces well into the nineteenth century) as follows: "To our way of seeing, old France is a space which is *difficult to master* because it is too vast, difficult to cross, difficult to watch over" (*L'Identité de la France: Espace et Histoire* [Paris: Arthaud-Flammarion, 1986], p. 97; italics mine).
8. References to *Dom Juan* in this paper are to Molière, *Oeuvres complètes,* ed. Robert Jouanny (Paris: Garnier, 1962), Vol. I.
9. Apostolidès, *Le Roi-Machine,* p. 54.
10. Robert Jouanny observes in his introduction to the play that Dona Elvira resembles "une amante racinienne" (*Oeuvres complètes,* I, 710).
11. Roland Barthes, *Sur Racine* (Paris: Editions du Seuil, 1963), p. 29.
12. Ibid., p. 43.
13. Aletta Biersack, "Local Knowledge, Local History: Gertz and Beyond," in *The New Cultural History,* ed. Lynn Hunt (Berkeley and Los Angeles: Univ. of California Press, 1989), pp. 87, 90.
14. Claude Lévi-Strauss, *La Portière jalouse* (Paris: Plon, 1985), p. 152.
15. Elias, *La Société de cour,* p. 86. On this point, I agree with Lionel Gossman who finds it hard to conceive of anyone finding anything "revolutionary" in the "banalities" of Don Louis (*Men and Masks: A Study of Molière* [Baltimore: Johns Hopkins Press, 1963], p. 17).
16. William Levitan, "Seneca in Racine," *Yale French Studies,* 76 (1989), 193.
17. Barthes, *Sur Racine,* pp. 17-20.
18. Phillipe Perrot, *Le Travail des apparences ou les transformations du corps féminin XVIIIe-XIXe siècle* (Paris: Editions du Seuil, 1984), p. 35.

LE MISANTHROPE

CRITICAL COMMENTARY

Dorothy F. Jones (essay date 1982)

SOURCE: "Love and Friendship in *Le Misanthrope*," in *Romance Notes,* Vol. XXIII, No. 2, Winter, 1982, pp. 164-69.

[*In the following essay, Jones explores the polarities of the characters in Molière's* Le Misanthrope.]

Two fundamental contrasts strike the audience of ***Le Misanthrope***: the contrast between Alceste and Célimène, and the contrast between Alceste and Philinte. Critics have been sensitive to the psychological, philosophical, and theatrical value of these polarities. "Alceste est l'exacte antithèse de Célimène,"[1] declares Jean Mesnard, while Jacques Guicharnaud defines the hero and his love as "deux univers soumis à quelque attraction réciproque, mais dont les éléments imcompatibles ne parviennent à aucun moment à fusionner."[2] Guicharnaud suggests that

Célimène's dramatic function is to "s'opposer point par point à Alceste sur le plan de l'amour, comme Philinte . . . sur le plan de l'amitié . . ." (p. 396).

Philinte, indeed, has been viewed almost exclusively as a foil to Alceste. "Rien ne fait paraître davantage une chose que celle qui lui est opposée,"[3] declared Donneau de Visé of the hero and his friend, in our earliest analysis of the play. Few critics since then have been able to resist taking sides is such a meeting of opposites. Gustave Michaut, in a lengthy ironic footnote, lists the crowd, from Rousseau on, who have opted either for intransigant Alceste or for accommodating Philinte.[4] Modern scholars, more sensitive since René Bray and W. G. Moore[5] to the purely theatrical value of this opposition, have remained equally impressed by it. "Le centre du drame, c'est le 'non' qu'Alceste oppose à Philinte" (pp. 380-381), says Guicharnaud, in discussing Act I, scene 2.

Less attention has been paid, however, not to what separates Alceste and Philinte but to the friendship that unites them. Some critics would claim that Philinte, "ce lymphatique et tiède personnage,"[6] is incapable of friendship, that his philosophical detachment cuts him off from human contact as effectively as Alceste's misanthropy. "Alceste hait les hommes, Célimène les méprise, Philinte s'en désintéresse" (p. 75), says Marcel Gutwirth. For the most part, however, spectators have been less severe. We simply tend to take the relationship between the pair for granted. Typically, Jean Mesnard, who discusses perceptively the extent to which friendship within the play is limited by self-interest and the desire to please, concludes: "Sans doute l'amitié de Philinte pour Alceste n'est-elle pas suspecte; mais Molière ne l'analyse pas: c'est une simple donnée de la pièce" (p. 871).

I suggest, on the contrary, that a proper acknowledgment of the relationship between Philinte and Alceste is crucial to our understanding of ***Le Misanthrope.*** Three critics in particular have taken steps in this direction. René Jasinski is impressed by Philinte's friendship for Alceste which he sees as one of those virtues that make him Molière's ideal. "On ne saurait trouver plus parfait ami," he declares, arguing that "il faut que nous ayons été déviés par une longue tradition d'outrances déclamatoires pour que l'on sente en général si peu la qualité d'un tel dévouement."[7]

Merlin Thomas is concerned not with Philinte's ideological rôle but with his effectiveness as a character on stage. He sees in Philinte's allusion to ***L'École des maris*** (v. 100) evidence that these "deux frères" are childhood friends, and argues from his experience as a director that "the first thing for the actor playing Philinte to establish is his relationship with Alceste. They are friends—in so far as Alceste is capable of friendship. From start to finish of the play Philinte does his best for Alceste. . . . And Alceste cannot do without Philinte."[8]

The relationship between Philinte and Alceste is brought into sharpest focus in a statement by Louis Jouvet. Advising his students on the interpretation of Act I, scene I, Jouvet insists:

> Dis-toi que, Alceste et Philinte, ce sont deux amis (chose qu'on ne montre jamais dans aucune représentation de la pièce d'ailleurs), mais toute la pièce repose sur cette amitié. L'étonnant, c'est l'histoire de ces deux amis, Pylade et Oreste, qui sont tombés dans le salon de Célimène. De ces deux amis, l'un est plus intelligent que l'autre dans la connaissance du monde et de la vie sociale et aperçoit très nettement les dangers que court l'autre, Alceste, tandis que celui-ci se dit: ce sont des dangers, entendu, mais j'aime suffisamment cette femme pour la ramener à des sentiments différents. ***Le Misanthrope,*** c'est d'abord ce drame-là.[9]

The particular merit of Jouvert's statement is to remind us that Alceste is after all involved in *two* relationships, not only *eros* but *philia.* The contrast between love and friendship is a common theme in 17th-century literature. One thinks, for example, of La Bruyère's tireless efforts to distinguish between *amour* and *amitié* in "Du Cœur." This distinction is implicit in ***Le Misanthrope*** and constitutes, I believe, a third contrast useful to our understanding of the play. The relation between Philinte and Alceste is in ironic opposition to the relation between Alceste and Célimène.

It is easy to see the quality of Alceste's love for Célimène as Racinian, as Jacques Guicharnaud for example has also already noted (p. 448). Egocentric, irrational, demanding, the force which pushes Alceste towards Célimène is as destructive as the passion that hounds Oreste. Erotic love leads Alceste to betray his truest self: "Efforcezvous ici de paraître fidèle," begs this champion of sincerity. "Et je m'efforcerai, moi, de vous croire telle" (v. 1389-1390). Even fulfilled, this love would not lead Alceste to authentic contact with others, only to a kind of idolatrous *solitude à deux.* "Que doit vous importer tout le reste du monde?" he aks Célimène (v. 1772), insisting that love means she be ready to "trouver tout en moi, comme moi tout en vous" (v. 1782). Alceste will not be saved from his misanthropy by his love for Célimène, and the most casual observer can see that the couple would be miserable together. The comic perspective of Molière's play should not blind us to the fact that erotic love, in the case of his hero, is presented as an essentially negative force.

The relationship with Philinte, on the other hand, offers Alceste the possibility for a truly redemptive contact with another human being. The friendship of this second *couple* is characterized by many of the qualities Alceste demands in human relations, most notably sincerity and authenticity. With Philinte, Alceste can be himself, as his constant explosions of ill humour testify, and with Alceste, Philinte abandons those "dehors civils" (v. 66) he claims are necessary for dealing with other people. Alceste's dream that "en toute rencontre / Le fond de notre cœur dans nos discours se montre" (v. 69-70) is in fact fulfilled when he and Philinte are together.

Philinte shows in his dealings with Alceste none of that flegmatic detachment which so irritated Rousseau[10] and which Philinte's own theories of social behaviour might lead us to expect. He intervenes constantly and bluntly to criticize in Alceste those faults he sees as harmful to his friend, and his physical pursuit of Alceste—"Je ne vous quitte pas" (v. 446)—from beginning to end of the play is the sign of his loving involvement.

Furthermore, friendship with Philinte opens the way to friendship with others. Alceste's love for Célimène merely drives him further into isolation as he seeks to retreat with her behind the wall of his misanthropy. His relationship with Philinte, on the contrary, moves him towards other people, not away from them. Philinte tries constantly to help his friend keep his place in the society that represents, whatever else, the sole opportunity for contact with fellow humans. His "faisons un peu grâce à la nature humaine" (v. 146) is not a mere lecture on social conformity; it is part of a loving campaign to keep his friend in touch with other people. His offer to sacrifice his own love for Eliante is his attempt, on the deepest level of generosity, to bring Alceste out of solitude into a relationship with another human being.

In theory Alceste himself is well aware of the distinction between erotic love and friendship. He sees his feelings for Célimène as irrational—"la raison n'est pas ce qui règle l'amour" (v. 248)—even as an "indigne tendresse" (v. 1751). Friendship on the other hand is a freely chosen relationship between equals: "Avec lumière et choix cette union veut naître" (v. 281), he tells Oronte. In fact, however, he is unable to recognize the difference. He brings to his own friendship with Philinte the same jealousy and desire for exclusiveness that mark his relationship with Célimène; and he is, saddest of all, unable to appreciate the special quality of the love that Philinte offers him.

It is fruitful to examine the dénouement of ***Le Misanthrope*** with these thoughts in mind. Alceste, like his Racinian counterpart, fails to capture and possess the one he loves, despite the help of his friend. Oreste, in the face of this failure, withdraws into madness and Alceste also prepares to reject reality—the world of social intercourse—to flee to the private *désert* of his dreams. This is a serious retreat, albeit foreshadowed from the play's beginning. Alceste abandons the possibility of erotic love—"Non, mon cœur à présent vous déteste" (v. 1779)—not only the *amour-passion* of his relationship with Célimène, but a potential *amour-estime* with Eliante. He breaks the network of ties, however superficial and frivolous, that bind him to the society of Célimène's salon, a charmed circle in which with all his brusqueness he had a place.

The true importance of this break is his rejection of Philinte's friendship. One by one the characters leave the stage—"C'est la fuite devant le dénouement qui en manifeste la tristesse," says Jacques Scherer (cited in Bray, p. 271), but the hero is not left alone: Eliante and Philinte do not join the general exodus. It is Alceste who, blind to the love they offer him, announces that he is "trahi de toutes parts" (v. 1803), turns his back on his friends and exits. It matters little whether, as Lionel Gossman argues, Alceste actually desires to be pursued.[11] The retreat dramatizes his basic inability to respond fully to friendship, to enter freely into authentic relationship with another human being.

The initiative remains with Philinte. Like Pylade, he rushes to the rescue of the disappointed lover, continuing the same affectionate pursuit of his friend with which he opened the play, and this at a moment when the fulfillment of his own desires with Eliante might well have led him into the more closed and exclusive world of *eros*. The love he shares with Eliante takes its place, however, within the generous framework of their mutual friendship for Alceste. The relationship of this third couple thus leaves to friendship the privileged position, in relation to erotic love, it holds throughout the play. *Philia,* in accordance with a long tradition, remains in ***Le Misanthrope*** the highest form of human love; and it is Alceste's rejection of this love which is the truest measure of his misanthropy. For charity, the love that enables humans to love each other as God loves them, there is no room in the secular universe of Molière's play.

Notes

1. "*Le Misanthrope*: mise en question de l'art de plaire," *Revue d'histoire littéraire* (Sept.-Déc. 1972), p. 873.
2. *Molière: une aventure théâtrale* (Paris: Gallimard, 1963), p. 453.
3. *Lettre écrite sur la comédie du "Misanthrope."*
4. *Les Luttes de Molière* (Geneva: Slatkine Reprints, 1968. Rpt. edit. Paris 1922-25), pp. 208-209.
5. *Molière: homme de théâtre* (Paris: Mercure de France, 1954) and *Molière, a new criticism* (Oxford: Clarendon Press, 1962, lst edit. 1949).
6. Marcel Gutwirth, *Molière ou l'invention comique* (Paris: Minard, 1966), p. 164.
7. *Le 'Misanthrope' de Molière* (Paris: A. Colin, 1951), p. 196 and p. 198.
8. "Philinte and Eliante," in W. D. Howarth and M. Thomas, *Molière: Stage and Study* (Oxford: Clarendon, 1973), p. 74. Thomas also makes a convincing case for the love between Philinte and Eliante.
9. *Molière et la comédie classique.* Coll. Pratique du théâtre (Paris: Gallimard, 1965), p. 13.
10. *Lettre à M. d'Alembert sur les spectacles.*
11. *Men and Masks: A Study of Molière* (Baltimore: Johns Hopkins, 1963), p. 83.

Patricia Francis Cholakian (essay date 1985)

SOURCE: "The 'Women Question' in Molière's *Misanthrope*," in *The French Review,* Vol. LVIII, No. 4, March, 1985, pp. 524-32.

[*In the following essay, Cholakian contends that Molière's* Le Misanthrope*'s underlying presumption is that women camouflage their true selves in order to become what men desire.*]

Molière's theater is generally seen as profeminist because it champions the cause of ingénues, like Agnès in ***L'Ecole des femmes,*** against the tyrannical power of an older male who seeks to prevent them from exercising their "natural" right in the choice of a mate.[1]

On the other hand ***Les Précieuses ridicules*** and ***Les Femmes savantes*** have often been considered anti-feminist because they ridicule women who seek to break away from the role assigned to them within marriage and the family and to invade the male world of words and ideas (speaking and knowing).[2] According to Bénichou, Molière thus confines women to the feminine domain of feeling, which he calls "l'accomplissement dans l'amour" or self-realization through love. Molière may be said, therefore, to favor woman's desire to follow the dictates of her emotions, so long as she does not challenge the superiority of men in the domain of the "word."[3]

This analysis does not seem to apply, however, to Molière's most elusive masterpiece, ***Le Misanthrope,*** for in it he portrays neither a harassed ingénue nor a pretentious blue-stocking. When, however, one asks how this play treats the "woman question," one realizes that its entire argument is based on the presupposition that women define their worth as individuals in terms of masculine admiration, whereas men possess an innate sense of their own superiority. This presupposition in turn determines the same sex and male/female relationships within the play. In other words, one finds here a substantiation of the Lacanian theory that women mask themselves in order to become what men desire: "C'est pour ce qu'elle [la femme] n'est pas qu'elle entend être désirée en même temps qu'aimée."[4] Furthermore, a study of how women use language in ***Le Misanthrope*** reveals the "word" as the main tool whereby they practice the art of deception.

There are three female characters in ***Le Misanthrope,*** Célimène, Arsinoé, and Eliante, all of whom are rivals for the affections of the misanthrope Alceste. The first, Célimène, is surrounded by flattering admirers who frequent her salon in the hope of persuading her to designate one of them as her favorite. This young widow of twenty is in no hurry, however, to declare herself or to marry.

In order to maintain this situation, she must secretly convince each man that he is the favorite, while committing herself to none of them. In this way she remains in control of the men whom she reduces to amorous servitude. Since as males they require exclusive rights over the woman of their choice, they find this situation intolerable. The play thus contains a power struggle arising from the men's need to know and Célimène's determination to keep them guessing.

Célimène is rebelling against the established social order by her refusal to designate a partner and to commit herself to a marriage in which she would be subject to the absolute authority of her husband (i.e., Alceste who would force her to live with him in the "desert"). But she cannot effectively liberate herself from male domination because of her emotional dependence on her suitors, who reassure her that she is desirable as a woman. Without their presence, Célimène would be nothing.[5]

Unlike Philaminte in ***Les Femmes savantes,*** therefore, Célimène never questions the basic assumption that men are superior to women. Rather than striving to liberate herself, Célimène is preoccupied with keeping all of her suitors constantly in her presence, ordering Alceste not to leave (II, 3) and nervously inquiring whether the two marquis have another appointment when she sees them moving in the direction of the door (II, 4). What is more, in her letters she is even willing to perjure herself to make sure that they do not desert her. When she speaks of Arsinoé's prudishness as a mask for her "affreuse solitude" (v. 862), she is revealing her own fear of being abandoned by the masculine sex.

The prude, Arsinoé, arrives as a messenger from the world outside the salon to warn the coquette that her flirtatiousness is endangering her reputation among "des gens de vertu singulière," who make sure that women do not break the moral code on which the male hierarchy is based. (In other words, Célimène's behavior carries with it the threat of polygamy and matriarchy).[6] In veiled terms, she delivers to the coquette what amounts to a threat; that is, if she does not give up "cette foule de gens dont vous souffrez visite,/Votre galanterie et les bruits qu'elle excite—" (vv. 889-90), it will be assumed by the virtuous people with whom Arsinoé identifies herself that Célimène is a woman of ill-repute: "Aux ombres du crime on prête aisément foi—" (v. 907). Unsuccessful herself in attracting male admiration, Arsinoé insinuates that Célimène is offering her admirers more than conversation: "Pensez-vous faire croire, à voir comme tout roule, / Que votre seul mérite attire cette foule?" (vv. 1005-06).

Arsinoé's real motive in coming to Célimène with this message is not, however, any genuine, if misguided, concern for either her virtue or her reputation. Arsinoé represents the forces of oppression that appear in Molière's other plays in the guise of such characters as Arnolphe, Tartuffe, and Harpagon, but the fact that these repressive forces here take the form of a woman is one more indication of the wide divergence between this play and those which follow the more traditional comic pattern outlined by Knutson.[7] The mask of the prude endows Arsinoé with a form of power. It allows her to exert a threat which will intimidate the woman whose glamorous and exciting existence she envies. Moreover, by its use she hopes to frighten Célimène into changing her ways. Should this happen, Arsinoé would have a better chance of winning for herself the man she covets: Alceste. Thus like Célimène, Arsinoé's real concern is with authenticating her existence through masculine admiration. Her conquest of Alceste will prove that she too, is an object of male desire and will enable her to recover her own sense of self-worth.

Arsinoé may be viewed as an archetypal figure: the older woman who, having passed the age of coquetry, has allied herself with the social order, which imposes monogamy, in order to thwart and frustrate her younger rival. As Céliméne herself realizes, the two are really different aspects of a woman's life cycle. The coquette eventually becomes a prude when she loses the power to control men with her sexual charms. Because Célimène and Arsinoé can see behind the masks which they wear to mystify the men whom they seek to attract, they are able to identify and define each other.[8]

The third woman in the play is Eliante, Célimène's cousin and companion. In the typical comedy, she should also be Célimène's confidante, but the play offers no glimpses of any private relationship between the two women. Instead, they appear to be strangely aloof from each other, and aside from Célimène's unsuccessful attempt to enlist Eliante's aid in fending off the combined attack of Orante and Alceste (V, 2), they never exchange any words at all. The reason for this is that both are completely absorbed in the men around them. It is with Philinte that Eliante shares her thoughts and feelings, not Célimène.

Eliante is also avowedly in love with Alceste and waiting patiently for him to tire of Célimène or for Célimène to tire of him. Philinte knows this, but offers to marry Eliante on the rebound, should her hope of winning Alceste fail; and Eliante agrees readily. For a poor relation like Eliante, marriage offers the only means by which she can establish an identity of her own. Whom she marries is secondary. Thus Eliante, the "wise" foil to Célimène, philosophically resigns herself to a loveless match rather than continue her existence as a single woman, without status. Like both Arsinoé and Célimène, she, too, is unable to envision a form of identity which is not validated by a relationship with a man.

In contrast, all the men in the play demonstrate a sense of themselves as superior individuals, well integrated into the social structure. Whereas Célimène and Eliante never converse, and she and Arsinoé can only communicate through insults, there are many instances in the play in which the male characters demonstrate their ability to cooperate with each other. In the case of the two pairs of male rivals, for example, disputes are settled according to pre-established gentlemanly codes of behavior. Oronte has recourse to the arbitration of marshalls to settle his quarrel with Alceste. Acaste and Clitandre contract a gentlemen's agreement to withdraw from seeking Célimène's favors should the other produce proof positive of her preference. When the two letters come to light, they keep their word and abandon her, while their friendship for each other remains intact. Even Oronte and Alceste promise to abide by Célimène's decision if she will choose between them (V, 2). Philinte likewise defers respectfully to Eliante's preference for his friend, thus complying with the code of the "honnête homme." This contrasts markedly with the way in which Arsinoé attempts to win Alceste away from Célimène. All the men in the play are thus bound by codes which honor fair play and respect the territorial rights of other men.

No such codes exist between the women in the play. Célimène takes great care to flatter all her friends in their presence, but she makes no effort to hide her true feelings from Arsinoé.[9] She parodies Arsinoé's hypocritical warning and counterattacks at her most vulnerable point, her age, thus establishing her sexual superiority and reducing Arsinoé's accusations to pathetic attempts to mask her own impotence. Since one of the main problems dealt with in the ***Misanthrope*** is the disparity between what people say *about* each other and what they say *to* each other, it is especially significant that only Célimène and Arsinoé drop the pretense of good manners to express their hostility openly. These jealous women do not bother to be polite to each other for long. Each recognizes in the other a member of an inferior caste—the female sex. Célimène flatters and manipulates her male friends because in her eyes they are of value. The female, who possesses no value in her eyes, is not worth flattering. Arsinoé likewise attacks her "friend" in the hope of winning a male prize. The entire exchange reinforces the stereotype of women as their own worst enemies.

Even Eliante, who is supposedly Célimène's closest friend demonstrates the inability of women to cooperate with each other. She does not back up Célimène when she begs her to save her from having to choose publicly between Alceste or Oronte, brushing her off with "je suis pour les gens qui disent leur pensée" (v. 1662).

What is more, none of the women in the play seems to possess an active sense of self-esteem. While Alceste demands to impose his will on the way others react to him—"Je veux qu'on me distingue" (v. 64)—Célimène sees herself as passive, powerless to change the way in which others think about her: "Puis-je empêcher les gens de me trouver aimable?" (V. 462). Likewise Arsinoé, lacking the courage of her convictions, must seek the backing of the anonymous group of virtuous folk, and Eliante in her long speech in II, 4 (vv. 711-30) never mentions her own feelings on the subject of love, casting her entire tirade in the masculine third person, speaking of "les amants" and "leur passion." The speaker remains carefully descriptive and passive. She offers no judgment of her own. It is the masculine "amants" who react to the *object* of their affections. How women regard the men they love is not her concern. Eliante's detached tone is in marked contrast with Alceste's next line, "Et moi, je soutiens, moi . . ." (v. 731).

In III, 1 we see that even the most foppish and silly of men do not base their identities on the opinions of women, as women base theirs on the opinions of men. When Acaste catalogues his reasons for self-satisfaction, the fact that he is "fort aimé du beau sexe" is far down on his list, well after even "les dents belles surtout." Wealth, birth, physical courage, intelligence, and literary acumen all precede (vv. 781-804). It goes without saying that when Oronte wants a valid opinion of his sonnet, he does not address himself to a woman but to a man. His ego is so strong, however, that when he fails to elicit the favorable critique he seeks from Alceste, he does not rewrite his sonnet; he demands an apology.

The most telling proof of women's need to mask themselves in compensation for their inferior status comes, however, at the level of their language, which they use in devious if not deceptive ways. In his seminal study, *Molière: une aventure théâtrale,* Jacques Guicharnaud gallantly attempts to prove that Célimène never actually lies to her suitors, because she is really speaking the language of preciosity, which they do not know how to interpret. She does not mean to deceive the suitors, she merely uses signs they are incapable of decoding. And so, the fact that Célimène has taken care to tell Alceste that she loves him does not necessarily imply that she will give up her other admirers for him: "Pour être différente de la logique masculine exclusive, cette logique féminine n'est pas obligatoirement signe de mauvaise foi."[10] Célimène's duplicity is thus excused in Guicharnaud's eyes because it is not premeditated. We have already seen that Célimène's pleasure is based on the admiration of a considerable number of males because she needs to prove her worth in the eyes of men, who alone have the power to validate a woman's existence. Guicharnaud shows that he is half aware of this fact when he speaks of a feminine logic different from masculine logic: i.e., the logic which requires that a woman shall cleave to one man and forsake all others. Nevertheless, it is difficult to accept Guicharnaud's conclusion that Célimène is ignorant and therefore innocent of the effect that her misleading words have on the men in her little group. Does she not notice that all her suitors take her words literally and believe her when she implies privately to each one that he is in fact her favorite? Were that the case, she would be remarkably insensitive to what is happening around her. Guicharnaud is right in perceiving that Célimène speaks a different language from the men in the play, a language which they cannot understand. But is that not because she does not want them to understand her?

Jouvet's pithy summary of the play: "C'est la comédie d'un homme qui veut avoir un entretien décisif avec une femme qu'il aime"[11] could be rephrased, "It is a comedy about a woman who avoids having a decisive discussion with anyone." A close reading of her skirmishes with Alceste reveals how adroitly she manages not to declare herself while continually holding out to him the hope that she has in fact already given him her heart. In II, 1 when Alceste demands to know what advantage he has over his rivals, she replies, "Le bonheur de savoir que vous êtes aimé." The response is already ambiguous, lacking as it does the qualifier which would confirm that he is the *only* one she loves; but when he presses for yet more assurance, Célimène huffily takes back her guarded avowal: "Hé bien! pour vous ôter d'un semblable souci, / De tout ce que j'ai dit, je me dédis ici" (vv. 511-12). In act IV, when Alceste confronts Célimène with the supposed letter to Oronte, she uses exactly the same tactic, first suggesting that the letter was written to a woman and then withdrawing her plausible explanation: "Non, il est pour Oronte" (V. 1365). Eventually, she bursts out in righteous indignation, "Allez, vous êtes fou dans vos transports jaloux, / Et ne méritez pas l'amour qu'on a pour vous" (vv. 1391-92), thus simultaneously tantalizing him with the admission that she loves him and withdrawing it as punishment for his doubts. She has maneuvered him into thinking he has received an encouraging message: since I do not find your love genuine, mine must be sincere. But in fact the message which he receives is not really the message which was sent; nor is the mystery of the real message ever revealed.

In Guicharnaud's view, Célimène is genuinely hurt by Alceste's refusal to believe in her love for him. According to him, the coquette has founded her happiness on a conception of the *Pays du Tendre* "dont chaque ville est habitée par un soupirant choisi; Alceste occupe la capitale."[12] Alceste, however, is unable to conceive of Célimène's hierarchy of suitors. According to Guicharnaud, Célimène is exactly what she appears to be and therefore has every right to be indignant when Alceste doubts her word.

This argument would be convincing did it not exclude the obvious fact that none of the suitors has any intention of taking his place within the "hierarchy" established by Célimène. Thus, Acaste is sure that he is not wasting his time in Célimène's salon (vv. 807-22) and Clitandre believes he possesses some "marque certaine / D'avoir meilleure part au cœur de Célimène" (vv. 801-02). Nor will Oronte accept second place: "Il me faut de votre âme une pleine assurance: / Un amant là-dessus n'aime point qu'on balance" (vv. 1589-90). In truth the only one who believes in the hierarchy of lovers is Célimène herself. Célimène's feminine language is a language which she alone understands. If her discourse is sincere, it must then be recognized as a monologue, for dialogue is not possible between people who do not speak the same language.

When Clitandre and Acaste arrive, each bearing a letter written by her to the other, the contradictory evidence can be compared and acted upon. It is clear that the purpose of these letters was to dissuade the addressees from abandoning Célimène. In order to accomplish this, she had to persuade each marquis of her affection for him. If, in fact she is really saying that she has a place for each in her hierarchy, she is nevertheless quite careful to word both letters in such a way that the recipient will assume that he is at the top.

It is difficult not to see in these repeated misunderstandings between her and her suitors the intent to gain her own ends—that is to keep them all near her, through the conscious manipulation of language. The salient quality of language for Célimène is ambiguity. It does not serve the function of communication, since its intent is not to purvey meaning, but to mystify.[13]

The grimacing mask of the prude precedes Arsinoé, as does her "faux voile." Célimène who sees through Arsinoé's pose indicts her rival for using language duplicitously to mislabel sexual attractiveness, naming it a "crime," in order to cover up the fact that she possesses no appeal of her own. Arsinoé wishes to make Célimène's conquest of Alceste into a "theft." She hides her jealous spite. In short, according to Célimène, Arsinoé is constantly sending false messages (vv. 854-72).

When Arsinoé enters the room, it becomes immediately apparent that what she says is not what she means. Instead, she offers to Célimène the option of interpreting her words in multiple ways which may signify either what they seem to mean or the exact opposite. Like Célimène, Arsinoé has learned the trick of placing the burden of interpretation on the listener: "Vous pouvez bien penser quel parti je sus prendre" (v. 893).[14]

Arsinoé's stated reason for her second appearance is equally at variance with its real intent. Entering with Acaste and Clitandre, who have come to confront Célimène with the two incriminating letters, she again makes a pretense of not believing what she has heard about Célimène:

> J'ai du fond de votre âme une trop haute estime Pour vous croire jamais coupable d'un tel crime; Mes yeux ont démenti leurs témoins les plus forts, Et, l'amitié passant sur les petits discords, J'ai bien voulu chez vous leur faire compagnie Pour vous voir vous laver de cette calomnie. (vv. 1675-82)

Her use of the word "fond" is particularly clever, since it introduces the possibility of a double interpretation and protects her from the accusation of judging her "friend" uncharitably. All the key words in this speech, *foi, estime, démenti, amitié, laver,* and *calomnie* also signify the opposite of their literal sense.

In these two scenes Arsinoé's hypocritical use of language distorts its meaning, but her use of the "word" to deceive goes even farther. She purposely misleads Alceste into believing that a letter addressed to her was in fact written to Oronte. (It is true that this point is never definitely resolved in the play, but since there is no evidence of any alliance between her and Oronte, it is difficult to see how she could have come into possession of a letter addressed to him. It is much more probable that Célimène's characteristically ambiguous question "Mais, si c'est une femme à qui va ce billet . . . ?" [v. 1344] does in fact signify the truth). Arsinoé knows that Célimène is leading all her suitors on with flattery and half-promises, but in order to communicate this truth, she must resort to a falsehood, thus causing further confusion to Alceste. Like Célimène, she sends a message which he cannot decode.

It should be noted, however, that Arsinoé's attempt to unmask the coquette actually fails. A false letter from one woman is given a false address by another. In this situation, Lacan's celebrated dictum that a letter always reaches its destination does not seem to apply, the reason being that women and not men are manipulating the "word."[15] It is two *men,* the little marquis, who, despite their effeminacy, manage to bring to light the truth about Célimène's mystifying use of language—thanks to their *gentlemen's* agreement. Even emasculated men have an edge over women.

The key to feminine discourse is produced by Eliante in her monologue (II, 4), the theme of which is the disparity between what women are and what they seem to the men who love them: "Jamais leur passion n'y voit rien de blâmable" (v. 713). The signifying characteristics of the woman who is loved are reinterpreted by her lover and given new signifiers: thinness becomes a good figure; plumpness becomes majesty; messiness becomes casualness; dishonesty intelligence; and stupidity becomes goodness. This explains the gap between lover and beloved, mystified and mystifier, signifier and signified, male and female. It is this communication gap that is at the heart of the play.

What Eliante, who speaks her mind, reveals in this passage, both Arsinoé and Célimène demonstrate: women and men do not use words in the same way. Unlike men, for whom a spade is a spade and a rose a rose, women assign ambiguous meanings to words. The result is that their listeners, or readers, hear what they want to hear, while remaining in doubt as to what is truly intended. Women thus deprive language of denotative meaning and so overload it with connotative meanings that the interlocutor cannot understand them. The result is the total confusion which permits women to authenticate their existence through their hold over men.

It is not my intention to speculate here as to Molière's own attitude toward his female protagonists. Whether he, too, felt privately that women should stay in their place and play out the roles assigned to them by tradition; or whether he realized that the social institutions that placed men in a superior position had forced women into devious and duplicitous behavior, is quite beside the point. What I have tried to demonstrate here is that ***Le Misanthrope*** draws a true and disturbing picture of the way women function toward members of both sexes in an androcentric society. If one is determined to wrest a commentary on this situation from the author himself, the empty stage on which the curtains falls at the end of the play may be a silent clue.

In any case, it is clear that no one wins in the world of ***Le Misanthrope***: not Alceste, who fails to dominate a creature who insists on her own pathetic version of freedom; not Célimène who loses the little world of mystery and illusion which she has created; not Arsinoé who, despite her attempt to ally herself with the forces of sexual repression, remains alone. Critics have sometimes pointed to the "second-best" marriage between Eliante and Philinte as a substitute "happy ending," but it is difficult to see how this sad match, founded from its inception on the devaluation of both spouses, can ever be anything but a dreary compromise.

In ***Le Misanthrope*** Molière portrays the inauthenticity of human relationships. Insofar as these relationships are male/female, this inauthenticity arises from women's lack of autonomous identity. Since male admiration is the only touchstone by which women verify their existence, they view themselves, and are viewed by others, as sexual objects. Thus they constantly manipulate those around them in order to arouse their desire. This in turn leads to "feminine" language, a perversion of the "word," and a total breakdown in communication between the sexes.

Notes

1. This view is shared by such disparate critics as Simone de Beauvoir, *Le Deuxiéme Sexe* (Paris: Gallimard, 1949) I, p. 180, and Paul Bénichou, *Morales du grand siècle* (Paris: Gallimard, 1948), pp. 311-13. Knutson explains Molière's attacks on male authoritarianism in terms of a comic mythos which suspends the principle of authority ruling the "highly ritualized and hierarchical society of 17th century France. . . ." Harold C. Knutson, *Molière: An Archetypal Approach* (Toronto and Buffalo: Toronto University Press, 1976), p. 19.
2. Lapeyre sees the pretentious language spoken by the *savantes* as an attempt to "dire autrement," which Molière chastises severely because "ce désir qui s'attaque à l'ordre ne peut créer que du désordre." Elizabeth Lapeyre, "*Les Femmes savantes:* une lecture aliénée," *French Forum* 6, No. 2 (May 1981), pp. 137-38.
3. In this regard, Domna Stanton argues that the "precious" language ridiculed by Molière never really existed. The satires of preciosity grew out of masculine fears that women were gaining control over language as a result of their preeminence in literary salons. "*Préciosité* and the Fear of Women," *Yale French Studies* 62 (1981), 107-34.
4. Jacques Lacan, "La Signification du phallus," *Ecrits* (Paris: Seuil, 1966), p. 694.
5. See Lionel Gossman, *Men and Masks* (Baltimore: Johns Hopkins, 1965), p. 91: "Apart from her masks Célimène is nothing, a pure seeing, transparent and opaque at the same time." What Gossman does not make explicit is that Célimène is nothing because she functions only as a sex object.
6. In his recent reexamination of *Le Misanthrope,* Gossman writes, "Arsinoé . . . has chosen the matronly role of active collaboration with the oppressor, identification with the male order, as the only effective means available to her of manipulating it." "The Art of Melancholy in the *Misanthrope*" *Theatre Journal* 34 (1982), p. 331.
7. See Knutson, *Molière,* p. 25.
8. The loathing self-recognition experienced by the two women in this scene coincides with Gilbert and Gubar's interpretation of the mirror symbol in *Snow White.* See "The Queen's Looking Glass" especially pp. 37-44 in *The Madwoman in the Attic: A Study of Women and the Literary Image in the Nineteenth Century* (New Haven: Yale University Press, 1979).
9. Brody noticed this in "*Don Juan* and *Le Misanthrope,* or the Esthetics of Individualism in Molière" *PMLA* 84 (1969) p. 572: "brutal personal truths are exchanged by the two most dishonest participants in the action."
10. Jacques Guicharnaud, *Molière: une aventure théâtrale* (Paris: Gallimard, 1963) p. 400.
11. Cited by A. Dudley, "Comment interpréter Molière," *L'Ere Nouvelle,* 20 juin 1938.
12. Guicharnaud, p. 400.
13. "L'amour se heurte en elle à une divinité plus ancienne, plus puissante que lui: *l'illusion.*" Marcel Gutwirth, *Molière ou l'invention comique* (Paris: Minard, 1966) p. 88.
14. "Arsinoé of course aims at investing a fiction with both a semblance of truth and the serenity of art." Brody, p. 573.
15. See Lacan, "Séminaire sur la lettre volée," *Ecrits,* p. 41.

Larry W. Riggs (essay date 1992)

SOURCE: "Another Purloined Letter: Text, Transparency, and Transcendence in *Le Misanthrope*," in *The French Review,* Vol. 66, No. 1, October, 1992, pp. 26-37.

[*In the following essay, Riggs, focuses on the character of Alceste and his attempts to discern text from reality in* Le Misanthrope.]

Alceste, the *Misanthrope,* is a man trying to escape from the jungle of social semiotics. His constant threats to retire to a *désert* are symptomatic of his desire to avoid the agony of watchfulness and waiting imposed on him by performative interaction with others. At the same time, he longs to be *present* in a potent and central way. He aspires to control the allocation of attention in his social circle, guaranteeing both admiration for himself and others' guilt-ridden submission to him. Like any person aspiring to dominate, Alceste must try to define the Other in order to delineate his own identity clearly and to found the desired hierarchy. This is where Célimène's letter comes in. The essence of the sexual encounter between Alceste and Célimène emerges through the confrontation occasioned by this "text within the text." Alceste's refusal of difference, his attempts to obliterate the Other, are exemplary of the solipsist's absorption of everything into the self. Alceste tries to absorb into himself the status of texts as privileged signifiers. The play challenges this status and shows that Alceste's denial of the difference between text and life reduces him to an object adequately defined by the word *misanthrope.* In creating the character of Alceste, Molière has anticipated our recent rediscovery of textuality and its relation to psychology and culture.

As is true in Poe's story, a letter here is central in what is in fact a problem of interpretation. We can say of Célimène's letter, which becomes a vital instrument in Alceste's effort to dominate and control Célimène, what Jacques Lacan has said of the other one: according to Lacan, in addition to having a particular content which may be evidence of something or other, the purloined letter has a structural place in a drama defining a relationship and repeating an archetype or paradigm ("La Lettre"). It ritualizes a structure and, therefore, a difference and a hierarchy. In Molière's play, Alceste would like to have the degree of mastery possessed by Poe's detective. The latter's superior lucidity and control are confirmed by his seeing the "hidden" letter. Alceste pretends that possessing Célimène's letter gives him a similarly penetrating gaze.

Being written documents, both letters fall within the modern valuation of documentary evidence over spoken communication as disclosure of truth. Alceste certainly finds it convenient to believe that Célimène has revealed her true essence, has inadvertently disclosed her inmost truth, in the letter. One suspects that writing, because of its seeming detachment from a performing body, is easier to take as "transparent" discourse. Once words have been conceived as objects, then persons can be defined as containers of truths that can be confessed, or extracted.

This suspicion is reinforced by the terms in which the letter is spoken about in the play. Arsinoé, in offering to show the letter to Alceste, says that it will provide a "pleine lumière" (l. 1126) on Célimène's character, a "preuve fidèle / De l'infidélité du cœur de votre belle" (ll. 1129-30). This promise complements Alceste's desire to position himself as the definitive moral consciousness for the play. Célimène, whom Alceste makes the representative of all that he abhors about humanity, will be fully disclosed, opened to the annihilating flame of Alceste's condemnation, by the letter. This revealing text, produced by Célimène's own hand, promises to complete and legitimate Alceste's paradigmatic conception of his relations with her and with society. I shall argue that this paradigm and, indeed, the identity Alceste is trying to constitute for himself, are themselves composed of texts. He wants to construct for himself an Archemedean point, an independent, lucid perspective which will enable him to manipulate without becoming entangled.

Alceste's hopes for this letter are clear in his statement to Arsinoé that only incontrovertible evidence can interest him: "Les doutes sont fâcheux plus que toute autre chose; / Et je voudrais, pour moi, qu'on ne me fît savoir / Que ce qu'avec clarté l'on peut me faire voir" (ll. 1122-24). He would like to condemn Célimène and then re-create her. The *auto da fé* he envisions, with Célimène condemned by his justice and redeemed by his grace, would illuminate *him* with the fire of her purification. He wants to wield an authority guaranteed and justified by the defectiveness of human nature as represented by Célimène. His attitude, particularly in his use of the terms *doute* and *lumière,* is quite Cartesian. Célimène corresponds to the nature to be penetrated and controlled by knowledge. Moreover, Alceste's ambition is clearly therapeutic.

These lines also show the emphasis on the *visual* in Alceste's attitude. He wants to gain permanent control by *mapping* his relations with Célimène, by reducing them to a fixed, visual structure. This visual analogue suggests that Alceste's misanthropy itself, as a definitive perspective on morally immobilized human objects, is a technique for escaping time and drama. It is also, as I shall demonstrate, a text.

At the same time, misanthropy appears as a virtually inevitable *cost* of elevating the idea of a sovereign self over obligations and relationships. Alceste reflects the aggressiveness and fear of Cartesian epistemology and absolutist politics.

Arsinoé's offer is irresistible to Alceste. The relationship with Célimène that such evidence permits him to envision constitutes him as just what he wants to be: a transcendent subject whose judgmental consciousness dominates and manipulates without becoming entangled. He sees the chance to escape, thanks to this written evidence, from doubt, from the problematics and drama of sign production and interpretation in society. The assumption that textual evidence is a transparent illumination of incontrovertible truth is dependent on conceiving visible language products as both a means to and a paradigm of control.

In fact, of course, this transaction between Alceste and Arsinoé highlights the contradictions and hypocrisies in Alceste's performance and permits us to begin appreciating his curious relationship to *texts* in general. The issue of Célimène's letter focuses attention on the question of interpretation. Thinking, or wanting to think, that he has certain proof of Célimène's perfidy—"de sûrs témoins" (l. 1128)—Alceste completely ignores the key issue of *motive.* He has begun by failing to consider Arsinoé's probable motives. She is, after all, Célimène's *rival.* The interesting result is that Arsinoé is able to use Alceste's desire for control to manipulate him. His need to solve the problem of doubt by processing Arsinoé's "information" through his pre-established conceptual matrix—the paradigmatic text actually encoding *his* motives—makes him both a victim and an example of the very same self-seeking insincerity he pretends to abhor.

Alceste's systematic attitude, or ideology—"Je *cherchais* le malheur qu'ont rencontré mes yeux" (l. 1292)—does not really solve the problem of interpreting signs. Like any such system, it merely creates pretexts for ignoring the problem by imposing pre-fabricated, absolute definitions. The combination of credulity and outrage with which Alceste first accepts and then uses the letter enables him to play, in the remainder of the action, the role assigned him by his ambition.

Having read the letter between Acts III and IV, Alceste fulminates without restraint throughout Act IV. Finding himself in possession of the *pretext* he has wanted pushes him on to a paroxysm of what amount to hackneyed, pseudo-tragic thunderings and lamentations. He will be shown to be at his most derivative and textual when trying to perform with greatest power and intensity.

In Act IV, ii, Eliante and Philinte raise the issue of interpretation, asking whether Alceste has not drawn conclusions about the letter's significance too quickly: "Avez-vous pour le croire un juste fondement?" (l. 1231); "Une lettre peut bien tromper par l'apparence" (l. 1241). He insists on ignoring this issue, however. He does not wonder why Célimène wrote what she did, even after, in Act IV, iii, she freely admits to having written it. Not wanting to face his interpretive responsibility, Alceste pretends that the letter's meaning is self-evident, and thus that his own reaction is not a motivated interpretation. He is sinking deeper and deeper into a morass of signs—into a pluralistic field of mimetic, manipulative, performative speeches and gestures. He would like to cut through this jungle, or rise above it. In his fulminations, he is railing against his ontological insecurity and the metaphysical emptiness of signs. He tries to impose a closure enthroning him as privileged signifier. In the process, his performance becomes an anthology of quotations and paraphrases from other texts.

Alceste seizes on written words because they appear to be separate from the context of erotic, pluralistic speech whose temptations and dangers are represented by Célimène, and which constantly reminds him that he is a speaking, interpreting body among other motivated bodies. In confronting written language, he can pretend that he and the words exist in a metaphysical "space" where he can play the judge/inquisitor. Alceste is trying to become the proprietor of a world converted into a "textual preserve" (Natoli 12). The apparent objectivity of the written words makes them seem transparent and, at the same time, makes Alceste's pretensions seem plausible. The myth of objectivity, however, constitutes both the "objective" world and its "objective" analyst. Much of what Alceste says in Act IV is quoted directly from the earlier "heroic comedy," ***Dom Garcie de Navarre.*** His textual evidence serves as pretext for his performance of what amounts to the script of offended God and wronged lover in Act IV, iii. That performance is virtually plagiarized from the earlier, more serious play. There is a supplementary irony in the fact that, as many in Molière's audience would have been aware, the earlier play had been a failure.

The desire to dominate leads directly to the implicit or explicit citing of authorities. The letter would most appropriately be chalked up to the kind of formulized effusiveness Alceste has criticized from the opening scene of the play. However, Alceste is trapped within the paradigm he has set up and which the letter seems to him to justify. His textual quotations from the role of Dom Garcie underline Molière's awareness that one is always the creature of the rhetorical techniques one takes up. Alceste is the prisoner of his text.

Alceste's grandiloquence cannot hide the fact that his point of departure is an interpretation motivated by the wish to say the things supposedly justified by the pretext. His response is a short-circuit. He believes he has achieved his ideal: a situation wherein "Le fond de notre cœur dans nos discourse se montre" (l. 70). Alceste is the perfect example of looking only for what one wants to find, or what one's method of search *can* find. He is the creature of his program for imitating God, of his "masterful" technique.

This is why he must ignore what Célimène *says* about the letter. For him, the letter is functioning scripturally: it seems to have "called" him and Célimène into the roles *he* has wanted for them. He takes the letter as a release from the ontological uncertainty of interacting with her. It seems definitive and does not argue. Alceste reflects here the tendency, growing in Western Europe since the late Middle Ages, not only to prefer written over oral evidence, but to use documents for stifling non-documentary claims. This reminds us of Orgon's love of binding texts in ***Le Tartuffe***: Orgon sees the drawing up of a marriage contract and *donation* as a means of making his will supreme in his household.

Socrates distrusted writing because it cannot *converse* (Greene 23). This is precisely why Alceste, like modern, text-based culture, prefers it. The rise of modern rule by written law permitted many a dispossession and many a forgery. It is true, but not obvious, that writing *is* communicative behavior, and as such is motivated by desires and fears.

Thus, Alceste tries to constitute himself definitively by treating the letter as constitutive of the "Célimène" to whom his prefabricated role will be an appropriate response. His speeches are, in addition to being plagiarized from another script, full of metaphors whose subtext is the discourse of Inquisition. They constantly repeat the structure of difference, the hierarchical relationship with Célimène, which the letter seems to him to have established. He is God and Judge, and she is *the* Sinner. Of course, the metaphors are no more transparent than the letter. They do not disclose or allude to any definitive truth. They merely repeat a claim whose basis is the documentary constitution of a mythic object to which he responds *as if* it were Célimène.

The textualized Alceste and Célimène need not and cannot communicate—or change—because they are entirely objectified by the language that has "called" them into existence. Having wished to escape from his own evanescence through time by escaping from the evanescence and drama of speech, Alceste *does* become objectified, but as a ridiculous type, not as a transcendent subject. As Walter Ong has said, sound is the most evanescent of perceptions, while vision favors immobility (*Psychodynamics* 29). Alceste wants to escape from the evanescent, agonistic realm of speech into the abstract world of texts. He projects the familiar, the predictable, onto the object of his anxious desire.

Alceste's attempted "scriptural" trickery is strikingly like the process whereby any religion's or ideology's rituals repeat a structure of difference. The appropriateness and indispensability of the ideology depend on textual sources and on the "monstrousness" of human nature when it has not been submitted to the operation of the ideology. Hobbes, whose denunciation of human nature was critical to the credibility of absolutism, and Bossuet, who spent fifteen years writing his *Politique tirée des propres paroles de l'Ecriture Sainte* to legitimate the French monarchy, come to mind in this connection. Alceste's "Jealous God" performance draws all of its textual precedents, from Dom Garcie to, perhaps, Scripture itself, into the comic anthology of scripts for self-interested, obscurantist, tyrannical performance.

All the elements of the script according to which Alceste likes to play come together in the intertextuality of his performance in Act IV. He wants an indissoluble partnership between a transcendent Alceste and a shameful, adoring Célimène. What he produces is grandiloquent comic chatter aimed at a "Célimène" he has in effect hallucinated. This chatter reduces him to a collection of intertexts hopelessly out of contact with Célimène and with life. Writing has here radically separated the "knower" from the "known." Alceste is merely a role. He is, in fact, *literature.* He is not even a dramatic character.

Instead of escaping semiosis by transcending contingent communication, Alceste has sunk below the level of relative individuality required for any communication at all. He is neither the exalted Object of others' admiration nor the Subject of their subjectivity. He is the simple emptiness of a conventionalized role, the futile fixity of a text. His uncritical absorption of the letter has activated a machinery of quasi-scriptural precedents. The relation with Célimène he desires would just institutionalize the repetition of a *misreading.* Shoshana Felman has said that the ego is an agency created to *misread,* to interpret experience as a confirmation, rather than a subversion, of the ego's seeming unity and solidity (61). I believe Molière would agree: Alceste's misreading of the letter, and of social relations in general, is necessary to the unity of his performance. In the end, his performance is nothing more than that rigid, monotonous, and unrewarding consistency.

Alceste is tempted to ignore motive—his own, Célimène's, and Arsinoé's—by the same aspect of texts emphasized by contemporary reader-response theory: the mutual absence of writer and reader that seems to confer on writing or print an "objective" existence it does not really have. Alceste does not consider the entire *context* of the letter as social communication. We are encouraged to do so. For example, Célimène was no doubt motivated to write what she did by something Alceste ought to see as the simple social imperative to be "insincere." She may well have felt it was necessary to flatter the letter's recipient. Paradoxically, he has to believe the letter is perfectly *sincere* in order to make use of it for his ultimate purpose. This is a clear indication of the false distinction he makes between oral and written communication. Here, Molière destroys the myth of text as somehow separate from struggle and power. The production and interpretation of writing are as agonistic as is oral communication.

Alceste tries to evade his responsibility for creating the "Célimène" to whom he is responding by repeating the myth of textual transparency: "Quoi! vous bravez ainsi ce témoin convaincant . . ." (l. 1336). He deals only with the Célimène he hallucinates, but he pretends to be impressed only by the most objective evidence. He is in a hurry to exercise the power he believes is inherent in his "knowledge." His behavior is a ritualized set of gestures. It is now clear, in fact, that his misanthropy amounts to a *technique,* a method, and that it is designed to ritualize and hierarchize a subject/object relation. However, like all techniques, it takes possession of him as he takes it up to apply it. As contemporary theory would have it—and as Molière evidently understood, though perhaps in different terms—the "I" which reads Célimène's letter is composed of previous readings.

All knowledge is interpretation or inference, and every inference is the captive of its motives. We are always shaped by the rhetoric in which we state our claims, and Alceste's particular version of the "objectivist myth" (Lakoff and Johnson 210) merely objectifies *him.* The use of the word *convaincant* indelibly inscribes Alceste's responsibility, but he fails to acknowledge that he has *chosen* to be convinced. What Alceste is seeking throughout the play is the power to name Célimène. All he can achieve is his own reduction to *le misanthrope.*

The ritual repetition designed to hide the subjectivity—the desire—at the origin of Alceste's misanthropy destroys his ability to communicate with and respond to the somewhat fluid outer world without making him independent of that world. This is emphasized by the constant conflict between Alceste's ambition and the succession of scenes, each of which—and, more particularly, the *relentless succession* of which—undermines his pose. The desire that causes him to see Célimène as reducible to a text reduces *him* to that degree of simplicity.

If the letter is evidence of anything, it is that social life is a continuing, inescapable interpretive problem. The letter's position in the exchange between Alceste and Arsinoé shows that "disclosures" are always motivated and therefore cannot be *clear.* It is Alceste's aggressive, even desperate will-to-understand the letter that is actually insincere and perfidious, because it motivates his partnership in Arsinoé's treacherous "disclosure" of a Célimène deserving condemnation. The structure to which the letter is really the key is that of Alceste's relation to Arsinoé, and in that he is merely a dupe.

Having seen the central importance of the letter, and of the fact that it is, precisely, a text, it is appropriate to look at the whole play with the issue of textuality explicitly in mind. The fact is that the derivative, or intertextual, aspect of Alceste's performance is pointed out in the play's first scene. This theme is established when Philinte says: "Je ris des noirs accès où je vous envisage, / Et je crois voir en nous deux, sous mêmes soins nourris, / Ces deux frères que peint ***l'Ecole des maris***" (ll. 98-100). This alerts us to Alceste's unoriginality and to the fact that those who interact with him are pressured toward unoriginality, too. Benjamin Bennett makes the point that this passage creates in us a double consciousness as regards the comparability of literary word and theater: the reference to an earlier play is, of necessity, a reference to literature; at the same time, theater *is* resistance to the systematizing, accumulating tendency of the literary word (2). Philinte's remark awakens our awareness of precisely this paradox in our spectatorship. More importantly, however, it prepares us to perceive that Alceste is inhabited by, or constituted from, an anthology of textual and rhetorical precedents. Like Alceste, the audience of drama must live an irremediable tension between continuity and contingency.

The second scene, the famous "sonnet scene," establishes another element in Alceste's relation to textuality. This scene is central to the play in a way that has nothing to do with the issue on which critics have most often focused: the quality of the poem Oronte asks Alceste to judge. The sonnet's real significance lies in the fact that, although he calls it "sottises" (l. 326), its rhetoric is a rehearsal of what will be Alceste's speeches to and about Célimène. His seemingly fierce anti-conformism and severe moralism turn out to be convergent with the hackneyed rhetoric of a conventional lover's lament. The sonnet's persona expresses impatience with waiting for a clear commitment from his mistress:

> L'espoir, il est vrai, nous soulage
>
> Et nous berce un temps notre ennui;
>
> Mais, Philis, le triste avantage Lorsque rien ne marche après lui! (ll. 315-18)

He expresses his fear that this situation will become permanent, and he threatens to die if it does:

> S'il faut qu'une attente éternelle
>
> Pousse à bout l'ardeur de mon zèle,
>
> Le trépas sera mon recours. (ll. 327-29)

Alceste has already expressed himself in analogous terms (ll. 240-42, 257). His quest for autonomy through definitive possession of Célimène corresponds to the sonnet's demand for a commitment, as his threat to withdraw to a desert of silence and isolation echoes its threat of suicide or death from despair. Alceste's entire performance converges with a poetic cliché. Oronte, then, is not merely Alceste's rival for Célimène; he is his *double*.

So, Alceste's efforts to "call" Célimène into a role complementary to the one he wants to play, his desire to "recruit" her into a partnership guaranteeing his autonomy, makes him the puppet of previous versions of the quest for ontological security. He is the creature, the prisoner, of an entire tradition. The succession of scenes in the play both emphasizes the repetitiveness of his behavior and reduces his would-be transcendence to the fragmented state of contingent Being.

Virtually every scene in which Alceste and Célimène appear together repeats the theme of the sonnet. Alceste is in a textual trap, and he tries to entangle Célimène in the textual toils. His wish to be what Felman calls a "self-possessed proprietor of knowledge" (84)—to become a transcendent subject by acquiring proof that the Other deserves to be a vilified object—is delusive. Moreover, Alceste's desire, like that of all the *ridicules,* reflects his need to dominate, but it also establishes *lack* at the center of his reality. He lusts for overwhelming presence, but absence defines him.

Jane Gallop speaks of the ego as a kind of "armor" (86). Alceste's predilection for expressions like "rompre en visière" (l. 96) to describe his relations with others suggests that Molière would have agreed. Not only is Alceste much like the ego constructed for essentially defensive reasons from texts, and given to reducing others to a textual fixity in order to misread them, but his literalistic reading of Célimène's letter recalls that consolidation of *priestly* power has often been based on literalistic misreadings of texts. The religious subtext of Alceste's inquisitorial metaphors emphasizes this connection. In all of his major plays, Molière is concerned to denounce the consolidation of power around ideological "readings" of reality (Riggs).

Like all objectivists, Alceste assigns fixed, inherent qualities to his object. Moreover, his choice of an abstraction like *sincérité* as supreme value already links him with modern, increasingly textual culture's propensity for legalistic abstractions over existential contexts or relationships as *foci* of loyalty (Williams 184). This also links him to a number of the other *ridicules.*

With this in mind, it is clear why Alceste constantly threatens to become *absent* from the scene or context of speech, why so much of his discourse emphasizes light and perspective, and why he feels threatened by words dissociated from textuality. Absence tempts him because he associates it with both powerful, definitive discourse—he imagines himself as both a *deus absconditus* and an ever-present judge—and safety from oral exchange.

He tries to defeat or escape from time as experienced in the struggles and evanescence of spoken communication by founding a secure, definitive knowledge and control on the structural fixity of texts.

Alceste would like, of course, to escape his own contingency, his own inexorable evanescence or movement toward death. He can do this only by "leaping" into a premature "death": he becomes the equivalent of a text. The *désert* which he associates with a glorious, vertical absence from context, with a privileged view, invades and destroys his *presence* in social life. Written discourse lacks full, existential context, and Alceste's performance is clearly an attempt to transcend context. The landscape of his desire is a desert. Molière shows us, again, why a would-be tyrant always becomes an object of the techniques that constitute the tyranny.

Misanthropy appears, now, as a consequence of elevating idea over relationship. It is the essence of what we may term a "positional consciousness," or definitive perspective: Alceste wants to map the moral universe into a permanently fixed structure reflecting an equally permanent hierarchization of his relations with others. He believes he has found the means of placing himself at the Archimedean point. He wants to occupy a fixed, and glorious, position in a synchronic paradigm, with no risk of "falling" back into the relativity of diachronic, oral drama. Spoken words, and their interpretations, are always modifications of existential situations (Ong, *Orality* 67). Such agonistic communication always engages the body as it engages motive and desire. Misanthropy is a blanket-condemnation of the contingent, pluralistic, and erotic in life. With structural fixity in a timeless visual "space" as the ideal, actual communicative behavior can only appear dangerous, corrosive, and degraded.

Alceste is not comfortable being a desiring body among other desiring bodies. Yet, his performance is occasionally interrupted by avowals of his desire. For example, in the play's first scene, Philinte points out that Célimène's character does not correspond with Alceste's stated principles. Alceste says: "En dépit qu'on ait, elle se fait aimer" (l. 232). There is a triple admission in this line. First of all, he concedes that his principles do not control even his own behavior. He also suggests that erotic attractiveness is an aspect of the temporal, dramatic experience he is, on the level of principle, trying to escape. Furthermore, he seems to admit that what he desires in Célimène is her *desirability,* or the prospect of triumphing over the others who desire her. This latter point is related, of course, to the fact that Alceste wants to monopolize Célimène's own capacity for desire and admiration, to capture her as Arnolphe believed he could capture Agnès.

In addition, and perhaps most fundamentally, there is the fact on which I have focused here: desire for Célimène promises a high probability that Alceste will wind up being justified in reciting his misanthropic script. It is well to keep in mind that another Moliéresque character, the Jupiter of ***Amphitryon,*** owns the kind of transcendence Alceste is seeking and apparently finds it boring. Jupiter voluntarily descends into the erotic, contingent context of drama. Drama constantly replaces the raggedness of being within the space of literature, it struggles against the myth that uniformity is possible and desirable. Molière's main characters *enact* this tension. They *are* the textual temptation.

If Alceste is constructing the landscape of his desire, then, as far as his consciousness is concerned, the desert of textualized abstraction carries the day over the burgeoning jungle of oral communication. The play's final Act merely confirms Alceste's commitment to his role. When Célimène is abandoned by her coterie—after they have discovered *textual* evidence of her contempt for them—Alceste continues to demand not only her love, but her promise to join him in his *désert* of non-communication. In fact, he merely continues to adumbrate the few possible variations on his script. The landscape of his desire is, precisely, the *désert* of anti-erotic, anti-corporal structure, a structure he identifies with triumph over contingency. It is the "desert" of open vistas structured by a fixed, dominant perspective. Alceste is an early would-be inhabitant of a world defined by visual analogues and energized by the prospect of dominating and manipulating the dense, echoing jungle of acoustic space.

Molière himself was sensitive on the issue of textuality: Abby Zanger has recently argued persuasively that Molière did not like the idea of publishing necessarily definitive scripts of his plays. What Alceste does is just what Molière did not want to do. As a man of the theater and a writer, Molière was both closely acquainted with and somewhat separate from the gathering forces of literary language and practice. He lived the tension between literature as progressive closure and drama as constant critique and subversion of codes. His major plays all deal with issues of textuality, and ***Le Misanthrope*** shows the evolution of a character into complete impasse under the influence of a scripturally sustained quest for permanence. Otto Mayr's book on the relations between machinery and cultural evolution in early modern Europe is a fascinating account of the growing importance of abstraction, reduction of natural processes to visual analogues, and the idea of conquering time and behavior. Alceste, as a character, involves us in considering the implications of this cultural trend. He is as much a Cartesian as a misanthropist. In fact, misanthropy, hostility to nature in the human, is inherent in the Cartesian identification of knowledge with control. Alceste's desire to remove doubts is motivated by the same wish for control and the same heroic conception of the self that permeates the *Discours de la méthode.*

Lacan's brief passage on Alceste in "Propos sur la causalité psychique" sees the character as confused between the language of the Subject and the language of Being. I have suggested that Molière was very much aware of issues like those Lacan was trying to articulate. As elsewhere in Molière's major comedies, the raggedness or discontinuity of Being constantly undermines the unitary pretensions of what we would now call would-be "transcendent subjects." Alceste's performance is inescapably oral: it takes place in the complex, interactive, erotic space of speech.

Alceste exemplifies the effects of what I will call "hegemonic metaphors": his discourse and his performance are dominated by a fund of metaphors based on Judeo-Christian theology. The Judeo-Christian elements are implicit in Alceste's hegemonic ambition. He plays God in his quasi-scriptural speeches in Act IV.

A metaphor, of course, always obscures the aspect of things on which it does not focus. Alceste never really perceives the actual Célimène or the actual nature of his relations with her. Such perception would require attentiveness not dominated by desire and the ambition to control. It would thus require that he accept his own contingency.

Alceste is mesmerized by the language that constitutes his role as surely as Orgon is mesmerized by Tartuffe, or the *femmes savantes* by Trissotin, and for similar reasons. He believes the text of the letter can justify the text of his performance, whose resemblance to a fixed text is precisely what makes it ridiculous. In this case, a letter cannot be the key to any definitive perspective because the letter itself is a problem in interpretation, not a revelation. Alceste cannot succeed as a supreme moral authority; he can only fail as one member of a semiotic community.

Works Cited

Bennett, Benjamin. *Theater as Problem: Modern Drama and Its Place in Literature.* Ithaca: Cornell UP, 1990.

Felman, Shoshana. *Jacques Lacan and the Adventure of Insight.* Cambridge: Harvard UP, 1987.

Gallop, Jane. *Reading Lacan.* Ithaca: Cornell UP, 1985.

Greene, William Chase. "The Spoken and the Written Word." *Harvard Studies in Classical Philology* 60 (1951): 23-59.

Kintgen, Eugene, Barry M. Kroll, and Mike Rose, eds. *Perspectives on Literacy.* Carbondale, IL: Southern Illinois UP, 1988.

Lacan, Jacques. "Propos sur la causalité psychique." *L'Evolution Psychiatrique* 1 (1947): 123-65.

———. "Le Seminaire sur 'La Lettre volée.'" *La Psychanalyse* 2 (1956): 1-44.

Lakoff, George, and Mark Johnson. *Metaphors We Live By.* Chicago: U of Chicago P, 1980.

Mayr, Otto. *Authority, Liberty, and Automatic Machinery in Early Modern Europe.* Baltimore: Johns Hopkins UP, 1986.

Natoli, Joseph. "Introduction." *Tracing Literary Theory.* Ed. J. Natoli. Urbana: U of Illinois P, 1987.

Ong, Walter J., S. J. *Orality and Literacy: The Technologizing of the Word.* London: Methuen, 1982.

———. "Some Psychodynamics of Orality." Kintgen et al. 28-43.

Riggs, Larry W. "La Raison de la plus folle est toujours la meilleure: Synthetic Language and the Hallucinations of Reason in *Les Femmes savantes.*" *Symposium* 41.3 (Fall 1987): 214-26.

Williams, Raymond. *Towards 2000.* London: Chatto and Windus, 1983.

Zanger, Abby. "Paralyzing Performance: Sacrificing Theater on the Altar of Publication." *Stanford French Review* 12.2-3 (Fall-Winter 1988): 169-86.

Noel Peacock (essay date 1990)

SOURCE: "Lessons Unheeded: The Denouement of *Le Misanthrope*," in *Nottingham French Studies,* Vol. 29, No. 1, Spring, 1990, pp. 10-20.

[*In the following essay, Peacock examines the ending of Molière's* Le Misanthrope, *contending that its paradoxical nature is representative of the comic, and not the tragic, dramatic genre.*]

'Le dénouement, quel qu'il soit, ne peut être que tragique'.[1] Horville's dark interpretation of the ending of ***Le Misanthrope*** is representative of a tradition in Molière criticism which is still widely accepted despite persuasive attempts to correct it.[2] Evidence, however meagre, from Molière's contemporaries indicates a comic ending. Montausier, who was thought at the time to have been a prototype of Alceste, claimed that he had become the butt of everyone's laughter. The first performance of the play provoked what Donneau de Visé termed 'rire dans l'âme'. The tragic lighting seems to have been introduced in productions after Molière's death featuring Baron in the title role. Baron's interpretation gained critical support in the eighteenth century from German classicists, particularly from Goethe, who viewed the play as a societal tragedy in which the noble Alceste is defeated in his struggle against the world.[3] The Romantics turned Alceste's separation from Célimène into a moment of supreme pathos. This interpretation was maintained in influential criticism in the early part of the twentieth century.[4] Over the last thirty years the ending has often been regarded as generically different from the rest of the play.[5] It has sometimes been considered to be unequivocally tragic and comparable with Racine's dénouements.[6]

The aim of this [essay] is to reaffirm the comic status of the dénouement. To do so, I shall attempt to define the 'action' of the play, and within the framework of that definition, examine those aspects of the ending which have given rise to a tragic interpretation—the main theme, the construction and the extent to which the characters experience 'enlightenment'.

The word 'action' has been the subject of much terminological confusion. It tends to be treated as a synonym of 'plot'. It does sometimes take on this meaning in seventeenth-century dramatic theory, for example, 'unity of action' signifies 'unification of plot'.[7] The restricted sense in which I am using the term is found, however, in some of the prefatory material and discussions on tragedy by Corneille and Racine. Here 'action', which is sometimes synonymous with 'subject', may be understood as the general concept in the mind of the dramatist; 'plot' is the external means at his disposal to convey this general concept to the audience.

In his first *Discours,* Corneille argued that the distinctions between tragedy and comedy were found in the different types of 'action':

> La comédie diffère donc en cela de la tragédie, que celle-ci veut pour son sujet une *action illustre, extraordinaire, sérieuse:* celle-là s'arrête à une *action commune et enjouée* (italics mine).[8]

In his preface to *Bérénice,* Racine stressed the magnitude of the 'action' in tragedy:

> Ce n'est point une nécessité qu'il y ait du sang et des morts dans une tragédie: il suffit que *l'action en soit grande,* que les acteurs en soient héroïques, que les passions y soient excitées, et que tout s'y ressente de cette tristesse majestueuse qui fait tout le plaisir de la tragédie (italics mine).[9]

The types of action chosen by Corneille were generally ones which would provoke admiration on the part of the audience; those chosen by Racine were of a kind which would arouse the emotions of pity and fear. For both dramatists, the 'action' of the play raised important moral issues: for example, in *Horace,* the 'action' concerns the dangers of excessive patriotism; in *Cinna,* the nature of power, the consequences of responsibility, the question of moral salvation. In *Andromaque* and *Phèdre,* matters of international significance provide the backcloth against which the private struggles of the characters are set. In both Corneille and Racine, the principal characters face 'grands périls' whereas in ***Le Misanthrope,*** Alceste and Célimène experience 'inquiétude' and 'déplaisirs'.[10]

The 'action' of ***Le Misanthrope*** is of two kinds: for most of the characters, it concerns the 'discovery' of Célimène's duplicity and their ultimate discomfiture; for the spectator, the 'action' is perceived through the characters' enactment, but issues in his or her perception of Alceste's and Célimène's inability to accept the lessons of experience. This 'action' is purely domestic: the public dimension, the prerequisite for tragic effect in Corneille and Racine, is missing. Alceste believes it is present. He elevates his lawsuit to a phenomenon of universal interest:

> Je verrai, dans cette plaiderie,
>
> Si les hommes auront assez d'effronterie,
>
> Seront assez méchants, scélérats et pervers,
>
> Pour me faire injustice aux yeux de l'univers (. . .)
>
> Et je veux qu'il demeure à la postérité,
>
> Comme une marque insigne, un fameux témoignage
>
> De la méchanceté des hommes de notre âge.
>
> (197-200, 1544-46)[11]

Alceste's love for Célimène is deemed by him to be a fatal attraction: '(. . .) ce fatal amour né de vos traîtres yeux! (. . .) il faut suivre ma destinée' (1384, 1417). The consequences of Alceste's legal setback and of his separation from Célimène do not, however, go beyond the confines of his own inner circle. The destiny of nations will not be affected by his decision to leave for his 'désert'! Critics have sometimes taken Alceste's self-assessment literally. The character behaves and talks as if he is in an 'action illustre'. Alceste thinks that his situation is tragic. But, as we shall see, it is the character, and not the author, who has misunderstood the *genre.*

The high social rank of the characters has also led critics to distinguish ***Le Misanthrope*** from most of Molière's plays. Some seventeenth-century dramatists and theoreticians suggested that the comic hero was of a lower status than his tragic counterpart:

> (. . .) la comédie ne parle que des [personnes] mediocres (. . .)[12]
>
> Dans la comédie, il [le poète] imite les actions des personnes de petite condition, ou tout au plus de médiocre (. . .)[13]
>
> (. . .) dans la Comédie, dont les Personnages sont pris du menu peuple, tous jeunes Débauchez, Esclaves fort empressez, Femmes étourdies, ou Vieillars fort affairez (. . .)[14]

Corneille, however, did not think high rank in itself indicative of a tragic 'action':

> Lorsqu'on met sur la scène un simple intrigue d'amour entre des rois, et qu'ils ne courent aucun péril, ni de leur vie, ni de leur État, je ne crois pas que, bien que les personnes soient illustres, l'action le soit assez pour s'élever jusqu'à la tragédie. Sa dignité demande quelque grand intérêt d'État, ou quelque passion plus noble et plus mâle que l'amour (. . .) et veut donner à craindre des malheurs plus grands que la perte d'une maîtresse (. . .) s'il ne s'y rencontre point de péril de vie, de pertes d'États, ou de bannissement, je ne pense pas que [le poème] ait droit de prendre un nom plus relevé que celui de comédie.[15]

For Molière and Corneille, the 'action' was more important than the social status of the characters in determining the *genre.* We shall see that in ***Le Misanthrope*** the characters' elevated social status does not prevent them from behaving like some of the self-deluded heroes in Molière's bourgeois comedies or even like the naïve protagonists of the farce tradition.

The dominant theme emerging from the 'action' is that of incompatibility. The ending of ***Le Misanthrope*** reveals a break with the convention of literary comedy. Normally a five-act literary comedy ended in the celebration of marriages:

> Le dénouement traditionnel de la comédie est un mariage, et même, de préférence, plusieurs mariages (. . .) Il semble que le double mariage soit le minimum acceptable pour un dénouement heureux et qu'on doive y arriver à tout prix.[16]

In the *comédie d'intrigue,* obstacles to the union of the main characters are removed and there is an atmosphere of reconciliation and of reunion. Molière had scope for such an ending to ***Le Misanthrope***: three potential couples are announced in the opening scenes. The only marriage to take place (between Philinte and Éliante) has been regarded as highly unsatisfactory:

> (. . .) le mariage plus ou moins 'bâclé' de Philinte et d'Éliante ne peut faire oublier la rupture survenue entre Alceste et Célimène.[17]

But such criticism ignores the comic 'action' of the play: Philinte and Éliante provide a yardstick against which we can evaluate the inability of others (particularly of Alceste and Célimène) to learn the lessons of experience.

The theme of incompatibility, which has been thought to contain tragic overtones in this play, may be viewed however as a subtle variation on one of the central themes of Old French Farce—that of the *mal-marié.* The theme is also prominent in a number of Molière's plays from ***La Jalousie du Barbouillé*** to ***Amphitryon.***[18] The *badin*'s defeat in the conjugal struggle was a traditional comic closure in Native French Farce. Farcical echoes in the ending of *Le* ***Misanthrope*** have not been explored by critics. Admittedly, Alceste's marital status is different from that of the *mari confondu.* The role of Alceste is also much more complex than that of the naïve husband. Yet Alceste's oft-frustrated attempts to come to an understanding with Célimène evoke the cuckolded husband's futile quest to prove his shrewish wife's infidelity. Alceste is spared the beating usually meted out to the *lourdaud.* The physical expressiveness of the farce endings is reproduced (appropriately enough for the more sophisticated play) in the verbal fisticuffs of the final scene.

The topsy-turvy world of farce is also recalled in the numerous proposals of marriage. The fact that the initiative is taken by women further reverses the literary convention. The first two overtures are met with brusque refusals. Arsinoé's proposal, thinly veiled as a means of allowing Alceste revenge on Célimène, is brutally anticipated by the titular hero:

> Ce n'est pas à vous que je pourrai songer,
>
> Si par un autre choix je cherche à me venger.
>
> (1721-22)

Célimène's offer, in response to Alceste's request to accompany him to his 'désert' ('Si le don de ma main peut contenter vos voeux, / Je pourrai me résoudre à serrer de tels noeuds; / Et l'hymen . . .' (1777-79)) provokes an even more categorical rejection: 'Non, mon coeur, à présent, vous déteste' (1779).

The final overture contrasts with the previous female demonstrations on the art of proposal. Éliante's subtle hypothesis feeds Philinte his cue:

> Et voilà votre ami, sans trop m'inquiéter,
>
> Qui, *si je l'en priais,* la pourrait accepter.
>
> (1797-98 italics mine)

Philinte's very positive acceptance couplet provides retrospectively an ironic focus on Alceste's failure. Their union is a counterpoint to the incompatibility of the Alceste/Arsinoé and Alceste/Célimène relationships.

The comic 'action' is also conveyed by the repetitive structure of the play. The fact that the dénouement derives closely from the preceding episodes has increased speculation as to the play's tragic qualities. In many of his five-act comedies, Molière has recourse to an outside agency to untie the complications of the plot: (see, for example, the *patres, rex* and *deus ex machina* endings of ***L'École des femmes, L'Avare, Tartuffe*** and ***Dom Juan***). In such plays, the seemingly fortuitous introduction of characters unfamiliar to the audience creates discontinuity and an atmosphere of fantasy. The structure of ***Le Misanthrope*** is, on the other hand, quite coherent. Even the two episodes which have been thought to be digressive provide an ironic anticipation of the dénouement. In Act I, scene 2, Molière suggests two potentially tragic endings to the play: the *persona* of Oronte's sonnet, tired of waiting in hope, contemplates suicide: 'S'il faut qu'une attente éternelle/ Pousse à bout l'ardeur de mon zèle,/Le trépas sera mon recours' (327-29). This is a far cry from Oronte's verbal bravura at the end of the play: 'J'y profite d'un coeur qu'ainsi vous me rendez,/Et trouve ma vengeance en ce que vous perdez' (1705-06). The heroic ending envisaged by the *persona* of Alceste's *chanson* contrasts with the latter's flight to his 'désert', unaccompanied by 'ma mie' but pursued by the happy couple, Philinte and Éliante. Similarly, the mutual self-congratulation of the *marquis,* in Act III, scene 1 is based on false premises. The pact they make to keep each other informed, which lessens the fortuitous nature of the letter-reading ceremony,[19] will ironically burst the bubble of their illusions.

The tight construction of ***Le Misanthrope*** has been equated with the linear progression of the tragic plot. The structure of Molière's play is nearer, however, to the symmetrical rhythm of farce. Comparison with the circular structure of ***George Dandin,*** which itself derives from Native French Farce,[20] would seem more appropriate. The ending of ***Le***

Misanthrope brings us full circle, back to the point of departure. Alceste's entrance in a state of high dudgeon parallels his exit; on both occasions he is pursued by the unrelenting Philinte. Alceste's final exit is merely the fifth of a series of departures which occur at the end of each act: at the end of Act I he storms off with Philinte in pursuit; at the end of Act III he leaves with Arsinoé in search of proof of Célimène's infidelity; at the end of Acts II and IV he is summoned to appear before the *maréchaux.* In addition, Alceste's repeated threats to leave (95-96; 143-44; 1486; 1521-24; 1573; 1762) give to his final gesture a certain theatricality which distances the audience from the interpretation Alceste places on his departure.

The repetitive, circular pattern conveys in the central character the rigidity and inelasticity which, for Bergson, was the hallmark of the comic hero.[21] Apart from the change in the relationship between Philinte and Éliante, any sixth Act could well be a repetition of the first Act. The fact that there have been a number of sequels to ***Le Misanthrope*** indicates how far we are from the closed world of Racine in which heroes and heroines are irrevocably separated, usually by death.

The comic 'action' of ***Le Misanthrope*** also implies a lack of 'recognition' on the part of the main characters. The extent to which the characters are 'enlightened' has been a contentious issue. Critics have tended to find the 'discovery' of Célimène's duplicity pathetic. In most Racinian plays, the principal source of pathos is the character's apprehension of a tragic destiny:[22] in *Bérénice,* the titular heroine is brought to a realization that she has misunderstood the situation Titus was in, and ultimately perceives the futility of her projected suicide; in *Phèdre,* Thésée is forced to recognize the folly of his hasty judgement (sending Hippolyte to his death on false circumstantial evidence); in *Mithridate,* the eponymous hero's discoveries are equally poignant: that Monime is in love with his son, Xipharès, that the latter has been disloyal to him in the avowal of his love for Monime and that the invasion of Italy has had disastrous consequences. However, both the device used to bring about 'recognition' in ***Le Misanthrope*** and the primarily intellectual nature of the 'discovery' made by most of the characters preserve the comic register.

The means used to bring about 'discovery', the exchange of letters, is found more frequently in comedy than in tragedy. The establishment of true identity by means of material objects was used by tragic dramatists like Quinault and Boyer. Corneille and Racine, however, rejected this kind of 'material discovery'.[23] Molière explored the comic possibilities afforded by the reading of letters on stage (there are fifteen instances in nine of his plays[24]). Six years after the creation of ***Le Misanthrope,*** he was to parody the device of 'material discovery' in Ariste's 'false letters' which serve to bring about a satisfying comic closure in ***Les Femmes savantes.***

The 'discovery' made by most of the characters in ***Le Misanthrope*** is primarily intellectual. The moral and psychological self-appraisal conducted by many Racinian heroes and heroines is absent. Some of the sequels to the play have tried to fill this *lacuna.* In Fabre d'Eglantine's *Le Philinte de Molière ou la suite du Misanthrope,* Alceste benefits from his solitude and becomes a virtuous provincial landowner, filled with a love of humanity. In his *conte, Le Misanthrope corrigé,* Marmontel draws a moral lesson from Alceste's discomfiture. Courteline's *La Conversion d'Alceste* focuses on the reformed *misanthrope*'s return from self-exile. In Molière's text, there is no indication of any conversion. On the contrary, Molière emphasises the characters' self-delusion. This is rendered comic by the incongruity between the language they use and the situation in which the author has placed them. The mental blindness of Acaste, Clitandre, Oronte and Arsinoé anticipates in varying degrees that of Alceste and Célimène.

There is a disparity between Acaste's uncritical self-portrait in Act III, scene 1 and the disparaging sketch of him by Célimène: 'je trouve qu'il n'y a rien de si mince que toute sa personne; et ce sont de ces mérites qui n'ont que la cape et l'épée' (Act V, scene 4). Acaste's use of familiar expressions ('A vous le dé, Monsieur' and 'Voici votre paquet' are, as Rudler has pointed out,[25] not recorded in the *Dictionnaire de l'Académie*) and of mercenary language ('des coeurs du plus haut prix') contradicts his earlier claim to good taste, which had already been called into question by his extended mercantile imagery in Act III, scene 1. His minatory tone and use of the word 'se consoler' belie his contention that he is not piqued by his 'discovery': 'Mais je ne vous tiens pas digne de ma colère' (1696). Clitandre shows no self-awareness in his juvenile threats of revenge on the portrait artist: 'Il suffit, nous allons, l'un, et l'autre, en tous lieux, / Montrer de votre coeur le portrait glorieux' (1693-94). The *petits marquis*'s complete about-turn (cf. their adulation of Célimène in the *scène des portraits*) shows their distorted optic.

Oronte, imitating the tragic hero, bemoans his lack of foresight and professes to have learned from his experience:

> Allez, j'étais trop dupe, et je vais ne plus l'être.
>
> Vous me faites un bien, me faisant vous connaître:
>
> J'y profite d'un coeur qu'ainsi vous me rendez (. . .)
>
> (1703-05)

Oronte's closing remarks reveal, however, the obliquity of his vision. He does not take cognizance of the corrections made of his style by both Alceste and Célimène: note his exaggeratedly precious: 'votre coeur, paré de beaux semblants d'amour, / A tout le genre humain se promet tour à tour!' his mercenary imagery: 'un bien', 'profite', 'conclure affaire'; the inadequate formulation 'je vous ai vu écrire' (Oronte has not actually seen Célimène writing the letters).[26] Moreover, Oronte's confession of his error of judgement is itself hybristic: note his conviction that Célimène will be the loser; that he himself has regained his freedom; and that he is the obstacle to the relationship between Alceste and Célimène.

Arsinoé, who seeks to 'enlighten' others regarding Célimène's duplicity, is paradoxically the least 'enlightened' from a moral or psychological standpoint. Her response to the disclosure of Célimène's double-dealing is pharisaical: note the comic irony of her quasi-exclamatory statement and rhetorical question: 'Certes, voilà le trait du monde le plus noir (. . .) Voit-on des procédés qui soient pareils aux vôtres?' Fired by jealousy, Arsinoé fails to perceive how Alceste has behaved towards Célimène: 'Un homme comme lui, de mérite et d'honneur, / Et qui vous chérissait avec idolâtrie (. . .)'; 'idolâtrie' ('adoration des faux Dieux' (Richelet)) can hardly be applied to Alceste's method of wooing! Alceste's brusque contradiction of Arsinoé's thumbnail sketch of him produces a *volte-face*. Arsinoé's eulogy gives way to vituperation (1725); elevated abstractions are replaced by vulgar expressions: 'avoir', 'rebut', 'marchandise' (1724, 1727). Her exhortation to Alceste to undeceive himself and to recognize his pride (1729) gives further comic irony to her lack of self-awareness (note the unconscious irony of 'émouvoir' (1710) and the double irony of: 'Et je brûle de voir une union si belle' (1732)).

Alceste comes nearest to the tragic hero's confession of human limitation. On three occasions he lays claim to 'enlightenment'. On the first occasion he declares his 'faiblesse' and his humanity:

> Et je vous fais, tous deux, témoins de ma faiblesse.
> Mais, à vous dire vrai, ce n'est pas encor tout,
>
> Et vous allez me voir la pousser jusqu'au bout,
>
> Montrer que c'est à tort que sages on nous nomme,
>
> Et que, dans tous les coeurs, il est toujours de l'homme.
>
> (1752-56)

His confession, however, does not have any humbling effect or lead to any reevaluation of his conduct. His humanity is illustrated ironically in his detailed elaboration: he apportions all the blame to Célimène and offers the paradoxical solution of 'fuir tous les humains' (1762). Alceste's 'discovery' of his weakness emerges from his imitation of the tragic hero's classical dilemma:

> Hé! le puis-je, traîtresse?
>
> Puis-je ainsi triompher de toute ma tendresse?
>
> Et quoique avec ardeur je veuille vous haïr,
>
> Trouvé-je un coeur en moi tout prêt à m'obéir?
>
> (1747-1750)

Alceste's dilemma is, however, a false one based on a misapprehension of his 'tendresse' and on a rationalisation of his temperamental peculiarity (as the subtitle suggests Alceste is an *atrabilaire*). His offer of clemency ('oublier vos forfaits (. . .) excuser tous les traits') is in no way magnanimous. It is undermined by the intransigence of his terms ('Pourvu que (. . .) c'est par là seulement') and by the brutal language in which he formulates his final rejection of Célimène: 'Non, mon coeur, à présent, vous déteste (. . .)' (1779). Such categorical expression jars with the idealised portrayal of his love for her:

> Puisque vous n'êtes point, en des liens si doux,
>
> Pour trouver tout en moi, comme moi tout en vous (. . .)
>
> (1781-82)

Alceste's casting of himself in the role of a seventeenth-century Tristan or Lancelot gives further emphasis to his blindness.

Alceste's second claim to 'enlightenment' is again expressed in the diction of the tragic hero:

> Je m'en sens trop indigne, et commence à connaître
> Que le Ciel, pour ce noeud, ne m'avait point fait naître.
>
> (1791-92)

The context makes this 'discovery' heavily ironic. Alceste's self-deprecatory tone is both a rationalisation of his failure with Célimène and a means of extricating himself from the extravagant proposal he had made to Éliante in Act IV, scene 2. His tragic diction is unnecessary as Éliante no longer wanted to marry him. (Alceste's lengthy justification of his rejection of Éliante is punctured by her laconic interruption: 'Vous pouvez suivre cette pensée' (1795).) A further irony arises from the timing of Alceste's diplomacy: if he had used such expression to Célimène the situation might well have been different.

Alceste's third 'discovery'—of the restorative properties of the 'désert'—is equally ironic. His moment of 'recognition' has been compared to a conversion to Jansenism.[27] His 'désert' would become a kind of religious retreat where he can find serenity. But Alceste has not suddenly seen the light: the structure of the play suggests that the 'désert' is for Alceste a kind of *idée fixe*. Moreover, Alceste's *contemptus mundi* lacks the self-abasement of the *solitaires*. The religious language, 'le désert ou j'ai fait voeu de vivre', is for Alceste merely a vehicle for self-martyrdom. Mortification and penitence would have been inflicted on Célimène and not on himself: 'C'est par là seulement que (. . .) Vous pouvez réparer le mal de vos écrits,' (1765-66). Alceste's vision of the 'désert' has also been situated within the pastoral tradition.[28] Alceste's retreat from Paris is not however in pursuit of the rustic simplicity and purity of an earlier age. Alceste is no pastoralist: he retires to his country house, not to kill venison for his beloved or to cultivate gallantry. Alceste has not the humour of the countryman; in addition, Célimène will be left behind. A third interpretation turns Alceste's final speech into a quasi-phenomenological, quasi-Sartrian discovery of the 'liberté de la conscience de l'identité'.[29] This anachronistic reading fails to take account of the context of Alceste's declaration of triumph.

Alceste's parting lines confirm that, like other monomaniacs, he has not evolved emotionally or morally, despite all his protestations of lucidity. His benediction of the marriage of Philinte and Éliante (1801-02) contains negative undertones: the emphasis on 'vrais contentements' and on 'garder' shows that he sees their marriage through the prism of his own disappointment. Heralded by the empty hyperbole to which we have become accustomed (1803-06), Alceste's exit is mock-tragic. His self-delusion is reflected in the final paradox: his search for freedom in separation from the rest of humanity. The root causes of Alceste's failure lie not in the 'gouffre où triomphent les vices' but primarily in himself: his extremism (both in language and in behaviour) in the polite society founded on principles of moderation and of tolerance; his self-righteousness, in his clearsightedness with regard to the sins of others, but cecity with regard to his own; his self-absorption in, as Guicharnaud has suggested,[30] Alceste's wish to make Célimène a female version of himself.

Molière dispels any doubt concerning the comic status of Alceste's final 'discovery' with Philinte's curtain line. Producers who have given a dark interpretation of the hero have generally omitted Philinte's couplet in order to give to Alceste the isolation appropriate to a tragic hero. But as Hope has observed, it is essential that Philinte should have the last word to remind us of the circularity of the play.[31]

Modern interpretations of ***Le Misanthrope*** have sometimes found 'tragic discovery' in Célimène. Her exit in Dux's influential production 'left not a dry eye in the house'.[32] Guicharnaud's magisterial study has given weight to the notion of a tragic Célimène:

> le personnage 'tragique' dans ***Le Misanthrope,*** ce n'est peut-être pas Alceste, c'est Célimène, car c'est vraiment elle qui tombe de haut (. . .) Au centre de la pièce, la compréhension dans la haine annonçait ce morceau de la fin où s'exprime la compréhension dans l'amour. Il n'empêche qu'une illumination de ce genre est unique dans le théâtre de Molière, elle se situe bien *au-delà* de la comédie dont le finale a été escamoté.[33]

Célimène does acknowledge her mistakes: 'Vous en êtes en droit (. . .) J'ai tort, je le confesse (. . .) je tombe d'accord de mon crime envers vous (. . .) vous avez sujet de me haïr' (1737-1746). But her expression of guilt is attenuated by the use of modal verbs: 'je dois vous paraître coupable (. . .) j'ai pu vous trahir'. Nowhere does she give unequivocal expression to the fact of her deception. Célimène chooses a form of words which she thinks will be acceptable to Alceste. Her muted confession can therefore be seen as an attempt to pacify him. In believing that a marriage with Alceste can be contracted with merely the mildest expression of contrition on her part she betrays a naïvety rarely perceived in the role by critics.

Any 'enlightenment' on the stage is experienced by Philinte and Éliante, who, we have seen, demonstrate a willingness to learn from the experience of others. Yet even they are not possessed of all knowledge. Philinte's final couplet shows a degree of ingenuousness in his determination to bring back to Paris Éliante's 'first love' and in his belief that he will be able to achieve this feat—a more probable scenario is that Alceste will return of his own accord to give full vent to his misanthropy.

I have tried to show that the dénouement completes the comic 'action'. Lessons go unheeded by all but Philinte and Éliante, and even they are not free from error. Apart from their wedding, nothing is resolved. The problems of character remain: the misanthropication of Alceste is more extreme; Célimène's duplicity has been temporarily checked but uncorrected; the *marquis* set off to air their grievances elsewhere; Oronte will seek a 'superior' audience to listen to his inept poetry. The characters are locked in circularity, not unlike the protagonists of the farce tradition. In one sense, the ending of ***Le Misanthrope*** is more pessimistic than that of any Racinian tragedy.[34] The underlying pessimism, however, does not call into question the comic status of the play: it merely illustrates the central paradox of the comic *genre.*

Notes

1. R. Horville, *Le Misanthrope de Molière* (Paris: Hatier: Profil d'une oeuvre, 1981), p. 70.

2. Notably by J. D. Hubert, *Molière and the Comedy of Intellect* (California: University of California Press, 1962); F. L. Lawrence, 'Our Alceste or Nature's? A Problem of Interpretation', *Revue des langues vivantes,* 38 (1972); A. Eustis, *Molière as Ironic Contemplator* (The Hague: Mouton, 1973); R. McBride, *The Sceptical Vision of Molière* (London: Macmillan, 1977); W. D. Howarth, *Molière: A Playwright and his Audience* (C.U.P., 1982). These interpretations have not gone unchallenged: see, for example, M. Gutwirth's refutation of Hubert's view that Alceste is a 'héros burlesque' ('Visages d'Alceste', *Oeuvres et critiques,* 6, i (1981), p. 80).

3. Goethe asks: 'Ob jemals ein Dichter sein Inneres vollkommener und liebenswürdiger dargestellt habe' (see H. R. Jauss, 'The Paradox of the Misanthrope', *Comparative Literature,* 35 (1983), p. 318).

4. For A. Thibaudet ('Le Rire de Molière', *Revue de Paris,* 29 (1922), 99-125), once the *marquis* have left 'on ne rit ni d'Alceste ni de Célimène, et la scène n'a plus rien de comique, elle est simplement humaine'; for J. Arnavon (*Le Misanthrope de Molière* (Paris: 1930), especially pp. 272-73) Alceste's exit is profoundly moving.

5. E.g. A. Adam, *Histoire de la littérature française* (Paris: Éditions mondiales, 1962), III, p. 343: 'la comédie tend vers le drame'; P. J. Yarrow, 'A Reconsideration of Alceste', *French Studies,* 13 (1959), 314-331, p. 328: 'Molière appears to have begun by intending Alceste to be a comic figure, but, in the heat of the composition, his original conception developed and broke through the bounds of comedy; the creature took hold of the creator,

and Molière came to sympathize more and more with Alceste, to make him more complex and human, possibly to put more and more of himself into him'; J. Guicharnaud, *Molière: une aventure théâtrale* (Paris: Gallimard, 1963), p. 483: 'En guise de finale, théâtralement satisfaisante, la pièce nous offre le spectacle tout humain d'une véritable agonie'; Simone Dosmond, 'Le Dénouement du *Misanthrope*: Une "source" méconnue?', *La Licorne,* VII (1983), 25-40, p. 25: 'L'exil de "l'homme aux rubans verts", l'humiliation publique infligée à la coquette qui demeure seule au milieu de son salon (presque) désert sont loin, en effet, d'engendrer l'euphorie qui caractérise, en principe, les dénouements de comédies. Ne pourrait-on pas, dès lors, considérer Molière comme le créateur d'un genre hybride: la comédie à fin malheureuse?'

6. E.g. J. Morel compares the ending of *Le Misanthrope* with that of *Bérénice* (see J. Dubu, 'Molière et le tragique', *XVII*[e] *Siècle,* 98-99 (1973), p. 53); J. Cairncross, *Molière bourgeois et libertin* (Paris: Nizet, 1963), p. 84: 'Au cinquième acte, le doute ne subsiste ni sur la situation elle-même, ni sur l'angle sous lequel Molière présente l'amour d'Alceste. Nous voilà dans le monde fermé et sombre de Racine, de la tragédie la plus émouvante'; A. Szogyi, *Molière abstrait* (Paris: Nizet, 1985), p. 108: 'Nulle part ailleurs la planète moliéresque n'est aussi tragiquement dénudée, livrée sans espoir au désaccord, au gaspillage tragique (. . .) *Le Misanthrope* est un duel à mort, un combat sans merci avant l'halali de sa coquette proie'.
7. See H. T. Barnwell, *The Tragic Drama of Corneille and Racine: An Old Parallel Revisited* (O.U.P., 1982), p. 168. For an illuminating analysis of the significance of 'action' in Corneille and Racine see in particular pp. 1-31.
8. P. Corneille, *Writings on the Theatre,* ed. H. T. Barnwell (Oxford: Blackwell, 1965), p. 9.
9. J. Racine, Preface to *Bérénice* in *Oeuvres,* ed. P. Mesnard (Paris: Hachette, 1865), II, p. 366.
10. See Corneille, op. cit., p. 10.
11. All quotations from *Le Misanthrope* are taken from G. Rudler's edition (Oxford: Blackwell, 1972). References are to line numbers.
12. J. Mairet, *Préface de La Silvanire ou La Morte—vive, Oeuvres* (Paris: Rocolet, 1631), vol. II.
13. J. Chapelain, *Opuscules critiques,* ed. A. C. Hunter (Paris: Droz, 1936), p. 130.
14. F. H. abbé d'Aubignac, *La Pratique du théâtre,* ed. P. Martino (Paris: Champion, 1927), p. 276.
15. Corneille, op. cit., pp. 8-9.
16. J. Scherer, *La Dramaturgie classique en France* (Paris: Nizet, 1950), pp. 139-40.
17. Dosmond, op. cit., p. 25.
18. See also for example: *Les Précieuses ridicules, Le Mariage forcé, Dom Juan, George Dandin.*
19. See J. L. Shepherd, III, 'Arsinoé as Puppeteer', *French Review,* 42 (1968-69), 262-71.
20. See my edition: *La Jalousie du Barbouillé et George Dandin* (Exeter: Textes littéraires, LV), 1984.
21. H. Bergson, *Le Rire* (Paris: Alcan, 1900).
22. See Barnwell, op. cit., pp. 159-78. I am using 'recognition', 'discovery', 'enlightenment' as synonymous and as an equivalent of Aristotle's *anagorisis.*
23. Ibid., pp. 164-66.
24. See R. Duchêne, 'Molière et la lettre', *Travaux de linguistique et de littérature,* XIII, 2 (1975), pp. 261-73.
25. See Rudler, ed. cit., p. 139.
26. Ibid.
27. Cf. Robinet, *Lettres en vers,* 12 juin 1666:

    Et ce *Misanthrope* est si sage,
    En frondant les moeurs de notre âge,
    Que l'on dirait, benoît lecteur,
    Qu'on entend un prédicateur.
    Aucune morale chrétienne
    N'est plus louable que la sienne (. . .)

    See G. Mongrédien, *Recueil des textes et des documents du XVII*[c] *siède relatifs à Molière* (Paris: Centre National de la Recherche Scientifique, 1965), I, p. 266. Modern criticism has revived this notion: see in particular M. Deutsch, 'Le vertige Alceste', in J. P. Vincent *et al., Alceste et l'Absolutisme: essais de dramaturgie sur Le Misanthrope* (Paris: Galilée, 1977), pp. 85-103; Dosmond (op. cit), who pictures Alceste as 'le nouveau compagnon de Nicole et de Lancelot'.
28. For further discussion of Christian and pastoral interpretations see L. Lerner, *The Literary Imagination* (Sussex: The Harvester Press, 1982), pp. 24-38.
29. G. A. Goldschmidt, *Molière ou la liberté mise à nu* (Paris: Julliard, 1973), p. 93.
30. Op. cit., p. 485.
31. Q. Hope, 'Molière's Curtain Lines', *French Studies,* 26 (1972), p. 148.
32. For a review of the production see R. W. Herzel, 'Much Depends on the Acting: the Original Cast of *Le Misanthrope*', *PMLA,* 95 (1980), 348-66 (especially 348-51).
33. Op. cit., pp. 473, 485.
34. See Barnwell's application of the paradox to tragedy (op. cit., particularly, pp. 249-50): 'Tragedy disturbs the order of the moral universe, but it also restores it'.

L'AVARE

CRITICAL COMMENTARY

Dorothy F. Jones (essay date 1988)

SOURCE: "The Treasure in the Garden: Biblical Imagery in *L' Avare*," in *Papers on French Seventeenth Century Literature,* Vol. XV, No. 29, 1988, pp. 517-28.

[*In the following essay, Jones emphasizes the importance of the symbolic garden treasure—representing both death and life—presented in Molière's* L'Avare.]

Harpagon's treasure—his "chère cassette"—has received considerable attention as a central symbol in ***L'Avare.*** "Cette petite cassette grise . . . est le personnage principal," declares Couton in his Pléiade edition of the play.[1] In their staging, directors such as Jacques Mauclair and Charles Dullin have emphasized the tie between the miser and his treasure. A famous photo of Dullin in the title role shows him cheek to cheek with his cassette, in a terrible parody of lovers united. More recently, in Roger Planchon's 1986 production, Harpagon falls sobbing across the cassette in a tearful embrace as the curtain drops. But an equally important symbol has gone largely unnoticed: the garden where Harpagon's treasure is buried throughout most of the play.

No garden appears in Molière's principal source, the *Aulularia* of Plautus. Euclion's pot of gold is hid not in his garden but in the hearth of his house, and he twice moves it in the course of the play. Far from being linked to a particular place, the treasure is in almost constant movement. Nor has the garden received much attention from directors and scene designers. No trace of it remains in Jean Vilar's abstract platform setting (TNP, 1952), or in Jacques Mauclair's claustrophobic interior (Comédie française, 1962), nor do the files of the Arsenal, with one exception, show its appearance in earlier productions. Even Planchon, who expands his set beyond the confines of Harpagon's house, makes no attempt to show the garden itself.[2]

Yet there are clear indications that the garden appeared in Molière's own *mise en scène*. "[Le] théâtre est une salle, et sur le derrière, un jardin," wrote Laurent Mahelot, describing the original set for ***L'Avare.***[3] Roger Herzel, basing his case on an analysis of Brissart's 1682 illustrations, argues convincingly that the garden was visible through an arch at the back of the stage throughout most of the play.[4] With this precedent in mind, both Jacques Arnavon and Charles Dullin gave the garden a central place in their own décor.[5] "En réalité," writes Arnavon, "le centre du décor, c'est ce jardin dont on parle incessamment et qu'on voit à peine parce que c'est la qu'est la cassette. Comme on n'y peut passer la scène, il est indispensable de le rappeler d'une manière ou d'une autre à chaque acte" (pp. 241-242). Arnavon's proposed sets show large bay windows at the back of the stage opening onto the greenery and light of a garden behind (pp. 242, 315). And in his inventive production of the play in 1940, Dullin places the wall of the garden, "épais et hérissé de défenses" and backed by large trees, downstage right in view of the audience. Justifying his staging, he writes: "Reprenant l'indication de Mahelot . . . j'ai donné dans la mise en scène plus de présence au jardin . . . En effet, ce jardin est un pole d'attraction. C'est là qu'Harpagon a enfoui son trésor. Il y va continuellement. Il en écoute tous les bruits. C'est du jardin que partiront ses cris de désespoir: 'Au voleur! au voleur!' C'est le lieu dramatique par excellence" (p. 16).

An analysis of the text of the play confirms this sense of the garden's importance. Seen or unseen, the garden is evoked in every act of ***L'Avare*** in text, *didascalie,* or gesture, as follows:

> Act I: The word is mentioned once by Harpagon and once in stage directions. ". . . Je ne sais si j'aurai bien fait d'avoir enterré dans mon jardin dix mille écus . . ." (I,4). "Il regarde vers le jardin" (I,5). Harpagon makes one exit to the garden and returns.
>
> Act II: Harpagon makes a second trip to the garden and returns. This time the word itself has been replaced by "mon argent": "Il est à propos que je fasse un petit tour à mon argent" (II,3).
>
> Act III: Harpagon makes no reference to the garden and no trips to it. But the garden is mentioned by Cléante, who exits to it with the lovers: "Je vais . . . conduire Madame dans le jardin, où je ferai porter la collation" (III,9).
>
> Act IV: Movement from the garden intensifies. We see three entrances: the lovers return from the garden (sc.1), followed later by La Flèche with the cassette (sc.6) and by Harpagon himself (sc.7). Two references in stage directions emphasize these last two entrances.
>
> Act V: There are no exits or entrances from the garden. The word itself reappears twice in the interrogation of Maître Jacques by Harpagon, who also refers to it as the "lieu où j'avais mis mon argent."

A number of observations occur here. The garden is never described. With one exception, every reference to it, verbal or gestural, associates it with money. It is for most of the play primarily "le lieu où j'avais mis mon argent" and Harpagon's obsessive exits—Dullin increases their number—show the strength of this "pole d'attraction." Physical movement to or from the garden appears in every act but one. It ceases abruptly at the end of Act IV when the cassette has been stolen. The appearance of La Flèche, "sortant du jardin, avec une cassette" (IV,6), is the visual climax of this link between treasure and garden. It is also the moment when the link between the two is broken, as the treasure passes into Cléante's hands. When the money is removed from the garden, Harpagon follows it onstage immediately, and his loss, significantly, is expressed largely in terms of spatial disorientation. Even the boundary of the ramp breaks down as he addresses the audience directly.

His "au voleur" tirade contains no fewer than thirteen spatial references, beginning with the frantic succession of five 'où?" which culminates in his "j'ignore où je suis, qui je suis . . . je suis enterré," as he becomes the lost treasure he himself had buried. No one enters or leaves the garden after this point in the play.

But in Act II, when the treasure is still safely underground, Harpagon does not enter the garden at all. In fact if one may accept Herzel's convincing reconstruction, the garden was not even visible to Molière's audience during that act, when a *ferme* would have been drawn across to conceal it temporarily from view (p. 947). This is the act when Mariane first appears (III,4), and Harpagon's attention is turned towards the young girl he plans to marry. This interruption of his exits to the garden suggests the strength of his involvement with her. But what is more important is that his place is taken by Cléante. In a moment which Gaston Hall describes as a "mime of death,"[6] Harpagon is knocked down by his servant. He recovers to hear his son announce, "Je vais faire pour vous, mon père, les honneurs de votre logis, et conduire Madame dans le jardin, où je ferai porter la collation" (III,9). For the first time the garden is associated not with Harpagon's sterile treasure, but with youth, love, and nurture.

This contrast seems to me the key to the rôle of the garden in the play. Cléante's garden is the archetypal garden of love and delight, associated throughout western literature with the body of woman, with fertility and nourishment.[7] It is the antithesis of Harpagon's dusty hiding place, that "terre lourde, sans soleil" which Robert Jouanny imagines.[8] When Cléante exits to the garden, he gathers about him all the company of lovers, and even Frosine, in a move towards fellowship and celebration. Harpagon's own exits to the garden are always solitary; each time he withdraws he turns his back on society, leaving behind onstage his son and daughter in Act I, his guest, Frosine, in Act II. Cléante's own sortie in Act III is short-lived—the lovers return at the beginning of Act IV with "Rentrons ici, nous serons beaucoup mieux" (IV,1)—but his brief possession of the garden is long enough to remind us of its true nature and the extent to which Harpagon has disfigured it. This reminder comes at the midpoint of the play, and only with Mariane's entrance. She is as naturally associated with the garden for her lover as is that other feminine symbol, the cassette, Harpagon's own grotesque mistress.

For Cléante, moreover, the garden is also the place of the "collation" he offers Mariane. This love feast of fruits, the "bassins d'oranges," "citrons doux," "confitures" is itself another archetypal image, the banquet—specifically, that nuptial feast which so often, in comedy, celebrates the union of lovers at the end of the play. Northrop Frye points out how such "festive ritual" is normally associated with the emergence of the new society which "crystallizes" around the hero (*Anatomy,* p. 163). Cléante's collation is set in ironic juxtaposition to the two other "nuptial banquets" which precede it in Act III: the empty meal which exists only in Maître Jacque's frustrated imagination ("il faudra quatre grands potages et cinq assiettes. Potages . . . Entrées . . . Entremets . . ."), and the inverted banquet which Harpagon plans for his fiancée, where the guests will be encouraged to eat as little as possible ("Il faudra de ces choses dont on ne mange guère . . ."). The parodic nature of these other meals is brought into focus by their contrast with the generous table Cléante spreads for his beloved in the garden.

The recurrent descriptions of Harpagon's *sécheresse* take on their full power if seen in the context of the garden. "Il n'est rien de plus sec et de plus aride que ses bonnes graces," says La Flèche of his master (II,4). Cléante speaks at the very beginning of the play of "cette sécheresse étrange où l'on nous fait languir" (I,2). Critics seem irresistibly drawn to images of dryness in describing Harpagon. "Harpagon flétrit tout ce qu'il touche," writes Jacques Copeau, "desséche tout ce qui l'entoure . . . les deux traits qui le caractérisent sont la sécheresse et la dureté." "Everything that comes into contact with him shrivels," says Quentin Hope. Harpagon is the parody of the true gardener. The seed he plants is lifeless, and his very burial of the gold, as Marcel Gutwirth points out, symbolizes his relationship to his wealth. "Cet or, il se charge de l'enterrer, d'immobiliser la somme de vie, d'activités, d'échanges, de bonheur possible qu'il contient."[9]

In contrast, the image most associated with the lovers is water. Almost all the lovers are rescued from the water, as is the "good father," Anselme, who arrives at the end of the play. There has been much discussion of this romanesque dénouement, in which the survivors of "that classical shipwreck"[10] are reunited. But few critics have commented on the fact that Harpagon's daughter Elise has also been saved from the waves, and that her rescue is the basis of her love for Valère. Only Cléante has for some reason been spared this experience. In Roger Planchon's production, exploitation of water as a symbol is carried beyond the text. The Act I tête-à-tête between Elise and Valère begins with an erotic tumble amid the flapping sheets in the household laundry, after which Elise clambers into a large wooden bathtub onstage to bathe. And at the end of the play, when the lovers triumph, the very wall of Harpagon's house crumbles, to reveal in a blaze of light the tossing waves of the shipwreck and rescue.

The garden is therefore the focus for a whole cluster of archetypal images in ***L'Avare,*** images which enrich a play that Molière's contemporaries complained was only written in prose. But the full power of these images emerges if we now replace them in the context of the religious tradition within which Molière wrote.

L'Avare is the only one of Molière's plays in which the protagonist's mania is one of the seven deadly sins. Avarice is treated with particular seriousness in the Bible, where love of money is presented as the antithesis of the love of God. "No one can serve two masters," we are told flatly in the New Testament, "You cannot serve God and money" (Matt. 6:24). The same polarity appears in the admonition not to "lay up . . . treasures on earth, where moth and rust consume and where thieves break in and steal" but to "lay up treasures in heaven," because "where your treasure is, there will your heart be also" (Matt. 6:19-21). Love of money is seen as idolatry, the worship of a false god (Col. 3:5, Eph. 5:5). In contrast, the biblical image most often used to express a right relationship with God is marriage. Israel is the beloved of Yahweh in the Old Testament, as the Church is the Bride of Christ in the New. The banquet is the celebration of this relationship, the symbol of communion in God's love. "He who has no money, come, buy and eat!" urges Isaiah (55:1), while in the New Testament the hungry are told they will be filled and the faithful are invited to the wedding feast of the Lamb (Matt. 22,25; Rev. 19:9). Spiritual death is often expressed in terms of dryness, the "dry and weary land where no water is" of the Psalms (63:1), or the desert wilderness where the Israelites turn from God to worship the golden calf in Exodus. Water has a dual role, as Northrop Frye points out (*Code,* p. 145). Symbol of death and chaos—there will be no more sea in the redeemed world of Revelation (21:1)—it is also the source of life, the "living water" which Christ offers the Samaritan woman and all those who thirst (John 4). The sacrament of baptism, within the Christian tradition, combines these two aspects: after an immersion which symbolizes the death of the old self, one rises from the water into new life and communion, symbolized in a new name. And what of the garden? From the garden of Eden to that of Gethsemane, from the "enclosed garden" which is the bride's body in the Song of Songs to the place where the risen Christ appears as a gardener to Mary Magdalene, this image is one of the most powerful recurrent symbols in the Bible, symbol of fruitfulness and new life, of God's concern for creation. "The city, the garden, and the sheepfold," says Northrop Frye, "are the organizing metaphors of the Bible and of most Christian symbolism" (*Anatomy,* p. 141).

Viewed against this biblical background, the dominant images of ***L'Avare*** take on new life. Critics have frequently commented on the basic polarity underlying the play. Judd Hubert speaks of "the incompatible worlds of love and avarice," of the "strong opposition between generosity and happiness on the one hand, avarice on the other," and concludes that "the entire comedy consists in artificially forcing together two series of mutually exclusive concepts and attitudes, only to have them break apart with increasing violence . . ." (pp. 32, 33). In contrast to this critical view, however, audiences themselves frequently have an initial sense of moral uneasiness. The play seems very black indeed: honest Maître Jacques is taught to lie, Valère pursues his love by hypocrisy and flattery, Cléante robs and blackmails his father. But the imagery, rooted in the Bible, counters this ambiguity and rights the balance, suggesting that the battle in the play is a more clearcut contest between good and evil than at first appears. Harpagon is not merely the rapacious Parisian bourgeois, but the worshiper of the golden calf, the idolater who will sacrifice all to a false god. When he sends his son to "boire un grand verre d'eau claire" (I,4), his gesture is not merely niggardly but a terrible parody of the love of God which Christ urges us to express by giving "even a cup of cold water" to "one of these little ones" (Matt. 10:42). The miserly meal Harpagon will serve his unwilling fiancée recalls in irony its biblical opposite, the banquet to which a generous God invites creation. Harpagon's *sécheresse* goes beyond the psychological to symbolize his spiritual death. The Bible reminds us that the cassette he has buried contains not only 10,000 écus but also his heart.

Thanks to this imagery, Cléante, Elise, Mariane and Valère—those who in contrast serve "le dieu qui porte les excuses de tout ce qu'il fait faire, l'Amour" (V,3)—can hardly help being on the side of the angels. Cléante's candied fruit becomes a true love feast, reflecting those nuptial banquets which celebrate God's love, spread in a garden which evokes the Creator of all life. Through her association with the garden, Mariane, unscathed by those dubious years of slavery on the high seas, remains the virginal bride of the Song of Songs, like that other Lady of the Garden whom her name recalls. Even La Flèche's theft of the cassette reminds us that Christ too, after all, will "come as a thief in the night" (1 Thess.5:2) to ensure the triumph of love. At the end of the play these lovers rise from the waters of death into new life, newly baptized as Neapolitan aristocrats, to enter marriages that symbolize in biblical terms not only their own union but that between God and creation.

The biblical imagery of the play thus reinforces the binary structure which gives ***L'Avare*** it unity. The comic conflict takes on a deeper resonance. This is particularly true of the play's central image, the treasure in the garden. In the Bible, treasure is, not surprisingly, a symbol of one's ultimate commitment. For Harpagon clearly the cassette is this treasure, and he endows his sterile gold with all the power of a god: "Mon cher ami . . . mon support, ma consolation, ma joie . . . sans toi il m'est impossible de vivre" (IV,7). The garden where the cassette is buried is for him primarily "le lieu où j'avais mis mon argent," an inviolate (so he hopes) space to which he withdraws from our sight like a priest entering the holy of holies. The cassette's sudden first appearance onstage in Act IV in the hands of La Flèche has all the power of an epiphany. But as the garden is transformed into its opposite, in a kind of baroque metamorphosis, by the arrival of Mariane and the true lovers in Act III, the cassette, unearthed, also changes its nature. Buried, it is a symbol of wasted life, of idolatrous and fearful commitment to the perishable. "Raised" up, ironically by La Flèche, it takes on a new "imperishable" identity, to use the terms in which Paul describes the Resurrection (I. Cor.15:42). In the hands of those who love, the cassette, described for the first time in Act IV not as money but as "le trésor de votre père," becomes a treasure of an opposite sort.

There are two major steps in this transformation. The first is the famous *quiproquo* of V,3, in which Harpagon accuses Valère of stealing the cassette, while Valère believes he is being accused of seducing Elise. Thanks to this comic misunderstanding, Harpagon's money is transformed into Elise, through the words of her lover: "C'est un trésor, il est vrai, et le plus précieux que vous ayez sans doute . . . Je vous le demande à genoux . . .". The second step occurs in the final scene of the play, when Cléante reappears. He offers to surrender the cassette in return for permission to marry Mariane. This transaction turns Harpagon's money almost literally into Cléante's bride to be, in an exchange which clearly contrasts commitment to the God who is Love with commitment to the god who is money. Both examples are thus symbolic expressions of the opposition inherent in the Bible's view of avarice as idolatry: one's treasure can be *either* God *or* money, not both.

No one enters the garden after the cassette has been removed. With their own treasure unearthed, the lovers are free to move elsewhere. They carry within themselves the promise of fruitfulness and new life. Led by their true father Anselme, they leave Harpagon's barren ground behind to be united offstage with an unseen and loving mother.

The treasure in the garden is thus the center of the group of biblical images which embody the themes and undergird the structure of ***L'Avare.*** The dual nature of this central image—symbol of death and symbol of life—is reinforced, finally, by its association with two parables well known to Molière's audience. In each, the image of buried money is a focus. The first is the parable of the talents. A master, we are told in Matthew 25:14-30, entrusts his property to his servants in the form of talents. Some use their gifts fruitfully, but one servant "was afraid" and "went and dug in the ground and hid his master's money." When the master returns, this "worthless servant" is condemned and his buried talent given to the faithful servants, "For to everyone who has will more be given, and he [sic] will have abundance; but from him who has not, even what he has will be taken away." The buried talent is a symbol of rejection of the abundant life offered by God in favor of a life immobilized, literally dead and buried, like the treasure which Harpagon, that other fearful servant, also hides in the ground. And at the end of the play, Harpagon, like the worthless servant, has also lost even what he had. His cassette has been returned to him, but his household is empty. Even Maître Jacques is no longer an ally. His children have transferred their allegiance to a true father and mother, and are ready, like the faithful servants of the parable, to "enter into the joy" of new and loving parents.

In the second parable, buried money has a positive value. "The kingdom of heaven," we are told, "is like treasure hidden in a field which a man [sic] found and covered up; then in his joy he goes and sells all that he has and buys that field" (Matt.13:44). For the lovers, those who "have abundance," Harpagon's wasted talent becomes this second treasure. Prepared, like Cléante, to give all they have to possess it, they serve a god Harpagon does not know, "le dieu qui porte les excuses de tout ce qu'il fait faire, l'Amour." At the end of ***L'Avare,*** through the power of love, Harpagon's sterile treasure in the garden becomes for these seekers of the kingdom the sign of new life, and the false god he worships yields to the true.

Notes

1. Molière, *Oeuvres complètes* (Paris: Gallimard, 1971), II, 513. Citations to *L'Avare* are to this edition. For a useful *état-présent* of studies of the play, see Barbara Alsip, "*L'Avare:* A History of Scholarship," *Oeuvres et critiques* VI, 1(été 1981), 99-110.
2. Photos of the Mauclair set may be found in many school editions: Bordas, Hatier, Larousse. For a brief description of the Vilar set, see M. Descotes, *Les grands rôles du théâtre de Molière* (Paris: PUF, 1960), 149.
3. *Le Mémoire de Mahelot,* ed. H. C. Lancaster (Paris: E. Champion, 1920), 118.
4. "The Décor of Molière's Stage: The Testimony of Brissart and Chauveau," *PMLA* 93 (Oct. 1978), 946-948.
5. *Notes sur l'interprétation de Molière* (Paris: Plon, 1923); *Molière, L'Avare: Mise en scène de Charles Dullin* (Paris: Seuil, 1946).
6. "Molière's Comic Images," *Molière: Stage and Study,* ed. W. G. Howarth and M. Thomas (Oxford: Clarendon, 1973), 54.
7. See Northrop Frye, *The Anatomy of Criticism* (Princeton, N.J.: Princeton University Press, 1957) and his *The Great Code: The Bible and Literature* (Toronto: Academic Press Canada, 1983).
8. Notice, *Molière, Théâtre complet* (Paris: Garnier, 1960), II, 236.
9. Molière, *Oeuvres,* éd. J. Copeau (Paris: A la cité des livres, 1928), VII, 102. Q. Hope, "Animals in Molière," *PMLA* 79 (Sept. 1964), 420. M. Gutwirth, *Molière ou l'invention comique* (Paris: Lettres modernes, 1966), 129. See also Ralph Albanese, "Argent et réification dans *L'Avare,*" *Esprit créateur* 21 (Fall 1981), 42: ". . . portrait fondé sur des images de stérilité et de sécheresse." J. Hubert, "Theme and Structure in *L'Avare,*" *PMLA* 75 (March 1960), 32: "Harpagon is frequently characterized by his *dureté* or *sécheresse.*" L . . ., "La Morale de Molière," *Le Molièriste* (mai 1883), 44: "l'avarice . . . dessèche et flétrit une âme humaine . . .".
10. M. Gutwirth, "The Unity of Molière's *L'Avare,*" *PMLA* 76 (1961), 363.

John McCann (essay date 1995)

SOURCE: "Harpagon: The Paradox of Miserliness," in *Papers on French Seventeenth Century Literature,* Vol. XXII, No. 43, 1995, pp. 555-69.

[In the following essay, McCann maintains that the character of Harpagon, of Molière's L'Avare, *rises above pure meanness.]*

Being mean is not funny. We despise those whom we consider to be tight-fisted. People such as Harpagon, therefore, are unpromising subjects for comedy. Yet, as Pierre Gaxotte has pointed out:

> Par bonheur, Molière a éclairé son homme de tant de façons, lui a prêté tant de postures que non seulement il fait rire de ce qui aurait pu paraître odieux, mais qu'Harpagon se trouve être de tous les temps, du nôtre comme du sien.[1]

Few would dispute this. The status of ***L'Avare,*** unlike ***Le Misanthrope,*** is in no doubt: it is a comedy. There is, as Gaxotte says, a density of characterization that raises Harpagon above mere meanness.

Robert McBride finds density of another kind. For him it is:

> the simultaneous perception of two self-contained but rationally incompatible ideas [that] characterizes through and through the purely intellectual form of Molière's comedy.[2]

The word "incompatible" is crucial here. Molière's other plays demonstrate McBride's definition. The titles often contain two ideas, one of which undermines the other. ***Le Bourgeois gentilhomme*** designates two incompatible social statuses. ***Le Médecin malgré lui*** boldly announces the disparity between appearance and reality as does ***Le Malade imaginaire.*** Yet ***L'Avare*** would appear to be an exception if we accept the definition of miserliness given by Sylvie and Jacques Dauvin:

> Le mot latin *avaritia* nous renseigne micux: il désigne un *vif désir de conserver,* mais surtout *d'acquérir* toujours plus.[3]

The acquisition and keeping of riches are on the face of it compatible. Harpagon's happiness depends on holding on to his riches and if possible increasing them. But happiness is not assured as can be gauged from his first monologue in I,iv:

> Certes ce n'est pas une petite peine que de garder chez soi une grande somme d'argent; et bienheureux qui a tout son fait bien placé, et ne conserve seulement que ce qu'il faut pour sa dépense. On n'est pas peu embarrassé à inventer dans toute une maison une cache fidèle; car pour moi, les coffres-forts me sont suspects, et je ne veux jamais m'y fier: je les tiens justement une franche amorce à voleurs, et c'est toujours la première chose que l'on va attaquer. Cependant je ne sais si j'aurai bien fait d'avoir enterré dans mon jardin dix mille écus qu'on me rendit hier. Dix mille ecus en or chez soi est une somme . . .
>
> *Ici le frere et le sœur paraissent s'entretenant bas.*
>
> O Ciel! je me serai trahi moi-meme: la chaleur m'aura emporté, et je crois avoir parlé haut en raisonnant tout seul.[4]

As the above demonstrates, the possession of money induces not pleasure but anxiety. The reason is that possession also brings with it a fear of loss. The whole environment becomes threatening and Harpagon even feels that he cannot trust himself to keep his money safe.

Herein lies the paradox of miserliness: Harpagon was much happier when he had given someone else his money. Furthermore, he acquired more riches since interest had to be paid on the loan. Consequently Harpagon spends much of the play trying to give his gold to someone else. This is why we find him funny. He is doing the opposite of what we expect a miser to do. For him it is indeed more blessed to give than to receive—but not quite in the way Christ intended.

Thus it is that this devil can quote scriptural precepts for his own ends:

> La charité, maître Simon, nous oblige à faire plaisir aux personnes, lorsque nous le pouvons. (II,ii)

It is not hard to imagine Harpagon bathing in a righteous glow. But his motivation is not charity or the desire to do good but his fear of losing his money and his desire to increase it. Harpagon is being hypocritical. Similarly, the contract with Cléante makes great play of fairness and willingness to oblige but it is only as the reading of the document proceeds that we have cause to realize what that generosity means. The contract concludes:

> Le tout, ci-dessus mentionné, valant loyalement plus de quatre mille cinq cents livres, et rabaissé à la valeur de mille écus, par la discrétion du prêteur. (II,i)

Harpagon is defining himself as a generous man while in reality being miserly. He tries to present what he believes is an attractive image of himself while satisfying a deep-seated need to protect his wealth. An obligation to repay—and Harpagon's questioning of Maître Simon shows that he makes sure of his potential debtor—is a stronger protection for his miser's hoard than his back garden can provide.

Moreover, as the Dauvins have pointed out, avarice also means increasing what riches you have and an interest-bearing loan satisfies this desire as well. Harpagon's version of generosity is, like his concept of charity, quite different from that of the rest of us. His vision is not shared by us. Yet it is coherent and logical in its own terms. As McBride has pointed out above, rationality is self-contained. The ideas are developed in accordance with logic but without reference to our shared reality. It is the incongruities arising from Molière's exploitation of this that enables us to see the humour in Harpagon. Miserliness is dressed in surprising and, to us, inappropriate forms of behaviour—just as Harpagon wears clothing that is not appropriate for the times in which he is living. This tension constitutes the unifying dynamic of the play.

An additional comic piquancy is added when miserliness is caught in its own stratagem and forced to comply with its outward show of generosity. This happens when Cléante admires his father's ring and gives it to Mariane so that she too may admire it. He then announces that his father wishes her to have it:

> N'est-il pas vrai, mon père, que vous voulez que Madame le garde pour l'amour de vous? (III,vii)

Unlike the encounter just discussed, Cléante wins this particular struggle between himself and his father by forcing upon the latter a pattern of behaviour similar to those which Harpagon uses to clothe his miserliness. The difference is that this takes Harpagon further than he would have gone of his own accord. He who normally says, according to La Flèche: "Je vous prête le bonjour" (II,v), would merely have lent the ring.

Yet the notion that giving is only a temporary lending eventually triumphs for Mariane ends the scene by saying:

> Pour ne vous point mettre en colère, je la garde maintenant; et je prendrai un autre temps pour vous la rendre. (III,vii)

Of her own accord, Marianne accepts the principle so dear to Harpagon whereby what is given must be returned. He is not alone in his values. In Harpagon's moral code ownership is inviolate and injustice occurs when the owner is deprived of what is rightfully his. This principle turns out to be the foundation of the play's moral universe.

Loss is the major threat to this moral order. Giving is a means by which Harpagon can control loss. He retains power over what he has given and can recover it. However, there are other forms of loss which he cannot control. Indeed, a sense of loss is at the heart of his personality as is attested by his daughter:

> Il est bien vrai que, tous les jours, il nous donne de plus en plus sujet de regretter la mort de notre mere, et que . . . (I,ii)

There is a suggestion here that Harpagon's wife was a restraining influence on his avarice or that she shielded her children from its effects. One could perhaps go further and suggest that it was the loss of his wife that triggered off his current behaviour in that it may have caused him to transfer his affections to something he believes more durable. In itself, her death is not perhaps a noteworthy fact given the mortality rates of the seventeenth century and the large number of widowers in Molière's plays. What is perhaps more significant is the patterning—the way death is woven into the lives of the major female characters.

If we take Harpagon's wife as our point of departure, we can discern a progression based on the closeness of the main female characters (excluding Frosine) to death. Thus the next in order is Mariane's mother. It is from Cléante that we first learn about her when he tells Elise about the young girl with whom he has fallen in love:

> Elle se nomme Mariane, et vit sous la conduite d'une bonne femme de mère qui est presque toujours malade, et pour qui cette aimable fille a des sentiments d'amitié qui ne sont pas imaginables. Elle la sert, la plaint, et la console avec une tendresse qui vous toucherait l'âme. (I,ii)

The impression that we have is of a woman in failing health—one who is not dead but whose life is in danger. Like Harpagon's wife she is not to be seen but unlike her, she is still alive.

The progression continues with the next generation. Mariane is presented on stage but not until halfway through the play. She is in some distress and when asked why by Frosine, she replies:

> Hélas! me le demandez-vous? et ne vous figurez-vous point les alarmes d'une personne toute prête à voir le supplice où l'on veut l'attacher? (III,iv)

Mariane, too, is under the shadow of death, albeit metaphorically. She strikes us as being a fragile creature, more passive than Elise:

> Mon Dieu! Frosine, c'est une étrange affaire, lorsque pour être heureuse, il faut souhaiter ou attendre le trépas de quelqu'un, et la mort ne suit pas tous les projets que nous faisons. (III,iv)

Mariane is a creature who is at the mercy of events and who has no control over them. It is ironic that she who sees marriage as a form of death in the first of the two quotations above, should, in the second, see death as her only means of liberation. In this respect she is the opposite of Harpagon, who seeks to preserve and acquire. She sees her future happiness depending on the loss of her husband.

Against this, Elise stands out as a much stronger character. She is present from the beginning of the play and although in many ways the helpless victim of Harpagon (her statement about the effect that her mother's death had on her father suggest that she has no power to reform him), she seems to be made of sterner stuff. We find out early on that she was in fact saved from drowning by Valère. Her escape suggests someone whose link to life is stronger. But even here, she is in a position of dependence, saved by Valère, her future husband, in a way that Harpagon could not do for his own wife. So, in this respect, Elise is like Mariane in that she cannot herself have any control over death.

The position of these women on a scale of encroaching mortality reinforces the notion that loss cannot be confined to money. If Harpagon is obsessed by the need to keep what he has within his control and indeed increase that which he has, this must be seen against the background of impermanency in the play. In his struggles, he is representative of a humanity living in a world where no-one can be sure that anything will last. Even the younger generation are not immune. The fragility of the younger women has already been mentioned but it goes further than that. Valère's very first words state the fear clearly:

> Hé quoi? charmante Elise, vous devenez mélancolique, après les obligeantes assurances que vous avez eu la bonté de me donner de votre foi? Je vous soupirer, hélas! au milieu de ma joie! Est-ce du regret, dites-moi, de m'avoir fait heureux, et vous repentez-vous de cet engagement où mes feux ont pu vous contraindre? (I,i)

Human affections, like human beings, are transient. Valère fears that he will lose Elise. Thus, like Harpagon, he does what he does in order to preserve that which he values. Just as Harpagon dons the deformed habits of generosity, so Valère dons the livery of the miser. This means not just that he wears a servant's clothes but rather that his actions, willingly or unwillingly, are made to conform to those we would expect of Harpagon at his meanest. Thus he upbraids the cook with: "il faut manger pour vivre, et non pas vivre pour manger" (III,i). He is acting as a miser would. Harpagon's deformation of this, his inability to get it right, is another example of the ambiguous behaviour trapped between meanness and generosity that is the wellspring of comedy in this play. Indeed, here Harpagon and Valère are mirror images of each other, one acting the generous man and the other the miser, and it is curious that the name that the young man has adopted is almost an anagram of "l'avare". Even if this is pure coincidence, the bond between the two men is very strong. Valère's independence is circumscribed by Harpagon and, as we see in I,v, he does not allow himself any thought that might contradict Harpagon.

Given this the *quiproquo* of V,iii acquires new resonances:

> VALERE: Non, Monsieur, ce ne sont point vos richesses qui m'ont tenté; ce n'est pas cela qui m'a ébloui, et je proteste de ne prétendre rien à tous vos biens, pourvu que vous me laissiez celui que j'ai.
>
> HARPAGON: Non ferai, de par tous les diables! je ne te le laisserai pas. Mais voyez quelle insolence de vouloir retenir le vol qu'il m'a fait!
>
> VALERE: Appelez vous cela un vol?
>
> HARPAGON: Si je l'appelle un vol? Un trésor comme celui-la!
>
> VALERE: C'est un trésor, il est vrai, et le plus précieux que vous ayez sans doute; mais ce ne sera pas le perdre que de me le laisser. Je vous le demande à genoux, ce trésor plein de charmes; et pour bien faire, il faut que vous me l'accordiez.

The comedy in this scene, as can be seen from the extract quoted above, derives from the fact that Valère's language of love is a series of metaphors taken from the world of finance. Normally, such expressions are treated as mere clichés but in this case the humour makes us look at them in a new light. Because Harpagon takes words like "trésor" literally and does not realize that in moving from the plural "biens" to the singular form "celui," Valère is moving on to a metaphorical plane, the audience is made aware of the two different levels of meaning and the metaphorical one is thrown into relief, thereby bringing to life the clichés: they have an intensity of meaning that they would not otherwise have. The result of this is that we are able to view Valère's passion in a new light. The metaphorical linking of love and miserliness cuts both ways. It is not just that Harpagon loves money the way a normal man loves a woman but also that Valère loves Elise the way a miser loves money. Harpagon and Valère love in the same way.

The similarities are pointed up from the start of the play. Elise has been restored to her father just as the loan has been repaid. Indeed she too is like a piece of property and his immediate preoccupation is to dispose of her to someone else on advantageous terms—just as he is trying to arrange for someone else to take his money. His method of safeguarding his gold until such time as he gives it away is to bury it and similarly, when he becomes aware that Valère seeks to possess his other treasure, he threatens to confine her: "Quatre bonnes murailles me répondront de ta conduite" (V,iv). This is the equivalent of burying the gold in the garden where no one can get it. For Valère, Elise is to be got from her father by stealth and stratagem. His courtship depends not on consent but on using trickery to persuade her father to give her up. His devious, roundabout conduct to acquire Elise is forced upon him just as Cléante is forced into borrowing against his expectations, without his father being aware of it.

But if Harpagon and Valère can be seen as trying to conserve, Cléante is someone who dissipates. Harpagon accuses his son of spending his money on fripperies:

> Je vous l'ai dit vingt fois, mon fils, toutes vos manières me déplaisent fort: vous donnez furieusement dans le marquis; et pour aller ainsi vêtu, il faut bien que vous me dérobiez. (I,iv)

Furthermore, his own servant, La Flèche, warns him about his extravagant lifestyle:

> Je vous vois, Monsieur, ne vous en déplaise, dans le grand chemin justement que tenait Panurge pour se ruiner, prenant argent d'avance, achetant cher, vendant à bon marché, et mangeant son blé en herbe. (II,i)

Cléante is presented here as the opposite of his father. Where the latter seeks to conserve wealth and increase it, he spends it and reduces it. The two most telling jibes are that he is like the marquesses, those useless parasites, and that he is eating the seed corn. He has no useful function in the present and his squandering jeopardizes the future.

But in seeking to conserve, Harpagon also places the future in doubt for while change may bring undesirable consequences, on the whole it is natural and an inevitable part of living. So, ironically, Harpagon's actions caused by his reaction to his wife's death are anti-life. He is inimical to the process of living. Significantly, the method of preserving the gold from harm is to bury it—just as we mark the deaths of family and friends by burying them.

Thus Harpagon is someone who seeks to arrest life. Mariane on entering his house feels the shadow of the gallows upon her. By retaining Elise's dowry, Harpagon is seeking to impede this natural flow of wealth from one generation to the next. Indeed, the pattern of marriages that he has arranged—himself to the young Mariane, Elise to Anselme and Cléante to a widow—is a mixing up of generations, a binding of young to old, so that there is no smooth transition of one to the other.

In such a context, Cléante's response to La Flèche is significant:

> Que veux tu que j'y fasse? Voila où les jeunes gens sont réduits par la maudite avarice des pères; et on s'étonne après cela que les fils soubaitent qu'ils meurent. (II,i)

As we have seen, Cléante is in his own way an enemy of the future, squandering its possibilities by his commitments. However, he is forced to do so by Harpagon's avarice. Furthermore, the father becomes the target of the son's hostility and in a final twist Cléante's subterfuge leads his father to join in his wish that the latter may soon die:

> MAITRE SIMON: Tout ce que je saurais vous dire, c'est que sa famille est fort riche, qu'il n'a plus de mère déjà, et qu'il s'obligera, si vous voulez, que son pere mourra avant qu'il soit huit mois.
>
> HARPAGON: C'est quelque chose que cela. (II,ii)

Like some character in a Greek tragedy, Harpagon is made to utter the words that unknown to him are a curse upon himself. But this is comedy and the outcome is quite different. Nonetheless these words are not just a throw-away joke. They have a point. Harpagon's reaction to the theft of his money is more than just hyperbole:

> Au voleur! au voleur! à l'assassin! au meurtrier! Justice, juste Ciel! je suis perdu, je suis assassiné, on m'a coupé la gorge, on m'a dérobé mon argent. (IV,vii)

The theft is seen not just in terms of loss but in terms of murder. Thus the money that Harpagon seeks to conserve and increase is not just symbolically representative of his daughter, it also stands for himself. To steal his money is to take Harpagon's life. What Harpagon really fears is his own death.

That is why he takes such delight when Frosine tells him that he will outlive his children. That is why he seeks to marry again and parades as he does in front of Mariane. He is refusing to accept the reality of a death that is part of life and is instead seeking to create a little world that will be within his control, a world where everyone will be like a debtor beholden to him. Without him, others are as nothing. They need him as a debtor needs a creditor, as Cléante needs his father, as Valère needs Harpagon. Need becomes the instrument by which Harpagon exercises control and ensures that his own existence is essential.

Yet this is a lie. Despite what he pretends, he is not attractive to Mariane and, as we have seen earlier, she is one of those wishing for his death. There is an air of unreality about the Harpagon household. Harpagon is a domestic tyrant unwilling to listen to the truth from Maître Jacques. Valère is not a real servant. He is in disguise in order to worm his way into Harpagon's good books and gain Elise:

> Vous voyez comme je m'y prends, et les adroites complaisances qu'il m'a fallu mettre en usage pour m'introduire à son service; sous quel masque de sympathie et de rapports de sentiments je me déguise pour lui plaire, et quel personnage je joue tous les jours avec lui, afin d'acquérir sa tendresse. J'y fais des progrès admirables; et j'èprouve que pour gagner les hommes, il n'est point de meilleure voie que de se parer à leurs yeux de leurs inclinations, que de donner dans leurs maximes, encenser leurs défauts, et applaudit à ce qu'ils font. (I,i)

Here we see Valère openly admitting that he is adopting the viewpoint of the miser. He seems to believe that he can do so and maintain his own integrity. He is only wearing a mask. But it is rather like Hamlet's antic disposition: the mannerism becomes indistinguishable from the reality. Valère is not just adopting the same point of view as Harpagon. His attitudes influence his actions. He runs the household in the miserly fashion that Harpagon wants and like his master he beats Maître Jacques. In short Valère is sucked into the world of Harpagon not against his will but because his stratagem has made him susceptible. Despite what he thinks Valère is not his own man. For all his cleverness he dances to Harpagon's tune.

Cléante is also drawn into this world of scheming and subterfuge. He attempts by devious means to borrow money. He fails not because he is unable to carry out the pretense but because he runs up against the deviousness of his father who similarly hides his true identity in order to lend money. Similarly, in IV,iii, Harpagon outwits his son, who is concealing his true feelings beneath a variety of subterfuges, by appearing to offer him Mariane's hand in marriage. What this scene shows is that creating false images of the self, acting out a role that is untrue to one's own nature is not a way of controlling the situation—there is always the risk of meeting a better actor. Indeed, in the two scenes that follow, the factitious reconciliation and its breakdown demonstrate that pretense is not a viable means of conducting affairs. The truth will out.

With this in mind, we may now consider the character of Frosine, who lives by intrigue. What Valère says of himself could apply to her. Flattery is liberally applied to Harpagon's ego. She boasts to La Flèche:

> Mon Dieu! je sais l'art de traire les hommes, j'ai le secret de m'ouvrir leur tendresse, de chatouiller leurs cœurs, de trouver les endroits par où ils sont sensibles. (II,iv)

However, Frosine's wiles are to no avail against Harpagon. She creates a picture of his own personal attractiveness and of Mariane's infatuation for him—but to no avail. Harpagon accepts what she has to offer but feels under no obligation to help her out of her financial difficulties. It is not just that Harpagon's love of money is greater than his love of flattery, but also that Frosine's stratagems depend on insincere flattery being paid for in sincere thanks, that is, real money. In this instance, she meets someone who, when the subject of money is mentioned, retreats further into his own world, where it is he who is in charge. At the end of the scene, the audience has the impression of two people moving in separate worlds, with Frosine excluded from Harpagon's:

> HARPAGON: Adieu Je vais achever mes dépêches.
>
> FROSINE: Je vous assure, Monsieur, que vous ne sauriez jamais me soulager d'un plus grand besoin.
>
> HARPAGON: Je mettrai ordre que mon carrosse soit tout prêt pour vous mener à la foire (II,v)

No matter how skillful Frosine is, Harpagon manages to escape her ploys. Her description of Mariane's imaginary dowry is a tour-de-force but it does not take in Harpagon:

> FROSINE: [. . .] De plus elle a une aversion horrible pour le jeu, ce qui n'est pas commun aux femmes d'aujourd'hui; et j'en sais une de nos quartiers qui a perdu, à trente et-quarante, vingt mille francs cette année. Mais n'en prenons que le quart. Cinq mille francs au jeu par an, et quatre mille francs en habits et bijoux, cela fait neuf mille livres; et mille écus que nous mettons pour la nourriture, ne voila-t-il pas par année vos douze mille francs bien comptés?
>
> HARPAGON: Oui, cela n'est pas mal; mais ce compte-là n'est rien du réel. (II,v)

What is particularly comic about this is that Frosine's accounting methods bear more than a passing resemblance to Harpagon's. As we saw in II,i, he attributes arbitrary values to junk and then just as arbitrarily reduces them so as to appear not to be taking advantage of the second party. Frosine is doing something similar. Mariane's economies are no more likely to produce money than selling the junk will. Frosine, however, has met her master, for Harpagon sees through the obfuscation.

Yet this interchange has resonances beyond the present context. It suggests that money saved is not real. Harpagon is a miser and one of the characteristics of the miser is not spending money. The quotation above makes us ponder the extent to which money saved by Harpagon and money saved by Mariane are different since neither will ever be spent. It is as though money only exists when it is put to use: either in spending or in usury. Money is unreal in itself. This is perhaps easier to accept in the late twentieth century when money is reduced to a promise on a piece of paper or information shifted from one area to another. It is only when translated into goods and services that we can have some appreciation of its value. So the money buried in Harpagon's garden is as much use to him as none at all. If he does not use it, he might as well not have it. The irony of the theft by La Flèche is that Harpagon is really no worse off than he was before. He has lost only that which he did not use.

This is the important difference between Harpagon and Cléante. At the time the play begins, the latter is prepared to use money for some purpose. Where previously, he had been content to buy fine clothes for himself, now he wants to help Mariane and her mother. The money will be used beneficially instead of lying uselessly in the ground, buried like a corpse, or merely serving to beget more money if put out to usury.

So, keeping money is just as pointless as Frosine's flatteries. Both are equally valueless. Frosine, far from being a master intriguer who is able to manipulate the world around her, is merely a creator of illusions that are insubstantial and have no impact on reality. Her plot to help the young people by impersonating a lady from Brittany, is just another such and stands just as much chance of succeeding. Deceptions in general cannot succeed in the moral universe created by this play. There is always reality breaking in or someone who is not taken in or who finds out. Until the end of the fourth act, it is Harpagon who manages to outwit the others. Yet even he cannot win all the time. He has attempted to build up a picture of himself as a poor man but no-one, least of all his children, is taken in. Finally, La Flèche spies on Harpagon and the latter's anxiety about his money betrays him so that he gives away the truth—the location of the treasure.

Manipulation is not a viable means of controlling one's destiny, of ensuring against loss. However, this is a comedy and despite the darker aspects of the play, the mood is humorous. Even when Harpagon is most cast down, that is when he loses his money, we still laugh. This is because we feel that the emotion and reaction are in excess of what the situation requires. We do not know but we strongly suspect that the strong box will be returned. We know that the object of Cléante's passion is not the money but Mariane and so we see the theft not as an end but as a means to an end.

What is most striking is that it is chance which permits La Flèche to steal the money. Indeed, by concentrating on the role of manipulation and control, there is a danger that we will overlook the role of chance in the play. Manipulation is an attempt to exploit cause and effect. For example, Frosine flatters Harpagon in the hope that it will cause him to give her money. Similarly, Cléante is able to give Mariane his father's ring because he knows how his words will produce certain effect in the old man. However, Harpagon does not lose the ring, as we have seen. Mariane promises to return it, an unexpected and indeed unprovoked gesture on her part. There is no reason for her to make the offer she does. The unexpected also plays an important part in preventing Cléante taking out a ruinous loan—though he does not see it in that light at the time. More importantly, it is chance that saves Elise's life when she is saved from drowning by a fortuitously present Valère. But this is an amoral force—if force it is—for it is by chance that Harpagon spies his son kissing Mariane's hand, thereby arousing his suspicions. Nevertheless, though change and the transience of human life bring about loss, they also give conjunctions of circumstances, opportunities that we must seize.

In a sense we are back with the second sense of miserliness as proposed by the Dauvins. It is possible to increase what we have but it implies that our own efforts are not enough. There has to be a favourable conjunction of circumstances, a moment when we are offered something we could not have expected. To live by manipulation is to live by exploitation, to become a Frosine. The latter gives nothing and has nothing to give. She is a complete parasite. This is why she is not involved in the working out of the dénouement. For her to have succeeded in her plan would have involved the younger generation in her intrigues and the foundations of their lives would have been based on manipulation. Similarly, it would have been inappropriate for Valère to have succeeded in worming his way into Harpagon's favours. Had he succeeded it would have been either because he was sufficiently like the old man to win his approval or sufficiently deceitful to outwit him. Neither situation promises well for the future.

The dénouement when it comes resolves the problems satisfactorily and unexpectedly. Anselme is an unlikely source of help. Indeed, the fact that he is the husband Harpagon had chosen for Elise, predisposes us against him. We imagine that if he is a friend of Harpagon, then he must be like him and have similar motivations. Indeed, the way Harpagon behaves when first introduced to Mariane, is subliminally used to build up a picture of Anselme. The truth is quite different. Yet though Ansleme is a key factor in the resolution of the play, his role is more of a catalyst than anything else. His presence causes the situation to be changed. Truth can at last be revealed, creating a number of opportunities to be taken advantage of:

> ANSELME: Le Ciel, mes enfants, ne me redonne point à vous pour être contraire à vos vœux. Seigneur Harpagon, vous jugez bien que le choix d'une jeune personne tombera sur le fils plutôt que sur le père. Allons, ne vous faites point dire ce qu'il n'est pas nécessaire d'entendre, et consentez ainsi que moi à ce double hyménée. (V,vi)

It is evident from this that Anselme accepts unquestioningly the forward movement of time. For there is nothing more natural than that life should move on from one generation to the next. His reaction is one of generosity. He gives his consent. As was pointed out earlier, it is one of the paradoxes of miserliness that in order for Harpagon to keep his money safe and indeed increase it, it was necessary for him to give it away. Similarly here, in order that life may be secured and humanity increase, it is necessary for Anselme to give up his claims on Elise and give his own daughter and son in marriage to the children of Harpagon. More importantly, it is necessary for the miser to give away his children.

Giving is the keynote of the finale of the play and Molière dresses it up in many different guises. To begin with there is the open-handed generosity of Anselme who consents to the younger generation giving themselves in marriage and paying the wedding expenses, Harpagon's suit and the officer. There is also Cléante, giving back that which was taken. More interesting is Harpagon. He too is part of the process of giving. Indeed he is an essential part both artistically and thematically. In the first instance his demands prevent the play degenerating into the mawkishly sentimental. A reformed Harpagon, brimming with the milk of human kindness, would not be credible. A Harpagon exploiting the situation is. But is he doing anything different from the other characters? He like them is simply taking advantage of the situation. It benefits him but, and this must not be overlooked, it benefits them. They are better off at the end of the play than at the beginning. In the case of Maître Jacques the situation is more ambiguous. Harpagon's "Pour votre paiement, voilà un homme que je vous donne a pendre" (V,vi) is a parody of the theme of giving but just as much a part of it all the same. Indeed, Harpagon's consent, his giving away of his family is crucial to the dénouement. Without it, no new family would be created. Thus, Harpagon's actions do not place him beyond the pale.

This is not, however, the opinion of critics such as Harold Knutson:

> Harpagon, however, is spared the humiliating retreat of Arnolphe. Instead, the lost *cassette* severs him from human reality. Society's place will be somewhere offstage; the world in front of us is now cold, lifeless, and metallic. The reunited family is imbued with the vision of the soon-to-be-found mother; what glows in Harpagon's mind is the image of more gold to be extorted from Anselme, and of the only form that woman can ever take in his vision of the world as objects to be amassed, "ma chère cassette."
>
> Like Argan and Monsieur Jourdain, Harpagon is protected from the sense of defeat by his very mania. But while the other two join the triumphant family, imparting joy to it in their own happiness, however illusory, Harpagon stands alone. Society has not expelled him, it has left him behind.[5]

"Extort" is a strong word not justified by the exchange between Harpagon and Anselme:

> HARPAGON: Je n'ai point d'argent à donner en mariage à mes enfants.
>
> ANSELME: Hé bien! j'en ai pour eux; que cela ne vous inquiète point.
>
> HARPAGON: Vous obligerez-vous à faire tous les frais de ces deux mariages?
>
> ANSELME: Oui, je m'y oblige; êtes-vous satisfait?
>
> HARPAGON: Oui, pourvu que pour les noces vous me fassiez faire un habit.

ANSELME: D'accord. Allons jouir de l'allégresse que cet heureux jour nous présente.

LE COMMISSAIRE: Holà! Messieurs, holà! tout doucement, s'il vous plaît: qui me payera mes écritures? (V,vi)

There is no indication in the original that Harpagon extorts any gold from Anselme. The money that he receives is his own, returned to him by Cléante. His first speech is merely an attempt to avoid spending money. His claim obviously is untrue but it is not a demand. Anselme offers to take upon himself Harpagon's responsibilities. The second speech is a question—which puts more pressure on Anselme but the sum involved must be less than for the marriage settlements. In neither case does Harpagon receive any money for himself. In the third speech, Harpagon does indeed state a condition but it is for a suit not money. Knutson's claim that Harpagon is thinking about all the gold he can extort from Anselme is not borne out by the text.

Nor is his claim that Harpagon is isolated. Anselme's "Allons jouir de l'allégresse" surely does not exclude the person he has just addressed. Rather, the first person plural includes Harpagon and extends the invitation beyond the pair of interlocutors to the other members of the two families. Such an interpretation fits the facts of the text much better—as can be seen from the reaction of the officer to what is going on. His "Messieurs" is obviously addressed to those whom he takes to be in charge, Anselme and Harpagon, and it is highly unlikely that he would call out to them to stop ("tout doucement") if what he was hearing or seeing did not lead him to believe that both of them were leaving or about to leave the scene. Thus, there can be no doubt that Harpagon is leaving not just to see his "chère cassette" but to join in the celebrations. He is anything but isolated. In fact, his condition that Anselme buy him a new suit is highly significant. Harpagon's clothes are old and out of date. They have served to mark him out from the rest of his family and are a statement of his being out of step with society. The new clothes will remedy that. They are a mark of his reintegration.

Yet he remains true to himself. He is coaxed into giving away his family but in a kinder, gentler way than was the case when he gave up his ring to Mariane. No-one loses. He is taking advantage of the situation as everyone else is. Like Anselme, he is giving consent but on his own terms. The paradox of miserliness is vindicated: in order to preserve and increase what one has, one must be prepared to give. The way a miser gives—while remaining what he is—is comic and adds to the humour of the piece. Harpagon gets what he wants, his "chère cassette" and for the first time in the play he is truly content. The play has a happy ending, as befits a comedy.

Notes

1. Pierre Gaxotte, *Molière* (Paris, 1977), p. 290.
2. Robert McBride, *The Sceptical Vision of Molière: A Study in Paradox* (London and Basingstoke, 1977), p. 14.
3. Sylvie and Jacques Dauvin, *Molière: L'Avare* (Frankfurt am Main and Paris, 1984), p. 51.
4. Molière, *Œuvres complètes,* edited by Georges Couton, Bibliothèque de la Pléiade, 2 vols (Paris, 1971), II, p. 524. All references are to this edition.
5. Harold C Knutson, *Molière: An Archetypal Approach* (Toronto and Buffalo, 1976), p. 102.

Michael S. Koppisch (essay date 1996)

SOURCE: "'Til Death Do Them Part: Love, Greed, and Rivalry in Molière's *L'Avare*," in *L'Esprit Createur,* Vol. XXXVI, No. 1, Spring, 1996, pp. 32-49.

[In the following essay, Koppisch discusses the role of greed and rivalry in Molière's L'Avare.*]*

Avarice has a dual function in ***L'Avare***: it is both the dominant character trait of Harpagon and the sign of a contagion that touches every aspect of his family's existence. From the moment he steps on stage, Harpagon is obsessed with money. His first words are to demand that La Flèche, his son's valet, leave immediately, lest the servant spy on him in the privacy of his own home and discover the whereabouts of his hidden treasure. The play ends with Harpagon eagerly awaiting the moment when he can see once again "ma chère cassette" (5.6).[1] By this time, his treasure has become the old man's only friend, "mon support, ma consolation, ma joie," he calls it (4.7). Harpagon's conviction that, deprived of his money, he can no longer carry on anchors the play's comic vision in a darker realm. Indeed the miser is, arguably, as unhappy before the theft of his ten thousand *écus* as he is after it. He frets constantly about how dangerous it is to have so much money around the house (1.4). Burying his money in the garden puts it out of sight, but not out of mind, for Harpagon is terrified that others may have guessed his secret. Were the true extent of his wealth to become known, he would fear for his life: "un de ces jours," he tells Cléante, "on me viendra chez moi couper la gorge, dans la pensée que je suis tout cousu de pistoles" (1.4). Harpagon's greed has turned his life into a nightmare.

It has also contaminated the social and moral order of his entire household. Ironically, Harpagon comes to a point when he tells the Commissaire investigating the theft of his box that "s'il [ce crime] demeure impuni, les choses les plus sacrées ne sont plus en sûreté" (5.1). If he fails to grasp that punishing the culprit will make no difference, he is, nonetheless, absolutely right about "les choses les plus sacrées." They have been tainted. As Louis Lacour, the editor of the reprinting of the play's original 1669 edition, says, "il nous semble assister à la décadence d'une famille."[2] Harpagon no longer fulfills the most elementary obligations of a father, preferring his money even to the life of his own daughter. Elise's revelation that she had been saved from drowning by Valère, whom Harpagon believes to be guilty of the theft, elicits from her father his nastiest line: "Tout cela n'est rien; et il valait bien mieux pour moi qu'il te laissât noyer que de faire ce qu'il a fait" (5.4). Paternal love has been banished from the repertoire of Harpagon's feelings. Paternal authority fares no better. Harpagon's children refuse to obey him, plot against their father's tyranny, lie to him. Harpagon mistreats his servants, who, in turn, wish their master no good. To defend themselves against Harpagon, members of his household adopt certain of his own worst flaws. This, finally, leaves the family on the brink of turmoil.

Jean-Jacques Rousseau centers his brief critique of ***L'Avare*** on precisely this tendency toward the disintegration of a family order:

> C'est un grand vice d'être avare et de prêter à usure; mais n'en est-ce pas un plus grand encore à un fils de voler son père, de lui manquer de respect, de lui faire mille insultants reproches, et, quand ce père irrité lui donne sa malédiction, de répondre d'un air goguenard, qu'il n'a que faire de ses dons?[3]

Although he makes no attempt to justify the rapacious Harpagon, the more dangerous transgression, in Rousseau's eyes, is the abrogation of filial duty. The threat represented by the machinations of a miser is limited. He might, at worst, make his children miserable until he mends his ways or dies. However, when the child treats his father just as the father treats him, the very order on which family relations are founded is called into question. The contours of the relationship between father and son become hazy in ***L'Avare,*** as Harpagon discredits himself and Cléante increasingly takes liberties with the role of father. Rousseau focuses on the dissolution of the special bond between father and son because this is a crisis both fundamental to the play's action and indicative of the chaos that threatens Harpagon's family.

Desire for riches invades every quarter of life in this household, bringing with it confusion and disorder. The discourse of love itself, usually free from such concerns, has been contaminated—directly and indirectly—by money. The first impediment to her love for Valère that Elise mentions is, of course, "l'emportement d'un père," but her real reservation is that Valère will have a change of heart, a "froideur criminelle dont ceux de votre sexe *payent* le plus souvent les témoignages trop ardents d'une innocente amour" (1.1; my emphasis). To his assurance that he, Valère, is different, Elise replies that all men sing the same tune: "Tous les hommes sont semblables par les paroles; et ce n'est que les actions qui les découvrent différents" (1.1). Distinguishing one man from another may not be as simple as it would seem. Similarities have, perhaps, more force—and are more troubling—than difference. And as for Valère's behavior, his own description of it makes one understand the young woman's hesitation. In order to be close to his beloved, Valère has insinuated himself into Harpagon's household by pretending to be a servant. Such a ploy may be justified in the name of love, but Valère has gone further than is prudent, hoping to seduce the father along with his daughter. His tactic is at best hypocritical, even though his adversary is a despicable old miser. Valère draws Elise's attention to the fact that he is merely playing a role, pretending to be something that he is not: "Vous voyez comme je m'y prends . . . sous quel masque de sympathie et de rapports de sentiments je me déguise pour lui plaire, et quel personnage je joue tous les jours avec lui . . ." (1.1). The goal is couched in terms of acquisition: "acquérir sa [Harpagon's] tendresse."

Valère, moreover, is pleased with himself for having succeeded famously in deceiving his future father-in-law: "J'y fais des progrès admirables," he gloats. Valère's self-satisfaction derives in part from his sense that he is acting on a principle in which he believes, but this principle reveals a singular cynicism: "et j'éprouve que pour gagner les hommes, il n'est point de meilleure voie que de se parer à leurs yeux de leurs inclinations, que de donner dans leurs maximes, encenser leurs défauts, et applaudir à ce qu'ils font" (1.1). Whether or not this role is played well matters little, he goes on. All men are taken in by flattery. It cannot be helped that "la sincérité souffre un peu au métier que je fais." "Un peu"? What might constitute "beaucoup"? In any event, Valère now enunciates a maxim not unrelated to Elise's initial concern that all men are alike: "mais quand on a besoin des hommes, il faut bien s'ajuster à eux; et puisqu'on ne saurait les gagner que par-là, ce n'est pas la faute de ceux qui flattent, mais de ceux qui veulent être flattés" (1.1). Refusing all responsibility for his dishonest behavior, Valère sweeps away a major difference between flatterer and flattered. Real guilt lies with the victim of flattery, rather than with its perpetrator. On at least one level—that of culpability—the difference between trickster and dupe has been reversed. The two may not be identical, but a barrier separating them has broken down. As differences crumble, the distinction between the noble, magnanimous Valère who saves Elise's life by risking his own and the wily pretender may also be called into doubt. At the very least, Valère has demonstrated that he is neither honesty and goodness incarnate nor an absolute scoundrel. Verbs often associated with financial dealings—"gagner," "acquérir"—signal the impact of money and greed on human relations in Harpagon's family, as Elise, at the end of this scene, implores Valère to do his best to "gagner l'appui de mon frère" (1.1).

Money impinges more directly on Cléante's love for Mariane. The young girl lives with her sick mother in a state of near penury. By discreetly providing for the family's financial needs, Cléante would like to lighten Mariane's burden: "Figurez-vous, ma sœur, quelle joie ce peut être que de relever la fortune d'une personne que l'on aime" (1.2). Only Harpagon's stinginess prevents his son from fulfilling this desire. Curiously, the sole way of expressing his love that occurs to Cléante is a gift of money: his father's tight-fistedness, he says, leaves him "dans l'impuissance de goûter cette joie, et de faire éclater à cette belle aucun témoignage de mon amour" (1.2). The juxtaposition of the words "impuissance" and "joie" suggests the strength of Cléante's feelings toward a father "[qui] s'oppose à nos désirs" (1.2). Cléante's choice of a gift in kind is not unique in Molière's theater. Dom Garcie de Navarre would have liked to bestow upon Done Elvire just such a present; Alceste harbors the same dream; and Orgon was so generous to Tartuffe that the impostor was able to return half of what he received without, apparently, noticing the loss. Could it be that Cléante, like those others and, indeed, his own father, might use money as a means of acquiring power? The suspicion cannot be proven. Nor, however, is Cléante so high-minded as to remove it from the realm of possibility. Money and love are, for better or for worse, inextricably linked in Cléante's mind.

The power of wealth on the imagination of Harpagon is, of course, overwhelming. Knowing full well that Mariane is not rich, he allows, somewhat vaguely, that "si l'on n'y trouve pas tout le bien qu'on souhaite, on peut tâcher de regagner cela sur autre chose" (1.4). Harpagon nevertheless hopes to extract a dowry from the mother of his intended. The contradiction is a glaring one but gives no pause to the miser, who insistently questions Frosine about whether she had explained that "il fallait . . . qu'elle [Mariane's mother] se saignât pour une occasion comme celle-ci" (2.5). That he would pursue a woman without visible wealth in itself shows the depth of his feelings for her. Still, he cannot conceive of a marriage that will not make him a richer man. For his children's marriages, money determines who the spouse will be. Elise is to wed Anselme, "dont on vante les grands biens" (1.4) and "[qui] s'engage à la prendre sans dot" (1.5). Cléante will become the husband of a widow, presumably rich. No value, no institution—love, marriage, family—is sacred where financial gain seems possible. The very institutions and beliefs on which Harpagon's existence is built are undermined by his overwhelming desire for wealth.

The breakdown of order is here vividly represented, as elsewhere in Molière's theater, by characters' resort to physical violence as a replacement for rational discourse. No sooner has he appeared on stage than Harpagon threatens La Flèche with a sound thrashing because the valet asks perfectly logical questions: "Tu fais le raisonneur. Je te baillerai de ce raisonnement-ci par les oreilles" (1.3). Jacques receives a beating for telling his master the truth (3.1) and, at the play's conclusion, is momentarily in danger of being hanged for having lied about the theft of the money box. Truth and falsehood incite the same reaction—violence. Poor Jacques also comes in for a beating by Valère, who, in his treatment of the servant, behaves exactly like Harpagon. When Cléante refuses to bow to parental authority by giving up Mariane, Harpagon's attempt to impose himself is violent: "Je te ferai bien me connaître, avec de bons coups de bâton" (4.3). All that guarantees his power over his son is the rod. Harpagon is regularly reduced to violence as he tries to shore up a crumbling order. After losing his treasure, he will go so far as to prescribe violent acts against himself as a means of uncovering the truth about the theft. Truth itself, apparently, cannot exist without the exercise of violence. The dilemma confronting Harpagon is simply that violence engenders greater violence and, ultimately, chaos, not an order that he can dominate from his position as head of the family. As the action of the play unfolds, turmoil overtakes Harpagon's household.

The old miser Euclio in Plautus' *Aulularia,* which is the primary source of Molière's play, shares Harpagon's obsession with a large fortune. Both have found for their daughters a suitor who does not insist on a dowry, both are unnecessarily suspicious of anyone who might conceivably rob them, both treat others, especially servants, rudely. Molière found in Plautus the idea for some of the best comic bits of his play. Harpagon's first encounter with La Flèche (1.3), the miser's famous monologue (4.7), and the extended misunderstanding between Harpagon and Valère over the theft (5.3) all have specific counterparts in the Latin play.[4] Molière has turned to Plautus with great profit. However, having found the givens of his plot in the Roman tradition, Molière proceeds to create a work that is in every way more radical than his model. Although the protagonists of the two plays suffer from the same malady, Euclio realizes that money is the cause of his woes and would almost prefer to be done with his riches rather than continue to be burdened by them. Nor does he allow money to destroy the good order of his household. Plautus' conception of the comic hero clearly leaves open the possibility of redemption from his madness. Euclio's obsession is less destructive than Harpagon's because it does not overwhelm every other value in his life. The single-mindedness of Harpagon, by contrast, is absolute.

This mania, whose intensity makes it so typical of Molière's theater, must be viewed in the context of another, more crucial addition to the plot of Plautus' play. Harpagon, unlike Euclio, is in love, and he loves the same woman as his son. The rivalry between father and son has a powerful impact upon affairs of the purse, as well as affairs of the heart. What Molière has done by changing Plautus in just this way is to shift the entire focus of his play away from the emphasis on a predetermined character trait that alone explains a character's dilemma. If only Euclio can be less greedy, master a flaw in his personality, all will once again be well. Lyconides will marry Phaedria, and Euclio will be freed from the suffering caused by his wealth. Although the text of the *Aulularia* is not complete, it is clear from the second argument that this is precisely what happens:

> Auro formidat Euclio, abstrudit foris.
> Re omni inspecta comressoris servolus.
> Id surpit; illio Euclioni sem refert.
> Ab eo donatur auro, uxore et filio.[5]

Such a resolution in ***L'Avare***—or in any other Molière play, for that matter—would be virtually unthinkable. Good Molièresque maniac that he is, Harpagon leaves the stage as he had stepped onto it, obsessed with his chest full of money. His final act is to have Anselme pay the Commissaire, which frees Harpagon to "voir ma chère cassette" (5.6). The miser remains unaltered, but turmoil does not ensue. In fact, a measure of order is restored to the household.

For, in ***L'Avare,*** the knot to be undone by the comic dénouement is not, as in Plautus' play, simply greed. Greed is, rather, the sign of a deeper malaise. Harpagon is already a wealthy man and has no ostensible reason to worry about his money. That he is incapable of putting aside, even for a moment, thoughts of it indicates how thoroughly Harpagon identifies himself with his money. Through his accumulated wealth and through it alone, is he able to relate to the world in which he lives. Harpagon's every human sentiment is filtered through his miserliness: "En un mot, il aime l'argent, plus que réputation, qu'honneur et que vertu" (2.4). This explains why he is, again in the words of La Flèche, "de tous les humains l'humain le moins humain" (2.4). The servant does not exaggerate. Harpagon's conception of himself depends upon his wealth. He is attached to his "chère cassette" in the same way as Monsieur Jourdain to social status or Argan to illness. His money itself is both real and unreal: real because it does indeed exist and unreal because it cannot, in and of itself, change his life. Not surprisingly, the money box remains buried in the garden throughout the play. To dig it up would change nothing. What money does allow Harpagon, however, is a way of asserting his control over others.

As the father of Cléante and Elise, Harpagon has by right a large role to play in deciding whom they will marry. Money solidifies his paternal authority by eliminating any uncertainty about an otherwise difficult decision. Valère prevaricates in his response to Harpagon's famous "sans dot": "Vous avez raison: voilà qui décide tout, cela s'entend . . . Ah! il n'y a pas de réplique à cela . . . Il est vrai: cela ferme la bouche à tout. *Sans dot*" (1.5). Harpagon believes every word of it. Rather than complicating the issue, financial considerations make good sense of it. Both power and right are on Harpagon's side. Cléante experiences his father as a tyrant and swears to his sister that unless things change, "nous le quitterons là tous deux et nous affranchirons de cette tyrannie où nous tient si longtemps son avarice insupportable" (1.2). At the heart of Harpagon's imperious control over the lives of his children is greed, "son avarice." Stinginess also sets him apart from everyone else in the play. Being a miser makes Harpagon different, and he must defend himself against attack on every side: "Je ne veux point avoir sans cesse devant moi un espion de mes affaires, un traître, dont les yeux maudits assiègent toutes mes actions . . ." (1.3). The military image of a siege translates perfectly the configuration of Harpagon's relations with others: they against me, a fortress of strength. As he himself puts it, even his children have joined the ranks of the enemy: "Cela est ètrange, que mes propres enfants me trahissent et deviennent mes ennemis" (1.4). By cunning or by force, the enemy must be defeated, brought under control, made subservient to a more powerful master.

Harpagon's strategy is a simple one, easily recognizable to readers of Molière. He will marry off his children to well-heeled mates from whom the family will, hopefully, benefit and keep Mariane for himself, pinching his pennies all the while. Needless to say, Cléante and his sister have ideas of their own about the future. In a curious way, Harpagon is right to see his children as his enemies, for they become rivals with him in a struggle over their own destiny. Elise takes badly the news of her father's intention that she marry Anselme. Going so far as to threaten suicide if forced to marry, she flatly rejects Harpagon's proposal. The dialogue between father and daughter is a model of imitative belligerence. Elise and Harpagon speak the same language, use the same words. All that distinguishes the words of one from the words of the other is an occasional direct negation of what has just preceded or will shortly follow. Harpagon's obstinacy is met by the obstinacy of his daughter, her tartness by his irony:

> *Elise*—Je vous demande pardon, mon père.
>
> *Harpagon*—Je vous demande pardon, ma fille.
>
> *Elise*—Je suis très humble servante au seigneur Anselme; mais, avec votre permission, je ne l'épouserai point.
>
> *Harpagon*—Je suis votre très humble valet; mais, avec votre permission, vous l'épouserez dès ce soir.
>
> *Elise*—Dès ce soir?
>
> *Harpagon*—Dès ce soir.
>
> *Elise*—Cela ne sera pas, mon père.
>
> *Harpagon*—Cela sera, ma fille.
>
> *Elise*—Non.
>
> *Harpagon*—Si.
>
> *Elise*—Non, vous dis-je.
>
> *Harpagon*—Si, vous dis-je.
>
> *Elise*—C'est une chose où vous ne me réduirez point.
>
> *Harpagon*—C'est une chose où je te réduirai.
>
> *Elise*—Je me tuerai plutôt que d'épouser un tel mari.
>
> *Harpagon*—Tu ne te tueras point, et tu l'épouseras.
>
> (1.4)

A standard comic technique—having two interlocutors contradict each other with much the same words—is more than a clever way of eliciting laughter. That both parties to the disagreement use the same language suggests a real identity between them. Each contradicts the other in the hope of having his—or her—own way. In this particular instance, Elise seems to be right and her father wrong, although the daughter should treat her father with more respect. Harpagon's behavior and Elise's response to it endanger the good order of the household by suggesting that there is a similar basis for parental authority and a child's disobedience. The duel ends in a draw, the father's authority challenged and no resolution of the quarrel in sight. Assuming opposite stances, Elise and Harpagon behave similarly. Their only recourse seems to be to a third party.

Valère's position as trusted servant of Harpagon and secret lover of Elise makes him at once an "ideal" choice as judge—father and daughter agree on his probity!—and the person least likely to be able to resolve the dispute. Without even knowing the subject of the quarrel, Valère declares Harpagon in the right: "vous ne sauriez avoir tort, et vous êtes toute raison" (1.5). As soon as the old man leaves the room, Valère explains to Elise that favoring Harpagon had merely been a ploy. Valère is really on Elise's side. Despite his double talk, he knows very well where his sympathy lies. So does the audience. At this early point in the play, it is neither necessary nor desirable that the conflict be resolved. Valère's duplicity, however, merely hides the fact that there is no rational resolution possible to the dilemma created by Harpagon's rivalry with his children. This unhappy truth will be apparent as Harpagon takes on his son.

Cléante explicitly—and cynically—recognizes his father's authority over him at the beginning of his first conversation with his sister: "je sais que je dépends d'un père, et que le nom de fils me soumet à ses volontés." But let there be no mistake about it: Cléante says this only "afin que vous ne vous donniez pas la peine de me le dire" (1.2). What he really wants is to check Harpagon's power. The son sees his father as an obstacle to success and will shortly learn that Harpagon is also his rival for the affection of Mariane. The two distinguishing comic features of Harpagon—his inappropriate love for Mariane and his preoccupation with money—both place him in rivalry with his son. It is this rivalry and its ramifications that motivate much of the action in Molière's play. Rivalry also leads directly to the disintegration of a family order founded on differences among members of the household.

The scene in which Cléante realizes that Maître Simon has arranged for him to borrow money at usurious rates from none other than his own father is reminiscent of the debate between Harpagon and Elise. Using the same comic device, Molière puts similar words into the mouths of his characters. This time, however, the similarity of the two characters is emphasized as each accuses the other of criminal behavior. Rather than contradicting each other, father and son see each other as mirror images of themselves. The dialogue blurs the distinction between usury and profligate borrowing:

> *Harpagon*—Comment, pendard? c'est toi qui t'abandonnes à ces coupables extrémités?
>
> *Cléante*—Comment, mon père? c'est vous qui vous portez à ces honteuses actions?
>
> *Harpagon*—C'est toi qui te veux ruiner par des emprunts si condamnables?
>
> *Cléante*—C'est vous qui cherchez à vous enrichir par des usures si criminelles?
>
> *Harpagon*—Oses-tu bien, après cela, paraître devant moi?
>
> *Cléante*—Osez-vous bien, après cela, vous présenter aux yeux du monde? (2.2)

The difference between borrower and lender, like that between flatterer and flattered, disappears as Harpagon and Cléante are reduced to the same level. When Cléante asks which of them is more guilty, Harpagon responds by ordering his son to leave. For there seems to be no clear-cut answer to that query.

At the moment he invites Mariane to his house and introduces her to his family, Harpagon is unaware that she and Cléante are in love and takes as mere impertinence his son's open opposition to Mariane's becoming "ma belle-mère" (3.7). Since she understands perfectly well what he really means, Mariane praises Cléante's honesty in expressing his feelings. His candor takes a curious turn as Cléante goes on to declare his love: "souffrez, Madame, que je me mette ici à la place de mon père, et que je vous avoue que je n'ai rien vu dans le monde de si charmant que vous" (3.7). To Harpagon's objection, Cléante retorts that "c'est un compliment que je fais pour vous à Madame" (3.7). What Cléante does in order to vie with his father is simply to replace him. Their struggle for the hand of Mariane results in the son's speaking for, standing in for the father. Harpagon recognizes this and resents it: "Mon Dieu! j'ai une langue pour m'expliquer moi-même, et je n'ai pas besoin d'un procureur comme vous" (3.7). His self-assertion is necessary if he is not to be eliminated altogether. The barrier between father and son, which should protect the role of each, is momentarily lowered in this scene—momentarily and dangerously. For Cléante does not stop at speaking for his father. Having taken the first step, he continues by presenting to Mariane a diamond ring taken from Harpagon's finger. The miser is beside himself at the thought of the expense of this gift but can do nothing to get it back without compromising his love. Rivalry, which could be expected to separate the factions, here does the opposite. In a sense, Cléante and Harpagon become one. Cléante wants Mariane to have the ring and forces it on her. Harpagon wants the opposite but dares not contravene his son's "generosity." On the surface, at least, the two act as one. The comic effect of the scene derives in part from Harpagon's impotence when faced with a rivalry that levels differences. In their dispute over money, Cléante and Harpagon behaved similarly. Where love is involved, Cléante slips into the role assumed by his father.

This unexpected effect of the rivalry between Cléante and Harpagon is what Rousseau found so disturbing. When it finally occurs to him that his son might also love Mariane, Harpagon tricks Cléante into admitting his passion and then orders him to give up his love. Cléante must also marry the woman his father has picked for him. In other words, Harpagon wants both to defeat his son and make him obedient to his father's will. Nowhere is Harpagon's desire for power more straightforwardly articulated.

Cléante's will, however, is no less strong. He refuses to acquiesce. On the contrary, the young man embraces rivalry with his father and the terrible struggle it implies: "je vous déclare, moi, que je ne quitterai point la passion que j'ai pour Mariane, qu'il n'y a point d'extrémité où je ne m'abandonne pour vous disputer sa conquête" (4.3). Recognizing the deadlock at which he has arrived with Cléante, Harpagon resorts to the order of difference upon which his whole existence has been founded: "Ne suis-je pas ton père? et ne me dois-tu pas respect!" (4.3). Cléante's response is devastating in its confirmation that rivalry has erased even this difference: "Ce ne sont point ici des choses où les enfants soient obligés de déférer aux pères, et l'amour ne connaît personne" (4.3). Love does not distinguish between father and son. Harpagon's threat to beat his son, his readiness to give in to violence, represents the irrational, chaotic state to which rivalry has reduced his family.

Once again, a third person is called upon to adjudicate the dispute. This time, Maître Jacques will be the judge. The role of justice in ***L'Avare*** is to prevent the onslaught of chaos by maintaining an order based on difference. By deciding that one party or the other is right, justice marks a distinction between the two. Harpagon's repeated choice of servants as mediators indicates how badly he wants to control events. It also undermines the potential efficacy of the system of justice, for it is unlikely that Harpagon would accept a judgment against himself rendered by a servant. The structure of the scene in which Harpagon and Cléante appear before Maître Jacques reveals why the power of justice to maintain differences is sapped by rivalry. Harpagon and Cléante present virtually identical cases. Both love a woman whom they want to marry, each is prevented from doing so by the importunities of the other. Harpagon thinks it wrong that Cléante will not obey him. Cléante accuses his father of a love inappropriate for a person of his advanced age. As if to underline their identity, Maître Jacques answers both Harpagon and Cléante in the same manner. To Harpagon's complaints about his son, he says: "Ah! il a tort." And to Cléante of his father, Maître Jacques declares: "Il a tort assurément" (4.4). For Maître Jacques, Harpagon and Cléante are identical in their stubbornness, and he treats them similarly. His would-be "resolution" to the dilemma is no less artificial or more satisfactory than had been the miser's peremptory dismissal of his son after their quarrel about money or Valère's hesitation to side with Elise against Harpagon come what may. Just as he had told each man that the other was wrong, Jacques also assures each that the other has capitulated. Harpagon is overjoyed to learn that his son will obey him, and Cléante believes that his father will let him marry Mariane. When, in the course of their reconciliation, they discover the truth, Harpagon curses his son, who answers with the phrase that incurred Rousseau's wrath:

> *Harpagon*—Et je te donne ma malédiction.
>
> *Cléante*—Je n'ai que faire de vos dons. (4.5)

The face of justice in this scene is altogether farcical. Maître Jacques is hardly a worthy judge of any cause, let alone one that concerns his master. On the other hand, the task of the real representative of justice, when he appears later in the play, will be no easier nor meet with any greater success.

As the difference between those who are right and those who are wrong becomes increasingly problematic, justice loses its capacity to function decisively. Harpagon thinks of nothing but hoarding money and is rightly accused of avarice by his family and servants. He, in turn, condemns them for going to the opposite extreme with their spendthrift ways. Money, in ***L'Avare,*** is a preoccupation shared by characters of every stripe. Their attitudes toward it divide them into two groups: Harpagon and the others. In the final analysis, however, it is impossible to say that right is on the side of one or the other. Rivalry between Harpagon and members of his family makes them all behave similarly, albeit in the name of opposing principles. The Commissaire, called by Harpagon to unravel the mystery of the theft of the strong box, makes no headway because Harpagon can give him no clues. Harpagon believes that everyone is guilty. To the reasonable question "Qui soupçonnezvous de ce vol?" his response is categorical: "Tout le monde" (5.1). Justice itself is ensnared in the net that Harpagon casts out, losing its special—and necessary—quality of disengagement and impartiality. Should the culprit not be found, Harpagon will lump justice together with all the other guilty parties: "si l'on ne me fait retrouver mon argent, je demanderai justice de la justice" (5.1). It is in the context of this leveling of all differences that Harpagon's famous monologue must be read.

Beside himself at the loss of his precious money box, Harpagon laments his fate. The tone and substance of his monologue, based on a similar speech of Euclio, reveal the depth of the crisis triggered by the theft. Without realizing it, Harpagon lays bare the truth of his situation. Money has meant far more to him than the financial security that comes with wealth. It has been his "cher ami . . . mon support, ma consolation, ma joie" (4.7). Life is worth living only if Harpagon can recover his money. Along with it, the miser has lost a firm grasp on himself. No longer can this most egotistical of creatures be certain who he is: "Mon esprit est troublé, et j'ignore où je suis, qui je suis, et ce que je fais" (4.7). The most telling manifestation of Harpagon's alienation is his absolute inability to make fundamental distinctions between various groups of people. Friends and enemies, servants and family members, all are dissolved into one single category: thief. Since all are identical, all are to be treated in the same way. Indeed, Harpagon does not even spare himself: "Je veux aller quérir la justice, et faire donner la question à toute la maison: à servantes, à valets, à fils, à fille, et à moi aussi" (4.7). The miser's own identity is lost in the undifferentiated mass of humanity subsumed under the name "voleur." Even the audience is included in his suspicions. His tirade pushes to the limit a tendency to suspect everyone, to deny distinctions that make it possible for society to function. Harpagon has always been distinguished by his wealth and the sense of power it has brought him. Now, however, his enemies mock him. Crazed, he stares at the audience and realizes that everyone is laughing at him: "Ils me regardent tous, et se mettent à rire" (4.7). His madness consists in his being swallowed up by their laughter. Harpagon becomes one of them, a thief. When he reaches out for the arm of a suspected culprit, it turns out to be his own arm that he has seized. This scene is not, as some have claimed, exaggerated.[6] It is, rather, the powerful comic representation of a crisis that is the natural outcome of imitative rivalry. He who would be superior to others is reduced to the same level as those he intended to dominate and, in the process, loses his own identity.

This is a kind of death, and Harpagon links the theft of his money to his own demise. The opening words of his monologue—"Au voleur! au voleur!"—are counterbalanced by "à l'assassin! au meurtrier!" (4.7). In the next lines, he equates being robbed with being "perdu," being "assassiné," and having his throat slit. More references to death than to the robbery occur in the first lines of Harpagon's speech, and the miser's last words are a threat of multiple executions followed by his suicide: "Je veux faire pendre tout le monde; et si je ne retrouve mon argent, je me pendrai moi-même après" (4.7). In other words, the monologue begins and concludes on the theme of death. Addressing his lost money, Harpagon gives vent to his despair: "sans toi, il m'est impossible de vivre. C'en est fait; je n'en puis plus; je me meurs, je suis mort, je suis enterré" (4.7). He looks for a savior to bring him back to life: "N'y a-t-il personne qui veuille me ressusciter, en me rendant mon cher argent, ou en m'apprenant qui l'a pris?" (4.7). Although the comic impact of Harpagon's obsession with death is undeniable, the presence of the spectre of death throughout the play makes it a powerful image.[7]

Harpagon is terrified of being killed, and his monologue in Act IV, with its repetition and intensification of much that he says elsewhere, is the culminating point of his fear. One of the reasons for which he resents Cléante's extravagant spending is that it might encourage people to think of Harpagon as a rich man, thereby endangering his life: "les dépenses que vous faites seront cause qu'un de ces jours on me viendra chez moi couper la gorge, dans la pensée que je suis tout cousu de pistoles" (1.4). Now precisely that has happened: "On m'a coupé la gorge" (4.7). Earlier, Harpagon would have liked to have the inventor of "ces grands hauts-de-chausses" hanged for an invention that can serve to hide stolen goods (1.3). Now the once-powerful master will hang himself after having others hanged for the crime. He shares their fate with those whom he would dominate. Like his chest, which he had "enterré dans mon jardin" (1.4), Harpagon in his unhappiness is now himself buried: "je suis enterré" (4.7).

Avarice is a fortification that Harpagon has erected to protect himself against the unknown and, ultimately, death. As La Flèche explains to Frosine, the very sight of a borrower, who might ask him to part with money, strikes Harpagon "par son endroit mortel" (2.4). Money is the miser's only defense against death. Therefore, he cannot take lightly the threat of losing it. What money does is give substance to an existence without other solid, visible underpinnings. Harpagon needs money for the same reason that Pascal's hunter needs the hare. Piling it up diverts his attention from his own emptiness. Riches serve him well as a basis for creating an identity different from that of others, and on this difference can be founded his conviction that he is superior to them. Molière, of course, knows as well as Pascal that even though Harpagon's wealth may be very real, the superiority that he would construct upon it is imaginary, always likely to crumble. And try as he might, Harpagon cannot suppress the truth. This is why he lives in constant fear of being robbed. The least suggestion that he might lose money brings him face to face with the possibility of his own annihilation. When La Merluche runs on stage and accidentally knocks Harpagon down, the miser is certain that his creditors have paid the lackey to do him in: "Ah! je suis mort," he cries as he falls (3.9). Robbery, for him, is the equivalent of murder.[8] If Harpagon's belief that he can avoid death by barricading himself behind his wealth is mad, it does, nonetheless, help explain his aberrant behavior.

Furthermore, the rivalry in which he engages with such fervor runs the risk of ending with the death, real or symbolic, of at least one of the combatants. To rob Harpagon of his money is to steal his identity, and, as he himself says, there is no reason to go on living without his money. Likewise, were he to lose the struggle of wills with his son, his identity as a superior being would be crushed. Cléante is not unaware of the mortal dimension of his battle with his father. The avarice of a father, he tells La Flèche, can reduce a son to wishing his father dead (2.1). Harpagon does not realize that he is himself the father in question when Maître Simon tells him that his prospective creditor "s'obligera, si vous voulez, que son père mourra avant qu'il soit huit mois" (2.2). His insouciant response—"C'est quelque chose que cela"—is loaded with irony. Nor is Cléante the only person who looks forward to Harpagon's death. Jokingly commenting on his youthfulness, Frosine assures the miser that he will live to a ripe old age: "Il faudra vous assommer, vous dis-je; et vous mettrez en terre et vos enfants, et les enfants de vos enfants" (2.5). In retrospect, her joke becomes less droll when later we hear her explain to Mariane that it would be "impertinent" of Harpagon not to die within three months of their marriage (3.4), thus making his wife a rich widow. What Frosine's comment suggests is that death awaits Harpagon whether he wins or loses his struggle with Cléante for the hand of Mariane. This rivalry, it would seem, inevitably degenerates into annihilation and death.

Death is present at every turn in ***L'Avare,*** and the existence of individual characters takes form around a core of resistance to it. In the first scene of the play, Elise evokes the day she might have drowned had not Valère saved her from the waves' fury. From that moment on, she has thought of nothing but Valère. This episode, in which she narrowly escaped death, has given meaning to her life. Mariane and her mother, who never appears on stage, have been haunted by the presumed death of the girl's father.

Shortly after discovering that his money has been stolen, Harpagon learns from Valère that Elise has agreed to marry him. Harpagon has lost both his money and his daughter. He does not trust his servants, his son has turned against him, and justice has no power to restore order: "Voiciun étrange embarras," says Frosine (5.4). Harpagon's household is on the brink of chaos.[9] Figuratively, at least, Harpagon is threatened with death: "On m'assassine dans le bien, on m'assassine dans l'honneur" (5.5). Anselme, to whom he says these words, will restore a measure of order. For he, quite by chance, turns out to be the long-lost father of Mariane and Valère, the "late" Dom Thomas d'Alburcy, whose family believed he had perished at sea while seeking exile from Naples. Dom Thomas, convinced that his family had perished as well, had come to France and taken up a new identity. He was about to seek consolation in a new family with Elise as his wife. With encouragement from Anselme and the promise from Cléante that his money will be returned, Harpagon consents to the marriage of his son to Mariane and his daughter to Valère. Overcome in love by the force of events, Harpagon clings all the more fiercely to his greed, insisting that Anselme give his children money for their weddings, underwrite the expenses of the weddings, buy him a new suit for the ceremony, and provide the Commissaire's salary.

At first blush, this conclusion to the play seems altogether artificial and, therefore, unsatisfactory. Only by pure coincidence is a semblance of order restored. However, the comic dénouement of ***L'Avare*** makes perfect sense and follows logically from everything that has preceded it. The return to order at the end of the play is literally snatched from the clutches of death. Had Dom Thomas really died, as well he might have under the circumstances and, indeed, as everyone thought he had, there might have been no resolution of the crisis possible without Harpagon's demise. Keeping out of the way of death has been at the root of the way in which Harpagon has organized life. To trick death, that ultimate destruction of the will, has been the miser's goal. He has made sense of a meaningless existence and averted a confrontation with the absence of meaning by avoiding death. The resurrection of Dom Thomas does that too, but it has no more finality either.

The comic resolution provided by Anselme is by no means a final one, and this, really, is the meaning of the end of ***L'Avare.*** If the "étrange embarras" can be eliminated only by the return to life of a man believed to have been long since dead, it is apparent that this "embarras" is resistant to all but the most powerful of remedies. Death will, in the end, overcome attempts to conquer it, and rivalry's relentless movement toward death cannot be stopped in its tracks. As in other plays of Molière, the monomaniac remains unrepentant and unreformed. A crisis of order in the household brought about by Harpagon's rivalry with his son has been narrowly averted. That his avarice has remained untouched by the momentary return to order leaves the permanent risk of a new and equally devastating crisis. ***L'Avare*** is among the more somber of Molière's plays. Not the least of the reasons for this is the clarity with which the play's conclusion demonstrates the destructiveness of the plague of rivalry.

Notes

1. Molière, *L'Avare,* in *Œuvres complètes,* ed. Georges Couton, 2 vols. (Paris: Gallimard, 1971), Vol. 2. The Couton edition is used throughout for citations from *L'Avare.*
2. Molière, *L'Avare,* ed. Louis Lacour (Paris: Librairie des Bibliophiles, 1976), vii.
3. Jean-Jacques Rousseau, *Lettre à M. d'Alembert,* in *Du Contrat social* (Paris: Garnier, 1962), 149-50.
4. See Couton's introduction to *L'Avare,* 508-09.
5. Plautus, *Aulularia or the Pot of Gold,* in *Plautus,* trans. Paul Nixon, 5 vols. (London and Cambridge, MA: William Heinemann and Harvard UP, 1916-38), 1, 232-33. "Anxious about his gold, Euclio hides it outside the house. Everything he does having been witnessed, a rascally servant of the girl's assailant [Lyconides] steals it. His master informs Euclio of it, and receives from him gold, wife, and son." (Euclio's daughter Phaedria is already pregnant by Lyconides, whence the "son.")
6. See Molière, *L'Avare,* in *Œuvres,* eds. Eugène Despois and Paul Mesnard, 13 vols. (Paris: Hachette, 1873-1900): "Molière, à l'exemple de Plaute, a cru qu'en cet endroit un peu d'exagération ne dépassait pas les droits de la comédie. Autrement peut-être, la scène risquait-elle d'être trop voisine du tragique" (7:175).
7. As Georges Couton has it, "Cela pue à la fois l'argent et le cadavre" (513).
8. Reference has already been made to Harpagon's monologue in Act IV, where he speaks of robbery and murder as one. Later, during his comic misunderstanding with Valère, Harpagon, still believing that Valère is a thief, calls his future son-in-law's crime "un assassinat de la sorte" (5.3). The image of assassination is used again in this way in 5.5.
9. As René Girard points out in *La Violence et le sacré* (Paris: Grasset, 1972), the breakdown of differences often leads to chaos.

FURTHER READING

Criticism

Cruikshank, John, ed. *French Literature and Its Background.* London: Oxford University Press, 1969, 187 p.

Considers the literary, intellectual, and social aspects of seventeenth-century France.

Hope, Quentin M. "Dramatic Techniques in *Les Précieuses Ridicules.*" In *Renaissance and Other Studies in Honor of William Leon Wiley*, edited by George Bernard Daniel, Jr., pp. 141-150. Chapel Hill: The University of North Carolina Press, 1968.

Surveys playwriting techniques first seen in *Les Précieuses Ridicules.*

Knutson, Harold C. *Molière: An Archetypal Approach.* Toronto: University of Toronto Press, 1976, 208 p.

An archetypal approach analyzing the comedy of Molière.

———. "Molière in Performance." *Papers on French Seventeenth Century Literature* IX, No. 16, (1982): 151-71.

Focuses on the theatrical aspects of Molière's work.

———. *The Triumph of Wit: Molière and Restoration Comedy.* Columbus: Ohio State University Press, 1988, 192 p.

Examines Molière's work using criteria normally associated with Restoration manners comedy.

Konstan, David. "A Dramatic History of Misanthropes." *Comparative Drama* XVII, No. 2 (1983): 97-123.

A study of the virtues and deficiencies of misanthropes in three dramas, including Molière's *Le Misanthrope.*

Lawrence, Francis L. "The Ironic Commentator in Molière's *Dom Juan,*" *Studi Francesi* XII, No. 35 (1968): 201-07.

Explores the obtrusive interplay between the hero and the buffoonish valet.

Moore, W. G. *Molière: A New Criticism.* London: Oxford University Press, 1949, 136 p.

Criticism of Molière's work as viewed from a Restoration-era perspective.

Powell, John S. "Music and the Self-Fulfilling Prophecy in Molière's *Le marriage forcé,*" *Early Music* XXI, No. 2 (1993): 213-30.

Explains how Molière wove music, comedy, and dance into an integrated play with manifold meanings.

Romero, Laurence. *Molière: Traditions in Criticism 1900-1970.* Chapel Hill: University of North Carolina Department of Romance Languages, 1974, 282 p.

Overviews critical studies of Molière from French, British, and American sources.

Zimbardo, Rose A. "Considering Comedy." *Modern Language Quarterly* 49 (1988): 65-72.

Lists problems presented by theories of comedy, evidenced by Zimbardo's perception of Knutson's inability to understand Molière.

Additional coverage of Molière's life and career is contained in the following sources published by the Gale Group: *DISCovering Authors; DISCovering Authors: British; DISCovering Authors: Canadian; DISCovering Authors Modules: Dramatists, Most-studied Authors; Literature Criticism From 1400 to 1800,* Vols. 10, 28.

Tirso de Molina
1580?-1648

(Born Gabriel Téllez) Spanish playwright of the Golden Age.

INTRODUCTION

Tirso de Molina was one of the four most famous and revered playwrights of Spain's Golden Age. De Molina was a disciple of the first, most famous, and most prolific of these dramatists, Lope de Vega. Although he is supposed to have written nearly 400 plays, not all are assuredly his writings, and today less than 90 are extant. Because de Molina's plays range from the highly comic to the tragic and because he wrote as much to serve principle as to please an audience, comparisons to Shakespeare are common. De Molina's greatest contribution to both life and letters is Don Juan, the character who first appeared in *El burlador de Sevilla* (1630; *The Trickster of Seville and the Stone Guest*).

BIOGRAPHICAL INFORMATION

De Molina was born Gabriel Téllez in Madrid around 1580. His parentage is uncertain, but he was probably the illegitimate son of a duke, a status that might account for de Molina's complaints about his lack of social position, the injustice of certain social conventions, and his dislike of nobility and hierarchy. He studied at the universities of Alcalá and Guadalajara. In 1601 he joined the large and noble Mercedarian Order in which he held high office, winning prestige as a theologian and acting as the Order's chronicler. In 1613 he relocated to Toledo, becoming a friar, and later moved to Santo Domingo. In 1621 de Molina traveled to Madrid, where he wrote a great many of his plays. He gook part in the literary celebration in 1622 for San Isidro—presided over by Lope de Vega—but did not win any prizes for the poetry he submitted. In 1625 de Molina was banished from the Junta de Reformación for alleged obscenities and was transferred to a remote friary in Trujillo where he served as Prior for three years. He was told never to write further plays or poems, and it appears he mostly followed this edict since most of his plays appear to have been written from 1605–1625, the latter being the date of his reprimand. At Trujillo, he served as official chronicler of the Order. During the thirties he was in Barcelona, Madrid, and Toldedo, and was again banished to a friary in Soria, where he became its Prior from 1645–47. He is said to have written three to four hundred plays in his lifetime. He died in Almazán in 1648.

MAJOR WORKS

De Molina initially depended greatly on his renowned contemporary, Lope de Vega, whose influence is evident in one of de Molina's earliest plays, *Los lagos de San Vicente* (1607; *The Miraculous Lakes of Saint Vincent*), which closely imitates de Vega's *Santa Casilda*. The progression from imitation to mastery can be seen in de Molina's body of work, which came to include comedies, tragedies, historical plays, and novels. De Molina is best known for his religious plays, the most significant of which are *El burlador de Sevilla* and *El condenado por desconfiado* (1624; *Damned for Despair*). *El burlador* is attributed with introducing the theme of Don Juan into European literature. Later, this theme became famous in world literature through Wolfgang Amadeus Mozart's opera *Don Giovanni*. De Molina also wrote many serious plays inspired by stories from the Old Testament, including *La venganza de Tamar* (1634; *The Vengeance of Tamar*). As a playwright of the Golden Age, de Molina had to concentrate on amusing his audience despite his serious subject matter. *Don Gil de la calzas verdes* (1611; *Don Gil in*

Green Breeches), in which de Molina uses the convention of women disguised as men, and *El vergonzoso en palacio* (1612; *The Shy Young Man at Court*) are among his most spirited comedies.

CRITICAL RECEPTION

The traditional, yet adventurous themes and memorable characters de Molina created throughout his career undoubtedly contributed to his literary significance during and since the Golden Age. His *El burlador de Sevilla* is generally considered his masterpiece, although his religious play *El condenado por desconfiado* also is much admired. His comedies employing the comic device of women disguised as men, including *Don Gil de la calzas verdes* and *El vergonzoso en palacio*, are admired for the depth of characterization given the female characters. His historical drama, *La prudencia en la mujer* (1622; *Prudence in a Woman*), depicting the reign of Queen Maria, garnered critical praise for its insight into Spanish politics and morality. Another strong female character of de Molina is the protagonist of *Marta la piadosa* (1615; *Pious Martha*), in which a woman employs deceitful tactics to flummox the rigid patriarchal establishment in order to marry the man of her choosing. His religious plays are often thought to be imitative and less successfully accomplished than the similarly themed plays of Lope de Vega. In fact, de Molina is considered second only to de Vega as the era's most significant writer.

PRINCIPAL WORKS

Plays

Los lagos de San Vicente [*The Miraculous Lakes of Saint Vincent*] 1607

El melancólico [*The Melancholiac*] 1610

Don Gil de la calza verdes [*Don Gil in Green Breeches*] 1611

El vergonzoso en palacio [*The Shy Young Man at Court*] 1612

Los cigarrales de Toledo [*The Country Houses of Toledo*] 1621

La prudencia en la mujer [*Prudence in a Woman*] 1622

El condenado por desconfiado [*Damned for Despair*] 1624

La huerta de Juan Fernández 1626

El burlador de Sevilla y convidado de piedra [*The Trickster of Seville and the Stone Guest*] 1630

La venganza de Tamar [*The Vengeance of Tamar*] 1634

Antona García 1635

Las quinas de Portugal [*The Arms of Portugal*] 1638

OVERVIEWS AND GENERAL STUDIES

Gerald E. Wade (essay date 1949)

SOURCE: "Tirso de Molina," in *Hispania*, Vol. XXXII, No. 2, May, 1949, pp. 131-40.

[*In the following essay, Wade discusses de Molina's life and work, focusing on how he used his genius to serve humanity.*]

Tirso de Molina (born Gabriel Téllez) died in 1648. The tercentenary of his death has occasioned a rebirth of interest in him and his work. Indeed, the resurgence of Tirsian scholarship began some years ago, in Spain, England, and the United States. The appearance of Doña Blanca de los Ríos' long-awaited volume on Tirso[1] was a climactic event that will have scholarly repercussion for years to come. The volume is the first of two which will contain Tirso's biography and the texts of all his plays; the second is scheduled to appear in 1949. The scholarly labors of Father Manuel Penedo, of Santiago Montoto, and of Fray Martín Ortúzar have contributed substantially to our knowledge of Tirso and his theater. In England, two commentators on Tirso and his art have produced recent contributions of genuine worth. Aubrey Bell's "Some Notes on Tirso de Molina"[2] is an attempt to review the major facts of Tirso's life and work; the essay has in general that authority and charm which Mr. Bell's efforts invariably possess, but it has also a number of features, whether in reference to Tirso's biography or to an appreciation of his plays, that, in the light of our very recent knowledge of him and his work, are of doubtful accuracy. Miss I. L. McClelland's essays in the *Bulletin of Spanish Studies*[3] have dealt stimulatingly, and with some profundity, with certain esthetic features of Tirso's art.

In the United States, Miss Ruth Lee Kennedy began some years ago a systematic study of Tirso's theater which has resulted in findings of exceptional importance for an understanding of him and his art. Miss Kennedy's essays have dealt with the background of his *comedias*, the social, economic, and political milieu that brought them forth, and her persistent effort to date his plays by throwing them against this background—truly a fundamental requisite for a comprehension of his work—has resulted in the accurate dating of a number of those whose dates have heretofore been uncertain.[4] Her recent study of ***La prudencia en la mujer*** (*PMLA* for December, 1948) illumines Tirso's attitude toward his dramatic material and his use of Spanish history to offer a lesson in government to the young Felipe IV; for the first time, Tirso becomes three-dimensional, a truly living person, placed in the framework of his time and its problems, a fearless fighter for decency in life and in government. Miss Alice H. Bushee and Sherman W. Brown[5] have made welcome contributions, while Otis H. Green and others have considered Tirso and his theater in a number of studies. Joaquín Casalduero's provocative study of the Don Juan theme[6] was received with great interest, but not all of his readers will agree with his ideas in the matter.

The immediate future of Tirsian scholarship both in the United States and abroad is bright. In Spain, Father Penedo will continue his contributions to *Estudios*; in particular, his proposed edition of the very significant *Historia de la Merced* of Tirso is awaited eagerly. Father Penedo and his fellow Mercedarians are publishing this year a special volume in memory of Tirso which contains studies written in Spain and in the United States. It will offer, among other matters, a bibliography of Tirso, compiled by Everett W. Hesse; it is hardly necessary to stress the importance of this first effort at a complete bibliography of the great Mercedarian. Miss Esmeralda Gijón is making a study of Tirso's style and language. In this country, Miss Kennedy will continue her studies in chronology and historical background; in collaboration with Courtney Bruerton, she plans an investigation of Tirso's versification. Miss Lorna Stafford and Miss Alice H. Bushee are completing a historical edition of ***La prudencia en la mujer***, and C. E. Anibal and I hope to offer a critical edition of the *Santa Juana* trilogy. It is in fact only proper that Tirso, the Spanish Shakespeare,[7] as he has been called, should receive sharply increased attention in the years to come. Mr. Bell has recently expressed again[8] the wonder of Tirso's relative neglect through the centuries, the indifference on the part of many students of Spanish literature toward the treasure that lies in his surviving plays.

These plays, including three *autos sacramentales,* number a tentative eighty-four, as published by Hartzenbusch in volume V of the *Biblioteca de autores españoles* and by Cotarelo in volumes IV and IX of the *Nueva Biblioteca de autores españoles.* Two other *autos* are in volume XVIII. But of the total number of eighty-six *comedias* and *autos*, one *comedia*, *La romera de Santiago*, has been claimed with apparent finality for Luis Vélez de Guevara[9], while another, *La reina de los reyes*, is now known to be of other authorship. This play, one of the twelve *comedias* of the much-discussed *Segunda Parte* of Tirso, has been shown by Santiago Montoto[10] to have been written by the Sevillan Hipólito Vergara; Sr. Montoto's significant discovery is, one may hope, the beginning of a solution of the *Segunda Parte* riddle which has always perplexed students of Tirso. Thus there are seventy-nine surviving *comedias* which may possibly have come from Tirso's pen, but of these, only fifty-one titles are his with complete certainty (the five *autos* are accepted without question as his). These were published in four of the five volumes or *Partes* which appeared between 1627 and 1636. Of the twelve *comedias* of the remaining *Parte*, the puzzling *Segunda*, four are Tirso's and the others of uncertain authorship, on the evidence of Tirso's own words in the dedicatory of the volume.[11] Thus fifty-five surviving *comedias* are quite surely of his authorship, and a number of others, perhaps as many as twenty-eight, came from his pen at least in part.

The most famous play which is usually ascribed to Tirso is ***El burlador de Sevilla***. But since it did not appear originally in any of Tirso's own volumes, it is still, in the final analysis, of debatable paternity. In some ways it is the most remarkable drama of the entire Golden Age; Miss McClelland, in two of her essays, gives it sufficient comment to bring out certain aspects of its deep significance for dramatic art. Moreover, this first of the Don Juan plays is a literary ancestor with a progeny far greater than that of any other play ever written; the Don Juan theme has surely appeared in all the civilized languages. Tirso's play has a number of technical faults and its text has been corrupted from the original probably more than Américo Castro has been willing to admit.[12] But its theme is still very much alive, and if it should eventually be granted to some other dramatist, the prestige that will accrue to him will be very great. It is unfortunate for Tirso's great reputation that not only the ***Burlador de Sevilla*** but also ***El Condenado por desconfiado***—the best-known religious play of the Golden Age—should be only doubtfully his. Fray Martín Ortúzar has recently argued for Tirso's paternity for the play by proposing that the ***Condenado***, written by a follower of the Thomist Zumel, could logically have come from Tirso's pen since Tirso was himself a follower of Zumel.[13] For the present we leave to those trained in theology the decision regarding the theological ideas of the ***Condenado***. Nor is there space here to consider the bearing these ideas may have on the authorship of the play. Fortunately for Tirso's fame, there is no doubt about his paternity of the most remarkable historical drama of the Golden Age, ***La prudencia en la mujer***, which testifies to Tirso's genius for creating character, a gift denied, in equal degree, to all other playwrights of the *Edad de oro*, but one which he has utilized to the full in a number of plays. At the same time, it shows Tirso's talent for the play thesis.

The enigma of his birth is still the most puzzling thing about Tirso de Molina. Here is one of the greatest playwrights of all time, and his parentage is still a matter of doubt. Scholars have been skeptical of the belief of Doña Blanca de los Ríos that he was a Girón, an illegitimate half-brother of Don Pedro, "el gran duque," as he came to be called. She bases her belief on a baptismal certificate which shows that a certain Gabriel, born in 1584 in the parish of San Ginés in Madrid, was given no surname except apparently that in a marginal notation later crossed out very thoroughly.[14] This marginal notation Sra. de los Ríos would read as "Gabriel Téllez Girón, hijo del Duque Osuna." The eminent scholar, Antonio Paz y Melia, she asserts, agreed completely with her in the reading of the notation. This was before the turn of the century, and the ink, presumably, had not blackened so much through action of the light as it has since. The most devastating attempt at a refutation of her reading was made by Artiles Rodríguez;[15] this scholar rejected her reading for the marginal notation and hence the Osuna paternity for Tirso.[16] Sr. Artiles, however, accepted the balance of the certificate as Tirso's, with the consequent assertion of his birth in 1584 in the parish of San Ginés, Madrid. Until further evidence of Tirso's parentage becomes available, it seems reasonable to agree with Sr. Artiles' conclusion. After most industrious search by Señora de los Ríos and others, no other certificate has been found which could reasonably be taken as Tirso's, and the one discovered in the parish of San Ginés may well become his by default, if for no other reason.[17] The date of 1584 is supported substantially by another document that records Tirso's age: a record of the beginning of his journey to the New World in 1616. The document in question is dated as of that year, and it gives Tirso's age as thirty-four. This figure would imply his birth in 1583 rather than in 1584, but the discrepancy is too slight to have importance in a day when documentation was much less careful than in our own.[18] Tirso, then, was born in Madrid, as he himself tells us more than once,[19] and almost certainly in 1584, as Doña Blanca's discovery indicates.[20] The years from 1584 to 1600 are blank for him; there has been discovered no record to tell where he was or what he was doing. Of his family we know only for certain that he had a sister, "parecida a él en ingenio y en desdichas."[21]

It is probable that Tirso's schooling was partly at the famous University of Alcalá, although there is no sure evidence of the fact.[22] Doña Blanca de los Ríos thinks that he may also possibly have attended the University of Salamanca.[23] His first documented activity is his entrance into the Mercedarian Order; this was in 1600 or 1601, as Father Penedo has lately shown.[24] The next documented date for his biography is the composition date of ***El vergonzoso en palacio***. This, presumably his first play, was written apparently in 1605 or 1606; again, it is Father Penedo who has presented the documents that seem to substantiate the fact.[25] Tirso thus began his playwriting at the age of twenty-one or two.

His dramatic activity continued until 1625, possibly with interruptions due to his trip to the New World in 1616 and, at other periods, because of his absorption in the affairs of his Order. In 1625 he was forbidden by Felipe IV's *Junta de Reformación* to write any more plays or verse.[26] The interdict has often been interpreted as springing from the *Junta*'s belief in the danger of Tirso's plays to public morals; actually, there are many reasons to believe that it was a weapon used against him by powerful enemies. As the daring, indeed, rash inditer of frequent attacks on powerful figures after 1621—as many of his plays make clear—Tirso was too bold and effective an enemy to be overlooked. The exile from Madrid that was a part of the interdict was one that, with intermissions, was to last the rest of his life. We know from his own words that he was the victim of persecution of the envious and the slanderous; it is clear that he was more than the victim of his own persecution complex; that he had very real enemies who were powerful enough to undo him.[27]

It is not probable that Tirso long observed the interdict against writing plays, although according to the preliminaries of his various ***Partes*** it is clear that he constantly needed the favor of powerful friends to gain permission for publishing them. He himself, in the preliminaries to his ***Tercera Parte***, twice stated that he had not written plays for ten years prior to its publication—this was in 1634. But it is hardly possible to take him literally. Cotarelo has pointed out that ***Desde Toledo a Madrid*** was "concluida o retocada después de 8 de julio de 1625"; that ***No hay peor sordo*** was composed "por los años de 1625," and that ***La huerta de Juan Fernández*** was written (or retouched?) in 1626.[28] Miss Kennedy agrees that ***No hay peor sordo*** was written late in 1625 or early in 1626, subsequent to the edict of the ***Junta de Reformación***, and suggests ***Habladme en entrando*** as another play of about that time.[29] Sra. de los Ríos reproduced in her *Enigma biográfico*, p. 64, a document showing that Tirso was given nine hundred *reales* in Trujillo in April of 1629 for three *comedias*; presumably these were of recent composition, since Tirso would have sold his older plays some time before. It is not known in what year he stopped writing for the stage; the year 1639 can no longer be accepted with assurance, since the supposedly holographic manuscript of ***Las quinas de Portugal***, dated in that year, is really not in Tirso's hand and hence is of uncertain composition date.[30]

From 1605 or 1606 until 1625, with a lapse of at least two years because of his Santo Domingo visit, Tirso, then, wrote more or less constantly for the stage. In the preliminaries to the ***Tercera Parte*** he states that he has written more than four hundred plays in twenty years, but this may be an exaggeration. It is now quite certain that he revised or at least retouched a number of plays, and the total which he wrote may have been considerably less than the four hundred he claimed. From 1625 on he wrote further plays to a total whose number is as yet unknown. The last year in which he composed a *comedia* was perhaps 1630 or 1631;[31] thereafter, there is no record of such production. Some of his plays, at least, were in great demand by the play producers; Sra. de los Ríos has published a document which reproduces a contract showing that on one occasion a play producer bought one of Tirso's *comedias* before it was completed.[32] A number of his *comedias* were produced again and again. He tells us, for instance, that ***El vergonzoso en palacio*** was played by many companies,[33] while the surviving *licencias* of the holographic *Santa Juana* reveal production in many of Spain's major cities over a number of years. The popularity of his plays from 1624 to 1628 has been attested by Henri Mérimée: during that period the play producers Roque de Figueroa, Juan Acacio and Jerónimo Amella all carried *comedias* by Tirso in their repertoires.[34]

Tirso wrote almost every type of play: comedy, tragedy, the palace play, the cloak and sword *comedia*, the play of intrigue, of history, of legend, of Biblical lore, of saints' lives, the psychological drama. His gift for the comic, which he seemed constitutionally incapable of resisting, even in his most serious plays, was unequalled; no other playwright's clowns were as funny as his. He attempted nothing original as far as the *comedia*'s formula was concerned, being content to follow his great master, Lope de Vega.[35] But within the formula he was superbly original in his gift for comedy and in his capacity to create character, especially that of women. It is of course untrue that Tirso could create only feminine character, a charge often made against him. He did find the feminine heart more an enigma than the masculine, and hence more of a challenge to his curious mind. His reputation for creating outstanding women characters has come largely from his most famous comic situation; that in which a man becomes merely a pawn in a determined woman's hands. ***Don Gil de las calzas verdes, La villana de Vallecas, La celosa de sí misma, Marta la piadosa, El amor médico*** represent the situation best of all his plays. Tirso wrote such plays largely because they are amusing and, at times, rather sensational, especially when the lady of the drama dons men's clothing and pursues her faithless lover. But it must also be true that Tirso saw Spanish society dominated by its women; Doña Blanca de los Ríos has suggested tht he wrote ***La mujer que manda en casa*** as an attack on Felipe III's Queen, Margarita de Austria, because he saw feminine dominance represented in the royal household itself.[36] Doctor Marañón has suggested[37] that even Don Juan was woman-dominated; that he was the victim rather than the victimizer of his intended prey. Be that as it may, it has intrigued students of Tirso that he, a priest, should be so interested in women and that he should understand them so well. Earlier commentators on the matter saw in this fact a suggestion of his libertinism; modern students of Tirso are entirely unwilling to accept the accusation, which is completely lacking in substantiation. Tirso was a priest from the age of sixteen or seventeen; as far as we know, his personal relationships with women were, from that age on, those that came normally from his priestly duties. That these duties permitted him to be somewhat worldly in the sense that he was not cloister-confined and that he was no doubt often in the company of women-folk and their men—as in ***Los cigarrales de Toledo***—is our good fortune; it has meant those superb dramas that so delight us today.

Tirso possessed a deep fund of theological knowledge, and this was given official recognition when he was granted the degree of *Maestro* by Pope Urban VIII in 1637.[38] His theology colors many of his writings; this is one reason for the consistent attribution to him of the doubtful ***Condenado por desconfiado***. Seemingly out of consonance with his theological bent are his oft-expressed cynicism (occasionally as brazen as that of the picaresque novel) and an apparent heartlessness that is at times diamond-hard. To offset this hardness one finds at times a deep tenderness which is unsurpassed in the history of the drama. A moralist, he was driven by an irresistible urge to attack fraud and corruption, insincerity and cant; it was this fearless assault on corruption in high places that must have been largely responsible for the interdict of 1625.

During the years of his dramatic activity and beyond them until at least the year 1639—the date of publication of the second part of his *Historia de la Merced*—Tirso was busy with the affairs of his Order. As his youthful capacity grew in the matters of his profession he was given responsibilities in keeping with it. He was one of those chosen to go to Santo Domingo on business of his Order; it must have been a coveted journey. While there he "read" three courses in theology, a responsible task. This New World activity made him eligible for the *presentatura*,[39] which was granted some time before June, 1618; he had been made *procurador* for Santo Domingo at some time before that date.[40] He became *Comendador* (Prior) of Trujillo in 1626, *cronista* of his Order in 1632, *Definidor de Castilla* in that same year, *Comendador de Soria* in 1647. His travels took him over a great part of the Spanish peninsula; his residence is documented in Madrid, Toledo, Soria, Trujillo, Cuenca, Almazán,[41] Zaragoza, and Cataluña, while he visited more or less briefly in Guadalajara, Valladolid,[42] Salamanca, and Sevilla. His plays make one suspect that he may have seen Galicia, Italy and Portugal, while parts of the ***Cigarrales de Toledo*** possibly suggest a visit to Sardinia.

Tirso de Molina lived one of the most useful lives of his generation. In a day when literary genius was superabundant, he excelled, and he used a great part of his genius for the service of his fellow men, whether directly in the duties of his Order or in many of his plays as a satirist-reformer. At times the moral tone of his writings distresses the modern reader because Tirso lived in a day of relatively low moral tone, and he was first of all a man of his time. Even though he was one of its most intelligent and brilliant spokesmen, he was not advanced beyond his generation in the major features of Golden Age ideology, especially those having to do with the internal and external politics of Spain. He was always a Spaniard, and yet on occasion he has achieved a Shakespearean-like universality through his deep understanding of the human heart. Tirso died in one of the remote convents of his Order, an exile from his beloved Madrid and Toledo, whether disillusioned and embittered by his apparent defeat at the hands of his implacable enemies we know not. His death, formerly dated as of March 12, 1648 and believed to have been in Soria, is now known to have occurred at Almazán in that year, and some time between February 20 and 24; the recent documentation of the fact is due to the valued efforts of Father Penedo[43].

Notes

1. Blanca de los Ríos de Lampérez, *Tirso de Molina. Obras dramáticas completas*. Madrid, 1946, 1.

2. See the *Bulletin of Spanish Studies*, XVII, 68 (October, 1940), 172-203.

3. See XVIII, 72 (October, 1941), 182-204; XIX, 76 (October, 1942), 148-163; XX, 80 (October, 1943), 214-231. Miss McClelland's essays, amplified and with the addition of much new material, have recently been published in one volume: *Tirso de Molina. Studies in Dramatic Realism*. (Liverpool Studies in Spanish Literature: Third Series), Liverpool, 1948.

4. For Miss Kennedy's articles, see the *Hispanic Review*, X, 2 (April, 1942), 91-115; X, 3 (July, 1943), 183-214; XI, 1 (January, 1942), 17-46; XII, 1 (January, 1944), 49-57.

5. See Miss Bushee's *Three Centuries of Tirso de Molina* (Philadelphia, 1939) and Mr. Brown's text edition of *La villana de Vallecas* (New York, 1948).

6. Joaquín Casalduero, "Contribución al estudio del tema de Don Juan en el teatro español," in *Smith College Studies in Modern Languages*, XIX, 3-4 (April-July, 1938).

7. The name was given him, no doubt, because of his profoundly human qualities, but there are at times verbal parallels as well that argue for a common source. For instance, Shakespeare's "All the world's a stage" has a striking parallel in Tirso. There seems, however, to be implied no borrowing on the part of either, but rather, a common source for both playwrights. The idea had become a commonplace one in classic times; see George Lyman Kittredge's edition of *As You Like It* (New York: Ginn and Company, 1939), xviii. Tirso's parallel is not consistent throughout with Shakespeare's, but a few lines are notably similar: Que es comedia nuestra vida, / y en ella representantes / cuantos contemplas vivientes; / con papeles diferentes / representan los mortales / ya púrpuras, ya sayales; / pero al fin es lo ordinario / que el sepulcro su vestuario / los desnude, y haga iguales . . . (*Deleytar aprovechando*, ed. 1635, I, folios 152, 153). I am indebted to Miss Kennedy for the location of the reference.

8. See note 2.

9. See F. E. Spencer and Rudolph Schevill, *The Dramatic Works of Luis Vélez de Guevara* (Berkeley, 1937), 110.

10. See his "Una comedia de Tirso, que no es de Tirso," in *Archivo Hispalense*, Sevilla, 2a. época, VII (1946), 18-19, pp. 99-107.

11. See Cotarelo, *Comedias de Tirso*, I (*Nueva Biblioteca de Autores Españoles*, IV, Madrid, 1906), lix, n.

12. See the Castro edition of the *Burlador* (*Clásicos castellanos*, Madrid, 1932), p. xviii.

13. See Father Ortúzar's "'El condenado por desconfiado' depende teológicamente de Zumel," *Estudios,* IV, 10 (enero-abril, 1948), 7-41. Father Ortúzar's is one of a recent series of articles on *El condenado*; see, for example, those by Fray Rafael María de Hornedo in *Razón y Fe*, 120 (mayo-agosto, 1940), 18-34, 170-191; 138 (diciembre, 1948), 636-646. The last-named article attempts to summarize the major writings on the theological intent of *El condenado*.

14. The certificate is reproduced photographically in Sra. de los Ríos' *El enigma biográfico de Tirso de Molina* (Madrid, 1928), 33-34, and also in her *Obras de Tirso de Molina,* I, lxxxvii.

15. Artiles Rodríguez's study, "La partida bautismal de 'Tirso de Molina,'" may be read in the *Revista de la Biblioteca, Archivo y Museos*, V (October, 1929), 403-411. C. E. Anibal made a digest and commentary on it in Hispania, XII (1929), 325-327.

16. Juan Millé Giménez, another commentator on Sra. de los Ríos' thesis for Tirso's paternity, accepted her reading of the birth certificate without question. In his review of her *El enigma biográfico de Tirso* in *Síntesis* (Buenos Aires, III, 27 [agosto, 1929], 367-368), he suggested that Tirso's father might well have been D. Juan Téllez Girón, of some thirty years of age, a poet, a soldier of the Armada in 1588, and a man of rebellious and adventurous humor. D. Juan had built a reputation for wildness. Sr. Millé thinks that the mother, Gracia Juliana, could have been an actress of easy virtue, and that such a double *ascendencia* would explain well some of the principal traits of Tirso's work.

It might be suggested that Tirso's own reticence about his birth is strong evidence for illegitimacy (though not necessarily that of a Girón). It may be that he said nothing about his paternity because he was too proud to claim it against his father's refusal to legitimize him. Of course everyone in Madrid knew who he was, and the "conspiracy of silence" which has obscured the information might seem to be a further indication that he was an illegitimate son of some high-born person. There is no record of his having been twitted about his birth, as Lope was twitted for the mediocrity of his parentage and his attempt to claim gentility. Sra. de los Ríos has remarked a number of times on Tirso's championing of the *segundón* and the *bastardo* in his plays, a significant circumstance. Again it seems that the tone of the various dedicatories of his works to his noble friends has perhaps less of the subservient in it than was common in that of some writers; that Tirso was addressing them more on a basis of equality. One must admit, however, that regardless of whether or not he was of noble parentage, his pride, one of his most positive traits, always kept him from abject servility; he was no Lope to do his contemptible act for another Sessa.

17. In her *El enigma biográfico*, Sra. de los Ríos chose not to confide in her readers the discovery of another baptismal certificate which her later *Obras de Tirso de Molina*, I contains. On page lxx of the *Obras* a footnote reproduces a certificate that states that a certain Gavriel Josepe López y Téllez was born in the parish of San Sebastián in Madrid on March 20, 1579. The Señora explains that this Gavriel could certainly not be Tirso; this, presumably, was her reason for failing to mention it in her *Enigma*. Scholars may well deplore her determination to keep silent so long about the certificate of 1579, but they will agree that of the two documents, the one dated 1584 is much more probably that of Tirso.

18. Sra. de los Ríos has reproduced the document photographically in the *Revista Nacional de*

Educación, II, 22 (Octubre, 1942), 102, *bis*. See also her essay accompanying the document: "La fecha del nacimiento de 'Tirso de Molina'," 101-114.

19. See Cotarelo, *Comedias de Tirso de Molina*, I, x.

20. The 1571 or 1572 date for Tirso's birth has been thoroughly discredited. Based on the authority of a statement on a portrait of him—the portrait itself is taken to be genuine—the date is now discarded and has been replaced in scholarly discussion by 1584 or 1583, depending on the individual student's willingness to accept the 1584 baptismal certificate as Tirso's. Karl Vossler's acceptance of the 1571 or 1572 date (see *Escorial*, Febrero, 1941, 167-186) is surprising in a critic of his deservedly great reputation.

21. See Cotarelo, *op. cit.*, xi. Miss Kennedy, in her *PMLA* study (see her footnote 29), would tentatively identify this sister as "doña María de San Ambrosio y Piña, monja en la Magdalena de Madrid." Sister María wrote one of the laudatory poems preceding the text of Tirso's *Los cigarrales de Toledo*.

22. See Cotarelo, *op. cit.*, xi-xii.

23. See her *Obras*, I, xxxix*b*, cix, cxvii*b*, n. 1.

24. P. M. Penedo, "Noviciado y profesión de Tirso de Molina (1600?-1601)," *Estudios*, I, 2 (mayo-agosto, 1945), 82-90.

25. P. M. Penedo, "El Fraile Músico de 'Los Cigarrales de Toledo,' de Tirso de Molina," *Estudios,* III, 9 (septiembre, 1947), 383-390. Father Penedo's date for the *Vergonzoso* supersedes that suggested by Sra. de los Ríos. In her *Obras de Tirso de Molina*, I, she states that the play was composed in 1611 or 1612; see her pp. xliv, xlvii, lxii, cx, 179, 298.

26. See Angel González Palencia, "Quevedo, Tirso y las comedias ante la Junta de Reformación," *Boletín de la Real Academia Espanola*, XXV, 43-84. The *acta* referring to Tirso is dated March 6, 1625 and reads as follows: "*Maestro Téllez, por otro nombre Tirso, que hace comedias.*—Tratóse del escándalo que causa un fraile mercedario, que se llama el Maestro Téllez, por otro nombre Tirso, con comedias que hace profanas y de malos incentivos y ejemplos. Y por ser caso notorio se acordó que se consulte a S. M. de que el confesor diga al Nuncio [several words were crossed out and replaced by "que mande a su Provincial"] le eche de aquí a uno de los monasterios más remotos de su Religión y le imponga excomunicación mayor *latae sententiae* para que no haga comedias ni otro ningún género de versos profanos. Y esto se haga luego."

27. For his own statement regarding the envy that pursued him, see, for example, *Antona García* (Cotarelo, I, 634a) where, as Miss Kennedy correctly suggests (*op. cit.*, footnotes 40, 86), the Castellano 7° is Tirso; or the *Cigarrales de Toledo* (ed. Said Armesto, 102). See also the statement of Avila, his supposed nephew, in the foreword to Tirso's *Tercera Parte* (Cotarelo, *op. cit.*, lvii, n.); it is of course Tirso rather than Avila who wrote the words. And Tirso's good friend Montalbán writes of the *maldicientes* who had been pursuing the former; see the *aprobación* of the *Quarta Parte* (*ibid.*, lxv, n.) See also *ibid.*, lxviii, the first two lines of the note of column *a*.

The question of Tirso's personal relationships is one which is yet to receive study; the investigation will inevitably bring rich reward in a more complete understanding of him and his theater. Tirso found it impossible to refrain from attacking his enemies in print, from giving advice to people in high places, including the King himself, from using his plays as propaganda for his friends. Miss Kennedy's *La prudencia* study reveals Tirso's noble reason for composing the play as advice for the young Felipe IV, while Otis H. Green's study of the Pizarro trilogy (*Hispanic Review*, IV, 201-225) shows a less admirable Tirso who deliberately distorted history in order to aid some friends. I have ready for publication a study of *Amar por razón de estado* and of the historical event that brought it forth; the study will demonstrate Tirso's awareness of and keen interest in the matters of current import that were agitating the Court. Tirso was always interested in what was going on about him; it was part of his armament to keep alerted for possible attack on the interests of his Order, and it was a part of his dramatic creed to use his talents in the *comedia* as propaganda for a cause he considered just.

28. Cotarelo, *Comedias de Tirso de Molina*, II, xvii, xxix; I, xliii, n. 2.

29. See her *PMLA* study, footnote 105.

30. For a denial of the holographic character of the *Quinas* manuscript, see "Notes on Tirso de Molina," *Hispanic Review*, VII, 71. Juan Antonio Tamayo has given the matter thorough study; see the *Revista de Bibliografía Nacional*, III (1942), Fascículos 1 and 2, 38-63. His findings are corroborative of those in the *Hispanic Review* reference.

31. For a consideration of the years of Tirso's dramatic activity, see the *Hispanic Review* reference of note 30. It was there suggested that *Amar por señas* was probably Tirso's first play. Miss Kennedy has dated this play as subsequent to 1620; see *Hispanic Review*, XI, 1 (January, 1943), 29-34. Since Father Penedo has shown that *El vergonzoso en palacio* was probably written in 1605 or 1606, this play should perhaps now be accepted as Tirso's first one.

32. See Blanca de los Ríos, "Trece documentos nuevos para completar la biografía de Tirso," *ABC*, December 23, 1934.

33. See the *Cigarrales de Toledo*, ed. Said Armesto, 339.

34. Henri Mérimée, *Spectacles et Comédiens à Valencia* (Toulouse-Paris, 1913), 169-178. The *Syxto* 5° of

page 173 is now known to be Tirso's *La elección por la virtud*, apparently written in 1612 and bought in September of that year by Juan Acacio (see the reference in note 32 above. The date 1632 for the document reproduced in the *ABC* article is an obvious misprint for 1612). Its *Segunda parte*, documented by Mérimée (*op. cit.*), has not survived.

35. To Lope he paid tribute publicly on a number of occasions; for example, in the epilogue to the *Vergonzoso en palacio* (*Cigarrales de Toledo, ed. cit.*, 128) and in his play *La fingida Arcadia*. There is, however, some doubt whether his comments in this play were intended purely as a tribute of praise and admiration; the thrusts at Lope's *Arcadia* which some of the characters make were perhaps too keenly satiric for Lope's liking.
36. See her *Obras de Tirso de Molina*, I, 440.
37. Dr. Gregorio Marañón, "Don Juan, apuntes para su biografía," in *Cinco ensayos sobre Don Juan*, Valencia, n.d., 199.
38. See *El enigma biográfico de Tirso de Molina*, 67.
39. *Engima biográfico*, 59. The *presentatura* was a theological degree equivalent to the *bachillerato*, asserts Sra. de los Ríos (*Obras de Tirso de Molina*, I, lxxvii). The 1780 Academy Dictionary states that it was a "título que se da en algunas religiones al teólogo, que ha seguido su carrera, y acabadas sus lecturas, está esperando el grado de Maestro. *Ad Magisterium presentatus*."
40. *Enigma biográfico*, 54.
41. *Op. cit.*, 53 *et passim*. For his residence and exile in Cuenca in 1640, see Blanca de los Ríos, "Aparece un importante documento de Tirso de Molina," *ABC*, August 22, 1946. The Almazán residence receives comment below.
42. Only recently has his Valladolid visit been documented. See P. M. Penedo, "Muerte documentada de Fray Gabriel Téllez en Almazán y otras referencias biográficas," *Estudios*, I, 1 (enero-abril, 1945), 203.
43. P. M. Penedo, *loc. cit.*

J. C. J. Metford (essay date 1950)

SOURCE: "Tirso de Molina's Old Testament Plays," in *Bulletin of Hispanic Studies*, Vol. XXVII, No. 107, July-September, 1950, pp. 149-63.

[*In the following essay, Metford examines de Molina's religious background, which compelled him to write about the Old Testament, and how his knowledge of the human mind transformed his plays into works of art.*]

Like most dramatists of the Golden Age, Tirso de Molina tried his hand at adapting for the stage stories from the Old Testament. Three *comedias* of this type, acknowledged to be his, survive, but it is conceivable that he wrote others in collaboration, or that some from his pen now pass under the name of other dramatists. His extant plays are: ***La Mejor Espigadera***, a re-creation of the ever popular history of Ruth; ***La Venganza de Tamar***, which turns on Amnon's incestuous passion (2 Samuel, xiii); and ***La Mujer que manda en casa***, a version of Jezebel's libidinous career (I Kings, xvi-xxii). These plays may be examined in two ways, either historically and comparatively, to determine their place in the long procession of Old Testament dramas and their relationship to similar works by other writers, or as isolated examples of Tirso's dramatic craft. It is proposed, in this article, to concentrate on the latter aspect—to ignore, for example, the superiority of ***La Mejor Espigadera*** to Horozco's earlier version of the same story, and the similarities and contrasts between ***La Venganza de Tamar*** and Calderón's *Los Cabellos de Absalón*, in order to emphasize the special value of these plays as specimens of Tirso's workmanship. Apart from their intrinsic merits, which place them high on the list of Tirso's best plays, they are interesting as revelations of the dramatist in action, selecting, rejecting and adding to his source-material in order to make the Old Testament come alive on the stage.

When he chose the subjects for these *comedias*, Tirso was, to some extent, following a convention. The continuous appearance of Old Testament plays throughout the Golden Age—and the many reprints of the best of them in the eighteenth century—testifies to their perennial popularity. Almost every company of strolling players had a few such works in its repertory, and any dramatist, hard-pressed for fresh material, was sure of success if he dressed up one of the conventional themes in the fashion of his day. The reason for this was to be found in the instinctive delight which the patrons of the theatre exhibited at the familiar represented through the medium of drama. As epics and ballads implanted the most colourful events in the national story in the minds of the people and thus gave rise to their enduring interest in historical dramas, so sermons, moral tracts and ecclesiastical art made them conversant with Biblical stories and accounted for the vogue of Biblical plays. The original impetus to represent the Bible in dramatic form derived from the association of the church with the stage. This was perpetuated in the New Testament plays of the Golden Age which continued to be linked with the great religious festivals—Tirso's ***La Vida de Herodes***, for example, although based on Josephus' account of Herod, is intended as an Epiphany play because it identifies the protagonist with the ruler who slaughtered the Innocents. The Old Testament plays, on the contrary, are as much historical as religious in intent, because Biblical history was regarded as the forerunner of the national story and thus as part of the cultural heritage. This is best seen in ***La Venganza de Tamar***, an episode in the life-story of David. Although basically religious, it is also historical. There are, indeed, hints in the construction that this play is the second of a trilogy written about David's reign, the first part of which is now lost, and the second embedded in the conclusion to Calderón's *Los Cabellos de Absalón*.

Apart from the fact that Old Testament plays were strongly favoured in the theatre, other considerations prompted Tirso's choice of subject. The three stories which he adapted revolved about outstanding women—Ruth, Jezebel and Tamar—thus providing him with the opportunity to indulge his unrivalled powers in the presentation of female characters. It is also possible that, in writing ***La Mujer que manda en casa*** and ***La Venganza de Tamar***, he was influenced by the possibilities that his source afforded for the treatment of subjects not normally considered suitable for the stage. In this he resembled the mediaeval artists who used such subjects as Adam and Eve before the Fall, and Susannah and the Elders, as the excuse for anatomical drawing. Tirso, fascinated by the depths to which human personality could sink when in the grip of unrestrained passion, was thus given licence to depict lust in all its ugliness without exposing himself to censure, for what was in the Bible could scarcely incur criticism. In any case, it is clear that he selected the stories advisedly, because they afforded him adequate scope for his peculiar insight into human character and motives.

"Tirso de Molina" was the pseudonymous disguise of Fray Gabriel Téllez. Do the plays then reveal characteristics which indicate that their author was a trained theologian and Biblical scholar who achieved positions of considerable importance in his Order? There are abundant manifestations of these facts in all three *comedias*. At every stage in the composition of the plays, the Mercedarian seems to have guided the hand of the dramatist. It goes without saying that nothing contrary to the Faith is allowed to creep into the text. In addition, no opportunity is missed to point a moral or to deliver a short homily on the consequences of evil conduct. A very real sympathy is shown in ***La Mejor Espigadera*** and in ***La Mujer que manda en casa*** with the sufferings of the poor during a famine, and the rich man is censured for gathering his produce into barns instead of sharing it with his less fortunate neighbours. Great prominence is given in ***La Venganza de Tamar*** to the Christian belief in forgiveness for those who truly repent and mend their ways—a dogma which is always to the fore in Tirso's plays and which is given its finest expression in *Tanto es lo de más como lo de menos*. Despite the enormity of his crime, Amnon is forgiven by his father and vows:

> Yo pagaré amor tan grande
> con no ofenderle desde hoy.

Unfortunately his repentance is not sincere. To test his resolution, Tirso invents an episode where Amnon meets the disguised Tamar but is not strong enough to resist temptation and is therefore punished for his fall from grace. ***La Mujer que manda en casa*** and ***La Mejor Espigadera*** are sermons on the need to preserve the true faith despite the opposition of the infidel: Naboth, like the Constant Prince, prefers to die rather than break the Almighty's precepts; Elijah maintains his orthodoxy in face of the victory of the prophets of Baal. Ruth's fidelity to her mother-in-law is not the main theme of Tirso's treatment, as it is in other versions of the story; the chief emphasis is placed on her conversion and her determination never to desert her new belief. Masalón (Mahlon) ignores his mother's warnings, renounces his faith in order to win a bride and dies a retributive death in the hands of a rival.

Evidence that the writer was also a Biblical scholar is provided by the introduction of explanatory notes at points in the text where the uninstructed might fail to comprehend the significance of the action. In ***La Mujer que manda en casa***, the audience is left in no doubt as to the implications of the worship of Baal and the nature of the rites conducted in the sacred groves: Naboth explains everything to his wife and thus to the spectators. In Ahab's proclamation ordering a general fast, Tirso adds in parentheses for the benefit of the ignorant: "como en Israel se acostumbra cuando se espera algún castigo riguroso". When Naboth refuses to yield his patrimony to the king, he gives chapter and verse in support of his contention:

> Gran señor, no ignoráis vos,
> que en su Levítico, Dios
> manda, por justos respetos,
> que no se puedan vender
> posesiones que en herencia
> toquen a la descendencia
> del primogénito; ver
> puede Vuestra Majestad
> en el vigésimo quinto
> capítulo si es distinto
> mi intento, de esta verdad

Similarly, Naomi, in ***La Mejor Espigadera***, enlarges on the custom which prevailed in Judah whereby the owner of the estate feasted with the threshers. When Boaz covers Ruth with his cloak, a few lines are added to make the symbolism clear. These annotations are not included to demonstrate the author's knowledge of Hebrew custom, but spring from his anxiety to make the story comprehensible, just as a good preacher takes care to expound his text, for the benefit of his congregation.

Tirso's scholarly training is also revealed in the extreme care with which he reproduces the Scriptural narrative. As far as possible he incorporated the actual words of his source into the text of the play, altering them, or making additions, sparingly, and generally only in deference to the demands of his verse-form. This method is best observed in scenes of great dramatic tension or in the climax of the story, precisely where the Bible is fullest and most explicit. This verbal fidelity to the source gave the plays the stamp of authenticity, for the audience, even if they were not in the habit of reading the Bible themselves, recognized words which were familiar to them through sermons and other forms of ecclesiastical teaching. Thus, in ***La Mujer que manda en casa***, the supernatural is made perfectly credible when narrated in strict conformity with the source:

. . . *Baja un ángel y déjale a la cabecera un vaso de agua y una tortilla de pan, y vuela*	. . . et ecce angelus Domini tetigit eum, et dixit illi: Surge et comede.
Ángel: Despierta y come.	Respexit, et ecce ad caput suum subcinericius panis, et vas aquae; comedit ergo, et bibit, et rursum obdormivit.
Elías: ¿Qué es esto? ¿Quimeras mi sueño fragua? Pero, un pan y un vaso de agua a mi cabecera han puesto. Reciente está, entre cenizas parece que se coció; el cielo lo sazonó. (*Come*).	
(*Duérmese y dentro dice el ángel*) Ángel: Despierta y come, que tienes mucho camino que andar.	Reversusque est angelus Domini secundo et tetigit eum, dixitque illi: Surge, comede: grandis enim tibi restat via.
Elías. . . . (*Despiértase, come y bebe*) Vuelo a comer, su apetito de nuevo me fortalece; vuelvo a beber, ya parece, desmayos, que resucito. Recobráos, pues, fuerzas mías, que en virtud de este manjar bien podremos caminar cuarenta noches y días. Al monte Oreb, siento yo, Señor, quo me encamináis	Qui cum surrexisset, comedit et bibit, et ambulavit in fortitudine cibi illius quadraginta diebus et quadraginta noctibus, usque ad montem Dei Horeb.

In most cases, the Bible narrative was characterized by simplicity of style and economy of words so that it had to be expanded considerably to make it suitable for the stage. When this was so, Tirso contrived to retain the spirit of the original by incorporating its phrases *passim* throughout the scene. This device may be illustrated by printing the Vulgate text of 2 Samuel xiii, 15-17 alongside the phrases which are to be found in Amnon's speech at the conclusion of Act III, Scene 1 of ***La Venganza de Tamar***. It is to be noted that, throughout this crucial scene—the incestuous rape of Tamar—Tirso is careful to conform strictly to the Biblical version, probably to protect himself from possible charges of meretricious exploitation of an unsavoury episode.

Vulgate	*La Venganza de Tamar*
Et exosam eam habuit Amnon odio magno nimis, ita ut majus esset odium, quo oderat eam, amore quo ante dilexerat. Dixitque ei Amnon: Surge, et vade.	Más es mi aborrecimiento que fué primero mi amor.
sed vocato puero, qui ministrabat ei, dixit: Ejice hanc a me foras, et claude ostium post eam.	¡Vete de aquí; salte fuera!
	Echadme de aquí esta víbora, esta peste.
	Llevadme aquesta mujer; cerrad la puerta tras ella.

Where it was difficult or impossible to reproduce all the incidents in the source in dramatic form, either on account of the limitations of the stage or because of nature of the action, Tirso compromised by using the device of reporting to the audience events assumed to take place off stage. This technique is best illustrated by ***La Mujer que manda en casa***. The Book of Kings is crammed with dramatic incidents, yet even Tirso, despite his ability to fill his plays with action, quailed before the variety of episodes which his source afforded him. He therefore selected the material which could best be presented on the stage of his day—the appearance of the Angel by the juniper tree, the story of Naboth's vineyard—and regretfully excluded such episodes as Elijah's departure for Heaven in a fiery chariot and the contest with the prophets of Baal on Mount Carmel which would tax the ingenuity of the most competent stage manager. Yet he was unwilling to forgo even the minutest detail of the Bible, story if he could contrive to introduce it into the play. Passing reference is therefore made to the miracle of the widow's son and to the magic cruse, but the most striking incidents are related at length by one of the characters who has supposedly witnessed them off stage. In such instances Tirso makes the account a close paraphrase of the Bible—*e.g.*, Jehu's relation of the events on Mount Carmel is a metrical version of 1 Kings xviii, 17-46.

It is probable that Tirso was so strikingly faithful to his source as much on account of the predilections of his patrons as from his natural disposition as a friar. His audience was as familiar as he with the details of the original and undoubtedly expected them to be presented with due veracity. The prestige of the Bible also demanded that it should be treated with far less freedom than would be permitted to the writer of historical plays. This reverence for the source and desire to conform to it as strictly as possible nevertheless betrayed Tirso into two cardinal weaknesses, from the standpoint of dramatic technique. He tended to dwell too long on an incident which was intrinsically dramatic but scarcely apposite to the ultimate purpose of his play. He also lacked courage to exercise his powers of selection and rigorously to exclude anything which did not directly contribute to the development of his theme. If the intention of ***La Venganza de Tamar*** is to demonstrate that death is the consequence of evil, then the sub-plot of Absalom's rebellion against David is an unnecessary complication which detracts from the dramatic force of Amnon's punishment for his sin against Tamar. The Book of Kings, based on an earlier history of Ahab's reign, was rewritten by a priestly author intent on emphasizing the religious struggle between Yahweh and Baal. It offered Tirso the ingredients of a powerful drama. Prerequisite for success was the ruthless exclusion of everything in the complicated Bible narrative which did not directly contribute to the unfolding of the conflict between the rival faiths, a conflict symbolized by the struggle between two outstanding personalities, Elijah and Jezebel. Tirso unwisely dwelt too long on episodes which were interesting in themselves but which used up his time, so that the important stages in the conflict had to be narrated instead of being dramatized. Consequently the play is not so effective as it might have become had Tirso been able to free himself from the trammels of his source.

Fray Gabriel Téllez is thus seen to have exercised careful supervision over the composition of the Old Testament plays, obliging the dramatist to consult the original, to reproduce it reverently and accurately and to explain the more recondite references for the enlightenment of the audience. But what of the part played by Tirso de Molina? Did the dramatist half of this dual personality not exert some influence on the construction of the plays? He may frequently be observed at work, lightening the touch of his religious counterpart, making the plays live as dramas instead of moral exhortations. Alterations in the source which are made in obedience to the exigencies of dramatic representation are an apt illustration of this point. Chronology is changed to increase the sense of drama. In the Bible Absalom's revenge for the outrage on his sister takes place after "two full years are past"; in the play it follows inexorably on the crime; Naomi's husband, who has sinned through greed, is killed by robbers before he can enjoy the prosperity which follows his son's marriage, whereas in the Bible he dies some time after this event. Changes are made in the story, the better to integrate the various strands in the plot. Jezebel, not Ahab, is responsible for building the groves to Baal in order to satisfy her inordinate desires; Naboth's death is due not so much to his refusal to yield his vineyard to the King as to his rejection of Jezebel's amorous proposals; the revens, as a measure of poetic justice, take the food from Ahab's table to feed Elijah by the Brook Kerith. Most notable of all are the additions to the Biblical material which the dramatist makes to bring the plays within the conventional formula of the *comedia*. Only a small proportion of the incidents in the plays are derived directly from the source. In ***La Venganza de Tamar***, six scenes out of forty-three are sufficient to render the Biblical text in dramatic form and the action attributable to the source does not begin until the second act. The familiar story of Ruth is not reached until the third act of ***La Mejor Espigadera***, the first two being devoted to the events leading to her marriage with Mahlon and his death. The history of Jezebel is narrated with a wealth of detail in the Book of Kings so that, in the case of ***La Mujer que manda en casa,*** Tirso had rather more to dramatize than in the other two plays, yet even here he contrived to introduce a great deal which is extraneous to his source and the product of his fertile imagination. Some of the additional material was evidently suggested by the source, but improved almost beyond recognition in the process of adaptation. The Bible, for example, contains the statement that David captured a finely ornamented crown. Tirso developed this into a magnificent scene in which Absalom is tempted to try on the crown and so reveal to his father his secret ambition to supplant him. The mention, which Tirso found in the Book of Kings, of the cannibalism practised by two women during a famine, is, in the same way, the source of the powerful scene in ***La Mejor Espigadera*** where Jaleel threatens to eat his child to save himself from death by starvation. Most of the supplementary material, however, is entirely Tirso's invention. Some of it comes from his stock-in-trade, such as the device, used in ***La Mejor Espigadera, La Mujer que manda en casa*** and ***El Vergonzoso en palacio***, whereby a confession of love is obtained through one of the characters feigning to dream. A fair proportion of the original scenes are concessions to the prevailing conventions which governed the composition of the *comedia*. This fact is best observed in the provision of low comedy to suit the tastes of Tirso's patrons. Yet, even in this, he shows great skill in developing the comedy naturally out of the action. He accomplishes this through the exploitation of rustic characters wherever the plot warrants their introduction. Thus, Ruth gleaning in the fields, Tamar seeking refuge on her brother's farm, Elijah hiding in the wilderness, provided the excuse for comic relief, but the appearance of countrymen speaking in dialect, misunderstanding strange words and indulging sometimes in bitter, sometimes gay humour was a natural concomitant of the plot. Whether the inventions are in obedience to dramatic formulae or made to eke out the Biblical incidents to fill the three acts of a *comedia*, one quality is strikingly evident in all Tirso's additions to his source: his inherently romantic temperament. Like Zorrilla, Tirso lived in a world of intrigue, midnight adventures and forlorn damsels. As, for Don Quixote, inns were castles and tavern-wenches high-born ladies, so, for the Mercedarian dramatist, the ordinary is transmuted into something rich and wonderful. Ruth is no longer a peasant "in tears amid the alien corn", but a princess whom Mahlon, a beggar because he has been robbed of his possessions, wins in the course of adventures appropriate to a Byzantine novel. In the Bible he dies a natural death, but in the play he is overthrown by his rival who thus takes revenge for his defeat in love. When Ruth first caught sight of Boaz in the play she thought he was the reincarnation of her first husband and Tirso made this more credible by having the same actor double the parts. He may have used this device to lessen the popular antipathy to a second marriage, but it is more than likely that he was acting in obedience to the dictates of a romantic imagination. For the same reason, he is not disposed to tell the episode of Naboth's vineyard as it is in the Bible—the struggle between a powerful king who wishes to improve his estate and a humble man who refuses to sell his patrimony. Complications are introduced to heighten the dramatic interest so that Naboth has not only to contend with Ahab but with the importunities of Jezebel, who makes him the object of her passion, and also with the jealous clamours of his own wife, who is wrongly convinced of Naboth's infidelity. In ***La Venganza de Tamar***, Amnon, unlike his namesake in the source, is not initially guilty of a sordid and incestuous passion. Seeking to satisfy his curiosity regarding the famed beauty of his father's wives, he scales the seraglio walls at midnight and is charmed by the voice and appearance of an unknown maiden whom he only later discovers to be his half-sister. Tirso thus constructed his Biblical plays in the same way as his other *comedias*. They were built as "arquitecturas del ingenio fingidas" and his powerful imagination gave them the "prodigies, adventures and intrigues in abundance" and the "wholly Romantic and chivalric" colouring which Sismondi found to be characteristic of Spanish literature in general.

When the Old Testament plays were presented on the stage, the audience must have been kept at a high pitch of expectancy. Incident follows incident with surprising rapidity; there is a constant succession of minor climaxes in the action; and interest is never allowed to flag because the outcome of each new turn of the story is anxiously awaited. As each episode was resolved, Tirso called up fresh complications from the inexhaustible depths of his imagination, so that the spectator's curiosity was constantly engaged as the play rushed breathlessly to its conclusion. It would seem unlikely that such a concentration of action at such a rapid pace would permit more than the slightest delineation of character, sufficient to carry the story but no more. Surprisingly, Tirso managed not only to present well-rounded personalities, but also to allow them to develop in the course of the action. Even the minor characters, no more than names in the Bible, come to life as clearly defined individuals—Elimelec, the personification of greed; Jehu, the upright soldier and instrument of God's vengeance on Jezebel; the subtle, villainous Jonadab who encourages Amnon in his evil ways: all these are vividly represented in the plays. As in all Tirso's works, the women characters in the Biblical plays reveal his insight into the workings of the feminine mind. Perhaps Ruth is the least interesting of them, especially in the concluding scenes where she is passively carrying out her mother-in-law's instructions, yet even she, in the first part of the play, acts with considerable charm as she uses her feminine powers to make Mahlon declare his passion and to compel her unwelcome suitor to find the man whom she really loves. It was implicit in Tirso's design that Tamar, although her "tragedia lastimosa" provided the plot, should not figure too prominently in the play and thus distract attention from the chief actors. She is nevertheless drawn with great sympathy and given a witty and engaging personality. Naomi and Jezebel are contrasted types, the former the vehicle of Tirso's didacticism and the latter the incarnation of a woman who is the slave to her passions. To present her as a human being and not an abstraction required considerable skill because of the proverbial villainies attributed to this female Herod. In Tirso's hands, she becomes less of a monstrosity and more of a psychological probability than she was in the popular mind. Resourceful, domineering over all with whom she is brought into contact, able to make her husband her abject servant, she obliges everyone except Naboth and the fiery prophet to pander to her will. There is more than a touch of Lady Macbeth in this masterful woman and Ahab's admiring outburst:

> ¡Qué pecho tan varonil te dió el cielo!

recalls Macbeth's equally approving "Bring forth men children only!" She attains true magnificence in the final scenes where she adorns herself in her finery, and, with assumed joyfulness, although there is terror in her heart, tries the power of her charms on Jehu. Tirso well knew how to create a part which gave a competent tragic actress unlimited scope for demonstrating her virtuosity. How grandly she could play the deserted queen as she listens to the doleful song which prophesies her death or as she sees in her mirror not the reflection of her own cruel beauty, but the bloody face of the man whom she has murdered!

The male characters are drawn with comparable skill, but two are outstanding because of their complexity. Amnon and David are among Tirso's greatest creations, a son and a father who, at first sight, are completely unlike, yet, on closer examination, are seen to represent two facets of the same temperament. In the play, David, although no longer in the prime of his powers, is still the hero, winning battles as in his youth. Amnon is the man of peace in an age of war, recalling Marlowe's Edward II. Even the servants comment on the contrast with his illustrious father which Amnon himself is the first to recognize:

> No soy soldado yo
> cual de él la fama pregona

and he prefers an hour spent in Jerusalem to all the campaigns that his father has won. From David, the sweet singer of psalms, he has inherited only his love of poetry:

> En esto quiero imitar
> a David. . . .

and this gift he develops as a consolation for his melancholy temperament. Whereas David has been a great lover, Amnon scorns women as faithless creatures with whom he could never be happy. Nevertheless the vein of passion which he has inherited from his father manifests itself in a totally unexpected way. He listens to his brother's lewd talk and is shocked by his loose attitude to women, ironically exclaiming "¡A la mujer de tu padre!" when Absalom speaks of seducing David's concubines, but their conversation excites his curiosity and he enters the women's quarters only to find himself ensnared by the love which he pretended to despise. Even then he could have saved himself from the consequences of a passion which he soon discovers to be impossible had he not inherited a grain of David's selfishness. In the fertile soil of Amnon's indolence this has grown into an uncontrollable desire always to have his own way:

> en dandole en la cabeza
> una cosa, no podrán
> persuadirle a lo contrario
> catorce pecadores. . . .

explains his servant. "Lo que apetezco, he de ejecutar" and "provecho es hacer mi gusto", says Amnon, from the first resigning himself to defeat in the age-old conflict between reason and bestial instincts—a struggle which greatly interested Tirso and which he describes with great skill in ***La Vida de Herodes***. Amnon's violent rejection of Tamar after his lust is satiated is thus made psychologically possible. Tirso has carefully built up a picture of an unusual personality, melancholy, poetic, the prey to his desires. He shows that such a character would naturally yield to the temptations which a stronger person would have resisted. The oppressive sense of sin operating on a hypersensitive nature causes the dramatic revulsion from the person who was once the object of an all-consuming love. What a tribute to Tirso's abilities that he is able to convey all this in the narrow limits of three *jornadas* filled with action!

In David, Tirso comes as near finding a tragic hero of classical stature as the genius of the *comedia*, with its blending of grave and gay, allowed. He dominates the play, for, even when he is not on the stage, he is constantly being mentioned by the other characters who go in fear of him. Tirso presents a warrior grown old but still capable of preserving his authority. All his life, he has dedicated his efforts to one end—to carve out a kingdom which he might bequeath to his son—but his is a tragedy of thwarted ambition. Amnon is killed by his brother in revenge for the outrage committed on Tamar; the rest of his sons flee from his household and the play is full of ominous hints as to their ultimate fate. In the end David is left alone with his possessions, now of no value to him because there is no one on whom he may bestow them. His tragedy is made even more poignant when he realizes that the loss of Amnon and the dissension within his household is punishment for the sin committed long before when he stole Uriah's wife. That David was prepared to forgive Amnon for the rape of Tamar is suggested by the source—Amnon's crime was by no means comparable to Oedipus' transgression, for, although Jewish law forbade marriage to a half-sister (Leviticus xviii, 9), there is evidence that it was permissible in David's time (*cf.* 2 Samuel xiii, 13)—but Tirso makes his readiness to come to terms with his sons undeniably pathetic. Such is his power to create character and to exploit the resources of histrionic talent that one is driven to ask whether, had he been subject to the discipline of the classical tragic formula, he might not have produced masterpieces comparable with the greatest European dramas. In all probability, this would never have come to pass, for his was a temperament which would brook no limitations. His best creations emerge incidentally, in great flashes of inspiration, as he works at a given theme.

This is perhaps the most significant fact that is derived from a study of the Old Testament plays. The friar in Tirso impelled him to write three plays which were intentionally didactic and of religious significance, but the dramatist in him transformed the results into works of art. The framework is the Bible narrative, but the adornments come from Tirso's rich fancy and his superlative knowledge of the human mind. The *comedia*, subject to certain conventions, but unrestricted and free of all rules, was the only medium suited to such a genius.

Chronology

La Mejor Espigadera and ***La Venganza de Tamar*** were published in 1634, in the *Parte Tercera* of Tirso's collected plays; ***La Mujer que manda en casa*** appeared in 1635, in the *Cuarta Parte*. A document discovered by Henri Mérimée[1] indicates that the first two plays existed in manuscript at least ten years before they were printed. It is the record, made in 1628 by a Valencian notary, of the *fabulas sive comedias* belonging to a company of players. These plays were impounded because their manager, Juan-Jerónimo Amella, or Almella, was unable to discharge a debt due to the *Teatro de la Olivera. Hieronymo Almella, fabularum Auctore, et domna Emanuela Henriquez, viuda* are cited as the principals. The lady is easily identified as the wife of Juan Bautista Valenciano, an actor-manager who was killed in a brawl in 1624.[2] Cotarelo y Mori reprinted the notice of his burial which he found in the register of a church in Madrid. It included words which echoed the phrase used by the Valencian notary: ". . . Enterróle su mujer Dª. Manuela Enríquez y Juan-Jerónimo Valenciano, hermano del difunto . . ."[3] There is little reason to doubt that this brother (whose remarkable likeness to Juan Bautista was exploited in Tirso's ***Los Hermanos parecidos***) was the Juan-Jerónimo Almella mentioned in Mérimée's document. The title *valenciano*, used by both brothers, was possibly no more than a locative, a nickname useful in Madrid but pointless in their native city, where Juan-Jerónimo would naturally revert to his patronymic, especially in matters involving legal proceedings. It is known that in July 1627, Juan Bautista's company—which apparently remained intact after his death and continued to use his name—was obliged to abandon certain performances in Valencia after five days—"per auer falta de gent."[4] The players are next heard of in April 1628, in Ciudad Rodrigo, but Almella is now their manager. They are invited once more to Valencia and a sum of money is advanced towards the cost of their journey.[5] Failure to repay part of this advance led to the seizure of the company's property, recorded by Mérimée. Among the plays on the notary's list was ***Tanto es lo de más como lo de menos***, published in the *Parte Primera*, 1627, with the note: "Representóla Juan Bautista". It has been questioned whether this refers to Juan Bautista Villegas or to the *valenciano*[6] but the fact that a manuscript of the play was part of the repertory of the latter's company resolves the doubt in favour of the *valenciano*. Moreover, of the five plays mentioned by Rennert as performed by Juan Bautista, four appear on the notary's inventory.[7] There is considerable justification, therefore, for the assumption that all the plays seized in Valencia had been performed in Juan Bautista's lifetime and were inherited by his wife as part of the property used for the reconstituted company when her brother-in-law succeeded her deceased husband as *autor de comedias*—otherwise the notary would not have mentioned her in the document. If this is so, then ***La Mejor Espigadera*** and ***La Venganza de Tamar***, both on the Valencia list, must have been written before Bautista's death in 1624. This must certainly be true in the case of ***La Venganza de Tamar*** because Tirso would scarcely have risked dealing with such an unsavoury subject after the ecclesiastical injunction of 1625.

Professor Ruth Lee Kennedy has stated that ***Tanto es lo de más como lo de menos*** was written in 1620, though possibly retouched later.[8] A verbal resemblance between that play and ***La Venganza de Tamar*** suggests that they were composed about the same period, although ***La Venganza***

de Tamar was written first. In ***Tanto es lo de más como lo de menos***, Nineucio drives the beggars out of his house, shouting:

> Echádmelos de aquí a palos;
> cerradme esas puertas todas.[9]

These lines are reminiscent of the scene where Amnon, overcome by loathing for Tamar, orders his servants:

> Llevadme aquesta mujer;
> cerrad la puerta tras ella.[10]

Here Tirso paraphrased the Bible: "Ejice hanc a me foras et claude ostium post eam." The words seem to have impressed themselves on Tirso's mind, for he also uses them in *La Vida de Herodes* when Herod orders Mariamne to be thrown into prison:[11]

> Cerrad esas puertas todas,
> llevadme de aquí esta infame.[12]

La Vida de Herodes also resembles ***La Venganza de Tamar*** in other respects: Antipatro's concern for his son (Act I, Scene iv) is similar to David's anxiety over Amnon's behaviour (Act II, Scene iv); Joab's misinterpretation of Tamar's innocent pretence of love for Amnon (Act II, Scene viii) is expanded into a dramatic climax where Herod is driven mad with jealousy when he mistakes the nature of the feigned love-play between his wife and Josefo (Act III, Scene viii). Tirso used similar scenes and situations in a number of plays. From the point of view of chronology, it is necessary to establish whether these repetitions tended to recur over a number of years or whether they were made within approximately the same period, but there is not sufficient evidence available regarding the dates of Tirso's plays for an accurate answer to be given to the question. The close similarities in these scenes and the verbal coincidence cited above would appear to confirm that ***La Vida de Herodes*** and ***La Venganza de Tamar*** were written about the same time. It is interesting to note in this connection that, in Lope de Vega's *El Mejor Alcalde el rey*, Act III, Scene v, the heroine is defended with the words ". . . Elvira no es Tamar. . . ." This suggests that the story of Tamar was topical because it had been played about the same time as Lope's play. This is dated 1620-23 by Morley and Bruerton.[13]

A convenient *terminus ante quem non* for the composition of ***La Vida de Herodes*** is provided by the fact that Tirso drew the plot of this play direct from the works of Josephus. The Jewish historian narrated the Herod-Mariamne story twice, in the *Antiquities* and in the *Jewish War*, the main difference in the accounts being that the command to kill Mariamne, should Herod fail to return to her, is given twice in the former and once in the latter work. Tirso's version resembles the *Jewish War* in this respect, but there are also indications that he was conversant with the *Antiquities*. Flavius Josephus was available to him in translation as well as in Latin, and the republication in Madrid, in 1616, of the Antwerp version of the *Jewish War* of 1557, seems to have given Tirso the idea for a play about Herod. Thus interested in Josephus, he evidently consulted the *Antiquities* for the account of David's reign and incorporated two of Josephus's variants from the Scriptural narrative in ***La Venganza de Tamar:***

(1) Act III, Scene xvi. *Absalón*: A Gesur huyendo voy que es su rey mi agüelo, y padre de nuestra injuriada madre.	Josephus, *Antiquities*, VII.[14] At Abesalomus in Gesuram ad avum maternum confugit, istius loci dynastam.

The relationship is not given in the Bible: "Porro Absalom fugiens, abiit ad Tholomai, filium Amniud, regem Gessur."[15]

(2) David, believing all his sons to be dead, is overcome by grief, but the sound of horses gives him new hope:

Act III, Scene xvii. Caballos suenan: ¿ si serán mis amados hijos éstos?	Josephus, *Antiquities*, VII. Interea vero sonitus equorum et venientum turba illos in se convertit.

The horses are not mentioned in the Bible: the lookout gives warning of the approach of a large body of men.

Except for a single instance in ***La Mujer que manda en casa*** where Josephus and Tirso make Elijah tell the prophets of Baal to call on their gods for help, whereas the Bible has "on their god", there is nothing to indicate that this play was composed under the influence of the *Antiquities*. In all other cases where Josephus differs from the Bible, Tirso follows the Bible, thus suggesting that ***La Mujer que manda en casa*** was written some time before he became interested in the Jewish historian as a source for his plays. No evidence is available to fix when before 1616 the play was likely to be composed.

In the cases of ***La Mejor Espigadera*** and ***La Venganza de Tamar***, it would appear that the earliest date for their composition would be 1616 and the latest 1624, the most probable period being around 1620, either just before or soon after ***Tanto es lo de más como lo de menos***.

Notes

1. *Spectacles et comédiens à Valencia*, Toulouse, Paris, 1913, pp. 175-8.
2. H. A. Rennert: *The Spanish Stage*, New York, 1909, p. 465.
3. N.B.A.E., Vol. IX, pp. xxiii b, xxxviii a.
4. Mérimée, *op. cit.*, pp. 194-5.
5. Cristóbal Pérez Pastor: *Nuevos datos acerca del histrionismo español*, Madrid, 1901, p.214.
6. See *Hispanic Review*, Vol. IX, 1941, p. 35, n. 59.
7. Rennert, *op. cit.*, p. 614.
8. *Hispanic Review*, Vol. XI, 1943, pp. 42-45.
9. N.B.A.E., Vol. IV, p. 126a.
10. *Op. cit.*, p. 425a.
11. Vulgate, 2 Regum, xiii, 17.

12. N.B.A.E., Vol. IX, p. 202a.
13. *The Chronology of Lope de Vega's Comedias,* New York, 1940, p. 368.
14. Flavii Josephi Hebraei *Opera Omnia*, Lipsiae, 1782, p. 765.
15. Vulgate. 2 Regum xiii, 37.

Gerald E. Wade (essay date 1982)

SOURCE: "Love, Comedia Style," in *Kentucky Romance Quarterly*, Vol. 29, No. 1, 1982, pp. 47-60.

[*In the following essay, Wade discusses how priests and other officials of the church wrote erotic Spanish comedies during the Golden Age in spite of the fact that moralists of the time opposed the subject.*]

The "aesthetics of the folk"[1] have determined not entirely but in large part the nature and content of literature. Thus when the folk affirm that all the world loves a lover, that the course of true love never runs smooth, or that love makes the world go 'round, the aphorisms, like those of similar nature, help to make understandable the inevitable recurrence of the love motif in much of the world's literature. Although this motif may be, and often is, treated seriously—and also tragically—[2] it is more usually, in what may be termed its surface treatment, given a comic texture. As stated by Benjamin Lehman,[3] comedy meets a need, and this in every age. It uses its accustomed devices to beget emotions, usually but not always mirthful, through the actions and utterances of the characters of a play or novel or short story, and this even though all comedy, including farce, is at bottom essentially serious. It is serious because it affords a more or less pleasing vision of reality that the average person takes for granted, and it makes an affirmation about life that corresponds with the vision of most of us that this is the way things are. It includes the feeling that we like to keep things agreeable, free from the threat of time and disruption. The ideology of the dramatists who composed Spain's Golden Age comedy reveals something of this vision. The result, in keeping with the first two sentences of this article, is drama of a comic type often constructed about the love of a boy and a girl, and the dramatic action has to do with their efforts to achieve a successful union by overcoming the obstacles placed in their way. Having for a brief time distorted the societal fabric by their resistence to the obstacles that work to prevent their union, the fabric is restored when they succeed. The audience will know that the first bliss of young love will not last forever, but this is of little consequence within the confines of the play, since the post-marital fortunes of the lovers are seldom included in it. The lovers are youthful, charming, and compelled toward their destiny, their physical oneness. This biological urge, this mating instinct, may be treated as comic and not as morally offensive for most of us. Indeed, it delights us; it is recognized as Nature's provision for the perpetuation of the human race, a consummation, again for most of us, not to be deplored. As Lehman suggests (p. 166), the carnival of ancient comedy thus persists, as does the sense of the ancient fertility rite.

The love portrayed in the *Comedia*, as has often been remarked, is usually quite physical. Two young people meet, assess each other's eligibility for mating, and there is instant love—the *Comedia* often tells us that love enters through the eyes and ears. There is little of what might be called the spiritual element of the lovers' mutual attraction; the psychological ingredients of their passion seldom receive more than a limited explication by the author.[4] For the sake of decorum, or because they had not been invented, the author usually but not always, avoids terms common in our time that are often applied by psychologists to love, its physical aspects and accompanying emotional states. There is no reason to believe that the *Comedia*'s audiences found less comprehensible an author's euphemisms rather than the blunter terms now used by psychologists, terms in our late 20th century so common as to appear in the news media.

Now the most intimate element of love-making, the sexual union of the lovers to be consummated soon after the final lines of the play, was looked upon by Spain's seventeenth-century moralists as sinful. Dominated by the Judeo-Christian ethic that had evolved through the centuries, society considered the sex act as an evil, one indeed that had to be endured by moralists and theologians but only grudgingly. The mutual attraction of the sexes in a *Comedia* was excoriated by those enemies of the theater throughout the century.[5] It is not possible to say with assurance when and why the belief that sexual indulgence is sinful originated, but one may reasonably assume that its evil repute grew from the abuse of the sexual union for pleasure, and this evil repute probably began not very long after man became man.[6] In any event, the Judeo-Christian concept of the sex act for Western peoples has been that it is an evil in itself. But despite this, sexual materials have served throughout the history of literature as titillating subject matter, and have provided a favored theme for the folk.

The *Comedia*, as students of the genre recall, was subject to censorship. The censor was required to attest that the play to which he gave approval contained nothing inimical to the Christian faith or doctrine. Thus the authors of the *Comedia* would seem to be required in principle to accept belief in the evil of the sexual act and that a play's subject matter that approved of it directly or by indirection was an attack on the faith. But despite this, the censorship accepted the genre's exploitation of the often used boy-meets-girl situation with its accompanying inference that the sexual union of the lovers would be morally and ecclesiastically permissible. This seeming paradox in the thinking of the dramatists and their audiences, as also that of the Church, had a partial and apparently, for them, a reassuring explanation in the conviction that the consummation of the lovers' affection was to be made acceptable by the churchly sacrament of marriage. This sacrament is of course still considered necessary and efficacious by orthodox Jews and Christians.

And so the Spanish folk, as those of other cultures, have through many centuries found their literature, as that of the *Comedia*, responsive to their felt need for the portrayal of their sexual impulses. The result is the inevitable note of eroticism that comedy more often than not took on in Golden Age drama. Using the standard definition, eroticism is an equivalent term for sexual excitement, and erotic materials of any sort are those that tend to incite genital stimulation. It follows that a person's fantasies and day dreams involving the subject of his or her sexual desire are erotic, and this element is always present in the boy-meets-girl situation so frequent in comedy. It is obvious that nothing in itself is erotic; that it becomes so in proportion as an individual's fantasies make it so.

There is thus in order the analysis of any *comedia* that has to do with a boy-meets-girl motif, and of the way in which the author manipulates his materials effectively to make them inoffensively acceptable to his popular audience. It is apparent that in his effort to arouse gential excitement in the persons of his audience, the author has their collaboration as "co-authors" with him; they exercise this activity more or less in proportion as the author's words and the actors' execution of their roles stimulate their erotic fantasies. Some authors used erotic materials more forthrightly than the decorum of other authors permitted. This matter has had comment in at least four recent articles by specialists in the *Comedia*.

The first of these was Professor R. R. MacCurdy's "The Bathing Nude in Golden Age Drama," an article that documented its title through pertient passages and references in a number of plays.[7] MacCurdy found Rojas to be the most frequent user of the bathing nude as a strip-tease device to titillate his audience. The emotions aroused in the audience are labeled as "lust," that is, an excessive sexual craving, in the usual definition of the term. (One observes that whereas "lust" denotes a moralistic attitude, eroticism does not have to imply a moralistic tone.) The second of the two articles, Sturgis Leavitt's "The Strip-Tease in Golden Age Drama," added to MacCurdy's study, and agreed that Rojas more than any other dramatist employed the device. The author also suggested that Tirso was the most parsimonious of the playwrights in his use of the strip-tease *topos*. Leavitt differed in his manner of approach from MacCurdy; the former employed a tone of banter with a linguistic style appropriate to that tone. He labeled the strip-tease as good fun and had little sympathy for the moralists who were offended by it. Quite correctly he pointed out that the device, in comparison with modern nudity on the stage and in the cinema is relatively decorous.[8] Neither of the two authors chose to see the sexual *topoi* that suffuse the *Comedia* as an expression of the aesthetic proposed in the present article, an expression that did its part in making of Golden Age drama a major component of much of the world's literature.

The third of the articles is that by Professor Mariano Pallarés Navarro, "Algunos aspectos sexuales en tres obras de Tirso de Molina."[9] Pallarés discusses some of the sexual and erotic elements in ***El burlador de Sevilla, El vergonzoso en palacio*** and ***Don Gil de las calzas verdes***. Following an introductory explanation of the social background of Tirso's time, the author describes the erotic content of the three plays named. He gives the terms and quotes passages for some of them that are of erotic content; all of them would come under the label of "deshonestidad," a term often used by those who decried the *Comedia*. The terms are "sexual," "erótico," "pasión," "gozar" (to enjoy the sex act), "amor carnal," "atracción física," "lograr la belleza" (i.e. of the admired female), "impulso [sexual] arrollador", "natural" (as applied to amorous passion), "desear," "apetito natural," "relación carnal," "capacidad sexual," "llamas tiranas [de amor]." Two terms of a sexual connotation that are used in one or another of the plays are "homosexualismo" and "hermafrodita." There are also terms of double meaning with sexual insinuations, and the overall lesson objected to by the moralists is that if love cannot be achieved by licit means, any stratagem that may work is acceptable. The punishment for violating the moral code (except for Don Juan) is negligible, if there is any at all, and the lesson is clear that Tirso's attitude toward the objections of the moralists to his sexualized comedies is that their opinion is of minor concern for him.

The fourth article is one of broader scope, a rather thorough study of the love element in Tirso's plays. The author is Professor Jaime Asensio, and the title of his study is "Casos de amor en la comedia de Tirso de Molina."[10] His theory of the Tirsian love concept—love is the Mercedarian's favored theme—was determined by the reading of thirty-eight plays. Asensio does not hesitate to affirm that the same concept obtains in most of the plays of the Golden Age.

Professor Asensio's article is deserving of more space than it can be given here. The nexus of his study is that the debased love concept made clear in Tirso's *comedias*—a concept that permeated all of society—had replaced the earlier and noble neo-Platonic idea of love about which the individual and society could construct a sense of order in the universe.[11] The debased concept made clear by Tirso's plays led to disorder. Thus Asensio sees Tirsian love as "enredo," "engaño," and hence "desorden." But when on page 19 he affirms that the Mercedarian's love concept is not a discovery of sensuality, he falls into a contradiction, since elsewhere (pages 9, 11, 24-27, 30-31), he accepts the erotic as a major component of the Tirsian formula. For Asensio Tirsian love is evil, and the problem takes on for him an approach he labels the Leibnitzian *periculum-salvatio* solution. This proposes that an evil person can be saved from his soul's peril only by the grace of God. Asensio blames the rejection of the neo-Platonic idea of love on the Church: through the doctrines formulated by the Council of Trent, Spanish Catholicism repudiated neo-Platonism because of this philosophy's pagan origin. This philosophy had been replaced by the idea that the individual should make his own decisions about good and evil. But since the individual of Tirso's time was incapable of making the difficult decisions affecting his spiritual wellbeing, he fell into error,[12] disillusionment and indecision, the *desengaño* of the "edad conflictiva."[13]

Asensio sees that the love life of a character of the *Comedia* is pursued under a social aegis that sanctions his actions. Hence for Asensio society was corrupt, a theory accepted as fact by students of the Golden Age. He adopts the thesis of J. A. Maravall that the *Comedia* supports the power structure of the time. Indeed, he goes so far, in a kind of extension of the Maravall thesis, as to suggest that it was not really life that disillusioned society and the individual; rather, it was the artifice of the *Comedia*, itself an *engaño*. One presumes that he means that the theater was only, as Aristotle proposed, an "imitation of an action." I find it hard to put the blame of the period's corruption in thought and action only on the *Comedia*, even though its influence was not small. I should feel obligated to think that the answer to the dilemma is that the authors of the drama reproduced most of the major aspects of their culture, but they also introduced other factors that offered new insights as part of their creative process.

And so we see that eroticism permeated the *Comedia*, as stated by the authors named above. The generalization is especially true for the boy-meets-girl kind of plot. To repeat, eroticism is sexual excitement, and erotic materials are those that excite genital stimulation. The process of excitement is originated by the day-dream fantasies of the individual concerned.

And thus we come to the point at issue, that is, the extent to which it may be shown in detail how the love of the *Comedia* depends directly on the *topos* of eroticism as this is observed in the psychological exploitation of that emotion's elements in a boy-meets-girl *comedia*. To explore the matter there is needed a *comedia* that comes close to perfection in its demonstration of the thesis concerned. There are many plays that might be recalled, but the one that seems to me to fulfill most adequately the conditions required is Tirso's ***La celosa de sí misma***. It is in this play that the erotic fantasies of the *primer galán* are so clearly—and amusingly—evident. The play, as it turns out, is not of the *mujer disfrazada de hombre* theme, and to most students of the *Comedia* is less well-known than others of Tirso's canon. But the action moves rapidly and is expertly manipulated for maximum audience reaction. The plot is intricate and its summary in a brief form is difficult. It will be necessary to omit those elements of the action that do not offer a direct contribution to the elucidation of the theme at hand. As occasion warrants, there will be comments to help make evident the action's erotic nature. The text of the play is that of Blanca de los Rís, *Tirso de Molina. Obras dramáticas completas*, 2 (Madrid: Aguilar, 1952), 1441-92.

As the play opens, don Melchor, a youthful Leonese, has just arrived in Madrid accompanied by his *lacayo* Ventura. Don Melchor, noble by birth but financially less than affluent, has come to meet in her home the girl to whom he has tentatively been affianced through an arrangement made by relatives. She will have a handsome dowry. She is also reportedly beautiful, and Melchor makes clear to the audience that this beauty must be a part of the girl's endowments if she is to meet his approval. It is apparent that Melchor, surely knowledgeable about women as a youth of his time must be in a day when the don Juan ideal of machismo applied to all young gentlemen worthy of the label, carries within him fantasies that are erotic: in his imagination he can picture the physical allurements that he hopes will be obvious as he first sees his bride-to-be.

It is a festal day and Melchor decides to attend mass before repairing to the home of his fianceé. The mass is to be heard in the nearby convent of the Victoria, a favored place for young people to congregate to see others of the opposite sex. Melchor is warned by the shrewd Ventura to watch out for city slickers and golddiggers, notoriously on the prowl for victims in this cosmopolitan and wicked metropolis.[14] Ventura offers a wager that before Melchor has a chance to meet his affianced, he will become the victim of a designing female. Melchor scoffs at the idea.

Melchor and Ventura hear mass, the latter in a nearby church. When they come together again, the former excitedly tells the *lacayo* that he had worshipped by the side of a beautiful female, and Ventura recalls his prediction of his master's victimization by a designing woman. He is aghast when the *galán* states that of the lady's person he had seen only a hand, but that this was so divinely formed that it is surely indicative of the beauty of her entire person. (The hand is of course a fetish, and will remain so throughout the play. Melchor's erotic fancies are already working at full speed.)[15] When the lady appears, Melchor addresses her in the exaggerated love language of the *Comedia*. At first opposed to his advances, the lady softens and agrees to meet him here on the following day. Of her person Melchor has seen no more than her hand: the lady is clothed in the fashion of the day with her entire person concealed.[16]

The scene shifts to the home of don Alonso, the father of the girl Melchor has come to see as his intended bride. This is Magdalena, and she appears changing her clothes. (It is this scene from Tirso that Leavitt recalled in his article on the strip-tease.) She tells her maid Quiñones of the handsome stranger she had seen a while ago at the Victoria convent, and she hopes that her intended husband may be as personable. Magdalena is of course the convent lady, and it is apparent that she has seen in him, the stranger, a husband, the head of her family and the father of her children; this although she may be only partly conscious of this train of thought. When Melchor appears, Magdalena is overjoyed in seeing her hope come true. But Melchor finds her unattractive; he is still bedeviled by the fantasized perfection of the lady at the convent. Magdalena, seeing that he is not attracted to her, is saddened, and is beginning to feel jealous of herself, as the play's title has it.

At the beginning of Act II Magdalena and Melchor met at the convent entrance. She is dressed in all-concealing mourning garb so as to keep her identity secret, but to him she shows her hand for identification. She tells him that she knows Magdalena, and she reproaches him for his fickleness yesterday: even though he was Magdalena's husband-to-be, he had told her, the convent lady, that he loved her. Melchor assures her of his love, and affirms his intention of renouncing Magdalena. Magdalena, on his insistence, now shows him one eye; this may be taken as a mild form of strip-tease. She then shows him the other eye: more strip-tease. As will be learned later, her eyes are black, a fact that Ventura observes but Melchor does not. Verily, as Shakespeare and others have told us, love is blind. Or perhaps, as St. Augustine expressed it in his "amabam amare," Melchor is in love with love. (The suggestion comes from de Rougemont, of reference in note 2.)

It turns out that Angela, one of Magdalena's friends, has seen Melchor, and determines to capture him.[17] By bribing Ventura, Angela discovers the details of the Melchor-Magdalena-convent lady situation. In the meantime, don Alonso, having learned of Melchor's involvement with the lady of the convent, becomes upset enough to reproach Melchor for his deceitful actions. Magdalena tells him that her father has arranged another marriage for her and leaves him. Disconsolate, Melchor determines to return home to León.

As Act III begins, Melchor is making preparation for the homeward journey, but receives a message to come to the convent. He goes there with Ventura, and finds Angela. She is dressed in mourning, posing as the convent lady. Urged to disclose an eye, she does so. Ventura exclaims that the eye is blue, and that yesterday's eye was black. Melchor refuses to believe this. Magdalena enters in mourning garb. She and Angela, each claiming to be the one Melchor loves, throw him into confusion. (Is Tirso hinting here that this is the function of the feminine sex?) Each girl agrees to expose a hand so Melchor may decide who is who, but when the brothers of the girls appear, the latter leave hurriedly, fearing recognition.

Melchor is told by a messenger to appear tonight to talk with the lady he loves at a window. He is, however, to come to Magdalena's window in order, says the messenger, that the lady's relatives may not discover what she is doing. Magdalena is not to be told of this in advance. Melchor shows up at the window, and is addressed by Magdalena in the role of the convent lady. She tells him that she can not go through with the marriage with Melchor because of family reasons, and she hopes he will marry Magdalena, her dear friend. Magdalena as the convent lady now draws back from the window, and reappears at once as herself. She tells him that because of his fickleness, she wants nothing from him. Don Alonso, having heard that a man is at Magdalena's window, comes into the street to investigate. Angela also appears, claims to be the promised bride, the lady at the convent. But Magdalena joins them in the street and in the ensuing conversation, everything is cleared up. Melchor, contrite, confesses his errors, and is accepted by Magdalena as her fiancé. Other marriages are arranged for the minor characters, and all ends as the *Comedia* of comic structure usually does.

The matter-of-fact recital of the play's action gives small indication of its exuberance and verve, its great store of vitality. There are frequent specimens of the author's characteristic humor, much of it expressed through Ventura's wit as he coins words, satirizes *culto* language, mocks his master's stupidity at not seeing the obvious in the fact that the women he pursues (or is pursued by) are one person. A part of what Tirso's audience found "spicy" are the homosexual hints on doña Blanca's pages 1476-77 and 1487-88; the inferences were meant to add to a feeling of naughtiness that enhanced audience response.[18] There is, however, a lack of the scatology found at times in Tirsian drama. There is no stage direction proposing how any one of the actors should do this or that scene, and it was up to the audience to respond adequately to whatever the actors gave them as the latters' interpretation of their roles. Physical decorum was apparently observed carefully; there is no indication that Melchor touched Magdalena except when he kissed her hand at the window. Thus the audience was required to use its imagination and fantasies in order to comprehend the situation, the basic eroticism. There can be no doubt that its members understood adequately what was going on. What it was that they missed that has been added by the psychologists in their study of eroticism is a matter not to be discussed here.

La celosa is a situation comedy, a "sitcom" somewhat like that of our modern theater. For this type of drama there is needed a series of actions that first of all lend themselves to a comic treatment. The erotic love theme has always been useful for this. Development of character is of minor concern. One searches in vain for a word or phrase that may tell us directly what any one of the persons is really like inside. They are types. Except for the servants, all are of the upper class, not particularly intelligent, and Melchor least of all. They are of "pure blood," and with the keen sense of personal honor to be found to an exaggerated degree in the *Comedia*. The men are presumably virile, although Tirso's treatment of the male in many of his plays may make one doubt this. The ladies are physically attractive, virtuous and *discretas*, this last term meaning that they have enough common sense to behave in a way befitting their sex and social position. In the final analysis a genteel or noble lady's worth as a candidate for marriage depended first of all on her virginal virtue, and next on the size of her dowry. Her beauty was an added element to be desired but not necessarily required. Hence Melchor's placing beauty first as his lady's most desirable trait was unrealistic for the ideas of the time. But the *autores* of the boy-meets-girl type of comedy usually saw to it that a sufficient degree of physical attractiveness was present in their nubile ladies to stimulate the erotic fantasies of their suitors and hence of the play's audience. And thus it has been in much of the world's literature, written to fill a folk need since literature's beginning.

Spain's seventeenth-century drama was sufficiently popular to meet that folk need, this being first of all concerned with a desire for entertainment.[19] A modern student who is beginning his study of the *Comedia* may be surprised to learn that churchmen formed part of the public that took pleasure in the drama, whether this be of a profane or of a religious nature. As observed in note 5, the Church supported the theater partly because of the latter's contributions to the hospitals, and as a consequence the Church gave to the acting profession a degree of respectability. Priests attended dramatic performances; they sat in a section reserved for them called a *desván* or *tertulia*. A picture of the section may be seen opposite page 193 in José Deleitó's book on the ways in which the public amused itself.[20] Deleitó (p. 285) remarks on the ease with which "lo eclesiástico y lo teatral" had "extrañas conexiones," and adds (p. 286), "Nada más frecuente que el tránsito de la iglesia al Teatro y de la escena al claustro." He goes on to relate how there were priests who renounced their calling to become actors. Some of them married. But there were also actors who took holy orders, just as there were dramatists like Lope, Mira, Moreto, Alonso Remón, Calderón—and of course Tirso—who did likewise.[21] One reason for the compatibility of Church and Theater was the latter's origin in the church in medieval times: priests acted in skits of religious content, written in Latin. Gradually this kind of drama went to the vernacular, became more worldly, and eventuated in the commercial theater.[22] But the compatibility of Church and Theater persisted despite this worldliness, and in Tirso's time both institutions had sympathy for each other.

It may be assumed that the distinction between what was morally acceptable and what was not was less sharply distinguished in the public—and the priestly—mind than we should expect to find in our own time. The seventeenth century was a difficult one for intellectuals. The dramatists were of course of that small and elitist group one of whose activities and functions was to seek freedom for the exploration and the exploitation of new areas such as the Lopean *Comedia*. Inhibited by the moral and theological absolutes of the Counter-Reformation—absolutes officially supported by the Church and State—the Establishment—intellectuals had to be careful not to go too far in their pursuit of new areas and ideas. As remarked above, the *Comedia* has been labeled by Maravall and Asensio as propaganda for the Establishment.[23] This charge cannot be refuted, although the *Comedia* was more than that. Nor should it be rejected out of hand, since one (even though only one) of the major functions of literature is to set down aspects and interpretations of its period's culture and thus to express the folk needs, as heretofore proposed. Among other things, literature is usually fashionable, and it was a fashion of the Establishment to support the theater. The *Comedia* was a favorite diversion of the young Felipe IV. Furthermore, the king was exaggeratedly fond of the other sex, and his erotic impulses helped to encourage the eroticism that was also fashionable in the culture. To find it in the theater, then, was not necessarily to be considered as deplorable, and this because of the fact (or in spite of it?) that the Establishment was, so to speak, playing both sides of the street: as seen, it supported on the one hand the cultural imperative of the Counter Reformation and, on the other, it fostered a theater (not to mention other institutions, such as prostitution) that undermined the moral code.[24] Theological doctrine has always had difficulties in its adoption, as our time so well illustrates.

To sum up, this article has assumed that literature is written to meet the folk needs of each generation. A major part of literature has been given over to the portrayal and interpretation of human love. This fits in well with the theory that reality is fundamentally comic rather than tragic. Since much of love is sexual in its nature, eroticism (that is, sexual excitement, originating in or accompanied by genital stimulation) is a necessary ingredient of the literary formula for the portrayal of love, especially so when this is concerned with the youthful emotions of the boy-meets-girl situation of comedy. The Spanish comedy of the Golden Age was more often than not given to this type of comedy and with the accompanying eroticism. This element survived in spite of the opposition of moralists, who saw in the erotic theater an evil that was forbidden by the Church of the Counter Reformation. The hand-in-glove compatibility of the Church and the Theater was explained in part by the fact of the origin of the Theater in the medieval Church, as also by the approval of the Establishment. Priests and other churchly people wrote erotic plays, apparently with no major twinge of conscience; they took pleasure in entertaining their audiences with the relatively decorous exploration of the complex of young love. The erotic element of youthful affection was made quite clear in Tirso's ***La celosa de sí misma*** as Melchor the *galán* exercised his sexual fantasies and day dreams as these were inspired by the mysterious lady he met at mass. The fundamental appeal of the boy-meets-girl theme is still of course very popular.[25]

Addenda

After this study had been completed there came to hand an article that had escaped my attention, Francisco Ayala's, "Erotismo y juego teatral en Tirso," in *Insula*, 19:214 (septiembre 1964), 1, 7. Ayala had just reread ***El vergonzoso en palacio*** and he recalls how Tirso had reprinted the play in the *Cigarral primero* of the ***Cigarrales de Toledo***; this printing had come after a number of years during which the play had become famous in Spain, Italy and America—or so Tirso states. Following its presentation in the *cigarral*, members of the smart set who were present—Tirso refers to them as "el más bello y ilustre auditorio que dio estimación al Taxo y sobervia a sus aguas"—discussed the play's merit and demerits as dramatic art. The only criticism of a major sort was that of the play's violation of the classic unities, although there was not a consensus about it. No remark was made about the eroticism which Ayala found as making up much of the *comedia*'s substance, although one of those present deplored Tirso's making wantons of the two daughters of the Duke of Aveiro. Apparently the Toledan smart set, male and female, found the eroticism acceptable; this is a further indication of the taste of Tirso's time. That at least some of the characters of the ***Cigarrales*** were living persons of the nobility has been established beyond reasonable doubt. See, for example, my "Tirso's ***Cigarrales de Toledo***: Some Clarifications and Identifications," *Hispanic Review*, 33 (July 1965), 246-72.

There came also to hand an expansion of Professor MacCurdy's article of reference in note 7: "Women and Sexual Love in the Plays of Rojas Zorrilla: Tradition and Innovation," *Hispania* 62:3 (May Sept. 1979), 255-65. The article adds substantially to the author's original study.

In an article in *BCom* 32:1 (Spring 1980), 3-9, "*El galán Castrucho*: Lope in the Tradition of Bawdy," Professor David M. Gitlitz offers a sprightly and informative comment on the subject of his title. He shows how the young Lope—*El galán Castrucho* is probably of 1598—pulls out all the stops and lets go with an uninhibited erotic and scatological kind of drama not often found in the *Comedia*. Gitlitz's article brings to mind an article of some years ago that I published in the *Homenaje a Guillermo Guastavino . . .* (Madrid: Asociación de bibliotecarios, archiveros y arqueólogos, 1974), pp. 347-60. The article, "Un breve comentario sobre dos comedias del siglo de oro," discusses two plays, the first of which is Lope's *El caballero del milagro*, composed between 1593 and 1598. The play's action takes place in Rome and is a picture of low life in which all the female characters are prostitutes. It is apparent that the youthful Lope, now in his thirties and an accomplished practitioner of the bawdy and the pornographic in his own life, introduces some of these elements into plays that are yet to receive attention. Gitlitz suggests that this kind of exaggerated erotica must have suffused the life of the times to an extent still not appreciated.

Notes

1. The words are taken from the Russian critic P. N. Berkov, as recalled by Robert C. Stephenson in the latter's essay on "Farce as Method." See *Comedy, Meaning and Form*, Robert W. Corrigan, ed. (Scranton, Pa.: Chandler, 1965), p. 317. The Stephenson essay was first published in *Tulane Drama Review*, 5:2 (1961), 85-93.

2. In his controversial *Love in the Western World,* first published in New York in 1940 as a Pantheon book and reprinted in 1956—the translation is by Montgomery Belgion—Denis de Rougemont traces the history of Western love as he understands it. Love as Eros, passion, often results in adultery and death, as in a model myth of the 12th and 13th centuries, that of Tristan and Iseult. It follows that for de Rougemont love is often tragic. The tragedy that springs from love is indeed a frequent motif of Western literature, but the discussion of love in the present article will take a different direction.

3. Lehman's discussion, "Comedy and Laughter," first published in the *Univ. of California Publications. English Studies,* 10 (U. of Cal. Press, 1959), 81-101, was reprinted on pp. 163 ff of the volume edited by Corrigan named in note 1.

4. This is not to say that the spiritual element is necessarily lacking in the lovers' emotions; indeed, we may assume its presence to a greater or lesser degree. This "spiritualized" love, at times labeled "neo-Platonic," is that which represents an effort to transcend physical desire. It will have comment below.

5. The moralists' disapproval of the theater resulted in its closing only twice, in 1598 and in 1646. The closings on other occasions came from other circumstances. This on the authority of N. E. Shergold in his *History of the Spanish Stage* (Oxford: Clarendon, 1967), p. 522. The theater's critics were made ineffective partly by the fact that hospitals were supported by theater funds. Furthermore, the yearly performances of the *autos sacramentales* were staged by professionals, and these performers could not make a living unless permitted to offer other types of drama during the theatrical season. Again, the actors and actresses, in spite of a notoriously unconventional life-style, took on a degree of respectibility as the seventeenth century progressed. Shergold (p. 523) reports on the increasingly tolerant attitude of the civil authorities and the Church, as is indicated, for example, by the permission for an actors' guild in 1631. The approving document was signed by the Cardinal Archbishop of Toledo, and the inaugural ceremonies included a sermon by the Bishop of Vermiglin.

6. For the orthodox Jew or Christian there is often involved in the evil repute of love the doctrine of original sin. This doctrine is tied in in some fashion with the story of Adam and Eve in Genesis 3. However, theologians through the centuries have not been able to come to a consensus about the specific nature of the act that may have caused this sin. The bibliography of the subject is formidable and is to be approached by the layman with caution. It is convenient to use the encyclopedias. One may, for example, read the *Encyclopedia Americana* (s.v. *Original Sin*) or *The New Catholic Encyclopedia* (s.v. *Original Sin; Sex; Fall of Man*). The *Americana* attempts an objective view, while that of the *New Catholic Encyclopedia* restricts itself to the Roman Catholic view of the issue.

7. MacCurdy's article is in *Romance Notes,* 1 (1959), 36-39.

8. Leavitt, "Strip-Tease . . ." in *Homenaje a Rodríguez Moñino* [no editors named], (Madrid, 1966), pp. 305-10.
9. Pallarés, "Algunos aspectos . . . ," *Kentucky Romance Quarterly*, 19:1 (1972), 3-15.
10. Asensio, "Casos de amor . . . ," *Cuadernos hispanoamericanos*, nos. 289-90 (julio-agosto, 1974), 1-33.
11. Asensio states that Tirso is not to be considered a theorist of love ("un teórico de amor"). If this means that the Mercedarian does not explicate a love theory in philosophical detail, this is of course correct. But the Tirsian idea of love as shown in the plots of his plays is quite clear, not to be mistaken. It is that love is erotic, as seen by the four scholars named.
12. As observed, Asensio faults the Counter Reformation doctrine in its rejection of neo-Platonism. Where was the individual to find salvation for his sins? Asensio makes clear his conviction that the Church and the government have the solutions for the problem of salvation in whatever way this problem might be solved. This is his solution in spite of his criticism above of the Church's lack of the capacity to formulate adequate norms because of its rejection of the neo-Platonic concept.
13. Asensio (p. 32) sees the multiple marriage device of the *Comedia* as a cure for the eroticism he deplores in the love of man and woman, and thus commends the churchly sacrament of marriage. The eroticism he finds objectionable is that which lacks the churchly sacrament.
14. The convent of the Victoria was close to the Calle Mayor, as doña Blanca states in a footnote to p. 1441. Ventura's remarks include the assertion that in that street love is sold "a varas, medida y peso," and we are reminded by E. Rodríguez Solís in his *Historia de la prostitución en España y América* (Madrid: Biblioteca Nueva, [1921?], p. 115 that, according to Mesonero Romanos there was in the Calle Mayor an "asiento de una mancebía célebre, sostenido por magnates de la corte, con lonjas y tiendas de objetos de plata y oro," and (p. 116) that it was "un lugar de citas para niñas picañas, busconas de manto y de daifas del agarro." The less than elevated moral tone of Tirso's Spain has been so often remarked upon that it needs no extended comment here. Let the assertions of Dr. Gregorio Marañón suffice. On p. 32 of his *El conde-duque de Olivares* (Madrid: Espasa Calpe, 1952), he refers to the youthful love exploits of that gentleman who was to become the *privado* of Felipe IV, and remarks: "Fueron, en suma, estos tiempos de [la vida del conde-duque] de pasión desordenada y cínica, muy al uso de la época." Again, on p. 206, Marañón refers to "la cruda fusión mística-sensual" of the spirit of the time, and goes on to suggest that the source of the attitude lay partly in the Spanish myths of the period, especially that of don Juan, "amasado en muerte y lujaria."
15. It may also be suggested that, amusingly enough, Melchor's attitude involves an approach to neo-Platonism in that his instant infatuation is inspired by the minimum of beauty he has observed—that of the lady's hand—and from that works upward in his imagination toward a fantasized vision of the idea of beauty as one and perfect, according to Plotinus (q.v. in *The Dictionary of Philosophy*, Dagobert D. Runes, ed. [New York: Philosophical Library, 1960]). For the Christian neo-Platonist the supreme Beauty would be God.
16. The all-concealing clothing of the time was permitted within the church. For street wear women were required by laws passed and always ignored to uncover their faces; the laws were intended to protect the public against disreputable females and men dressed as women who had criminal activities in mind. Modern commentaries on the laws are multiple. See, e.g., the Rodríguez volume cited in note 14, p. 115 ff; also A. de León Pinelo, *Anales de Madrid* (Madrid: CSIC, 1971), p. 316.

    Not only could the hand serve an erotic purpose; the exposed female foot could be a fetish, an inspiration for the amorous fantasies of an admiring male. One may read the amusing and informative article on the matter by A. David Kossoff, "El pie desnudo: Cervantes y Lope," in *Homenaje a William L. Fichter*, A. David Kossoff and José Amor y Vázquez, eds. (Madrid: Castalia, 1971), pp. 381-86. It may be suspected that during Spain's seventeenth century any part of the female anatomy could, when exposed, become an object of male admiration. Our play wll do its part in making this clear.
17. Angela is a little on the odd side. In Act I we are told that she disdains all men because, deploring her descent from Adam, she is upset at having as an ancestor one who had the shamelessness to appear naked before his wife. Again, having learned from Magdalena of the latter's planned marriage, she exclaims that she cannot understand how a girl can stand before a priest and a group of wedding guests and say "yes" to a man. The girl who can do this, she opines, is either *libre y animosa* or lacking in intelligence. Angela's budding love for Melchor has obviously changed her mind about the desirability of a husband.
18. Naughtiness adds to the dramatic effect. Virtue as a dramatic motif is colorless. Audiences feel in witnessing naughtiness a vicarious pleasure without risking their own punishment. As Valle-Inclán wrote in his *Sonata de Primavera*, the best part of sanctity are the temptations.
19. Comedy, as in our play, is often an escape mechanism, a "trip" into a kind of never-never land where untoward and amusing events happen and

turn out as they should in an idealized world. Piquancy is added to *La celosa* by the probability that Tirso, as in certain other of his plays, was using it partly to tease prominent persons of the nobility. He was also perhaps recalling a scandal that had been imperfectly hushed up in the court circle. See my "*La celosa de sí misma* de Tirso de Molina," in the Fichter homage volume of reference in note 16.

20. José Deleito y Piñnuela, *También se divierte el pueblo* (Madrid: Espasa Calpe, 1944).

21. A recent checking of Cayetano Alberto de la Barrera's *Catálogo . . . del teatro antigue español* (Madrid: Rivadeneyra, 1860) revealed 1,012 separate entries of names of playwrights who had each written one or more plays. Of these, 92 were churchmen, 12 were women (10 of them nuns). Thus, about 10 percent of the dramatists had churchly connections.

22. See Shergold, op. cit., Chaps. 1 and 2.

23. Cf. my review of José María Díez, *Sociología de la comedia españols del siglo XVII* (Madrid: Cátedra, 1976) in the *Bulletin of the Comediantes* (Spring, 1979), pp. 76-77.

24. At this point one might expatiate on the *desengaño* of the baroque period, the disillusionment that, among other causes, arose from two that come to mind: the uncertainty among the people as to what was or was not morally wrong and, as a corollary to this, their inability to overcome the lusts of the flesh. No space may be given here to pursue further the element of *desengaño*; it has had considerable discussion in the scholarly literature. The reader may choose to give thought to the matter as it arises in my article "Spain's Golden Age Culture and the *Comedia*," in *Hispania*, 61:4 (December 1978), 832-50.

25. The popularity of the theme has meant its persistence in drama from the ancient Greeks on. Northrop Frye, in his *Anatomy of Criticism* (Princeton: Univ. Press, 1957), p. 163, reminds us of this fact and of other fundamentals of comedy: The basis of all modern comedy is to be found in Greek New Comedy, as transmitted by Plautus and Terence. "What normally happens is that a young man wants a young woman, that his desire is resisted by some opposition [. . .], and that near the end of the play some twist in the plot enables the hero to have his will. In the first place, the movement of comedy is usually a movement from one kind of society to another. At the beginning of the play the obstructing characters are in charge of the play's society, and the audience recognizes that they are usurpers. At the end of the play the device in the plot that brings the hero and heroine together causes a new society to crystallize around the hero, and the moment this crystallization occurs is the point of the resolution of the action, the comic discovery, the *anagorisis* or *cognitio*. The appearance of this new society is frequently signalized by some kind of party or festive ritual, which either appears at the end of the play or is assumed to take place immediately afterward. Weddings are most common." The reader will recognize *La celosa*'s formula in the above, changed in minor ways. In passing, and in reference to Tirso's well-known *Don Gil de las calzas verdes*, it is recalled with amusement how in that *comedia* the boy-wants-girl formula has become girl-wants-boy and she gets him after removing the obstructions in her path (as Magdalena gets Melchor). And so in *Don Gil* it is the girl who is the "hero," while the *galán* is a kind of anti-hero who is mocked. One recognizes that Melchor of *La celosa* has a narrow escape from mockery (if he escapes at all), and that Tirso is, in his own way, calling into question the machismo of the Spanish male of his time. (In *El burlador de Sevilla* Don Juan's machismo sends him to Hell.)

A colleague who graciously took time from a busy schedule to read the present article agreed on the whole with its conclusions, but wondered to what extent Tirso regarded his Melchor as a ninny worthy only of mockery. The consultant sees in Melchor's *idée fixe* toward the convent lady's hand the kind of rigidity that Bergson regarded as the essence of the comic personality. In my reply I acknowledged the consultant's penetrating assessment of Melchor's character, even though my agreement with the assessment is not complete. Melchor is indeed not very bright. I also suggested that Melchor represents Tirso's liking for the weak male, one dominated by his female antagonist, as recalled just above in my reference to *Don Gil*. I also recalled that some years ago I proposed the possibility that perhaps Tirso was expressing his belief that the Spanish male of the century was sufficiently enslaved by his obsession with sex that he (Tirso) may have seen Spain as governed from the bedroom. In any event, different readers may see different things in *La celosa* just as they make variant interpretations of any piece of literature. One may pointedly recall Emile Zola's remark that "a work of art is a corner of nature seen through a temperament."

Henry W. Sullivan (essay date 1985)

SOURCE: "Love, Matrimony and Desire in the Theatre of Tirso de Molina," in *Bulletin of the Comediantes*, Vol. 37, No. 1, Summer, 1985, pp. 83-99.

[*In the following essay, Sullivan concludes that the totality of de Molina's true views on love cannot be determined from his plays.*]

Tirso studies have been historically bedevilled by a range of problems so various and intransigent that scholars have been understandably reluctant to address large aspects of his drama (such as the theme of love) with any confidence. I am referring to the almost total absence of firm dates of composition for the *comedias* (despite Ruth Lee Kennedy's lifelong efforts) and the consequent lack of any reliable chronology. The authorship of a large number of his plays has also been challenged (most sweepingly by Margaret Wilson), including many major ones: ***El burlador de Sevilla; El condenado por desconfiado; El rey don Pedro en Madrid; Los amantes de Teruel*** among a dozen others.[1] The facts of Tirso's birth, parentage and early life have given rise to a controversy that has raged for almost a hundred years without achieving a resolution, and what is known of the rest of his life is sketchy. As new material comes to light, it tends to fill out our picture of the Mercedarian friar, but not the writer. Other critics such as Cotarelo y Mori and Da. Blanca de los Ríos have dismissed as a fiction the existence of the nephew, Francisco Lucas de Avila, who edited the *Partes* II-V of his *comedias* in the 1630's. If true, this skeptical claim would destroy the most obvious theory for the transmission of Tirso's texts from MS to print.

In order to come to grips with an issue as central as the love interest presented in the works of this major dramatist, I have decided to suspend temporarily the problems outlined above by privileging theory above neo-Positivistic archivalism and by looking at the systems of thought implicit in the texts themselves. There are some risks involved in this procedure. We know enough about the fashionable love theories of the day and the climate of theological opinion to set rough ideological parameters for the thought of Tirso de Molina. The next step is to decide how far his own ideas fit or do not fit into these conventional molds. The use of Lacan's theories on Desire, however, is another matter. In discussing the historically determined thought-systems to be presented in sections I and II, the basic interplay will be between Tirso's own ideas and those of his age. In section III, the basic interplay will be between those ideas present in Tirso's texts and our understanding of those texts here and now in the late twentieth century. As we shall see, however, Lacan claimed that his account of the structure of the human psyche was valid for all mankind-the-language-user. If we accept (at least provisionally) this concept of diachronic validity, then the behavior and motivation of Tirso's characters may be analyzed in terms of Lacanian Desire for the very considerable enlightenment that such analysis brings. The reader must be the judge of the results. These will be presented in book-length form in the near future under the title *Love, Matrimony and Desire in the Theater of Tirso de Molina*.

The Mercedarian priest and polygraph Fray Gabriel Téllez (1581?-1648) is best known to posterity as the creator of the defiant seducer Don Juan Tenorio or—in his Italian incarnation—Don Giovanni. Don Juan, however, is only the most celebrated example in the Mercedarian's theater of erotic love and sexual *élan* expressed in unusual, not to say deviant, form. More than any other Spanish playwright, Tirso felt drawn to the portrayal of pathological human desire and superhuman energy on the stage, and in so doing became the greatest dramatist of character in the Golden Age. The purpose of my 1976 study, *Tirso de Molina & the Drama of the Counter Reformation*, was to examine Tirso's special relationship to the philosophical and theological controversies of the late sixteenth century, linking these to his dramatic themes, as well as to his "Baroque" technique and language. There was little room in that treatment for a discussion of interpersonal relationships between characters. I wish now, however, to scrutinize more closely Tirso's attitude towards love and matrimony, and his portrayal of the broader human phenomenon of desire.

The objective of my projected study, then, is to set out in systematic fashion the theoretical bases of Tirso's views on love, matrimony and desire, in a way which will isolate and explain the idiosyncratic nature of these views. Love intrigue and the many faces of desire did, it is true, constitute a perennial and indispensable element of all Golden-Age drama. Tirso was no exception here, but it is the bizarre sexual behavior of his men and women protagonists which has struck successive observers and critics as unique.[2] Now if love and desire assume strange guises in Tirso, we may ask *why* this is so. What does it mean? How can it be analyzed? And in a broader sense, can perversity or pathology tell us something about normalcy?

The unwieldy mass of dramatic materials extant from the Spanish seventeenth century (80 plays by Tirso alone, for example; many thousands more by his contemporaries) makes comprehensive or *singulatim* treatment of love in the *comedia* a difficult, if not impossible, task. What is required is some theoretical key or framework which would bring this random mass of data under control. But *qua* Tirso de Molina, the literary artist who inherited the late-Renaissance love conventions of Spain; and *qua* Fray Gabriel Téllez, the Mercedarian churchman who inherited the late-Renaissance, neo-Scholastic theology of Spain, Tirso himself has provided us with this key. I have been able to discern at least five distinct theories (or subsystems) of love in his theater (courtly, neo-Platonic, mystic, atomistic, love in relation to the honor code); and his comments on the sacrament of marriage, on consanguinity, papal dispensation of impediments, clandestinity, and the canonical legitimacy of marital union, have left us a complex theological deposition on the theory of matrimony. Furthermore, almost all sexual variations with regard to the object of desire that have been documented in modern psychoanalytic literature are also to be found in his theater. Much the most fruitful theoretical approach to the analysis of these sexual aberrations, I believe, is suggested by the thought of the late French psychoanalyst Jacques Lacan (1901-1981). Tirso emerges from this Lacanian scrutiny as a brilliant pre-Freudian analyst, whose frankness, remarkable insight and love of the bizarre led him to an arresting picture of the movements of the psyche which was far ahead of its time.

A partial apology for this kind of hybrid methodology can be made on the basis of its theoretical newness. Though there has been a profound and far-reaching renewal of literary theory during the last decade or so in North America, its effect on Golden-Age theater studies has been limited. The dominant trends in our field are still: 1) neo-Positivistic (editing of texts, establishing facts of biography, bibliography and sources; studies on the physical realities of playhouse construction or staging); or 2) aesthetic-formalist (studies of imagery, verse-pattern frequency, analyses of rhetorical strategies and intertextual influences; semiotics and structuralism); or 3) neo-Aristotelian (thematico-structural analysis of plays in relationship to dramaturgical properties such as Unity of Action, poetic justice, the recognition of guilt by the guilty, etc.). My proposed theoretical approach is drawn straight out of the epoch in question (Renaissance theories of love; theology of matrimony), as well as from the insights of modern, post-Structuralist psychoanalysis (Jacques Lacan). This "ancient and modern" theoretical confluence is, I hope to show, mutually self-corroborating, and no analysis of Spanish drama has yet been attempted along these lines.

I—Theories of Love in the Theater of Tirso de Molina

Though in our modern day, few people subscribe consciously to a specific theory of love, the Renaissance was, so to say, "in love with love" itself. No epoch speculated more actively and abundantly on love's nature, its origins and its meaning. A variety of competing theoretical subsystems grew up therefore, especially in Spain. The first of these, chronologically speaking, was the Medieval courtly-love system (with its beginnings in twelfth-century France). In his celebrated *Allegory of Love* (1936), C.S. Lewis characterized this system by its pseudo-feudal worship of women (i.e., humility and courtesy), by its adultery, and the "religion of love."[3] To this list, I would add the conception of love as ever unsatiated, ever increasing desire.[4] The tantalizing dimension of nonsatisfaction is achieved in courtly literature by the invention of divisive obstacles, leading to the lover's near-perpetual separation. The courtly-love theory produced a mannered stylization of amatory rhetoric in fifteenth-century Castilian poetry (the *cancioneros*). It made its appearance in the Spanish drama as an articulate system in the pioneer eclogues of Juan del Encina, as Antony van Beysterveldt has convincingly shown.[5]

Tirso's major play on the theme of courtly love is his poetic tragedy, ***Los amantes de Teruel***, a Medieval love-legend conveniently updated by Tirso to the reign of Charles V (1520-1555). It displays all the psychological fingerprints of the courtly view of passion. Don Diego Marsilla and Isabel de Segura have been lovers since childhood. In the eyes of Isabel's father, however, Marsilla's lack of fortune makes him ineligible as a husband. The father therefore consents to a time limit or *plazo* of three years and three days before which Marsilla must make his fortune. Marsilla chooses a life of reckless, semi-suicidal soldiering in North Africa under Charles V. He distinguishes himself, but worldly profit and spoils of war seem to elude him. Rewarded finally by a grateful Emperor, Marsilla returns to Spain perilously close to the deadline, only to discover Isabel the bride of the scheming Don Gonzalo, who has convinced her through trickery that her soldier-lover is dead. Confronting Isabel at last in her bridal chamber and demanding a final kiss, Marsilla is rebuffed and falls dead at Isabel's feet. She, distracted with grief at his funeral in turn, throws herself upon Marsilla's corpse and dies.

This play, often reminiscent of *Romeo and Juliet* in its story and intense poetry, shows the hero as the perfect courtly lover by his absolute service of Isabel, his reckless deeds performed in her name, and the heretical elevation of his passion over the injunctions of Christian morality. In a characteristically Tirsian twist, the courtly themes of adultery and separation are fused in his version of the tale. The Mercedarian pushes the motif of separation to such an extreme that the lovers never actually meet onstage at all until the end of the last act. This is arguably a partial dramatic weakness in terms of character-drawing, but it preserves faithfully the courtly tradition of keeping the lovers divided and in a state of ever unsatiated desire. But the one, long-postponed moment of the lovers' reunion also permits Tirso paradoxically to introduce the companion motif of adultery. When Marsilla finally enters Isabel's bridal chambers, she is, of course, now a married woman, not his paramour. Hence, to ask for a passionate kiss from the erstwhile betrothed is an adulterous request, and she refuses not out of a lack of compassion but out of her sense of duty as a newlywed wife. An underlying irony of the play, therefore, is that, as long as the lovers' passion is licit, they are never together to enjoy it, and, when they are reunited, circumstances have rendered this same passion adulterous.

Much is made in the play of ill omens and a sense of star-crossed doom. Since this atmosphere is established early on, it suggests at first an element of predeterminism in the play's action. On the other hand, the characters do not themselves seem convinced that the stars are entirely to blame, and, as usual in Tirso, we should seek the true elements of causality in their personalities. The thrust of the play seems far more to suggest that the sources of doom are to be found in the lovers' common death-wish and their exorbitant attitudes to life and passion. Indeed, the minor characters express surprise at their extravagance. Thus Tirso distances himself from the theory of love dramatized in ***Los amantes de Teruel*** and, in his stress on external Fate as the displacement of unconsciously willed self-destruction, he implicitly chides the absurdity and extremism of courtly love's emotional surrender.

The neo-Platonic love system came to Renassiance Spain from indigenous Judaic sources and from fifteenth-century Italy, notably Ficino, and was diffused in popularising works such as Castiglione's *Il Cortegiano* (1528) and León Hebreo's *Dialoghi di Amore* (1535). Most educated

Spaniards of the sixteenth century read Italian, but for those who did not *Il Cortegiano* was accessible in Boscán's translation (1534) and the *Dialoghi di Amore* in the translations of Micer Carlos Montesa (1582) or the Inca Garcilaso (1590). Plato's teachings concerned *eros*, or desirous love, as a process of stepwise contemplation that could aspire, at the lowest level, to immortality through offspring; on a higher plane to the ethical life and sound public institutions; to the enrichment of philosophy and science, or, finally, to a supreme beatific vision of eternal and supercosmic beauty as the "Form of Good" which stands at the head of all other Forms. In its neo-Platonic popularisations, love was held to be desire for a beautiful person; thence a contemplation of the beauty *per se* in this beloved and, finally, a contemplation of the Idea or divine essence of Beauty itself. These ideas lent themselves easily to elaboration in the Spanish pastoral novel, in the sonnets of Herrera or in the popular theater (Lope's *Fuenteovejuna*, for example).

For Tirso, however, who stood back in sardonic distance from the Idealisms of the Renaissance, the notion that physical desire or *eros* sought its consummation in the mystic contemplation of unalloyed, or even divine Beauty was an absurd affectation. This is clear in his superb comedy ***La celosa de sí misma***, where the veiled Magdalena coquettishly bares and then conceals her gloved hand in a Madrid church to the gaze of Melchor, unaware that he is her newly arrived fiancée. Melchor conceives an aberrant, fetishistic passion for this hand, a fact which exasperates his maneservant and provides much of the play's humor. In particular, when Magdalena is later presented to him as his fiancée, he finds her beauty inferior to that of the veiled woman in the church, the bogusly named Condesa de Chirinola; so that Magdalena is paradoxically her own rival, or "the woman jealous of herself" of the title.

And yet the ideological assumptions behind Melchor's behavior derive from an extravagant neo-Platonism. Though Magdalena never removes her veil, Melchor imagines that her hand is the paradigm of her unseen face; that the whole of the mystery woman's body must be as beautiful as the single part. The Platonic imagery pervades the play and is clear in Melchor's words in Act II:

> D. Melchor: Por la luz pura y divina
> que amante adoro y no veo,
> que os juzgo por maravilla
> de la belleza . . .
> (II, v, 1464b)[6]

But we cannot be in much doubt about Tirso's attitude towards this view of love. As Dr. Premraj Halkhoree has written: "The structure of the play exposes the limitations and ultimate absurdity of the literary neo-Platonic view. It is because the Condesa is the ideal woman that Melchor loves her, and this, in turn, is why Magdalena wants to be the Condesa and is angry in III, xvii when Melchor agrees to marry Magdalena. But Magdalena's identification with the Condesa is only possible for so long as the latter remains the abstract Platonic ideal, without an identity. A man cannot marry an abstract concept of beauty, however, and that is why Melchor's marriage to the Condesa is an impossibility."[7]

The mystic-love system flowered suddenly in Spain in the sixteenth century, two centuries after its apogee in the rest of Europe. A number of Tirso's plays take this system as the basis for portraying the relationship of men and women to God. St. Thomas Aquinas had argued that man's highest purpose on earth was to know God through reason. Duns Scotus, on the other hand, argued that man's purpose was to love God through the will. In dramas such as ***Quien no cae, no se levanta*** and ***La ninfa del cielo***, Tirso followed the noetic-ecstatic writings of St. John of the Cross and other Spanish divines and—in a remarkable fusion of Thomist and Scotistic traditions—demonstrated that mystic love was a medium of actual knowledge of God.

Now while the doctrinal nuances of this view are novel, a play such as ***La ninfa del cielo*** shows Tirso's limited ability to convey the supernatural convincingly in stage terms. His great insight into humanness is here actually at odds with his capacities for abstraction and theological demonstration. The heroine, doomed by her erratic sexual conduct, can retrieve her honor only in a providential death and mystic marriage with Christ. True to himself and to the prevailing Baroque sensibility of the day, Tirso also injected a lurid vein of material sensuality into the religious ecstasy of these plays. But his finest mystical achievement is probably his trilogy on the career of Santa Juana: a regenerative woman, who moves society towards her without force, intrigue, or even self-awareness.[8]

A fourth subsystem was the neo-Scholastic or "atomistic" theory of love. In ***El amor médico*** and other comedies, Tirso applied the Scholastic tradition of "faculty" psychology and the topology of the soul to love. This was an attempt to analyse the separate faculties of the rational soul as conceived of by theologians—memory, understanding, will, imagination and the rest—as an account of sensation and cognition in general. According to the atomistic theory, love was an emotion stimulated by solid particles or an influx absorbed through the eyes. Sancho de San Ramón, Yvonne David-Peyre and others have shown that Tirso displayed a more than common understanding of medicine, pathology and psychosomatic illness.[9] Since Spanish physicians of the sixteenth century such as Gómez Pereira, Huarte de San Juan and Miguel Sabuco combined their medical observations with naturalistic philosophy, it is not surprising to see materialist touches in Tirso's atomistic account of the sensation of love. The notion of love as a stream of contiguous solid bodies, optically absorbed, is both materialist and implicitly anti-Idealist.

Of all the subsystems of love so far discussed, this seems to be the only one which Tirso took seriously. Extra evidence for this statement is provided by an excellent article of F.G. Halstead published in 1943.[10] In that article, Halstead argues that Tirso linked his optical love-system with belief in astrology or supernatural forces. According to Halstead, Tirso questioned whether the subject's free-will had the power to resist the influx of love. Tirso elsewhere states that, when the normal social conventions or bonds of friendship are broken, this can only be legitimized by the plea of love or the will to power.[11] Thus, this favored system, though it took its remote origins in Medieval spiritualism, acquired for Tirso strong materialist, naturalist, and even determinist implications.

Fifth and last, Tirso constantly brought love up against the obligations of the notorious honor code. This burdensome system not only fused the idea of woman as a proprietary love-object with sexual jealousy in general, but also extended the field of concern to include the male's preoccupation with social appearances in the eyes of other men, specifically his reputation, and even his identity. Duelling, and blood vengeance for real or imagined slights, inevitably accompanied this view of sexual relations. Again, while Tirso paid lip-service to this honor code, he also obliquely undermined it, mocking the rigidity and absurdity of its conventions.

This comes through, for example, in his famous *comedia de enredo*, ***Don Gil de las calzas verdes***. Don Martín, the hero, and the irascible Don Juan are rivals for the love of Doña Inés. In a remarkable scene in the middle of the play (II, viii), Don Juan confronts Don Martín and demands satisfaction in a duel. The torpid and duplicitous Martín, however, responds with a string of casuistical arguments instead of drawing his sword: that Inés must choose the lucky man and, if it be Juan, there is no cause for a fight; that if she wishes to obey her father and marry Martín, then why should Martín risk a sure thing and leave her prematurely widowed, etc.? If he *should* succeed in winning Inés, suggests the phlegmatic Martín finally to an astounded Juan, then they can fix an appointment for a duel one month hence. It is very hard to imagine a Calderonian gallant reacting in this way to a situation where his reputation and valor were obviously at stake.

II—Neo Scholastic Doctrines on Matrimony in Tirso's Theater

The theology of matrimony became a burning issue in Spain after the final sessions of the Council of Trent (1563). While Catholics argued that marriage was a sacrament that conferred grace, Luther and later Protestant theologians rejected this. A second major problem was the prevalence of secret or clandestine marriages. Though these were severely and repeatedly prohibited in the West by conciliar law and pontifical decrees throughout the Middle Ages, there was no law requiring the presence of a priest for a valid marriage. The prohibition thus became ineffective. Secretly but validly married couples were able to separate and successfully enter new unions in the presence of a priest. Others lived in concubinage while pretending to be secretly married.[12]

In an effort to put an end to such abuses, the Council of Trent enacted its revolutionary *Tametsi* decree in 1563. It declared marriages invalid unless contracted in the presence of the bishop or the parish priest (usually the pastor of the domicile of one of the spouses), or another priest authorized by either of them, and in the presence of at least two other witnesses.

Yet, as with so many of the Tridentine decrees, *Tametsi* did not bring controversy on marriage to an end. There ensued, inspired by the inner impulses of the minoritarian Catholic reform and the goadings of the iconoclastic Protestant Reformers, a veritable Golden Age of literature on the theory of matrimony (1585-1635). The three masterpieces of this literature were, significantly, all composed by Spaniards: Pedro de Ledesma, *De magno matrimonii sacramento* (1592); Thomás Sánchez S.J., *De sancto matrimonii sacramento* (1602); and Basilio Ponce, *De sacramento matrimonii* (1624).

In the years of Tirso's artistic maturity as a playwright, that is, from about 1605 to 1625, the issues of marriage as sacrament and the validity of clandestine union were vigorously debated. Across the sweep of his dramas, Tirso reexamined the canonical niceties of the whole matter (betrothal, wedding, consummation; consanguinity, impediments, dispensation, etc.) and tended to adopt positions minimizing the legal obstacles. Matrimony in Fray Gabriel Téllez's dramatic world is usually *preceded* by sexual relations, not a Christian sacrament as it is in Lope. Some 20-odd Tirsian *comedias* take as their starting-point the consummation of a union contracted under promise of marriage, but without either betrothal or nuptials. The comic action then shows how the abandoned woman (always dressed as a man) pursues and wins back her fickle lover. The plays' endings imply, by the final sanction of official recognition, that the original promise of the parties, the matter (i.e., the bodies of the spouses), and the ministers (i.e., the contracting parties) contained all elements necessary to the sacrament. Indeed, this very argument was made at Trent by Antonio di Gragnano (Sullivan, *Tirso*, p. 26).

In such plays as ***El pretendiente al revés***, Tirso investigates the legality of clandestine marriage; here Carlos and Sirena have met secretly at night for over a year (I, vi) and regard their union as licit. In many plays, Tirso takes on the delicate issues of incest and consanguinity (***La venganza de Tamar, Averígüelo Vargas, El castigo del penséque***). In his Pizarro trilogy, for instance, he seems to admit consanguinity in the second degree. In ***La huerta de Juan Fenández***, prospective cross-cousin and uncle-niece marriages are favorably reviewed.

One of the most interesting of Tirso's lucubrations on the validity of matrimony is ***La república al revés***, a turbulent drama set in the reign of the eighth-century Byzantine Empress Irene.[13] Early on in the play, her restless son Constantino takes over the reins of power. Irene has prearranged a dynastic marriage for him with Carola, the daughter of the King of Cyprus. On greeting her at the betrothal ceremony, however, Constantino is smitten by the beauty of her lady-in-waiting Lidora, and, against his mother's wishes and all political discretion, insists on making Lidora his Imperial consort. All parties, however, including the Senate (II, ii, 398-99), consider the betrothal ceremony legally binding. But when the young Emperor instructs his henchman Leoncio to make sure it is Lidora who occupies the bridal-chamber that night instead of Carola, a further complication arises. Himself besotted with Lidora, Leoncio proposes to usurp the Emperor's place; he engineers events so that Constantino unknowingly consummates his relationship with Carola in the darkness of night. Leoncio spends the night with Lidora.

Depending on one's legal point of view, Constantino is now a bigamist inasmuch as he has a legal wife, Carola (whom he spurns), and a common-law wife, Lidora (with whom he cohabits). When Carola informs the stunned Constantino that she is pregnant with his child (II, viii, 402-03), he refuses to believe it, and Carola considers herself the victim of a plot to convict her of adultery. This would permit Constantino grounds for a divorce. Meanwhile, depending on one's point of view, Lidora is now committing adultery with Clodio, her lover, who is posing as her brother. Finally, when a son is born to Carola, Irene takes possession of the Empire in the name of this grandson. This act tends to reinforce the legitimacy of the parents' union, since the latter materially affects the Imperial succession. Throughout the play, therefore, although there is no marriage ceremony and Constantino explicitly and sincerely rejects the union from the start, Tirso upholds the legality of the bride's intention and the inadvertent consummation as sufficient grounds for a canonically valid marriage.

Notes

1. See Margaret Wilson, *Tirso de Molina* (Boston: Twayne, 1977), and my review in *Journal of Hispanic Philology*, 3, no. 1 (1978), 97-99.
2. Cf. Mario Penna, *Don Giovanni e il mistero di Tirso* (Turin: Rosenberg e Sellier, 1958); the remarks of Mario Méndez Bejarano reproduced in J. Sanz y Díaz, *Tirso de Molina* (Madrid: C.B.E., 1964), pp. 213-14; and Henry W. Sullivan, "Tirso de Molina: dramaturgo andrógino," in Maxime Chevalier, ed., *Actas del V Congreso Internacional de Hispanistas*, 2 vols. (Brodeaux: Institut des Etudes Ibériques et Iberoaméricaines, 1977), 811-18.
3. Cf. C.S. Lewis, *The Allegory of Love: A Study of Medieval Tradition* (London: Oxford University Press, 1953 ed.), pp. 2; 12-123.
4. Cf. A.J. Denomy, *The Heresy of Courtly Love* (New York: Declan X McMullen, 1947), p. 20. See also T.A. Kirby, "Courtly Love," in Alex Preminger ed., *Princeton Encyclopedia of Poetry and Poetics* (Princeton: Princeton University Press, 1974), p. 157b.
5. This is the general thesis of Antony van Beysterveldt, *La poesía amatoria del siglo XV y el teatro profano de Juan del Encina* (Madrid: Insula, 1972).
6. All citations are from the standard edition of Da. Blanca de los Ríos Lampérez, *Tirso de Molina: Obras dramáticas completas*, 3 vols. (Madrid: Aguilar, 1946-58), and are quoted by act, scene, page and column numbers.
7. See the unpublished doctoral thesis of Dr. Premraj Halkhoree, "Social and Literary Satire in the Comedies of Tirso de Molina," Edinburgh, 1969, at p. 103.
8. See Nazario Ruano, "Tirso de Molina el último gran fraile," in *Desnudez: Lo místico y lo literario en San Juan de la Cruz* (Mexico City: Polis, 1962), pp. 293-309.
9. Cf. Rafael Sancho de San Román, "La medicina y los médicos en la obra de Tirso de Molina," *Estudios de Historia de la Medicina Española*, 2, no. 1 (1960), 1-71, and his "El quéhacer médico en la obra de Tirso de Molina," *Boletín de la Medicina de la Sociedad Española de Historia de la Medicina*, 2, no. 4 (1962). See also Yvonne David-Peyre, "Un Cas d'observation clinique chez Tirso de Molina," *Les Langues Néo-Latines*, 4 (1971), 2-22, also translated as "Un caso de observación clínica en Tirso de Molina," *Asclepio*, 20 (1968), 221-23.
10. See Frank G. Halstead, "The Optics of Love: Notes on a Concept of Atomistic Philosophy in the Theatre of Tirso de Molina," *PMLA*, 58 (1943), 108-21.
11. This sentiment is expressed in *Cómo han de ser los amigos* (II, ii, 287). See my *Tirso de Molina and the Drama of the Counter Reformation* (Amsterdam: Editions Rodopi N.V., 1976; 2nd ed. 1981), p. 110, note 11.
12. Cf. "Marriage, Canon Law of" in the *New Catholic Encyclopedia* (New York etc.: McGraw-Hill, 1967), IX, 277a.

Jean S. Chittenden (essay date 1987)

SOURCE: "The Monarch/Mother in the 'Comedias' of Tirso de Molina," in *Crítica Hispánica,* Vol. 9, Nos. 1-2, 1987, pp. 39-49.

[*In the following essay, Chittenden studies the development of female characters in de Molina's plays, outlining their roles and comparing them with one another.*]

As critics have frequently noted, the presence of the *madre* in the *comedia* is very rare. As a matter of fact, among the 256 female characters in the 61 plays that we know to have been written by Tirso de Molina, there are only 15 *madres* whose role as a mother plays a significant part in the development of the drama. Reigning female monarchs are likewise scarce, there being only 13 in Tirso's *comedias.* In the category of monarch/mother we find only four: Irene, in ***La república al revés;*** Tetis, in ***El Aquiles***; Elena, in ***El árbol del mejor fruto***; and María de Molina, in ***La prudencia en la mujer***. Each of these women shows herself to be a strong character, who, in her concern for his future, counsels her son wisely and well. In this study I shall give a brief outline of the role of each of these personages in the drama in which she appears, compare the four with Tirso's female characters in general and with each other, and discuss the probable chronology and evolution of the monarch/mother in Tirso's works.

It is noteworthy that these four plays have historical or mythological settings which explain in large part the presence of the monarch/mother. ***La república al revés,*** according to the introduction of Doña Blanca de los Ríos Lampérez, is "un trozo de Historia novelada" (1: 375). It is the story of the Greek ruler, Irene, who has acted as empress during the minority of her son Constantino IV, and who subsequently is arrested by her son, who gives the order that she be put to death by the garrote. Ultimately Irene is saved by Tarso, a shepherd, and by the Greek soldiers who support her because Constantino has proved to be a ruthless and tyrannical ruler who persecutes Christians and lets robbers and adulterers go free. Finally Irene judges everyone, ordering that Constantino be imprisoned and his eyes put out, although his wife, Carola, begs that he be forgiven. Irene responds to her, "Juez de la causa de Dios / he de ser; no me enternezco / con ruegos; llevadle preso / a una torre" (3.20). The play ends as Irene returns to the palace, with order now restored in the kingdom.

El Aquiles, which is Tirso's only play based on a mythological theme, tells of how Tetis, Achilles' mother, abets him in a love affair with Deidamia in order to keep his mind off war and fighting and thereby protect his life. Because Deidamia has been promised to another by her father, King Licomedes, Tetis plots for Achilles to gain admission to the palace by dressing as a woman and posing as Deidamia's cousin. This ruse is successful, and soon Deidamia realizes that her "cousin" is really Achilles in disguise. They become lovers, but at the end of the play Ulysses finds Achilles and shames him into revealing that he is a man, convincing him to go off to fight against Troy.

The plot of ***El árbol del mejor fruto*** concerns Elena and her son, Cloro, a shepherd who bears a striking resemblance to Constantino, the son of the Roman Emperor Constancio. When Constantino is killed by some robbers, the Emperor comes for his body and sees Cloro, whereupon Elena reveals to him that he is their son, born before Constancio married another. Cloro, incidentally, has always believed that he is more than just a shepherd. Constancio makes Elena his empress; Cloro, who is now called Constantino, is recognized as emperor and goes off to fight Magencio, who has taken Rome in an effort to make himself emperor. Cloro accepts Christ, defeats the forces of Magencio and then sets out for Jerusalem with Elena to look for the cross made of wood from the Tree of Life (*El Árbol de la Vida*) of the Garden of Eden on which Christ was crucified. Elena tortures a Jew named Judas in order to make him reveal the whereabouts of the cross, and then she and Cloro, along with several others, go to find it. The play ends praising Christ and the cross, *el árbol del mejor fruto*. Judas becomes a Christian and Elena is to have a great church built on the spot where they found the cross.

The best known of these four dramas, ***La prudencia en la mujer***, is based on the *Crónica de don Fernando Cuarto*, attributed to Fernán Sánchez de Tovar. It deals with the period after the death of Sancho IV in 1295, when his widow, Doña María de Molina, acted as regent for her son Fernando IV, and with the early days of Fernando's reign. The queen overcomes plots by various nobles, led by Don Enrique and Don Juan, to usurp the throne; an attempt to have Fernando poisoned by Ismael, a Jewish doctor; and the ingratitude and hostility of her son, influenced by the unscrupulous nobles. Through all of these problems María remains unwavering and strong, and finally at the end she is vindicated, the scheming nobles flee or are exiled, and Fernando remains on the throne.

There is general agreement among scholars who study the *comedia* that Tirso created the most true to life and well drawn female characters to be found in that genre. Manuel de Montoliú says of him:

> parece haber estudiado perfectamente la complicada y enigmática alma femenina. Sus mujeres astutas, intrigantes, resueltas y apasionadas contrastan vivamente con sus hombres tímidos, que se resignan a ser juguete del bello sexo. Y es que la fogosidad de las pasiones femeninas, que muchas veces queda oculta bajo la capa de las conveniencias sociales, sólo es conocida en toda su realidad en el secreto de la confesión, y Gabriel Téllez, rico de estas lecciones aprendidas en el ejercicio de su ministerio, encontró en el teatro un campo para desplegar el conocimiento así adquirido de la complicada alma femenina. (596)

This opinion is shared by many others, such as Karl Vossler, who notes in Tirso a certain tendency toward the emancipation of women (114), and Melveena McKendrick, who says "And no one would deny that Tirso had a taste for the creation of female characters with remarkable resources of personality" (201).[1]

Although among Tirso's female characters there are some who are almost superhuman and Amazon-like in their strength, the majority of his women are coquettish, cunning, and occasionally unscrupulous in achieving their ends. One thinks of Marta la Piadosa pretending to have taken a vow of chastity in order to avoid marrying the man her father has chosen for her, or of the cleverness and deceit of Jusepa in *Por el sótano y el torno* in finding a way to meet a suitor from the house across the road. The four monarch/mothers stand in contrast to these more covert schemers in their open resolve and perseverence in trying to help their sons, regardless of the consequences for them personally.

In comparing our four monarch/mothers with each other, one quickly notes many similarities. As has just been stated, they have in common their devotion to their sons and their determination to help them by both word and deed. They are all strong willed and forceful characters. Each speaks of her concept of herself as a mother, gives advice and counsel to her son, guards his life and happiness, to some degree incurs his ingratitude or wrath, and ultimately puts duty above all else.

The degree of hostility on the part of the four sons ranges from the complaints of Achilles and Cloro to the order of the imprisonment of Doña María by Fernando and Constantino's command that his mother be killed. Achilles, who blames Tetis for having left him to be raised by Quirón, says to her:

> El ser primero
> te debo, pues que nací
> de ti, pero no el postrero,
> que del sustento adquirí. (1.6)[2]
> . . . . .
> A Quirón me encomendaste;
> forma quejas, madre, de él
> si tan diverso me hallaste,
> que yo estimo ser cruel
> en más que ser tu hijo. (1.6)

Cloro bemoans the fact that he does not know who his father is, saying "pues nunca mi ingrata madre / me ha dicho quién es mi padre" (1.3). Later he calls Elena "rigurosa madre" and expresses again his anger that she will not reveal his father's name (1.7).

Irene receives much more cruel treatment from Constantino, who gives this order to Andronio:

> Corre
> donde mi madre está presa
> y con diligencia y priesa,
> dentro de la misma torre
> la da un garrote. (2.3)

In ***La prudencia en la mujer*** Fernando likewise deals harshly with his mother, speaking to Don Juan:

> Pues sois ya mi mayordomo,
> y estáis, Infante, agraviado,
> tomad a mi madre cuentas,
> hacelda alcances y cargos
> de las rentas de mis reinos:
> y si no igualan los gastos
> a los recibos, prendelda. (3.6)

He later comes to realize, however, that Don Juan and the other nobles have raised false accusations against Doña María.

The wisdom and loyalty of the monarch/mothers is seen in the way they advise their sons in order to help them solve their problems. Tetis tells Achilles to dress as a woman in order to be with Deidamia and win her affection. In an amusing scene Achilles practices walking on high heels, curtsying to the king, and learning how to act as a "lady" of the court. Tetis says to him:

> Todo es fácil a quien ama.
> Cuando estés en la presencia
> del Rey, haz la reverencia
> que te he enseñado de dama;
> vuélvela a ensayar aquí. (2.1)

She adds:

> Hijo, en la dificultad
> tu ciego amor te ha metido;
> ten con las acciones cuenta
> que te enseñé. (2.1)

Elena supports Cloro in his new found Christian faith and urges him to look for the cross, saying, "Hijo, el cielo es en tu ayuda. / Por la señal vencerás / de la cruz: no esperes más" (2.6).

Later, she exhorts him to continue his search:

> Hijo, Cristo es el Eterno;
> quien no le adora se ofusca;
> la cruz soberana busca,
> noble asombro del infierno:
> vamos a Jerusalén. (2.10)

Irene gives sound advice to Constantino as to how to be a good emperor. She hands him a sword, a globe, and a cross. Upon giving him the globe she reveals her apprehension about his capacity to rule, cautioning him:

> Tenlo bien, siendo prudente,
> que con la prudencia sola
> gobernarás bien tu gente,
> porque como el mundo es bola
> rodaráse fácilmente.
> La Cruz que ves de ese modo,
> es la ley de Dios, y estima
> su ley, a que te acomodo,
> que por aqueso está encima,
> porque Dios es sobre todo. (1.2)

The fullest and most comprehensive advice is given by Doña María to Fernando. In a scene that reminds one of Polonius and Laertes, she says to him:

> El culto de vuestra ley,
> Fernando, encargaros quiero;
> que éste es el móvil primero
> que ha de llevar tras sí al rey;
> y guiándoos por él vos,
> vivid, hijo, sin cuidado,
> porque no hay razón de estado
> como es el servir a Dios.
> Nunca os dejéis gobernar
> de privados, de manera
> que salgáis de vuestra esfera,
> ni les lleguéis tanto a dar
> que se arrojen de tal modo
> al cebo del interés,
> que os fuercen, hijo, después
> a que se lo quitéis todo.
> Con todos los grandes sed
> tan igual y generoso

que nadie quede quejoso
de que a otro hacéis más merced:
tan apacible y discreto,
que a todos seáis amable;
mas no tan comunicable
que os pierdan, hijo, el respeto. (3.1)

She further warns him to respect and cheer his vassals, not to let the court jesters counsel him, to value his armed forces, and to choose wise doctors in whom he has confidence.

The above-mentioned similarities among these four characters relate chiefly to positive traits. It is in the differences that we find the more negative characteristics. Everett Hesse speaks of two aspects of the mother archetype in the *comedia*—the benevolent and the malevolent. He says, "Its malevolent aspect can be destructive; having received life from Mother-Earth people are ultimately buried in her in death. The act of involvement in another person's affairs can be carried to an extreme by a domineering mother who prevents her child from having a life of its own" (72). According to Hesse, Tetis serves as an excellent example of this negative side—"a monster who seeks to dominate her son, forcing him to don feminine garb. In [this play] we see the mythological fight between mother and son in which the growing power of the male corresponds to the increasing awareness of his identity" (70-71). This view of Tetis does not take into account her motherly love and concern for Achilles' safety and well being. Her reaction when Achilles chides her for entrusting his upbringing to Quirón and threatens to go off to war reveals her affection for him:

¡Ay hijo del alma mía!
Ese valor ha de ser
mi muerte, y yo he de perder,
perdiéndote, mi alegría. (1.7)

Although the other three mothers do not dominate their sons to such a degree—indeed María de Molina and Irene withdraw to the country in order to give their sons a free hand—both Irene and Elena exhibit other negative characteristics. Elena believes that the end justifies the means as she has Judas tortured in order to make him reveal the place where the cross can be found. Her cruelty is somewhat mitigated by the fact that Judas is converted to Christianity and thereby redeemed at the end, and that the traitor, Lisinio, is resusitated from the dead and likewise saved through Christian forgiveness. For her part, Irene shows little sympathy as she punishes her son's treacherous acts by ordering his eyes put out and sending him to prison at the end of ***La rúpublica al revés***, in spite of Carola's plea for mercy. Her sense of justice prevails over her motherly affection, and she shows herself to be a severe and firm judge.

It is more difficult to find flaws in María de Molina's character. In addition to advising her son well and showing great regard for his welfare, she is also a very self-sacrificing mother, selling all of her jewels and even her most treasured wimple in order to have the money that Fernando needs. A compassionate person, throughout the play she forgives those who plot against her, in contrast to Irene and Elena. Although her forgiveness of her enemies might be perceived as a sign of weakness, in my opinion it stands as a fine example of the Christian spirit.

Turning to the chronology and evolution of the monarch/mother, we are faced with the problem of dating Tirso's plays. Doña Blanca sets the probable date of ***El Aquiles*** at 1611 or 1612 and the date of ***El árbol del mejor fruto*** at 1621. Ruth Lee Kennedy places ***La república al revés*** at 1615 or 1616 and concludes that ***La prudencia en la mujer*** was written between 1621 and 1623, with the strong likelihood that the date of composition was August of 1622.[3]

In an examination of the development of the monarch/mother from Tetis and Irene to Elena and María de Molina, one finds certain foreshadowings of the characters of Elena and María in the two earlier personages. Doña Blanca refers to Tetis as "deidad mitológica con alma de madre cristiana. Una de las madres que aparecen como en esbozo desde el amanecer del teatro de Tirso" (1: 1895). Elena is a much more fully delineated character than Tetis as she supports and abets Cloro in his search for the cross, even after his wife leaves him because he has been converted to Christianity. In so doing, she proves herself to be a devoted Christian mother, the fulfillment of the figure suggested by Tetis.

Even more striking, however, are the similarities between Irene and María. As we have already seen, they have in common their strong wills, their loyalty to their sons, their giving advice to their sons, and their having been rejected by their sons. Additionally, as Doña Blanca notes, there are several other ways in which the two plays are alike (1: 377-78). Ernest Templin and Ion Agheana have, in fact, mentioned these plays as an example of Tirso's self-plagiarism.[4] Both Irene and María retire to the country, where they are greeted enthusiastically by the peasants. Both of them praise the simple rural life and speak of its joys in contrast to the more complex life of the court. Finally, in each play, the young king at one point is hidden in a tree in order to protect him from his enemies.

A careful analysis of these four queens, then, leads to the conclusion that María is, indeed, the culmination of the monarch/mother that Tirso sketched out in his earlier plays. Tetis and Irene, in particular, serve as prototypes for María, who appears as the intelligent, prudent, magnanimous, self-sacrificing and forceful ideal Christian mother. María herself says that she is a woman with three souls when she speaks to the disloyal nobles:

Si porque es el rey un niño
y una mujer quien le ampara,
os atrevéis ambiciosos
contra la fe castellana;
tres almas viven en mí:
la de Sancho, que Dios haya;
la de mi hijo, que habita

en mis maternas entrañas,
y la mía, en quien se suman
esotras dos: ved si basta
a la defensa de un reino
una mujer con tres almas. (1.2)

In speaking of ***La prudencia en la mujer***, McKendrick says that it is "concerned, not with female leadership as are Lope's [plays], but with leadership in general and/or with individuals, with human beings, who are called or who force their way to leadership" (199). She continues, "The focus [in this play] is much wider. In dealing with remarkable individuals, it embraces, not half the human race, but mankind as a whole" (199).

Several critics of the *comedia* have suggested that the virtuous and majestic María de Molina is a representation of the Virgin Mary.[5] Certainly as a woman of high moral standards, a chaste widow, the defender of the crown and the faith, and a symbol of loyalty and trust, María embodies the ideals and qualities associated with the Blessed Virgin, and, of course, she even bears the same name. It is for these reasons, perhaps, that she endures as a great patriotic and religious figure for Spaniards of all times.

Notes

1. For additional comments by critics about Tirso's female characters, see Vossler 111-14.
2. All quotations are from the three volume collection of Tirso's works edited by Doña Blanca de los Ríos Lampérez.
3. For Doña Blanca's dating of *El Aquiles,* see 1: 1887; for *El árbol del mejor fruto*, see 3: 309. Kennedy dates *La república al revés* in her article in *Reflexión 2; La prudencia en la mujer*, in the *PMLA* article.
4. Agheana mistakenly attributes the examples taken from *La república al revés* and *La prudencia en la mujer* to Wade's article on self-plagiarism in Tirso, rather than to Templin. Templin's article on this case of Tirso's self-plagiarism supposes *La prudencia en la mujer* to precede *La república al revés* and therefore assumes that the latter is derived from the former.
5. Among those espousing this view are Moir (96); MacCurdy, in the introduction to his edition of the play (28); and Margaret Wilson (93-94). Agheana sees her as symbolizing Spain and as a "timeless moral symbol" (50).

Works Cited

Agheana, Ion Tudor. *The Situational Drama of Tirso de Molina*. Madrid: Playor, 1973.

Hesse, Everett. "The Mother Archetypes in the *Comedia.*" *Proceedings of the Second Annual Golden Age Spanish Drama Symposium*. 8-10 March, 1982. El Paso: The University of Texas at El Paso (1982): 62-72.

Kennedy, Ruth Lee. "*La prudencia en la mujer* and the Ambient that Brought It Forth." *PMLA* 63 (1948): 1131-90.

———."Tirso's *La república al revés* and Its Debt to Mira's *La rueda de la fortuna.*" *Reflexión 2* 2 (1973): 39-50.

McKendrick, Melveena. *Woman and Society in the Spanish Drama of the Golden Age*. London and New York: Cambridge University Press, 1974.

Montoliú y de Togores, Manuel. *Literatura castellana*. Barcelona: Cervantes, 1929.

Téllez, Gabriel (Tirso de Molina). *El burlador de Sevilla y convidado de piedra* and *La prudencia en la mujer*. Ed. Raymond R. MacCurdy. New York: Dell, 1965.

Téllez, Gabriel (Tirso de Molina). *Tirso de Molina: Obras dramáticas completas*. Ed. Doña Blanca de los Ríos Lampérez. 3 vols. Madrid: Aguilar, 1946-58.

Templin, Ernest H. "Another Instance of Tirso's Self-plagiarism." *Hispanic Review* 5 (1937): 176-80.

Vossler, Karl. *Lecciones sobre Tirso de Molina.*Madrid. Taurus, 1965.

Wade, Gerald E. "Tirso's Self-Plagiarism in Plot." *Hispanic Review* 4 (1936): 55-65.

Wilson, Edward M. and Duncan Moir. *A Literary History of Spain. The Golden Age: Drama 1492-1700*. London: Benn, 1971.

Wilson, Margaret. *Tirso de Molina*. Boston: Twayne, 1977.

David H. Darst (essay date 1988)

SOURCE: "Tirso de Molina's Idea of 'Tragedia,'" in *Bulletin of the Comediantes*, Vol. 40, No. 1, Summer, 1988, pp. 41-52.

[*In the following essay, Darst concludes that de Molina's use of the word* tragedia *is more in line with Medieval Latin tradition than Aristotelian precepts.*]

Tirso de Molina's authorship of more than 80 extant dramas makes him the most prolific playwright of his time after Lope de Vega and Pedro Calderón de la Barca. Tirso's plays cover the entire spectrum of dramatic groups, which modern critics have labelled with generic names like *comedias de costumbres, comedias de capa y espada, comedias de santos, comedias mitológicas*, and *comedias histórico-legendarias*. His opinions about the theater of his time are well-known, because in his prose miscellany ***Cigarrales de Toledo*** (1624) he presented a brilliant defense of the *comedia nueva* and its privilege to imitate the contemporary mores and customs of the natural world rather than those of the ancient world described by Aristotle and Horace (Darst 83-106). Specifically, Tirso defended the right to ignore the previously venerated rules of length (both physical time and the unity of 24 hours), verisimilitude (mixture of noble and peasant characters, historicity, licentious portrayals of noble-born people), place (specifically, that the events in a play must transpire in one locale), and decorum (especially sexual deviations) by appealing to the ubiquitous "licencia de Apolo."

It is clear, then, that Tirso rejected outright the bulk of received opinion about theater. Given this fact, one should be able to assume that the Mercedarian would also spurn the nomenclature associated with Aristotelian and Horatian criticism, especially words associated with the specific genres of tragedy and comedy. It is possible to determine in a general way Tirso's notion of what these expressions meant by examining the generic terms he used in the last lines of his plays to describe the events dramatized on stage. In effect, a study of the last several lines of the 82 plays in Blanca de los Ríos's *Obras dramáticas completas* reveals that Tirso preferred the designations *comedia*, which he appended to 15 plays, *historia*, used for 13 plays, and *ejemplo,* used for 11 plays. He also used rarely the terms *tragedia*, in four plays, *parte*, in three plays, and *tradición*, *suceso*, and *novela*, each in one play. Thirty three of the plays in question have no specific designation, although most of these do have the title of the work in the last lines. While the nimiety of *comedia, historia*, and *ejemplo* is of great significance in any development of an aesthetics of Tirsian dramaturgy, this present study will undertake solely the task of determining Tirso's meaning and use of the word *tragedia.* It will attempt to show that the Mercedarian's use of the designation was as opposed to Aristotelian-Horatian ideas on theater as was his prose defense of drama in general in the ***Cigarrales de Toledo***. The results of this study will also hopefully defuse the polemic among present-day critics concerning the purported "problem" of Spanish tragedy (MacCurdy, ch. 1), since it will show that Classical precepts cannot properly be applied to the plays that Tirso and his fellow dramatists called *tragedia*.

The four plays under scrutiny are ***Los amantes de Teruel*** (c. 1615), ***Amazonas en las Indias*** (c. 1630), ***Escarmientos para el cuerdo*** (c. 1620), and ***La venganza de Tamar*** (c. 1620). ***Los amantes de Teruel*** develops the Romeo and Juliet theme. Marsilla and Isabel are secretly in love, but discover that Rufino, Isabel's father, is planning to marry his daughter to Don Gonzalo, the local millionaire. Marsilla exacts a promise from Rufino to delay the wedding for three years and three days so that Marsilla can become rich enough to marry Isabel. Rufino agrees and Marsilla departs to seek his fortune fighting against the Arabs. He succeeds, but arrives in Teruel a day late, although in time to see his beloved leave the church on the arm of Don Gonzalo. With nothing more to live for, Marsilla literally drops dead at the feet of Isabel. The next day, at his funeral, she throws herself on his body to die also from frustrated love.

Amazonas en las Indias dramatizes the controversial political fortunes of Gonzalo Pizarro in Peru. Pizarro returns from an expedition to the Amazon river to find his brother (the more famous Francisco) assassinated and Diego de Almagro in full rebellion against the Spanish Crown. Pizarro helps the royal chancellor Vaca de Castro in subduing Almagro, and then retires to his estate in the Peruvian mountains. Meanwhile, the viceroy Blasco Núñez Vela passes strict laws against slavery and imprisons many of Gonzalo's conquistador friends, causing the Lima hierarchy to arrest the viceroy and to ship him back to Spain. The rebels name Gonzalo Pizarro the governor of Lima, and attempt to make him king of the Incas. Gonzalo refuses to join the rebellion, but is nevertheless arrested and executed by the royal authorities.

Escarmientos para el cuerdo dramatizes the fortunes of Manuel de Sosa, who seduced Doña María de Silva in Portugal and then left with their son, Diaguito, for Goa, where he married Leonor de Sá and fathered another son. María arrives in Goa to claim her fiancé and discovers his double life. Manuel, forced to choose between the two women, again tricks María and sails with Leonor and both children for Portugal. The ship founders, however, and the family is forced to bargain for food and water with African savages, who nevertheless eventually slaughter them all.

La venganza de Tamar is the well-known Biblical story of Amón's infatuation for his half-sister Tamar. He brutally rapes her and then refuses to have anything more to do with her. David, suspecting that Tamar's brother Absalón will seek vengeance, tries to intercede on his son's behalf, but to no avail. Absalón and Tamar trick Amón into coming to a village feast and then murder him at the banquet table.

The final verses of these dramas display a style and vocabulary appropriate to the disastrous endings. In ***Los amantes de Teruel***, Rufino observes, over the bodies of the star-crossed Marsilla and Isabel, that "esta tragedia que veis, / y yo lloro, causa amor" (1: 1397). In *Escarmientos para el cuerdo*, a mariner calls the deaths of Manuel de Sosa, his wife Leonor, and their two children at the hands of African cannibals "el más trágico suceso / que conservaron anales / que desdichas escribieron," and exclaims at the sight of the bodies of Leonor and the young Diaguito:

> Aquí si pueden los ojos
> sufrir del scita fiero
> espectáculo tan triste,
> está el teatro funesto
> (*Descubre a doña Leonor, ya difunta, y a Diaguito ensangrentado.*)
> en que la ciega fortuna
> tragedia eterniza el tiempo
> para escarmiento de amantes,
> y éste es el acto postrero. (3: 259)

La venganza de Tamar ends with the Autor declaring: "Y de Tamar la historia prodigiosa / acaba aquí en tragedia lastimosa" (3: 404). Finally, ***Amazonas en las Indias*** closes with:

> Este fue el fin lastimoso de don Gonzalo; la fama de lo contrario ha mentido. La malicia, ¿qué no engaña? Lea

> historias el discreto que ellas su inocencia amparan, y supla en esta tragedia, quien lo fuere, nuestras faltas. (3: 734)

One can make a number of deductions from the use of words like these at the end of the four plays in question. All four dramas present rigorously historical facts taken from bonafide sources. ***La venganza de Tamar*** has Biblical sources (2 sam.) and owes much to Flavius Josephus's *Antiquities of the Jews*. ***Los amantes de Teruel*** was a popular legend at the time previously dramatized by Rey de Artieda, from whom Tirso borrowed entire speeches and scenes. ***Escarmientos para el cuerdo*** follows a verse chronicle in Portuguese by Jerónimo Corte Real. ***Amazonas en las Indias,*** although laced with mythic lore concerning Amazons, traces faithfully the rise and fall of Gonzalo Pizarro during the Spanish conquest of Peru. The plays are more than mere history, however, because they end with what are essentially very pathetic events, and they are usually sad from at least the middle of the play to the close. All the works also end in the death of the protagonist, which is not true for any of the plays Tirso designated solely *historia* except for ***Tan largo me lo fiáis*** (whose "esta verdadera historia" line [2:633] is replaced in the printed version by the title ***"El convidado de piedra"***; [2:686]). The manner of death is unimportant, so it is not a factor in the denomination of the dramas as tragedies. Likewise, there does not appear to be any cause and effect relationship between the moral character of the protagonist and his demise. Nobility of spirit coupled with a self-blinding tragic flaw, as prescribed by traditional Aristotelian criticism, does not justify the deaths of Marsilla, Manuel, or Gonzalo Pizarro. It may be possible to show that their actions in some way may have contributed to their bad luck; but one cannot say that because Manuel tricked his first fiancée he died with his sons and second wife in the desert, or that Marsilla committed any particular sin that caused him to arrive a day late, or that Gonzalo Pizarro should not have been so loyal to his king. Marsilla dies mysteriously of love, as does Isabel. Gonzalo goes willingly to be decapitated for crimes against the State he did not commit. He, like Marsilla, is totally innocent. Manuel and Leonor die at the hands of savages in Africa. She is certainly not guilty of any specific misdeed, and he repents convincingly of his selfish acts with María. Amón, on the other hand, does rape his sister; and the manner of his death, with knife and fork in his hands at a banquet table, reflects, through the technique of *contrapassio*, his sin of the appetites. Nonetheless, the last lines give the emphasis to David's grief that Absalón should have murdered his brother thusly out of vengeance: "Llorará David / como Jacob, en sabiendo / si a Josef mató la envidia, / que a Amón la venganza ha muerto" (3:404). In all but this last play, the author makes it quite clear that the deaths are due more to bad luck than to a sinful act or some subtle hamartia on the part of the protagonist. Throughout ***Escarmientos para el cuerdo***, Manuel experiences presages of his ill fortune (like the fall he takes in the middle of the second Act) and declaims his "desventura," "fortuna," "desdicha," and "hado." Gonzalo Pizarro's impending death is a leitmotif in ***Amazonas en las Indias*** because the Amazon, Menalipe, is a pythoness who constantly foretells what another character in the play will eventually call "la muerte desdichada / del español más valiente" (3:734). Marsilla is beset continually by bad timing, since he always arrives too late to receive the boons he feels should be his; and he repeatedly complains against Fortune and Luck. Amón is in a different category, since he is the only one of the four who is brutally and suddenly murdered. Marsilla, Manuel, and Gonzalo all accept death as the result of their presaged fate. The deaths of the first two, in fact, almost could be considered suicides; and Gonzalo willingly decided to die rather than to have himself crowned king of Peru.

In terms of Aristotelian tragedy, the four plays lack all the critical precepts. The Greek lexicon simply does not apply to the plays Tirso called *tragedia*. Clearly, then, for Tirso the term *tragedia* is not of Aristotelian-Horatian lineage; yet the four plays do have much in common, and their author at the least put them together in a genre he considered to justify the use of the word *tragedia*. Indeed, Tirso's utilization of the term is of an ancestry as pure and noble as that associated with the Aristotelian usage; for by the time the Mercedarian began to write the plays in question, two very different meanings for *tragedia*, as it applies to drama, had become popular. One was the recently discovered Aristotelian meaning with its three unities, its insistence on cause and effect, and its unique nomenclature of spoudaios, hamartia, and catharsis that was introduced into Spain by Alonso López Pinciano and continued by Francisco Cascales and Jusepe Antonio González de Salas. Most modern scholars, whose names and works are legion, have used the Aristotelian notions of these Spanish thinkers when they applied the term *tragedia* to plays by Golden Age dramatists (Moir). Yet there was another, better-known, meaning at the time for *tragedia* which has received very little attention. It is the popular sense of the word that evolved from the Latin grammarians through the Medieval thinkers to the Golden Age writers, these latter using it to present a "modern" idea of serious drama opposed to the "ancient" one based on Aristotle and the Classical unities.

The major Latin source on tragedy is the *De Fabula* by a fourth-century grammarian named Evanthius which was always included with the *De Comedia* of Donatus in the commentaries on Terence. The pertinent section of what Evanthius wrote is as follows:

> Of the many differences between tragedy and comedy, the foremost are these: In comedy the fortunes of men are middle-class, the dangers are slight, and the ends of the actions are happy; but in tragedy everything is the opposite—the characters are great men, the fears are intense, and the ends disastrous. In comedy the beginning is troubled, the end tranquil; in tragedy events follow the reverse order. And in tragedy the kind of life is shown that is to be shunned; while in comedy the kind is shown that is to be sought after. Finally, in comedy the story is always fictitious; while tragedy often has a basis in historical truth.[1] (43)

The second most important source is the late fourth-century grammarian Diomedes, who had written in his *Artis Grammaticae* the famous dictum that "tragedy concerns heroes embracing adverse fortune:" *tragoedia est heroicae fortunae in adversis comprehensio*, which he credited to one Theophrastus (487). Diomedes also gave the etymology for the word tragedy, "which back then authors of tragedy called TRAGOS, that is 'goat,' the reward which was offered for the song"[2] (487), which Diomedes substantiated by citing from Horace's *Ars Poetica* the verses that begin "the poet who first competed in tragic song for a paltry goat" (*carmine quo tragico vilem certavit ob hircum*, v. 220).

The most popular purveyor of these notions to the Renaissance was Dante Alighieri, who included an amalgam of the Latin definitions in his letter to Can Grande:

> Now comedy is a certain kind of poetical narration which differs from all others. It differs, then, from tragedy in its subject-matter, in that tragedy at the beginning is admirable and placid, but at the end or issue is foul and horrible. And tragedy is so called from *tragos*, a goat, and *oda*; as it were a "goat-song," that is to say foul like a goat, as appears from the tragedies of Seneca. Whereas comedy begins with sundry adverse conditions, but ends happily, as appears from the comedies of Terence. And for this reason it is the custom of some writers in their salutation to say by way of greeting: "a tragic beginning and a comic ending to you!" Tragedy and comedy differ likewise in their style of language; for that of tragedy is high-flown and sublime, while that of comedy is unstudied and lowly.[3] (200-01)

In Spain the first commentators of Tragedy all use the words from this Medieval Latin tradition. Juan de Mena followed Dante closely when he wrote in the mid-fifteenth century: "Tragédico es dicha la escritura que habla de altos hechos y por bravo y soberbio y alto estilo, la cual manera siguieron Homero, Virgilio, Lucano y Estacio; por la escritura tragédica, puesto que comienza en altos principios, su manera es acabar en tristes y desastrados fines" (*Preceptiva* 53). Hernán Núñez later in the century used the same materials and incorporated the words of Diomedes: "La definición de la tragedia según Diomedes gramático es ésta: *tragedia est heroicae fortunae in adversis comprehensio*, que quiere decir: la tragedia es materia de los casos adversos y caídas de grandes príncipes, por lo cual siempre los fines tiene lúgubres y tristes" (*Preceptiva* 56).

Throughout the sixteenth century these definitions of Evanthius and Diomedes continued to be the sources for the declarations on tragedy by Bartolomé de Torres Naharro (*Preceptiva* 61), Lupercio Leonardo de Argensola (*Preceptiva* 63, 65, 67) and Juan de la Cueva (*Preceptiva* 70-71). If these men were aware of an Aristotelian definition of tragedy based on other principles, they did not inform their readers of it. The literary scholars were also evidently unimpressed by Aristotle, if Sebastián de Covarrubias Orozco can be accepted as a representative figure. When he penned his definition of *tragedia* for his *Tesoro de la lengua castellana o española* (1611), he used exclusively the words of Evanthius (973), as he used solely those of Donatus for his definition of *comedia* (341-42). Nevertheless, Alfredo Hermenegildo, a leading scholar on sixteenth-century tragedy, seems oblivious to the origins for these writers' remarks (although he does acknowledge the imitation of Senecan drama). Hermenegildo illogically uses the later Aristotelian critics to explain Renaissance tragedy, despite the fact that these early tragedians never mentioned Aristotle and the seventeenth-century Aristotelians never mentioned the early tragedians.

The arguments concerning the Aristotelian notions of spoudaios, decorum, peripeteia, anagnorisis, catharsis, hamartia, and the Classical unities that López Pinciano, Cascales, and González de Salas present in their books are well known (Darst 83-106) and need no review here. Suffice it to say that these three critics toe the line on Aristotelian tragedy, offering very little new material not already discussed by the Italian theorists of the previous century. One could, nevertheless, logically expect their ideas to influence heavily the words and terminology of the Golden Age writers; but such is not the case. In fact, the seventeenth-century commentators of Tirso's generation seem to be as unaware of Aristotle's thoughts on the matter as were their sixteenth-century counterparts. Luis Alfonso de Carballo (*Preceptiva* 93), Juan de la Cueva (*Preceptiva* 121), Cristóbal de Virués (*Preceptiva* 122), Carlos Boyl (*Preceptiva* 154), and Lope de Vega (*Preceptiva* 127-28) all utilize exclusively the Latin definitions of tragedy. Lope, for example, who knew Aristotle and cited Robortello's commentaries, referred to the word *tragedia* only to make fun of it, and this in spite of attaching to 42 of his extant dramas the words *tragedia* or *tragicomedia* (Morby). In his *Arte nuevo de hacer comedias*, he used *tragedia* three times; and in all cases it was in the term's Latin sense. Comedy, said Lope, "trata / las acciones humildes y plebeyas, / y la tragedia las reales y altas" (vv. 58-60). "La *Ilíada* / de la tragedia fue famoso ejemplo, / a cuya imitación llamé epopeya / a mi *Jerusalem* y añadí 'trágica'" (vv. 89-92). "Por argumento la tragedia tiene / la historia, y la comedia el fingimiento" (vv. 111-12). In his introduction to *Las Almenas de Toro*, dedicated to Guillén de Castro, the Fénix commented that "la comedia imita las humildes acciones de los hombres, como siente Aristóteles, y Robertollo Utinense comentándole: *at vero tragedia praestantiores imitatur*; de donde se sigue la clara grandeza y superioridad del estilo" (3: 766). Yet Lope followed this statement with the observation that the present drama was not one: "Pero como en esta historia del Rey don Sancho, entre su persona y las demás que son dignas de la tragedia, por la costumbre de España, que tiene ya mezcladas, contra el arte, las personas y los estilos, no está lejos el que tiene, por algunas partes, de la grandeza referida, de cuya variedad tomó principio la tragicomedia" (3: 767). Finally, in the prologue to his *El castigo sin venganza*, Lope called the play a *tragedia*, "advirtiendo que está escrita al estilo Español, no por la antiguedad Griega, y seueridad Latina, huyendo de las sombras, Nuncios, y Coros; porque el gusto puede mudar los preceptos, como el vso los trages, y el tiempo las costumbres" (121). None of these references have anything to do with Aristotle's definition of tragedy, nor do they even take seriously the idea of tragedy. On the contrary, they tend to negate the genre's very existence by proposing a mixture of forms (epic and tragedy in the *Arte nuevo,* comedy and tragedy in the two prologues).

Tirso, for his part, never made any statements at all about *tragedia* other than those that surround the use of the word in his plays. There he wrote "rigor de los hados inconstantes" (1: 1397), "el más trágico suceso / que conservaron anales / que desdichas escribieron," "espectáculo tan triste," "teatro funesto," "espectáculo tan triste" (3: 259-60), "historia prodigiosa . . . / . . . lastimosa" (3: 404), "muerte desdichada," "desgracias," "fin lastimoso" (3: 734). All of these phrases document that the Mercedarian was using the notion in the Medieval Latin tradition rather than the Classical Greek one. Diomedes, Evanthius, and Dante couch the tragic action in terms opposite from the comic action and stress the unhappy ending of a true historical event: *exitus funesti, heroicae fortunae in adversis comprehensio, in fine sive exitu est foetida et horribilis, de historia fide.* Tirso follows their example and even their language when he describes these plays he designated *tragedia.*

If there is any relation at all between Aristotelian ideas—including those about tragedy—and Tirso's dramaturgy, it is probably in the plays in which the Mercedarian placed the word *ejemplo: Como han de ser los amigos, La ninfa del cielo, El celoso prudente, Ventura te dé Dios, hijo, La adversa fortuna de don Alvaro de Luna, Quien da luego da dos veces. El condenado por desconfiado, Celos con celos se curan, Quien no cae no se levanta, La firmeza en la hermosura*, and *La mujer que manda en casa* (a play in which Abdías predicts a "trágico fin a tu casa" [1: 623] for Jezabel, and Raquel calls the murder of Nabot "la impiedad más lasciva, / la más bárbara tragedia / la crueldad más inaudita" [1: 624]). These are for the most part serious works, and many fit within the use of the key term *ejemplo* by Jusepe Antonio González de Salas who, when defining it, wrote: "La semejanza en los trabajos y la comparación siempre los hizo leves. Doctrina que ninguno ignora, experimentada en el propio desconsuelo; así está expuesta nuestra vida triste a desventuras. Templarán pues los humanos las pasiones suyas con aquellos Ejemplos pintados en la tragedia, que comparados a sus desdichas, podrán ellas parecer menores" (1: 27).

A good case to show how closely tied the notions of *ejemplo* and *tragedia* must have been at the time is the peroration in *La adversa fortuna de don Alvaro de Luna.* In a manuscript written and signed by Antonio Mira de Amescua, the lines read "y acaba aquí la tragedia / de la embidia y la fortuna" (Sánchez-Arce 151); but in a contemporary player's copy (MS 16546 BN) the lines read "y acaba aquí el gran exemplo / de la embidia y la fortuna" (Sánchez-Arce 204). Tirso de Molina's edition of the play, published in his *Segunda parte* (1635), reads "y con este triste ejemplo / de la envidia y la fortuna" (1: 2039). Whatever the circumstances were between the composition of the two early texts, Tirso evidently did not consider the Don Alvaro play a *tragedia* when he published it but rather one that would present a moral example to the spectators.

In conclusion, Tirso de Molina's use of the word *tragedia* is not in line with the Aristotelian precepts of tragedy as they have been known since the Renaissance; rather it follows the popular Medieval Latin tradition embodied in the famous lines *tragedia est heroicae fortunae in adversis comprehensio.* While Aristotle's ideas about tragedy can certainly apply to Tirso's serious works in a universal, critical way, since the tragedy of man described by Aristotle is universal, it would be fallacious to use them *ad litteram* because Tirso never recognized Aristotle's authority on the matter; nor do the words of Alonso López Pinciano, Francisco Cascales, and Jusepe Antonio González de Salas serve much good when examining the plays Tirso named tragedies, since at least he and Lope de Vega never cited these authors nor showed any influence from them. Tirso and Lope utilize words and impressions that developed from the "modern" tradition of Donatus, Evanthius, Diomedes, and Dante; so it is to them that scholars can go to ascertain the historical basis for the idea of tragedy held by Tirso de Molina and his contemporaries.

Notes

1. *Inter tragoediam autem et comoediam cum multa tum imprimis hoc distat, quod in comoedia mediocres fortunae hominum, parui impetus periculorum laetique sunt exitus actionum, at in tragoedia omnia contra, ingentes personae, magni timores, exitus funesti habentur; et illic prima turbulenta, tranquilla ultima, in tragoedia contrario ordine res aguntur; tum quod in tragoedia fugienda uita, in comoedia capessenda exprimitur; postremo quod omnis comoedia de fictis est argumentis, tragoedia saepe de historia fide petitur* (1: 21).

2. *Tragoedia est heroicae fortunae in adversis comprehensio. A Theophrasto ita definita est. . . . Quonaim olim actoribus tragicis TRAGOS, ita esta hircus, praemium cantus proponebatur* (487).

3. *Et est comoedia genus quoddam poëticae narrationis, ab omnibus aliis differens. Differt ergo a tragoedia in materia per hoc, quod tragoedia in principio est admirabilis et quieta, in fine sive exitu est foetida et horribilis; et dicitur propter hoc a "tragos" quod est hircus, et "oda" quasi cantus hircinus, id est foetidus ad modum hirci, ut patet per Senecam in suis tragoediis. Comoedia vero inchoat asperitatem alicuius rei, sed eius materia prospere terminatur, ut patet per Terentium in suis comoediis. Et hinc consueverunt dictatores quidam in suis salutationiibus dicere loco salutis, "tragicum principium, et comicum finem." Similiter differunt in modo loquendi: elate et sublime tragoedia;*

> *comoedia vero remisse et humiliter, sicut vult Oratius in sua Poetica . . .* (200-01).

Works Cited

Cascales, Francisco. *Tablas poéticas.* Ed. Benito Brancaforte. Madrid: Espasa-Calpe, 1975.

Covarrubias Orozco, Sebastián de. *Tesoro de la lengua castellana o española.* Madrid: Turner, 1977.

Dante Alighieri. *Epistolae: The Letters of Dante.* Trans. Paget Toynbee. Oxford: Clarendon, 1966.

Darst, David H. *IMITATIO: Polémicas sobre la imitación en el siglo de oro.* Madrid: Orígenes, 1985.

Diomedes. *Artis Grammaticae. Grammatici Latini.* Ed. Henrich Keil. Hildesheim: Olm, 1961.

Evanthius. *De Fabula. Commentum Terenti.* Ed. Paul Wessner, 6 vols. Leipzig: Teubner, 1902. Trans. O.B. Hardison. *Classical and Medieval Literary Criticism.* New York: Ungar, 1974.

González de Salas, Jusepe Antonio. *Nueva idea de la tragedia antigua.* 2 vols. Madrid: Antonio de Sancha, 1778.

Hermenegildo, Alfredo. *La tragedia en el renacimiento español.* Barcelona: Planeta, 1973.

López Pinciano, Alonso. *Philosophía antigua poética.* Ed. Alfredo Carballo Picazo. 3 vols. Madrid: CSIC, 1973.

MacCurdy, Raymond R. *The Tragic Fall: Don Alvaro de Luna and Other Favorites in Spanish Golden Age Drama.* Chapel Hill: NCSRLL, 1978.

Moir, Duncan. "The Classical Tradition in Spanish Dramatic Theory and Practice in the Seventeenth Century." *Classical Drama and Its Influence: Essays Presented to H.D.F. Kitto.* Ed. M.J. Anderson. New York: Barnes, 1965. 193-228.

Molina, Tirso de [Gabriel Téllez]. *Obras dramáticas completas.* Ed. Blanca de los Ríos. 3 vols. Madrid: Aguilar, 1946-58.

Morby, Edwin S. "Some Observations on *Tragedia* and *Tragicomedia* in Lope." *Hispanic Review* 11 (1943): 185-209.

Preceptiva dramática española del renacimiento y el barroco. Ed. Federico Sánchez Escribano and Alberto Porqueras Mayo. Madrid: Gredos, 1965.

Sánchez-Arce, Nellie E., ed. *La segunda de don Aluaro [adversa fortuna de don Alvaro de Luna].* México: Jus, 1960.

Vega Carpio, Lope Félix de. *Las almenas de Toro. Obras escogidas.* Ed. F.C. Sainz de Robles. 3 vols. Madrid: Aguilar, 1961-64.

———;. *El castigo sin venganza.* Ed. C.A. Jones. Oxford: Pergamon, 1966.

Catherine Larson (essay date 1989)

SOURCE: "New Clothes, New Roles: Disguise and the Subversion of Convention in Tirso and Sor Juana," in *Romance Languages Annual*, Vol. 1, 1989, pp. 500-04.

[*In the following essay, Larson considers the implications of cross-dressing in the comedies of de Molina and Sor Juana.*]

In an article on role change in Calderonian drama, Susan Fischer reminds us that that the "essence of the theater is change—the theoretically temporary metamorphosis of an actor into a character he is to portray onstage" (73). What we find in any number of Golden Age plays is the literalization of that metaphor, in which characters assume other roles in addition to those assigned by the dramatist, often utilizing disguises to accomplish the role change. In the theater of the Golden Age, the convention of the woman who dresses like a man was relatively commonplace, reflecting a liberating experience in all senses of the word: male clothing facilitated admittance into a world that would otherwise be closed to the female characters of the *comedia*, allowing them to travel freely within a restrictive, patriarchal society and to take greater control over their own destinies. In that sense, when female characters donned male clothes, they changed not only their physical appearance, but their entire dramatic definitions. They assumed new roles as the result of their change of costume, moving from states of helpless passivity to ones of independence and control, qualities normally associated more with the masculine than with the feminine.

The use of this convention is tied to the relationship between characters and audiences. In the *comedia*, disguise was generally considered impenetrable; this means that other characters onstage could not see through the disguise, even though the audience might be fully aware of the deception. The convention, then, forms part of the larger issue of defining an audience's experience with a play. The notion of the willing suspension of disbelief extends to cover the situation of the *mujer vestida de hombre*, so that the audience, while noting the deception, simultaneously accepts the multiple role playing as part of the entire possible world created onstage.

Carmen Bravo-Villasante has discussed at length the *comedia* convention of the *mujer vestida de hombre*, particularly its two most popular manifestations, the woman in love who is trying to reunite with her beloved—the case we will examine here—and the more male-oriented *mujer heroica-guerrera* (15). Yet, much less common in the *comedia* than the appearance of the woman dressed as a man was that of the man who dressed as a woman.[1] The reasons for this contrast are certainly obvious: the hint of homosexuality as well as a concomitant disinterest on the part of a male in assuming the role of a second-class citizen would make the *hombre vestido de mujer* a rare entity, indeed. Still, the convention was turned on its head in a few Golden Age plays. The idea of the world turned upside down is precisely what unites these two versions of the same theme.[2] In both cases, wearing the clothing of the opposite sex signals a carnavalesque attitude, in which cross-dressing suggests the crossing of sexual barriers, liberation, and a general subversion of social norms.

This phenomenon is not unique to Golden Age comedy; a classic example of its use in a serious drama is that of Rosaura in *La vida es sueño*. The present study, however, looks at two representative Golden Age comedies: Tirso's ***Don Gil de las calzas verdes*** and Sor Juana's *Los empeños de una casa*. Tirso plays with the convention of the woman dressed as a man, while Sor Juana inverts the technique with a male who dons women's clothing. As we will see, the two plays have much in common, but the convention—already a type of inversion—can also be inverted again in innumerable permutations, allowing for a closer examination of the entire notion of identity and role playing in the theater of the Golden Age.

Tirso's ***Don Gil de las calzas verdes*** carries the *mujer vestida de hombre* convention to a parodic extreme. Doña Juana, who had been jilted by her lover, dresses like a man in order to allow her freedom of movement and to facilitate her plans to avenge her lost honor. In assuming the role of Don Gil, Juana deceives her lover and her servant, causes two women to fall in love with her, and eventually wins back the hand of the unfaithful Don Martín. Throughout the comedy, Doña Juana delights in her deception, knowingly and willfully challenging the behavioral norms of society much like a female Don Juan Tenorio.[3] The *enredos* that all of this role playing produces lead to a climax in which not only Doña Juana, but three other characters simultaneously claim that they are Don Gil de las calzas verdes, a character who is not really a character at all, but Doña Juana's invention, a fiction.

Juana's own role playing is also multiple: in addition to dressing as a man, Juana also assumes the role of a woman, Doña Elvira, as part of her scheme. She therefore moves between three separate roles in the course of the play: she is Juana, Gil, and Elvira—man and woman, avenger and victim, aggressive and passive, real and illusory—all in one.

Although Doña Juana is able to fool all of her peers until the end of the play, the *gracioso*, her servant Caramanchel, notes that there is something strange associated with his mistress. In this sense, Caramanchel is able to penetrate the disguise that Juana has donned; her true identity is not totally masked. Caramanchel sees Don Gil as a kind of hermaphrodite, embodying both male and female qualities:

> Capón sois hasta en el nombre;
>
> * * *
>
> ¡Qué bonito que es el tiple moscatel!
>
> * * *
>
> Aquí dijo mi amo hermafrodita que me esperaba . . .
> (1718b-1719a)

Scholars who have analyzed this farce tend to see the division within Doña Juana as representative of a larger issue: the conflict between the love and vengeance themes.[4] Although Juana arrives in Madrid vowing to avenge her stained honor, critics such as Everett Hesse and David Darst have noted that Juana's real, interior motivation is her love for Don Martín and her desire to force him to marry her. Darst observes that

> the pants Juana wears, which visibly represent her decision to pursue Martín in an active and forceful way, are green, a color representative, not of vengeance, but of hope. . . . There is thus an optical appearance to Juana that belies her verbal expressions of vengeance. (74)

Nonetheless, Darst also sees in Doña Juana a woman unaware of this underlying motivation and of her divided self. His allusions to the character's weak "qualities and characteristics typical of womankind—confusion, variability, deceit; in short, a never ending changing of forms" (73) indicate a perspective that would tend to negate the strengths others have found in her characterization. Thus, according to Darst, the climax of the play signals a Pyrrhic victory for Doña Juana, because

> the multiplication of the Gil disguise represents a complete decomposition of Juana's mastery of the role, since she never expected the Gils to reproduce as they did, and cannot possibly hope to control them all in the future. (82)

Still, Doña Juana has been able to accomplish her goal; the play ends with the real (and witnessed) promise of marriage from Don Martín. It is only in the mouth of the *gracioso* that Tirso leaves us with a question regarding the characterization of his protagonist: when Juana finally confesses to Caramanchel that she really is a woman, he replies, "Eso bastaba / para enredar treinta mundos" (1762b).

Sor Juana's *Los empeños de una casa* generally follows the Calderonian model of the *comedia de enredo* or *de capa y espada*, although her play also offers a few twists that could only have come from this Mexican nun. The plot involves a brother and sister, each of whom pursues—and is pursued by—others. Sor Juana has one of the female characters recount elements of the dramatist's own life story, including the conflict that arises when an intelligent woman tries to exert control over her own destiny. Like many other Golden Age plays of this type, the action of the comedy is ultimately about such issues as control, since the series of *enredos* that complicate the dramatic action results from multiple attempts to manipulate other characters in the name of love and for the game of love.

One technique that serves these love battles between the sexes is the use of disguise. A number of characters use disguises, with examples ranging from the *mujer tapada* convention to those in which men disguise themselves to carry out an abduction. Night scenes also function to create an atmosphere of confusion, as characters repeatedly bump into one another in the dark, mistaking the identities of others in the process. The quintessential example of disguise, however, appears in the most humorous scene of the play. It involves the *gracioso*, Castaño, who decides to wear women's clothing so that he can leave the house undetected and unchallenged. In this scene, Castaño dresses on stage in an inverted strip tease, talking not merely to himself, but to the ladies in the audience:

> Lo primero, aprisionar me conviene la melena, (I.319-20)
>
> * * *
>
> Ahora entran las basquiñas. ¡Jesús, y qué rica tela! No hay duda que me esté bien, porque como soy morena me está del cielo lo azul. (I.327-31)
>
> * * *
>
> Temor llevo de que alguno me enamore. (I.405-6)
>
> * * *
>
> ¿Qué les parece, señoras, este encaje de ballena? (I.349-50)
>
> * * *
>
> Dama habrá en el auditorio que diga a su compañera:—Mariquita, aqueste bobo al Tapado representa. Pues atención, mis señoras, que es paso de la comedia, (I.377-82)

Castaño's onstage dressing functions on a number of levels; its self-referentiality underlines the notion of role playing, in which the actor, first seen preparing for his role, then steps out of that role to speak directly to the audience. As each piece of clothing is added, the audience witnesses Castaño's transformation into a woman, but the *gracioso* also subverts that characterization by breaking role, calling attention to the use of convention in the theater, and reminding the audience that they are only attending the performance of a play.

Castaño's comic cross-dressing scene therefore deals with a number of weighty issues. In subsequent scenes, however, he seems to enjoy his new role as woman so much that he flirts shamelessly, until, at the end of the play, two men are ready to fight over "her"; Castaño asks the audience, "Miren aquí si soy bello, / pues por mí quieren matarse" (1196-97). Castaño's experience with dressing in women's clothes is clearly intended to function as a principal source of humor for the play. Still, this male who dresses like a woman also helps the audience explore the relationship between the sexes, as well as the very nature of the theater.

What happens in these two plays when women dress as men and men as women? Among many other things, this type of role reversal undercuts traditional views of gender roles in Golden Age society—or at least in *comedia* representations of that society. Tirso presents a woman intent on taking control of her own destiny, even if such an act requires her to leave her home, dress as a man, court other women, and even propose marriage to them. This characterization inverts the vision of the typical *comedia dama*, confounding the masculine and the feminine in a baroque fusion of illusion and reality. Sor Juana turns the convention of the *mujer vestida de hombre*—already an inversion of the norm—upside down by having a male character dress like a woman. When Tirso and Sor Juana use this specific type of role playing, they achieve any number of similar effects, both for the other characters on stage and for the audience.

One obvious result of such role playing is the incorporation of a self-conscious, metadramatic attitude within the dramatic text, since the wearing of new clothes and the adoption of new roles lead to a kind of role playing within the role. Richard Hornby describes such layered role playing as "an excellent means of delineating character. . . . Even when the role within the role is patently false, the dualistic device still sets up a feeling of ambiguity and complexity with regard to the character" (67). This multiple role play projects multiple ironies upon the text, explores areas of gender identification, and raises such existential questions as those dealing with the nature of human identity; Hornby observes:

> Theatre, in which actors take on changing roles, has, among its many other functions, the examination of identity. For the individual, theatre is a kind of identity laboratory, in which social roles can be examined vicariously. . . . Role playing within the role sets up a special acting situation that goes beyond the usual exploration of specific roles; it exposes the very nature of role itself. The theatrical efficacy of role playing within the role is the result of its reminding us that all human roles are relative, that identities are learned rather than innate. (68, 71-72)

Hornby's comments, which emphasize the connections between human identity and the theater, underscore the role playing found in the examples of this study.[5]

Everett Hesse sees the role playing that occurs in ***Don Gil de las calzas verdes*** as related to the concept of the play within the play, in which disguise performs a dual function:

> la técnica de una comedia dentro de un drama se desarrolla como una mascarada, una especie de *commedia dell'arte* en que los personajes (sobre todo Juana) parecen improvisar el diálogo para dominar la acción en cualquier cambio inesperado. En la mascarada se emplean disfraces no sólo para ocultar la identidad sino también los verdaderos motivos de los personajes.(49)

Other critics have concurred with Hesse's assessment; Henry Sullivan suggests that Tirso's protagonists are fond of producing

> theatrical tableaux to influence other characters and . . . assume spurious roles to mystify and manipulate opponents. Such play-acting was seen as a complex of goal-directed energy, will and practical intelligence that

As the play proceeds, however, it is the old King who emerges as the tragic figure, torn between his love for his children and dismay at their behaviour, incapable any more of exercising either his judgement or his authority. We are left at the end with the poignant image of the once great and powerful king lamenting the murder of his beloved first son, a murder precipitated by his own partisan compulsion to put mercy before justice. The last line of his speech, invoking as it does the murderer Absalón, reminds the audience that the full course of this tragedy is not yet run.

It has been suggested that the action of ***La venganza de Tamar*** unfolds against a contemporary political background characterized by the upheavals that surrounded the succession of Philip IV to the throne of Spain in 1621; Tirso undoubtedly saw the death of Philip III as marking the end of stability and prosperity for Spain.[6] But a contemporary audience's interest would have been captured mainly by its powerful handling of a particularly gripping, familiar biblical story. The full-length plays on biblical and doctrinal themes by seventeenth-century Spanish dramatists constitute a significant proportion of the theatre's total output. Lope proved their popularity and other dramatists followed his example in providing the *corrales* with plays which could unequivocally boast of providing instruction along with entertainment. The theatre as a result became in a way a self-appointed instrument of the faith, providing an extra dimension to the religious life of Spain that at once reflected and stimulated popular devotion and afforded the theatre some protection from the attacks of ecclesiastical and moral reformers. This allowed churchmen to become enthusiastic patrons of the *corrales* and of course a significant number of dramatists were themselves men of God: of the three major playwrights both Lope and Calderón became playwright-priests, while Tirso was from the start of his career a friar. Technically the religious plays they wrote do not constitute a category apart. They were performed in the *corrales* before the usual audiences and were written to the familiar *comedia* pattern. They speak the standard language of love and honour, they are full of action, excitement and passion, with *graciosos* who provide touches of comedy, and they employ all the conventions and devices of the secular plays. They even use sexual excitement as a legitimate channel of moral instruction, as can be seen in Tirso's ***La mujer que manda en casa*** and Calderón's *La devoción de la cruz* (*Devotion to the Cross*). To all intents and purposes they take place in a world whose ethos is recognizably that of seventeenth-century Spain. The liberties they took with their material often attracted the opprobrium of the theatre's critics but their audiences, of course, loved them.

The *comedias de santos*, saints' plays, form a coherent group within this larger body. These normally portray, with considerable artistic licence, the conversion or martyrdom of famous figures from hagiographic history and legend, but the special dramatic potential inherent in the theme of conversion inspired bolder, freer creations as well. There are as a result a number of very striking plays which depict not only the conversion and salvation of criminals but conversely the descent into crime of men and women who have been travelling the road to sainthood. This chiastic movement between the two poles of criminality and sanctity baffled, even shocked commentators until A. A. Parker convincingly argued that the plays present problems which are in fact psychological and social (in the widest sense) rather than religious, and therefore essentially moral not dogmatic.[7] Banditry in the Golden-Age drama is unquestionably a means of personal self-assertion and not of sociopolitical reform as it tends to be in other literatures. The psychological and philosophical justification of the apparently melodramatic plots, Parker claimed, is to be found in the proverb 'The greatest sinners make the greatest saints', which implies that temperamental energy is a prerequisite both of great good and great evil, and in the aphorism 'Corruptio optimi pessima' which encapsulates the Thomist principle that evil follows from the inversion or distortion of good.

The most famous and the finest of these plays is Tirso's magnificently grim ***El condenado por desconfiado (Damned for Despair)***,[8] a complex play which seems to confirm Parker's interpretation of the psychology of the saints and bandits plays but which has in addition an important contemporary theological dimension. Tirso uses the psychology of sin and repentance to confront in an unusually direct way for the theatre two of the dominant religious problems of the age—the question of justification by faith or good works and the related question of free will and divine grace. Even within Catholicism there was such fierce disagreement between Jesuits and Dominicans over the relationship between free will and divine grace that in 1611 the exasperated Inquisition forbade the publication of any more works on the subject of grace. In 1607 the Pope's pronouncement that both sides were free to defend their opinions had been jubilantly greeted in Madrid with fireworks and bull-fights. When Tirso dramatized these problems some years later he was dealing not with some technical squabble over abstractions but with a topic of still passionate concern.

The play tells the story of two young men. Paulo is a hermit who to save his soul has spent ten years of penance and prayer in the wilderness. One night he has a terrifying nightmare of Hell which impels him to beg God to reveal his spiritual fate. Seeing his chance, the Devil appears in the guise of an angel to tell him that his fate will be that of a certain Enrico. Paulo complacently assumes that Enrico must be a saintly man and is horrified to discover that he is a dyed-in-the-wool villain. Overwhelmed by bitterness and despair he avenges himself on God by becoming a murderous bandit himself. Unable to believe that either Enrico or he himself can now be saved he meets a violent death at the hands of the law and goes unrepentant to Hell. What he did not know was that Enrico himself has never lost faith in the possibility of redemption; just before Enrico's execution his ailing father, whom he loves, respects and supports, prevails upon him to repent and he is saved. The Devil's ambiguous prophecy has proved both true and untrue; whether or not the Devil himself knew that Enrico would in fact escape his clutches remains an intriguing question mark.

The play's theological position *vis-à-vis* the *De auxiliis* controversy is elusive, perhaps intentionally so; in a way it compromises by emphasizing both faith and responsibility. Its practical message of faith, hope and charity, however, is clearly spelt out. So, too, are Paulo's sins: doubt in the efficacy of repentance, arrogance in trying to preempt his own fate and lack of charity in his judgement of Enrico. The power of the play comes from Tirso's masterly ability to give dramatic life to these ideas by showing us two men gambling for the highest stakes of all—eternity. Even for us now the play succeeds in making this issue as dramatically real and immediate as any threat of physical death; its impact on an audience of seventeenth-century believers is not difficult to imagine. The work's fascination lies partly in the startling outcome,[9] partly in the understandable uncertainty and confusion generated in Paulo, and in Act III in Enrico as well, by the difficulty of telling the real from the counterfeit, of distinguishing between false voices and true. There is fascination too in the contrary characters of Paulo and Enrico, both psychological adolescents, the one rebelling against an apparently unjust God, the other against all restraints upon his own will. Our reactions to each are complicated. In Paulo we recognize the rational intellectual, eager to know, incapable of blind faith and irrational hope, believing in fair and logical connections between crime and punishment, effort and reward. We understand the insecurity, self-doubt and almost pathological fear which lead to his calculating attempt to buy himself salvation and then erupt into the fateful nightmare. At the same time we lose patience with his meanness of spirit, his wilful over-interpretation of the Devil's prophecy,[10] his obdurate rejection of hope in the face of all encouragement and, above all, his refusal throughout to accept responsibility for himself and his fate. As for the presumptuous Enrico, we detest his mindless violence and bully-boy ways, but we respect his spiritual courage and are moved by his tenderness towards his father and most of all we admire his complete acceptance of responsibility for what happens to him. He recognizes that forgiveness is there, that it is up to him ask for it or not. Paulo, on the contrary, is guilty even at the end of a crucial failure of understanding: when assured that Enrico has been saved he sees no need to repent, confident that he will automatically share the same fate.

The abdication of control over his own destiny, together with his incapacity for love—love of God, his neighbour or himself—makes of Paulo the lesser man, for all Enrico's wickedness. Not only theologically but psychologically and dramatically as well, the play's outcome is entirely convincing and consistent. The fact that it leaves us harbouring more sympathy than we probably ought to feel for the pessimist, the man temperamentally incapable of faith, is a reflection of Tirso's tendency to create characters which overflow the containing ideas of the age. It is certainly the inadequate, anguished Paulo, unable to the last to see that the salvation he hungers for lies all along within his own grasp, who remains most vividly with us; the scene in Act III in which he dons his hermit's garb once more and desperately tries to persuade an impatient Enrico to repent has a quite extraordinary intensity.

As becomes its subject the play is sparely written. Dramatically and theatrically it operates entirely through the stark power of its parallel enactment of two conflicting ideologies and two opposed temperaments in a situation where Hell's flames await the one who has misunderstood the nature of redemption. There are virtually no concessions to public taste. Both men are in their different ways insufferable and apart from the stricken Anareto, Enrico's father and for him a sort of God-figure, the play is full of objectionable individuals. There is no real love interest—Enrico has a sharp but unsavoury moll who plays a minor role. Apart from a few intense speeches of Paulo's, more elaborate as becomes his intellectual and contemplative nature, the play's language is correspondingly pared down and direct. The work has as its structural basis an elegant symmetry, the symmetry of its protagonists, each with his servant, the symmetry of its supernatural adversaries—the Devil and the Good Shepherd—or inner voices, and the criss-cross symmetry of the saints and bandits theme. Its final theatrical effects are appropriately awe-inspiring and balanced: Enrico's soul soars heavenward supported by angels, Paulo disappears in flames through a trapdoor in the stage. The popularity of doctrinal drama in Spain was due in no small measure to such spectacular climaxes.[11]

The play that makes truly magnificent drama out of Christian ideas and reveals the eternal human preoccupations they contain was Spain's distinctive contribution to European drama. Tirso's most famous play ***El burlador de Sevilla o El convidado de piedra (The Trickster of Seville or The Stone Guest)*** is another masterly example.[12] Less openly dogmatic than ***El condenado por desconfiado,*** it is, for all that it gave Europe one of its legendary lovers, don Juan, another eschatological work. Here, however, presumption, bombast, and over-confidence end up not in Heaven but in Hell. The don Juan of popular imagination—compulsive, irresistible lover, intellectual and social rebel—is a composite figure, the result of many subsequent versions and variations. Tirso's original is very different—a brothel-creeper, a trickster, a predator, a betrayer of promises, friends and hospitality, a murderer even—who delights not in seducing women but, more sinisterly, in dishonouring and humiliating them. He wins their favours either by bribery or outright deception. He is not a rebel but a criminal within the system, exploiting his social privileges to further his own ends, believing in divine retribution but foolhardy enough to think that youth is an insurance against it. He prates about his honour when in fact he is everything that is dishonourable; he believes in the rules but regards himself as above them.

As the alternative titles of the play indicate, the work has two main strands which converge in don Juan's consignment to Hell: that of the trickster and that of the stone guest. We are shown four of don Juan's sexual japes. He makes love to the Duchess Isabela in the King's palace by pretending to be her fiancé; he seduces a fishergirl, Tisbea, under solemn promise of marriage (regarded as binding by the conventions of the theatre); he tries to take his best friend's place in his mistress doña Ana's bed when the lovers arrange a tryst to consummate their passion, and finally he desecrates a sacrament by seducing the bride, Aminta, on her wedding night under promise of marriage to himself—'the choicest trick of all'. This essentially episodic plot is given cohesion and sustained tension by don Juan's obliviousness to the gravity of his actions. His catchphrase whenever he is warned that he will one day be called to account for his crimes, 'Tan largo me lo fiáis' ('You certainly allow me extended credit'—*fianza* being a financial and legal term meaning credit or bailbond) becomes the play's leitmotif, reminding us that while don Juan thinks time is on his side (penance, he thinks, is for the infirm and the aged) it is in fact rushing him onwards towards his doom. The time bomb is triggered when don Juan scornfully invites to dinner the sepulchral statue of doña Ana's father, don Gonzalo, killed while defending his daughter from don Juan's predations. That night a thundering on the door announces the arrival of the terrifying guest, who sits at the table but remains silent in the face of don Juan's flippant bravado and his servant Catalinón's hysterical attempts at conversation. Only when he and don Juan are left alone does he speak, to invite don Juan to dine with him in return the following night in his chapel and only after the statue has left does don Juan collapse into terror. Persuading himself that it was all a figment of his imagination and that not to turn up the following night would be a sign of cowardice, don Juan decides to go. After a meal of vipers and scorpions, vinegar and gall, during which don Juan remains defiant to the end, the statue offers don Juan his outstretched hand. He takes it, only to be fatally overpowered by its burning, crushing grip, refused the absolution he begs for and swallowed up into the tomb, never to re-emerge. As he disappears, the statue booms out, 'This is God's justice: as man sows therefore shall he reap.'

While Tirso took don Juan's catchphrase and the idea of the stone guest from oral tradition (the exchange of invitations between a living man and a corpse belongs to European folklore),[13] don Juan was his own creation. Tirso's conception of the character has a moral and ethical emphasis absent from don Juan the myth figure, symbol of sexual energy and individualistic self-assertion. There is undoubtedly an incontrovertible fascination in don Juan's brazen recklessness in the play, in his refusal of fear in the face of the supernatural, in his sense of himself as archetypal man; when he refuses to let Isabela light a lamp to see his face and she cries out in alarm '¿Quién eres, hombre?' ('Who are you, man?'), his answer is 'Un hombre sin nombre' '(A man without a name'). And herein the seeds of the myth lie. Tirso's don Juan, however, as bringer of chaos and confusion, with his sinister arrogance, his delight in power and control, his cynicism and slippery duplicity, assumes an aura that is more than human. When he appears in Aminta's bedroom and she remonstrates '¿En mi cuarto a estas horas?' ('In my bedroom at this hour?'), he replies 'Éstas son las horas mías' ('These hours are mine'). Night is his element; it is no coincidence that the play opens in the dark and that, like some earlier Count Dracula, don Juan resists the light. It is not only we who catch a whiff of the Devil: described by his uncle as a snake—the Devil's symbol—he is explicitly called Lucifer by that man of judgement and conscience, his servant Catalinón, when he commiserates with the wretched Aminta. Defiant to the end, he is greater in death than in life; it is in defeat that he commands our admiration. He is one of the few Golden-Age characters who swamp the action that contains them. He is too big for the play and hence has had to leave it behind.

His ultimate sin is Lucifer's own—he challenges God himself, unaware that he is playing with hell-fire. Fire consequently provides the play's dominant imagery, linking as it does the ideas of sexual lust and destruction. Don Juan uses vocabulary of fire to describe not only his passions but his contempt for the world—'que el mundo se abrase y queme' ('Let the world burn and go up in flames')—and significantly he uses the same words in reverse when he is crushed by the statue—'¡Que me quemo! ¡Que me abraso!' ('I am in flames! I burn!'). When he disappears the whole chapel goes up in flames; the destroyer is destroyed, the consumer consumed; Hell has claimed its own. It is a cataclysmic ending to a cataclysmic struggle. Don Juan has defied God's law as well as man's, pitting the power of youth and noble birth against the power of time and divine retribution. He has scoffed at death and it is therefore a dead man who calls in the debts he thought he could pay at his own convenience. The relationships he has violated are, with a little manoeuvring and papering over the cracks, re-established in a socially acceptable way. But there is no complacency in this ending. Few characters emerge with honour from the events the play portrays, and peasantry and aristocracy alike are depicted with a pervasive irony.

This gives the play a unity of tone and vision which, together with the themes of deception and deferred payment, and the metaphors of the bailbond, fire and personified death, knits the four episodes into a dramatic whole. The work has not the structural perfection of ***El condenado por desconfiado***. Of the women, the proud self-assertive Tisbea is the only one in whom any dramatic conflict takes place, and even so the thematic parallelism between her character and don Juan's—she delights in making men suffer as he does women—is never developed. Once more we see Tirso's imagination straining against the discipline of the *comedia* form. For all this, the work is a magnificent achievement, thematically and poetically tightly coherent, theatrically stunning, with a larger than life protagonist of extraordinary potency who was to step out of the work and capture the imagination of the world in a way unrivalled by any other dramatic creation. In consigning don Juan to Hell, Tirso ironically gave him the gift of immortality: the theologian in Tirso would have disapproved but the artist would certainly have rejoiced.

Tirso is the only seventeenth-century dramatist who compares with Lope and Calderón in terms both of sustained achievement and outstandingly memorable individual plays. Distinctive as their typical creations are, they habitually combine theatrical impact, thematic weight and mastery of language in a way not matched consistently by any other dramatist. Nonetheless, Lope's lessons were successfully applied and developed by a number of other gifted dramatists capable of producing plays of the first order. It must be emphasized that the drama during Lope's theatrical hegemony did not stand still. Not only was there a general move, led by Lope himself, towards greater artistic control, but there were as the years went by certain developments from which Lope remained aloof: a marked growth in the satirical content of plays, and the visible influence on some dramatists (not Tirso) of the complex, Latinate language of Góngora's major poetic works, the *Fábula de Polifemo y Galatea* (1613) and the *Soledades* (1614). There was a certain tendency, too, to sensationalism, exaggeration and stylization, a move away from realism into the fantastic and mannered. Satire apart, Lope's followers were walking the path that would lead to Calderón.

Notes

1. See David H. Darst, *The Comic Art of Tirso de Molina* (Chapel Hill, 1974); I. T. Agheana, *The Situational Drama of Tirso de Molina* (New York, 1972); Ruth L. Kennedy, *Studies in Tirso de Molina, I: The Dramatist and his Competitors, 1620-26* (Chapel Hill, 1974); I. L. McClelland, *Tirso de Molina: Studies in Dramatic Realism* (Liverpool, 1948); S. Maurel, *L'univers dramatique de Tirso de Molina* (Poitiers, 1971); Henry W. Sullivan, *Tirso de Molina and the Drama of the Counter Reformation* (Amsterdam, 1976); and Margaret Wilson, *Tirso de Molina* (Boston, 1977).
2. In his *Los cigarrales de Toledo* and in a scene interpolated for the purpose in his play *Antona García*.
3. See Ruth L. Kennedy, '*La prudencia en la mujer* and the Ambient that Brought it Forth', *Publications of the Modern Languages Association*, 63 (1948), 1131-90.
4. J. C. J. Metford, 'Tirso de Molina and the Conde-Duque de Olivares', *BHS*, 36 (1959), 15-27; and Ruth L. Kennedy, 'La perspectiva política de Tirso en *Privar contra su gusto*, y la de sus comedias posteriores', *Homenaje a Tirso de Molina* (Revista Estudios, Madrid, 1981), 199-238.
5. Marie Gleeson Ó Tuathaigh, 'Tirso's Pizarro Trilogy: A Case of Sycophancy or Lèse-Majesty?', *BCom*, 38 (1986), 63-82.
6. See A. K. G. Paterson (ed.), *La venganza de Tamar* (Cambridge, 1969), 28.
7. In an essay first published in Spain in 1949, republished as 'Bandits and Saints in the Spanish Drama of the Golden Age', *Critical Studies of Calderón's Comedias*, ed. J. E. Varey, vol. 19 of *The Comedias of Calderón,* ed. D. W. Cruickshank and J. E. Varey (London, 1973), 151-68. See also Melveena McKendrick, 'The *bandolera* of Golden-Age drama: a symbol of feminist revolt', *Critical Studies of Calderón's Comedias*, 169-90.
8. Authorship has been disputed but the play is now generally accepted as Tirso's. For the background to the play, see Daniel Rogers' introduction to his edition (Oxford, 1974).
9. Tirso anticipates the audience's surprise, referring them at the end to two theological sources for the events he describes.
10. Paulo consistently holds that what the 'angel' said was that if Enrico were damned he would also be damned, whereas if Enrico were saved then that would be his fate too. This is in fact his own reading of the Devil's words, born, like the Devil's appearance itself, of his own obsession.
11. In addition to Parker's article, among the many studies of the play are I. L. McClelland, *Tirso de Molina: Studies in Dramatic Realism*; C. V. Aubrun, 'La comédie doctrinale et ses histoires de brigands. *El condenado por desconfiado*', *BHisp*, 59 (1957), 137-51; T. E. May, *El condenado por desconfiado.* I. The enigmas. II. Anareto', *BHS*, 35 (1958), 138-56; C. A. Pérez, 'Verosimilitud psicológica de *El condenado por desconfiado*', *Hispanófila,* 27 (1969), 1-21.
12. The play has a complicated textual history and may not in fact be Tirso's although it is generally accepted as his. For a discussion of the play and bibliography see Daniel Rogers, *Tirso de Molina: El burlador de Sevilla*, Critical Guides to Spanish Texts (London, 1977).
13. See Dorothy McKay, *The Double Invitation and the Legend of Don Juan* (Stanford and London, 1943).

EL CONDENADO POR DESCONFIADO

CRITICAL COMMENTARY

Teresa Scott Soufas (essay date 1990)

SOURCE: "Religious Melancholy (Tirso)," in *Melancholy and the Secular Mind in Spanish Golden Age Literature,* University of Missouri Press, 1990, pp. 37-63.

[*In the following excerpt, Soufas concentrates on de Molina's* El condenado por desconfiado *and its character Paulo who, in Soufas' essay, clearly defines the seventeenth-century understanding of religious melancholy.*]

> In truth it was melancholy that the devil breathed into Adam at the time of his fall: melancholy which robs a man of his ardour and faith.
>
> *St. Hildegard of Bingen*

The epigraph above calls attention to the importance of melancholy in the religious and the moral teachings against sin. St. Hildegard of Bingen concentrates on the origin of melancholy, which she describes as simultaneous with the commission of Original Sin. In her account, the twelfth-century saint focuses on the moment when Adam ate the forbidden apple and the melancholy humor in his blood curdled, "as when a lamp is quenched, the smouldering and smoking wick remains reeking behind . . . the sparkle of innocence was dulled in him, and his eyes, which had formerly beheld heaven, were blinded, and his gall was changed to bitterness, and his melancholy to blackness."[1] Hers is a description of melancholia that represents an important medieval articulation of the link between the humoral condition and the spiritual, ethical, and moral issues which continue to be raised 450 to 500 years later by the Renaissance doctors and scientists in their multifaceted treatises on melancholy. The beliefs that began to emerge in the later sixteenth century and blossomed full-blown in the seventeenth echo her insistence upon the moral responsibility incumbent upon the melancholic and those administering to him or her to seek relief and/or cures through medical and theological means.

The Renaissance expository writers reiterate as well St. Hildegard's insistence upon the all-pervasive quality of melancholy as a nearly universal affliction. In her view, melancholia is Adam's punishment and thus the "incurable hereditary evil" to which all human beings are vulnerable, while in the early seventeenth century, Burton likewise writes: "thou shalt soon perceive that all the world is mad, that it is melancholy."[2] Such notions reinforce the tradition of melancholy as a concern in moral teachings and associate it with the pride and thirst for forbidden knowledge as the basis of humanity's Fall. This is a dimension that finds an almost full reverberation in the intellectual scope of the literary representation of melancholy in the seventeenth century, when emphasis was placed on the melancholic's illicit use of the mind in both secular and spiritual matters.

The religious melancholic is an individual whose depiction in Renaissance literature evinces his or her ties to ethical and medical notions that date back to the early centuries of Christianity. That depiction reaches a height of scientific focus in the late sixteenth and early seventeenth centuries, when the medico-scientific writers like Alfonso de Santa Cruz and Pedro Mercado include references to it or provide related case histories.[3] Burton's examination of the syndrome in his *Anatomy of Melancholy* is the first extensive secular coverage of the subject, and it serves as a compendium of an age-old topic frequently written about by officials of the Christian Church. Burton's chapter on religious melancholy appears in the *Anatomy* from its earliest edition (1621) and, though certainly not widely circulated in Spain, it is coextensive with certain Spanish dramatic representations of the same spiritual/humoral condition. I choose to concentrate on one such work, Tirso de Molina's ***El condenado por desconfiado***, for two reasons. First, its range of possible dates of composition has been postulated between 1615 and 1625.[4] These dates situate the drama in that period of heightened literary interest in melancholy when Tirso and other writers had more frequent opportunities for exposure to notions about aspects of religious melancholy and its evolution from the earlier sinful condition known as *acedia* that Burton also summarizes during approximately the same period. Second, ***El condenado por desconfiado*** is a play in which its author scrutinizes the majority of the questions surrounding the topic of religious melancholy, including the complex and varying elements of despair, neglect, idleness, delusions, and vulnerability to the Devil's persuasion that melancholics were believed to suffer and that continued to characterize the notion of *acedia* from the Middle Ages through the Renaissance.[5]

As a character clearly defined within the framework of the seventeenth-century understanding of religious melancholy, Tirso's ascetic hermit Paulo in ***El condenado por desconfiado*** has much in common with such diverse figures of history and fiction as the gods of Olympus, the fourth-century monks living with Evagrius in the Egyptian desert, and countless other historical and literary personalities believed to suffer from a pathological melancholy system. Part of the background of Tirso's characterization of Paulo involves the terminological evolution of *acedia*, a word used very early to describe the tedium afflicting the monks of Alexandria as a consequence of the monotony of their routine, which causes, among other things, restlessness, dejection, and a wish to leave the monastic life altogether. Lyman looks back even further to the Homeric stories about the Olympian life, in which the literal definition of *acedia*, "uncaring," had been "inadvertently institutionalized in the leisure world of the Greek deities" whose hedonistic life gave way to gloomy disillusionment and immoral pursuits that contaminated as well the mortals with whom they interacted.[6] Through the writings of John Cassian, the monastic vice of *acedia* was introduced into the Latin West and passed through transformations during the Middle Ages, becoming associated and even interchangeable with the deadly sin of sloth. Thus it was eventually a danger for persons of any profession.

A new emphasis was placed on the internal mental state and emotions as causes of *acedia*; now seen as a weakness of the spirit, religious melancholy was likewise connected to *tristitia*, thereby gaining a psychological basis as well, as Siegfried Wenzel explains. He further contends: "In this process *acedia* came to be understood as man's culpable aversion against the divine good—a conception with which the emphasis on the vice's mental aspects and the more 'spiritualized' view reached its culmination."[7] Paralleling this cycle was another, for the Scholastics characterize *acedia* as a sin occupying a position between sins of the spirit and those of the body. Other moralists group *acedia* with the carnal vices of lust and gluttony because of its pathological connection to one's need for rest and sleep, exaggerated in the physical listlessness often evident in the melancholic. The demonasticization of *acedia*, its internalization, and its categorization as a "vice of the spirit" as well as a "vice of the flesh" occurs, nevertheless, over the whole of the Middle Ages, and Wenzel ultimately concedes a tripartite categorization—"monastic, Scholastic, and popular"—which, he tells us, "can be localized with some accuracy in time, and even more, in literary genre." He adds, however, that "never did a later form completely replace an earlier one. The laicization . . . of the vice in the twelfth and thirteenth centuries did not entail the total loss of monastic elements . . . and the concept of *acedia* one meets in the fourteenth and fifteenth centuries is a comprehensive one, embracing elements from all stages of *acedia*'s past life."[8]

As is the case with scholarly melancholics, their religious counterparts are also solitary thinkers, and Tirso depicts his accidic monk as prideful in his contemplation. The emphasis on the "mental aspects" involved in one's "culpable aversion against the divine good" to which Wenzel refers is at the heart of what Tirso portrays in ***El condenado por desconfiado***.[9] The play dramatizes the dialectical response on the part of its author to the epistemological struggle over the perceived strength or danger inherent in the active melancholy mind. The play also addresses a related point made by Sullivan concerning the composite nature of Golden Age dramatic presentations that encompass "the basic antagonisms of the Counter Reformation itself, i.e., Renaissance liberation in conflict with a medievalizing reaction; the *comedia* was a theater that restated medieval values, but explored the scope of human freedom without being able to help itself."[10] Tirso's transvalued treatment of the melancholy mentality portrays Enrico the bandit as a counterpart to the religious melancholic Paulo, for Enrico exhibits numerous traits of melancholy criminality that were also thought to plague the religious melancholic once he or she had despaired of salvation. Like two complementary character studies of distinct but related melancholic disorders, Paulo and Enrico dramatize what the more scientific writers record in their treatises, but these two diverge in their eventual responses to their afflictions. Understanding the context of melancholy within which Tirso develops the action, theme, imagery, and characterization in this play provides a means of reading the work that accounts for its canonicity in seventeenth-century terms.

In the nonliterary studies of *acedia*, the authors comment upon the concept in its more secular context through its connection to humoral melancholy. Those pseudo-scientific writers of the sixteenth and seventeenth centuries who do address the topic of religious melancholy as a discrete type describe it as marked by despair over one's salvation and failure to pursue or to finish good works. Certain characteristics became associated with the religious individuals whose melancholy symptoms were either the result or, conversely, the cause of their devout lifestyle; insufficient or unfit diet, fasting, and other such hardships of a strict religious life were thought either to produce or to exacerbate the physiological symptoms of the disorder. So, too, the solitude which melancholics are said to seek as well as the darkness of a cave or a monastic cell are part of the hermit's ambience. Cristóbal Acosta asserts in his late sixteenth-century *Tratado en contra y pro de la vida solitaria* (Treatise against and for the solitary life) that "melancholía no os faltará, que allende la vuestra natural, la divina scriptura llama triste al que vive solo y sin compañía" (you will not lack melancholy, for besides your natural melancholy, divine scripture labels sad the one who lives alone and without company).[11] The study and meditation associated with melancholy is often described as a cause of heightened anxiety and a weakening of faith and convictions in the religious. In their melancholic states, they convince themselves of their own eternal damnation and the impossibility of ever receiving God's grace and redemption.

Murillo, in particular, regards the religious as especially susceptible to melancholia. With references to Pliny, he includes those "dados a los estudios, y a la Religion" (those given to study and to Religion) in the category that also encompasses the "Insanos, Melancholicos, y Maniacos" (Insane, Melancholics, and Maniacs), adding that these individuals are known popularly as "alumbrados" (illuminati) and are "callados, tristes, y excordes" (quiet, sad, and mentally unbalanced). The blending of medical and moral notions evident in the majority of the expository works is clearly articulated in Murillo's study, as certain sections dealing with the cure of melancholy diseases attest. He posits, for example, "que los Medicos no curen el cuerpo, antes que este curada el alma con el Santissimo Sacramento de la Penitencia, y Sagrada comunion, y confession Sacramental . . . y es gran desdicha lo que en esto passa, que muchos Medicos . . . por dezir a los enfermos que se confiessen en tiempo, se hallan con ellos muertos, no sin grande cargo de sus conciencias" (that the Physicians do not cure the body, before the soul is cured with the Holy Sacrament of Penitence, and Holy communion, and Sacramental confession . . . and it is very unfortunate what happens in this matter, for many Doctors . . . by telling the sick people to confess, find that they die, not without great charge to their consciences). He further counsels physicians that they recognize the link between disease and sin (an echo of St. Hildegard's account of the origin of melancholy) and so the doctor must consider "si acaso la enfermedad que se padece es causada, y le vino al enfermo por sus pecados: porque es de Fe Catolica, que por nuestros pecados enfermamos muchas vezes" (if by chance the illness suffered is caused and comes to the patient through his sins: because it is part of the Catholic Faith that due to our sins we become sick many times). He adds, however: "Mas aunque el Demonio pueda causar enfermedades innumerables, puede el Medico, como instrumento de la Divina Iusticia, o qualquiera otro varon de vida inculpable, (pie & devote), ahuyentar a los Demonios" (But although the Devil may cause innumerable diseases, the Doctor, as an instrument of Divine Justice, or any other man of guiltless life, "devoutly," can drive away Devils).[12] The physician's task is thus diverse and combines both ethical and scientific fields.[13] Murillo cites the exhortation *nosce teipsum* as an important moral underpinning to his arguments about the religious melancholics, explaining: "el que fuere perfectamente sabio, se conocera perfectamente a si mismo . . . y assi, como se puede afirmar que se cognosca perfectamente el Melancholico, o Maniaco, que con sus propias manos se quita la vida" (he who may be perfectly wise, will know himself perfectly . . . and so, as one can affirm that the Melancholic or the Maniac knows himself perfectly, for with his own hands he ends his life).[14] The despair and self-destructive tendencies (in both a physical and spiritual sense) are therefore an inherent danger in the melancholy self-contemplation that needs to be tempered and redirected by means of theological and medical ministering.

Tirso's characterization of Paulo in the play undeniably entails the traditional conception of *acedia*. The isolated life based on a routine of meditation and sparse diet, the latter highlighted through the complaints of Paulo's servant Pedrisco, is indeed what has occupied the hermit for ten years. His initial attack of despair, moreover, follows a period of sleep, and his subsequent rancor and neglect of his duty to God are, as Daniel Rogers asserts, in keeping with the vices that St. Thomas associates with *acedia*.[15] The blending of the accepted notion of *acedia* with that of the humoral disorder of melancholy must, however, be considered. What Paulo does and says and the visual and poetic imagery attendant upon his behavior reflect this blend of psychological, physiological, and ethical factors.

As the play begins, Paulo expresses his preference for solitude and darkness:

> ¡Dichoso albergue mío! Soledad apacible y deleitosa, que en el calor y el frío me dais posada en esta selva umbrosa.
>
> (My happy refuge! Peaceful and delightful solitude, that in the heat and the cold gives me shelter in this dark forest.)[16]

In the medical books, as in their artistic literary counterparts, an affinity for solitary darkness is often mentioned in descriptions of melancholy characteristics. The associated metaphorical suggestions link melancholy with that darkness of mind which the dark humor brings about as well as that physical darkness in which melancholics prefer to stay or which might worsen their already fearful nature. Murillo writes, for example:

> espantanse, y assombranse estos melancholicos, como lo hazen los muchachos en las tinieblas, y obscuridades, y entre los crecidos, y mancebos, los indoctos, y rudos; porque de la manera que las tinieblas exteriores, casi a todos los hombres les dan pavor, y miedo, si no es que son muy ossados, o enseñados: assi de la misma manera, el color del humor melancholico viene a hazer tener temor con tinieblas, y obscuridad, cubriendo con sombra, o assombrando el celebro, demanera, que lo que parece que se colige de Galeno, es, que la causa destos sympthomas, miedo, y tristeza, mas es el color del humor, que no la destemplança de las qualidades.
>
> (These melancholics become frightened and startled, as do children in the shadows and in darkness, and among older people and youths, the uneducated and the uncultured; because in the way that external darkness shocks and frightens almost all people; if they are not very brave or educated: thus the color of the melancholic humor causes fear by shadows, darkness, covering with shade, or by startling the brain, so it seems that what we can summarize from Galen is that the cause of these symptoms, fear, and sadness, is the color of the humor rather than the irregularity of the qualities.)[17]

The tradition of *acedia* and the vulnerability of religious persons, in particular hermits, to melancholia makes the references to solitude and darkness significant in the case of a figure purportedly living such a reclusive life. St. Hildegard's references to the darkness of the descent of sin and melancholy on humanity are also recalled by such passages.

Thus, although Paulo's monologue seems to express the *beatus ille* topos, it more appropriately indicates to the audience the melancholic condition that afflicts him. The intensity of Paulo's statements builds through the first four stanzas of his speech to the point where he shouts:

> ¿Quién ¡Oh celeste velo! aquestos tafetanes luminosos rasgar pudiera un poco para ver . . . ?(1.21-24)
>
> (Who, Oh celestial veil! could tear a little bit these luminous curtains in order to see . . . ?)

Again, there is an echo of Hildegard's metaphorical explanation of melancholy, which posits Adam's loss of innocence as an inability to look into heaven, a privilege that had formerly been his. Paulo suggests his parallel experience of wishing to duplicate the prelapsarian privilege that nevertheless cannot be reclaimed by humanity, whom he figuratively represents in this moment of blasphemous pride. He hastens to add, however, "¡Ay de mí! Vuélvome loco" (Woe is me! I am going crazy [1.24]), thereby identifying his own underlying instability and linking himself from the beginning of the play with the state of *locura* which, like *manía*, the sixteenth- and seventeenth-century scientists use as a synonym for *melancolía*.

His outburst displays as well the ecstatic state that melancholia was thought capable of triggering in the religiously devout, for as Lawrence Babb asserts: "Melancholy symptoms of a religious character include many rapturous fancies."[18] As is typical of religious melancholics, Paulo's thoughts turn to the question of his own meriting of salvation and to the threatening "puertas del profundo" (doors to hell [1.36]). Furthermore, his last sentence before leaving the stage ("Ved que el hombre se hizo / de barro vil, de barro quebradizo" [Understand that man was made of common clay, of fragile clay]; 1.75-76) carries with it the traditional biblical teaching but also hints at the connection between the humor melancholy and the earth, its mate among the natural elements.

The hermit's words end with his entrance into one of the mountain grottoes and are followed by the vociferous complaints of his only servant and companion Pedrisco. The *gracioso* bemoans specifically the bad diet that robs him, and presumably his master, of sound health. Outlining the regimen the two men follow and the emotional consequence it has for both at times, he says:

> Aquí penitencia hacemos, y sólo yerbas comemos, y a veces nos acordamos, de lo mucho que dejamos por lo poco que tenemos. (1.112-16)
>
> (Here we do penance, and we only eat herbs, and at times we remember, how much we left behind for the little that we have.)

Pedrisco's complaints, though comical in presentation because of their stress on his interest in creature comforts, nevertheless emphasize repeatedly his sadness, "triste fin me pronostico" (I predict a sad end for myself [1.81]), and lamenting further ("memorias me hacen llorar" [memories make me cry]; 1.124): "ya está todo perdido" (now everything is lost [1.132]). Pedrisco thus sets the mood for Paulo's next monologue, which itself begins "¡qué desventura! / Y ¡qué desgracia, cierta, lastimosa!" (What misfortune! / And what certain and regrettable bad luck! [1.139-40]). It is this frame of mind which dominates Paulo throughout the rest of the play, and this scene, moreover, subtly suggests that the entryways through which the hermit and his servant pass into their respective caves are analogous to the doors to hell ("puertas del profundo") which Paulo dreads in his first speech. The dark abyss, however, is a mental and emotional one, linked nevertheless to the physical world through his melancholy physiology but leading to eternal spiritual damnation because of the obsessive despair upon which he seizes.

The immediate cause of Paulo's fear and sadness, the two emotions most characteristic of melancholia, is his nightmarish dream vision of "la muerte cruel" (cruel death) and the final judgment upon his condemned soul. Having described the unsettling images, Paulo relates his concerns in terms that reinforce his identity as a religious melancholic: "Con aquella fatiga y aquel miedo / desperté" (I awoke with that fatigue and that fear [1.177-78]). He emphasizes at once the physical weariness associated with *acedia* and the fright of melancholia. He then goes on to describe the classical traits of one so afflicted:

> . . . aunque temblando, y no vi nada si no es mi culpa, y tan confuso quedo, que si no es a mi suerte desdichada, o traza del contrario, ardid o enredo, que vibra contra mí su ardiente espada, no sé a qué atribuya. (1.178-83)
>
> (. . . although trembling, and I saw nothing if not my guilt, and so confused do I remain, that if it is not to my wretched luck, or trick, ruse, or intrigue of Satan, who moves his burning sword against me, I do not know to what to attribute it.)

His doubts and self-recrimination are accompanied by repetitive despairing questions: "¿Heme de condenar, mi Dios divino, / como ese sueño dice, o he de verme / en el sagrado alcázar cristalino?" (Am I to condemn myself, my divine God, / as that dream says, or will I find myself / in the sacred crystal palace? [1.185-87]); "¿qué fin he de tener?" (what end must I have? [1.189]); "¿He de ir a vuestro Cielo, o al infierno?" (Will I go to your Heaven, or to hell? [1. 192]).

Of particular interest to Renaissance expository writers are the powers ascribed to melancholics who are said to be able to see into the future and experience rapturous visions. In Spain, most treatises on melancholy reflect their authors' refusal to accept such purported powers, and express instead another popular Renaissance notion that the devil preys more frequently upon melancholic individuals and is responsible for their visions of damnation. In his appended section about these supposed prophetic powers, Freylas directly addresses the connection between the devil and melancholy, saying, "es cierto que se junta el demonio con el humor melancolico, porque halla en el muy grande disposicion para hazer grandes danos, como es persuadir a que se ahorquen, o desesperen de la misericordia de Dios" (it is certain that the devil joins himself to the melancholy humor, because he finds in it a very great disposition to do great harm, like persuading melancholics to hang themselves, or to despair of God's mercy).[19] Murillo likewise writes "el Demonio se alegra con el humor Melancholico" (the Devil rejoices in the Melancholic humor). He goes into great detail in his arguments meant to discourage belief in the purported abilities of melancholics to prophesy and to speak languages never studied (particularly Latin), citing many ancient and contemporary sources about the devil's intervention in such cases.[20] These sorts of expressions by Spanish expository writers are commonplaces in the tradition of melancholy as the *balneum diaboli* that many of their European contemporaries also record.

In his discussion of this phenomenon, Babb includes references to similar statements by Philip Barrough, Johann Weyer, Robert Burton, André Du Laurens, and others.[21] Jackson, who devotes an entire chapter in his study to beliefs about the purported supernatural powers enjoyed by melancholics and their presumed sources, explains that the issuing of prophesy by melancholy persons had varyingly been through a transformation of the Platonic theory of divinely inspired madness in combination with the Aristotelian theories about the superior capabilities of the melancholic mind. Numerous medical writers acknowledge the strength of such a tradition, but they often relegate the prophetic visions to the realm of pathological delusion.[22] Certainly, the Spanish physicians who are more generally Galenic in their approach to melancholy support this kind of assessment.

Dramatizing a similar view of such melancholic abilities of prophecy, Tirso represents the devil's sway upon Paulo's diseased melancholy mind. Like several of the physicians, however, Tirso makes plain that God allows the devil's trickery. The devil in ***El condenado por desconfiado*** is able to influence Paulo, but only after the experience of his frightening dream, which intensifies the connection between the hermit and melancholia. Freylas, for instance, writes: "el que [tiene abundancia de] melancolia visita con los suenos los muertos, y sepulcros, y . . . cosas negras y tristes" (he who [has an abundance of] melancholy visits the dead in dreams, as well as graves, and . . . dark and sad things).[23] In addition, Murillo discusses at length the melancholy fixations and obsessions that befall an overly melancholy mind because of both fear and the devil's intervention. The effects he describes seem particularly applicable to Paulo:

> Ay algunas personas tan escrupulosas por razon de la complexion melancholica, y fria, que estan dispuestas para el temor, y assi las mugeres melancholicas, y los hombres que padecen esta enfermedad estan mas sugetos a esta passion, porque el temor, y la frialdad aprietan el corazon, y de alli se dispone la imaginacion a concebir el mal que esta por venir, y por flaqueza de la cabeça quando esta con lesion, como sucede en los melancholicos, o el Demonio los despierta, y atiza, el que puede mover los humores melancholicos, con permision de Dios, y la imaginacion puede ser enganada, y tener demasiadamente alguna cosa, o por abstinencias, vigilias, y asperezas, o compania de personas escrupulosas.
>
> (There are some persons who are so scrupulous because of their cold and melancholic makeup that they are disposed to fear. Thus many melancholic women, and the men who suffer from this disease, are quite subject to that passion, because fear and coldness press upon the heart. In this way, one's imagination is prepared to conceive some future evil. And, as happens with melancholics, either some weakness in the head as when it has been wounded, or the Devil, with God's permission, wakes and stirs in them that which can move the melancholic humors and the imagination can be deceived, putting excessive emphasis on some thing: abstinence, vigils, mortification, or the company of pious people.)[24]

So it is that, in his monk's routine, Paulo is overly susceptible to cold fear and even more so once his body is affected by what was thought to be the cooling influence of sleep. The devil, who has received permission from "el Juez más supremo y recto" (the most supreme and just Judge [1.230]) to deceive, and thus test, Paulo, has been able to exacerbate his fearful thoughts about the future. The consequences are dire, for, not availing himself of the suggested remedies for his pathological condition—described, for example, by Murillo as confession, medical advice, and, in particular, recourse to God's grace—Paulo does not reverse the process.[25] The devil appeals to him through his senses in a physical visitation as well. The hermit's imagination receives this sensory information, but his overly active melancholy intellect is not able to interpret correctly the information offered. The natural tendencies he has toward pride and rumination become symptoms of his disease, and he progressively takes on more and more of the most negative qualities of pathological melancholia whose sufferers are "soberbios, altivos, renegadores, astutos, doblados, injuriosos, y amigos de hazer mal, y vengativos, y los que tienen el ingenio mas agudo, suelen ser acedos, colericos, y malcontentos" (prideful, haughty, ill-tempered, crafty, deceitful, insulting, vengeful, and fond of doing evil, and those who have the most astute wit, are usually disagreeable, angry, and malcontent).[26] On the authority of numerous Renaissance discussions of religious melancholy, Babb asserts: "Such [persons] often develop a dreadful melancholy which provokes them to commit monstrous crimes."[27]

Upon learning from the devil in angel's guise that his fate is to be that of the stranger Enrico, Paulo makes clear that he is experiencing the "impious delusions of divine favor" that many expository writers label as the devil's inspiration.[28] The hermit declares: "Algún divino varón, / debe de ser: ¿quién lo duda?" (He must be some saintly man, / who can doubt it? [1.289-91]), and "¡Gran santo debe de ser! / Lleno de contento estoy" (He must be a great saint! / I am full of happiness [1.321-22]). His statement about contentment should, of course, be taken ironically, since his words and behavior provide evidence instead of his religious melancholia. La Puerta de la Mar, the site to which Paulo is directed in order to observe Enrico, is, moreover, symbolically linked to melancholy through connection with Saturn and one of his realms of influence, the sea. It also recalls the "puertas del profundo" that Paulo earlier dreaded.

The result of the devil's message is in the short run a more hopeful, though deluded, discourse on Paulo's part, rhetoric that lasts only until he observes Enrico and learns that this man is a hardened criminal with a record of multiple crimes. Other melancholy symptoms then begin to become evident in Paulo's demeanor. Abandoning all hope of salvation, he yields to the more violent side of his melancholy nature and suffers alternations between the so-called hot and cold characteristics that the pathological melancholic can experience as a consequence of a strong show of emotion. The result is a series of alternating cycles of violence, overwhelming fear, and incapacitating sadness that plague him during the rest of the play. The fires of hell which Paulo anticipates thus correspond to the more manic and violent activities upon which he embarks, though he heads for the mountains, made of earth and therefore symbolic of melancholy. He declares to Pedrisco: "En el monte hay bandoleros: / bandolero quiero ser" (In the mountains there are bandits: / I want to be a bandit [1.979-80]), adding further that in comparison to Enrico "[t]an malo tengo de ser / como él, y peor si puedo" (I want to be as bad / as he, and worse if I am able [1.984-85]). The inner heat of his agitated pathological adust state is apparent and he exclaims at one point: "Rayo del mundo he de ser" (I will become a thunderbolt of the world [1.998]), while at another, "Fuego por la vista exhalo" (I exhale fire through my eyes [2.1427]). He likewise continues to express his pride, describing the course his villainy will take: "Más que la Naturaleza / he de hacer por cobrar fama" (In order to gain fame / I must outdo Nature [2.1438-39]).

Following his intentions to lead the evil life that corresponds to the eternal damnation he expects, Paulo dramatizes the perversion of his will's action by means of his unhealthy intellect. He never completely relents in his certainty of condemnation and proves that his melancholy susceptibility to the devil's suggestion is more profound than is his faith in God's grace. He listens to but does not believe the angelic messenger sent to advise him to repent and accept God's forgiveness. Paulo's adherence to a conviction that his fate is predetermined is, of course, an unacceptable stance from the point of view of the Zumelian theology that Tirso follows.[29] The potential for physiological determinism inherent in humoralism is likewise rejected by the ethical notions of the physicians writing on melancholy, for measures to relieve the various melancholy disorders are nearly always aimed at restoring the patient to a state of balance (Huarte, of course, is a notable exception), physically and mentally, and overcoming the effects of the offending humor. Indeed, the humoral tendencies that render Paulo prone to melancholic despair, criminality, emotional imbalance, and excessive pride are aspects of his personality which Renaissance medicine teaches can be controlled. As Tirso presents him, then, there is no reason to assume that Paulo is inherently unable to break out of his cycle of religious melancholy. It is, however, a mistake to assume that the hermit needs merely to exercise reason's control over his passions, for like other melancholy characters in Spain's Golden Age, Paulo is a figure whose thought process is depicted as dangerous because he thinks too much.

The ruminations of a melancholy mind that the expository writers warn against are thus very much a part of Paulo's traits. The deeper and more pathological his melancholy, the more powerful becomes his tendency to think, and the more profound becomes his despair. His arguments for turning to the life of crime that Enrico leads, for example, are evidence of his consciously made decision to do so:

> si su fin he de tener, tenga su vida y sus hechos; que no es bien que yo en el mundo esté penitencia haciendo, y que él viva en la ciudad con gustos y con contentos, y que a la muerte tengamos un fin. (1.970-77)
>
> (If I must have his end, let me have his life and deeds; for it is not right that I do penance in the world, while he lives in the city with pleasures and happiness, and that in death we have the same end.)

He pursues his goal of evil with full conviction, affirming at one point: "Pues hoy verá el cielo en mí / si en las maldades no igualo / a Enrico" (Well then today heaven will see in my actions / if I do not equal Enrico / in evil [2.1424-26]). Paulo is thus cognizant of what he does and even reasons through his rejection of salvation. His melancholy temperament, of course, predisposes him to his initial despairing reaction to the dream in his cave, but Tirso, with Renaissance sensibility, develops him as an individual whose physical and psychological natures are interdependent and whose moral shortcomings cannot be categorized as merely the results of uncontrolled emotion or weak rationality.

The other important character in ***El condenado por desconfiado*** who is portrayed within the broad context of melancholy is Enrico. He initially exhibits the extreme violence, cruelty, and treachery associated with the melancholy villains who populate so many of the Elizabethan works examined by Babb and Lyons. Enrico's characterization is manipulated by Tirso to trace this bandit's evolution from destructive behavior in the first two acts to the fearful and sad melancholy contemplation of a captured prisoner in act 3. Enrico thus provides a significant figure against which to measure Paulo. The young villain begins the play in the same sphere of violence into which the hermit moves, but at the end, he is in a frame of mind which approximates that of Paulo in his earlier ascetic existence. Paulo dramatizes the consequences of despair and religious melancholy that culminate in violence and damnation. Enrico enacts the positive outcome that remains a possibility for Paulo and for any sinner who undertakes a contemplative self-examination for the correct reasons and accepts the limitations of the human intellect in comparison with God's grace. Tirso's transvaluation of melancholy thus provides two characters whose respective melancholy imbalances lead eventually to two completely different kinds of contemplation, one that brings about the damnation of a figure of devotion and the other the salvation of a murderous criminal.

Lyons describes melancholy villains as "plotting revengers" who derive "great enjoyment from [their] villainies." This is the case with Enrico in Tirso's play, for in act 1 he makes a festive occasion of the recounting of crimes among his band of accomplices (scene 11). Lyons further explains that "[d]isenchantment with the world and disillusionment over their failure in it are understood to make such characters amenable to any kind of villainy."[30] Babb adds that in Elizabethan England writers regarded the melancholic's criminal bias as very dangerous "because melancholy sometimes endows men with great acumen, which presumably may be turned to evil uses."[31] Though Tirso does not refer to the birth of his bandit as having occurred under Saturn's astrological influence, as do some of the English playwrights with regard to their villainous characters,[32] Enrico claims "Yo nací mal inclinado, / como se ve en los efetos / del discurso de mi vida" (I was born with bad tendencies, / as is seen in the effects / of the passage of my life [1.724-26]). Tirso nevertheless suggests the connection between Enrico's criminality and the disposition with which he is born, elements that reinforce the characteristics of Saturnine melancholy as then understood as well as the melancholic's ability to overcome such inclinations.

Enrico proceeds to deliver a long monologue on his evil deeds, which encompass his entire life: ". . . haciendo / travesuras cuando niño, / locuras cuando mancebo" (. . . committing mischief as a child, / folly as a youth [1.737-39]). During the play his sustained criminality is depicted through descriptions of his robberies, swindles, and even murders. In accord with the definitions of melancholy villains, Enrico likewise expresses his misanthropy in terms of a reaction against his failures: "Quedé pobre y sin hacienda, / y como enseñado a hacerlo, / di en robar de casa en casa" (I was left poor and without property, / and having learned how to do so, / I turned to robbing house after house [1.748-50]). His evil, like Paulo's, is also consciously undertaken, a fact that he emphasizes with such boasts as: "Por hacer mal solamente / he jurado juramentos / falsos, fingiendo quimeras" (Only in order to do evil / have I committed perjury / inventing fantastic ideas [1.828-30]). He adds further:

> No digo jamás palabra si no es con un juramento, con un "pese" o un "por vida", porque sé que ofendo al cielo. (1.844-47)
>
> (I never say a word if it is not with a curse, with a "may the Devil take me" or "God damn me" because I know that I offend heaven.)

Enrico continues with the claim that he has never been to Mass nor, finding himself in danger, has he ever confessed "ni invocado a Dios eterno" (nor invoked the eternal God [1.851]). His rejection of good and his embrace of wrongdoing and violence are similar to the course of action the despairing Paulo will soon undertake at the end of act 1 with the determination: "Los pasos pienso seguir / de Enrico" (I plan to follow the footsteps / of Enrico [1.1010-11]).

Neither man, however, denies a belief in God. Paulo even prays "Señor, perdona / si injustamente me vengo" (Lord, forgive me / if I avenge myself unjustly [1.1002-3]), just before he heads into the mountains to become a *bandolero*. Enrico declares his underlying hope of eventual salvation when he addresses Paulo and chides him for his lack of faith: "Desesperación ha sido / lo que has hecho, y aun venganza / de la palabra de Dios" (What you have done / is desperate, and even vengeance, / against the word of God [2.1971-73]). He adds, furthermore:

> mas siempre tengo esperanza en que tengo de salvarme; puesto que no va fundada mi esperanza en obras mías, sino en saber que se humana Dios con el más pecador, y con su piedad se salva. (2.1996-2002)
>
> (But I always have hope that I will be saved; although my hope is not based on my works, but rather on knowing that God is humane with the greatest sinner, and through His pity he is saved.)

Tirso therefore uses his reprobate Enrico as the mouthpiece of the most positive message in the play. Through the melancholy villain, the dramatist underscores the hope for all sinners who must understand that salvation is a gift bestowed on unworthy recipients by a loving and forgiving Deity.

An important point also to be made in comparing Enrico and Paulo involves an issue addressed by the scientists and moralists who consider religious melancholy and its characteristic despair—as opposed to a genuine sense of sin—akin to the distinctions made by ascetic writers between "a positive and a negative kind of tristitia, the former leading to penance and salvation, the latter to death."[33] This is the very issue upon which the Englishman Timothy Bright focuses in his *Treatise of Melancholie* and is the difference eventually enacted by Enrico and Paulo and the ends to which they progress. The lifelong criminal finally acknowledges his sins and asks for forgiveness while the one-time holy man is seen burning in the flames of hell because of his despair. Unlike Enrico, Paulo recognizes too late his error in relying solely upon his own interpretation of deceptive evidence and not enough upon God's promises.

Tirso clearly depicts a physiological and mental shift in Enrico once the young man is apprehended by the authorities and put into prison for the murder of the governor. Though in the beginning of his stay in jail he exhibits more violent tendencies, even killing one of the guards and threatening his former lover with renewed abuse because she has married another rogue, his surroundings come to reflect and enhance the internal changes in him brought about by the physical conditions as well as the thoughts and emotions he is experiencing. This depiction also recalls another notion about *acedia* and anger. As Lyons points out, "[i]n schemes of the sins, anger was a cause of *acedia*."[34] Her references to Chaucer and Dante call attention to two passages that seem to announce the association Tirso subtly insinuates through the feelings and behavior of Enrico. In the "Parson's Tale," Chaucer writes: "Envye and Ire maken bitternesse in herte, which bitternesse is mooder of Accidie."[35] Dante likewise pairs "l'anime de color cui vinse l'ira" (the souls of those whom anger overcame) in the Fifth Circle of Hell with those "che sospira, / e fanno pullular quest'acqua al summo" (who sigh and make the water bubble on the surface). This group explains to their observer: "Tristi fummo / nell'aere dolce che dal sol s'allegra, / portando dentro accidioso fummo" (We were sullen in the sweet air that is gladdened by the sun, bearing in our hearts a sluggish smoke) and they are sunk in black sludge—an appropriate reminder of the connection between *acedia* and melancholy.[36]

After his angry outbursts, Enrico finds himself removed from his cell to a deeper dungeon chamber, a place that physically intensifies a growing inner coldness that is presumably caused by the adustion of the humors from his outburst of anger, jealousy, and violence. The stage directions indicate that he is now in "Un calabozo" (a dungeon [p. 180]), and whereas he had earlier shared a cell with Pedrisco (now a member of Paulo's band of marauders) Enrico is, at present, in solitude. He begins scene vi with a speech that evinces his increasingly fearful melancholy state:

> En lóbrega confusión ya, valiente Enrico, os veis, pero nunca desmayéis; tened fuerte corazón. (3.2232-35)

(In gloomy confusion now, brave Enrico, you find yourself, but do not lose heart; keep a strong heart.)

Almost immediately he hears the voice of the devil, who chooses this moment, when Enrico is his most melancholically contemplative and suggestive, to try to win another victory by delusion and persuasion. Enrico's initial reaction is one of heightened fear: "Esta voz me hace temblar. / Los cabellos erizados / pronostican mi temor" (This voice makes me tremble. / My hairs stand on end / and foretell my fear [3.2241-43]). Fear begins to dominate him, as he repeatedly makes clear: "tanto temor me da" (I am so afraid [3.2253]); "¡qué confuso abismo! / No me conozco a mí mismo, / y el corazón no reposa" (What a confusing abyss! / I do not recognize myself, / and my heart does not rest [3.2258-60]); and "Un sudor frío / por mis venas se derrama" (A cold sweat flows / through my veins [3.2271-72]). His ultimate response at this point is an intellectual one as he calls upon his own mental powers for answers: "¿Qué me dices, pensamiento?" (What do you have to say to me, thought? [3.2285]).

Unlike Paulo, who privileges the devil's messages above even those from an angelic shepherd, Enrico listens and heeds the counsel of a heavenly second voice that opposes the devil's urging to escape through an apparent breach in the prison wall. Though the bandit wavers in his decision when he learns that he will soon be hanged for his crimes, he eventually does confess his sins. His aged father Anareto rebukes him for, among other things, his "loco pensamiento" (insane thinking [3.2465]), but in the old man's presence Enrico dies a Christian death. Paulo, on the other hand, dies unconfessed and unsaved, and Pedrisco comments upon the outcome:

> Las suertes fueron trocadas. Enrico, con ser tan malo, se salvó, y éste al infierno se fué por desconfiado. (3.2899-2902)
>
> (Their fates were switched around. Enrico, although so bad, saved himself, and this one went to hell because of his lack of faith.)

Notes

1. In Jackson, *Melancholia and Depression*, 326. See also Jean Starobinsky's discussion of St. Hildegard's writings on melancholy and original sin, in *History of the Treatment of Melancholy*, 35.
2. Burton, *Anatomy of Melancholy*, 28.
3. Santa Cruz, "Diagnostio et cura affecctuum melancholicorum," 35-36 and Mercado, *Dialogos de Philosophia*, fol. Xiiii.
4. Henryk Ziomek, *A History of Spanish Golden Age Drama*, 93.
5. Babb, *Elizabethan Malady*, 47-54; Jackson, *Melancholia and Depression*, 72. A particularly accessible sixteenth-century Spanish account of the dangers of melancholia for members of monasteries and convents written by one from their ranks is found in St. Teresa of Avila's *Las fundaciones*, ed. Guido Mancini (Madrid: Iter Ediciones, 1970), 86-90.
6. Standford M. Lyman, *The Seven Deadly Sins*, 14-15.
7. Siegfried Wenzel, *The Sin of Sloth: "Acedia" in Medieval Thought and Literature*, 174-76.
8. Ibid., 170-71, 179; see also Starobinski, 31-35, 325-41 and Jackson, *Melancholia and Depression*, 65-77, 325-41.
9. Henry W. Sullivan discusses what he considers Tirso's consistent depiction of the privileged status accorded the individual will and its freedom in the pursuit of personal goals. He asserts: "This subordination of intellect, energy and ethical nicety to the attainment of an end determined by the individual will may be termed an ethical voluntarism. . . . Tirsian *voluntad* desires ends and employs manipulative, intelligent cunning to obtain that end" (*Tirso de Molina and the Drama of the Counter Reformation*, 171). I would, nevertheless, argue that the intellect is not subordinated to the will in melancholy characters such as Paulo, for in Tirso's straightforward representation of the faculties of the rational soul—the reason, the memory, and the will—it is the reason or the intellect that contemplates and interprets what is good and what is evil and then informs the will of its determination. The will, which desires the good and rejects the evil, causes physical action toward the good through the sensitive passions and thus functions as the primary controlling agent in the human soul. It is, however, important to understand the essential role of the intellect in the determination of good toward which the will moves. As in all cases of melancholy, the reasoning process of the mind is disrupted in various ways, and the manipulative energies of the religious melancholic, like those of the scholar, are better understood as originating in the overly contemplative intellect. Certainly, the ends sought by Paulo are very much products of his melancholic intellect.
10. Ibid., 63.
11. *Tratado*, not paginated.
12. Murillo y Velarde, *Aprobacion de ingenios*, fols. 21v, 29r, 28r, 33v.
13. Babb, *Elizabethan Malady*, 19, views medicine and psychology as interconnected in the Renaissance.
14. *Aprobacion de ingenios*, fol. 21r.
15. Daniel Rogers, "Introduction" to *El condenado por desconfiado*, by Tirso de Molina, 24.
16. Tirso de Molina, *El condenado por desconfiado,* ed. Ciriaco Morón and Rolena Adorno, act 1, verses 1-4. Subsequent references (act and verse) will be cited in the text.
17. *Aprobacion de ingenios*, fol. 98v.

18. Babb, *Elizabethan Malady*, 48.
19. Freylas, *Conocimiento, curacion y preservacion*, section not paginated.
20. *Aprobacion de ingenios*, fols. 31r, 30r-33r.
21. Babb, *Elizabethan Malady*, 48-49.
22. On the supernatural powers of melancholics, see *Melancholia and Depression*, 325-41; on pathological delusion, see 327-28.
23. *Conocimiento, curacion y preservacion*, section not paginated.
24. *Aprobacion de ingenios*, fols. 73v-74r.
25. Ibid., fol. 29r.
26. Ibid., fol. 38r.
27. Babb, *Elizabethan Malady*, 48.
28. Ibid., 49.
29. For a cogent discussion, see Sullivan, *Drama of the Counter Reformation*, 13-69.
30. Lyons, *Voices of Melancholy*, 23, 35.
31. Babb, *Elizabethan Malady*, 84.
32. Some of the examples of this practice are noted in Babb, *Elizabethan Malady*, and include Robert Greene's Duke Valdracko in *Planetomachia* and Conrade in Shakespeare's *Much Ado About Nothing*. See Babb's discussion of melancholy villains (85-91).
33. Jackson, *Melancholia and Depression*, 68; see also Babb, *Elizabethan Malady*, 52.
34. Lyons, *Voices of Melancholy*, 63.
35. In *The Canterbury Tales*, ed. A. C. Cawley, 575.

EL BURLADOR DE SEVILLA

CRITICAL COMMENTARY

Archimede Marni (essay date 1952)

SOURCE: "Did Tirso Employ Counterpassion in His *Burlador de Sevilla*?" in *Hispanic Review*, Vol. XX, No. 2, April, 1952, pp. 123-33.

[*In the following essay, Marni considers the question of whether or not counterpassion (the principal that considers if a punishment fits a crime) was used in de Molina's* El burlador de Sevilla.]

The spiritual damnation of Don Juan by Tirso de Molina posed no problem either to the famous Mercedario himself or to his contemporary fellow-Christians. For them it was a simple matter of dogma. Divine justice dooms unrepentant mortal sinners to everlasting punishment.[1] But does not Don Juan express repentance?

> Deja que llame quien me confiese y absuelva,

he cries, only to be told

> No hay lugar; ya acuerdas tarde,

and to feel, immediately thereafter, the pangs of hell:

> ¡Que me quemo! ¡Que me abraso! ¡Muerto soy![2]

The modern reader is inclined to ask: "Did God deal fairly with Don Juan?" And there is further cause for modern uneasiness in this matter. It would even appear that the Lord, the all-mighty Judge, rejecting the standard rules of chivalry and fair play, had recourse to *deceit* in meting out His punishment. In the scene in which Don Juan has kept his promise to come to dinner with the statue, we read:

Don Juan. Ya he cenado; haz que levanten la mesa.

Don Gon. Dame esa mano; no temas, la mano dame.

Don Juan. ¿Eso dices? ¿Yo, temor? ¡Que me abraso! ¡No me abrases con tu fuego . . . no me aprietes! (pp. 288-289).

But Don Gonzalo does not let him go. Instead, the *burlador* dies and sinks into Hell.

The deceit we have mentioned, especially as contained in the *no temas* of Don Gonzalo, seems evident, and could be singled out as incompatible with the Christian concept of God. Such being the case, and without wishing to take upon himself the role of an *advocatus Dei*, one may suggest a possible solution of the problem by calling attention to the principle of *counterpassion* as employed by Dante in choosing the *kind* of punishment bestowed upon the denizens of the *Inferno*. Not that we wish to claim an influence on Tirso by the great Italian poet. It may be true, however, that if Fr. Gabriel Téllez was the *gran teólogo*[3] that most of his commentators have seen in him, he must have come upon the idea of counterpassion either in his reading of St. Thomas' commentary on the Fifth Book of Aristotle's *Ethics*, or in his other theological studies.[4] Counterpassion may be defined as the principle whereby justice demands that a sin receive retribution first and foremost in *kind*, "that the penalty should be of the same sort as the injury inflicted."[5] But in order to clarify and limit the meaning of the term to the needs of this paper, it may be sufficient to recall how Dante used it, bearing in mind at the same time that some of the best examples abandon the realm of the physical for the more elusive psychological and spiritual. An excellent specimen of the latter type presents itself to the poet immediately upon crossing the portals of Hell. A pandemonium assails his ears:

> Diverse lingue, orribili favelle,
> parole di dolore, accenti d'ira,

voci alte e fioche, e suon di man con elle
facevano un tumulto, il qual s'aggira
sempre in quell'aura sanza tempo tinta,
come la rena quando turbo spira.

It comes from people who in life had been either lukewarm or neutral, mingled together to form the numberless throng

. . . di coloro
che visser sanza infamia e sanza lodo.[6]

According to Dante, such men and women, far from being calm and collected on earth, are subconsciously in constant agitation and turmoil, pursued and driven on by an ever-present fear of being disturbed. Thus by choosing the way of inaction they have really cast themselves in such spiritual unrest that, when they reach their proper place in Hell, their true state is made manifest. For, as the poet continues:

E io, che riguardai, vidi una insegna
che girando correva tanto ratta,
che d'ogni posa mi parea indegna;
e dietro le venìa sì lunga tratta
di gente, ch'io non averei creduto
che morte tanta n'avesse disfatta . . .
Questi sciaurati, che mai non fur vivi,
erano ignudi, stimolati molto
da mosconi e da vespe ch'eran ivi. (*Inf.*, III, 52-66.)

Thus counterpassion is used both to disclose the real spiritual nature of these wretches and to prescribe their fitting punishment. A second example that we may recall concerns the punishment meted out to tyrants and conquerors. In life these criminals have reveled in bloodshed. Consequently, in death their just punishment consists of being confined perpetually in a river of boiling blood (*Inf.*, XII, 100-139.) A third and last case, one in which the poet makes sure that his readers shall not let pass un-noticed the source of the type of punishment he chooses for the various sins, deals with the Provençal poet Bertran de Born. Tradition reports him as having aroused young Henry of England against his own father, Henry II. Dante meets Bertran in the ninth pouch of the Eighth Circle, where dwell the sowers of discord, that is, those who have severed what nature has united.

Io vidi certo, ed ancor par ch'io 'l veggia,
un busto sanza capo andar sì come
andavan li altri della trista greggia;
e 'l capo tronco tenea per le chiome,
pèsol con mano a guisa di lanterna . . .
Quando diritto al piè del ponte fue,
levò 'l braccio alto con tutta la testa,
per appressarne le parole sue,
che fuoro: "Or vedi la pena molesta . . .
E perchè tu di me novella porti,
sappi ch' i' son Bertram dal Bornio, quelli
che diedi al Re giovane i ma' conforti
Io feci il padre e 'l figlio in sè rebelli . . .
Perch'io parti' così giunte persone,
partito porto il mio cerebro, lasso!,
dal suo principio ch'è in questo troncone
Così s'osserva in me lo contrapasso." (*Inf.*, XXVIII, 118-142.)

Summing up, in all three of the above passages it is to be noted that: 1. The quality of the punishment is given prominence over the quantity. 2. Taken allegorically, these episodes, as do most of the others portrayed in the *Inferno*, represent evil men, not so much as they are in Hell, but as they actually live on earth. 3. The validity of the justice involved, the counterpassion, is confirmed only because the sinners have commited their crimes of their own free will.[7]

If Tirso's paternity of ***El condenado por desconfiado*** were universally accepted, one could cite with more confidence some passages extremely applicable to our discussion, since they treat explicitly of the spiritual state of sinners both in life and death. Again an example from the *Inferno* by way of clarification. Appalled by the inhuman aspect of treachery, Dante wonders how a person guilty of such a sin can remain alive, that is, continue as a member of the human community. As a matter of fact, he doesn't, as Dante is told upon reaching Tolomea, the second last place he visits in Hell. Here the explanation is given how it is that Branca Doria, who "as yet is not dead, but eats and drinks, and sleeps and puts on garments," has actually been there for several years already:

sappie che tosto che l'anima trade
come fec'io, il corpo suo l'è tolto
da un demonio, che poscia il governa
mentre che 'l tempo suo tutto sia volto.
Ella ruina in sì fatta cisterna. (*Inf.*, XXXIII, 129-133.)

Similarly in the ***Condenado,*** Tirso on three different occasions refers to Enrico as a body whose soul has left it, and is already suffering the torments of Hell:

Paulo. A éste han llamado Enrico
Pedrisco. Será otro.
¿Querías tú que fuese este mal hombre,
que en vida está ya ardiendo en los infiernos?

And ten verses below:

Pedrisco. Mire y calle,
que somos pobres, y este *desalmado*
no nos eche en la mar.

Finally, six pages later:

Pedrisco. Pues aqueste ya está ardiendo
en los infiernos.[8]

In other words, as far as Pedrisco is concerned, and unbeknown to him (but perhaps not so to Tirso de Molina!), Enrico represents a perfect example of Aristotelian-Thomistic counterpassion. The equation that like begets like, or better still, that like *is* like is clearly portrayed. Fiendish Enrico behaves like a devil because it *is* the devil who is in control of his body while his soul "ya está ardiendo en los infiernos."

Transferring this to the case of Don Juan, it follows that if it may be proved that Fr. Gabriel Téllez looked upon him as a *desalmado*, as one already in Hell, then no deceit could have been involved in the oft-quoted "dame esa mano." Don Gonzalo's request and his action in dragging him down with the sinking tomb would exist in the play merely as a symbol, and solely for the benefit of the un-indoctrinated spectator.

The ***Burlador*** contains much more internal evidence of counterpassion, whether intentional or subconscious, than the ***Condenado.*** Indeed, the play opens with a clear-cut example of its use even in lay justice. It concerns the way the King of Naples reacts towards Duchess Isabela upon discovering her moral transgression. With utter indifference to her presence, he orders Don Pedro to take her in custody. This slight hurts her pride, so she addresses the King saying:

> Gran señor, volvedme el rostro.

To which the King significantly replies:

> Ofensa a mi espalda hecha
> es justicia y es razón
> castigalla a espaldas vueltas. (p. 173.)

That is to say, both justice and reason find it equitable that the transgression be punished in *kind*. Isabela has of her own free will decided to ignore the obligation and courtesy she owes to her king. Consequently, counterpassion dictates that she receive disregard and discourtesy from him in his administration of justice.[9] The two following examples are, most likely, more indicative of Tirso's pattern of thinking or imagination than of intentional counterpassion, but still they hold to the theme that like begets like. One appears at the end of the first *Jornada*, where Tisbea, by this time a much wiser woman, exclaims:

> Yo soy la que hacía siempre
> de los hombres burla tanta;
> que siempre las que hacen burla,
> vienen a quedar burladas. (p. 210.)

The other is found in the comment of Catalinón upon being told by Don Juan that he intends to deceive Doña Ana:

> No lo apruebo.
> Tú pretendes que escapemos
> una vez, señor, burlados;
> que el que vive de burlar
> burlado habrá de escapar
> pagando tantos pecados
> de una vez. (p. 227.)

Of similar import is the striking parallel in phraseology between the utter indifference with which the *burlador* is willing to visit the world with fire and brimstone provided he (or his friends in evil) gain his evil purposes, and the retributory mode of his death. Upon being informed by the Marqués de la Mota that Doña Ana, who loves the *marqués*, has been destined by the king for another man's hand, Don Juan gives his friend the following advice:

> Quien tan satisfecho vive
> de su amor, ¿desdichas teme?
> Sacalda, solicitalda,
> escribilda y engañalda,
> y el mundo se abrase y queme. (p. 224)

Little suspecting, however, that much sooner than he had anticipated, he was going to need practically the same identical words for himself, as the stony hand of the Comendador refused to let his go:

> Don Juan. ¡Que me quemo! ¡Que me abraso! (p. 289.)

Counterpassion plays, likewise, an important, if not decisive, role in the search for a solution to two major problems arising in the death scene of the ***Burlador***. The first has been already mentioned—the presumed deceit involved in Don Gonzalo's "Dame esa mano, no temas." The second has to do with the denying of a confessor *in extremis* to Don Juan.

In asking for Don Juan's hand, even if with a deceitful intention, the Comendador was acting fully in accordance with the principle of counterpassion, since he was dealing with a man who had made deception the norm of his moral life. Indeed, on at least three occasions Don Juan had given his hand in false faith.

> dame, duquesa, la mano (p. 166),

he said to Isabela when the latter called for help upon discovering her betrayal. And to the hesitating Aminta his false words were:

> dame esa mano[10]
> y esta voluntad confirma con ella;

and again a few verses below:

> Juro a esta mano, señora . . .
> de cumplirte la palabra. (p. 259.)

As for the deceitful intention attributed to Don Gonzalo when he asked Don Juan not to be afraid to give him his hand, an intention justified by the often quoted "no temas," it may be properly claimed that the two words were spoken for quite a different reason. There seems to be justification that they were uttered with a taunting feeling of scorn, since Don Gonzalo felt convinced that the *burlador* was a coward at heart. In fact, he told him so at least on two occasions. Once as he lay dying:

> Seguiráte mi furor;
> que es traidor, y el que es traidor
> es traidor porque es cobarde. (p. 238.)

And once again at the church when Don Juan came to keep his supper date:

> Don Gon. El muerto soy, no te espantes.
> No entendí que me cumplieras
> la palabra, según haces
> de todos burla.

Don Juan. ¿Me tienes
en opinión de cobarde?

Don Gon. Sí, que aquella noche huíste
de mí cuando me mataste. (p. 286.)

The second problem, the denying of a confessor to Don Juan, even though he asked for one, involves more significant theological issues. Consequently, it may find in the principle of counterpassion a more solid theological explanation, at least as far as the Aristotelian-Thomistic concept of Justice envisaged it. Basically, it is one entailing the efficacy of sufficient grace. In other words, just to what point may a sinner persist in his evil doing, confident that Divine Mercy will not remain deaf to his death-bed repentance, a repentance perhaps arising more through fear than real contrition? In the case of Buonconte da Montefeltro, whom Dante meets in the Ante-Purgatory, among those who through violent death have postponed repentance until extremely late, the Italian poet opines that it is never too late to repent. Or, as the devil put it when he came to take away the soul of the well-known sinner, Buonconte:

O tu del ciel, perchè mi privi?
Tu te ne porti di costui l'etterno
per una lacrimetta che 'l mi toglie. (*Purg.*, V, 105-107.)

On the other hand, not all those who have treated the problem seem to have been so lenient as Dante. For instance, St. Augustine has been quoted by Martín de Azpilcueta as doubting the *real* (but not the presumptive) salvation of those who seek confession after delaying until death is upon them. Of greater significance to the present discussion, however, is Azpilcueta's own opinion, since he was both a Spaniard and practically a contemporary of Tirso de Molina. In his *Manual de confesores y penitentes* we find the following passage so decisively applicable to the case of the *burlador*:

> . . . se engañan muchos pẽsando, q̃ qualquier dolor, y herir de pechos, y qualquier *Miserere mei,* basta para el perdõ de los pecados mortales, y es contriciõ: pues para ello es menester arrepentimiẽto tã generoso y qualificado como està dicho. Ni repugna a esto q̃ los q̃ muerẽ estãdo en pecado mortal sin confesiõ, se presumẽ morir arrepentidos, y cõtritos, si muestrã algunas señales dello, como si piden cõfessiõ, o jurã obedecer a los mandados de la yglesia: o si no pueden hablar, leuãtan las manos al cielo, o hierẽ los pechos, como lo dize Host. Porq̃ esto es verdad, para effecto de presumir, q̃ murierõ cõtritos, y de no denegarles la absoluciõ de la descomuniõ, ni la sepultura. Pero no, pa. effecto de morir delãte de Dios verdaderamẽte cõtritos, si dtro de sus almas no tuvierõ arrepẽtimiw̃to en la manera susodicha qualificado.[11]

Don Juan had waited too long before asking for a confessor. He did not even ask for one immediately upon feeling the hellish fire pervade his whole being. Instead he attempted to defend himself and punish the statue of the rash Comendador as he had done in life by murdering the real one. He cries out:

Con la daga he de matarte.

And only when he realizes that he is striking a vain apparition:

Mas ¡ay! que me canso en vano
de tirar golpes al aire,

does he beg:

Deja que llame
quien me confiese y absuelva. (p. 289.)

Don Gonzalo, however, is not a mere man. He has already told Don Juan:

No alumbres, que en gracia estoy. (p. 277.)

He is in contact with the Infinite and is not obliged, as St. Augustine is, to *presume*. He *knows* that Don Juan's request for confession does not come from an *aborrecimiento del pecado*, and so is perfectly justified in refusing him a confessor.

Taken from the point of view of counterpassion, the refusal is quite as valid, if not more so, since it approaches the problem less with respect to Divine Mercy, than as a basic case of Divine Justice, if we bear in mind the definition of counterpassion as the principle whereby the penalty should be of the same sort as the injury inflicted. It is *just* that Don Juan be refused the opportunity to confess, since on repeated occasions he has sneered at the idea of taking time to do so. Even his own father's warning that some day it might be too late proved completely useless:

Don Diego. Mira que, aunque al parecer
Dios te consiente y aguarda,
su castigo no se tarda,
y que castigo ha de haber
para los que profanáis
su nombre, que es jüez fuerte
Dios en la muerte.
Don Juan. ¿En la muerte?
¿Tan largo me lo fiáis?[12]
De aquí allá hay gran jornada.

Don Diego. Breve te ha de parecer. (p. 231.)

And it proved to be *breve*, indeed!

Thus, by the exercise of his Free Will in evil actions, and by this obstinate persistence in them, the *burlador* has so plunged himself in sin that as one reads the play, the impression is gained that Tirso looked upon him, too, as a *desalmado,* as he had done with Enrico in the ***Condenado***. The association of Don Juan's name, or person, with that of the devil appears early in the play. Don Pedro first suggests the relationship as he informs Octavio of what has taken place in the King's palace soon after the deception of Doña Isabela:

pero pienso que el Demonio
en él tomó forma humana. (p. 178.)

In the same act, Don Juan himself utters a verse, as he begins the siege of Tisbea, that in its figurative meaning may be frought with tragic irony, as he says to her:

DON JUAN. Muerto soy.

TISBEA. ¿Cómo, si andáis?

DON JUAN. Ando en pena, como veis. (p. 195.)

Next, it is Batricio who, on seeing Don Juan appear as the uninvited guest at his wedding feast, feels like uttering "retro, Satanas" as he complains:

Imagino
que el demonio le envió. (p. 244.)

Finally, his servant, Catalinón, who we may be justified in believing was as close to his master as any other living person, and on whose judgment we should rely with complete confidence, calls Don Juan by his right name when, in apostrophising the luckless betrothed of Aminta, he says:

¡Desdichado tú que has dado
en manos de Lucifer! (p. 246.)[13]

Such then, is the real person Fray Gabriel Téllez has portrayed—a devil incarnate, who, living up to his nature, is first and foremost a *deceiver*, and who gloats over his evil nature. One may conclude that, by the Aristotelian-Thomistic concept of Justice as counterpassion, the words:

Dame esa mano;
no temas, la mano dame,

imply no deceit.

Notes

1. See below, quotation from Azpilcueta, for a justification of this statement.
2. Tirso de Molina, *El burlador de Sevilla*, ed. Américo Castro, Clásicos Castellanos (Madrid, 1932), p. 289. All future references to the *Burlador* will be to this edition.
3. The theological erudition of Tirso is commonly recognized among his critics. While in Santo Domingo, Tirso "leyó tres cursos de teología," as Castro states (ed. cit., p. viii).
4. For a succinct discussion of counterpassion, see Alan H. Gilbert, *Dante's Conception of Divine Justice* (Durham, N. C., 1925).
5. Gilbert, op. cit., p. 76.
6. *Inferno*, III, 25-36, ed. Giuseppe Vandelli, Società Dantesca Italiana (Milano, Hoepli, 1929). All future references to the *Divina Commedia* will be to this edition.
7. This point must be borne in mind presently when we shall examine the various examples of counterpassion, and the death scene, in the *Burlador*.
8. Tirso de Molina, *La prudencia en la mujer, El condenado por desconfiado* (Buenos Aires, Espasa-Calpe, 1943), pp. 124 and 130. The word *desalmado*, underscored by this writer, can have only a spiritual meaning since Enrico is still alive.
9. The inseparable inter-relation between free will, justice, and counterpassion must not be lost sight of from now on.
10. Note that these are the exact words that Don Gonzalo addresses to the *burlador* in the death scene (p. 276).
11. Martín de Azpilcueta, *Manual de confesores y penitentes* (Barcelona, 1567), p. 7. The writer is indebted for this quotation and suggestion for its use and application to Professor Otis H. Green.
12. This has been Don Juan's standard answer to anyone who has seen fit to warn him of the inevitable retribution. Undoubtedly it has been a kind of leitmotif with which Tirso has stressed his central idea that finally time will not be available for Don Juan's repentance.
13. Arturo Farinelli has already seen in Don Juan the Devil himself. He states in his "*Don Giovanni, note critiche*": "Non patteggia col demonio perchè è demonio egli stesso." *Gior. Stor. d. Lett. Ital.*, XXVII, 2.

Frank Sedwick (essay date 1955)

SOURCE: "*El Burlador*, *Don Giovanni*, and the Popular Concept of Don Juan," in *Hispania*, Vol. XXXVIII, No. 2, May, 1955, pp. 173-77.

[*In the following essay, Sedwick concludes that neither de Molina's* El burlador *nor Mozart's* Don Giovanni *ultimately define the concept of Don Juan.*]

Tirso de Molina's ***Burlador de Sevilla*** is, among other things, a drama of the collective erotic subconscious, a Renaissance glorification of manly beauty and individual courage, and a baroque theological tragedy. [A paper read at the 36th Annual Meeting of the AATSP, New York, December 29-30, 1954.] Mozart's *Don Giovanni* portrays a *burlador burlado*, amateurishly gross in the art of love, and sketchily depicted by the librettist, Lorenzo Da Ponte. Mozart's music notwithstanding, Da Ponte lacked the tools for giving sufficient substance to an opera potentially the culmination of a great human and literary theme. Then, too, Tirso's great figure would necessarily lose its magic force in the atmosphere of Figaro. Yet the popular concept of Don Juan, the connotation which the man on the street has for him, is neither tragic nor comic, neither the *burlador* of Tirso nor the *burlador burlado* of Da Ponte and Mozart.

Let us first define the "popular concept" of Don Juan and then proceed to seek its source. To the man on the street,

Don Juan means "lady's man," a hero to be identified with the inner romantic life of each individual as a suppressed ideal, a man to be envied. I formulated this definition after I had put a question to each of eighteen people, men and women, not likely to be well educated, including such everyday people as a barber, a truck driver, a grocery clerk, and a salesgirl in a small store. The question was: "What does the statement 'He is a Don Juan' mean to you?" If there was a significant reply, I followed it with the query: "Where do you think the expression 'Don Juan' comes from?" Sixteen of the eighteen answered the first question to the general effect that a Don Juan was a "lady's man." To two it meant nothing. As to the second question, none of the sixteen had any idea of the specific origin of the expression; four offered the correct "guess" that it was taken from "some book." None knew precisely which book or books, although three thought that it was Spanish. None had ever heard of the opera *Don Giovanni* or of ***El burlador de Sevilla***.

The favorable conception of Don Juan today as a man of charm to whom women are strongly and quickly attracted has come to exist despite the customary treatment of the theme in which Don Juan invariably gains his conquests, and hence his reputation, by deceit rather than through pure charm, his magnetic personality notwithstanding. It is almost impossible to find a Don Juan work in which the libertine gains his end with no trickery involved, even though he has a certain personal allurement capable of stimulating affection at first. The scholar knows Don Juan too well to admire him openly, but the mass-man envies Don Juan because *he knows only the favorable unearned increment of Don Juan's personality*.

To seek the source of universal popular Donjuanism is to begin by examining the origin of the legend and then by tracing its circuitous route in Europe through the centuries as a drama for the stage. It is lost effort to affirm either that the theme of the debauchee originates with Tirso, or in Lope de Vega's *Dineros son calidad*, or in Juan de la Cueva's *El infamador*, or that it goes back to a fifteenth-century auto *El ateista fulminado*, or to a Leonese *romance* "Pa' misa diba un galán," or that it is recorded first in Ovid's *Ars Amandi*. Without doubt this very elementary theme of all themes must have been one of the first, in one form or another, not only in all literature, but also in universal folklore. Indeed, one author, Dorothy E. MacKay, in a book entitled *The Double Invitation in the Legend of Don Juan*, points out the abundance of Don Juan legends in the *Romancero*, as well as the fact that the "double invitation" was well established in tradition long before the time of Tirso. Until the appearance of the MacKay work in 1943, the only intensive investigation of this legend was that done by Menéndez Pidal in *Sobre los orígenes de "El convidado de piedra"* in 1906.

Tirso was the first writer to treat effectively and profoundly the religious element in connection with the intrepid seducer. The whole of his play was original, even if the parts were not. Still Tirso's success has been largely aleatory, for it is more his means that has been elaborated upon, the machinations of Don Juan, than his end, the moral. The critics, however, are still not in agreement as to the true meaning of the specific kind of power complex with which Tirso endowed his Don Juan. Ramiro de Maeztu intimates that Don Juan is an atheist; Guillermo Díaz-Plaja's thesis is that the *burlador* is merely a worshipper of women who is typical of the Neoplatonism and *dolce stil nuovo* of the Renaissance; Marañón states that the fact that Don Juan is not attracted to women as individuals, but rather as a genus, indicates his immaturity and adolescence; Farinelli even attempts to prove that Don Juan is of Italian origin. Said Armesto accepted this challenge to a polemic and tried to vindicate the originality of Don Juan in favor of Spain. His view was seconded by Unamuno, who further declared Don Juan to be, within Spain, of Galician, not Sevillian, origin. Yet Unamuno frequently noted the etymological relationship between *Tenorio* and *tenor*—tenor—and in Unamuno's play *El hermano Juan*, Don Juan is impotent and feminine, while his women are the seductresses, not the seduced. Only a partial list of those who have published significant books or essays on the *Burlador* would include such other names as: John Austen, Hans Heckel, Cotarelo y Mori, Schroeder, Agustín, Gendarme de Bévotte, Casalduero, Boelte, Castro, Gillet, Grau, Osma, Menéndez y Pelayo, Spitzer, Muñoz Peña, Ríos de Lampérez, Templin, Bergamín, Lomba, Rank, and even Kierkegaard. Nearly every scholar of note in the field of Hispanic letters ultimately has something to say concerning Don Juan.

After the first edition of Tirso de Molina's ***El burlador de Sevilla*** in 1630, the legend became known in Italy through the dramas of Giacinto Cicognini and Onofrio Giliberto, with later fame reserved for Goldoni's *Don Giovanni Tenorio*. In France, versions of the legend by Dorimon and Villiers preceded Molière's well-known *Don Juan, ou Le festin de pierre*, dated 1665. Molière's play was followed by dramas with the same theme by no less than ten French imitators from 1669 up to 1921. In Spain and in Spanish America, Zorrilla's *Don Juan Tenorio* has been a much more successful imitation of the legend than two other Spanish plays by Alonso Cordova y Maldonado and Antonio de Zamora. From England we have Shadwell's *The Libertine*, Shaw's *Man and Superman*, and Byron's long poem *Don Juan*, although the last two can hardly qualify as traditional Don Juan works. Various German, Dutch, Scandinavian, and Russian Don Juans have appeared from time to time. Depending on his taste, the reader today can find nearly any kind of Don Juan: hypocrite, amiable, converted, saved, effeminate, aged, degenerate, or acquaintance of Faust. There are at least nine major paintings on the theme, including one Goya, and innumerable musical versions.

Nowadays the most often-seen musical version of Don Juan is that of Mozart's opera *Don Giovanni*, presented for the first time on October 29, 1787, at Prague. Five unimportant Italian musical versions of the legend preceded Mozart's opera, but Mozart and Da Ponte imitated only one in detail. It was the Giuseppe Bertati (composer)-Giovanni Bertati (librettist) little-known opera *Don Giovanni Tenorio, o sia Il convitato di pietra*, given first at Venice only nine months before Mozart's opera appeared. Da Ponte followed much of the Gazzaniga libretto scene by scene, used most of the characters, giving some of them different names, and duplicated the dialogue of borrowed scenes almost word for word. Incidentally, one of the rare copies of the libretto to Gazzaniga's opera may be found in the Library of Congress. It is, however, Mozart's opera which has become famous, and Gazzaniga's which has been all but forgotten.

Several literary critics who have commented on Don Juan in opera agree with a number of music critics that Mozart's *Don Giovanni* was intended to be, and is a stirring tragedy, this despite the fact that Mozart himself classified it as *dramma giocoso*. Jacinto Grau, for example, in his *Don Juan en el drama*, 1944, admits that *Don Giovanni* has comical elements but he asserts that ". . . el milagroso genio de Mozart adivina la grandeza del Burlador y tras . . . el pateismo irónico de la escena del cementerio, con Leporello, el Comendador y Don Juan, nos da en el último acto, una honda enocion profundamente dramática. . . ." Christopher Benn, a music critic, complains in his book *Mozart on the Stage*, 1945, that the modern audience does not take *Don Giovanni* seriously enough. He says: "A production of *Don Giovanni* must aim not merely at good presentation of Mozart's music, but at making the opera as a whole convincing to the modern audience." His point of view that this opera "should send a cold shiver down the back" is not an uncommon one among opera critics. Actually the opera has strayed as far in spirit from its Tirso Molinan ancestry as have all the other versions. Mozart's *Don Giovanni* is not convincing as a tragedy, nor can it be prescribed to be so simply because the opera does have a leitmotif suggesting tragic overtones in the music. Also one should bear in mind how very much of the story and dialogues are taken from the Gazzaniga libretto, which makes not the slightest pretense of tragedy.

It should be apparent to anyone who has read Tirso and heard Mozart's opera that the intrigues and amorous adventures of Don Giovanni are incontrovertibly more humorous than those of Tirso's Don Juan. For example, one clever scene in the opera is the exchange of cloaks between Don Giovanni and the servant Leporello in order to strand Leporello with Elvira. At the very beginning of the opera, the enumeration of the *catalogo delle belle* establishes the mirthful atmosphere, so that by the time Don Giovanni tricks Masetto into a beating the audience will surely snicker. In spite of all his bravado, Don Giovanni of the opera often takes on the aspect of the henpecked husband who attempts to philander—and unsuccessfully.

The most salient feature of this operatic Don Juan is that he is constantly foiled, although he has more free rein than in Tirso and at least as much as he has in any of the interim works. There are neither Tirso's Don Diego, nor Don Pedro, nor King, nor any strong male figures, as there are for example in Molière and Goldoni, to keep him in check or at least to admonish him. Mozart's foppish Ottavio is surely no threat; the Commendatore dies early in the first act; Leporello is wholly subservient; and the peasant Masetto, the only male capable of antagonizing Don Giovanni, is consumed by his own jealousy and too much handicapped by his low social status to be an effectual avenger or even reprover. It will be remembered that in Tirso, Doña Ana is the only one of the four female victims who escapes consummated ravishment by Don Juan, if his dying words to the statue can be believed: "A tu hija no ofendí, / Que vió mis engaños antes." Apparently Don Juan has conquests in all the other versions, but in Mozart's opera Don Giovanni has not one single success! One has the impression that the libertine of the opera is playing the game for the fun of it, that he does not have to win to be satisfied. In other words, he is an amateur; and his catalogue, evaluated on the basis of his present accomplishments, is a fiction. He is not interested in Elvira. Anna informs Ottavio that she has resisted Don Giovanni successfully, as in Tirso, and Don Giovanni fails on each occasion to conquer the peasant girl Zerlina. The result is that Mozart's Don Juan fails to live up to his reputation and, furthermore, emerges from each situation as the *burlador burlado*. Indeed it seems incongruous to find in the opera a libertine who actually is jealous when, after the exchange of cloaks with his servant, Leporello makes love to Elvira with too much zeal. That Don Juan should experience jealousy at all is a serious alteration of his traditional character. So much does Tirso's tiger shrink to Mozart's mouse that only tradition justifies the intervention of the supernatural at the end. Mozart's Don Juan, therefore, cannot be the one definitive of Donjuanism in the popular concept, nor can his opera be as tragic as the overtones in the music suggest, or even as somber as many believe it to be.

Probably moved by their enthusiasm for the opera, some interpreters of Mozart, among them Edward Dent, Christopher Benn, and Pierre Jean Jouve, give one the impression that both the definitive form and popular conception of Don Juan stem from Mozart's *Don Giovanni*. Nothing could be farther from the truth in consideration of the little currency which opera in general enjoys, as well as the fact that Mozart's Don Juan does not match the popular concept of Don Juan. Even few opera-goers know that *Giovanni* is Italian for *Juan*, or rather, if they do know, they attach no significance to it. It follows that the majority of opera lovers, both lay students and musicians, know little of the history or meaning of the Don Juan legend which they are seeing enacted. *Don Giovanni* is heard as just another opera, not as the musical interpretation of a famous legend; and the audience does not recognize its own popular conception of a Don Juan, a "lady's man," in Mozart's Don Giovanni, for it is not there.

What, then, is the origin of the popular concept of Don Juan, the hero, the suppressed ideal who is envied by men and to whom women are attracted? Surely it is not Tirso's play, little known even among Spaniards. Although the Don Juan of Molière has travelled somewhat farther than the other Don Juans, the rest of the many French Don Juans, like the German and Italian ones, are best known in their own regions, and little abroad except by *literati*. The English ones of Shaw and Byron are only points of departure for philosophical thought and have little to do with the traditional form of the legend. Mozart's opera *Don Giovanni* is probably the most universally-known version of the legend. Even though the Don Juan of Mozart is weaker, that is, less convincing as a tragic character, than the libertine of some of Mozart's predecessors, still because music can express better than literature all the necessary dash and vigor of Don Juan, the score gives the lines of the libretto a somewhat stronger libertine and, strong or weak, surely a picturesque one. Another picturesque and often-seen Don Juan is the *Don Juan Tenorio* of Zorrilla, the most popular Don Juan for Spanish-speaking people, being the expected dramatic presentation on the occasion of All Saints' Day, everywhere a national institution. Yet the fact is inescapable that Zorrilla's Don Juan is scarcely known outside of Spain and Spanish America. What remains, then, as the source of universal popular Donjuanism? Only the synthesis of all the various Don Juans. Don Juan of the popular concept is not derived from the opera, from Tirso, or from any one source, rather from all the sources together, and possibly with deeper roots in the folkloric aspects of the theme quite uninfluenced by any Don Juan play. This is evident when one considers that the man on the street's connotation for Don Juan, "lady's man," has no basis in any one literary work.

The thesis proposed, therefore, is that neither Tirso's play nor Mozart's opera may be designated the single, or even principal, source from which the popular concept of Don Juan emanates. This concept is best approximated by the synthesis of all Don Juan works, and—most important of all—with an added increment of personality not to be found in any single work. In other words, no writer has yet portrayed the Don Juan whom you and I knew before we began to read books and hear operas.

Bruce W. Wardropper (essay date 1957)

SOURCE: "*El Burlador de Sevilla*: A Tragedy of Errors," in *Philological Quarterly,* Vol. XXXVI, No. 1, January, 1957, pp. 61-71.

[*In the following essay, Wardropper presents an in-depth discussion of de Molina's* El burlador de Sevilla.]

"Todo este mundo es errar."[1]

The point about Tirso's Don Juan is, not that he is a profligate, but that he is a deceiver, a source of error. He broadcasts *burlas* about Spain and Italy. *Burlas* are contrived *engaños*, the opposite of *veras*. In Part I of *Don Quixote* the knight is the victim of a series of *engaños*, more or less fateful misunderstandings; but in Part II, especially in the events at the court of the Duke and Duchess, he is the victim of *burlas*, deliberately engineered misunderstandings. The aristocrats' pleasure, in their *casa de plazer*, is the fruit of mischief, of *la malicia*—the Satanic force in the allegory of the time. In this sense Don Juan too is Satanic:[2] out of malice he perverts the idea of truth held by others. ***El burlador de Sevilla***, then, like *Don Quixote, La vida es sueño, El criticon, Los sueños*, and so many other seventeenth-century Spanish works, is concerned with nothing less than an examination of the nature of truth, and man's perennial failure to apprehend it and live up to it.

Don Juan's motive in deceiving is the same one that caused the Duke and Duchess to establish an elaborate house and household of deception: selfish pleasure. The *burla* is a deceit practised for amusement, for sport; its object is to entertain. Thus Don Juan boasts:

> Sevilla a voces me llama
> *el Burlador*, y el mayor
> gusto que en mí puede haber
> es burlar una mujer
> y dejalla sin honor (II, 268-72).

El gusto, the hedonistic principle that Lope first equated with *lo justo*, and later opposed to it:[3] this is the primary motive of Don Juan, as it was of the Comendator in *Fuente Ovejuna*. In each case the result of identifying pleasure with justice is libertinage, *confusión*, anarchy.[4]

Don Juan's *burlas* are directed against all that is most sacred in the social order. He is an iconoclast, upturning conventional secular morality. Whereas the *pícaro* does not possess or understand "la negra que llaman honra,"[5] Don Juan appreciates and possesses it, but perversely seks to destroy it. As a result he is destroyed by honor.

Don Juan is a man of honor except in his dealings with women. Catalinón makes this clear in an aside:

> Como no le entreguéis vos
> moza o cosa que lo valga,
> bien podéis fiaros dél,
> que, cuanto en esto es cruel,
> tiene condición hidalga (II, 160-4).

In the game of seduction this occasionally honorable man will, nevertheless, use honor as a weapon against even a male opponent. The onslaught on Aminta is successful because her *novio* Batricio leaves the field, believing, through Don Juan's suggestion, that he has been dishonored by his wife-to-be. Don Juan exults:

> Con el honor le vencí,
> porque siempre los villanos
> tienen su honor en las manos,
> y siempre miran por sí . . .
> que el honor se fué al aldea
> huyendo de las ciudades (III, 101-4; 107-8).

With women, of course, the *burla* is successful because Don Juan, deemed to be a man of honor by his victims, gives a word he has no intention of keeping. He promises unequivocally and shamelessly; it is only when he is asked to swear that he allows himself a private escape clause. He does not hesitate to say to Tisbea:

> y te prometo de ser
> tu esposo (I, 930-1).

But when she agrees to be fully his only

> bajo la palabra y mano
> de esposo (I, 941-2),

he has to parody the formula of secret marriage or, as the Scots say, marriage by covenant:[6]

> Juro, ojos bellos,
> que mirando me matáis,
> de ser vuestro esposo (I, 942-4).

An oath taken on someone's beautiful eyes may deceive, but it does not bind. Soon he will try the same trick on Aminta, swearing by her hand. And when she insists on an oath containing a greater risk of perjury, he makes his false step:

> ruego a Dios
> que a traición y alevosía
> me dé muerte un hombre . . . muerto:
> que, vivo, ¡Dios no permita! (III, 279-82)

This aside, a mental reservation, is as much a joke as swearing by Tisbea's eyes. But, unfortunately for Don Juan, he has invoked the name of God, and his deceitful behavior has clashed for the first time with a realm of absolute truth and absolute power. For God has the power of miracles, and can turn this joke against its perpetrator.

But just as divine justice seizes on this step to punish Don Juan, honor—the secular moral code—catches him out too. For Don Juan, with men of his own social rank, keeps his word. Catalinón, a great believer in marriage as a remedy for the youthful sowing of wild oats, urges his master to go to the wedding that has been arranged with Isabela, instead of to the stone feast; Don Juan replies indignantly:

> ¿No ves que di mi palabra? (III, 867).

and rushes to his doom. Ironically, this word were better not kept. But Don Juan's honor was at stake. He has accepted the invitation proudly, insisting to the ghost that he is what at least four women know he is not: a man of his word and a gentleman.

> Honor
> tengo, y las palabras cumplo,
> porque caballero soy (III, 641-3).

If it is anything, honor is a part of the fabric of mutual trust that gives stability to the social order. It is supposed to make predictable the behavior of the *caballero* who claims to be honorable. Don Juan succeeds in his deceits precisely because he destroys the conventions on which human coexistence is based. His conduct thus threatens the whole social order. But in the same way his conduct is made possible because the social order has already been more or less corrupted; for Don Juan is, more than an eccentric phenomenon, a symptom. He is the greatest, not the sole, *burlador*; the Marqués de la Mota and other rakes run close on his heels. A rotten society has spawned these men who, knowing truth, despise it. For this reason ***El burlador de Sevilla*** carries a bitter social criticism.

The chief target is the institution of favoritism, *la privanza*. And the point about *la privanza* is that, while the King has an undoubted right to raise whom he pleases to positions of authority, those so favored have an especially hard moral responsibility: they must subordinate personal feelings to the public good. In other words, royal favorites should not themselves have favorites. But human nature being what it is, they do in fact give special treatment to their friends and relatives. A *privado* is therefore, almost by definition, one who betrays the royal trust. This doctrine, familiar to readers of Quevedo, is carefully enunciated in the play.

Both in Spain and in Naples the courts are dominated by relatives of Don Juan—Don Diego, his father, and Don Pedro, his uncle. This fact allows the deceiver to operate with impunity in both kingdoms. It also accounts for the atmosphere of political corruption that is apparent in the play. While there is nothing wrong with the social order itself, there is something wrong with those who head and administer it. And the error of these men is, not political, but ethical. Expediency, disguised as prudence, has replaced the moral judgment in them.

So in the first scene—in Naples—a picture is drawn of a realm governed by pleasure-seeking and expediency. When things go too far, when pleasure exceeds its limits, neither the King nor Don Pedro appeals to a moral principle: they simply try to save appearances. The King tries to hush up, in the name not of honor but of prudence,[7] the scandalous duping of the Duchess Isabela. Don Pedro disobeys the King's order to arrest the malefactor for reasons of family solidarity, and is thereby led to a series of lies and injustices which include the false accusation of the Duke Octavio, righted by the further wrong of allowing him to escape, in contravention of the royal command. Don Pedro tells Octavio that he is presumed to be guilty (knowing full well that it is his nephew who is really the guilty one), and yet explains to him the circumstantial evidence against him,

> por si acaso me engaño (I, 276).

In this way a highly placed official loses without qualms his personal integrity as a noble.[8]

Don Juan comes to count on receiving favors from favorites. He is sure that the law will never catch up with him:

Si es mi padre
el dueño de la justicia,
y es la privanza del rey,
¿qué temes? (III, 163-6)

If the law had intervened there would have been less tragedy. Don Juan would have committed fewer crimes and—what is more important, given the theological intent of the play—fewer sins. Fewer persons would have been involved in tragic situations of his making.

Thus, even from an ethical, non-social point of view, it would have been better if Don Juan had run afoul of the law. This is the meaning of Catalinón's reply to the question just quoted:

De los que privan
suele Dios tomar venganza
si delitos no castigan (III, 166-8).

Malefactors may be sure of ultimate divine punishment, but it is God's will that a preliminary temporal punishment should be meted out in this world.[9] Don Juan's career of debauchery is a clear example of how others are led to immorality when a sinner is left immune. In a certain sense the play is a plea for law enforcement.

Don Juan, then, deceives in a deceit-full society. It is hardly necessary to add that he also deceives himself. His self-deception—the distortion of his own moral values—is best studied in the situations calling for bravery. His courage is first established when he risks his life to save Catalinón from the waves. But this brave act is a consequence of his basic error: the assumption that death will not catch up with him until he is an old man. Bravery in Don Juan turns out to be a kind of rashness: a failure to estimate the odds against him, the result of a perverted sense of values. Catalinón admits his fear of attending the stone feast. Don Juan mocks him, asking, since he fears Don Gonzalo dead, what he would do if he were alive (III, 548-50). He crects this particular question into a general principle:

el temor y temer muertos
es más villano temor;
que si un cuerpo noble vivo,
con potencias y razón
y con alma, no se teme,
¿quién cuerpos muertos temió? (III, 678-83)

This, of course, makes nonsense of conventional beliefs. One is supposed to be afraid of the noumenal, as Catalinón is. The fact, and Don Gonzalo dying recognizes it, is that Don Juan is really a coward:

Seguiráte mi furor,
que eres traidor,
y el traidor es traidor porque es cobarde (II, 545-7).

At the end, in the presence of mortality, Don Juan is afraid:

¡Valgame Dios! todo el cuerpo
se ha bañado de un sudor,
y dentro de las entrañas
se me hiela el corazón (III, 664-7).

But he still maintains his fiction of fearlessness: "Yo, temor?" (III, 948) Rejection of this error, a frank recognition that there are times when men ought to be afraid, would have saved not only his life but his soul. It is probably admitted fear—of the Lord, of the noumenal—that saves Catalinón.

Don Diego's error consists in being too much a father, and too little a magistrate. The King decides to marry off and exile Don Juan, rather than punish him more severely, because of his father's merits:

y agradezea
sólo al merecimiento de su padre (II, 20-1).

Later, he bestows still one more dubious honor on the son, creating him Count of Lebrija, again because of the father's past services:

Merecéis mi favor dignamente,
que si aquí los servicios ponderamos,
me quedo atrás con el favor presente (III, 705-7).

Don Juan's treatment is based, not on what he is, but on what his father has done. He lives beyond the law in a reflected favor.

Now Don Diego sees nothing wrong in this. He consistently uses his influence at court to intervene in his son's behalf. He even has a certain grotesque pride in Don Juan's "tantas y tan extrañas mocedades" (II, 43). Too late he realizes his son's true nature. He is, as much as any of the deceived women, the dupe of Don Juan. Only when the evidence of wickedness accumulates is he disillusioned:

¡Ay hijo! ¡Qué mal me pagas
el amor que te he tenido! (III, 783-4)

Finally, when he consents to the execution of his son (III, 1023-7) he has forfeited the King's trust:

¡Esto mis privados hacen! (III, 1028)

What, fundamentally, is the King shocked at? Not at the human failing that causes Don Diego to shield his erring son, but rather at his basic assumption that youth excuses all excesses. This theme—the overindulgence of age for youth, and youth's disrespect for age—runs through the play. The elderly feel that young men must be allowed to sow their wild oats. In this attitude is another of the relaxations of strict justice of which Don Juan takes advantage. With his uncle he actually invokes the principle himself:

Mozo soy y mozo fuiste;
y pues que de amor supiste,
tenga disculpa mi amor (I, 62-4).

Don Pedro, in the name of *mocedades*, lets him escape. "Esa mocedad te engaña," (I, 117) he observes futilely, not realizing that it is he who has been deceived by a youthful guilt that he believes to be—somehow—innocence. Don Diego and Octavio almost draw swords on this same issue.

> OCTAVIO Eres viejo.
> DON DIEGO Ya he sido mozo en Italia.
>
> . . . . .
>
> OCTAVIO No vale *fuí*, sino soy.
> DON DIEGO Pues fuí y soy. *(Empuña.)* (III, 764-5; 770-1)

The point of this debate lies in the theological "message" of the play: that, since death comes unexpectedly, every moment may be one's last; that youth is as subject to sudden death as age; that repentance and absolution may not be possible at the moment of death.

To be a reminder of this fact is Catalinón's function. He is the voice of Don Juan's conscience, a constant reminder of death. The first time he fulfills his purpose, on the occasion of the seduction of Tisbea—

> Los que fingís y engañáis
> las mujeres desa suerte
> lo pagaréis en la muerte (I, 903-5)—

he provokes the famous response that becomes the principal refrain of the play: "¡Qué largo me lo fiáis!" Unperturbed, he continues to sermonize on these lines:

> Tú pretendes que escapemos
> una vez, señor, burlados,
> que el que vive de burlar
> burlado habrá de escapar
> pagando tantos pecados
> de una vez.
>
> DON JUAN ¿Predicador te vuelves, impertinente? (II, 308-13)

But each time he reminds his master "que hay castigo, pena y muerte" (III, 181) he hears the creditor's reply:

> Si tan largo me lo fiáis,
> vengan engaños.[10]

The imagery always calls to mind a system of banking. Don Juan never denies his debt—to God, not to society!—but always assumes that the foreclosure date will somehow never come round.[11]

Catalinón frequently uses, as above, the first person plural. He identifies himself with his master in their life of deceit. He is an observer, a *mirón*, of the game of seduction:

> y por mirón no querría
> que me cogiese algún rayo
> y me trocase en ceniza (III, 172-4).

Just as the rooter for a successful player may claim, by custom, a part of the gain, a *barato*, so he, watching a losing player, may expect to pay part of the penalty. He wonders if he can escape scot free:

> ¿Mas si las forzadas viene
> n a vengarse de los dos? (III, 518-9)

But his sense of solidarity with his master does not blind him to the truth. He could feel pity for the victims of the *burlas* (II, 723, etc.). He was aware that the obverse of a *burla* is tragedy:

> Graciosa burla y sucinta,
> mas siempre la llorará [Aminta] (III, 442-3).

Eventually, perhaps because he is sympathetic, perhaps because of dramatic necessities, he escapes being dragged down to hell with Don Juan.

If Catalinón has erred, it is only by association. He is, fundamentally, a good man; perhaps that is the significance of his name.[12] But it is important to realize that, among the principal characters, he is exceptional. Most of the others err, either morally or in judgment. This has been sufficiently demonstrated for Don Juan, and his father and uncle. It remains to be shown that the women are as much the victims of self-deception as of Don Juan's deceits. The theme that women, in their trust of men, are naïve and prone to disillusionment is announced in the first scene: Isabela mistakes, not the intentions of her lover, but his very identity.[13] And the theme, in the characteristic manner of this play, is restated as a refrain:

> ¡Mal haya la mujer que en hombres fía! (III, 394, etc.)

El burlador de Sevilla is full of these significant refrains, for it is conceived as much lyrically as dramatically.

Tisbea, the next victim, has erred in rejecting suitable lovers of her own social class, in "killing them with disdains" (I, 461). She commits the same mistake as Laurencia, in *Fuente Ovejuna,* and Diana, in *El desdén con el desdén.* Her frigidity in love is transformed by her encounter with Don Juan into the chastizing fire of unrequited sexual desire, against which she cries out in her final refrain:

> ¡Fuego, zagales, fuego, agua, agua!
> ¡Amor, clemencia, que se abrasa el alma! (I, 999-1000 etc.)

But she also placed too much trust in lustful man. The fearful refrain,

> ¡Plega a Dios que no mintáis! (I, 613, etc.)

reveals her misgivings: she trusts a perjurer's word against her better judgment.

Aminta, the most difficult of Don Juan's conquests, insists on extracting from him an oath taken on the name of God. Yet even she fails to recognize the duplicity in the man's manner.

¡Qué mal conoces
al Burlador de Sevilla! (III, 299-300),

comments Don Juan. She is blinded by his assertion that he is a *caballero* (III, 235). But it is she who has just told Belisa that

La desvergüenza en España
se ha hecho caballería (III, 131-2).

Batricio, her *novio*, has a truer picture of the *caballero*, in his repeated rhyming of this word with "mal agüero" (II, 672-3, etc.). But he is ashamed into a sense of inferiority—and thus into an unreasonable trust—of Don Juan when he finds himself constantly reprimanded, like a child, with the words "grosería, grosería" (III, 24, etc.).

Among the objects of Don Juan's attention only Doña Ana is realistic. She does not, like Isabela, mistake the intruder's identity (II, 516-9). Nor does she, like Tisbea and Aminta, fall a prey to flattery—possibly for lack of time, because her father, unlike Don Juan's, does not hesitate to seek temporal justice, even if he must be killed in the process. At any rate Don Juan is able later to assure the ghost:

A tu hija no ofendí,
que vió mis engaños antes (III, 963-4).

Doña Ana and her father, Don Gonzalo, are the only ones to triumph over Don Juan: they hold firm to an unselfish moral principle, honor. But since in Don Juan's Spain justice is partial they must triumph in death.

For the other characters in this tragedy of errors there is no moral victory, only bitter disillusionment, the conviction of a great truth. Don Juan had contracted a debt of sin that should have been repaid in full before the *plazo* expired. But only the Banker knew the expiry date. And having failed to pay, by repentance and absolution,[14] Don Juan lost all his assets: life itself and hope of salvation. The voices from the dead pronounced the moral: debts must be repaid, because credit expires:

Que no hay plazo que no llegue
ni deuda que no se pague.

* * *

Esta es justicia de Dios:
quien tal hace, que tal pague (III, 932-3; 957-8)

After such a message the mass wedding of the victims, sinners all, must have been a grave affair.

Notes

1. *El burlador de Sevilla y convidado de piedra,* Act II, verse 513: while this verse may be a later interpolation it is true to the spirit of the play.—All quotations are given, by Act and verse, from the edition by Américo Castro in Tirso de Molina, *Obras*, I (Madrid, 1910, Clásicos Castellanos).
2. Tirso's Don Juan is, of course, something less than Satanic in the Baudelairean sense. Consider, however, his advocacy of *la malicia* when he tells Aminta that, if her marriage to Batricio is not consummated,

   por engaño o por malicia puede anularse (III, 264-5).
3. Cf. R. Menéndez Pidal, *De Cervantes y Lope de Vega* (Buenos Aires, 1940), pp. 92-93.
4. See my study of *Fuente Ovejuna*, to appear in *Studies in Philology*.
5. *Lazarillo de Tormes*, Tratado III.
6. Justina Ruiz de Conde, in *El amor y el matrimonio secreto en los libros de caballerías* (Madrid, 1948), gives a good account of the historical and literary vogue of secret marriage. After it is banned by the Council of Trent as an abuse, it survives as a literary convention. In Scottish law, uninfluenced by the Counter-Reformation, it lasted until 1935.
7. Esto en prudencia consiste" (I, 24).
8. Don Pedro's rôle in this scene is in marked contrast to Clotaldo's rapidly-reached decision to turn over for execution one whom he presumes to be his son. In *La vida es sueño* Clotaldo and Rosaura are the only characters consistently faithful to unselfish principles. Clotaldo's loyalty and obedience to the King, even to the point of being willing to sacrifice a newly found blood tie, save him from the general *desengaño* and punishment at the end.
9. Don Diego keeps remitting to God the punishment that it is his duty to mete out. Cf. especially Act II, Scene XI, which ends with the verse (424): "A Dios tu castigo dejo."
10. III, 182-3. The lesson is repeated so often that Don Juan attains a reflex blunt awareness of death in the moments before he sins; but his immediate repudiation of the warning is equally automatic. Cf. the confusion of values in his "prayer" before seducing Aminta:

    Estrellas que me alumbráis, dadme en este engaño suerte, si el galardón en la muerte tan largo me lo guardáis (III, 117-20).
11. This interpretation of the phrase "¡Tan largo me lo fiáis!"—the obvious one—is clearly expounded in Karl Vossler, *Escritores y poetas de España* (Madrid, 1944), p. 62.
12. Catalinón, as various textual allusions make clear, is a name with a meaning. Successive generations of editors have stated, without justification, that it means "coward." Frank Sedwick (*Bulletin of the Comediantes*, VI [1954], No. 2, 4-6) correctly refutes this interpretation. Professor Leo Spitzer, consulted by me, supported the theory that the name is a compound of *Catalina* (on the analogy of *Marica>maricón*). This leaves the semantic problem

of what *Catalina* suggested in popular speech in Tirso's time. Correas gives a saying alluding to the saint's goodness: "'Una santa Catalina,' por santa y buena: es una santa Catalina; parecía una santa Catalina: pensábamos que era una santa Catalina" (Samuel Gili Gaya, *Tesoro lexicográfico, s.v.* Catalina). Possibly Catalinón suggested something like "tin god" to seventeenth-century readers. Bruno Migliorini, *Dal Nome proprio al nome comune* (Genève, 1927), does not discuss the problem of Catalinón.

13. A completely pessimistic view of woman is taken by all of the male characters: cf. vv. I, 153-6; 356-8; II, 53-4; III, 727, etc. Catalinón describes his master as the "castigo de las mujeres" (I, 897), which implies their guilt. The *burla* is woman's just punishment, as Tisbea confesses:

    Yo soy la que hacía siempre de los hombres burla tanta; que siempre las que hacen burla, vienen a quedar burladas (I, 1015-8).

    It may be that the error of Octavio, who has nothing good to say about women, lies in the exaggeration with which he attributes all his woes to Isabela and her sex: "Huyendo vengo el fiero desatino / de una mujer," he says (II, 53-4). But he would scarcely have blamed Isabela if she had gone to bed with him, her official lover. This would have been fornication, however, in Christian law. His rage against Isabela is directed at her having been duped, at her having made a not too simple mistake in identifying her lover!

14. At the end he beseeches Don Gonzalo: "Deja que llame / quien me confiese y absuelva." The reply is: "No hay lugar; ya acuerdas tarde" (III, 966-8).

Everett W. Hesse (essay date 1981)

SOURCE: "Tirso's Don Juan and the Opposing Self," in *Bulletin of the Comediantes*, Vol. 33, No. 1, Spring, 1981, pp. 3-7.

[*In the following essay, Hesse examines the possibility that the characters Don Juan and Catalinon in de Molina's* El burlador de Sevilla *may represent a single psychological entity.*]

Some years ago Otto Rank studied the psychological interdependence of master and servant in Mozart's opera Don Giovanni.[1] He views the Don and his servant Leporello as a single psychological entity. In his role as confidant, companion and servant, Leporello makes all kinds of admonitions which Don Giovanni permits because he has need of him. What Rank has done for an understanding of the relationship between Don Giovanni and Leporello has prompted me to investigate whether a similar relationship exists between Don Juan and Catalinón in Tirso's ***El burlador de Sevilla***.

Don Juan and Catalinón may be regarded as characters completely distinct one from the other as separate individuals (like Don Quijote and Sancho), or they may be considered from a psychoanalytic perspective as complementary parts of a unified whole. That is, they resemble two projections of the same human personage seen as two because they are out of focus, much like what happens when one looks through the lens of a camera and sees two images, images that have not been brought into focus as one. This concept is not made explicit by the author but is implied in the way each character reacts on the other. This reduction of two characters into one is therefore to be considered latent rather than manifest.

Don Juan represents the id, the instinctual, appetitive nature of man. Catalinón stands for the superego in both of its principal capacities, that of a censoring conscience dictating abstinence and the idealistic ego which imposes honorable duties and noble standards of conduct.[2] Don Juan and Catalinón thus may and do quarrel; in fact Don Juan strikes his servant across the mouth for his moralizing but nothing can undo the tie that binds them together. The *burlador* as protagonist, or as agonist, thus has his double in the person of the play's *gracioso*. As is conventional in the *comedia*, the *gracioso* is a subordinate character in some way attached to the protagonist as friend or attendant, one whose function it is, as a kind of double, to play a portion of the composite role of the protagonist. This role as double is, during the more serious conflicts, that of an ironical buffoon.

It is recalled that an oft-observed phenomenon of literature is its depiction of endopsychic conflict as of an interpersonal nature; the seemingly separate characters represent psychological forces at odds. There is apparent a kind of defense mechanism by which an individual separates a part of the self from that which he wishes to escape. Don Juan's refusal to accept an indivisible oneness of his personality may be a part of his attempt to flee that aspect of it that fears the consequences of his being caught and thereby of terminating his pleasure. This is part of the self in Don Juan which he finds detestable in Catalinón and which he tries to exclude from his own personality.

As Gerald E. Wade has pointed out in his edition of the play, the exact meaning of the name Catalinón has eluded commentators.[3] It seems to connote a person lacking in courage, a fearful individual, a timid soul. It is an attribute which Don Juan detests, especially when Catalinón's warnings and advice would interfere with the master's pleasure. This gives rise to Don Juan's well-known response, "¡Qué largo me lo fiáis!" (905). Don Juan implies that he has no fear of carrying out his plan to seduce women because of his "condición," and concludes that "Catalinón con razón / te llaman" (906-7). Catalinón timidly consents to his master's profligacy, but as for himself, ". . . en burlar mujeres / quiero ser Catalinón" (908-9).

Throughout ***El burlador de Sevilla*** one gets an impression of Don Juan's valor. Don Gonzalo too notices it, "valiente estás" (2709), at a point near the crisis. But a closer scrutiny reveals that Don Juan's valor is merely a façade behind which lurks an inner fear common to all humankind. It is the manifestation of a defiance that essays an important role in compensating for that fear which seems almost indiscernible in the early part of the play but which becomes more evident in the latter reaches of the work. If Don Juan is as brave as he claims to be, then why does he refuse to identify himself in the first seduction? In reply to Isabela's query, "¿. . . quién eres, hombre?" he conceals his identity behind the mask of sexual anonymity, "¿Quién soy? Un hombre sin nombre" (14-15). Is it not fear which makes him respond in kind to the king's request for his identity? ". . . Quién ha de ser? / Un hombre y una mujer" (22-23). Another instance of his fear occurs as he again seeks refuge behind the mask of anonymity when Don Juan forbids Catalinón to disclose his identity to Tisbea, "Si te pregunta quién soy, / di que no sabes . . ." (681-2).

Fear is an unpleasant and often strong emotion caused by anticipation or awareness of danger. It implies anxiety and usually a loss of courage. The basic split in Don Juan's personality is caused by the desire to hide his fear and appear as a fearless and bold person contemptuous of danger. Before exploring the opposing self, let us consider some other factors.

Don Juan also suffers from a fragmented personality. There is a certain narcissistic tendency in his boasting, ". . . caballero soy" (42). As a caballero, he promises to keep his word and accepts the statue's invitation to supper (2442-4, 2458-9, 2669). Catalinón tags his master as "el burlador de España" (1488) to which Don Juan replies, "tú me has dado gentil nombre" (1489), probably because it titillates his ego.

Then there is a lack of sincerity in his false humility when he kneels before his uncle and surrenders his sword (102). Also, his confession of guilt, while true, serves to screen his hypocrisy (111). He adds an element of truth to convince Don Pedro of his contriteness when he confesses his seduction of Isabela by having posed as the Duke Octavio (71). Again, he masquerades as a repentant sinner asking for forgiveness on the pretext of his youth and reminding his uncle of his own youthful adventures (61-4). Don Juan's true feelings contradict his outward display of repentance and are found in the asides (115, 119-120).

Another element of his personality is his desire for power which in the play seems to be related to feelings of status and dominance. The male heterosexual, being under the influence of sexual-identity images, as we have observed above, is preoccupied with the opposite sex as a 'sexual object' to be dominated. Since Don Juan sees the other only in a generic context of sex object, he cannot relate to her as truly other, that is, as a person. He cannot consider her as an equal in a sexual sense any more than he can consider Batricio as his equal in a social sense. Don Juan conquers Batricio because the latter is of inferior rank, "con el honor le vencí" (1924). Don Juan accepts the statue's challenge to protect his standing as a "caballero." This attitude establishes his male identity by means of domination, usually accompanied by violence. These components of Don Juan's personality, his narcissism, his lack of sincerity and his desire for power all are related to his display of "courage" or fearlessness and contrast sharply with Catalinón's fearfulness. Following Stoller, G. E. Wade has discussed Don Juan's fear of bisexuality, even if this means stooping to sexual perversion.[4] We now turn to a more detailed scrutiny of the opposing self in Don Juan's personality, that facet which he tries to avoid and which the author represents in Catalinón, who serves as a kind of alter ego or superego to his master.

Catalinón disapproves of the new deceit already gestating in his master's mind. The servant fears that one day the *burlador* will be *burlado*. Don Juan will not heed Catalinón's admonition since he claims he is not a coward, "y al cobarde hace el temor" (1361). After he is stabbed and before he dies, Don Gonzalo accuses Don Juan of being a coward and a traitor, ". . . el que es traidor / es traidor porque es cobarde" (1586-7).

Don Juan's decision to consult Aminta's father regarding a marriage is highly ironic. It is a piece of bravado on Don Juan's part, designed to heighten the irony of his seduction of Aminta with the father's apparent approval. It is also a kind of defense mechanism that could be employed in case he were arrested later. Does not this desire for "security" arise from his fear of being caught? He knows beforehand of the damage to Aminta's reputation ("pero antes de hacer el daño / le pretendo reparar" *[1922-23]*), but he persists in his plan for the sheer sadomasochistic pleasure he intends to derive from his encounter. Don Juan is vexed by Catalinón's "temores extraños" (1999), and the threat of death and hell (1994). Don Juan cannot face the bad news of an impending disaster, and angered by Catalinón's admonition, he slaps his servant on the face (2221).

Don Juan begins to display outward signs of fear for the first time in Act Three. The stage directions (between 2334-35) indicate his mental state as "turbado." Catalinón and the other servants exhibit a paralyzing fear in this scene and Don Juan reproves them several times for it. "¡necio y villano temor!;" "necio temblar;" and "necio temer!" (2351; 2360; 2364). When the statue indicates that all must leave, Catalinón warns Don Juan not to remain. But the latter with his customary bluster remarks, "¡A ser yo Catalinón . . . !" (2428), which again revives the notion of a timid and fearful person, perhaps even a coward. Don Juan will give his word as a caballero to accept the invitation to supper the next night. Testing Don Juan's courage, Don Gonzalo allays his fears with "no temas," to which Don Juan in his egoism replies, "¿Yo temor?" (2445-6). After the statue leaves, the stage directions read, ". . . y queda D. Juan con pavor" (between 2464-65). Now D. Juan begins to feel the affects of fear, "¡Válgame Dios! Todo el cuerpo / se ha bañado de un sudor" (2465-66). He felt a cold chill in his heart when the statue took his hand

and it burned like the fires of Hell (2469-72). Then he rationalizes that his fear is a product of his mind:

> Pero todas son ideas
> que da la imaginación,
> el temor y temer muertos
> es más villano temor;
> que si un cuerpo noble, vivo,
> con potencias y razón
> y con alma, no se teme,
> ¿quién cuerpos muertos temió? (2477-84).

Don Juan, who hitherto had considered himself the epitome of courage, more and more exhibits the fear of danger in his confrontation with the unknown, and his behavior in these last scenes reveals a nervousness and an anxiety manifested earlier only by Catalinón. Don Juan accepts the challenge to bolster his ego and his narcissism, "porque se admire y espante / Sevilla de mi valor" (2487-8). If earlier he needed to prove his masculinity, now he needs to prove his valor in the face of a gnawing fear.

On meeting Don Juan in the chapel, the statue reassures him with, ". . . no te espantes" (2690). And when Don Juan inquires if Don Gonzalo considered him a coward, the latter answers in the affirmative. Don Juan as much as admits his fear, "hui de ser conocido" (2697). During the bizarre meal, Don Juan feels an icy chill in his heart (2740), which he admits in an aside, "(un hielo el pecho me parte)." Once again the statue seeks to reassure him, "no temas; la mano dame" (2750). Denying his fear to the last, Don Juan extends his hand in a display of daring that belies his true feelings, "¿Eso dices? ¿Yo temor?" (2751).

Don Juan and Catalinón are subject doubles who play a friendly role as secret sharers rather than that of bitter antagonists in spite of an occasional quarrel and a buffet. Nevertheless, a disharmony exists between them at the narrative level as Catalinón is constantly nagging his master about his sexual behavior. They are antithetical or opposing selves in that Don Juan does not share feelings of moral guilt expressed by Catalinón. Rather, it is a question of fearlessness versus fearfulness until events push Don Juan toward sharing some feelings of anxiety and fear that his servant had previously experienced. At that point in the play the double becomes a single as Don Juan gathers together, albeit too late, the opposing segments of his personality. Throughout, Don Juan employs a defense mechanism by which he attempts to segregate himself from that part of his personality that he loathes and which he finds in Catalinón. But Don Juan's fearlessness turns to fearfulness when he loses control of the action and, unable to cope with his problem, he calls for confession, ". . . deja que llame / quien me confiese y absuelva" (2770-1). Tirso's play read thus implies a psychological dimension hitherto unexplored.

Notes

1. Otto Rank, *Don Juan. Etude sur le Double* (Paris, 1932).
2. José F. Montesinos, "Algunas observaciones sobre la figura del donaire en el teatro de Lope de Vega," in his *Estudios sobre Lope de Vega*, Nueva edición (Salamanca: Anaya, 1967), pp. 21-64, considers the "figura del donaire" as something akin to a *voz* in an opera to serve as a contrast to the *galán*. Montesinos specifically mentions our play, "Graciosos ha habido en el teatro español, como el Catalinón de Tirso, que por razones de contraste han tenido que ser voceros de la más acendrada moral católica."

   Joaquín Casalduero, *Contribución al estudio del tema de Don Juan en el teatro español* (Madrid: Porrúa, 1975) points out the *galán-gracioso* duality in the play but neither he nor Montesinos was aware of the psychological dualism inherent in the play and which I intend to develop in this paper.
3. *El burlador de Sevilla y convidado de piedra* (New York: Scribner's, 1969), Note 880. All verse references are to this edition.
4. Gerald E. Wade, "The Character of Tirso's Don Juan of *El burlador de Sevilla*: A Psychoanalytic Study," *BCom*, 31 (Spring, 1979), 33-42. Wade bases his study of Don Juan's character on Robert J. Stoller, M. D., *Perversion: The Erotic Form of Hatred* (New York: Pantheon Books, 1975). See also his study, "The Character of Don Juan in *El burlador de Sevilla*," in *Hispanic Studies in Honor of Nicholson B. Adams*. J. E. Keller and K. L. Selig, eds. (Chapel Hill: University of North Carolina Press, 1966), pp. 167-178.

Elizabeth Teresa Howe (essay date 1985)

SOURCE: "Hell or Heaven? Providence and Don Juan," in *Renascence*, Vol. XXXVII, No. 4, Summer, 1985, pp. 212-19.

[*In the following essay, Howe compares de Molina's* The Trickster of Seville and the Stone Guest *to Zorilla's* Don Juan Tenorio, *concluding that although the Don Juan plays have very different endings, Don Juan receives the proper punishment in both.*]

In Spanish theater, a reversal of the protagonists' expectations marks the two principal plays which feature Don Juan Tenorio as the hero. In the seventeenth-century version by Tirso de Molina, ***The Trickster of Seville and the Stone Guest***, Don Juan pursues his anarchic pleasures confident that salvation is only a deathbed confession away. He acts with impunity throughout the play, ignores the repeated admonitions of others, and ultimately finds damnation rather than salvation in the final apotheosis. On the other hand, in the nineteenth-century Romantic version by José de Zorrilla, *Don Juan Tenorio*, the hero acts out his role expecting damnation for his crimes only to be taken in hand and led to salvation by Doña Inés. These different endings prompt the present discussion, for in each play the dramatist presents a Providential design which is completed in the final destiny of the two Don Juans. At the same time, each playwright intertwines doctrinal considerations in the fabric of his play so that the story of Don Juan speaks to larger questions than the eternal reward or punishment of a single libertine.

If, as Lane Cooper maintains, "there is . . . but one agency against which a . . . hero may not hope to contend—and that is the poet . . . [since he], not destiny, controls the action," (82, 83) then the playgoer must concede that the playwright is himself the ultimate providence of the world he creates on stage. Nevertheless, each playwright brings to his work his own beliefs and so imbues it directly or indirectly with his notion of the Providential design to be depicted in the unfolding action of the play.

Certainly the Mercedarian monk, Gabriel Téllez (better known to Spanish playgoers as Tirso de Molina), reflects in ***The Trickster of Seville and the Stone Guest*** the theological debates concerning Providence, predestination, and free will current in seventeenth-century Spain. Leo Weinstein offers the most succinct explanation of such theories for the contemporary reader. Some scholars regard the play as an implicit refutation of the Molinist doctrine concerning free will and salvation, upholding instead the "strict constructionist" view propounded by Aquinas. Rather than a dry, theological argument transposed to the stage, however, Tirso's play personalizes the controversy by depicting a man of flesh and blood insatiably indulging his appetites, confident that somehow he can "beat the devil" in the end. The ordering of events on stage manifests Tirso's interpretation of these disputes by means of an intricate pattern of foreshadowing and symbolism.

The opening scenes of ***The Trickster*** introduce the words and actions which inevitably point to Don Juan's final end. As the play begins, the darkened set reveals the muffled figure of a man confronting the bewildered noblewoman, Isabela. He replies to her desire to light a candle "to convince my soul / of the good that is coming" by responding: "I'll douse the light if you do" (***Trickster***, I.I.i.23). He identifies himself only as "a man without a name." In these few lines, the playwright prepares the audience for the denouement by cloaking the figure of Don Juan in anonymity and obscurity. Juxtaposed with him is the noblewoman who, while hardly an innocent figure in the seduction, uses references to light ("glories," "truths," "light") to underscore the contrast between good and evil. When Don Juan closes the scene by commanding Isabela to give him her hand ("Give me your hand, Duchess"), he symbolizes the seducer's power over women and anticipates the final scene where the stone guest makes a similar and fatal demand of him: "Give me your hand. / Don't be afraid. Give me your hand!" (III. VII.xxi). The initial request for the lady's hand is but the first of many throughout the play, for Don Juan seals his promise of marriage to Tisbea by stating: "This is my hand and my word" (I. V.xvi.50) just as he seals the fate of the young bride, Aminta, by requesting her hand (III.I.vii.85). The seducer's consistent abuse of this simple gesture of friendship and honor makes the Comendador's command in the final scenes a truly fitting retribution for the reprobate.

As the play progresses, Don Juan becomes increasingly Satanic-like. Thus, what Tirso hints at in the opening scenes becomes clearer as the action unfolds. Don Pedro, his uncle, muses that "the devil himself / took human form in him" (I.II.ix.33), an observation the protagonist seems to echo when he tells Tisbea that "from that hellish sea / I am cast into your shining heaven" (I.III.xii.40). The demonic comparisons resonate with each other to illuminate his character, a man seduced by his own sense of power and determined by his fate. Thus, his abuse of the handshake not only symbolizes his power to seduce women but also his increasing contempt for all civil authority and social mores. When, prior to dishonoring Aminta, he remarks that the villagers "always have their honor in their hands / and they are always looking out for it" (III.I.iii.80), he manifests his contempt for law and order. What one "has in hand," one controls, yet it is inevitably Don Juan who takes matters in hand (Orozco, 786). The unwillingness or inability of society to take in hand the rebellious protagonist is also established early in the first act.

Having successfully compromised the lady's honor in the first scene, Don Juan next demonstrates his ability to manipulate the civil authorities. Taken into custody by an armed guard led coincidentally by his uncle, he manages to escape with his kinsman's help. Don Juan's disregard for society's laws manifests itself in anti-social behavior which the temporal authorities are unwilling or unable to curb. The king tries to redress the wrongs committed by his errant nobleman, but he proves powerless either to control or to punish Don Juan. The failure of temporal authorities necessitates the direct intervention of the divine into the secular realm in order to castigate the sinner and to restore harmony. Through the instrumentality of a "*diabolus ex machina*, God intervenes in the affairs of men. In rejecting Don Juan's plaintive cry for a last minute confession, the stone guest reminds him that "This is God's justice. / Whatever you do, you pay for" (III.VII.xii).

The statue's rebuff of the protagonist, like his request for the nobleman's hand, is the culmination of a series of similar admonitions uttered throughout the play. Don Juan's uncle warns him of divine punishment as do his servant, Catalinón, and the women whom he betrays. All are turned aside by the blithe rejoinder, "How long you give me credit!" which bespeaks the protagonist's misplaced confidence in his own invincibility. Like the fatal auguries of Greek drama, the repeated warnings directed at Don Juan fall on deaf ears. Weinstein points out that Don Juan's procrastination embodied in the "How long" tag transforms the story from that of a licentious seducer to one of divine retribution inexorably approaching the presumptuous sinner (16). In sum, "Tirso condemns neither a devil nor a saint, but a man who, in accordance with his own theological precepts, could have and should have saved himself" (Fernández, 45). Don Juan's infernal end serves notice not only to the sinful who presume too greatly on the mercy of God to forgive their transgressions, but it is also a warning to temporal authority who tacitly accepted his disorderly behavior. In damning eternally Don Juan, Tirso implicitly upholds St. Thomas Aquinas' doctrine concerning man's ultimate end: "since a rational creature has, through its free choice, control over its actions, . . . it is subject to divine providence in an especial manner: for something is imputed to it as a fault, or as a merit, and accordingly there is given to it something of punishment or reward" (*Summa*, I.Ia.20.ii).

Tirso's nineteenth-century Romantic counterpart, José de Zorrilla, emphasizes instead eternal reward through divine mercy in his version of the legend. Sub-titled a "religious-fantastic drama in two parts," the play presents Don Juan in a form that recalls his predecessor while at the same time altering the character and the message. Zorrilla's Don Juan remains both seducer and social outcast, but with a Romantic flair for action. Nevertheless, as the sub-title indicates, the playwright balances religious questions against the fantastic qualities of the Romantic rebel.

Emulating Tirso's opening scene, the Romantic Zorrilla presents a protagonist "nameless" in disguise but with a curse on his lips. A series of scenes follow in which Don Juan's dual nature as seducer and rebel is neatly synthesized. Claiming victory in a year-long wager with his friend, Don Luis de Mejía, Don Juan catalogs an incredible list of conquests and adventures which firmly establishes his ignoble reputation while laying the foundation for his ultimate demise. Witness to his boasting are his father, Don Diego, and his intended father-in-law, Don Gonzalo de Ulloa, both of whom are outraged at what they hear. Each in turn chastises him—Don Gonzalo with a curse which proves prophetic and Don Diego with the warning that God will punish him for his misdeeds.

Dialogue and circumstances thus recall the earlier play by Tirso even as they expand on it. Don Juan Tenorio begins as a man without a name, but, as Carlos Feal points out, "Zorrilla's Don Juan insistently affirms his name . . . [He] becomes the man who portrays himself, who plays the role that other men, other Don Juans before him have helped create" (378). At the same time, Zorrilla's Don Juan glories in his abilities, boasting to Don Luis that he will complete his seductions of women from every social strata:

> . . . because I promise you
> that with the novice I'll also bed
> the lady of some friend
> who's just about to wed. (*Tenorio*, I.I.xii.145)

His boast not only confirms his role as trickster, but also his disregard for the rules of social order represented by Don Gonzalo and Don Diego. When Don Juan chooses to ignore the admonitions of divine retribution awaiting such licentious behavior, his father hurls a final epithet comparing the young libertine to the devil: "children like you / are sons of Satan" (I.I.xiii.149).

Other characters, including Don Juan, take up the theme through the course of the play when they intimate that the protagonist is the devil incarnate. Zorrilla emphasizes this association in the title of Act IV, Part I: "The Devil at the Gates of Heaven." As the quintessential rebel against all authority, Satan is a logical extension of the Romantic hero pursuing self-gratification in defiance of social restraint. Don Juan's intentions to seduce a bride on the eve of her wedding and a novice about to take vows both draw attention to the almost demonic forces which motivate him, emphasizing his likeness to Satan. Ironically, these intentions prove Don Juan's undoing as villain and "doing," if you will, as redeemed hero.

The key to Don Juan's salvation lies in the innocent Doña Inés, the woman to whom he was betrothed, but who is now about to be professed as a nun. While Don Juan utilizes the good offices of Brígida, the young woman's maid, to seduce her, Doña Inés feels a presentiment that her destiny and that of the protagonist are intertwined when she remarks: "Heaven joined / our two destinies / and engendered in my soul this fatal longing" (I.II.iii. 182). While Zorrilla appears to espouse a faulty theology concerning salvation both at this point in the play and at the conclusion, Feal presents a symbolic reading of this section that addresses the problems raised.

> This transformation of Don Juan begins to manifest itself in his conversation with the go-between Brígida. He talks of tearing Inés 'from the arms of Satan' (I.II.ix), but it is he himself who has been compared to Satan. In reality, he must tear Inés away from his own satanism—or Donjuanism. In other words, it is he who must extricate himself from Satan's grasp. These lines can be better understood if one thinks of Inés as symbolically representing Don Juan's soul, as she clearly does at the end of the play. Thus Juan and Inés are saved together (or, had one been condemned, the other would have been condemned as well). (377)

The playwright cleverly lays the foundation for just such a symbolic reading of the play in a number of references to Doña Inés. In her conversation with Don Juan, for example, Brígida describes her mistress as a "poor caged heron / born within this very cage" (I.II.ix. 167). On the one hand, the comparison describes the sheltered existence Doña Inés has experienced up to now. On the other, however, it evokes the language of religion which envisions the soul held captive by the body in this earthly existence. Zorrilla emphasizes the religious imagery in the letter of Don Juan to Doña Inés. In it, the protagonist states that "the heavens joined / the destinies of us both" then goes on to address her as "heart of my heart," "light of my eyes," and "Inés of my soul" (I.III.iii). While such language reflects the excesses of amorous rhetoric, it also sets the stage for the intertwined destinies of the two characters.

The conversion of Don Juan occurs during the famous couch scene when the seducer himself is seduced by a higher love. Doña Inés alludes to the strange, magnetic attraction he exercises over her, remarking that "Perhaps Satan put in you / his captivating look / his seductive tongue / and the love that denied God" (I.IV.iii. 197). When she succumbs to his blandishments, he again addresses her as "my soul," then succumbs himself to the stirrings of a genuine love which she has aroused in him. He professes his faith in God even as he rejects his past behavior when he states:

> It isn't Satan, Doña Inés
> who places this love in me;
> it is God, who desires because of thee
> to win me for Himself, per chance.
> . . . I feel in your presence
> capable even of virtue. (I.IV.iii. 198)

The amorous scene is soon shattered, however, by the sudden appearance of Don Gonzalo, the Comendador, who demands satisfaction from Don Juan for dishonoring his daughter. Don Gonzalo rebuffs the hero's attempts to beg the father's pardon and humble himself. Instead, the outraged father insults him. When Don Juan reminds the Comendador that his salvation may depend on Doña Inés, Don Gonzalo ridicules him. The duel which follows results in the Comendador's death at the hero's hands. Don Juan expresses his despair at this turn of events when he laments that heaven has deserted him at the very moment of his conversion. As Part One of the play closes, he deserts the grief-stricken Doña Inés, convinced that he has lost both love and eternal salvation.

Between the end of Part One and the beginning of Part Two five years elapse, a period in which the protagonist has apparently continued his wanton ways. When he reappears he learns that Doña Inés has died and that society's condemnation of him remains unaltered. As in Part One, the events of Part Two transpire in the course of a single night. The final scene reunites the three principal characters in a demonstration of the mercy of God and an apotheosis of love. Vestiges of Tirso's play are evident in the graveyard setting, the presence of the vengeful stone guest, and the foreboding request for Don Juan's hand which the Comendador makes. Don Juan's steadfast refusal to believe that God will still forgive him increases the tension. Throughout the play, however, he has consistently misread the signs put before him by Providence. Early in the play, for example, he laughs off Don Luis' suggestion that the price of his wager to seduce Doña Ana and Doña Inés will be his life. Yet when another guest in the form of Doña Inés' ghost explains that God has, indeed, joined their fates, Don Juan finally throws himself on His mercy. Through *diosa ex machina*, Don Juan is saved from hell and led to salvation. As Feal observes, "Inés is the true redeemer, or intercessor in Don Juan's redemption, and is thus associated with the Virgin Mary. Like the Virgin of Catholic theology, Inés intercedes between man and God" (381).

Zorrilla dramatically turns the tables on the Don Juan legend. In doing so he skillfully combines religious and Romantic motifs. While Tirso's *trickster* presumes that time is on his side only to be condemned for his excesses, Zorrilla's Don Juan is convinced that salvation is denied him only to discover heaven through the intercession of a virtuous woman. In a Romantic exaggeration, Zorrilla suggests that even Satan might be saved. Hector R. Romero finds in Zorrilla's resolution of the play a Molinist reply to Tirso's ending, for the Romantic Don Juan does use his free will to repent not once but twice (15, 16). Whether the playwright had in mind the theological question concerning free will and predestination that inspired Tirso's work is debatable. Still, he concludes in keeping with Catholic orthodoxy which exalts God's mercy. As Aquinas observes: "God acts mercifully, not indeed by going against His justice, but by doing something more than justice. . . . Hence, it is clear that mercy does not destroy justice, but in a sense is the fulness thereof" (*Summa*, I.Ia.2e.iii). Zorrilla shows God "doing something more than justice" when he ties the fate of Doña Inés to that of Don Juan. Her willingness to suffer even damnation with him convinces the hero both of the depth of Inés love and of God's mercy. That is his salvation.

Both plays deal with the design of Providence. Each Don Juan is warned of the need to repent, but both seriously misread the signs given them. The *trickster* continues his licentious ways confident he can confess in time, only to be brought up short by God's justice. Zorrilla's Don Juan Tenorio underestimates the power of grace as a result of the death of the Comendador and the loss of Doña Inés, only to be surprised by God's mercy. Both learn in the moment of death that nothing is determined in the unfolding of man's life. Through literal "*dei ex machina*," the playwrights effectuate their Providential designs. Justice and mercy are the two facets of divine Providence; each receives its just due in the two Don Juan plays.

Works Consulted

Abrams, Fred. "The Death of Zorilla's Don Juan and the Problem of Catholic Orthodoxy." *Romantic Notes* 6 (1964).

Aquinas, Thomas. *Providence and Predestination, Truth, Questions 5 and 6*. Chicago: Regnery, 1961.

———. *Summa theologiae*. V Cambridge: Blackfriars; New York: McGraw, 1964-1976.

Cooper, Lane. *The Poetics of Aristotle, It's Meaning and Influence*. Boston: Marshall Jones, 1923.

Feal, Carlos. "Conflicting Names, Conflicting Laws: Zorilla's Don Juan Tenorio." *PMLA* 96 (1981).

Fernández-Turienzo, Francisco. "*El Convidado de piedra*: Don Juan pierde el juego." *HR* 45 (1977).

Gonzáles, Angel Custodio, ed. *Don Juan: El burlador de Sevilla por Tirso de Molina. Don Juan Tenorio per José Zorilla*. Santiago de Chile: Zig-Zag, 1947. Selections translated by Elizabeth Teresa Howe.

Orozco, D. Sebastián Covarrubias. *Tesoro de la lengua castellana o española*. Madrid: Turner, 1977.

Romero, Hector R. "Consideraciones teológicas y románticas sabre la muerte de Don Juan en la obra de Zorrila." *Hispano* 54 (1975).

Weinstein, Leo. *The Metamorphoses of Don Juan.* Stanford: Stanford UP, 1959.

Peter W. Evans (essay date 1986)

SOURCE: "The Roots of Desire in *El Burlador de Seville*," in *Forum for Modern Language Studies*, Vol. XXII, No. 3, July, 1986, pp. 232-45.

[*In the following essay, Evans discusses how de Molina, through his characters and language, exposes the cruelty and horror of human desire in* El burlador de Sevilla.]

El burlador de Sevilla shares with Tirso's other plays a preoccupation with stereotypes of role and gender, but whereas, say, in ***El castigo del penséque, La mujer por fuerza***, and ***La firmeza en la hermosura*** his focus is on viragos and timid or inept men, in this play attention is fixed primarily on an ideal of virility that had taken root throughout Europe by the beginning of the seventeenth century. As the *burlador* not just of Sevilla but also of España (p.655a), Don Juan seems in some respects through one particular dimension of his complex persona to embody a nation's stereotype of the virile man. While virility is allowed a temporary and illusory status as a symbol of assault on the stabilities and decay of civilised life, Tirso is nevertheless plainly in sombre mood in ***El burlador de Sevilla***. More despairing of human achievement, glancing more anxiously than in the comedies at the darker patterns of life, Tirso is here simultaneously excavating—at the metaphysical level—human fears of the unknown, of the supernatural, and of death, and also highlighting—at the socio-political level—the seamier side of Empire, probing the social and ideological sources of moral decay. The play is a reversal of the notion found so ofteny in Golden Age literature that men and women are capable of self-transcendence through love, the self's privileged access to recognition of the divine structure of the universe. In a play full of dazzling baroque technique and eerie suggestion, Tirso exposes through Don Juan's vampiric, insatiable and fatal thirst for sexual conquest, the cruelty and horror of desire.

Like Lope, who perhaps had fewer reservations about celebrating the ideal of the Superman, an age's oneiric projection of its own unconscious aspirations to divinity, Tirso adopts an ambivalent attitude to his protagonist's exploits, to the release through his dramatised heroism of a nation's inner quest. There are plays—such as the Pizarro trilogy—whose male characters recall the less ambiguous panegyrics of, for instance, Guillén de Castro's Cid plays, but in many of the great comedies, where the narrative frequently hinges on female lessons in humility, responsibility and sensitivity, Tirso displays a lower degree of tolerance for the Superman. In ***El pretendiente al revés***, the Duke of Brittany is taught that he cannot trample over others, especially not his wife, whom he insensitively attempts to use as an ally in his seduction of another woman; in ***Don Gil de las calzas verdes*** Don Martín learns that he cannot easily extricate himself from a relationship with a woman whom he has compromised and whom he may have made pregnant; ***El Aquiles*** and ***El melancólico*** reveal the extent to which a less rigid definition of role and gender, a tolerance of a certain degree of male feminisation, a little more of the *gentle* man and somewhat less of the *macho* man, is more acceptable in the pursuit not only of personal but also of social relationships. ***El Aquiles*** and ***El melancólico*** both concentrate on men straining to live up in public to the ideals of stereotyped virility.

In ***El burlador de Sevilla,*** too, such moral considerations underlie the play's imaginative structures, but before reaching them one is expected to focus momentarily on the amoral appeal of *brío* and the freedom from convention it seems so thrillingly to promise.

It has sometimes been fashionable to treat the play in a way suggesting that its naïve purpose was simply to construct an Aunt Sally of a character whose sole *raison d'être* is to be condemned in the name of virtue. Morality plays, sermons, tracts are of course the true homes of simple moral lessons, certainly not ***El burlador de Sevilla***, a play, like much else Tirso wrote, that thrives on ambiguity and paradox. Don Juan is a sort of Everyman, "el pequeño mundo del hombre", a site for the release and interplay of conflicting attitudes, desires, ambitions, ideals, aspirations and fears. For that reason he is not only an "hombre sin nombre" (p.634b), a representative of all men, but also the simultaneously nameless and over-named impersonator of Don Octavio, the Marqués de la Mota, Hector, Aeneas, and various other ideals, shabby or respectable, of heroism, nobility and virility. Put another way, he is the phantom, in some senses the monstrous incarnation, of his interlocutors' fears and desires and, by extension, the "other" self of the audience, the dream embodiment of our fears and desires. After all, he is at once all these characters and none of them, a screen on whom expectations, desires and illusions are projected, a shadowy figure assuming the shapes and fancies of a hollow world full of conforming mediocrities denied individuality.

There are narrow functional and psychological senses in which Don Juan is, as an "hombre sin nombre", the impostor or "other" of these characters and, in consequence, of course, of ourselves. But he is also, in a wider sense, all that civilisation regards as "other" and refuses to recognise in itself. In connection with the first, largely dramatic and psychological issue it may be useful to recall Ovid; the second may benefit from a reading of Freud.

As A. K. G. Paterson has noted, there are countless echoes of Ovid throughout Golden Age art, particularly Tirso's. In presenting us with a character in flux, the play indirectly recalls the *Metamorphoses*, but it is also full of veiled references to the *Ars Amatoria*. The advice to all dedicated seducers to learn the advocate's verbal arts, to cultivate making outrageous and impossible promises to one's victims, to override embarrassment at betraying one's closest friends, for instance, are only three examples of Ovid's hidden presence in the play. But perhaps even more significant than these is the passage in the same text where Ovid suggests that the most successful seducer will be he who, acting like a kind of Proteus, can turn himself into an endless variety of shapes and selves:

> Qui sapit, innumeris moribus aptus erit,
> Utque leves Proteus modo se tenuabit in undas,
> Nunc leo, nunc arbor, nunc erit hirtus aper.
> His iaculo pisces, illa capiuntur ab hami:s
> His cava contento retia fune trahunt.

In being Octavio, Mota, Hector, Aeneas and "Don Juan Tenorio", the latter a self-dramatisation of a social ideal, Don Juan is Tirso's Proteus, the scourge of stability and convention, the emblem of a civilisation's ideological contradictions. He is at once the crystallisation of civilised *creencias*, and a character eager for the glare for publicity (for "notoriety" as Gaseno's far from contemptible metathesis in the "Tenorio/notorio" pun [p.680b] makes clear). Purely in psychological terms Don Juan is plainly not to be treated exclusively as an example of Juan Huarte de San Juan's choleric man. He includes the choleric man in his repertoire of selves but, as a character capable of variation and inconsistency, he is the dramatisation of a notion of human identity expressed perhaps most provocatively by Pico dell Mirandola in *De dignitate hominis*: "Quis hunc nostrum chamaeleonta non admiretur?"

But in so far as Don Juan is Tirso's spokesman for society, there is clearly a desire to articulate the positive as well as the negative features of Golden Age life, its aspirations as well as its repressions. As so many have noticed, Don Juan is characterised by the demonic, but what still remains to be underlined is that his *loco amor*, in some senses the symbol for a way of life, stems as much from *doctrina*, which one might more narrowly define as the repressions of his background—which are only implicit in the play—as from his own idiosyncratic personality, which in any case is a composite of living and literary ideals and commonplaces. The investigation of the origins and nature of repression is nowhere more brilliantly undertaken than in Freud's work, most notably *Totem and Taboo* and *Civilisation and Its Discontents*.

There Freud illustrates the ways through which in responding to social drives towards the control of sexuality and aggression, civilisation not uncharacteristically succeeds in overstepping the mark and achieves a surplus repression. But the repressed reappears, sometimes in monstrous form. On this reading, Don Juan the bestial demon, a character in metamorphosis from man to beast, the insatiable *áspid, serpiente*, of transgression and desire, is himself the reappearance of repressed instinct, a dramatisation of the revolt by the unconscious against the excesses of civilisation, a clash perhaps best epitomised by the tense relationship between Don Juan and Don Diego, his father. The relationship between these two characters has at least two dimensions of serious relevance to this issue: the first is related to the purely personal, psychologically realistic intimacy between a father and son, of the kind Golden Age drama specialised in sometimes so brilliantly (Enrico and Anareto, Pedro and Juan Crespo and so on). In these exchanges between father and son we note a certain degree of affection, goodwill, and naturally, of concern. But beneath all this there lies in ***El burlador de Sevilla*** a second dimension of conceptual implications, centring on the ideological struggle that is only dimly apprehended by Don Diego and Don Juan as they confront each other on the battleground of family honour.

Here Tirso depicts the clash of instinct, particularly the libido, against the law of the father, more specifically the law of surface values, of order, propriety, decorum and loveless marriages based on property, of class and hierarchies. Don Juan's paroxysms of sexual indulgence are in some respects expressions of Tirso's conviction that we are all at some time or another in our lives tempted to transgress, to yield to excess and outrage, simply in order to feel truly alive.

Though Don Juan is the character most identified with the negative snake/devil imagery, it is worth noting that these associations are regularly made by others (e.g. p.637a, p.639b, p.641a, p.664b, p.665b, p.666b), and that, moreover, they are deliberately used by Tirso as a means of typifying society at large. There is even a *calle* de la Sierpe (p.659b). This pattern emphasises the point that Don Juan is a social hyperbole, a heightened dramatic synecdoche of the values and contradictions of his background. The imagery is not intended to set him apart, but rather to give him a context which the audience will recognise in broader, social terms as his real place of definition. The same is true of the images of childhood and immaturity.

The early attempt to vindicate Don Juan's "irresponsibility" on the grounds of *mocedad* (p.652a), naturally tunes in with the age's devotion to *brío*, to which Don Juan himself before the Comendador's statue draws attention: ". . . tengo brío / y corazón en las carnes" (p.683a) Cervantes, in *Don Quijote,* part one, to take only one other example from the period, puts the case with precisely the same degree of equivocation as Tirso when he describes his own hero's behaviour like this:

> Decía esto con tanto brío y denuedo, que infundió un terrible temor en los que le acometían; y así por esto como por las persuasiones del ventero, le dejaron de tirar; y el dejó retirar a los heridos, y tornó a la vela de sus armas, con la misma quietud y sosiego que primero.

Tirso's invocation of *brío* is not the only echo of *Don Quijote* in the ***Burlador***: there are many Cervantine touches here, as elsewhere in Tirso's work, but particular mention could be made too of Catalinón's aping of Sancho's desire to be a governor in hoping through his master to become one day a count. Pressing the Cervantine analogies a little further it is just possible from one point of view to argue that Don Juan is in some respects the heir to Don Quijote, or perhaps even St Teresa herself, in the way he hurls himself with such vigour into his chosen field of exploits. The audience is expected temporarily to suspend moral judgment and to become instead awe-struck by the tonic sight of Don Juan's frenzied vitality and natural insubordination, his refusal to contemplate submission, his flouting of convention and his undistracted dedication to selfish needs and desires. In the pursuit of his vocation he has the outrageous fanaticism and unbending will of Don Quijote and St Teresa, recalling in the process Tirso's casual assault on *pusilanimidad* in the prologue to the ***Cigarrales de Toledo***. In mythic terms he is also a version of Prometheus (at one point in the play Don Juan is actually described as a giant [p.639b]), following the pattern so lucidly and suggestively phrased by Marcuse when he talks of the "predominant culture-hero" as the "trickster and (suffering) rebel against the gods, who creates culture at the price of perpetual pain". Yet it is clearly not Tirso's purpose to make us wholly sympathetic to his Satanic hero. Don Juan's primary function is to stir the audience into recognising the social hypocrisies masking the undeniable truths of existence.

At a trivial level, the reverse side of all this *brío* is of course, as Deibe has argued, an appalling immaturity. Don Juan is the negative twin of the hero who dares test the limits of life. Creating endless roles for himself which ultimately succeed only in distancing himself from any substantial and life-enhancing values, he victimises women to the glory of his narcissistic omnipotence, oblivious of his own rapidly withering humanity. Like so many of Tirso's other *niño*, admittedly less malign, heroes (like Rodrigo in *El castigo del penséque*), he fails to progress beyond a retarded notion of love's nature and wealth. Yet once again, as with the devil imagery, the play is careful to use *niño* vocabulary and its figurative resonances not to isolate Don Juan, for *amor niño*, it should be remembered, is a concept first mentioned by the King of Naples (p.637b), and subsequently embroidered by Octavio (p.638a). The point is simply that Tirso is quite clearly determined to argue that his devil-child is a horrifying product of the age, a brilliantcomplex image of a culture's social and moral contradictions. This is not to argue that Tirso, a more or less respectable Friar in the Order of Mercy, is writing radical drama with programmes for reform, merely that as one of the age's most gifted and profound dramatists, he is compelled to express what he clearly sees as the ironies and failures of a hopelessly muddled culture still reeling from the effects of expulsion from Paradise. Tirso is Golden Age society's dramatic barometer of conscious repression and unconscious desire.

It may not be entirely platitudinous to recall that ***El burlador de Sevilla***, like any work of art, is a texture of interwoven threads, some new, some borrowed, some inherited, all in some senses fashioned by history and culture. The "intertextual" contexts of the play include, as I have argued, Ovid, Cervantes, Pico della Mirandola, Juan Huarte de San Juan, but also, quite clearly, both Lope de Vega, whose general influence on subsequent drama in Spain needs no further comment here, and Seneca. Seneca's influence on Golden Age dramatists, like Juan de la Cueva and Rojas Zorrilla, both of whom had a profound taste for atrocities, has largely been noted, but Lope and Tirso, normally admired for their greater sense of decorum, are not incapable of Senecan horror and savagery themselves. The severing of heads in *El mayordomo de la Duquesa de Amalfi*, *El bastardo Mudarra* and *Fuenteovejuna*, the supernatural moments of *El rey don Pedro en Madrid* and ***El burlador de Sevilla***, are scenes of almost unexampled outrage, clearly relying on Senecan antecedents. The stone guest—though in some ways, as Terence May and Pidal have argued, reincarnations of ancient European legends—is closely modelled on Senecan figures of revenge of the kind described by Andromanche in *The Trojan Women*, who return to torment their mortal enemies. The formula of pagan revenge tragedy is transformed here into its Christian equivalent, where alongside the secular revenge sought by the victimised women (Tisbea uses the word "venganza" [p.672b]), there is the spectacle of a higher revenge taken by the stone guest who, still bearing some of the pagan, Senecan hallmarks, embodies seventeenth-century notions of divine justice that are at least partly inspired by the Old Testament text "Vengeance is mine, and I will repay". The all too pitifully human thirst for retaliation and retribution in this life, described by Bacon in the essay on revenge as the pursuit of "wild justice", is contrasted with divine justice, the only kind of revenge which will not prove to be, as Ford puts it, in *'Tis Pity She's a Whore*, "its own executioner".

The lamentable shortcomings of a civilisation's systems of order and belief, coupled with Don Juan's brazen exposure of its hypocrisies, his unhesitating gratification of the urges of his primal will, and his singleminded, playful, commitment to self-indulgence (life is a game to Don Juan, for "en el juego / quien más hace gana más" [p.675a]), all combine to reduce the impact of the conventional moral lesson which, of course, in many respects the play teasingly offers. So, though he is consumed by demonic tendencies, and though he is condemned, as Parker argues, as a betrayer—sent, we must therefore assume on Dante's assurance, to the very heart of hell for this vilest of sins—Don Juan is Tirso's, perhaps the Golden Age's, most outrageous monster not simply because of his own contempt for anything that does not serve his own inescapably selfish purposes, but also because, as he passes like a whirlwind of aggressive, infernal desire through every level of society, he reveals that the monstrous, the diabolical, is by no means restricted to easily-constructed scapegoat figures of eccentricity. Tirso allows one to wonder whether in seventeenth-century Spain the monstrous had become almost banal in its diffusion.

None of these remarks is intended to suggest, however, that Don Juan is Tirso's creation of an invariably knowing *eiron*, deliberately or crusadingly denouncing the prim tyranny of seventeenth-century life and ideology. Rather, that as an ambivalent character of mixed youthful vitality and diabolical corruption he is the play's paradoxical figure of disenchantment and smugness, of revolt and subjugation, of repression and desire, a character, in contrast to society's greater hypocrites, mercifully immune from the prig's urge to dispense moral blandishments and pseudo sentiment.

As he sets about making his conquests this structural principle of ambiguity, a feature designed to provoke in the audience a dual attitude of empathy and detachment, Don Juan forces us to be content with neither an exclusively romantic view of him as a daring embodiment of Renaissance *brío*, nor with a predominantly theological notion of him as a conventional personification of evil. Tirso allows one to be as repelled by his moral squalor as drawn to the positive side-effects of his admittedly unwitting social critique. What Calderón perhaps tried with varying degrees of success to do with some of his *auto* devils, Tirso strikingly achieves through his portrayal of Don Juan in ***El burlador de Sevilla***: the creation of a character, like Milton's Satan, or Shakespeare's Richard III, who is alternatively irresistible and repellently evil, another of the characters one might add to A. P. Rossiter's list of "angels with horns". Though we are expected to include moral judgments in the range of responses we make to the sensuous pleasures and intellectual challenges of ***El burlador de Sevilla***, we make them against the background of the clashing voices of theology and morality. This is, as Paterson has remarked of another play by Tirso, the drama of experience, not of theological debate.

While most spectators would deplore Don Juan's scandalous and shocking victimisation of Tisbea, Aminta, Isabela and Ana, few would not also feel some sympathy, however transient, for his shameless urge to disrupt the normality of universally frantic quests for monogamous unions. At a frivolous level the play generally satirises the fetishisation of female virginity (a topic most eloquently but, by today's standards, somewhat hysterically treated in Vives' *Instrucción de la mujer cristiana*), practised by *comedia* lovers devoted to the double standard. Though as a matter of convention, and perhaps some urgency, nuptials are being arranged for him, Don Juan never interrupts his relentless celebration of the transgression of marriage, the violation of its sanctity, and the exposure of the humbug of scores of *comedia* unions. "Burlar una mujer y dejarla sin honor" (p.656b) has, naturally, an overridingly offensive tone, but if one looks beyond literal meanings, one can see an unmistakable assault on sanctimonious contemporary attitudes to sexuality, usually imposed by men on unsuspecting or bewildered women. From one point of view, there is quite possibly a literary joke in Don Juan's siege of marriage, perhaps a moment for Tirso to reveal the arbitrariness of a dramatic device used conveniently as a way of cloaking a play's multiple thematic problems and various contradictions, a tired convention which serves at once to articulate the audience's wish-fulfilments and also, as Walter Kerr puts it, to allow everyone to go home. Yet Tirso's spirit of transgression, embodied in Don Juan, extends beyond purely literary satire: Don Juan's recklessness seems designed to make one probe, or at least question, the respective foundations of social and moral certainties.

An atmosphere of repression shrouds the entire play, and since women are its primary victims, it is worth scrutinising the extent to which they are already vulnerable to exploitation even before Don Juan's predatory intervention in their lives. Though all four women are depicted in ways that are designed to reveal negative sides to their character, it is probably unproductive to argue, like Deibe, that they are deliberately cast in a predominantly unfavourable light so as to fit in with his allegedly "frailuna" and "misogynistic" view of women. Where he does expose the negative features in the pshychology of the play's women Tirso is at pains to excavate their origins. The case of Isabela is especially illuminating from this point of view.

Most significant is the way Tirso uses her as a way of drawing attention to the silencing of women in public life. In other plays Tirso's splendid *ingenio*-touched women are seen overcoming their silencing through recourse to charades, disguises, feignings and other ruses: the woman dressed as man in ***Don Gil de las calzas verdes***, masquerading as another woman in ***La villana de Vallecas***, pretending to be devout and above carnality in ***Marta la piadosa***, or deaf to love in ***No hay peor sordo . . .***, are all vivid examples of Tirso's concentration on the release of women's voices through *ingenio*. But through Isabela in ***El burlador de Sevilla*** Tirso prefers not to concentrate on the ingenious woman's dependence on wit as a means of self-expression, choosing instead to focus on the act of silencing itself.

Isabela has been making love to Don Juan, whom she mistakes for Don Octavio, her lover, and when she finally discovers her error she succeeds in rousing the palace residents, last of whom is the king himself. He accepts Don Pedro's false account of the truth, and what begins as a family plot to conceal Don Juan's involvement in the incident (he is Don Pedro's nephew), soon becomes an unconscious male conspiracy to deny a woman the right to give her own version of the outrage. Isabela twice attempts to speak for herself, but on each occasion she is silenced by the "dead hand of a patriarch":

> Rey: Idos, y guardad la puerta
> de esa cuadra. Di, mujer:
> ¿qué rigor, qué airada estrella
> te incitó que en mi palacio,
> con hermosura y soberbia,
> profanases sus umbrales?
> Isabela: Señor . . .
> Rey: Calla, que la lengua
> no podrá dorar el yerro
> que has cometido en mi ofens
> a. ¿Aquél era el Duque Octavio?
> Isabela: Señor . . .
> Rey: No importan fuerzas,
> guardas, criados, murallas,

fortalecidas almenas
para amor, que la de un niño
hasta los muros penetra. (p.637b)

The speech structures, the dismissive, insulting tone of the king's language are all part of a larger pattern of tyranny over women, unmistakably signposted later on in the play when in her absence Isabela's destiny is summarily but decisively fixed by Don Diego and the King of Spain. Such silencing gives a particularly ironic perspective to the remark made by Don Pedro to Don Octavio as he recounts the incidents at the palace, when at one point he remarks, "voces de mujer oímos" (p.639b). In such circumstances it is small wonder that women are sometimes driven to self-centred, negatively "monstrous" ways.

The silencing of Isabela contrasts sharply with the release of Tisbea's voice. Her brilliant opening speech is the expression primarily of revelry in freedom, not just from love but for its own sake. This is the licence of pastoral, the consolation of solitude in the airy expanses of nature, and as she develops her theme the audience, sharing through her language the pleasures of the country, finds welcome relief from the stifling figurative darkness of the previous scene in Naples. Her speech convinces us that like the *burlador* Tisbea seeks and imagines she is privileged to ignore social convention. Like Don Juan, she is a transgressor though, by contrast, a monster apparently of sexual abstinence. Tisbea is one of Tirso's strong, rare, prodigious heroines, thrillingly monstrous, displaying through the baroque flights of her language her confident, self-conscious independence and a studied, vivifying eccentricity. Her vocabulary of transgression is a sign of her inner strength, and as we hear her speak we see her framed by the sea, her place of definition, the eternal feminine, the pre-civilised cradle of life itself, though also of course of love and of oblivion. While we admire Tisbea's spirited allegiance to an ideal of freedom, we simultaneously fret over her seemingly inflexible disavowal of her own erotic instincts. We cannot help but feel that like other victims of self-delusion, she is misguidedly desecrating the sacred place of an invisible but powerful goddess, Aphrodite herself. Her denial of love in the setting of the goddess of love's own domain is as striking and as arrogantly foolhardy as Don Juan's rejection of God's law in the cemetery. Tisbea's meeting with Don Juan by the seashore is the equivalent of Don Juan's encounter with the stone guest amid the tombstones, a refusal by mere mortals to admit that there is more to life than is dreamt of, paraphrasing Hamlet, in their philosophies, and significantly in both settings stone imagery plays a crucial part in Tirso's figurative and narrative patterns.

As if anticipating the stone imagery connected with Don Gonzalo in Act III, Tisbea first talks of precious stones—the sea, according to her mercenary perceptions, is like an infinity of sapphires—and then describes herself as a rock. The references to sapphires warn us that Tisbea, like Aminta, is not uncontaminated by court or town values, and we are left to suppose that she may be additionally attracted to Don Juan through the promise of social advancement. But Tisbea is also stony, or rocky, because she is a creature of nature, a prodigy of elemental freedom. Moreover, beyond these drives there are, from another point of view, the negative implications of her flinty attitudes to love. These are primary and perhaps easily accessible meanings, but there are at least two other important implications of Tirso's use of language at this point in the play. First, if Tisbea is stony she is clearly destined, by analogy with the play's other character of stone, to be an avenger. But where Don Gonzalo is in one respect the living conceit of God's revenge, Tisbea is in some senses fated to be an avenger of exploited women. Second, and less positively, her stoniness suggests not physical but social and ideological immobilisation. While on the one hand Don Gonzalo's immobilisation is the timelessness of eternity, and, on the other, Don Juan's is the stasis of desire, Tisbea's is the paralysis brought about by *esquivez* and, perhaps to a lesser extent, of an unacknowledged appetite for both wealth and social status.

The curious aspect of Tisbea's soliloquy is that although she revels in her immunity from love, her language is nevertheless characterised by detailed evocations of the sensuous and tangible features of nature's delights. The communicative or ideational aspects of her speech inform us of her relief and satisfaction in *esquivez*, but its poetic dimensions—in Jakobson's sense—tell us something different and even contradictory. Following Freud we might want to say that taken as a whole her speech (pp.640-42) dramatises the clash between conscious restraint and unconscious transgression: the vocabulary of kissing ("sus riberas besa"), precious stones ("zafiros . . . aljófar"), and eroticism, particularly through fish imagery ("necio pececillo"), competes with the language of lofty seclusion ("obeliscos de paja / mi edificio coronan . . ." etc.). This language of transgression complements the play's insistent use of verbal and visual food imagery, and it is noticeable that Tisbea herself speaks of love as "una fruta sabrosa". Food as a substitute for erotic pleasure is, of course, a topos of ancient and modern literature alike. So despite her intentional protestations we know from the language she uses almost in spite of herself that Tisbea is not immune to desire. For such a woman a man characterised only by gentlemanly qualities ("medido en las palabras / liberal en las obras / sufra do en los desdences / modesto en las congojas" as Anfriso might well be [p.641b]), and by an imposing physique, cannot on those grounds alone be seriously entertained as a lover. Anfriso clearly lacks that elusive inner blaze of passion that Don Juan alone seems capable of igniting.

However, despite the contradictions, Tisbea is at least a shade freer than Isabela, a step closer to independence in an idealised life so far infected as little as possible by the snares and confusions of civilization. Some way from Utopia, she can still at least here in the seclusions of nature, as poor Isabela could not, speak and articulate her dreams and desires. That seems to be the primary significance of her leisurely and perhaps unconscious recourse in the language of excess. Spared some of the more debilitating forms of social and psychological oppression, she is nevertheless, as her ambivalent soliloquy makes clear, not entirely exempt from the repressions and corruptions of civilised life. The dismantling of Tisbea's language reveals a woman unconsciously formulating perceptions and expectations of sexual fulfilment, all of which find their natural expression in the monstrous form of Don Juan.

Where by comparison with Isabela she had seemed through her gifted use of language in some respects independent and powerful, Tisbea pales almost into insignificance beside Don Juan whose access to real power, symbolised once more through language, is supreme. Daniel Rogers rightly notes that Don Juan's speeches are, to say the least, concise. By comparison with Tisbea's magnificent monologue, they are in some respects minimal. In a play where he did not hesitate to use long speeches of baroque dimensions—not only through Tisbea, but also in the Lisbon speech—whenever they were felt to be necessary dramatically, Tirso clearly sought through Don Juan's comparatively reticent linguistic idiosyncrasies not only to suggest the self-absorption of the narcissist, the self-sufficient tyrant of love showing no sign of immersion in the other reality of his partner, but also to indicate that having power *de facto* as a man the *burlador* has no need for perorations. It is sufficient for him, as a man, merely to look in order to exercise that power.

Tirso was clearly fascinated by language. ***Palabras y plumas***, for instance, is full of commentary on language not only as a medium at once rich and impoverished but also as an instrument of power. Language there is frequently used in the service of tyranny, and the play is full of characters who are masters of rhetoric, repeatedly sabotaging meaning with linguistic virtuosity. Characters lead counterfeit lives through words but, significantly it is a woman, the play's principal female character Matilde, who inveighs against "palabras" in an important speech. In ***El burlador de Sevilla*** the play's women are once again our guides to the pitfalls of language: Aminta complains that Don Juan is a *lisonjero* who is full of "retóricas mentiras" (p.670b); so too does Tisbea even in the paradoxical remark "mucho habláis cuando no habláis" (p.644a).

Aminta's words are shorn of ambiguity, since they simply draw attention to the manipulations of rhetoric; but if, on the other hand, one looks at Tisbea's remark, one can detect at least two rich layers of meaning crucial to the play's over-all structure. First, even though Don Juan is verbally thrifty he clearly depends to some extent on the implied expansive aura of his Satanic appearance, the kinetics and visual presence that arouse the repressed longings of a sensual woman. But second, as Don Juan is not actually silent it is quite clear that what he does say, however brief, is skilfully aimed at his interlocutors' most vulnerable emotional targets. In fact a nobleman's simple marriage proposal to a peasant girl of the seventeenth century (the actual historical context of the play is, of course, set back in time) would seriously have tempted thoughts of a life of luxury to swamp all other considerations and sensible objections to the folly of a union contracted on the basis of a rash promise. To such a peasant girl the gravity of these spare words, the "palabras de marido" (p.650b), as Tisbea puts it, might have exceeded by far damage to psychological resistance inflicted by the most highly-wrought baroque conceits of love. Like Isabela, who mistook Don Juan for her own lover Octavio, Tisbea and Aminta are blinded by what they see, perceiving only the hallucinatory shape of their own dreams of status and wealth, suddenly embodied in the living form of Don Juan. Like Isabela's confusion—to the point where she remains, even when they are in bed together we must presume, ignorant of Don Juan's true identity—the mistaken view taken by Tisbea and Aminta of Don Juan is a symbol of their limited moral and psychological perception. The incident involving Isabela and Don Juan belongs to a long line of literary "bed tricks", that goes at least as far back as *Genesis* 19:33. In Tirso's work, related tricks of perception—where characters fail to recognise friends or relations, or are persuaded to accept strangers as acquaintances—are also very common (***El celoso prudente*** and ***El castigo del penséque*** contain interesting examples). One should resist the temptation to regard these as instances of Tirso's far-fetched and unrealistic notions of human behaviour, and instead be prepared to view them as dramatic conventions used as a way of underlining failures in perception, devices for drawing the attention of the audience to the all too human contexts of illusion. They give yet more proof, if any were needed, of the *comedia*'s transgression of realism, and in the particular case of Tirso's dramatic art, they reveal an endless fascination with the processes through which we make sense of reality, as knowledge, anxiety, or prejudice construct the distorting lenses of our inner vision. Isabela's image of Don Juan, like Tisbea's and Aminta's, is in some senses the equivalent in this play of Don Quijote's view of the barber's basin on that rainy day in La Mancha.

In all three cases in this play the women's responses are largely conditioned by their repressive social contexts. Moreover, as he is society's agent of desire, Don Juan not only excites the erotic—as well as the more materialistic—urges of his victims, he also acts as the implacable scourge of love, the cruel judge who punishes the very women whom he has deliberately set out not only to stimulate but also, through encouragement of sexual indulgence, in some respects to liberate. Both Catalinón and Tisbea draw attention to his punitive role:

> CATALINÓN: Ya sé que eres
> castigo de las mujeres . . .
>
> TISBEA: . . . Reparo en que fue castigo
> de amor el que he hallado en ti. (p.648b, p.649a)

There are psycho-social elements in Don Juan's treatment of women. Broadly speaking, his psychological drive seems to originate in a pre-Sadean, conviction that sexual pleasure is inseparable from tyranny; the social origins of this attitude are the well-known Judaeo-Christian strictures. Of the latter we are offered more than a glimpse, but what is particularly revealing is the way in which at the slightest excuse men trot out all the usual misogynistic abuse. The anger displayed by Octavio, one of Don Juan's most successful impersonations, suggests that an unconscious rage, nurtured by centuries of irrational vilification of women, society's scapegoats for a wider *malaise*, may well be an important component of Don Juan's motivation in victimising women. The easy rage and misogyny of Octavio and Batricio are well captured by Tirso in the following speeches:

> Octavio: Marqués, yo os quiero creer.
> Ya no hay cosa que me espante;
> que la mujer más constante
> es, en efeto, mujer . . .
> ¡Ah, veleta! ¡Débil caña!
> A más furor me provoco,
> y extrañas provincias toco
> huyendo desta cautela . . . (p.640b)
> Batricio: Al fin, al fin es mujer . . .
> que el honor y la mujer
> son malos en opiniones . . . (p.667a)

As "Don Juan"—as opposed to when he is masquerading as Don Octavio or the Marqués de la Mota—Don Juan victimises women in four easy stages: he first woos and excites them beyond resistance through his "lisonjeras palabras"; he then fetishises them, so as to maintain his emotional distance; he then seduces them; and he finally punishes them through desertion. The third crucial stage of fetishisation, the stage that ensures his unthreatened superiority, his wilful commitment to sexual conquest without real personal involvement, is unwittingly highlighted by Tisbea. While commenting, on first setting eyes on him, on his status, prowess and assumed moral qualities ("excelente, gallardo, noble y galán caballero" [p.643b]), she primarily draws attention to herself, conditioned of course into doing so by the tradition of centuries, as a pleasurable object of gaze: "ya podéis *ver*, en brazos de una mujer" (p.643b). Tisbea is victim to the prejudices of a theory of expression and kinetics that goes back as far as Aristotle (compare, for instance, Gracián's remarks in *Cris*; IV of *El Criticón*), though Tirso might have been more familiar with Quintilian: "por el semblante y modo de andar se conoce el estado de ánimo . . ." When Don Juan describes a woman he seems to echo Tisbea's own view of how a man should look at a woman: he comments on "buenos ojos" and "blancas manos" (the *comedia galán*'s staple mode of response), and the imagery of sight, in so far as it is applied to women, is recurrent throughout the play (particularly p.666a). But the whole issue of the way in which he and through him we ourselves habitually look at women—male or female spectators—is brought directly to our attention through a crucial remark made in Act III by Catalinón:

> . . . De los que privan
> suele Dios tomar venganza
> si delitos no castigan,
> y se suelen en el juego
> perder también los que miran.
> Yo he sido mirón del tuyo,
> y por mirón no querría
> que me cogiese algún rayo
> y me trocase en ceniza. (p.668b)

While Don Juan is at once a narcissist and a fetishist (a narcissist because he is preoccupied with his reputation which will grow in proportion to the number of women he seduces, and a fetishist because he reduces women to the status of desirable objects, Catalinón, as a *gracioso*, the conventional *alter ego* of the audience, is also a voyeur. While Don Juan's characterisation is an elaborate conceit for the intermingling of energy and devilry, a disturbing dramatic device designed to plunge the audience into the realms of the primitive, to make one tremble at the prospect of the unknown and, on these grounds, an embodiment of the reappearance of repressed instinct, a symbol, in short of hyperactivity, Catalinón is a reluctant man of action, a symbol of perception. When he defines himself as not just a spectator at Don Juan's *burlas* but as a *mirón* as well, the real spectators in the theatre reflect on the circumstances which make them, too, even if only temporarily, *mirones*.

The concept of voyeurism is related to the notion of *impertinencia* which, Cervantes, for one, analysed so brilliantly in *El curioso impertinente*. In ***El burlador de Sevilla*** Don Juan describes Catalinón as an *impertinente* (p.657a), though we might feel that it is a case of the pot calling the the kettle black. Ripio also defines Octavio as an *impertinente* (p.638a). If Catalinon is a *mirón* at Don Juan's *burlas* against women, to what extent are we, whom he represents, not also in some ways *mirones*, in the pejorative sense, as well? Are we perhaps *mirones* taking pleasure from looking at the spectacle of the *castigo* of women who have dared exercise their sexuality and eroticism? The brilliance of the play is not that Tirso is crudely joining in the misogynistic outcry against women, seeking to make them pay for man's expulsion from paradise, but that through this highly self-conscious method of Catalinón's *mise-en-abŷme* we are made to reflect even more deeply on the play's issues, and to catch ourselves applauding perhaps with unconscious and unrecognised sado-masochistic tendencies those who punish our own repressed, formerly unconscious but now recognised desires. Through Catalinón, too, we are forced to look at what we have created: on the one hand, subjugated, socially and ideologically confused women, and, on the other, demonic men intoxicated and demented by forbidden yet condoned desires.

James Mandrell (essay date 1988)

SOURCE: "Language and Seduction in *El Burlador de Seville*," in *Bulletin of the Comediantes*, Vol. 40, No. 2, Winter, 1988, pp. 165-80.

[*In the following essay, Mandrell analyzes the language of* El burlador de Sevilla, *focusing on de Molina's concerns with how the linguistics of the play affected seventeenth-century Spanish society.*]

Critical wisdom holds that the four seductions in Tirso de Molina's ***El burlador de Sevilla y convidado de piedra*** are important in an external, referential sense and in an internal, structural one, that they serve to prove a point regarding Spanish society in general as well as to establish the structural frame and dramatic rhythm within the *comedia*. The social point of the seductions is straightforward enough: Don Juan respects neither the conventions of his own class (the nobility) nor those of his inferiors (the peasantry). Women of all classes qualify as potential objects of his desire. This fact, along with the division of the quartet of women into two noblewomen (the Duquesa Isabela and Doña Ana) and two *villanas* (Tisbea and Aminta), allows for a special kind of symmetry of action in the drama. Don Juan moves from the a seduction of an aristocrat to the seduction of a peasant, accomplishing his goal with apparently equal ease. So when Don Juan flees from Doña Ana, the third of his victims, it is only to be expected that he will end up with Aminta, since earlier he quite literally fell into Tisbea's arms while fleeing from the consequences of his seduction of Isabela. The drama is organized around the symmetry of the four seductions, around the way one seduction logically follows another.[1]

Despite the apparent symmetries of structure, action, and dialogue, there are subtle differences between and among the episodes involving the four women in ***El burlador de Sevilla*** that encourage a far different reading of the function of seduction in the drama. Repetition of the act of seduction is not meaningful only in a formal sense, only insofar as it underscores the symmetry of action and dialogue and drives home the point about the wages of sin. Rather, seduction, because of its prominence and predominantly linguistic cast vis-à-vis the promise, suggests the linguistic issues that will be elaborated and eventually resolved during the course of the *comedia*.[2] Moreover, these scenes of seduction serve as a significant index of Don Juan's progression through and development in the drama, since each individual seduction is carefully presented in such a way as to complement the preceding action and to provide more information about how Don Juan achieves his goal in a society that would normally repress him.

This means that Don Juan's transgressions are not just cumulative, serial aggravations that add up to his punishment, but, rather, that they constitute a progressively complex exploration of the nature of language as it functions in the world, as Don Juan's tool in seduction, and, finally, as his undoing. In what follows, I wish to explore the linguistic implications of seduction as presented in this drama, relating them to concerns pertinent to seventeenth-century Spanish society and religious orthodoxy. My reading of ***El burlador de Sevilla*** will demonstrate the ways in which Tirso was profoundly concerned with language and its role in the world, its capacity to create and to establish certain truths as well as to deceive.

I

The linguistic concerns of ***El burlador de Sevilla*** are apparent from the earliest moments of the drama. Opening *in medias res* with the final moments of a lovers' rendezvous, the first scene demonstrates the crucial importance of the promise for the success of Don Juan's endeavors. Furthermore, this scene quickly establishes the two fundamental enigmas on which the subsequent action will be based:

> Isabela. Duque Octavio, por aquí
> podrás salir más seguro.
>
> Don Juan. Duquesa, de nuevo os juro
> de cumplir el dulce sí.
>
> Isabela. Mi gloria, ¿serán verdades,
> promesas y ofrecimientos,
> regalos y cumplimientos,
> voluntades y amistades?
>
> Don Juan. Sí, mi bien.
>
> Isabela. Quiero sacar una luz.
>
> Don Juan. Pues, ¿para qué?
>
> Isabela. Para que el alma dé fe
> del bien que llego a gozar.
>
> Don Juan. Mataréte la luz yo.
>
> Isabela. ¡Ah, cielo! ¿Quién eres, hombre,?
>
> Don Juan. ¿Quién soy? Un hombre sin nombre.
>
> Isabela. ¿Que no eres el duque?
>
> Don Juan. No. (1-16)[3]

The role played by the promise in this scene is patently obvious: one form of "enjoyment" is exchanged for another as Don Juan swears once again ("de nuevo") to "cumplir el dulce sí" in return for Isabela's favors. The two questions posed by this scene are also obvious: who is the "hombre sin nombre" and how did he succeed in getting into the Duquesa's bedchamber.

Don Juan's identity is not, in fact, revealed until much later in the first act, after the conclusion of the scenes involving the Duquesa. But this does not mean that the character who seduced the Duquesa remains anonymous. When his uncle undertakes to punish the man who was caught in the Neapolitan palace, he learns that the culprit is none other than his nephew. To Don Pedro's demand, "¡Di quién eres!" Don Juan insolently replies, "Ya lo digo: / tu sobrino" (53-54). Yet Don Pedro neither addresses nor refers to Don Juan by name. Identity is established first and foremost by means of blood ties, and Don Juan remains an "hombre sin nombre" throughout these opening scenes, indeed, up until Catalinón reveals various details about the *burlador*'s family as well as his name to

Tisbea at the beginning of the second scene of seduction (570-78). With the unexpected help of his name and noble lineage—unexpected since the *burlador* enjoins Catalinón in this same scene to keep his name a secret after the manservant has already given Tisbea the full particulars (679-84)—Don Juan proceeds with his plan to seduce the *pescadora*.

This second seduction not only reveals the name of the *burlador*, it also shows Don Juan to good advantage in terms of his facility with the spoken word. (One should also note that Tisbea is an equally adept speaker.) The linguistic implications of this scene do not, however, pertain only to the *burlador*, since it is the controlling force of language as it functions in society as a system of exchange mutually agreed upon by Don Juan and Tisbea that is revealed here. As the peasant astutely remarks, "Mucho habláis." Don Juan, not to be outdone, replies even more smoothly, "Mucho entendéis" (695). The one flatters the other's gift of speech, the second flatters the powers of comprehension of the first. If there is any doubt as to this emphasis, Tisbea tells Don Juan, "Yo a ti me allano / bajo *la palabra* y mano / de esposo" (938-40; emphasis mine). Later, after she has been tricked, she laments, "Engañóme el caballero / debajo de fe y *palabra*" (1017-18; emphasis mine). Don Juan gives his word in this exchange as he did in the first instance, but he does so without intending to fulfill the desire of the other individual involved.

Although we are somewhat closer to understanding the first scene of the drama—since the identity of the "hombre sin nombre" is now known—we still do not know precisely how Don Juan gained access to the Duquesa's chambers, even though it seems clear that language is somehow implicated in the entire process. The question of "how" remains a mystery only until the third seduction, Don Juan's encounter with Doña Ana. The stage is set for this *burla* when Don Juan and the Marqués de la Mota scheme together to play a trick on Beatriz, a woman of questionable honor. In order to fool Beatriz into thinking that Don Juan is the Marqués, the latter gives his cape to the *burlador*. The plan is for Don Juan to present himself to Beatriz, to pretend that he is the Marqués, and to enjoy the woman's favors.

Earlier in these scenes involving the Marqués and Doña Ana, however, Don Juan was entrusted by one of Doña Ana's ladies to deliver a missive to his aristocratic friend. His curiosity piqued by the "papel," Don Juan opened the note and read of Doña Ana's desire that the Marqués should come to her under the cover of night, wearing his red cape, in order to make love to her and thereby to thwart her father's plans to marry her to another man, one she does not love. Unable to resist the opportunity offered to him, Don Juan relays the message, but not the missive itself, adding one piece of misleading information not found in the original "papel": that the Marqués is to present himself at Doña Ana's door at midnight and not at eleven o'clock as suggested in the letter. Don Juan has thus created the conditions for a far more cleverly vile *burla* than the one that he and the Marqués had planned together. Instead of going to the home of Beatriz, Don Juan goes to the home of the beloved Doña Ana, where he is assured of gaining access, since he is wearing the Marqués' red cape. This third seduction comes to an abrupt end when Doña Ana realizes that the man in the red cape is not the Marqués. Her cries for help bring her father Don Gonzalo; and Don Juan is forced to kill the Comendador in order to escape.

Doña Ana's seduction resembles the opening scene of ***El burlador de Sevilla*** insofar as neither scene of seduction in which a noblewoman is involved shows Don Juan at work.[4] Rather, each scene is brought to a close within the play even as the events leading up to those final moments are external to the drama *per se*, meaning that the point of the first and third seductions would seem to be the discovery of the imposter and not the actual fact of the seduction, Tirso, however, makes one significant addition to the presentation of the third seduction: although the play does not portray the seduction of Doña Ana, it does represent the events leading up to Don Juan's entry into the house of the Ulloas. The inclusion of these scenes involving Don Juan, the Marqués, Catalinón, and Doña Ana's servant provide us with the answer to the second question posed by the opening scene of the drama. How does Don Juan gain access to a noblewoman's chamber? He does so both by being an especially adept opportunist who successfully manipulates the personalities and the intricate events surrounding him, and by being a skillful actor.[5] Still more important, Don Juan, as an actor, takes his cues from a *written text*, in this instance, Doña Ana's letter.

The essence of Doña Ana's letter furnishes the *burlador* with his next role in the drama, it provides him, ironically enough, with his next *papel*. Enclosed in the *papel* sent to the Marqués is a dual message that is fully apprehended by Don Juan in his role as its bearer. So when Don Juan says of the appearance of the letter, "A mí el papel ha llegado / por la estafeta del viento" (1308-09), he not only comments on the unexpected manner in which the letter (*papel*) for the Marqués materializes, but also on the way another role (*papel*) "arrives." To the question of how Don Juan gains access to the noblewomen we must answer that the *burlador* is not just an actor, he is a masterful interpreter of the *written* word.

Yet the *papel* not only provides Don Juan with the role he plays in the third seduction, it also provides him in the fourth seduction with the means by which he convinces Batricio that Aminta had already promised herself to the *burlador*. As Don Juan explains to Batricio, "Al fin, Aminta, celosa, / o quizá desesperada / de verse de mi olvidada / y de ajeno dueño esposa, / esta carta me escribió / enviándome a llamar, / y yo prometí gozar / lo que el alma prometió" (1864-71). Don Juan again assumes the role intended for another, this time portraying a wronged lover. In the context of this new seduction, Don Juan becomes the *papel*'s destination, the lover, and Batricio is cast as the wrongful and unwanted husband—and all of this is attributed to the hand of the most likely illiterate Aminta. While Don Juan is adept at intercepting and representing *papeles*, he is equally skilled in reinterpreting those texts and roles with another end in mind.

Don Juan's skill as an actor—as an interpreter and reinterpreter of the written word—is developed in the fourth and final seduction in the domain of the spoken word and social discourse, conflating the presentation of Don Juan's *modus operandi* in the second and third seductions (where, in the seduction of Tisbea, the discussion centered around questions of the spoken word and, in the case of Doña Ana, the question at hand pertained to a written text). During the pastoral interlude of the scenes involving Aminta and her wedding party, the fourth victim says upon hearing Don Juan's seductive words. "No sé que diga; / que se encubren tus verdades con retóricas mentiras" (2051-53). Her averment of doubt points to the inherently linguistic aspects of the *burlador*'s skills, and to the fact that Don Juan seduces when the moment is most propitious for the exercising of his facility with the spoken word. Like Tisbea, Aminta exacts a promise from her would-be lover, in response to which Don Juan solemnly swears, "Juro a esta mano, señora, / . . . / de cumplirte la palabra" (2068-70).

Seduction in ***El burlador de Sevilla*** appears, first, to be much more than a structural device and, second, to have much more to do with questions of language than is usually acknowledged. As seduction is related to the promise, it suggests certain types of contractual obligation that are not specific to sexual relations between men and women but, rather, that have as much or more to do with society as a whole. Thus, we must look at other aspects of the *comedia* if we are to understand the ways in which Don Juan's linguistic facility allows him to deal with the world at large.

II

The reinscription of Don Juan's linguistic facility and of his reliance on a textual model takes place primarily in the context of his interactions in the exclusively male world of affairs of state and honor in a progression similar to his development over the course of the four seductions. This progression takes shape in a series of increasingly violent skirmishes and encounters between the *burlador* and his male antagonists, beginning with the King of Naples and his men who intrude during the final moments of the rendezvous with Isabela. In the first instance of such an encounter, Don Juan's perfidy is opposed to the moral rigor of the Rey de Nápoles. In the scenes involving Tisbea, on the other hand, Don Juan has brief—and in appearance not hostile—contact with the fishermen, including Tisbea's suitor, Anfriso. With his attempt on the honor of Doña Ana, the nature of the affront to traditional mores intensifies, resulting in Don Juan's open combat with Don Gonzalo. Finally, with the seduction of Aminta, the second and third scenes of seduction collapse into one as Don Juan tricks Batricio, the husband, and enters into his plans with the help of Aminta's father, Gaseno: "Pero antes de hacer el daño / le pretendo reparar; / a su padre voy a hablar / para autorizar mi engaño. / Bien lo supe negociar; / gozarla esta noche espero. / La noche camina, y yo quiero / su viejo padre llamar" (1904-11).

The situation of the opening scene is recapitulated in the last seduction in inverse fashion. Where Don Juan committed an affront to the King and had to be duly punished, he now proceeds by receiving the father's blessing. What appears to be an act of submission before the authority of another is, in fact, another *burla*. Don Juan will trick the father much in the same way that he tricked Batricio and will play on the avarice of both the father and the daughter. Like the scenes of seduction, these confrontations between and among the male characters follow a carefully plotted path in which specific moments and conflicts are reworked, seemingly to Don Juan's advantage.

Moreover, as a counterpoint to these encounters between and among the many male characters, Tirso inserts several scenes in which the Rey de Castilla decides affairs of state and social well-being with various officials of his kingdom. Don Juan's irreverence in the face of authority is not, then, surprising, particularly in view of other events in the play and the nature of the action overall. Still more significant is the way that this authority reveals itself and takes shape in ***El burlador de Sevilla*** and the dramatic world therein, since it bears a close relationship to Don Juan's linguistic facility. In contrast to Don Juan's empty promises, performatives devoid of any intent to fulfill the letter of his word, the commands of the Kings of Naples and Spain embody an obvious intent to impose their individual will on the events and lives under their jurisdiction.[6] The royal edicts emanate from the putative central force in the drama to affect all under their rule. That Don Juan disrepects and disobeys these edicts and their bearers is significant on the level of plot. But, because Don Juan disregards *both* the force of the promises that he makes *and* the authority embodied in the directives of others, the linguistic cast of the seductions carries over into Don Juan's dealings in the world of men.

The two lines of inquiry in ***El burlador de Sevilla*** outlined thus far (the one associated with the seductions proper and serving to reveal Don Juan as an actor, the other deriving from Don Juan's dealings with figures of worldly authority) converge and come into sharp focus in Don Juan's encounters with the sepulchral statue of the Comendador. Like the *burlador*'s exchanges with the other male characters, his dealings with the statue reveal the hierarchical ordering of this world. Furthermore, this series of exchanges succeeds in placing the *burlador* in a situation in which he must make and keep a promise. The result of his *burla* is a reciprocal invitation that Don Juan, giving his word as a "caballero," promises to honor. In a recapitulation of all that has transpired between the *burlador* and his female victims, Don Juan promises to dine at the Ulloa chapel.

At the same time, this encounter brings into focus the other skirmishes and encounters between Don Juan and the male characters of the drama. A representation of Doña Ana's father (and in crassly psychoanalytic terms, the Oedipal "father" that Don Juan killed in order to possess the "mother") and an agent of God, the statue functions as an overdetermined avatar of the Father. He thereby recalls the previous exchanges between father and sons, and not just those between the *burlador* and Don Diego and Gaseno, the two other fathers in the drama, but those involving the other male figures, too, since Don Pedro Tenorio also plays a protective role not unlike that of a real or even a surrogate father. Even Anfriso can be included in this schema, since he is described by Tisbea as "un pobre *padre* / de mis males testigo" (2199-2200); the fact that Anfriso is her suitor and will later become her husband does not obviate his function as figure of paternal authority for Tisbea.[7] In meting out divine justice, then, the Statue serves to emphasize blood ties, as at the opening of the drama: he represents all of the various "father" figures, and functions as a symbolic father, in the role of what Jacques Lacan has called the "paternal metaphor" or "nom du père."[8]

Guy Rosolato defines the paternal metaphor in this way: "Personne distincte, c'est-à-dire perçue comme capable de faire alterner sa parole et son désir, il devient l'autorité interdictrice. Auteur originel et autonome des lois, il en devient le principe, pour être crainte admiré, puisque l'enfant lui délègue par la toute-puissance de ses pensées un pouvoir sans limites, quoique obscur dans ses raisons, qui protège et punit."[9] Particularly in his guise as an agent of *Dios*, the symbolic father embodies and adumbrates the complex set of laws by which society—and the individual as constituted in society—is controlled. This set of laws, rather, this authority, is not only materially *real* but also *symbolic*, manifest in those conventional systems of signs within which action and social interaction take place, including and appearing most obviously in the powers that determine the uses and ends of language.

In ***El burlador de Sevilla,*** the Statue is both an agent of God's will, a supernatural *verbe de Dieu*, and a kind of synecdoche, representing as he does all of the father figures in the *comedia*. Thus, he assumes the terrestrial role of the divine "figure of the Law." By holding Don Juan to a promise, the Statue tacitly holds him answerable for *all* of his promises; and the fact that Don Juan discovers a linguistic loophole in the form of intention does him little good.

Still, the issue of Don Juan's intent is, of course, central to the linguistic questions that we have been discussing, as is the Statue's symbolic role. Behind Don Juan's promises to his female victims there was no intent at all, or, rather, there was the intent *not* to honor the *appearance* of intent inherent in the performance of a promise. When Don Juan swears to "cumplir el dulce sí" his intention is completely otherwise. Don Juan's sins against society are, therefore, not so much sins of carnality as they are sins of *linguistic* perversion. In this regard the Marqués de la Mota is hardly any better than his friend and cohort; and Doña Ana's attempt to betray the honor of her family—and her father's word—is equally symptomatic of a widespread social problem. Don Juan's failure to keep his promises thus threatens the social fabric in a society in which speech is the one essential way of making a contract.[10]

Emphasis on the spoken word and verbal contracts derives in part, perhaps, from the relative illiteracy of the Spanish population (although the literacy rate in sixteenth- and early-seventeenth-century Spain was, in fact, higher than originally thought[11]). But this emphasis probably derives as well from the power of the Church in Spanish society, from patristic theories of the sign, and from the importance of these theories for the religious doctrines associated with the sacraments, the linguistic aspects of which are most apparent, and most pertinent for this discussion, in the sacrament of marriage.[12] Matrimony is the only sacrament in which the two individuals directly involved act as the ministers of the sacramental rite. It is, therefore, a form of contractual agreement effected in language, one accomplished by a pair of individuals who act as instruments of Christ in the granting of their consent. Matrimony also has worldly importance apart from the role it plays in religious and spiritual life and apart from the strictly biological function of reproduction that it both institutionalizes and monitors. As Augustine teaches, "Habeant conjugia bonum suum, non quia filios procreant, sed quia honeste, quia licite, quia pudice, *quia socialiter procreant*, et procreatos pariter, salubriter, instanter educant, quia thori fidem invicem servant, quia sacramentum connubii non violant."[13] The enactment of the marriage rite constitutes the performance of a verbal contract that has a bearing on all society in that it "procreates" on a social level. This sacramental rite is thereby present in day-to-day life as a part of conventional contracts and exchanges. Don Juan, by freely promising to many without, in fact, intending to honor any of the promises, by perverting the linguistic basis of religious doctrine on the sensitive issue of the sacrament of marriage, contravenes and profanes not only those doctrines and sacraments but also menaces the very foundations of society.

The chaos created by Don Juan—erotic and linguistic—is therefore justly punished. The sheer magnitude and number of his misdeeds render him dangerous, even fatal. There is, however, an element of scapegoating involved in the meting out of this just recompense.[14] As we have noted, Don Juan is hardly the only deceitful individual in the world portrayed in ***El burlador de Sevilla***, a fact that Bruce W. Wardropper succinctly sums up in one phrase, "Don Juan deceives . . . in a deceit-full society."[15] So, even though Don Juan is not and cannot be mistaken for the innocent victim of sacrificial ritual, neither is he the only character in the *comedia* deserving of punishment. He is not merely a perpetrator of evil, but also a victim insofar as he pays for the sins and transgressions of others as well as for his own misdeeds. In this way, his actions serve to unify society against him and his death restores unity to society itself. Finally, Catalinón's timely announcement of the *burlador*'s even more timely demise allows the king to set the world immediately to right by ordering everyone to marry: "¡Justo castigo del cielo! / Y agora es bien que se casen / todos, pues la causa es muerta, / vida de tantos desastres" (2852-55).

This movement to marriage *en masse*, towards the nuptials of Octavio and Isabela, Anfriso and Tisbea, the Marqués and Doña Ana, and the consummation of the marriage of Batricio and Aminta, is, of course, a convention of Golden Age *comedias*. But despite the conventional nature of this final scene, we must note that, for all of the havoc that he wreaked, Don Juan himself instigated this happy ending. As a kind of destructive erotic force in the world, the *burlador* either channeled existing or incited new attractions, acting very much like a seventeenth-century version of the Platonic *daemon*, Eros, or, in his Roman guise, Cupid.[16] Isabela, for instance, is so unsure of her suitor that she must ask him to swear once more to uphold his promise to marry her *after* he, or the man playing his part, has "enjoyed" her favors. The other noblewoman in the drama, Doña Ana, finally gives herself up to her lover the Marqués when it appears that she is to be married by her father and her king to someone else: Don Juan. Tisbea, a prime example of the *mujer esquiva*, shuns all suitors only to fall victim to her arrogant pride. By attempting to marry above herself, she is an easy mark for Don Juan's promises. In this way, too, Aminta falls into Don Juan's trap, although initially with some misgivings. If it seems, then, that the *burlador* disrupts the harmony of an idyllic world, destroys happy conjugal unions, the truth is, in fact, otherwise. Only at the end of the anarchical path stretching from Italy to Spain is matrimony resurrected as the symbol of social harmony, since it is only after Don Juan's perfidy that Octavio, the Marqués, the prideful Tisbea and greedy Aminta, set aside their individual desires and content themselves with their lot as part of a union leading to some common good.

Don Juan thereby serves a social function in two senses. First, he unifies society against him and assumes the collective burden of guilt. Second he engenders the conditions by which desire is directed towards matrimony in socially productive ways. Although Don Juan may not seem to play strictly a positive role in the world portrayed by Tirso in ***El burlador de Sevilla***, he does serve a significant social function by showing how love construed in terms of Christian matrimony can bring individuals into closer union with the deity and can thus benefit the common good of all mankind. Like his mythical forebear, Eros, Don Juan is a daemonic force in the world, the means by which Tirso's all too human souls are led to a sacramental union. Don Juan's failed promises are contradicted by the potential good of the four mutual promises to be made at the end of the drama. In this way, the inquiry into the uses, abuses, and ends of language is brought to an end. The character who relies on the written word for his cues is duly punished; and the rest of society reaffirms its sustained commitment to social order by means of verbal contracts. It would not be misleading to identify Don Juan with Freud's Eros or "life instinct," as the force that, "by bringing about a more and more far-reaching combination of the particles into which living substance is dispersed, aims at complicating life and at the same time, of course, preserving it."[17]

III

It is important to see that the lesson of Tirso's *comedia* is not merely a moral one but that it also pertains to the crucial relationships between sign and referent and between word and deed so prominent in current discussions of literature. Tirso's play advocates nothing less than the fidelity of a performative action and proposes as inevitable the connection between literature and the world. The consequences of this assertion are significant for understanding the precise nature of a written text in a world of spoken language, since, although Doña Ana's letter signifies, in and of itself, both seduction (because it invites the Marqués to enjoy [*gozar*] "tu esperanza . . . y el fin de tu amor" [1336-37]) and the making of a promise ("y yo prometí gozar lo que el alma prometió" [1870-71]), it takes on its real meaning only once it is brought into the realm of the spoken word and human action. In other words, a *papel* is meaningful only *in potentia* and its meaningful nature remains a merely potential force until it is acted upon, just as, in fact, Don Juan acts upon the contents of Doña Ana's letter and acts within the parameters that it establishes. The written text assumes a worldly force when it has been drawn into the world by the action and discourse it engenders. This in turn underscores the impact of Tirso's *comedia* in that it, too, transcends its status as a text only when it is performed; thereby, it functions as a meaningful force in the world when it engenders, through its performance, human action.

The concept of seduction with which we began, either when construed traditionally in terms of sexual seduction or when read as an unproblematic structural device, fails to apprehend and to interpret fully those linguistic dimensions of the drama that we have been discussing here. Rather, seduction is presented in ***El burlador de Sevilla*** in its more etymologically strict sense, as a "leading astray" (Latin, *se* + *ducere*) as a *linguistic* seduction dependent on the worldly complexity of making empty promises. As such, the seductions in this *comedia* serve to emphasize what is at stake in various aspects of speech, the danger of breaches in a previously agreed upon linguistic economy being, of course, nothing less than the collapse of social order. It seems to me that this is the point at which ***El burlador de Sevilla*** can be read as following upon ideas in Juan de la Cueva's *El infamador* (1581), since Leucino's defamations affect society in ways similar to Don Juan's perversions of the promise; and Tirso's *comedia* finds its rightful place in a literary culture obsessed with the relations between language and literature on the one hand and with reality on the other.

In conclusion, it is important to note that the recent trends in criticism that would radically separate literature from the world, or a word from its worldly referent, exercise the same type of seduction practiced by Don Juan in that such approaches rely on a rhetoric that is forceful yet nonetheless skeptical of its worldly import. In terms of such an analysis, ***El burlador de Sevilla***, a work initially intended as a meaningful and instructive commentary on the linguistic vices of society, as a literary demonstration of the possibly incompatible ends to which language might be applied, might well result in a formally analyzed "text" ironically imprisoned within that selfsame system of deception that it would have—that it *should have*—exposed. But these limitations can be avoided. Recognition and recuperation of the worldly importance of language restores to Tirso's *comedia* the lessons pertaining to linguistic aspects of seduction that it so carefully adumbrates and exemplifies.

Notes

1. For an elaboration of this point of view, along with a discussion of the concomitant social implications, see A. A. Parker's seminal "The Spanish Drama of the Golden Age: A Method of Analysis and Interpretation." *The Great Playwrights*, ed. Eric Bentley (New York: Doubleday, 1970). 1: 694. See also Joaquín Casalduero, "Introducción," *El burlador de Sevilla y convidado de piedra*, Letras Hispánicas, 58, 3rd ed. (Madrid: Cátedra, 1978) 13-23, for a structural interpretation of seduction in the drama. I will cite *El burlador de Sevilla* from an advance copy of the forthcoming edition by James A. Parr (Madrid: Taurus); all references will be given in the text by line number.
2. On the notion of the promise in Don Juan, see: Joaquín Casalduero, *Contribución al estudio del tema de Don Juan en el teatro español* (1938: rpt. Madrid: Porrúa Turanzas, 1975) 19-39; Xavier A. Fernández, "Estudio Preliminar," *El burlador de Sevilla y convidado de piedra* (Barcelona: Alhambra. 1978) 18-25; and Shoshana Felman, *Le Scandale du corps parlant. Don Juan avec Austin ou la séduction en deux langues* (Paris: Seuil, 1980), which serves as a touchstone for my own analysis of the promise in *El burlador de Sevilla.*
3. Useful commentary on this opening scene includes: Manuel Durán and Roberto González Echevarría, "Luz y oscuridad: La estructura simbólica de *El burlador de Sevilla." Homenaje a William L. Fichter. Estudios sobre el teatro antiguo hispánico y otros ensayos*, ed. A. David Kossoff and José Amor y Vázquez (Madrid: Castalia, 1971), 201-09; and Arturo Serrano Plaja, "Un no de Don Juan y un no a Don Juan. (Notas sobre *El burlador de Sevilla," Segismundo* 9 (1973): 17-32. Since criticism on *El burlador de Sevilla* is voluminous I will cite only those studies that are crucial to my own interpretation.
4. In fact, there is some question as to whether or not Doña Ana is actually seduced and early commentators are as confused as more recent critics. Wardropper, for instance, seems to think not, but there has been continuing discussion. See Wardropper, "*El burlador de Sevilla*: A Tragedy of Errors," *PQ* 36 (1957): 70; Vicente Cabrera, "Doña Ana's Seduction in *El burlador de Sevilla.*" *BCom* 26 (1974): 49-51; Luis González-del-Valle, "Doña Ana's Seduction in *El burlador de Sevilla*: A Reconsideration," *BCom* 30 (1978): 42-45; and José M. Ruano de la Haza, "Doña Ana's Seduction in *El burlador de Sevilla*: Further Evidence Against," *BCom* 32 (1980): 131-33.
5. On Don Juan as an actor see Daniel Rogers, *Tirso de Molina: 'El burlador de Sevilla'*;, Critical Guides To Spanish Texts, 19 (London: Grant and Cutler, 1977), 33; and Henry Sullivan, *Tirso de Molina and the Drama of the Counter Reformation*, 2nd ed. (Amsterdam: Rodopi, 1981), 77.
6. On the notion of the performative in language see J. L. Austin, *How To Do Things with Words*, ed. J. O. Urmson and Marina Sbisà, 2nd ed. (Cambridge: Harvard UP, 1975), especially 4-11.
7. This is one point at which I part company with Parr's fine edition. Parr emends this line of the *comedia* to read, "Un pescador, Anfriso, y un pobre padre / de mis males testigo" (2199). Obviously, the traditional reading of this line, which I give in the text, complements my reading of the drama and I therefore use it here.
8. On Lacan's notion of the "nom du père" see the following: "Fonction et champ de la parole et du langage," "D'une préliminaire à tout traitement possible de la psychose," and "Subversion du sujet et dialectique du désir dans l'inconscient freudien" in *Ecrits*, La Champ Freudien (Paris: Seuil, 1966), 266-322, 531-84 and 793-828, respectively.
9. *Essais sur le symbolique*, Collection Connaissance de L'Inconscient (Paris: Gallimard, 1969), 39.
10. There is an explicit indictment of written agreements in *La estrella de Sevilla* (Act 2, scene 4) in which two characters discuss a "contract" that is to be taken out on a third character. On this aspect of *La estrella de Sevilla* see Elias L. Rivers, "The Shame of Writing in *La estrella de Sevilla*," *Folio* (1980): 105-17. A modified version of this article appears in Rivers' *Quixotic Scriptures: Essays on the Textuality of Hispanic Literature* (Bloomington: Indiana UP, 1983), 79-87.
11. Recent studies indicate that the literacy rate in sixteenth- and early-seventeenth-century Spain probably ranged between 50% and 65%. See: P. Berger, "La Lecture en Valence, 1474 à 1504," *Mélanges de la Casa de Velázquez* 11 (1975): 99-118; M.-C. Rodríguez and B. Bennassar. "Signatures et niveau culturel des témoins et accusés dans les procès d'inquisition du ressort du tribunal de Tolède (1525-1817) et du ressort du tribunal de Cordove (1595-1632)," *Cahiers du Monde*

Hispanique-luso-brasilien 31 (1978): 17-47; C. Larquié, "L'Alphabétisation à Madrid en 1650," *Revue d'Histoire Moderne et Contemporaine* 28 (1981): 132-57; J. E. Gelabert González, "Lectura y escritura en una ciudad provinciana del siglo XVII: Santiago de Compostela," *BH* 84 (1982): 264-90; J. N. H. Lawrance. "The Spread of Lay Literacy in Late Medieval Castile," *BHS* 62 (1985): 79-94.

12. A sacrament is the sensible sign of Christ's love for and union with the Church. The making of a sacrament entails both an action and the speaking of words in order to provide the possibility of grace and redemption. To translate this into the terminology with which we have been discussing *El burlador de Sevilla*, sacraments are a kind of performative, a complex action that takes place in language, in which the words spoken during the course of the accompanying action and the action itself join to form a sensible or visible sign of this process. The word both empowers and embodies the sacrament, which, despite its oral and transient nature is nonetheless powerful throughout all time: "Nam et in ipso verbo, aliud est sonus transiens, aliud virtus manens" (Augustine, *In Joannis Evangelium* 80, 3, *Patrologiae cursus completus: Series latina*, ed. J.-P. Migne, 221 vols. [Paris: 1844-90], 35 [1845]: col. 1840).

13. *De Sancta Virginitate* 12, 12, *Patrologiae cursus completus*, 40 (1887): col. 401.

14. On scapegoating and the scapegoat mechanism in myth and ritual see René Girard, *La violence et la sacré*; (Paris: Grasset, 1972); *"To double business bound": Essays on Literature, Mimesis and Anthropology* (Baltimore: Johns Hopkins UP, 1978); and *Le Bouc émissaire* (Paris: Gallimard, 1982).

15. "A Tragedy of Errors" 65.

16. In Plato's *Symposium*, Socrates explains how he learned of Eros from Diotima:

    "What then is Love?" I asked; "Is he mortal?" "No." "What then?" "As in the former instance, he neither mortal nor immortal, but is a mean between the two." "What is he, Diotima?" "He is a great spirit [*daemon*] and like all spirits he is an intermediary between the divine and the mortal." "And what," I said, "is his power?" "He interprets between gods and men . . . through Love all the intercourse and converse of gods with men, whether they be awake or asleep, is carried on." (202d, e; 203a; I cite from the *Symposium*, trans. Benjamin Jowett, *The Dialogues of Plato*, 4th ed. [Oxford: Clarendon Press, 1954], 1: 504-55)

    In this context, it is instructive to consider the story of Cupid and Psyche in Apuleius' *The Golden Ass*, bks. 4-6 (a fine discussion of which is to be found in James Tatum's *Apuleius and 'The Golden Ass'*; [Ithaca: Cornell UP, 1979], especially 49-68). Here, Cupid (Eros, love) is the daemonic force by which the human soul (psyche) can be bound to the gods in love and can thereby achieve immortality.

17. See Sigmund Freud, *The Ego and the Id, The Standard Edition of the Complete Psychological Works of Sigmund Freud*, ed. and trans. James Strachey in collaboration with Anna Freud (London: Hogarth Press, 1954), 19: 40.

Judith H. Arias (essay date 1990)

SOURCE: "Doubles in Hell: *El Burlador de Sevilla* Y *Convidado de Piedra*," in *Hispanic Review*, Vol. 58, No. 3, Summer, 1990, pp. 361-77.

[*In the following essay, Arias examines why both Don Juan and the Commander perish in de Molina's* El burlador de Sevilla, *concluding that the violence committed by the Commander in the name of God is no more than Don Juan's violence committed in vain.*]

Tirso de Molina's ***El burlador de Sevilla y convidado de piedra*** (c. 1630) is a play with a deceptively simple happy ending. After sinning against society and against God throughout the four adventures that compose the dramatic action, Don Juan finally meets with his just fate in the flames of hell. In the closing scene, the King heralds the return to social order by ordaining the marriage of Don Juan's victims; the source of the community's problems, he proclaims, has been dealt his just punishment from Heaven:

> ¡Justo castigo del cielo!
> Y agora es bien que se casen
> todos, pues la causa es muerta,
> vida de tantos desastres. (3.1057-60)

Here we see what critics commonly confirm: that the force of divine justice impels the play's particularly prominent movement from "order disturbed to order restored," a movement which Arnold Reichenberger identifies as typical of the comedia in general (307).

One problem, however, obscures our understanding of this divine justice. Since the premiere of ***El burlador*** nearly 360 years ago, commentators have virtually ignored the question of why the Commander, a messenger of God, perishes in the flames together with Don Juan. In fact, critics for the most part continue to weave their interpretations of the dramatic events as though this apparent philosophical inconsistency did not exist. The present study endeavors to shed light on this problem, first by exploring the reasons why we persist in minimizing the double damnation and then by illustrating why the incident is central to a more profound understanding of the play's underlying organization and significance. I shall show that the resolution of ***El burlador*** perpetuates a mythological lie at the same time that it allows a glimpse of the heretofore unrecognized ethnological truth which this lie encumbers. René Girard's theory concerning the violent origins of religion and the victimary mechanism upon which society is based suggests the way of finally unveiling this truth.

It is curious that our critical understanding of the play's resolution mirrors the King's own perception of the happy ending. Similarly, our disregard for the significance of the Commander's fate duplicates the reaction of the single dramatic witness to the catastrophe, Catalinón. A close look at the text reveals that the King's knowledge of Don Juan's death is based upon Catalinón's secondhand account of the incident. After escaping the flames in the chapel that devour both the Commander and Don Juan, Catalinón scurries to the palace to relate the strange tale of his master's fate. Don Juan's victims, his father, and the King listen in wonder as the servant tells how he saw the vivified statue take Don Juan by the hand and squeeze the very life out of him, saying he was acting in accordance with God's will. Catalinón then seals his version of the story by repeating the Commander's own words: "Dios / me manda que así te mate, / castigando tus delitos. / Quien tal hace que tal pague" (3.1047-50). Like all representation, Catalinón's account of the catastrophe entails a degree of distortion: he says nothing of the fire within the statue nor of the Commander's and Don Juan's dual descent into those flames. He ignores these details; their meaning does not penetrate. Instead, by repeating the statue's words, the servant prompts his listeners to believe that the Commander was indeed a messenger sent from heaven to kill the guilty sinner in punishment for his crimes, the instrument of divine justice responsible for the ultimate triumph of good over evil. Future audiences of ***El burlador***, like Catalinón's own audience, unquestioningly perpetuate this mistaken belief.

Reichenberger lends authority to the conventional perception when he says that the Spanish playwright of the comedia "may be and often is a priest, . . . but not a prophet or seer (*vates*) who sees farther than his public and points towards new goals but dimly perceived by his audience" (306). Just prior to Reichenberger's comments in the late 1950s, however, critics were beginning to identify elements in Tirso's play that intimate a heretofore unperceived complexity of meaning. In *The Approach to the Spanish Drama of the Golden Age*, Alexander A. Parker notes that each of Don Juan's adventures entails the progressive breaking down of the institutions and beliefs that unite the community; his behavior, Parker suggests, is not the merely capricious exercise in sexual revelry it appears to be (13; see also Rodríguez). And in "***El Burlador de Sevilla***: A Tragedy of Errors," Bruce Wardropper argues that if Don Juan's conduct threatens the social order, it is only because the community is already corrupt (64; see also Aubrun; Ruiz Ramón; Lundelius). Parker's and Wardropper's germinal observations corroborate the suggestion that the playwright's vision and that of his public are not one and the same, that in fact Tirso gives dramatic form to a truth that Catalinón and the society of ***El burlador***, as well as the play's commentators and audiences, sorely wish to ignore. The breadth of this truth exceeds what commentators are prone to judge as the limited terrain of the comedia in general; it concerns the universal and timeless problem of human violence.

Traditionally, interpretations of ***El burlador*** focus on questions which involve either contemporary religious orthodoxy or the problem of the origins of the supernatural episode. On the one hand, commentators view the play as an exemplary drama belonging to the tradition of the propaedeutic literature of the times, the Catholic Reformation started in 1563 by the edicts of the Council of Trent. In its historical context, the meaning of the drama hinges on the theological controversy over the doctrines of predestination and free will. Américo Castro sums up the traditional view that the play's underlying problem concerns whether man can live sure of divine grace since destiny rules over his ultimate fate, or whether he must work toward salvation through the practice of good deeds and virtue (14).[1] On the other hand, the episode of the vivified statue has been a focal point of interest ever since Arturo Farinelli, Víctor Said Armesto, and Georges Gendarme de Bévotte began the chauvinistic search for its origins in Spanish and European folklore. Without detracting from the value of these two dominant critical perspectives, it must be noted that commentators have lost sight of the play's overall mythological organization. They have not explored its sacrificial theme and, in particular, the implications of its sacrificial resolution.

Nevertheless ***El burlador*** is clearly a sacrificial drama. As René Girard would see it, the generative and organizing force behind the themes and motifs of the play is the scapegoat mechanism which culminates in sacrifice. In *Violence and the Sacred* Girard explains his thesis that the process of scapegoating, or unanimous victimization, is at the heart of religious beliefs and prohibitions and, ultimately, of all human institutions. It is, he believes, the generating source, or structuring device, of all world mythologies. According to the Girardian theory, scapegoating provided the means for ensuring the peaceful continuity of societies in the earliest stages of development. Primitive communities discharged the aggressiveness and wrongdoings of individual members of a social group onto a single victim, thereby diverting the threat of escalating violence within the group onto a random substitute. The expulsion or murder of the scapegoat served to bring the potentially destructive situation under control, to eliminate the contagion of internal violence, and to restore social order. The victim, who was initially charged as the cause of social disintegration, became in retrospect the cure for the same ills with which he was charged. Unaware that its own collective transfer occasioned the solution for internal dissension and violence, the primitive community endowed its victim with the power to cure those ills; it sanctified the victim, thus giving birth to what would become the notion of god. Eventually, ritual sacrifices emerged as a form of imitating or recreating the scapegoat process, which the community remembered as its source of peace. The memory of collective violence and expulsion of the surrogate victim, as Girard summarily says, "is preserved, but concealed under the veils of ritual sacrifice which falsifies the nature of the crisis and moralizes the scapegoat mechanism. At later stages in culture," he adds, "the function of the ritual is taken over by literature" (*Violence* 201).

There appears to be an explicit parallel between the scapegoat process as Girard describes it, and the dramatic action of ***El burlador***. The trend in recent studies of the play has in fact begun to expose the similarities by challenging the Manichaean notion of good and evil as these two forces appear in opposition throughout the play. Don Juan continues to emerge as the unchristian sinner who is guilty of crimes against both God and the community. But critics now agree that Don Juan's victims, far from being innocent as once assumed, actually form part of a corrupt society in which pride, arrogance, lust, envy, greed, dishonesty, favoritism, and hypocrisy prevail as norms of behavior. As Francisco Ruiz Ramón shows in "Don Juan y la sociedad del Burlador," corruption pervades all levels of the society from the countryfolk of the provinces to the nobles in the royal palace; gender is not a discriminating factor nor is the King himself exempt. At the end of the play, nevertheless, the members of this society are unanimous in their charge that Don Juan is the sole cause of their problems. His "miraculous" death at the hands of the "messenger of God" not only appeases their demand for just retribution but achieves the cathartic effect of cleansing the community of its own sins and guilt and of reaffirming the members' own mistaken sense of righteousness—a catharsis which sympathetic audiences and readers of the play also experience. At the same time, Don Juan's death provides the occasion for the marriage of victims and rivals, which amounts to a reconfirmation of faith in the institutions that define the community. His immolation, like that of the sacrificial victim in primitive societies, sets the stage for the restoration of social order. The happy ending thus marks the beginning of a period of renewed social harmony while Don Juan emerges not only as the source but also the cure of the community's problems. His at once pernicious and beneficent nature is perpetuated to this day by artists and critics who either romanticize Don Juan's heroic proportions or censure the violence that he incarnates. The essential ambiguity of the figure, characteristic of any scapegoat, has become proverbial.

Further evidence of the parallel between the scapegoat mechanism and the dramatic action of ***El burlador*** arises in the crisis which leads to the sacrificial solution, and which Don Juan's actions provoke. Although much commentary centers on Don Juan's sexual behavior, his sexuality serves not only to divert our attention away from the less obvious motivating force that impels his actions (the subject of a forthcoming study) but also to veil the less obvious characteristic that defines the real essence of his being. Don Juan's own words in the opening scene of the play point to this characteristic: as he makes his debut into the world of literary fiction, he boldly proclaims, "¿Quién soy? Un hombre sin nombre" (1.15). His later behavior confirms that Don Juan's refusal here to identify himself cannot be explained in psychological terms alone as a renunciation of the "law of the Name-of-the-Father," as Jacques Lacan argues (qtd. in Sullivan 94) but can be better understood in terms of a rejection of the system of nomenclature in general. In saying that he is a man without a name, Don Juan denies the process that makes possible the separation of subject and object and thus provides the basis for the system of differentiation upon which human knowledge resides. His iconoclasm persists throughout the play, from his first to his final adventure, as he makes a mockery not only of the father / son relation, but also of the relation between subject and king, man and woman, and man and God. He further disregards class distinctions, rules of hospitality, bonds of friendship, the institution of marriage, and respect for the dead. At the same time that Don Juan ravages social customs, laws, and institutions, he refuses to acknowledge humanity's most fundamental categories of thought: past and future, sin and virtue, sacred and profane. In a word, Don Juan progressively destroys the system of biological, cultural, and ontological distinctions that defines the human community and provides for its peaceful coexistence and development. He incarnates the very spirit of social violence.

The *ex-abrupto* opening of ***El burlador***, the repetition of fleeting sexual adventures and flight, the incessant switching of matrimonial partners, the disregard for the unities of time and space, and the abrupt changes in tone from dramatic to lyric to comic all reflect Don Juan's own Dionysian behavior. His extreme iconoclasm, which structure and theme reinforce, sets into motion the social crisis which precipitates the play's victimary resolution. As Girard would see it, the events preceding this resolution constitute the dramatic reenactment of a "sacrificial crisis," a crisis in which forms of social violence tend to eliminate all differences within a cultural unit and thereby threaten its very existence:

> The sacrificial crisis can be defined . . . as a crisis of distinctions—that is, a crisis affecting the cultural order. This cultural order is nothing more than a regulated system of distinctions in which the differences among individuals are used to establish their identity and their mutual relationships. . . . Order, peace, and fecundity depend on cultural distinctions; it is not these distinctions but the loss of them that gives birth to fierce rivalries and sets members of the same family or social group at one another's throats. (*Violence* 49)

Girard calls this leveling of cultural differences "undifferentiation," a theme which emerges from multiple levels of ***El burlador***. Tirso captures the spirit of the crisis of distinctions in the closing scenes of the play. On the one hand, categorical distinctions disappear: the vivified statue is evidence of a disregard for the distinction between life and death, the demonic meal in the chapel betrays a rupture in the boundary between infernal and divine, and the vengeful, deceitful, and violent behavior of the "messenger of God" challenges the Christian understanding of what constitutes good and evil. On the other hand, the gathering of nobles and countryfolk at the palace of Seville signals the collapse of cultural distinctions: father turns against son (3.1023-27), subjects ignore the conventions of decorum in the presence of their king (3.759-60), a fisherwoman befriends a Duchess (3.1106), a country maiden appears as a courtesan on the arm of a Duke (3.827-30). The indiscriminate crowd is unanimous, moreover, in its rejection of Don Juan; everyone speaks of his or her desire for revenge and retribution. The feeling is that if the situation is not quickly resolved, the pandemonium will lead to all out violence. At the same time, the shifting of scenes between the palace, and the inn and church where Don Juan's encounters with the vivified statue occur, suggests that a supernatural solution is at hand.

Tirso in fact suggests the probability of such a solution at intervals throughout the play, each time Don Juan's father, servant, and victims warn him that he must eventually come to terms with divine justice. In addition, the textual portrayal of an ineffectual king precludes the possibility of a judicial solution to the crisis. The judicial system, after all, as Girard says, "can only exist in conjunction with a firmly established political power" (*Violence* 23). And the King of Castille, as Ruiz Ramón says, plays the role of nothing more than a vulgar matchmaker (89). It is thus not surprising that when the King finally orders that Don Juan be seized and killed (3.1022), the sacrificial solution is already set into motion by the intervention of the Commander's vivified statue. The demonic inversion of the imagery of sacrifice surrounding the last communal meal as well as Don Juan's immolation in the chapel (altar) only serve to further highlight the sacrificial theme.

On this basis, the play appears to be a thinly-veiled Christianized dramatization of a sacrificial rite. But if ***El burlador*** were merely a Christian representation of sacrifice cast in the theological mold and concurring with the understanding of its time, then Charles V. Aubrun would be correct in judging the supernatural denouement as a badly integrated afterthought. Tirso's play is not such a drama, however, precisely because of the supernatural episode. As the remainder of this study endeavors to show, the intervention and eventual fate of the stone statue in fact exposes the psychology of the mechanism of sacrifice, thus planting the seeds for its very demystification.

In a sacrificial context as Girard describes it, the alternation of roles between sacrificer and victim serves to reveal their fundamental lack of difference (see "To double business"). With this in mind, it is interesting to note that Tirso insists on the themes of role reversal and alternation to the extent that his insistence can hardly be fortuitous. The reciprocal invitation to dinner, in which Don Juan and the Commander respectively double as both host and guest, is one obvious case in point. Another striking example occurs in the scene in which the statue lures Don Juan to his death: here the Commander imitates the same deceitful behavior, gestures, and language the *burlador* previously employed in his own adventures throughout the play (see Allain). The underlying identity of the Commander and Don Juan, which a Girardian view of the role reversals suggests, is confirmed in the climactic moment of the play when the antagonists perish together as doubles in the flames of hell. The dual title of the play highlights the structural and thematic coherence of the work by intimating this eventual doubling. Nevertheless, in spite of the textual insistence on alternation, role reversal, and reciprocity, Charles Aubrun suggests the duplicity of the dinner scenes is superfluous; Archimede Marni dismisses the duplicity of the Commander's behavior on the grounds of the religious concept of justice as counterpassion; and critics in general ignore the episode of the double damnation.

The themes of role reversal, alternation, reciprocity, and doubling all highlight the essential absence of difference between Don Gonzalo and Don Juan, divine messenger and sinner, sacrificer and victim. These themes also reinforce the predominate theme of undifferentiation, or the leveling of distinctions which provokes the social crisis that culminates in sacrifice. In addition, the supporting themes emphasize the infernal circularity of the process of revenge in which the Commander engages, as will be explained. And finally, in a still more general sense, role reversal, alternation, reciprocity, and doubling all underscore the notion of substitution as the basis for the practice of sacrifice. In other words, the themes reflect the process of sacrificial substitution whereby the society seeks to deflect its own violence upon the victim. As we see then, these intertwining themes constitute a remarkable thematic cluster whose unity is founded in sacrificial victimization.

Perhaps the principal difficulty with the resolution of Tirso's play does not arise from the text after all, but from interpretations that fail to distinguish between the mythological and the Christian elements which converge in the text.[2] The most disturbing paradox of the resolution is the forthright association between the sacred and violence—an association which belongs distinctively to mythological consciousness. The Commander's role as a messenger of God openly links the issue of divine justice with revenge, deceit, and murder: the statue tricks Don Juan into taking his hand, ignores his plea for divine absolution and the chance for a final confession, kills the unsuspecting victim, and imputes his murderous act to divine injunction. His behavior points to the essential characteristic of the mythological quality of the sacred, which "is its dual nature," as Girard explains. "[I]t is both harmful and beneficial. It leaves the impression of a double transcendence, a paradoxical conjunction, because we understand [the duality] from a Christian perspective considered by us to be the norm, whereas in fact it is unique" (*Scapegoat* 199).

Our failure until now to come to terms with the Commander's fate appears to be the result of viewing his behavior from a Christian perspective rather than as evidence of the persistence of ancient beliefs. Most commentators do injustice to the text by ignoring the Commander's fate altogether. Some resort to the slanted rationalization of Daniel Rogers, for example, who says "there is no indication that Don Gonzalo, having delivered his charge into hell, will himself be obliged to stay there" (144). Others, like Archimede Marni, dispense with the problem while explaining the Commander's unchristian conduct on the grounds of what they call the Aristotelian-Thomistic concept of counterpassion, a sophisticated rendering of the "eye for an eye" code of justice. They show that Don Juan's punishment is made to fit his crimes but no one extends this observation to the Commander's own fate. Each of these commentators misses the point. They fall victim to the divine messenger's own game of taking his violence seriously and thus they entrap themselves within the same sacrificial system that the play and its participants represent. Such responses not only obscure the perspective necessary to understand the problem at hand, the critics' reliance on religious orthodoxy to explain the Commander's violent behavior also provides a revealing example of how religion shelters us from confronting the truth of violence, just as the Girardian theory maintains.

Although it is true that Tirso shows the primitive "eye for an eye" principle controls retaliation, he is unambiguous in condemning the Commander's own use of violence to deter violence. In the end, Tirso leaves no room to justify or to dismiss this conduct, for the play's self-professed instrument of divine justice perishes with the guilty sinner in the flames. We must finally recognize, then, that the text means precisely what it says: the Commander suffers the same punishment as Don Juan; he burns in hell. Consequently, if the Commander is an instrument of divine justice, he is also a victim of that justice. If he is a messenger of God sent to ensure the triumph of good over evil, he is also a part of the evil over which the good eventually triumphs.

The textual association statue/vengeance/God sheds light on this problem. The obvious nature of the vivified statue's evil is vengeance and this becomes apparent in the second act of the play. As he lies dying, Don Gonzalo's sole concern is his desire for revenge; with his last breath he threatens Don Juan that his fury will follow him (2.542). At the end of the play, the vivified statue fulfills this threat. The fire raging within the statue is metaphorically a desire for vengeance so terrible and omnipotent that it survives death itself. The statue's fire is also real to the extent that it eventually destroys his antagonist. It seems clear, then, that the Commander's statue embodies the spirit of vengeance. He represents the unchristian desire for revenge which consumes each of Don Juan's victims as they gather at the palace and which is, moreover, deeply ingrained not only in seventeenth-century Spanish society but in the human community of all times and places. This view suggests that our understanding of the statue's origins must be tied not only to the medieval legends and ballads in which he appears but to a far earlier time in the history of the human race. Perhaps he is linked in the memory of society with the notion of the graven images of stone that man placed between himself and God, or perhaps even with the notion of death by stoning whereby no one person is responsible for the crime.

We must, accordingly, question the notion that the statue is a messenger of God, as he claims, and suspect instead that he represents the community and is a product of its own illusions. As he appears in ***El burlador***, the avenging statue is in fact a typical product of mythical thought, which conceives of the sacred and violence and of life and death as a single essence (see Cassirer). He is a consequence of the thinking that hypostatizes forces and activities as its means of engendering mythical explanations of the world and, in this particular instance, as its means of avoiding the burden of its own guilt. Just as Venus is love and beauty, and Vulcan is the forming principle at work in the universe, the vivified statue, as Tirso presents him, is vengeance.

On this basis, one might assume that the supernatural intervention of the Commander is not linked primarily with miracle, as traditional commentaries maintain. The statue does not belong to the Christian realm of the miraculous, which ordinarily involves the element of faith and the intervention of God, but to the world of mythological monsters where anything can turn into anything else, where the boundary between life and death is nonexistent, and where the direct intervention of ambivalent gods is a common occurrence. If we wish, nevertheless, to follow through with the interpretation of the statue's intervention along the lines of miracle, we can argue that the miraculous occurs not with the appearance of the statue but with his disappearance into the flames. His damnation is tantamount to God's denial of the self-appointed messenger and to His rejection of the responsibility for the vengeance and violence that the statue attributes to Him. In leaving the Commander to burn with the unchristian sinner, God reveals their essential similarity at the same time that He returns the burden of vengeance/violence back to man and woman, who are its true originators and perpetrators. He leaves humankind to its own devices.

If we slightly adjust the focus of Wardropper's thesis of "El tema central de ***El burlador de Sevilla***," that the theme of the drama concerns the miraculous intervention of God because human justice does not work, we reveal an essential insight. God does not intervene through the mediation of the avenging statue because the King and the judicial system are inadequate to deal with the problem at hand. After all, the King does not seriously try to deal with Don Juan until the end of the play, when he finally orders that the *burlador* be seized and killed. Instead, God intervenes to destroy the statue which embodies the self-righteous illusion that the society has created out of its own desire for vengeance. Vengeance is the system of human justice which necessitates the intervention of God to ensure its destruction.

All this explains why the Commander's damnation serves to demystify his own rationale. The incident reveals the means by which humanity conceals from itself the human origin of its own violence (*Violence* 161). The projection of vengeance/violence onto the supernatural statue and the statue's subsequent projection of vengeance/violence onto God merely duplicate the process by which the human community avoids responsibility for this burden and seeks to justify this evil. The solution is infallible, for violence is first imputed to a supernatural monster and then to God Himself, always to an element outside the realm of human jurisdiction and control. Thus we can begin to understand Girard's thesis that "violence is the heart and secret soul of the sacred" (*Violence* 31). The statue's own violent conduct carried out in the name of God, as well as our dismissal of it on the basis of religious dogma, in essence, demonstrates this truth.

The text, moreover, speaks for itself in revealing the Commander's, and our own, mistaken perception of the workings of divine justice in ***El burlador***. It shows that the "eye for an eye" dictum understood as a principle for action ignores the fact that the retaliatory code serves also as an *a posteriori* statement on the fate of those who adopt it. In other words, the text shows that the violence which revenge perpetuates inevitably ends in the destruction of both parties. The Commander's own words testify to the fact that he becomes a victim of the same divine law he self-righteously espouses. When the statue is about to kill Don Juan, he says, "Ésta es justicia de Dios: / quien tal hace que tal pague" (3.956-57). When he later descends into the flames with Don Juan, the Commander repeats the same words: "Ésta es justicia de Dios: / quien tal hace que tal pague" (3.973-74). In the first instance, we understand the aphorism to mean that the *burlador* himself is finally deceived, tricked into paying with his life the price for his sinful ways. In the second instance, however, the meaning changes as the words paradoxically become a commentary on the Commander's own fate. The statue is consumed by his own fire; he alone is responsible for his own death. As Girard says, "[t]he very weapons used to combat violence are turned against their users. Violence is like a raging fire that feeds on the very objects intended to smother its flames" (*Violence* 31). At this point in the drama, we must either dismiss the episode as nonsense, or finally recognize the universal law that violence inevitably will return to the perpetrator. The other option, Catalinón's, of ignoring the Commander's fate, is no longer open to us.

Textual indications of the statue's association with hell, which precede and foreshadow the catastrophe, confirm that the Commander's damnation is neither incidental nor an oversight on the part of the dramatist. Prior to leaving the inn where the first dinner scene takes place, the statue asks for Don Juan's hand and assures him there is nothing to fear. "¿Eso dices? ¿Yo temor?" answers Don Juan extending his hand; "Si fueras el mismo infierno / la mano te diera yo" (3.645-47). Immediately afterwards, he ponders the infernal nature of his antagonist but quickly dismisses his premonition as a figment of his imagination:

> Cuando me tomó la mano,
> de suerte me la apretó,
> que un infierno parecía
> jamás vide tal calor.
> Un aliento respiraba,
> organizando la voz,
> tan frío, que parecía
> infernal respiración.
> Pero todas son ideas
> que da la imaginación: (3.668-77)

When Don Juan returns to the chapel to comply with the reciprocal invitation to dinner, his "imaginary" fears prove to be prophetic. At the Commander's request, he raises a tombstone to discover their meal of scorpion, vipers, and fingernails, items which folklorist Dorothy Mackay equates with the popular conception of hell's horrors. It is hardly fortuitous that the Commander refers to these items as "*nuestros* manjares" (3.921; emphasis added). Don Juan unwittingly alludes once again to demonic imagery, saying to his host: "Comeré / si me dieses áspid a áspid / cuantos el infierno tiene" (3.2725-27). After the meal in the chapel, which by now has undeniable associations as an anteroom of hell rather than a house of God, the statue once again asks for Don Juan's hand and deceptively reassures him there is nothing to fear. "¿Eso dices? ¿Yo temor?" repeats Don Juan, echoing his response of their previous encounter. This time his reply ends not with the same fatuous boast but with the terrified realization that the statue's fire is burning him: "¡Que me abrasas! ¡No me abrases con tu fuego!" (3.946-50). Moments later, chapel, avenger, and victim are engulfed in the flames.

All in all, the textual evidence linking the avenging statue with hell is irrefutable. The Commander's attribution onto God of his own violence and vengeance is a self-righteous delusion which his own damnation serves to expose. The monologue in which Don Juan describes the statue's infernal presence, the parallel dialogue of the two dinner scenes depicting him as a diabolic figure, the fiendish food and setting over which he presides, and the fact that the fire which eventually destroys both antagonists arises from within the statue all leave little room to question his identity not as a messenger of God but as hell itself. Our commentary finally allows us to understand his disappearance into the flames as an extraordinary event to the extent that it manifests, in ever so brief an instant, the convergence of mythology with Christianity: it reveals that vengeance, the life force of the sacrificial system upon which mythology rests, is hell.

In conclusion, my study has shown that the play's movement from the disturbance of order to the restoration of order is a reenactment of the scapegoat mechanism triggered in primitive societies by a social crisis of distinctions. As violence increasingly threatens the well-being and structure of the community, the resentment and desire for revenge among its members come to rest on a single individual and dissipate with his death, thus providing for the return to order. Tirso's drama presents a prime example of Girard's thesis that ritual sacrifice takes over the function of the scapegoat mechanism and that literature eventually takes on the function of this ritual. In the process, these rites moralize the workings of the mechanism, a process which ***El burlador*** decisively reflects but only ostensibly endorses.

What is truly remarkable about this play is that it is a sacrificial drama in which Tirso establishes the guilt of the victim at the same time that he denounces the innocence of the avenger and of the community he represents. It is a drama that begins to expose the sacrificial mechanism. The incident of the statue's damnation lifts the play's mechanism of concealment briefly to reveal the truth that Catalinón does not see and that the commentators' rationalizations of the Commander's unchristian behavior further veil. This truth, as I have shown, concerns the process of the sacralization of violence and the illusory nature of the process of revenge which seems to generate this violence. It concerns our inability to comprehend human violence, an inability to come to terms with it, a refusal to assume responsibility for it. Tirso quickly conceals these truths with the play's sacrificial ending, however, for in the final solution he reverts to the very mechanism that the Commander's damnation begins to dismantle. But in so doing, he points to still another truth, which is the ethnological reality that social order depends upon victimization.

The ending of Tirso's drama thus appears to contradict the notion implicit in the concept of counterpassion that violence is of a dual essence: that the sinner Don Juan exhibits a bad violence which must be punished while the Commander's good violence is to be condoned on the grounds that it reflects the will of God. Actually both bearers of violence are condemned to the flames. This means that the difference between their behavior is arbitrary; it suggests that the "divine" justice that entails deceit, vengeance, and murder is our own creation. In other words, the belief that imputes revenge and sacrifice to divine injunction is but another of the many ways we have of rationalizing human violence. It is an illusion, as Girard's theory explains, shared by members of a persecuting crowd whose vengeful gods are born of a desire to justify the crowd's own violence.[3]

Notes

1. I address this aspect of the play in my current study, "The Theological Language of Tirso in *El burlador* and *El condenado*."
2. One of the most challenging aspects of Girard's theory is his thesis that Christianity is not merely one myth among the world mythologies. On the subject of revelation and the Gospels, see *The Scapegoat* 100-11; *Things Hidden* 180-262. See also Schwager's study of the gradual revelation throughout the Judaeo-Christian Scriptures of God's rejection of violence, vengeance, and sacrifice.
3. A part of this study was originally presented at the Colloquium on Vengeance organized by the Program of Interdisciplinary Research, Stanford University, 27-29 Oct. 1988. I wish to thank Professor Cesáreo Bandera for his generosity in discussing the ideas of this work with me, and Professors Juan Bautista Avalle-Arce and René Girard for their own generous support, suggestions, and criticism concerning my current research and writing.

Works Cited

Allain, Mathé. "El burlador burlado: Tirso de Molina's Don Juan." *Modern Language Quarterly* 27 (1966): 174-84.

Aubrun, Charles V. "Le Don Juan de Tirso de Molina: essai d'interprétation." *Bulletin of Hispanic Studies* 49 (1957): 26-61.

Cassirer, Ernst, *Mythical Thought*. Trans. Ralph Manheim. New Haven: Yale UP, 1955. Vol. 2 of *The Philosophy of Symbolic Forms*. 3 vols. 1955-1957.

Castro, Américo. Introduction. *Cinco Ensayos sobre Don Juan*. Ed. Américo Castro. Santiago: Cultura, 1937.

Farinelli, Arturo. "Cuatro palabras sobre Don Juan." In *Homenaje a Menéndez y Pelayo*. Vol. 1. Madrid: Librería General de Victoriano Suárez, 1899. 205-22.

Gendarme de Bévotte, Georges. *La Légende de Don Juan: son évolution dans la littérature dès origines au romantisme*. 1906. Geneva: Slatkine Reprints, 1970.

Girard, René. "To double business bound." In *Essays on Literature, Mimesis, and Anthropology*. Baltimore: Johns Hopkins UP, 1988.

———. *The Scapegoat*. Trans. Yvonne Freccero. Baltimore: Johns Hopkins UP, 1986.

———. *Things Hidden since the Foundation of the World*. Trans. Stephen Bonn and Michael Metteer. Stanford: Stanford UP, 1987.

———. *Violence and the Sacred*. Trans. Patrick Gregory. Baltimore: Johns Hopkins UP, 1986.

Lundelius, Ruth. "Tirso's View of Women in *El burlador de Sevilla*." *Bulletin of the Comediantes* 27 (1975): 5-14.

MacKay, Dorothy. *The Double Invitation in the Legend of Don Juan*. Stanford: Stanford UP, 1943.

Marni, Archimede. "Did Tirso Employ Counterpassion in His *Burlador de Sevilla?*" *Hispanic Review* 20 (1952): 123-33.

Parker, Alexander A. *The Approach to the Spanish Drama of the Golden Age*. London: Hispanic and Luso-Brazilian Councils, 1957.

Reichenberger, Arnold G. "The Uniqueness of the *Comedia*." *Hispanic Review* 27 (1959): 303-16.

Rodríguez, Alfred. "Tirso's Don Juan as Social Rebel." *Bulletin of the Comediantes* 30 (1978): 46-55.

Rogers, Daniel. "Fearful Symmetry: The Ending of *El Burlador de Sevilla*." *Bulletin of Hispanic Studies* 41 (1964): 141-59.

Ruiz Ramón, Francisco. "Don Juan y la sociedad del burlador de Sevilla: La crítica social." In *Estudios sobre teatro español y clásico contemporáneo.* Madrid: Fundación Juan March y Cátedra, 1978. 71-95.

Said Armesto, Víctor. *La leyenda de Don Juan: Orígenes poéticos de "El Burlador de Sevilla y convidado de piedra."* Madrid: Librería de los Sucesores de Hernando, 1908.

Schwager, Raymond. *Must There Be Scapegoats? Violence and Redemption in the Bible.* Trans. Maria L. Assad. San Francisco: Harper, 1987.

———. "The Theology of the Wrath of God." In *Violence and Truth: On the Work of René Girard.* Ed. Paul Dumouchel. Stanford: Stanford UP, 1988. 44-52.

Sullivan, Henry W. "Love, Matrimony, and Desire in the Theatre of Tirso de Molina." *Bulletin of the Comediantes* 37 (1985): 83-99.

Téllez, Gabriel [Tirso de Molina]. *El burlador de Sevilla y convidado de piedra.* In *Tirso de Molina: Comedias.* Ed. Américo Castro. Madrid: Espasa-Calpe, 1970. 147-256.

Wardropper, Bruce W. "*El Burlador de Sevilla:* A tragedy of Errors." *Philological Quarterly* 36 (1957): 61-71.

———. "El tema central de *El burlador de Sevilla.*" *Segismundo* 17-18 (1973): 1-8.

Raymond Conlon (essay date 1990)

SOURCE: "The 'Burlador' and the 'Burlados': A Sinister Connection," in *Bulletin of the Comediantes,* Vol. 42, No. 1, Summer, 1990, pp. 5-22.

[In the following essay, Conlon examines the role of Don Juan in de Molina's El burlador de Sevilla *suggesting that Don Juan's lack of motive or purpose in his cruelty towards women indicates that he symbolizes all male characters.]*

El burlador de Sevilla begins with an error or, more precisely, a misidentification. In a darkened passageway of the palace of the king of Naples, Lady Isabela, who has just become Don Juan's first conquest in the play addresses the *Burlador* as "Duque Octavio." Isabela is not alone in identifying Don Juan as Octavio: Viewers seeing the play for the first time would make the same mistake. They would have no reason to doubt that the man on stage is Octavio, and would continue to believe him to be the Duque until Isabela recognizes her error and disabuses them. To viewers the confusion of identities of Don Juan and Octavio might well suggest some symbolic connection between the two figures. They could conclude that Don Juan and Octavio share some fundamental likeness, one which could only emerge in such a tenebrous setting, after the blackness of night had obscured the characters' obvious differences. Subsequent misidentifications between Don Juan and the other *burlados* Mota and Batricio, might bring this one to the minds of these spectators, who could conclude that the ***Burlador*** is linked in some subtle but basic way with all of the men he "victimizes," and that confusions between the *Burlador* and the *burlados* symbolize that link between them. The repeated misidentifications might even lead viewers to believe that the tie between each victim and his victimizer is so strong that Don Juan functions as some sort of surrogate for each of these men.[1] Because of the conspicuous role misogyny plays in the behavior of the *burlados* and Don Juan,[2] viewers might reasonably infer that the *Burlador*'s surrogacy in some fashion involves this sentiment, the specific surrogate acts being Don Juan's sexual humiliations of his "victims" women.

Apparently accepting the surface victimizer-victim connection between Don Juan and the *burlados*, critics of ***El burlador*** have said little about the existence of the more subtle, subterranean tie between them. This oversight may be traceable to an underestimation of the psychological dimension of the misogynic utterances of the *burlados.* Despite the particularly insistent and venomous character of these comments, scholars have paid insufficient attention to what they reveal about the men who make them, their psychology, which is the basis of the link between the *burlados* and Don Juan. Instead, these vituperations are sometimes accepted as authorial statements, the play's last word on the moral nature of women.

This is the case even in an essay by Ruth Lundelius described as the "best" discussion of the play's vision of women (Singer 67)[3] and, in the closest thing we have to a study of the *burlados* and their bond with Don Juan, two essays (one an adaptation and expansion of the other) by Carlos Feal Deibe. Lundelius uses comments by two of the *burlados*, Batricio and Octavio (and other male figures) to support her assessment of ***El burlador de Sevilla*** as the work of a "serious misogynist" (13), which offers an "ignominious characterization" (6) of its female figures, whom it "radical[ly] censure[s]" (6).[4] She appears to overlook entirely the psychological motives of Batricio and Octavio for their low opinion of women, without entertaining the notion that they—not the women whom they excoriate—are the focus of the playwright's attention and scorn. With little psychological analysis, Feal Deibe also records the sexually hostile observations of two of the *burlados*, Mota and Octavio, as evidence that the women in the play are "ser[es] luciferino[s], . . . proyeccion[es] amplificada[s] de la figura de Eva" (*En nombre* 10).[5] Even when he does descry the pathological root of a figure's view of women, as in his discussion of Batricio, this critic fails to see how the character's psychology discredits the observations Batricio makes about his bride, Aminta, and women in general. Observing, for example, that Batricio's belief in the faithlessness of Aminta is really an expression of a deeprooted general fear of women ("*El burlador* . . ." 310), Feal Deibe nonetheless interprets Aminta's behavior more or less as Batricio does: Aminta is ready to submit to the first man she meets and has a buried sexual desire for Don Juan ("*El burlador* . . ." 311).

Just as Feal Deibe and Lundelius tend to ignore the psychological roots of the *burlados*' sexually malicious comments, they overlook the ways in which the play undercuts the specific misogynic criticisms these men make—that women are unfaithful and lascivious. This oversight is surprising, inasmuch as these charges are refuted by the behavior of the women closest to these men, their lovers. The first charge is contradicted by the loyalty of the women: None is naturally faithless; two sleep with Don Juan believing him to be their lovers, the third only after her lover has rejected her. Repudiating the second accusation is the fact that these women must be seduced in ways which, as we have just seen, make absolutely clear that each is at heart monogamous. To escape the conclusion that the circumstances surrounding the sexual surrender of these women mitigate their culpability Lundelius must resort to glibness: "Of course, for the sake of the play they [the three lovers of the *burlados* and Tisbea] must be susceptible and they must be tricked, for without 'burlas' there would be no 'burlador'" (13).[6]

Behind Lundelius' and Feal Deibe's belief that the author has placed his imprimatur on the accusations leveled at the women in this play—and indeed, all women—lies a methodological error: the tendency to equate the meaning of the play with the view held by the largest and most vocal bloc of its characters. Thus, since almost all of the male figures articulate a morally critical view of women so must the play. Such an assumption tends to transform characters into a chorus which *informs* the audience which theme the playwright is communicating. This interpretation of Tirso's artistry ignores two important points of drama: 1. A fiction central to most modern plays is that characters possess independent personalities, psychological autonomy—a fiction which crumbles when particular characters are obviously functioning as the poet's spokesmen. 2. A play's theme often emerges not so much from characters' actions or words directly but from the viewer's inferences about the characters' *motives* for those actions or words. Of course some characters in plays do directly communicate themes, like the shepherd/angel in Tirso's own ***El condenado por desconfiado***,[7] or Tiresias in *Oedipus Rex*, or indeed the chorus in Greek plays, but in such cases their words are not—as are those of the *burlados* here—undercut by psychological analysis or refuted by the behavior of other characters. Moreover, as the above examples show, when characters enjoy a special status which endows their speeches with explicit thematic significance there is often something in their role which alerts the audience to this fact—the shepherd/angel's irrelevance to the action of the play and the transparently allegorical character of his speech; the unusual social function of Tiresias; and the traditional narrative role of the chorus. Not only is there nothing about the *burlados* which grants their views particular authority, but, as we have seen, the play specifically undercuts their words.

Besides denying the *burlados* moral authority, the dramatic undermining of their misogynic observations raises an important question: Why do these men have such hostility to women? Here, just as in real life, a stubborn insistence on an attitude contradicted by reality, especially one hostile to a large sector of humanity, points to the presence of volcanic psychological forces lying beneath that attitude. The specifically sexual character of the *burlados*' misogyny (all their hostile remarks about women relate to female sexual duplicity or promiscuity) strongly suggests that they are dominated by a fear, conscious or unconscious, of the female in her sexual role. These characters are, then, like many others in Tirso's theatre sexually obsessed figures (Sullivan "Tirso . . ." 811). They are different, however, in that they are not driven by desire (Sullivan "Love, Matrimony . . ." 95), a need to consummate an erotic impulse, but taken over by a fear of the object of their sexual attachment (i.e., women). In each of the three male figures this sexual terror takes the form of sexual hostility and leads them away from the normal course of male-female sexual relations.

It is this unhealthy, sexually rooted misogyny which ties the *burlados* to the *burlador*. Don Juan's sexual humiliations of their women symbolically express the misogynic ire of the *burlados*, complementing their unrealized fear and hostility towards all women. His purposeless cruelty to women enacts the *burlados*' baseless distrust of them. Obviously the misogynic link between *Burlador* and *burlados* is not a causal one, nor of course are the participants aware of its existence; rather it is a symmetrical balance of impulse and expression, observed only by the viewer, which universalizes misogyny.

That Don Juan in his humiliations of the women in this play functions as an extension of Mota, Batricio, and Octavio is suggested by the unusual way he "seduces" their women—impersonating the nobles Octavio and Mota and replacing the peasant Batricio with his bride. *Burlas* involving impersonation occur in other Tirsian plays; often, as here, they employ some variation of a device called *engañar con la verdad* (Templin 193), which sometimes reveals hidden sexual predilections and unacknowledged sexual identities.[8] In ***El burlador de Sevilla*** the "*engaños*" are the impersonations by Don Juan of the *burlados* with the women romantically connected to these men; the "*verdad*," the fact that these impersonations symbolize the likeness in attitude of *Burlador* and *burlados* toward the women involved and possibly women in general. When, for example, Don Juan seduces Isabela by pretending to be her lover, Octavio, Don Juan expresses not only his own contempt for this woman but Octavio's. Octavio has the same dishonorable motives towards Isabela as the *Burlador*: He disdains any legitimate link with her, desiring her only to satisfy his passion. Don Juan's assumption of the roles and identities of the *burlados* points to a fundamental irony in the play: Don Juan's *burlas* serve the unconscious desires of the men he "humiliates."

Perhaps the most complex misogynic surrogate relationship exists between Don Juan and the Marqués de Mota, the *burlado* whose hostility towards women is the most repressed and expressed the most obliquely. Mota's animus towards women is suggested in an unusual way: by his prurient interest in and encyclopedic knowledge of the misfortunes of Seville's prostitutes. He has an unnatural fascination in their ageing, their diseases, their loss of hair and teeth, and their professional afflictions generally. One can easily imagine how, with a cruel smile, a contemporary actor could have communicated the unhealthy passion which lay behind this figure's arcane knowledge, as he recounted how Inés "el tiempo la desterró" (II, 172); how Teodora, only "se escapó del mal francés / por un río de sudores" (II, 181-182); how Blanca is "sin blanca ninguna" (II, 199); and how Constanza "lampiña de frente y ceja" (II, 175). The pathetic vanity of this last trollop, who, hearing herself called "vieja" (II, 176) thought she had heard "bella" (II, 177), is the stuff of his anecdotes.

The apparent pleasure Mota takes in discussing the degradation of the streetwalkers he presumably patronizes links him with men and women who, because of feelings of guilt for their sexual impulses, deflect their disgust at themselves onto their real or imagined sexual partners. Such "projection" defends them against their revulsion at their own physical desires (White and Gilliard 85). Since such hostility characteristically reflects the pressure moral censure exerts inwardly (A. Freud 119), it would seem from the perverse quality of the pleasure the misfortunes of these women obviously afford Mota that his attraction to them provokes intense psychological discomfort. The male's transference of his sexual disgust with himself to his female partner is a phenomenon which interests Tirso, as his psychologically piercing portrait of Amón in ***La venganza de Tamar*** powerfully demonstrates,[9] and he depicts it here also. Mota makes prostitutes the symbol as well as the vessel of his own corruption, and then "punishes" them mentally by the pleasure which he apparently takes in their decay. Loathing them for their power to "make him" commit sin, he is driven to discuss them in such a way as to deny them any human feelings or human worth, and apparently takes comfort in the knowledge that they are rotting away.[10]

Mota's feelings towards prostitutes are complicated and contradictory. Although driven by his resentment of these women to punish them mentally, he is, obviously, also attracted to them. In addition to his display of intimate knowledge of the seven about whom Don Juan queries him, without prompting he expatiates a second time on Seville's women of the night (II, 462-65; 467-474). His ambivalence about prostitutes, loathing them and desiring them, links him with those men pathologically drawn to prostitutes whom Freud describes as "fixat[ed] on the phantasies formed by the boy in puberty" (172).[11] Such men exhibit the same contradictory reactions to prostitutes as those displayed by many adolescent males who visit these women: "a mixture of longing and horror" (S. Freud 171), desire and disgust. Like the youth awakened to the pleasures of the flesh by such women, Mota seems to have an insatiable appetite for their delicious but tainted fruit. For Mota, as for the boys, the passions these women stir up make them a grave menace.[12] He sees their activities as reenactments of the temptation and fall: They are Eves (II, 471) who offer a man a fatal "*bocado*" (II, 472) which turns him into an Adam (II, 468).

The specifically immature quality of Mota's sexual pathology is also communicated by his *perros muertos*.[13] *burlas* in which, Mota has a friend replace him in a mistress' bed without her knowledge. Their boyish quality alone points to his sexual immaturity: they reduce sexuality to a nasty game which pits a couple of males against an unsuspecting female. The sexual sharing of a woman also suggests emotional fixation. Its vaguely bisexual character particularly recalls the undefined sexual world, half-homosexual, half-heterosexual, common in male adolescence (S. Freud 44-45). The resentment of the female as sexual figure, which the pranks' malicious quality reveals, is an observable trait of adolescent boys who often disguise their sexual fear and desire of females by acts of hostility.

That Motas' *perros muertos* are adolescent and misogynic is perhaps apparent; less apparent is how they complement the Marqués' interest in prostitutes. Mota, to expunge his own guilt and express his resentment of women, punishes prostitutes by discoursing on the sufferings they incur in their profession. The "punishment" he metes out, however, being neither direct nor active, lacks a personal stamp; thus it can not purge him of his "sin." The *perros muertos* are directly hostile acts towards women and, therefore, possess greater exculpatory powers.

The psychological function of these pranks, like the *burlas* of many characters in Tirso's theatre, is the release of repressed emotion, some basic insecurity or fear (Templin 195). The intensity of this insecurity is suggested by the frequency with which he engages in such pranks. He boasts that "dimos anoche un cruel" (II, 208) and he plans for "esta noche "ten[er] ciertos otros dos" (II, 209).

The two aspects of Mota's personality which we have established as misogynic—his interest in the decay of prostitutes and his joy in *perros muertos*—are the two which bind him to Don Juan. Mota's initial discourse on Seville's demimonde are in response to questions from the *Burlador*, questions which make clear that Don Juan is intimate with the same women as Mota. Their dialogue establishes that the two men have like reactions to these women. To the mockingly cruel description of the ageing of one prostitute by Mota, "A Vejel se va" (II, 169),[14] Don Juan adds an equally cruel riposte: Vejel is "buen lugar para vivir [ella] (II, 170). If Mota is obsessed with the decay of Constanza, Don Juan goes a step further and queries if she "irá a morir" (II, 173). Finally, both men discuss women in the skin trade in literally non-human terms, with Mota and Don Juan speaking of "abadejo[s]" (II, 189) and "trucha[s] (II, 188), slang terms for prostitutes and courtesans (MacCurdy 115n), but which, of course, literally mean codfish and trout. Just as the subject of prostitutes and their conditions are first raised by Don

Juan, so he also introduces the subject of *perros muertos* with the question: "Marqués, ¿qué hay de perros muertos?" (II, 206).

This second activity, the *perros muertos*, powerfully dramatizes the link between Mota and Don Juan. As envisioned by Mota, Don Juan is to impersonate him in one of these jests: "La mujer ha de pensar que soy él" (II, 507). To make the two men indistinguishable in the dark—the indispensable condition of the *perro muerto* being played on Mota's mistress, Beatriz—Mota lends Don Juan his red cape which identifies both men as the Marqués to Doña Ana.[15] The two impersonations, the two acts of sexual malice, are connected: the impersonation with Ana fulfils the malicious spirit of the proposed impersonation with Beatriz, which was never carried out. The link between the *perro muerto* and the *burla* and the indistinguishability of Mota and Don Juan suggest that the *Burlador* is a surrogate for Mota with Ana, as he was supposed to have been with Beatriz, enacting the hostility that the Marqués feels toward female sexuality and thus, unconsciously, towards Ana, for sexually enticing him. Since, as Feal Deibe observes, the cape was not lent to seduce Doña Ana but Beatriz, the two women become linked (*En nombre* 16). Their mutual identity in these misogynic pranks symbolizes the similarity of attitude towards women generally of the two men. All women are to Don Juan what his prostitutes and his mistresses are to Mota, and Don Juan's *burlas* are the Marqués' *perros muertos*, with both men punishing their sexual partners for no apparent sin but their sexuality.

The misogyny in Mota which makes Don Juan an appropriate sexual replacement for the Marqués is present in the other two *burlados* as well. The feckless peasant Batricio communicates his responses towards women—distrust and fear—by the terror the notion of sexual dishonor strikes in him.[16] That these feelings come to the surface as soon as Batricio learns of Don Juan's presence at his wedding, before the *Burlador* has said or done anything, points to their unconscious character: They are long festering infections buried in some deep and vital place in Batricio's spirit, brought to the surface by Don Juan (Conlon "Batricio . . ." 88). Learning that a nobleman has come to his wedding, Batricio immediately concludes that this is a "mal agüero" (II, 671), and that the stranger's presence "quita gusto y celos da" (II, 673). Batricio himself reveals an awareness of the irrational, unconscious character of his suspicions as his conscious mind struggles to put down this misogynic insurrection from some lower psychological depth asking "¿de qué me aflijo yo?" (II, 678). The protests of his rational, conscious mind cannot prevail against the dark misogyny unleashed by Don Juan's presence, and is silenced by the sixfold repetition of the cry, "mal agüero, mal agüero." He is quickly consumed psychologically by his unconscious misogyny which, once ignited, burns out of control. Surface joy becomes apprehension, apprehension becomes fear, fear becomes doubt, and doubt conviction. At the arrival of Don Juan, Batricio is overcome by a vague foreboding and jealousy; the seating of the *Burlador* at the wedding table makes Batricio feel "conden[ado] a celos" (II, 702). After Don Juan takes Batricio's seat, the groom declares that his wedding is a "culebra" (III, 44) (Conlon "Batricio" 87).

The sense that some pre-existing terror has taken hold of Batricio is further suggested by the way he expresses his feelings about women and honor—frenetically, desperately, one clichéd platitude tumbling atop another: "que el honor y la mujer / son malos en opiniones" (III, 83-84); "mujer entre mala y buena, / que es moneda entre dos luces" (III, 95-96); "la mujer en opinión / siempre más pierde que gana, / que son como la campana, / que se estima por el son (III, 85-88).

Nothing Aminta says or does justifies such distrust. In fact, her behavior reveals deep love and desire for Batricio.[17] Batricio's misgivings do not concern Aminta personally, but only as she is a member of the female sex. His is a deductive distrust—'all women are perfidious, Aminta is a woman, therefore. . . .' His thinking becomes explicit when Don Juan claims to be her lover. Batricio blames her treachery on the inherent moral frailty of her gender: "al fin es mujer" (III, 68) he sighs.

Because Batricio "knows" that he will be betrayed by Aminta, his relationship with Don Juan takes on an almost explicitly surrogate character. Batricio is so clearly relieved to be rid of Aminta, to learn that she is to join Don Juan in what was supposed to have been his, Batricio's, marriage bed (Feal Deibe "*El burlador*" 310) that he tells Don Juan: "Si tú en mi eleción lo pones, / tu gusto pretendo hacer" (III, 81-82) and wishes that the nobleman: "Gózala, señor, mil años" (III, 97). These bizarre expressions of well wishing (especially the first with its explicit linking of Don Juan's pleasure with Aminta to Batricio's desires, and balance of the first and second person pronouns and conjugations), suggest strongly that Don Juan and Batricio have a tacit accord. Batricio's part in the agreement is a simple one: he must be a gracious loser. His graciousness comes naturally to him, as Batricio is genuinely beholden to Don Juan for providing him the excuse to shun the roles of lover and of husband. The surrogate role of Don Juan is symbolized on stage when, immediately after this exchange, Belisa, Aminta's maid, hears Don Juan and thinks he is Batricio: ". . . pienso que viene, / que nadie en la casa pisa / de un desposado, tan recio" (III, 137-39).[18] Shortly after, Aminta, hearing the *Burlador*, asks: "¿Quién llama a Aminta? / Es mi Batricio?" (III, 201-02). Batricio's displacement by Don Juan bears striking resemblances to Mota's. Like that one, it not only expresses the *burlado*'s feelings about women and the sexual threat they pose but shields him from this menace: Because of Don Juan's "graciosa burla" (III, 441) of Aminta, over which she will cry forever ("siempre la llorará": III, 443), Batricio will be free of any fear for his honor.

As we have seen, misogyny is so powerful and profound a psychological force in ***El burlador de Sevilla*** that it obscures differences in characters as unlike as Mota and Don Juan and Batricio and Don Juan. Beneath the skin of Octavio, a noble, courses the blood of the peasant Batricio (Martin 277). Like Batricio, Octavio, in John Varey's words, is "willing to believe the worst of womankind" (214). When he discovers that Isabela has given herself to another man, he, like Batricio, attributes his beloved's actions not to an individual deficiency on her part but to woman's endemic moral frailty: "la mujer más constante / es, en efeto, mujer" (I, 357-358). His exclamations moments before, "¡Oh, mujer! Ley tan terrible / de honor" (I, 339-40) establish that the fear of woman's perfidy makes the weight of honor as insupportable to him as it is to Batricio. Like Batricio, finally, his distrust of his mistress precedes any grounds she may provide for his distrust. In his first appearance on stage (before he learns of Isabela's liaison with Don Juan), he speaks of his jealous condition. Its intensity is such that to describe it he resorts to phrases used to depict the sufferings of mariners desperate for lack of a sailing wind, "en calma" (Castro 155), and souls in purgatory, "siempre en pena" (MacCurdy 99). His "pensamientos de Isabela" (I, 203), his desire to "guarda[r] ausente y presente / el castillo del honor" (I, 207-208) [lo] tienen . . . *en calma*" (I, 204), and "siempre *en pena*" (206).

Octavio and Batricio share an abhorrence of marriage (Feal Deibe, *En nombre* 24). Batricio flees this union with Aminta because it seems to promise inevitable sexual humiliation. Octavio is equally hostile to the idea of marrying Isabela. He desires only, in his servant Ripio's phrase, "amor[es] impertinente[s]" (I, 210). With Isabela, he seeks, ". . . porfialla, / regalalla y adoralla, / y aguardar que se rindiera" (I, 224-26). He becomes enraged when Ripio suggests that he marry Isabela, denouncing his man as "necio" (I, 231), and deriding marriage as fit only for "lacayo[s] o lavandera[s]" (I, 232).[19]

Octavio's hostility to the notion of marrying her, articulated in this exchange, makes explicit the illicit character of his passion for Isabela. This quality is connected in a significant way to Don Juan's seduction of Isabela, as her dialogue with the *Burlador* immediately after the seduction establishes. It makes clear that she surrendered herself to him because the man she took to be Octavio promised to marry her. Don Juan's pledge to wed her ("Duquesa, de nuevo os juro / de cumplir el dulce sí" (I, 3-4)) and her response "¿Mis glorias serán verdades, / promesas y ofrecimientos . . . ?" (I, 5-6) indicate that the *Burlador* used the promise of marriage to persuade Isabela to sleep with him. This is underscored by his phrase "de nuevo," a reference to a pledge of marriage which could only have taken place earlier in the seduction. Seeing and hearing this, viewers would conclude that, as Don Juan pleaded and cajoled, he became aware of Isabela's wish to wed Octavio and exploited that desire. Realizing this, the audience would then see a connection between the refusal of Octavio to wed Isabela and Don Juan's impersonation of him. Don Juan is successful with Isabela because he seems to offer her what Octavio denies her—a legitimate union.[20] This connection means that the *Burlador*'s deceitful vow not only manifests his own cynicism towards the feelings of women but mirrors and is contingent upon the Count's for its expression.

The links between the actions of Don Juan and the hostility to women of Octavio and the other *burlados* remind us that the shadowy figure Don Juan is as much a function as a character.[21] His function, as several readings of the play have demonstrated, is to punish women (Feal Deibe *"El burlador . . ."*; 301; Wardropper 69; Valbuena Prat 110-11). And the crime for which women must suffer is their sexuality. This sin demands humiliation because, in one way or another, male humiliation is what uncontrolled female sexual expression threatens. Before the perfunctory mass betrothals at the end of the play, each of the offending females undergoes a particular abasement. With Isabela the sinner is made to hate the sin and herself. She "es de llorar mientras tuviere vida" (III, 336) because "en la esparcida voz [está su] agravio" (III, 334). Ana is banished to the convent *de las Descalzas* (III, 692) where, surrounded by virgins of marble and those of flesh and blood, she may contemplate her descent into depravity. A particularly demeaning humiliation is apportioned to Aminta. This victim continues to believe Don Juan's promise of marriage: "estas dos semanas, / no ha de caer en el chiste" (III, 437-438).

In addition to punishing women, Don Juan's seduction-impersonations serve yet another more subtle role: they vitalize the preconceptions of the *burlados* concerning female lasciviousness and treachery.[22] By making or appearing to make these women sleep with him and betray their lovers, Don Juan bolsters the *burlados*' convictions about women. Because of Don Juan each of these men can confidently say to himself, "la mujer más constante / es, en efeto, mujer" (I, 357-58).

The breakdown in the conventional opposition between victim and victimizer, which we have just seen, along with the realization of Don Juan's functional quality, helps explain an important mystery surrounding ***El burlador de Sevilla*** and its protagonist—the motiveless quality of Don Juan's actions, the fact that he is not driven by any articulated passion, anger, hatred, or sexual need to humiliate women. His actions seem unmotivated precisely because they are not so much personally his but symbolic expressions of the poison infecting the *burlados* (and perhaps the other misogynists in the play as well) with whom he is unwittingly involved in a complicitous union. These men are the spirit of misogyny in the culture, and he is their agent.[23] Through his actions, Don Juan of course also symbolizes misogyny; in fact, precisely because of the purposelessness and motivelessness of his cruelty towards women, he is the supreme example of this impulse.[24]

Notes

1. The presence and function of other "secret sharer" relationships have been observed in Tirsian drama.

For a discussion of the links between Don Juan and Catalinón in *El burlador de Sevilla,* see Hesse; between a noble and a peasant in *El vergonzoso en palacio*, see Conlon "Sexual Passion and Marriage . . ." (9).

2. Bruce Wardropper observes, "A completely pessimistic view of woman is taken by all of the male characters" (69). See also Ayala (8).
3. Singer claims that Lundelius' analysis of the women in the play is "so essentially correct [as to be] difficult to argue against" (67).
4. Comments by other figures critical of women also accepted by Lundelius as the equivalent of thematic statements include Catalinón's reference to his master as "el castigo de las mujeres." She maintains that this line "implies the . . . guilt" (12) of the women Don Juan seduces. Her conclusions made a few sentences later, that, in the moral vision of this play their humiliations are "richly merited punishments" (12), in part builds on that quotation. Just as the psychology of the *burlados* was sacrificed to make them into spokesmen for the author, a critical element of Catalinón's dramatic characters, his role as *gracioso*, is ignored here. Overlooked is the fact that since the *gracioso* figure characteristically employs comic hyperbole, *castigo* does not necessarily suggest moral censure in this context; it perhaps merely signifies punishment in a vague and jocular sense, as in, "This job is the punishment for my sins." There is no obvious reason why it should be taken more literally than the *gracioso*'s description of Don Juan as the "langosta de mujeres" (II, 436), or more seriously than his suggestion that a public pronouncement should warn the women of Spain of the danger Don Juan represents (II, 435-444).
5. The doubtful logic and unsubstantiated assertions Feal Deibe employs to maintain the position that women in *El burlador de Sevilla* are sexually corrupt point to the tenuousness of the misogynic interpretation of this play. In his discussion of Ana, for example, he connects two facts: that Ana has returned from Lisbon and that "Lisboa" 'Lisbon' is the name of the red light district of Seville. He concludes that since "ha pasado precisamente a Sevilla desde Lisboa [Ana]" (*En nombre* 14), it follows that she "se confunde con 'lo peor de Portugal'" (*En nombre* 15). He attempts to turn Aminta into an Eve figure by connecting the name of the town, Dos Hermanas, where the peasant woman lives, with a reference made in a discussion between Mota and Don Juan to two sisters who are prostitutes. He concludes: "la novia de Dos Hermanas debe, de algún modo, asociarse con esas dos pecadoras" (*En nombre* 17). His argument for the corruption of Isabela—that she unconsciously wishes to be seduced by Don Juan (*En nombre* 10) is not supported by textual evidence. It ignores, moreover, the conspicuous fact that she does not know that she is sleeping with Don Juan, as her address to "Duque Octavio" makes clear.
6. Explicitly in the case of Lundelius' study, and perhaps implicitly in the work of other critics who insist that the view of the *burlados* and the play's other misogynists represents that of the *burlador*'s creator, is the desire to counter the notion that Tirso is one of "the more extravagant admirers and champions of womankind" (Lundelius 5) common in earlier scholars, notably Blanca de los Ríos. The need to right a distortion, an overemphasis on but one tendency in Tirsian drama, is well taken, but does not justify a Newtonian counter—distortion which interprets Tirso's women as Eve-like, or morally spineless, or lascivious. The women Don Juan deceives are not spotless paragons of feminine virtue, but none is sluttish or promiscuous, and each wishes to be faithful to one man. True, as some critics are quick to point out, the women in the play are willing to surrender themselves sexually to the men they hope to marry, but this would hardly make them despicable to a contemporary audience. Many admirable unmarried women in Spanish literature of this period give themselves to men, including such agreeable Tirsian heroines as Madalena in *El vergonzoso en palacio*, Doña Juana in *Don Gil de las calzas verdes,* and Doña Violante in *La villana de Vallecas*.

   Those who see Tirso's women either as expressions of a rosy benevolence to or a blind resentment of females on their creator's part do a disservice to the most astute and sensitive student of the female psyche in Golden Age drama. He invests the female characters in *El burlador* with faults—Isabela is calculating, Ana headstrong, Tisbea self-satisfied and Aminta credulous, but these faults do not make them damnable to their creator, guilty of the suspicions of the *burlados* or deserving of the humiliations by Don Juan.
7. The authorship of both *El condenado por desconfiado* and *El burlador de Sevilla,* though traditionally accepted as Tirso's, is controversial. A detailed defense of Tirso's paternity of either play is quite beyond the scope of this essay, but a major reason for including both works in the Mercedarian's canon is the extraordinary psychological perspicacity they demonstrate. No dramatist of the Golden Age reveals such insight into the human mind as Tirso, and no playwright is so capable of so subtly implying the existence of a functioning unconscious mind from individual, sometimes, seemingly unrelated traits of a character's behavior and speech as he does with the *burlados* here and with Paulo and Enrico in *El condenado por desconfiado*.

   A motif of *El burlador de Sevilla* which, as will be discussed in the text, links it with other plays by Tirso is sexual deviancy—Mota's prurient obsession with prostitutes, Octavio's indignant rejection of licit sexuality, Batricio's eager acceptance of the role of cuckold, and Don Juan's gratuitous cruelty to women. Among Golden Age dramatists this interest in the sexually aberrant is singularly conspicuous in Tirso (Sullivan "Tirso . . ." 811). In particular, the indirect manifestation of sexually aberrant attitudes and behavior, sexual deviancy as expressions of some unconscious impulse or dread, such as we see here, points to the pen of Tirso as to no other dramatist of the *Siglo de Oro*.

For a discussion of the controversy over the authorship of *El burlador de Sevilla*, see the bibliography on the subject in Claramonte 67-68.

For a discussion of the psychology of the characters in *El condenado por desconfiado*, see Conlon "Enrico . . . ," Darst, and Pérez.

8. An example of this is in *El vergonzoso en palacio*. There Madalena, pretending to slumber, communicates her sexual desire for her tutor by feigned sleep talking. In another variation of "engañar con la verdad" in the same play, Madalena's sister, Serafina, exposes a heretofore unacknowledged aspect of herself, when, rehearsing for a holiday play the role of a jealous man, she loses control of herself and passionately kisses her lady-in-waiting, Juana.

9. Amón, immediately after he has raped his sister Tamar, excoriates her in the most vile terms calling her "arpia" (III, 4), "ponzoña" (III, 7), monstruo" (III, 9), and "veneno" (III, 2). He then asks these rhetorical questions: "¿Qué yo te quise es posible?" (III, 11); and "¡Quién por no verte ni oirte / sordo naciera y sin ojos!" (III, 39-40). This diatribe ends with this order to his servants: "Echadme de aquí / esta víbora, esta peste" (III, 79-80).

10. In Gerald Wade's psychoanalytical study of Don Juan, he observes that a "preference for prostitutes," according to the psychiatrist Robert J. Stoller, is a "cryptoperversion." In many cases the "perverse person sees . . . [these] creature[s as being] without humanity[.]" and he "delight[s]" in "humiliat[ing]" (35) them. While Wade does not mention Mota specifically, the application of this description to this character is obvious.

11. Mota's characteristic use of projection is itself a form of fixation. In this respect, according to Anna Freud, he is like "a number of people [who] remain arrested in the development of the superego and never quite complete the internalization of the critical process" (119). Whereas in normal people "vehement indignation at someone else's wrongdoing is the precursor" of self-criticism, in the fixated individual it is a "substitute for guilty feelings on its own account" (119).

12. The reactions which Mota displays occur in adolescents who consort with prostitutes because their sexual contacts provoke insupportable psychological tensions from barely repressed unconscious associations and impulses (S. Freud 171). A major tension arises because youths begin to see their mothers as prostitutes of sorts, concluding that "the difference between [their] mother[s] and whore[s] is not after all so very great, since basically they do the same thing" (S. Freud 171). Freud perceives that the adolescents' "unconscious relation" between their response to prostitutes and their feelings for their mothers produces in them (and, presumably, in fixated adult men) the sort of intense ambivalence we see in Mota (170).

13. The precise definition of "dar perro muerto," according to the *Diccionario de Autoridades*, is as follows: "Se toma también por el engaño ú daño que se padece en algun ajuste ò contrato, ò por la incomodidád u desconveniencia que se tiene, esperando por mucho tiempo a alguno, o para que execute alguna . . . cosa" (232). In this play, the term is specifically used in terms of cheating prostitutes, according to some editors of *El burlador* like MacCurdy (116n) and Oliver Cabañes (161n). However, two points suggest that the woman involved here, Beatriz, is a mistress, not a prostitute. First, there is no mention of cheating her out of money; second, if she were merely involved with Mota on a financial basis, it would not be important—and thus a *burla*—that she believe Don Juan to be Mota. The psychological dimension of the bed trick here is emphasized by its lack of any utilitarian purpose. Unlike the use of this device in other plays of this period (such as Shakespeare's *All's Well that Ends Well*, where Helena employs it to reclaim her husband, Bertram), there is no practical need being served here.

14. According to Castro, Vejel refers to the village Vejer de la Frontera in Cádiz, and is a play on the word for aged "*vejez*" (194n).

15. That the dramatic function of the cape is, by identifying its wearer as Mota, to link Don Juan and Mota seems obvious. This is underscored by Don Juan himself when, seeing Mota, he observes: "Luego que la capa vi, / que érades vos conocí" (II, 453-54). It is definitely not a "phallic symbol," as Feal Deibe asserts ("*El burlador* . . ." 307), because in shape and function it clearly bears no resemblance or analogical connection to the male organ.

16. For a detailed discussion of Batricio's behavior from a psychoanalytical point of view, see Conlon "Batricio. . . ."

17. To interpret Aminta, as Lundelius does, as a "giddy, silly girl" who succumbs to Don Juan "after a little flattery and a few tactical lies" (11) ignores the central irony of the whole episode in Dos Hermanas: It is not Aminta who has been seduced by Don Juan's lies but Batricio. She capitulates to Don Juan only after he brings home to her the awful truth that "que [la] olvida" Batricio (III, 226).

In his discussion of Aminta, Serge Maurel points out how the circumstances of her seduction lessen her responsibility morally and indict those around her. He observes that Aminta's surrender to Don Juan is ultimately the consequence of her abandonment by her father and Batricio, "par ceux qui auraient mission de la protéger" (570), who "ne s' opposent aux prétentions du seigneur" (571). Maurel's conclusion about the seduction of Aminta by Don Juan, that "les démissions des autres font sa victoire facile" (571) is difficult to dispute.

18. Feal Deibe asserts that the confusion of Don Juan and Batricio here "revela, al menos inconscientemente, su deseo [de Aminta] de acoger a don Juan" (*En nombre* 19). His reasoning—that a grammatical ambiguity in the speech of Belisa confusing Don Juan with Batricio—symbolizes not an important likeness the two men share but the perfidy of Aminta is illogical on its face. The fact that Don Juan does not disguise himself with Aminta bolsters this position, this critic asserts, because it indicates her desire for Don Juan (*En nombre* 19). This whole argument ignores the obvious facts that the peasant woman seeks to be faithful to Batricio, repeatedly expresses her feeling for him, and apparently has a deep desire to be married to him, but in the end comes to the painful conclusion that he has abandoned her.

19. Given Octavio's feelings, his betrothal to Isabela (like the other betrothals) at the end of the play seems to be one more example of a theme common in Tirso's drama—the cynicism of marriage as a social institution. For a discussion of marriage in Tirso, see Ruiz Ramón 211.

20. Since she offers no textual substantiation, Lundelius' assertion that Doña Isabela "had expected to surrender [to Duque Octavio on this occasion], though only on condition of his 'palabra de matrimonio'" (8) is presumably based on the fact that she meets Don Juan in the dark and would not have done so except for a planned sexual assignation. This is mere dramatic backtracking to action which took place before the play began, without anything actually said during the play to justify it. Moreover, this thesis raises three questions: How did Don Juan know about the tryst? How did he arrange to replace Octavio? And finally, why does Octavio make no mention of this assignation after he learns of Isabela's "betrayal"?

21. Ayala suggests something like this when he observes: "'carece' de una psicología [Don Juan], en contraste con los que lo rodean . . . dentro de la misma obra" (9).

22. Feal Deibe seems to be making a similar point when he observes that a function of Don Juan is to be "la medida en que la culpa se proyecta totalmente en la mujer" ("*El burlador* . . ." 301).

23. Peter Evans in an undeveloped observation hints at this idea, but limits its application to one character: "The anger [towards women] displayed by Octavio, one of Don Juan's most successful impersonations, suggests that an unconscious rage nurtured by centuries of irrational vilification of women, society's scapegoats for a wider *malaise,* may well be an important component of Don Juan's motivation in victimizing women" (243-44).

24. The author wishes to thank his brother Thomas Conlon for his generous editorial assistance and suggestions in this essay.

Works Cited

Ayala, Francisco. "Burla, burlando . . ." *Asomante* 17 (1961): 7-15.

Claramonte, Andrés de. *El burlador de Sevilla.* Ed. Alfredo Rodríguez López-Vázquez. Kassel: Reichenberger, 1987.

Conlon, Raymond. "Batricio in *El burlador de Sevilla*: The Pathology of Sexual Honor." *Don Juan: The Metamorphosis of a Theme.* Eds. George E. Gingras and Josep Sola-Solé. Washington, DC: Catholic University Press, 1988. 86-94.

———. "Enrico in *El condenado por desconfiado:* A Psychoanalytical View." *RCEH* 10, no. 2 (1986): 173-182.

———. "Sexual Passion and Marriage—Chaos and Order in Tirso de Molina's *El vergonzoso en palacio.*" *Hispania 71, no.1 (1988): 8-13.*

Darst, David H. "The Thematic Design of El condenado por desconfiado." *KRQ*, 21 (1974): 483-494.

Diccionario de Autoridades. Real Academia Española. 1737.

Evans, Peter W. "The Roots of Desire in *El burlador de Sevilla.*" *FMLS* 23, no.3 (1986): 232-245.

Feal Deibe, Carlos. "*El burlador* de Tirso y la mujer." *Symposium* 29 (1975): 300-313.

———. "*El burlador* de Tirso: Demonio y víctima expiatoria." *En nombre de Don Juan.* Phila.-Amsterdam: Benjamin, 1984. 9-34.

Freud, Anna. *The Ego and the Mechanisms of Defense.* London: Hogarth, 1968.

Freud, Sigmund. *Five Lectures on Psycho-Analysis*[;]*Leonardo da Vinci and Other Works.* Ed. and translator James Strachey. Vol. II of *The Standard Edition of the Complete Works of Sigmund Freud.* London: Hogarth, 1957. 24 vols. 1953-74.

Hesse, Everett W. "Tirso's Don Juan and the Opposing Self." *Theology, Sex and the Comedia and Other Essays.* Madrid: Porrúa, 1982. 62-69.

Lundelius, Ruth. "Tirso's view of Women in *El burlador de Sevilla.*" *BCom* 21 (1975): 5-13.

Martin, Jean Eleanor. "A Consideration of the Role of Honor in Tirso de Molina's *El burlador de Sevilla.*" *KRQ* 27, no. 3 (1980): 272-280.

Maurel, Serge. *L'Univers dramatique de Tirso de Molina*. Poitiers: Univ. de Poitiers, 1971.

Pérez, Carlos A. "Verosimilitud psicológica de *El condenado por desconfiado*." *Hispanófila* 27 (1966): 1-21.

Rogers, Daniel. *Tirso de Molina: El burlador de Sevilla*. London: Tamesis, 1977.

Ruiz Ramón, Francisco. *Historia del teatro español*. 5a ed. Madrid: Cátedra, 1983.

Singer, Armand E. "Don Juan's Women in *El burlador de Sevilla*." *BCom* 33 (1981): 67-71.

Sullivan, Henry W. "Love, Matrimony and Desire in the Theatre of Tirso de Molina." *BCom* 37, no. 1 (1985): 83-99.

———. "Tirso de Molina: Dramaturgo Andrógino." *Actas del quinto congreso internacional de hispanistas*. Bordeaux: Instituto de Estudios Ibéricos e Iberoamericanos, University of Bordeaux, 1977. 811-18.

Templin, Ernest. "The *burla* in the Plays of Tirso de Molina." *HR* 8 (1940): 15-201.

Tirso de Molina. *El burlador de Sevilla*, 6a ed. Ed. Américo Castro. Madrid: *Clásicos Castellanos*, 1958.

———. *El burlador de Sevilla* [.] *La prudencia en la mujer*. Ed. Juan Manuel Oliver Cabañes. Barcelona: Plaza & Janes, 1984.

———. *El burlador de Sevilla* in *Spanish Drama of the Golden Age*. Ed. Raymond R. MacCurdy. Englewood Cliffs, NJ: Prentice Hall, 1971.

———. *La venganza de Tamar*. Ed. A.K.G. Paterson. Cambridge. Cambridge University Press, 1969.

Valbuena Prat, Angel. *Historia del teatro español*. Barcelona: Planeta, 1956.

Varey, John E. "Social Criticism in *El burlador de Sevilla*." *Theatre Research International* 2 (1977): 197-221.

Wade, Gerald E. "The Character of Don Juan of *El burlador de Sevilla*: A Psychoanalytical Study." *BCom* 31 (1979): 33-42.

Wardropper, Bruce W. "*El burlador de Sevilla:* A Tragedy of Errors." *PQ* 36 (1957): 61-71.

White, Robert and Robert Gilliard. *Elements of Psychopathology*. N.Y.: Grune and Stratton, 1975.

FURTHER READING

Criticism

Bushee, Alice. "The Five Partes of Tirso de Molina," *Hispanic Review III*, no. 2 (1935): 89-102.

An article focusing on the rarity of de Molina's Partes.

Green, Otis H. "New Light on Don Juan: A Review Article," *Hispanic Review IX*, no. 4 (1941): 89-102.

A review of Josquín Casalduero's book Contribución al estudio del tema de Don Juan en el treatro español, which takes a very broad, scholarly look at the theme of Don Juan.

Halstead, Frank G. "The Attitude of Tirso de Molina Toward Astrology," *Hispanic Review IX*, no. 4 (1941): 89-102.

An article attempting to understand de Molina's ideology and views on freewill.

Morley, S. G. "Character Names in Tirso de Molina," *Hispanic Review XXVIII*, no. 2 (1959): 222-227.

A superficial analysis of names used in de Molina's plays.

Sola-Solé, Josep M., and George E. Gingras, ed. *Tirso's Don Juan: The Metamorphosis of a Theme* Washington, D.C.: The Catholic University of America Press, 1988.

An in-depth study of de Molina's life and work.

Wilson, Margaret. *Tirso de Molina*. Boston: Twayne Publishers, 1977.

A collection of papers from an international symposium on de Molina, featuring a broad range of topics concerning de Molina's life and works.

Additional coverage of de Molina's life and career is contained in the following source published by the Gale Group: *Hispanic Literature Criticism: Supplement*, Vol. 1.

Megan Terry
1932-

American playwright.

INTRODUCTION

Considered among the first dramatists to embrace feminist causes and avant-garde techniques, Terry's work often presents female characters in situations that test them or require them to challenge their own gender preconceptions. In other plays, Terry explores the psyches of such societally marginalized characters as battered women, teenagers, the elderly, and prisoners. As a director of many of her own works, Terry advocates a community theater approach in which she sometimes recruits individuals from the audience or from the streets outside the theater to act. Her philosophy of each participant bringing their "own reality" to the play, along with her use of space and music, are among the key identifiers of her work.

BIOGRAPHICAL INFORMATION

Born in Seattle, Washington, Terry became fascinated with the theater when she was seven years old after attending her first live production. Determined theater would be her career, Terry mounted theatrical productions in her neighborhood and school, serving as actor, writer, director, designer, and set builder. While still in high school, she interned with the Seattle Repertory Playhouse where she worked with director Florence James and actor Burton James, whose political views influenced Terry's later dramas. As a student at the University of Edmonton, Terry immersed herself in set design and technical direction, skills that later affected her approach to theatrical writing. After completing college, Terry continued to write and produce dramas, some of which were performed at New York City's Open Theatre. The experimental environment at the Open Theatre helped Terry conceive her plays as a series of action blocs rather than sequential scenes. She also began using her scripts as starting points for dialogue and action and allowed the participants to ad lib their parts.

MAJOR WORKS

Terry's prolific writing resulted in the production of more than fifty plays and numerous awards. *The Magic Realists* (1969) signalled Terry's experimentation with postmodern techniques, which included songs and dream sequences. Her first success and perhaps best-known play, *Viet Rock* (1966), is generally regarded as the first rock musical as well as the first drama about the Vietnam conflict. Despite its topicality and popularity, *Viet Rock* received mixed reactions to its innovative form and antiwar message. *Viet Rock* is also noted for Terry's use of "transformational drama," a highly influential postmodern technique she defines as "a dramatic action composed of brief sequences that are suddenly transformed into different sets of characters and circumstances." In contrast to her previous work, *Approaching Simone*, which received the 1970 Obie Award for best play, received wide acclaim from critics. The play portrays the life of philosopher Simone Weil, who, at age thirty-four, committed suicide by starvation to protest World War II soldiers starving at the front line. During the 1970s, Terry wrote several plays concerning family, societal, and gender issues, including *Hothouse*, *Pioneer*, *American King's English for Queens*, and *Goona Goona*. Family scenarios used in her 1978 play *American King's English for Queens* demonstrate the sexism Terry perceives as inherent in the English language, and the 1979 play *Goona Goona* depicts the abuse that occurs in some families.

CRITICAL RECEPTION

Although she received favorable notices for her one-act plays *Calm Down Mother* (1966) and *Keep Tightly Closed in a Cool Dry Place* (1966), *Viet Rock* was the first of Terry's plays to receive serious critical notice. While some critics found the play's use of rock music and subversive politics offensive and amateurish, others applauded Terry's use of such innovative theatrical techniques as nonlinear time and refusal to maintain the play's action within the confines of the stage. The play, however, was highly influential, inspiring other musicals, including the well-known play *Hair*. *Approaching Simone*, however, was received enthusiastically by critics, many of whom admired the humane themes Terry employed. In her play *Hothouse*, inspired by her relationships with her mother and grandmother, Terry explores the expectations society places on female behavior. While admiring her treatment of feminist themes, some critics faulted Terry's reliance on autobiographical material. In contrast to the negative reviews *Hothouse* received, Terry's *Babes in the Bighouse* (1974) was lauded: the plays use of humor and satire was considered by critics as an inspired means to portray potentially controversial issues of sexuality and the degradation of female prisoners.

PRINCIPAL WORKS

Plays

Beach Grass 1955
The Dirt Boat 1955
Go Out and Move the Car 1955
Seascape 1955
New York Comedy: Two 1961
Eat at Joe's 1963
Ex-Miss Copper Queen on a Set of Pills 1963
When My Girlfriend Was Still All Flowers 1963
Calm Down Mother: A Transformation Play for Three Women 1966
Keep Tightly Closed in a Cool Dry Place 1966
Viet Rock: A Folk War Movie 1966
Comings and Goings: A Theatre Game 1967
The Gloaming, Oh My Darling: A Play in One Act 1967
Changes 1968
Home: Or Future Soap 1968
Jack-Jack 1968
The Key Is on the Bottom 1968
Massachusetts Trust 1968
The People vs. Ranchman 1968
Sanibel and Captiva 1968
The Magic Realists 1969
One More Little Drinkie 1969
The Tommy Allen Show 1969
Approaching Simone: A Drama in Two Acts 1970
American Wedding Ritual Monitored/Transmitted by the Planet Jupiter 1972
Choose a Spot on the Floor 1972
Grooving 1972
Off Broadway Book 1972
Nightwalk 1973
St. Hydro Clemency; or, A Funhouse of the Lord: An Energizing Event 1973
Susan Perultz at the Manhattan Theatre Club 1973
All Them Women 1974
Babes in the Bighouse: A Documentary Fantasy Musical About Life Inside a Women's Prison 1974
Couplings and Groupings 1974
Fifteen Million Fifteen Year Olds 1974
Henna for Endurance 1974
Hospital Play 1974
Hothouse 1974
The Narco Linguini Bust 1974
The Pioneer 1974
Pro Game; The Pioneer: Two One-Act Plays 1974
We Can Feed Everybody Here 1974
Women's Prison 1974
Pioneer 1975
100,001 Horror Stories of the Plains 1976
Women and Law 1976
Brazil Fado: You're Always with Me 1977
Lady Rose's Brazil Hide Out 1977
Sleazing Toward Athens 1977
Willie-Willa-Bill's Dope Garden, A Meditation in One-Act on Willa Cather 1977
American King's English for Queens 1978
Attempted Rescue on Avenue B: A Beat Fifties Comic Opera 1979
Goona Goona 1979
Advances 1980
Fireworks 1980
Janis Joplin 1980
Flat in Afghanistan 1981
Katmandu 1981
The Trees Blew Down 1981
Winners: The Lives of a Traveling Family Circus and Mother Jones 1981
Kegger 1982
Mollie Bailey's Traveling Family Circus: Featuring Scenes from the Life of Mother Jones 1983
Amtrak 1988
Headlights 1988
Retro 1988
Body Leaks 1990
Breakfast Serial 1991
Do You See What I'm Saying? 1991
Sound Fields: Are We Hear 1992

AUTHOR COMMENTARY

Megan Terry (essay date 1977)

SOURCE: "Two Pages a Day," in *The Drama Review*, Vol. 21, No. 4, December, 1977, pp. 60-4.

[*In the following essay, Terry discusses her passion for writing and her everyday, artistic life.*]

I was bused to the theatre at the age of seven. There was a program, sponsored by the Junior League, to bring children to live theatre. I lived in a small fishing village outside of Seattle; it was a long bus ride, but it changed my life. Professional actors, who had worked together for twenty years under the direction of Mrs. Florence Bean James (who had studied with Stanislavsky) were playing *Rumplestiltskin*. That was it. I fell in love.

As soon as I was allowed to go about on my own (fourteen), I went back to that theatre and hung around and begged to clean johns and sort nuts and bolts until they took me into the company.

Mrs. James and her actor husband, Burton, inspired me to write for the theatre. They always hoped a playwright would emerge from their theatre. When I joined, I was more interested in design. But watching her direct and teach acting, I got hooked on all aspects of theatre. I was fascinated by her sense-memory exercises and her classes in improvisation.

Watching improvisations, I saw that the actors would be sometimes marvelous; the improvisation would be more real than life, but it was also fragile—difficult to repeat and keep that "living" quality. I started to try to write down some of the improvisations with the thought that if the structure could be secured and dialog written the actors could have a tighter scenario and be relieved of the "playwriting" part of their work. They would be freer to fly in their art. And the improvisation could stay fresh. This wasn't so easy to do, and I think it took me ten years of trying before I got good at it.

In college and on my own, I studied fine arts, theatrical design and costume. I was swept away for a time by the Collagists. I believe the experience of working in collage for five years influenced the way I put plays together later on. I think of "building" or "making" a play.

I bought a lot of wire "in" and "out" boxes at the Salvation Army, and each is loaded with notes. Sometimes these notes turn into plays, and sometimes I have to empty them into larger boxes marked "notes." I have many cards with possible titles stashed in drawers around the house.

Sometimes a title comes first, sometimes last, sometimes that's all that comes. I buy pens by the gross. Notepads are in every room, pocket, purse. There is always paper in the typewriter.

I write a lot from life. I *listen* to characters and write down what they say. They usually surprise me. The way people speak is music to me. I collect language. I've trained my ear over the years, both out of pleasure and a desire to save what I'm hearing. I imagine I can hear the inner person via the rhythms of a person's sentence structure. I try to be as faithful as I can to individual rhythms when I'm writing.

I love to write. The act of writing gives me almost as much pleasure as lovemaking. I can write as long as my energy holds out—sometimes two days and nights at a time, sometimes eight to ten hours, sometimes only two pages, then I take a nap, wake up, drink a giant cup of Irish breakfast tea with a cinnamon stick and write twenty-four more hours.

I have a one-inch-by-two-inch section of masking tape on the left-hand side of my typewriter. I have written on the tape "Two Pages." That means to me that my only requirement to earn bread and board and to be relieved of guilt for each day of my life, all I have to hand in to myself, is two pages of new material. It may be on anything, but notebook writing doesn't count. It must be writing that can actually be worked into a now or future play. When I have a deadline to meet, either one of my own or one commissioned, I up the number of pages from five to ten to twenty. Two pages a day, two times 365, adds up to enough pages for anyone.

Typing is an unnatural act. I got "D" in typing in high school. When I realized later on that I was more into writing than design, acting or directing, I had to relearn typing. Not an easy job. I'm athletically coordinated, but I couldn't type. Why? I still don't know. It was necessary for me to conquer this mechanical defect, or I could never have moved ahead as a writer. I have memories of banging my head on the typewriter and crying from frustration and anger at my ineptness. This was the basis of early writing blocks. But I found the writing was always there, ready to show itself on the page if I could only get the mechanical problems out of the way. The only thing to solve it was to force myself to take junk jobs in insurance companies and engineering firms as a temporary typist to build my speed. This worked, but took longer than I thought.

That pain is all behind me now. I have since beaten to death one Royal and two Olympias. Now I have a strong IBM Selectric at home and another in the lighting booth at the theatre. I go to work with the actors and do the warm-up exercises with them, then go up to the lighting booth to write scenes for whatever play we're into—usually at the rate of a scene a day or every two days, depending on how much research is involved. This is in addition to the personal assignments I have given myself or outside commissions from other groups. The act of writing is no longer a pain, but now a physical joy akin to hang gliding.

Cappuccino first thing in the morning. I jump into sweat clothes and take the dogs to the park. Back inside, a long hot shower; then I choose clothing according to what I plan to write. For aggressive scenes, blue jeans; for tender scenes, love scenes, I dress in silk.

After the first burst of writing, it's time to start dinner for the company. I usually cook a giant soup or stew for the members of our household every three of four days. I think of my main career as that of a cook. Writing occurs in between stirring and chopping, serving, and watching my friends eat. After the soup or stew is started, I move back and forth from the typewriter to the stove, stirring, tasting, adding spices, more vegetables, experimenting with lower and lower heat.

I never stop working on a show we have in performance or in our permanent repertoire because I am always learning new things about the piece from the audience. I cut, add, or rewrite after consultation with our director Jo Ann Schmidman and the company. I stop working on the *written* text once a play is published, but if new editions come out, I incorporate any changes we've developed that will, in my opinion, make the play play better.

Now we are doing developmental work for a play, a rock samba musical I'm writing, set in Brazil. The first impulse to write this show came from an interview Janis Joplin gave to the press. She had gone to Brazil for Mardi Gras, hitchhiked up the coast of Brazil, and somehow kicked junk. No one knows anything else about that period in her life. I put on her records again today and try to write drafts of scenes that have her beat as their basis.

Megan Terry with Kathleen Betsko and Rachel Koenig (interview date 1987)

SOURCE: An interview in *Interviews with Contemporary Women Playwrights*, Beech Tree Books, 1987, pp. 377-401.

[*In the following interview, Betsko and Koenig cover an array of topics including how Terry describes her creative process to the message the author would like to convey to the world.*]

Megan Terry was born July 22, 1932, in Seattle, Washington. A founding member of The Open Theater and The New York Theatre Strategy, she is now Literary Manager and Playwright-in-Residence at the Omaha Magic Theatre. Ms. Terry has written more than sixty plays, including ***X-Rayed-iate, Family Talk, Porch Visit, Above It: Speculations on the Death of Amelia Earhart, Family Circus: Featuring Scenes from the Life of Mother Jones, Fifteen Million Fifteen-Year-Olds, High Energy Musicals from the Omaha Magic Theatre, Kegger, Objective Love, American King's English for Queens, Brazil Fado, 100,001 Horror Stories of the Plains, Babes in the Bighouse, Hothouse, Nightwalk*** (with Jean-Claude van Itallie and Sam Shepard), ***American Wedding Ritual, The Tommy Allen Show, Approaching Simone, Keep Tightly Closed in a Cool Dry Place, Comings and Goings, Calm Down Mother, Eat at Joe's*** and ***The Magic Realists.*** Ms. Terry graduated from the University of Washington, earned certificates in directing, acting and design from the Banff School of Fine Arts, and won a Fellowship to Yale.

[Kathleen Betsko and Rachel Koenig]: You've written a cornucopia of plays, had hundreds of productions worldwide and share administrative and artistic responsibilities at the Omaha Magic Theatre. When do you find time to write?

[Terry]: Whenever I have to. Helping to run a theater is like running a small business, so the writing has to get squeezed in whenever it can. I used to write two pages a day when things were calmer, but sometimes I have to write ten. I buy pens by the gross.

You still write by hand, then?

I always have paper in three typewriters. Two down at The Magic Theatre and one at home. And I must have pens. I always seem to be on the move.

Describe your creative process. How does a play begin in your mind?

In many different ways. I was trained in fine arts and went into theater first as a designer and performer. Sometimes it's an image, or the entire set. Sometimes I draw the set first and then write scenes to go in it. Other times, characters start speaking and acting in my mind, and then I become like a secretary to the characters and type as fast as I can to get it all down.

When you work on a topic that requires research, do you begin the research or the writing first?

No set way. ***Approaching Simone*** [1970] took me fifteen years to get together because I had to do a lot of research. Many of her [Simone Weil's] books were out of print, and I had to comb rare-book libraries. The greatest thing that happened as a result of doing the play was that the publishers brought Simone Weil's work out again in paperback.

Your play **Brazil Fado** *[1977] is peppered with news reports. Are those taken from real incidents?*

Yes, from *The Omaha World Herald, The Christian Science Monitor*, and *The New York Times*.

Rosalyn Drexler uses news clippings, current events, weird items in her work, too. Why do you?

In ***Brazil Fado*** I wanted to say a few things about the continuing tragedies in Central and South America.

It's a fascinating play.

Can you tell me why nobody's doing it?

You're making a connection in **Brazil Fado** *between an American couple playing torture games and torture in the world at large. Do you think, in this conservative era, anybody wants to buy a play on that subject?*

Not even other women producers, unfortunately. But we have no problem producing such plays for our Omaha audience.

In Magic Dust, *the newspaper your theater publishes and distributes in the community, you reported on your attendance at the Open Theater Conference at Kent State University in December 1983. You say most students have never heard of Joe Chaikin and the Open Theater.*

Even the head of the Drama Department there managed to stay away! [Laughter] That was always the case, too, when we were on tour with the Open Theater. Very rarely did the drama people—the people who were teaching in theater departments—ever show up at our performances! Isn't that amazing? It's unbelievable to me that the Open Theater has stayed alive in people's minds as long as it has! . . . One of the problems is that many *critics* are looking through a rearview mirror. I think they only read *The New York Times* and each other. They don't know what's happening in the *world*. And they're so negative. Even the supportive critics think nothing's happened since the sixties. But almost everyone who was in the Open Theater is now running a company of their own today. People such as Jo Ann Schmidman, Paul Zimet, Ellen Madden, Shami Chaikin, Ray Berry, Ralph Lee, Tina Shepard, Sam Shepard, Jean-Claude van Itallie, Gwen Fabricant, James Barbosa and Barbara Van are all growing and developing incredible new work. But several critics who attended that conference think that the only new thing is performance art. They don't do their homework.

What was the most important thing about the conference for you?

I think we realized that we were all meant to be together when we were. We realized we loved one another and we respected one another. That the work *was* important, and it was still ongoing in our heads and in the work we're doing now. It was a *fabulous* affirmation. Some of us had not seen each other for ten years! So you can imagine there was advance trepidation. People wondered if some of the old friction would arise, but none did. We've matured. It *is* possible to grow up! [Laughter] We were so *young* then! And we were working in the dark! We were uncovering things that were extremely dynamic and scary. Some of the early problems we had were just part of the process. We cried for joy when we saw one another. It was very heady to realize we'd made a great contribution to the growth of our field and to the artistic development of one another.

What do you think that generation of theater people learned from the fifties, from the early work of The Living Theatre? And then what do you think the seventies learned from the sixties?

I've written a play which I haven't released that deals with the late fifties. Obviously, nobody's ready to even consider it yet. Theater is a conservative art necessarily because it deals with living human beings having to get along with one another to bring something about.

Theater lags behind the other arts?

Yes—it has to—because discoveries have to be made in the other art forms before they can be assimilated into theater. Since painting or poetry is a one-to-one thing, it can develop faster. It's my opinion that American painting, poetry and jazz reached their zenith in the fifties. And that had to happen before the theater could take off. The theater conserves and accumulates, and the sixties couldn't have happened the way it did if such exciting work hadn't arrived in the fifties in the other art forms. Witness the amazing success of the exhibit of late fifties and early sixties painting entitled *BLAM!* at the Whitney [Museum of American Art]. Young people are going to that exhibit and coming out reeling with energy and ideas from that time. For too long people have believed the conservative propaganda that nothing happened in the fifties but Eisenhower's golf swing. Also, the sixties would have been different had Kennedy not been shot. The assassination was a catalyst that brought together and then exploded an astounding energy in theatrical art.

Are there particular people of that fifties generation that influenced you?

The American musical theater . . . the Beat Generation poets, [Gary] Snyder, [Jack] Kerouac, [Allen] Ginsberg . . . the painters [Robert] Rauschenberg, Red Grooms, [Claes] Oldenburg, Jackson Pollock, Helen Frankenthaler.

And of the musicians?

Anita O' Day . . . Sara Vaughan . . . Lambert Hendricks and Ross, Kenny Berrel Trio . . . I was very into jazz and Elvis Presley rock 'n roll!

What happened to theater in the sixties? What was breaking down, changing?

Up until the sixties, the American theater for the most part was an imitation—except for musicals—of the European theater. The Oedipus complex vis-à-vis Mother England was very strong. People went to the theater to learn how to behave, so they could continue an upwardly mobile climb. How to dress, how to smoke cigarettes with *élan*, how to mix drinks while looking seductive, et cetera—how to look WASP. We in the Open Theater and other groups were not interested in "getting ahead" in the old way. We wanted to get somewhere with ourselves, our art and with each other. We wanted a richer, a "realer" life. I feel we democratized the theater. We began to put every kind of American on the stage. I wanted to write plays where it didn't matter what you looked like as long as you had the talent to play it. Also, we were a generation of people educated by those who had survived World War II and come back to teach. World War II gave us as a people a global view. Up to then, in spite of World War I, we'd been insular. We now belonged to the whole world.

And now do we think the world belongs to us?

I think the Russians have made a very clear statement, lately, about *that*. The world is split in two. What happened to the [1984] Olympics in Los Angeles is continuing evidence. [The Soviet Union refused to send competitors to the games.]

How did the democratization of the theater during the sixties affect the seventies?

In the late fifties, early sixties, people came from all over America to New York. And they weren't welcome in the existing Broadway theater. So people like Lanford Wilson, Joe Chaikin, Irene Fornes, Julie Bovasso and all the rest of us who had been told we weren't tall enough, short enough, or thin enough got fed up, and in American entrepreneurial fashion started our own theaters. All these young people were idealists! With fine training. The models in our head were those of the Moscow Art Theatre, the Group Theatre. The Group Theatre ideal evolved into the Actors Studio, and, because of their directors going into film, put Americans in *film* on a *global* scale. But there was, to our minds, no *real* American *theater*. Previously playwrights had appeared to the popular mind only one at a time. In the beginning was O'Neill. Then Tennessee Williams. Then Miller. Edward Albee was the last of the "lone" playwrights. The sixties was an incredible explosion of thirty-five talented writers showing up in New York. And nobody knew how to deal with them! Critics have a Messiah complex! Their brains are too tiny to hold more than one talent in their minds at a time. Michael Feingold [*The Village Voice*], Jack Kroll [*Newsweek*] and Sylvie Drake [*The Los Angeles Times*] are different. They love *theater*. They're in it *with* us. Unfortunately, many other critics seem bent on using the stuff of theater as raw material for their own careers in a way that demonstrates they're not *part* of the field.

Why do you think they're always bemoaning the lack of political plays?

Yet when one appears, they don't recognize it. They're always asking for "language." But when Stephen Berkoff arrived with *Greeks*, or Maria Irene Fornes with *Fefu and Her Friends*, they couldn't hear it! . . . I don't know why most of them think there can only be *one* writer at a time to sum up an age! America is *vast*. There are many Americas. If you tour this country, you find that out very quickly. Yet critics tend to put the playwright up on the cross. They allow one or two successes, and then they fire napalm. The pressure is horrendous. I'm fearful for Sam Shepard now. You *know* you have to worry when your face appears on the cover of a national magazine. [Laughter]

Do you make a distinction between theater critics that review for the media and academic theater criticism?

I just heard three marvelous papers at Stanford University. Dr. Margaret Wilkerson on Lorraine Hansberry, Dr. Beverly Beyers-Pevitts and Dr. Rosemary Curb on an array of writers. Their criticism is useful, even inspiring, to a writer.

What elements of criticism are useful to you?

To have the thoughts of minds of their caliber paying attention to writing and writers, their creative comparisons, turns lights on in my head; I see things I hadn't thought of before. New possibilities for plays form in my mind. It drives me forward. Whereas, the other kind of criticism makes me think, "*What* am I *doing*? I'm going to go back to crab fishing!" [Laughter]

What about the regional critics versus the New York critics?

I'm thinking of Richard Christianson of *The Chicago Tribune*, Chris Koyamo of *Chicago Magazine* and Joan Bunke of *The Des Moines Register*. They bring a terrific education, a love of theater, concern and a disciplined but considered point of view to their writing. Sylvie Drake, Dan Sullivan and John Mahoney of *The Los Angeles Times*, Bernard Weiner of *The San Francisco Chronicle*, Mike Steel of *The Minneapolis Tribune* and Helen Krich Chinoy and Linda Walsh Jenkins, academic critics, are people who are joining in a partnership with the writer. There is an attitude in New York that critics and playwrights shouldn't talk to one another! Weird.

But you once traveled three thousand miles across country with a critic, didn't you?

Elliot Norton of *The Boston Herald-American*. He had panned my play, ***Approaching Simone***. Among other things, he called the play "pagan." It was a trip sponsored by the American Theatre Association. We ended up falling in love with one another . . . as human beings. He has a right to his opinion. We became friends because we saw one another in action, helping to teach young writers.

You discovered your mutual concerns.

Right. The future.

Walter Kerr, in a [November 23,] 1966 article in The New York Times, *lashed out at your antiwar play,* **Viet Rock**, *while heaping praise upon Jean-Claude van Itallie's* America, Hurrah *in the same article. The headline said, "One Succeeds, the Other Fails. Why?"*

He attacked me two Sundays in a row. That's when Jean-Claude and I were both playwrights in the Open Theater. But he couldn't kill the play. He closed it in New York, but it was translated into every major language and was proclaimed in every major, and many minor, cities all over the world, and it repaid its backers every cent.

Do you think that the critical vitriol increased because you directed **Viet Rock** *yourself?*

Well, I was picketed by a group of directors besides everything else! Because I wouldn't join the Directors' Guild.

In addition, you kept the critics away on opening night?

No, that was a bad move on the part of the producer. For the sake of keeping the play running. This producer told me if he had it all to do over again, he never would have let the critics come at *all*. [Laughter] He could have kept it running for a year. We had standing room only. The place was packed every night until Kerr's second Sunday drubbing appeared in *The Times*. Then the phones went dead. Before that, they'd been ringing off the walls; people were throwing themselves in my arms and the actors' arms crying every night after the show, but Kerr managed to kill it.

If all producers united, kept the critics away for a month, would theater criticism as we know it—the "hit or bomb" syndrome—change? One critic of **Viet Rock**, *Whitney Bolton [in the November 15, 1966 issue] of* The Morning Telegraph, *said, ". . . I cannot deny [the producers] their right to close the first performance here to us. For that matter, I would think that there is no existing law demanding that newspaper and magazine critics be admitted gratis to any production. Producers in their exercises of rights certainly can deny us admission on the customary cuff and can demand that we buy our seats when and if available. For all producers to follow this pattern would be to send us (the critics) to the showers and that might not be a bad thing."*

Well, maybe it could be done. But reviewers—I'm not talking about critics—feel that they have to protect the public. Especially as the costs of tickets rise. So they're on the side of the public, not the side of the writers. You've got to remember that. Broadway is just a showcase for television now. Broadway is no longer the place I was taught about when I went to college, i.e., the place where The Theater was kept alive, the Theater of Ideas. A place where one could be in touch with human feelings, where you could see yourself, where society could see itself. Broadway is now a place for the tourists to go and be beguiled by stagecraft. They're giving standing ovations to strobe lights!

Will you talk a little bit about Florence James, who she is and how she influenced your career?

She's past ninety now and in a nursing home, though her mind is still extremely sharp. Until five years ago, even though she was blind, she still went to the theater where she worked and gave notes. She'd won a scholarship as a young woman to the Moscow Art Theatre, where she met and studied with Stanislavsky and was influenced greatly by Vaktangov and Meyerhold. She shared all her education with us in the theater she and her husband, Burton W. James, founded in Seattle. I joined as a teenager and was especially swept away by the staging ideas and constructivist sets of Meyerhold. Mrs. James was our director and acting teacher, and her husband was a great actor. She was a powerful director and a powerful intellect.

Do you think that having a great woman as an early role model was helpful to you?

Definitely. But it wasn't only Florence's influence. It was my mother, my grandmothers, my aunts, my great-aunts, my mother's cousins. Fantastic women. I love to be with them. I go home several times a year just so I can hang out with them! They're all beautiful and bright, witty, full of the devil. Terrific singers.

We read that your great-grandmother crossed the country with her seven children.

Yes, by covered wagon, without her husband. He was on the job elsewhere as an Indian scout. I only found out about it recently. You see, I come from a pioneer culture, so I'm kind of different from people raised in the East. Women worked side by side with the men. I was taught to build houses. I worked alongside my father and grandfather. We built several houses together. My grandfather was a great engineer who built bridges and railroads. I grew up using tools. I think that's important. Not enough women get to use tools, not even kitchen tools! There's too much isolation among women nowadays. The culture I grew up in, the women were always in the kitchen together. Incredible cooperation, preparing family reunions with lots of joking and singing at huge parties. There was a conference in Kansas City a couple of weeks ago where Dr. Marlene Springer was speaking about a prairie diary she's editing with her husband. It described how the women in Kansas would hurry up and get all their housework done in the morning so in the afternoon they could go porch visiting! They'd sit and rock and pass the time. Then along came the telephone and the porch visiting stopped! And women missed the physical presence of one another. They were seeing men but only hearing each other on the telephone. When there was a special event in the community and all the women would see one another, there'd be an incredible reunion, they'd just rush to hug, and then exchange passionate letters afterwards. Some people have misinterpreted or inferred sexual significance to this, but actually they were just starved for the plain sight of one another! There also had been many instances on the prairies of women committing suicide because of isolation and loneliness. We tend to forget the important reinforcement that physical presence can bring. I find that's an extra dividend of writers' conferences for women. We can give strength and reinforcement to one another. We're going to work with the Springers on creating a new play out of their diary findings for next season, and of course we're calling it ***Porch Visiting***.

What do you say to those people who say that by holding women's conferences we're excluding half of the population?

Men were free to come. Several men were featured speakers. There were only three men in the audience, but it certainly was open to them. I wonder why the other half of the population isn't where *our* action is.

You teach playwriting. Are you spreading the word about women dramatists?

Constantly. Recently, I taught Emily Mann's *Still Life* at a university in Minnesota. My students were *outraged* that they'd never heard of this play, nor the work of Maria Irene Fornes, nor Roz Drexler, Rochelle Owens, Adrienne Kennedy, Sybil Pearson, Caryl Churchill, Pam Gems, Ntozake Shange, Julie Bovasso, Jo Ann Schmidman, Tina Howe. They knew none of these people, and they were getting their master's degrees! They were really angry by the time I finished with them. [Laughter]

You mentioned earlier that the theater world had been used to plodding along with one significant playwright at a time. Then, suddenly, in the sixties, thirty-five new ones flooded the scene. Was that the group Fornes told us about? The New York Theatre Strategy?

Yes, there were thirty-five of us—men and women.

It started out as an all-female group originally, though, didn't it?

We couldn't raise any money! Foundations said we had no track record. And we said: We women have five hundred seventy-five thousand years of track record! They didn't give any money until we got the men in there, though.

You said that you had always wanted to write for women, yet you began writing long before the Women's Movement.

[Laughing] I'd been an actor! I gave directors a hard time because I would change my lines. I'd been trained via the Stanislavsky method; I always wrote interior dialogues for my characters and elaborate descriptions of what my character was doing before my entrance. Often I'd substitute my lines for what was in the text—but only for writers who, in my opinion, hadn't written well enough. However, I was more than happy to learn my lines when I was playing Shaw, O'Casey or Synge. But I didn't get to play them often enough. Finally I decided, "The hell with this! I'm going to start writing!"

And that's where your playwriting began?

Partly. I'd watch actors do great improvisations in workshops and acting classes at the Seattle Repertory Playhouse. Many times their work seemed better than the lines they were trying to learn. But I really started to write when I saw most actors couldn't repeat a great improvisation unless they were also writers. Some actors are great storytellers, and this gift could be transferred into writing.

How did you manage to harness the spontaneous vitality of the improvisation and translate that into a text?

I was trained in improvisation as an actor and so I internalized that way of working as a writer. Also, I've been a painter, sculptor and theater designer; laying down ideas, then ripping them up or moving them around was part of my method of work, so I didn't get lost in the linear.

So how many drafts do you normally go through before you publish a text?

Some come out perfect the first time . . . ***Comings and Goings*** [1966]. Others, like ***Hothouse*** [1971], take ten years of drafts.

When you said earlier that you always wanted to write for women, did you mean parts for actresses? Or did you mean write for the women in the audiences?

Both. So many of the interesting roles are for the men. These roles may show many facets of a character—thus the men playing these roles may stretch themselves and show their power as the character and themselves—while the women characters may have only one aspect to project. This may be all the play requires, but the actress does not get a workout and the audience sees only a one-sided woman.

Do you think Aristotelian rules are at all relevant to women dramatists?

Yes, know them and then you can play with them. You don't have to be controlled by them. They're there to use, like building blocks, and you can move them around in any way you want to.

So you don't think women's experience demands new forms of writing?

No. But I personally love new forms and I've created some new forms. I'm essentially a fan of the new, but the oldest form can be just fine—if you fill it with the truth as you see it. Put your experience into any form that's comfortable, or create one that's perfect for you.

Do you see your work as influencing the writing of male playwrights?

Tom Eyen told me after he saw ***Calm Down, Mother*** [1965], he ran home and wrote *The White Whore and the Bit Player*. Many other writers have told me that my work gives them courage.

What did you mean when you said, "Theater is like medicine: It was started by women and usurped by men"?

Storytelling. Mothers telling stories to babies. The first teaching was, is through storytelling. Kitchen sink drama didn't become "art" until men started doing it. Women were writing domestic dramas for thirty, forty years before John Osborne.

Even Joe Papp has said he doesn't want any more "kitchen sink" drama in his theater [New York Shakespeare Festival]. Just as we are becoming more prolific, our most common settings—the kitchen, the bedroom—have become passé;.

And men have been out in the "real" world. Look what trouble this so-called real world has brought us.

No woman playwright has ever been considered a literary "great." Why?

The day *that* happens playwriting will no longer be called an art. The same thing happens in business. The minute women infiltrate a job, men turn their backs on it. It no longer has currency.

Will you describe what The Omaha Magic Theatre is doing in terms of self-publishing of plays?

We published our plays for ten years, and we've been recently rewarded for this industry by attracting Broadway Play Publishing, Inc., of New York City. They bring out our work now. It was a mind-bending experience learning the mechanics of self-publishing. But we did it!

You've been trying to encourage women playwrights to send you their bibliographies so that you can drop them off at theaters around the country?

Yes, also so that we can keep in touch. In addition, I do many seminars at universities where I can share this information. There is no such thing as substantial book royalties for a playwright. Photocopying has done away with that. All you can hope for is production royalties. That's why I've asked other writers for their bibliographies—that news is essential to send out into the world—to the young and to potential producers.

Perhaps this book can carry the message to women playwrights to get those bibliographies to you.

Someone should publish a bibliography of all the women writers and give them free to libraries. Then the young people, and we who care, can find out what each other's doing.

What will it take to stop this state-by-state isolation in America? Do you think that New York will always be the heart of theater?

The theatrical energy is no longer in New York, except when it's residing in writers like Irene Fornes and Ping Chong, or writer/performers like Meredith Monk. The energy now is Chicago, San Francisco, Omaha, Minneapolis, Los Angeles, Seattle.

And Louisville?

Once a year. But the theater is decentralizing. The next century belongs to the Pacific Rim and the Hispanics. Asia is rising. The Spanish are rising again. We're split into two worlds now, clearly. Maybe that's what happened with men and women, too? But we must work to bring about a balance.

There are some people who feel that there is a renewed but more covert war going on between men and women now . . . a deeper malaise setting in, separating us.

I think that men are negative because women are positive and on the rise! It's driving the men crazy! Martha Boesing, [playwright and founder of At The Foot of the Mountain Theater] was telling me that in the thousand plays she receives each year, most have hopeful endings! [Laughs] Women are feeling positive and forward-looking. Plays men are writing often end with everybody dead, dying or neurotic to the point of no return.

What can we do to heal this polarization?

Live your life as if the revolution had been a success!

You certainly do. Tell us about the touring aspect of the Magic Theatre.

We tour the Midwest six months of the year, and we take our other plays with us to sell as we go. We've sold the work developed at our theater by mail order, too, all over the United States and, in fact, the world.

Has the Magic Theatre been addressing the issues of nuclear war?

Jo Ann Schmidman, our artistic director, wrote a marvelous piece called *Velveeta Meltdown*. We staged it in Central Park here and more than five hundred people came. The people of Omaha turned out for Mondale yesterday. When he said he was for a nuclear freeze, a cheer went up through the park that I'm surprised you didn't hear all the way back in New York. We have the SAC Air Force Base here. Omaha is the A-number-one target. Nebraska and Wyoming were told to accept the MX missiles.

Are they torn between having jobs and getting rid of these weapons?

No. Farm people don't want their land wrecked, nor do they want to be targets.

You've opened up dialogues between your theater and the community. Your play **Kegger** *[1982] discussed teenage alcoholism and toured Nebraska. What were the results of this particular effort?*

We're catalysts in the community. Communities keep in touch with us via our touring network. Everyone is working now to find ways to have chemical-free fun. They've formed positive peer-pressure groups within the schools to let kids know it's okay *not* to drink. One of the things that the Magic Theatre Company learned—doing research with neurosurgeons, neuropsychologists and biologists—is that people under the age of twenty-five lack an enzyme to deal with alcohol. That's why kids deteriorate so fast when they get heavily into booze and drugs. What might take eighteen *years* to ruin an adult will take eighteen months for a kid. But it takes a while to get this information through to kids. We were asked to take ***Kegger*** into a Lutheran college, a very conservative school, because they found their students were having keggers every night! The kids were coming to class drunk. After another performance of ***Kegger*** at a large state university, some of the professors came to us afterward and said, "You know you've really opened our eyes. We didn't know why the kids were sleeping in class, or why their grades were falling off." It never crossed their minds that they were drunk or hung over! It's a long education process. One of the big causes of this drinking is that kids don't think they're going to *see* [age] twenty-five. Many of the young people I interviewed really believe that we're all going to blow up, and that they might as well have their good times while they can!

Are your playwriting students politically aware?

You might get one out of fifty who sees the bigger picture. When they're under twenty-one they're still having a lot of problems with interpersonal relationships, with their families. . . . They have to work their family play out of their systems first. And some of the students I met are working three jobs.

Is this despair in the young—drinking, and so on—stopping the kids from writing?

At no time in history have so many people been writing plays. I had ten in a recent university group, and all ten of them could write. They had me working overtime to prepare for them. They were all bright; some were in a kind of negative despair, but not all. There is no lack of talent. We've just got to give kids a better world to live in.

Do you feel that there's a necessity for regional theaters and playwrights to start forming the sort of alliances that the Omaha Magic Theatre has created with Nebraska communities?

More theaters are willing to do that than a lot of writers may realize. I belong to the American Theatre Association, and I find a lot of community theaters are looking to affiliate with writers. Many universities are eager to produce new works of playwrights who are willing to work with their students. I think too many writers are sitting around waiting for Godot. The National Endowment for the Arts has done everything it can to encourage new works in the last ten years. And these efforts have paid off. Every proposal I've read from theaters all around the country has a new play production or development program. It's up to the writer now to go get affiliated or start her own theater. If you don't like the way a theater does things, then start your own, Babe! This is the land of entrepreneurs. If you read the tax laws, they're all written for the small business people. If the writer can see himself or herself as a small businessperson, the sky's the limit.

In the Magic Theatre's Statement of Purpose, we see that you're not separating art from business. You are encouraging everyone to learn the business side.

If you don't, you go under! Besides, if you don't know where money comes from, you get arrogant and begin to think the world owes you a living.

Where would playwrights go to gather these entrepreneurial skills?

You can start by starting. You can go and offer yourself to a small theater company. Every small theater company in this country needs talent. Learn it by doing it.

And that would include learning to write a grant?

That is the biggest pain in the neck. Everyone with writing skills should be learning to write grants and helping out that way. At The Magic Theatre we share the chore around so that everyone gets to learn what that "pain in the neck" is and sees where their salary comes from.

When were you first able to earn a living from your plays?

Strangely enough, with ***Viet Rock*** in 1966.

Did you see any of the foreign productions of that play?

No, but they sent me photos of it, from Tokyo, Germany . . .

Calm Down, Mother*'s being translated into Cantonese.*

Yes, it's being produced in Hong Kong. I can't tell you what a high that's given me. I have been intrigued by China since I was a child.

Do you have any plans to go to China?

Yesterday, we got a call from Korea. They want us to come to their next International Theater Festival. If we get to Korea, then perhaps we can tour China.

Would you talk about the theme of dominance and submission that crops up so often in your work? Why is this subject so compelling to you?

Well, I think you have to *submit* to art. [Laughter] One must submit the ego to the work, or the work never gets done. That's the positive side of submission. The only utopias that ever lasted very long were those where people submitted to an idea greater than the individual.

Isn't that surrender rather than submission? Is there a difference?

Yes. Surrender used that way implies bliss as well as loss of self. Submission, on the other hand, means against your will you do thus and so because you are forced by either superior strength or psychological power. Sorting this out is important for mental health, and I believe my plays have healing powers.

Your work constantly addresses the power struggles of human beings. Where does this obsession come from?

It started in grade school, being very bright in class. There were two boys as bright as I, and we were friends. I had one of those rare experiences of going to school with the same friends from first to the eighth grade. But by the eighth grade the teachers stopped calling on me, even though they knew I knew the answers. When I got into high school, that was it. It didn't matter how bright the girls were, only the boys were called on; you could see them being groomed for leadership.

Did you feel angry about that?

Oh, yes! But I was still very naïve when I was a freshman in high school. The other members of the freshman class urged me to stand up in an assembly and criticize the student council! Which I did. And there was an incredible silence. Later I found out—when I was a senior—that all the boys in the Student Council were offended and they collectively agreed *never* to take me out! [Laughter] They'd made a pact. I found out at an early age that when a woman opens her mouth there are consequences!

Was that the theme you were dealing with in your play **Attempted Rescue on Avenue B** *[1977]?*

If you show your power you'll get killed.

How have you protected yourself?

I think being Irish provides a certain protection, and strong women to look to in my family. My family has always been behind me one hundred thousand percent. My mother always told me I was beautiful and brilliant. She still does.

What were the factors that led up to you leaving New York and divorcing yourself from the commercial theater?

I saw that there were two worlds and I didn't have to live in the negative one. And I also realized I didn't have to be "the woman" behind "the man."

Yes. That subject is also dealt with in **Attempted Rescue**. *What kinds of sacrifices are necessary for women artists, do you think?*

I don't think one has to make any. It's all in the way you look at the world. It's just a matter of organizing your time.

Are you organized?

I must be, because I get *enough* done; but I feel that I only accomplish one-tenth of what I'm capable of.

So a women doesn't have to sacrifice her personal relationships to be a committed artist?

Not at all!

Chinese playwright Bai Fengxi might disagree, I think. She bases much of her work around this very question. Can a woman have a full-time career as well as a happy marriage and family life?

Perhaps her traditions place intolerable burdens on her. But we're a young country, and women raised here should be able to shrug off a lot of society's pressures.

How different an experience was it for you to go off and work with someone like Jo Ann Schmidman in Omaha after the New York scene?

It was very different. Because she liked everything I wrote! That was *really* different! I mean, reinforcing! It took me a long time to believe her, because she was so accepting with her generous policies and attitude. Plus she's a great director! I'm a pretty good director, but after I saw her directing I had sense enough to back off from directing and write more. She's also an amazing performer. She's the only actor Joe Chaikin ever put directly into the Open Theater without a probation period. She's the first director I've worked with who has been raised totally on television. She's visually literate. She physicalizes my work in ways that I would never have dreamed of! I have a terrific ear, but she has wonderful visual sense.

So you have a true collaboration, then, between writer and director?

Yes. We also write together. This piece we're working on now, ***X-rayed-iate*** [1984], is really her child. I wrote most of the text, but the concept, the structure, the movement of it is hers.

Here in New York we sense a growing barrier between playwrights and directors.

The director is a recent phenomenon, you know, in the last hundred years.

You've described yourself as a benevolent dictator. Are you autocratic as a director in the rehearsal setting?

In the sense that we have to open on a certain date, on time, you know. I expect people to be punctual at rehearsals and pay attention. I was involved in too many situations in the past where there was excessive talking and not enough action. Sometimes you can talk something to death and never get any work done. In that sense, you need to know when to be a dictator, to make sure that the work gets done. A director constantly has to strengthen the self-image of the actors. There's been something rotten going on in American theater for a long time. Artists don't believe in their own talents! One is constantly having to reassure them. I mean, it was true in the Open Theatre, and it's still true with these kids coming out of school, today. They don't know how to work, they don't know where to work. Not only do they not know how to work on a role, they don't know how to pick up a hammer! The culture that I was raised in, the work ethic of the pioneer culture, has disintegrated. You spend two thirds of your time teaching people how to work. If actors came knowing how to work, if they had a sense of themselves, that they had a right to work, it would be peaches and cream.

Staying on the subject of director autocracy, what about playwrights like Susan Yankowitz, who was barred from rehearsals of her play Knife in the Heart *at Williamstown. Isn't that taking dictatorship too far?*

I said *benevolent* dictatorship. I didn't know that was still going on. If it is, then direct your own work. Shaw did it. Irene Fornes is the best director of her own work. I know that in the old days a director used to take the writer across the street to the bar to get him drunk! [Laughter]

Do you believe that there's a female aesthetic in playwriting?

A female aesthetic could only happen if the next generation of women were raised all together on a desert island. We've been taught by men!

So you don't think the innovations of women are in any way organic?

I really don't. How would you measure it?

We don't know. That's why we're asking women playwrights this question. What we do know, after reading tons of women's plays and hundreds of their reviews, is that there are certain elements common to all: Many of their plays are woman-centered, with a much higher percentage of female roles than plays by men.

This will probably continue until the balance is redressed. But after there's a balance, and we have female characters living up there on the stage that we haven't had for a long time, that may all change.

Tell us why you decided on cross-gender casting in **Babes in the Bighouse** *[1974]?*

We thought that was a very clear way for men to learn how to empathize with women. After the performances, men said, "*Now* I understand what you women are talking about!" By putting a man in a dress, in the same constraints as the women characters in the play, it became clear to the men in the audience what women were up against. Earlier we'd learned, while playing a boys' high school, that the boys in the audience only paid attention to what male characters said. Men are socialized to respond to a male body and a male voice; from an early age they seem to be trained to discount what women say. There were terrific laugh lines that women had in the play, but the audience would only laugh if a male character said something funny. That's how we found out boys wouldn't pay attention to what women said. By having men play women in ***Babes***, we got men to pay attention to what the play was saying. But we didn't have to change the writing. And this was in 1974!

Will you tell us a bit about your experience bringing theater to inmates in prison?

Any time we need an ego boost, we can play a prison and become reenergized. There are no masks. If they like the show, they're with you all the way—talking to the stage, calling out terrific, appropriate, additional lines and giving our performers standing ovations at the end. Then we have amazing discussions. They have a lot of time to think in jail, and they sincerely want to help solve society's problems.

Do you have any problems getting your Nebraska audience to accept the sexuality in your plays?

We don't have any trouble with people out here! They are farmers or they've been close to the farm. They deal with animals, procreation, the elements and nature. I think that people are too rarified in New York. They've been too long away from animals and plants and trees.

Megan, do you think the voices of the black women playwrights have fallen silent in the last few years?

There's nothing silent about [Ntozake] Shange. Some new writers are writing realistic plays—choosing Lorraine Hansberry as their model rather than Adrienne Kennedy or Shange, who are poets as well as playwrights.

Shange's experimenting in performance art. She feels that's a viable way to keep her poetry alive. But she's had some difficulty getting some things produced.

It seems to me *Spell #7* is an even stronger piece than *colored girls*, but Shange said the same men who produced *colored girls* didn't get behind her second play. Women are going to have to put one another forward. There's got to be more support among women for women's work. I think black women have a hard time getting hold of each other's work and need to find a way to share their work faster.

Will you explain what happened when Actors Equity Association forbade its members to appear in showcases of your work?

That was a result of a series of misunderstandings. There was a showcase of my play ***Hothouse*** [1974], in which ten actors took part. The Showcase Code states that if a play is moved from Off Off Broadway after its twenty-one performances the original actors must be retained in the cast or paid two weeks' salary. Then it was done again, produced by several of the original actors but with five or six replacements, at The Truck and Warehouse Theatre [in New York's East Village]. The actors begged me to sign a paper that they said was only a formality. They said they loved the show and wanted to do it again because they thought it would bring them to the attention of agents and producers. By this time about sixteen different people had been in and out of the play. The play was picked up by the Chelsea Theatre; they intended to give it a first-class production. The problems arose because the Chelsea management wanted to cast their own people in the play. I was happy with the first group who had played it at the Circle Rep Workshop. Barbara Rosoff had directed and Arden Fingerhut had created a stunning lighting design. But now there was a new director, a new producer, and they had their own vision. I argued and persuaded, but the Chelsea group would allow the retention of only one of the original actors. That person they fired after four days. Naturally, that person and those other actors were distressed, and so was I. Some of those actors complained to their union, and their union sent me a bill for over five thousand dollars and told me I was in effect blacklisted in New York City until that bill was paid.

I have not paid the bill. And I would advise playwrights not to sign a showcase form. It prevents subsequent performances of a play, because the play will become encumbered with this type of lien. Recently Equity has further complicated the code to make one pay not only theatrical salaries, but TV and film salaries, too, before they will allow the play to be performed. It seemed to me that if their union was a true union the new actors hired by Chelsea could have refused the jobs in favor of the creators of the roles. But this argument went nowhere with Equity. I offered to pay Equity twenty-five dollars a week for the rest of my life to help bring down this bill, but they wouldn't accept that. Where they thought I would dig up five thousand dollars just so I could have my plays done in New York City, I don't know. But I haven't had any problems getting productions in other cities.

You once said that playwrights subsidize the theater.

All artists have subsidized this culture since the beginning!

Don't most people feel that it is the artists who are subsidized, and not vice versa?

The average middle-class salary is thirty-five thousand a year, and the tiny percentage of artists who get five thousand are considered to be subsidized? There's been subsidy for artists only in the last fourteen years, anyway. The people at the National Endowment for the Arts, and some of the private foundations, work very hard to share money around, pitiful few dollars that there are. When I'm on one of those "deciding-who-gets-what" committees, I feel like I'm shredding pennies. Isn't it strange that this American culture has valued everything but the people who create something out of thin air? What is left when a civilization dies? Only its art and a few tool fragments.

What's the playwright's responsibility to society?

To critique that society, the perceived world and beyond. Beckett, for instance, critiques "being." You must always guard against being coopted.

What was your first conception of a writer?

I don't know, because I had such a miserable education. It was through other writers and painters that I learned to write. And through struggle. When you read what Lorca did and said before they shot him, when you think of the artists who made the effort to communicate with us. . . . Look what things they went through so we could open our minds. All the people who went to their deaths. . . . We owe them a lot.

What do you wish to convey to the world through your plays?

That life is possible. I'm always fighting against inertia. Art is about taking action. The essential core of theater is action. I believe in taking creative action. What else is there to do?

What advice do you have for young women in high school and college who are thinking about becoming a playwright?

Do it. See all kinds of performance, from polka dances to basketball games. Do you know what I miss in the world? Singing. There's a lot of noise, but there isn't enough singing lately. Don't you miss the women singers of the sixties? You have to turn on country music to hear a woman sing now. We don't have enough new singers. I'm still writing musicals, and I wish there were more singers.

What contributions do you feel that you've made in changing the form of the American musical?

I proved rock music worked on the stage. No one would believe it, or even allow it. Certainly I speeded up exposition. You don't have to sit for two acts anymore to get to the heart of a play or musical.

You once said that the form of the play is the least important thing, that those who are obsessed with structure have received too much schooling. Telling the truth, you said, is far more important than form. Do you believe that content dictates form?

I used to believe that, but I've been proved wrong. [Laughter] Because people have revitalized old forms! By putting another kind of content in it. If you're telling the truth, it grabs people. I think form is fashion. I just happen to love fashion.

Is that why you've mastered so many different forms of playwriting?

I love creating, and seeing if something will work. I like to keep building myself out on farther and farther ledges. I like to defy gravity.

Would you say that your major concern as a writer is the continuity of the family?

My biggest resentment about war, besides the obvious destruction, is how it wrecks families. Our family was destroyed by World War II, our extended family.

Your play **Hothouse** *dealt with this subject.*

I don't know if it dealt with it enough. Did it make the point?

[KB]: It speaks to me personally, having been raised in Coventry, England, in wartime and having my own family torn apart by war.

Maybe we can make other kinds of structures to take the place of the extended family. People these days seem to desire community more than romantic love.

[RK]: Ideas of community were brought to a renaissance in the sixties and seventies. Now, as we move through the eighties, everyone has become more individual, more career-oriented. We hear many young women describe themselves as "post-feminists." Their goal is to make thirty thousand dollars a year when they get out of school.

Young women are writing to me using the words *make it.* What does that mean? I don't know. I guess they are concerned about making enough money. For whom? In whose eyes? Wait till they make it and find out nobody cares. We're living in a kind of glitter time. You know what it reminds me of? Restoration comedy.

Some of the women playwrights don't want to be aligned politically with women anymore. They say, "I'm not a feminist, I'm a humanist." Or, "I don't want to be called a woman playwright."

They don't want to be ghetto-ized.

How do you feel about being "ghetto-ized?"

It's a danger. I told the feminists I wouldn't write their party line, either. I made a big speech to a large Midwest feminist group; I told them it was my duty to criticize everything, including them, and a whole bunch of people in hobnailed boots walked out.

And yet no one looks at a book exclusively devoted to male playwrights' interviews—and there are many of them—and says, "Look at those poor guys—they're ghettoized. . . ."

You're right. This came up last week at [a] Stanford University [conference on women in theater]. There were eight women's plays being presented. And there were no male characters in their plays. And one woman in the audience got up and said, "I don't like all this lesbian writing, where's love between the sexes?" Out of eight plays—only *one* had a lesbian character, and that play was an uproarious comedy. But this woman labeled all the work, work dealing with all sorts of female characters trying to solve many sorts of problems, in a pejorative way. On the positive side, I'm impressed that feminists can write so well. I witnessed some great writing there. But where were the male characters? This question took over the audience. It was like a mob psychology of the early seventies! After having this wonderful experience—fresh, funny, very moving writing—suddenly the whole audience took up what this woman was saying. Martha Boesing, [playwright] and I had to put a stop to it. Finally, I had to say, "Look. David Mamet just won the Pulitzer Prize, but you wouldn't think of asking him why there were no women in *Glengarry Glen Ross*." The minute a woman writes about what women are talking about when the men aren't around, people jump on them. Including other women. But I don't want to be perceived as writing only for women. I'm writing for the whole human race! I feel responsible for the past, present *and* the future!

We see feminism as embodying humanism, not separate from it.

I've noticed, at these conferences where some men have been speaking out, that a lot of American males perceive feminists as separatists. They want to dismiss all women's work if they think they're not going to be allowed to be an equal part of the audience.

Isn't that male anger precisely why some women are reluctant to call themselves feminists?

They're afraid of male retaliation. After all, who holds the purse strings?

Are you talking about censorship?

And grant giving.

You've said you don't object to being called a feminist.

Why should I object?

So what does feminism mean to you personally?

I want to redress the balance! If a Martian came here to visit our culture, it would think it was visiting a homosexual society. Men run everything.

Your play **American King's English for Queens** *[1978], explores sexism in the language of criticism. Do you think women's plays are critiqued with a different vocabulary than men's plays?*

I don't think the critics feel that they're doing this. They think they're being fair, that they're just applying a literary standard.

If a man and a woman playwright, of equal craft, put a readily recognizable character on stage, why is the woman's character called a "stereotype" and the man's an "archetype"?

How they take care of their own. Isn't it wonderful?

Why is an angry play by a woman conceived of as "bitter"? Yet an angry play by a man is . . .

A "blockbuster"!

Are the women getting accused of bad craft when, in fact, it's the content that's upsetting to the critics?

If you analyzed these plays, scene by scene, would the craft of the women's plays hold up?

We think so. Especially in the case of a Caryl Churchill, an Emily Mann, Fornes, Drexler, Owens, Farabough, et cetera. A common critical term used to describe innovative women's work is "nonplay."

They want a fried egg. A beginning, a middle and an end, with a rising climax. A male orgasm.

Well, then, let's go back to your play **American King's English for Queens** *and your attack on sexism in the language.*

Just go listen in the supermarket to how people talk to their children. It'll make your hair stand on end.

The cruelty?

Yes. Roles and attitudes toward the self are shaped within the family by how one is spoken to.

What were the audience discussions like after **American King's English for Queens***?*

Exciting and intense, and that's where we got the idea for ***Goona Goona*** [1979], from the discussions after ***American King's English for Queens***. We began to explore all the ways we talk to one another.

But **Goona Goona** *was about family violence. What's the connection?*

The violence in the language led to the discovery of actual physical violence going on at home. I mean this one door opened, and other doors just kept opening beyond that. Discussions after ***Kegger*** have led to our next piece, which will be about family communication. People found out that they're not only having a hard time talking to one another, they can't even talk to themselves in their own heads anymore. We've found a whole group of scholars who work with us, share their expertise and research to build plays for our audiences. The audience tells us what they want to deal with. We do one piece a year, which we think of as lending our skills to give voice to community concerns. The other seven plays we produce are for our own and our audience's artistic growth.

The Magic Theatre, from what we've read, seems to be financially successful, too. You've combined art, community outreach and business rather well.

And we've never had a deficit.

If local corporations subsidize you or give grants—say, for instance, a place like Campbell's soup, which is based in your area—does that inhibit doing a play about the problems at a Campbell's soup plant?

I understand that Campbell's soup is one of the best places for women to work. There may be difficulties in other places with other companies, but we haven't had any problems with corporations, because the things we've been writing about are the things that employees who work for them want to talk about!

We heard you use these wonderful soft sculptures in your plays. Diane Degan designs them?

And Sora Kim. We all design them. We have a large group of Midwest painters and sculptors who work with us on all our shows. We also have three composers in residence. When I designed ***Goona Goona***, I designed the whole house as a gigantic quilt. I designed the costumes as a combination of puppets and football uniforms with padding so the actors wouldn't get hurt. They had to hit each other with baseball bats while depicting family violence.

Do you get many requests from other states for your scripts that deal with family and community problems?

Yes. The biggest difficulty right now is getting it down on paper fast enough to meet the demand. Right now I'm trying to get ***Objective Love, Goona Goona, Kegger***, and ***Fifteen Million Fifteen-Year-Olds*** completed, so that we can share them around. We're constantly bombarded with requests for these scripts. We expect to have most of them ready by the end of the summer. In Xerox form. Our earlier plays have been brought out by Broadway Play Publishing, Inc.

Megan, what message would you most like to send round the world?

It's worth it to make a life in art. I want to tell everybody it's *possible* and it's worth it. I've lived long enough now to see what happens to people who don't follow their hearts.

Megan Terry (lecture date 1989)

SOURCE: "Anybody Is as Their Land and Air Is," in *Studies in American Drama, 1945-Present*, Vol. 4, 1989, pp. 83-90.

[*In the following lecture, Terry discusses her life in theater, focusing on the need of individuals to give of themselves in order to make a difference in the world.*]

I think it's more fun to think in groups than alone with a typewriter. Maybe that's why, of all the writing fields, I chose playwriting. My mind has always worked faster than my typewriter. At times I lay this malady to the fact that I got a "D" in typing in high school and may not belong in this technological age. Contrary to popular belief, typing isn't natural to all women.

Most of my early life was spent in trees, because I was into building treehouses. By the time I was 12, I'd built a subdivision and I'm proud to say most of my friends preferred to live in my treehouse than with their parents, except when it rained. I think skill in the use of tools is a good prerequisite for playwriting.

The lay of the land dictates the placement of towns, the path of railroads, the direction of the interstate, and has been known to inspire poems, songs, novels, paintings, laments, loneliness, several wars, and both possessive and altruistic love.

In some ways the artist is a distiller of the landscape. I use the term artist in all its definitions. Some artists go beyond reflecting, meditating on, or collecting the look of the landscape in their work, and preserve and transmit it in such a way that they become stewards and guardians. The people working for a clean environment have an easier case to make because of evidence collected and recorded by artists who show in their art how perfect the land and environment once was. Don't let anyone tell you that an artist works only for art or for oneself. You are at the center of civilization. Indeed you demonstrate through your work what a *civilized* being is. When I look back at my own education, I see that I educated myself, mainly by studying the great plays that have been handed down to us since the Greeks.

It's probably possible to educate yourself well through intense attention to any of the arts. To have qualified and inspired teachers is, of course, an added luxury . . . and I trust those here today are enjoying this luxury.

An educated woman is a relatively new development on our cultural landscape. Another thing we have now is longevity. Death from childbirth is no longer the great killer of American women it once was. We have a chance to live longer and think longer and create longer than our great-grandmothers. Our great-grandmothers possibly couldn't let themselves think in this way. Two of my great-grandmothers are buried out here on the plains. They died in childbirth. Each of them made a great deathbed speech to their little children who gathered around for the last good-bye, a speech of love and instruction that carried these children through a lifetime of hardship, to triumphs of various scale.

My mother's mother was a poet, a secret poet, whose poems were discovered after her death. She felt writing was time stolen from her family, so she hid her work. But she willed her poems to me. This gift had a profound effect on a 13-year-old. My grandmother gave me a charge and a vocation. She saved me from confusion and she saved me time. I knew what I would do with my life. As I watched my friends flounder and change their minds a hundred times, I knew in my deepest heart that I would be a writer. Never underestimate the power you have with the generations coming after you. If we are to make things better for other artists, we must take an interest in them at an early age and support them and their work.

I can truthfully say that geography in a sense drove me straight into writing. Geography in the sense of dirt.

I worked in the fields as a child. In grade school I picked strawberries for 25 cents a flat. We all looked forward to attaining high school age because then we'd be allowed to work in the bulb fields. These were commercial flower bulbs: tulip, daffodil, and narcissus. High school girls could make a dollar an hour in the bulb fields. Boys weren't welcome there—it was said they didn't have the patience to be thorough enough. Eight dollars for eight hours. The idea of making eight dollars a day was heady. You could buy good school clothes and save up for a second-hand car on that money. But after two and a half months on my hands and knees digging in the wet soil, my fingernails felt like they were being exquisitely tortured with instruments five times worse than bamboo splinters. Every night it took two hours of soaking to get the mud out from under my nails. Each night on the ride home in the closed, dusty van with the other exhausted girls, I found myself praying for a way out of my immediate geography. The last straw came the next week when my money was cut to 75 cents an hour because I led the group in singing to make the time pass. The boss didn't think working and singing could be done without the work suffering. I was defiant and wanted to prove the work went better. So I kept singing and though my production increased, I was cut to 50 cents an hour. That night, while soaking out the mud, I reread my grandmother's poems. The next morning I quit my job and I've been writing ever since.

In reflecting on what I might tell you so that we could have a dialogue, I realized that lately I'm very happy in my work with the Omaha Magic Theatre. It wasn't always the case. When I first started to try to write, many times the frustration of not getting onto the paper what I could see in my head and feel in my heart caused me to cry a lot. Once the frustration was so overwhelming I banged my head on my typewriter. I survived, but the typewriter had to be traded in.

It makes me smile today when I look back on that distraught person who wanted more than anything in the world to have a life in art. Now I'm living it, and I'm thrilled because at that time, I didn't think I'd ever be happy on this plane. I realize also that in these strange times it's not too cool to be happy, but it's a fact.

What's the source of this happiness?

For me, it's meaningful work, within a community of artists who work for love of their art and who work to make this art accessible to the community in which they live. And I feel I'm doing it with them in the geography where I chose to live. The attainment of personal happiness, however, doesn't make me feel I can turn my back on the world. The energy that happiness brings permits me to fight better than ever, with a clearer eye and a less strangulating tension than in the past. When I lived in New York, I used to have a terrible recurring dream—I dreamed I was in a concentration camp. Everytime I tried to speak, a soldier would approach with a length of barbed wire; if I persisted in speaking, the soldier would wrap the barbed wire around my throat and twist it until I couldn't breathe. I haven't had that nightmare since I moved to Omaha.

This new freedom came about because I took action to remake my life. I got the energy for that action from the women's movement. I've lived there now for 15 years. My friends on both coasts ask me, "Megan, what on earth are you doing in Nebraska?" I answer, "I'm living a real life." I chose to move there—or did I? The influence of my grandparents and their experiences with this landscape had a profound effect on me during my growing up years on the West Coast. Even though they thought they were now living in "God's country" in the Northwest, it was the prairie they talked about more and more as they aged. Their prairie homes became "Paradise Lost" to me. They were great story tellers. Their experiences growing up there shaped their characters. They were strong and independent beings, each of them. They had walked or had ridden in covered wagons from Iowa, Minnesota, and Nebraska across the Oregon Trail to the state of Washington, where they built homes, established farms and businesses, and raised their families.

My poet grandmother, the eldest of 13, went with her mother and the younger children west. Her father, an Indian scout for the Army, showed up once a year wherever they were, to make another baby and then ride on. Often when I'm on tour with the Omaha Magic Theatre, I imagine I'm retracing my grandmother's path—Wyoming, western Nebraska, the Platte River, the Missouri. I block out the telephone poles and look at her world. She went west because she wanted to get as close to the sea as she could get.

What drew me back? Sunlight. Endless sky. It's necessary for me to have light. Since living in Nebraska, I've written five times as much as any place I've lived. To me there's something energizing about the quality of the light there. In the spring when we're on tour in Iowa, the sight of the lambs, the piglets, the calves with their mothers in the fields, the rolling green: I identify with this, and though it doesn't appear literally in my work, the energy, comfort, and connection with it is what keeps me working.

The opportunity to know more people, really know them, is also an important fuel to my writing. I found when I reached puberty that I'd fallen in love with the whole human race. I wanted to know each one. I wanted to know and be close to as many people as I possibly could. I remember standing at the bus stop, looking intently at each person, wondering who that person was, what did they feel, what did they think about what they felt, what were their lives like? I was in despair; I felt I could never know them because I was too shy. There I was, hopelessly in love with human beings and unable to speak to them with ease.

Theatre gave me a structure to deal with this love. Theatre helped me find a way to be with people on a day-to-day basis. Playing other characters helped me get closer to people I could only observe but not really know. Moving into writing helped me to get inside characters and love people by making portraits of them within my plays. In the Midwest, touring to all the little towns we play, I get to meet more and more people. Thus, I've been able to keep my love affair going.

Some of the first plays I wrote when I finally settled there had to do with my grandparents. When I had them with me, I didn't know I was a writer, or I would have tape-recorded their stories. Once there, their stories came back to me. If I felt this way about my people, I wondered if the other members of the Omaha Magic Theatre wanted to get some of their families' stories into a play—and sure enough, the whole company did. We went out and interviewed grandparents and great-grandparents and put the results together into a total musical piece called ***100,001 Horror Stories Of The Plains***. Within this framework, I was able to re-create my great-grandmother's death-bed charge to her seven sons, and to write about the Sunday afternoon my grandfather and grandmother met and fell in love at first sight on an outing to dig for arrowheads along the Snake River. In this way I could keep my people alive for myself and for others.

One of my dear writer friends lost her mother at a young age. When she met my mother she was so taken with her, she offered to buy her from me. I wasn't ready to sell my mother, but it did cause me to take a closer look. My friend was right—my mother is remarkable. I wrote her into the play ***Hothouse*** and sent a copy to my friend. My friend could take strength from my mother's essence, and it gave my mother a kick, too. I was afraid to show her the play, but after she read it, she called me immediately, laughing and sounding like a girl. She said, "I love it, it's me, I feel rejuvenated." Now whenever she gets feeling too much the great-granny, she rereads the play and feels young again.

We talk to our audiences wherever we go. We write one show a year to give voice to community concerns, or as in the case of ***Horror Stories***, to celebrate the community. ***American King's English For Queens*** grew out of an examination of how we use the English language in speaking to one another, children, and young people, to socialize them and prepare them for their roles in society. We wanted to do this because we felt that it's the accumulation of everyday attitudes in our communication with one another that shapes how we think about ourselves; the audible landscape of our language tends to shape gender roles.

We asked scholars in the Missouri Valley area to give us seminars on linguistics, English, anthropology, the history of language, etc., to get ourselves ready to produce this play. I had to write the text, but everyone in our company was involved with the seminars over a period of seven months. There are very bright people working out there, affiliated with universities, colleges, or doing independent research, and they are generous in sharing their discoveries with us. After each performance we have long talks with our audience, led by humanities scholars and members of the company. During these discussions we get the subjects for our next big community piece. We do from eight to ten productions a year, one of which we think of as lending our writing, art, and theatre skills to community concerns.

It was in western Nebraska in the seventies that we first heard vivid and terrifying accounts of spouse and child abuse.

A neighbor of a farm family in trouble rose to recount how her friend had been nailed to a cross by her husband in the basement of the farm home and kept there alive for three months. She survived because her children brought her food and water. Later when that husband died, there was no mourning at his funeral, but relief on the part of the immediate family and the concerned neighbors. Isolation, and inability to deal with anger in healthy ways, had brought on such conditions. After this story came out, others poured forth. They dealt with child abuse, incest, teenage suicide. . . .

We slowly made our way back to Omaha, reeling from this information. We'd heard the accounts with our own ears, but it was still hard to grasp. We called in a new group of scholars to check with them. They informed us this was not going on only on isolated farms, but in upwardly mobile families, who are isolated because of affluence and mobility. There are many kinds of geography. It also turned out that the scholars in Omaha and in other Missouri Valley areas were doing some of the most advanced primary research into spouse and child abuse. They were eager to share their knowledge with us, and so a new play that we called ***Goona Goona*** began to be formed from first-hand accounts and quantified data.

In discussions after performances of ***Goona Goona***, audiences in every state and from every economic strata asked us now to tackle the problems that young people face in dealing with alcohol—our so-called "legal" drug. Strangely enough, ***Kegger***, the play that holds the results of our findings, has something to do with geography, too. Kids have to drive somewhere to hold their keggers, and once there they have to consume all the evidence. As you know, this creates a problem in finding a safe way home.

Another motivation to tackle this subject came from discussions with prisoners. Whenever we play a college or community for money, we play the local prison free. Ninety percent of the women and men claimed they committed their crimes while under the influence. Additionally, they said they are emotionally no more than 10 or 12. They started with booze at such an early age that the quest for self was totally interrupted and arrested. That was the fact that rocked me. They had no idea who they were or why they were.

We set to work to make a play to help ourselves, our community, and our young people. I was able to get to know hundreds of young citizens from the Midwest. We interviewed kids from every kind of background. I wrote the play from their point of view and in their language. The play has received reactions from praise to blame, but we played it for three years, and now other theatres around the country are touring it. These plays are in existence because of our response to the geography of our touring, our questioning, and our listening in our contact with concerned and caring people all over the Midwest. That's another thing about the people who live in this landscape. They aren't afraid to try to solve problems. They're used to rolling up their sleeves to deal with nature, animals, with themselves. If they can't solve the problems alone, they're willing to work with others. This is inspiring to me. We have seen people come together as a result of discussions after our performances to create a shelter for battered women, to raise money for support teams to aid battered children, to work as a community to find creative alternatives to the senseless killing of teens on the highways.

We stay close to our audience. We get to know them, we build relationships over the years. We teach people in small communities how to produce arts events. When they have a success bringing us to town, then they feel able to bring in other artists, poets, painters, dancers, musicians. . . . Touring supports the actors and artists within our company and enables us to do eight other plays a year that we want to do for our own growth and to lead our audiences.

Our learning then proceeds geometrically. This is how the structure of our kind of theatre can serve an art form. It can also be seen as a rewarding social yet formal structure for aesthetic, emotional, and intellectual interaction among diverse people who might not have met in any other context. The added bonus I receive is to exercise and pursue my lifelong intense interest in individuals and families. I'm no longer that waif waiting at the bus stop looking longingly for contact and communion with strangers, but am now an integrated, productive member of an ever-growing community. I proved to myself that alienation does not have to be a permanent state. You can reach out, share, confide, and exercise your innate powers. Whether you embrace and/or transcend your gender and geography, do take action *to give* of your talent and skills *to others*. This is how you *can* make a difference in the quality of life for *yourself*, your *colleagues*, your *community*, your *region*, your *country*, and possibly the history of your art.

Judith Babnich (interview date 1992)

SOURCE: An interview in *The University of Mississippi Studies* in *English*, Vol. X, 1992, pp. 191-203.

[*In the following interview, Terry discusses her play* Turn Your Headlights On.]

In 1969 Jo Ann Schmidman, a young actress, founded a theatre in Nebraska amid the rolling plains of middle America. She named it the Omaha Magic Theatre and described it as a place open to everyone. Its initial goal was to produce four new musicals by untried American writers and composers each year, and by so doing, to attract new American playwrights to Omaha. The group assembled by Schmidman included actors, actresses, directors, writers, and technicians, all devoted to the process of theatre, all offering a living example of alternative theatre.

In the twenty years it has been in existence, the Omaha Magic Theatre has proven to be one of the few working alternative theatres in this county. Since it was founded, the theatre has been a highly "avant-garde" experimental theatre, a strictly feminist theatre and its present status a humanist theatre, exploring meaningful social issues. Regardless of the labels—avant garde, experimental, feminist, humanist—which Schmidman dislikes, the Magic Theatre is first and foremost a professional theatre which is driven by a need to produce the highest quality artistic work and by so doing make their audiences think. Dedicated to fostering humanism, the Magic Theatre wants to effect social change and have an impact making the world a better place to live. While commercial theatre tends to view its audiences in dollar signs, the Magic Theatre truly cares about the people who attend their performances and not about how much money they are going to make.

Megan Terry, playwright in residence since 1974, has written the majority of Magic Theatre plays. Author of over fifty plays, including one of the first Vietnam plays, ***Viet Rock***, Terry has received all the major playwrighting awards. She is the recipient of the ABC Yale University and Guggenheim fellowships and has also been awarded the silver medal for "Distinguished Contribution to and Service in American Theatre" by the American Theatre Association. Before working with the Magic Theatre, Terry worked with the Open Theatre and the New York Strategy.

She first became acquainted with the Magic Theatre when she met Schmidman in 1970 at Boston University. Having worked in New York as a playwright for the Open Theatre, she came to Boston at the request of the University.

> I was commissioned to go to Boston University to write the centennial production, and they brought me out all their star actors. And I said, "No, no. I have to see the whole school if I'm going to write this play I have in mind." And I devised a series of group improvisations, and Jo Ann turned out to be the strongest, most exciting performer in the whole school. And I said, that's the one I'll write the play around. And they all fainted, because she had not played a role in a mainstage production, and she was a senior. I thought it was terrible. What they thought were their best actors were boring people to me. They were competent soap type actors, but they were not able to do anything that I could write, they couldn't have sustained it. And the exercise, of course, wasn't about theatre, it was about real energy . . . so the friendship started and that's what brought me to Omaha.

The play Terry wrote for the University was the award-winning ***Approaching Simone***, wherein she chronicled the story of Simone Weil, the French philosopher-activist-mystic. Her production proved to be highly successful, winning her an Obie Award for Best Off-Broadway Play of 1970.

Throughout her career Terry has continued to receive recognition for her playwrighting. Just recently she was awarded a $20,000 National Endowment of the Humanities playwrighting fellowship. "It was a great joy to receive the award. Now the Theatre won't have to pay me a salary. We can hire more people to help out and more people can realize their potential. It frees up money." The fellowship assistance also frees up Terry's time to complete several writing projects she has not had the time to finish. One of her projects that she was able to complete is her current play ***Headlights*** which was first produced by the Arkansas Summer Theatre Academy in July of 1988 and, then in April of 1989 at the Omaha Magic Theatre under the direction of Schmidman. For the past few years the company has toured the play throughout the Midwest. Still believing that theatre can educate and uplift, Terry has continued to write plays that have a strong social message. In ***Headlights*** she struggled with the all pervasive problem of illiteracy in this county. A 1982 Census Bureau survey revealed that 13% of adults in this country cannot read. One out of eight American have difficulty reading a street sign or the label on a medicine bottle. Adding to the problem is the nearly 49% high school drop out rate which, in many cases, is directly related to problems of literacy.

Alarmed by these frightening statistics, Terry chose to illuminate the problem in a challenging, optimistic way. In addition to investigating the problems of the illiterate, the play also helped "the audience relive the experience of learning how to read."

Through song, dance and narration, Terry's play tells the story of a group of characters, ranging in age from teenagers to grandparents, who are all unwilling to come to grips with their reading problems. All encounter embarrassing situations over their inability to read. Fifteen-year-old Matt is unable to quit high school to work in a motorcycle plant because he can't read the job application form. Songwriter

Hilary, hoping to find fame in Denver, ends up in Omaha because she can't read a map. Salesman Eddie is powerless to help his little daughter pass second grade reading because he can't read himself. By the end of the play, all three characters became involved in literacy programs where they learn to turn their "headlights on" through the warmth and dedication of a volunteer teacher who works "one on one" with each of them.

This past January the company performed ***Headlights*** at Wichita State University. During their stay on campus, I interviewed Megan Terry. The following are portions of my January 26, 1990 interview with Terry.

[Judith Babnich]: The first production of **Headlights** *was staged by The Arkansas Children's Theatre under the direction of Bradley Anderson. How did that production come about?*

[Megan Terry]: He called me up.

Did he know who you were? Your work?

No. He found an ad that we placed in *Theatre For Youth Today*, a periodical that serves the youth theatre movement in America. It's tied up with the International Theatre Association for Young People. I've been invited to speak at their conventions and I'm on their board of directors. But anyway, our theatre took an ad in that magazine about some of our youth plays ***Dinner's in the Blender*** and ***Sleazing Toward Athens***. Bradley saw that ad and he asked me if any of my playwrighting friends would want to write a play on literacy because Southwestern Bell was putting up $4,000 to commission a play on the subject. I immediately said I was interested. I said yes before I knew how much money was involved. I had been thinking about the subject anyway.

Prior to the call?

Yes. It was certainly in the air. Some students coming to our theatre as young interns have grave difficulty in reading and writing. They can't read maps, that's why Hilary in the play ends up in Omaha when she thinks she's going to Denver because she can't read maps and she can't read road signs.

I can't read maps.

So, you know. I found out I had to navigate on tour because I was getting so frustrated and angry because whoever was driving was getting us lost and you know how much time that adds to a trip. So I just had to start teaching map reading and do it myself until we got enough people who could. So the problem of illiteracy has been on my mind for many, many years. The play is also a celebration of my grandmother's spirit. She was a volunteer teacher. It was through her that I became fascinated by the volunteers, the people who give of their time to teach one on one. They're all a great variety of people and they do it for many reasons but they get a great deal back, especially spiritual. Their spiritual bank gets filled when they work this way. Great and deep friendships develop through being a volunteer tutor in a literacy program.

What was your grandmother like?

Mary Jane Henry was a fantastic teacher and she was also the town midwife and doctor. Everyone went to her. They went to Mrs. Henry when they needed advice, when they needed to give birth, when they were ill. She also taught in the school. She had all ages in one room.

Was she a trained doctor?

No. She learned all of this on her own. She had no more education than anyone else. Her schooling ended at age eighteen, but she was just brilliant. She was working in this coal mining town where it was full of people from Eastern Europe: Czechs, Hungarians, Romanians, Greeks, Yugoslavians, and Polish. None of these people could speak English. The coal companies encouraged families to send their children into the mines at the age of eight and nine. They would take the boys and this just tore my grandmother apart. So she decided the best way to help the children continue their education was to teach the parents English. So she would work with the mothers teaching them English while she was also teaching their children in school as a way to keep the kids in school and progressing. One of her students, that she was very proud of, became an Attorney General of the United States. If it wasn't for my grandmother, he would have gone into the mines and never been heard of again. So I grew up hearing all these stories.

So the problem of illiteracy is a subject that your grandmother first acquainted you with?

Right, and also I had my degree in education. I've always been interested in the struggle.

Your degree is in education and not theatre?

That's right. I graduated from the University of Washington, Seattle. I went there and then I went up to Canada for a couple of years and went to the University of Alberta in the School of Fine Arts. But I came back and finished at the University of Washington. To get a degree in education you had to go five years.

Why didn't you major in theatre?

I didn't respect the theatre department at the time that I was at that school. I had practically been raised at the Seattle Repertory Playhouse so I had been in professional theatre from an early age. When I was seven I saw an incredible production of a play for children that I totally fell in love with theatre and never looked back. When I was a teenager, I scratched on the door until they let me in. And I learned so much from these people that by the time I got to college, they looked like kindergartners to me. Every minute that I wasn't at the University I was over at the Playhouse. The theatre was headed by a woman director, Florence Dean James, and her husband who was the leading actor in the company, Burton James. They were two of the most generous, talented, far-seeing, educated, civilized human beings I've ever met in my life. And from them I got a tutorial education in the Greeks, in Shakespeare, the Scandinavians, and the Russian playwrights and designers. They turned me on to directors such as Meyerhold and to the great constructivest designers. So here I am fifteen years old studying constructivism that's only now coming into people consciousness.

But you still got your degree in education.

To quiet my families fears.

Elementary ed?

Yes. Third grade. I did my student teaching with third graders. It was a riot.

I bet you were a lively teacher.

I was so in love with my students and they fell in love with me. I couldn't bear teaching third grade because I didn't want to send them on to the next year.

So you flunked them all.

Oh, I couldn't stand the idea of losing my children every year. The practice of teaching, which I got A+ for and a superior rating and all kinds of awards, showed me that I emotionally couldn't bear it. That's why I've always loved being in a theatre company and being with people year after year. It satisfies my emotional needs and my intellectual needs. I come from a huge family and theatre gives you the chance to re-create the family in your own image. Keep the idea of the extended family going. My mother was the youngest of thirteen. And her mother was the eldest of thirteen. On my father's side, my grandfather was one of sixteen. So you can imagine our family reunions were out of this world. We had to rent a giant community hall to be all together. And they are all musical and great storytellers from the Irish tradition. So I grew up being totally entertained all the time and I want to keep it going.

Getting back to **Headlights** *and how the play evolved, what happened after you agreed to write the play?*

I started doing formal research by first contacting the Literary Council.

How were you able to do that?

The wife of one of our Omaha cast members, Marge Farmer, is a great teacher of reading. She's in demand all over this continent and South America. She's always flying somewhere to teach other teachers how to teach reading, especially in the Hispanic world. She helped me deal with the Literacy Council. I also called my friend Phyllis Jane Rose, the former artistic director of Foot of the Mountain in Minneapolis and she did field research for me in Minneapolis. The whole theatre company plus Bradley Anderson went out with tape recorders in Arkansas and interviewed people who had been through the literacy program, the students and the teachers. So I have all these wonderful tapes to base the play on. The one scene in the play where the father tries to romance the teacher to get her to pass his daughter really is my father's story.

Your dad did that?

My second grade teacher was gonna fail me because of poor reading skills. I was the top reader in the first grade. In the second grade, for some reason, I had a personality conflict with the teacher. I was in the top reading group called the Stars or the Bluebirds or something like that. It was the beginning of the school year . . . I'll never forget this. I can see the page of the book, everything. There's a picture of a mother walking with her two children and the title of the story began with a "W". I knew the work "Mother", but I didn't know the first word. I went up to the desk and pointed to this first work asking the second grade teacher what it was and she said, "Go back to your seat. You sound that word out yourself." The only word that I knew that began with a "W" that was that long was "window". I thought, "If she calls on me, what am I going to say?" And of course she knew I didn't know the word. So when it came time for reading session she called on me. I'll never forget. I was red in the face. My body was in a total sweat. I put my hand in a fist and filled my pencil tray with sweat from my hands. I had a total panic attack.

So young to have your first panic attack.

Seven years old. Terrible. Gee whiz. So of course the only thing I could croak out was "Window Mother" and everybody laughed. She just points, "Go immediately to the Busy Bees. Your seat is changed." I went from the first seat in the room to the last seat in the room. Total humiliation. Total.

So your dad came in?

She threatened to fail me and my father, who is just an incredible guy, women would just faint at the sight of him, tried to romance the teacher to get me through.

And you go through?

I passed, thanks to my dad.

So after you've gathered all this information, then did you go to Arkansas?

No. They mailed me up the tapes and I interviewed people here. And of course I interviewed myself and all my family. I have so many teachers in my family. I just had huge resources, plus we had very intelligent creative people here in Omaha. I had several Humanities Scholars to consult with. I'm still working with the Humanities Scholars. They will now give more feed back from the finished script and the production and there will probably be revisions. It's a continually evolving process to create the script. Adding and subtracting new materials, as you learn more.

Did you go to Arkansas at all?

No. But I was in constant communication and they mailed me boxes of tapes.

Did you go down for the production?

No, because we were doing our own production here, so I didn't get to see their production. I do know that they used all the children in their academy ranging in age from seven to older teens and they also used their faculty and their permanent company as the adults. I wanted to write a piece that could use up forty-five children that they were working with through the summer in their acting program. They have an institute, an acting institute for young people at the Arkansas Childrens Theatre, which is under the umbrella of the Arkansas Arts Center. And they have composers there. Their set design was very fascinating. They built a gigantic skating ramp. The kids could roller skate and ride their bikes on it and skateboard. I designed the play to use elements of performing art and to also make it possible for a whole community to put on the play. The play is quite versatile. I wanted to write it to appeal to all age groups.

So it's not a children's play.

No. Well what is a children's play? I don't know what a children's play is. It's a play about literacy and all ages can be in it if they want to. Or adults can play the kids. You can do it in many different styles. You could do it totally without props. You could do it in total naturalism. You could do it in the Omaha Magic Theatre style which is "on-beyond-zebra," the way Jo Ann did.

On-beyond-zebra. Can you define what that is?

Well just on-beyond-zebra. It's the way Jo Ann directs. She is able to inspire the designers, the composers and the actors to push beyond what their normal mode of expression would be. So when all of this comes together, it's a hybrid. It's a new kind of thing.

Where does the word zebra come from?

The word "z". You know in those A B C books, and then the last word is usually zebra. So when you get to the end of the possibilities there is still a step beyond.

Moving to the area of theme, what ideas or messages did you want to get across to the audience?

The basic idea, basic motivation that gave me the energy to write the play is the worry and compassion for people who can't read. The quest for finding answers to life's questions of "Who am I?" "What am I doing here?" is much harder for someone who can't read. People who can read have access to the great minds of the past, through their account or their diaries, their books, their novels or anything collected and saved for us through the generations. To have access to this information aids the quest for the self. To be able to commune with yourself, to deal with yourself in this world as you find it. To have that interrupted, or blighted or stopped, it seems to me a pity, a great loss, a tragedy. A tragedy because you arrived here with a bundle of possibilities and if you don't have the tools to unlock the possibilities of your own mind what do you do? You may end up going around and around in a maze. And I believe that human beings have a basic drive to be good and to contribute to other human beings. We seem to be quite social animals who, for the most part, derive great pleasure from inner action with other human beings and contributing to the welfare of the community. Certainly we have some negative fringe elements that pop up here and there. For fifteen years, we've played prisons and I've met these so called "fringe elements" and I find 99 percent of them have a drive toward goodness and wanting to get better and contribute to culture. So if you are illiterate, even though you have an incredibly high I.Q., you are closed off from all the possibilities of civilization as being human. Your growth is stunted, and that's a tragedy to me. But that's what gave me the driving energy to complete the project. I have seventeen projects I'm working on right now. I completed this one because the idea of being able to help people out of that kind of darkness, through writing a play that may stimulate them to seek help through illiteracy councils or on their own, however that may be, seemed to me a worthwhile thing to do. Plus it was a chance to examine what is this thing that we take for granted, this ability to read and write.

And we do.

When I was teaching in the little grades, I saw the struggle. One of the greatest struggles a human being goes through, at the age of five, six and seven, is learning to read and write. It takes great effort, application. It's a fascinating struggle. During the final scene of the play I address this issue by equating books with boulders.

Can you explain that?

The struggle to learn to read and write is like trying to push a boulder that outweighs you a hundred fold, up a hill. But when you break through the code and begin to understand then the boulder carries you. Once you can read, you're not confined. Your mind can travel anywhere. You can go anywhere. Even if you're in prison, you can go anywhere. A woman who came to one of our shows works in a rest home. She said of the eighty-seven people there, only two read still. One is ninety-four and the other one is in her eighties or something. She said, "Those people aren't in a rest home. They take their books and they travel out of there every single day. And they go anywhere they want, backward and forward in time. Into the future, into a romance. They have adventures because the other people who either never could read or have stopped reading or have forgotten how to read are like vegetables and are depressed. They have lost their freedom." One of my basic interests ever since I was a child is an interest in freedom, and that's why I love this country, and our constitution. And I like to reiterate the idea of what our rights are, and our blessings and then what we owe one another. The idea of losing your freedom and not even ever knowing it is a tragedy. Another theme I wanted to pursue in the play was to celebrate the volunteer, the one who gives of her or his time to help another person out of this cage that they're in. I think these are unsung heroes and they deserve praise and thanks from the community at large. Forty-nine percent of our young people are dropping out of school between kindergarten and twelfth grade. No wonder we're having economic difficulties in the world. As anyone who pays casual attention to television and newspapers realizes, the Germans and the Japanese are beating us to death economically around the world. If we're gonna compete and even hold our own, we must be an educated populous. We must have people who can read and write and communicate with another. Not just English. We have to know the nuances of other cultures and we have got to know their languages. Otherwise we're gonna sink right down and become the fourth world.

The fourth world? What do you mean?

This idea of America becoming the fourth rate power does not set well with me. Coming from a pioneer culture, I have a very competitive spirit. My people had to be competitive to have made it from the old country to America in difficult times, to establish themselves, to push forward. They even went from the east coast to the west coast in wagon trains. But coming out of that culture, I have also lived through the times when America was born at the height of the depression. People were living on the beaches in shacks and huts and cardboard boxes. I remember it vividly. Then the war came and the mobilization. All the men in our family and all the men in our neighborhood were going to war. I've seen America become the first rate power of the world and now have lived long enough to see it beginning to fail and fall and falter. I don't like that at all. I love competition. I love sport. I love all my playwrighting friends who keep writing so well it stimulates me to keep writing . . . trying to write at the top of my personal best. I feel that I should make a contribution to this country. It is like a patriotic act to do this play and work on it and show it as many places as we can. I hope hundreds of plays will be written on this subject from many different angles, points of view, styles. Our small theatre company cannot make that much of a dent. We need many theatre companies doing this work and we need to give support to the literacy councils and to other people struggling. We need to support the people who want to learn to read, and want to join the rest of us and be interactive and productive citizens. But also for the joy of knowing people from the past. The great thing about libraries is you may not get along in your immediate vicinity but you can find someone who lived in another century that you might click with. One of the cast members during our early workshops commented that some of their best friends are dead. They are authors of books they love. But they are speaking to us now. We're all contemporaries as long as we can access each others minds. So it's not lost. You know the old thought of "those who do not study history are condemned to repeat it", goes for personal things too. The ability to read doesn't mean that everybody has to become an Einstein or a Gertrude Stein, but that you can just get along with yourself and your family. Reading enhances and enriches your life in general in so many areas.

But there are a lot of people who can read, and just don't. That's a problem also.

As Mark Twain put it, "The man who doesn't read good books has no advantage over the man who can't read."

Many teachers have this problem with their students. They prefer to watch videos and t.v. rather than read.

The path of life is also an anathema to me. I think that's why I love theatre because it's about action. About taking action, solving problems. We need to educate our people to the joys of some problem solving. It is fun to solve a problem, and theatre is constant problem solving. I think that a lot of people don't realize that that's one of the great benefits of self education that you get from being in theatre. It teaches you to make decisions, to solve problems, to make choices.

To be on time. The show must go on.

Right. Good work habits. Inner action. Working at group bonding. It is a marvelous thing for women to get those skills. Men have it easily in sport. Women have been held back because they haven't had that early training in group bonding and group work, inner action and inner dependence. And the support, and the warmth and affection that you get from working in that group and the struggles too. But it's a wonderful part of life. It's an extra. Theatre is usually thought of in aesthetic terms or art terms or entertainment terms but they don't consider the social inner active part of the theatre.

I think that's a reason why a lot of people are involved in theatre.

It's a wonderful structure for people who are shy to enter into a group. It's a great way to be a contributing member of a culture as well as developing ones art and aesthetic skills. And that's that basic part of theatre that really feeds me and keeps me in it. I think that creativity could be channeled into any art form or scientific form, or political form. But what I love about theatre is the social aspect. I also love the spiritual part of it. I see rehearsal as a spiritual practice because of the repetitiveness of devotion that it requires. The honesty, the constantly bearing your soul and sharing your inner most feelings and thoughts and who you are with the audience is a spiritual practice, both in the acting concept and the writing part of it. It really deeply satisfies me. First of all, I think the church just deals with one aspect of a human being. Theatre deals with all aspects of the possibilities of being human.

Felicia Hardison Londré (essay date 1996)

SOURCE: An interview in *Speaking on Stage: Interviews with Contemporary American Playwrights*, edited by Philip C. Konlin and Colby H. Kullman, The University of Alabama Press, 1996, pp. 138–49.

[*Below, Londré provides a brief overview of Terry's career followed by a 1989 interview covering an array of topics.*]

From her days as a founding member of the Open Theatre in New York (1963–67), to her current activities as resident playwright and literary manager of the Omaha Magic Theatre, Megan Terry has used the stage to tell the truth for and about the communities in which she worked, while her innovations in theatrical form have emerged from the creative process itself. The community of seventeen actors and four writers that made up the Open Theatre provided the impetus for ***Viet Rock*** (1966), her best-known play of the Vietnam War period. Today she draws upon the concerns of the Midwest communities that the Omaha Magic Theatre visits on tour, demonstrating in her plays the possibility of change through "creative action."

Megan Terry is the author of over sixty plays and the recipient of numerous awards, including the Stanley Award, an ABC-Yale University Fellowship, two Rockefeller Grants, an Earplay Award, a Creative Artists Public Service Grant, and a Guggenheim Fellowship.

Terry's way of creating a script by "playing with the elements of theatre" actually pioneered certain techniques that we associate with theatre of the 1960s, some of which have been absorbed into standard theatre practice: the involvement of actors in shaping a work for performance; the expansion of American musical comedy form to include rock music; borrowing clichés of the mass media; having actors leave the performance space to interact with audience members; and using "transformations." Terry's work is emblematic of the 1960s, a decade in which many idealistic young talents turned their backs on the commercial theatre and devoted themselves instead to exploring alternative venues and forms. In the explosion of activity—happenings, street theatre, guerilla theatre, the work of Joseph Chaikin and the Open Theatre, the Bread and Puppet Theatre, the San Francisco Mime Troupe, the Living Theatre, the Performance Group, and many others—perhaps the only common characteristic was the breakdown of traditional Aristotelian dramatic structure. Terry's transformations may be considered one of the more successful alternative forms that appeared in that heady era.

Terry developed her transformational technique and honed the script for ***Viet Rock*** through her work with members of the Open Theatre in a series of all-day Saturday workshops devoted to exploring the subject of violence, particularly as manifested in the war that was dominating the media. During that six-month process in 1965-66 she used improvisation as a tool to explore the group's confusion, anger, fears, and hope (for the optimistic Terry, there is always hope). ***Viet Rock*** actualizes her experimentation with constructing a dramatic action composed of brief sequences that are suddenly transformed into different sets of characters and circumstances. Exploring the social ramifications of the war from multiple points of view, the rock musical opens with the actors playing children's games, which segue into the inevitable cops and robbers, cowboys and Indians; these build to the sounds and actions of real war. An explosion cues their transformation into mothers cuddling their male babies. The "babies" are stripped to their shorts, and this transforms them into draftees lined up for an army physical, for which the women play the doctors. In the course of the play the same actors become senators, war protesters, Vietnamese, and various other characters. The use of transformation, as opposed to a motivationally connected narrative, allows for greater compression, rapid pacing, freedom to digress and to comment through counterpoint, and unlimited perspectives on the topic.

Viet Rock opened at Cafe La Mama on 21 May 1966, was taken to New Haven that fall to open the professional theatre season at Yale University, and had a sixty-two performance Off-Broadway run. Terry recalls that "one of the best things ***Viet Rock*** did was bring a lot of very bright people into the theatre" (David Savran, *In Their Own Words: Contemporary American Playwrights* [New York: Theatre Communications Group, 1988], 249).

Viet Rock illustrates another of Terry's abiding concerns: the role of language in human power struggles. According to Phyllis Jane Rose, the play was "meant to be a catalogue of clichés, conscientiously chosen to demonstrate the disparity between the reality of war and contemporary American attitudes toward it, attitudes expressed in habitual media-propagated language" ("Megan Terry," *Twentieth-Century American Dramatists, Part 2: K-Z*, ed. John MacNicholas *Dictionary of Literary Biography* [Detroit: Gale Research, 1981], 7:284). The sergeant drilling his GIs repeatedly calls them "girlies," as if to reinforce his authority by verbally reducing his recruits to the lowest status he can conceive. Indeed, sexism in language became the subject of an entire play, ***American King's English for Queens*** (1978). "English can be like bullets," Terry told David Savran (250). That work then led to ***Goona Goona*** (1979), a play about family violence arising from violence in language. As Terry observed,

"Roles and attitudes toward the self are shaped within the family by how one is spoken to" (Kathleen Betsko and Rachel Koenig, *Interviews with Contemporary Women Playwrights* [New York: Beech Tree, 1987], 387).

A feminist perspective came to the fore in Terry's dramatic biography of Simone Weil, ***Approaching Simone*** (1970), which won an Obie award for the best play of 1969-70. Terry's move to Omaha in 1974 to join Jo Ann Schmidman's Magic Theatre signaled the growing importance of theatre outside New York. "In the seventies, maybe our style scared people, but now we find people are beginning to crave it," Terry has said. "I think that the more our culture gets fragmented, the more people want a feeling of community and contact." Thus her current work, as she explains in the following interview (conducted on 21 March 1989 and amplified in January 1994), grows out of the needs she perceives in her adopted community and the surrounding region.

[Londré]: To start with something biographical, could you tell me a little about your work at La Mama and how you arrived at your transformational technique?

[Terry]: Ellen Stewart let me do a play a month at La Mama, and that led to ***Viet Rock***. We did ***Magic Realists***, ***Comings and Goings***, and opened ***Viet Rock*** on Armed Forces Day in May 1960. ***Magic Realists*** was the only play that didn't grow out of workshops with Joseph Chaikin and the Open Theatre. Regarding the transformation, a lot of things came together. I was trained in creative dramatics at the University of Washington and worked a lot with children. I ran a playschool in Canada for two years, and I learned a lot about transformations from them. Another influence on transformations comes from American stand-up comedy—the impressionists, people who can switch from one character to another—plus the cartoons—Bugs Bunny and Tom and Jerry. Then there was Gertrude Stein and the cubists, the collagists. Put them all together! The first transformations were done in New York in ***Calm Down Mother***. Then we, the Open Theatre, did a double bill of ***Calm Down Mother*** and ***Keep Tightly Closed***. There were influences from Joseph Chaikin, who had worked with Nola Chilton, who had been influenced perhaps by Viola Spolin.

Are you still using the technique?

If the material demands it. At Omaha Magic Theatre we develop one or two pieces a year that have no set characters. In plays like ***Sea of Forms*** and ***Walking through Walls***, which I wrote with our artistic director Jo Ann Schmidman, the actors constantly transform, because those plays develop themes rather than characters—themes like the unity of all forms or how to break down internal or external barriers.

Is it important to you as a playwright to work closely with actors?

I like it because I was brought up in the theatre. I love actors and the social interaction. I have my typewriter down here, and I like to work here. I find that actors stimulate me very much. I adore actors, and I adore the art and craft of acting. I love to be up close.

Does your method of working combine the typewriter and the cassette recorder?

No. No, I really don't record what they say. But I see *how* things work. What's interesting about actors is their souls. When they find their gestures, you can see how much they can do, and then see how many lines or speeches I can cut. I learned to edit from watching actors. What they can do is a substitute for words. I find, when I'm judging a lot of playscripts in a contest, that many writers haven't the foggiest notion about editing their work. The plays are overwritten.

What do you look for in a new playwright?

A voice. A clear, fresh voice or point of view that really wakes you up, something that only that one writer knows and can convey and that makes you understand things in new ways. I look for theatrical power, hypnotic energy, and the psychic news. We have a bias toward avant-garde work.

I understand you have something called a community-problem play. What is that like?

Well, we listen to community concerns. This is what's supporting our art. It supports all the rest of the work we do. It's the opposite of what they taught me in playwriting class in college, for example, that "art and politics don't mix." But actually what has supported us for the last fifteen years are plays like ***Babes in the Bighouse***, which deals with women in prison, and ***American King's English for Queens***, which shows how children are socialized by the way adults speak to them, how gender roles are developed through the way children are talked to and how they internalize pronouns. We talk a lot, at great length actually, about the play in every community where we play, on the road or here in Omaha. We have a discussion afterward to get the audiences thinking. Out of that kind of work came ***Goona Goona***, which deals with spouse and child abuse. Out of the discussions after ***Goona Goona*** performances came ***Kegger***, which deals with young people drinking and driving. In those discussions the audience said, "The reason we drink is because we can't talk to one another," and out of that discussion came ***Dinner's in the Blender***, which deals with impossible and possible ways for families to communicate. It's just moved on like that. The production of ***Kegger*** supported our company for three years. We even had to organize a second company to deal with the demand. And now that it's been published, it's being done all over the country. It's been done in Maryville, Missouri, in Los Angeles, and by Dallas Children's Theatre and will be done by San Francisco New Conservatory Children's Theatre and the Virginia Children's Theatre.

Is there any difference in audience response between Omaha and the small towns you visit on tour?

The difference is that on tour the whole town comes, unless there's a basketball game.

Is the script adapted for different communities, or is it pretty much set after the Omaha performances?

We toured our version around the Midwest, so it was the same in Iowa, the Dakotas, Nebraska, Kansas. What they did in Dallas was change the slang to keep up with the local language, and they changed certain place names. Also I encouraged them to go out and listen to the music that their young people listen to. Then I encouraged them to rearrange the music to carry the local beat. Our Midwest rock translated perfectly into rap music for Dallas. They put it to a Spanish beat for L. A. We prepare study guides and send them out. We get a lot of help in developing the plays and study guides from humanities scholars, some from Nebraska and some from Iowa. We take scholars with us on the road, and they help with the discussions after the show. It is an interdisciplinary project during the development of the play. Then we take scholars from different disciplines with us on tours. For instance, one scholar is a historian and talks with the community about the history of alcohol, which is fascinating! We hear how alcohol developed because grain was rotting and they needed to do something with the grain to create another cash crop, so they invented alcohol. Then they had to invent corks so alcohol could be transported from one place to another without evaporating. It's just so amazing, the things we learn. At other places we've had a neurosurgeon, a neuropsychiatrist, who explains what happens to you physiologically. We've also learned about alcohol in prisons, because every time we played a college or community center we played a local prison too. And that's where we got firsthand testimony. Prisoners would say, "You know, I started drinking when I was eleven or twelve, and so emotionally I'm still eleven or twelve." I think this kind of arrested emotional and intellectual development is so tragic. The quest for the self arrested by drugs and alcohol is a sad and tragic state for a person to be in. It's another kind of stunted prisoner.

You say you perform inside the prisons?

Yes. We started doing that with the Open Theatre. And we perform on Indian reservations, in community centers, colleges, halfway houses, high schools—we play a lot of gymnasiums.

Would you describe your work as "political theatre," or is there another term for it?

I'd call it "social action theatre," because it's a catalyst for a community to talk together about how to solve a problem. For instance, one town decided that, instead of having a senior prom where all the kids drank, as they usually did, they would buy up tons of red paint and let the kids paint the town red.

What did they paint!?

They painted the whole town. All the exteriors. It was a very small town.

And this was your doing?

We were just the catalyst for it. They figured it out for themselves.

Do your local reviewers see your work as art or politics?

They don't care—it's just a play. It doesn't matter whether it's art or politics. It's a catalyst for the community. Some communities were able to get together and create halfway houses and safe houses for battered women and abused children after we played ***Goona Goona***, for instance. Now we're doing a piece called ***Head Light***, which deals with literacy. I've done a lot of research for it, worked with the literacy council. And again scholars will help with leading audience discussions after the performance and help us to develop and finalize a good study guide for schools and communities and literacy councils to use in conjunction with our visit.

How do you begin your work on a play like that? Does the research come first?

First there's the stimulus from audience discussions, accounts by honest eyewitnesses, or people who are involved in helping people in trouble, or the victims themselves. When I find that the same themes keep coming up, that's when I get going and start my research.

At what point do you know you are ready to sit down at the typewriter?

When the shape of the play takes place in my mind. When I can see that shape or when the characters start talking to me, when they take on a life of their own—then I can write the play. I revise it during rehearsals and also on the road. Some plays start out twice as long as they end up. So I subtract. Then I add materials stimulated by the audience. It's a process of adding and subtracting. Mostly subtracting.

Why is music such an important element in all your plays?

I love to have music around me. I come from a very musical family. Every time we had a family party, everyone sang and played and even sang in five-part harmony. We have many wonderful young composers here. You know, Kansas City and Omaha are the homes of jazz. So I can have any combination of soft jazz or hard rock and roll. There are a lot of very creative composers here. We have composers ranging from a Charles Ives disciple to a synthesizer/industrial rock musician to a reggae musician. According to the feeling of the piece, we can call on anywhere from one to six composers. We have five on ***Head Light***. It's plain fun to have music in a play.

I've noticed this upbeat, positive attitude of yours that comes through in other interviews, like the one with David

Savran in In Their Own Words. Does your optimism ever hamper you from really grappling with problems in your plays?

Gee, I don't know. I want other people to be as happy as I am, I guess. I get upset when they don't get the chance. There are quite a lot of young people depressed these days. People in their twenties. I can't understand being depressed in your twenties. But I see a lot of it in my travels

How do you keep your optimism while dealing with the serious problems you confront in your work?

I don't know, maybe it's because of my pioneer background. I feel very close to a pioneer culture. My people went from Illinois, Minnesota, Iowa, Nebraska, to the West Coast. And before that they came across the seas from Ireland. So I know that you can keep moving forward to get where you want to go. I still feel very close to that. I was lucky enough to know my great-grandparents. They lived into their nineties. So growing up hearing all the stories they could tell—going against the elements, going through the Civil War, coming West, and surviving, and then establishing themselves there—it's just all part of my environment. Knowing that is very important. I mean, many people have no idea who their grandparents are. You know, our so-called affluence has created this modern mobility, but people don't know who they are. The extended family has been decimated by the automobile and upward mobility. It really disturbs me to see young people floundering, because I knew what I wanted to do at an early age. I was lucky enough to live three blocks from a great theatre. A theatre that took me in as a young teenager and taught me theatre arts and crafts and a respect for our field.

Do you separate your personal life from your professional life, or are they totally integrated?

They're totally integrated. I think of our theatre as extended family. I like to have people of all ages around me. We have people from high school age to a sixty-seven-year-old sculptor working on our shows. When people come to the Magic Theatre, they always marvel at the cross section of ages—onstage *and* in the audience.

Do you ever crave to work with the classics?

Oh, I love the classics. The Greeks, the French, the Irish, the Scandinavians, the Russians.

But your theatre doesn't produce them?

Everyone else does though. We might get around to it one day, but there's so much good new work to do. We've been presenting plays from the 1960s along with fresh, new work.

Describe what you believe were the most significant changes between the American theatre of the 1950s and the theatre of the 1960s.

The 1960s marked an explosion of playwriting styles. One reason for this was because at least thirty-five strong playwrights arrived and began to show their work in New York within the same time period. It was the kind of creative combustion that hadn't been seen since Greek and Elizabethan times. Sheer numbers of challenging writers with many different points of view were in the same geographical location. I believe this could take place because of some excellent teaching that had gone on in the universities by the people who had fought in World War II. They came back to their students with a global view and a new sense of American power and energy in the world. Before this playwrights seemed to arrive in the national consciousness one at a time. But this new group of playwrights realized they were a group. Some realized this because they literally received energy from one another, and others, because their audiences were telling them it was so. And yet others hated to hear it from people who were then starting to write about the theatre, the way they had previously written about politics. It was like sport to show our work to one another and almost play "can you top this" with each new play.

Another physical fact that made this possible was that our theatres were literally within walking distance of one another. When I say that playwrights arrived one at a time, it seems sometimes that it was true and at other times that the people who were writing about the American theatre of the 1950s and before could only see or hear that one person at a time. They didn't seem to be able to hold more than one writer in their consciousness, that is, one O'Neill, then one Tennessee Williams, then one Arthur Miller, etc. There were other people writing at this time, but then a writer had to make a big, big Broadway impression to take up enough psychic space to be able to be hailed as *the* American playwright. In the 1960s we realized we weren't welcome on Broadway, but we had confidence. We started our own theatres and found directors and actors of like minds, colleagues, who would work in collaboration, in groups where the actor was treated as a cocreator, not as an employee or interpreter. This attitude or practice made for a completely different dynamism in performance. The 1960s audiences responded to this, and we were off and flying. Our work and ideas took over the decade, and soon American theatre production ideas and playwriting seemed to be leading the world. These ideas cross-pollinated with many other cultures.

What influences do you see the 1960s having on theatre of the 1990s?

I feel now in the 1990s much of this early interaction is now coming to a new fruition. Evidence is already on our stages, on world stages with more on the horizon. I believe the American theatre of the 1950s was the culmination of European influence on American playwriting. For instance, I believe the American theatre of the absurd is the end of that cycle, not a beginning. Many important playwrights are represented in an excellent collection, edited by Poland and Mailman, *The Off-Off Broadway Book*. Here you will find the work of many strong writers who are still at work today: John Guare, Rochelle Owens, Maria Irene Fornes, Ronald Tavel, Rosalind Drexler, Kenneth Bernard, Jean-Claude van Itallie, and myself among many others. Recently we produced double bills of plays by many of these writers. One written in the 1960s and one written in the last two years. We didn't tell our audiences which were which, and we found they couldn't tell the difference. Each of the plays seemed fresh to them; all seemed to them to have been written that morning. This tells me that it's time for a reevaluation of all of the work of these writers and that a concerted effort should be made to bring their work to wider audiences. We try hard to get the news of the writers we admire out to others who may be interested in producing this exciting work. We have published a book to help with this, *Right Brain Vacation Photos: Twenty Years of Omaha Magic Theatre Productions*. It is our hope that the production possibilities shown in the photos and samples of text will stimulate more productions for these productive 1960s writers, as well as the new writers we have been producing. Included in the book are instructions and addresses for contacting the writers. At our theatre many Ph.D. candidates come from all over the world to visit, to observe our work, and to pore over our archives. In time they will get the word out, and there will be more productions of the works of this fecund period, as well as productions of the many subsequent works of these writers. Nearly all are still writing, and many are writing now at the top of their form.

In what ways were the playwrights of the 1960s distinctly American?

The 1960s writers and the 1960s productions have a distinctive American voice. I should say "voices," because there are many Americans, and the 1960s began to demonstrate this fact. The cultural diversity of our country and our heritage began to become known then. These ideas have been taken up by all the other media and most of our social and political institutions.

How would you characterize 1960s contributions to directing and acting?

There were great advances made in direction, acting, and production design in the 1960s. A synthesis and cross-pollination from discoveries in other media and art were coming into the theatre. You can see fruition of these seminal ideas in much of the performance art of the last ten years and now on Broadway in productions such as *Tommy*, as well as in opera and the new wave festivals at the Brooklyn Academy of Music, that is, [in the work of] Robert Wilson, Laurie Anderson, and Karen Finley and in the current work of the Omaha Magic Theatre. Ideas from the last hundred years in art and design have come into the theatre. Some of these ideas are amplified, modified, and expanded by the use of electronic media and by the application of image projection possibilities on a large scale. Now you can see that the designer, too, has been brought to join the creative, producing team as a cocreator who makes as strong a statement about the theme or ideas of the play as the playwright, director, and performer. Sometimes one person may wear all these hats, sometimes a creative team, but all work together to bring new power into our field and thus more enjoyment to the audience that makes the effort to go out to the theatre and join in with the creative interaction possible in this evolving art form.

How would you evaluate theatre of the 1960s in light of your work and interests of the 1980s and 1990s?

The theatre of the 1960s—the energy of it and the ideas of it—the plays themselves, the productions, many of which I saw, are still in my mind. I know that I was privileged to be alive then and to be a part of it and to have it embroidered into the fiber of who I am. Not a day goes by that some young person doesn't come to our theatre to ask me what the 1960s were really like—to sit with me, to hear the stories of those who were the shakers and movers then but are putting it down now. I believe there will be an entire reevaluation of that period and that the positive discoveries will be given their proper honor in our formal histories. The 1960s will always be with us. That decade, which I believe is one of the longest decades in history, wasn't really over until 1975, when the Vietnam War was stopped. That war marked the fact that we live in a global village, and it brought about the rediscovery of the facts that we truly are, not only our sister and brother's keeper, but that we had only a short time to relearn to be the stewards of our planet.

Over the last several years what have been your major goals for the Omaha Magic Theatre? How have your roles as director-playwright-producer helped you fulfill those goals?

These past several years have been crucial ones of trying to survive. Our funding has shrunk, not only from public and private entities, but colleges and universities also have barely enough funds for their own arts programs. To secure touring dates takes ten times the effort that it did in the mid-1980s. We have to keep our company going, and we have to make new work for our audiences. And we feel a strong desire to keep growing as artists. We feel an obligation to serve our field through outreach and education, to share with the young and with other artists some of what we have learned. We are seeing theatres folding across the nation. It takes everything we've learned and more hours than we can count anymore to do the work to keep OMT alive. But we've managed to live into our twenty-fifth year as a theatre that produces *only* new work. It doesn't get easier. What sustains us is that we know that in the 1960s we created a new theatre, and that through this theatre we made worldwide friends for our theatre and for our country and ourselves. We still have these friends, and we are adding new ones all the time. We must be doing something right, because there is a steady stream of young artists and seasoned scholars coming to our door. We have managed to build a touring and residency season for our new collaborative works. We keep going by building new works that will challenge and refresh our company and our audience. We use every skill we have and borrow, through advice, those we don't possess. In some ways theatre is an ideal situation because one must constantly learn to keep doing it at all. The brain and body get maxed out every day. Theatre is not only an art form, it is a form where to stay alive you have to constantly solve new problems, and that is the fun of it and the head-banging part of it. I am privileged to work with very great and generous artists and colleagues, like our artistic director, Jo Ann Schmidman, and our designer, Sora Kimberlain, and an expanding team of young and mature artists. Theatre is still fun, and it is still the hardest thing that there is to do. We create something out of nothing, we artists. We don't use up resources; we recycle and rearrange and thus create new resources, self-renewing, to fire ourselves and warm the souls of those who are dedicated to serve and/or take sustenance from this art form.

OVERVIEWS AND GENERAL STUDIES

Bonnie Marranca and Gautam Dasgupta (essay date 1981)

SOURCE: "Megan Terry," in *American Playwrights: A Critical Survey, Vol. 1*, by Bonnie Marranca and Gautam Dasgupta, Drama Book Specialists, 1981, pp. 183-92.

[*In the following excerpt, Marranca and Dasgupta critique Terry's career, focusing on the author's use of various styles.*]

Megan Terry began her theatrical career in the mid-fifties in Seattle, Washington, where she first had her plays produced and worked as a director and actor. But it was her work as a member of The Open Theater from 1963 to 1968 that brought her to prominence. In the mid-sixties Terry ran a playwrights' workshop for that company in which many of her own plays were developed. Since 1971 she has been working with the Omaha Magic Theatre, founded in 1969 by another former Open Theater member, Jo Anne Schmidman.

Terry's work in the theatre is characterized by her use of "transformations," an approach to acting which reached its dramatic high point in productions of The Open Theater, but which she has experimented with since the mid-fifties. Transformations are defined by a nonpsychological, action and image-oriented conception of character which negates the notion of a fixed reality or situation in favor of the continuous displacement of one reality with another.

Besides Terry's early work with transformations, they grew from several sources, namely Viola Spolin's theatre games, the work of Nola Chilton, and Second City techniques—acting strategies based on "games" and "role-playing." As an acting idea (and an approach to the creation of a text), transformations have been an important development in performance theory in the American theatre, the first significant break with the Stanislavsky system.

Not all of Terry's plays are transformation plays, however. She has written in several styles which include naturalism (***Hothouse***), satirical comedy (***The Tommy Allen Show***), and absurdism (***The Gloaming, Oh My Darling, The Magic Realists***). Many of the plays are musicals (***Viet Rock, Massachusetts Trust, Brazil Fado***). Generally they are loose, free-form structures that agitate for unconventional modes of dramaturgy.

Whatever the form, Terry tends thematically to explore social issues in contemporary American society: the Viet Nam war (***Viet Rock***), crime (***The People vs. Ranchman***), politics (***Massachusetts Trust***), sexism (***American Kings English for Queens***). She is interested in ways in which society fuels itself on deception. But the plays do not propagate a doctrinaire political point of view; instead they lean toward more abstract treatments of subject matter, frequently through comedic means.

Terry's characters are usually outsiders, people struggling to keep their individuality in a system which pushes them to conform to the status quo. The theme of dominance-submission runs through many of the plays and the characters have rich fantasy lives which help them triumph over banal or oppressive surroundings (***Keep Tightly Closed in a Cool Dry Place***). Because of the emphasis on transformations and the absence of conventional plots, characters easily create realities for themselves.

Terry has, throughout her career, tried to embrace new forms, though her most successful works are the transformation plays. Her plays tax the capabilities of actors by requiring rapid and frequent changes of character and situation, and a great deal of physical work (***Comings and Goings, Viet Rock***). Usually they need few technical effects and hardly more than a few ramps and props.

Not mere formal exercises, however, the works explore human relations in a variety of circumstances, ranging from contained domestic settings to more epic-style scenes. Many of them are specifically about women and their relationships to other women and to society. If some of the plays are more consciously feminist in perspective (***Approaching Simone, Hothouse***), others nevertheless depict female imagery (***The Gloaming, Oh My Darling, Sanibel and Captiva***). Terry's drama is dominated by characters victimized by others or by the "system"—characters for whom she shows a great deal of compassion.

This is evident from her earliest work in the theatre, ***Ex-Miss Copper Queen on a Set of Pills***, which unfolds as an encounter between two garbage scavengers, B.A. and Crissie, and a stoned, down-and-out young woman. It takes place just before dawn on New York's Lower East Side. B.A. and Crissie meet Copper Queen on one of their morning routines, and though not very bright themselves, they outsmart the newcomer and run away with her shabby fur coat. The play ends with the trusting Copper Queen—who describes herself as an ex-beauty contest winner from Montana and the mother of an illegitimate child taken from her by her own parents—waiting on the street for the two women. They have promised to let her look after the "baby" they pretend to be wheeling in their dump-heap carriage.

A highly sentimental play in the realistic mode, ***Copper Queen*** attempts to show how feelings of trust and affection can exist in an urban atmosphere of degradation, a dominant theme in many of the plays of Terry's contemporaries, though the strong may overpower the weak in the fight for survival. It also offers characters whose lives of fantasy energize the mundane reality of their existence, a frequent theme in Terry's work. Still, this is a minor play for a writer who had not yet begun to work in her more exciting transformation style.

Transformations first surface in ***Keep Tightly Closed in a Cool Dry Place***, a play which focuses on three men—Jaspers, Gregory, and Michaels—in a prison cell. Far from the prison melodrama one might anticipate from its setting, ***Keep Tightly Closed*** is not a conventional play with a story, but more a fragment of a possible narrative. In a series of rapid transformations it shifts realities in which the men—all of them jailed, it appears, for the murder of Jaspers' wife (that may or may not be true)—continually create new identities for themselves.

The play is framed by scenes in which the men act out the routine, mechanized aspects of their lives. But in between there are a number of transformational scenes which help the characters transcend their environment. They "become" General Custer, an Indian chief, a soldier at war, figures in Captain John Smith's Jamestown, drag queens, movie gangsters, and criminals reenacting the murder of Jaspers' wife. At other times they are simply themselves, trying to cope with the terror of confinement.

These improvisational-style scenes—developed by The Open Theater, which premiered the play—are acted out in a variety of styles that encompass naturalism, camp, vaudeville, gangster movies, costume epics, melodrama, and abstraction. Uninterested in the psychological probing of her characters, Terry instead devises a series of images that flow together, in an effort to explore confinement, dependency, domination-submission, ritual, friendship, deprivation, and loneliness—all of the emotional conditions that characterize a prisoner's life—through action rather than plot. The men, in other words, are defined by the "roles" they play in the transformations.

This continual exchange of one reality for another proposed by the transformation reflects the modern temper. It is a notion of dramatic character that revels in action, fragmentation, and the divided self—unlike naturalism and its insistence on story and character built through the accumulation of emotional and intellectual details which conspire to make a composite of a total, unified theory of self.

In conventional drama aspects of a character are successively peeled away, ultimately revealing the defining center of a personality. In transformational plays, however, as many aspects of the self are revealed as there are layers. The audience is forced in conventional theatre to sit passively and watch the drama develop onstage, while the audience for an innovative transformational play is invited to actively and continually adjust its expectations of "reality" onstage.

Keep Tightly Closed in a Cool Dry Place, though not the most skillful of transformation plays, is a good example of the style's radical approach to character, plot construction, and acting. All of these will reach their fullest potential in Terry's most accomplished play in this style, ***Viet Rock***.

Another transformation of the same period, 1966, is ***Comings and Goings***, which its author calls a "theatre game." Indeed, this series of about thirty successive transformations illustrates how important the notion of "play" is to the concept of transformation.

Comings and Goings explores various ways He and She relate to one another: sexually, emotionally, socially. Scenes take place at home, in a night club, a diner, a police station, and outdoors, among other places. The dialogue is deliberately ordinary and concise (often one word exchanges) to set up the reality of a situation.

The short scenes flow smoothly into and out of each other, unlike the more fragmented ***Keep Tightly Closed in a Cool Dry Place***, which was tied to a narrative structure while often growing out of the final image of the previous scene or from its dialogue. He and She, not always human beings, are even called upon to become inanimate objects—a plug and a socket, a pencil and list, two galaxies—as was frequently the case in the sixties, when American actors first began on a wide scale to experiment with alternatives to naturalistic acting. Often, especially in The Open Theater, this meant a highly physicalized, non-psychological treatment of character in the sparest of settings.

Comings and Goings, referred to by Terry in a Note prefacing the play as "a trampoline for actors and director," is perhaps a highly polished series of skits about role-playing rather than a play, and that is not to belittle this transformation, which calls for virtuosic acting *con brio*. It is, after all, about acting—that is, gesture, tone of voice, facial expression, attitude, movement.

One of the highlights of the piece is the scene in the diner between a customer and a waitress, which is played in five different ways ranging from casual transaction to sexual encounter. In other scenes Terry has He and She—who, incidentally, have been played by more than two actors—reverse positions in a scene or repeat the same dialogue with different actions.

Comings and Goings is bright, original, witty, and unpretentious. Unfortunately, it is so rooted in the theatrical experimentation of the sixties that now it seems more an acting exercise that reveals its age than a piece for the permanent dramatic repertoire. Still, it accomplished what it set out to do, and that is perhaps all one should ask of it.

In a totally different vein is ***The Gloaming, Oh My Darling***, which grew out of a section of an earlier fragmentary play, ***Calm Down Mother***. In this absurdist-style work two old women pass their time in a nursery home, intertwining memory and fantasy for as long as they can resist death. They alternately fight, console, insult, hurt, and charm one another when they aren't fooling with "Mr. Birdsong," the object of their sexual fantasies. In fact, much of their fantasy life revolves around sex. When Mrs. Tweed says, "I hear a man's voice," Mrs. Watermellon replies, "It's your longing."

In ***Gloaming*** all time flows in a continuous present which Terry attempts to imbue with a special female presence. The actual situation of the play reflects the triumph of the human spirit against death, an unfeeling nurse, and the visits of grotesque family members. ***The Gloaming, Oh My Darling*** embodies themes that are important to Terry, showing particular interest in female imagery, but it is too sentimental to succeed as absurdism, dramatic territory she has never seemed very comfortable in.

Sanibel and Captiva, a later radio play, continues the absurdist attempt to slightly more successful ends. In this one-act poetic drama an elderly husband and wife are fishing, their conversation orchestrated with the sounds of the surf, gulls, minahs, a barking dog, a car approaching, an airplane overhead.

In the play, which reflects the influence of Beckett, Terry succeeds in creating a certain amount of ambiguity and sensuality, but it is less arresting as a dramatic experience than the transformation plays. These action-oriented works seem better suited to Terry's temperament than the reflective, more static dramas. Terry's manipulation of imagery is plainly more inventive than her dialogue. Finally, if the development of character becomes too central in the play, she has a tendency to fall into sentimentalizing.

Transformations are the driving force behind Terry's antiwar play, ***Viet Rock***, which developed in an Open Theater workshop she conducted (1965-66). A counterculture musical termed by the author "a folk war movie," ***Viet Rock*** combines marching cadences and the frug to the accompaniment of bitterly satiric rock music.

> When the bombs fall
> The Viets rock and rock
> When the napalm bursts
> Then the Viets roll.

Viet Rock is a political play but not an ideological one, even as Terry makes her sympathies known in the structure of images which coalesce around the various themes the play develops in its nonnarrative movement. She presents a panoramic sweep of conflicting attitudes toward the war (military, domestic, governmental, protest)—not the war itself. Alternating parody and sentiment, moments of joy and those of disaster, Terry's view of America—far from Norman Rockwell's uncomplicated portraits—evolves from its advertising slogans, antiwar chants, rock and roll dances, and movie-style gestures, all of them set in relief against the militaristic, sexist, racist machine that grinds out soldiers for a war in Southeast Asia. The result is a broadly satiric rock musical style that indeed gave a new shape to the new expression characterizing the political, social, and cultural upheavals of the sixties.

In ***Viet Rock*** scenes move rapidly from one event to another, emphasizing the social aspect of events without regard for conventional laws of space and time. When the play opens the actors are in a circle on the floor, which breaks apart in an instant transformation as the male actors become babies and the female actors their mothers. This image soon gives way to the scene of an army physical, then the women becoming mothers and sweethearts saying goodbye to young soldiers, then men in drill formation, and so forth. All of these scenes occur quickly after a situation has been established, so that a large number of perspectives can be shown.

Since Terry tends to disregard gender roles where possible, women play soldiers and become airplanes; they are also shown in active protest against the war. In the final scene of Act I—in which a Senate hearing takes place—the actors take turns playing senators and witnesses; when an actor finishes his place as one character, he quickly becomes another. There is no development of character because the style of the play does not allow for it, and reality is not fixed, character never rigidified. ***Viet Rock*** embodies the frenzy, passion, and conflict of a certain period in American life in a style that echoed the fragmentation of the times.

Viet Rock also reflects many of the experimental theatre techniques of its era—not only in the transformational style it represents but in its rock musical form (the play is a contemporary of *Hair*), the highly physical demands it makes on actors, its need for audience contact, the structure of choral configurations, the improvisational, open shape, and literal development of imagery.

On the thematic level it represents the sense of engagement exemplified by many of the theatre groups who were performing during the war in Viet Nam. In recent years, and with the end to the war, politics has given way to more formalistic, perceptual explorations of theatre.

Though ***Viet Rock*** seems dated now from a stylistic point of view, in its time it provided a strong communal experi-

ce of political protest. The final scene of the play—in which the "dead" rise up, walk through and touch the audience in a "celebration of presence"—is typical of theatrical experiences of the sixties when theatre companies made a special effort to emphasize the shared experience of theatre, disregarding the space between actor and audi-ce. That was perhaps the significance of **Viet Rock** as a lay—not its politics, which are more an emotional war than an analysis of it.

d Terry continues her interest in ues, but to less successful ackles the theme of ggest that in a fantasies is a

time she does not rely on transformations as an organizing principle. Instead, she offers a three-part structure, at the center of which is a television talk show parody; Parts One and Three are autonomous environments for the audiences to wander in. In Part One the audience, as if at a carnival, walks through a series of rooms before the play begins: "Room of Strange Walls and Floors," "Room of Mirrors," "Room of the War Toys," "Chekhov Room," "Tai Chi Room"; in Part Three actors' "Speeches on the Cross" are accompanied by individual torture scenes.

The middle section of **Tommy Allen** is the actual TV talk show—complete with commercials—done in a satirical revue style. Tommy Allen (the character is played by four men and women) has as his guests a country-western singer, suburban housewife, child molester, and gay comedian whose shenanigans—interspersed with commercials for dope, vaginal deodorant, and violence—make day Night Live seem innocuous in comparison. Ter-ica is a country degraded by its perversion of nd ruled by consumerist ethics—a land f to death. Its inhabitants are adrift in lk and unfulfilling relationships. g," says Tommy 2.

is not always excess of real

essay date 1984)

egan Terry: Mother of American Feminist eminist Theatre, Macmillan, 1984, pp. 53-76.

ollowing excerpt, Keyssar explores Terry's ary impact on feminist theater; contending that rk does not invite radical revolution but instead attention to the power of women.]

ce the early sixties Megan Terry has been a sustaining force in feminist drama, nurturing other American women playwrights and continually extending the reaches of her own plays. Captivated by theatre from the age of fourteen, Terry, now in her early fifties, has written more than fifty dramas most of which have been both produced and published. Reviewers whose attention is fixed on New York commercial successes tend to ignore Terry's work, but she has received public recognition and support over the last twenty years from numerous foundations and government offices. As playwright in residence of the Omaha Magic Theatre since 1970, she has, with the Magic Theatre's artistic director and founder Jo Ann Schmidman, been able to sustain one of America's most innovative theatres for more than fourteen years.

Terry's own definitions of feminist drama are deliberately broad: "anything that gives women confidence, shows themselves to themselves, helps them to begin to analyze

it the orma-and the e merely tre, musi-**English for** linguistic and "wild child" iety. gic Theatre is **Brazil** rmation style. In this

310

d ees " is z are , after central keep the deception mily. This is

ehold is Jody's y her. She seems s his promise of a

stable, conformist future in the hope of a better life at home. Roz is right when she remarks of David, "He's not our kind of people." By rejecting him Jody refuses the opportunity to run from the degradation of her environment and create the possibility of a new life for herself. Home is a "hothouse" which stifles emotional growth and personal independence, but marriage may be another kind of entrapment, hints Terry.

If marriage is shown as a bourgeois alternative, a kind of bondage, the brutal conditions Jody faces living with her mother and grandmother and their various boyfriends are glossed over, even dismissed, in favor of Terry's "thesis." The fact of showing women without men interests Terry, even though the prospect of young Jody living with these two women, who spend all their time drinking, is disheartening and presents a false sense of support if one thinks of them serving as role models.

Intellectually, Terry is being fair when she insists that women turn to each other and away from men who try to brutalize and dominate them (Jack and Roz) or remold them (David and Jody), but she hangs her premise on some pretty shaky characters. ***Hothouse*** doesn't make as strong a feminist statement as it apparently sets out to, and it is disappointing to see Terry fall prey at this stage of her career (perhaps it is an old play?) to old-fashioned psychologizing and simple notions of fate, heredity, and environment (now she is in O'Neill territory). ***Hothouse*** is an unsatisfying representation of family life, all the more so because it fits potentially provocative subject matter to a conventional form, conventionally and falsely fashioned.

Terry moves into a nonnaturalistic world in another recent play which uses transformations. In her opening speech of ***American Kings English for Queens*** Silver Morgan, a young girl raised by prairie dogs until she was taken at seventeen into the Connell family home, asks, "Do you think like you talk, or talk like you think?" Terry's play, performed by the Omaha Magic Theatre, sets out to explore the ramifications of that question in the style of musical fantasy.

A series of scenes conspire to offer lessons—the play is a teaching tool, it seems—about the uses and abuses of language, sex roles, concepts of romance, and the socialization process. The lessons are self-conscious and simplistic, as if ***American Kings English*** were prepared for grade school audiences. Whatever insight Terry has [illegible] offer on the imaginative possibilities of language whe[illegible] resists rigid socialization dissipates in the inanity o[illegible] dialogue and in banal song lyrics. Here even transf[illegible] tions, which Terry has used elsewhere to exp[illegible] imagistic and structural potential of her plays, a[illegible] illustrative or functional. Caught in a mix of s[illegible] cal comedy, and didacticism, ***American King[illegible] Queens*** is a lackluster attempt at uniting [illegible] feminist thought—not to mention th[illegible] theme—in a critique of contemporary so[illegible]

Another new play from the Omaha M[illegible] ***Fado***, a return to the earlier transf[illegible]

satirical musical that evolves simultaneously as [illegible] plays—one taking place in an American home, the other i[illegible] a TV news station—Terry sets out to examine the Brazilian socio-political situation in the context of American society.

Unless it is done in the style of the grotesque or black humor, a play that combines scenes of torture with Carmen Miranda-type numbers is hardly likely to succeed a[illegible] serious politics. Aside from its trivializing of the thema[illegible] material, and its ineffectual attempts to comment on e[illegible] Brazilian or American society, ***Brazil Fado*** lac[illegible] organization and focused energy of the best transfo[illegible] plays. It is marred by a certain tackiness [illegible] indulgence that, unfortunately, has characteri[illegible] work with the Omaha Magic Theatre.

Sadly, Megan Terry's most recent efforts h[illegible] her achievements with The Open Thea[illegible] tending more and more to be shapel[illegible] Where transformations once gave a [illegible] the plays, they now seem to have[illegible] tiveness. Terry hasn't found a ne[illegible] rent work the structural foundat[illegible] truth about most of the adven[illegible] prominence in the sixties—a[illegible] important experimental w[illegible] not maintained its earlie[illegible] tion.

Helene Keyssar [illegible]

SOURCE: "M[illegible] Drama," in [illegible]

[*In the* [illegible] *extraor*[illegible] *her w*[illegible] *calls*[illegible]

S[illegible]

whether it's a positive or negative image, it's nourishing'. Her plays, however, consistently reveal a precise criticism of stereotyped gender roles, an affirmation of women's strength, and a challenge to women to better use their own power. In Terry's plays we witness a sustained yet never repetitive development of transformation as the central convention of feminist drama. 'Transformation', she asserts, 'reveals to us an efficient universe. Nothing is lost—it's just transformed.'

Born in Seattle, Washington, on 22 July 1932, Terry 'hung around' a community theatre until its director, Florence Bean James, took her in and she began to work on set construction and design. For Terry, the concept of transformation and its development as a key technique of her dramaturgy began with this early training in design and collage; she still thinks of what she does as a kind of architectural process in which she 'builds' plays.

Despite her father's refusal to pay for her education because she would not join a sorority, she took a BA in education at the University of Washington. Her studies included creative dramatics, taught by her cousin Geraldine Siks. Growing up, she had loved cartoon characters and impersonators; working with young children who naturally used role transformation in their daily play led her to think that adult plays could be written that used the same process.

Terry left Seattle in 1956 when a double bill of one of her first plays and a play by Eugene O'Neill was lambasted by local critics. She promised her father on her departure that if she had not made it in the theatre by the time she was thirty-five, she would give up and become a teacher. For the next ten years, she endured the struggles of a young, unknown playwright in New York, a life enriched and complicated in the early sixties by her association with Joseph Chaikin, Peter Feldman, Maria Irene Fornes, Barbara Vann, and more than a dozen other young actors, writers and directors who were rejecting the stylistically and commercially 'closed' theatre of Broadway to create what they soon called the Open Theatre. Many of the original Open Theatre company members had been trained by Nola Chilton, whose teaching emphasised the freeing of the individual actor's body and voice through exercises that focused on imagined objects and sensations. Even more important to the development of Megan Terry's work, however, was the structure given to daily workshops by transformation exercises originally created by a Chicago artist and teacher, Viola Spolin. Spolin's theatre games meshed perfectly with Terry's vision of a theatre in which actors created and altered the world in front of the audience, relying on their own resources of body, voice and imagination.

In its first few years, from 1963 until 1966, the Open Theatre was a set of workshops, led by different members of the company, including Terry. By the spring of 1964, Terry had drafted a new one-act play, ***Calm Down Mother***, inspired by her Open Theatre Workshops. That summer, on a month's Rockefeller Foundation Grant at the Office for Advanced Drama Research in Minneapolis, she revised this as well as an earlier, full-length drama, ***Hothouse***, and another one-act play, ***Ex-Miss Copper Queen on a Set of Pills***, written when she first arrived in New York. In that one month of Minneapolis heat, she also wrote another one-act play, ***Keep Tightly Closed in a Cool Dry Place***. The three one-act plays became part of the Open Theatre's repertory and were first performed by the company in 1965 at the Sheridan Square Playhouse which the company rented for public performances.

Hothouse is unmistakably drawn from an earlier period of Terry's life and work (although it was not actually produced until 1974, by which time it seemed outdated to some reviewers). Set in a fishing village near Seattle in 1955, it is the only one of her plays that could be called a conventional, realistic drama. In contrast to most well-made modern plays, however, the central characters are women, and the world of the play is distinctively female. Three generations of women from one family inhabit a small house in which an uncountable number of houseplants seem to have taken over the living space. Ma, the grandmother of the group, is a spirited, not-so-old lady, who has 'started again'—with men, booze and life itself—so many times that she's lost count. Her daughter Roz spends much of her time drinking, swearing and making love to one man or another. Jody, Roz's daughter, is caught between the invigorating but crazy life of her female family and the naïve passion of her university-student lover, David. Each of the women has and wants her man, and much of the play revolves around the pending divorce of Roz and Jack, Jody's here-again, gone-again father.

Much like Shelagh Delaney's *Lion in Love*, Terry's ***Hothouse***, while realistic in its detail and dialogue, relies little on narrative development, and instead builds a distinctively female environment. The experience of watching either of these plays has more in common with that of listening to a jazz trio than with witnessing Ibsenesque modern drama. Already in ***Hothouse***, Terry's extraordinary ability to make every word a gesture is apparent. Hers is not the skill (or inclination) of the eighteenth-century playwrights who strove to differentiate characters through language; rather, more like Samuel Beckett than any other notable predecessor or contemporary, Terry's words function on stage as physical actions, as mediations that gradually change the people who speak and the relations between them.

Hothouse reveals a political coherence between the assertiveness of the language and the speaking voice. Terry's women defy expectations of ways women talk, especially to each other. Jody, Roz and Ma are acerbic, witty and candid; they make us laugh as few female stage characters do. But they have not simply been allowed access to the male domain of verbal aggression. The lines these women speak express thoughts inseparable from feelings; these are intelligent people whose perspicacity reveals rather than conceals caring. When, at the end of the play, Roz gazes down at Jody who has crumpled into an exhausted sleep, she claims both her connection to and her separation from her daughter:

> Roz: My glass is empty. Who's the bartender around here? . . . Don't be mad at me, Jody? Jody? I love you more than anything in the world. You hear that? You never have to do without love, Angel. . . . You were so little. Look at you now. Tall and pretty. As tall as your old lady. And a hell of a lot smarter. A hell of a lot.

Hothouse none the less has as much in common with the predecessors of feminist drama as it does with Terry's subsequent work and the other plays that come to define contemporary feminist drama. Like almost all of Western drama, the strategy of ***Hothouse*** pivots around a covenant of expectation between audience and characters: the implicit promise is that at some point, usually near the end of the play, a recognition scene will occur in which a character reveals herself or himself in some new way to us and to another in the world framed on stage. In this process of revelation, both the character and the spectator learn something new about who each is. In the classic example, Oedipus endures a series of such recognitions and revelations, discovering step by step who he is and, in our witnessing of these illuminations, we assumedly discover something of who we are. The revelation of erotic attraction in Hellman's *The Children's Hour* functions strategically in an almost identical way.

The structure of ***Hothouse*** sustains this basic pattern. Both Jody and Roz are caught in elemental confusions about their own identities. Jody seeks self-definition through David's love for her, but finally discovers that she 'can't live off feelings of other people'; to find herself, she must acknowledge both her separateness and her ties to the women who have reared her. Roz, in turn, must acknowledge her identity as a mother, and must reveal her love for her daughter. That she initially does so half-drunk, with Jody asleep, is a resistance to the recognition scene and a source of partial frustration for the audience. But a moment later, as the play ends, the traditional convention is completed: Jody awakes in her mother's arms, returns Roz's embrace and welcomes the outside world to participate:

'Come in Bugs . . . Come in Flies.'

Such recognition scenes at once assert and resist change. In the terms of ancient Greece, it is through such moments that one comes to 'know thyself'. This, of course, implies that there is some primary, core 'self' in each human being, and that the process of becoming a better person is one of shedding delusions and defences, of making the hidden seen. Within such a framework, progress is ironically a movement backwards in history, a matter of retrieval and purification, and, finally and essentially, a matter not of transformation of the self but of acceptance. It is the individual will that makes recognitions possible; context and relationships with others may inhibit or inspire the process but are secondary agents.

If one's goal as a playwright is to inspire radical alterations in human actions, then the 2500-year-old dramaturgical fixation on the recognition scene might well be viewed as a prison. The 1960s were a time when a major shift in the structure of drama became possible. But possibility is not the same as necessity, and for many male playwrights there was no compulsion to reject the old forms. (There are, of course, exceptions, like Samuel Beckett and Harold Pinter.) For women, or at least for women who saw that self-awareness and self-discovery were only first steps towards change, it was crucial that a new way be found. A theatre that genuinely included women had to take as a central convention, the overt display of people becoming other.

In this context, the work that Megan Terry produced in the mid-sixties was genuinely experimental, a struggle and testing of a whole new way of doing theatre. In the plays that follow ***Hothouse*** recognition scenes vanish, and in their place appear series of transformations. Instead of characters gradually and painfully discovering their true selves, actors take on one role only to discard that role in front of the audience for another. What was always true of theatre—that the human being could in this arena transcend her or himself—now became not just an unquestioned aesthetic principle but a manifestation of political and aesthetic struggle.

Within a short period of time in the mid-sixties, Terry produced half a dozen plays in this new transformational mode. The one-act ***Ex-Miss Copper Queen on a Set of Pills*** reveals its earlier roots and suggests the transition between the more conventional strategy employed in ***Hothouse*** and the transformational structure that would inform all of Terry's subsequent work. In ***Ex-Miss Copper Queen*** three marginal women meet on the street somewhere on the Lower East Side in New York City. The character known only as 'Copper Queen' is an embodiment of a dramatic transformation: as she lies half-drunk, half-drugged on a front step at the beginning of the play, we see both the naïve beauty queen that she was ten years before and the bedraggled streetwalker she has become at twenty-six. As Copper Queen sips her wine and talks to the pavement—half-succeeding in animating it—two old women, B.A. and Crissie, appear. B.A., the more assertive of the two, wears three wigs, each a different colour and suggestive of a different age; each woman wears a rubber glove on one hand; Crissie wears a white lace glove on her other hand. The two women are scavengers. They salvage items of value from the garbage of the city streets, placing the retrieved items in an ancient but polished pram. Like Copper Queen, their appearances are perplexing and defiant of categorisation.

During the brief encounter of these three women, Copper Queen tells her story of decline from riches to rags, from innocence to brutal experience. Her success in a beauty contest in Butte, Montana, had transported her to New York, where she lost a second contest and became pregnant. Helpless, she yielded to her parents' plan that they rear the child as their own, while she stayed as far away as possible. The tale is of a transformation, but in this play, the alteration of character remains within the familiar mode of narration of past events. We do, however, witness a hint of a destructive form of transformation in the ironic tranquillity that emerges from Copper Queen as her various pills take effect.

As in ***Hothouse***, it is not so much what happens, but the nature of the bond established among the women that is important in this play. Each of the women is elusive, unfixed in any history or type. What connects each to the others and to us is their fierce determination to work and their pride in their own endurance. Within this very limited and particular group, collecting garbage and whoring are legitimate. Just as the pram is transformed from a traditional sentimental object to an efficient work tool, so work itself and its relation to women is at least redefined.

Terry's next three plays move more completely into the transformational mode. ***Keep Tightly Closed in a Cool Dry Place*** begins with an archetypical transformation in which the three male actors combine to become a machine. Consistent with Viola Spolin's urgings that change be developmental, the actors make a transition from the machine image to prisoners in a cell by moving in 'a military manner' to their bunks. During the one hour in which we witness these three men in their jail cell, we learn that all three have been convicted of murder of the wife of one of the men. In her production notes, Terry makes clear that the script is deliberately ambiguous as to whether a murder has been committed and if so, who is responsible for it. In contrast to some dramatic works, however, where ambiguity is intended as a device to challenge the audience, Terry's intention was at least as much to create a challenge to the players and directors 'to decide what matters to you'. The script stands as a score for actors who must, in Terry's words, 'come to understand that they are connected with one another by muscle, blood vessels, nervous structure—impulses felt by one member may be enacted by another'. In the final sequence of the play the three men lock arms facing outwards in a circle and turn like a machine wheel chanting 'And roller and roller and roller, And rocker and rocker and rocker.' This image captures the interdependence as well as the constraints of the prison these men inhabit.

Calm Down Mother, written during this same period and often hailed as the first truly feminist American drama, embraces the transformational form even more persistently than does ***Keep Tightly Closed in a Cool Dry Place***, but it is also an obvious complement to the latter work. ***Calm Down Mother*** calls for three women players, who are named in the cast of characters simply as 'Woman One', 'Woman Two' and 'Woman Three'. As in ***Keep Tightly Closed*** Terry has here moved into a theatrical style that unhesitatingly focuses on the actors; in the manner of the 'poor theatre' heralded by Jerzy Grotowski, the play is set on a bare stage, with the only props being four straight chairs. As the lights come up on the three women 'clustered together to suggest a plant form', we hear a taped speech in the voice of an amused gentlewoman describing the evolution of three one-celled creatures from passive life in the sea to rooting on the land.

At the close of this speech, one of the women breaks from the group structure, walks towards the audience and identifies herself as Margaret Fuller. The abrupt transition, different from the more flowing transformations that characterise other experimental work in the sixties, is the first appearance of Terry's own distinctive signature. The woman's brief speech also contains a quotation from Fuller that identifies Terry's own hope for women in this and other plays. 'I'm Margaret Fuller,' Woman One begins. 'I know I am because from the time I could speak and go alone, my father addressed me not as a plaything, but as a lively mind.'

For most women, however, it is difficult to know oneself as a 'living mind', and the montage of scenes that follow in ***Calm Down Mother*** catches moments in that struggle for a variety of women characters. Structurally, each of the scenes is similar in its triangulation of interaction among three women and in a common tension between generation, between mothers and daughters, symbolic or literal. In one early scene, two older women, sisters who run a Brooklyn delicatessen, become nostalgic when a young female customer enters whose hair reminds them of their own youth and their mother. In another scene, one woman lies still on the floor while her two daughters meet in a distant city and acknowledge their mother's impending death from bone cancer. This crisis allows the 'strong' sister to reveal her own vulnerability.

While Terry centres on mother-daughter relationships, she does not sentimentalise them. In the penultimate scene of the play, two sisters fight about the morality of contraception, and their mother, after attempting to stop their argument, rejects the daughter who advocates the pill. 'You're no daughter of mine,' Ma cries, 'Pack your things.' That line resonates through the final scene in which all three actresses paradoxically declare their self-sufficiency and their identification with reproduction: 'The eggies in our beggies [*sic*] are enough . . . Are enough . . . Are enough.'

This last scene serves as an ironic counterpart to Margaret Fuller's assertion of the struggles to be a 'living mind', and also unites the varied transformational devices used to move one scene into another. Some of these transformations, links between sets of characters and contexts, are abrupt freezes in which the end of one scene is held, then released into a new context. Most of the transformations exploit a gesture or emotional beat to allow the passage of the actresses from one role to another. At the end of a nursing-home scene, the two patients, already objectified by their context, become mechanical subway doors, through which the third woman, the nurse in the previous scene, tries to pass. During the movement pattern, the women chant 'Please keep your hands off the doors.' What makes this transformation effective is that it picks up on one motif from the previous scene—the mechanisation of the lives of these women patients—and then creates a context in which a motif of the next scene about three prostitutes is ironically announced in 'keep your hands off'. By the end of the play, Terry has brought the audience to accept persistent change in the bodies, voices and roles of each actress. The image of three women, smiling sweetly at us while they touch their bellies, breasts and sides and chant 'Our bodies, our bellies . . . our funnies . . . our eggies' seems perfectly right.

Terry employs a number of similar devices in ***Comings and Goings***, a play that like ***Calm Down Mother***, was and remains central to feminist drama. Although many of the roles in ***Comings and Goings*** can be played by two women *or* two men, this play's tension emerges from pairings of many kinds and focuses particularly on male-female relationships. Class is not explicitly an issue here, but power and its relationship to gender roles are key issues to the conflicts that occur repeatedly in the play.

The opening scenes in ***Comings and Goings*** attune the spectator to the language-based transformations of this play. Like many of Terry's dramas, this one unveils the rituals that structure and inform our daily lives. The context of the opening of ***Comings and Goings*** is the awakening of a couple to a new day. The key lines exchanged between the two are 'Time to get up', and 'In a minute'. Stage directions suggest that this scene be repeated a number of times with the actors reversing roles and lines. In performance, actors stress the different meanings and infinite variety of interactions possible by varying modes of deliverance. 'Time to get up' can be spoken cheerfully, reluctantly or commandingly, and 'in a minute' can be a refusal, an acceptance or even a seductive invitation to return to bed.

The elemental frame for this opening scene sets up the performance strategy of displacement that structures ***Comings and Goings***. Stage directions urge repetition of some scenes, and require that the entire company be prepared to play any role at any time. As many devices have been used to accomplish this as there have been performances. Some companies have labelled performers with numbers or names and put those labels in a hat to be randomly drawn by members of the audience. Other companies have used an onstage stage manager to decide the moments when one performer will replace another and/or to decide who replaces whom. In some productions an arrow on a wheel has been spun by members of the company and/or members of the audience. Whichever device is used to provoke change, transformations occur both within and between scenes. Describing this outside of the context of a performance might lead to the conclusion that ***Comings and Goings*** is fragmented and disruptive in production. In fact, however, with any well-rehearsed company the continual exchange of actors, while emphasising the concept of improvisation within a frame, is accomplished very fluidly.

Comings and Goings is strikingly successful in performance precisely because its theme and its form are inseparable. It is a play about role definitions and role change which relies on theatrical role transformations to move the play forward. Each of the mini-scenes presents a moment of encounter between two people, in which the tension of change, of coming and going, is central. Individual control over the scene is a crucial issue of content as well as of performance. In one segment towards the middle of the play, for example, a waitress and customer enact a common ritual of ordering food; by the repetition and variation of interpretation, at times the waitress appears to be the servant to the customer, whereas in other presentations the customer is at the mercy of the waitress.

In addition to calling attention to improvisation, ritual and role-playing as basic elements of theatre, ***Comings and Goings*** stresses the particular relationship of social roles to gender roles. In most of the scenes a predictable male-female relationship sets the frame but awaits violation or criticism. The restaurant scene, for example, illuminates gender roles by alternating control between the waitress and the customer; differences in inflection as well as reversal of the source of identical lines of dialogue make the waitress either servant or expert. As male and female performers replace each other within scenes, it becomes impossible to dismiss unequal power relations between men and women as 'merely' a matter of individual greed or condescension. We come to see that it is the roles we have defined for men and women that determine domination.

Again paradoxically, ***Comings and Goings*** is not simply a condemnation of social and gender roles in contemporary society. Indeed, the experience of the play for both performers and audience is constantly joyous. While the scenes portray a world in which human beings are persistently alienated from each other, unable to acknowledge each other's needs and desires, the uncertainty for any performer of when she or he will be on and each's responsibility for every role demonstrates an ensemble process in which each member is dependent on the other in a positive and constructive manner. The performance transcends the world portrayed and makes the mode of playing appealing to the spectator.

A similar juxtaposition of sharp political criticism with intoxicating energy in performance characterised productions of ***Viet Rock***, the play that brought Terry fully to public attention. Written in 1966 in conjunction with her Saturday Workshop at the Open Theatre, ***Viet Rock*** was one of the first plays to confront the war in Vietnam and the first rock musical ever written. First performed on 25 May 1966 by members of the Open Theatre at Café La Mama the importance of the play was at first blurred by the more successful opening during the same season of another Open Theatre production, Jean Claude van Italie's *American Hurrah*. It was not, in fact, until after ***Viet Rock*** received high praise on European tours that it received respectful attention in the United States.

Viet Rock is a difficult play—both to perform and to witness—but it gradually overcame its initially negative response and lingered on in numerous productions, in the growing antiwar consciousness of many Americans, and in its dramaturgical effects on contemporary theatre. Subtitled 'A Folk War Movie', it fulfils that title both in its obvious satire of scenes from war movies and its evocation of known and newly created American rituals. The opening circle, in which actors gradually rise from prone positions like spokes of a wheel, bounce, then fling themselves around the stage floor, typifies the explosive conjoining of lyrical and satirical attitudes that permeates the play. The human circle is accompanied first by a male voice singing the lyrics of the play's theme-song 'Viet Rock' and then by a taped voice that begins 'Things could be different. Nobody wins. We could be teams of losers.'

Following the opening circle of ***Viet Rock*** is an 'instant transformation' of the kind Terry employed in ***Calm Down Mother*** and ***Comings and Goings***: male actors become baby boys and female actors become mothers who then 'lovingly' undress the males down to their underclothes. Subsequent scenes relentlessly survey the variety of contexts that comprised the Vietnam war for Americans. We see army physicals, soldiers departing for Vietnam confronted by antiwar protesters, women burning in the final stages of death, soldiers parachuting into Vietnam and arriving mistakenly in 'Love's quicksand' in Shangri-La. The long central scene is set 'back home' at a US Senate hearing of the war that ends Act I with the ironic singing of 'America the Beautiful'.

Act II begins with the oral presentation of letters 'sent' between soldiers and the mothers back home. It then cuts, in Brechtian fashion, back to the American soldiers in Vietnam; male actors play the Americans, while female actors play South Vietnamese soldiers. At the end of the play, we are returned to an explosion and a circle, but this time the circle is tangled, 'the reverse of the beautiful circle of the opening image', and there is no sound but a 'deathly silence'.

Terry criticises war and the values that are a context for it. She misses no chance to note the sexism of the military: the Sergeant demeans his men deliberately by calling them 'girlies', the interchangeability of the weak is designated clearly by the casting of women as Vietnamese soldiers, and 'Mom' is perceived by the men as a correlative for sentiment. Because these gestures remind us that female attributes are commonly used derogatorily, they suggest a particularly feminist perspective.

Equally pertinent to the development of a feminist dramaturgy is the insistent sounding of song in this play. For Terry, as was the case for Bertolt Brecht, music renews the possibility of a poetic theatre, a theatre that at once engages and 'alienates' the audience. Here, and in some of her other plays, songs perform two apparently antithetical tasks: they transcend ordinary discourse through melody and metaphor while providing a frame in which the harshest sort of criticism can occur. Music intoxicates. It is capable of transforming not the actors but the audience. When that possibility is exploited as Terry and subsequent feminist dramatists rediscovered, it can be conjoined with words that lead us in our 'transformed' state to think differently about the world. It is thus difficult to refrain from singing 'America the Beautiful' at the end of Act I of ***Viet Rock***, but as we do so, it is equally hard to avoid recognition of the lie this war gave to that song.

The tension and public attention provoked by the productions of ***Viet Rock*** and *America Hurrah* led to significant changes in the Open Theatre's structure. The company abolished its assortment of workshops and, with the help of a Ford Foundation Grant, decided to focus all its work on one collaborative effort under Chaikin's direction. With this change of direction, Megan Terry gradually moved out on her own, writing, with increasingly precise language, dramas that unabashedly questioned the American dream and its corruption in the hands of the greedy and mendacious. The domineering male power structure loomed large in Terry's ***The People vs. Ranchman*** and ***Massachusetts Trust***, and women who were just beginning to address their position in American society welcomed these plays.

One of her most intriguing scripts from the late sixties was a television drama, ***Home***, produced in 1968 by public television. The play envisions a futuristic world in which overpopulation has created small, isolated, dense communities that live in tiny cubicles from birth to death. All groups are overseen by an external controlling power that regulates everything from food to reproduction. A rare instance of a drama fully conceived for video, ***Home***'s environment *is* its source of power and conflict. For the television production, fold-up beds were installed in walls, and one wall contained a large, circular television screen surrounded by cameras. Television and control were thus the medium and the message.

This apparent divergence from Terry's theatrical work retains many elements of her previous dramaturgy. While the characters remain constant throughout the ninety-minute production, the day is ritualistically divided into segments, and when Central Control commands, new activities are instantly initiated. Women dominate the internal space, both in number (of the nine onstage characters, five are female) and in the urgency of their presence. But power ultimately resides in the male voice of Central Control, and the 'intruder' who eventually penetrates the cubicle is a man. The play ends in a rock song, reminiscent of the final songs of both ***Viet Rock*** and ***Comings and Goings***.

Terry's next leap as a playwright came in 1969-70 with the creation of the Obie-award winning drama ***Approaching Simone***. The Simone of the title is Simone Weil, the French writer and martyr who starved herself to death in 1943 at the age of 34. Terry had been intrigued by Weil since she first came to know of her in the fifties. Her goal in writing the play, Terry told one Interviewer, was to place Simone's heroic spirit, her enormous will, in front of other women: '*Then* people will say, "My God, it *is* possible; women *are* free to do this and *can*."'

This focus on one complex, transcendent woman is unique among Terry's works, but the playwright's signature remains vivid in the deployment of the rest of the cast, an ensemble who repeatedly transform into characters from Simone's life and externalisations of Simone's pleasures and pain. Terry's architectural, episodic style lends itself well to a biographical drama, in which the epiphanic as well as the ordinary moments of Simone's life and death are equally embraced. Some of Weil's power lay in her own words and the poetry she loved, both of which Terry caresses in the play, but equally remarkable are the visual metaphors that evoke Simone's construction and destruction of herself. A familiar theatre exercise in which the entire company lifts one member takes on particular force in Act II when the entire cast suddenly appears to raise and caress Simone's body, which is wracked with both physical and spiritual agony. Each actor in the company removes and puts on a piece of Simone's clothing, in a haunting attempt to take on her pain. But no one can remove Simone's pain, and in the end the ensemble vanishes. Simone is left in a pinpoint of light that slowly, slowly fades to black.

Few theatrical images of the last twenty years have been as compelling as this last moment of ***Approaching Simone***, and, for the first time, critics were fully appreciative of Terry's success. Instead of exploiting this success to turn to commercial theatre, however, Terry joined with five other women playwrights in 1972 to form the Women's Theater Council. This group, which included Fornes, Drexler, Bovasso, Kennedy and Owens as well as Terry, came together to demonstrate the existence of feminist drama and to support each other as well as other playwrights in achieving productions of plays that arose from women's visions. As a formal body, the Council was short lived, but it did serve to establish a network that has continued into the 1980s.

For Terry, the establishment of the Women's Theater Council and its successor, the Theater Strategy Group, did not suffice as an environment in which to pursue her own commitments to an experimental, community-based theatre in which women could thrive. In 1968, one of Terry's colleagues from the Open Theatre, Jo Ann Schmidman, had returned to her native Omaha, Nebraska, where she had established a new more central, storefront theatre, the Omaha Magic Theatre (OMT). The goal of the theatre was to effect social change: 'We want to have an impact on the community of Omaha, Nebraska. We believe that change is possible here. There's responsiveness.' Terry visited the OMT in 1970, and thus began a lasting association with the company. By 1974, while productions of her plays were blossoming throughout the country, she had moved her resident to Omaha, where she has remained ever since as resident playwright.

An early aim of the OMT according to Terry and Schmidman was 'to crash some barriers for women'. But at first, the company, which was and remains open to anyone who wants to participate, attracted mostly male actors, writers and musicians. Then in 1974, following Terry's move to Omaha and perhaps because of the increasing force of the women's movement, the desired feminist orientation of the theatre began to be realised and OMT was able to focus on plays about women by women.

The play that served as one catalyst for this change was Terry's ***Babes in the Bighouse***, one of the first big successes of the OMT and one of Terry's most provocative dramas. Set in a woman's prison, ***Babes*** is a 'documentary musical fantasy' that interweaves clichéd public notions of life in a women's prison with documentary material drawn from prison interviews and visits. Songs and stories reveal the internal lives of the inmates. When the OMT performs the play, the audience is seated on at least two sides of the playing area; for the original production, audience members entered the theatre and were immediately confronted by brightly-coloured metal scaffolding arranged in two tiers to represent double-decker prison cells. The actors, who repeatedly transform from inmates to guards and matrons, address many of their speeches directly to the audience, and often more than one activity and discourse occur simultaneously. Despite moments of comic relief and the characteristic inclusion of song and dance, for the audience the experience of ***Babes in the Bighouse*** is undeniably troubling.

Throughout this play the prison world strains towards the audience, threatening yet reminding us that we are on the outside. The inmates first present themselves in a grotesque version of our projections of 'bad women': costumes for the opening utilise a wild mixture of corsets, feathers, long gloves, leather, spike heels and heavy make-up. The performers replace these costumes with simple housedresses and colourful band uniform jackets for most of the play, but the ambience of hostility of many kinds is sustained by the starkness and vulgarity of the language and the raw physical violence that repeatedly flashes or hints its presence. There is no comfort for the audience in the stripping of new inmates or the fight between two characters named El Toro and Jockey over the attentions of another prisoner. It is crucial, however, to ***Babes***'; intentions, that the most aggressive and distressing actions of the production are not predictable prison behaviours but are the stories the women tell us of their past and present anguish.

With ***Babes in the Bighouse,*** Terry's development of a distinctive feminist dramaturgy achieves a new force and cohesion. In a gesture similar to one Caryl Churchill would make in Britain a few years later, Terry and Schmidman cast men as well as women in the roles of the female prisoners and matrons, and by their own account this led the entire company to a more rigorous study of 'women's speech patterns, their physical and emotional behaviors and just how it is to be a woman.' Here, as with Churchill's *Cloud Nine*, there is no campiness or hidden grin in the performance of female roles by men; rather, we quickly accept from the all-female context of the women's prison that our perceptions of gender are based on social roles, gestures and styles.

Transformations also take on a more precise and fluid form in this play. According to the stage directions, the dominant dramatic image for ***Babes*** is 'How the Women Walk'. As spectators, we experience the walks of the performers as a continuous chord that permeates each scene. The walks serve as the occasion for transformations of one character to another, and they visually express the condition of being a woman 'in prison'. Changes in characters are facilitated and underlined by the physical rhythm of the walking movement itself.

Four years after writing ***Babes in the Bighouse***, during which time she had written and helped produce another six plays for the OMT, Terry turned her attention to another kind of prison for women, the more pervasive confinement of the English language. Entitled ***American King's English for Queens***, this 'musical in two acts' reveals the many sides of sexism in the uses and abuses of American English by a 'typical' American family. In the first act, we see the Connell family at home in their ordinary, daily rituals. The second act sharpens the focus and suggests new possibilities for a language of cooperation and genuine communication through the invasion of the family by Silver Morgan, a seventeen-year-old feral child.

The first hint we are given of the play's direction is a wonderfully funny yet tense scene in which Mom Connell insists, carelessly, on referring to a rabbit as 'he'. Jaimie, her young daughter, is confused and frustrated by the pronoun, because her mother's consistent reference to the rabbit as male contradicts her understanding that rabbits have lots of babies. Her mother never comes to appreciate the source of her daughter's distress, and Jaimie can only escape her confusion by asking 'If all the rabbits are boys, are all the cats girls?'

The most irritating character in the play is Dad who sets the drama's tones and tensions by his constant admonitions that his family must speak 'proper' English. For Dad, 'proper' means the absence of slang and the use of correct grammar, but he fails to see that within those rules language users make continuous decisions that shape the world in sexist terms. Dad does learn, however, and, by the end of the play, is able to ask 'Do you think like you talk?' The question is never explored in its philosophical intricacies, but it does lead the audience to agree that although language may initially define our humanness, the ways we use language determine what kinds of human beings we are and can be.

Like many of Terry's most recent plays, ***American King's English for Queens*** addresses central feminist issues in terms that are accessible to any spectator. On the page, these concerns sometimes seem simplistically articulated as when Susu, the oldest daughter, explains to her siblings that 'We'll have to think of a way we can teach her [Silver, the feral girl] to talk without making her feel that being a girl is not as good as being a boy.' But in performance, Terry's controlled use of dramatic conventions creates a more subtle context for the verbal statements. Transformations appear again, this time both to show different aspects of Mom's dreams and to demonstrate the changes in Silver Morgan. And the OMT's discovery of the possibilities of soft sculpture, of sets created out of the traditional female art of quilting, adds a meaningful, striking dimension to the spectator's experience.

American King's English for Queens is indicative of the kind of path that Terry and the OMT have taken in recent years and of one possible route for feminist theatre. This path is characterised by the desire to engage the largest possible community and to do so through lightly comic, colourful, song-filled confrontations with social problems that concern every American family. One of Terry's most recent dramas, ***Kegger***, pursues this route by confronting adolescent drinking; another OMT production, *Running Gag*, takes a number of light-hearted pokes at the current American obsession with jogging.

Neither of these plays directly addresses the economic and political structures that some feminists find it crucial to confront. For more than twenty years, Megan Terry has illuminated the lives of American women through her drama. Although she is a critic of sexism, violence, materialism and social corruption, her work does not call for a radical social revolution as much as it calls attention to the enormous strength she perceives in women, especially in the ability to will transformations. Hers is explicitly not a Marxist understanding of culture or society; in a distinctly American fashion, she protests inequality and injustice but does not analyse society in terms of class and economic oppression. But by utilising an ever-evolving set of feminist theatrical conventions and by putting in front of an audience a genuinely free ensemble that persistently emphasises the value of collaborative work and of women's work, Terry's dramas do suggest the possibility of transforming the texture if not the structure of everyday life. For Megan Terry, 'the real news is not that women are down, are victims, but that women are in good health and making it'. And at least in Omaha, Nebraska, feminist drama is in good health and making it, too.

Kathleen Gregory Klein (essay date 1984)

SOURCE: "Language and Meaning in Megan Terry's 1970s 'Musicals'," in *Modern Drama*, Vol. XXVII, No. 4, December, 1984, pp. 574-83.

[*In the following essay, Klein concentrates on the meaning and power of the language in Terry's musicals.*]

American King's English for Queens is the most clearly articulated of Megan Terry's language plays of the 1970s, explicitly concerned with the ways in which the text and context of language mold thinking, seeing, and believing. In four full-length plays, ***Tommy Allen Show, Babes in the Bighouse, Brazil Fado*** and ***American King's English for Queens***—all "musicals" performed at the Omaha Magic Theatre—although ostensibly savaging television, Middle American family life, marriage, sex, or prison, Terry challenges the perceptions molded by language itself and the clichés about language as a vehicle for communication. Whereas words seldom say what they mean, the reverse (that they mean what they say) is often true. What is conveyed between characters onstage, or between them and the audience, is seldom confined by either the connotative or denotative meanings of the words used; and yet these deliberately chosen words and phrases are capable of creating meaning for both speaker and auditor.

Using the notorious American snipe hunt as a metaphor in ***American King's English for Queens***, Terry identifies the parameters of language-meaning discourse. But action and reaction also create a context for meaning which either validates or rejects language's implications. Two features are vital to Terry's context for language: the transformations which illuminate the shifting realities purported to have acknowledged meanings; and the songs which redefine the circumstances of the characters and storyline seriously or mockingly. Unlike the absurdists, Terry does not investigate language to devalue it, nor meaning to abandon it, nor action to replace them both. Instead, all of her challenges testify her reluctance to allow the idea of meaninglessness to mask the uses made of language, action, and meaning.

From Martin Esslin's early appraisal of the absurdists to Ronald Hayman's 1979 summary of their efforts, critics, playwrights and directors alike have acknowledged that the last thirty years of drama have been primarily, not only antiart or antitheatre, but also antilanguage.[1] They posit the notion that it is impossible to communicate at all, by whatever means attempted; or that language is an unacceptable vehicle for successful communication; or that language communicates what the speaker had not meant; or, at best, that what language can communicate is extremely limited and probably not worth the attempt anyway. The most respected playwrights of our time have leaned toward minimization; some de-emphasize language to convey meaning through action, while others script both language and action in the most limited ways. Beckett's dramatic works quite clearly follow the latter pattern: in *Waiting for Godot*, language and movement frequently contradict each other, what had come before, or what was clear to the audience; in the later works, bodies are lost in urns or behind curtains, and brief, disconnected phrases (or even sounds and musical notes) replace comprehensible speech. Pinter is committed to the same reconsideration of communication, frequently allowing his characters a torrent of words, often emphasizing silences as strongly as the language which surrounds them: Pinter thinks of "talk" as covering over silence. In *Theatre and Anti-Theatre,* Hayman examines how, in the same period, three important directors—Peter Brook, Jerzy Grotowski, and Joseph Chaikin—turned away from language-meaning parallels.[2] Separately, these directors evolved practices which accommodated their beliefs that language, being culture specific, could not communicate as successfully as movement, more universal. In short, the absurdists and their successors seem to have perceived language (words, sentence structure, constructions) as meaningful to the speaker and the auditor—though seldom, if ever, having the same meaning. What they seem less willing to grant is the meaning accorded to language by social practice. Where this influence is acknowledged by the absurdists, it is used in ironic ways—e.g., greetings and other socially ritualistic exchanges in *Godot, Happy Days, The Birthday Party*—often recognized by the characters as well as the audience.

In the four full-length musicals named above, Terry admits that a speaker does not always say what she or he means, but does mean what she or he says: something is communicated by language. And in a structured world, socialized auditors recognize general language use as well as irony, clichés, and stereotypes to which they react.[3] These responses may have been conditioned by the social climate, and the word choice of the speaker or the verbal response of the listener may not actually correspond with what they believe themselves to be saying, but these factors do not lessen communication. Normal utterances, lacking the precision of poetry's language choice, expand rather than contract the range of communication, especially when joined with action rather than separated from it.

For most speakers and listeners, language (i.e., a word for something) defines, identifies, or places an object so that it can be discussed without consideration of what the word means in any precise way. For example, the female human being may be identified by either of two terms—"woman" or "girl"—which distinguishes one from the other by differences in age; however, ordinary usage does not differentiate them that way, as is obvious when a group of middle-aged women is called "the girls." In more ordinary use, terms like "lady," which has overtones relating to behavior, or "gal," which is both the female equivalent of "guy" and a frequent variant of "girl," carry their overtones implicitly from speaker to listener. Neither they nor the audience are aware of these meanings, treating them as natural extensions of the terms requiring no explicit acknowledgment.

American King's English for Queens poses a series of questions about language and gender; its form and impact are basically feminist. "What is the difference between boys and girls or women and men?" leads to "What is appropriate behavior for these sex-differentiated people?" and culminates in "What is the social place for girls and boys or men and women?" "English is such an expressive language," Silver Morgan says in the play's first scene.[4] The all-American family, the Connells, have captured her in a snipe hunt from the prairie-dog town where she was raised. The great snipe-hunt fantasy serves here to define the limits of language and its meaning. If there is no such animal as a snipe, as we know, then the Connell children cannot find one; but whatever is captured on a snipe hunt must obviously be a snipe. Played by a woman, Silver looks like a woman; conditioned by her upbringing, she thinks she is a prairie dog; but described as the "only one in captivity" (p. 51) and worth "at least twenty-five thousand, if not a hundred million" (p. 72), she/it must be a snipe. The family response to Silver Morgan arises not from what they see or think, but from what they call her.

This process of eliciting meaning from the words used to talk about something dominates the Connells. The only boy in the family, Doug refuses to play a careers game with his sisters because he might have to be a ballerina or stewardess. When he draws cards for "good personality" or "bad makeup," he is threatened by the careers his sisters propose: nurse, teacher, or model. The "simple game" becomes a "stupid girl's game" as his rejection of the game becomes a rejection of all girls with whom he associates stupidity and criticism: "Girls are crazy! Girls are crazy! Lazy-crazy!" (p. 29). Doug and his father consistently distinguish the household by gender:

> DAD: You women outnumber us five to two. (p. 72)
>
> DOUG: But two men against five women? (p. 73)

Yet eleven-year-old Katie proposes that they are "seven human beings" (p. 73), although Doug is not sure: "Are we human beings and men too?" (p. 73). Both men acquiesce slowly and reluctantly to this dual status and the proposed team effort of raising Silver Morgan. Dad's earlier lyrics associating "you sissies, girls and dinks / Couldn't shoot a chink in a holler. . . ." (p. 45) show how he feels about girls by the ways he names them: they join the apparently prejudice-free term "girls" with the highly charged, pejorative terms "sissy," "dink," and "chink," so that "girl" is no longer a value-neutral term. Because this is true, Dad must teach Doug how to behave like a man:

> Now here is the way a man stands.
>
> You must hold yourself like a man. (DOUG *follows too literally and holds his crotch.*)
>
> You protect your sisters.
>
> Men don't cry. If you cry I'll make you wear your sisters' clothes to school. Good . . . good . . . You look cool! (pp. 37-39)

Men's behavior is seen as a function of what they are called: Doug is a boy at nine years old, but when called a "man," he can *be* one. Crucial to the meaning of "man" is its negative, i.e., not-girl, the ultimate degradation. Not only Doug acknowledges what Dad is teaching him, but Mom and his sisters recognize the same connotations surrounding the terms "man" and "girl," reacting at one point by inverting them to "boys" and "women." Simply as a result of this name change, the females feel stronger and more unified while the males feel threatened.

This assignment of meaning occurs in the transformations as words are given visual reality. When Mom sings about her lost life while chopping stew vegetables, she is trapped by a net the full width of the stage:

> Somewhere in this murk of me
>
> There really may still lurk a me
>
> Who's free
>
> (*Kids drape a net over* MOM'*s head and hold ends like ladies-in-waiting.*)
>
> What is she like?
>
> And where did she go
>
> For the last twenty years or so?
>
> (*Kids spin* MOM *in net, beat her with vegetables.*) (p. 29)

Trapped in her own stew, Mom gets stuffed with a carrot and tormented with celery. The limits on her life, her imagination, and her opportunities are presented more clearly to the audience than to the characters; their impact is clear and direct. Here, action is meaning.

Babes in the Bighouse, set in a women's prison, uses all the B-movie implications of its title directly and in reverse. Notably, the tension between prisoners and guards is diluted by visitors from the community who are urged to rethink their attitudes about the institution and disregard some of the prisoners' complaints because of so-called changes in the system:

> I want to welcome you to our campus. I think some of you may have noticed the new sign just to the right of the front gate: "Women's State Correctional Facility." The legislature was kind enough to vote us a new name *this* year and we were able to paint a new sign with the materials left over from repairing our "Adjustment Center." In the dark ages of penology, there *was* a place where inmates were confined for punishment, which our charges referred to as "solitary confinement," or euphemistically, as "the hole." But since the sociological-anthropo-sensitivity-psychiatric revolution has brought us into this new age of enlightenment—and thus more humane treatment geared toward rehabilitation—what *used* to be called "the hole" is now a gaily painted place where inmates who may be feeling upset may go to meditate—alone—away from the *hubbub* of correctional life.[5]

But the prisoners are not confused by talk; nor are the audience, having already been told by one of the inmates:

> They got a hole in here—they call it "The Adjustment Center." They want everything here to sound like a hospital or a school so you'll think that with a new name somethin's changed around here. No matter how many times they call it a "campus," this place is still a joint. (I, 1)

Because they understand the rules, the prisoners also recognize how to avoid them. Since reading aloud from a dirty book is forbidden, they mock the regulations by proposing to circumvent them: Jockey offers to "croon a dirty book to you. They couldn't take it away, hey? No, there'd be nothing for 'em to confiscate. Nothing to go against me in my file for the parole board, because it would go right out into the air" (II, 32). This strategy reverses the previous notions of language and meaning whereby saying makes it so; in this case, "saying" goes right out into the air because regulations acknowledge written words as though the obscenity were in either the writing down or the reading rather than the action described. (It is ironic that in this lesbian setting the sexual aggressor in Jockey's dirty book is male and the narrative directly parallels those in *Playboy* or erotic romances.)

The play consistently stresses the confusion among language, behavior, and meaning which the authority figures and the prisoners manipulate. Language is a weapon in the hands of both. Having just refused a new prisoner's correction of her name in the records from Bessie to Betsy, the Matron calls roll to which each inmate responds: "Mamie Eisenhower . . . Ida Lupino . . . Happy Ford . . . Betty Rockefeller . . . Tricia Diet-Rite . . . Amy Carter . . . Marlena Dexadrine" (II, 2-3). Emphasizing her arrogant stance, a prisoner later turns aside the Matron's entrapping question "When did you stop engaging in homosexual behavior?" with a twist on the question's classic form: "When I stopped beating my husband" (II, 19). As they comprehend the power struggle between themselves, both groups try to hold an advantage through language as well as action.

The operational defining of the term "lady" appears half-a-dozen times in the play. Like its extended form "Christian ladies," the word is used by the guards to categorize approved behavior they hope to promote. "Ladies," apparently by definition, do not act smart, do get respect; they do not fight like men, do have their hair curled at a beauty parlor. Viciously the Doctor, who had injected one angry prisoner with a muscle relaxant which affects breathing, identifies the term: "Do you promise you will become a feminine person, demure and self-controlled? To smile whenever you see me walk by? To control your temper and learn to walk like a sexy woman?" (II, 27). In short, a "lady" is exactly what two inmates had previously claimed—"a prostitute." This emphasis on isolated bits of behavior, while different from the standard, societally accepted definition, nonetheless focuses on the same aspect—behavior which restricts the ways in which women can act. It becomes clear that this redefinition is a feature of the prison authority's lexicon when an inmate, wanting to shower more than once a week, appeals to the "ladylike" nature of her request. She is ignored. Her listeners know exactly what they understand the term to mean; all other definitions, especially by prisoners, can be disregarded.

In this play, transformations illuminate meaning for the audience as the actors become one another, shifting from prisoner to guard to visitor, and being treated by others onstage or behaving themselves according to the parts they play: they become what they are named. No one needs to have the precise natures of the terms "guard" or "prisoner" explained to her; even the audience share the social meanings of these terms automatically. Through the transformations, the actors and audience participate in the apparently different but essentially limited roles available to women in the Bighouse. Because no fixed identity is attached to any actor or character, the woman becomes the women. Their survival and satisfaction are group functions; each relies implicitly and explicitly on the others; each knows that she can rely on the others' recognition of her identity and its meaning.

Transformations like those of ***Babes*** and the split-stage presentation of ***Brazil Fado*** elaborate more clearly than specific language the meaning of the latter work. Two scenes play simultaneously: one, in an American bedroom, is a bizarre sex scene with sadomasochistic components juxtaposed against the second, in a Brazilian TV station, with news reporters broadcasting information about political repression in Brazil. The dramatic irony resulting from the audience's simultaneous awareness of both and the effect of secondary dialogue provide meaning as a counterpoint to language. While armed Brazilian police brutally beat a local family on one stage, the American couple, Danielle and Barton, move toward sexual orgasm as he whips her with the head of a mop and tantalizes her with a rubber shower attachment on the other stage. Abruptly, she insists, "It's gross."[6] She is referring neither to the torture nor to the sexual activity, however, but to her unbreakable habit of chewing on her lips. The contrast between the lovers' routine and the reports of torture unrealistically sung in a Carmen Miranda style makes both appear ludicrous and serious.

The "newscasters" are continually transformed into Fred Astaire and Ginger Rogers dancing a tango, the stereotyped Latin spitfire Carmen Miranda, the Bride of Frankenstein, brutal police, cowed peasants, corporate spokespersons, tortured prisoners, pornography salespersons, guerrillas, or government officials. With as few as four actors playing all these roles, the frequency of the transformations keeps the audience from settling into any familiar pattern of expectation. This unpredictability adds to the impact of the statements made by the various characters; they are simultaneously more and less shocking and believable. The transformations also give the newscasters opportunity to overuse the jargon of each group (identified by language choices, clothing, and behavior). The Finance Minister rationalizes in governmentalese:

> The use of torture is very prejudicial to our world-wide economic progress and the improvement of our financial system. . . . We believe that economic expansion will solve our internal social problems, but to bring this about, we still need three or four years of social stability at home. (p. 16)

The educational jargon is equally contrived:

> This statement I want to share with you children, comes from a primary resource group of what are known in the adult world as "political prisoners." (p. 17)

The business world, smothered in style rather than interested in content, is similarly structured:

> (*Warm Announcer Approach*) This is the only time the sponsors will interrupt this program about the terrible things going on in Brazil. We feel it's more important for you the public to be aware of the terrible tortures going on in Brazil than to be interrupted all the time by commercial messages. We'll keep our message short as a riding crop, tight as a bit in your teeth. (pp. 20-21)

The advertisement which follows, juxtaposed with Barton and Danielle's continued sexual activity, is for "*Obedience,* an S and M extravaganza. . . . Humiliation, spanking, bondage, only fifty dollars for a six-month trial offer" (p. 21). The melodies used to sing reports of death and torture are light and upbeat, contradicting the words used; the groups' jargon and clichés are persistently used. "*Newscasters . . . march upstage left on hands and feet, bellies up, like ants and sing*":

> They'll never call me Nero
> (*March in Place*) In my country's uniform.
> (*March Left*) When I turn the thumbscrew
> I do so as a hero. (p. 31)

When one newscaster challenges another about their reports, she is told: "If I listened to what I read, I might respond, and if I responded I would get angry, and then I would get depressed that I couldn't do anything about it, and then I would get exhausted, and face would get puffy. I would look terrible on camera. I would lose my job" (p. 30). If people do think as they talk rather than the reverse, as proposed in ***American King's English for Queens***, then the newscasters seem to be clinging to jargon and scoobedo to keep from acknowledging the meaning of what they are saying.

The power of language is clearly recognized by this repressive dictatorship; censorship is one of its primary aims. Reports of seized letters being written to the Free World by political prisoners are themselves cut off. Censored newspapers are filling their blank columns with poetry. "Thus all Brazilians enjoy classical culture with . . . what's left of the news . . . I mean what's right with the news . . . rather, the news that's fit to . . . still be in print" (p. 10), according to a news announcer transformed to a terrorist with a paper bag over his head. Despite all this, the barrage of information directed at the audience through language and movement, delivered by a rapidly transforming cast, is unmistakable and obvious in its meaning.

Terry clearly recognizes the role of television in contemporary life and the fascination of Americans' response. As a molder of ideas and reactions, an influence on attitudes, it outdistances all other media. Its pronouncements, entertainment, and very existence are accepted with seriousness. The earliest of these four plays, ***Tommy Allen Show***, is a superb parody of every TV talk show ever produced in America. There are four Tommy Allens (one woman, two men, and two people in a horse costume), multiple announcers, guests named Mrs. Assbite and Child Molester, and commercials for Avon's "Pussy Off," the Trinity, and the High Heaven Heroin Company. Its plug is aimed at a growing audience:

> And for the kids, try our Johnny Junkie Kit, with a complete set of toy works, black jack, rubber tube, monogrammed spoon, and a little pink pail to throw up in. . . . Ages three to six. For the girls, needles and heroin bags for Barbie and Ken, and a little prostitute outfit for Barbie when she has to support Ken's habit, and a drag costume for Ken when Barbie is too sick to stroll. Remember, buy your junk only from authorized dealers of the High Heaven Heroin Company.[7]

Nothing escapes commercialization and the hard sell. To "quit," "sleep more," or "dream/escape," Tommy Allen 1 fantasizes aloud as a "commercial for his dreams" plays in the movie area of the studio, showing him in a nightshirt, using stylized gestures, running through a forest, between trees, and into a lake. His fantasy is making love, gathering plastic bottles from the beach, learning to take out the garbage, and finally, smiling angelically while he is beaten by police with billy clubs. Announcer 3, who cannot believe Tommy 1 would want to escape "(*pointing to the audience*) All this," tries to interrupt the dream fantasy by calling his name; he is helped by Tommy 2's question: "What's the best way to get the crud out of your belly button?" Interrupting his dream program, Tommy 1 delivers the answer in his "best commercial selling voice," concluding with the standard plea: "Don't go away folks, we'll be right back." As the fantasy ends—"Hello, folks, we're back"—Tommy 1's dream is reduced from whatever meaning it might have had for him or others to a device filled with nonsequential, unrelated attention-grabbing statements designed to elicit an immediate, if empty, sense of identification or response from the audience both in the studio and at home (p. 44). Parodying the American dream fantasy, the ***Show*** demonstrates how easily images and language manipulate the listeners.

The ***Show*** suggests that people are often dragged along by the force and flow of words rather than using language thoughtfully, that language and meaning can exist in the public sphere as though unassociated with their speakers or creators. The television commercials, selling either "good" or "evil," have this kind of independent life, even as "real" TV commercials tout the typical and normal American family as consisting of male and female parents with two or three children (some of each sex) while statistics demonstrate that fewer than ten percent of American families fit this norm: the autonomous meaning of TV advertising's words and actions convinces ninety percent of the population that it is unusual. The ubiquitous "informed source," "unnamed spokesperson," or "highly placed official" of contemporary news releases is a speaker similarly separated from the language and meaning attributed to her or him.

Tommy 3, who first sings in imitation of Streisand, Dietrich, and Garland, and plays with her microphone like

Tina Turner, begins her monologue by acknowledging the relationship between thinking and speaking. When she meets people, her conversation switches to certain automatic responses; she talks but does not think. This habit has led her to more than the boredom she admits; she has apparently forgotten how to think. Because the social exchanges of "how was your day?, how was school?, etc." (p. 45) fit so many situations, she has been able to convey greeting, interest, concern or friendship to a listener as conditioned by language conventions as she. When Tommy 3 tries to explain how she began to think and to notice what was around her, she is interrupted by the TV laugh track at points which make a potentially serious comment merely laughable. Hearing the laugh track, the audience are supposed to assume that her monologue—like its standard late-night model—is an extended joke. Whether they see the humor or not, they laugh: no one wants to be singled out as the one who missed the punch line when laughter indicates apparent understanding of the apparent joke.

Television's lunacy is easily parodied; it is separate from life's, yet reflects it while claiming to represent it. These three positions of outside, reverse, and duplicate are often mistaken for the thing which is rather than the thing which is as it is. So too with language. Obviously, words do not exist in a vacuum; they have a societal status, are rarely idiosyncratic for speaker or listener, and often mean what the speaker would not acknowledge having said. Both spoken and heard, of course, they have the capacity to influence those who use them. Communication, however defined, is achieved through language as well as through action; people mean what they say, even when they do not realize it. Language with its various auras influences individual and societal behavior. As Terry's musicals insist, it is never without meaning or power.

Notes

1. Martin Esslin, *The Theatre of the Absurd*, rev. ed. (Woodstock, N.Y., 1973).
2. Ronald Hayman, *Theatre and Anti-Theatre: New Movements Since Beckett* (New York, 1979).
3. See such extensions of the Whorf-Sapir position as Anthony Wootton, *Dilemmas of Discourse* (New York, 1976), an examination of sociological interpretations of language; or M.A.K. Halliday, *Language as Social Semiotic* (Baltimore, 1978), on the social interpretation of language and meaning.
4. Megan Terry, *American King's English for Queens* (Omaha, c. 1978), p. 3; hereafter cited parenthetically in the text.
5. Megan Terry, *Babes in the Bighouse* (Omaha, c. 1984), Act I, pp. 4-5; hereafter cited parenthetically in the text.
6. Megan Terry, *Brazil Fado* (Omaha, c. 1978), p. 9; hereafter cited parenthetically in the text.
7. Megan Terry, *The Tommy Allen Show*, in *Scripts*, 2 (December 1971), 37-61, passage from 41; hereafter cited parenthetically in the text.

June Schlueter (essay date 1987)

SOURCE: "*Keep Tightly Closed in a Cool Dry Place*: Megan Terry's Transformational Drama and the Possibilities of Self," in *Studies in American Drama, 1945-Present*, Vol. 2, 1987, pp. 59-69.

[*In the following essay, Schlueter discusses how Terry's transformational drama acknowledges the extent to which the self is shaped by modern culture.*]

> In order "to make it," we need to make images of ourselves. We compose ourselves from the cultural models around us. We are programmed into a status hunger. Once we have masked ourselves with the social image suitable to a type, we enter the masquerade of the setup. Even the masquerade of our ethnic and sex roles permeates our life so thoroughly that many of us are afraid to give them up. In giving them up we fear we would be giving up our identity, and even life itself.
>
> (Chaikin 13)

Joseph Chaikin's comment represents part of his response to what he and others involved in the Open Theatre of the 1960s called the "setup." In advertising for an "ingenue," a "leading lady," a "character actress," a "male juvenile character," and so on, trade papers reflected a disturbing coincidence between theatre and society: both based their vocabulary of character on the stereotype. Both assumed there were "fixed ways of telling one person from another" and found security in institutionalizing that assumption. As a consequence, Chaikin points out, "Each element of the societal [or theatrical] disguise, the acceptable image, can be assessed on an almost absolute and exploitative scale of values: 'It is better to be Caucasian'; 'it is better to be heterosexual and male'; 'it is better to be rich'; 'it is better to be Protestant'" (12-14).

Megan Terry's early transformation plays—***Eat at Joe's, Calm Down Mother, Keep Tightly Closed in a Cool Dry Place, Comings and Goings***, and ***Viet Rock***—represent a further response of the Open to the "setup." Abjuring the rigidity of appointed and anointed roles, the Open made transformational drama a staple of its early repertory, creating theatrical exercises and plays in which actors shifted freely and suddenly from one character, situation, time, or objective to another. As Terry's colleague Peter Feldman put it, "Whatever realities are established at the beginning are destroyed after a few minutes and replaced by others. Then these are in turn destroyed and replaced" (201). From the perspective of two decades of subsequent theatre, it should now be clear that Terry's work with transformation challenged more than the individual actor seeking versatility and range. In freeing the actor from the prescriptiveness of the assigned role, transformational drama challenged the prevailing character of realistic theatre, which reinforced social and theatrical expectations. Terry's work in neutralizing fixed assumptions, dismantling the stereotype, and reevaluating the institutional hierarchy proved seminal in forming emerging principles and modes of New York's alternative theatre.

Chief among these emerging principles was Off-Broadway's conception of character. Until Beckett's *Waiting for Godot* startled Broadway in 1956; until Joseph Cino opened the Cafe Cino in 1958; until the Becks went public with the Living Theatre in 1959, with Jack Gelber's *The Connection*; until Edward Albee turned to playwriting, staging *The Zoo Story* in New York in 1960; until Ellen Stewart opened La Mama in 1962; and until the Open Theatre became a presence in 1963, the prevailing mode of American drama was realism. The principle of construction was the cause-and-effect relationship, the plot proceeding neatly through units of action that raised a dramatic question, satisfied that question, and raised another, even as a dominant dramatic question sustained itself throughout the play. Character became clear through motive, often discovered in a past event that justified a character's present perversions. The social-psychological-moral paradigm pursued by Ibsen in *A Doll House* and *Ghosts* remained the model for serious postwar American drama, which placed its faith in causality and its attendant claims.

Modern American drama took little notice of Pirandello's radical assault on the theatre in 1923, when *Six Characters in Search of an Author* rocked its Paris audience and changed Europe's theatrical vocabulary. In his 1953 study of *"Modernism" in Modern Drama*, Joseph Wood Krutch needed only to append a brief chapter on American drama, asking how modern it was, even while he was expressing moral outrage over Pirandello. The Italian playwright, he argued, of all the moderns, made "the most inclusive denial of all, namely, the denial that the persistent and more or less consistent character or personality which we attribute to each individual human being, and especially to ourselves, really exists at all" (77). For Krutch, the "dissolution of the ego" that Pirandello's plays present obviated all moral systems, "since obviously no one can be good or bad, guilty or innocent, unless he exists as some sort of continuous unity" (78).

Krutch's reaction might well be justified if one assumes the moral function of theatre, in which case consistency, plausibility, and growth are all essential elements of the continuous self. But a play, as Megan Terry and others have shown, might also be designed to play with the epistemological question of how the self takes form, without identifying a self that is morally accountable, psychologically consistent, or socially defined.

Transformational drama acknowledges the multiple and shifting selves that at any moment or collection of moments constitute a developing self, placing that composite in a context that is itself shifting. The consequence is a drama of perception analogous to a Picasso painting of a woman's profile seen in the same canvas as the woman's frontal view. Neither has priority, neither negates the other, both suggest the complexity of the dynamic process that we can only tentatively call the self. Moreover, transformational drama acknowledges the extent to which the modern self is shaped by popular culture—advertising, movies, fictional heroes, romanticized history, TV commercials—the stereotypes provided by the media that steal into ordinary lives and shape expectations. In its involvement with media propaganda as the living artifacts of our culture, transformational drama becomes a kind of found art, a collage of the objects that incipiently form, reform, and transform models of self. And, finally, though transformational drama of necessity negates Krutch's concept of an identifiable and continuous self, it curiously affirms the relationships between self and others that Krutch's more traditional analysis of character would also assert. As Feldman points out in his "Notes for the Open Theatre Production," rehearsals for ***Keep Tightly Closed*** began with improvisations dealing with "dependency, enclosure and isolation" (199). And as Bonnie Marranca notes in her study of *American Playwrights*, ***Keep Tightly Closed*** explores "confinement, dependency, domination-submission, ritual, friendship, deprivation, and loneliness" (185). Terry's approach to these relationships is, of course, different from Ibsen's, but, like realistic drama, it affirms the invariables of human experience. Unlike the dominant paradigm, however, transformational drama accommodates and affirms the variables as well.

Any of Terry's transformation plays might serve to illustrate the Open's contribution to redefining dramatic character, though her technique is not always the same. In ***Comings and Goings***, randomly selected actors replace other actors, often in mid-sentence, and are themselves replaced, continually subverting the identification of actor and character or of audience and character. In ***Calm Down Mother***, three actresses assume changing roles, becoming first one character and then another. In ***Viet Rock***, the technique, as Richard Schechner describes it, is variously employed: "In the opening scene the actors become, in rapid sequence, a human, primordial flower, mothers and infants, army doctors and inductees, inductees and mothers. In the Senate Hearing scene actors replace other actors within the framework of a single scene" (16). In ***Keep Tightly Closed in a Cool Dry Place***, not only do the three inmates change into other characters as the play progresses, but the situation being dramatized changes as well. Schechner sees Terry's techniques in ***Keep Tightly Closed*** as accomplishing three functions: "They explode a routine situation into a set of exciting theatrical images; they reinforce, expand, and explore the varieties of relationships among the three men; they make concrete the fantasies of the prisoners" (13). It is this play, mounted at the Open Theatre in 1965 in a double bill with ***Calm Down Mother***, that I find most diverse, most fascinating, and most representative of the potential and the impact that Terry's work with transformational drama has had on the American theatre. I would like to look at the transformations in that play more closely and then offer some comments on Terry's contribution to off-Broadway's redefinition of the definition of self.

Keep Tightly Closed in a Cool Dry Place, like all transformation plays, does not ask its actors to find some coincidence between themselves and the characters they are portraying, nor does it ask its actors to create subtexts.

In place of this psychological work, it offers a sequence of opportunities for verbal and nonverbal behavior, each involving an abrupt shift in roles. Transformational drama is clearly both a challenge and an opportunity for the actor wanting to see himself or herself not as a trade magazine type but as an actor capable of moving with facility among diverse roles. Yet transformational drama is not simply "for the actors," as Gerald Weales suggests in his unappreciative assessment of Terry's work (240). Transformational drama, like all drama, is for the audience, whose response to the abrupt changes the form demands helps create this alternative model of presenting dramatic character, one that says more about the epistemology of character, onstage and off, than realistic drama can.

The three men who share a prison cell in ***Keep Tightly Closed***, all sentenced for their part in the collective murder of Jaspers's wife, provide a centering situation—not necessary for transformational drama but immensely effective here. Jaspers, an attorney in his thirties, hired Michaels to hire Gregory to murder his wife so he could collect half a million dollars in insurance payoffs. Though Gregory accomplished the deed, he was apprehended, offering a confession that implicated the other two as well. Now cellmates, Michaels has taken refuge in illness, Gregory in dreams and orgasms, and Jaspers is restless and angry. Though confined as the other two are, the lawyer still attempts to exercise his authority and to employ whatever strategy might help him get free. He bullies Michaels into agreeing to torture Gregory. When Michaels frustrates Gregory by repeating everything he says, Jaspers offers calculated comfort, advising the humiliated man not to sign the confession when he is upset. Still later, he contrives to get Gregory to join him in persuading Michaels to confess.

As the drama of Jaspers's power struggle progresses, the three remind themselves of the circumstances that led to their incarceration. At one point, Jaspers assumes the role of prosecuting attorney/judge/arresting officer, interrogating Gregory and attempting to reshape the arrest and trial into the scenario he would have liked to see. The three speak of the murder, reproaching and comforting one another, and Gregory tells stories: one of a dream he had of raping a woman, the other a fantasy of a woman who swallowed a snake's egg and was eaten away inside by the snake. Though arranged with no special respect for chronology or causality, each of the episodes in the centering situation contributes to the audience's conception of the three cellmates: Jaspers is arrogant, authoritative, angry. Michaels, a server rather than a leader, is burdened by conscience and compassion. Gregory is a weak but dangerous sexually-preoccupied underling.

But if presentation of the socially-psychologically-morally recognizable character were all transformational drama achieved, it would be indistinguishable in effect from realistic drama. What is special about transformational drama is that it provides multiple perspectives through providing alternate situations and roles. In ***Keep Tightly Closed***, the centering situation, which itself admits recollection, wishful thinking, and fantasy, is punctuated repeatedly by actions among other characters outside the cell, played by the same three actors. Hence at one point Jaspers becomes General Custer, Michael a bluecoat, and Gregory their Indian victim. At another, the three become characters in a Jamestown drama, with a dying fifteen-year-old begging for water from Captain Smith. In one especially chilling vignette, Gregory recreates the moments in Jaspers's kitchen immediately preceding the crime, while Jaspers becomes his soon-to-be-murdered wife and Michaels his eight-year-old son. Three times, the trio become mechanical devices, and in one sequence they are transformed into a vaudeville trio, drag queens, and movie gangsters.

In none of the transformations is an audience to see the three as Rosalind playing Ganymede playing Rosalind (Shakespeare, *As You Like It*) or Solange playing Claire while Claire plays Madam (Genet, *The Maids*), even when Gregory as the murderer replays the kitchen drama. For each transformation, the three actors, not the characters, assume different roles or join in the mechanical representation of a container, a lead pencil, and a labeling machine—all identifiable through the prescriptions and restrictions spoken by the actors. Even if the transformation is completely convincing, however, and the audience understands that Jaspers is not General Custer or the dying boy but that the actor has merely shifted roles, its perception of character changes in a number of ways. For one thing, as Chaikin points out, the wearing of a disguise affects the actor: "In former times acting simply meant putting on a disguise. When you took off the disguise, there was the old face under it. Now it's clear that the wearing of the disguise changes the person. As he takes the disguise off, his face is changed from having worn it" (6). The face that is changed from having worn the disguise is the face the audience sees. Though an audience understands that it is not Jaspers who is playing General Custer but an actor shifting roles, the afterimage of the character that actor has just played necessarily informs the next. Hence an audience's perception of Custer is affected by the afterimage of Jaspers, and the afterimage of Custer, in turn, changes the audience's perception of Jaspers. As the actor who plays Jaspers assumes other roles as well, the layering multiples: images and afterimages combine in a densely layered portrait that challenges the clear, sharp outlines of the realistically drawn face.

Moreover, as it is creating the Picasso face, transformational drama is also engaging, even exploiting, the special double vision that an audience brings to every theatrical experience. While the transformation requires the actor to abandon one role for another, at the same time it plays on the knowledge that an audience never achieves the same abandonment. Though willing by convention to believe the masquerade and to enter the fiction of the play, an audience watching Olivier playing Lear never forgets that it is watching both Olivier and Lear. Nor do recidivist playgoers discard their recollection of Olivier playing Hamlet when they watch Olivier playing Lear or, for that matter, their image of Olivier playing Hamlet when they watch Jacobi in that role. Transformational drama demands that the audience not only be aware of the multiplicity of selves generated by a multiplicity of roles but that it become an active participant in the process of definition and redefinition that never ends.

Were we talking of ***Comings and Goings***, which shifts arbitrarily from one situation to the next and randomly appoints actors to assume specific roles, we might stop our discussion here, without attention to context. But ***Keep Tightly Closed*** presents a nuclear trio of characters whose prison experience is central to the play. Given this centering situation, it is safe to assume that Terry's choices of transformations in ***Keep Tightly Closed*** are not random but are chosen for their specific content to contribute both to an audience's perception of Jaspers, Michaels, and Gregory and to its understanding of how character takes form. In shifting to the situation with Custer, a bluecoat, and a redskin, for example, Terry provides a vignette that might well have served as a subtext or a preparatory improvisation for the trio had the group been operating under the Method. Jaspers—arrogant, authoritative—changes into the General, "buckles on sword, tips hat forward, climbs on horse, gallops in circle, comes back to Michaels," and commands; "Tie that redskin up." Michaels, who followed Jaspers's orders in securing a hired murderer, now changes into the obedient bluecoat, responding with a "Yes, sir!" Gregory, who is about to be interrogated by Jaspers and coerced into signing a confession, becomes the Indian, laughing derisively and refusing to sign the treaty even when tortured (163-4). Or Jaspers, exhausted from Gregory's refusal to sign, becomes a fifteen-year-old dying in Jamestown: "Please, water . . . a taste . . . only one . . . then I'll ask for nothing more . . . a drop. . . ." The others take verbal jabs at the absent Captain Smith, creating a portrait of a hellish old "piss-pot"—not unlike Michaels's and Gregory's perception of Jaspers—and cursing the day they "signed on this voyage." As the lad's life fades, Gregory becomes Captain Smith, assuming the position of authority figure and father (173-4). In both cases, history provides an analogy that works through association of the relationships and emotions of the past with those of the present. In this duo of vignettes, the actor (and, by association, Jaspers) becomes both father and son, tormentor and tormented, the dominant figure and the submissive one.

If history provides a subtext for the centering situation, so also do the collection of offbeat characters recognizable to any contemporary audience: the vaudeville trio, drag queens, and gangsters. Earlier I spoke of how at times the prisoners discuss and act out events of the recent past, sometimes reshaping them in response to their needs, and how Gregory, when encouraged by Michaels, speaks of his dream and, on his own initiative, tells the story of the woman whom an interior snake emaciated and killed. In describing two of the play's alternate situations—the General Custer and Captain vignettes—I spoke of shifting situations and roles, in which the audience is asked to think of the historical characters and relationships in the context of the centering situation and the characters and relationships of the centering situation in the context of the historical vignettes. When, halfway through the drama, Terry has the actors wrap themselves in a prison blanket, lock arms, and break into a song and dance, then shift into a vignette as drag queens, then into one as gangsters, she is introducing another order of transformation, one that crosses the line between the centering situation and the alternate situation through more than analogy. In these vignettes, the actors retain their identities as Jaspers, Michaels, and Gregory even as they engage in the transformation, so that style and tone reflect the drag queen or gangster even as content betrays their prison identities. The shift between role playing and transformation is subtle and ill defined, a tactic that requires the audience to think of the three cellmates at the same time it is thinking of the offbeat figures.

Here again, we have relationships similar to those profiled in the historical vignettes: Jaspers becomes the dominant queen; joined by Michaels, he torments Gregory, who tries to swallow an embarrassing love note. But "Swinging Woolf's" love note was "sent to this cell" (179), apparently by a prisoner, or perhaps by a guard, attracted to one of the three cellmates. In the gangster vignette, Michaels's movie gangster discusses his seduction of Gregory's movie gangster as he primed him for the murder assignment. To Michaels's gangster's "I buy lots of slobs drinks when I want a few laughs," Gregory's gangster, or Gregory, replies, "Some laugh. You're in for life for a few laughs. You aren't laughing now" (180).

These offbeat vignettes comment as well on the peculiar way in which a uniquely modern character, both national and individual, takes form. These products of Hollywood—singers and dancers, drag queens, and movie gangsters—are merely another part of the propaganda machine that advertises for an ingenue or a leading lady. These seemingly harmless representations of humanity are surface rather than substance, which, through mass dissemination, acquire legitimacy of form. Terry's introduction of these recognizable pieces of Hollywood celluloid wrenches us away from the individual confinement of the prisoners and reminds us of the social and personal confinements that media stereotyping prescribes.

The culminating vignette of the play, in which Jaspers becomes a preacher, his cellmates altar boys, and then the three become father and sons, brings together the centering situation, the transformation vignettes, and the vignettes in which role playing and transformation are difficult to divide. Having just tried to persuade Gregory to help him get Michaels to confess, the actor playing Jaspers, or Jaspers, changes abruptly into a preacher, speaking before a congregation about a man "in our midst" (194) accused of murdering his wife. After delivering an exhausting sermon that warns the congregation of impending losses and urges community as a countering strength, the preacher collapses into the arms of Michaels and Gregory, who become Jaspers's eight-year-old son, Richard, and his ten-year-old, Mark. Both offer comfort to their father, assuring him that "Mommie's in heaven" (196); then all three engage in a chanting prayer to "Our father, Our Father" (197-98).

In his notes to the Open Theatre production, Feldman remarks that he took it that "Jaspers' mind cracks completely at the end, and the 'Dearly Beloved' speech shows him in the midst of a wild, pseudo-religious, ecstatic delusion" (204). Yet Walters's notes reveal that he told his actor not to play Jaspers playing a priest but simply to play a priest (208). That the two directors approached the moment with opposing assumptions suggests the complexity of this culminating vignette, in which a preacher who looks just like Jaspers says what Jaspers would have said had Jaspers been in the pulpit—or in which Jaspers himself (or a Jasper who has lost touch with himself) orates. The figure in the pulpit is at once a preacher before his congregation, one of any number of TV evangelists (Feldman used a Cardinal Cushing oration as his model [204]), Jaspers in prison adopting the role of a preacher, and a mentally incompetent Jaspers who has collapsed under the moral weight of confinement, isolation, and loss. The vignette curiously accommodates the social-psychological-moral inscriptions of realistic drama, urging affirmation of the invariables of human relationships and experience that the previous vignettes individually and collectively record. But it departs from the realistic model in not yielding to the static face. This shifting portrait of Jaspers provides a stage image not of the morally accountable, psychologically consistent, socially-defined self that Krutch values but of the dynamic process of character formation and the multiple layers that constitute an anatomy of self.

Terry's understanding of transformational drama as more than an acting exercise, as an opportunity to explore with intelligence and with force the modes of self-definition in a contemporary arena, helped move American theatre beyond the cliche. A decade after Terry's work with transformational drama at the Open, Sam Shepard, acknowledged high priest of off-Broadway, framed a note to actors in *Angel City*: Instead of the idea of a "whole character" with logical motives behind his behavior which the actor submerges himself into, he should consider instead a fractured whole with bits and pieces of characters flying off the central scheme. Collage construction, jazz improvisation. Music or painting in space (qtd. in Gilman xv-xvi). Shepard might have been describing Terry's transformational drama, created a decade earlier at the Open.

If Terry's work with redefining character has found legitimacy in the American theatre, so also has it been influential in feminist theatre. Helen Keyssar, who has written on women playwrights of the last two decades, calls Terry the mother of American feminist theatre (53). Today's Terry, in residence at the Omaha Magic Theatre, where she and Joanne Schmidman have created new theatre for nearly twenty years, calls herself a feminist—and a humorist, and a humanist, and, most importantly, a theatre person (Leavitt 286). Yet her motherhood rightly began in the sixties at the Open, not only because she was writing plays for and about women but because she was writing transformational drama. That form's theatrical efforts at dismantling the stereotype, freeing the actor from the prescriptiveness of an assigned role, and reevaluating the institutional hierarchy speak with force to the comparable goals of feminism. Terry's work in neutralizing fixed assumptions helped prepare off-Broadway for the gender deconstructions of the burgeoning phenomenon we now call feminist theatre. In an interview with Diane Leavitt in 1977, Terry spoke of her desire to "explore the possibilities of what a woman could be." She remarked, "We don't know what a woman could be like because we've had so many outlines and definitions forced upon us" (288).

Terry dedicated ***Keep Tightly Closed*** to Chaikin, whose words began this paper. Perhaps it would be appropriate to end as well with a quotation from Chaikin's *The Presence of the Actor*: "The joy in theatre comes through discovery and the capacity to discover. What limits the discoveries a person can make is the idea or image he [or she] may come to have of himself [or herself]" (1). Terry's transformational drama is a theatre of discovery, in which all things, and joy, are possible.

Works Cited

Chaikin, Joseph. *The Presence of the Actor: Notes on the Open Theater, Disguises, Acting, and Repression*. New York: Atheneum, 1972.

Feldman, Peter. "Notes for the Open Theatre Production." *Viet Rock: Four Plays by Megan Terry*. New York: Simon and Schuster, 1967. 199-206.

Gilman, Richard. Introduction. *Seven Plays*. By Sam Shepard. New York: Bantam Books, 1981. xi-xxvii.

Keyssar, Helen. *Feminist Theatre: An Introduction to Plays of Contemporary British and American Women*. London: Macmillan, 1984.

Krutch, Joseph Wood. *"Modernism" in Modern Drama: A Definition and an Estimate*. Ithaca, NY: Cornell UP, 1953.

Leavitt, Dinah L. "Megan Terry: Interview." *Women in American Theatre: Careers, Images, Movements: An Illustrated Anthology and Sourcebook*. Ed. Helen Krich Chinoy and Linda Walsh Jenkins. New York: Crown, 1981. 285-92.

Marranca, Bonnie, and Gautam Dasgupta. "Megan Terry." *American Playwrights: A Critical Survey*. Vol. 1. New York: Drama Books Specialists, 1981. 183-92.

Schechner, Richard. "The Playwright as Wrighter." Introduction. *Viet Rock: Four Plays by Megan Terry*. New York: Simon and Schuster, 1967. 7-18.

Terry, Megan. *Keep Tightly Closed in a Cool Dry Place. Viet Rock: Four Plays by Megan Terry*. New York: Simon and Schuster, 1967. 153-98.

Walter, Sidney S. "Notes for the Firehouse Theatre Production." *Viet Rock: Four Plays by Megan Terry*. New York: Simon and Schuster, 1967. 206-09.

Weales, Gerald. *The Jumping-Off Place: American Drama in the 1960's*. London: Macmillan, 1969.

Judith Babnich (essay date 1988)

SOURCE: "Megan Terry and *Family Talk*," in *The Centennial Review*, Vol. XXXII, No. 3, Summer, 1988, pp. 296-311.

[*In the following essay, Babnich provides an in-depth discussion of Terry's* Family Talk, *including an interview with the author.*]

I

For the last ten years Megan Terry, playwright in residence at the Omaha Magic Theatre since 1974, has been writing plays focused on themes of particular interest to the American family. Her newest musical comedy, ***Family Talk***, is the fourth in a series of plays tackling the problems of domestic life. Common to all these plays is Terry's concern of "how are we going to get closer to one another and get a feeling of forward momentum as a family?"[1] Terry believes the actual process of being an effective family has been in deep trouble for a long time and she hopes her plays will suggest possible solutions.

Her interest in the family as a main subject for her plays began in 1977 with ***American King's English for Queens (AKEFQ)*** which investigates the ways language shapes male and female roles within the family. She wove her play around the central question, "Do you think like you talk or talk like you think?"[2]

The story revolves around the Connell family: Daniel Connell (Dad), an ambitious business executive in his 40s; Julia Connell (Mom), his wife, a homemaker in her late 30s; and their four children Susu, 16, Kate, 11, Doug, 9, and Jaimie, 6. Dad, who has worked in a corporate office all his life, now fears that his job might be lost due to cutbacks. Mom, filled with fantasy and frustration, remembers Dad's broken courtship promises and cries in her veal stew. The children throughout the play harass each other and pester their parents. The central event of the play occurs when Mom and Dad send the children off on a snipe hunt, that legendary pastime. Instead of a snipe, the kids catch Silver Morgan, a human being raised by prairie dogs. Never taught the English language, Morgan can speak only in barks and chirps. The children for the remainder of the play try to teach Morgan to speak their language and become one of the Connells. The problem, however, is that the Connells do not all speak the same English. Daddy Connell speaks the authoritarian language of the male business world, Mommie echoes her husband's language, and the children wallow in sex-oriented words and ideas.

In 1979 Terry wrote ***Goona Goona***, a play about violence within the family. This new musical comedy asked the question, "Do we look like goons to our children?"[3] The story line centers on the affluent West Omaha family known as the Goons. The father, Dr. Granville Goon, an "M-Deity" is a workaholic surgeon by day and a wife and child beater by night. June Goon is his quaalude-popping wife. Imprisoned in their expensive home, she tries to escape her life through pill-induced euphoria and sleep. The children Gaga and Garfield, who try to love their parents, are confused and bewildered by their beatings. The youngest child, the hyper-violent Gogo Goon, is kept in chains all the time so as not to hurt himself or his family. Rounding out the family is sadistic Grandmother Goon who at one point in the play scrubs her grandchildren's backs with steel wool before forcing them into a boiling bath.

Hearing the cries of agony from the Goon household but afraid to call the police are the two snoopy neighbors, Mr. and Mrs. Marriott. Their dilemma, and one of the major questions of the play, is that even though there is something seriously wrong next door, should they become involved in someone else's domestic problems? Appearing at various moments in the play are the three visiting nurses whose job it is to keep an eye on reports of family abuse. As they travel around the community they provide factual information about abuse for the audience. Toward the end of the play, the Nurses and the Police do try to deal with the Goon's problem, but because of professional standards and red tape, it's too late to help. Gogo Goon eventually kills his parents, grandmother and the visiting nurses.

The third of Terry's family plays is the 1981 ***Kegger***. Billed as an educative, preventative piece, ***Kegger*** examines alcohol use and abuse among teenagers. Most of the action of the play occurs at a keg party, where many young teens, due to peer pressure, not only drink but become totally inebriated. Once in this intoxicated state the teens begin their litany of why they drink and how much each of them can drink. In the early morning hours the party finally ends and many of the nauseated participants who drank too many "purple passions" are faced with the dilemma of driving home drunk.

Interwoven into the play's structure are monologues or what Terry called "testimonies" from teenage alcoholics, recovered teenage alcoholics, and their parents. It is through these testimonies that Terry shows the myriad of effects of heavy drinking on the teenager. Oftentimes alcohol does more damage to the growing body in its effects on emotional development, growth of judgment, and logic skills.

II

In ***Family Talk*** Terry investigates the breakdown of communication within the nuclear family. A focus of this work is to explore problems of familial interaction in a world of video domination. The family's "hypnotic routines" play a pivotal role in character development and theme.

Family Talk, like all of Terry's plays, is written as a series of transformations. An alternative to realistic playwriting, the transformational style involves a change of realities, of time, place, and character which is considered a major innovation in both playwriting and acting style. It violates linear plot development (with a beginning, middle, and end) and well-defined characters. Transformational theatre has an entirely different kind of construction. Plays are more circular, intuitive, and personal. The audience's usual habit of identifying actor and character is challenged and broken. Characters continually transform into other characters.

Richard Schechner, in the introduction to Terry's book *Viet Rock and Other Plays*, commented that an audience member's attention while watching Terry's transformational theatre is "divided between the virtuosity of the group of performers (an appreciation of 'pure performance') and a close scrutiny of the action which seems almost abstract when stripped of its usual actor-character identification".[4] In trying to evaluate Terry's plays Schechner further added: ". . . Miss Terry's plays in print do not have the same authority as, say, the texts of Arthur Miller; and this lack of authority is to the play's advantage. The texts remain 'pretexts' for productions; their staging should not be a recreation so much as a reconstruction."[5] This important point must always be considered when transformational plays are read. The script does not give an adequate idea of the play because so much depends on the actors' movements and characterizations.

In addition to being transformational, all of Terry's plays are written as comedies that are full of parody and satire and never intended to be dogmatic or propagandistic. Said Jo Ann Schmidman, founder of The Omaha Magic Theatre, "The work we do is entertainment . . . fun and light, even though the subject matter may often be heavy."[6] In essence, Terry's plays are a combination of pure entertainment and a social message, a difficult but most effective combination to achieve.

Dedicating ***Family Talk*** "to the evolution and constant redefinition of the American family," Terry depicts the stereotypical suburban family: mother, father and five children ranging from seven to sixteen years of age.[7] The Kraaz family has lost the fundamental ability to communicate. An exasperated mother Kraaz calls her family to dinner in Act I, and is answered by an almost commercial-like singsong unison reply from her T.V.-dominated children—"That's O.K. Mom, put it in the microwave." After persistent, thwarted attempts, such as banging her pots and pans to get her family's attention, she takes drastic action and unplugs and apparently breaks the television.

> MOM: I'm sick of eating alone.
>
> GREGG: Be right there, Mom.
>
> MOM: You always say that.
>
> DIANE: Be right there, Mom.
>
> MOM: From now on you can cook your own dinner.
>
> DAVEY: Thanks, Mom.
>
> MOM: You know what we're having for dinner tonight? Baked alligator and swamp rat souffle.
>
> ALL: Make mine rare, Mom.
>
> MOM: Molten lava has rolled all the way from Hawaii and is eating away at the dining room table.
>
> ALL: One more minute, Mom.
>
> MOM: *(Puts bucket over head, makes menacing cutting gesture with arms and moves into family room to cut the T.V. cord.)* One . . . two . . . three . . . four . . . five . . . six . . . seven . . .
>
> *(Electrical malfunction sound and lights black out as cord is cut.)*
>
> KIDS: MOM!
>
> GREGG: What'd you do?
>
> KIDS: Mom?
>
> DAVEY: The TV's broken.
>
> KIDS: Mom!
>
> DAVEY: You broke the TV.[8]

Without the drone of the T.V. to distract them, the Kraaz children are forced to communicate with their parents.

Throughout Act I the family confronts familiar problems: television, name calling, overly authoritarian parents, and a teenage daughter who lives for the phone. Electronic entertainment infiltrates every aspect of their lives, even driving a wedge between Mr. and Mrs. Kraaz. Caught up in being the breadwinner, father Kraaz loses himself in the newspaper during his off hours, and a simple shopping trip to a Nebraska furniture mart erupts into a spousal fight.

> MOM: Going shopping with you is the most terrifying thing a person could ever attempt to do!
>
> DAD: It's not my fault you lose your glasses! You always undercut yourself by losing your glasses.
>
> MOM: I never lose my glasses.
>
> DAD: I know—you've just "mislaid" them.
>
> MOM: I've just . . . *You* always lose your keys!
>
> DAD: And you always find them for me.
>
> MOM: That's right.
>
> DAD: I'd find your glasses for you, but I'm afraid of the alligators in your purse.
>
> MOM: Don't try to make me laugh when I'm feeling so hurt.
>
> DAD: You're not the only one who gets hurt.

Mom: That Nebraska Furniture Mart was a snake pit.

Dad: I thought it would make you happy.

Mom: Why would you think it would make me happy to go further into debt?

Dad: Those plane tickets put us in debt.

Mom: My dad was sick, I thought he was going to die. I had to go to him; I had to help Mother. She had to live on Valium the whole time. She could never have gone through it without my help.

Dad: I'm not begrudging you your trip to help your folks. I'm only pointing out where the extra debt came from.

Mom: And I'll pay it off, every cent!

Dad: Calm down. I'm not Scrooge. What's going on here? I took you out to buy you a present and we end up one step from the divorce court.

Mom: A new stove isn't my idea of romance.

Dad: Oh, no. That's it! I'm going for a run.[9]

To relieve his frustration Dad jogs around the block and Mom plunges into a deep depression that even her sympathetic children cannot alleviate.

A particularly strong scene demonstrating the verbal and physical abuse among siblings is that of thirteen-year-old Jennifer on the telephone. Each of the other kids is holding onto multicolored wires attached to Jennifer's symbolic phone which is a baby doll with a mouthpiece attached to its head. Throughout this scene the children prey on Jennifer and eventually tangle her up like a captured animal. Mom intervenes only to have yet another argument with her daughter.

An acting motif used throughout is the image of a constant swirling haze symbolic of the chaos in the family. Throughout the first act the actors grope aimlessly about trying to communicate their dilemma. They are constantly moving in directionless patterns literally bumping into each other as they search for an answer. Complementing this swirling movement is the occasional use of a specially rigged microphone (vocoder) that electronically distorts the actor's voices.

The stage environment, designed by Diane Ostdiek, consisted of a large monopoly board-like floor cloth with such designated areas as: "Danger—Mom at Work," "Fallout Zone" and "Zombie Land" and central to the action is a large abstract television set. Due to its placement, the T.V. takes on an ever present God-like focus. The entire ground cloth is framed in a blue outstrip known as the "Stargazing Strip." This area is critical to the set and production. When domestic life becomes too overwhelming, Kraaz family members escape to the "Stargazing Strip" to get away and think. A limited but selective number of props were used in the production. Five large gallon white paint containers without handles were used in several clever ways. Kraaz children could disappear or hide by placing the buckets over their heads. The containers also doubled as furniture and weapons.

Appreciating this dramatic production requires understanding why and how it was written. The themes for the play come from feedback from many of the OMT's touring audiences. It is a regular practice for the company to conduct audience discussions after performances both in Omaha and on tour. According to Terry, "It was those discussions that made it clear that domestic violence and teen drinking were symptoms of a deeper problem: that families can't communicate."[10] The recurrent theme of the family and communication skills came from consulting counselors, psychologists and communication experts.

According to Terry, television is America's fantasy life, catapulting us into an unreal world, such as shows that glorify the rich and powerful as do *Dallas* and *Dynasty*. These shows give us what we lack in our real life, while ***Family Talk*** tries to restore what we have lost through our infatuation with television—a delight in others' efforts to achieve and grow.

What Terry has done in ***Family Talk*** is not simply focus on a shattered family but rather emphasize the elements of reconciliation and communication that heal and make the family whole. As a result, Terry has focused her new play on a positive theme: improving communication within the family. During Act II the family resolves to conduct weekly meetings and Bible readings. These proposals are almost cliché in our society; however, for a family that wants to care for and support one another, they can be powerful tools for personal family transformation.

III

This past year I was fortunate enough to attend a performance of this innovative production and interview Ms. Terry about her play and also her work in recent years. The following are excerpts from that interview.

[Babnich]: Could you elaborate more on ways the audiences helped you write **Family Talk?**

[Terry]: I have taped all the discussions over the years, and the prevailing concern of most people is how are we going to get close to one another and get a feeling of forward momentum as a family group? People would get up and say, "My husband won't talk to me." Other people would say, "I have a teenage son that I might as well not have, because he never speaks. I put food on the table and he takes it to his room." The young people say to us: "If I don't speak in a certain way my mom won't speak to me, because I have to speak perfectly. Perfect means her way." Throughout all the discussions we kept hearing the same sort of things. Parents kept asking, "Where does it all start? What can we do before our kids start digging through our bags to take money to go out and buy a six-pack of beer?" And the idea that kept coming up over again was talk. Simple as that, we need to start talking together which is certainly more easily said than done. So I decided instead of writing a play and just saying, "Well here's the problem, folks; we're going to dump another problem in your lap," I said, "Do you suppose I could write a play on how to do something right and would anyone come if I did? Is there any way to put positive role modeling on the stage?"

And you decided yes.

I decided I'm going to fight it out. We called all the successful family counselors in town. Omaha has been in the forefront of a lot of work with families with kids in trouble. So, we took these people to lunch and picked their brains and asked, "What works?" Each one of them had a different way of dealing with the family group, and many of them were having success.

What did you learn from these counselors?

The family has been in deep trouble. All of the counselors we talked to are making a fortune because this is true. But I think Americans are recognizing the problem and many people are working to find ways to strengthen the family, to redefine it, to accept all the different kinds of families we have. The old-fashioned nuclear family of the '50s is a kind of myth. There's a huge increase of single person households of people living together, of single parent households, mixed households, and divorced persons. We have to say we're a big country with big arms and we have to embrace all these things and validate whatever way it is people are getting together. We need to let go of the old myths that are hurtful and rigid and yet find what was good in the old-fashioned family and try to revive it and support it, as it can be applied to our newly defined family. Some people have accused me of totally going soft but it seems to me that if there are things that are valid in the old fashioned family and things that work, like developing good manners and listening to one another and taking turns, then we should use them. We have so much chaos in life today. How do you train yourself to be more available to yourself? The big struggle that I've always had is between my animal self and my civilized self and trying to get these in harmony so we can both go forward as one. It seems to me that the family is one place where an individual can get a good grounding in how to deal with his or her self.

You mentioned earlier, that you are not in the habit of giving solutions in your plays. Could you tell me more about that?

I always feel it is cheating to give direction. I'm such a democrat. I always say that if I lay out the facts people will be intelligent enough to make up their own minds and know what to do. But I see some people are so bewildered they need more clues.

What type of solution did you propose in **Family Talk?**

To agree that everyone get together at least once a week and have some time together to really exchange feelings, thoughts, plans and ways of going forward. Otherwise we were finding that people just stayed isolated all through the whole development of the family. They all went off or got married and they still didn't know each other. And then the family reunions or holidays were excruciating times, and I think a lot of people can relate to that. A lot of people suffer severe anxiety having to go back and be with their families again if these things haven't been worked through at an early age. Sometimes I think we're a nation of disaster freaks judging by the news and what other people are writing. The big risk now is not death, destruction or disaster but compassion. It is a revolutionary tact to show tenderness, warmth and the fact that love and coming together is possible. It is possible to be close, to sing in harmony, to cry and laugh together. We need these positive images. It seems as if the whole planet is on the verge of chaos.

Do you think **Family Talk** *will help the plight of the family?*

Well, some of the counselors and families (especially those who have experienced the play together as a family) have said it will. But, I have no idea. A good percentage of the audience say that it makes them feel good and that maybe there's hope and new ways to do things. I remember a young family who, after the show was over, took a long time before getting up from their chairs. I walked over to them and the father said, "Thank you for the show, we have a lot to digest." He found a lot of things that they were going to go home and try to use and help each other move forward better as a group.

Moving on to the subject of playwriting and the production itself, how did you begin to write **Family Talk***? The last time we talked was in 1980. Has your approach to writing changed since then? Do you work from an outline?*

No. Once I have an idea I rush out to a typewriter. I have typewriters stashed here and there. For ***Family Talk*** I had lots and lots of scenes. We used only a third or close to half of what I'd written.

How long did it take you to write that first group of scenes?

It's hard to know, somewhere between four to five months.

In some of your earlier plays, **Viet Rock** *and* **Babes in the Bighouse**, *scenes were written in workshop with the help of the actors. Did you use this method for Family Talk?*

After compiling all the research I then went home and wrote a script. Once I had a working script I brought it to workshop where Jo Ann and a group of 35 people read it through a couple of times and then we put it away for two months.

Did you do that on purpose?

Yes, and we didn't touch it again.

Did you do something else?

No, the workshops continued. We met four times a week without the script. This is how we always work, really. I write independently of Jo Ann while she independently evolves the play structure. During workshop I listened to people's family stories too, but it was more like getting "essences of warmth" rather than using anything direct, anything specific. During the workshops we were also touring ***Mud*** and ***Kegger.***

What happened after the two months of workshop?

We went back to the script and then it was a matter of ordering scenes and fitting in discoveries we made in workshop.

By this time did you have a completed script to give the actors?

No. The actors trust Jo Ann so well that I don't think they suffered any anxiety. We've worked together for so long that Jo Ann had no problem taking a scene and staging it, regardless of where it was going to be placed in the body of the play. The cast would kid me a lot about how the play was going to end. We started working on the play in October of 1985 and I didn't have a final scene until New Year's Eve. In fact, I wrote two different endings before I settled on the family meeting.

Was the order of scenes set by January?

No, we were still changing things around. Jo Ann looked at all the scenes and we had a lot of discussions about how the play should start. At first she didn't like the scene I wrote but after she worked on it and created her own way of introducing the scene then she liked it.

When I was watching the play I felt that the dissonant underlying music complemented the chaotic movement on stage. As in the past, were you also involved in writing the music?

I wrote the lyrics for four songs: "Exceptional", "How to Exasperate A Mother", "I write a Thousand Letters" and "The Dream Song." Jo Ann, John Sheehan, and Joe Budenholzer wrote the other tunes.

I noticed that the musical score combined different musical styles from country western rock and roll, to abstract polytonal melodies. How would you describe the music?

Jo Ann and I, in working with different types of composers, mix the styles. Rather than having one musical voice, which is typical of a traditional musical, we have several. John's music is what I suppose critics call no music. It's very dramatic, sort of like avant-garde opera, and it effectively shows dream states on the stage. His music worked very well in depicting the underside of the family, the chaotic stages, the fragmentation, the disparate qualities. Joe's music was used during the times of family harmony. His final song, "Quality Time," was a mixture of folk and country; it was very warm, simple and easy.

What have you been doing since 1980?

Working hard! We've been working here constantly 18 hours a day.

Do you still feel good about working and living in Omaha?

Yes!

Any regrets that you're not in New York?

No. The last time I was in New York I was amazed at how I couldn't wait to get back to Omaha.

What bothered you about New York and the theatre scene?

It's just so hard to move around there and the commercial theatre work isn't good.

What do you think is the future for commercial theatre?

They've priced themselves out of existence and into absurdity. They're going to have to retrench. As you know, our top ticket price is $5, so people can afford to see live theatre. If commercial theatre doesn't do something to get young people back into the theatre, the commercial theatre will die because they are not creating audiences for the future.

What do you think the future of alternative theatre is?

It will probably always be led by people who are not satisfied with what they see elsewhere, by people who have a better vision, a vision of what they want to see on the stage so they put it there themselves. There will always be people like that and they'll be coming out of who knows where and not necessarily New York. Where did Grotowski develop? Not in New York. Eugenio Barba or Dario Fo didn't work in New York City either. Name all the great theatre artists who don't work in New York City and you see that you don't have to be in New York City to do good work. That's one thing I say when I speak to young people; you don't have to go into exile to be an artist anymore because of the work done by the National Endowment for the Arts and the State Arts Councils and now Corporate Giving for the Arts. You can be an artist wherever you want to pitch your tent. If you love the landscape in which you were raised and that feeds you as an artist, then you should stay there and make your art there. When I was growing up you had to go to Hollywood or New York, but that's not true anymore. Besides, New York has also priced itself out of existence because of the rents. In the 1960s I paid $25 a month for this coldwater flat that is now going for $1050, and three families are living in it. The young people can't afford to live in New York anymore. So they're going to Minneapolis, Omaha, Seattle, or Denver because they can afford to live there and make work happen.

As a final question, Megan, what does the future hold for you?

I'm always writing and rewriting. I never quit rewriting until it's published and then if I get a chance at another edition I write and rewrite some more. I've just finished rewriting one of my past plays, ***Sleazing Toward Athens***, which is about the clash of materialism with the humanities on today's commuter campuses.

So you're going to keep on writing and rewriting?

I'll never live long enough to develop all the ideas I have. I have an idea a minute. I guess I'll just have to leave a lot of them on computer discs for other people to explore if they wish to do so.

Notes

1. Personal interview with Megan Terry, 3 May 1986.
2. Megan Terry, *American King's English for Queens* (Omaha, Nebraska: Omaha Magic Theatre Press, 1978), p. 1.
3. *"Goona Goona," The Jewish Press.* 23 November 1979, p. 13.
4. Megan Terry, *Viet Rock and Other Plays*. New York: Simon and Schuster, Inc., 1967, p. 1.
5. Terry, p. 1.
6. Personal interview with Jo Ann Schmidman, 21 February 1980.
7. Portions of the plot synopsis are taken from my review of *Family Talk* published in the May issue of *Theatre Journal*, 1987.
8. Megan Terry, *Family Talk*, (Omaha, Nebraska: *Omaha Magic Theatre Press*, 1986), pp. 3-4.
9. Terry, pp. 40-41.
10. Terry Interview.

Jan Breslauer and Helene Keyssar (essay date 1989)

SOURCE: "Making Magic Public: Megan Terry's *Traveling Family Circus*," in *Making A Spectacle: Feminist Essays on Contemporary Women's Theatre*, edited by Lynda Hart, The University of Michigan Press, 1989, pp. 169-80.

[*In the following essay, Breslauer and Keyssar examine Terry's* Mollie Bailey's Traveling Family Circus, *a play that shows people how to make a difference in their world.*]

When Megan Terry moved to the Omaha Magic Theater in 1974, she began a new phase of the feminist discourse she had begun to shape in the experimental theatre of the 1960s. The energy that she had directed for more than a decade toward collaborative production endeavors, primarily in New York City with the Open Theater, now became more precisely focused on joint endeavors with her colleague, Jo Ann Schmidman, and on efforts to engage and address the local community in Omaha. While Terry was one of the few feminist playwrights to have had her work from the sixties and early seventies published, after 1974 fewer of her texts were commercially printed, even though she and the Omaha Magic Theater made serious efforts to arrange for low-cost script publication and willingly made copies of new scripts available to anyone who asked. Awareness of Terry's work since 1974 has also been limited because, although the Omaha Magic Theater has toured extensively in the Midwest and occasionally on the East and West Coasts, it has remained remote from the mainstream Boston-New Haven-New York-Washington, D.C. theatre circuit.

It is not, therefore, surprising, that when, in the 1980s, the press discovered the "new women playwrights," Megan Terry was ignored or overlooked. At the same time, there is good reason to claim, as one of us did in *Feminist Theatre*,[1] that Terry is the "mother of American feminist theatre." Evidence for this claim abounds in Terry's more than fifty plays. As a body of work, these dramas have explored a wide range of feminist issues: production and reproduction, the language of patriarchy, gender roles inside and outside the family, the victimization and heroism of women, and the pain and power of women in a repressive society are all essential elements of Terry's dramatic discourse. Her plays persistently criticize and subvert specific institutions and events in American society—from the war in Vietnam to the hypocritical behavior of parents toward adolescents—but these critiques are not merely casual gestures at topical issues or facile assaults on patriarchy and sexism. Rather, they are specifications of a vision that emphasizes a transformation of morality as the basis of social and political change.

Although critical of the particular instances of violence and oppression against women, Terry's plays have never insisted, as has the work of some feminists working in other media, that revolution is necessary in order to improve the stature of women in society. Her objections to inequality are not usually couched in terms of an economic system that creates such situations, but rather emerge as protests against individual circumstances, institutional corruption, or verbal and conceptual distortions, notably common in occurrence as these may be. Even, for example, in a play like ***Babes in the Bighouse*** (1979), which harshly condemns both the treatment of women prisoners and, metaphorically, the pervasive imprisonment of women in the codes and practices of modern society, the challenge is to the audience's sense of responsibility and dignity, not to the economic and political systems that support such prisons. Terry's outlook in this regard has been archetypically American and may be a strategic choice given that her audience, too, is, for the most part, assertively American. Enacting her own feminist version of American romanticism, Terry has chosen in most of her plays to highlight the positive, though incremental, change that is available: women, in her dramas, are "alive and well" and on the way to doing even better.

This belief that things can be better took form in Terry's work as magic even before she joined forces with the theater of that name. ***Calm Down Mother*** (1965), one of Terry's first plays to be explicitly concerned with women as women, depicts the tensions as well as the attachments between mothers and daughters, but ends with a ritual-like chant that invokes woman's reproductive capabilities as a source of difference and almost mystical strength. ***Viet Rock*** (1966) concluded in "deathly silence," but the intense ambiance of community in the acting ensemble deliberately encouraged spectators to believe that they—we—could overcome the various oppressions represented and enacted in that war. The most memorable moment in ***Approaching Simone*** (1970) occurs when each member of the acting company takes on a piece of Simone's clothing, symbolically taking on her pain and her struggle for women's freedom. Simone Weil, like theater itself in Terry's hands, is a model, but, as dramatized, her heroism can join her to others rather than separate her from them.

It is possible, then, to comprehend Terry's move to Omaha, Nebraska, as a geographical expression of her conviction that possibilities exist outside the norm. It is also important to note that this move came at the beginning of a decade that was to see both the rise and the retrenchment of feminism, including, in the eighties, a new generation of women content to identify themselves as "post-feminists." From the retrospective view of 1988, however, those changes are dated, and even for some who embraced "post-feminism," that label is showing itself not only as inaccurate but invidious.

As if sensing such a trend in the offing, Terry's 1983 collaboration with JoAnne Metcalf, ***Mollie Bailey's Traveling Family Circus: Featuring Scenes from the Life of Mother Jones***, represented a new and increasingly politicized direction for her drama. Retaining the basic optimism of her previous work, while venturing into one of the most contested arenas of contemporary American society, Terry dares in ***Mollie Bailey's Traveling Circus*** to show the possibility of authentic communication and mutual support between two types of successful women who, in today's world, would appear to be unyielding foes. The central figures and the orchestrators of events in this drama are Mollie Bailey and Mother Jones, both born in the nineteenth century, the former out of Terry's imagination, the latter out of history. In Terry's staged world, Mother Jones, a political activist, socialist, and organizer for the rights of women and children, is not the evil enemy but the star performer and ally of Mollie Bailey, a woman who is a traditional housewife and, ironically, the ringmistress of a traveling "family" circus.

In this world, dramaturgically and politically, transformation and possibility are key motifs, as they have been throughout Terry's work,[2] but their explicit presence has been augmented by an increased attention to the social-political cosmos. The onstage transformations that were oppositional conventions in Terry's dramas of the sixties (and that became accepted theatrical practice in American experimental theatre before vanishing, in the seventies, from the work of most male playwrights) are revitalized in ***Mollie Bailey's Traveling Circus*** as circus feats. More eloquently than in Terry's previous work, these transformations are also now the feats of American women recovering and reconstructing their history. Even the production history of this drama diverged from the pattern Terry had established in the previous decade: first produced in the Plays in Process series of the Mark Taper Forum in Los Angeles, ***Mollie Bailey's Traveling Family Circus*** was then produced at California Institute of the Arts and in Santa Barbara, California, before appearing onstage "at home" at the Omaha Magic Theater.

The prologue to ***Mollie Bailey's Traveling Circus*** signals the ironic tone and mythic frame for this play. Suspended on a wide trapeze or platform held aloft by "invisible" stagehands, two Celtic queens, who are, simultaneously, Mollie Bailey and Mother Jones, are crossing the Irish Sea on a raft in the midst of a fierce storm. Lashed to their raft are other, unconscious members of their tribe. Mother Jones's opening line—"Did you lash down the males?"—instantly establishes the inversion of conventional power relations between men and women; the men are not only physically subjugated to the women but are treated as sexual types, as "males." (A few lines later, Mother Jones confirms this conception when she reassures Mollie that they will reach land with at least one male "in good condition.") The prologue also establishes a mother-daughter relationship between Mother Jones and Mollie Bailey: literally fulfilling the role suggested by her ironic, historical name, "Mother" Jones commands, instructs and nurtures Mollie, who, in turn, proclaims her love for "Mother" and her confidence that she will be empowered by her mother's attachment and support:

> Mollie. Mother, I love you so. Let me stand against the storm and spell you. If you hold my hand I'll be able to feel the way to steer. (P. 2)

Theatrically and culturally, this prologue is at once familiar and disconcerting. The sea-storm setting and the playful echo of "Take in the topsail" in "lash down the males" blatantly recall Shakespeare's *The Tempest*, which, like Terry's play, is situated in both the historical context of the discovery of the new world and the mythical context of a separate space of spectacle where time and place are magically construed. The raft of the two Celtic queens is a far cry, however, from the sailing ship of *The Tempest*, and the two women steering the raft's course would have had no place, even as passengers, on Shakespeare's all-male ship. Perhaps even more unsettling, where Gonzalo ended the prologue of *The Tempest* longing for any piece of dry land, Mother Jones bypasses an island, seeking greener fields. Contrary to gender stereotypes, the men of *The Tempest* quickly lose patience, blame others, and surrender to fear and chaos, whereas Mother Jones concludes the prologue of the contemporary drama warmly reassuring Mollie that "If we're not in trouble, we're not going in the right direction."

The right direction in ***Mollie Bailey's Traveling Family Circus*** is rarely straight forward, or straight backward. In keeping with many contemporary feminist plays, this prologue and the two acts that follow exploit theater's liberty with time and place to conjoin previously disconnected elements of culture and history. Such temporal and spatial reconfigurations orient the spectator toward alternative ways of viewing the present and the past. Terry has subverted conventional representations of chronology and history repeatedly in her work, beginning with ***Calm Down Mother***, but the particular juxtaposition in ***Mollie Bailey's Traveling Family Circus*** of a historical figure with a fictional character has even more striking affinities with several of Caryl Churchill's dramas than with Terry's own previous work.

Churchill's *Top Girls*, like Terry's ***Mollie Bailey's Traveling Circus***, begins with an imagined ritual of passage that requires a new understanding of gender roles. The similar emphases in Terry's and Churchill's dramaturgies on unprecedented historical representations and on explicit intertextual gestures suggest that the most potent emergent element of feminist theater may not be the recovery of women's history but what Mother Jones calls "getting into trouble," and what I have elsewhere described as doing dangerous history.[3] Where many feminist endeavors, in the theater and in other media, have aimed to recuperate women's history as an inspirational resource for women and men, dangerous historical explorations seek not only to recover the forgotten achievements of women but also to examine the conditions under which gender conflicts have repeatedly arisen and repeatedly been resolved such that women have remained subordinate to men. Dangerous historians, and dramatists doing dangerous history, confront the illusions of the past, including those that conceal women's complicity in the recurrent subjugation of women to men. Dangerous history also refuses to ignore women's violence at key moments in that history. The processes and effects of doing dangerous history in drama are increasingly evident not only in plays by Churchill and Terry, but in other feminist dramas such as Wendy Kesselman's *My Sister in This House* (1982), Louise Page's *Salonika* (1982), Ntozake Shange's *Three Pieces* (1981) and Sharon Pollock's *Blood Relations* (1981).

If, then, Terry's prologue to ***Mollie Bailey's Traveling Circus*** is a warning that we are about to enter the realm of dangerous history, it is therefore appropriate that the setting into which Mother Jones and Mollie Bailey are lowered for acts 1 and 2 is a circus, a place whose attraction is inseparable from its embrace of danger. That Terry sets this play in a circus is at once a logical extension of her long-term association of magic, theater, and spectacle and an assertion that what has once been implicit in her own dramaturgy and in American culture will now become explicit, theatrically and substantively. At least in modern societies, the circus is the ultimate world of possibilities, paradoxes, and perversions; it is a reminder of the lost world of carnival, a world that Soviet cultural critic M. M. Bakhtin has recalled to our attention as the locus of folk humor and unofficial culture in Western societies from the Greeks through the Renaissance.[4] Because the circus separates the audience from the performer/participants, it is not a true carnival, but in its irreverent conjoining of laughter and fear, its deployment of popular imagery, its love of exaggeration, its pleasure in the grotesque, and the promiscuity of its attachments, the circus, like the Rabelaisian novels that attracted Bakhtin's attention, signifies a symbolic opposition to the dominant values and practices of patriarchal societies.

Mollie Bailey's circus partakes of these essential attributes, but it also evokes a uniquely American understanding of circus: an exotic incarnation of the American rags to riches dream in which anyone can be anything and all is attainable. The American circus is the archetypical carnival that we run away to join, hoping to belong to a world in which our fantasies become real and we're freed from normative constraints. So Terry, in ***Mollie Bailey's Traveling Family Circus***, dreams for us, envisioning a society with new rules that embrace diversity. Once we enter this world, it will metamorphosize us in such a way that we neither want nor are able to return to our previous lives.

Traditionally, and in Terry's play, the circus is the realm of a liberated Saturnalia in which identity is redefined. As in most forms of carnival, the masters may become servants and vice versa, but there are possibilities even beyond this. Anyone can become anyone, then, in turn, become someone else. Identity is no longer fixed, especially when performers adopt new personages for their various "acts" or roles within the performance as a whole. Combining a familiar circus routine and a transformation technique often used in the sixties and seventies by improvisational theatre companies like the San Francisco Mime Troupe and Paul Sills's Story Theater, Terry is able to stress this fluidity of identity in ***Mollie Bailey's Traveling Family Circus*** with far less stylistic self-consciousness than in her previous works: within the circus setting, one man can stand on another's shoulders to play the Father; the Mother can be similarly performed; the actress and the actor playing Mollie and her husband, Gus, can grow older and younger within a minute's time; other actors in the company can transform from trapeze artists to canaries. The circus setting naturalizes these transformations because within the bounds of circus the notion of who one is within the group is in Heraclitian flux: age, gender, and authority are constantly redefined.

The circus not only has performers who transcend the circumscription of labels, it also has clowns, indefatigable warriors who conquer the impossible, recovering from falls that in everyday life would bring men and women down. Mollie Bailey herself displays some of the attributes of the clown in the first scenes of act 1, when, as she introduces her children, "endless streams of people seem to keep coming out from under her skirt." And, although the circus life is controlled by metaphors of the family, often with the ringmaster as patriarch, in this play, Mollie Bailey is ringmistress and a matriarch who is able to share her power without diminishing it.

Mollie's ability to share her power is explicitly attributed in the play to her gender identity, but the drama suggests that, even for a woman as strong as Mollie, this might not be possible in the ordinary world. The circus, however, is, also, importantly, a cooperative, a collective in which interdependence is all, and, frequently, a matter of life and death.[5] The benefits of cooperative effort are announced in the prologue of ***Mollie Bailey's Traveling Family Circus***, but it is in the arena of the circus itself that the particular possibilities and originality of the cooperation between Mollie Bailey and Mother Jones are revealed.

Following two scenes that introduce the audience for the circus (and the drama) to Mollie Bailey's personal history of escape from an authoritarian father to love, marriage, and centerstage in "Women's Eternal Circus," Mollie, as ringmistress, introduces "for the first time anywhere" an act that "has never been staged in America or on the continent." The "act" is a scene from nineteenth-century American history, starring Mother Jones, and, as Terry blatantly reminds us, this is not a scene commonly played on the stages of American history or theater. In stark contrast to the frivolity and resurrection symbology of the initial circus scenes, Mother Jones first appears as a herald of death, carting the dead bodies of four children on top of coffins in a procession of carts drawn by old women. The image recalls the travels of other famous and weary souls, particularly the journeys of Brecht's Mother Courage with her wagons and children who die in the face of overwhelming adversities. In a speech to the audience, Mother Jones narrates the story, which is, indeed, a true story, of the epidemic that took the lives of her husband and four children. She tells of her grief, then sings to us of her determination to "find a way to fight for the living." As Mollie made a new life for herself with Gus and the circus after leaving her parents, Mother Jones reincarnates life from death. What Mollie does for a nuclear family, Mother Jones creates for the communal family of the poor and oppressed.

By embracing theater's ability to realize the impossible, to blur borders between the "real" and the imagined, Terry creates a dream juxtaposition of the lives of two outstanding women from history "who didn't know each other, [but who allow us to] know more about ourselves by knowing them."[6] This juxtaposition sharpens the sad irony of Mother Jones's name: it was not until after she had lost her four children and husband to a yellow fever epidemic and had become an extraordinarily successful labor organizer that Mary Harris Jones became known as "Mother" Jones. The lives and works of Mother Jones and Mollie Bailey are thus inverses each of the other, but are also analogues; both demonstrate the force of nurturing activities and the empowerment possible through what anthropologist Nancy Chodorow has called "the reproduction of mothering." (I am thinking here of mothering, not as the institution that presently determines women's experience, but as it might be imagined in a non-gender-biased society.)

By showcasing Mother Jones, Mollie Bailey reveals her to be an object of her admiration, though there is never any suggestion that Mollie is dissatisfied with her own life. Notably absent is any indication of competition between the two women. Instead, mutual respect and collaboration between Mother Jones and Mollie Bailey implies a personalized version of the triumph of a feminism based on responsibility and attachment to others over a patriarchal social system grounded in ideas of rights and competition. This is not a feminism that excludes men, that requires an alternative lifestyle or is biologically constrained. The dialogue between Mollie and her husband, Gus, emphasizes that the pleasure they take in the life and family they have created for themselves is informed rather than threatened by Gus's recognition of Mollie's strength. And Mollie can be strong and still value "clean family fun" and a "down-home good time show."

Equally important, Mollie Bailey can be strong in her ways while fully acknowledging the different strengths of Mother Jones, whom we see in the first act as an "agitator, aggravator, hellraiser," crusading against starvation wages for child and women laborers. Mollie attempts to delight little children and provide them with the gift of laughter and life while Mother Jones struggles for downtrodden children and fights the police. But while Mollie's voice is sweet and often expressed in song and Mother Jones's voice is harsh and inclined to cursing, each woman is able to hear the other, and neither sees herself or the other as victim.

The episodic, non-narrative structure of the play supports the audience's understanding of the differences as well as the interdependencies between Mollie Bailey and Mother Jones. After Mollie's initial introduction in act 1 of the "Mother Jones act," scenes from the life of Mother Jones are intercut with scenes from Mollie's life. The connections between these scenes are often not explicitly articulated by an on-stage character, but are implicit in the similarities or contrasts between the events in Mother Jones's life and those in Mollie Bailey's. Two scenes in act 1, for example, juxtapose Mother Jones's instruction of a young soldier with Mollie's instruction of her daughter. Functioning much like an Eisensteinian montage in film, the audience learns from the collision between the two scenes more than from the separate content of either situation.

On a larger scale, act 1 and act 2 of ***Mollie Bailey's Traveling Family Circus*** have only a minimal narrative relation to each other but interanimate each other by contrasts and continuities of roles and themes. Where Mollie was the initiating voice of act 1, it is Mother Jones who begins act 2, and, notably, it is now Mother Jones who uses song to present her message. Her song repeats a refrain: "I was born in Revolution . . ." that reminds us of the changes in her life and in the historical context of her life, but that also reassures us of some continuity: ". . . And I'll never leave you. . . . Til we've seen these troubles through." Like Brecht's women, when she is not changing herself,

Mother Jones is the emissary of change; and like Brecht's Widow Begbick (*Man Is Man*) and Jenny (*Threepenny Opera*), as well as Mother Courage, Mother Jones's survival and success are predicated on her adaptability. Unlike Brecht's women characters, however, Terry's bringers of change are not only changed themselves by circumstances but are also able to transform themselves.

This openness to change is as true of Mollie as it is of Mother Jones. Mollie transforms herself most obviously by leaving home and then creating her circus/family. The actress's onstage transformations from middle-aged woman to young girl and then again to older woman heighten and defamiliarize these commonplace changes, giving them dramatic equivalence with the radical alterations of Mother Jones's life. This is not to say that Terry conflates the tragedies of Mother Jones's life with the traumas of growing up and separation from parents, but that the models of change we are offered range, importantly, from the heroic to the ordinary. Mollie's attitude toward change, rather than her circumstances, provide a way to understand our own capacity to transform ourselves. She has a propensity for change, she tells us: "I was born when I was already ten thousand years old."

Mollie also celebrates complexity and eventually dismisses the archetypal purity ascribed to women; by so doing, she suggests we do the same. When her son, Eugene, presents his intended bride for her consideration, Mollie destroys his expectations of what is to be thought valuable:

> Eugene. She'll expand me! She has a beautiful soul, so clean, so pure, so white.
>
> Mollie. (*To audience and all*) Right away I'm alarmed!
>
> Eugene. But those are all perfect qualities. . . . She has a clean soul.
>
> Mollie. Then don't marry her.
>
> Eugene. I don't understand you.
>
> Mollie. You can marry her if her soul is as patched as our tent. (P. 31)

Mollie again invokes the circus as a source of imagery and meaning when she goes on to explain to Eugene her position on freedom from the tyranny of perfection:

> You think to sell us your bride by showing only her pure points. That's not what circus is all about. Where are the falls? Falling and almost falling and recovering from falling. That's our job. (Pp. 32-33)

From a lifetime of "acts" inside the bigtop of Mollie Bailey-Mother Jones's Family of Women's Eternal Circus, Mollie has learned the lesson with which she concludes her sermon to her son: "If the soul is a soul that is whole, it must be made up of all aspects, dark and light, of the human/animal possibilities." Stage directions indicate that Eugene is frightened by his mother's exhortation. No wonder, since what Mollie proposes is no less than a dismantling of the secure matrix of role-playing on which society has come to depend. Perhaps most threatening, Mollie's admonitions are pointedly addressed to her son at the moment he wishes to marry, and they are called forth, specifically, by Eugene's unquestioning assumption of the value of a pure soul.

Eugene's vision of a perfect marriage modifies the patriarchal stereotype by insisting on his own purity as well as that of his bride-to-be, but Mollie's revisionist gender values call not only for equality but for transformations of values for both men and women. Authentic transformations necessarily bring a genuinely brave new world. Eugene senses the terror of the unknown in this projected cultural revolution, and his explosion: "Mother. . . . You ask for everything!" is not unlike the shriek of the isolated daughter in Caryl Churchill's *Top Girls*, whose final cry is "afraid."

Mollie's only fear, the fear that grounds her advice to her son, is of a life lived without risk. As she explains in her final "introduction" of Mother Jones, Mollie admires and wants her audience to "experience" Mother Jones because, "Mother Mary Harris Jones is one first-class risk-taker. . . . " She and Mother Jones each have "a different way of living in this world" and "a different philosophy of life," Mollie continues, but with or without the labels and diverse "philosophies" of capitalism and socialism, of homemaker and agitator, as mothers, they share an understanding that "sometimes to minimize the danger, you have to take risks" (42).

Mollie Bailey and Mother Jones each acknowledge for themselves and for the audience that "history" as we know it is as much a human creation as any other enterprise. The task, therefore, is to rewrite a history that will enable rather than circumscribe those that come to be influenced by it. In the past, men have written the histories, but in the world of Terry's play, Mollie is the author of herself and of her story, a story that is unlike that of many authors because it is not, finally, a monologue but a dialogue. Aware that others will be suspicious of this mode of telling, and will demean her and her story as "woman's work," when you come to watch her circus, you will hear her say:

> Some people have put forward the notion that women don't know how to organize, don't know how to make decisions, don't understand logic, nor can they even tell a story with a beginning and a middle and an end. I confess, to the last accusation, because the way I see it the story has no beginning and it not only hasn't ended for me, it's always starting all over again. (P. 41)

Speaking here for the first time in the play "for women," Mollie's "confession" affirms the episodic, circular structure of her circus and of the play itself, while simultaneously reclaiming Terry's basic belief in the regenerative powers of women and the epiphanic stories they tell. Life does go on in Mollie's stories: in the final scene of the play, Mollie's husband, Gus, dies in the arms of the couple's very pregnant daughter, Minnie. Terry then deploys the most theatricalized transformation of the drama to play this motif out fully: all of the actors drape garments on Mollie that before our eyes, change her into a seventy-five-year-old woman. The individual women, Mollie Bailey and Mother Jones, are as vulnerable to time's tolls as we are, but in parting from the audience, speaking in one voice for the first time, they encourage us: "Go on—go on and open / Open that door you've never opened before!"

Mollie Bailey's Traveling Family Circus: Featuring Scenes from the Life of Mother Jones ends on this chord, but the legacies of Mollie and Mother Jones do not. They are part of a re-engendered society and of a new history in which lives and acts transform rather than simply end. In this play, as in her previous work, Terry pushes boundaries, but here she not only imagines anew a universe in which people may effect their own transfigurations, she also takes the risk of reconfiguring the terrian of women's relations to each other. The ordinary moments of our contemporary lives are made extraordinary both by replacing women in history and by imagining difference among women as well as between men and women as a source of strength rather than weakness. In Terry's hands, familiar dramatic tools and cultural practices are made strange and magical by combining signs and conventions from differing forms of discourse and diverse value systems. The songs, transformational acting techniques, dialogic discourse, and wondrous feats of ***Mollie Bailey's Traveling Family Circus*** together make everyday existence alien, but rather than making us remote from our own society, they urge us to reenter our own worlds through new doors.

Like a magician who is freed to show the audience how she pulls the rabbit out of the hat, Terry, like Mollie Bailey and Mother Jones, shows women and men *how* to work to make a difference. Mother Jones and Mollie Bailey will, indeed, "be back again," to haunt us and inspire us, as will all the previously hidden struggles, defeats, and triumphs of women when today's women own their pasts as their inheritance, an inheritance that is rightfully ours but for which we also must accept the dangers of responsibility.

Notes

1. Helene Keyssar, *Feminist Theatre* (London: Macmillan, 1984, 1986), 53-76.
2. For a different introduction to the idea of transformation in Terry's dramas, see June Schlueter, "*Keep Tightly Closed in a Cool Dry Place*: Megan Terry's Transformational Drama and the Possibilities of Self," in *Studies in American Drama: 1945-Present*, vol. 2, 59-69.
3. Helene Keyssar, "Hauntings: Gender and Drama in Contemporary English Theatre," *Amerikanische Studien*, December 3-4, 1986, 461-68.
4. Mikhail Bakhtin, *Rabelais and His World* (Bloomington, Ind.: Indiana University Press, 1984), especially 432-74.
5. Op cit. 153, 255-56. Bakhtin comments frequently on what he calls the "wholeness" or collectivity of carnival. For example, "The individual feels that he is an indissoluble part of the collectivity, a member of the people's mass body. In this whole, the individual body ceases to a certain extent to be itself; it is possible, so to say, to exchange bodies, to be renewed (through change of costume and mask)" (255). We might note that this description of the spirit of carnival is similar to Nietzsche's notion of the Dionysian in *The Birth of Tragedy*.
6. Megan Terry, author's note to script of *Mollie Bailey's Traveling Circus: Featuring Scenes from the Life of Mother Jones* (New York: Broadway Play Publishing, 1983).

Additional coverage of Terry's life and career is contained in the following sources published by the Gale Group: *Contemporary Authors* Vols. 77–80; *Contemporary Authors Biographical Series* Vol. 3; *Contemporary Authors New Revision Series* Vol. 43; *Contemporary Literature Criticism* Vol. 19; and *Dictionary of Literary Biography* Vol. 7.

How to Use This Index

The main references

Calvino, Italo 1923-1985 .... **CLC 5, 8, 11, 22, 33, 39, 73; SSC 3**

list all author entries in the following Gale Literary Criticism series:

BLC = *Black Literature Criticism*
CLC = *Contemporary Literary Criticism*
CLR = *Children's Literature Review*
CMLC = *Classical and Medieval Literature Criticism*
DA = *DISCovering Authors*
DAB = *DISCovering Authors: British*
DAC = *DISCovering Authors: Canadian*
DAM = *DISCovering Authors: Modules*
  DRAM: *Dramatists Module;* ***MST:*** *Most-Studied Authors Module;*
  MULT: *Multicultural Authors Module;* ***NOV:*** *Novelists Module;*
  POET: *Poets Module;* ***POP:*** *Popular Fiction and Genre Authors Module*
DC = *Drama Criticism*
HLC = *Hispanic Literature Criticism*
LC = *Literature Criticism from 1400 to 1800*
NNAL = *Native North American Literature*
NCLC = *Nineteenth-Century Literature Criticism*
PC = *Poetry Criticism*
SSC = *Short Story Criticism*
TCLC = *Twentieth-Century Literary Criticism*
WLC = *World Literature Criticism, 1500 to the Present*

The cross-references

See also CANR 23; CA 85-88; obituary CA116

list all author entries in the following Gale biographical and literary sources:

AAYA = *Authors & Artists for Young Adults*
AITN = *Authors in the News*
BEST = *Bestsellers*
BW = *Black Writers*
CA = *Contemporary Authors*
CAAS = *Contemporary Authors Autobiography Series*
CABS = *Contemporary Authors Bibliographical Series*
CANR = *Contemporary Authors New Revision Series*
CAP = *Contemporary Authors Permanent Series*
CDALB = *Concise Dictionary of American Literary Biography*
CDBLB = *Concise Dictionary of British Literary Biography*
DLB = *Dictionary of Literary Biography*
DLBD = *Dictionary of Literary Biography Documentary Series*
DLBY = *Dictionary of Literary Biography Yearbook*
HW = *Hispanic Writers*
JRDA = *Junior DISCovering Authors*
MAICYA = *Major Authors and Illustrators for Children and Young Adults*
MTCW = *Major 20th-Century Writers*
SAAS = *Something about the Author Autobiography Series*
SATA = *Something about the Author*
YABC = *Yesterday's Authors of Books for Children*

Literary Criticism Series Cumulative Author Index

See also CLR 6; DA3; MAICYA; SATA 100; YABC 1

Anderson, C. Farley
See Mencken, H(enry) L(ouis); Nathan, George Jean

Anderson, Jessica (Margaret) Queale 1916- .... **CLC 37**
See also CA 9-12R; CANR 4, 62

Anderson, Jon (Victor) 1940- . **CLC 9; DAM POET**
See also CA 25-28R; CANR 20

Anderson, Lindsay (Gordon) 1923-1994 .... **CLC 20**
See also CA 125; 128; 146; CANR 77

Anderson, Maxwell 1888-1959 ...... **TCLC 2; DAM DRAM**
See also CA 105; 152; DLB 7, 228; MTCW 2

Anderson, Poul (William) 1926- ..... **CLC 15**
See also AAYA 5, 34; CA 1-4R, 181; CAAE 181; CAAS 2; CANR 2, 15, 34, 64; CLR 58; DLB 8; INT CANR-15; MTCW 1, 2; SATA 90; SATA-Brief 39; SATA-Essay 106

Anderson, Robert (Woodruff) 1917- .... **CLC 23; DAM DRAM**
See also AITN 1; CA 21-24R; CANR 32; DLB 7

Anderson, Sherwood 1876-1941 .... **TCLC 1, 10, 24; DA; DAB; DAC; DAM MST, NOV; SSC 1; WLC**
See also AAYA 30; CA 104; 121; CANR 61; CDALB 1917-1929; DA3; DLB 4, 9, 86; DLBD 1; MTCW 1, 2

Andier, Pierre
See Desnos, Robert

Andouard
See Giraudoux, (Hippolyte) Jean

Andrade, Carlos Drummond de ..... **CLC 18**
See also Drummond de Andrade, Carlos

Andrade, Mario de 1893-1945 ...... **TCLC 43**

Andreae, Johann V(alentin) 1586-1654 .... **LC 32**
See also DLB 164

Andreas-Salome, Lou 1861-1937 .. **TCLC 56**
See also CA 178; DLB 66

Andress, Lesley
See Sanders, Lawrence

Andrewes, Lancelot 1555-1626 .... **LC 5**
See also DLB 151, 172

Andrews, Cicily Fairfield
See West, Rebecca

Andrews, Elton V.
See Pohl, Frederik

Andreyev, Leonid (Nikolaevich) 1871-1919 .... **TCLC 3**
See also CA 104; 185

Andric, Ivo 1892-1975 .... **CLC 8; SSC 36**
See also CA 81-84; 57-60; CANR 43, 60; DLB 147; MTCW 1

Androvar
See Prado (Calvo), Pedro

Angelique, Pierre
See Bataille, Georges

Angell, Roger 1920- .... **CLC 26**
See also CA 57-60; CANR 13, 44, 70; DLB 171, 185

Angelou, Maya 1928- ... **CLC 12, 35, 64, 77; BLC 1; DA; DAB; DAC; DAM MST, MULT, POET, POP; WLCS**
See also AAYA 7, 20; BW 2, 3; CA 65-68; CANR 19, 42, 65; CDALBS; CLR 53; DA3; DLB 38; MTCW 1, 2; SATA 49

Anna Comnena 1083-1153 .... **CMLC 25**

Annensky, Innokenty (Fyodorovich) 1856-1909 .... **TCLC 14**
See also CA 110; 155

Annunzio, Gabriele d'
See D'Annunzio, Gabriele

Anodos
See Coleridge, Mary E(lizabeth)

Anon, Charles Robert
See Pessoa, Fernando (Antonio Nogueira)

Anouilh, Jean (Marie Lucien Pierre) 1910-1987 .... **CLC 1, 3, 8, 13, 40, 50; DAM DRAM; DC 8**
See also CA 17-20R; 123; CANR 32; MTCW 1, 2

Anthony, Florence
See Ai

Anthony, John
See Ciardi, John (Anthony)

Anthony, Peter
See Shaffer, Anthony (Joshua); Shaffer, Peter (Levin)

Anthony, Piers 1934- ... **CLC 35; DAM POP**
See also AAYA 11; CA 21-24R; CANR 28, 56, 73; DLB 8; MTCW 1, 2; SAAS 22; SATA 84

Anthony, Susan B(rownell) 1916-1991 .... **TCLC 84**
See also CA 89-92; 134

Antoine, Marc
See Proust, (Valentin-Louis-George-Eugene-) Marcel

Antoninus, Brother
See Everson, William (Oliver)

Antonioni, Michelangelo 1912- .... **CLC 20**
See also CA 73-76; CANR 45, 77

Antschel, Paul 1920-1970
See Celan, Paul
See also CA 85-88; CANR 33, 61; MTCW 1

Anwar, Chairil 1922-1949 .... **TCLC 22**
See also CA 121

Anzaldua, Gloria 1942-
See also CA 175; DLB 122; HLCS 1

Apess, William 1798-1839(?) .... **NCLC 73; DAM MULT**
See also DLB 175; NNAL

Apollinaire, Guillaume 1880-1918 . **TCLC 3, 8, 51; DAM POET; PC 7**
See also Kostrowitzki, Wilhelm Apollinaris de
See also CA 152; MTCW 1

Appelfeld, Aharon 1932- .... **CLC 23, 47**
See also CA 112; 133; CANR 86

Apple, Max (Isaac) 1941- .... **CLC 9, 33**
See also CA 81-84; CANR 19, 54; DLB 130

Appleman, Philip (Dean) 1926- .... **CLC 51**
See also CA 13-16R; CAAS 18; CANR 6, 29, 56

Appleton, Lawrence
See Lovecraft, H(oward) P(hillips)

Apteryx
See Eliot, T(homas) S(tearns)

Apuleius, (Lucius Madaurensis) 125(?)-175(?) .... **CMLC 1**
See also DLB 211

Aquin, Hubert 1929-1977 .... **CLC 15**
See also CA 105; DLB 53

Aquinas, Thomas 1224(?)-1274 ... **CMLC 33**
See also DLB 115

Aragon, Louis 1897-1982 . **CLC 3, 22; DAM NOV, POET**
See also CA 69-72; 108; CANR 28, 71; DLB 72; MTCW 1, 2

Arany, Janos 1817-1882 .... **NCLC 34**

Aranyos, Kakay
See Mikszath, Kalman

Arbuthnot, John 1667-1735 .... **LC 1**
See also DLB 101

Archer, Herbert Winslow
See Mencken, H(enry) L(ouis)

Archer, Jeffrey (Howard) 1940- ..... **CLC 28; DAM POP**
See also AAYA 16; BEST 89:3; CA 77-80; CANR 22, 52; DA3; INT CANR-22

Archer, Jules 1915- .... **CLC 12**
See also CA 9-12R; CANR 6, 69; SAAS 5; SATA 4, 85

Archer, Lee
See Ellison, Harlan (Jay)

Arden, John 1930- ..... **CLC 6, 13, 15; DAM DRAM**
See also CA 13-16R; CAAS 4; CANR 31, 65, 67; DLB 13; MTCW 1

Arenas, Reinaldo 1943-1990 . **CLC 41; DAM MULT; HLC 1**
See also CA 124; 128; 133; CANR 73; DLB 145; HW 1; MTCW 1

Arendt, Hannah 1906-1975 .... **CLC 66, 98**
See also CA 17-20R; 61-64; CANR 26, 60; MTCW 1, 2

Aretino, Pietro 1492-1556 .... **LC 12**

Arghezi, Tudor 1880-1967 .... **CLC 80**
See also Theodorescu, Ion N.
See also CA 167

Arguedas, Jose Maria 1911-1969 ... **CLC 10, 18; HLCS 1**
See also CA 89-92; CANR 73; DLB 113; HW 1

Argueta, Manlio 1936- .... **CLC 31**
See also CA 131; CANR 73; DLB 145; HW 1

Arias, Ron(ald Francis) 1941-
See also CA 131; CANR 81; DAM MULT; DLB 82; HLC 1; HW 1, 2; MTCW 2

Ariosto, Ludovico 1474-1533 .... **LC 6**

Aristides
See Epstein, Joseph

Aristophanes 450B.C.-385B.C. ..... **CMLC 4; DA; DAB; DAC; DAM DRAM, MST; DC 2; WLCS**
See also DA3; DLB 176

Aristotle 384B.C.-322B.C. ... **CMLC 31; DA; DAB; DAC; DAM MST; WLCS**
See also DA3; DLB 176

Arlt, Roberto (Godofredo Christophersen) 1900-1942 ..... **TCLC 29; DAM MULT; HLC 1**
See also CA 123; 131; CANR 67; HW 1, 2

Armah, Ayi Kwei 1939- . **CLC 5, 33; BLC 1; DAM MULT, POET**
See also BW 1; CA 61-64; CANR 21, 64; DLB 117; MTCW 1

Armatrading, Joan 1950- .... **CLC 17**
See also CA 114; 186

Arnette, Robert
See Silverberg, Robert

Arnim, Achim von (Ludwig Joachim von Arnim) 1781-1831 .... **NCLC 5; SSC 29**
See also DLB 90

Arnim, Bettina von 1785-1859 ..... **NCLC 38**
See also DLB 90

Arnold, Matthew 1822-1888 .... **NCLC 6, 29, 89; DA; DAB; DAC; DAM MST, POET; PC 5; WLC**
See also CDBLB 1832-1890; DLB 32, 57

Arnold, Thomas 1795-1842 .... **NCLC 18**
See also DLB 55

Arnow, Harriette (Louisa) Simpson 1908-1986 .... **CLC 2, 7, 18**
See also CA 9-12R; 118; CANR 14; DLB 6; MTCW 1, 2; SATA 42; SATA-Obit 47

Arouet, Francois-Marie
See Voltaire

Arp, Hans
See Arp, Jean

Arp, Jean 1887-1966 .... **CLC 5**
See also CA 81-84; 25-28R; CANR 42, 77

Arrabal
See Arrabal, Fernando

Arrabal, Fernando 1932- .. **CLC 2, 9, 18, 58**
See also CA 9-12R; CANR 15

Arreola, Juan Jose 1918- ...... **SSC 38; DAM MULT; HLC 1**
See also CA 113; 131; CANR 81; DLB 113; HW 1, 2

Arrick, Fran .... **CLC 30**
See also Gaberman, Judie Angell

Artaud, Antonin (Marie Joseph) 1896-1948 .... **TCLC 3, 36; DAM DRAM**
See also CA 104; 149; DA3; MTCW 1

Arthur, Ruth M(abel) 1905-1979 .... **CLC 12**
See also CA 9-12R; 85-88; CANR 4; SATA 7, 26

Artsybashev, Mikhail (Petrovich) 1878-1927 .... **TCLC 31**
See also CA 170

Arundel, Honor (Morfydd) 1919-1973 .... **CLC 17**
See also CA 21-22; 41-44R; CAP 2; CLR 35; SATA 4; SATA-Obit 24

Arzner, Dorothy 1897-1979 .... **CLC 98**

Asch, Sholem 1880-1957 .... **TCLC 3**
See also CA 105

Ash, Shalom
See Asch, Sholem

Ashbery, John (Lawrence) 1927- . **CLC 2, 3, 4, 6, 9, 13, 15, 25, 41, 77, 125; DAM POET; PC 26**
See also CA 5-8R; CANR 9, 37, 66; DA3; DLB 5, 165; DLBY 81; INT CANR-9; MTCW 1, 2

Ashdown, Clifford
See Freeman, R(ichard) Austin

Ashe, Gordon
See Creasey, John

Ashton-Warner, Sylvia (Constance) 1908-1984 .... **CLC 19**
See also CA 69-72; 112; CANR 29; MTCW 1, 2

Asimov, Isaac 1920-1992 .... **CLC 1, 3, 9, 19, 26, 76, 92; DAM POP**
See also AAYA 13; BEST 90:2; CA 1-4R; 137; CANR 2, 19, 36, 60; CLR 12; DA3; DLB 8; DLBY 92; INT CANR-19; JRDA; MAICYA; MTCW 1, 2; SATA 1, 26, 74

Assis, Joaquim Maria Machado de
See Machado de Assis, Joaquim Maria

Astley, Thea (Beatrice May) 1925- . **CLC 41**
See also CA 65-68; CANR 11, 43, 78

Aston, James
See White, T(erence) H(anbury)

Asturias, Miguel Angel 1899-1974 ... **CLC 3, 8, 13; DAM MULT, NOV; HLC 1**
See also CA 25-28; 49-52; CANR 32; CAP 2; DA3; DLB 113; HW 1; MTCW 1, 2

Atares, Carlos Saura
See Saura (Atares), Carlos

Atheling, William
See Pound, Ezra (Weston Loomis)

Atheling, William, Jr.
See Blish, James (Benjamin)

Atherton, Gertrude (Franklin Horn) 1857-1948 .... **TCLC 2**
See also CA 104; 155; DLB 9, 78, 186

Atherton, Lucius
See Masters, Edgar Lee

Atkins, Jack
See Harris, Mark

Atkinson, Kate .... **CLC 99**
See also CA 166

Attaway, William (Alexander) 1911-1986 .... **CLC 92; BLC 1; DAM MULT**
See also BW 2, 3; CA 143; CANR 82; DLB 76

Atticus
See Fleming, Ian (Lancaster); Wilson, (Thomas) Woodrow

Atwood, Margaret (Eleanor) 1939- . **CLC 2, 3, 4, 8, 13, 15, 25, 44, 84; DA; DAB; DAC; DAM MST, NOV, POET; PC 8; SSC 2; WLC**
See also AAYA 12; BEST 89:2; CA 49-52; CANR 3, 24, 33, 59; DA3; DLB 53; INT CANR-24; MTCW 1, 2; SATA 50

Aubigny, Pierre d'
See Mencken, H(enry) L(ouis)

Aubin, Penelope 1685-1731(?) .... **LC 9**
See also DLB 39

Auchincloss, Louis (Stanton) 1917- . **CLC 4, 6, 9, 18, 45; DAM NOV; SSC 22**
See also CA 1-4R; CANR 6, 29, 55, 87; DLB 2; DLBY 80; INT CANR-29; MTCW 1

Auden, W(ystan) H(ugh) 1907-1973 . **CLC 1, 2, 3, 4, 6, 9, 11, 14, 43; DA; DAB; DAC; DAM DRAM, MST, POET; PC 1; WLC**
See also AAYA 18; CA 9-12R; 45-48; CANR 5, 61; CDBLB 1914-1945; DA3; DLB 10, 20; MTCW 1, 2

Audiberti, Jacques 1900-1965 .... **CLC 38; DAM DRAM**
See also CA 25-28R

Audubon, John James 1785-1851 . **NCLC 47**

Auel, Jean M(arie) 1936- .... **CLC 31, 107; DAM POP**
See also AAYA 7; BEST 90:4; CA 103; CANR 21, 64; DA3; INT CANR-21; SATA 91

Auerbach, Erich 1892-1957 .... **TCLC 43**
See also CA 118; 155

Augier, Emile 1820-1889 .... **NCLC 31**
See also DLB 192

August, John
See De Voto, Bernard (Augustine)

Augustine 354-430 ...... **CMLC 6; DA; DAB; DAC; DAM MST; WLCS**
See also DA3; DLB 115

Aurelius
See Bourne, Randolph S(illiman)

Aurobindo, Sri
See Ghose, Aurabinda

Austen, Jane 1775-1817 ..... **NCLC 1, 13, 19, 33, 51, 81; DA; DAB; DAC; DAM MST, NOV; WLC**
See also AAYA 19; CDBLB 1789-1832; DA3; DLB 116

Auster, Paul 1947- .... **CLC 47, 131**
See also CA 69-72; CANR 23, 52, 75; DA3; DLB 227; MTCW 1

Austin, Frank
See Faust, Frederick (Schiller)

Austin, Mary (Hunter) 1868-1934 . **TCLC 25**
See also CA 109; 178; DLB 9, 78, 206, 221

Averroes 1126-1198 .... **CMLC 7**
See also DLB 115

Avicenna 980-1037 .... **CMLC 16**
See also DLB 115

Avison, Margaret 1918- .... **CLC 2, 4, 97; DAC; DAM POET**
See also CA 17-20R; DLB 53; MTCW 1

Axton, David
See Koontz, Dean R(ay)

Ayckbourn, Alan 1939- .... **CLC 5, 8, 18, 33, 74; DAB; DAM DRAM; DC 13**
See also CA 21-24R; CANR 31, 59; DLB 13; MTCW 1, 2

Aydy, Catherine
See Tennant, Emma (Christina)

Ayme, Marcel (Andre) 1902-1967 .. **CLC 11; SSC 41**
See also CA 89-92; CANR 67; CLR 25; DLB 72; SATA 91

Ayrton, Michael 1921-1975 .... **CLC 7**
See also CA 5-8R; 61-64; CANR 9, 21

Azorin .... **CLC 11**
See also Martinez Ruiz, Jose

Azuela, Mariano 1873-1952 . **TCLC 3; DAM MULT; HLC 1**
See also CA 104; 131; CANR 81; HW 1, 2; MTCW 1, 2

Baastad, Babbis Friis
See Friis-Baastad, Babbis Ellinor

Bab
See Gilbert, W(illiam) S(chwenck)

Babbis, Eleanor
See Friis-Baastad, Babbis Ellinor

Babel, Isaac
See Babel, Isaak (Emmanuilovich)

Babel, Isaak (Emmanuilovich) 1894-1941(?) .... **TCLC 2, 13; SSC 16**
See also CA 104; 155; MTCW 1

Babits, Mihaly 1883-1941 .... **TCLC 14**
See also CA 114

Babur 1483-1530 .... **LC 18**

Baca, Jimmy Santiago 1952-
See also CA 131; CANR 81, 90; DAM MULT; DLB 122; HLC 1; HW 1, 2

Bacchelli, Riccardo 1891-1985 .... **CLC 19**
See also CA 29-32R; 117

Bach, Richard (David) 1936- .... **CLC 14; DAM NOV, POP**
See also AITN 1; BEST 89:2; CA 9-12R; CANR 18; MTCW 1; SATA 13

Bachman, Richard
See King, Stephen (Edwin)

Bachmann, Ingeborg 1926-1973 ..... **CLC 69**
See also CA 93-96; 45-48; CANR 69; DLB 85

Bacon, Francis 1561-1626 .... **LC 18, 32**
See also CDBLB Before 1660; DLB 151

Bacon, Roger 1214(?)-1292 .... **CMLC 14**
See also DLB 115

Bacovia, George .... **TCLC 24**
See also Vasiliu, Gheorghe
See also DLB 220

Badanes, Jerome 1937- .... **CLC 59**

Bagehot, Walter 1826-1877 .... **NCLC 10**
See also DLB 55

Bagnold, Enid 1889-1981 ..... **CLC 25; DAM DRAM**
See also CA 5-8R; 103; CANR 5, 40; DLB 13, 160, 191; MAICYA; SATA 1, 25

Bagritsky, Eduard 1895-1934 .... **TCLC 60**

Bagrjana, Elisaveta
See Belcheva, Elisaveta

Bagryana, Elisaveta 1893-1991 .... **CLC 10**
See also Belcheva, Elisaveta
See also CA 178; DLB 147

Bailey, Paul 1937- .... **CLC 45**
See also CA 21-24R; CANR 16, 62; DLB 14

Baillie, Joanna 1762-1851 .... **NCLC 71**
See also DLB 93

Bainbridge, Beryl (Margaret) 1934- . **CLC 4, 5, 8, 10, 14, 18, 22, 62, 130; DAM NOV**
See also CA 21-24R; CANR 24, 55, 75, 88; DLB 14; MTCW 1, 2

Baker, Elliott 1922- .... **CLC 8**
See also CA 45-48; CANR 2, 63

Baker, Jean H. .... **TCLC 3, 10**
See also Russell, George William

Baker, Nicholson 1957- . **CLC 61; DAM POP**
See also CA 135; CANR 63; DA3; DLB 227

Baker, Ray Stannard 1870-1946 .. **TCLC 47**
See also CA 118

Baker, Russell (Wayne) 1925- .... **CLC 31**
See also BEST 89:4; CA 57-60; CANR 11, 41, 59; MTCW 1, 2

Bakhtin, M.
See Bakhtin, Mikhail Mikhailovich

Bakhtin, M. M.
See Bakhtin, Mikhail Mikhailovich

Bakhtin, Mikhail
See Bakhtin, Mikhail Mikhailovich

Author Index

See also AAYA 16; CA 5-8R; CAAS 18; CANR 11, 56; CLR 3; DLBY 81; INT CANR-11; MAICYA; MTCW 1; SATA 6, 68
Bowen, Elizabeth (Dorothea Cole) 1899-1973 .... **CLC 1, 3, 6, 11, 15, 22, 118; DAM NOV; SSC 3, 28**
See also CA 17-18; 41-44R; CANR 35; CAP 2; CDBLB 1945-1960; DA3; DLB 15, 162; MTCW 1, 2
Bowering, George 1935- .... **CLC 15, 47**
See also CA 21-24R; CAAS 16; CANR 10; DLB 53
Bowering, Marilyn R(uthe) 1949- ... **CLC 32**
See also CA 101; CANR 49
Bowers, Edgar 1924- .... **CLC 9**
See also CA 5-8R; CANR 24; DLB 5
Bowie, David .... **CLC 17**
See also Jones, David Robert
Bowles, Jane (Sydney) 1917-1973 .... **CLC 3, 68**
See also CA 19-20; 41-44R; CAP 2
Bowles, Paul (Frederick) 1910-1999 . **CLC 1, 2, 19, 53; SSC 3**
See also CA 1-4R; 186; CAAS 1; CANR 1, 19, 50, 75; DA3; DLB 5, 6; MTCW 1, 2
Box, Edgar
See Vidal, Gore
Boyd, Nancy
See Millay, Edna St. Vincent
Boyd, William 1952- .... **CLC 28, 53, 70**
See also CA 114; 120; CANR 51, 71
Boyle, Kay 1902-1992 .... **CLC 1, 5, 19, 58, 121; SSC 5**
See also CA 13-16R; 140; CAAS 1; CANR 29, 61; DLB 4, 9, 48, 86; DLBY 93; MTCW 1, 2
Boyle, Mark
See Kienzle, William X(avier)
Boyle, Patrick 1905-1982 .... **CLC 19**
See also CA 127
Boyle, T. C. 1948-
See Boyle, T(homas) Coraghessan
Boyle, T(homas) Coraghessan 1948- ... **CLC 36, 55, 90; DAM POP; SSC 16**
See also BEST 90:4; CA 120; CANR 44, 76, 89; DA3; DLBY 86; MTCW 2
Boz
See Dickens, Charles (John Huffam)
Brackenridge, Hugh Henry 1748-1816 .... **NCLC 7**
See also DLB 11, 37
Bradbury, Edward P.
See Moorcock, Michael (John)
See also MTCW 2
Bradbury, Malcolm (Stanley) 1932- .... **CLC 32, 61; DAM NOV**
See also CA 1-4R; CANR 1, 33, 91; DA3; DLB 14, 207; MTCW 1, 2
Bradbury, Ray (Douglas) 1920- ... **CLC 1, 3, 10, 15, 42, 98; DA; DAB; DAC; DAM MST, NOV, POP; SSC 29; WLC**
See also AAYA 15; AITN 1, 2; CA 1-4R; CANR 2, 30, 75; CDALB 1968-1988; DA3; DLB 2, 8; MTCW 1, 2; SATA 11, 64
Bradford, Gamaliel 1863-1932 ..... **TCLC 36**
See also CA 160; DLB 17
Bradley, David (Henry), Jr. 1950- . **CLC 23, 118; BLC 1; DAM MULT**
See also BW 1, 3; CA 104; CANR 26, 81; DLB 33
Bradley, John Ed(mund, Jr.) 1958- . **CLC 55**
See also CA 139
Bradley, Marion Zimmer 1930-1999 .... **CLC 30; DAM POP**
See also AAYA 9; CA 57-60; 185; CAAS 10; CANR 7, 31, 51, 75; DA3; DLB 8; MTCW 1, 2; SATA 90; SATA-Obit 116
Bradstreet, Anne 1612(?)-1672 ..... **LC 4, 30; DA; DAC; DAM MST, POET; PC 10**
See also CDALB 1640-1865; DA3; DLB 24
Brady, Joan 1939- .... **CLC 86**
See also CA 141
Bragg, Melvyn 1939- .... **CLC 10**
See also BEST 89:3; CA 57-60; CANR 10, 48, 89; DLB 14
Brahe, Tycho 1546-1601 .... **LC 45**
Braine, John (Gerard) 1922-1986 .... **CLC 1, 3, 41**
See also CA 1-4R; 120; CANR 1, 33; CDBLB 1945-1960; DLB 15; DLBY 86; MTCW 1
Bramah, Ernest 1868-1942 .... **TCLC 72**
See also CA 156; DLB 70
Brammer, William 1930(?)-1978 ..... **CLC 31**
See also CA 77-80
Brancati, Vitaliano 1907-1954 ...... **TCLC 12**
See also CA 109
Brancato, Robin F(idler) 1936- .... **CLC 35**
See also AAYA 9; CA 69-72; CANR 11, 45; CLR 32; JRDA; SAAS 9; SATA 97
Brand, Max
See Faust, Frederick (Schiller)
Brand, Millen 1906-1980 .... **CLC 7**
See also CA 21-24R; 97-100; CANR 72
Branden, Barbara .... **CLC 44**
See also CA 148
Brandes, Georg (Morris Cohen) 1842-1927 .... **TCLC 10**
See also CA 105
Brandys, Kazimierz 1916- .... **CLC 62**
Branley, Franklyn M(ansfield) 1915- .... **CLC 21**
See also CA 33-36R; CANR 14, 39; CLR 13; MAICYA; SAAS 16; SATA 4, 68
Brathwaite, Edward (Kamau) 1930- .... **CLC 11; BLCS; DAM POET**
See also BW 2, 3; CA 25-28R; CANR 11, 26, 47; DLB 125
Brautigan, Richard (Gary) 1935-1984 . **CLC 1, 3, 5, 9, 12, 34, 42; DAM NOV**
See also CA 53-56; 113; CANR 34; DA3; DLB 2, 5, 206; DLBY 80, 84; MTCW 1; SATA 56
Brave Bird, Mary 1953-
See Crow Dog, Mary (Ellen)
See also NNAL
Braverman, Kate 1950- .... **CLC 67**
See also CA 89-92
Brecht, (Eugen) Bertolt (Friedrich) 1898-1956 .... **TCLC 1, 6, 13, 35; DA; DAB; DAC; DAM DRAM, MST; DC 3; WLC**
See also CA 104; 133; CANR 62; DA3; DLB 56, 124; MTCW 1, 2
Brecht, Eugen Berthold Friedrich
See Brecht, (Eugen) Bertolt (Friedrich)
Bremer, Fredrika 1801-1865 .... **NCLC 11**
Brennan, Christopher John 1870-1932 .... **TCLC 17**
See also CA 117
Brennan, Maeve 1917-1993 .... **CLC 5**
See also CA 81-84; CANR 72
Brent, Linda
See Jacobs, Harriet A(nn)
Brentano, Clemens (Maria) 1778-1842 .... **NCLC 1**
See also DLB 90
Brent of Bin Bin
See Franklin, (Stella Maria Sarah) Miles (Lampe)
Brenton, Howard 1942- .... **CLC 31**
See also CA 69-72; CANR 33, 67; DLB 13; MTCW 1
Breslin, James 1930-1996
See Breslin, Jimmy
See also CA 73-76; CANR 31, 75; DAM NOV; MTCW 1, 2
Breslin, Jimmy .... **CLC 4, 43**
See also Breslin, James
See also AITN 1; DLB 185; MTCW 2
Bresson, Robert 1901- .... **CLC 16**
See also CA 110; CANR 49
Breton, Andre 1896-1966 . **CLC 2, 9, 15, 54; PC 15**
See also CA 19-20; 25-28R; CANR 40, 60; CAP 2; DLB 65; MTCW 1, 2
Breytenbach, Breyten 1939(?)- . **CLC 23, 37, 126; DAM POET**
See also CA 113; 129; CANR 61; DLB 225
Bridgers, Sue Ellen 1942- .... **CLC 26**
See also AAYA 8; CA 65-68; CANR 11, 36; CLR 18; DLB 52; JRDA; MAICYA; SAAS 1; SATA 22, 90; SATA-Essay 109
Bridges, Robert (Seymour) 1844-1930 .... **TCLC 1; DAM POET; PC 28**
See also CA 104; 152; CDBLB 1890-1914; DLB 19, 98
Bridie, James .... **TCLC 3**
See also Mavor, Osborne Henry
See also DLB 10
Brin, David 1950- .... **CLC 34**
See also AAYA 21; CA 102; CANR 24, 70; INT CANR-24; SATA 65
Brink, Andre (Philippus) 1935- ...... **CLC 18, 36, 106**
See also CA 104; CANR 39, 62; DLB 225; INT 103; MTCW 1, 2
Brinsmead, H(esba) F(ay) 1922- ..... **CLC 21**
See also CA 21-24R; CANR 10; CLR 47; MAICYA; SAAS 5; SATA 18, 78
Brittain, Vera (Mary) 1893(?)-1970 . **CLC 23**
See also CA 13-16; 25-28R; CANR 58; CAP 1; DLB 191; MTCW 1, 2
Broch, Hermann 1886-1951 .... **TCLC 20**
See also CA 117; DLB 85, 124
Brock, Rose
See Hansen, Joseph
Brodkey, Harold (Roy) 1930-1996 .. **CLC 56**
See also CA 111; 151; CANR 71; DLB 130
Brodskii, Iosif
See Brodsky, Joseph
Brodsky, Iosif Alexandrovich 1940-1996
See Brodsky, Joseph
See also AITN 1; CA 41-44R; 151; CANR 37; DAM POET; DA3; MTCW 1, 2
Brodsky, Joseph 1940-1996 .... **CLC 4, 6, 13, 36, 100; PC 9**
See also Brodskii, Iosif; Brodsky, Iosif Alexandrovich
See also MTCW 1
Brodsky, Michael (Mark) 1948- ...... **CLC 19**
See also CA 102; CANR 18, 41, 58
Bromell, Henry 1947- .... **CLC 5**
See also CA 53-56; CANR 9
Bromfield, Louis (Brucker) 1896-1956 .... **TCLC 11**
See also CA 107; 155; DLB 4, 9, 86
Broner, E(sther) M(asserman) 1930- .... **CLC 19**
See also CA 17-20R; CANR 8, 25, 72; DLB 28
Bronk, William (M.) 1918-1999 ...... **CLC 10**
See also CA 89-92; 177; CANR 23; DLB 165
Bronstein, Lev Davidovich
See Trotsky, Leon
Bronte, Anne 1820-1849 .... **NCLC 4, 71**
See also DA3; DLB 21, 199
Bronte, Charlotte 1816-1855 ..... **NCLC 3, 8, 33, 58; DA; DAB; DAC; DAM MST, NOV; WLC**
See also AAYA 17; CDBLB 1832-1890; DA3; DLB 21, 159, 199
Bronte, Emily (Jane) 1818-1848 .. **NCLC 16,**

Author Index

35; DA; DAB; DAC; DAM MST, NOV, POET; PC 8; WLC
See also AAYA 17; CDBLB 1832-1890; DA3; DLB 21, 32, 199

Brooke, Frances 1724-1789 .... **LC 6, 48**
See also DLB 39, 99

Brooke, Henry 1703(?)-1783 .... **LC 1**
See also DLB 39

Brooke, Rupert (Chawner) 1887-1915 ..... **TCLC 2, 7; DA; DAB; DAC; DAM MST, POET; PC 24; WLC**
See also CA 104; 132; CANR 61; CDBLB 1914-1945; DLB 19; MTCW 1, 2

Brooke-Haven, P.
See Wodehouse, P(elham) G(renville)

Brooke-Rose, Christine 1926(?)- ..... **CLC 40**
See also CA 13-16R; CANR 58; DLB 14

Brookner, Anita 1928- .... **CLC 32, 34, 51; DAB; DAM POP**
See also CA 114; 120; CANR 37, 56, 87; DA3; DLB 194; DLBY 87; MTCW 1, 2

Brooks, Cleanth 1906-1994 ...... **CLC 24, 86, 110**
See also CA 17-20R; 145; CANR 33, 35; DLB 63; DLBY 94; INT CANR-35; MTCW 1, 2

Brooks, George
See Baum, L(yman) Frank

Brooks, Gwendolyn 1917- .... **CLC 1, 2, 4, 5, 15, 49, 125; BLC 1; DA; DAC; DAM MST, MULT, POET; PC 7; WLC**
See also AAYA 20; AITN 1; BW 2, 3; CA 1-4R; CANR 1, 27, 52, 75; CDALB 1941-1968; CLR 27; DA3; DLB 5, 76, 165; MTCW 1, 2; SATA 6

Brooks, Mel .... **CLC 12**
See also Kaminsky, Melvin
See also AAYA 13; DLB 26

Brooks, Peter 1938- .... **CLC 34**
See also CA 45-48; CANR 1

Brooks, Van Wyck 1886-1963 .... **CLC 29**
See also CA 1-4R; CANR 6; DLB 45, 63, 103

Brophy, Brigid (Antonia) 1929-1995 . **CLC 6, 11, 29, 105**
See also CA 5-8R; 149; CAAS 4; CANR 25, 53; DA3; DLB 14; MTCW 1, 2

Brosman, Catharine Savage 1934- ... **CLC 9**
See also CA 61-64; CANR 21, 46

Brossard, Nicole 1943- .... **CLC 115**
See also CA 122; CAAS 16; DLB 53

Brother Antoninus
See Everson, William (Oliver)

The Brothers Quay
See Quay, Stephen; Quay, Timothy

Broughton, T(homas) Alan 1936- ... **CLC 19**
See also CA 45-48; CANR 2, 23, 48

Broumas, Olga 1949- .... **CLC 10, 73**
See also CA 85-88; CANR 20, 69

Brown, Alan 1950- .... **CLC 99**
See also CA 156

Brown, Charles Brockden 1771-1810 .... **NCLC 22, 74**
See also CDALB 1640-1865; DLB 37, 59, 73

Brown, Christy 1932-1981 .... **CLC 63**
See also CA 105; 104; CANR 72; DLB 14

Brown, Claude 1937- .... **CLC 30; BLC 1; DAM MULT**
See also AAYA 7; BW 1, 3; CA 73-76; CANR 81

Brown, Dee (Alexander) 1908- . **CLC 18, 47; DAM POP**
See also AAYA 30; CA 13-16R; CAAS 6; CANR 11, 45, 60; DA3; DLBY 80; MTCW 1, 2; SATA 5, 110

Brown, George
See Wertmueller, Lina

Brown, George Douglas 1869-1902 .... **TCLC 28**
See also CA 162

Brown, George Mackay 1921-1996 . **CLC 5, 48, 100**
See also CA 21-24R; 151; CAAS 6; CANR 12, 37, 67; DLB 14, 27, 139; MTCW 1; SATA 35

Brown, (William) Larry 1951- .... **CLC 73**
See also CA 130; 134; INT 133

Brown, Moses
See Barrett, William (Christopher)

Brown, Rita Mae 1944- ...... **CLC 18, 43, 79; DAM NOV, POP**
See also CA 45-48; CANR 2, 11, 35, 62; DA3; INT CANR-11; MTCW 1, 2

Brown, Roderick (Langmere) Haig-
See Haig-Brown, Roderick (Langmere)

Brown, Rosellen 1939- .... **CLC 32**
See also CA 77-80; CAAS 10; CANR 14, 44

Brown, Sterling Allen 1901-1989 ..... **CLC 1, 23, 59; BLC 1; DAM MULT, POET**
See also BW 1, 3; CA 85-88; 127; CANR 26; DA3; DLB 48, 51, 63; MTCW 1, 2

Brown, Will
See Ainsworth, William Harrison

Brown, William Wells 1813-1884 .. **NCLC 2, 89; BLC 1; DAM MULT; DC 1**
See also DLB 3, 50

Browne, (Clyde) Jackson 1948(?)- .. **CLC 21**
See also CA 120

Browning, Elizabeth Barrett 1806-1861 . **NCLC 1, 16, 61, 66; DA; DAB; DAC; DAM MST, POET; PC 6; WLC**
See also CDBLB 1832-1890; DA3; DLB 32, 199

Browning, Robert 1812-1889 . **NCLC 19, 79; DA; DAB; DAC; DAM MST, POET; PC 2; WLCS**
See also CDBLB 1832-1890; DA3; DLB 32, 163; YABC 1

Browning, Tod 1882-1962 .... **CLC 16**
See also CA 141; 117

Brownson, Orestes Augustus 1803-1876 .... **NCLC 50**
See also DLB 1, 59, 73

Bruccoli, Matthew J(oseph) 1931- .. **CLC 34**
See also CA 9-12R; CANR 7, 87; DLB 103

Bruce, Lenny .... **CLC 21**
See also Schneider, Leonard Alfred

Bruin, John
See Brutus, Dennis

Brulard, Henri
See Stendhal

Brulls, Christian
See Simenon, Georges (Jacques Christian)

Brunner, John (Kilian Houston) 1934-1995 .... **CLC 8, 10; DAM POP**
See also CA 1-4R; 149; CAAS 8; CANR 2, 37; MTCW 1, 2

Bruno, Giordano 1548-1600 .... **LC 27**

Brutus, Dennis 1924- .... **CLC 43; BLC 1; DAM MULT, POET; PC 24**
See also BW 2, 3; CA 49-52; CAAS 14; CANR 2, 27, 42, 81; DLB 117, 225

Bryan, C(ourtlandt) D(ixon) B(arnes) 1936- .... **CLC 29**
See also CA 73-76; CANR 13, 68; DLB 185; INT CANR-13

Bryan, Michael
See Moore, Brian

Bryant, William Cullen 1794-1878 . **NCLC 6, 46; DA; DAB; DAC; DAM MST, POET; PC 20**
See also CDALB 1640-1865; DLB 3, 43, 59, 189

Bryusov, Valery Yakovlevich 1873-1924 .... **TCLC 10**
See also CA 107; 155

Buchan, John 1875-1940 ... **TCLC 41; DAB; DAM POP**
See also CA 108; 145; DLB 34, 70, 156; MTCW 1; YABC 2

Buchanan, George 1506-1582 .... **LC 4**
See also DLB 152

Buchheim, Lothar-Guenther 1918- ... **CLC 6**
See also CA 85-88

Buchner, (Karl) Georg 1813-1837 . **NCLC 26**

Buchwald, Art(hur) 1925- .... **CLC 33**
See also AITN 1; CA 5-8R; CANR 21, 67; MTCW 1, 2; SATA 10

Buck, Pearl S(ydenstricker) 1892-1973 .. **CLC 7, 11, 18, 127; DA; DAB; DAC; DAM MST, NOV**
See also AITN 1; CA 1-4R; 41-44R; CANR 1, 34; CDALBS; DA3; DLB 9, 102; MTCW 1, 2; SATA 1, 25

Buckler, Ernest 1908-1984 .. **CLC 13; DAC; DAM MST**
See also CA 11-12; 114; CAP 1; DLB 68; SATA 47

Buckley, Vincent (Thomas) 1925-1988 .... **CLC 57**
See also CA 101

Buckley, William F(rank), Jr. 1925- . **CLC 7, 18, 37; DAM POP**
See also AITN 1; CA 1-4R; CANR 1, 24, 53; DA3; DLB 137; DLBY 80; INT CANR-24; MTCW 1, 2

Buechner, (Carl) Frederick 1926- .... **CLC 2, 4, 6, 9; DAM NOV**
See also CA 13-16R; CANR 11, 39, 64; DLBY 80; INT CANR-11; MTCW 1, 2

Buell, John (Edward) 1927- .... **CLC 10**
See also CA 1-4R; CANR 71; DLB 53

Buero Vallejo, Antonio 1916- .... **CLC 15, 46**
See also CA 106; CANR 24, 49, 75; HW 1; MTCW 1, 2

Bufalino, Gesualdo 1920(?)- .... **CLC 74**
See also DLB 196

Bugayev, Boris Nikolayevich 1880-1934 .... **TCLC 7; PC 11**
See also Bely, Andrey
See also CA 104; 165; MTCW 1

Bukowski, Charles 1920-1994 .. **CLC 2, 5, 9, 41, 82, 108; DAM NOV, POET; PC 18**
See also CA 17-20R; 144; CANR 40, 62; DA3; DLB 5, 130, 169; MTCW 1, 2

Bulgakov, Mikhail (Afanas'evich) 1891-1940 . **TCLC 2, 16; DAM DRAM, NOV; SSC 18**
See also CA 105; 152

Bulgya, Alexander Alexandrovich 1901-1956 .... **TCLC 53**
See also Fadeyev, Alexander
See also CA 117; 181

Bullins, Ed 1935- .... **CLC 1, 5, 7; BLC 1; DAM DRAM, MULT; DC 6**
See also BW 2, 3; CA 49-52; CAAS 16; CANR 24, 46, 73; DLB 7, 38; MTCW 1, 2

Bulwer-Lytton, Edward (George Earle Lytton) 1803-1873 .... **NCLC 1, 45**
See also DLB 21

Bunin, Ivan Alexeyevich 1870-1953 .... **TCLC 6; SSC 5**
See also CA 104

Bunting, Basil 1900-1985 ... **CLC 10, 39, 47; DAM POET**
See also CA 53-56; 115; CANR 7; DLB 20

Bunuel, Luis 1900-1983 . **CLC 16, 80; DAM MULT; HLC 1**
See also CA 101; 110; CANR 32, 77; HW 1

Bunyan, John 1628-1688 .. **LC 4; DA; DAB; DAC; DAM MST; WLC**
See also CDBLB 1660-1789; DLB 39

See also CA 21-24R; 146; CANR 23, 61, 79; DA3; DLB 85, 124; MTCW 1, 2
Canfield, Dorothea F.
See Fisher, Dorothy (Frances) Canfield
Canfield, Dorothea Frances
See Fisher, Dorothy (Frances) Canfield
Canfield, Dorothy
See Fisher, Dorothy (Frances) Canfield
Canin, Ethan 1960- .... **CLC 55**
See also CA 131; 135
Cannon, Curt
See Hunter, Evan
Cao, Lan 1961- .... **CLC 109**
See also CA 165
Cape, Judith
See Page, P(atricia) K(athleen)
Capek, Karel 1890-1938 .. **TCLC 6, 37; DA; DAB; DAC; DAM DRAM, MST, NOV; DC 1; SSC 36; WLC**
See also CA 104; 140; DA3; MTCW 1
Capote, Truman 1924-1984 ...... **CLC 1, 3, 8, 13, 19, 34, 38, 58; DA; DAB; DAC; DAM MST, NOV, POP; SSC 2; WLC**
See also CA 5-8R; 113; CANR 18, 62; CDALB 1941-1968; DA3; DLB 2, 185, 227; DLBY 80, 84; MTCW 1, 2; SATA 91
Capra, Frank 1897-1991 .... **CLC 16**
See also CA 61-64; 135
Caputo, Philip 1941- .... **CLC 32**
See also CA 73-76; CANR 40
Caragiale, Ion Luca 1852-1912 .... **TCLC 76**
See also CA 157
Card, Orson Scott 1951- .... **CLC 44, 47, 50; DAM POP**
See also AAYA 11; CA 102; CANR 27, 47, 73; DA3; INT CANR-27; MTCW 1, 2; SATA 83
Cardenal, Ernesto 1925- ...... **CLC 31; DAM MULT, POET; HLC 1; PC 22**
See also CA 49-52; CANR 2, 32, 66; HW 1, 2; MTCW 1, 2
Cardozo, Benjamin N(athan) 1870-1938 .... **TCLC 65**
See also CA 117; 164
Carducci, Giosue (Alessandro Giuseppe) 1835-1907 .... **TCLC 32**
See also CA 163
Carew, Thomas 1595(?)-1640 . **LC 13; PC 29**
See also DLB 126
Carey, Ernestine Gilbreth 1908- ..... **CLC 17**
See also CA 5-8R; CANR 71; SATA 2
Carey, Peter 1943- .... **CLC 40, 55, 96**
See also CA 123; 127; CANR 53, 76; INT 127; MTCW 1, 2; SATA 94
Carleton, William 1794-1869 .... **NCLC 3**
See also DLB 159
Carlisle, Henry (Coffin) 1926- .... **CLC 33**
See also CA 13-16R; CANR 15, 85
Carlsen, Chris
See Holdstock, Robert P.
Carlson, Ron(ald F.) 1947- .... **CLC 54**
See also CA 105; CANR 27
Carlyle, Thomas 1795-1881 . **NCLC 70; DA; DAB; DAC; DAM MST**
See also CDBLB 1789-1832; DLB 55; 144
Carman, (William) Bliss 1861-1929 .... **TCLC 7; DAC**
See also CA 104; 152; DLB 92
Carnegie, Dale 1888-1955 .... **TCLC 53**
Carossa, Hans 1878-1956 .... **TCLC 48**
See also CA 170; DLB 66
Carpenter, Don(ald Richard) 1931-1995 .... **CLC 41**
See also CA 45-48; 149; CANR 1, 71
Carpenter, Edward 1844-1929 ...... **TCLC 88**
See also CA 163
Carpentier (y Valmont), Alejo 1904-1980 .... **CLC 8, 11, 38, 110; DAM MULT; HLC 1; SSC 35**
See also CA 65-68; 97-100; CANR 11, 70; DLB 113; HW 1, 2
Carr, Caleb 1955(?)- .... **CLC 86**
See also CA 147; CANR 73; DA3
Carr, Emily 1871-1945 .... **TCLC 32**
See also CA 159; DLB 68
Carr, John Dickson 1906-1977 .... **CLC 3**
See also Fairbairn, Roger
See also CA 49-52; 69-72; CANR 3, 33, 60; MTCW 1, 2
Carr, Philippa
See Hibbert, Eleanor Alice Burford
Carr, Virginia Spencer 1929- .... **CLC 34**
See also CA 61-64; DLB 111
Carrere, Emmanuel 1957- .... **CLC 89**
Carrier, Roch 1937- .... **CLC 13, 78; DAC; DAM MST**
See also CA 130; CANR 61; DLB 53; SATA 105
Carroll, James P. 1943(?)- .... **CLC 38**
See also CA 81-84; CANR 73; MTCW 1
Carroll, Jim 1951- .... **CLC 35**
See also AAYA 17; CA 45-48; CANR 42
Carroll, Lewis ... **NCLC 2, 53; PC 18; WLC**
See also Dodgson, Charles Lutwidge
See also CDBLB 1832-1890; CLR 2, 18; DLB 18, 163, 178; DLBY 98; JRDA
Carroll, Paul Vincent 1900-1968 ..... **CLC 10**
See also CA 9-12R; 25-28R; DLB 10
Carruth, Hayden 1921- .... **CLC 4, 7, 10, 18, 84; PC 10**
See also CA 9-12R; CANR 4, 38, 59; DLB 5, 165; INT CANR-4; MTCW 1, 2; SATA 47
Carson, Rachel Louise 1907-1964 . **CLC 71; DAM POP**
See also CA 77-80; CANR 35; DA3; MTCW 1, 2; SATA 23
Carter, Angela (Olive) 1940-1992 .... **CLC 5, 41, 76; SSC 13**
See also CA 53-56; 136; CANR 12, 36, 61; DA3; DLB 14, 207; MTCW 1, 2; SATA 66; SATA-Obit 70
Carter, Nick
See Smith, Martin Cruz
Carver, Raymond 1938-1988 .... **CLC 22, 36, 53, 55, 126; DAM NOV; SSC 8**
See also CA 33-36R; 126; CANR 17, 34, 61; DA3; DLB 130; DLBY 84, 88; MTCW 1, 2
Cary, Elizabeth, Lady Falkland 1585-1639 .... **LC 30**
Cary, (Arthur) Joyce (Lunel) 1888-1957 .... **TCLC 1, 29**
See also CA 104; 164; CDBLB 1914-1945; DLB 15, 100; MTCW 2
Casanova de Seingalt, Giovanni Jacopo 1725-1798 .... **LC 13**
Casares, Adolfo Bioy
See Bioy Casares, Adolfo
Casely-Hayford, J(oseph) E(phraim) 1866-1930 ..... **TCLC 24; BLC 1; DAM MULT**
See also BW 2; CA 123; 152
Casey, John (Dudley) 1939- .... **CLC 59**
See also BEST 90:2; CA 69-72; CANR 23
Casey, Michael 1947- .... **CLC 2**
See also CA 65-68; DLB 5
Casey, Patrick
See Thurman, Wallace (Henry)
Casey, Warren (Peter) 1935-1988 ... **CLC 12**
See also CA 101; 127; INT 101
Casona, Alejandro .... **CLC 49**
See also Alvarez, Alejandro Rodriguez
Cassavetes, John 1929-1989 .... **CLC 20**
See also CA 85-88; 127; CANR 82
Cassian, Nina 1924- .... **PC 17**
Cassill, R(onald) V(erlin) 1919- .. **CLC 4, 23**
See also CA 9-12R; CAAS 1; CANR 7, 45; DLB 6
Cassirer, Ernst 1874-1945 .... **TCLC 61**
See also CA 157
Cassity, (Allen) Turner 1929- ...... **CLC 6, 42**
See also CA 17-20R; CAAS 8; CANR 11; DLB 105
Castaneda, Carlos (Cesar Aranha) 1931(?)-1998 .... **CLC 12, 119**
See also CA 25-28R; CANR 32, 66; HW 1; MTCW 1
Castedo, Elena 1937- .... **CLC 65**
See also CA 132
Castedo-Ellerman, Elena
See Castedo, Elena
Castellanos, Rosario 1925-1974 ..... **CLC 66; DAM MULT; HLC 1; SSC 39**
See also CA 131; 53-56; CANR 58; DLB 113; HW 1; MTCW 1
Castelvetro, Lodovico 1505-1571 .... **LC 12**
Castiglione, Baldassare 1478-1529 ..... **LC 12**
Castle, Robert
See Hamilton, Edmond
Castro (Ruz), Fidel 1926(?)-
See also CA 110; 129; CANR 81; DAM MULT; HLC 1; HW 2
Castro, Guillen de 1569-1631 .... **LC 19**
Castro, Rosalia de 1837-1885 . **NCLC 3, 78; DAM MULT**
Cather, Willa
See Cather, Willa Sibert
Cather, Willa Sibert 1873-1947 ..... **TCLC 1, 11, 31; DA; DAB; DAC; DAM MST, NOV; SSC 2; WLC**
See also Cather, Willa
See also AAYA 24; CA 104; 128; CDALB 1865-1917; DA3; DLB 9, 54, 78; DLBD 1; MTCW 1, 2; SATA 30
Catherine, Saint 1347-1380 .... **CMLC 27**
Cato, Marcus Porcius 234B.C.-149B.C. .... **CMLC 21**
See also DLB 211
Catton, (Charles) Bruce 1899-1978 . **CLC 35**
See also AITN 1; CA 5-8R; 81-84; CANR 7, 74; DLB 17; SATA 2; SATA-Obit 24
Catullus c. 84B.C.-c. 54B.C. .... **CMLC 18**
See also DLB 211
Cauldwell, Frank
See King, Francis (Henry)
Caunitz, William J. 1933-1996 .... **CLC 34**
See also BEST 89:3; CA 125; 130; 152; CANR 73; INT 130
Causley, Charles (Stanley) 1917- ...... **CLC 7**
See also CA 9-12R; CANR 5, 35; CLR 30; DLB 27; MTCW 1; SATA 3, 66
Caute, (John) David 1936- .. **CLC 29; DAM NOV**
See also CA 1-4R; CAAS 4; CANR 1, 33, 64; DLB 14
Cavafy, C(onstantine) P(eter) 1863-1933 .... **TCLC 2, 7; DAM POET**
See also Kavafis, Konstantinos Petrou
See also CA 148; DA3; MTCW 1
Cavallo, Evelyn
See Spark, Muriel (Sarah)
Cavanna, Betty .... **CLC 12**
See also Harrison, Elizabeth Cavanna
See also JRDA; MAICYA; SAAS 4; SATA 1, 30
Cavendish, Margaret Lucas 1623-1673 .... **LC 30**
See also DLB 131
Caxton, William 1421(?)-1491(?) .... **LC 17**
See also DLB 170

Colegate, Isabel 1931- .... **CLC 36**
See also CA 17-20R; CANR 8, 22, 74; DLB 14; INT CANR-22; MTCW 1
Coleman, Emmett
See Reed, Ishmael
Coleridge, M. E.
See Coleridge, Mary E(lizabeth)
Coleridge, Mary E(lizabeth) 1861-1907 .... **TCLC 73**
See also CA 116; 166; DLB 19, 98
Coleridge, Samuel Taylor 1772-1834 .. **NCLC 9, 54; DA; DAB; DAC; DAM MST, POET; PC 11; WLC**
See also CDBLB 1789-1832; DA3; DLB 93, 107
Coleridge, Sara 1802-1852 .... **NCLC 31**
See also DLB 199
Coles, Don 1928- .... **CLC 46**
See also CA 115; CANR 38
Coles, Robert (Martin) 1929- .... **CLC 108**
See also CA 45-48; CANR 3, 32, 66, 70; INT CANR-32; SATA 23
Colette, (Sidonie-Gabrielle) 1873-1954 .... **TCLC 1, 5, 16; DAM NOV; SSC 10**
See also CA 104; 131; DA3; DLB 65; MTCW 1, 2
Collett, (Jacobine) Camilla (Wergeland) 1813-1895 .... **NCLC 22**
Collier, Christopher 1930- .... **CLC 30**
See also AAYA 13; CA 33-36R; CANR 13, 33; JRDA; MAICYA; SATA 16, 70
Collier, James L(incoln) 1928- .... **CLC 30; DAM POP**
See also AAYA 13; CA 9-12R; CANR 4, 33, 60; CLR 3; JRDA; MAICYA; SAAS 21; SATA 8, 70
Collier, Jeremy 1650-1726 .... **LC 6**
Collier, John 1901-1980 .... **SSC 19**
See also CA 65-68; 97-100; CANR 10; DLB 77
Collingwood, R(obin) G(eorge) 1889(?)-1943 .... **TCLC 67**
See also CA 117; 155
Collins, Hunt
See Hunter, Evan
Collins, Linda 1931- .... **CLC 44**
See also CA 125
Collins, (William) Wilkie 1824-1889 .... **NCLC 1, 18**
See also CDBLB 1832-1890; DLB 18, 70, 159
Collins, William 1721-1759 . **LC 4, 40; DAM POET**
See also DLB 109
Collodi, Carlo 1826-1890 .... **NCLC 54**
See also Lorenzini, Carlo
See also CLR 5
Colman, George 1732-1794
See Glassco, John
Colt, Winchester Remington
See Hubbard, L(afayette) Ron(ald)
Colter, Cyrus 1910- .... **CLC 58**
See also BW 1; CA 65-68; CANR 10, 66; DLB 33
Colton, James
See Hansen, Joseph
Colum, Padraic 1881-1972 .... **CLC 28**
See also CA 73-76; 33-36R; CANR 35; CLR 36; MAICYA; MTCW 1; SATA 15
Colvin, James
See Moorcock, Michael (John)
Colwin, Laurie (E.) 1944-1992 ... **CLC 5, 13, 23, 84**
See also CA 89-92; 139; CANR 20, 46; DLBY 80; MTCW 1
Comfort, Alex(ander) 1920-2000 ..... **CLC 7; DAM POP**
See also CA 1-4R; CANR 1, 45; MTCW 1
Comfort, Montgomery
See Campbell, (John) Ramsey
Compton-Burnett, I(vy) 1884(?)-1969 .... **CLC 1, 3, 10, 15, 34; DAM NOV**
See also CA 1-4R; 25-28R; CANR 4; DLB 36; MTCW 1
Comstock, Anthony 1844-1915 ..... **TCLC 13**
See also CA 110; 169
Comte, Auguste 1798-1857 .... **NCLC 54**
Conan Doyle, Arthur
See Doyle, Arthur Conan
Conde (Abellan), Carmen 1901-
See also CA 177; DLB 108; HLCS 1; HW 2
Conde, Maryse 1937- ... **CLC 52, 92; BLCS; DAM MULT**
See also BW 2, 3; CA 110; CANR 30, 53, 76; MTCW 1
Condillac, Etienne Bonnot de 1714-1780 .... **LC 26**
Condon, Richard (Thomas) 1915-1996 ... **CLC 4, 6, 8, 10, 45, 100; DAM NOV**
See also BEST 90:3; CA 1-4R; 151; CAAS 1; CANR 2, 23; INT CANR-23; MTCW 1, 2
Confucius 551B.C.-479B.C. . **CMLC 19; DA; DAB; DAC; DAM MST; WLCS**
See also DA3
Congreve, William 1670-1729 .... **LC 5, 21; DA; DAB; DAC; DAM DRAM, MST, POET; DC 2; WLC**
See also CDBLB 1660-1789; DLB 39, 84
Connell, Evan S(helby), Jr. 1924- .... **CLC 4, 6, 45; DAM NOV**
See also AAYA 7; CA 1-4R; CAAS 2; CANR 2, 39, 76; DLB 2; DLBY 81; MTCW 1, 2
Connelly, Marc(us Cook) 1890-1980 . **CLC 7**
See also CA 85-88; 102; CANR 30; DLB 7; DLBY 80; SATA-Obit 25
Connor, Ralph .... **TCLC 31**
See also Gordon, Charles William
See also DLB 92
Conrad, Joseph 1857-1924 .. **TCLC 1, 6, 13, 25, 43, 57; DA; DAB; DAC; DAM MST, NOV; SSC 9; WLC**
See also AAYA 26; CA 104; 131; CANR 60; CDBLB 1890-1914; DA3; DLB 10, 34, 98, 156; MTCW 1, 2; SATA 27
Conrad, Robert Arnold
See Hart, Moss
Conroy, Pat
See Conroy, (Donald) Pat(rick)
See also MTCW 2
Conroy, (Donald) Pat(rick) 1945- .. **CLC 30, 74; DAM NOV, POP**
See also Conroy, Pat
See also AAYA 8; AITN 1; CA 85-88; CANR 24, 53; DA3; DLB 6; MTCW 1
Constant (de Rebecque), (Henri) Benjamin 1767-1830 .... **NCLC 6**
See also DLB 119
Conybeare, Charles Augustus
See Eliot, T(homas) S(tearns)
Cook, Michael 1933- .... **CLC 58**
See also CA 93-96; CANR 68; DLB 53
Cook, Robin 1940- ...... **CLC 14; DAM POP**
See also AAYA 32; BEST 90:2; CA 108; 111; CANR 41, 90; DA3; INT 111
Cook, Roy
See Silverberg, Robert
Cooke, Elizabeth 1948- .... **CLC 55**
See also CA 129
Cooke, John Esten 1830-1886 .... **NCLC 5**
See also DLB 3
Cooke, John Estes
See Baum, L(yman) Frank
Cooke, M. E.
See Creasey, John
Cooke, Margaret
See Creasey, John
Cook-Lynn, Elizabeth 1930- . **CLC 93; DAM MULT**
See also CA 133; DLB 175; NNAL
Cooney, Ray .... **CLC 62**
Cooper, Douglas 1960- .... **CLC 86**
Cooper, Henry St. John
See Creasey, John
Cooper, J(oan) California (?)- .... **CLC 56; DAM MULT**
See also AAYA 12; BW 1; CA 125; CANR 55; DLB 212
Cooper, James Fenimore 1789-1851 .... **NCLC 1, 27, 54**
See also AAYA 22; CDALB 1640-1865; DA3; DLB 3; SATA 19
Coover, Robert (Lowell) 1932- .... **CLC 3, 7, 15, 32, 46, 87; DAM NOV; SSC 15**
See also CA 45-48; CANR 3, 37, 58; DLB 2, 227; DLBY 81; MTCW 1, 2
Copeland, Stewart (Armstrong) 1952- .... **CLC 26**
Copernicus, Nicolaus 1473-1543 .... **LC 45**
Coppard, A(lfred) E(dgar) 1878-1957 .... **TCLC 5; SSC 21**
See also CA 114; 167; DLB 162; YABC 1
Coppee, Francois 1842-1908 .... **TCLC 25**
See also CA 170
Coppola, Francis Ford 1939- .. **CLC 16, 126**
See also CA 77-80; CANR 40, 78; DLB 44
Corbiere, Tristan 1845-1875 .... **NCLC 43**
Corcoran, Barbara 1911- .... **CLC 17**
See also AAYA 14; CA 21-24R; CAAS 2; CANR 11, 28, 48; CLR 50; DLB 52; JRDA; SAAS 20; SATA 3, 77
Cordelier, Maurice
See Giraudoux, (Hippolyte) Jean
Corelli, Marie 1855-1924 .... **TCLC 51**
See also Mackey, Mary
See also DLB 34, 156
Corman, Cid 1924- .... **CLC 9**
See also Corman, Sidney
See also CAAS 2; DLB 5, 193
Corman, Sidney 1924-
See Corman, Cid
See also CA 85-88; CANR 44; DAM POET
Cormier, Robert (Edmund) 1925- . **CLC 12, 30; DA; DAB; DAC; DAM MST, NOV**
See also AAYA 3, 19; CA 1-4R; CANR 5, 23, 76; CDALB 1968-1988; CLR 12, 55; DLB 52; INT CANR-23; JRDA; MAICYA; MTCW 1, 2; SATA 10, 45, 83
Corn, Alfred (DeWitt III) 1943- ..... **CLC 33**
See also CA 179; CAAE 179; CAAS 25; CANR 44; DLB 120; DLBY 80
Corneille, Pierre 1606-1684 ... **LC 28; DAB; DAM MST**
Cornwell, David (John Moore) 1931- .... **CLC 9, 15; DAM POP**
See also le Carre, John
See also CA 5-8R; CANR 13, 33, 59; DA3; MTCW 1, 2
Corso, (Nunzio) Gregory 1930- .. **CLC 1, 11**
See also CA 5-8R; CANR 41, 76; DA3; DLB 5, 16; MTCW 1, 2
Cortazar, Julio 1914-1984 .. **CLC 2, 3, 5, 10, 13, 15, 33, 34, 92; DAM MULT, NOV; HLC 1; SSC 7**
See also CA 21-24R; CANR 12, 32, 81; DA3; DLB 113; HW 1, 2; MTCW 1, 2
Cortes, Hernan 1484-1547 .... **LC 31**
Corvinus, Jakob
See Raabe, Wilhelm (Karl)
Corwin, Cecil
See Kornbluth, C(yril) M.
Cosic, Dobrica 1921- .... **CLC 14**
See also CA 122; 138; DLB 181

Dillard, R(ichard) H(enry) W(ilde) 1937- .... **CLC 5**
See also CA 21-24R; CAAS 7; CANR 10; DLB 5
Dillon, Eilis 1920-1994 .... **CLC 17**
See also CA 9-12R, 182; 147; CAAE 182; CAAS 3; CANR 4, 38, 78; CLR 26; MAICYA; SATA 2, 74; SATA-Essay 105; SATA-Obit 83
Dimont, Penelope
See Mortimer, Penelope (Ruth)
Dinesen, Isak .... **CLC 10, 29, 95; SSC 7**
See also Blixen, Karen (Christentze Dinesen)
See also MTCW 1
Ding Ling .... **CLC 68**
See also Chiang, Pin-chin
Diphusa, Patty
See Almodovar, Pedro
Disch, Thomas M(ichael) 1940- .. **CLC 7, 36**
See also AAYA 17; CA 21-24R; CAAS 4; CANR 17, 36, 54, 89; CLR 18; DA3; DLB 8; MAICYA; MTCW 1, 2; SAAS 15; SATA 92
Disch, Tom
See Disch, Thomas M(ichael)
d'Isly, Georges
See Simenon, Georges (Jacques Christian)
Disraeli, Benjamin 1804-1881 . **NCLC 2, 39, 79**
See also DLB 21, 55
Ditcum, Steve
See Crumb, R(obert)
Dixon, Paige
See Corcoran, Barbara
Dixon, Stephen 1936- .... **CLC 52; SSC 16**
See also CA 89-92; CANR 17, 40, 54, 91; DLB 130
Doak, Annie
See Dillard, Annie
Dobell, Sydney Thompson 1824-1874 .... **NCLC 43**
See also DLB 32
Doblin, Alfred .... **TCLC 13**
See also Doeblin, Alfred
Dobrolyubov, Nikolai Alexandrovich 1836-1861 .... **NCLC 5**
Dobson, Austin 1840-1921 .... **TCLC 79**
See also DLB 35; 144
Dobyns, Stephen 1941- .... **CLC 37**
See also CA 45-48; CANR 2, 18
Doctorow, E(dgar) L(aurence) 1931- .... **CLC 6, 11, 15, 18, 37, 44, 65, 113; DAM NOV, POP**
See also AAYA 22; AITN 2; BEST 89:3; CA 45-48; CANR 2, 33, 51, 76; CDALB 1968-1988; DA3; DLB 2, 28, 173; DLBY 80; MTCW 1, 2
Dodgson, Charles Lutwidge 1832-1898
See Carroll, Lewis
See also CLR 2; DA; DAB; DAC; DAM MST, NOV, POET; DA3; MAICYA; SATA 100; YABC 2
Dodson, Owen (Vincent) 1914-1983 .... **CLC 79; BLC 1; DAM MULT**
See also BW 1; CA 65-68; 110; CANR 24; DLB 76
Doeblin, Alfred 1878-1957 .... **TCLC 13**
See also Doblin, Alfred
See also CA 110; 141; DLB 66
Doerr, Harriet 1910- .... **CLC 34**
See also CA 117; 122; CANR 47; INT 122
Domecq, H(onorio Bustos)
See Bioy Casares, Adolfo
Domecq, H(onorio) Bustos
See Bioy Casares, Adolfo; Borges, Jorge Luis
Domini, Rey
See Lorde, Audre (Geraldine)
Dominique
See Proust, (Valentin-Louis-George-Eugene-) Marcel
Don, A
See Stephen, SirLeslie
Donaldson, Stephen R. 1947- .... **CLC 46; DAM POP**
See also CA 89-92; CANR 13, 55; INT CANR-13
Donleavy, J(ames) P(atrick) 1926- ... **CLC 1, 4, 6, 10, 45**
See also AITN 2; CA 9-12R; CANR 24, 49, 62, 80; DLB 6, 173; INT CANR-24; MTCW 1, 2
Donne, John 1572-1631 .... **LC 10, 24; DA; DAB; DAC; DAM MST, POET; PC 1; WLC**
See also CDBLB Before 1660; DLB 121, 151
Donnell, David 1939(?)- .... **CLC 34**
Donoghue, P. S.
See Hunt, E(verette) Howard, (Jr.)
Donoso (Yanez), Jose 1924-1996 .. **CLC 4, 8, 11, 32, 99; DAM MULT; HLC 1; SSC 34**
See also CA 81-84; 155; CANR 32, 73; DLB 113; HW 1, 2; MTCW 1, 2
Donovan, John 1928-1992 .... **CLC 35**
See also AAYA 20; CA 97-100; 137; CLR 3; MAICYA; SATA 72; SATA-Brief 29
Don Roberto
See Cunninghame Graham, Robert (Gallnigad) Bontine
Doolittle, Hilda 1886-1961 ...... **CLC 3, 8, 14, 31, 34, 73; DA; DAC; DAM MST, POET; PC 5; WLC**
See also H. D.
See also CA 97-100; CANR 35; DLB 4, 45; MTCW 1, 2
Dorfman, Ariel 1942- ..... **CLC 48, 77; DAM MULT; HLC 1**
See also CA 124; 130; CANR 67, 70; HW 1, 2; INT 130
Dorn, Edward (Merton) 1929- .. **CLC 10, 18**
See also CA 93-96; CANR 42, 79; DLB 5; INT 93-96
Dorris, Michael (Anthony) 1945-1997 .... **CLC 109; DAM MULT, NOV**
See also AAYA 20; BEST 90:1; CA 102; 157; CANR 19, 46, 75; CLR 58; DA3; DLB 175; MTCW 2; NNAL; SATA 75; SATA-Obit 94
Dorris, Michael A.
See Dorris, Michael (Anthony)
Dorsan, Luc
See Simenon, Georges (Jacques Christian)
Dorsange, Jean
See Simenon, Georges (Jacques Christian)
Dos Passos, John (Roderigo) 1896-1970 ..... **CLC 1, 4, 8, 11, 15, 25, 34, 82; DA; DAB; DAC; DAM MST, NOV; WLC**
See also CA 1-4R; 29-32R; CANR 3; CDALB 1929-1941; DA3; DLB 4, 9; DLBD 1, 15; DLBY 96; MTCW 1, 2
Dossage, Jean
See Simenon, Georges (Jacques Christian)
Dostoevsky, Fedor Mikhailovich 1821-1881 .... **NCLC 2, 7, 21, 33, 43; DA; DAB; DAC; DAM MST, NOV; SSC 2, 33; WLC**
See also DA3
Doughty, Charles M(ontagu) 1843-1926 .... **TCLC 27**
See also CA 115; 178; DLB 19, 57, 174
Douglas, Ellen .... **CLC 73**
See also Haxton, Josephine Ayres; Williamson, Ellen Douglas
Douglas, Gavin 1475(?)-1522 .... **LC 20**
See also DLB 132
Douglas, George
See Brown, George Douglas
Douglas, Keith (Castellain) 1920-1944 .... **TCLC 40**
See also CA 160; DLB 27
Douglas, Leonard
See Bradbury, Ray (Douglas)
Douglas, Michael
See Crichton, (John) Michael
Douglas, (George) Norman 1868-1952 .... **TCLC 68**
See also CA 119; 157; DLB 34, 195
Douglas, William
See Brown, George Douglas
Douglass, Frederick 1817(?)-1895 . **NCLC 7, 55; BLC 1; DA; DAC; DAM MST, MULT; WLC**
See also CDALB 1640-1865; DA3; DLB 1, 43, 50, 79; SATA 29
Dourado, (Waldomiro Freitas) Autran 1926- .... **CLC 23, 60**
See also CA 25-28R, 179; CANR 34, 81; DLB 145; HW 2
Dourado, Waldomiro Autran 1926-
See Dourado, (Waldomiro Freitas) Autran
See also CA 179
Dove, Rita (Frances) 1952- ...... **CLC 50, 81; BLCS; DAM MULT, POET; PC 6**
See also BW 2; CA 109; CAAS 19; CANR 27, 42, 68, 76; CDALBS; DA3; DLB 120; MTCW 1
Doveglion
See Villa, Jose Garcia
Dowell, Coleman 1925-1985 .... **CLC 60**
See also CA 25-28R; 117; CANR 10; DLB 130
Dowson, Ernest (Christopher) 1867-1900 .... **TCLC 4**
See also CA 105; 150; DLB 19, 135
Doyle, A. Conan
See Doyle, Arthur Conan
Doyle, Arthur Conan 1859-1930 ... **TCLC 7; DA; DAB; DAC; DAM MST, NOV; SSC 12; WLC**
See also AAYA 14; CA 104; 122; CDBLB 1890-1914; DA3; DLB 18, 70, 156, 178; MTCW 1, 2; SATA 24
Doyle, Conan
See Doyle, Arthur Conan
Doyle, John
See Graves, Robert (von Ranke)
Doyle, Roddy 1958(?)- .... **CLC 81**
See also AAYA 14; CA 143; CANR 73; DA3; DLB 194
Doyle, Sir A. Conan
See Doyle, Arthur Conan
Doyle, Sir Arthur Conan
See Doyle, Arthur Conan
Dr. A
See Asimov, Isaac; Silverstein, Alvin
Drabble, Margaret 1939- ..... **CLC 2, 3, 5, 8, 10, 22, 53, 129; DAB; DAC; DAM MST, NOV, POP**
See also CA 13-16R; CANR 18, 35, 63; CDBLB 1960 to Present; DA3; DLB 14, 155; MTCW 1, 2; SATA 48
Drapier, M. B.
See Swift, Jonathan
Drayham, James
See Mencken, H(enry) L(ouis)
Drayton, Michael 1563-1631 .... **LC 8; DAM POET**
See also DLB 121
Dreadstone, Carl
See Campbell, (John) Ramsey
Dreiser, Theodore (Herman Albert) 1871-1945 ... **TCLC 10, 18, 35, 83; DA; DAC; DAM MST, NOV; SSC 30; WLC**

Eddison, E(ric) R(ucker) 1882-1945 .... **TCLC 15**
See also CA 109; 156
Eddy, Mary (Ann Morse) Baker 1821-1910 .... **TCLC 71**
See also CA 113; 174
Edel, (Joseph) Leon 1907-1997 . **CLC 29, 34**
See also CA 1-4R; 161; CANR 1, 22; DLB 103; INT CANR-22
Eden, Emily 1797-1869 .... **NCLC 10**
Edgar, David 1948- . **CLC 42; DAM DRAM**
See also CA 57-60; CANR 12, 61; DLB 13; MTCW 1
Edgerton, Clyde (Carlyle) 1944- ..... **CLC 39**
See also AAYA 17; CA 118; 134; CANR 64; INT 134
Edgeworth, Maria 1768-1849 ... **NCLC 1, 51**
See also DLB 116, 159, 163; SATA 21
Edmonds, Paul
See Kuttner, Henry
Edmonds, Walter D(umaux) 1903-1998 .... **CLC 35**
See also CA 5-8R; CANR 2; DLB 9; MAICYA; SAAS 4; SATA 1, 27; SATA-Obit 99
Edmondson, Wallace
See Ellison, Harlan (Jay)
Edson, Russell .... **CLC 13**
See also CA 33-36R
Edwards, Bronwen Elizabeth
See Rose, Wendy
Edwards, G(erald) B(asil) 1899-1976 .... **CLC 25**
See also CA 110
Edwards, Gus 1939- .... **CLC 43**
See also CA 108; INT 108
Edwards, Jonathan 1703-1758 ..... **LC 7, 54; DA; DAC; DAM MST**
See also DLB 24
Efron, Marina Ivanovna Tsvetaeva
See Tsvetaeva (Efron), Marina (Ivanovna)
Ehle, John (Marsden, Jr.) 1925- ..... **CLC 27**
See also CA 9-12R
Ehrenbourg, Ilya (Grigoryevich)
See Ehrenburg, Ilya (Grigoryevich)
Ehrenburg, Ilya (Grigoryevich) 1891-1967 .... **CLC 18, 34, 62**
See also CA 102; 25-28R
Ehrenburg, Ilyo (Grigoryevich)
See Ehrenburg, Ilya (Grigoryevich)
Ehrenreich, Barbara 1941- .... **CLC 110**
See also BEST 90:4; CA 73-76; CANR 16, 37, 62; MTCW 1, 2
Eich, Guenter 1907-1972 .... **CLC 15**
See also CA 111; 93-96; DLB 69, 124
Eichendorff, Joseph Freiherr von 1788-1857 .... **NCLC 8**
See also DLB 90
Eigner, Larry .... **CLC 9**
See also Eigner, Laurence (Joel)
See also CAAS 23; DLB 5
Eigner, Laurence (Joel) 1927-1996
See Eigner, Larry
See also CA 9-12R; 151; CANR 6, 84; DLB 193
Einstein, Albert 1879-1955 .... **TCLC 65**
See also CA 121; 133; MTCW 1, 2
Eiseley, Loren Corey 1907-1977 .... **CLC 7**
See also AAYA 5; CA 1-4R; 73-76; CANR 6; DLBD 17
Eisenstadt, Jill 1963- .... **CLC 50**
See also CA 140
Eisenstein, Sergei (Mikhailovich) 1898-1948 .... **TCLC 57**
See also CA 114; 149
Eisner, Simon
See Kornbluth, C(yril) M.
Ekeloef, (Bengt) Gunnar 1907-1968 .... **CLC 27; DAM POET; PC 23**
See also CA 123; 25-28R
Ekelof, (Bengt) Gunnar
See Ekeloef, (Bengt) Gunnar
Ekelund, Vilhelm 1880-1949 .... **TCLC 75**
Ekwensi, C. O. D.
See Ekwensi, Cyprian (Odiatu Duaka)
Ekwensi, Cyprian (Odiatu Duaka) 1921- .... **CLC 4; BLC 1; DAM MULT**
See also BW 2, 3; CA 29-32R; CANR 18, 42, 74; DLB 117; MTCW 1, 2; SATA 66
Elaine .... **TCLC 18**
See also Leverson, Ada
El Crummo
See Crumb, R(obert)
Elder, Lonne III 1931-1996 .... **DC 8**
See also BLC 1; BW 1, 3; CA 81-84; 152; CANR 25; DAM MULT; DLB 7, 38, 44
Eleanor of Aquitaine 1122-1204 .. **CMLC 39**
Elia
See Lamb, Charles
Eliade, Mircea 1907-1986 .... **CLC 19**
See also CA 65-68; 119; CANR 30, 62; DLB 220; MTCW 1
Eliot, A. D.
See Jewett, (Theodora) Sarah Orne
Eliot, Alice
See Jewett, (Theodora) Sarah Orne
Eliot, Dan
See Silverberg, Robert
Eliot, George 1819-1880 .... **NCLC 4, 13, 23, 41, 49, 89; DA; DAB; DAC; DAM MST, NOV; PC 20; WLC**
See also CDBLB 1832-1890; DA3; DLB 21, 35, 55
Eliot, John 1604-1690 .... **LC 5**
See also DLB 24
Eliot, T(homas) S(tearns) 1888-1965 . **CLC 1, 2, 3, 6, 9, 10, 13, 15, 24, 34, 41, 55, 57, 113; DA; DAB; DAC; DAM DRAM, MST, POET; PC 5; WLC**
See also AAYA 28; CA 5-8R; 25-28R; CANR 41; CDALB 1929-1941; DA3; DLB 7, 10, 45, 63; DLBY 88; MTCW 1, 2
Elizabeth 1866-1941 .... **TCLC 41**
Elkin, Stanley L(awrence) 1930-1995 .... **CLC 4, 6, 9, 14, 27, 51, 91; DAM NOV, POP; SSC 12**
See also CA 9-12R; 148; CANR 8, 46; DLB 2, 28; DLBY 80; INT CANR-8; MTCW 1, 2
Elledge, Scott .... **CLC 34**
Elliot, Don
See Silverberg, Robert
Elliott, Don
See Silverberg, Robert
Elliott, George P(aul) 1918-1980 .... **CLC 2**
See also CA 1-4R; 97-100; CANR 2
Elliott, Janice 1931- .... **CLC 47**
See also CA 13-16R; CANR 8, 29, 84; DLB 14
Elliott, Sumner Locke 1917-1991 ... **CLC 38**
See also CA 5-8R; 134; CANR 2, 21
Elliott, William
See Bradbury, Ray (Douglas)
Ellis, A. E. .... **CLC 7**
Ellis, Alice Thomas .... **CLC 40**
See also Haycraft, Anna (Margaret)
See also DLB 194; MTCW 1
Ellis, Bret Easton 1964- ... **CLC 39, 71, 117; DAM POP**
See also AAYA 2; CA 118; 123; CANR 51, 74; DA3; INT 123; MTCW 1
Ellis, (Henry) Havelock 1859-1939 .... **TCLC 14**
See also CA 109; 169; DLB 190
Ellis, Landon
See Ellison, Harlan (Jay)
Ellis, Trey 1962- .... **CLC 55**
See also CA 146
Ellison, Harlan (Jay) 1934- . **CLC 1, 13, 42; DAM POP; SSC 14**
See also AAYA 29; CA 5-8R; CANR 5, 46; DLB 8; INT CANR-5; MTCW 1, 2
Ellison, Ralph (Waldo) 1914-1994 ... **CLC 1, 3, 11, 54, 86, 114; BLC 1; DA; DAB; DAC; DAM MST, MULT, NOV; SSC 26; WLC**
See also AAYA 19; BW 1, 3; CA 9-12R; 145; CANR 24, 53; CDALB 1941-1968; DA3; DLB 2, 76, 227; DLBY 94; MTCW 1, 2
Ellmann, Lucy (Elizabeth) 1956- .... **CLC 61**
See also CA 128
Ellmann, Richard (David) 1918-1987 .... **CLC 50**
See also BEST 89:2; CA 1-4R; 122; CANR 2, 28, 61; DLB 103; DLBY 87; MTCW 1, 2
Elman, Richard (Martin) 1934-1997 .... **CLC 19**
See also CA 17-20R; 163; CAAS 3; CANR 47
Elron
See Hubbard, L(afayette) Ron(ald)
Eluard, Paul .... **TCLC 7, 41**
See also Grindel, Eugene
Elyot, Sir Thomas 1490(?)-1546 .... **LC 11**
Elytis, Odysseus 1911-1996 ...... **CLC 15, 49, 100; DAM POET; PC 21**
See also CA 102; 151; MTCW 1, 2
Emecheta, (Florence Onye) Buchi 1944- . **CLC 14, 48, 128; BLC 2; DAM MULT**
See also BW 2, 3; CA 81-84; CANR 27, 81; DA3; DLB 117; MTCW 1, 2; SATA 66
Emerson, Mary Moody 1774-1863 .... **NCLC 66**
Emerson, Ralph Waldo 1803-1882 . **NCLC 1, 38; DA; DAB; DAC; DAM MST, POET; PC 18; WLC**
See also CDALB 1640-1865; DA3; DLB 1, 59, 73, 223
Eminescu, Mihail 1850-1889 .... **NCLC 33**
Empson, William 1906-1984 .. **CLC 3, 8, 19, 33, 34**
See also CA 17-20R; 112; CANR 31, 61; DLB 20; MTCW 1, 2
Enchi, Fumiko (Ueda) 1905-1986 ... **CLC 31**
See also CA 129; 121; DLB 182
Ende, Michael (Andreas Helmuth) 1929-1995 .... **CLC 31**
See also CA 118; 124; 149; CANR 36; CLR 14; DLB 75; MAICYA; SATA 61; SATA-Brief 42; SATA-Obit 86
Endo, Shusaku 1923-1996 .... **CLC 7, 14, 19, 54, 99; DAM NOV**
See also CA 29-32R; 153; CANR 21, 54; DA3; DLB 182; MTCW 1, 2
Engel, Marian 1933-1985 .... **CLC 36**
See also CA 25-28R; CANR 12; DLB 53; INT CANR-12
Engelhardt, Frederick
See Hubbard, L(afayette) Ron(ald)
Engels, Friedrich 1820-1895 .... **NCLC 85**
See also DLB 129
Enright, D(ennis) J(oseph) 1920- . **CLC 4, 8, 31**
See also CA 1-4R; CANR 1, 42, 83; DLB 27; SATA 25
Enzensberger, Hans Magnus 1929- . **CLC 43; PC 28**
See also CA 116; 119
Ephron, Nora 1941- .... **CLC 17, 31**

See also CA 135; 147
Feinstein, Elaine 1930- .... **CLC 36**
See also CA 69-72; CAAS 1; CANR 31, 68; DLB 14, 40; MTCW 1
Feldman, Irving (Mordecai) 1928- ... **CLC 7**
See also CA 1-4R; CANR 1; DLB 169
Felix-Tchicaya, Gerald
See Tchicaya, Gerald Felix
Fellini, Federico 1920-1993 .... **CLC 16, 85**
See also CA 65-68; 143; CANR 33
Felsen, Henry Gregor 1916-1995 .... **CLC 17**
See also CA 1-4R; 180; CANR 1; SAAS 2; SATA 1
Fenno, Jack
See Calisher, Hortense
Fenollosa, Ernest (Francisco) 1853-1908 .... **TCLC 91**
Fenton, James Martin 1949- .... **CLC 32**
See also CA 102; DLB 40
Ferber, Edna 1887-1968 .... **CLC 18, 93**
See also AITN 1; CA 5-8R; 25-28R; CANR 68; DLB 9, 28, 86; MTCW 1, 2; SATA 7
Ferguson, Helen
See Kavan, Anna
Ferguson, Samuel 1810-1886 .... **NCLC 33**
See also DLB 32
Fergusson, Robert 1750-1774 .... **LC 29**
See also DLB 109
Ferling, Lawrence
See Ferlinghetti, Lawrence (Monsanto)
Ferlinghetti, Lawrence (Monsanto) 1919(?)- .... **CLC 2, 6, 10, 27, 111; DAM POET; PC 1**
See also CA 5-8R; CANR 3, 41, 73; CDALB 1941-1968; DA3; DLB 5, 16; MTCW 1, 2
Fern, Fanny 1811-1872
See Parton, Sara Payson Willis
Fernandez, Vicente Garcia Huidobro
See Huidobro Fernandez, Vicente Garcia
Ferre, Rosario 1942- .... **SSC 36; HLCS 1**
See also CA 131; CANR 55, 81; DLB 145; HW 1, 2; MTCW 1
Ferrer, Gabriel (Francisco Victor) Miro
See Miro (Ferrer), Gabriel (Francisco Victor)
Ferrier, Susan (Edmonstone) 1782-1854 .... **NCLC 8**
See also DLB 116
Ferrigno, Robert 1948(?)- .... **CLC 65**
See also CA 140
Ferron, Jacques 1921-1985 ... **CLC 94; DAC**
See also CA 117; 129; DLB 60
Feuchtwanger, Lion 1884-1958 .... **TCLC 3**
See also CA 104; DLB 66
Feuillet, Octave 1821-1890 .... **NCLC 45**
See also DLB 192
Feydeau, Georges (Leon Jules Marie) 1862-1921 ..... **TCLC 22; DAM DRAM**
See also CA 113; 152; CANR 84; DLB 192
Fichte, Johann Gottlieb 1762-1814 .... **NCLC 62**
See also DLB 90
Ficino, Marsilio 1433-1499 .... **LC 12**
Fiedeler, Hans
See Doeblin, Alfred
Fiedler, Leslie A(aron) 1917- . **CLC 4, 13, 24**
See also CA 9-12R; CANR 7, 63; DLB 28, 67; MTCW 1, 2
Field, Andrew 1938- .... **CLC 44**
See also CA 97-100; CANR 25
Field, Eugene 1850-1895 .... **NCLC 3**
See also DLB 23, 42, 140; DLBD 13; MAICYA; SATA 16
Field, Gans T.
See Wellman, Manly Wade
Field, Michael 1915-1971 .... **TCLC 43**
See also CA 29-32R
Field, Peter
See Hobson, Laura Z(ametkin)
Fielding, Henry 1707-1754 ... **LC 1, 46; DA; DAB; DAC; DAM DRAM, MST, NOV; WLC**
See also CDBLB 1660-1789; DA3; DLB 39, 84, 101
Fielding, Sarah 1710-1768 .... **LC 1, 44**
See also DLB 39
Fields, W. C. 1880-1946 .... **TCLC 80**
See also DLB 44
Fierstein, Harvey (Forbes) 1954- ... **CLC 33; DAM DRAM, POP**
See also CA 123; 129; DA3
Figes, Eva 1932- .... **CLC 31**
See also CA 53-56; CANR 4, 44, 83; DLB 14
Finch, Anne 1661-1720 .... **LC 3; PC 21**
See also DLB 95
Finch, Robert (Duer Claydon) 1900- .... **CLC 18**
See also CA 57-60; CANR 9, 24, 49; DLB 88
Findley, Timothy 1930- . **CLC 27, 102; DAC; DAM MST**
See also CA 25-28R; CANR 12, 42, 69; DLB 53
Fink, William
See Mencken, H(enry) L(ouis)
Firbank, Louis 1942-
See Reed, Lou
See also CA 117
Firbank, (Arthur Annesley) Ronald 1886-1926 .... **TCLC 1**
See also CA 104; 177; DLB 36
Fisher, Dorothy (Frances) Canfield 1879-1958 .... **TCLC 87**
See also CA 114; 136; CANR 80; DLB 9, 102; MAICYA; YABC 1
Fisher, M(ary) F(rances) K(ennedy) 1908-1992 .... **CLC 76, 87**
See also CA 77-80; 138; CANR 44; MTCW 1
Fisher, Roy 1930- .... **CLC 25**
See also CA 81-84; CAAS 10; CANR 16; DLB 40
Fisher, Rudolph 1897-1934 . **TCLC 11; BLC 2; DAM MULT; SSC 25**
See also BW 1, 3; CA 107; 124; CANR 80; DLB 51, 102
Fisher, Vardis (Alvero) 1895-1968 .... **CLC 7**
See also CA 5-8R; 25-28R; CANR 68; DLB 9, 206
Fiske, Tarleton
See Bloch, Robert (Albert)
Fitch, Clarke
See Sinclair, Upton (Beall)
Fitch, John IV
See Cormier, Robert (Edmund)
Fitzgerald, Captain Hugh
See Baum, L(yman) Frank
FitzGerald, Edward 1809-1883 ...... **NCLC 9**
See also DLB 32
Fitzgerald, F(rancis) Scott (Key) 1896-1940 .... **TCLC 1, 6, 14, 28, 55; DA; DAB; DAC; DAM MST, NOV; SSC 6, 31; WLC**
See also AAYA 24; AITN 1; CA 110; 123; CDALB 1917-1929; DA3; DLB 4, 9, 86; DLBD 1, 15, 16; DLBY 81, 96; MTCW 1, 2
Fitzgerald, Penelope 1916-2000 ...... **CLC 19, 51, 61**
See also CA 85-88; CAAS 10; CANR 56, 86; DLB 14, 194; MTCW 2
Fitzgerald, Robert (Stuart) 1910-1985 .... **CLC 39**
See also CA 1-4R; 114; CANR 1; DLBY 80
FitzGerald, Robert D(avid) 1902-1987 .... **CLC 19**
See also CA 17-20R
Fitzgerald, Zelda (Sayre) 1900-1948 .... **TCLC 52**
See also CA 117; 126; DLBY 84
Flanagan, Thomas (James Bonner) 1923- .... **CLC 25, 52**
See also CA 108; CANR 55; DLBY 80; INT 108; MTCW 1
Flaubert, Gustave 1821-1880 .. **NCLC 2, 10, 19, 62, 66; DA; DAB; DAC; DAM MST, NOV; SSC 11; WLC**
See also DA3; DLB 119
Flecker, Herman Elroy
See Flecker, (Herman) James Elroy
Flecker, (Herman) James Elroy 1884-1915 .... **TCLC 43**
See also CA 109; 150; DLB 10, 19
Fleming, Ian (Lancaster) 1908-1964 . **CLC 3, 30; DAM POP**
See also AAYA 26; CA 5-8R; CANR 59; CDBLB 1945-1960; DA3; DLB 87, 201; MTCW 1, 2; SATA 9
Fleming, Thomas (James) 1927- ..... **CLC 37**
See also CA 5-8R; CANR 10; INT CANR-10; SATA 8
Fletcher, John 1579-1625 .... **LC 33; DC 6**
See also CDBLB Before 1660; DLB 58
Fletcher, John Gould 1886-1950 .. **TCLC 35**
See also CA 107; 167; DLB 4, 45
Fleur, Paul
See Pohl, Frederik
Flooglebuckle, Al
See Spiegelman, Art
Flying Officer X
See Bates, H(erbert) E(rnest)
Fo, Dario 1926- .... **CLC 32, 109; DAM DRAM; DC 10**
See also CA 116; 128; CANR 68; DA3; DLBY 97; MTCW 1, 2
Fogarty, Jonathan Titulescu Esq.
See Farrell, James T(homas)
Follett, Ken(neth Martin) 1949- .... **CLC 18; DAM NOV, POP**
See also AAYA 6; BEST 89:4; CA 81-84; CANR 13, 33, 54; DA3; DLB 87; DLBY 81; INT CANR-33; MTCW 1
Fontane, Theodor 1819-1898 .... **NCLC 26**
See also DLB 129
Foote, Horton 1916- .... **CLC 51, 91; DAM DRAM**
See also CA 73-76; CANR 34, 51; DA3; DLB 26; INT CANR-34
Foote, Shelby 1916- ... **CLC 75; DAM NOV, POP**
See also CA 5-8R; CANR 3, 45, 74; DA3; DLB 2, 17; MTCW 2
Forbes, Esther 1891-1967 .... **CLC 12**
See also AAYA 17; CA 13-14; 25-28R; CAP 1; CLR 27; DLB 22; JRDA; MAICYA; SATA 2, 100
Forche, Carolyn (Louise) 1950- ..... **CLC 25, 83, 86; DAM POET; PC 10**
See also CA 109; 117; CANR 50, 74; DA3; DLB 5, 193; INT 117; MTCW 1
Ford, Elbur
See Hibbert, Eleanor Alice Burford
Ford, Ford Madox 1873-1939 . **TCLC 1, 15, 39, 57; DAM NOV**
See also CA 104; 132; CANR 74; CDBLB 1914-1945; DA3; DLB 162; MTCW 1, 2
Ford, Henry 1863-1947 .... **TCLC 73**
See also CA 115; 148
Ford, John 1586-(?) .... **DC 8**
See also CDBLB Before 1660; DAM DRAM; DA3; DLB 58
Ford, John 1895-1973 .... **CLC 16**
See also CA 45-48

See also CA 125
Fukuyama, Francis 1952- .... **CLC 131**
See also CA 140; CANR 72
Fuller, Charles (H., Jr.) 1939- .... **CLC 25; BLC 2; DAM DRAM, MULT; DC 1**
See also BW 2; CA 108; 112; CANR 87; DLB 38; INT 112; MTCW 1
Fuller, John (Leopold) 1937- .... **CLC 62**
See also CA 21-24R; CANR 9, 44; DLB 40
Fuller, Margaret .... **NCLC 5, 50**
See also Fuller, Sarah Margaret
Fuller, Roy (Broadbent) 1912-1991 . **CLC 4, 28**
See also CA 5-8R; 135; CAAS 10; CANR 53, 83; DLB 15, 20; SATA 87
Fuller, Sarah Margaret 1810-1850
See Fuller, Margaret
See also CDALB 1640-1865; DLB 1, 59, 73, 83, 223
Fulton, Alice 1952- .... **CLC 52**
See also CA 116; CANR 57, 88; DLB 193
Furphy, Joseph 1843-1912 .... **TCLC 25**
See also CA 163
Fussell, Paul 1924- .... **CLC 74**
See also BEST 90:1; CA 17-20R; CANR 8, 21, 35, 69; INT CANR-21; MTCW 1, 2
Futabatei, Shimei 1864-1909 .... **TCLC 44**
See also CA 162; DLB 180
Futrelle, Jacques 1875-1912 .... **TCLC 19**
See also CA 113; 155
Gaboriau, Emile 1835-1873 .... **NCLC 14**
Gadda, Carlo Emilio 1893-1973 ...... **CLC 11**
See also CA 89-92; DLB 177
Gaddis, William 1922-1998 .. **CLC 1, 3, 6, 8, 10, 19, 43, 86**
See also CA 17-20R; 172; CANR 21, 48; DLB 2; MTCW 1, 2
Gage, Walter
See Inge, William (Motter)
Gaines, Ernest J(ames) 1933- ..... **CLC 3, 11, 18, 86; BLC 2; DAM MULT**
See also AAYA 18; AITN 1; BW 2, 3; CA 9-12R; CANR 6, 24, 42, 75; CDALB 1968-1988; CLR 62; DA3; DLB 2, 33, 152; DLBY 80; MTCW 1, 2; SATA 86
Gaitskill, Mary 1954- .... **CLC 69**
See also CA 128; CANR 61
Galdos, Benito Perez
See Perez Galdos, Benito
Gale, Zona 1874-1938 .... **TCLC 7; DAM DRAM**
See also CA 105; 153; CANR 84; DLB 9, 78, 228
Galeano, Eduardo (Hughes) 1940- . **CLC 72; HLCS 1**
See also CA 29-32R; CANR 13, 32; HW 1
Galiano, Juan Valera y Alcala
See Valera y Alcala-Galiano, Juan
Galilei, Galileo 1546-1642 .... **LC 45**
Gallagher, Tess 1943- ..... **CLC 18, 63; DAM POET; PC 9**
See also CA 106; DLB 212
Gallant, Mavis 1922- . **CLC 7, 18, 38; DAC; DAM MST; SSC 5**
See also CA 69-72; CANR 29, 69; DLB 53; MTCW 1, 2
Gallant, Roy A(rthur) 1924- .... **CLC 17**
See also CA 5-8R; CANR 4, 29, 54; CLR 30; MAICYA; SATA 4, 68, 110
Gallico, Paul (William) 1897-1976 .... **CLC 2**
See also AITN 1; CA 5-8R; 69-72; CANR 23; DLB 9, 171; MAICYA; SATA 13
Gallo, Max Louis 1932- .... **CLC 95**
See also CA 85-88
Gallois, Lucien
See Desnos, Robert
Gallup, Ralph
See Whitemore, Hugh (John)
Galsworthy, John 1867-1933 ... **TCLC 1, 45; DA; DAB; DAC; DAM DRAM, MST, NOV; SSC 22; WLC**
See also CA 104; 141; CANR 75; CDBLB 1890-1914; DA3; DLB 10, 34, 98, 162; DLBD 16; MTCW 1
Galt, John 1779-1839 .... **NCLC 1**
See also DLB 99, 116, 159
Galvin, James 1951- .... **CLC 38**
See also CA 108; CANR 26
Gamboa, Federico 1864-1939 .... **TCLC 36**
See also CA 167; HW 2
Gandhi, M. K.
See Gandhi, Mohandas Karamchand
Gandhi, Mahatma
See Gandhi, Mohandas Karamchand
Gandhi, Mohandas Karamchand 1869-1948 .... **TCLC 59; DAM MULT**
See also CA 121; 132; DA3; MTCW 1, 2
Gann, Ernest Kellogg 1910-1991 .... **CLC 23**
See also AITN 1; CA 1-4R; 136; CANR 1, 83
Garber, Eric 1943(?)-
See Holleran, Andrew
See also CANR 89
Garcia, Cristina 1958- .... **CLC 76**
See also CA 141; CANR 73; HW 2
Garcia Lorca, Federico 1898-1936 . **TCLC 1, 7, 49; DA; DAB; DAC; DAM DRAM, MST, MULT, POET; DC 2; HLC 2; PC 3; WLC**
See also Lorca, Federico Garcia
See also CA 104; 131; CANR 81; DA3; DLB 108; HW 1, 2; MTCW 1, 2
Garcia Marquez, Gabriel (Jose) 1928- .... **CLC 2, 3, 8, 10, 15, 27, 47, 55, 68; DA; DAB; DAC; DAM MST, MULT, NOV, POP; HLC 1; SSC 8; WLC**
See also Marquez, Gabriel (Jose) Garcia
See also AAYA 3, 33; BEST 89:1, 90:4; CA 33-36R; CANR 10, 28, 50, 75, 82; DA3; DLB 113; HW 1, 2; MTCW 1, 2
Garcilaso de la Vega, El Inca 1503-1536
See also HLCS 1
Gard, Janice
See Latham, Jean Lee
Gard, Roger Martin du
See Martin du Gard, Roger
Gardam, Jane 1928- .... **CLC 43**
See also CA 49-52; CANR 2, 18, 33, 54; CLR 12; DLB 14, 161; MAICYA; MTCW 1; SAAS 9; SATA 39, 76; SATA-Brief 28
Gardner, Herb(ert) 1934- .... **CLC 44**
See also CA 149
Gardner, John (Champlin), Jr. 1933-1982 . **CLC 2, 3, 5, 7, 8, 10, 18, 28, 34; DAM NOV, POP; SSC 7**
See also AITN 1; CA 65-68; 107; CANR 33, 73; CDALBS; DA3; DLB 2; DLBY 82; MTCW 1; SATA 40; SATA-Obit 31
Gardner, John (Edmund) 1926- .... **CLC 30; DAM POP**
See also CA 103; CANR 15, 69; MTCW 1
Gardner, Miriam
See Bradley, Marion Zimmer
Gardner, Noel
See Kuttner, Henry
Gardons, S. S.
See Snodgrass, W(illiam) D(e Witt)
Garfield, Leon 1921-1996 .... **CLC 12**
See also AAYA 8; CA 17-20R; 152; CANR 38, 41, 78; CLR 21; DLB 161; JRDA; MAICYA; SATA 1, 32, 76; SATA-Obit 90
Garland, (Hannibal) Hamlin 1860-1940 .... **TCLC 3; SSC 18**
See also CA 104; DLB 12, 71, 78, 186
Garneau, (Hector de) Saint-Denys 1912-1943 .... **TCLC 13**
See also CA 111; DLB 88
Garner, Alan 1934- .... **CLC 17; DAB; DAM POP**
See also AAYA 18; CA 73-76, 178; CAAE 178; CANR 15, 64; CLR 20; DLB 161; MAICYA; MTCW 1, 2; SATA 18, 69; SATA-Essay 108
Garner, Hugh 1913-1979 .... **CLC 13**
See also CA 69-72; CANR 31; DLB 68
Garnett, David 1892-1981 .... **CLC 3**
See also CA 5-8R; 103; CANR 17, 79; DLB 34; MTCW 2
Garos, Stephanie
See Katz, Steve
Garrett, George (Palmer) 1929- . **CLC 3, 11, 51; SSC 30**
See also CA 1-4R; CAAS 5; CANR 1, 42, 67; DLB 2, 5, 130, 152; DLBY 83
Garrick, David 1717-1779 ...... **LC 15; DAM DRAM**
See also DLB 84
Garrigue, Jean 1914-1972 .... **CLC 2, 8**
See also CA 5-8R; 37-40R; CANR 20
Garrison, Frederick
See Sinclair, Upton (Beall)
Garro, Elena 1920(?)-1998
See also CA 131; 169; DLB 145; HLCS 1; HW 1
Garth, Will
See Hamilton, Edmond; Kuttner, Henry
Garvey, Marcus (Moziah, Jr.) 1887-1940 .... **TCLC 41; BLC 2; DAM MULT**
See also BW 1; CA 120; 124; CANR 79
Gary, Romain .... **CLC 25**
See also Kacew, Romain
See also DLB 83
Gascar, Pierre .... **CLC 11**
See also Fournier, Pierre
Gascoyne, David (Emery) 1916- ..... **CLC 45**
See also CA 65-68; CANR 10, 28, 54; DLB 20; MTCW 1
Gaskell, Elizabeth Cleghorn 1810-1865 .. **NCLC 70; DAB; DAM MST; SSC 25**
See also CDBLB 1832-1890; DLB 21, 144, 159
Gass, William H(oward) 1924- . **CLC 1, 2, 8, 11, 15, 39, 132; SSC 12**
See also CA 17-20R; CANR 30, 71; DLB 2, 227; MTCW 1, 2
Gassendi, Pierre 1592-1655 .... **LC 54**
Gasset, Jose Ortega y
See Ortega y Gasset, Jose
Gates, Henry Louis, Jr. 1950- .... **CLC 65; BLCS; DAM MULT**
See also BW 2, 3; CA 109; CANR 25, 53, 75; DA3; DLB 67; MTCW 1
Gautier, Theophile 1811-1872 . **NCLC 1, 59; DAM POET; PC 18; SSC 20**
See also DLB 119
Gawsworth, John
See Bates, H(erbert) E(rnest)
Gay, John 1685-1732 . **LC 49; DAM DRAM**
See also DLB 84, 95
Gay, Oliver
See Gogarty, Oliver St. John
Gaye, Marvin (Penze) 1939-1984 .... **CLC 26**
See also CA 112
Gebler, Carlo (Ernest) 1954- .... **CLC 39**
See also CA 119; 133
Gee, Maggie (Mary) 1948- .... **CLC 57**
See also CA 130; DLB 207
Gee, Maurice (Gough) 1931- .... **CLC 29**
See also CA 97-100; CANR 67; CLR 56; SATA 46, 101
Gelbart, Larry (Simon) 1923- ... **CLC 21, 61**
See also CA 73-76; CANR 45

Author Index

Gogol, Nikolai (Vasilyevich) 1809-1852 .... **NCLC 5, 15, 31; DA; DAB; DAC; DAM DRAM, MST; DC 1; SSC 4, 29; WLC**
See also DLB 198

Goines, Donald 1937(?)-1974 . **CLC 80; BLC 2; DAM MULT, POP**
See also AITN 1; BW 1, 3; CA 124; 114; CANR 82; DA3; DLB 33

Gold, Herbert 1924- .... **CLC 4, 7, 14, 42**
See also CA 9-12R; CANR 17, 45; DLB 2; DLBY 81

Goldbarth, Albert 1948- .... **CLC 5, 38**
See also CA 53-56; CANR 6, 40; DLB 120

Goldberg, Anatol 1910-1982 .... **CLC 34**
See also CA 131; 117

Goldemberg, Isaac 1945- .... **CLC 52**
See also CA 69-72; CAAS 12; CANR 11, 32; HW 1

Golding, William (Gerald) 1911-1993 . **CLC 1, 2, 3, 8, 10, 17, 27, 58, 81; DA; DAB; DAC; DAM MST, NOV; WLC**
See also AAYA 5; CA 5-8R; 141; CANR 13, 33, 54; CDBLB 1945-1960; DA3; DLB 15, 100; MTCW 1, 2

Goldman, Emma 1869-1940 .... **TCLC 13**
See also CA 110; 150; DLB 221

Goldman, Francisco 1954- .... **CLC 76**
See also CA 162

Goldman, William (W.) 1931- ..... **CLC 1, 48**
See also CA 9-12R; CANR 29, 69; DLB 44

Goldmann, Lucien 1913-1970 .... **CLC 24**
See also CA 25-28; CAP 2

Goldoni, Carlo 1707-1793 .... **LC 4; DAM DRAM**

Goldsberry, Steven 1949- .... **CLC 34**
See also CA 131

Goldsmith, Oliver 1728-1774 . **LC 2, 48; DA; DAB; DAC; DAM DRAM, MST, NOV, POET; DC 8; WLC**
See also CDBLB 1660-1789; DLB 39, 89, 104, 109, 142; SATA 26

Goldsmith, Peter
See Priestley, J(ohn) B(oynton)

Gombrowicz, Witold 1904-1969 ... **CLC 4, 7, 11, 49; DAM DRAM**
See also CA 19-20; 25-28R; CAP 2

Gomez de la Serna, Ramon 1888-1963 .... **CLC 9**
See also CA 153; 116; CANR 79; HW 1, 2

Goncharov, Ivan Alexandrovich 1812-1891 .... **NCLC 1, 63**

Goncourt, Edmond (Louis Antoine Huot) de 1822-1896 .... **NCLC 7**
See also DLB 123

Goncourt, Jules (Alfred Huot) de 1830-1870 .... **NCLC 7**
See also DLB 123

Gontier, Fernande 19(?)- .... **CLC 50**

Gonzalez Martinez, Enrique 1871-1952 .... **TCLC 72**
See also CA 166; CANR 81; HW 1, 2

Goodman, Paul 1911-1972 .... **CLC 1, 2, 4, 7**
See also CA 19-20; 37-40R; CANR 34; CAP 2; DLB 130; MTCW 1

Gordimer, Nadine 1923- .... **CLC 3, 5, 7, 10, 18, 33, 51, 70; DA; DAB; DAC; DAM MST, NOV; SSC 17; WLCS**
See also CA 5-8R; CANR 3, 28, 56, 88; DA3; DLB 225; INT CANR-28; MTCW 1, 2

Gordon, Adam Lindsay 1833-1870 .... **NCLC 21**

Gordon, Caroline 1895-1981 ...... **CLC 6, 13, 29, 83; SSC 15**
See also CA 11-12; 103; CANR 36; CAP 1; DLB 4, 9, 102; DLBD 17; DLBY 81; MTCW 1, 2

Gordon, Charles William 1860-1937
See Connor, Ralph
See also CA 109

Gordon, Mary (Catherine) 1949- .. **CLC 13, 22, 128**
See also CA 102; CANR 44; DLB 6; DLBY 81; INT 102; MTCW 1

Gordon, N. J.
See Bosman, Herman Charles

Gordon, Sol 1923- .... **CLC 26**
See also CA 53-56; CANR 4; SATA 11

Gordone, Charles 1925-1995 .... **CLC 1, 4; DAM DRAM; DC 8**
See also BW 1, 3; CA 93-96, 180; 150; CAAE 180; CANR 55; DLB 7; INT 93-96; MTCW 1

Gore, Catherine 1800-1861 .... **NCLC 65**
See also DLB 116

Gorenko, Anna Andreevna
See Akhmatova, Anna

Gorky, Maxim 1868-1936 ... **TCLC 8; DAB; SSC 28; WLC**
See also Peshkov, Alexei Maximovich
See also MTCW 2

Goryan, Sirak
See Saroyan, William

Gosse, Edmund (William) 1849-1928 .... **TCLC 28**
See also CA 117; DLB 57, 144, 184

Gotlieb, Phyllis Fay (Bloom) 1926- . **CLC 18**
See also CA 13-16R; CANR 7; DLB 88

Gottesman, S. D.
See Kornbluth, C(yril) M.; Pohl, Frederik

Gottfried von Strassburg fl. c. 1210- .... **CMLC 10**
See also DLB 138

Gould, Lois .... **CLC 4, 10**
See also CA 77-80; CANR 29; MTCW 1

Gourmont, Remy (-Marie-Charles) de 1858-1915 .... **TCLC 17**
See also CA 109; 150; MTCW 2

Govier, Katherine 1948- .... **CLC 51**
See also CA 101; CANR 18, 40

Goyen, (Charles) William 1915-1983 .... **CLC 5, 8, 14, 40**
See also AITN 2; CA 5-8R; 110; CANR 6, 71; DLB 2; DLBY 83; INT CANR-6

Goytisolo, Juan 1931- .. **CLC 5, 10, 23, 133; DAM MULT; HLC 1**
See also CA 85-88; CANR 32, 61; HW 1, 2; MTCW 1, 2

Gozzano, Guido 1883-1916 .... **PC 10**
See also CA 154; DLB 114

Gozzi, (Conte) Carlo 1720-1806 ... **NCLC 23**

Grabbe, Christian Dietrich 1801-1836 .... **NCLC 2**
See also DLB 133

Grace, Patricia Frances 1937- .... **CLC 56**
See also CA 176

Gracian y Morales, Baltasar 1601-1658 .... **LC 15**

Gracq, Julien .... **CLC 11, 48**
See also Poirier, Louis
See also DLB 83

Grade, Chaim 1910-1982 .... **CLC 10**
See also CA 93-96; 107

Graduate of Oxford, A
See Ruskin, John

Grafton, Garth
See Duncan, Sara Jeannette

Graham, John
See Phillips, David Graham

Graham, Jorie 1951- .... **CLC 48, 118**
See also CA 111; CANR 63; DLB 120

Graham, R(obert) B(ontine) Cunninghame
See Cunninghame Graham, Robert (Gallnigad) Bontine
See also DLB 98, 135, 174

Graham, Robert
See Haldeman, Joe (William)

Graham, Tom
See Lewis, (Harry) Sinclair

Graham, W(illiam) S(ydney) 1918-1986 .... **CLC 29**
See also CA 73-76; 118; DLB 20

Graham, Winston (Mawdsley) 1910- .... **CLC 23**
See also CA 49-52; CANR 2, 22, 45, 66; DLB 77

Grahame, Kenneth 1859-1932 ..... **TCLC 64; DAB**
See also CA 108; 136; CANR 80; CLR 5; DA3; DLB 34, 141, 178; MAICYA; MTCW 2; SATA 100; YABC 1

Granovsky, Timofei Nikolaevich 1813-1855 .... **NCLC 75**
See also DLB 198

Grant, Skeeter
See Spiegelman, Art

Granville-Barker, Harley 1877-1946 .... **TCLC 2; DAM DRAM**
See also Barker, Harley Granville
See also CA 104

Grass, Guenter (Wilhelm) 1927- . **CLC 1, 2, 4, 6, 11, 15, 22, 32, 49, 88; DA; DAB; DAC; DAM MST, NOV; WLC**
See also CA 13-16R; CANR 20, 75; DA3; DLB 75, 124; MTCW 1, 2

Gratton, Thomas
See Hulme, T(homas) E(rnest)

Grau, Shirley Ann 1929- . **CLC 4, 9; SSC 15**
See also CA 89-92; CANR 22, 69; DLB 2; INT CANR-22; MTCW 1

Gravel, Fern
See Hall, James Norman

Graver, Elizabeth 1964- .... **CLC 70**
See also CA 135; CANR 71

Graves, Richard Perceval 1945- ..... **CLC 44**
See also CA 65-68; CANR 9, 26, 51

Graves, Robert (von Ranke) 1895-1985 .... **CLC 1, 2, 6, 11, 39, 44, 45; DAB; DAC; DAM MST, POET; PC 6**
See also CA 5-8R; 117; CANR 5, 36; CDBLB 1914-1945; DA3; DLB 20, 100, 191; DLBD 18; DLBY 85; MTCW 1, 2; SATA 45

Graves, Valerie
See Bradley, Marion Zimmer

Gray, Alasdair (James) 1934- .... **CLC 41**
See also CA 126; CANR 47, 69; DLB 194; INT 126; MTCW 1, 2

Gray, Amlin 1946- .... **CLC 29**
See also CA 138

Gray, Francine du Plessix 1930- ... **CLC 22; DAM NOV**
See also BEST 90:3; CA 61-64; CAAS 2; CANR 11, 33, 75, 81; INT CANR-11; MTCW 1, 2

Gray, John (Henry) 1866-1934 ..... **TCLC 19**
See also CA 119; 162

Gray, Simon (James Holliday) 1936- .... **CLC 9, 14, 36**
See also AITN 1; CA 21-24R; CAAS 3; CANR 32, 69; DLB 13; MTCW 1

Gray, Spalding 1941- ... **CLC 49, 112; DAM POP; DC 7**
See also CA 128; CANR 74; MTCW 2

Gray, Thomas 1716-1771 ...... **LC 4, 40; DA; DAB; DAC; DAM MST; PC 2; WLC**
See also CDBLB 1660-1789; DA3; DLB 109

Grayson, David
See Baker, Ray Stannard

Grayson, Richard (A.) 1951- .... **CLC 38**
See also CA 85-88; CANR 14, 31, 57

Greeley, Andrew M(oran) 1928- .... **CLC 28; DAM POP**

See also BW 1, 3; CA 111; 125; CANR 79; DLB 50, 221
Harper, Michael S(teven) 1938- .. **CLC 7, 22**
See also BW 1; CA 33-36R; CANR 24; DLB 41
Harper, Mrs. F. E. W.
See Harper, Frances Ellen Watkins
Harris, Christie (Lucy) Irwin 1907- . **CLC 12**
See also CA 5-8R; CANR 6, 83; CLR 47; DLB 88; JRDA; MAICYA; SAAS 10; SATA 6, 74; SATA-Essay 116
Harris, Frank 1856-1931 .... **TCLC 24**
See also CA 109; 150; CANR 80; DLB 156, 197
Harris, George Washington 1814-1869 .... **NCLC 23**
See also DLB 3, 11
Harris, Joel Chandler 1848-1908 .. **TCLC 2; SSC 19**
See also CA 104; 137; CANR 80; CLR 49; DLB 11, 23, 42, 78, 91; MAICYA; SATA 100; YABC 1
Harris, John (Wyndham Parkes Lucas) Beynon 1903-1969
See Wyndham, John
See also CA 102; 89-92; CANR 84
Harris, MacDonald .... **CLC 9**
See also Heiney, Donald (William)
Harris, Mark 1922- .... **CLC 19**
See also CA 5-8R; CAAS 3; CANR 2, 55, 83; DLB 2; DLBY 80
Harris, (Theodore) Wilson 1921- .... **CLC 25**
See also BW 2, 3; CA 65-68; CAAS 16; CANR 11, 27, 69; DLB 117; MTCW 1
Harrison, Elizabeth Cavanna 1909-
See Cavanna, Betty
See also CA 9-12R; CANR 6, 27, 85
Harrison, Harry (Max) 1925- .... **CLC 42**
See also CA 1-4R; CANR 5, 21, 84; DLB 8; SATA 4
Harrison, James (Thomas) 1937- .... **CLC 6, 14, 33, 66; SSC 19**
See also CA 13-16R; CANR 8, 51, 79; DLBY 82; INT CANR-8
Harrison, Jim
See Harrison, James (Thomas)
Harrison, Kathryn 1961- .... **CLC 70**
See also CA 144; CANR 68
Harrison, Tony 1937- .... **CLC 43, 129**
See also CA 65-68; CANR 44; DLB 40; MTCW 1
Harriss, Will(ard Irvin) 1922- .... **CLC 34**
See also CA 111
Harson, Sley
See Ellison, Harlan (Jay)
Hart, Ellis
See Ellison, Harlan (Jay)
Hart, Josephine 1942(?)- ...... **CLC 70; DAM POP**
See also CA 138; CANR 70
Hart, Moss 1904-1961 .... **CLC 66; DAM DRAM**
See also CA 109; 89-92; CANR 84; DLB 7
Harte, (Francis) Bret(t) 1836(?)-1902 ... **TCLC 1, 25; DA; DAC; DAM MST; SSC 8; WLC**
See also CA 104; 140; CANR 80; CDALB 1865-1917; DA3; DLB 12, 64, 74, 79, 186; SATA 26
Hartley, L(eslie) P(oles) 1895-1972 .. **CLC 2, 22**
See also CA 45-48; 37-40R; CANR 33; DLB 15, 139; MTCW 1, 2
Hartman, Geoffrey H. 1929- .... **CLC 27**
See also CA 117; 125; CANR 79; DLB 67
Hartmann, Sadakichi 1867-1944 .. **TCLC 73**
See also CA 157; DLB 54
Hartmann von Aue c. 1160-c. 1205 .... **CMLC 15**
See also DLB 138
Hartmann von Aue 1170-1210 ..... **CMLC 15**
Haruf, Kent 1943- .... **CLC 34**
See also CA 149; CANR 91
Harwood, Ronald 1934- .... **CLC 32; DAM DRAM, MST**
See also CA 1-4R; CANR 4, 55; DLB 13
Hasegawa Tatsunosuke
See Futabatei, Shimei
Hasek, Jaroslav (Matej Frantisek) 1883-1923 .... **TCLC 4**
See also CA 104; 129; MTCW 1, 2
Hass, Robert 1941- . **CLC 18, 39, 99; PC 16**
See also CA 111; CANR 30, 50, 71; DLB 105, 206; SATA 94
Hastings, Hudson
See Kuttner, Henry
Hastings, Selina .... **CLC 44**
Hathorne, John 1641-1717 .... **LC 38**
Hatteras, Amelia
See Mencken, H(enry) L(ouis)
Hatteras, Owen .... **TCLC 18**
See also Mencken, H(enry) L(ouis); Nathan, George Jean
Hauptmann, Gerhart (Johann Robert) 1862-1946 ...... **TCLC 4; DAM DRAM; SSC 37**
See also CA 104; 153; DLB 66, 118
Havel, Vaclav 1936- . **CLC 25, 58, 65; DAM DRAM; DC 6**
See also CA 104; CANR 36, 63; DA3; MTCW 1, 2
Haviaras, Stratis .... **CLC 33**
See also Chaviaras, Strates
Hawes, Stephen 1475(?)-1523(?) .... **LC 17**
See also DLB 132
Hawkes, John (Clendennin Burne, Jr.) 1925-1998 . **CLC 1, 2, 3, 4, 7, 9, 14, 15, 27, 49**
See also CA 1-4R; 167; CANR 2, 47, 64; DLB 2, 7, 227; DLBY 80, 98; MTCW 1, 2
Hawking, S. W.
See Hawking, Stephen W(illiam)
Hawking, Stephen W(illiam) 1942- . **CLC 63, 105**
See also AAYA 13; BEST 89:1; CA 126; 129; CANR 48; DA3; MTCW 2
Hawkins, Anthony Hope
See Hope, Anthony
Hawthorne, Julian 1846-1934 .... **TCLC 25**
See also CA 165
Hawthorne, Nathaniel 1804-1864 . **NCLC 39; DA; DAB; DAC; DAM MST, NOV; SSC 3, 29, 39; WLC**
See also AAYA 18; CDALB 1640-1865; DA3; DLB 1, 74, 223; YABC 2
Haxton, Josephine Ayres 1921-
See Douglas, Ellen
See also CA 115; CANR 41, 83
Hayaseca y Eizaguirre, Jorge
See Echegaray (y Eizaguirre), Jose (Maria Waldo)
Hayashi, Fumiko 1904-1951 .... **TCLC 27**
See also CA 161; DLB 180
Haycraft, Anna (Margaret) 1932-
See Ellis, Alice Thomas
See also CA 122; CANR 85, 90; MTCW 2
Hayden, Robert E(arl) 1913-1980 .... **CLC 5, 9, 14, 37; BLC 2; DA; DAC; DAM MST, MULT, POET; PC 6**
See also BW 1, 3; CA 69-72; 97-100; CABS 2; CANR 24, 75, 82; CDALB 1941-1968; DLB 5, 76; MTCW 1, 2; SATA 19; SATA-Obit 26
Hayford, J(oseph) E(phraim) Casely
See Casely-Hayford, J(oseph) E(phraim)
Hayman, Ronald 1932- .... **CLC 44**
See also CA 25-28R; CANR 18, 50, 88; DLB 155
Haywood, Eliza (Fowler) 1693(?)-1756 .... **LC 1, 44**
See also DLB 39
Hazlitt, William 1778-1830 ..... **NCLC 29, 82**
See also DLB 110, 158
Hazzard, Shirley 1931- .... **CLC 18**
See also CA 9-12R; CANR 4, 70; DLBY 82; MTCW 1
Head, Bessie 1937-1986 ... **CLC 25, 67; BLC 2; DAM MULT**
See also BW 2, 3; CA 29-32R; 119; CANR 25, 82; DA3; DLB 117, 225; MTCW 1, 2
Headon, (Nicky) Topper 1956(?)- ... **CLC 30**
Heaney, Seamus (Justin) 1939- .... **CLC 5, 7, 14, 25, 37, 74, 91; DAB; DAM POET; PC 18; WLCS**
See also CA 85-88; CANR 25, 48, 75, 91; CDBLB 1960 to Present; DA3; DLB 40; DLBY 95; MTCW 1, 2
Hearn, (Patricio) Lafcadio (Tessima Carlos) 1850-1904 .... **TCLC 9**
See also CA 105; 166; DLB 12, 78, 189
Hearne, Vicki 1946- .... **CLC 56**
See also CA 139
Hearon, Shelby 1931- .... **CLC 63**
See also AITN 2; CA 25-28R; CANR 18, 48
Heat-Moon, William Least .... **CLC 29**
See also Trogdon, William (Lewis)
See also AAYA 9
Hebbel, Friedrich 1813-1863 .... **NCLC 43; DAM DRAM**
See also DLB 129
Hebert, Anne 1916-2000 .... **CLC 4, 13, 29; DAC; DAM MST, POET**
See also CA 85-88; CANR 69; DA3; DLB 68; MTCW 1, 2
Hecht, Anthony (Evan) 1923- .... **CLC 8, 13, 19; DAM POET**
See also CA 9-12R; CANR 6; DLB 5, 169
Hecht, Ben 1894-1964 .... **CLC 8**
See also CA 85-88; DLB 7, 9, 25, 26, 28, 86
Hedayat, Sadeq 1903-1951 .... **TCLC 21**
See also CA 120
Hegel, Georg Wilhelm Friedrich 1770-1831 .... **NCLC 46**
See also DLB 90
Heidegger, Martin 1889-1976 .... **CLC 24**
See also CA 81-84; 65-68; CANR 34; MTCW 1, 2
Heidenstam, (Carl Gustaf) Verner von 1859-1940 .... **TCLC 5**
See also CA 104
Heifner, Jack 1946- .... **CLC 11**
See also CA 105; CANR 47
Heijermans, Herman 1864-1924 ... **TCLC 24**
See also CA 123
Heilbrun, Carolyn G(old) 1926- ..... **CLC 25**
See also CA 45-48; CANR 1, 28, 58
Heine, Heinrich 1797-1856 ...... **NCLC 4, 54; PC 25**
See also DLB 90
Heinemann, Larry (Curtiss) 1944- . **CLC 50**
See also CA 110; CAAS 21; CANR 31, 81; DLBD 9; INT CANR-31
Heiney, Donald (William) 1921-1993
See Harris, MacDonald
See also CA 1-4R; 142; CANR 3, 58
Heinlein, Robert A(nson) 1907-1988 . **CLC 1, 3, 8, 14, 26, 55; DAM POP**
See also AAYA 17; CA 1-4R; 125; CANR 1, 20, 53; DA3; DLB 8; JRDA; MAICYA; MTCW 1, 2; SATA 9, 69; SATA-Obit 56
Helforth, John
See Doolittle, Hilda

Hellenhofferu, Vojtech Kapristian z
See Hasek, Jaroslav (Matej Frantisek)
Heller, Joseph 1923- . **CLC 1, 3, 5, 8, 11, 36, 63; DA; DAB; DAC; DAM MST, NOV, POP; WLC**
See also AAYA 24; AITN 1; CA 5-8R; CABS 1; CANR 8, 42, 66; DA3; DLB 2, 28, 227; DLBY 80; INT CANR-8; MTCW 1, 2
Hellman, Lillian (Florence) 1906-1984 .. **CLC 2, 4, 8, 14, 18, 34, 44, 52; DAM DRAM; DC 1**
See also AITN 1, 2; CA 13-16R; 112; CANR 33; DA3; DLB 7, 228; DLBY 84; MTCW 1, 2
Helprin, Mark 1947- ...... **CLC 7, 10, 22, 32; DAM NOV, POP**
See also CA 81-84; CANR 47, 64; CDALBS; DA3; DLBY 85; MTCW 1, 2
Helvetius, Claude-Adrien 1715-1771 . **LC 26**
Helyar, Jane Penelope Josephine 1933-
See Poole, Josephine
See also CA 21-24R; CANR 10, 26; SATA 82
Hemans, Felicia 1793-1835 .... **NCLC 71**
See also DLB 96
Hemingway, Ernest (Miller) 1899-1961 ... **CLC 1, 3, 6, 8, 10, 13, 19, 30, 34, 39, 41, 44, 50, 61, 80; DA; DAB; DAC; DAM MST, NOV; SSC 1, 25, 36, 40; WLC**
See also AAYA 19; CA 77-80; CANR 34; CDALB 1917-1929; DA3; DLB 4, 9, 102, 210; DLBD 1, 15, 16; DLBY 81, 87, 96, 98; MTCW 1, 2
Hempel, Amy 1951- .... **CLC 39**
See also CA 118; 137; CANR 70; DA3; MTCW 2
Henderson, F. C.
See Mencken, H(enry) L(ouis)
Henderson, Sylvia
See Ashton-Warner, Sylvia (Constance)
Henderson, Zenna (Chlarson) 1917-1983 .... **SSC 29**
See also CA 1-4R; 133; CANR 1, 84; DLB 8; SATA 5
Henkin, Joshua .... **CLC 119**
See also CA 161
Henley, Beth .... **CLC 23; DC 6**
See also Henley, Elizabeth Becker
See also CABS 3; DLBY 86
Henley, Elizabeth Becker 1952-
See Henley, Beth
See also CA 107; CANR 32, 73; DAM DRAM, MST; DA3; MTCW 1, 2
Henley, William Ernest 1849-1903 . **TCLC 8**
See also CA 105; DLB 19
Hennissart, Martha
See Lathen, Emma
See also CA 85-88; CANR 64
Henry, O. .... **TCLC 1, 19; SSC 5; WLC**
See also Porter, William Sydney
Henry, Patrick 1736-1799 .... **LC 25**
Henryson, Robert 1430(?)-1506(?) ..... **LC 20**
See also DLB 146
Henry VIII 1491-1547 .... **LC 10**
See also DLB 132
Henschke, Alfred
See Klabund
Hentoff, Nat(han Irving) 1925- .... **CLC 26**
See also AAYA 4; CA 1-4R; CAAS 6; CANR 5, 25, 77; CLR 1, 52; INT CANR-25; JRDA; MAICYA; SATA 42, 69; SATA-Brief 27
Heppenstall, (John) Rayner 1911-1981 .... **CLC 10**
See also CA 1-4R; 103; CANR 29
Heraclitus c. 540B.C.-c. 450B.C. . **CMLC 22**
See also DLB 176
Herbert, Frank (Patrick) 1920-1986 ...... **CLC 12, 23, 35, 44, 85; DAM POP**
See also AAYA 21; CA 53-56; 118; CANR 5, 43; CDALBS; DLB 8; INT CANR-5; MTCW 1, 2; SATA 9, 37; SATA-Obit 47
Herbert, George 1593-1633 .... **LC 24; DAB; DAM POET; PC 4**
See also CDBLB Before 1660; DLB 126
Herbert, Zbigniew 1924-1998 .... **CLC 9, 43; DAM POET**
See also CA 89-92; 169; CANR 36, 74; MTCW 1
Herbst, Josephine (Frey) 1897-1969 .... **CLC 34**
See also CA 5-8R; 25-28R; DLB 9
Heredia, Jose Maria 1803-1839
See also HLCS 2
Hergesheimer, Joseph 1880-1954 .. **TCLC 11**
See also CA 109; DLB 102, 9
Herlihy, James Leo 1927-1993 .... **CLC 6**
See also CA 1-4R; 143; CANR 2
Hermogenes fl. c. 175- .... **CMLC 6**
Hernandez, Jose 1834-1886 .... **NCLC 17**
Herodotus c. 484B.C.-429B.C. ..... **CMLC 17**
See also DLB 176
Herrick, Robert 1591-1674 .... **LC 13; DA; DAB; DAC; DAM MST, POP; PC 9**
See also DLB 126
Herring, Guilles
See Somerville, Edith
Herriot, James 1916-1995 .... **CLC 12; DAM POP**
See also Wight, James Alfred
See also AAYA 1; CA 148; CANR 40; MTCW 2; SATA 86
Herris, Violet
See Hunt, Violet
Herrmann, Dorothy 1941- .... **CLC 44**
See also CA 107
Herrmann, Taffy
See Herrmann, Dorothy
Hersey, John (Richard) 1914-1993 .. **CLC 1, 2, 7, 9, 40, 81, 97; DAM POP**
See also AAYA 29; CA 17-20R; 140; CANR 33; CDALBS; DLB 6, 185; MTCW 1, 2; SATA 25; SATA-Obit 76
Herzen, Aleksandr Ivanovich 1812-1870 .... **NCLC 10, 61**
Herzl, Theodor 1860-1904 .... **TCLC 36**
See also CA 168
Herzog, Werner 1942- .... **CLC 16**
See also CA 89-92
Hesiod c. 8th cent. B.C.- .... **CMLC 5**
See also DLB 176
Hesse, Hermann 1877-1962 . **CLC 1, 2, 3, 6, 11, 17, 25, 69; DA; DAB; DAC; DAM MST, NOV; SSC 9; WLC**
See also CA 17-18; CAP 2; DA3; DLB 66; MTCW 1, 2; SATA 50
Hewes, Cady
See De Voto, Bernard (Augustine)
Heyen, William 1940- .... **CLC 13, 18**
See also CA 33-36R; CAAS 9; DLB 5
Heyerdahl, Thor 1914- .... **CLC 26**
See also CA 5-8R; CANR 5, 22, 66, 73; MTCW 1, 2; SATA 2, 52
Heym, Georg (Theodor Franz Arthur) 1887-1912 .... **TCLC 9**
See also CA 106; 181
Heym, Stefan 1913- .... **CLC 41**
See also CA 9-12R; CANR 4; DLB 69
Heyse, Paul (Johann Ludwig von) 1830-1914 .... **TCLC 8**
See also CA 104; DLB 129
Heyward, (Edwin) DuBose 1885-1940 .... **TCLC 59**
See also CA 108; 157; DLB 7, 9, 45; SATA 21
Hibbert, Eleanor Alice Burford 1906-1993 .... **CLC 7; DAM POP**
See also BEST 90:4; CA 17-20R; 140; CANR 9, 28, 59; MTCW 2; SATA 2; SATA-Obit 74
Hichens, Robert (Smythe) 1864-1950 .... **TCLC 64**
See also CA 162; DLB 153
Higgins, George V(incent) 1939-1999 .... **CLC 4, 7, 10, 18**
See also CA 77-80; 186; CAAS 5; CANR 17, 51, 89; DLB 2; DLBY 81, 98; INT CANR-17; MTCW 1
Higginson, Thomas Wentworth 1823-1911 .... **TCLC 36**
See also CA 162; DLB 1, 64
Highet, Helen
See MacInnes, Helen (Clark)
Highsmith, (Mary) Patricia 1921-1995 ...... **CLC 2, 4, 14, 42, 102; DAM NOV, POP**
See also CA 1-4R; 147; CANR 1, 20, 48, 62; DA3; MTCW 1, 2
Highwater, Jamake (Mamake) 1942(?)- .... **CLC 12**
See also AAYA 7; CA 65-68; CAAS 7; CANR 10, 34, 84; CLR 17; DLB 52; DLBY 85; JRDA; MAICYA; SATA 32, 69; SATA-Brief 30
Highway, Tomson 1951- ...... **CLC 92; DAC; DAM MULT**
See also CA 151; CANR 75; MTCW 2; NNAL
Higuchi, Ichiyo 1872-1896 .... **NCLC 49**
Hijuelos, Oscar 1951- .... **CLC 65; DAM MULT, POP; HLC 1**
See also AAYA 25; BEST 90:1; CA 123; CANR 50, 75; DA3; DLB 145; HW 1, 2; MTCW 2
Hikmet, Nazim 1902(?)-1963 .... **CLC 40**
See also CA 141; 93-96
Hildegard von Bingen 1098-1179 . **CMLC 20**
See also DLB 148
Hildesheimer, Wolfgang 1916-1991 . **CLC 49**
See also CA 101; 135; DLB 69, 124
Hill, Geoffrey (William) 1932- ..... **CLC 5, 8, 18, 45; DAM POET**
See also CA 81-84; CANR 21, 89; CDBLB 1960 to Present; DLB 40; MTCW 1
Hill, George Roy 1921- .... **CLC 26**
See also CA 110; 122
Hill, John
See Koontz, Dean R(ay)
Hill, Susan (Elizabeth) 1942- ... **CLC 4, 113; DAB; DAM MST, NOV**
See also CA 33-36R; CANR 29, 69; DLB 14, 139; MTCW 1
Hillerman, Tony 1925- . **CLC 62; DAM POP**
See also AAYA 6; BEST 89:1; CA 29-32R; CANR 21, 42, 65; DA3; DLB 206; SATA 6
Hillesum, Etty 1914-1943 .... **TCLC 49**
See also CA 137
Hilliard, Noel (Harvey) 1929- .... **CLC 15**
See also CA 9-12R; CANR 7, 69
Hillis, Rick 1956- .... **CLC 66**
See also CA 134
Hilton, James 1900-1954 .... **TCLC 21**
See also CA 108; 169; DLB 34, 77; SATA 34
Himes, Chester (Bomar) 1909-1984 . **CLC 2, 4, 7, 18, 58, 108; BLC 2; DAM MULT**
See also BW 2; CA 25-28R; 114; CANR 22, 89; DLB 2, 76, 143, 226; MTCW 1, 2
Hinde, Thomas .... **CLC 6, 11**
See also Chitty, Thomas Willes
Hine, (William) Daryl 1936- .... **CLC 15**
See also CA 1-4R; CAAS 15; CANR 1, 20; DLB 60

See also CA 108; CANR 48
Hostos, E. M. de
See Hostos (y Bonilla), Eugenio Maria de
Hostos, Eugenio M. de
See Hostos (y Bonilla), Eugenio Maria de
Hostos, Eugenio Maria
See Hostos (y Bonilla), Eugenio Maria de
Hostos (y Bonilla), Eugenio Maria de 1839-1903 .... **TCLC 24**
See also CA 123; 131; HW 1
Houdini
See Lovecraft, H(oward) P(hillips)
Hougan, Carolyn 1943- .... **CLC 34**
See also CA 139
Household, Geoffrey (Edward West) 1900-1988 .... **CLC 11**
See also CA 77-80; 126; CANR 58; DLB 87; SATA 14; SATA-Obit 59
Housman, A(lfred) E(dward) 1859-1936 ... **TCLC 1, 10; DA; DAB; DAC; DAM MST, POET; PC 2; WLCS**
See also CA 104; 125; DA3; DLB 19; MTCW 1, 2
Housman, Laurence 1865-1959 ...... **TCLC 7**
See also CA 106; 155; DLB 10; SATA 25
Howard, Elizabeth Jane 1923- .... **CLC 7, 29**
See also CA 5-8R; CANR 8, 62
Howard, Maureen 1930- .... **CLC 5, 14, 46**
See also CA 53-56; CANR 31, 75; DLBY 83; INT CANR-31; MTCW 1, 2
Howard, Richard 1929- .... **CLC 7, 10, 47**
See also AITN 1; CA 85-88; CANR 25, 80; DLB 5; INT CANR-25
Howard, Robert E(rvin) 1906-1936 . **TCLC 8**
See also CA 105; 157
Howard, Warren F.
See Pohl, Frederik
Howe, Fanny (Quincy) 1940- .... **CLC 47**
See also CA 117; CAAS 27; CANR 70; SATA-Brief 52
Howe, Irving 1920-1993 .... **CLC 85**
See also CA 9-12R; 141; CANR 21, 50; DLB 67; MTCW 1, 2
Howe, Julia Ward 1819-1910 .... **TCLC 21**
See also CA 117; DLB 1, 189
Howe, Susan 1937- .... **CLC 72**
See also CA 160; DLB 120
Howe, Tina 1937- .... **CLC 48**
See also CA 109
Howell, James 1594(?)-1666 .... **LC 13**
See also DLB 151
Howells, W. D.
See Howells, William Dean
Howells, William D.
See Howells, William Dean
Howells, William Dean 1837-1920 . **TCLC 7, 17, 41; SSC 36**
See also CA 104; 134; CDALB 1865-1917; DLB 12, 64, 74, 79, 189; MTCW 2
Howes, Barbara 1914-1996 .... **CLC 15**
See also CA 9-12R; 151; CAAS 3; CANR 53; SATA 5
Hrabal, Bohumil 1914-1997 ...... **CLC 13, 67**
See also CA 106; 156; CAAS 12; CANR 57
Hroswitha of Gandersheim c. 935-c. 1002 .... **CMLC 29**
See also DLB 148
Hsun, Lu
See Lu Hsun
Hubbard, L(afayette) Ron(ald) 1911-1986 .... **CLC 43; DAM POP**
See also CA 77-80; 118; CANR 52; DA3; MTCW 2
Huch, Ricarda (Octavia) 1864-1947 .... **TCLC 13**
See also CA 111; DLB 66
Huddle, David 1942- .... **CLC 49**
See also CA 57-60; CAAS 20; CANR 89; DLB 130
Hudson, Jeffrey
See Crichton, (John) Michael
Hudson, W(illiam) H(enry) 1841-1922 .... **TCLC 29**
See also CA 115; DLB 98, 153, 174; SATA 35
Hueffer, Ford Madox
See Ford, Ford Madox
Hughart, Barry 1934- .... **CLC 39**
See also CA 137
Hughes, Colin
See Creasey, John
Hughes, David (John) 1930- .... **CLC 48**
See also CA 116; 129; DLB 14
Hughes, Edward James
See Hughes, Ted
See also DAM MST, POET; DA3
Hughes, (James) Langston 1902-1967 . **CLC 1, 5, 10, 15, 35, 44, 108; BLC 2; DA; DAB; DAC; DAM DRAM, MST, MULT, POET; DC 3; PC 1; SSC 6; WLC**
See also AAYA 12; BW 1, 3; CA 1-4R; 25-28R; CANR 1, 34, 82; CDALB 1929-1941; CLR 17; DA3; DLB 4, 7, 48, 51, 86, 228; JRDA; MAICYA; MTCW 1, 2; SATA 4, 33
Hughes, Richard (Arthur Warren) 1900-1976 .... **CLC 1, 11; DAM NOV**
See also CA 5-8R; 65-68; CANR 4; DLB 15, 161; MTCW 1; SATA 8; SATA-Obit 25
Hughes, Ted 1930-1998 . **CLC 2, 4, 9, 14, 37, 119; DAB; DAC; PC 7**
See also Hughes, Edward James
See also CA 1-4R; 171; CANR 1, 33, 66; CLR 3; DLB 40, 161; MAICYA; MTCW 1, 2; SATA 49; SATA-Brief 27; SATA-Obit 107
Hugo, Richard F(ranklin) 1923-1982 .... **CLC 6, 18, 32; DAM POET**
See also CA 49-52; 108; CANR 3; DLB 5, 206
Hugo, Victor (Marie) 1802-1885 ... **NCLC 3, 10, 21; DA; DAB; DAC; DAM DRAM, MST, NOV, POET; PC 17; WLC**
See also AAYA 28; DA3; DLB 119, 192; SATA 47
Huidobro, Vicente
See Huidobro Fernandez, Vicente Garcia
Huidobro Fernandez, Vicente Garcia 1893-1948 .... **TCLC 31**
See also CA 131; HW 1
Hulme, Keri 1947- .... **CLC 39, 130**
See also CA 125; CANR 69; INT 125
Hulme, T(homas) E(rnest) 1883-1917 .... **TCLC 21**
See also CA 117; DLB 19
Hume, David 1711-1776 .... **LC 7, 56**
See also DLB 104
Humphrey, William 1924-1997 .... **CLC 45**
See also CA 77-80; 160; CANR 68; DLB 212
Humphreys, Emyr Owen 1919- ...... **CLC 47**
See also CA 5-8R; CANR 3, 24; DLB 15
Humphreys, Josephine 1945- .... **CLC 34, 57**
See also CA 121; 127; INT 127
Huneker, James Gibbons 1857-1921 .... **TCLC 65**
See also DLB 71
Hungerford, Pixie
See Brinsmead, H(esba) F(ay)
Hunt, E(verette) Howard, (Jr.) 1918- . **CLC 3**
See also AITN 1; CA 45-48; CANR 2, 47
Hunt, Francesca
See Holland, Isabelle
Hunt, Kyle
See Creasey, John
Hunt, (James Henry) Leigh 1784-1859 .... **NCLC 1, 70; DAM POET**
See also DLB 96, 110, 144
Hunt, Marsha 1946- .... **CLC 70**
See also BW 2, 3; CA 143; CANR 79
Hunt, Violet 1866(?)-1942 .... **TCLC 53**
See also CA 184; DLB 162, 197
Hunter, E. Waldo
See Sturgeon, Theodore (Hamilton)
Hunter, Evan 1926- . **CLC 11, 31; DAM POP**
See also CA 5-8R; CANR 5, 38, 62; DLBY 82; INT CANR-5; MTCW 1; SATA 25
Hunter, Kristin (Eggleston) 1931- .. **CLC 35**
See also AITN 1; BW 1; CA 13-16R; CANR 13; CLR 3; DLB 33; INT CANR-13; MAICYA; SAAS 10; SATA 12
Hunter, Mary
See Austin, Mary (Hunter)
Hunter, Mollie 1922- .... **CLC 21**
See also McIlwraith, Maureen Mollie Hunter
See also AAYA 13; CANR 37, 78; CLR 25; DLB 161; JRDA; MAICYA; SAAS 7; SATA 54, 106
Hunter, Robert (?)-1734 .... **LC 7**
Hurston, Zora Neale 1903-1960 . **CLC 7, 30, 61; BLC 2; DA; DAC; DAM MST, MULT, NOV; DC 12; SSC 4; WLCS**
See also AAYA 15; BW 1, 3; CA 85-88; CANR 61; CDALBS; DA3; DLB 51, 86; MTCW 1, 2
Huston, John (Marcellus) 1906-1987 .... **CLC 20**
See also CA 73-76; 123; CANR 34; DLB 26
Hustvedt, Siri 1955- .... **CLC 76**
See also CA 137
Hutten, Ulrich von 1488-1523 .... **LC 16**
See also DLB 179
Huxley, Aldous (Leonard) 1894-1963 ... **CLC 1, 3, 4, 5, 8, 11, 18, 35, 79; DA; DAB; DAC; DAM MST, NOV; SSC 39; WLC**
See also AAYA 11; CA 85-88; CANR 44; CDBLB 1914-1945; DA3; DLB 36, 100, 162, 195; MTCW 1, 2; SATA 63
Huxley, T(homas) H(enry) 1825-1895 .... **NCLC 67**
See also DLB 57
Huysmans, Joris-Karl 1848-1907 .. **TCLC 7, 69**
See also CA 104; 165; DLB 123
Hwang, David Henry 1957- . **CLC 55; DAM DRAM; DC 4**
See also CA 127; 132; CANR 76; DA3; DLB 212; INT 132; MTCW 2
Hyde, Anthony 1946- .... **CLC 42**
See also CA 136
Hyde, Margaret O(ldroyd) 1917- .... **CLC 21**
See also CA 1-4R; CANR 1, 36; CLR 23; JRDA; MAICYA; SAAS 8; SATA 1, 42, 76
Hynes, James 1956(?)- .... **CLC 65**
See also CA 164
Hypatia c. 370-415 .... **CMLC 35**
Ian, Janis 1951- .... **CLC 21**
See also CA 105
Ibanez, Vicente Blasco
See Blasco Ibanez, Vicente
Ibarbourou, Juana de 1895-1979
See also HLCS 2; HW 1
Ibarguengoitia, Jorge 1928-1983 ..... **CLC 37**
See also CA 124; 113; HW 1
Ibsen, Henrik (Johan) 1828-1906 .. **TCLC 2, 8, 16, 37, 52; DA; DAB; DAC; DAM DRAM, MST; DC 2; WLC**
See also CA 104; 141; DA3

Author Index

Author Index

DLB 15, 100, 160; JRDA; MAICYA; MTCW 1, 2; SATA 13, 100
Lewis, Janet 1899-1998 .... **CLC 41**
See also Winters, Janet Lewis
See also CA 9-12R; 172; CANR 29, 63; CAP 1; DLBY 87
Lewis, Matthew Gregory 1775-1818 .... **NCLC 11, 62**
See also DLB 39, 158, 178
Lewis, (Harry) Sinclair 1885-1951 . **TCLC 4, 13, 23, 39; DA; DAB; DAC; DAM MST, NOV; WLC**
See also CA 104; 133; CDALB 1917-1929; DA3; DLB 9, 102; DLBD 1; MTCW 1, 2
Lewis, (Percy) Wyndham 1882(?)-1957 .... **TCLC 2, 9; SSC 34**
See also CA 104; 157; DLB 15; MTCW 2
Lewisohn, Ludwig 1883-1955 .... **TCLC 19**
See also CA 107; DLB 4, 9, 28, 102
Lewton, Val 1904-1951 .... **TCLC 76**
Leyner, Mark 1956- .... **CLC 92**
See also CA 110; CANR 28, 53; DA3; MTCW 2
Lezama Lima, Jose 1910-1976 ... **CLC 4, 10, 101; DAM MULT; HLCS 2**
See also CA 77-80; CANR 71; DLB 113; HW 1, 2
L'Heureux, John (Clarke) 1934- .... **CLC 52**
See also CA 13-16R; CANR 23, 45, 88
Liddell, C. H.
See Kuttner, Henry
Lie, Jonas (Lauritz Idemil) 1833-1908(?) .... **TCLC 5**
See also CA 115
Lieber, Joel 1937-1971 .... **CLC 6**
See also CA 73-76; 29-32R
Lieber, Stanley Martin
See Lee, Stan
Lieberman, Laurence (James) 1935- .... **CLC 4, 36**
See also CA 17-20R; CANR 8, 36, 89
Lieh Tzu fl. 7th cent. B.C.-5th cent. B.C. .... **CMLC 27**
Lieksman, Anders
See Haavikko, Paavo Juhani
Li Fei-kan 1904-
See Pa Chin
See also CA 105
Lifton, Robert Jay 1926- .... **CLC 67**
See also CA 17-20R; CANR 27, 78; INT CANR-27; SATA 66
Lightfoot, Gordon 1938- .... **CLC 26**
See also CA 109
Lightman, Alan P(aige) 1948- .... **CLC 81**
See also CA 141; CANR 63
Ligotti, Thomas (Robert) 1953- ..... **CLC 44; SSC 16**
See also CA 123; CANR 49
Li Ho 791-817 .... **PC 13**
Liliencron, (Friedrich Adolf Axel) Detlev von 1844-1909 .... **TCLC 18**
See also CA 117
Lilly, William 1602-1681 .... **LC 27**
Lima, Jose Lezama
See Lezama Lima, Jose
Lima Barreto, Afonso Henrique de 1881-1922 .... **TCLC 23**
See also CA 117; 181
Limonov, Edward 1944- .... **CLC 67**
See also CA 137
Lin, Frank
See Atherton, Gertrude (Franklin Horn)
Lincoln, Abraham 1809-1865 .... **NCLC 18**
Lind, Jakov .... **CLC 1, 2, 4, 27, 82**
See also Landwirth, Heinz
See also CAAS 4
Lindbergh, Anne (Spencer) Morrow 1906- .... **CLC 82; DAM NOV**
See also CA 17-20R; CANR 16, 73; MTCW 1, 2; SATA 33
Lindsay, David 1878-1945 .... **TCLC 15**
See also CA 113
Lindsay, (Nicholas) Vachel 1879-1931 .... **TCLC 17; DA; DAC; DAM MST, POET; PC 23; WLC**
See also CA 114; 135; CANR 79; CDALB 1865-1917; DA3; DLB 54; SATA 40
Linke-Poot
See Doeblin, Alfred
Linney, Romulus 1930- .... **CLC 51**
See also CA 1-4R; CANR 40, 44, 79
Linton, Eliza Lynn 1822-1898 ...... **NCLC 41**
See also DLB 18
Li Po 701-763 .... **CMLC 2; PC 29**
Lipsius, Justus 1547-1606 .... **LC 16**
Lipsyte, Robert (Michael) 1938- .... **CLC 21; DA; DAC; DAM MST, NOV**
See also AAYA 7; CA 17-20R; CANR 8, 57; CLR 23; JRDA; MAICYA; SATA 5, 68, 113
Lish, Gordon (Jay) 1934- . **CLC 45; SSC 18**
See also CA 113; 117; CANR 79; DLB 130; INT 117
Lispector, Clarice 1925(?)-1977 ..... **CLC 43; HLCS 2; SSC 34**
See also CA 139; 116; CANR 71; DLB 113; HW 2
Littell, Robert 1935(?)- .... **CLC 42**
See also CA 109; 112; CANR 64
Little, Malcolm 1925-1965
See Malcolm X
See also BW 1, 3; CA 125; 111; CANR 82; DA; DAB; DAC; DAM MST, MULT; DA3; MTCW 1, 2
Littlewit, Humphrey Gent.
See Lovecraft, H(oward) P(hillips)
Litwos
See Sienkiewicz, Henryk (Adam Alexander Pius)
Liu, E 1857-1909 .... **TCLC 15**
See also CA 115
Lively, Penelope (Margaret) 1933- . **CLC 32, 50; DAM NOV**
See also CA 41-44R; CANR 29, 67, 79; CLR 7; DLB 14, 161, 207; JRDA; MAICYA; MTCW 1, 2; SATA 7, 60, 101
Livesay, Dorothy (Kathleen) 1909- .. **CLC 4, 15, 79; DAC; DAM MST, POET**
See also AITN 2; CA 25-28R; CAAS 8; CANR 36, 67; DLB 68; MTCW 1
Livy c. 59B.C.-c. 17 .... **CMLC 11**
See also DLB 211
Lizardi, Jose Joaquin Fernandez de 1776-1827 .... **NCLC 30**
Llewellyn, Richard
See Llewellyn Lloyd, Richard Dafydd Vivian
See also DLB 15
Llewellyn Lloyd, Richard Dafydd Vivian 1906-1983 .... **CLC 7, 80**
See also Llewellyn, Richard
See also CA 53-56; 111; CANR 7, 71; SATA 11; SATA-Obit 37
Llosa, (Jorge) Mario (Pedro) Vargas
See Vargas Llosa, (Jorge) Mario (Pedro)
Lloyd, Manda
See Mander, (Mary) Jane
Lloyd Webber, Andrew 1948-
See Webber, Andrew Lloyd
See also AAYA 1; CA 116; 149; DAM DRAM; SATA 56
Llull, Ramon c. 1235-c. 1316 .... **CMLC 12**
Lobb, Ebenezer
See Upward, Allen
Locke, Alain (Le Roy) 1886-1954 . **TCLC 43; BLCS**
See also BW 1, 3; CA 106; 124; CANR 79; DLB 51
Locke, John 1632-1704 .... **LC 7, 35**
See also DLB 101
Locke-Elliott, Sumner
See Elliott, Sumner Locke
Lockhart, John Gibson 1794-1854 . **NCLC 6**
See also DLB 110, 116, 144
Lodge, David (John) 1935- .. **CLC 36; DAM POP**
See also BEST 90:1; CA 17-20R; CANR 19, 53; DLB 14, 194; INT CANR-19; MTCW 1, 2
Lodge, Thomas 1558-1625 .... **LC 41**
Lodge, Thomas 1558-1625 .... **LC 41**
See also DLB 172
Loennbohm, Armas Eino Leopold 1878-1926
See Leino, Eino
See also CA 123
Loewinsohn, Ron(ald William) 1937- .... **CLC 52**
See also CA 25-28R; CANR 71
Logan, Jake
See Smith, Martin Cruz
Logan, John (Burton) 1923-1987 ...... **CLC 5**
See also CA 77-80; 124; CANR 45; DLB 5
Lo Kuan-chung 1330(?)-1400(?) .... **LC 12**
Lombard, Nap
See Johnson, Pamela Hansford
London, Jack .... **TCLC 9, 15, 39; SSC 4; WLC**
See also London, John Griffith
See also AAYA 13; AITN 2; CDALB 1865-1917; DLB 8, 12, 78, 212; SATA 18
London, John Griffith 1876-1916
See London, Jack
See also CA 110; 119; CANR 73; DA; DAB; DAC; DAM MST, NOV; DA3; JRDA; MAICYA; MTCW 1, 2
Long, Emmett
See Leonard, Elmore (John, Jr.)
Longbaugh, Harry
See Goldman, William (W.)
Longfellow, Henry Wadsworth 1807-1882 .. **NCLC 2, 45; DA; DAB; DAC; DAM MST, POET; PC 30; WLCS**
See also CDALB 1640-1865; DA3; DLB 1, 59; SATA 19
Longinus c. 1st cent. - .... **CMLC 27**
See also DLB 176
Longley, Michael 1939- .... **CLC 29**
See also CA 102; DLB 40
Longus fl. c. 2nd cent. - .... **CMLC 7**
Longway, A. Hugh
See Lang, Andrew
Lonnrot, Elias 1802-1884 .... **NCLC 53**
Lopate, Phillip 1943- .... **CLC 29**
See also CA 97-100; CANR 88; DLBY 80; INT 97-100
Lopez Portillo (y Pacheco), Jose 1920- .... **CLC 46**
See also CA 129; HW 1
Lopez y Fuentes, Gregorio 1897(?)-1966 .... **CLC 32**
See also CA 131; HW 1
Lorca, Federico Garcia
See Garcia Lorca, Federico
Lord, Bette Bao 1938- .... **CLC 23**
See also BEST 90:3; CA 107; CANR 41, 79; INT 107; SATA 58
Lord Auch
See Bataille, Georges
Lord Byron
See Byron, George Gordon (Noel)
Lorde, Audre (Geraldine) 1934-1992 ...... **CLC 18, 71; BLC 2; DAM MULT, POET; PC 12**

Mauriac, Francois (Charles) 1885-1970 .... **CLC 4, 9, 56; SSC 24**
See also CA 25-28; CAP 2; DLB 65; MTCW 1, 2
Mavor, Osborne Henry 1888-1951
See Bridie, James
See also CA 104
Maxwell, William (Keepers, Jr.) 1908- .... **CLC 19**
See also CA 93-96; CANR 54; DLBY 80; INT 93-96
May, Elaine 1932- .... **CLC 16**
See also CA 124; 142; DLB 44
Mayakovski, Vladimir (Vladimirovich) 1893-1930 .... **TCLC 4, 18**
See also CA 104; 158; MTCW 2
Mayhew, Henry 1812-1887 .... **NCLC 31**
See also DLB 18, 55, 190
Mayle, Peter 1939(?)- .... **CLC 89**
See also CA 139; CANR 64
Maynard, Joyce 1953- .... **CLC 23**
See also CA 111; 129; CANR 64
Mayne, William (James Carter) 1928- .... **CLC 12**
See also AAYA 20; CA 9-12R; CANR 37, 80; CLR 25; JRDA; MAICYA; SAAS 11; SATA 6, 68
Mayo, Jim
See L'Amour, Louis (Dearborn)
Maysles, Albert 1926- .... **CLC 16**
See also CA 29-32R
Maysles, David 1932- .... **CLC 16**
Mazer, Norma Fox 1931- .... **CLC 26**
See also AAYA 5; CA 69-72; CANR 12, 32, 66; CLR 23; JRDA; MAICYA; SAAS 1; SATA 24, 67, 105
Mazzini, Guiseppe 1805-1872 .... **NCLC 34**
McAlmon, Robert (Menzies) 1895-1956 .... **TCLC 97**
See also CA 107; 168; DLB 4, 45; DLBD 15
McAuley, James Phillip 1917-1976 . **CLC 45**
See also CA 97-100
McBain, Ed
See Hunter, Evan
McBrien, William (Augustine) 1930- .... **CLC 44**
See also CA 107; CANR 90
McCabe, Patrick 1955- .... **CLC 133**
See also CA 130; CANR 50, 90; DLB 194
McCaffrey, Anne (Inez) 1926- .... **CLC 17; DAM NOV, POP**
See also AAYA 6, 34; AITN 2; BEST 89:2; CA 25-28R; CANR 15, 35, 55; CLR 49; DA3; DLB 8; JRDA; MAICYA; MTCW 1, 2; SAAS 11; SATA 8, 70, 116
McCall, Nathan 1955(?)- .... **CLC 86**
See also BW 3; CA 146; CANR 88
McCann, Arthur
See Campbell, John W(ood, Jr.)
McCann, Edson
See Pohl, Frederik
McCarthy, Charles, Jr. 1933-
See McCarthy, Cormac
See also CANR 42, 69; DAM POP; DA3; MTCW 2
McCarthy, Cormac 1933- .... **CLC 4, 57, 59, 101**
See also McCarthy, Charles, Jr.
See also DLB 6, 143; MTCW 2
McCarthy, Mary (Therese) 1912-1989 ..... **CLC 1, 3, 5, 14, 24, 39, 59; SSC 24**
See also CA 5-8R; 129; CANR 16, 50, 64; DA3; DLB 2; DLBY 81; INT CANR-16; MTCW 1, 2
McCartney, (James) Paul 1942- ..... **CLC 12, 35**
See also CA 146
McCauley, Stephen (D.) 1955- .... **CLC 50**
See also CA 141
McClure, Michael (Thomas) 1932- .. **CLC 6, 10**
See also CA 21-24R; CANR 17, 46, 77; DLB 16
McCorkle, Jill (Collins) 1958- .... **CLC 51**
See also CA 121; DLBY 87
McCourt, Frank 1930- .... **CLC 109**
See also CA 157
McCourt, James 1941- .... **CLC 5**
See also CA 57-60
McCourt, Malachy 1932- .... **CLC 119**
McCoy, Horace (Stanley) 1897-1955 .... **TCLC 28**
See also CA 108; 155; DLB 9
McCrae, John 1872-1918 .... **TCLC 12**
See also CA 109; DLB 92
McCreigh, James
See Pohl, Frederik
McCullers, (Lula) Carson (Smith) 1917-1967 .. **CLC 1, 4, 10, 12, 48, 100; DA; DAB; DAC; DAM MST, NOV; SSC 9, 24; WLC**
See also AAYA 21; CA 5-8R; 25-28R; CABS 1, 3; CANR 18; CDALB 1941-1968; DA3; DLB 2, 7, 173, 228; MTCW 1, 2; SATA 27
McCulloch, John Tyler
See Burroughs, Edgar Rice
McCullough, Colleen 1938(?)- .... **CLC 27, 107; DAM NOV, POP**
See also CA 81-84; CANR 17, 46, 67; DA3; MTCW 1, 2
McDermott, Alice 1953- .... **CLC 90**
See also CA 109; CANR 40, 90
McElroy, Joseph 1930- .... **CLC 5, 47**
See also CA 17-20R
McEwan, Ian (Russell) 1948- .. **CLC 13, 66; DAM NOV**
See also BEST 90:4; CA 61-64; CANR 14, 41, 69, 87; DLB 14, 194; MTCW 1, 2
McFadden, David 1940- .... **CLC 48**
See also CA 104; DLB 60; INT 104
McFarland, Dennis 1950- .... **CLC 65**
See also CA 165
McGahern, John 1934- .. **CLC 5, 9, 48; SSC 17**
See also CA 17-20R; CANR 29, 68; DLB 14; MTCW 1
McGinley, Patrick (Anthony) 1937- . **CLC 41**
See also CA 120; 127; CANR 56; INT 127
McGinley, Phyllis 1905-1978 .... **CLC 14**
See also CA 9-12R; 77-80; CANR 19; DLB 11, 48; SATA 2, 44; SATA-Obit 24
McGinniss, Joe 1942- .... **CLC 32**
See also AITN 2; BEST 89:2; CA 25-28R; CANR 26, 70; DLB 185; INT CANR-26
McGivern, Maureen Daly
See Daly, Maureen
McGrath, Patrick 1950- .... **CLC 55**
See also CA 136; CANR 65
McGrath, Thomas (Matthew) 1916-1990 .... **CLC 28, 59; DAM POET**
See also CA 9-12R; 132; CANR 6, 33; MTCW 1; SATA 41; SATA-Obit 66
McGuane, Thomas (Francis III) 1939- .... **CLC 3, 7, 18, 45, 127**
See also AITN 2; CA 49-52; CANR 5, 24, 49; DLB 2, 212; DLBY 80; INT CANR-24; MTCW 1
McGuckian, Medbh 1950- ... **CLC 48; DAM POET; PC 27**
See also CA 143; DLB 40
McHale, Tom 1942(?)-1982 .... **CLC 3, 5**
See also AITN 1; CA 77-80; 106
McIlvanney, William 1936- .... **CLC 42**
See also CA 25-28R; CANR 61; DLB 14, 207
McIlwraith, Maureen Mollie Hunter
See Hunter, Mollie
See also SATA 2
McInerney, Jay 1955- .. **CLC 34, 112; DAM POP**
See also AAYA 18; CA 116; 123; CANR 45, 68; DA3; INT 123; MTCW 2
McIntyre, Vonda N(eel) 1948- .... **CLC 18**
See also CA 81-84; CANR 17, 34, 69; MTCW 1
McKay, Claude . **TCLC 7, 41; BLC 3; DAB; PC 2**
See also McKay, Festus Claudius
See also DLB 4, 45, 51, 117
McKay, Festus Claudius 1889-1948
See McKay, Claude
See also BW 1, 3; CA 104; 124; CANR 73; DA; DAC; DAM MST, MULT, NOV, POET; MTCW 1, 2; WLC
McKuen, Rod 1933- .... **CLC 1, 3**
See also AITN 1; CA 41-44R; CANR 40
McLoughlin, R. B.
See Mencken, H(enry) L(ouis)
McLuhan, (Herbert) Marshall 1911-1980 .... **CLC 37, 83**
See also CA 9-12R; 102; CANR 12, 34, 61; DLB 88; INT CANR-12; MTCW 1, 2
McMillan, Terry (L.) 1951- ...... **CLC 50, 61, 112; BLCS; DAM MULT, NOV, POP**
See also AAYA 21; BW 2, 3; CA 140; CANR 60; DA3; MTCW 2
McMurtry, Larry (Jeff) 1936- . **CLC 2, 3, 7, 11, 27, 44, 127; DAM NOV, POP**
See also AAYA 15; AITN 2; BEST 89:2; CA 5-8R; CANR 19, 43, 64; CDALB 1968-1988; DA3; DLB 2, 143; DLBY 80, 87; MTCW 1, 2
McNally, T. M. 1961- .... **CLC 82**
McNally, Terrence 1939- .. **CLC 4, 7, 41, 91; DAM DRAM**
See also CA 45-48; CANR 2, 56; DA3; DLB 7; MTCW 2
McNamer, Deirdre 1950- .... **CLC 70**
McNeal, Tom .... **CLC 119**
McNeile, Herman Cyril 1888-1937
See Sapper
See also CA 184; DLB 77
McNickle, (William) D'Arcy 1904-1977 .... **CLC 89; DAM MULT**
See also CA 9-12R; 85-88; CANR 5, 45; DLB 175, 212; NNAL; SATA-Obit 22
McPhee, John (Angus) 1931- .... **CLC 36**
See also BEST 90:1; CA 65-68; CANR 20, 46, 64, 69; DLB 185; MTCW 1, 2
McPherson, James Alan 1943- . **CLC 19, 77; BLCS**
See also BW 1, 3; CA 25-28R; CAAS 17; CANR 24, 74; DLB 38; MTCW 1, 2
McPherson, William (Alexander) 1933- .... **CLC 34**
See also CA 69-72; CANR 28; INT CANR-28
Mead, George Herbert 1873-1958 . **TCLC 89**
Mead, Margaret 1901-1978 .... **CLC 37**
See also AITN 1; CA 1-4R; 81-84; CANR 4; DA3; MTCW 1, 2; SATA-Obit 20
Meaker, Marijane (Agnes) 1927-
See Kerr, M. E.
See also CA 107; CANR 37, 63; INT 107; JRDA; MAICYA; MTCW 1; SATA 20, 61, 99; SATA-Essay 111
Medoff, Mark (Howard) 1940- .. **CLC 6, 23; DAM DRAM**
See also AITN 1; CA 53-56; CANR 5; DLB 7; INT CANR-5
Medvedev, P. N.
See Bakhtin, Mikhail Mikhailovich
Meged, Aharon
See Megged, Aharon

See also CA 81-84; CANR 33, 61; DA3; MTCW 1, 2; SATA 62
Nash, (Fredric) Ogden 1902-1971 . **CLC 23; DAM POET; PC 21**
See also CA 13-14; 29-32R; CANR 34, 61; CAP 1; DLB 11; MAICYA; MTCW 1, 2; SATA 2, 46
Nashe, Thomas 1567-1601(?) .... **LC 41**
See also DLB 167
Nashe, Thomas 1567-1601 .... **LC 41**
Nathan, Daniel
See Dannay, Frederic
Nathan, George Jean 1882-1958 .. **TCLC 18**
See also Hatteras, Owen
See also CA 114; 169; DLB 137
Natsume, Kinnosuke 1867-1916
See Natsume, Soseki
See also CA 104
Natsume, Soseki 1867-1916 ...... **TCLC 2, 10**
See also Natsume, Kinnosuke
See also DLB 180
Natti, (Mary) Lee 1919-
See Kingman, Lee
See also CA 5-8R; CANR 2
Naylor, Gloria 1950- ... **CLC 28, 52; BLC 3; DA; DAC; DAM MST, MULT, NOV, POP; WLCS**
See also AAYA 6; BW 2, 3; CA 107; CANR 27, 51, 74; DA3; DLB 173; MTCW 1, 2
Neihardt, John Gneisenau 1881-1973 .... **CLC 32**
See also CA 13-14; CANR 65; CAP 1; DLB 9, 54
Nekrasov, Nikolai Alekseevich 1821-1878 .... **NCLC 11**
Nelligan, Emile 1879-1941 .... **TCLC 14**
See also CA 114; DLB 92
Nelson, Willie 1933- .... **CLC 17**
See also CA 107
Nemerov, Howard (Stanley) 1920-1991 .. **CLC 2, 6, 9, 36; DAM POET; PC 24**
See also CA 1-4R; 134; CABS 2; CANR 1, 27, 53; DLB 5, 6; DLBY 83; INT CANR-27; MTCW 1, 2
Neruda, Pablo 1904-1973 . **CLC 1, 2, 5, 7, 9, 28, 62; DA; DAB; DAC; DAM MST, MULT, POET; HLC 2; PC 4; WLC**
See also CA 19-20; 45-48; CAP 2; DA3; HW 1; MTCW 1, 2
Nerval, Gerard de 1808-1855 . **NCLC 1, 67; PC 13; SSC 18**
Nervo, (Jose) Amado (Ruiz de) 1870-1919 .... **TCLC 11; HLCS 2**
See also CA 109; 131; HW 1
Nessi, Pio Baroja y
See Baroja (y Nessi), Pio
Nestroy, Johann 1801-1862 .... **NCLC 42**
See also DLB 133
Netterville, Luke
See O'Grady, Standish (James)
Neufeld, John (Arthur) 1938- .... **CLC 17**
See also AAYA 11; CA 25-28R; CANR 11, 37, 56; CLR 52; MAICYA; SAAS 3; SATA 6, 81
Neville, Emily Cheney 1919- .... **CLC 12**
See also CA 5-8R; CANR 3, 37, 85; JRDA; MAICYA; SAAS 2; SATA 1
Newbound, Bernard Slade 1930-
See Slade, Bernard
See also CA 81-84; CANR 49; DAM DRAM
Newby, P(ercy) H(oward) 1918-1997 .... **CLC 2, 13; DAM NOV**
See also CA 5-8R; 161; CANR 32, 67; DLB 15; MTCW 1
Newlove, Donald 1928- .... **CLC 6**
See also CA 29-32R; CANR 25
Newlove, John (Herbert) 1938- .... **CLC 14**
See also CA 21-24R; CANR 9, 25
Newman, Charles 1938- .... **CLC 2, 8**
See also CA 21-24R; CANR 84
Newman, Edwin (Harold) 1919- ..... **CLC 14**
See also AITN 1; CA 69-72; CANR 5
Newman, John Henry 1801-1890 . **NCLC 38**
See also DLB 18, 32, 55
Newton, (Sir)Isaac 1642-1727 ...... **LC 35, 52**
Newton, Suzanne 1936- .... **CLC 35**
See also CA 41-44R; CANR 14; JRDA; SATA 5, 77
Nexo, Martin Andersen 1869-1954 .... **TCLC 43**
Nezval, Vitezslav 1900-1958 .... **TCLC 44**
See also CA 123
Ng, Fae Myenne 1957(?)- .... **CLC 81**
See also CA 146
Ngema, Mbongeni 1955- .... **CLC 57**
See also BW 2; CA 143; CANR 84
Ngugi, James T(hiong'o) .... **CLC 3, 7, 13**
See also Ngugi wa Thiong'o
Ngugi wa Thiong'o 1938- . **CLC 36; BLC 3; DAM MULT, NOV**
See also Ngugi, James T(hiong'o)
See also BW 2; CA 81-84; CANR 27, 58; DLB 125; MTCW 1, 2
Nichol, B(arrie) P(hillip) 1944-1988 . **CLC 18**
See also CA 53-56; DLB 53; SATA 66
Nichols, John (Treadwell) 1940- ..... **CLC 38**
See also CA 9-12R; CAAS 2; CANR 6, 70; DLBY 82
Nichols, Leigh
See Koontz, Dean R(ay)
Nichols, Peter (Richard) 1927- .. **CLC 5, 36, 65**
See also CA 104; CANR 33, 86; DLB 13; MTCW 1
Nicolas, F. R. E.
See Freeling, Nicolas
Niedecker, Lorine 1903-1970 ... **CLC 10, 42; DAM POET**
See also CA 25-28; CAP 2; DLB 48
Nietzsche, Friedrich (Wilhelm) 1844-1900 .... **TCLC 10, 18, 55**
See also CA 107; 121; DLB 129
Nievo, Ippolito 1831-1861 .... **NCLC 22**
Nightingale, Anne Redmon 1943-
See Redmon, Anne
See also CA 103
Nightingale, Florence 1820-1910 .. **TCLC 85**
See also DLB 166
Nik. T. O.
See Annensky, Innokenty (Fyodorovich)
Nin, Anais 1903-1977 .... **CLC 1, 4, 8, 11, 14, 60, 127; DAM NOV, POP; SSC 10**
See also AITN 2; CA 13-16R; 69-72; CANR 22, 53; DLB 2, 4, 152; MTCW 1, 2
Nishida, Kitaro 1870-1945 .... **TCLC 83**
Nishiwaki, Junzaburo 1894-1982 .... **PC 15**
See also CA 107
Nissenson, Hugh 1933- .... **CLC 4, 9**
See also CA 17-20R; CANR 27; DLB 28
Niven, Larry .... **CLC 8**
See also Niven, Laurence Van Cott
See also AAYA 27; DLB 8
Niven, Laurence Van Cott 1938-
See Niven, Larry
See also CA 21-24R; CAAS 12; CANR 14, 44, 66; DAM POP; MTCW 1, 2; SATA 95
Nixon, Agnes Eckhardt 1927- .... **CLC 21**
See also CA 110
Nizan, Paul 1905-1940 .... **TCLC 40**
See also CA 161; DLB 72
Nkosi, Lewis 1936- . **CLC 45; BLC 3; DAM MULT**
See also BW 1, 3; CA 65-68; CANR 27, 81; DLB 157, 225
Nodier, (Jean) Charles (Emmanuel) 1780-1844 .... **NCLC 19**
See also DLB 119
Noguchi, Yone 1875-1947 .... **TCLC 80**
Nolan, Christopher 1965- .... **CLC 58**
See also CA 111; CANR 88
Noon, Jeff 1957- .... **CLC 91**
See also CA 148; CANR 83
Norden, Charles
See Durrell, Lawrence (George)
Nordhoff, Charles (Bernard) 1887-1947 .... **TCLC 23**
See also CA 108; DLB 9; SATA 23
Norfolk, Lawrence 1963- .... **CLC 76**
See also CA 144; CANR 85
Norman, Marsha 1947- .... **CLC 28; DAM DRAM; DC 8**
See also CA 105; CABS 3; CANR 41; DLBY 84
Normyx
See Douglas, (George) Norman
Norris, Frank 1870-1902 .... **SSC 28**
See also Norris, (Benjamin) Frank(lin, Jr.)
See also CDALB 1865-1917; DLB 12, 71, 186
Norris, (Benjamin) Frank(lin, Jr.) 1870-1902 .... **TCLC 24**
See also Norris, Frank
See also CA 110; 160
Norris, Leslie 1921- .... **CLC 14**
See also CA 11-12; CANR 14; CAP 1; DLB 27
North, Andrew
See Norton, Andre
North, Anthony
See Koontz, Dean R(ay)
North, Captain George
See Stevenson, Robert Louis (Balfour)
North, Milou
See Erdrich, Louise
Northrup, B. A.
See Hubbard, L(afayette) Ron(ald)
North Staffs
See Hulme, T(homas) E(rnest)
Norton, Alice Mary
See Norton, Andre
See also MAICYA; SATA 1, 43
Norton, Andre 1912- .... **CLC 12**
See also Norton, Alice Mary
See also AAYA 14; CA 1-4R; CANR 68; CLR 50; DLB 8, 52; JRDA; MTCW 1; SATA 91
Norton, Caroline 1808-1877 .... **NCLC 47**
See also DLB 21, 159, 199
Norway, Nevil Shute 1899-1960
See Shute, Nevil
See also CA 102; 93-96; CANR 85; MTCW 2
Norwid, Cyprian Kamil 1821-1883 .... **NCLC 17**
Nosille, Nabrah
See Ellison, Harlan (Jay)
Nossack, Hans Erich 1901-1978 .... **CLC 6**
See also CA 93-96; 85-88; DLB 69
Nostradamus 1503-1566 .... **LC 27**
Nosu, Chuji
See Ozu, Yasujiro
Notenburg, Eleanora (Genrikhovna) von
See Guro, Elena
Nova, Craig 1945- .... **CLC 7, 31**
See also CA 45-48; CANR 2, 53
Novak, Joseph
See Kosinski, Jerzy (Nikodem)
Novalis 1772-1801 .... **NCLC 13**
See also DLB 90

Author Index

See also CA 116; 121; CANR 78

Oskison, John Milton 1874-1947 . **TCLC 35; DAM MULT**
See also CA 144; CANR 84; DLB 175; NNAL

Ossian c. 3rd cent. - .... **CMLC 28**
See also Macpherson, James

Ostriker, Alicia (Suskin) 1937- ...... **CLC 132**
See also CA 25-28R; CAAS 24; CANR 10, 30, 62; DLB 120

Ostrovsky, Alexander 1823-1886 . **NCLC 30, 57**

Otero, Blas de 1916-1979 .... **CLC 11**
See also CA 89-92; DLB 134

Otto, Rudolf 1869-1937 .... **TCLC 85**

Otto, Whitney 1955- .... **CLC 70**
See also CA 140

Ouida .... **TCLC 43**
See also De La Ramee, (Marie) Louise
See also DLB 18, 156

Ousmane, Sembene 1923- .. **CLC 66; BLC 3**
See also BW 1, 3; CA 117; 125; CANR 81; MTCW 1

Ovid 43B.C.-17 . **CMLC 7; DAM POET; PC 2**
See also DA3; DLB 211

Owen, Hugh
See Faust, Frederick (Schiller)

Owen, Wilfred (Edward Salter) 1893-1918 ... **TCLC 5, 27; DA; DAB; DAC; DAM MST, POET; PC 19; WLC**
See also CA 104; 141; CDBLB 1914-1945; DLB 20; MTCW 2

Owens, Rochelle 1936- .... **CLC 8**
See also CA 17-20R; CAAS 2; CANR 39

Oz, Amos 1939- .... **CLC 5, 8, 11, 27, 33, 54; DAM NOV**
See also CA 53-56; CANR 27, 47, 65; MTCW 1, 2

Ozick, Cynthia 1928- .... **CLC 3, 7, 28, 62; DAM NOV, POP; SSC 15**
See also BEST 90:1; CA 17-20R; CANR 23, 58; DA3; DLB 28, 152; DLBY 82; INT CANR-23; MTCW 1, 2

Ozu, Yasujiro 1903-1963 .... **CLC 16**
See also CA 112

Pacheco, C.
See Pessoa, Fernando (Antonio Nogueira)

Pacheco, Jose Emilio 1939-
See also CA 111; 131; CANR 65; DAM MULT; HLC 2; HW 1, 2

Pa Chin .... **CLC 18**
See also Li Fei-kan

Pack, Robert 1929- .... **CLC 13**
See also CA 1-4R; CANR 3, 44, 82; DLB 5

Padgett, Lewis
See Kuttner, Henry

Padilla (Lorenzo), Heberto 1932- ... **CLC 38**
See also AITN 1; CA 123; 131; HW 1

Page, Jimmy 1944- .... **CLC 12**

Page, Louise 1955- .... **CLC 40**
See also CA 140; CANR 76

Page, P(atricia) K(athleen) 1916- .... **CLC 7, 18; DAC; DAM MST; PC 12**
See also CA 53-56; CANR 4, 22, 65; DLB 68; MTCW 1

Page, Thomas Nelson 1853-1922 ...... **SSC 23**
See also CA 118; 177; DLB 12, 78; DLBD 13

Pagels, Elaine Hiesey 1943- .... **CLC 104**
See also CA 45-48; CANR 2, 24, 51

Paget, Violet 1856-1935
See Lee, Vernon
See also CA 104; 166

Paget-Lowe, Henry
See Lovecraft, H(oward) P(hillips)

Paglia, Camille (Anna) 1947- .... **CLC 68**
See also CA 140; CANR 72; MTCW 2

Paige, Richard
See Koontz, Dean R(ay)

Paine, Thomas 1737-1809 .... **NCLC 62**
See also CDALB 1640-1865; DLB 31, 43, 73, 158

Pakenham, Antonia
See Fraser, (Lady) Antonia (Pakenham)

Palamas, Kostes 1859-1943 .... **TCLC 5**
See also CA 105

Palazzeschi, Aldo 1885-1974 .... **CLC 11**
See also CA 89-92; 53-56; DLB 114

Pales Matos, Luis 1898-1959
See also HLCS 2; HW 1

Paley, Grace 1922- .... **CLC 4, 6, 37; DAM POP; SSC 8**
See also CA 25-28R; CANR 13, 46, 74; DA3; DLB 28; INT CANR-13; MTCW 1, 2

Palin, Michael (Edward) 1943- .... **CLC 21**
See also Monty Python
See also CA 107; CANR 35; SATA 67

Palliser, Charles 1947- .... **CLC 65**
See also CA 136; CANR 76

Palma, Ricardo 1833-1919 .... **TCLC 29**
See also CA 168

Pancake, Breece Dexter 1952-1979
See Pancake, Breece D'J
See also CA 123; 109

Pancake, Breece D'J .... **CLC 29**
See also Pancake, Breece Dexter
See also DLB 130

Panko, Rudy
See Gogol, Nikolai (Vasilyevich)

Papadiamantis, Alexandros 1851-1911 .... **TCLC 29**
See also CA 168

Papadiamantopoulos, Johannes 1856-1910
See Moreas, Jean
See also CA 117

Papini, Giovanni 1881-1956 .... **TCLC 22**
See also CA 121; 180

Paracelsus 1493-1541 .... **LC 14**
See also DLB 179

Parasol, Peter
See Stevens, Wallace

Pardo Bazan, Emilia 1851-1921 .... **SSC 30**

Pareto, Vilfredo 1848-1923 .... **TCLC 69**
See also CA 175

Parfenie, Maria
See Codrescu, Andrei

Parini, Jay (Lee) 1948- .... **CLC 54, 133**
See also CA 97-100; CAAS 16; CANR 32, 87

Park, Jordan
See Kornbluth, C(yril) M.; Pohl, Frederik

Park, Robert E(zra) 1864-1944 .... **TCLC 73**
See also CA 122; 165

Parker, Bert
See Ellison, Harlan (Jay)

Parker, Dorothy (Rothschild) 1893-1967 . **CLC 15, 68; DAM POET; PC 28; SSC 2**
See also CA 19-20; 25-28R; CAP 2; DA3; DLB 11, 45, 86; MTCW 1, 2

Parker, Robert B(rown) 1932- .... **CLC 27; DAM NOV, POP**
See also AAYA 28; BEST 89:4; CA 49-52; CANR 1, 26, 52, 89; INT CANR-26; MTCW 1

Parkin, Frank 1940- .... **CLC 43**
See also CA 147

Parkman, Francis Jr., Jr. 1823-1893 .... **NCLC 12**
See also DLB 1, 30, 186

Parks, Gordon (Alexander Buchanan) 1912- .... **CLC 1, 16; BLC 3; DAM MULT**
See also AITN 2; BW 2, 3; CA 41-44R; CANR 26, 66; DA3; DLB 33; MTCW 2; SATA 8, 108

Parmenides c. 515B.C.-c. 450B.C. . **CMLC 22**
See also DLB 176

Parnell, Thomas 1679-1718 .... **LC 3**
See also DLB 94

Parra, Nicanor 1914- ..... **CLC 2, 102; DAM MULT; HLC 2**
See also CA 85-88; CANR 32; HW 1; MTCW 1

Parra Sanojo, Ana Teresa de la 1890-1936
See also HLCS 2

Parrish, Mary Frances
See Fisher, M(ary) F(rances) K(ennedy)

Parson
See Coleridge, Samuel Taylor

Parson Lot
See Kingsley, Charles

Parton, Sara Payson Willis 1811-1872 .... **NCLC 86**
See also DLB 43, 74

Partridge, Anthony
See Oppenheim, E(dward) Phillips

Pascal, Blaise 1623-1662 .... **LC 35**

Pascoli, Giovanni 1855-1912 .... **TCLC 45**
See also CA 170

Pasolini, Pier Paolo 1922-1975 . **CLC 20, 37, 106; PC 17**
See also CA 93-96; 61-64; CANR 63; DLB 128, 177; MTCW 1

Pasquini
See Silone, Ignazio

Pastan, Linda (Olenik) 1932- .... **CLC 27; DAM POET**
See also CA 61-64; CANR 18, 40, 61; DLB 5

Pasternak, Boris (Leonidovich) 1890-1960 .... **CLC 7, 10, 18, 63; DA; DAB; DAC; DAM MST, NOV, POET; PC 6; SSC 31; WLC**
See also CA 127; 116; DA3; MTCW 1, 2

Patchen, Kenneth 1911-1972 . **CLC 1, 2, 18; DAM POET**
See also CA 1-4R; 33-36R; CANR 3, 35; DLB 16, 48; MTCW 1

Pater, Walter (Horatio) 1839-1894 ... **NCLC**
See also CDBLB 1832-1890; DLB 57, 156

Paterson, A(ndrew) B(arton) 1864-1941 .... **TCLC 32**
See also CA 155; SATA 97

Paterson, Katherine (Womeldorf) 1932- .... **CLC 12, 30**
See also AAYA 1, 31; CA 21-24R; CANR 28, 59; CLR 7, 50; DLB 52; JRDA; MAICYA; MTCW 1; SATA 13, 53, 92

Patmore, Coventry Kersey Dighton 1823-1896 .... **NCLC 9**
See also DLB 35, 98

Paton, Alan (Stewart) 1903-1988 ..... **CLC 4, 10, 25, 55, 106; DA; DAB; DAC; DAM MST, NOV; WLC**
See also AAYA 26; CA 13-16; 125; CANR 22; CAP 1; DA3; DLB 225; DLBD 17; MTCW 1, 2; SATA 11; SATA-Obit 56

Paton Walsh, Gillian 1937-
See Walsh, Jill Paton
See also AAYA 11; CANR 38, 83; DLB 161; JRDA; MAICYA; SAAS 3; SATA 4, 72, 109

Patton, George S. 1885-1945 .... **TCLC 79**

Paulding, James Kirke 1778-1860 . **NCLC 2**
See also DLB 3, 59, 74

Paulin, Thomas Neilson 1949-
See Paulin, Tom
See also CA 123; 128

Paulin, Tom .... **CLC 37**
See also Paulin, Thomas Neilson
See also DLB 40

Pausanias c. 1st cent. - .... **CMLC 36**

Paustovsky, Konstantin (Georgievich) 1892-1968 .... **CLC 40**
See also CA 93-96; 25-28R

Pavese, Cesare 1908-1950 . **TCLC 3; PC 13; SSC 19**
See also CA 104; 169; DLB 128, 177

Pavic, Milorad 1929- .... **CLC 60**
See also CA 136; DLB 181

Pavlov, Ivan Petrovich 1849-1936 . **TCLC 91**
See also CA 118; 180

Payne, Alan
See Jakes, John (William)

Paz, Gil
See Lugones, Leopoldo

Paz, Octavio 1914-1998 . **CLC 3, 4, 6, 10, 19, 51, 65, 119; DA; DAB; DAC; DAM MST, MULT, POET; HLC 2; PC 1; WLC**
See also CA 73-76; 165; CANR 32, 65; DA3; DLBY 90, 98; HW 1, 2; MTCW 1, 2

p'Bitek, Okot 1931-1982 ... **CLC 96; BLC 3; DAM MULT**
See also BW 2, 3; CA 124; 107; CANR 82; DLB 125; MTCW 1, 2

Peacock, Molly 1947- .... **CLC 60**
See also CA 103; CAAS 21; CANR 52, 84; DLB 120

Peacock, Thomas Love 1785-1866 . **NCLC 22**
See also DLB 96, 116

Peake, Mervyn 1911-1968 .... **CLC 7, 54**
See also CA 5-8R; 25-28R; CANR 3; DLB 15, 160; MTCW 1; SATA 23

Pearce, Philippa .... **CLC 21**
See also Christie, (Ann) Philippa
See also CLR 9; DLB 161; MAICYA; SATA 1, 67

Pearl, Eric
See Elman, Richard (Martin)

Pearson, T(homas) R(eid) 1956- ..... **CLC 39**
See also CA 120; 130; INT 130

Peck, Dale 1967- .... **CLC 81**
See also CA 146; CANR 72

Peck, John 1941- .... **CLC 3**
See also CA 49-52; CANR 3

Peck, Richard (Wayne) 1934- .... **CLC 21**
See also AAYA 1, 24; CA 85-88; CANR 19, 38; CLR 15; INT CANR-19; JRDA; MAICYA; SAAS 2; SATA 18, 55, 97; SATA-Essay 110

Peck, Robert Newton 1928- ... **CLC 17; DA; DAC; DAM MST**
See also AAYA 3; CA 81-84, 182; CAAE 182; CANR 31, 63; CLR 45; JRDA; MAICYA; SAAS 1; SATA 21, 62, 111; SATA-Essay 108

Peckinpah, (David) Sam(uel) 1925-1984 .... **CLC 20**
See also CA 109; 114; CANR 82

Pedersen, Knut 1859-1952
See Hamsun, Knut
See also CA 104; 119; CANR 63; MTCW 1, 2

Peeslake, Gaffer
See Durrell, Lawrence (George)

Peguy, Charles Pierre 1873-1914 . **TCLC 10**
See also CA 107

Peirce, Charles Sanders 1839-1914 .... **TCLC 81**

Pellicer, Carlos 1900(?)-1977
See also CA 153; 69-72; HLCS 2; HW 1

Pena, Ramon del Valle y
See Valle-Inclan, Ramon (Maria) del

Pendennis, Arthur Esquir
See Thackeray, William Makepeace

Penn, William 1644-1718 .... **LC 25**
See also DLB 24

PEPECE
See Prado (Calvo), Pedro

Pepys, Samuel 1633-1703 .... **LC 11, 58; DA; DAB; DAC; DAM MST; WLC**
See also CDBLB 1660-1789; DA3; DLB 101

Percy, Walker 1916-1990 ..... **CLC 2, 3, 6, 8, 14, 18, 47, 65; DAM NOV, POP**
See also CA 1-4R; 131; CANR 1, 23, 64; DA3; DLB 2; DLBY 80, 90; MTCW 1, 2

Percy, William Alexander 1885-1942 .... **TCLC 84**
See also CA 163; MTCW 2

Perec, Georges 1936-1982 .... **CLC 56, 116**
See also CA 141; DLB 83

Pereda (y Sanchez de Porrua), Jose Maria de 1833-1906 .... **TCLC 16**
See also CA 117

Pereda y Porrua, Jose Maria de
See Pereda (y Sanchez de Porrua), Jose Maria de

Peregoy, George Weems
See Mencken, H(enry) L(ouis)

Perelman, S(idney) J(oseph) 1904-1979 .... **CLC 3, 5, 9, 15, 23, 44, 49; DAM DRAM; SSC 32**
See also AITN 1, 2; CA 73-76; 89-92; CANR 18; DLB 11, 44; MTCW 1, 2

Peret, Benjamin 1899-1959 .... **TCLC 20**
See also CA 117; 186

Peretz, Isaac Loeb 1851(?)-1915 . **TCLC 16; SSC 26**
See also CA 109

Peretz, Yitzkhok Leibush
See Peretz, Isaac Loeb

Perez Galdos, Benito 1843-1920 . **TCLC 27; HLCS 2**
See also CA 125; 153; HW 1

Peri Rossi, Cristina 1941-
See also CA 131; CANR 59, 81; DLB 145; HLCS 2; HW 1, 2

Perlata
See Peret, Benjamin

Perrault, Charles 1628-1703 .. **LC 3, 52; DC 12**
See also MAICYA; SATA 25

Perry, Anne 1938- .... **CLC 126**
See also CA 101; CANR 22, 50, 84

Perry, Brighton
See Sherwood, Robert E(mmet)

Perse, St.-John
See Leger, (Marie-Rene Auguste) Alexis Saint-Leger

Perutz, Leo(pold) 1882-1957 .... **TCLC 60**
See also CA 147; DLB 81

Peseenz, Tulio F.
See Lopez y Fuentes, Gregorio

Pesetsky, Bette 1932- .... **CLC 28**
See also CA 133; DLB 130

Peshkov, Alexei Maximovich 1868-1936
See Gorky, Maxim
See also CA 105; 141; CANR 83; DA; DAC; DAM DRAM, MST, NOV; MTCW 2

Pessoa, Fernando (Antonio Nogueira) 1888-1935 ..... **TCLC 27; DAM MULT; HLC 2; PC 20**
See also CA 125; 183

Peterkin, Julia Mood 1880-1961 ..... **CLC 31**
See also CA 102; DLB 9

Peters, Joan K(aren) 1945- .... **CLC 39**
See also CA 158

Peters, Robert L(ouis) 1924- .... **CLC 7**
See also CA 13-16R; CAAS 8; DLB 105

Petofi, Sandor 1823-1849 .... **NCLC 21**

Petrakis, Harry Mark 1923- .... **CLC 3**
See also CA 9-12R; CANR 4, 30, 85

Petrarch 1304-1374 .... **CMLC 20; DAM POET; PC 8**
See also DA3

Petronius c. 20-66 .... **CMLC 34**
See also DLB 211

Petrov, Evgeny .... **TCLC 21**
See also Kataev, Evgeny Petrovich

Petry, Ann (Lane) 1908-1997 .. **CLC 1, 7, 18**
See also BW 1, 3; CA 5-8R; 157; CAAS 6; CANR 4, 46; CLR 12; DLB 76; JRDA; MAICYA; MTCW 1; SATA 5; SATA-Obit 94

Petursson, Halligrimur 1614-1674 .... **LC 8**

Peychinovich
See Vazov, Ivan (Minchov)

Phaedrus c. 18B.C.-c. 50 .... **CMLC 25**
See also DLB 211

Philips, Katherine 1632-1664 .... **LC 30**
See also DLB 131

Philipson, Morris H. 1926- .... **CLC 53**
See also CA 1-4R; CANR 4

Phillips, Caryl 1958- . **CLC 96; BLCS; DAM MULT**
See also BW 2; CA 141; CANR 63; DA3; DLB 157; MTCW 2

Phillips, David Graham 1867-1911 .... **TCLC 44**
See also CA 108; 176; DLB 9, 12

Phillips, Jack
See Sandburg, Carl (August)

Phillips, Jayne Anne 1952- .... **CLC 15, 33; SSC 16**
See also CA 101; CANR 24, 50; DLBY 80; INT CANR-24; MTCW 1, 2

Phillips, Richard
See Dick, Philip K(indred)

Phillips, Robert (Schaeffer) 1938- ... **CLC 28**
See also CA 17-20R; CAAS 13; CANR 8; DLB 105

Phillips, Ward
See Lovecraft, H(oward) P(hillips)

Piccolo, Lucio 1901-1969 .... **CLC 13**
See also CA 97-100; DLB 114

Pickthall, Marjorie L(owry) C(hristie) 1883-1922 .... **TCLC 21**
See also CA 107; DLB 92

Pico della Mirandola, Giovanni 1463-1494 .... **LC 15**

Piercy, Marge 1936- ... **CLC 3, 6, 14, 18, 27, 62, 128; PC 29**
See also CA 21-24R; CAAS 1; CANR 13, 43, 66; DLB 120, 227; MTCW 1, 2

Piers, Robert
See Anthony, Piers

Pieyre de Mandiargues, Andre 1909-1991
See Mandiargues, Andre Pieyre de
See also CA 103; 136; CANR 22, 82

Pilnyak, Boris .... **TCLC 23**
See also Vogau, Boris Andreyevich

Pincherle, Alberto 1907-1990 ... **CLC 11, 18; DAM NOV**
See also Moravia, Alberto
See also CA 25-28R; 132; CANR 33, 63; MTCW 1

Pinckney, Darryl 1953- .... **CLC 76**
See also BW 2, 3; CA 143; CANR 79

Pindar 518B.C.-446B.C. .. **CMLC 12; PC 19**
See also DLB 176

Pineda, Cecile 1942- .... **CLC 39**
See also CA 118

Pinero, Arthur Wing 1855-1934 .. **TCLC 32; DAM DRAM**
See also CA 110; 153; DLB 10

Pinero, Miguel (Antonio Gomez) 1946-1988 .... **CLC 4, 55**
See also CA 61-64; 125; CANR 29, 90; HW 1

Pinget, Robert 1919-1997 ...... **CLC 7, 13, 37**

See also CA 85-88; 160; DLB 83
Pink Floyd
See Barrett, (Roger) Syd; Gilmour, David; Mason, Nick; Waters, Roger; Wright, Rick
Pinkney, Edward 1802-1828 .... **NCLC 31**
Pinkwater, Daniel Manus 1941- ...... **CLC 35**
See also Pinkwater, Manus
See also AAYA 1; CA 29-32R; CANR 12, 38, 89; CLR 4; JRDA; MAICYA; SAAS 3; SATA 46, 76, 114
Pinkwater, Manus
See Pinkwater, Daniel Manus
See also SATA 8
Pinsky, Robert 1940- ...... **CLC 9, 19, 38, 94, 121; DAM POET; PC 27**
See also CA 29-32R; CAAS 4; CANR 58; DA3; DLBY 82, 98; MTCW 2
Pinta, Harold
See Pinter, Harold
Pinter, Harold 1930- . **CLC 1, 3, 6, 9, 11, 15, 27, 58, 73; DA; DAB; DAC; DAM DRAM, MST; WLC**
See also CA 5-8R; CANR 33, 65; CDBLB 1960 to Present; DA3; DLB 13; MTCW 1, 2
Piozzi, Hester Lynch (Thrale) 1741-1821 .... **NCLC 57**
See also DLB 104, 142
Pirandello, Luigi 1867-1936 .... **TCLC 4, 29; DA; DAB; DAC; DAM DRAM, MST; DC 5; SSC 22; WLC**
See also CA 104; 153; DA3; MTCW 2
Pirsig, Robert M(aynard) 1928- .. **CLC 4, 6, 73; DAM POP**
See also CA 53-56; CANR 42, 74; DA3; MTCW 1, 2; SATA 39
Pisarev, Dmitry Ivanovich 1840-1868 .... **NCLC 25**
Pix, Mary (Griffith) 1666-1709 .... **LC 8**
See also DLB 80
Pixerecourt, (Rene Charles) Guilbert de 1773-1844 .... **NCLC 39**
See also DLB 192
Plaatje, Sol(omon) T(shekisho) 1876-1932 .... **TCLC 73; BLCS**
See also BW 2, 3; CA 141; CANR 79; DLB 225
Plaidy, Jean
See Hibbert, Eleanor Alice Burford
Planche, James Robinson 1796-1880 .... **NCLC 42**
Plant, Robert 1948- .... **CLC 12**
Plante, David (Robert) 1940- ..... **CLC 7, 23, 38; DAM NOV**
See also CA 37-40R; CANR 12, 36, 58, 82; DLBY 83; INT CANR-12; MTCW 1
Plath, Sylvia 1932-1963 .... **CLC 1, 2, 3, 5, 9, 11, 14, 17, 50, 51, 62, 111; DA; DAB; DAC; DAM MST, POET; PC 1; WLC**
See also AAYA 13; CA 19-20; CANR 34; CAP 2; CDALB 1941-1968; DA3; DLB 5, 6, 152; MTCW 1, 2; SATA 96
Plato 428(?)B.C.-348(?)B.C. .. **CMLC 8; DA; DAB; DAC; DAM MST; WLCS**
See also DA3; DLB 176
Platonov, Andrei
See Klimentov, Andrei Platonovich
Platt, Kin 1911- .... **CLC 26**
See also AAYA 11; CA 17-20R; CANR 11; JRDA; SAAS 17; SATA 21, 86
Plautus c. 251B.C.-184B.C. .. **CMLC 24; DC 6**
See also DLB 211
Plick et Plock
See Simenon, Georges (Jacques Christian)
Plimpton, George (Ames) 1927- ...... **CLC 36**
See also AITN 1; CA 21-24R; CANR 32, 70; DLB 185; MTCW 1, 2; SATA 10
Pliny the Elder c. 23-79 .... **CMLC 23**
See also DLB 211
Plomer, William Charles Franklin 1903-1973 .... **CLC 4, 8**
See also CA 21-22; CANR 34; CAP 2; DLB 20, 162, 191, 225; MTCW 1; SATA 24
Plowman, Piers
See Kavanagh, Patrick (Joseph)
Plum, J.
See Wodehouse, P(elham) G(renville)
Plumly, Stanley (Ross) 1939- .... **CLC 33**
See also CA 108; 110; DLB 5, 193; INT 110
Plumpe, Friedrich Wilhelm 1888-1931 .... **TCLC 53**
See also CA 112
Po Chu-i 772-846 .... **CMLC 24**
Poe, Edgar Allan 1809-1849 .... **NCLC 1, 16, 55, 78; DA; DAB; DAC; DAM MST, POET; PC 1; SSC 34; WLC**
See also AAYA 14; CDALB 1640-1865; DA3; DLB 3, 59, 73, 74; SATA 23
Poet of Titchfield Street, The
See Pound, Ezra (Weston Loomis)
Pohl, Frederik 1919- .... **CLC 18; SSC 25**
See also AAYA 24; CA 61-64; CAAS 1; CANR 11, 37, 81; DLB 8; INT CANR-11; MTCW 1, 2; SATA 24
Poirier, Louis 1910-
See Gracq, Julien
See also CA 122; 126
Poitier, Sidney 1927- .... **CLC 26**
See also BW 1; CA 117
Polanski, Roman 1933- .... **CLC 16**
See also CA 77-80
Poliakoff, Stephen 1952- .... **CLC 38**
See also CA 106; DLB 13
Police, The
See Copeland, Stewart (Armstrong); Summers, Andrew James; Sumner, Gordon Matthew
Polidori, John William 1795-1821 . **NCLC 51**
See also DLB 116
Pollitt, Katha 1949- .... **CLC 28, 122**
See also CA 120; 122; CANR 66; MTCW 1, 2
Pollock, (Mary) Sharon 1936- .... **CLC 50; DAC; DAM DRAM, MST**
See also CA 141; DLB 60
Polo, Marco 1254-1324 .... **CMLC 15**
Polonsky, Abraham (Lincoln) 1910- .... **CLC 92**
See also CA 104; DLB 26; INT 104
Polybius c. 200B.C.-c. 118B.C. ..... **CMLC 17**
See also DLB 176
Pomerance, Bernard 1940- .. **CLC 13; DAM DRAM**
See also CA 101; CANR 49
Ponge, Francis 1899-1988 . **CLC 6, 18; DAM POET**
See also CA 85-88; 126; CANR 40, 86
Poniatowska, Elena 1933-
See also CA 101; CANR 32, 66; DAM MULT; DLB 113; HLC 2; HW 1, 2
Pontoppidan, Henrik 1857-1943 ... **TCLC 29**
See also CA 170
Poole, Josephine .... **CLC 17**
See also Helyar, Jane Penelope Josephine
See also SAAS 2; SATA 5
Popa, Vasko 1922-1991 .... **CLC 19**
See also CA 112; 148; DLB 181
Pope, Alexander 1688-1744 .. **LC 3, 58; DA; DAB; DAC; DAM MST, POET; PC 26; WLC**
See also CDBLB 1660-1789; DA3; DLB 95, 101
Porter, Connie (Rose) 1959(?)- .... **CLC 70**
See also BW 2, 3; CA 142; CANR 90; SATA 81
Porter, Gene(va Grace) Stratton 1863(?)-1924 .... **TCLC 21**
See also CA 112
Porter, Katherine Anne 1890-1980 .. **CLC 1, 3, 7, 10, 13, 15, 27, 101; DA; DAB; DAC; DAM MST, NOV; SSC 4, 31**
See also AITN 2; CA 1-4R; 101; CANR 1, 65; CDALBS; DA3; DLB 4, 9, 102; DLBD 12; DLBY 80; MTCW 1, 2; SATA 39; SATA-Obit 23
Porter, Peter (Neville Frederick) 1929- .... **CLC 5, 13, 33**
See also CA 85-88; DLB 40
Porter, William Sydney 1862-1910
See Henry, O.
See also CA 104; 131; CDALB 1865-1917; DA; DAB; DAC; DAM MST; DA3; DLB 12, 78, 79; MTCW 1, 2; YABC 2
Portillo (y Pacheco), Jose Lopez
See Lopez Portillo (y Pacheco), Jose
Portillo Trambley, Estela 1927-1998
See also CANR 32; DAM MULT; DLB 209; HLC 2; HW 1
Post, Melville Davisson 1869-1930 . **TCLC 39**
See also CA 110
Potok, Chaim 1929- . **CLC 2, 7, 14, 26, 112; DAM NOV**
See also AAYA 15; AITN 1, 2; CA 17-20R; CANR 19, 35, 64; DA3; DLB 28, 152; INT CANR-19; MTCW 1, 2; SATA 33, 106
Potter, Dennis (Christopher George) 1935-1994 .... **CLC 58, 86**
See also CA 107; 145; CANR 33, 61; MTCW 1
Pound, Ezra (Weston Loomis) 1885-1972 . **CLC 1, 2, 3, 4, 5, 7, 10, 13, 18, 34, 48, 50, 112; DA; DAB; DAC; DAM MST, POET; PC 4; WLC**
See also CA 5-8R; 37-40R; CANR 40; CDALB 1917-1929; DA3; DLB 4, 45, 63; DLBD 15; MTCW 1, 2
Povod, Reinaldo 1959-1994 .... **CLC 44**
See also CA 136; 146; CANR 83
Powell, Adam Clayton, Jr. 1908-1972 .... **CLC 89; BLC 3; DAM MULT**
See also BW 1, 3; CA 102; 33-36R; CANR 86
Powell, Anthony (Dymoke) 1905-2000 .... **CLC 1, 3, 7, 9, 10, 31**
See also CA 1-4R; CANR 1, 32, 62; CDBLB 1945-1960; DLB 15; MTCW 1, 2
Powell, Dawn 1897-1965 .... **CLC 66**
See also CA 5-8R; DLBY 97
Powell, Padgett 1952- .... **CLC 34**
See also CA 126; CANR 63
Power, Susan 1961- .... **CLC 91**
See also CA 145
Powers, J(ames) F(arl) 1917-1999 ... **CLC 1, 4, 8, 57; SSC 4**
See also CA 1-4R; 181; CANR 2, 61; DLB 130; MTCW 1
Powers, John J(ames) 1945-
See Powers, John R.
See also CA 69-72
Powers, John R. .... **CLC 66**
See also Powers, John J(ames)
Powers, Richard (S.) 1957- .... **CLC 93**
See also CA 148; CANR 80
Pownall, David 1938- .... **CLC 10**
See also CA 89-92, 180; CAAS 18; CANR 49; DLB 14
Powys, John Cowper 1872-1963 .. **CLC 7, 9, 15, 46, 125**
See also CA 85-88; DLB 15; MTCW 1, 2
Powys, T(heodore) F(rancis) 1875-1953 .... **TCLC 9**
See also CA 106; DLB 36, 162
Prado (Calvo), Pedro 1886-1952 .. **TCLC 75**

Author Index

Author Index

Smith, A(rthur) J(ames) M(arshall) 1902-1980 .... **CLC 15; DAC**
See also CA 1-4R; 102; CANR 4; DLB 88
Smith, Adam 1723-1790 .... **LC 36**
See also DLB 104
Smith, Alexander 1829-1867 .... **NCLC 59**
See also DLB 32, 55
Smith, Anna Deavere 1950- .... **CLC 86**
See also CA 133
Smith, Betty (Wehner) 1896-1972 ... **CLC 19**
See also CA 5-8R; 33-36R; DLBY 82; SATA 6
Smith, Charlotte (Turner) 1749-1806 .... **NCLC 23**
See also DLB 39, 109
Smith, Clark Ashton 1893-1961 ...... **CLC 43**
See also CA 143; CANR 81; MTCW 2
Smith, Dave .... **CLC 22, 42**
See also Smith, David (Jeddie)
See also CAAS 7; DLB 5
Smith, David (Jeddie) 1942-
See Smith, Dave
See also CA 49-52; CANR 1, 59; DAM POET
Smith, Florence Margaret 1902-1971
See Smith, Stevie
See also CA 17-18; 29-32R; CANR 35; CAP 2; DAM POET; MTCW 1, 2
Smith, Iain Crichton 1928-1998 ...... **CLC 64**
See also CA 21-24R; 171; DLB 40, 139
Smith, John 1580(?)-1631 .... **LC 9**
See also DLB 24, 30
Smith, Johnston
See Crane, Stephen (Townley)
Smith, Joseph, Jr. 1805-1844 .... **NCLC 53**
Smith, Lee 1944- .... **CLC 25, 73**
See also CA 114; 119; CANR 46; DLB 143; DLBY 83; INT 119
Smith, Martin
See Smith, Martin Cruz
Smith, Martin Cruz 1942- ... **CLC 25; DAM MULT, POP**
See also BEST 89:4; CA 85-88; CANR 6, 23, 43, 65; INT CANR-23; MTCW 2; NNAL
Smith, Mary-Ann Tirone 1944- ...... **CLC 39**
See also CA 118; 136
Smith, Patti 1946- .... **CLC 12**
See also CA 93-96; CANR 63
Smith, Pauline (Urmson) 1882-1959 .... **TCLC 25**
See also DLB 225
Smith, Rosamond
See Oates, Joyce Carol
Smith, Sheila Kaye
See Kaye-Smith, Sheila
Smith, Stevie .... **CLC 3, 8, 25, 44; PC 12**
See also Smith, Florence Margaret
See also DLB 20; MTCW 2
Smith, Wilbur (Addison) 1933- .... **CLC 33**
See also CA 13-16R; CANR 7, 46, 66; MTCW 1, 2
Smith, William Jay 1918- .... **CLC 6**
See also CA 5-8R; CANR 44; DLB 5; MAICYA; SAAS 22; SATA 2, 68
Smith, Woodrow Wilson
See Kuttner, Henry
Smolenskin, Peretz 1842-1885 ...... **NCLC 30**
Smollett, Tobias (George) 1721-1771 .. **LC 2, 46**
See also CDBLB 1660-1789; DLB 39, 104
Snodgrass, W(illiam) D(e Witt) 1926- .... **CLC 2, 6, 10, 18, 68; DAM POET**
See also CA 1-4R; CANR 6, 36, 65, 85; DLB 5; MTCW 1, 2
Snow, C(harles) P(ercy) 1905-1980 .. **CLC 1, 4, 6, 9, 13, 19; DAM NOV**
See also CA 5-8R; 101; CANR 28; CDBLB 1945-1960; DLB 15, 77; DLBD 17; MTCW 1, 2
Snow, Frances Compton
See Adams, Henry (Brooks)
Snyder, Gary (Sherman) 1930- .... **CLC 1, 2, 5, 9, 32, 120; DAM POET; PC 21**
See also CA 17-20R; CANR 30, 60; DA3; DLB 5, 16, 165, 212; MTCW 2
Snyder, Zilpha Keatley 1927- .... **CLC 17**
See also AAYA 15; CA 9-12R; CANR 38; CLR 31; JRDA; MAICYA; SAAS 2; SATA 1, 28, 75, 110; SATA-Essay 112
Soares, Bernardo
See Pessoa, Fernando (Antonio Nogueira)
Sobh, A.
See Shamlu, Ahmad
Sobol, Joshua .... **CLC 60**
Socrates 469B.C.-399B.C. .... **CMLC 27**
Soderberg, Hjalmar 1869-1941 .... **TCLC 39**
Sodergran, Edith (Irene)
See Soedergran, Edith (Irene)
Soedergran, Edith (Irene) 1892-1923 .... **TCLC 31**
Softly, Edgar
See Lovecraft, H(oward) P(hillips)
Softly, Edward
See Lovecraft, H(oward) P(hillips)
Sokolov, Raymond 1941- .... **CLC 7**
See also CA 85-88
Solo, Jay
See Ellison, Harlan (Jay)
Sologub, Fyodor .... **TCLC 9**
See also Teternikov, Fyodor Kuzmich
Solomons, Ikey Esquir
See Thackeray, William Makepeace
Solomos, Dionysios 1798-1857 ...... **NCLC 15**
Solwoska, Mara
See French, Marilyn
Solzhenitsyn, Aleksandr I(sayevich) 1918- .... **CLC 1, 2, 4, 7, 9, 10, 18, 26, 34, 78; DA; DAB; DAC; DAM MST, NOV; SSC 32; WLC**
See also AITN 1; CA 69-72; CANR 40, 65; DA3; MTCW 1, 2
Somers, Jane
See Lessing, Doris (May)
Somerville, Edith 1858-1949 .... **TCLC 51**
See also DLB 135
Somerville & Ross
See Martin, Violet Florence; Somerville, Edith
Sommer, Scott 1951- .... **CLC 25**
See also CA 106
Sondheim, Stephen (Joshua) 1930- . **CLC 30, 39; DAM DRAM**
See also AAYA 11; CA 103; CANR 47, 68
Song, Cathy 1955- .... **PC 21**
See also CA 154; DLB 169
Sontag, Susan 1933- ... **CLC 1, 2, 10, 13, 31, 105; DAM POP**
See also CA 17-20R; CANR 25, 51, 74; DA3; DLB 2, 67; MTCW 1, 2
Sophocles 496(?)B.C.-406(?)B.C. .. **CMLC 2; DA; DAB; DAC; DAM DRAM, MST; DC 1; WLCS**
See also DA3; DLB 176
Sordello 1189-1269 .... **CMLC 15**
Sorel, Georges 1847-1922 .... **TCLC 91**
See also CA 118
Sorel, Julia
See Drexler, Rosalyn
Sorrentino, Gilbert 1929- . **CLC 3, 7, 14, 22, 40**
See also CA 77-80; CANR 14, 33; DLB 5, 173; DLBY 80; INT CANR-14
Soto, Gary 1952- . **CLC 32, 80; DAM MULT; HLC 2; PC 28**
See also AAYA 10; CA 119; 125; CANR 50, 74; CLR 38; DLB 82; HW 1, 2; INT 125; JRDA; MTCW 2; SATA 80
Soupault, Philippe 1897-1990 .... **CLC 68**
See also CA 116; 147; 131
Souster, (Holmes) Raymond 1921- .. **CLC 5, 14; DAC; DAM POET**
See also CA 13-16R; CAAS 14; CANR 13, 29, 53; DA3; DLB 88; SATA 63
Southern, Terry 1924(?)-1995 .... **CLC 7**
See also CA 1-4R; 150; CANR 1, 55; DLB 2
Southey, Robert 1774-1843 .... **NCLC 8**
See also DLB 93, 107, 142; SATA 54
Southworth, Emma Dorothy Eliza Nevitte 1819-1899 .... **NCLC 26**
Souza, Ernest
See Scott, Evelyn
Soyinka, Wole 1934- .. **CLC 3, 5, 14, 36, 44; BLC 3; DA; DAB; DAC; DAM DRAM, MST, MULT; DC 2; WLC**
See also BW 2, 3; CA 13-16R; CANR 27, 39, 82; DA3; DLB 125; MTCW 1, 2
Spackman, W(illiam) M(ode) 1905-1990 .... **CLC 46**
See also CA 81-84; 132
Spacks, Barry (Bernard) 1931- .... **CLC 14**
See also CA 154; CANR 33; DLB 105
Spanidou, Irini 1946- .... **CLC 44**
See also CA 185
Spark, Muriel (Sarah) 1918- ... **CLC 2, 3, 5, 8, 13, 18, 40, 94; DAB; DAC; DAM MST, NOV; SSC 10**
See also CA 5-8R; CANR 12, 36, 76, 89; CDBLB 1945-1960; DA3; DLB 15, 139; INT CANR-12; MTCW 1, 2
Spaulding, Douglas
See Bradbury, Ray (Douglas)
Spaulding, Leonard
See Bradbury, Ray (Douglas)
Spence, J. A. D.
See Eliot, T(homas) S(tearns)
Spencer, Elizabeth 1921- .... **CLC 22**
See also CA 13-16R; CANR 32, 65, 87; DLB 6; MTCW 1; SATA 14
Spencer, Leonard G.
See Silverberg, Robert
Spencer, Scott 1945- .... **CLC 30**
See also CA 113; CANR 51; DLBY 86
Spender, Stephen (Harold) 1909-1995 ... **CLC 1, 2, 5, 10, 41, 91; DAM POET**
See also CA 9-12R; 149; CANR 31, 54; CDBLB 1945-1960; DA3; DLB 20; MTCW 1, 2
Spengler, Oswald (Arnold Gottfried) 1880-1936 .... **TCLC 25**
See also CA 118
Spenser, Edmund 1552(?)-1599 .... **LC 5, 39; DA; DAB; DAC; DAM MST, POET; PC 8; WLC**
See also CDBLB Before 1660; DA3; DLB 167
Spicer, Jack 1925-1965 .... **CLC 8, 18, 72; DAM POET**
See also CA 85-88; DLB 5, 16, 193
Spiegelman, Art 1948- .... **CLC 76**
See also AAYA 10; CA 125; CANR 41, 55, 74; MTCW 2; SATA 109
Spielberg, Peter 1929- .... **CLC 6**
See also CA 5-8R; CANR 4, 48; DLBY 81
Spielberg, Steven 1947- .... **CLC 20**
See also AAYA 8, 24; CA 77-80; CANR 32; SATA 32
Spillane, Frank Morrison 1918-
See Spillane, Mickey
See also CA 25-28R; CANR 28, 63; DA3; DLB 226; MTCW 1, 2; SATA 66
Spillane, Mickey .... **CLC 3, 13**
See also Spillane, Frank Morrison

Author Index

See also AITN 1; CA 1-4R; CANR 9, 58; DLB 185; INT CANR-9; MTCW 1, 2
Tallent, Elizabeth (Ann) 1954- .... **CLC 45**
See also CA 117; CANR 72; DLB 130
Tally, Ted 1952- .... **CLC 42**
See also CA 120; 124; INT 124
Talvik, Heiti 1904-1947 .... **TCLC 87**
Tamayo y Baus, Manuel 1829-1898 . **NCLC 1**
Tammsaare, A(nton) H(ansen) 1878-1940 .... **TCLC 27**
See also CA 164; DLB 220
Tam'si, Tchicaya U
See Tchicaya, Gerald Felix
Tan, Amy (Ruth) 1952- . **CLC 59, 120; DAM MULT, NOV, POP**
See also AAYA 9; BEST 89:3; CA 136; CANR 54; CDALBS; DA3; DLB 173; MTCW 2; SATA 75
Tandem, Felix
See Spitteler, Carl (Friedrich Georg)
Tanizaki, Jun'ichiro 1886-1965 .. **CLC 8, 14, 28; SSC 21**
See also CA 93-96; 25-28R; DLB 180; MTCW 2
Tanner, William
See Amis, Kingsley (William)
Tao Lao
See Storni, Alfonsina
Tarantino, Quentin (Jerome) 1963- .... **CLC 125**
See also CA 171
Tarassoff, Lev
See Troyat, Henri
Tarbell, Ida M(inerva) 1857-1944 . **TCLC 40**
See also CA 122; 181; DLB 47
Tarkington, (Newton) Booth 1869-1946 .... **TCLC 9**
See also CA 110; 143; DLB 9, 102; MTCW 2; SATA 17
Tarkovsky, Andrei (Arsenyevich) 1932-1986 .... **CLC 75**
See also CA 127
Tartt, Donna 1964(?)- .... **CLC 76**
See also CA 142
Tasso, Torquato 1544-1595 .... **LC 5**
Tate, (John Orley) Allen 1899-1979 . **CLC 2, 4, 6, 9, 11, 14, 24**
See also CA 5-8R; 85-88; CANR 32; DLB 4, 45, 63; DLBD 17; MTCW 1, 2
Tate, Ellalice
See Hibbert, Eleanor Alice Burford
Tate, James (Vincent) 1943- .... **CLC 2, 6, 25**
See also CA 21-24R; CANR 29, 57; DLB 5, 169
Tauler, Johannes c. 1300-1361 ..... **CMLC 37**
See also DLB 179
Tavel, Ronald 1940- .... **CLC 6**
See also CA 21-24R; CANR 33
Taylor, Bayard 1825-1878 .... **NCLC 89**
See also DLB 3, 189
Taylor, C(ecil) P(hilip) 1929-1981 ... **CLC 27**
See also CA 25-28R; 105; CANR 47
Taylor, Edward 1642(?)-1729 .... **LC 11; DA; DAB; DAC; DAM MST, POET**
See also DLB 24
Taylor, Eleanor Ross 1920- .... **CLC 5**
See also CA 81-84; CANR 70
Taylor, Elizabeth 1912-1975 .... **CLC 2, 4, 29**
See also CA 13-16R; CANR 9, 70; DLB 139; MTCW 1; SATA 13
Taylor, Frederick Winslow 1856-1915 .... **TCLC 76**
Taylor, Henry (Splawn) 1942- .... **CLC 44**
See also CA 33-36R; CAAS 7; CANR 31; DLB 5
Taylor, Kamala (Purnaiya) 1924-
See Markandaya, Kamala
See also CA 77-80
Taylor, Mildred D. .... **CLC 21**
See also AAYA 10; BW 1; CA 85-88; CANR 25; CLR 9, 59; DLB 52; JRDA; MAICYA; SAAS 5; SATA 15, 70
Taylor, Peter (Hillsman) 1917-1994 . **CLC 1, 4, 18, 37, 44, 50, 71; SSC 10**
See also CA 13-16R; 147; CANR 9, 50; DLBY 81, 94; INT CANR-9; MTCW 1, 2
Taylor, Robert Lewis 1912-1998 ..... **CLC 14**
See also CA 1-4R; 170; CANR 3, 64; SATA 10
Tchekhov, Anton
See Chekhov, Anton (Pavlovich)
Tchicaya, Gerald Felix 1931-1988 . **CLC 101**
See also CA 129; 125; CANR 81
Tchicaya U Tam'si
See Tchicaya, Gerald Felix
Teasdale, Sara 1884-1933 .... **TCLC 4**
See also CA 104; 163; DLB 45; SATA 32
Tegner, Esaias 1782-1846 .... **NCLC 2**
Teilhard de Chardin, (Marie Joseph) Pierre 1881-1955 .... **TCLC 9**
See also CA 105
Temple, Ann
See Mortimer, Penelope (Ruth)
Tennant, Emma (Christina) 1937- . **CLC 13, 52**
See also CA 65-68; CAAS 9; CANR 10, 38, 59, 88; DLB 14
Tenneshaw, S. M.
See Silverberg, Robert
Tennyson, Alfred 1809-1892 .. **NCLC 30, 65; DA; DAB; DAC; DAM MST, POET; PC 6; WLC**
See also CDBLB 1832-1890; DA3; DLB 32
Teran, Lisa St. Aubin de .... **CLC 36**
See also St. Aubin de Teran, Lisa
Terence c. 184B.C.-c. 159B.C. .... **CMLC 14; DC 7**
See also DLB 211
Teresa de Jesus, St. 1515-1582 .... **LC 18**
Terkel, Louis 1912-
See Terkel, Studs
See also CA 57-60; CANR 18, 45, 67; DA3; MTCW 1, 2
Terkel, Studs .... **CLC 38**
See also Terkel, Louis
See also AAYA 32; AITN 1; MTCW 2
Terry, C. V.
See Slaughter, Frank G(ill)
Terry, Megan 1932- .... **CLC 19; DC 13**
See also CA 77-80; CABS 3; CANR 43; DLB 7
Tertullian c. 155-c. 245 .... **CMLC 29**
Tertz, Abram
See Sinyavsky, Andrei (Donatevich)
Tesich, Steve 1943(?)-1996 .... **CLC 40, 69**
See also CA 105; 152; DLBY 83
Tesla, Nikola 1856-1943 .... **TCLC 88**
Teternikov, Fyodor Kuzmich 1863-1927
See Sologub, Fyodor
See also CA 104
Tevis, Walter 1928-1984 .... **CLC 42**
See also CA 113
Tey, Josephine .... **TCLC 14**
See also Mackintosh, Elizabeth
See also DLB 77
Thackeray, William Makepeace 1811-1863 . **NCLC 5, 14, 22, 43; DA; DAB; DAC; DAM MST, NOV; WLC**
See also CDBLB 1832-1890; DA3; DLB 21, 55, 159, 163; SATA 23
Thakura, Ravindranatha
See Tagore, Rabindranath
Tharoor, Shashi 1956- .... **CLC 70**
See also CA 141; CANR 91
Thelwell, Michael Miles 1939- .... **CLC 22**
See also BW 2; CA 101
Theobald, Lewis, Jr.
See Lovecraft, H(oward) P(hillips)
Theodorescu, Ion N. 1880-1967
See Arghezi, Tudor
See also CA 116; DLB 220
Theriault, Yves 1915-1983 ... **CLC 79; DAC; DAM MST**
See also CA 102; DLB 88
Theroux, Alexander (Louis) 1939- ... **CLC 2, 25**
See also CA 85-88; CANR 20, 63
Theroux, Paul (Edward) 1941- .... **CLC 5, 8, 11, 15, 28, 46; DAM POP**
See also AAYA 28; BEST 89:4; CA 33-36R; CANR 20, 45, 74; CDALBS; DA3; DLB 2; MTCW 1, 2; SATA 44, 109
Thesen, Sharon 1946- .... **CLC 56**
See also CA 163
Thevenin, Denis
See Duhamel, Georges
Thibault, Jacques Anatole Francois 1844-1924
See France, Anatole
See also CA 106; 127; DAM NOV; DA3; MTCW 1, 2
Thiele, Colin (Milton) 1920- .... **CLC 17**
See also CA 29-32R; CANR 12, 28, 53; CLR 27; MAICYA; SAAS 2; SATA 14, 72
Thomas, Audrey (Callahan) 1935- .. **CLC 7, 13, 37, 107; SSC 20**
See also AITN 2; CA 21-24R; CAAS 19; CANR 36, 58; DLB 60; MTCW 1
Thomas, Augustus 1857-1934 .... **TCLC 97**
Thomas, D(onald) M(ichael) 1935- . **CLC 13, 22, 31, 132**
See also CA 61-64; CAAS 11; CANR 17, 45, 75; CDBLB 1960 to Present; DA3; DLB 40, 207; INT CANR-17; MTCW 1, 2
Thomas, Dylan (Marlais) 1914-1953 .... **TCLC 1, 8, 45; DA; DAB; DAC; DAM DRAM, MST, POET; PC 2; SSC 3; WLC**
See also CA 104; 120; CANR 65; CDBLB 1945-1960; DA3; DLB 13, 20, 139; MTCW 1, 2; SATA 60
Thomas, (Philip) Edward 1878-1917 .... **TCLC 10; DAM POET**
See also CA 106; 153; DLB 98
Thomas, Joyce Carol 1938- .... **CLC 35**
See also AAYA 12; BW 2, 3; CA 113; 116; CANR 48; CLR 19; DLB 33; INT 116; JRDA; MAICYA; MTCW 1, 2; SAAS 7; SATA 40, 78
Thomas, Lewis 1913-1993 .... **CLC 35**
See also CA 85-88; 143; CANR 38, 60; MTCW 1, 2
Thomas, M. Carey 1857-1935 ...... **TCLC 89**
Thomas, Paul
See Mann, (Paul) Thomas
Thomas, Piri 1928- .... **CLC 17; HLCS 2**
See also CA 73-76; HW 1
Thomas, R(onald) S(tuart) 1913- ..... **CLC 6, 13, 48; DAB; DAM POET**
See also CA 89-92; CAAS 4; CANR 30; CDBLB 1960 to Present; DLB 27; MTCW 1
Thomas, Ross (Elmore) 1926-1995 . **CLC 39**
See also CA 33-36R; 150; CANR 22, 63
Thompson, Francis Clegg
See Mencken, H(enry) L(ouis)
Thompson, Francis Joseph 1859-1907 .... **TCLC 4**
See also CA 104; CDBLB 1890-1914; DLB 19
Thompson, Hunter S(tockton) 1939- .... **CLC 9, 17, 40, 104; DAM POP**

See also BEST 89:1; CA 17-20R; CANR 23, 46, 74, 77; DA3; DLB 185; MTCW 1, 2

Thompson, James Myers
See Thompson, Jim (Myers)

Thompson, Jim (Myers) 1906-1977(?) .... **CLC 69**
See also CA 140; DLB 226

Thompson, Judith .... **CLC 39**

Thomson, James 1700-1748 .. **LC 16, 29, 40; DAM POET**
See also DLB 95

Thomson, James 1834-1882 .... **NCLC 18; DAM POET**
See also DLB 35

Thoreau, Henry David 1817-1862 . **NCLC 7, 21, 61; DA; DAB; DAC; DAM MST; PC 30; WLC**
See also CDALB 1640-1865; DA3; DLB 1, 223

Thornton, Hall
See Silverberg, Robert

Thucydides c. 455B.C.-399B.C. ... **CMLC 17**
See also DLB 176

Thumboo, Edwin 1933- .... **PC 30**

Thurber, James (Grover) 1894-1961 . **CLC 5, 11, 25, 125; DA; DAB; DAC; DAM DRAM, MST, NOV; SSC 1**
See also CA 73-76; CANR 17, 39; CDALB 1929-1941; DA3; DLB 4, 11, 22, 102; MAICYA; MTCW 1, 2; SATA 13

Thurman, Wallace (Henry) 1902-1934 .... **TCLC 6; BLC 3; DAM MULT**
See also BW 1, 3; CA 104; 124; CANR 81; DLB 51

Tibullus, Albius c. 54B.C.-c. 19B.C. .... **CMLC 36**
See also DLB 211

Ticheburn, Cheviot
See Ainsworth, William Harrison

Tieck, (Johann) Ludwig 1773-1853 .... **NCLC 5, 46; SSC 31**
See also DLB 90

Tiger, Derry
See Ellison, Harlan (Jay)

Tilghman, Christopher 1948(?)- ...... **CLC 65**
See also CA 159

Tillich, Paul (Johannes) 1886-1965 .... **CLC 131**
See also CA 5-8R; 25-28R; CANR 33; MTCW 1, 2

Tillinghast, Richard (Williford) 1940- .... **CLC 29**
See also CA 29-32R; CAAS 23; CANR 26, 51

Timrod, Henry 1828-1867 .... **NCLC 25**
See also DLB 3

Tindall, Gillian (Elizabeth) 1938- ..... **CLC 7**
See also CA 21-24R; CANR 11, 65

Tiptree, James, Jr. .... **CLC 48, 50**
See also Sheldon, Alice Hastings Bradley
See also DLB 8

Titmarsh, Michael Angelo
See Thackeray, William Makepeace

Tocqueville, Alexis (Charles Henri Maurice Clerel, Comte) de 1805-1859 . **NCLC 7, 63**

Tolkien, J(ohn) R(onald) R(euel) 1892-1973 .... **CLC 1, 2, 3, 8, 12, 38; DA; DAB; DAC; DAM MST, NOV, POP; WLC**
See also AAYA 10; AITN 1; CA 17-18; 45-48; CANR 36; CAP 2; CDBLB 1914-1945; CLR 56; DA3; DLB 15, 160; JRDA; MAICYA; MTCW 1, 2; SATA 2, 32, 100; SATA-Obit 24

Toller, Ernst 1893-1939 .... **TCLC 10**
See also CA 107; 186; DLB 124

Tolson, M. B.
See Tolson, Melvin B(eaunorus)

Tolson, Melvin B(eaunorus) 1898(?)-1966 .... **CLC 36, 105; BLC 3; DAM MULT, POET**
See also BW 1, 3; CA 124; 89-92; CANR 80; DLB 48, 76

Tolstoi, Aleksei Nikolaevich
See Tolstoy, Alexey Nikolaevich

Tolstoy, Alexey Nikolaevich 1882-1945 .... **TCLC 18**
See also CA 107; 158

Tolstoy, Count Leo
See Tolstoy, Leo (Nikolaevich)

Tolstoy, Leo (Nikolaevich) 1828-1910 . **TCLC 4, 11, 17, 28, 44, 79; DA; DAB; DAC; DAM MST, NOV; SSC 9, 30; WLC**
See also CA 104; 123; DA3; SATA 26

Tomasi di Lampedusa, Giuseppe 1896-1957
See Lampedusa, Giuseppe (Tomasi) di
See also CA 111

Tomlin, Lily .... **CLC 17**
See also Tomlin, Mary Jean

Tomlin, Mary Jean 1939(?)-
See Tomlin, Lily
See also CA 117

Tomlinson, (Alfred) Charles 1927- .. **CLC 2, 4, 6, 13, 45; DAM POET; PC 17**
See also CA 5-8R; CANR 33; DLB 40

Tomlinson, H(enry) M(ajor) 1873-1958 .... **TCLC 71**
See also CA 118; 161; DLB 36, 100, 195

Tonson, Jacob
See Bennett, (Enoch) Arnold

Toole, John Kennedy 1937-1969 .... **CLC 19, 64**
See also CA 104; DLBY 81; MTCW 2

Toomer, Jean 1894-1967 .. **CLC 1, 4, 13, 22; BLC 3; DAM MULT; PC 7; SSC 1; WLCS**
See also BW 1; CA 85-88; CDALB 1917-1929; DA3; DLB 45, 51; MTCW 1, 2

Torley, Luke
See Blish, James (Benjamin)

Tornimparte, Alessandra
See Ginzburg, Natalia

Torre, Raoul della
See Mencken, H(enry) L(ouis)

Torrence, Ridgely 1874-1950 .... **TCLC 97**
See also DLB 54

Torrey, E(dwin) Fuller 1937- .... **CLC 34**
See also CA 119; CANR 71

Torsvan, Ben Traven
See Traven, B.

Torsvan, Benno Traven
See Traven, B.

Torsvan, Berick Traven
See Traven, B.

Torsvan, Berwick Traven
See Traven, B.

Torsvan, Bruno Traven
See Traven, B.

Torsvan, Traven
See Traven, B.

Tournier, Michel (Edouard) 1924- ... **CLC 6, 23, 36, 95**
See also CA 49-52; CANR 3, 36, 74; DLB 83; MTCW 1, 2; SATA 23

Tournimparte, Alessandra
See Ginzburg, Natalia

Towers, Ivar
See Kornbluth, C(yril) M.

Towne, Robert (Burton) 1936(?)- .... **CLC 87**
See also CA 108; DLB 44

Townsend, Sue .... **CLC 61**
See also Townsend, Susan Elaine
See also AAYA 28; SATA 55, 93; SATA-Brief 48

Townsend, Susan Elaine 1946-
See Townsend, Sue
See also CA 119; 127; CANR 65; DAB; DAC; DAM MST

Townshend, Peter (Dennis Blandford) 1945- .... **CLC 17, 42**
See also CA 107

Tozzi, Federigo 1883-1920 .... **TCLC 31**
See also CA 160

Traill, Catharine Parr 1802-1899 . **NCLC 31**
See also DLB 99

Trakl, Georg 1887-1914 ..... **TCLC 5; PC 20**
See also CA 104; 165; MTCW 2

Transtroemer, Tomas (Goesta) 1931- .... **CLC 52, 65; DAM POET**
See also CA 117; 129; CAAS 17

Transtromer, Tomas Gosta
See Transtroemer, Tomas (Goesta)

Traven, B. (?)-1969 .... **CLC 8, 11**
See also CA 19-20; 25-28R; CAP 2; DLB 9, 56; MTCW 1

Treitel, Jonathan 1959- .... **CLC 70**

Trelawny, Edward John 1792-1881 .... **NCLC 85**
See also DLB 110, 116, 144

Tremain, Rose 1943- .... **CLC 42**
See also CA 97-100; CANR 44; DLB 14

Tremblay, Michel 1942- .... **CLC 29, 102; DAC; DAM MST**
See also CA 116; 128; DLB 60; MTCW 1, 2

Trevanian .... **CLC 29**
See also Whitaker, Rod(ney)

Trevor, Glen
See Hilton, James

Trevor, William 1928- . **CLC 7, 9, 14, 25, 71, 116; SSC 21**
See also Cox, William Trevor
See also DLB 14, 139; MTCW 2

Trifonov, Yuri (Valentinovich) 1925-1981 .... **CLC 45**
See also CA 126; 103; MTCW 1

Trilling, Diana (Rubin) 1905-1996 . **CLC 129**
See also CA 5-8R; 154; CANR 10, 46; INT CANR-10; MTCW 1, 2

Trilling, Lionel 1905-1975 ..... **CLC 9, 11, 24**
See also CA 9-12R; 61-64; CANR 10; DLB 28, 63; INT CANR-10; MTCW 1, 2

Trimball, W. H.
See Mencken, H(enry) L(ouis)

Tristan
See Gomez de la Serna, Ramon

Tristram
See Housman, A(lfred) E(dward)

Trogdon, William (Lewis) 1939-
See Heat-Moon, William Least
See also CA 115; 119; CANR 47, 89; INT 119

Trollope, Anthony 1815-1882 .. **NCLC 6, 33; DA; DAB; DAC; DAM MST, NOV; SSC 28; WLC**
See also CDBLB 1832-1890; DA3; DLB 21, 57, 159; SATA 22

Trollope, Frances 1779-1863 .... **NCLC 30**
See also DLB 21, 166

Trotsky, Leon 1879-1940 .... **TCLC 22**
See also CA 118; 167

Trotter (Cockburn), Catharine 1679-1749 .... **LC 8**
See also DLB 84

Trotter, Wilfred 1872-1939 .... **TCLC 97**

Trout, Kilgore
See Farmer, Philip Jose

Trow, George W. S. 1943- .... **CLC 52**
See also CA 126; CANR 91

Troyat, Henri 1911- .... **CLC 23**
See also CA 45-48; CANR 2, 33, 67; MTCW 1

Trudeau, G(arretson) B(eekman) 1948-
See Trudeau, Garry B.
See also CA 81-84; CANR 31; SATA 35
Trudeau, Garry B. .... **CLC 12**
See also Trudeau, G(arretson) B(eekman)
See also AAYA 10; AITN 2
Truffaut, Francois 1932-1984 .. **CLC 20, 101**
See also CA 81-84; 113; CANR 34
Trumbo, Dalton 1905-1976 .... **CLC 19**
See also CA 21-24R; 69-72; CANR 10; DLB 26
Trumbull, John 1750-1831 .... **NCLC 30**
See also DLB 31
Trundlett, Helen B.
See Eliot, T(homas) S(tearns)
Tryon, Thomas 1926-1991 . **CLC 3, 11; DAM POP**
See also AITN 1; CA 29-32R; 135; CANR 32, 77; DA3; MTCW 1
Tryon, Tom
See Tryon, Thomas
Ts'ao Hsueh-ch'in 1715(?)-1763 .... **LC 1**
Tsushima, Shuji 1909-1948
See Dazai Osamu
See also CA 107
Tsvetaeva (Efron), Marina (Ivanovna) 1892-1941 .... **TCLC 7, 35; PC 14**
See also CA 104; 128; CANR 73; MTCW 1, 2
Tuck, Lily 1938- .... **CLC 70**
See also CA 139; CANR 90
Tu Fu 712-770 .... **PC 9**
See also DAM MULT
Tunis, John R(oberts) 1889-1975 .... **CLC 12**
See also CA 61-64; CANR 62; DLB 22, 171; JRDA; MAICYA; SATA 37; SATA-Brief 30
Tuohy, Frank .... **CLC 37**
See also Tuohy, John Francis
See also DLB 14, 139
Tuohy, John Francis 1925-1999
See Tuohy, Frank
See also CA 5-8R; 178; CANR 3, 47
Turco, Lewis (Putnam) 1934- .... **CLC 11, 63**
See also CA 13-16R; CAAS 22; CANR 24, 51; DLBY 84
Turgenev, Ivan 1818-1883 ... **NCLC 21; DA; DAB; DAC; DAM MST, NOV; DC 7; SSC 7; WLC**
Turgot, Anne-Robert-Jacques 1727-1781 .... **LC 26**
Turner, Frederick 1943- .... **CLC 48**
See also CA 73-76; CAAS 10; CANR 12, 30, 56; DLB 40
Tutu, Desmond M(pilo) 1931- .... **CLC 80; BLC 3; DAM MULT**
See also BW 1, 3; CA 125; CANR 67, 81
Tutuola, Amos 1920-1997 ..... **CLC 5, 14, 29; BLC 3; DAM MULT**
See also BW 2, 3; CA 9-12R; 159; CANR 27, 66; DA3; DLB 125; MTCW 1, 2
Twain, Mark 1835-1910 ..... **TCLC 6, 12, 19, 36, 48, 59; SSC 34; WLC**
See also Clemens, Samuel Langhorne
See also AAYA 20; CLR 58, 60; DLB 11, 12, 23, 64, 74
Tyler, Anne 1941- . **CLC 7, 11, 18, 28, 44, 59, 103; DAM NOV, POP**
See also AAYA 18; BEST 89:1; CA 9-12R; CANR 11, 33, 53; CDALBS; DLB 6, 143; DLBY 82; MTCW 1, 2; SATA 7, 90
Tyler, Royall 1757-1826 .... **NCLC 3**
See also DLB 37
Tynan, Katharine 1861-1931 .... **TCLC 3**
See also CA 104; 167; DLB 153
Tyutchev, Fyodor 1803-1873 .... **NCLC 34**
Tzara, Tristan 1896-1963 ..... **CLC 47; DAM POET; PC 27**
See also CA 153; 89-92; MTCW 2
Uhry, Alfred 1936- . **CLC 55; DAM DRAM, POP**
See also CA 127; 133; DA3; INT 133
Ulf, Haerved
See Strindberg, (Johan) August
Ulf, Harved
See Strindberg, (Johan) August
Ulibarri, Sabine R(eyes) 1919- .... **CLC 83; DAM MULT; HLCS 2**
See also CA 131; CANR 81; DLB 82; HW 1, 2
Unamuno (y Jugo), Miguel de 1864-1936 . **TCLC 2, 9; DAM MULT, NOV; HLC 2; SSC 11**
See also CA 104; 131; CANR 81; DLB 108; HW 1, 2; MTCW 1, 2
Undercliffe, Errol
See Campbell, (John) Ramsey
Underwood, Miles
See Glassco, John
Undset, Sigrid 1882-1949 .... **TCLC 3; DA; DAB; DAC; DAM MST, NOV; WLC**
See also CA 104; 129; DA3; MTCW 1, 2
Ungaretti, Giuseppe 1888-1970 .. **CLC 7, 11, 15**
See also CA 19-20; 25-28R; CAP 2; DLB 114
Unger, Douglas 1952- .... **CLC 34**
See also CA 130
Unsworth, Barry (Forster) 1930- ... **CLC 76, 127**
See also CA 25-28R; CANR 30, 54; DLB 194
Updike, John (Hoyer) 1932- . **CLC 1, 2, 3, 5, 7, 9, 13, 15, 23, 34, 43, 70; DA; DAB; DAC; DAM MST, NOV, POET, POP; SSC 13, 27; WLC**
See also CA 1-4R; CABS 1; CANR 4, 33, 51; CDALB 1968-1988; DA3; DLB 2, 5, 143, 227; DLBD 3; DLBY 80, 82, 97; MTCW 1, 2
Upshaw, Margaret Mitchell
See Mitchell, Margaret (Munnerlyn)
Upton, Mark
See Sanders, Lawrence
Upward, Allen 1863-1926 .... **TCLC 85**
See also CA 117; DLB 36
Urdang, Constance (Henriette) 1922- .... **CLC 47**
See also CA 21-24R; CANR 9, 24
Uriel, Henry
See Faust, Frederick (Schiller)
Uris, Leon (Marcus) 1924- .... **CLC 7, 32; DAM NOV, POP**
See also AITN 1, 2; BEST 89:2; CA 1-4R; CANR 1, 40, 65; DA3; MTCW 1, 2; SATA 49
Urista, Alberto H. 1947-
See Alurista
See also CA 45-48, 182; CANR 2, 32; HLCS 1; HW 1
Urmuz
See Codrescu, Andrei
Urquhart, Guy
See McAlmon, Robert (Menzies)
Urquhart, Jane 1949- .... **CLC 90; DAC**
See also CA 113; CANR 32, 68
Usigli, Rodolfo 1905-1979
See also CA 131; HLCS 1; HW 1
Ustinov, Peter (Alexander) 1921- ...... **CLC 1**
See also AITN 1; CA 13-16R; CANR 25, 51; DLB 13; MTCW 2
U Tam'si, Gerald Felix Tchicaya
See Tchicaya, Gerald Felix
U Tam'si, Tchicaya
See Tchicaya, Gerald Felix
Vachss, Andrew (Henry) 1942- ..... **CLC 106**
See also CA 118; CANR 44
Vachss, Andrew H.
See Vachss, Andrew (Henry)
Vaculik, Ludvik 1926- .... **CLC 7**
See also CA 53-56; CANR 72
Vaihinger, Hans 1852-1933 .... **TCLC 71**
See also CA 116; 166
Valdez, Luis (Miguel) 1940- . **CLC 84; DAM MULT; DC 10; HLC 2**
See also CA 101; CANR 32, 81; DLB 122; HW 1
Valenzuela, Luisa 1938- .... **CLC 31, 104; DAM MULT; HLCS 2; SSC 14**
See also CA 101; CANR 32, 65; DLB 113; HW 1, 2
Valera y Alcala-Galiano, Juan 1824-1905 .... **TCLC 10**
See also CA 106
Valery, (Ambroise) Paul (Toussaint Jules) 1871-1945 .. **TCLC 4, 15; DAM POET; PC 9**
See also CA 104; 122; DA3; MTCW 1, 2
Valle-Inclan, Ramon (Maria) del 1866-1936 .... **TCLC 5; DAM MULT; HLC 2**
See also CA 106; 153; CANR 80; DLB 134; HW 2
Vallejo, Antonio Buero
See Buero Vallejo, Antonio
Vallejo, Cesar (Abraham) 1892-1938 ...... **TCLC 3, 56; DAM MULT; HLC 2**
See also CA 105; 153; HW 1
Valles, Jules 1832-1885 .... **NCLC 71**
See also DLB 123
Vallette, Marguerite Eymery 1860-1953 .... **TCLC 67**
See also CA 182; DLB 123, 192
Valle Y Pena, Ramon del
See Valle-Inclan, Ramon (Maria) del
Van Ash, Cay 1918- .... **CLC 34**
Vanbrugh, Sir John 1664-1726 .... **LC 21; DAM DRAM**
See also DLB 80
Van Campen, Karl
See Campbell, John W(ood, Jr.)
Vance, Gerald
See Silverberg, Robert
Vance, Jack .... **CLC 35**
See also Vance, John Holbrook
See also DLB 8
Vance, John Holbrook 1916-
See Queen, Ellery; Vance, Jack
See also CA 29-32R; CANR 17, 65; MTCW 1
Van Den Bogarde, Derek Jules Gaspard Ulric Niven 1921-1999 .... **CLC 14**
See also CA 77-80; 179; DLB 19
Vandenburgh, Jane .... **CLC 59**
See also CA 168
Vanderhaeghe, Guy 1951- .... **CLC 41**
See also CA 113; CANR 72
van der Post, Laurens (Jan) 1906-1996 .... **CLC 5**
See also CA 5-8R; 155; CANR 35; DLB 204
van de Wetering, Janwillem 1931- . **CLC 47**
See also CA 49-52; CANR 4, 62, 90
Van Dine, S. S. .... **TCLC 23**
See also Wright, Willard Huntington
Van Doren, Carl (Clinton) 1885-1950 .... **TCLC 18**
See also CA 111; 168
Van Doren, Mark 1894-1972 .... **CLC 6, 10**
See also CA 1-4R; 37-40R; CANR 3; DLB 45; MTCW 1, 2
Van Druten, John (William) 1901-1957 .... **TCLC 2**
See also CA 104; 161; DLB 10
Van Duyn, Mona (Jane) 1921- ..... **CLC 3, 7, 63, 116; DAM POET**

Author Index

DC Cumulative Nationality Index

DC Cumulative Title Index

Title Index

Title Index

Title Index

Title Index

Title Index

ISBN 0-7876-3141-8